Macroeconomics

Macroeconomics: Imperfections, Institutions, and Policies

Wendy Carlin and David Soskice

OXFORD
UNIVERSITY PRESS

OXFORD
UNIVERSITY PRESS

Great Clarendon Street, Oxford OX2 6DP

Oxford University Press is a department of the University of Oxford.
It furthers the University's objective of excellence in research, scholarship,
and education by publishing worldwide in

Oxford New York

Auckland Cape Town Dar es Salaam Hong Kong Karachi
Kuala Lumpur Madrid Melbourne Mexico City Nairobi
New Delhi Shanghai Taipei Toronto

With offices in

Argentina Austria Brazil Chile Czech Republic France Greece
Guatemala Hungary Italy Japan Poland Portugal Singapore
South Korea Switzerland Thailand Turkey Ukraine Vietnam

Oxford is a registered trade mark of Oxford University Press
in the UK and in certain other countries

Published in the United States
by Oxford University Press Inc., New York

British Library Cataloguing in Publication Data
Data available

Library of Congress Cataloging in Publication Data
Data available

Typeset by Newgen Imaging Systems (P) Ltd., Chennai, India
Printed in Great Britain
on acid-free paper by
Ashford Colour Press Ltd., Gosport, Hampshire

ISBN 978-0-19-877622-2

10 9 8 7 6 5 4 3

For Andrew and Niki

■ PREFACE

1 Audience

This book provides a wide audience with access to modern macroeconomics. The core audience is undergraduates who already have some background in macroeconomics. It is also designed for graduate students, academic economists, and economists working in policy making and the private sector who want an introduction to major changes that have taken place in modern macroeconomics. Knowledge of economics has become increasingly central to courses in political science and public policy and this book will be used there as well.

Throughout the book, we emphasize the role that *imperfections* play in labour, product, and financial markets in short-, medium-, and long-run macroeconomics. *Institutions* and *policies* feature heavily in the book. By institutions we mean both the broad rules of the game within which the players in the economy operate and the key organizations. Central banks function according to the prevailing monetary policy framework and set monetary policy taking into account the behaviour of the private sector. Employers and employees operate within a set of labour market institutions in which unions may bargain over wages and where there are rules governing hiring and firing. Financial market institutions impinge on investment decisions by firms and on the behaviour of households. Governments implement fiscal policy within a fiscal policy framework. They also design and implement labour market, education, innovation, and competition policies. The large players in the economy may act strategically in their own interest and we analyse the macroeconomic impact of this.

2 What this book offers

- **to undergraduates studying economics**

It is likely that you were attracted to economics because it offers the prospect of understanding big questions about how the world works. Why has inflation been such a major problem in some countries at some times but now seems very low and stable in many countries? Do exchange rates matter for unemployment? Why is a country like the UK that had poor macroeconomic performance twenty years ago performing much better in recent years? Why are Germany and Japan performing so poorly? What are the likely consequences for other countries of a major hike in commodity and oil prices as a consequence of China's rapid growth? How did some countries get to be rich while others remain poor? Will the transition economies catch up with the rest of the European Union?

Just as when studying industrial economics you expect to be able to discuss competition policy debates, or, in labour economics, to participate in debates about the minimum wage or migration, in macroeconomics you should be able to discuss the following: deflation in Japan, the merits of euro membership for the recent accession countries of the EU, the causes and consequences of the USA's widening current account deficit, the likely consequences for unemployment of an acceleration of productivity growth, the role of education in economic growth, and so on.

This book gives you a systematic way of thinking about questions like these. You will end up with a model that you can use yourself to understand macroeconomic behaviour and policy issues in the real world. In whatever job you get, whether working in a start-up high tech company or in a family business, in a voluntary sector organization, for an investment bank, or for the ministry of foreign trade, you want the confidence to be able to interpret national and international economic trends and the policy debate. Such confidence is built in this book because it integrates the different components of macroeconomics and then shows in Chapters 17 and 18 how the model can be used to understand a whole range of performance and policy issues in Europe, Japan, and the USA in the last thirty years. You may want to take a look at these chapters before starting on the rest of the book.

Going beyond courses in macroeconomics, the book has core material for courses in the economics of growth, money and banking, labour economics, the economics of unemployment, international monetary economics, and the economics of monetary integration.

- **to graduate students in economics**

This book is based on the mainstream monetary macro model used in current research in universities and central banks. Modern monetary macroeconomics uses what is often called the 3-equation New Keynesian model, where the three equations are

- the *IS* curve
- the Phillips curve (*PC*) and
- an optimizing monetary policy rule (*MR*).

Built around this core, the book provides you with a reference back to intuitive and less formal explanations of the 3-equation model and of each of its components. To facilitate the forward linkage to more advanced treatments, we show in Chapter 15 how the model can be built up from microfoundations with forward-looking optimizing economic agents who have rational expectations.

The book also provides a rigorous coverage of growth theory—both exogenous and endogenous. There is a comprehensive chapter on the Solow–Swan model with an appendix that introduces Ramsey savings. We emphasize the characteristics of steady states, how the economy moves from one steady state to another, and how the model can be used to test empirically for whether economies are converging. Diagrams and intuitive explanations complement the formal derivations of the key results. We provide a unified treatment of endogenous growth models and explain how a simplified version of the Schumpeterian growth model works. We illustrate the rich variety of questions about growth and institutions that Schumpeterian models address. These chapters serve as a springboard for going on to more technical analysis and provide a stimulus for thinking about many applied questions.

- **to graduate students in political science and public policy**

This book provides a self-contained treatment of modern macroeconomics that is accessible to graduate students of political science and public policy who have the basic mathematical competences described below. The approach incorporates the presence of market imperfections and includes coverage of a wide range of policy instruments. It is designed to highlight the role in macroeconomics of differences across countries in institutions—from the labour market to the financial system—and is well suited for the study of economic performance and policy within specific political contexts. In the chapter on Political Economy, we explain in detail the standard tools of analysis that are used in political economy and their application to well-known problems including the credibility of central banks, political business cycles, the role of union coordination on wage bargaining to solve collective action problems, and voting models. This chapter includes a self-contained introduction to much of the game theory that is needed in macro political economy.

- **to professional economists**

The applied chapters on performance and policy in Europe, Japan, and the USA and on unemployment provide overviews of recent developments and empirical analyses within the framework of contemporary monetary macroeconomics. With its emphasis on how central banks behave and, more broadly, on institutions and policies, the book can be used as a refresher for those parts of macroeconomic theory that are most relevant for economists working on real-world problems. Although we develop the 3-equation New Keynesian model as the new core of the short- to medium-run model, we show how it links to the traditional macro workhorses such as *IS/LM* and the Mundell–Fleming model.

3 Approach

We begin from the assumption that our first task is to provide a model that can be used to understand macroeconomic behaviour and policy issues. As well as being plugged into the real world, the book is firmly connected to contemporary developments in macroeconomics so it opens up access to more advanced literature and courses.

3.1 The current consensus

Consensus in macroeconomics has often been elusive but the common ground is much wider now than has been the case in previous decades. A striking illustration of this can be found in the titles of two influential articles published in the late 1990s, which argue for a similar mainstream monetary macro model: 'The New Neoclassical Synthesis and the Role of Monetary Policy' and 'The Science of Monetary Policy: A New Keynesian Perspective'.[1] We like the New Keynesian label because whereas the neoclassical aspects of the model are standard methodological features of contemporary economic modelling, the term 'Keynesian' refers to the fact that such models allow for 'prolonged departures of economic activity from its optimal level as a consequence of instability in aggregate spending'.[2]

---

[1] Goodfriend and King (1997) and Clarida, Gali, and Gertler (1999). Also Woodford (2003).
[2] Woodford (1999).

There is broad agreement that a fully satisfactory macroeconomic model should be based on optimizing behaviour by micro agents, that individual behaviour should satisfy rational expectations, and that the model should allow for wage and price rigidities. The 3-equation (*IS-PC-MR*) model is the basic analytical structure in much of contemporary macroeconomics. The three equations are derived from explicit optimizing behaviour on the part of the monetary authority, price setters, and households in imperfect product and labour markets and in the presence of some nominal rigidities.

In the mainstream macro model that we present in this book:

- Business cycles are driven by shifts in aggregate demand (and we contrast this with the Real Business Cycle model in which supply shocks drive the cycle).
- Output and employment are affected by fluctuations in aggregate demand because of nominal rigidities that prevent wages and prices adjusting rapidly.
- The central bank is modelled as actively adjusting the interest rate in response to shocks to the economy so as to achieve its inflation target.
- Aggregate demand fluctuations shift the economy away from the equilibrium rate of unemployment.
- The equilibrium rate of unemployment (ERU) is the outcome of imperfectly competitive labour and product markets—there is involuntary unemployment at the ERU.
- Supply shocks shift the equilibrium rate of unemployment (ERU) and institutional and policy differences across countries imply different ERUs.

Although the 3-equation New Keynesian model is the basis for our short- and medium-run model, we aim to analyse real-life economic performance so we include a richer treatment of macroeconomic processes than is often the case in the formal microfounded New Keynesian models. Examples include the following:

- how institutional differences in wage setting affect macroeconomic outcomes
- a number of mechanisms through which multiple equilibria can emerge and hysteresis can operate, including coordination failures and capacity utilization effects
- how the flow approach to the labour market can be integrated with the wage- and price-setting model
- explanations for acyclical or weakly procyclical real wages
- problems with using an interest rate based monetary rule
- the role of the credit channel for monetary policy
- how imperfect information produces liquidity constraints in consumption and enhances the importance of retained profits for investment behaviour
- short- and long-run effects of fiscal policy and the logic of fiscal policy rules
- the interaction of rational expectations in financial markets with slow adjustment in goods markets to produce exchange rate overshooting
- causes and consequences of segmentation in international goods markets

- short- and medium-run analysis of interdependent economies, i.e. beyond the small open economy model
- the strategic interaction between the central bank and large wage setters and the consequences for equilibrium unemployment.

In the case of each variation in institutions, policy, or behaviour, we show how the basic *IS-PC-MR* model can be modified to include it.

3.2 How to study and teach the 3-equation model

This book introduces a new graphical 'baseline' version of the 3-equation (*IS-PC-MR*) model, as its core element. In the graphical presentation of the *IS-PC-MR* model, the *IS* diagram is placed vertically above the Phillips diagram, with the monetary rule represented in the latter along with the Phillips curves. The aggregate supply side is modelled using imperfect competition and the Phillips curves are derived explicitly from the behaviour of wage and price setters. The Phillips curves are the constraint that the central bank faces when deciding how best to set policy in response to a shock to the economy. The central bank chooses its preferred combination of output and inflation along the Phillips curve that it faces. It then uses the *IS* curve to calculate what interest rate it must set so that aggregate demand moves to the desired level.

The *IS-PC-MR* graphical analysis is particularly useful for explaining the optimizing behaviour of the central bank and for analysing its reactions to a wide variety of disturbances to the economy. Users can see and remember readily where the key relationships come from and are therefore able to vary the assumptions about the private sector or the behaviour of the policy maker. For example, we can see what happens if the central bank is made independent and is more averse to inflation than the government or if wages are more responsive to unemployment (e.g. if we want to compare two countries, in one of which unions are important and in the other they are not).

In order to use the graphical model, it is necessary to think about the economics behind the three key relationships and the processes of adjustment. One of the reasons *IS-LM* got a bad name is that it too frequently became an exercise in mechanical curve shifting. In the framework presented here, in order to work through the adjustment process, you have to engage in the same forward-looking thinking as the policy maker. We also encourage the sketching of the time paths of key variables as the economy moves from one equilibrium to another.

3.2.1 Why diagrams are essential

Despite the development of the 3-equation (*IS-PC-MR*) model, Hicks's famous *IS-LM* model of 1937 supplemented by Friedman's expectations-augmented Phillips curve is often the basic model taught to undergraduates (often referred to as *IS-LM-AS* or *IS-LM-PC*). But while it provides a basic general equilibrium macro model, key components have been sidelined by developments in economic theory and practice, and the 3-equation model has superceded it in graduate teaching. Undoubtedly the longevity of *IS-LM* has been due to the fact that its graphical method provides students with an integrated model that they can manipulate. Although the use of equations in intermediate macroeconomics texts has increased, diagrams retain a central place. In our view, this is for good reason. When developing an understanding of economics, it is very important not only to understand about equilibria and comparative statics but also to discuss how the economy might adjust from one equilibrium to another. To do this mathematically diverts attention from economics to mathematical methods. Diagrams help to develop economic intuition, i.e. they help you to get a feel for how the economy will respond to different shocks and policies within a systematic framework.

The book is based on the assumption that different readers gain different insights from mathematical, verbal, and graphical reasoning. So the book makes use of them all. Our view is that they reinforce each other, but it is quite possible, for example, to use the book with little emphasis on the equations.

3.3 Dealing with the open economy

An important characteristic of the book is that it offers a comprehensive and coherent treatment of the open economy. We move from the Mundell–Fleming model with fixed prices in the small open economy to an integrated approach to medium term inflation adjustments and then to interdependent economies. Again, we make use of a core diagram to provide a unified organizing framework for dealing with both theoretical and applied questions.

3.4 How to use the model to answer new questions

Once the open economy model has been covered, you will be able to use it to answer questions like this one: what is the likely effect of a country's involvement in a war abroad? The first step is to identify the nature of the shock and then to work out the new short-run equilibrium and the likely path of adjustment to it. How will the private sector respond and should policy be adjusted in the light of the shock? This is an aggregate demand shock: government purchases rise and this will push employment and output up. The consequences for inflation will depend on where unemployment is relative to the equilibrium rate. This will also feed into the central bank's decision about whether monetary policy should be adjusted (Chapter 5). The parallel development of the short- and medium-run model for the open economy in Chapters 9 and 10 allows the open economy aspects to be incorporated: e.g. what is the import content of government war-related purchases? The exchange rate regime in place will affect the analysis of the short-run impact (how will the exchange rate react under flexible rates?), whether consideration of central bank behaviour is relevant, and how inflation will respond. Different methods of financing the war-related expenditure may affect its impact on the economy and the discussion of tax versus bond based deficit financing in Chapter 6 is relevant. Next, we should consider whether involvement in the war could have medium-run consequences, i.e. for the supply-side of the economy (Chapter 4). One line of argument would follow from the assessment that the war may affect international commodities' prices, e.g. by interrupting the supply of oil. This would produce a negative external supply shock as analysed in Chapter 11.

4 Prerequisites and technical level

We assume readers have a familiarity with macroeconomics such as provided by a principles course. We use algebra and some simple calculus but explain the methods and the results verbally and graphically as well. We introduce the use of logs and exponential functions at the beginning of Chapter 13, because they are used in the theory of growth. Chapters 15 and 16 are designed more for a graduate audience and more maths is used. However, verbal and graphical explanations are still provided.

5   Chapter by chapter structure

CHAPTER 1 provides motivation for the main models presented in the book by identifying a set of key questions in macroeconomics. Since the book aims to show how the models can be brought to bear on contemporary performance and policy issues, cross-country data is presented—both in relation to the short- and medium-run issues and in terms of growth and the world distribution of income.

PART 1 consists of five chapters, which present the short- and medium-run macro model. CHAPTERS 2 and 3 set out the building blocks of the macro models beginning with aggregate demand and supply and then incorporating inflation, the Phillips curve, and the monetary rule. By the end of CHAPTER 3, the *IS-PC-MR* model is in place. The mainstream model of business cycles as fluctuations around the equilibrium rate of unemployment driven by aggregate demand shocks is contrasted with the real business cycle model. In the real business cycle model, supply shocks produce business cycles and over the course of the cycle, the fluctuations in employment reflect the choices made by workers responding to changing opportunities in the labour market.

The major institutional and policy determinants of equilibrium unemployment are analysed in CHAPTER 4. These include how wages and prices are set under imperfect competition, the influence on equilibrium unemployment of government policies, the role of different institutional arrangements for wage setting, explanations for hysteresis, and how the flow approach to the labour market can be integrated with the model of wage and price setting to enrich the analysis of equilibrium unemployment. The central bank's monetary policy rule is derived as an optimal policy rule in CHAPTER 5 and the problems of inflation bias and time inconsistency are explained. In CHAPTER 6, the macroeconomic roles of fiscal policy are presented: the provision of automatic stabilizers, the use of discretionary policy to complement monetary policy in stabilization, and the requirement to maintain a sustainable burden of public debt.

PART 2 has two chapters that deal with consumption, investment, money, and finance. The aim is to show how standard microfounded models influence the interpretation of the *IS*, the *LM*, and the *MR*. In CHAPTER 7, there is a more detailed analysis of consumption and investment behaviour. In each case the optimizing behaviour of forward-looking households or firms is used to derive respectively a consumption and an investment function, which are compared with the simple macroeconomic functions used in PART 1. In CHAPTER 8, there is a more detailed analysis of the different kinds of assets in the economy and the role of information problems in explaining the existence and role of financial institutions.

In PART 3, an integrated model for the analysis of the open economy is developed. CHAPTER 9 is concerned with the short-run analysis of a small open economy. It presents the traditional Mundell–Fleming model and incorporates financial openness by assuming perfect capital mobility and asset substitutability in the form of the uncovered interest parity condition. Price setting in the open economy, exchange rate overshooting, and the implications of dropping the assumptions of a small economy, perfect capital mobility, and perfect asset substitutability are examined. CHAPTER 10 extends the model from the short to the medium run by introducing the analysis of inflation. We use a core open economy diagram to show the goods market equilibrium (i.e. the open economy *IS*), the supply side (i.e. the equilibrium rate of unemployment in the open economy), and the trade balance. This graphical approach allows us:

(1) to analyse the contrasting short-run responses of the small open economy under fixed and flexible exchange rates to a given fiscal or monetary policy change or aggregate demand shock;

(2) to show that the medium-run equilibrium with constant inflation following a given shock is independent of the exchange rate regime.

CHAPTER 11 shows the versatility of the graphical approach by looking at aggregate demand, external trade and external supply shocks in the open economy. It also extends the *IS-PC-MR* model to the open economy showing how an inflation-targeting central bank responds to an aggregate demand shock. CHAPTER 12 goes beyond the typical scope of a macro course by looking at the analysis of interdependent economies.

In PART 4, there are two chapters on growth that provide a thorough treatment of both exogenous and endogenous growth models. CHAPTER 13 concentrates on the theory and empirics of the Solow–Swan model of exogenous growth and the issues surrounding convergence. CHAPTER 14 provides an introduction to a range of endogenous and Schumpeterian models of growth. We compare different channels through which endogenous growth may operate—knowledge spillovers from the accumulation of physical capital, investment in human capital, and investment in R&D. We show how the Schumpeterian model can help us to understand how institutions affect growth, both in countries at the world technology frontier and in poor countries.

PART 5 consists of two chapters: the microfoundations of the New Keynesian model in CHAPTER 15 and a chapter on political economy. CHAPTER 15 provides a systematic microfounded treatment of the key features of the New Keynesian model. Within the same framework, we investigate several models that produce multiple medium-run unemployment equilibria. These include models of hysteresis processes, and models in which workers value not only consumption and leisure but also fairness, which results in the existence of a range of equilibrium employment rates. CHAPTER 16 is on Political Economy. This focuses on the use of game theory to analyse government and central bank behaviour. Both chapters are self-contained in the sense that they do not assume prior knowledge of specific models or techniques, other than simple calculus. All of the game theory needed for CHAPTER 16 is provided in the chapter.

The book finishes up in PART 6 with two applied chapters. Although reference is made throughout the book to examples of particular historical episodes and to empirical evidence, the aim of PART 6 is to show how the models in the book can be used in a sustained exploration of performance and policy. CHAPTER 17 takes the period from 1990 and uses the models to provide an interpretation of major performance and policy issues in a set of OECD economies: from German unification, through the creation of EMU, to British economic performance, the US boom, and the Japanese doldrums. CHAPTER 18 focuses on a key performance problem—that of unemployment—and shows the usefulness of the models in helping to understand the empirical patterns and widely cited empirical studies. The applied chapters do not rely on the more advanced material in PART 5.

On a few occasions more difficult material is presented that may be skipped without loss of continuity. These sections are indicated by an asterisk.

Two kinds of exercises are provided at the end of each chapter—a set of so-called checklist questions that test for understanding of the key concepts in the chapter by focusing on common confusions and misunderstandings and a second set of exercises, some of which are open-ended questions for discussion and others are problems. Further material is available on the book's website and we encourage other instructors to provide teaching material related to the book that can be made available to all on the website. This book can be used as a core text in a number of different courses and some illustrative examples are provided below.

Chapters

1   Motivation for Macroeconomic Models
2   Aggregate Demand, Aggregate Supply, and Business Cycles
3   Inflation, Unemployment, and Monetary Rules
4   Labour Markets and Supply-Side Policies
5   Monetary Policy
6   Fiscal Policy
7   Consumption and Investment
8   Money and Finance
9   The Open Economy in the Short Run
10   Inflation and Unemployment in the Open Economy
11   Shocks and Policy Responses in the Open Economy
12   Interdependent Economies
13   Exogenous Growth Theory
14   Endogenous and Schumpeterian Growth
15   New Keynesian Microfoundations
16   Political Economy
17   Performance and Policy in Europe, the USA, and Japan
18   Unemployment: Institutions, Shocks, and Policies

Possible course structures

Intermediate macroeconomics

Core macroeconomic model: *Chapters 1–4*
Monetary and fiscal policy: *Chapters 5, 6*
Consumption, investment and money: *Selective use of Chapters 7, 8*
Open economy: *Chapters 9 (except section 6), 10, 11*
Reference to applications: *Chapters 17, 18*
Introduction to growth theory and facts: *Chapter 1 section 2 and selective use of Chapter 13*

Advanced macroeconomics

New Keynesian microfoundations: *Chapter 15*
Microfoundations of consumption and investment: *Selective use of Chapters 7, 8*
Microfoundations of credit constraints (Townsend model): *Chapter 8 section 3.2*
Exogenous growth and convergence: *Chapter 13*
Endogenous and Schumpeterian growth: *Chapter 14*
Topics in political economy: Selective use of *Chapter 16*

Labour economics: macro

Competitive and imperfectly competitive labour markets: *Chapter 2 sections 5, 6*
Labour markets and supply side policies: *Chapter 4*
Efficiency wages: *Appendix to Chapter 15*
Microfoundations: *Selective use of Chapter 15*
Empirical and policy analysis: *Chapter 18*

Money and banking

Money and finance: *Chapter 8*
Review of money in short- and medium-run macro models: *Chapter 2 section 3; Chapter 3 sections 2, 3*
Monetary policy: *Chapter 5*
Examples of monetary policy-making from Europe, USA, and Japan: *Chapter 17*
Modelling time-inconsistency as a game: *Chapter 16 section 1*

International monetary economics

Review of the open economy model: *Chapters 9–11*
Extension to the large open economy, imperfect capital mobility, and imperfect asset substitutability: *Chapter 9 section 6*
Modelling interdependent economies: *Chapter 12, Chapter 16 section 5*
Reference to applications: *Chapters 17*

Growth

Introduction to growth theory and facts: *Chapter 1 section 2*
The concept of the growth rate: *Chapter 13 section 1*
The Solow–Swan model and steady state growth: *Chapter 13 sections 2, 4* (including technical progress)
Growth accounting: *Chapter 13 section 3*
Theory and empirical analysis of convergence: *Chapter 13 section 5*
Models of endogenous growth: *Chapter 14 section 1*
Schumpeterian growth models and applications: *Chapter 14 section 2*

Unemployment

Review of core model: *Chapter 2 section 5, 6; Chapter 4; Chapter 10*
Models of hysteresis: *Chapter 15 sections 7–9*
Applied analysis of unemployment in OECD economies: *Chapter 18*

Economics of OECD

Introduction: *Chapter 1*

Review of core model: *Chapters 3–6*

Review of open economy macroeconomics: *Chapters 9–11*

Europe: *Chapter 17 sections 1–3; Chapter 18*

USA: *Chapter 17 section 4; Chapter 18*

Japan: *Chapter 17 section 5*

Macroeconomics of EMU

Introduction to the analysis of a currency union: *Chapter 11 section 6*

Historical background: *Chapter 17 section 2*

Monetary policy: *Chapters 3, 5; Chapter 17 section 3*

Fiscal rules: *Chapter 6 section 5*

Deeper analysis: *Chapter 12 section 4*

Political economy

Self-contained introduction to game theory methods used in political economy: *Chapter 16*

Monetary policy and time-inconsistency: *Chapter 16 section 1*

Fiscal and monetary policy conflicts: *Chapter 16 section 2*

Reputation: *Chapter 16 section 3*

Voting games and political business cycle models: *Chapter 16 section 4*

Games between interdependent economies: *Chapter 16 section 5*

■ MACROECONOMICS

"At last, an advanced undergraduate book which maps theory to facts. The theory, from the new Keynesian model of fluctuations to Schumpeterian models of growth, is sound. The applications, from European unemployment to the Japanese slump, highly revealing. You will enjoy every chapter, and become a good macroeconomist in the process."

Olivier Blanchard, Class of 1941 Professor, Massachusetts Institute of Technology

"The best way to learn economics is to have a textbook which develops a theoretical framework interactively with practical questions. *Macroeconomics: Imperfections, Institutions and Policies* does just this. The book is based on the mainstream monetary macro model which is now widely used by both academics and policy-makers. In a straightforward manner, it shows how this model can be used to address an enormous variety of practical questions without heavy use of mathematical technique. This is modern macroeconomics for undergraduates, post-graduates and business economists alike."

Stephen Nickell, School Professor of Economics, LSE;
Member of the Monetary Policy Committee, Bank of England

"When teaching intermediate macroeconomics in Harvard during the past years, I deeply felt that existing textbooks were all lacking: 1) proper microeconomic foundations linking important notions such as the Keynesian consumption function, the investment accelerator, the Phillips curve, the possibility of persistent (involuntary) unemployment, to precise sources of imperfections in the product, labor, or financial markets; 2) a suitable treatment of growth theory that can shed light on observed convergence and divergence patterns across countries and also on how growth policies should be designed—or what they can achieve—in various countries at different stages of development. Being the first comprehensive attempt at filling these gaps, the Carlin–Soskice macroeconomics textbook should be used by any instructor who wants to bring her students to the frontier of modern macroeconomics while at the same time remaining fully accessible to a broad undergraduate audience."

Philippe Aghion, Robert C. Waggoner Professor of Economics, Harvard University

"Imperfect competition, knowledge-based growth, inflation-targeting central banks and many other central features of modern economic systems have recently been integrated into the heart of macroeconomic theory. Carlin and Soskice do the profession a great service by writing a textbook that makes these developments accessible to undergraduates. The book presents macroeconomics at its best—as a useful framework for analyzing important questions."

Peter Howitt, Lyn Crost Professor of Social Sciences, Brown University

"What makes Carlin and Soskice invaluable is both their clarity and their commitment to helping the reader understand the intuitions that lie behind the models. Furthermore, there is constantly an attempt to make the work relevant to practical questions of public policy. . . .They tackle the impact of German Reunification, EMU, British economic performance, the 1990s US boom, and the long-standing Japanese recession. There is a major final chapter addressing the issues of unemployment, especially among the larger nations of Continental Europe. The authors approach these questions through the penetrating analytical lens of their framework, critically address the empirical evidence and come up with sometimes novel conclusions to the conventional wisdom."

Professor John Van Reenen, Director, Centre for Economic Performance,
London School of Economics

"Macroeconomics needs to be exciting and contemporary. Too often it becomes an area of difficulty and confusion for students. This book is to be welcomed for its very clear vision of what contemporary macroeconomics is about and its careful exposition leading the student to this."

Dr Mary Gregory, Oxford University

■ ACKNOWLEDGEMENTS

This book has been a major undertaking and we have relied on the contributions of many people. Our greatest debt is to Andrew Glyn for his unwavering support for the project and for his intellectual input.

Matthew Harding is co-author of the two chapters on economic growth, provided research assistance with Chapters 1 and 8, and contributed a great deal of useful criticism and new perspectives on many other parts of the book. Friends and colleagues have generously provided us with feedback, suggestions, and ways to improve the analysis. For help and encouragement over a number of years, we are particularly grateful to Nicholas Rau, as well as to Christopher Allsopp and David Vines. At a late stage David Romer played an invaluable role in clarifying some key arguments. We have received comments and suggestions from, or had valuable discussions with, Outi Aarnio, Philippe Aghion, Gian Luigi Albano, Marcus Alexander, Bruno Amable, Aqib Aslam, Orazio Attanasio, Andrea Bassanini, V. Bhaskar, Richard Blundell, Andrea Boltho, Maxim Bouev, Helen Callaghan, Robin Cubitt, Thomas Cusack, Michel De Vroey, Adriana Di Liberto, Steve Dowrick, John Driffill, Christian Dustmann, Donatella Gatti, Giacomo De Giorgi, Georg von Graevenitz, Liam Graham, Rachel Griffith, Bob Hancke, Bernd Hayo, Cameron Hepburn, Steiner Holden, David Howell, Steffen Huck, Torben Iversen, Esteban Jaimovich, Sujit Kapadia, Campbell Leith, Sara Lemos, Andrew Lilico, Deborah Mabbett, Gareth Macartney, Steve Machin, Massimo Di Matteo, Colin Mayer, Ian McDonald, Costas Meghir, Edward Nelson, Tom Ogg, Terry O'Shaughnessy, Nicholas Oulton, Nicola Pavoni, Malcolm Pemberton, Laura Povoledo, Daniel Rogger, Bob Rowthorn, Paul Seabright, Stephen Smith, Margaret Stevens, Jérôme Vandenbussche, and Donald Verry. Andrew Lilico provided research assistance on Chapters 7 and 8 and Giacomo De Giorgi completed and checked the outline answers to the questions.

Andrew Glyn, Nick Bloom, Steve Dowrick, David Howell, and Luca Nunziata kindly made their data available to us.

William Wachtmeister edited most of the chapters and greatly improved their readability. Martin Davies has read the text from beginning to end and picked up many errors and confusions.

For their assistance with technical matters in computing and graphics, we are indebted to Georg von Graevenitz and John McGlynn. Tessa and Jonathan Glyn and Joan Carlin worked on the preparation of the final manuscript. The administrative staff in the Economics Department at UCL have supported the project in countless ways. Many thanks also to the Wissenschaftszentrum für Sozialforschung in Berlin, where we had many conversations about the basic ideas, and to Hannelore Minzlaff and Ilona Köhler for splendid assistance.

Many cohorts of students at UCL have shaped the book through their questions, their frustrations and their enthusiastic course evaluations. This is equally true of several cohorts of graduate students at the Scuola Superiore Sant'Anna in Pisa. Students in universities in several countries have been using the draft chapters available on the internet and have sent in queries and suggestions.

Our editor Tim Page at OUP sympathetically allowed us the time to work out our approach to our satisfaction. We received excellent reviewers' reports, which have improved the text markedly. We are very grateful to Nicola Bateman for her efficiency and responsiveness during the production process.

Andrew, Tessa, and Jonathan Glyn have remained cheerfully optimistic that the book would get finished and have done a great job at keeping work in its proper perspective. Niki Lacey provided a delightful and intellectually stimulating environment in London, helped from time to time by Juliet, Dan, William, Lou, and Gill.

■ CONTENTS

LIST OF FIGURES

■ LIST OF TABLES

◼ ABBREVIATIONS

AGR   annual growth rate

ALMP   active labour market policies

APK   average product of capital

APL   average product of labour

APR   annual percentage rate

BP   balance of payments

BR   best response

CB   central bank

CCA   common currency area

CRS   constant returns to scale

DRS   decreasing returns to scale

DSGE   Dynamic Stochastic General Equilibrium

EAPC   expectations augmented Phillips curve

ECB   European Central Bank

EMU   European Monetary Union

ERM   Exchange Rate Mechanism

ERU   equilibrium rate of unemployment

EU   European Union

GDP   gross domestic product

GEMU   German Economic and Monetary Union

GNP   gross national product

GSP   gross state product

ICT   information and communications technology

IMF   International Monetary Fund

IRS   increasing returns to scale

LERU   long-run equilibrium rate of unemployment

LOP   law of one price

LTU   long-term unemployment

MIT   Massachusetts Institute of Technology

MPK   marginal product of capital

MPL   marginal product of labour

MR   monetary rule

MRW	Mankiw, Romer, and Weil
MV	market value
NAIRU	non-accelerating inflation rate of unemployment
nbfi	non-bank financial institution
NCBM	neoclassical benchmark model
NHW	non-human wealth
NKPC	New Keynesian Phillips curve
NMM	new macro model
OCA	optimal currency area
OECD	Organization for Economic Cooperation and Development
PBE	Perfect Bayesian Equilibrium
PC	Phillips curve
p.a.	per annum
p.c.	per capita
PFPR	prudent fiscal policy rule
PIH	permanent income hypothesis
PPP	purchasing power parity
PS	price setting
PSD	public sector deficit
PWT	Penn World Tables
R&D	research and development
RBC	real business cycle
RULC	relative unit labour cost
RWR	real wage rigidity
SAS	short-run aggregate supply
SBTP	skill-biased technical progress
SGP	Stability and Growth Pact
SGPE	subgame perfect equilibrium
SIPC	Sticky Information Phillips curve
TFP	total factor productivity
UCL	University College London
UIP	uncovered interest parity
VAT	value added tax
WS	wage setting
ZIRP	zero interest rate policy

1 Motivation for Macroeconomic Models

This book aims to provide models that can be used to understand a wide range of macro-economic behaviour and policy issues and to explain how different countries perform and how performance changes over time. We use two broad kinds of models: one is an integrated model for analysing the output, unemployment, inflation, exchange rate nexus of problems and the other is used for analysing growth. The choice of models is motivated by their usefulness in framing key questions that face macroeconomists. The questions include:

- How are the levels of output and employment determined and why do they fluctuate?
- Why does inflation occur and when should we worry about it?
- How does government policy affect inflation and unemployment?
- Why is unemployment higher for lengthy periods of time in some countries than in others?
- How do trade, international financial markets, and exchange rates affect employment and inflation?
- Why are some countries rich and others poor?
- Why are some countries catching up with the leaders and others not?

To explain how episodes of high unemployment or runaway inflation can occur requires us to understand how the wage and price setters in the economy behave as well as the government and the central bank. Countries differ widely in how their labour markets are organized—how important are these differences for explaining patterns of unemployment? Governments differ in how they manage economic policy. In many countries, monetary policy has been separated from the government and delegated to an independent central bank. A dozen European countries have dispensed with national monetary policy altogether by joining the European Monetary Union. In many countries, unions and employers' organizations are involved in wage setting. How would we expect these differences in institutional arrangements to influence performance?

In the analysis of growth, some models emphasize the role of the accumulation of capital—both physical capital and human capital. Others highlight the importance of innovative entrepreneurial activities. To account for the vast differences in the success with which countries have raised living standards, the role of economic policy and institutional arrangements for promoting investment and entrepreneurial activity needs to be addressed.

In the rest of this chapter, we put flesh on the bones of the questions posed above by first setting out in a schematic way how to model the short- to medium-run macro-economy. We motivate the core components of the model with empirical data showing cross-country trends in the key variables. In the second section, we do a parallel exercise for the long-run analysis by presenting some stylized facts and sketching the main ways that growth has been modelled.

1 Output, unemployment, and inflation

The aim of this section together with Chapters 2 to 4 is to set out a macroeconomic model for short- and medium-run analysis that is both reasonably simple and reasonably realistic. It has to be realistic if it is to provide a framework for analysing real-world macroeconomic problems. The model is a simple version of the New Keynesian model that is used in contemporary central banks and in modern monetary macroeconomics. This so-called 3-equation model consists of the *IS* curve that models aggregate demand, the *PC* or Phillips curve that represents the imperfectly competitive supply side of the economy, and the *MR* or monetary rule that captures the behaviour of an inflation-targeting central bank.

The overview seeks to show how the different elements of short- and medium-run macroeconomics fit together to influence the level of output and the rate of inflation. In the three chapters that follow, we present the bare bones of a closed economy. We give a basic rationale for the main features of macroeconomic behaviour on the demand and supply sides of the economy. This provides us with the tools for analysing business cycles and trends in unemployment.

The model that we set out in this section and in the next three chapters will allow us to begin to answer questions like these:

- How does a change in consumer confidence due to a collapse in the stock market affect the economy?

- What is the impact on output and inflation of changes in government policy such as changes in taxation or government expenditure or a change in monetary policy or in employment regulation?

- If the internet and globalization affect product market competition, what would we expect to be the macroeconomic impact?

- How do institutions like unions or an independent central bank affect inflation or unemployment?

What do we mean by 'impact on the economy' or 'macroeconomic implications'? We mean the impact on output, employment, the price level, and inflation. Our basic model must therefore provide us with the means to answer the following questions:

- Question 1. How is the *actual* or current level of output and employment in the economy determined?

- Question 2. What determines the level of employment in the economy at which inflation is stable? We call this the medium-run *equilibrium* level of employment.

- Question 3. How and why does the economy tend to adjust from its current position towards the medium-run equilibrium and what factors influence the speed and smoothness of adjustment?

Once we have a systematic way of answering these three questions, we can tackle a whole range of disturbances to the economy and assess the policy options available to the government or the central bank. There is, however, an important caveat. The real-world economies that we are interested in are open ones because they trade with other countries and are connected to international financial markets. This means that it is often unrealistic to use a closed economy model when dealing with an applied problem. On the other hand, we can easily lose sight of the wood for the trees if too many facets are introduced at once. The model is extended to the open economy in Chapters 9–11.

1.1 Assumptions and terminology

Before we begin, it is useful to clarify some assumptions and terms. On a first reading, the significance of all the distinctions that are drawn here may not be apparent. But reference back to this section may prove useful when reading through the overview of the model.

One special feature of macroeconomics is that the behaviour of a number of different kinds of economic actor or agent—such as households, firms, governments, unions, central banks—has to be taken into account simultaneously. Individuals make decisions to enter the labour force, to save, and to spend. They respond to job offers, to the interest rate, to changes in their current income level, and in the value of their accumulated wealth. Firms alter levels of production as demand for their output fluctuates, they set prices, and make investment decisions. Firms may also set wages or do so through joint negotiations with workers or with unions. Both households and firms will be sensitive to government tax, spending, and interest rate policy. And their behaviour will reflect not only the current state of economic variables but also how they expect the level of these variables—such as the interest rate, the tax rate, or wages—to move in the future.

In macroeconomics, the *aggregate supply side* refers to the supply of goods and services. The supply side consists of:

- the factors of production, which are 'labour' and 'capital'. The supply of and demand for labour and capital are part of the supply side.
- the technology through which the inputs of labour and capital are transformed into output.
- the way in which the incomes (wages and profits) that workers and firms receive are determined.

The *aggregate demand side* refers to the aggregate—or economy-wide—demand for goods and services. The aggregate demand for goods and services consists of:

- consumption demand
- investment demand
- demand stemming from government purchases.

Consumption demand refers to the expenditure by individuals on goods and services—spending is on both durable products such as a music system or a sofa and on non-durable products such as a concert or a loaf of bread.

Investment demand refers to expenditure on capital goods (machinery, equipment, and buildings). Most of the additions to the total amount (or stock) of machinery, equipment, and buildings in the economy reflect the investment expenditure by firms, where investment also includes the building up of inventories of materials or of finished goods. But new housing and spending by the government on machinery, equipment, and buildings (e.g. infrastructure such as roads or new school buildings) are also part of total investment.

Government spending on salaries (e.g. teachers, police) and purchases of goods (e.g. hospital supplies, ammunition for the army) and of services (e.g. contract cleaning and waste disposal) constitute 'government demand'.

Because the real-world economy is complex, it is necessary to make many simplifying assumptions when building a macroeconomic model. One method of simplifying is to think of some kinds of decisions and changes in economic variables taking place in the *short run*, others in the *medium run*, and yet others in the *long run*. Although there are no hard and fast rules about how the short, medium, and long run should be defined, we shall often use the following distinctions.

We think of the *short run* as the period during which output and employment can change but before prices and wages respond to the changes in output and employment. It is a familiar feature of the world that wages and prices are usually adjusted periodically, e.g. once or twice a year, rather than in response to changes in demand. We can therefore devote all of our attention in the short-run analysis to the determinants of the level of aggregate demand, output, and employment, assuming that wages and prices are given. When we say 'prices and wages are given', this is a way of referring to two short-run situations. Most straightforwardly, it means that prices and wages are fixed; the terms 'sticky' and 'rigid' are used interchangeably with 'fixed'. Assuming that prices and wages are given can also refer to the situation in which prices and wages are rising by a constant amount each year—e.g. by 2% per annum. In both of these cases, the key assumption is that in the short run the level of wages and prices or the rate of change of wages and prices does not respond to changes in the level of output. This assumption means that in the short-run analysis, it is aggregate demand that determines the level of output and employment. The short run should be thought of in terms of months rather than years.

We think of the *medium run* as the period during which wages and prices can respond to changes in output and employment and in which the supply side of the economy adjusts to establish a medium-run equilibrium in which inflation is constant once again. For the most part, we continue to assume (as for the short run) that the capital stock of the economy and the labour force are fixed. This means that the total amount of machinery and equipment is constant and so is the level of technology. We do not investigate changes in the population growth rate or allow for migration. This means that the central component of the supply side is the *labour market*—i.e. the deployment of the existing labour force on the existing capital stock in the economy. In the medium-run analysis, therefore, our attention is focused on the behaviour of wage and price setters: at what level of output and employment will wage and price setters be in equilibrium in the sense that there is no upward or downward pressure on wages or prices?

We shall see that it is reasonably straightforward to incorporate in the medium-run analysis an investigation of the *consequences* of changes in technology such as changes in productivity growth. But to investigate the *causes* of productivity growth and why it might change, we need to extend the analysis to the *long run*. We turn our attention to this in the second section of this chapter, which introduces growth theory. In the long-run analysis, we allow for growth in the population, in the physical capital stock (machinery and equipment), human capital stock (skills of workers), and improvements in technology.

At various points in the book, we make reference to the case of *perfectly competitive* markets. But we often work with a more general model with market imperfections. We interpret market imperfections very broadly to include not only the exercise of market power but also the consequences of the lack of complete information, such as the inability of employers to observe how hard a worker is working. For some questions we shall see that both models work in essentially the same way, but for other questions the results are different.

In this introductory section, we provide a bird's eye view of how the different bits of short- and medium-run macroeconomics fit together. We focus on macroeconomic outcomes in terms of output, unemployment, and inflation; and on the role of government fiscal policies (i.e. spending and taxation) and monetary policies. The aim here is to convey the general idea rather than to set out every step of the argument. The details are provided in the next three chapters. When working through the detail, it may be useful to return to the overview to see the bigger picture.

1.2 Fluctuations in output and employment

One concern of macroeconomists is with the causes and consequences of short-run fluctuations in economic activity. By short-run, we mean year-to-year or quarter-to-quarter fluctuations. Fig. 1.1 shows the quarterly growth rate of output for the United States since the end of the Second World War. Booms with strong growth of output and recessions with sharp contractions are evident: the swing from peak to trough and back again is called the business cycle. The figure also shows a comparison of annual growth rates of output for the United States and France from 1981 to 2003. A similar pattern of booms and recessions is revealed for both countries, but it is also clear that the peaks and troughs of the business cycle do not always coincide for these two economies.

In the short run, the level of output in the economy depends on the level of aggregate demand for goods and services. The standard '*IS/LM* model' is a useful starting point for understanding the factors that influence the level of aggregate demand and hence the level of output and employment in the short run. As we shall see, it is reasonable to assume that prices and wages are given in the short run. This means that we can concentrate on how quantities (i.e. output and employment) adjust to changes in the demand for goods and services. As we noted above, it is convenient in a macro model to look at the factors that determine aggregate consumption expenditure (by thinking about the influences on the spending and savings decisions of consumers) and aggregate investment expenditures

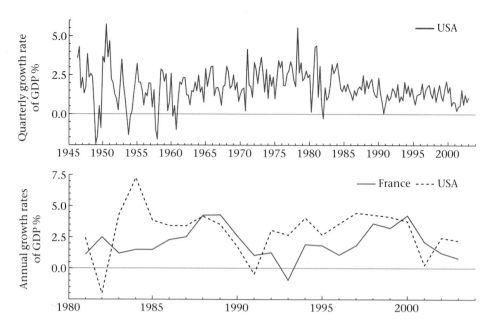

Figure 1.1 Quarterly growth rate of GDP for the United States GDP, 1945 to 2003 and annual growth rates of GDP for France and USA, 1981 to 2003

Source: US Dept of Commerce: Bureau of Economic Analysis: National Accounts Data, INSEE, and EIU.

(by identifying the determinants of the decisions of firms to change their stock of capital equipment). The government is a direct source of aggregate demand through its purchases of goods and services. The government authorities (including the central bank) have an indirect influence over the level of aggregate demand by their choice of tax rates and the interest rate.

1.3 Unemployment: international comparisons

Economists and policy makers are interested in what determines output and employment not only in the short run but over longer periods as well. We focus on the latter by looking at the trends presented in Fig. 1.2. Two questions arise immediately: why do different countries appear to have different unemployment rates and why are there persistent trends in unemployment in some countries?

The top panel of Fig. 1.2 shows the monthly unemployment rate for the USA from 1948 to 2003. The lower panel shows the annual unemployment rate for the United States and the average for the four large European economies (Germany, France, the UK, and Italy) from 1960 to 2003. There has been a trend of rising unemployment from the 1970s to the 1990s in Europe, which is reflected by the data for the big four European economies. There is a striking difference between the evolution of European and US unemployment. The idea of a roughly constant equilibrium unemployment rate looks more plausible for the United States than for Europe. In the United States, unemployment fluctuates a lot

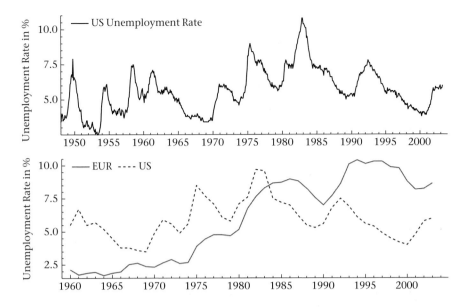

Figure 1.2 Monthly unemployment rate for the USA 1948 to 2003 and comparison of the unemployment rates for the USA and Europe, 1960 to 2003

Source: Federal Reserve Economic Data: St. Louis Fed and US Bureau of Labor Statistics: Foreign Labor Statistics.

Note: EUR is average of France, Italy, UK, and Germany (West Germany before 1991).

but it appears to have fluctuated around a rate of about 6% since the 1960s. European unemployment was well below that of the USA until the 1980s.

Fig. 1.3 shows the unemployment rates for France, Germany, Italy, Japan, Sweden, the UK, and the USA for the same time period (using the USA as a comparison benchmark in each picture). All of these countries exhibit significant variability in their unemployment experience over the past four decades. The UK followed the same trend rise in unemployment as much of Europe (France, Germany, Italy) from the early 1970s to the early 1980s. But since then, there has been a downward trend that was interrupted but not halted by the recession of the early 1990s. By contrast in Sweden, there was very low unemployment to the end of the 1980s followed by a dramatic jump in unemployment to the European average in the early 1990s, which has subsequently been reversed. Japan exhibited extremely low levels of unemployment compared to the other countries until the early 1990s, while recent years have seen a fairly strong ascending trend. These charts show changes in unemployment that persist over time and big differences across countries. They motivate the notion of a medium-run unemployment rate, in which changes over time and differences across countries are associated with variations in supply-side structure.

1.4 Modelling medium-run unemployment

We begin by contrasting how the aggregate supply side is presented in the competitive model and in the more general model with market imperfections. Many readers will be

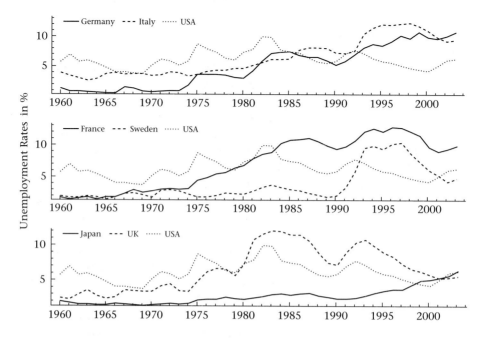

Figure 1.3 Unemployment rates for some of the major OECD economies, 1960 to 2003

Source: US Bureau of Labor Statistics: Foreign Labor Statistics.

Note: Germany is West Germany before 1991 and United Germany from 1991.

familiar with competitive models from their knowledge of microeconomics. In a competitive model of the labour market, we say that the labour market clears. This means that the real wage (i.e. the value of the wage in terms of the consumer goods it can buy) adjusts so that the demand for labour by firms is equal to the supply of labour by individuals. At the market-clearing real wage, firms are in equilibrium in the sense that at the prevailing real wage, it would not be profitable for them to employ any more labour. Conversely if they employed less labour, then they could increase their profits by raising employment. At the market-clearing real wage, there is also an equilibrium from the point of view of workers. At the prevailing real wage, more labour will not be supplied; equally if less labour was supplied, workers would be better off if they supplied more.

The only kind of unemployment that exists in the competitive equilibrium is *voluntary* unemployment. If workers derive more utility (i.e. happiness, pleasure) from being unemployed given the existing real wage than they would from working then they *choose* not to work and this is voluntary unemployment. The unemployed would prefer the leisure and no wage as compared with the alternative of working and receiving the prevailing real wage. The voluntarily unemployed may be searching for a job offering better wages and or conditions.

We shall call the rate of unemployment that corresponds to the market-clearing level of employment in the economy (i.e. when labour supply is equal to labour demand) the *competitive equilibrium rate of unemployment*.

1.4.1 **Imperfect competition model**

In contrast to the competitive model, we use a more general model in which the equilibrium in the labour market does not necessarily coincide with market clearing. One important consequence is that there can be *involuntary* unemployment even at equilibrium. In the competitive model, wages and prices emerge through the process of market clearing. For example, in a perfectly competitive product market, each firm faces the market price and chooses its level of output where its marginal cost is equal to the market price. By contrast, in the imperfect competition model, we can talk of wage-*setters* and price-*setters*. If there is imperfect competition in the product market, this means that prices are set by firms and firms earn 'supernormal' profits because they have some market power. This means that the price is set by the firm above the level of its marginal cost: the difference between the price and the marginal cost is the profit the firm makes.

With imperfect competition in the labour market, money wages will be set by employers or by unions or by both through negotiation. The importance of unions in wage setting in OECD countries is demonstrated in Table 1.1. Across the 30 countries that belong to the OECD, the average percentage of employees with wages covered by collective bargaining agreements is 60%. Clearly the USA is atypical in the limited role played by collective bargaining in wage setting. As the table illustrates, the influence of collective bargaining on wages is often considerably stronger than the rates of trade union membership.

The real wage for an individual will depend both on the outcome of wage setting and on the outcome of price setting across the economy. At any given level of employment, the real wage consistent with wage-setting behaviour in an imperfectly competitive labour market will typically be higher than that in a perfectly competitive labour market. Why is that? One explanation is that in a unionized workplace, the collective bargaining power of employees will normally result in a wage that is higher than the minimum an employee would be prepared to work for.

Table 1.1 The importance of unions in wage setting: OECD countries

	Trade Union Membership (%)				Collective bargaining coverage (%)		
	1970	1980	1990	2000	1980	1990	2000
France	22	18	10	10	80+	90+	90+
Germany	32	35	31	25	80+	80+	68
Italy	37	50	39	35	80+	80+	80+
Japan	35	31	25	22	25+	20+	15+
Sweden	68	80	80	79	80+	80+	90+
United Kingdom	45	51	39	31	70+	40+	30+
United States	27	22	15	13	26	18	14
OECD: 30 countries	**42**	**47**	**42**	**34**	**67**	**66**	**60**

Notes: For detailed notes, see Table 3.3, OECD *Employment Outlook* (2004).
% refer to number of employees.
Figures with a + sign represent lower-bound estimates.
Source: Table 3.3, OECD *Employment Outlook* (2004).

What is meant by equilibrium in the labour market in the imperfect competition model? It means that wage and price setters in the economy are in equilibrium, in the sense that at the current real wage and level of employment, they have no incentive to change their behaviour. There is one level of employment and rate of unemployment at which both wage and price setters accept the prevailing real wage. This is the *imperfectly competitive equilibrium rate of unemployment*. We shall see that imperfections in the labour or product market have the effect of raising unemployment above the rate in a competitive equilibrium. Although this is consistent with the fall in UK unemployment from the 1980s as union power declined and the markets became more competitive, it does not square with the low unemployment in highly unionized Sweden throughout most of the period. We shall need to enrich the model to account for such facts. This is done in Chapter 4.

1.5 Inflation

Imagine an economy that has constant inflation. In terms of our discussion so far, such an economy is in a medium-run equilibrium, which we shall call the equilibrium rate of unemployment or *ERU*. Wage and price setters are content with the prevailing real wage and there is no pressure from either side to adjust wage or price increases: inflation is therefore constant. If we now suppose that aggregate demand rises, output and employment will rise in the short run and unemployment will be pushed below the *ERU*. We would expect wage and price setters to react to this. This is because with fewer unemployed workers available, workers will be in a stronger bargaining position in the labour market and real wages will have to rise to satisfy their aspirations. Hence, the current real wage in the economy is now lower than the real wage with which wage setters will be satisfied. As a result, wage setters raise money wages in an attempt to achieve the higher expected real wage. But if wages go up, then price setters will not be in equilibrium. Higher wages raise costs for firms. To maintain their profits, firms will tend to raise their prices. An increase in aggregate demand that raises output and employment above the equilibrium level therefore leads to a rise in inflation.

This immediately raises the question of whether there is a lasting trade-off between inflation and unemployment: can the lower unemployment and higher inflation be sustained by the government setting its policy to achieve this? The discussion of the labour market suggests that this is unlikely. The fact that there is no lasting trade-off does not depend on whether the labour market is competitive. In a competitive labour market, if employment is higher than the level at which labour supply and demand are equal, the real wage will either be too low to maintain this level of employment from the labour supply side or too high for such employment to be profitable for firms (i.e. from the labour demand side). With wage and price setting agents, there is a parallel result. We can see this by extending our earlier example. Unemployment is below the *ERU* and inflation has gone up. Are wage and price setters in equilibrium? They are not: since inflation has gone up, the living standards of workers (i.e. their real wages) have been reduced below the level they will accept in the conditions of a tight labour market. At the next opportunity, wage setters will therefore raise money wages by more and inflation will rise further.

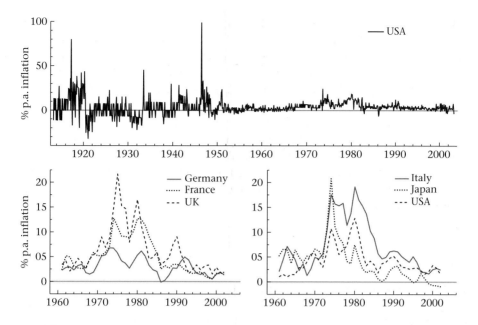

Figure 1.4 Inflation of consumer prices in the USA monthly, 1913–2003 and annually in some OECD economies, 1960 to 2003
Source: OECD.

Fig. 1.4 shows the inflation rate for France, Germany, Italy, Japan, the UK, and the USA. The first panel shows the monthly series of changes in the consumer price index for the USA covering most of the twentieth century. A particularly striking element is the relative smoothness of the series after 1950 compared with the large episodes of inflation and deflation in the pre-war period. As with the unemployment data, there are striking differences between the countries and also interesting patterns over time. One feature that shows up clearly in the post 1960 comparisons is the generally low level of German inflation—as compared with both the United States and Italy. Especially in Italy, but also in the United States, France, and the UK, there are two low-inflation eras at the beginning and the end of the forty-year period. In between there is more than a decade of high and variable inflation, with Italian inflation hitting rates of 20% p.a. in the mid-1970s and again in the early 1980s. One is led immediately to ask why the high inflation era was so much more pronounced in Italy than in Germany, why inflation rose so high, and what brought about the reduction in inflation from the mid-1980s and its convergence with German inflation by the end of the 1990s. Japan presents an equally fascinating challenge as we ponder the economic reasons behind its inflation experience, which reached levels over 20% p.a. in the 1970s and negative figures in recent years.

1.6 Inflation and monetary policy

Monetary policy is set in many different ways. In some countries and historical periods, monetary policy was directed to reducing unemployment; in others, it was oriented to an

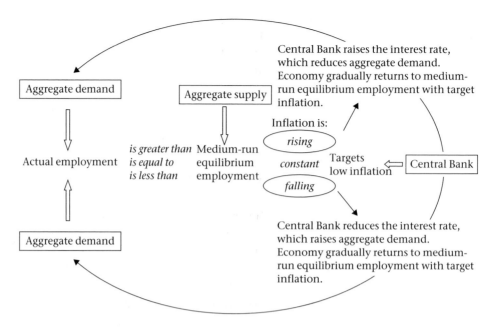

Figure 1.5 Schematic view of the short- and medium-run model

inflation target. Countries have also switched between fixed and flexible exchange rate regimes and we shall see in Chapter 9 that this is a change in monetary policy regime. Here we take the approach to monetary policy used now by many central banks to illustrate the interconnection between the aggregate demand and supply sides of the economy and policy.

Suppose that the central bank's policy is to set the interest rate so as to steer the economy to a low target rate of inflation. In response to a surge in inflation, we would expect to see it put up the interest rate. This would produce a fall in aggregate demand as investment spending responded to the increase in the interest rate (i.e. in the cost of borrowing). The cut-back in investment would lead in turn to lower aggregate demand and a fall in output. Unemployment would go up and inflationary pressure would diminish.

Fig. 1.5 provides a schematic overview of the short- and medium-run macro model. In the left hand side, the role of 'aggregate demand' and 'aggregate supply' are summarized. The components of aggregate demand determine the level of output and employment in the short run. The structural features of the economy on the supply side determine the medium-run equilibrium rate of unemployment (*ERU*). In the third panel, the implications for inflation are shown: if actual unemployment is equal to the *ERU*, then inflation will remain constant and the central bank will do nothing. With unemployment below the *ERU*, inflation is rising and vice versa for unemployment above the *ERU*. An increase in inflation above the central bank's target will trigger a rise in the interest rate; a fall in inflation will trigger an easing of monetary policy with a lower interest rate. In the right hand panel, the reaction of the central bank to inflation rising above or falling below the inflation target is shown. The looping arrows depict the feedback from the central bank's monetary policy rule to aggregate demand. This illustrates how a central bank uses a monetary policy rule to hold inflation close to a low target value. A glance at Fig. 1.4 highlights, however, that we shall need to investigate why episodes of high inflation and of deflation such as those depicted there occur.

1.7 Summary

We can summarize the key results that we shall derive in detail in the next three chapters as follows:

(1) Levels of employment and output in the short run are determined by the level of aggregate demand in the economy.

(2) There is a unique medium-run equilibrium rate of unemployment at which inflation is constant (the *ERU*). At this rate of unemployment, the expected real wage that arises from wage-setting decisions is equal to the real wage that results from the price-setting decisions of firms. Institutional and structural features on the supply side of the economy will determine the equilibrium rate of unemployment.

(3) In general, there is involuntary unemployment at the equilibrium rate of unemployment in the sense that there are workers prepared to work at the existing real wage who cannot get jobs. In the special case of perfectly competitive markets, there is no involuntary unemployment. In both cases, a fall in aggregate demand will lead to higher unemployment: this is involuntary.

(4) If the level of aggregate demand produces a rate of unemployment below the *ERU*, inflation will be rising. If unemployment is above the equilibrium rate, inflation will be falling.

(5) We shall see that if policy makers are targeting inflation, then the economy will tend to return to equilibrium unemployment following an unexpected rise or fall in aggregate demand. The speed with which the economy returns to the equilibrium will depend on how well markets and institutions in the economy work and on the decisions of policy makers.

2 Economic growth

2.1 The world income distribution

There are just two periods in world history during which there was a sustained growth in living standards. The first occurred in China between the eighth and the twelfth centuries, where a modest rate of growth took living standards to a level not attained in Europe until the eighteenth century.[1] The Chinese experience demonstrates that the initiation of a growth process does not entail its continuation indefinitely: in spite of its early experience

---

[1] See Maddison (1998). This is also available along with many other resources on economic growth on Angus Maddison's home page: www.eco.rug.nl/~Maddison/.

of growth, China entered the post-Second World War period as one of the world's poorest countries.

The second phase of sustained growth is a very recent phenomenon and began in Europe. A sustained increase in living standards started in Europe some time after 1500, but it was initially very slow. During the first two centuries it averaged only about 0.1% per annum, which translates into a 22% increase in income per capita over the entire period. Economic progress slowly gathered momentum, averaging 0.2% per annum during the 1700–1820 period, while from the early nineteenth century it began to grow by about 1% per annum, allowing for a doubling in the standard of living in seventy years. Growth rates that consistently reached above 1% per annum were only recorded after 1870. Yet the century and a quarter of sustained growth since then has had spectacular effects, transforming life for people in the countries that have stepped on to the growth elevator and creating a yawning gap between the 'haves' and the 'have nots'. The dramatic increase in world inequality is illustrated by the fact that in 1900, average income per head in Western Europe, the USA, and Japan was about five times higher than in Africa; now it is fifteen times higher.

Fig. 1.6 uses the Penn World Tables 6.1[2] to look at the distribution of average per capita income across countries in the world in 1960 and 2000. GDP per head of the population is measured at constant prices and at Purchasing Power Parity (PPP) adjusted exchange rates to enable average living standards to be compared across countries. In Fig. 1.6, country averages of GDP per capita are measured relative to the United States, i.e. the USA = 1. In 1960 the world's poorest country, Tanzania, had an average per capita GDP level of $382 per annum (i.e. just above $1 per day), while China's was $682 and the United States had per capita GDP of $12,273. Today, Tanzania is still the world's poorest country at $482 per capita GDP while the United States enjoys $33,293 per capita GDP.[3] Other examples of current GDP per capita levels are: United Kingdom $22,190 per capita, Romania $4,285 per capita, China $3,747 per capita, and Uganda $941.

Average growth in the United States was about 1.8% per annum from 1870 to 2000. If the average growth rate in the USA had been one percentage point lower over that period, and thus comparable to those achieved by India or Pakistan (over most of that period), its per capita GDP in 2000 would have only reached about $9,000, which would have meant a current level of economic performance roughly similar to that of Mexico or Poland. If on the other hand the USA had enjoyed growth rates only one percentage point higher than the actual one, and thus comparable to the average growth rate of Japan or Taiwan for most of that period, its GDP per capita levels would have been almost four times higher than they are now. These examples[4] illustrate how small differences in growth rates produce large effects in terms of the standard of living when they persist for long periods of time.

Fig. 1.6 shows on the left the frequency distributions of the average GDP per capita of countries of the world in 1960 and 2000, where average GDP per capita is measured relative to the USA (=1). It is immediately obvious that the vast bulk of countries are to

---

[2] The Penn World Tables and the supporting documentation describing the method of analysis and data-gathering process can be accessed at http://pwt.econ.upenn.edu/.

[3] In fact the United States only comes in second and Luxembourg is the world's richest country with $43,989 per capita GDP.   [4] Barro and Sala-i-Martin (2004). Chapter 1 provides a more detailed discussion.

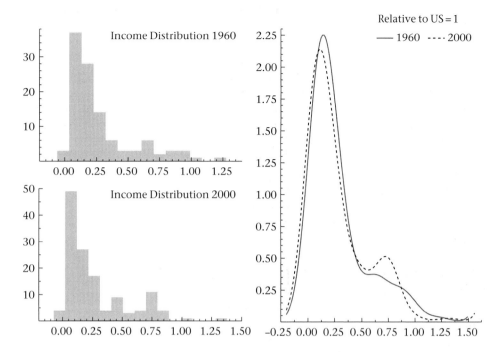

Figure 1.6 The world income distributions in 1960 and 2000 (by country). Kernel density estimates of the world income distribution in 1960 and 2000 using real GDP per capita at constant prices and relative to US = 1

Source: PWT 6.1.

be found with levels of average income way below that of the USA. The so-called kernel distribution in the right-hand panel is a different method of using the same information presented in the histograms on the left.[5] Looking at the right hand panel, we can see the way the world cross-country income distribution has changed between 1960 and 2000. First we notice a bimodal pattern, meaning that it now looks as if it has two peaks at the ends, while in 1960 it only had one. We also notice that the distribution in 2000 is slightly wider than it was in 1960. These are signs that over time as some countries have become richer and others poorer, the world has become increasingly more clustered between rich and poor countries.[6]

A different question is what has happened to the distribution of income across the peoples of the world, rather than across countries. In the past twenty years, some of the most populous countries such as China and India have grown faster than the rich countries and this has had the effect of pulling large numbers of people out of poverty.[7]

---

[5] It was derived by first plotting the different values of relative income in the form of a histogram as shown in the panel in the left hand side of Fig. 1.6. The method of kernel smoothing effectively averages and connects points that are close by to generate an estimate of the distribution which is smooth and makes more use of the underlying information than does a histogram.   [6] Jones (1997).

[7] For a recent overview and explanation of different methods of calculating the world income distribution, see Sutcliffe (2004).

This hints at powerful changes that occurred over the past four decades as the world witnessed both growth miracles and growth disasters, coupled with a profound tranformation of the political landscape and the collapse of many African economies under the burden of the AIDS epidemic. The extent of economic inequality between today's world economies becomes even more striking when we are reminded that in the developing world over 790 million people do not have enough food to eat and 1.3 billion people do not have access to safe drinking water. Almost half of the world's population survives on less than $2 a day. In Asia the number of people living in poverty, on less than $1 a day, fell from 420 million to around 280 million even when taking into account the financial meltdown of the late 1990s. In Eastern Europe on the other hand the number of people living on less than $1 a day has increased by a factor of twenty.[8]

Today most of the OECD countries together with some of the Asian economies find themselves at the top of the world's income distribution. In 1960 however we witness Latin American countries like Argentina, Uruguay, and Venezuela in the top 25 countries, whereas none are in the top 25 in 2000. Similarly, some Asian countries like China, India, Indonesia, and Pakistan that were in the bottom 25 countries in 1960 experienced sufficient growth to move well outside this group. Differences in economic growth rates have ranged from 6% p.a. for Taiwan to −1.8% p.a. for Zambia and have dictated the winners and losers of the last few decades.

In Fig. 1.7 we plot the relative per capita incomes of economies in 1960 and 2000 against the 45 degree line. Points that lie relatively close to the diagonal represent countries that have seen very little change in *relative* living standards over the past few decades compared to the USA. Points that lie above the diagonal represent countries that have experienced positive relative rates of economic growth. The plot also shows that within the cluster of points in the lower left corner, representing the poor countries of the world, many have experienced a deterioration in their relative position. Only very few countries that have had relatively low incomes per capita in 1960 have seen a significant improvement in their relative living standards, and can thus be identified as growth miracles. These form the loose cluster of points to the left of the 45 degree line and include most of the Asian economies but also Botswana, Mauritius, Cyprus, and Romania. Countries represented by points to the extreme right of the 45 degree line correspond to economies that have seen a deterioration of their relative position over the past few decades and are thus labelled as growth disasters. Notable examples include Chad, Iraq, and Venezuela.

Given the varied performance of countries as shown in Fig. 1.7, we naturally face the question of what the prospects are for the evolution of the income distribution in the future. Specifically, is there any hope that the world's poorest economies will catch up with the world's richest ones? We construct Fig. 1.8 by plotting the growth rate in per capita GDP over the period 1960 to 2000 against the log value of per capita GDP in 1960. This plot is a simple example of an attempt to explore the concept of economic convergence and corresponds to an old economic hypothesis that countries which start off poor ought to grow faster and thus catch up with the richer ones. If the countries that are initially poor are to catch up, there should be a *negative* relationship in the graph, with

---

[8] For a more detailed treatment of economic inequality see the World Bank's World Development Indicators www.worldbank.org/data/wdi2005/. See also www.un.org/millenniumgoals/.

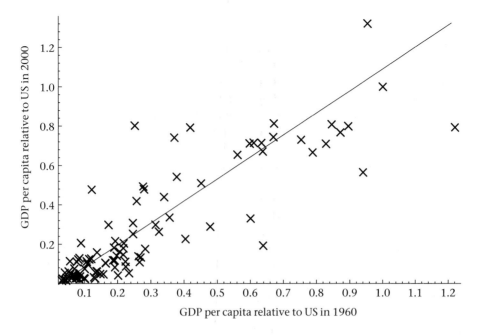

Figure 1.7 Scatter plot of relative incomes per capita in 2000 and 1960
Source: PWT 6.1.

countries on the left hand side (poor at the outset) having the high growth rates (located at the top) and vice versa for countries that are initially rich. We have also plotted the best fit line corresponding to the sample regression and we observe a small *positive* slope. However, we should note that the points are widely dispersed, and indeed if we perform a statistical test we obtain the result that the slope parameter is not significantly different from zero. Thus, we cannot confidently conclude that there is divergence on the basis of this data, but there is clearly no sign of convergence across countries.

However, if we were to perform the same analysis on subsamples of the data set, such that the countries that we include are relatively similar in terms of their economic, social, political, or historical experience we will obtain a strong negative relationship between the growth rate of income and the initial starting position, thus confirming the convergence hypothesis. In Chapter 13 we shall explore these ideas further by distinguishing between the concepts of unconditional and conditional convergence.

2.2 The stylized facts of economic growth

Early empirical work on economic growth by a number of economists such as Nicholas Kaldor, Simon Kuznets, and William Baumol uncovered a number of robust facts about the process of economic growth; facts that were deemed stable enough across countries and time to be used as the cornerstone of modern economic growth theory. They have been used as a guide to inform model building but also as a test of consistency for any new model that had to justify its existence by how its theoretical results would fit these

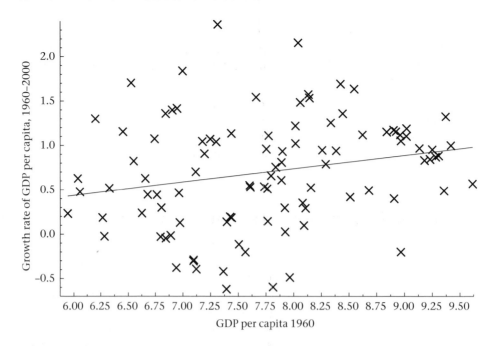

Figure 1.8 Is there cross-country convergence? Scatter plot of growth rates of GDP per capita between 1960 and 2000 against the initial level of GDP per capita in logs
Source: PWT 6.1.

stylized facts. Over the years, growth theory has attracted a large number of talented economists and both our theoretical understanding of the engine of economic growth and our collection of empirical facts has grown significantly. Here we shall note the classic stylized facts of economic growth that have guided economists over the past half-century, while augmenting the list with some of the newer empirical findings. As we learn the mechanics of both exogenous and endogenous growth theory and then explore the microfoundations of growth by looking at models of innovation in Chapters 13 and 14, we shall return to this section to verify our understanding of economic growth by explaining to what extent our models fit these stylized facts:

(1) Large discrepancies between both levels and growth rates of per capita income persist across countries and across time.

(2) In the long run economies exhibit a *balanced growth path*, that is output per capita and capital per capita grow at roughly constant positive growth rates over time.

(3) The real rate of return to capital is approximately constant over the long run, while real wages grow at a rate close to that of output per head. From (2) and (3) it follows that the ratio of capital to output shows no trend over time and the shares of capital and labour in total income stay roughly constant.

(4) High investment rates in both physical capital and formal education are closely related to high living standards.

(5) Low population growth is associated with high living standards.

(6) Technological progress associated with product market innovation is the main driving force behind the long-run growth of living standards in the leader country (or countries).

(7) Political, social, institutional and historical factors affect the long-run economic performance of an economy and are associated with differences in growth rates across countries. Such factors help to predict which countries have converged to high levels of GDP per capita and which countries have not.

2.3 Growth and diminishing returns to factor accumulation

In the light of the stylized empirical facts of economic growth we can turn to the theoretical models. One place to begin is to focus on what determines the *level* of output per worker. In our discussion of the short and medium run, we focused on a single factor of production, labour. We assumed that the amount of capital equipment available to the worker was fixed. When we move to the long run, we would expect differences in levels of output per worker across countries to depend on the amount of capital equipment available. As we shall see, human capital should also be included. Human capital refers to abilities and skills that people can acquire. The term human 'capital' is used to highlight the analogy with physical capital: investment only takes place if current consumption is sacrificed and resources are devoted to acquiring capital goods instead. Similarly, resources and time must be devoted to the accumulation of human capital through education, training, or learning on the job. In addition to the quantity of factors of production available per worker, both technology and efficiency will matter as well.

The neoclassical theory of economic growth was developed simultaneously in 1956 by Robert Solow (in the USA at MIT) and Trevor Swan (in Australia) and it focused on systematizing the role of factor accumulation in growth. The capital stock had grown dramatically during the first half of the twentieth century and provided the empirical backdrop to this modelling. The essence of the Solow–Swan model is that a country's level of output per head would be higher if there was a higher level of capital equipment per worker. In moving from a low level of capital per worker to a higher level of capital per worker, output per worker would be growing. However, although more investment would raise the *level* of output per worker (and hence living standards), the model predicts that more investment would only raise the *growth rate* of living standards temporarily. Why? The answer lies with the assumption that there are diminishing returns to physical investment. Having one computer will improve your output; having two may raise your average output by facilitating back-ups and allowing you to continue working when the first one crashes but it is unlikely to double your output.

Suppose the economy has had a particular level of output per head for some time. Suddenly, a bigger share of income is devoted to investment and this is maintained forever. The Solow–Swan model predicts that more capital-intensive techniques of production will be adopted. Output per worker will go up. But with each increase in capital intensity, the bonus in terms of higher output per worker diminishes. But why can the higher investment share not pay for a continuously rising capital intensity? The reason is that part of the capital stock disappears every year through depreciation so that eventually the feeble improvement in output will not generate sufficient extra savings to keep raising the capital intensity. After some time, the economy will therefore come to a new equilibrium and the level of output per worker will once more remain constant.

A number of issues are raised by this result:

- The model itself cannot account for the persistent growth of living standards that has been experienced in the last two centuries. The Solow–Swan model can be amended by including a particular kind of technical progress: if technology is improving year on year without using up any resources, we can say that there is exogenous technical progress. In that case, the initial situation described above would be one in which output per head rises at this constant, exogenous rate. When investment goes up, there is a period during which output per head rises faster than the rate of exogenous technical progress because of the increase in capital intensity that is taking place. Eventually, the economy will return to the original rate of growth, but with living standards at a higher level than would have been the case in the absence of the shift to higher investment. However, the steady growth of living standards is not explained by any economic mechanism *inside* the model and this seems unsatisfactory.

- The model helps to explain why there should be a positive relationship between output per head and capital per head. But does it predict correctly by how much a rise in capital per head will raise output per head? As we shall see in more detail in Chapter 13, it does not.

This question, in turn, focuses attention on

(1) the need to include human as well as physical capital as a factor of production in the growth model

(2) whether all countries have access to the same technology and

(3) whether even if they do, the technology can be used efficiently.

If human capital is included alongside physical capital in the Solow–Swan model, the predictions of the model better match the stylized facts. Indeed the Solow–Swan model augmented by the inclusion of human capital provides a powerful starting point for thinking about the determinants of the growth of countries that have caught up with the productivity leader. The USA came out of the Second World War as the undisputed world leader in output per capita. But by the mid-1980s, more than a dozen countries in Europe plus Australia, New Zealand, Canada, and Japan had substantially narrowed the gap. Levels of human and physical capital per head had become similar to those in the USA. But the Solow–Swan model is less successful in providing an explanation for the failure of lots of other countries to converge toward the living standards of the rich ones. And it cannot contribute to the explanation of persistent growth of output per head in the productivity leader since the only source in the Solow–Swan model is 'exogenous technical progress', which by definition is not explained.

2.4 Growth and constant returns to factor accumulation

Dissatisfaction with the role of exogenous technical progress in the Solow–Swan model motivated a new approach to growth theory called endogenous growth. As we have seen it is the assumption of diminishing returns to the accumulation of capital—physical and/or human—that prevents persistent growth of living standards in the Solow–Swan model. The mechanics of creating endogenous growth are straightforward: drop the assumption of diminishing returns to the accumulation of capital and replace it with an assumption of constant returns. If the benefits to growth from higher investment do not diminish then it seems intuitively plausible that if the economy devotes a higher share of income to investment, this raises the growth rate of output per capita permanently. This transforms a process of exogenous growth in the Solow–Swan model into one of endogenous growth.

In our example of the two computers, the idea of diminishing returns to the accumulation of capital is attractive so one challenge for proponents of endogenous growth is to come up with explanations for why returns to factor accumulation might not diminish. One influential idea focuses on human capital and argues that acquiring more education and training allows us to learn more. If the link between our existing human capital and our ability to learn more is sufficiently strong, then endogenous growth is possible: spending more time in education can raise the growth rate permanently. However, one might think that investing in education would eventually come up against the limits of human capacity. Perhaps more promising is the notion that higher investment in innovative activities (e.g. research and development) could allow for the continuous improvement in productivity.

As we shall see in Chapters 13 and 14 although there is a sharp *theoretical* difference between the Solow–Swan model of exogenous growth and the more recent theories of endogenous growth, once the Solow–Swan model is extended to include a broader concept of capital than simply buildings and machinery, many of the *empirical* predictions of the two sorts of model are similar. The so-called augmented Solow–Swan model predicts that countries with lower levels of GDP per capita will grow faster than the countries at the technological frontier and will therefore eventually converge to the richer ones. But if convergence is very slow because the returns to the accumulation of physical plus human capital diminish much more slowly than do the returns to physical capital alone, this process will look quite similar to endogenous growth.

By modelling how technology is transferred from technology leaders to laggards, both kinds of growth model can be brought closer to explaining real-world problems. One important idea is that poor countries can only take advantage of the technology used in more advanced countries if they have sufficient human capital. This helps to explain why some countries have been able to catch up and others have not.

2.5 Innovation and incentives: Schumpeterian growth

To go further in understanding growth it is necessary to look more closely at the incentives for innovation. The Austrian economist Joseph Schumpeter, writing early in the twentieth century, argued that innovations could sustain long-run growth and that institutions are important for creating the appropriate incentives for firms to engage in innovative activities. Why is investment in innovations different from investment in physical capital? The answer is that ideas are different from fixed capital: once an idea has been developed, my use of it does not prevent you from using it too. By contrast, if I am using my computer, you cannot use it simultaneously. Because ideas are 'non-rival' in this way, there has to be some method of creating an incentive for firms to invest time and resources in producing the innovation: if not then they will not be able to recover the costs incurred. Patents are a formal method of ensuring a period of monopoly for the innovating firm but other more informal methods of retaining secrecy about innovations are also common. In the Schumpeterian model, countries can be trapped with low levels of GDP per capita because the institutional structures are not conducive to taking advantage of spillovers in innovation from rich countries. This is investigated further in Chapter 14. Extensions of the Schumpeterian model allow us to explore the implications for innovation and growth of product market competition, of how financial markets are organized, and of other structural and institutional characteristics of the economy.

This chapter is a taster for what is to come. It hints at the way tractable models can help us to make sense of the big questions of macroeconomics.

■ QUESTIONS

Checklist questions

(1) Explain to a non-economist the difference between 'consumption' and 'investment'.

(2) Explain to a non-economist the difference between 'aggregate supply' and 'aggregate demand'.

(3) Comment on three aspects of Fig. 1.1.

(4) Provide a concise summary of the evolution of the unemployment rate in the United States as compared with that in one European economy from 1960 to 2000.

(5) What is meant by the statement that in a competitive economy, unemployment is voluntary? Explain how the labour market can be in equilibrium although there is involuntary unemployment.

(6) Comment on three aspects of Table 1.1.

(7) Comment on three aspects of the lower panels of Fig. 1.4.

(8) How would you explain to a non-economist the relationship between the rate of unemployment, the rate of inflation, and the central bank's monthly decision about whether to change the interest rate?

(9) What is the connection between the concept of diminishing returns to capital and the hypothesis that poor countries grow faster than rich ones?

(10) 'A rise in savings reduces GDP.' 'A rise in savings raises living standards but not the long-run growth rate.' 'A rise in savings raises the growth rate permanently.' Explain in words the logic of each of these statements.

Questions for discussion

QUESTION A. Why might the words of macroeconomic policy-makers be as important as their deeds?

QUESTION B. In the early 1990s, communist governments fell across Central and Eastern Europe and the Soviet Union. The state control over the economy ended and market mechanisms were introduced. A widely held view at the time was that the prevalence of inefficiency and lack of dynamism in the planned economies would be replaced by rapid 'catch-up' growth. Instead all the countries experienced a collapse in GDP, with positive growth rates only appearing in the mid-1990s in Central and Eastern Europe and the late 1990s in the former Soviet Union. Using the ideas introduced in this chapter, discuss the possible role of imperfections, institutions, and policies in explaining why the reality of transition did not match the early optimism.

PART ONE

The Macroeconomic Model

2 Aggregate Demand, Aggregate Supply, and Business Cycles

This chapter begins the process of setting out the short- to medium-run macro model. The first aim of the chapter is to explain how the level of output and employment is determined by the level of aggregate demand in the short run—i.e. when wages and prices are sticky. This provides a model of the business cycle, i.e. how the level of output and employment fluctuates in response to changes in aggregate demand. We begin with the standard approach of introducing the goods market equilibrium and then the money market equilibrium in the *IS/LM* model. The *IS* refers to the goods market and the *LM* to the money market. There are two broad ways of thinking about how monetary policy is implemented by governments or central banks and hence about the usefulness of the *LM* analysis. On the one hand, the government or central bank can be modelled as implementing monetary policy through its control over the level or the growth rate of the money supply. We shall see that this approach is best handled using the *LM*. On the other hand, the government or central bank can be seen as setting the interest rate so as to stabilize the economy and steer it toward an inflation target. This is the so-called monetary rule (*MR*) approach developed in Chapter 3.

Given the increasing prevalence of monetary rules in monetary policy-making, the question arises as to why should we bother with presenting the *LM* analysis at all?

- First, if we are to understand why governments and central banks have moved toward the use of monetary rules, it is useful to have a sound understanding of the *LM* approach as a benchmark. Moreover, even if the central bank is using the *MR* approach, the *LM* still exists since it represents equilibrium in the money market.

- Second, the *LM* approach is helpful in analysing problems of deflation—i.e. when prices are falling in the economy. Even if the central bank uses a monetary rule to adjust the interest rate to achieve an inflation target, we need to understand the circumstances under which this may be ineffective. An important example is the situation where the nominal interest rate is close to zero and the economy is characterized by a falling price level, as has characterized the Japanese economy for nearly a decade.

- Third, as we shall see in Chapter 9, much open economy analysis is conducted using the *IS/LM* model.

All three reasons suggest that even if the *LM* is less relevant for practical policy analysis than was once thought, it remains a useful modelling tool. The *IS/LM* model can be used for analysing the determinants of output in the short run when the government controls the money supply. It also provides components that are useful later on. We shall see that the *IS* curve is a key part of the 3-equation *IS-PC-MR* macro model developed in Chapter 3 for use with a monetary rule.

In the second part of this chapter, the focus shifts from aggregate demand to aggregate supply. As we shall see, in the medium run, wages and prices respond to changes in the level of activity (i.e. to changes in output and employment). The second task of the chapter is therefore to pin down the determinants of the medium-run level of employment at which the labour market is in equilibrium and pressures for wages and prices to change are absent. The integration of the short- and medium-run components is introduced in the final section of the chapter through the use of the aggregate demand and aggregate supply framework.

We contrast the explanation of business cycle fluctuations based on shifts in aggregate demand in the presence of sticky wages and prices on which we concentrate in this book with a completely different one, where it is shifts on the supply side of the economy such as technological change that produce booms and recessions. This second approach is called the Real Business Cycle model.

1 Aggregate demand

To understand how the level of output is determined in the short run, we look for the sources of changes in the aggregate demand for output. The short run is defined here as the period during which prices and wages are given. There are a number of ways of explaining why prices and wages might not respond *immediately* to changes in demand. Institutional arrangements normally mean that wages are reviewed periodically and not continuously. A common argument in support of price stickiness is that there are costs associated with changing prices, which are referred to as menu-costs. It is also useful to remember that it is profitable for firms in imperfectly competitive markets to increase output in response to higher demand even if the price remains unchanged. For the moment, we just assume that wages and prices are sticky—they do not respond to changes in employment or output in the short run. A more detailed discussion of the implications of price and wage behaviour for macroeconomics is presented in Chapter 15. The following terms are used by different authors to refer to this assumption: 'nominal rigidity', 'sticky wages, prices', 'fix-price'.

The standard model that is used to summarize the way in which the level of output is determined by aggregate demand in the short run (i.e. with sticky wages and prices) is the *IS/LM* model.[1] It consists of two parts: the goods market and the money market. We think of a short-run equilibrium in the economy as a situation in which both the goods and the money market are in equilibrium. The goods market part is labelled *IS* after the '*Investment-Savings*' version of the goods market equilibrium condition: planned investment must be equal to planned savings for equilibrium in the goods market. The money

---

[1] The model was introduced by John Hicks in 1937 (Hicks 1937). For a concise and interesting discussion of its origins and impact, see Leijonhufvud (1987).

market part is labelled *LM* after the equality between money demand (*L*iquidity) and *M*oney supply when the money market is in equilibrium. In *IS/LM* equilibrium, the level of output (and employment) and the interest rate are constant.

The model is useful because it allows us to work out what happens to output and to the interest rate when there is a change in aggregate demand or when the government changes its policies. On the *IS* side, we can analyse:

- shifts in consumption or investment
- changes in fiscal policy, i.e. in government expenditure or taxation.

On the *LM* side, we can analyse:

- shifts in money demand
- changes in monetary policy, e.g. in the money supply.

2 **The goods market: the *IS* curve**

The *IS* curve shows the combinations of the interest rate and output level at which there is equilibrium in the goods market. For goods market equilibrium, the aggregate demand for goods (and services) must equal the supply. Since we assume that wages and prices are fixed, the supply of output will adjust to any change in aggregate demand.

Aggregate demand refers to the planned real expenditure on goods and services in the economy as a whole. Equilibrium requires that planned real expenditure on goods and services is equal to real output:

$$y^D = y, \qquad \text{(goods market equilibrium)}$$

where y^D is planned real expenditure and y is real output.

Aggregate demand is made up of planned expenditure on consumption and investment by the private sector and planned government spending. It can be written as

$$y^D = c(y, t, \text{wealth}) + I(r, A) + g \qquad \text{(aggregate demand)}$$

where c is consumption, I is investment, and g is government spending, all in real terms. t is total taxation, r is the real rate of interest, and A refers to other (non-interest rate) determinants of investment. In general, we use lower case letters to refer to real variables and upper case ones to refer to nominal variables so y is real output and Y is output in money terms (e.g. in euros or dollars). However, this is not always possible: we use i for the nominal interest rate and I for real investment.

Some important features of the short-run macroeconomic model can be shown most easily if we assume linear functions. We shall use a simple linear consumption function that says consumption is a function of current post-tax (i.e. disposable) income and other factors such as wealth that are summarized in a term labelled autonomous consumption, which is assumed to be constant:

$$c = c_0 + c_y(y - t) \qquad \text{(consumption function)}$$

where c_0 is autonomous consumption and c_y is the constant proportion of current disposable income that is consumed: $0 < c_y < 1$. The term c_y is called the marginal propensity to consume out of disposable income. Disposable income is income minus taxation $(y - t)$. t is the total tax revenue, and if we take a linear tax function, then

$$t = t_y y \qquad \text{(tax function)}$$

where $0 < t_y < 1$. Thus if we substitute the tax function into the consumption function and rearrange the terms, the consumption function is:

$$c = c_0 + c_y(1 - t_y)y.$$

A notable feature of this consumption function is that consumption is affected by the current level of activity in the economy. In Chapter 7, we look at the microfoundations of consumption behaviour to see why current *and expected future* income are likely to be relevant for consumption expenditure. The simplest way to incorporate the insights of the forward-looking model of consumption is by including in c_0 the determinants of expected future income. The consumption function shifts when expected future income changes. The empirical evidence discussed in Chapter 7 confirms that current and expected future income influence current consumption.

Investment is assumed to depend negatively on the real rate of interest and positively on expected future profitability, the determinants of which are proxied by the term A. The simple idea is that firms are faced with an array of investment projects, which are ranked by their expected return. If the interest rate falls, then this reduces the cost of capital and makes some projects profitable that would not otherwise have been undertaken. Similarly, if the expected return on projects rises (because there is a surge of optimism in the economy), then at any given interest rate, more projects will be undertaken. We can write this investment function:

$$I = I(r, A). \qquad \text{(investment)}$$

It is sometimes handy to use a linear form, $I = A - ar$, where a is a constant. Expectational or confidence factors are often considered crucial determinants of investment behaviour. This would imply that shifts of the investment function arising from changes in A could be of greater significance than movements *along* the investment function in response to interest rate changes. A deeper examination of investment behaviour based on microeconomic foundations is to be found in Chapter 7.

The *IS* curve is defined by the goods market equilibrium condition $(y^D = y)$. To derive an explicit form for the *IS* curve, we use the linear versions of the consumption and investment functions and substitute them into the planned expenditure equation:

$$y^D = c_0 + c_y(1 - t_y)y + A - ar + g. \qquad \text{(planned expenditure)}$$

The planned expenditure equation is then substituted into the goods market equilibrium condition. We rearrange, using the fact that in the goods market equilibrium, $y^D = y$, and replacing $(1 - c_y)$ by the marginal propensity to save, s_y, to define an equilibrium locus of combinations of the interest rate and output:

$$y = \frac{c_0 + A + g}{1 - c_y(1 - t_y)} - \frac{a}{1 - c_y(1 - t_y)} \cdot r$$

$$= \frac{1}{1 - c_y(1 - t_y)} \cdot [c_0 + (A - ar) + g]$$

$$= \underbrace{\frac{1}{s_y + c_y t_y}}_{\text{multiplier}} \cdot [c_0 + (A - ar) + g].$$

The *IS* curve states that for a given interest rate the level of investment is fixed; to this level of investment is added autonomous consumption and government spending; and the associated level of output is found by multiplying the sum by the constant, $\frac{1}{s_y + c_y t_y}$, which is known as the multiplier. Savings and taxation both represent leakages from the feedback from income to expenditure. The reason that the tax leakage (t_y) is multiplied by c_y is that only that part of tax revenue that would have been spent constitutes an extra leakage over and above savings. The *IS* curve is downward sloping because a low interest rate generates high investment, which will be associated with high output. By contrast, when the interest rate is high, investment and hence equilibrium output is low.

The *IS* curve is derived graphically in Fig. 2.1. At r_H, investment ($I_0 = A - ar_H$), autonomous consumption and government spending are shown. Multiplying $I_0 + c_0 + g_0$ by the multiplier gives output equal to planned expenditure, y_0, on the *IS* curve. Using the same logic, at a low interest rate, planned expenditure will be high owing to high investment. Goods market equilibrium dictates a correspondingly high output level.

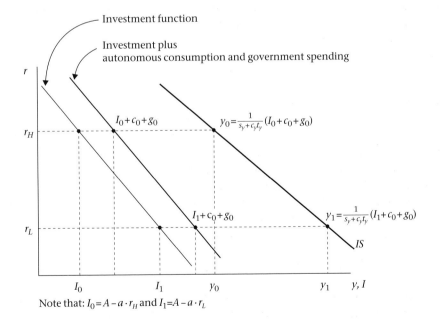

Figure 2.1 Deriving the *IS* curve

Using the *IS* curve equation and the diagram, we can separate the determinants of the slope and position of the *IS* curve into three groups.

(1) Any change in the size of the *multiplier* will change the slope of the *IS* curve. For example, a rise in the propensity to consume will increase the multiplier, making the *IS* flatter: it rotates counter-clockwise from the intercept on the vertical axis.

(2) Any change in the *interest sensitivity of investment* (a) will lead to a consequential change in the slope of the *IS* curve: a less interest-elastic investment function will be reflected in a steeper *IS* curve.

(3) Any change in *autonomous consumption* or in *government expenditure* (c_0, g) will cause the *IS* curve to shift by the change in autonomous spending times the multiplier. A change in the variable A in the investment function also shifts *IS*.[2]

Policy can be used to manipulate the *IS* curve through channels 1 and 3. For example, if income tax is proportional, i.e. if $t = t_y y$, a lower tax rate increases the size of the multiplier and, as in 1 above, swings the *IS* to the right, making it flatter. Any change in government spending will shift the *IS* in the manner described in (3) above.

A feature of the *IS* model of the goods market is that quantities adjust through the multiplier process to take the economy to a stable short-run equilibrium. For example, a fall in planned investment leads to a multiple contraction of output and employment until the level of income has fallen to the extent required to make saving equal to the lower level of investment. Initially, income falls by the fall in investment, ΔI. As the result of the fall in income and assuming $t_y = 0$, consumption declines by $\Delta c = c_y \Delta I$. This fall in consumption in turn reduces income, and in the next round consumption falls once more: $\Delta c = c_y(c_y \Delta I) = c_y^2 \Delta I$. To calculate the total drop in income, we sum the series:[3]

$$\Delta y = \Delta I + c_y \Delta I + c_y^2 \Delta I + c_y^3 \Delta I + \cdots$$
$$= (1 + c_y + c_y^2 + c_y^3 + \cdots)\Delta I$$
$$= \frac{1}{1 - c_y} \cdot \Delta I$$
$$= \frac{1}{s_y} \cdot \Delta I = \text{multiplier} \times \Delta I$$

The change in output is equal to the multiplier (i.e. $1/s_y$) times the change in investment.

---

[2] In the Appendix to this chapter, we show how the statements 1-3 can be made precise in the case of linear functions by working through the algebra and geometry of the *IS* curve.

[3] This is the sum of a geometric series. We want to find an expression for the series $1 + c_y + c_y^2 + c_y^3 + \cdots$, which we call x. If we put

then

$$x = 1 + c_y + c_y^2 + c_y^3 + \cdots \tag{2.1}$$

and if we subtract 2.2 from 2.1, we have

$$c_y \cdot x = c_y + c_y^2 + c_y^3 + \cdots \tag{2.2}$$

$$x(1 - c_y) = 1$$

$$\Rightarrow x = \frac{1}{1 - c_y}.$$

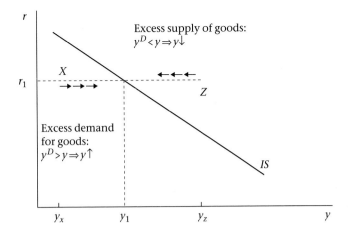

Figure 2.2 Adjustment to goods market equilibrium: excess demand at point X leads to a rise in output; excess supply at point Z leads to a fall in output

Another way of focusing on quantity adjustment to a new goods market equilibrium is to characterize positions off the IS curve (Fig. 2.2). At point X with output y_x, to the left of the IS curve, there is excess demand in the goods market because at the interest rate r_1, planned expenditure is equal to y_1. With aggregate demand in excess of output, stocks will fall and output will rise until $y = y^D$ on the IS curve.

3 The money market: the *LM* curve

The LM curve represents the combinations of the interest rate and output at which the money market is in equilibrium, so the focus here is on the way the money market works. Throughout the chapter, it is assumed that the central bank controls the money supply—we model central banks using an interest rate based monetary rule in Chapter 3.

3.1 Demand for money

A common confusion that arises when first studying macroeconomics is between the decision to save and the decision to hold money. The decision to save refers to the use that is made of the flow of income. Of the income received in any given period (e.g. a month) from working and from other sources such as interest income, there is a proportion that is saved and a proportion that is consumed. If consumption exceeds income, then the individual is dissaving—i.e. they are borrowing and accumulating debts.

What then is the 'demand for money'? Whereas the saving decision is an income allocation decision, the demand for money is a decision about the *form* in which to hold your *wealth*. Should you hold it as money or as another asset? To answer this it is necessary to know the difference between money and other assets. When someone asks how much money you have, you might answer by counting the notes or coins in your wallet or you might include the balance in your cheque account because you have instant access to this money by writing a cheque or using a debit card. You might also add in the balances on your other higher interest bank accounts—the 'term' accounts for which you have to give a certain notice period if you want to withdraw money without a penalty. All of these are money and they range from a narrow definition (notes and coins) to a broad one (term deposits). As we move from narrow to broad money, there is a gain in the interest return and a loss in liquidity.

Note that throughout the discussion of money demand and money supply, the relevant interest rate is the *nominal* interest rate, *i*. One characteristic common to all forms of money is that it is a very or fairly liquid asset and therefore indispensable for carrying out transactions in the economy. Second, if you have €1,000 in your account, then as long as you do not withdraw any of it, the value in money terms does not fall. This means that money is 'capital-safe' in *nominal* terms. If the money is in an interest bearing account, then the nominal amount will rise as interest accrues.

3.1.1 Money and bonds

Although some forms of money do pay interest, there are other assets available in the economy that offer a higher return than a term deposit as long as you are prepared to take on some risk. In addition to supplying money, the government can borrow from the general public by selling government bonds. The key difference between government bonds and money is that bonds are not 'capital-safe' in nominal terms: if there is a rise in the rate of interest, then the market value of the bond falls.

To understand the inverse relationship between the market price of a bond and the interest rate, consider a bond that is issued by the government at a face value of €100, and that pays €5 per annum in perpetuity. If the market interest rate is 4%, then the price the bond will sell for in the market (the market price) will be such as to make the yield of €5 represent a market return of 4%. The market value of the bond will be €x, where $0.04x = 5$; i.e., $x = 5/0.04 = $ €125. An interest rate lower than 5% implies a market value higher than the face value of the bond. If the interest rate is even lower at, say, 2%, then $x = 5/0.02 = $ €250 and similarly, if the interest rate is higher at, say 8%, then the market value is €62.50. There is an inverse relationship between the market value of the bond (i.e. the price at which it will sell in the market) and the market interest rate. It is clear that only if the interest rate is 5%, is the market value of the bond exactly equal to its face value. So unlike €100 in cash, the nominal market value of a €100 bond will go up whenever the nominal interest rate falls and vice versa.

3.1.2 Demand for money versus bonds

Consider the choice between holding one's assets in the form of money or in bonds, for example, from the perspective of a business deciding how to manage its cash. (As we shall see in Chapter 8, the discussion is not fundamentally different when additional assets such as equities are introduced.) Money is needed in order to carry out transactions in a market economy. Since desired transactions vary with the level of income, so will the demand for money. But the cost of holding assets in the form of money is that interest income is foregone. A rise in the interest rate will shift the balance of advantage in favour of interest-bearing assets including bonds.

We can summarize the demand for money as follows:

$$\frac{M^D}{P} = L(y, i), \qquad\qquad \text{(demand for money)}$$

where i is the *nominal* interest rate. We return to the question of the difference between the real interest rate, r, that features in the *IS* equation and the nominal interest, i, that features in the money market. We are dealing here with the 'L' part of the 'LM', where the 'L' refers to the demand for liquidity. A rise in the level of income, holding the interest rate unchanged, will raise the demand for money (i.e. $\partial L/\partial y > 0$) and a rise in the interest rate, holding the level of income unchanged will lower the demand for money (i.e. $\partial L/\partial i < 0$). Note that the demand for money is expressed in real terms i.e. (M/P) since it is normally assumed that a rise in the price level will raise the nominal demand for money in proportion.

Just as in the analysis of the goods market, it is sometimes helpful to express the demand for money as a linear function of the level of income and the interest rate:

$$\frac{M^D}{P} = L(y, i) = \underbrace{\bar{l} - l_i i}_{\text{asset demand}} + \underbrace{\frac{1}{v_T} \cdot y}_{\text{transactions demand}}, \qquad \text{(demand for money)}$$

where $\bar{l}, v_T$ and l_i are positive constants. The term $(\bar{l} - l_i i)$ reflects the asset motive for holding money and the term $(\frac{1}{v_T} \cdot y)$ reflects the transactions motive for holding money. In the famous theory called the Quantity Theory of Money, the only determinant of the demand for real money balances is the level of output. In other words, only the transactions motive is present. The Quantity Theory of Money can be stated as: $\frac{M^D}{P} = \frac{1}{v} \cdot y$, where v is the constant velocity of circulation. We use the now standard more general demand for money function in which the transactions demand is only one part of the demand for money. Hence, although the transactions velocity, v_T is constant, the overall relationship between money demand and output is not: it will vary with changes in the interest rate.

3.1.3 Asset and speculative motives

Two of the explanations given for the inverse relationship between the demand for money and the interest rate are known as the asset motive and the speculative motive. Both relate to the choice between holding money and bonds. Keynes argued for the relevance of the speculative motive as follows: if an individual believes that the current interest rate is above the level she considers normal, then she will expect the interest rate to fall to normal in due course. Under these circumstances, she will choose to hold financial assets over and above the money required for transactions in the form of bonds. She does this because she will expect to reap a capital gain on the bonds when the interest rate falls to its normal level. The converse would be true for a current interest rate believed to be below normal. Keynes believed that the subjective assessment of the normal interest rate would vary across the population, producing a smooth inverse relationship between the interest rate and the aggregate demand for speculative balances. Moreover a central implication of Keynes's argument is that expectations drive financial markets and that shifts in expectations have a self-fulfilling character. If bondholders suddenly believe that the interest rate will be higher in the future than they had previously believed, they will expect capital losses and will sell their bonds, driving bond prices down and interest rates up—the expectation of a rise in the interest rate is fulfilled. This feature of financial markets is of great importance for monetary policy.

A more general rationale for the negative dependence of the demand for money on the interest rate was developed by James Tobin in 1958. Instead of assuming, as had Keynes, that each individual is certain about what she expects the future rate of interest on bonds to be, Tobin focused on the implications of investor uncertainty. In the simplest version of Tobin's model, risk-averse[4] individuals allocate their portfolio between a riskless asset that pays no interest (money) and a risky one with a positive expected return (bonds). The individual's utility depends positively on the return from holding the asset and negatively on the risk of holding it. To maximize utility, the individual will hold a mixture of the two assets, trading off the benefits of a higher expected return against the associated risk according to her own preferences. A higher interest rate would lead her to substitute bonds for money (reduce the demand for money) because the higher expected return would offset the additional risk incurred. This produces an inverse relationship between the demand for money and the interest rate. A more detailed discussion of the speculative and asset motives can be found in Chapter 8.

3.2 Money market equilibrium

Money market equilibrium requires the demand and supply of money to be equal:

$$\frac{M^D}{P} = \frac{M^S}{P},$$ (money market equilibrium)

money demand = money supply

where the demand for money depends on the nominal interest rate and the level of output, as defined above, and the supply of money is assumed to be fixed by the monetary authorities at $\overline{M^S}$. In Chapter 8, we examine critically the assumption that the monetary authority can fix the supply of money; for now, we assume that this is possible. This assumption allows us to develop a useful benchmark model. If we substitute the demand for money function and the fixed money supply into the equilibrium condition,

$$L(y, i) = \frac{\overline{M^S}}{P},$$ (money market equilibrium)

we can define an upward sloping locus of money supply equal to money demand equilibria—the *LM* curve in the interest rate-output diagram.

The upward-sloping *LM* curve can be explained as follows. At a low level of income, the transactions demand for money is low because less money has to be held to finance

---

[4] Someone is risk averse if, when offered a fair bet, would refuse it; i.e., if offered the choice between receiving €100 with certainty or the chance of €200 (or zero) on the outcome of the toss of a fair coin, the individual would always take the certain €100. In other words, the individual prefers a *certain* value of €100 to an uncertain return with an *expected* value of €100.

transactions. Since the supply of money is fixed, for supply to equal demand in the money market, there must be a correspondingly high asset (or speculative) demand for money. A low interest rate will ensure this, since the returns from bondholding relative to the risks involved are low. The converse argument associates a high income level with a high interest rate.[5]

Using a linear demand for money function, there is a neat way of deriving the *LM* curve so that it is easy to see how shifts in the demand for money or changes in the interest sensitivity of the demand for money or changes in the money supply will affect the *LM* curve. The method is shown in Fig. 2.3 in two steps. Working through this diagram is a

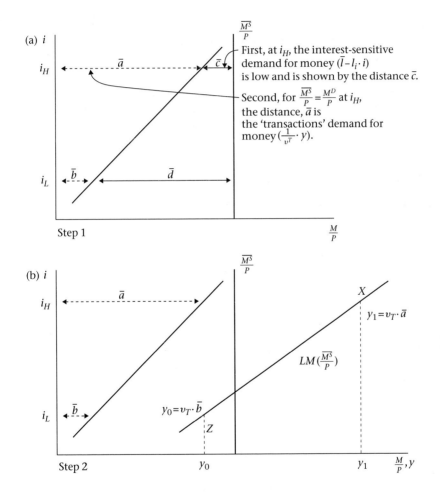

Figure 2.3 Deriving the *LM* curve

[5] The explicit form of the *LM* equation using the linear demand for money function is:

$$i = \frac{1}{l_i} \cdot \left(\bar{l} - \frac{\overline{M^S}}{P} \right) + \frac{1}{l_i} \cdot \frac{1}{v_T} \cdot y. \qquad \text{(LM equation)}$$

good method of securing your understanding of:

- the transactions demand for money and the role of v_T,
- the asset (or speculative) demand for money and the role of l_i;
- the role of the level of the money supply set by the central bank or the government, $\overline{M^S}$ and
- the equilibrium condition in the money market: $L = \frac{\overline{M^S}}{P}$.

In step 1, draw in the vertical real money supply line.[6] Now, draw in the interest-sensitive component of the demand for money 'backwards', i.e. relative to the money supply line as shown in Fig. 2.3. As we know, when the interest rate is high, the demand for money for asset purposes will be low (in the diagram, this is the distance $\bar{c}$). Now make use of the money market equilibrium condition: $\frac{\overline{M^S}}{P} = \bar{l} - l_i i + \frac{1}{v_T} \cdot y$. For money market equilibrium, asset demand for money $\left(\bar{l} - l_i i\right)$ plus the transactions demand for money ($\frac{1}{v_T} \cdot y$) are equal to the money supply. Hence we can see how large the transactions demand for money must be for money market equilibrium at the interest rate i_H in Fig. 2.3. This is shown as the distance $\bar{a}$. Once we know the transactions demand for money that is associated with the interest rate, i_H, i.e. the distance $\bar{a}$, then since v_T is a constant, it is straightforward to take the second step of calculating the level of output, y, that is consistent with generating this demand for money: $y_1 = v_T \times$ (transaction demand for money at i_H). This fixes the level of output, y_1, at which the money market is in equilibrium when the interest rate is i_H: point X in the bottom panel. Point Y can be derived in the same way. By joining points X and Y the 'LM curve' is drawn.

From the derivation of the *LM* curve, there are four ways in which the position and/or the slope of the *LM* curve can be affected.

(1) A change in the *transactions velocity of circulation*. The transactions velocity of circulation, v_T, is the constant reflecting the proportional relationship between income and the demand for *transactions* balances. It is the number of units of income that one unit of transactions balances can finance. Any rise in the transactions velocity as the result of financial innovation (e.g. introduction of credit cards, development of non-bank financial institutions) will rotate the *LM* to the right (clockwise), making it flatter.

(2) A change in the *interest sensitivity of the asset demand for money, l_i*. A more interest-sensitive demand for money, reflecting the fact that small changes in the interest rate will have large effects on the portfolio mix between money and bonds, will produce a flatter *LM* curve.
- A special case arises when the interest-sensitive demand for money becomes perfectly elastic, in which case, the *LM* curve becomes horizontal. The simplest interpretation of this is in terms of speculative demand: if it is the case that no one believes that the normal interest rate is lower than the actual interest rate, $\hat{i}$, then the speculative demand for money is perfectly elastic at $\hat{i}$ because nobody is prepared to use spare cash

---

[6] If you want to see what happens if the *supply* of money is also sensitive to the interest rate, you can modify the method at this point.

balances to further bid up the bond price. Under such conditions, the interest rate is so low that everyone believes it will rise to its normal level (opinions will differ on what that normal level is). In Fig. 2.3, if $\hat{\imath} = i_L$, the interest-sensitive money demand and the *LM* curves would turn horizontal at i_L. This is the famous 'liquidity trap' case, to which we return at the end of section 4.2 (see Fig. 2.6).

(3) A change in the *money supply*. An increase in the money supply will shift the *LM* curve to the right, since at any interest rate, with a given asset demand for money, a higher money supply will require higher transactions balances to bring money demand into line with the higher supply. A higher output level will generate the higher transactions demand.

(4) A change in the *price level*. For a given interest rate, with a higher price level, the available transactions balances can only finance a lower amount of output. The *LM* curve shifts to the left.

The simple mathematics and geometry of the *LM* curve required to specify statements 1–4 are presented in the Appendix to this chapter.

At a point such as *X* above the *LM* curve in Fig. 2.4, with the output level, y_0 and interest rate i_X, money balances are too high for money market equilibrium. We can see that the disequilibrium could be eliminated either by a rise in the level of output or by a fall in the interest rate. When there is excess supply of money (excess demand for bonds), the excess money balances are channelled into the bond market, the bond price is bid up, and the interest rate reduced (recall the earlier discussion of the inverse relationship between the interest rate and the price of bonds). The converse situation of excess demand for money is true of a point such as *Z* below the *LM* curve. This will be cleared by the sale of bonds, which pushes down the bond price and raises the interest rate.

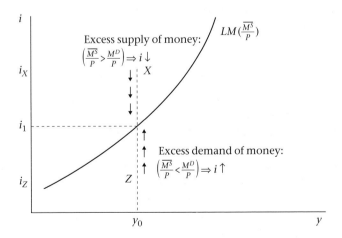

Figure 2.4 Adjustment to money market equilibrium: excess supply of money at point *X* leads to a fall in the nominal interest rate; excess demand for money at point *Z* leads to a rise in the nominal interest rate

4 Putting together the *IS* and the *LM*

By combining the goods and money markets, the interest rate and the short-run equilibrium level of output for a given price level are determined. Before that, there is one tricky problem that needs to be addressed. In the derivation of the *IS* curve, it is the *real* interest rate, *r*, that is relevant since investment spending depends on the real rate of interest. In the derivation of the *LM* curve, it is the *nominal* interest rate, *i*, that is relevant since the demand for money depends on the nominal interest rate.

4.1 Real and nominal interest rates

To clarify why it is the real rather than the nominal interest rate that affects real expenditure decisions in the economy, think about a firm considering an investment project. A higher money or nominal rate of interest will not impose a greater real burden on the firm if it is balanced by correspondingly higher inflation because the expected profits from the investment project will be higher in money terms and the balance between the real cost and the real return on the project will not have changed.

The real interest rate is defined in terms of *goods* and the nominal interest rate, in terms of *money*. Thinking of a consumer good, the real rate of interest, *r*, is how much extra in terms of this good would have to be paid in the future in order to have one of the goods today: $1 \text{ good}_t = (1 + r)\text{good}_{t+1}$, where the subscript *t* refers to today and $t + 1$ to one period later. The nominal rate of interest is how much extra in euros would have to be paid in the future in order to have one euro today: $1 \text{ €}_t = (1+i)\text{€}_{t+1}$. If goods prices remain constant then it is clear that the real and nominal interest rates are the same: if you lent one euro today, you would be able to buy $(1 + r)$ goods in the future. In general,

$$1 + r = (1 + i) \cdot \frac{P}{P^E_{t+1}},$$

where it is the expected price level in the future (P^E_{t+1}) that comes into play since at time *t*, we do not know what the price level will be at $t + 1$. If we use the following definition of expected inflation:

$$\pi^E = \frac{P^E_{t+1} - P}{P},$$

then

$$\frac{P}{P^E_{t+1}} = \frac{1}{1 + \pi^E}.$$

By rearranging the above expression, it follows that

$$(1 + r) = \frac{(1 + i)}{(1 + \pi^E)}.$$

and therefore that

$$r = \frac{i - \pi^E}{1 + \pi^E}.$$

When expected inflation is low, the denominator of this expression is close to 1 and we have the standard approximation for the relationship between the real and the nominal rate of interest:

$$i \approx r + \pi^E.$$

Inflation expectations will drive the divergence between the real and nominal interest rates. It should be noted that only one of these three terms is observable: the nominal interest rate, i. The real interest rate can be estimated from historical data on the nominal interest rate and the rate of inflation: this gives a measure of the so-called *ex post* real rate of interest. Alternatively, an *ex ante* measure can be derived from a model that is able to predict inflation. Finally, if bonds have been issued in the economy that are protected against inflation because the face value is indexed by the rate of inflation, then the yield on such a bond is a real rate of interest and can provide a third measure. But there are only a few countries that have issued index-linked or inflation-proof bonds (UK in 1981, the USA in 1997, France in 1998).

4.2 The *IS/LM* model

So as to avoid (temporarily) the problem of the *IS* depending on the real and the *LM* on the nominal interest rate we concentrate on how the *IS/LM* model works when the real and nominal rates are identical. This requires us to assume that inflation is zero and is expected to remain so. To remind us that two different interest rate concepts are involved, we draw the *IS/LM* diagram with both 'r' and 'i' on the vertical axis. We shall return to show how to amend the *IS/LM* model when inflation is different from zero in Chapter 3.

Now that both the *IS* and the *LM* relationships have been derived, the short-run equilibrium interest rate and level of output will be determined by the intersection of the two curves. To see how the *IS/LM* model works, the initial *IS/LM* equilibrium is disturbed by changing one of the exogenous variables. First, we consider the character of the new short-run equilibrium and as a second, we discuss the likely adjustment of the economy to it. The path of adjustment of the economy in the face of a disturbance will depend on the speed of adjustment in each market. The most plausible simple assumption is that money market disequilibria are cleared very rapidly in relation to disequilibria in the goods and services market. In the *IS/LM* diagram, this means that the economy returns to the relevant *LM* curve rapidly—the adjustment occurs through changes in the price of bonds in the financial markets and therefore in market interest rates. Goods market adjustment takes place less quickly since it involves adjustments to production and employment.

We look at two examples of government policy changes. In the first example (Fig. 2.5), government spending rises. The new *IS* is *IS*(g_1) to the right of the original one. The new short-run equilibrium is at the point A': output is higher and so is the interest rate. Higher government spending will generate higher aggregate demand and a higher output level.

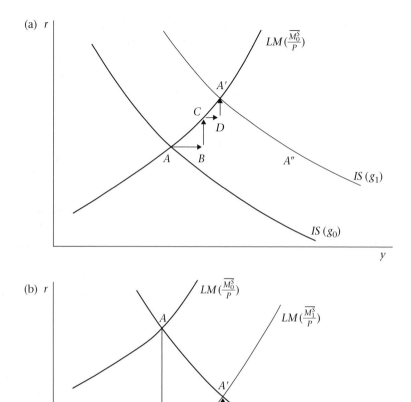

Figure 2.5 Comparative statics in the *IS/LM* model: sluggish adjustment in the goods market and rapid adjustment in the money market
(a) Fiscal policy: rise in government spending
(b) Monetary policy: rise in the money supply

Higher incomes will mean a higher demand for money but since monetary policy is unchanged (i.e. the *LM* curve remains fixed), a higher interest rate will be required in the new equilibrium to dampen the asset demand for money.

Let us now think about the likely process of adjustment to the new equilibrium. In the first instance, the rise in government spending produces excess demand for goods and results in unplanned inventory decumulation or in longer waiting times for services. If the rise in demand is sustained, then employment is increased. The economy moves from A to B. The rise in real income associated with higher output boosts the transactions demand for money, with the result that there is excess demand for money balances at *B*. Bonds are sold, causing the bond price to fall and the interest rate to rise (*B* to *C*). The rise in the interest rate dampens the excess demand for goods by reducing investment demand; nevertheless, at *C* there remains excess demand owing to increased consumption associated with the multiplier effects of the rise in government spending. Output and employment rise further (*C* to *D*). The adjustment process continues until the new equilibrium at *A'* is attained. The full multiplier expansion of output (*A* to *A''*) does not occur because when there is a fiscal expansion without any change in the money supply, the increase in the interest rate causes a fall in interest-sensitive spending. The implications of financing an increase in government expenditure by (i) taxation, (ii) bond finance as in the above example, and (iii) money finance are compared using the *IS/LM* model in Chapter 6.

In the second example (Fig. 2.5), the government or central bank increases the money supply through the use of open market operations. This means that it enters the money market purchasing bonds in exchange for newly printed money. The *LM* curve shifts to the right to $LM(\frac{\overline{MS}}{P})$. Once again, we first consider the new short-run equilibrium which has a higher level of output and a lower interest rate. With a higher money supply, the higher demand for money in the new equilibrium will require a lower interest rate. A lower interest rate will be associated with a higher level of investment and output (point *A'* in the lower panel of (Fig. 2.5)).

We turn now to the adjustment from point *A* to the new short-run equilibrium at *A'*. The immediate effect of the monetary authority's action is to create excess supply of money; the implied excess demand for bonds raises bond prices and lowers the interest rate. The economy moves from *A* to *B*, immediately attaining the new money market equilibrium along $LM(\frac{\overline{MS_1}}{P})$. The fall in the interest rate creates excess demand in the goods market by stimulating investment. Higher investment demand pushes up output and employment; raising output from *B* to *C*. At *C*, there is once again money market disequilibrium as excess *demand* for money accompanies the rise in output. The interest rate rises (*C* to *D*). Adjustment of output and the interest rate will continue until the new equilibrium at *A'* is reached.

Fig. 2.6 shows why expansionary monetary policy may not raise output even in the short run. If the interest rate is *î*, the *LM* curve is flat. When the central bank enters the money market to purchase bonds, there is no impact on the price of bonds: if everyone believes the only direction for the interest rate in the future is up, this implies they believe that bond prices will fall. Bondholders therefore willingly sell bonds at the existing price, being indifferent between money and bonds as the prospective capital loss on bonds just offsets the interest received, with the result that there is no rise in the bond price and no fall in the interest rate. The economy is in a liquidity trap where new money pumped into the economy is willingly held as money balances. The central bank is therefore powerless to use monetary policy to shift the economy to a higher level of output. For decades the case of the liquidity trap was viewed as a theoretical possibility with little practical relevance but the re-emergence of an era with very low nominal interest rates in the 1990s has revived interest in it. Since the nominal interest rate cannot fall below zero, the notion that everyone believes the interest rate will rise becomes plausible. The liquidity trap plays a role in the analysis of the long Japanese slump in the 1990s and is discussed further in Chapters 5 and 17.

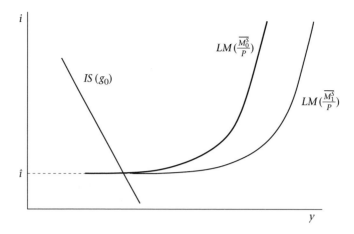

Figure 2.6 The liquidity trap

5 Aggregate supply

We turn now to setting out systematically the structure of the supply side of the economy that will be used to create an integrated short- and medium-run model. We begin by noting briefly how the supply side looks in a competitive model before moving to the more general model of imperfect competition with which we mainly work.

5.1 Equilibrium in the competitive labour market

In the competitive labour market the demand for labour and the supply of labour depend on the real wage. The downward-sloping labour demand curve shows the labour demanded at a given real wage. With a fixed capital stock, as we assume is the case in the short and medium run, output is a positive function of the level of employment, i.e.

$$y = f(E),$$

where f is the short- (and medium-) run production function. The standard assumption is that the production function is characterized by diminishing returns, which means that as more workers are employed, the increment in output declines. In short, the marginal product of labour, which can be written as $\frac{\partial y}{\partial E}$ or MPL declines as employment rises. The labour demand curve is often referred to as the MPL curve since under perfect competition, firms take the real wage as given and employ labour up to the point at which the marginal product of labour is equal to the real wage.

The supply of labour is upward sloping and is derived from the optimizing behaviour of households as they allocate their time between work and leisure to maximize their utility. The real wage is taken as given and the worker chooses the amount of labour to supply.

In a competitive labour market, the market clears, establishing the market-clearing real wage and level of employment. This is shown in Fig. 2.7 with the real wage w_0 and employment, E_{CE} (for *Competitive Equilibrium*). Any temporary displacement of the economy

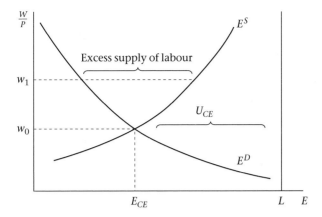

Figure 2.7 Equilibrium in the competitive labour market: equilibrium values of the real wage and employment

from equilibrium is assumed to be eliminated by a movement in real wages. For example, if the real wage rises above the market-clearing level (due say, to an unexpected fall in the price level), then labour supply exceeds labour demand at that real wage (w_1). The excess supply of labour will result in falling money wages until the unique competitive equilibrium is re-established with the real wage at w_0 and employment at E_{CE}. In this model, the only people who will be unemployed will be those *voluntarily* unemployed in the sense that at the going real wage, they prefer searching for a job or leisure over the goods obtainable through working. In Fig. 2.7, the labour force, which can be thought of as the maximum amount of labour that could be supplied, is shown by the vertical line. The competitive equilibrium rate of unemployment is U_{CE}/L, where L is the labour force, i.e. the sum of the employed and the unemployed. It is important to remember that the economy is at a welfare optimum in the competitive equilibrium so the voluntary unemployment that exists does not signify a problem. Rather, it reflects the choice by workers about whether and how much to work at the existing real wage.

6 Supply side in the imperfect competition model

A major task of macroeconomics is to analyse the causes and consequences of *involuntary* unemployment. Unless there are imperfections in the labour market, it is not possible for there to be involuntary unemployment when the labour market is in equilibrium, since wages would fall to clear the market. This is prevented in an imperfectly competitive labour market in which the wage is set either by employers, by unions, or as a result of bargaining between employer and union. Labour is not bought and sold in a spot market (like wheat); there are wage contracts that set the wage above the market-clearing level. As we have seen in Chapter 1, collective bargaining affects wage setting for a substantial proportion of workers in most OECD countries (see Appendix Table 4.1, Chapter 4 for the extent to which workers' wages are covered by collective bargaining in the full list of OECD countries.) Even in the absence of unions, problems of motivating workers to work efficiently mean that wages are set by employers above the market-clearing level. In imperfectly competitive product markets, firms set prices with a mark-up over their costs. The real wage is therefore the outcome of wage- and price-setting decisions across the economy. In an open economy model, the price level of imports will also affect wage and price setting but this issue is not addressed until later. The first section of Chapter 10 can be read in parallel with this section to see how the openness of the economy affects wage setting, price setting, and equilibrium unemployment. In the imperfect competition model, the *ERU* is the unemployment rate at which the real wage is consistent with the real wage expectations of both wage and price setters.

6.1 Wage setting

Under imperfect competition, there is an upward-sloping wage setting (*WS*) curve that is the counterpart of the labour supply curve in the competitive model. Because of labour market imperfections, the wage setting curve lies above the labour supply curve. In Fig. 2.8, if the real wage is equal to w_1, then the competitive labour supply is E_1. But with labour market imperfections, w_1 will be set at the lower level of employment, E_0 despite the fact that an additional number of workers ($E_1 - E_0$) would be prepared to work at that wage. Similarly, if $E = E_0$, then this supply of labour is consistent with a real wage of w_0, but under imperfect competition, a higher wage, w_1, is set at that level of employment.

Conditions in the labour market are the key determinant of the 'wage setting real wage'. In terms of money wages, the wage setting equation is

$$W = P \cdot b(E) \qquad \text{(wage equation)}$$

where P is the price level, E is the level of employment and b is a rising function of employment. When wages are set by unions, employers, or through bargaining, it is the

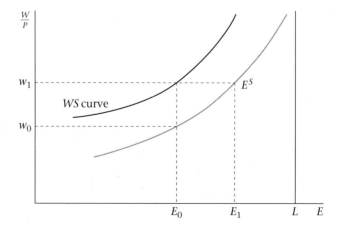

Figure 2.8 The wage setting real wage curve: *WS* curve and the labour supply curve

nominal (i.e. money) wage that is fixed. However, workers will evaluate wage offers in terms of the *real* wage that they are expected to deliver—i.e. it is the money wage relative to the expected consumer price level that affects the standard of living and hence the worker's utility.

Assuming that the actual and expected price level are equal, the wage equation can be written in terms of real wages to define the upward-sloping wage-setting curve in the labour market diagram (see Fig. 2.8):

$$w^{WS} = b(E), \qquad \text{(wage-setting real wage)}$$

where $w^{WS} \equiv W/P$.

The excess of the real wage on the *WS* curve above that on the labour supply curve at any level of employment is the mark-up per worker (in real terms) associated with labour market imperfections.

Two common interpretations of this mark-up, both relying on imperfect competition, are

(1) wage setting by unions and

(2) efficiency wage setting by firms.

6.1.1 Wage setting by unions

In unionized workplaces, wages are set through negotiations between the employer and the union. A simplified model of union wage setting takes the case of the so-called monopoly union, where the union can unilaterally set the wage. The union sets the wage in the interests of its members, who are concerned with both the real wage and employment. It aims to strike a balance between (i) too high a wage, which will push up the price of the firm's product and decrease demand for the firm's output and hence employment and (ii) too low a wage, which will fail to use the union's monopoly power to secure better living standards. This results in the union setting a wage at a given employment level that is higher than the competitive wage (the difference is referred to as the union wage mark-up) and produces a positively sloped wage setting curve that lies above the competitive labour supply curve. The details of how to derive the wage setting curve in the monopoly union model are set out graphically in Chapter 4 and in more detail in Chapter 15.

6.1.2 Efficiency wage setting by firms

Efficiency wage setting is quite different: here it is firms that set wages. At first sight, it is counter-intuitive that an employer should voluntarily set a wage above the minimum at which it can hire labour in the market. The argument is that by setting a wage above the competitive one, the employer is able to retain a well-qualified and cooperative workforce. The term 'efficiency' wages arises from the notion that the firm sets a wage that allows it to efficiently solve its motivation, recruitment, and/or retention problems. These problems arise because it is generally not possible to specify fully what a worker does, i.e. the employer cannot observe accurately the worker's effort. The employer must therefore use the wage to motivate the worker to perform well. As the labour market tightens, i.e. as unemployment falls, it becomes more difficult for the firm to solve these problems because workers can easily leave the firm and find work elsewhere. The result is that the employer sets a wage above the competitive wage and this 'efficiency' wage rises as unemployment falls. This is therefore a second way of understanding the wage setting curve. The details of how to derive the wage setting curve in efficiency wage models can be found in the appendix to Chapter 15 and can be understood without reading the rest of Chapter 15.

6.2 Price setting

Under perfect competition, the real wage implied by competitive pricing by firms is the marginal product of labour (or labour demand) curve. Firms take the market price, P, and set it equal to their marginal cost:

$$P = MC$$
$$= \frac{W}{MPL}$$
$$\Rightarrow \frac{W}{P} = MPL.$$

By contrast, under imperfect competition, firms set a price to maximize profits. The mark-up on marginal cost will depend on the elasticity of demand: as the elasticity of demand rises, the mark-up falls until we get to the special case of perfect competition where the elasticity of demand is infinite.

If we take the simplest case of monopoly, then profits are maximized when marginal revenue is equal to marginal cost. If the (absolute value of the) elasticity of demand (ϵ, called epsilon) is constant, then there is a constant mark-up greater than one of $\frac{\epsilon}{\epsilon-1}$ and we have the standard monopoly pricing formula:

$$P = \frac{\epsilon}{\epsilon - 1} \cdot \frac{W}{MPL}$$

and the price-setting real wage is:

$$\frac{W}{P} = \frac{\epsilon - 1}{\epsilon} \cdot MPL.$$

Fig. 2.9 illustrates the *PS* curve in the monopoly case: because $\frac{\epsilon-1}{\epsilon} < 1$, the price-setting real wage is a fraction of the marginal product of labour.

More generally, any type of product market imperfection causes the *PS* curve to lie below the competitive labour demand curve. The excess of the real wage on the labour demand curve above that on the *PS* curve at any level of employment is the supernormal profits per worker (in real terms) associated with the imperfect competition in the product market.

We shall normally use a horizontal rather than a downward-sloping *PS* curve. As we have seen, switching from perfect to imperfect competition does not in itself lead to a

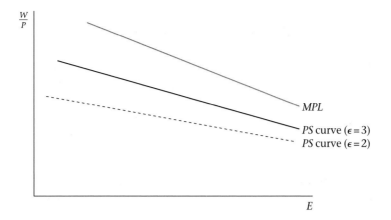

Figure 2.9 Relationship between the *MPL*, the price elasticity of demand, and the *PS* curve

horizontal *PS* curve. Additional assumptions are required. Three alternatives are:

• if the marginal product of labour is constant (which implies that it is equal to the average product) and the mark-up is constant, the price-setting real wage is equal to a constant fraction of labour productivity.

• if the marginal product of labour declines but the mark-up is counter-cyclical (i.e. the mark-up shrinks as employment rises) then the *PS* curve will flatten. The mark-up would be counter-cyclical if for example, new entry was encouraged by a boom, heightening product market competition.

• if firms set their prices using a rule of thumb, basing their price on their average costs over the business cycle (i.e. as the economy moves from recession to boom and vice versa) the *PS* curve would also flatten. Such a 'normal cost pricing' rule might result from firms wishing to limit the extent to which they modify their prices in response to changes in cost associated with changes in demand. Frequent price changes in response to changes in demand are costly in themselves (these are the so-called menu costs of price changes) and firms may also wish to avoid them for strategic reasons.

When looking explicitly at different patterns of how the real wage moves over the course of the business cycle or at the implications of supply-side policies for real wages, we should consider the more general downward-sloping *PS* curve. In other cases, it is more straightforward to use a flat *PS* curve. The flat *PS* curve offers a useful simplification because it implies that firms do not change their prices in response to fluctuations in output (in line with our assumption of sticky prices in the short run); rather, they change their prices only when their costs change, e.g. as a consequence of a change in wages. On the reasonable assumption that wage changes occur relatively infrequently (e.g. at the annual wage round or the periodic wage review in the case of individual contracts), it is wage changes that provide the natural trigger for the end of the short run in the model.

In this baseline case, we use simple assumptions to deliver a flat *PS* curve: a constant marginal product and a constant mark-up. Given these assumptions, if firms set prices to deliver a specific profit margin, then the fixed amount of output per worker is split into two parts: profits per worker and real wages per worker. The real wage implied by pricing behaviour is therefore constant and the *PS* curve is flat. Price setting can then be summarized as the marking up of unit labour costs by a fixed percentage, $\widehat{\mu}$ (pronounced 'mew' hat) on unit labour costs,

$$P = (1 + \widehat{\mu}) \left(\frac{W}{\lambda} \right), \qquad \text{(mark-up pricing rule)}$$

where unit labour costs are the cost of labour per unit of output i.e. $W \times E$ divided by y. We define $\frac{y}{E}$ (output per worker) as λ (lambda, labour productivity).

It is handy to express the mark-up in a slightly different way when setting up the macro model. If we let $\mu = \widehat{\mu}/(1 + \widehat{\mu})$, then the pricing equation can be written as

$$P = \frac{1}{1 - \mu} \cdot \frac{W}{\lambda}, \qquad \text{(price-setting equation)}$$

where we refer to μ as the mark-up from now on. This means that as the extent of competition faced by the firm increases, the size of the mark-up falls. Dividing each side by P and rearranging, gives

$$\lambda = \mu \cdot \lambda + \frac{W}{P}$$

output per head = real profits per head + real wages per head.

In other words, given the mark-up, the level of labour productivity, and the money wage, the price level set by firms implies a specific value of the real wage. This is the price-setting real wage (see Fig. 2.10):

$$w^{PS} = \frac{W}{P} = \lambda \cdot (1 - \mu). \qquad \text{(price-setting real wage)}$$

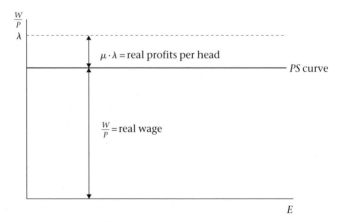

Figure 2.10 The price-setting real wage curve: *PS* curve

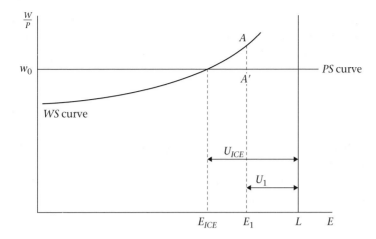

Figure 2.11 Equilibrium employment and unemployment: U_{ICE} and E_{ICE}

6.3 Equilibrium in the labour market under imperfect competition

The labour market under imperfect competition is characterized by an upward-sloping *WS* curve and a flat or downward-sloping *PS* curve. The labour market is in equilibrium where the curves cross (see Fig. 2.11):

$$w^{WS} = w^{PS}$$
$$b(E) = \lambda \cdot (1 - \mu),$$

(labour market equilibrium, imperfect competition)

and defines the unique equilibrium level of employment E_{ICE}, where $_{ICE}$ stands for 'imperfect competition equilibrium'. The associated equilibrium rate of unemployment (the *ERU*) is U_{ICE}/L, where L is the labour force.

The assumption that prices are set straight after wages (i.e. without a lag) means that the real wage is always on the *PS* curve whereas as noted above, workers are on the *WS* curve believing that the current price level is at its expected level. To take an example, suppose that employment rises to E_1 as a consequence of an expansionary fiscal policy. At the next wage setting round, this provokes a money wage rise as wage setters aim for point A. However, the immediate adjustment of prices to the cost increase means that prices rise in line with the wage increase and the economy moves to point A'. The timing assumption means that the economy is normally on the *PS* curve; if $P > P^E$, workers will be on the *PS* curve to the right of the equilibrium and if $P < P^E$, they will be on the *PS* curve to the left of the equilibrium. It follows that if lags in price setting were introduced, the real wage would lie in between the *WS* and *PS* curves.

The contrast between the competitive and imperfectly competitive equilibrium rates of unemployment is shown in Fig. 2.12, which superimposes the *WS* and *PS* curves on the labour market diagram showing the competitive labour supply and marginal product of labour curves. The *WS* curve lies above the labour supply curve to reflect the market imperfection. Similarly, the *PS* curve lies beneath the marginal product of labour curve

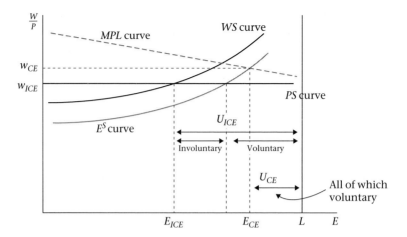

Figure 2.12 Concepts of unemployment

if there is imperfect competition in the product market: with firms making supernormal profits, workers will be paid less than their marginal product.

If the labour market is imperfectly competitive, unemployment at the *ERU* (equilibrium rate of unemployment) will necessarily include some involuntary unemployment. In other words, there will be individuals prepared to take a job at the going real wage who are unable to find a vacancy. How do we know this? The labour supply curve indicates the real wage at which an individual is prepared to work. Since the labour supply curve lies beneath the wage setting curve, we know that there are people who would be willing to work at the real wage, w_{ICE}, who are not employed when employment is at its equilibrium level, E_{ICE}.

Since there is involuntary unemployment at U_{ICE}, it is not the 'ideal' rate from a welfare perspective. Rather, given the institutions and practices in the economy that lie behind the wage and price setting curves, the *ERU* is the unemployment rate that constitutes an equilibrium in the sense that wage and price setters have no reason to change their behaviour. The split between involuntary and voluntary unemployment in the imperfect competition model is shown in the diagram.[7]

The equilibrium rate of unemployment is the outcome of structural or supply-side features of the economy that lie behind the wage setting and price-setting curves. It can therefore in principle be changed by supply-side policies or structural changes. For example, changes in legislation to weaken trade unions could lead to a reduction of union bargaining power and this would lower the expected real wage that could be negotiated by workers at any level of unemployment, lowering $b(E)$ and shifting the *WS* curve down. Holding all other features of the economy constant, this would lower the equilibrium rate of unemployment. Alternatively, an increase in the degree of product market competition—as a result, say, of changes in the application of competition policy or because the internet makes it easier to compare prices—would produce a lower profit

---

[7] For a recent exploration of different concepts of unemployment, see de Vroey (2004*a*). A summary can be found in de Vroey (2004*b*).

margin (μ) and a higher real wage at each level of employment (the *PS* curve would shift up). Similarly, any government policy change that affects wage- and price-setting outcomes will shift equilibrium unemployment. Policies related to unemployment benefits, taxation, labour, and product market regulation and incomes accords are all relevant. It is thus easy to imagine that international differences in policy and in institutional structures produce differences in equilibrium unemployment. We return to analyse supply-side shifts in Chapter 4.

7 Aggregate demand and aggregate supply

In many presentations of short- and medium-run macroeconomics, the two components of aggregate demand and supply are brought together using a diagram with the price level on the vertical axis and output on the horizontal one. We shall not make extensive use of this diagram in this book because it is not a particularly good way of analysing shocks and policy responses. However, it does serve a couple of useful purposes: first, it provides a simple way of seeing how the price level is determined and second it provides another lens through which macro models can be compared.

7.1 Aggregate demand: from the *IS/LM* diagram to the *AD* curve

The goods and money market equilibrium conditions can be transfered to a diagram with the price level on the vertical axis and output on the horizontal axis. In the top panel of Fig. 2.13, the economy begins at point *A*. (Note that the *LM* curve is indexed by the real money supply: $\frac{\overline{M^s}}{P_1}$, which means that the position of the *LM* curve is fixed by the real money supply defined by $\frac{\overline{M^s}}{P_1}$.) Next, we hold the nominal money supply constant and lower the price level to P_0: the new money market equilibrium is shown by $LM(\frac{\overline{M^s}}{P_0})$. The increase in the value of the real money balances in the hands of the public creates disequilibrium in the money market: with 'too much money', households rebalance their portfolios by buying bonds. This pushes up the bond price and lowers the interest rate. This is known as the 'Keynes effect'. The new equilibrium is at point *B* with higher output. The equilibria at *A* and *B* are mapped into the diagram beneath with *P* on the vertical and *y* on the horizontal axis. The combined goods and money market equilibria for different price levels produce the *AD* curve as shown. It follows from this derivation that anything that shifts the *IS* or *LM* curves, apart from a change in the price level, shifts the *AD* curve.

The *AD* curve has a completely different character from a demand curve in a microeconomic market, where the demand curve relates the quantity demanded to the price of a particular commodity.[8] By contrast, the *AD* curve represents two sets of equilibrium conditions. When the price level *P* changes, it disturbs the equilibrium in the money market, which triggers a change in behaviour that leads the interest rate to change. This in

---

[8] Why does a lower price level *not* mean that people are better off and therefore buy more? The fallacy in this argument is that a lower general price level implies lower money incomes in the economy since these make up the price level. Hence a lower price level does not imply higher real incomes and spending.

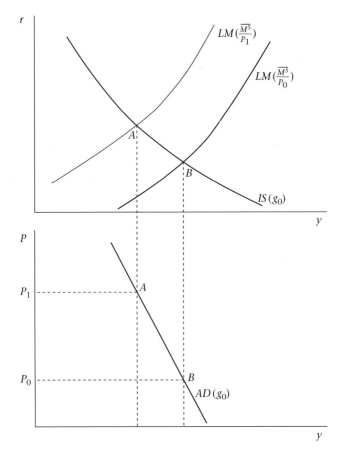

Figure 2.13 Deriving the *AD* curve

turn creates a disequilibrium in the goods market and output changes as equilibrium is restored.

We have already encountered indirectly the case in which a fall in the price level is *not* associated with a rise in output: the liquidity trap. If the *LM* curve is horizontal, then a fall in *P* shifts the horizontal section of the *LM* to the right and the interest rate does not change. The reason is that households are happy to hold on to the higher real money balances because they believe that the interest rate can fall no further. Under such circumstances, falling prices fail to stimulate the economy. This is one way of interpreting the Japanese slump in the early 2000s.

When Keynes argued for the relevance of the liquidity trap in the 1930s, some economists responded by claiming that even if the interest rate did not respond to a fall in the price level, there was another route to the revival of demand. The so-called Pigou effect depends on the response of consumption to changes in real wealth. If the Pigou effect is at work, falling prices raise real wealth and stimulate consumption thereby restoring the downward slope to the *AD* curve. But there seems to be a reverse

Pigou effect at work in Japan, where it is reported that falling prices leads consumers to hoard money in the expectation that prices will fall even further: consumption is postponed and not boosted.

7.2 Aggregate supply: from the labour market diagram to the *AS* curve

Information about the labour market equilibrium can also be transferred into the so-called *AD-AS* diagram. In both the competitive and imperfectly competitive models, there is a unique employment level consistent with labour market equilibrium. The short-run production function is used to convert that level of employment into the medium-run equilibrium level of output. Since the labour market equilibrium is defined in real terms, changes in the price level do not affect the equilibrium.

The aggregate supply curve is therefore vertical at y_{CE} or y_{ICE}, which is at the output level y_0 in Fig. 2.14. The diagram can be interpreted as representing either the competitive or the imperfectly competitive case. A rightward shift in the aggregate demand curve because of a rise in autonomous consumption, for example, would be associated with labour market equilibrium only at the unchanged y_{CE} or y_{ICE}. If the price level jumps up as shown in Fig. 2.14, then the economy moves straight from A to Z.

This special case of the immediate adjustment of wages and prices is summarized by the *AD* curve combined with a vertical *AS* curve. An economy of this kind experiences fluctuations in output only as a consequence of changes on the supply-side since fluctuations in aggregate demand shift the *AD* curve (e.g. fiscal policy, monetary policy, or private sector shocks), which affects the price level but not output and employment. We return to Fig. 2.14 below, but first, we look more closely at a model of business cycles where they are driven by the supply side.

7.3 Two approaches to business cycles

7.3.1 The Real Business Cycle model: supply shocks

The idea that the fluctuations in employment that we observe in the economy as it moves from recession to boom and back again are due purely to supply-side factors rather than to fluctuations in aggregate demand is central to the so-called Real Business Cycle (RBC) model.[9] In this model, the labour market is *always* in equilibrium. We shall see that this contrasts with the situation in a model in which the business cycle is driven by fluctuations in aggregate demand where in a boom, employment is above the equilibrium and in a recession, employment is below it. In the RBC model, it is supply-side factors such as changes in technology that drive the business cycle. To see how this works, we assume that in Fig. 2.15, the economy is initially at point A. A positive technology shock such as a wave of innovation, then shifts the marginal product of labour curve to the right (to MPL_H) and the economy moves to point B: this is a boom. The opportunity for workers to earn higher wages as a consequence of the new technology, leads them to

---

[9] The Nobel Prize in economics in 2004 was awarded to the economists that developed the real business cycle approach: Finn Kydland and Edward C. Prescott. Their prize lectures and other useful material can be found at: http://nobelprize.org/economics/laureates/2004/.

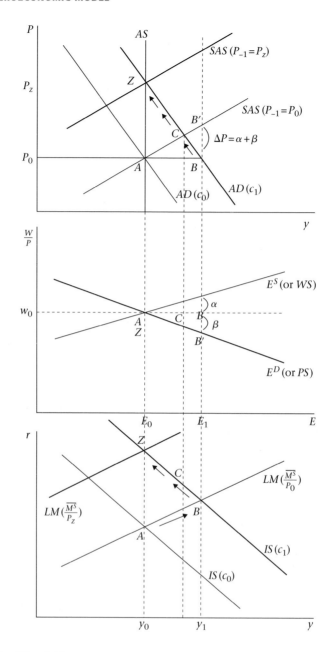

Figure 2.14 The *AD* and *AS* curves

supply more labour, i.e. to move up the labour supply curve. *B* is therefore also a position of labour market equilibrium. A negative supply shock, e.g. a sudden scarcity of a key raw material, would take the economy into a recession as the *MPL* curve shifted to the left leading to a new equilibrium at point *C*. At *C*, workers choose to supply less labour. The fall in employment is entirely voluntary in the sense that given the new circumstances

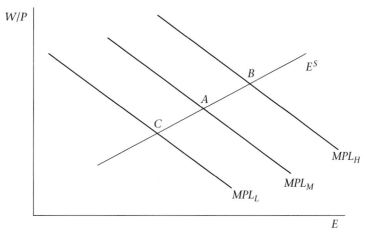

Figure 2.15 The Real Business Cycle model: equilibrium fluctuations due to technology shocks

facing them following the leftward shift in the marginal product of labour curve, workers choose to supply less labour. Workers choose to shift the timing of their supply of labour in response to the shifts in demand by working more in good times and less in bad times. This is called the 'intertemporal substitution of labour'.

Many economists remain sceptical about the idea that

- supply-side forces are the dominant source of business cycle fluctuations and that
- business cycles are purely 'equilibrium' phenomena.

As we shall see in Chapters 13 and 14, technological change plays the key role in explanations of the long-run growth of living standards. However, it seems less plausible that fluctuations in the rate of technical progress lie behind the pattern of booms and recessions that characterize economies. When an economy recovers from a recession, productivity typically rises relative to its long-run trend, with the reverse characterizing a recession. However, this does not mean that it is technical change that is causing the boom and recession—a simpler explanation consistent with the aggregate demand-based view of business cycles is that when aggregate demand falls, firms hold on to workers in the hope that the recession will be short-lived. It is costly to hire and fire workers so labour hoarding is to be expected. This will produce the outcome that productivity falls in recessions (employment is reduced by less than output falls) and rises in booms.

From Fig. 2.15, it is clear that for the RBC mechanism to be able to explain the substantial changes in employment that take place over the business cycle, a small change in the real wage must lead to a large change in the supply of labour, i.e. the labour supply curve needs to be very elastic. However, this does not fit the empirical evidence, which shows that for the main earner in the household, the intertemporal elasticity of labour supply is quite low.[10] Although the RBC approach is not the mainstream view of

---

[10] Recent evidence is presented in Ham and Reilly (2002) and in French (2004).

what drives business cycles it has had a major influence on the methodology of modern macroeconomics at the research frontier. This is discussed in more detail in Chapter 15.

7.3.2 Business cycles: aggregate demand shocks plus sticky wages and prices

At the opposite extreme from a world of rapidly adjusting wages and prices is the *IS/LM* model, where we assume that wages and prices do not adjust at all in the short run. Returning to Fig. 2.14, the sluggish adjustment of nominal wages and of prices implies the economy does not move directly from A to Z in response to an aggregate demand shock. In Fig. 2.14, the short-run adjustment due to the rightward shift of the *IS* curve is shown in the bottom panel and in the *AD-AS* diagram as the movement from A to B with the price level unchanged at P_0 in the top panel. It is clear from the middle panel that the labour market is not in equilibrium when employment is at E_1.

The short run comes to an end as wages and prices begin to adjust in response to the disequilibrium in the labour market. The nature of the disequilibrium is clear: the prevailing real wage, w_0, is on neither the labour supply nor labour demand curve in the competitive interpretation of Fig. 2.14; nor is it on the *WS* or the *PS* curve in the imperfectly competitive interpretation. The real wage is too *low* to elicit a supply of labour E_1 and too *high* for the employment of E_1 workers to be profitable. Under imperfect competition, wage setters will not be satisfied with a real wage of w_0 if employment is as high as E_1; and if the higher employment is accompanied by falling marginal productivity, then the profit margin cannot be maintained if the real wage remains at w_0. (If the *PS* curve was flat, price-setters would still be in equilibrium at B but wage setters would not.)

One way of explaining what happens once wages and prices begin to adjust is to assume that money wages go up by α—we assume this is interpreted as a real wage increase based on their view of the prevailing price level. But subsequently, prices rise by $\alpha + \beta$ to restore equilibrium on the price-setting side of the labour market. This leaves the economy at point B' in the labour market and *AD-AS* diagrams.[11]

The line through A and B' in the *AD-AS* diagram defines a short-run aggregate supply curve, the $SAS(P_{-1} = P_0)$. The *SAS* curve is indexed by last period's price level, P_{-1} to capture the assumption that when the money wage rises, the implications for the real wage are interpreted by workers in terms of the pre-existing price level, P_0. The slope of the *SAS* depends on the size of α and β and hence on the slope of the labour supply and labour demand curves (or the *WS* and *PS* curves). A flat *PS* curve produces a flatter *SAS* (since $\beta = 0$).

In fact, the economy moves from point B to C rather than to B' because of the impact of the higher price level on aggregate demand. A rise in the price level leads to a fall in the real money supply and the interest rate rises, reducing aggregate demand (the *LM* shifts left; the economy moves north-west up the *AD* curve). When the economy is at point C, the disequilibrium in the labour market is smaller than before but has not completely disappeared. The adjustment from C to Z occurs through the upward shifting of the

---

[11] We make the simplifying assumption that money wages change first and that prices change immediately afterwards. This implies that the real wage is on the labour demand (or *PS*) curve. By introducing different lags in wage and price adjustment, the real wage during the adjustment from B to Z can be anywhere between the labour demand curve and the labour supply curve or the *PS* and *WS* at the prevailing level of employment. Differences in lag patterns affect the real wage/ employment outcomes as the economy adjusts from B to Z.

SAS curves as the higher price level is incorporated into the next period's labour market decisions. Eventually, the price level rises to P_z and the $SAS(P_{-1} = P_z)$ crosses the *AS* curve at *Z*. At *Z*, equilibrium is restored in the labour market.

To summarize, when the *IS/LM* model is combined with sluggish adjustment on the supply side, the results of a positive *IS* shock are as follows:

- the *IS* curve shifts to the right and output and employment rise with the price and wage level unchanged in the short run. This is a business cycle boom. (To analyse a recession, work through the case of a negative *IS* shock.)

- in the labour market, there is disequilibrium and eventually wages and prices move in response.

- the higher price level leads in turn to a reduction in aggregate demand via the 'Keynes effect'.

- workers update the price level on the basis of which they behave, which shifts the *SAS* upwards.

- in the long run, equilibrium is restored with unemployment at the *ERU*, a higher real interest rate (and a change in the composition of output from investment to, in this example, consumption), and a higher price level.

As a final example it is interesting to consider two policy experiments—a change in the nominal money supply, $\overline{M^s}$ and a fiscal expansion. A monetary expansion shifts the *LM* curve and the *AD* curve to the right. The new medium-run equilibrium is at the *ERU*, real wages are unchanged, and the price level and nominal wage level are higher. In the *IS/LM* diagram, the new and old equilibria coincide: the impact of the increase on the money supply on the *LM* curve is reversed by the subsequent rise in the price level. By contrast, after a fiscal expansion, output returns in the medium run to its initial level, but its composition is different as the higher government spending crowds out some interest-sensitive private expenditure.

8 Conclusions

In this chapter, we have come quite a long way in setting out a macroeconomic model for short- and medium-run analysis. We can summarize the findings of the chapter as follows:

- In the short run, the level of employment and output is determined by the level of aggregate demand, which is analysed using the *IS/LM* model. This means that business cycles, i.e. booms and recessions, are due to fluctuations in the level of aggregate demand. Such fluctuations affect employment and output because of the nominal rigidities in the economy, i.e. the stickiness of wages and prices.

- Equilibrium in the labour market occurs where the labour supply and labour demand curves cross in a competitive economy and where the price-setting and wage setting curves cross in an imperfectly competitive economy. At the competitive equilibrium, any unemployment is voluntary, whereas at the imperfectly competitive equilibrium, there is a mixture of voluntary and involuntary unemployment.

• The wage-setting curve lies above the labour supply curve and it will be further above it the greater are the imperfections in the labour market. Similarly, the price-setting curve lies below the marginal product of labour curve and it will be further below the greater are the product market imperfections. With labour and/or product market imperfections, the equilibrium unemployment rate is higher than the competitive one. Structural and institutional features of the labour and product markets including government regulation affect the slope and position of the *WS* and *PS* curves.

• The aggregate demand and aggregate supply sides of the model are brought together in the *AD-AS* model. Under normal circumstances, the *AD* curve is downward sloping because a lower price level leads to the rebalancing of portfolios and a fall in the interest rate, which stimulates demand. The *AD* curve is vertical if there is a liquidity trap.

• There is a vertical aggregate supply curve at the level of output associated with labour market equilibrium. If prices and wages adjust immediately to any aggregate demand shock, the economy moves vertically up or down the *AS* curve and unemployment remains at the *ERU*. However, we normally assume there is no adjustment of wages and prices in the short run. When adjustment does take place, the economy moves along the *SAS* curve, which shows how wages adjust given the pre-existing price level; prices are assumed to adjust immediately after wages. The *SAS* shifts upwards and the economy eventually reaches the medium-run equilibrium.

• When the economy is in labour market equilibrium (at the *ERU*), the price level is the outcome of the factors that determine aggregate demand and aggregate supply: a shift on either side implies a new price level at labour market equilibrium. A change in the money supply leads to a new medium-run equilibrium characterized by a pure change in the price level with no change in either the level or composition of output.

• The economy fluctuates around the *ERU* as a result of shifts in aggregate demand (i.e. due to factors incorporated in the *IS* or *LM* curves). Business cycles are therefore disequilibrium phenomena. In the perfectly competitive economy, all unemployment when the economy is at the supply-side equilibrium is voluntary; involuntary unemployment arises in the short run when a fall in aggregate demand leads to a reduction in employment below equilibrium, i.e. while prices and wages are fixed. In the imperfect competition model, there is a mixture of voluntary and involuntary unemployment at the *ERU* and there is a rise in involuntary unemployment when a fall in aggregate demand pushes output and employment below the equilibrium.

• A completely different interpretation of business cycles is provided by the Real Business Cycle model. According to the RBC approach, fluctuations on the supply side lie behind cycles. Shifts in the *MPL* curve due to technology shocks generate cycles. These cycles are equilibrium phenomena since the economy is always in labour market equilibrium, irrespective of whether employment is buoyant or depressed. There is no involuntary unemployment.

To take the analysis of business cycles closer to that of contemporary economies, we need to incorporate inflation and an inflation-targeting central bank into the model. This is done in Chapter 3.

▨ QUESTIONS

Checklist questions

(1) What is the *IS* curve? Why does it slope downward? Why does an increase in government spending shift it to the right? What happens to the *IS* curve when the marginal propensity to consume rises? [Explain using words and either diagrams or equations; see the Appendix for the equations.]

(2) Assume that the interest rate is constant. Explain in words what happens when there is an increase in government spending. In so doing, explain the concept of the multiplier.

(3) What is the *LM* curve and why does it slope upward? What happens to the *LM* curve when (*a*) there is an increase in the demand for money (at a given level of income and interest rate); (*b*) the interest elasticity of the demand for money rises?

(4) Briefly explain why it is the real interest rate that is relevant for the *IS* curve and the nominal interest rate for the *LM* curve.

(5) Provide two different explanations for why the *PS* curve may be flat.

(6) Why is the *WS* curve upward sloping (*a*) when wages are set by unions and (*b*) when wages are set by firms?

(7) What is being assumed about the timing of wage setting and price setting that enables us to say that the economy is always on the *PS* curve but only on the *WS* curve in a medium-run equilibrium? What timing assumptions would deliver the result that the economy is always on the *WS* curve but only on the *PS* curve in a medium-run equilibrium?

(8) Discuss the plausibility of the assumptions in the previous question. Discuss the implications of the timing assumptions for the way real wages move in response to fluctuations in aggregate demand.

(9) What are the similarities and differences between the characteristics of labour market equilibrium under perfect as compared with imperfect competition?

(10) Show the likely effects on price- and/or wage setting behaviour as reflected in the *WS*/*PS* diagram of the following:
 (*a*) workers become more worried about losing their jobs at any given level of employment
 (*b*) the government intervenes to protect domestic firms from foreign competition
 (*c*) higher social security contributions paid by employers

(*d*) a reduction in the proportion of employees covered by union wage agreements (e.g. as the result of a decline in industries in the economy that are heavily unionized).

(11) In the context of tripartite negotiations between unions, employers' associations, and the government, union bosses strike a deal whereby they agree to make lower wage demands. Show the effect in the *WS/PS* diagram if they do so in return for:

(*a*) a reduction in the length of the working week so that workers finish at lunchtime on Fridays (assume that wages and productivity on the vertical axis are measured per week)

(*b*) statutory improvements in working conditions that boost morale.

(12) Does the aggregate demand curve for the whole economy slope down for the same reason as does the demand curve for DVDs?

(13) Explain why the long-run aggregate supply curve is vertical but the short-run one is not.

Problems and questions for discussion

QUESTION A. In an *IS/LM* model of the economy, why does the slope of the *IS* curve matter for macrocononomic policy analysis? Choose a policy instrument that will change the slope of the *IS* and explain why. What can you conclude from this example about how fiscal and monetary policy may interact?

QUESTION B. Suppose that there is a large temporary fall in private sector investment. What would you expect the effect of this to be? What would you expect to determine how long the effect lasts?

QUESTION C. Use the *IS/LM* model and compare the short-run implications of the use of two different monetary policies. Policy 1 is to keep the interest rate constant and Policy 2 is to keep the money supply constant. Choose a private sector '*IS*' shock that depresses the level of equilibrium output. Compare the implications for output of the use of Policies 1 and 2. Now choose a private sector '*LM*' shock that lowers equilibrium output and complete the same exercise as above. If the authorities are interested in stabilizing the economy, would you recommend that they adopt Policy 1 or Policy 2?

QUESTION D. Real wages are mildly procyclical in most industrial economies. Explore which models of wage and price formation and which sources of fluctuations in economic activity are consistent with this observation.

QUESTION E. Keynes emphasizes the weakness of the self-equilibrating forces in a capitalist economy and highlights the role of government in stabilization. Milton Friedman argues that Keynes's influence on public policy was enormous:

Keynes believed that economists (and others) could best contribute to the improvement of society by investigating how to manipulate the levers actually or potentially under control of the political authorities so as to achieve desirable ends, and then persuading benevolent civil servants and elected officials to follow their advice. The role of voters is to elect persons with the right moral values to office and then let them run the country.[12]

---

[12] Friedman (1997).

Think about Friedman's argument and consider what it suggests is the proper role for economists in policy making. Do you agree with him?

■ APPENDIX: SIMPLE MATHS OF *IS/LM*

The *IS* curve

Assume that the consumption, investment, and tax functions are linear:

$$c = c_0 + c_y(y - t),$$

where c_0 is autonomous consumption and c_y is the constant proportion of current disposable income that is consumed: $0 < c_y < 1$;

$$t = t_y y, \qquad\qquad \text{(tax function)}$$

where $0 < t_y < 1$. Thus if we substitute the tax function into the consumption function and rearrange the terms, the consumption function is:

$$c = c_0 + c_y(1 - t_y)y. \qquad\qquad \text{(consumption function)}$$

The investment function is

$$I = A - ar, \qquad\qquad \text{(investment function)}$$

where a is a constant. In goods market equilibrium,

$$y = y^D$$
$$= c_0 + c_y(1 - t_y)y + A - ar + g.$$

Solving for y gives:

$$y = \frac{c_0 + A + g}{s_y + c_y t_y} - \frac{a}{s_y + c_y t_y} \cdot r. \qquad\qquad \text{(IS curve)}$$

Construct the *IS* curve in $r - y$ space by first setting $r = 0$ to get the intercept of the *IS* curve on the y-axis (Fig. 2.16); when $r = 0$,

$$y = \frac{c_0 + A + g}{s_y + c_y t_y};$$

similarly for the intercept of the *IS* curve on the r-axis; when $y = 0$,

$$r = \frac{c_0 + A + g}{a}.$$

(1) Change in the size of the multiplier: An increase in the multiplier has no effect on $\frac{c_0 + A + g}{a}$ with the result that the r-intercept is unaffected. A rise in the multiplier simply shifts $\frac{c_0 + A + g}{s_y + c_y t_y}$ to the right along the horizontal axis. The *IS* rotates counter-clockwise, as shown in Fig. 2.16.

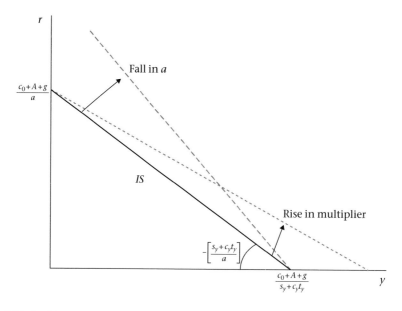

Figure 2.16 The *IS* curve

(2) Change in the interest-sensitivity of investment: A reduction in the interest-sensitivity of investment has no effect on the y-intercept; it simply shifts $\frac{c_0+A+g}{a}$ up the vertical axis. The *IS* curve rotates clockwise, as shown in Fig. 2.16.

(3) Change in the components of autonomous spending: An increase in c_0, A, or g produces a parallel outward shift of the *IS* curve since its slope is unchanged.

The *LM* curve

Assume that the demand for money function is linear and write it in real terms:

$$\frac{\overline{M^S}}{P} = \bar{l} - l_i i + \frac{1}{v_T} \cdot y.$$

Solving for i gives,

$$i = \frac{\bar{l} - \frac{\overline{M^S}}{P}}{l_i} + \frac{1}{v_T l_i} y. \qquad (LM \text{ curve})$$

Construct the *LM* curve in $i - y$ space by first setting $i = 0$ to get the intercept of the *LM* curve on the y-axis (Fig. 2.17); when $i = 0$,

$$y = v_T \left(\frac{\overline{M^S}}{P} - \bar{l} \right);$$

similarly for the intercept of the *LM* curve on the i-axis; when $y = 0$,

$$i = \frac{\bar{l} - \frac{\overline{M^S}}{P}}{l_i}.$$

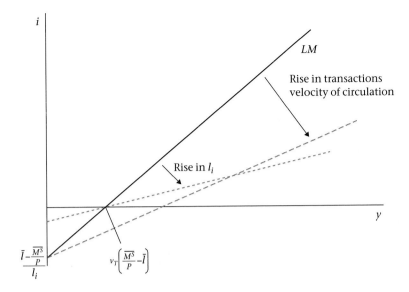

Figure 2.17 The *LM* curve

(1) Change in the transactions velocity of circulation: A rise in the transactions velocity of circulation v_T as the result for example of financial innovation means that the intercept of the *LM* with the vertical axis is unchanged while the intersection with the horizontal axis moves to the right. Thus the *LM* rotates clockwise, becoming flatter, as shown in Fig. 2.17.

(2) Change in the interest sensitivity of the demand for money: A rise in l_i, the interest sensitivity of the demand for money, has no effect on the intercept of the *LM* with the y-axis. It shifts the intercept with the vertical axis upward. Thus the *LM* rotates in a clockwise direction about the horizontal intercept, becoming flatter (Fig. 2.17).

(3) Change in the money supply: A rise in the money supply shifts the *LM* rightwards with no change in the slope. The size of the shift will be $v_T(\Delta M^S/P)$.

(4) Change in the price level. A rise in the price level shifts the *LM* leftwards with no change in the slope. The size of the shift will be $v_T(M^S/\Delta P)$.

3 Inflation, Unemployment, and Monetary Rules

The aim of this chapter is to move beyond the models presented in Chapter 2 so that we can analyse inflation and the monetary rules that are used by contemporary central banks—i.e. when the central bank sets the interest rate to stabilize the economy around an inflation target. In order to do this, we first introduce Phillips curves and show how they are derived from the labour market diagram. The key to understanding the Phillips curves is that when unemployment is at the equilibrium level, inflation is constant; when unemployment is lower, inflation goes up and when unemployment is higher, inflation goes down. This suggests that it might be possible to run the economy at lower unemployment but with a higher rate of inflation. However, as we shall see, such a trade-off is only possible in the short run because wage setters are concerned about the real wage and they will react when their real wage is eroded by inflation by pushing up their wage claims. In the long run, there is no trade-off between unemployment and inflation: this is shown by a vertical long-run Phillips curve.

Central banks are now typically viewed as operating monetary policy through adjusting the interest rate in order to keep the economy close to its inflation target at the equilibrium level of output. Since inflation is only constant at equilibrium output, this appears logical. The reason the central bank plays an active role in managing the economy is because the economy is subject to all kinds of disturbances that shift either inflation away from its target or output away from the equilibrium level or both. These shocks or disturbances produce changes in inflation that are persistent and costly to eliminate so there is a case for the central bank intervening to try to minimize the fluctuations.

If we take as an example a rightward shift of the *IS* curve as the result of an investment boom, this will push inflation up. The higher inflation will get incorporated into future wage- and price-setting decisions and will only be squeezed out of the economy by a period of unemployment above the equilibrium. The aim of the central bank is to minimize the cost to the economy of this shock in terms of the higher inflation caused by it and the higher unemployment required to reduce it. It will raise the interest rate so as to dampen aggregate demand and guide the economy back toward target inflation and equilibrium unemployment. This behaviour of the central bank is often described as the use of a 'reaction function' or monetary policy rule.

By combining the Phillips curve, the *IS* curve and the central bank's monetary rule, we have the so-called 3-equation model, *IS-PC-MR*. This model is a textbook version of the one used in contemporary central banks and in more advanced treatments of monetary macroeconomics. In Chapter 5, monetary policy is explored in greater depth and we investigate problems that can arise with the use of an interest rate based monetary policy rule.

In section 1, the Phillips curve is developed and the consequences of inflation inertia are explained. In section 2, the 3-equation model is presented. The central bank's monetary rule is derived and the *IS-PC-MR* model is used to analyse inflation and aggregate demand shocks. We look at the relative costs of 'cold turkey' and 'gradualist' disinflation strategies. In section 3 we look at how the inflation rate at the medium-run equilibrium is determined under two contrasting monetary policies: the interest rate based monetary rule and a policy where the central bank targets the money supply. Section 4 shows how inflation can be analysed using the standard *IS/LM* model.

In this chapter, we model the supply side using imperfectly competitive labour and product markets and adopt the simplification that the *PS* curve is flat. This makes the examples more straightforward and rarely makes a difference to the basic mechanisms under review but when it does, this is pointed out. An Appendix to the chapter presents a famous model of inflation and unemployment using a competitive labour market and a central bank that targets the growth of the money supply. This is Milton Friedman's model of the 'natural rate of unemployment' and is provided so the reader can see the parallels with the model presented in the chapter.

1 Inflation and Phillips curves

Inflation is the rate of change of prices, which means the price level today reflects the pattern of past inflation. Unless inflation is negative, which is called deflation, the price level does not fall. If P is today's price level and P_{-1} is last period's price level, then the rate of inflation over the past year is π:

$$\pi \equiv \frac{P - P_{-1}}{P_{-1}}.$$

Fig. 1.4 in Chapter 1 displays the inflation rates in several countries from the 1960s to the present: whilst inflation in the past decade has been low at 2 to 3% in many of the OECD countries, it was much higher often at rates between 10 and 20% in the 1970s. Policy makers are concerned about inflation. High inflation tends also to be volatile and this creates uncertainty and undermines the way in which prices convey information. As we shall see, it is costly to reduce high inflation—i.e. an increase in unemployment is normally required to bring inflation down. These reasons lie behind the so-called inflation-targeting regimes of central banks. For a fuller discussion of inflation and its costs, see Chapter 5. The objective of this section is to explore the origins of inflation and inflationary pressure.

1.1 Inflation inertia

In this chapter we introduce an important assumption used for modelling of inflation expectations and inflation inertia. The weight of evidence that has accumulated on inflation dynamics in many countries over the past decades suggests that changes in output (and employment) are followed by changes in inflation, which is summarized by saying that output leads inflation.[1] Consistent with this evidence is a standard model in which inflation depends on

- past inflation, π_{t-1},

- the gap between current unemployment and the *ERU*.

Some recent models have suggested to the contrary that inflation leads output— i.e. inflation goes up not because output has gone up but rather, inflation goes up in anticipation of a future increase in output. This means that the increase in inflation is observed before the increase in output takes place. One such model is introduced in section 1.7. However there is no strong empirical evidence to support replacing the standard view with this one.

There are two broad interpretations of the past inflation term: one in terms of expectations and the other in terms of inertia. In this book, we mainly use the second. However, a common way of rationalizing the inclusion of past inflation is to assume that wage setters expect inflation this period to continue to be what it turned out to be last period. This is interpreted as an example of the *adaptive formation of expectations*. As applied to inflation, expectations are formed adaptively when expected inflation this period is equal to last period's expected rate of inflation plus a correction term to take account of the amount by which last period's forecast was proved wrong:

$$\pi^E = \pi^E_{-1} + a(\pi_{-1} - \pi^E_{-1}), \qquad \text{(adaptive expectations)}$$

where a is a positive constant less than or equal to one. If past forecasting mistakes are fully corrected so that $a = 1$, we have

$$\pi^E = \pi_{-1}. \qquad \text{(simple adaptive expectations)}$$

This form of adaptive expectations therefore provides an interpretation of the lagged inflation term, π_{-1}, as a determinant of inflation. However, this is an unintelligent and thus implausible way of forming expectations: why look entirely to the past when forming a view about the future?

A more palatable and realistic interpretation of why past inflation is included as a determinant of inflation is in terms of the inertia that characterizes wage and price setting in a complex economy. A common view is that wage setters incorporate past inflation into their current money wage claim in order to make up for any erosion in living standards (i.e. in the real wage) that has taken place since the previous wage round. We shall generally assume that wage setters are not able to incorporate expected *future* changes to inflation in their current bargain. The theoretical and empirical debate about inflation inertia and expectations hypotheses is reviewed in Chapter 15, where a more general model that includes *both* past inflation and expected future inflation is developed.

In this chapter, we work with the standard model in which the inflation inertia term is defined as $\pi^I = \pi_{-1}$. Since 'inertial' inflation sounds rather clumsy, we often refer to

---

[1] For recent evidence, see Christiano, Eichenbaum, and Evans (2005); also Estrella and Fuhrer (2002), and Muellbauer and Nunziata (2004).

lagged inflation and denote it by π^I to emphasize the role of inertia in its interpretation. We have:

$$\pi = \pi^I + \alpha(y - y_e)$$

$$\underset{\text{current inflation}}{\pi} = \underset{\text{inflation inertia}}{\pi_{-1}} + \underset{\text{output gap}}{\alpha(y - y_e)}.$$

(inertia-augmented Phillips curve)

This is the inertia-augmented Phillips curve. When the lagged inflation term is interpreted as reflecting expected inflation on the assumption of adaptive expectations ($\pi^E = \pi_{-1}$), the term Expectations-augmented Phillips curve is used:

$$\pi = \pi^E + \alpha(y - y_e)$$

$$\underset{\text{current inflation}}{\pi} = \underset{\text{expected inflation}}{\pi_{-1}} + \underset{\text{output gap}}{\alpha(y - y_e)}.$$

(expectations-augmented Phillips curve)

We now turn to extending the macro model by deriving the Phillips curves.

1.2 Deriving Phillips curves

As we have seen in Chapter 2, there is a unique unemployment rate at which the labour market is in equilibrium. At this equilibrium, the *WS* and *PS* curves cross, which means both wage and price setters are content with the prevailing real wage and have no incentive to alter their behaviour. Our task here is to examine the link between unemployment and inflation: why is inflation constant at the equilibrium rate of unemployment and why, when unemployment deviates from equilibrium, will this be accompanied by changing inflation?

We begin with a numerical example in which inflation in the economy is 4% per year and unemployment is at the *ERU*: employment is E_1 and the real wage is w_1 (see Fig. 3.1).

Money wages are set so that the *WS* curve represents the real wage. To keep the real wage constant at w_1, wage setters require a money wage rise that will make up for the rise in prices over the past year. Since prices have risen by 4% (i.e. lagged inflation is 4%), money wage rises of 4% will therefore be set. Firms then set prices according to their pricing rule. Since prices are set as a constant mark-up on unit labour costs (W/λ), this depends on how much unit labour costs have risen. Since

$$P = (1 + \hat{\mu}) \cdot \frac{W}{\lambda},$$

$$\frac{\Delta P}{P} = \frac{\Delta W}{W} - \frac{\Delta \lambda}{\lambda}.$$

In the simple case where average labour productivity (λ) is constant, the only determinant of changes in unit labour costs is money wage changes:

$$\frac{\Delta P}{P} = \frac{\Delta W}{W}.$$

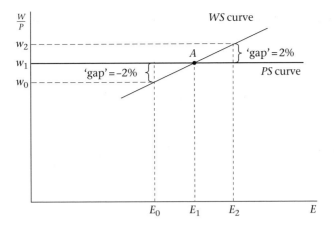

Figure 3.1 Upward pressure on inflation when employment is above equilibrium employment; downward pressure on inflation when employment is below equilibrium employment

Table 3.1 Constant, rising, and falling inflation

Inflation (% per year) and employment					
Period	Employment	Lagged inflation	'gap'	Wage inflation	Price inflation
0	E_1	4	0	4	4
Case 1: Constant inflation					
1	E_1	4	0	4	4
2	E_1	4	0	4	4
3	E_1	4	0	4	4
Case 2: Rising inflation					
1	E_2	4	2	6	6
2	E_2	6	2	8	8
3	E_2	8	2	10	10
Case 3: Falling inflation					
1	E_0	4	−2	2	2
2	E_0	2	−2	0	0
3	E_0	0	−2	−2	−2

Money wages have risen by 4% and so unit labour costs have risen by 4%. Therefore firms must raise prices by 4% in order to keep their profit margin unchanged. We have deduced that price and wage inflation remain unchanged at 4% per year and the economy remains at point A (see Fig. 3.1). This is illustrated as Case 1 in Table 3.1.

Suppose now that employment is at E_2, which is higher than the equilibrium and that lagged inflation is 4%. With employment of E_2, the real wage on the WS curve lies 2% above w_1 (shown by the 'gap' in Fig. 3.1 and Table 3.1). Money wages will have to be raised by 4% to keep the real wage unchanged; they will be raised by another 2% to take the real wage up to w_2 on the WS curve (money wages will rise by 4% + 2% = 6%). With a money wage rise of 6%, firms will increase prices by 6% so as to preserve their profit margin. Thus, we observe wage and price inflation of 6%—i.e. inflation is higher than in the previous period. The other thing to note is that since wages and prices have risen by the same amount, the real wage is w_1 and not the w_2 anticipated by wage setters.

Unemployment lower than the ERU is associated with a rise in inflation from 4% to 6%. But inflation will not remain at 6% because the labour market is not in equilibrium. The real wage outcome was w_1 yet wage setters require a real wage of w_2. When wages are next set, the 'catch-up' wage increase is 6% to cover past inflation so money wages will rise by 8% to take the real wage to w_2. In turn, prices will be raised by 8%. We observe the phenomenon that unemployment below the equilibrium rate is associated with rising inflation (see Table 3.1).

If we take the converse case of unemployment above the ERU and employment of E_0, the same reasoning gives the result that inflation is falling. At high unemployment, workers' power in the labour market is weakened, which is reflected in the positive slope of the WS curve. At employment of less than E_1, the WS curve is below the PS curve. In such a situation, the increased competition for jobs means workers will not be able to get money wage increases of the full 4% that would maintain their real wage. The money wage increase set by wage setters is 4% minus the 'gap' of 2%, i.e. 2%. With their costs rising by 2%, firms raise their prices by 2%, keeping their profit margins unchanged. Thus inflation falls to 2% (see Table 3.1). Since wages and prices have increased by the same amount, nothing happens to the real wage. In the following period, the negative gap between the WS curve and the prevailing real wage persists. Once again, the market conditions mean that wage setters will be unable to maintain the real wage of w_1: the money wage increase is 2% minus the 2% gap, i.e. money wages will not rise at all. In period 3, as we can see in the table, money wages and prices fall by 2%. Unemployment above the ERU is accompanied by falling inflation.

These results can be illustrated using a Phillips curve diagram. This has inflation on the vertical axis and output on the horizontal one. Just like the SAS curves of Chapter 2, which refered to the price *level* not the inflation rate, the Phillips curves are intimately related to the wage-setting and price-setting curves and are best understood when drawn on a diagram directly below the WS/PS diagram (see Fig. 3.2).

In reality, there is not a one-for-one relationship between a rise in output and a fall in unemployment. When output rises, workers who have been kept on the pay-roll but have not been fully employed (e.g. working shorter than normal hours) may be fully utilized with the result that higher output does not—at least initially—entail a rise in employment. This is called labour hoarding. Second, even if employment rises, unemployment does not necessarily fall if the new jobs are taken by those who were not previously in the labour force. People of working age who are neither employed nor unemployed are called economically inactive and the decision of whether or not to participate in the labour market is responsive to economic conditions.

The combination of labour hoarding and changes in the labour force mean that a 1% change in output growth above or below its trend tends to be associated with respectively a fall or rise in the unemployment rate of less than 0.5 percentage points. This empirical relationship between changes in the growth rate relative to its trend and changes

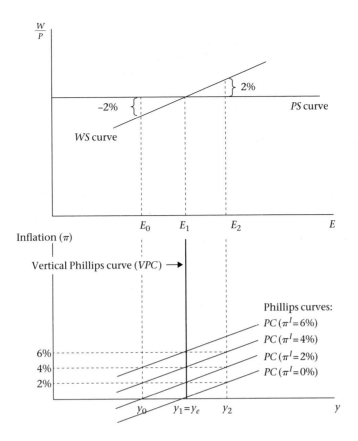

Figure 3.2 Deriving the Phillips curves

in the unemployment rate is called Okun's Law. The responsiveness of unemployment to changes in growth is lower in countries with tighter regulations on hiring and firing (as observed in many continental European countries) and with stronger traditions of lifetime employment, such as is characteristic of Japan. For ease of exposition, we shall nevertheless show changes in employment and unemployment moving one-for-one with changes in output.

An inertia- or expectations-augmented Phillips curve is defined as a feasible set of inflation and output pairs for a given rate of lagged inflation, $\pi^I = \pi_{-1}$. We construct the Phillips curves for the examples in Table 3.1. With $\pi^I = \pi_{-1} = 4\%$, we have identified three feasible inflation and output pairs: at $E_1, \pi = 4\%$; at $E_2, \pi = 6\%$; and at $E_0, \pi = 2\%$. This is the Phillips curve for $\pi^I = 4\%$ and we show it in Fig. 3.2. To emphasize that the Phillips curve is only defined for a given π^I, it is labelled $PC(\pi^I = 4\%)$.[2] Using the data in Table 3.1, we can plot the other Phillips curves and they are shown in Fig. 3.2.

---

[2] Note that in the alternative interpretation of the role of lagged inflation in the Phillips curves, expected inflation is equal to lagged inflation ($\pi^E = \pi_{-1}$) and the family of Phillips curves (e.g. $PC(\pi^E = 4\%)$) is described as 'expectations augmented'.

Each Phillips curve is defined by two characteristics:

(1) the lagged inflation rate, which is equal to the past inflation rate and fixes the height of the Phillips curve on a vertical line above the level of output associated with the *ERU*, and

(2) the slope of the *WS* curve, which fixes its slope.[3] The Phillips curves will be steeper if the *WS* curve is steeper and vice versa.

As well as a diagrammatic representation of Phillips curves, it is useful to express them in equation form as in section 1.1. We have argued that money wages increase by lagged inflation plus an amount to close the percentage gap between the existing real wage (i.e. on the *PS* curve) and the real wage on the *WS* curve. Prices increase by the same amount as wages. The percentage gap is a function of the difference between current and equilibrium employment; in addition, with constant productivity, employment and output are proportional, so for simplicity we shall use the simple linear expression:

$$\pi = \pi^I + \alpha(y - y_e)$$

$$\underset{\text{current inflation}}{\pi} = \underset{\text{inflation inertia}}{\pi_{-1}} + \underset{\text{output gap}}{\alpha(y - y_e)} \tag{3.1}$$

where α is a positive constant. The deviation of output from the medium-run equilibrium should be thought of in percentage terms (this is approximately equal to the difference between y and y_e if they are measured in logs). If output is above the medium-run equilibrium, then $y - y_e$ is positive and this will raise inflation above last period's inflation. Similarly if $y - y_e$ is negative, inflation will fall below last period's inflation; only with $y = y_e$ is inflation constant at last period's rate. We can see from this expression that the Phillips curve shifts up or down whenever lagged inflation changes and that its slope depends on α, which in turn reflects the slope of the *WS* curve.

1.3 Phillips's original curve

We now consider the interesting case where average inflation in the economy over many years is zero and the economy is buffeted about by unpredictable or random shocks to aggregate demand. By random, we mean that some shocks are positive and some are negative so that output is sometimes above and sometimes below the *ERU*. If these shocks are short-lived, it is reasonable to expect that wage setters view a temporary rise in prices as a fleeting experience and do not incorporate past inflation into their wage claims. If so, the economy would be observed at the points shown in Fig. 3.3. This is one way to present the original 'Phillips curve' published by A. W. Phillips using data for the UK between 1861 and 1957.[4] Fig. 3.4 reproduces Phillips's plot for the period between 1861 and 1913. Note that since Phillips has unemployment on the horizontal axis measured from left to right, the Phillips curve is downward sloping.

---

[3] Note that if the *PS* curve was downward sloping, the slope of the Phillips curve would be steeper, reflecting the slope of both the *WS* and the *PS* curves. This mirrors the discussion in Chapter 2 about the slope of the *SAS* curve.　　[4] Phillips (1958).

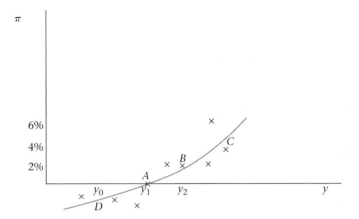

Figure 3.3 The 'original' Phillips curve

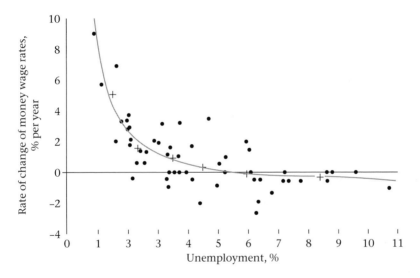

Figure 3.4 Phillips' original curve: UK 1861–1913
Source: Economica, 1958.

1.4 Phillips's original curve may exist but it cannot be exploited

Having seen a Phillips curve of the original type, we ask the following question:

- Can the government use policy to shift the economy from its customary position at point A to a higher level of activity at point B (in Fig. 3.3)? The policy maker may be tempted to do so in order to reduce unemployment at the cost of a small rise in inflation.

Suppose that the government increases the money supply (to shift the *LM* curve to the right). The interest rate falls and output is raised via higher investment spending. Unlike the random shocks that shifted the economy from A to D to B to C to A etc. in the world of the original Phillips curve, we have here a quite different situation: the government is seeking to *keep* output at y_2 because it prefers a situation with lower unemployment even if there is some inflation. Eventually, the tendency for the economy to be near point B is likely to figure in the calculations of workers—i.e. they will build the 2% p.a. inflation into their wage claims: expected inflation will rise from zero to 2% p.a. At this point, the long-run trade-off between inflation and unemployment disappears because the Phillips curve shifts up. If the government persists with its policy of holding output at y_2, the Phillips curve will continue to shift up as in Case 2 in Table 3.1 and the lower unemployment will be associated with ever-increasing inflation.

This example provides an important illustration of something in economics called the Lucas critique.[5] While the relationship originally estimated by Phillips seemed to suggest the existence of a trade-off between inflation and unemployment, this collapsed as soon as the government tried to exploit it. A stable Phillips curve only existed because governments did not systematically try to make use of it! The conclusion that the policy maker cannot choose any point other than one on a vertical line above the level of output at the *ERU*, has led to the notion of a vertical long-run Phillips curve. This is a useful reminder when analysing policy, and is shown in the Phillips curve diagram as *VPC*. It may be noted, that if governments cease to try to run the economy at unemployment below the *ERU*, the original Phillips curve of a stable trade-off may well reappear in the data.

1.5 Disinflation is costly

An important implication of the Phillips curve, $\pi = \pi_{-1} + \alpha(y - y_e)$, is that if the authorities wish to reduce the rate of inflation, there will be a cost as there will be a period in which unemployment is above the *ERU*. We assume that the economy is in a situation in which inflation is high and constant; unemployment is at the *ERU*. If inflation is to be *lower* than it was last period, unemployment must be pushed up *above* the *ERU*. This is because—as the Phillips curve shows—inflation is equal to what it was last period plus an amount that depends on how far the economy is from the *ERU*. Remember that a slacker labour market with higher unemployment means that the current real wage cannot be maintained and this will trigger lower wage and price inflation. Another way to put this is that when unemployment is above the *ERU*, there is a negative gap between the *WS* curve and the *PS* curve.

From the Phillips curve equation,

$$\pi = \pi_{-1} + \alpha(y - y_e)$$
$$\Rightarrow (\pi - \pi_{-1}) = \alpha(y - y_e)$$
$$\text{If } (\pi - \pi_{-1}) < 0,$$
$$\text{then } \alpha(y - y_e) < 0$$
$$\Rightarrow y < y_e.$$

[5] This was one of the contributions for which Robert Lucas was cited in the award of the Nobel prize in 1995 (Lucas (1976)).

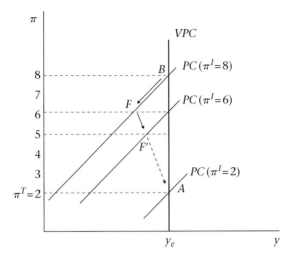

Figure 3.5 Disinflation is costly

We can also demonstrate the point using an example and a diagram.[6] In Fig. 3.5, the economy is at point B with high inflation of 8% (on $PC(\pi^I = 8)$). It is assumed that the central bank wishes to reduce inflation to its target rate, which is 2%. The Phillips curve shows the feasible inflation and output pairs, given last period's inflation, of 8%. The only points on the curve with inflation below 8% are to the left of B, i.e. with higher unemployment. With Phillips curves like this, disinflation will always be costly. It should be clear that if the influence of the past on wage setters could be wiped away, then the possibility of a costless disinflation emerges: this amounts to saying that the policy maker could shift the $PC(\pi^I = 8)$ down, e.g. to $PC(\pi^I = 2)$. In this case, the economy would jump from B to A.

Returning to the Phillips curve $PC(\pi^I = 8)$, we assume that the central bank has chosen to raise unemployment to point F. Inflation falls to 6% and a new Phillips curve $PC(\pi^I = 6)$ arises. The central bank can then choose a point on $PC(\pi^I = 6)$, point F'. This leads to a downward shift in the Phillips curve, which is not shown. Eventually, the objective of inflation at 2% is achieved and the economy remains at the ERU.

1.6 Disinflation and central bank preferences

Although any point on the initial Phillips curve such as $PC(\pi^I = 8)$ in Fig. 3.5 is feasible, the question naturally arises as to which point along this curve the central bank would choose when implementing a policy of disinflation. We assume that the aim of the central bank is to get the economy to the ERU with an inflation rate of 2%.[7] At one extreme, the

---

[6] Note that we have specified a linear Phillips curve, which is reflected in the diagram. In section 2.6 we return to question of the implications of linear as compared with convex Phillips curves.

[7] This sounds innocent enough but as we shall see in Chapter 5, if the central bank aims for an unemployment rate *below* the ERU, it will not be able to get inflation down to its target of $\pi^T = 2\%$. This is known as the inflation-bias problem of monetary policy.

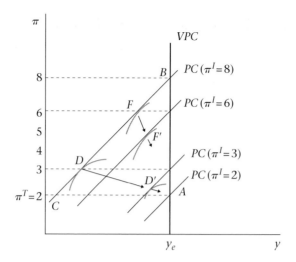

Figure 3.6 Disinflation and central bank preferences

central bank could choose point C (see Fig. 3.6). This brings inflation down to the target in the next period but at the cost of a steep rise in unemployment as indicated by the low output at point C. Once inflation has fallen to 2%, the Phillips curve shifts to $PC(\pi^I = 2)$ and the central bank can safely cut the interest rate to stabilize output at y_e. The economy would move from B to C to A.

A less harsh approach would be for the central bank to choose point F as in the case discussed above. The fall in inflation and the rise in unemployment in the first period would be less than if C were chosen. We can see that as we change the preferences of the central bank from a lower to a higher willingness to sacrifice a rise in unemployment in order to get a given reduction in inflation, we move along the Phillips curve from B to C. We summarize this by saying that the inflation aversion of the central bank rises as it chooses a point closer to C.

The central bank's preference between a deviation of inflation from π^T or of unemployment from the *ERU* can be represented with indifference curves. The indifference curves of two different central banks are shown in Fig. 3.6. The indifference curves of the more inflation-averse central bank are flatter. This central bank chooses point D and the other one chooses point F on $PC(\pi^I = 8)$. The more inflation-averse central bank chooses D because it is willing to sacrifice a bigger increase in unemployment to get inflation down by more. When the Phillips curve shifts down, the central bank chooses its preferred position where the indifference curve is tangential to the new Phillips curve and in this way the economy adjusts to point A. The inflation averse-central bank guides the economy down the path from D to A. In exactly the same way, the less inflation-averse central bank with steeper indifference curves guides the economy down the path from F to A. For both central banks, since their most preferred position is with $\pi = \pi^T$ and $y = y_e$, the indifference curves shrink to a point at A. The derivation of the central bank indifference curves is explained in detail in Chapter 5; a graphical illustration is all that is required here.

1.7 Costless disinflation and rational expectations

We noted above that if the influence of the past on wage setters was absent, it would be possible for the economy to jump from point B to point A in Fig. 3.5 without any rise in unemployment. What additional assumptions about the economy do we need to make in order to eliminate the cost of disinflation?

- inflation inertia is absent. This means there are no nominal rigidities in the economy in wage- or price-setting behaviour or institutions that operate to produce inflation inertia. And adaptive expectations play no role in wage setting. Instead, the so-called *rational expectations hypothesis* holds. Hence, we have

$$\pi = \pi^E + \alpha(y - y_e) + \epsilon$$

  where ϵ (called epsilon) is a random shock term.

- when the central bank announces a new low inflation target, π^T, this is believed by all market participants. Another way to say this is that the central bank's policy announcement is credible. For the target to be credible, it must be consistent with

$$\pi = \pi^T + \epsilon$$

  i.e with inflation remaining constant at the target, apart from unforeseen shocks.

Rational expectations of inflation mean that the only difference between what agents in the economy expect inflation to be and what it turns out to be is something random: they do not make systematic errors. Another way to express this is that the agent's subjective expectation of inflation is equal to the 'objective' expectation given all the available information about the structure of the economy and about policy that is available at the time the expectation is formed. Because all of the information available is used in forming the expectation, there is no correlation between the error term and the information available when the expectation is formed. When applied to inflation in our model, the rational expectations hypothesis means that:

$$\pi^E = E\pi = E(\pi^T + \epsilon) = \pi^T + E\epsilon = \pi^T$$
$$\therefore \pi^E = \pi^T, \qquad \text{(rational expectations of inflation)}$$

where E is the 'objective' expected value and the Phillips curve is now:

$$\pi = \pi^T + \alpha(y - y_e) + \epsilon. \qquad \text{(Phillips curve; rational expectations)}$$

This says that with rational expectations, when output is at equilibrium, inflation is at target apart from a random shock. We can express this another way, by rearranging as follows

$$y - y_e = \frac{1}{\alpha}(\pi - \pi^T - \epsilon)$$

$$= \frac{1}{\alpha}\left(\pi - \pi^E\right).$$

$$\text{Hence, } y = y_e + \underbrace{\frac{1}{\alpha}\left(\pi - \pi^E\right)}_{\text{inflation surprise}} \tag{3.2}$$

$$= y_e + \xi,$$

(Lucas surprise supply equation)

where ξ (pronounced 'ksi') is a random error. This is called the Lucas surprise supply equation after its originator, Robert Lucas.[8] Output only deviates from equilibrium when there is a surprise to inflation (or more generally to the price level). 'Surprise' or unanticipated inflation is normally interpreted as pushing output away from equilibrium because a firm will find it difficult to know whether this is a rise in economy-wide inflation or in the price of its product relative to the general price level. If it is a rise in economy-wide inflation, then the firm will not want to make a supply response; however, if the higher inflation reflects a rise in demand for the firm's product relative to other firms, it will want to increase its supply. In general, it will not be possible for firms to distinguish with certainty between a general and a relative price change with the result that some increased supply response will occur following an inflation 'surprise'.

We should note the possibility that wage and price setters may suspect that an increase in inflation is the result of a deliberate attempt of the central bank or the government to run the economy at unemployment below the equilibrium, so doubts may surface about the credibility of the inflation target. This is another way of expressing the discussion in section 1.4 about the Lucas critique and whether the Phillips curve trade-off can be exploited by the government. In such a case, we say that the inflation target of 2% is not credible. Even with rational expectations and in the absence of inflation inertia, there would not be a costless drop in inflation: rather, the government would have to demonstrate its preference for lower inflation even at the cost of a rise in unemployment by choosing a point to the left of B in Fig. 3.5. The issue of the credibility of monetary policy is explored in more depth in Chapter 5.

We can summarize by saying that in a world where available information is used by all market participants to form their expectations (rational expectations), where there are no sources of inflation inertia and where government commitment to the inflation target is credible, then random shocks to inflation known as surprises will lead output to deviate from its equilibrium level. This means, in contrast to the standard model with inflation inertia, that there will not even be temporary movements along the Phillips curve in response to announced changes in government policy: disinflation will not be costly. The following distinction between the two approaches should also be noted:

- when using inertia-augmented Phillips curves, causality goes from a deviation in output from equilibrium (e.g. because of a change in aggregate demand) to a change

---

[8] Lucas (1972, 1975). For a very clear discussion, see Hoover (1988).

in inflation relative to lagged inflation.

$$\Delta AD \rightarrow \Delta y \text{ relative to } y_e \rightarrow \Delta \pi \text{ relative to } \pi_{-1}$$

- in the Lucas surprise supply equation, causality goes from a deviation in inflation from its expected value to a change in output relative to equilibrium.

$$\Delta \pi \text{ relative to } \pi^E \rightarrow \Delta y \text{ relative to } y_e.$$

The Lucas supply equation highlights the fact that under the assumptions of rational expectations, policy credibility, and the absence of inflation inertia, since it is only unanticipated changes in inflation that can affect output, systematic monetary policy is ineffective in altering the level of activity in the economy. There is also no need for systematic policy because the economy returns directly to equilibrium once a shock to inflation has disappeared. These are strong assumptions. As we shall see in the rest of this chapter and in Chapter 5, because of the presence of inflation inertia, a variety of economic disturbances shift the economy shift the economy away from equilibrium and it does not return costlessly to equilibrium of its own accord. As a consequence, central banks do engage in systematic monetary policy to stabilize the economy.

2 Monetary rules and the 3-equation *IS-PC-MR* model

We are now in a position to introduce the so-called 3-equation model. The three equations are:

(1) the IS equation,
(2) the Phillips curve equation, and
(3) the monetary rule derived from the government or central bank's policy trade-off between output and inflation.

In this chapter, the emphasis is on gaining familiarity with the 3-equation model by using diagrams. The equations are set out for the sake of clarity. In Chapter 5, a more extensive analysis of monetary policy that makes use of the equations is undertaken and in Chapter 15, the further steps needed to develop the more sophisticated versions of this model that have become the workhorse of modern monetary macroeconomists are explained. Here we emphasize the development of a good intuitive feel for the adjustment processes.

We have already shown the *IS* and the Phillips curves in diagrams and set them out in explicit equation form. The monetary policy rule has not yet appeared explicitly in a diagram or as an equation. However, as we shall see in the next section, the monetary policy rule can be represented in the Phillips curve diagram by joining the points F, F', A in Fig. 3.5. Similarly, in Fig. 3.6, if we join the points F, F', A, we have the monetary policy rule for a less inflation-averse central bank and for a more inflation-averse central bank by joining the points D, D', and A.

2.1 **The 3-equation model:** *IS-PC-MR*

Before focusing on the monetary policy rule, we summarize the *IS* equation and Phillips curve equation in the form most useful for the analysis of shocks and policy responses.

(1) The *IS equation* will take a slightly simpler form from that in section 2 of Chapter 2. The simplification is to write it as $y = A - ar$, where A is the sum of exogenous multiplied-up demands (thus including private and public sector exogenous demand), and r is the real rate of interest:

$$y = A - ar. \qquad \text{(IS equation)}$$

We will moreover be particularly interested in the real rate of interest that equates y to y_e. This is defined as r_S, the stabilizing rate of interest:

$$y_e = A - ar_S. \qquad \text{(stabilizing interest rate)}$$

It can be seen that r_S changes whenever A or y_e changes. Assuming that A and y_e do not change, the y_e equation can be subtracted from the *IS* equation to get

$$y - y_e = -a(r - r_S). \qquad \text{(IS, output gap form)}$$

The difference between current and equilibrium output is known as the output gap. Given that the exogenous components of aggregate demand are unchanged, this equation makes clear that output will deviate from equilibrium to the extent that the interest rate differs from the stabilizing interest rate. This way of representing the *IS* equation is especially well suited to understanding the way that a monetary rule works. The central bank is going to choose the interest rate so as to influence the output gap as it seeks to achieve its stabilization objective. It is important to note that the central bank cannot bring about an instantaneous change in output by altering the interest rate. It takes time for interest rate changes to feed through to affect investment and output. We look at this in more detail in Chapter 5.

(2) The *inertia-augmented Phillips curve equation, PC,* needs no modification:

$$\pi = \pi_{-1} + \alpha(y - y_e). \qquad \text{(Phillips curve, } PC)$$

(3) The third equation, the *monetary rule, MR,* is derived from the central bank's output-inflation trade-off, discussed in the last section. This can be written as

$$y - y_e = -b(\pi - \pi^T). \qquad \text{(monetary rule, } MR)$$

This equation shows the combination of output and inflation that the central bank will choose given the Phillips curve that it faces. When inflation is high, the central bank will choose to reduce aggregate demand (by raising the interest rate) in order that inflation will come down. From Fig. 3.6, we can see that a higher b is associated with a more inflation-averse central bank.

To construct the *MR* line in a diagram, we simply take a Phillips curve and find the central bank's best output-inflation combination along the Phillips curve. This amounts to finding the tangency between the central bank's indifference curves and the relevant Phillips curve constraint that it faces: by joining up these points of tangency, the *MR* is formed. At each point of tangency, the *MR* equation will hold. Note also that the *MR* line will go through $y = y_e$ and $\pi = \pi^T$. For example, in Fig. 3.6 the *MR* for the more inflation-averse central bank would be found by joining up the points D, D', and A and that for the less inflation-averse central bank by joining up points F, F', and A.

The key to understanding the role of the *MR* line in macroeconomic analysis is that it shows the path along which the economy will be guided by the actions of the central bank to take it back to equilibrium output at target inflation. Whenever the economy is shifted away from the (y_e, π^T) equilibrium by an aggregate demand or supply shock, the job of the monetary authority is to use a change in the interest rate to get the economy onto the *MR* line; once on the line, it must continue to adjust the interest rate until the economy returns to (y_e, π^T). It is easy to show this in the Phillips diagram (Fig. 3.7). We first look at the case where inflation has risen above target to 6% shown by point B. Point B is on the Phillips curve $(PC(\pi^I = 6\%))$ and this shows the trade-off along which the central bank can choose its preferred point. To get inflation back to the target of 2%, output is going to have to fall below equilibrium. The *MR* line shows that the central bank will choose point F: it does this by raising the interest rate so that aggregate demand falls, taking output below y_e. Once the economy is on the *MR* line, adjustment back to point Z is easy to follow: with inflation of 5%, the new Phillips curve that the central bank faces is the one labelled $PC(\pi^I = 5\%)$ and the central bank will choose point F'. The process of step-by-step adjustment takes the economy to point Z.

In the case of a fall in inflation below target, the process works in the same way. If inflation falls to zero (point B'), this defines the Phillips curve $(PC(\pi^I = 0))$ and the central bank's preferred point is G: note that with inflation having fallen below target, aggregate demand will have to be raised by the central bank so that output goes above

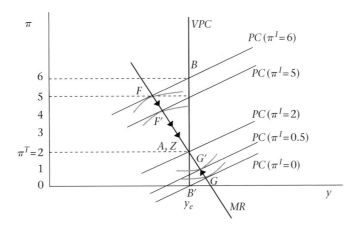

Figure 3.7 The monetary rule: the *MR* line

equilibrium in order to push inflation back up to 2%. Adjustment along the *MR* line to point *Z* occurs through exactly the same sequence of events as in the previous case. In Chapter 5, we explain why the government would try to keep inflation at a low but positive level, such as 2%—and would be keen to act to get the economy onto the *MR* line from a position such as *B*.

Once the *MR* line is well understood, it is a short step to bring together the monetary rule in the Phillips diagram with the *IS* curve so as to show explicitly the interest rate the central bank must set at each stage in order to deliver the required level of aggregate demand. This introduces no new concepts. It is simply a matter of going from the chosen output level on the *MR* line to the *IS* curve to see the interest rate that the central bank must set.

Why is the *MR* line shown in the Phillips diagram? Although it is possible to depict the monetary rule in the *IS* diagram, it is not our preferred method of presentation. The reason is that the essence of the monetary rule is to identify the central bank's best policy response given the Phillips curve it faces. To do this, we need to know:

- the central bank's preferences between output and inflation deviations (this can be represented by indifference curves as we have seen) and
- the *objective* trade-off between output and inflation shown by the Phillips curves.

Both of these appear in the Phillips diagram. Moreover, by working in the Phillips diagram, the direct input to the monetary rule of the structure of the supply side, which determines the position of the vertical Phillips curve and the slope of the inertia-augmented Phillips curves is kept to the forefront. Once the central bank has calculated its desired aggregate demand response by using the relevant Phillips curve and indifference curve, we shall see it is straightforward to go up to the *IS* diagram and discover what interest rate must be set in order to achieve the desired level of output.

In practice, the central bank sets the *nominal* interest rate but it does this in order to choose the real interest rate on the *IS* curve that will deliver its chosen level of aggregate demand. The real interest rate is the short-term real interest rate, r. The central bank can set the nominal interest rate directly but since the expected rate of inflation is given in the short run, the central bank is assumed to be able to control r indirectly. In the next section, the 3-equation model is made more concrete by taking different kinds of shocks and seeing how to analyse the implementation of the monetary policy rule to stabilize the economy in each case.

2.2 An inflation shock

An inflation shock is straightforward to analyse using the 3-equation model and indeed we simply set out more explicitly the analysis that we have already done in Fig. 3.7. The top diagram in Fig. 3.8 is the *IS* diagram, the bottom one is the Phillips diagram. Of the three equations the *IS* equation is shown in the top diagram, and the monetary rule (*MR*) and Phillips curves in the bottom one. We start at point *A* with $y = y_e$ and inflation at the target of 2%. We assume that there is an inflationary shock to the economy, which pushes inflation up to 4%. The economy moves to point *B* on PC ($\pi^I = 4$).

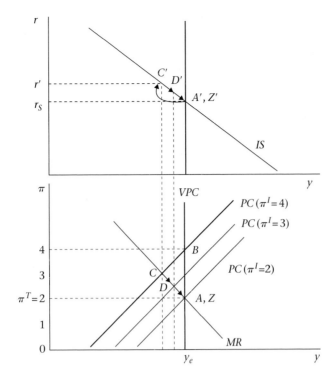

Figure 3.8 Inflation shock and the monetary rule

We can see explicitly that the central bank chooses the interest rate r' on the *IS* curve (point C') to achieve point C on the Phillips curve ($PC(\pi^I = 4)$). In the next period, the Phillips curve shifts down as a result of the fall in inflation: the new Phillips curve is indexed by $\pi^I = 3$ (i.e. it intersects the *VPC* at y_e with $\pi = 3\%$). Thus, the economy is guided down the *MR* line to the south-east as the central bank implements the monetary policy rule. We can also see the path down the *IS* curve as the central bank reduces the interest rate back toward the stabilizing interest rate, r_S. Eventually the economy returns to equilibrium output with target inflation at point Z. Note that the central bank behaves in an active, although rule based fashion: frequent adjustments of the interest rate are required by the monetary policy rule.

2.3 A temporary demand shock

We assume that the economy starts off in equilibrium with output at the equilibrium and inflation at the target rate of 2% (see Fig. 3.9). The economy is then disturbed by a temporary aggregate demand shock. By a temporary aggregate demand shock, we mean that the *IS* curve that reflects the shock is *IS'* and remains at *IS'* for only one period. Output is pushed up so that $y' > y_e$. The consequence of output above y_e is that inflation will rise above target—in this case to 4%. This defines the Phillips curve ($PC(\pi^I = 4)$) along which the central bank must choose its preferred point: point C. By going vertically up

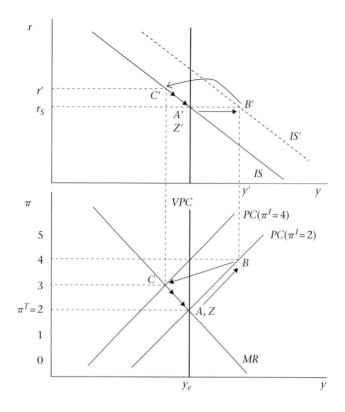

Figure 3.9 Temporary aggregate demand shock and the monetary rule

to point C' in the IS diagram, the central bank can work out that the appropriate interest rate to set is r'. The subsequent adjustment path down the MR line to point Z is exactly as described in the case of the inflation shock.

To summarize, the economy is shifted from A to B as a result of the aggregate demand shock. This rise in output builds a rise in inflation above target into the system. Because of inflation inertia, this can only be eliminated by pushing output below and (unemployment above) the equilibrium. The central bank therefore raises the interest rate in response to the aggregate demand shock because it can work out the consequences for inflation. It must raise the interest rate in order to depress interest-sensitive demand and reduce output. The central bank is forward looking and takes all available information into account.

2.4 A permanent demand shock

In the case of a permanent demand shock the IS curve shifts to IS' and stays there.

The economy starts in equilibrium with output at equilibrium and inflation on target at 2%. In the IS diagram, the initial stabilizing rate of interest is r_S. The IS curve shifts rightwards to IS'. Just as with the temporary demand shock, output goes up to y': the economy is at point B in the Phillips diagram and at B' in the IS diagram (Fig. 3.10).

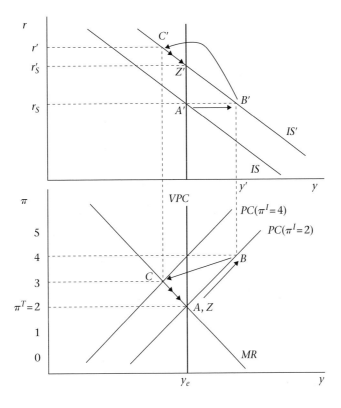

Figure 3.10 Permanent aggregate demand shock and the monetary rule

The subsequent analysis in the Phillips diagram is exactly as in the previous case: the only difference concerns the *IS* diagram. Because the *IS* shock is a permanent one, the stabilizing interest rate has risen to r'_S. With higher exogenous demand, a higher real interest rate is required to dampen interest-sensitive demand so that output is equal to y_e. Similarly, in order to get the economy onto the *MR* line at point C, the central bank has to set the interest rate at r', considerably higher than was necessary in the case of the temporary demand shock. Once the economy is at points C and C', adjustment along *MR* and *IS'* takes place in the usual way. The new equilibrium is at point Z in the Phillips diagram and at point Z' in the *IS* diagram. In Chapter 4, we shall examine how a supply shock can be analysed using the 3-equation model.

2.5 The *MR* line and the real interest rate

To illustrate that an inflation-targeting central bank sets the nominal interest rate in order to achieve a particular *real* interest rate, we return to the example in Fig. 3.10. As we have already seen, to steer inflation back to the target following the permanent demand shock, the central bank raises the interest rate and the economy moves to C and C'. This is a rise in the real interest rate from r_S to r'.

We contrast this with two alternatives: keeping the *real* interest rate unchanged and keeping the *nominal* interest rate unchanged. If the central bank keeps the *real* interest rate unchanged at r_S, then output remains at y' above the equilibrium and inflation will continue to rise as the Phillips curve shifts upward each period. If the central bank keeps the *nominal* interest rate unchanged, the economy moves from B' to a point on the new *IS* curve (*IS'*) to the south-east of point B'. The reason is that the rise in inflation signalled by the persistence of output above y_e reduces the real interest rate: with a given nominal interest rate and higher inflation, the real interest rate falls. In other words, if $i = r + \pi^E$, then $r = i - \pi^E$ so a higher π^E reduces r below r_S. A fall in the real interest rate will boost output further, taking the economy even further away from the inflation target.

This example illustrates that it is the real interest rate that the central bank is focused on when setting the nominal rate: when responding to the increase in expected inflation associated with the shift of the *IS* curve, the central bank takes account of the effect of higher expected inflation on the real interest rate and pushes the nominal rate up sufficiently to take this into account.

2.6 Sacrifice ratios and disinflation strategies

We have seen that the immediate response of a more inflation-averse central bank to an inflation shock is to dampen output by raising the interest rate by more than would a less inflation-averse one. It is willing to see a sharper rise in unemployment to get a faster fall in inflation. And this means that unemployment can in consequence return more rapidly to equilibrium. The terms 'cold turkey'[9] or 'shock therapy' are sometimes applied to this strategy and are contrasted with a more gradualist approach in which unemployment rises by less but the process of disinflation takes longer. An interesting question is whether cumulative unemployment is higher under cold turkey or gradualism: in other words, if we add up the unemployment rates in every period after the inflation shock until inflation returns to target and unemployment to equilibrium, with which strategy will there have been a higher total amount of unemployment?

We shall see that if the Phillips curves are linear and parallel, the cumulative amount of unemployment to achieve the reduction of inflation to target is the same under both strategies. In other words in this case, the sacrifice ratio (cumulative unemployment to achieve a given reduction in inflation) is independent of the degree of inflation aversion of the central bank.

To illustrate this, assume a government operates a simple monetary rule

$$y - y_e = -b(\pi - \pi^T)$$

where b reflects the toughness of response to an inflation rate above its target. Intuitively, the tougher is the government, the bigger will be the increase in unemployment in response to an expected inflation shock. On the other hand the bigger the

---

[9] The analogy is to the treatment of alcohol or drug addiction: a cold turkey strategy reduces drug intake dramatically at the outset whereas a gradualist treatment, reduces it slowly. The choice thus ranges between severe discomfort for a short time or less pain for a longer period of time.

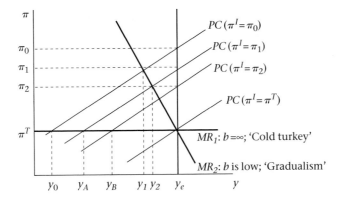

Figure 3.11 Disinflation strategies and sacrifice ratios: 'cold turkey' vs. 'gradualism'

increase in unemployment, the quicker will be the return of the economy to equilibrium with $\pi = \pi^T$. It is therefore unclear how the total amount of unemployment over time (i.e. cumulative unemployment) relates to b. But under a quite simple assumption it turns out that cumulative unemployment is independent of b. This assumption is that inertia augmented Phillips curve is linear:

$$\pi = \pi^I + \alpha(y - y_e)$$

with

$$\pi^I = \pi_{-1}.$$

The proof can be shown geometrically Fig. 3.11. First we assume maximum toughness on the part of the government so that $b = \infty$: its preference is to bring inflation back to target immediately, irrespective of the rise in unemployment that this entails. This implies that the monetary rule is horizontal as shown by MR_1. Suppose that initially the economy is in equilibrium with inflation equal to the target and that there is then an upward shock to the inflation rate i.e. $\pi^I = \pi_0 > \pi^T$. With MR_1 output falls from y_e to y_0 as the sharp rise in the interest rate takes effect. π falls from π_0 to π^T; next period therefore $\pi^I = \pi^T$, so the central bank can safely cut the interest rate back to the stabilizing interest rate and output rises back to y_e. If we measure unemployment by the difference of actual output from equilibrium output, then there is unemployment of $y_e - y_0$ for one period, after which unemployment is zero again: hence cumulative unemployment is simply $y_e - y_0$.

Now assume that the government has a more lenient monetary rule, MR_2. As a result of the inflation shock, output is cut from y_e to y_1 so that in the first period after the shock unemployment is $(y_e - y_1)$. Inflation is π_1, and this implies in the next period that π^I falls from $\pi^I = \pi_0$ to $\pi^I = \pi_1$. Using MR_2 the Phillips curve with $\pi^I = \pi_1$ implies that output rises from y_1 to y_2. This means that unemployment in the second period is $(y_e - y_2)$. Hence cumulative unemployment after two periods is $(y_e - y_1) + (y_e - y_2)$.

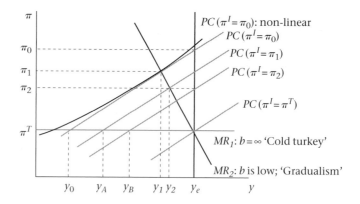

Figure 3.12 Sacrifice ratios and convex Phillips curves

The proof of the assertion that cumulative unemployment does not depend on the value of b can now be seen from the diagram (Fig. 3.11). $(y_e - y_1)$ is exactly $(y_A - y_0)$ on the horizontal axis; $(y_e - y_2)$ is exactly $(y_B - y_A)$. It can be seen that if we add the unemployment created in each subsequent period in the gradualist case to $(y_A - y_0) + (y_B - y_A) + \ldots$, the total is exactly $(y_e - y_0)$; in other words, it is equal to cumulative unemployment in the 'cold turkey' case with $b = \infty$. Since this demonstration did not depend on the particular value of b we used, it is true for any positive value of b.

The proof depends critically on the linearity of the Phillips curves. If a small increase in unemployment has a disproportionately larger effect on inflation than a bigger increase in unemployment (or vice versa) the result does not hold. This is shown in Fig 3.12. Let us assume that the linear Phillips curves are still a good approximation in the region of MR_2, the less inflation-averse monetary rule. This means they can be used as before to calculate the cumulative unemployment as $(y_e - y_0)$. To see what happens when the Phillips curves are convex, we use the monetary rule with $b = \infty$ and the black Phillips curve for $\pi^I = \pi_1$. This convex Phillips curve reflects the empirical finding that inflation becomes less sensitive to a rise in unemployment the higher unemployment is. It is not difficult to see that this implies a reduction in output greater than the fall to y_0. Hence cumulative unemployment with a more inflation-averse monetary rule will be greater than with a weaker one. The intuition is that the strategy of a very inflation-averse central bank of reducing inflation down to the target very fast will be more costly than a gradualist one if it is the case that inflation responds less to a rise in unemployment when unemployment is high: pushing unemployment up very high takes it into the region where its effect on wage-setting behaviour is more limited.

In summary, with non-linear Phillips curves of this kind, the sacrifice ratio is higher for a more inflation-averse central bank. With linear Phillips curves, the reduction of inflation to target has the same total unemployment cost—only the time pattern of the unemployment differs: high for a short period versus lower over a longer period. When the Phillips curves become flatter at higher unemployment, the welfare calculation is more complicated—a cold turkey strategy produces a more rapid return of the economy to target inflation but at greater cumulative unemployment cost than does a gradualist strategy. We return in Chapter 5 to discuss the empirical evidence that relates to sacrifice ratios.

3 Inflation at the medium-run equilibrium

3.1 Two monetary policies

3.1.1 Interest rate rule (*MR* approach)

In the 3-equation model, as long as the central bank's objective is to stabilize the economy around the *ERU*,[10] inflation at the medium-run equilibrium is equal to the target set by the central bank. The characteristics of the monetary policy rule ensure this.

- In the 3-equation model, in the medium-run equilibrium, $\pi = \pi^T$ if the central bank seeks to stabilize unemployment around the *ERU*.

If the central bank changes its inflation target, then the new medium-run equilibrium will be identical to the old one, except that inflation is at the new target rate. As we have seen, if the inertia in inflation can be eliminated, then the economy moves directly to the new equilibrium. However, on our normal assumption that the central bank is constrained to choose a point on the inertia-augmented Phillips curve, it will have to raise the interest rate to set the economy on the path toward the new inflation target. There will be a phase of costly disinflation before the new inflation target is achieved.

3.1.2 Money supply rule (*LM* approach)

When extending the *IS/LM* model to the medium run, we assume that the growth rate of the money supply is under the control of the central bank. Reasons why this may not be as easy as it sounds are explored in Chapter 8. Assuming that it is possible, we show that the growth of the money supply determines the rate of inflation in the medium-run equilibrium. We assume the approximation holds so that:

$$i = r + \pi^E$$

and note that at a medium-run equilibrium, $\pi = \pi^E$ so that

$$i = r + \pi.$$

Next, we take the money market equilibrium condition:

$$\frac{M^S}{P} = L(i, y) \qquad\qquad (LM)$$
$$= L(r + \pi, y)$$

and consider the situation at a medium-run equilibrium. The level of output is determined by the intersection of the *WS* and *PS* curves at y_e. The *IS* curve is fixed by the aggregate demand side of the economy. Hence, the real interest rate associated with y_e is fixed at r_S. Since by definition of the medium-run equilibrium, π is constant, the real demand for

---

[10] As noted earlier, if its unemployment objective is more ambitious than this, an inflation bias arises leaving inflation at the *ERU* above the target. This is explained fully in Chapter 5.

money (i.e. L) is also constant. The implication of the requirement that the money market is in equilibrium is that the real supply of money must also be constant. To keep the real money supply constant, the price level P must grow at the same rate as the nominal money supply, which is under the control of the authorities. We use the symbol γ (called gamma) to denote 'growth rate', so γ_M is the growth rate of the money supply. Assume it is constant at $\overline{\gamma_M}$:

$$\overline{\gamma_M} = \frac{M - M_{-1}}{M_{-1}},$$

which implies that

$$\pi = \overline{\gamma_M},$$

where the bar over γ_M is used to emphasize that the growth rate of the money supply is exogenous.

- When the IS/LM model is extended to the medium run, the medium-run equilibrium is characterized by a constant inflation rate equal to the constant growth rate of the money supply set by the central bank, i.e. $\pi = \overline{\gamma_M}$.

3.2 How the *MR* relates to the *LM* curve

Before returning to a traditional analysis of monetary policy and inflation using the IS/LM diagram, we ask what is the relation between the MR approach and the LM approach? And what role does the LM curve play in the 3-equation model? There are two key points. First, the approach to use depends on the type of monetary policy the government uses. If the government (or the central bank) is using an *interest-rate based monetary rule* so as to steer the economy to its inflation target, the correct model is the 3-equation model with the MR. This is often called an inflation-targeting regime.

But as we have just noted, the government could alternatively use a money supply rule (as did some governments in the 1970s and 1980s). The most common money supply rule is to set a target for the growth rate of the money supply, $\overline{\gamma_M}$. Another possibility is to hold the nominal money supply constant, at $\overline{M^S}$. A *money supply rule* (or monetary-targeting regime) requires that we use the LM curve approach.

Second, the LM condition does not disappear when the MR approach is being used. Here we need to distinguish between (*a*) the LM condition, which means that the demand for and supply of money are equal and (*b*) the money supply rule, which assumes that the money supply is set exogenously. The LM condition is

$$\frac{M^S}{P} = L(i, y). \tag{3.3}$$

This in itself says nothing about how the money supply, M^S, is fixed.[11] It simply states the equilibrium condition that the demand for and supply of money are equal. This must

---

[11] As we shall see in Chapter 8, in the world in which the central bank sets the interest rate, the causality goes from $i \to L \to M \to H$ whereas in the traditional LM model, causality is reversed: from $H \to M \to i$, where H is high-powered money.

always hold, apart from in the very short run, irrespective of whether the government is using a money supply rule or an interest rate based monetary rule. This is because when operating a monetary rule, the central bank's operations have to ensure that the money market is in equilibrium—otherwise the interest rate would not remain at the desired level. In an inflation-targeting regime, the *LM* curve is present in the background. In the diagram, it goes through the intersection of the *IS* curve and the interest rate set by the central bank but it plays no role in fixing the position of the economy in terms of output, inflation, or the interest rate.

4 Inflation in the *IS/LM* model

The *IS/LM*-model presents a different picture of policy making from the 3-equation *IS-PC-MR* model. The government or central bank is not modelled as using a monetary policy rule in the sense of a reaction function to respond to shocks. The term reaction function reflects the fact that the *MR* incorporates an assessment of the implications of any shock and a 'formula' for reacting that takes account of the structure of the supply and demand sides of the economy. When using an *MR*, the central bank is forward looking, forecasting the implications for inflation of any disturbance to the economy and setting the interest rate so as to guide the economy back to equilibrium. By contrast, the use of a money supply rule implies that monetary policy is passive.

It was explained in the previous section that the medium-run equilibrium only differs in the two models by what determines the medium-run equilibrium rate of inflation: this is the inflation target in the *IS-PC-MR* model and the growth rate of the money supply in the *IS/LM* model. Hence, when the economy is subjected to a shock, the new medium-run equilibrium will be identical in both models—assuming the supply sides are the same and that the growth rate of the money supply is the same as the inflation target in the *IS-PC-MR* model.

However, the adjustment path with a money supply rule will be somewhat different from the one we have analysed in the *IS-PC-MR* model. This is because in the *IS/LM* model, the central bank is assumed to stick to a constant money supply growth rate throughout. The real interest rate then changes as the result of the interaction between the central bank's fixed money supply growth and the evolution of inflation. If we take the case of a permanent aggregate demand shock, adjustment takes place in the *IS/LM* model as follows:

(1) Following the shift of the *IS* curve to the right, the rise in output drives up the demand for money. In the short run, inflation and the money supply growth rate are constant and equal to each other: the real money supply is constant. Hence the *LM* curve stays fixed and the higher money demand leads to the sale of bonds, a fall in the price of bonds, and a rise in the interest rate. This is the movement along the *LM* curve to its intersection with the new *IS* curve.

(2) Higher output and employment lead to a rise in inflation as shown by the Phillips curve. This will reduce the real money supply (since prices rise faster than does the money

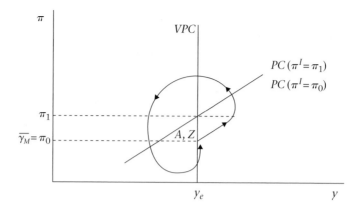

Figure 3.13 Aggregate demand shock: central bank holds money growth rate constant

supply) and cause the *LM* curve to shift to the left. This dampens demand as the interest rate rises.

(3) Since inflation has gone up but must end up back at its original level in the new medium-run equilibrium, the inertia in inflation implies that output will have to fall below y_e during the adjustment process. Inflation falls only when $y < y_e$.

(4) A spiral-shaped adjustment path in the Phillips curve diagram will be traced as the economy moves first to the north-east and then in a counter-clockwise spiral back to the equilibrium (see Fig. 3.13).

The adjustment path is more protracted in the *IS/LM* model than with the interest rate based monetary policy rule because when the central bank uses a monetary policy rule, it actively intervenes to guide the economy to the new medium-run equilibrium once it is on the disinflation path (e.g. from C' to Z' in Fig. 3.10). As inflation comes down, the central bank steps in and cuts the interest rate. The details of adjustment using the *IS/LM* model are set out in the appendix.

5 Conclusions

In this chapter, a framework has been set out within which shocks and policies affecting the economy can be systematically investigated. To the elements assembled in Chapter 2 to analyse aggregate demand (the *IS* curve, and the *LM* curve) and aggregate supply (the *WS* and *PS* curves and the *ERU*), we have added the Phillips curves and the monetary rule, *MR*.

The Phillips curves are used to analyse processes of inflation. The original Phillips curve depicted a stable empirical relationship between unemployment and inflation. However if a policy maker tries to exploit this relationship by choosing a lower unemployment rate in exchange for putting up with a higher rate of inflation, the stable relationship will disappear. If there are no lags in wage and price setting and wage and price setters are able to make the best use of the information available to them, a policy maker cannot choose a rate of unemployment below the *ERU* without the consequence of ever-increasing inflation. For the policy maker, therefore, the Phillips curve is vertical.

However, if past inflation plays a role in wage setting there will be a trade-off between inflation and unemployment—until the next round of wage setting. This is shown by Phillips curves that are indexed by lagged inflation and therefore shift up as π^I rises and down as π^I falls. The slope of these Phillips curves reflects the slope of the *WS* curve (and also the slope of the *PS* curve, if it is not horizontal): a steeper *WS* curve implies a stronger response of inflation to a change in unemployment for a given π^I.

One implication of Phillips curves of the form:

$$\pi = \pi_{-1} + \alpha(y - y_e)$$

is that disinflation is costly: unemployment has to rise above the *ERU* for inflation to fall.

We expressed the central bank's monetary rule, *MR*, in terms of its chosen combination of output and inflation given the Phillips curve it faces:

$$y - y_e = -b(\pi - \pi^T). \qquad\qquad \text{(monetary rule, } MR\text{)}$$

This is shown in the Phillips diagram.

The *IS* curve is added to the Phillips curve and the monetary rule to form the so-called 3-equation *IS-PC-MR* model. The *IS* curve plays two roles: it shifts in response to shocks to autonomous aggregate demand and it shows the interest rate that the central bank must choose in order to implement its monetary policy (i.e. as shown by the chosen point on the *MR* line). The model can be used to analyse the impact on inflation and unemployment of different kinds of shocks and to explore how the central bank will react to stabilize the economy. We can summarize the working of the *IS-PC-MR* model by taking the case of a temporary positive aggregate demand shock:

(1) An upward shift in consumer confidence leads to a rise in output and a fall in unemployment below the *ERU*.

(2) Lower unemployment in turn implies that inflation will rise above the central bank's target.

(3) The central bank raises the interest rate. It will set an interest rate high enough to push unemployment above equilibrium in order to bring inflation back down to the target.

(4) Once the economy is on the *MR* line, the central bank will gradually reduce the interest rate and the economy will return to the *ERU* with the interest rate once more at its stabilizing level, r_S, and inflation at target.

When the Phillips curve is added to the *IS/LM* model, we can analyse shocks under the assumption that the central bank is targeting the growth rate of the money supply. The two models, *IS-PC-MR* and *IS/LM* work in broadly similar ways and in the medium run inflation is equal to

• the central bank's inflation target if it uses an interest rate based monetary rule and

• the growth rate of the money supply when the central bank targets money growth.

Institutional features of the economy may prevent it swiftly returning to equilibrium following a disturbance. The monetary rule is an example of the active intervention of the central bank to steer the economy back toward equilibrium. The monetary rule will become ineffective if the nominal interest rate approaches zero: other policy instruments will be needed.

■ QUESTIONS

Checklist questions

(1) Use a diagram with the labour market in the upper panel and the inflation-output diagram beneath and show Phillips's long-run trade-off between inflation and unemployment. Explain what happens if the government decides to choose a lower unemployment rate on the basis that it is prepared to accept a higher rate of inflation.

(2) Give two examples of behaviour that are consistent with the hypothesis of rational expectations but not with that of adaptive expectations and vice versa. How can one decide which hypothesis applies in a particular instance of behaviour?

(3) Explain carefully all the assumptions that are being made in the claim that 'disinflation is costly'.

(4) Explain the Lucas supply equation stating clearly the role that is played by imperfect information. Contrast Lucas's model with Friedman's model in the Appendix where imperfect information also plays a role.

(5) Describe what happens in the economy following an inflation shock in the following cases: (*a*) the central bank cares only about avoiding increased unemployment; (*b*) the central bank cares only about its inflation target; (*c*) the central bank cares about both increased unemployment and about achieving its inflation target.

(6) Following a temporary negative aggregate demand shock, why does unemployment go below the *ERU* before the economy returns to medium-run equilibrium?

(7) Make a case for the use of an interest rate based monetary policy rule by evaluating the pros and cons of two other monetary rules:
(*a*) maintaining a constant nominal interest rate and
(*b*) maintaining a constant growth rate of the money supply.

(8) Explain what is meant by the sacrifice ratio in general and rank the alternative policies in question 5 in terms of the sacrifice ratio involved.

(9) If the central bank's monetary policy is an interest rate based rule, what determines the money supply? What happens to the economy if there is a sudden fall in the demand for money?

(10) What factors affect the speed with which the economy returns to medium-run equilibrium following a negative aggregate demand shock in the *IS/LM* model?

Problems and questions for discussion

QUESTION A. What factors influence the change in the unemployment rate associated with a given fall in output below trend? If the economy is experiencing rapid structural change, with employment shifting to different sectors (e.g. from 'old economy' to 'new economy' ones), how would you expect this to affect your answer to the first question? Could this account for the so-called 'jobless recoveries' discussed in the United States following the recessions in the early 1990s and early 2000s? [Useful reference: Groshen and Potter (2003).]

QUESTION B. Would you attribute the disappearance of the original stable Phillips curve to a change in the behaviour of workers or of the government?

QUESTION C. 'In medium run equilibrium, the real rate of interest depends on fiscal policy but not on monetary policy.' Do you agree? Does your answer apply to the nominal interest rate?

QUESTION D. 'Inflation is always and everywhere a monetary phenomenon.' 'Inflation reflects supply-side behaviour.' 'An expansionary fiscal policy leads to inflation.' Take each statement separately and provide an evaluation of it. Would you conclude that policy to control inflation should be in the hands of a committee representing central bankers, representatives of wage and price setters and the government? Explain.

■ **Appendix**

Inflation in the competitive model: Friedman's model

In his presidential address to the American Economics Association in 1967, Milton Friedman laid out a simple and highly influential macroeconomic model.[12] With competitive markets, it is quite difficult to explain why unemployment would differ from the natural rate. Friedman's explanation centres on the notion of misperception on the part of workers. Using the idea of imperfect information, he was able to explain why the economy could deviate temporarily from the natural rate of unemployment. In simple terms, the logic of the model generates results parallel to those presented in this chapter. There is a unique unemployment rate at which inflation is constant—the 'natural rate'. If unemployment is below that natural rate, then inflation will be increasing and vice versa. There is a vertical Phillips curve at the natural rate of unemployment, which implies that there is no long-run trade-off between unemployment and inflation. In the shorter run there is a trade off in which unemployment below the natural rate is attainable at the cost of rising inflation.

An example helps to show how the main results are derived and how they are represented by the vertical and expectations-augmented Phillips curves. In Fig. 3.14, the economy begins at the natural rate with zero inflation. Initially the economy is at the natural rate with a real wage of w_e, and we assume that the government wants to try to reduce unemployment further. The government uses its policy instruments to keep the level of real aggregate demand higher than the natural level of output. It is clear that, for workers to supply the E_1 amount of labour required to produce the output demanded, they will require a higher real wage of w^*. On the other hand, firms will demand E_1 workers *only* if the real wage is lower at w_1.

How can this apparent contradiction be resolved? The existence of demand for output in excess of supply produces rising prices. The rise in prices takes the price level above its expected level. For firms

---

[12] Published as Friedman (1968).

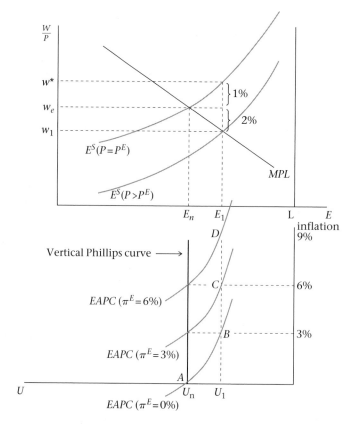

Figure 3.14 Competitive model: the natural rate of unemployment and the Phillips curves

who are aware of the rise in the price of their own output, it means a fall in the real wage to w_1 and higher demand for labour. But because of their inability to observe the actual price index for the bundle of *consumption* goods, workers are assumed to base their labour supply decision on the *expected* real wage, where they use prices from previous periods to form their expectation of prices this period. In other words, labour supply is $E^s = E^s(w^E)$, rather than $E^s = E^s(w)$, because of the inability of workers to observe the current price level. The expected real wage is $w^E = W/P^E$, which can be written as

$$w^E = \frac{W}{P^E} = \frac{W}{P} \cdot \frac{P}{P^E}.$$

Hence the labour supply equation is

$$E^s = E^s \left(\frac{W}{P} \cdot \frac{P}{P^E} \right)$$

and any change in P/P^E shifts the labour supply curve.

Fig. 3.14 shows the case where the actual price level exceeds the expected price. If $P > P^E$, then the labour supply curve will shift to the right because it is the workers' belief (based on their expectations) that the real wage is higher than it actually is and more labour will be supplied. For example, with the real wage w_1, when price expectations conform with the facts *ex post* (i.e. when $P = P^E$), the labour supply curve is $E^s(P = P^E)$ and labour supplied would be E_n.

If however, as in our example, prices are above the expected price level on which the labour supply decision is taken (i.e. if $P > P^E$), then the labour supply curve is $E^s(P > P^E)$ and labour supplied will be E_1. In our example, we shall assume that the real wage has fallen by 2% from w_e to w_1 (see Fig. 3.14). We can see from the diagram that in our example, the expected real wage must have risen by 1% for the labour E_1 to be supplied. It is easy to deduce that if workers were expecting zero inflation (based on past experience), then a money wage increase of 1% would amount to an expected wage increase of 1%. But firms will only employ E_1 workers if prices rise by 3% so as to lower the actual real wage by 2%. To summarize, the economy can shift from the natural rate to higher employment if inflation rises. Poor information on the part of workers leads them to confuse a money wage increase of 1% for a real wage increase of 1% when in fact real wages fall by 2%. Only through an unanticipated rise in the price level (in this case by 3%) can the illusion be created that the real wage has risen, when in fact it has fallen.

Friedman argued that in the following period, workers would update their inflation expectations. In the model presented in the chapter, a change in past inflation led to a shift in the Phillips curve. In Friedman's model, the Phillips curves are called expectations-augmented Phillips curves and shift up whenever there is a change in expected inflation. Friedman assumed that expectations are formed in a backward-looking way, i.e. adaptive expectations. In the following period, if workers update their inflation expectations based on past experience, expected inflation will have changed from zero to 3%. For workers to continue to supply labour at the level of E_1, money wages will have to rise by expected inflation of 3% *plus* 3% to take the real wage from the actual level in period zero of w_1 up to w^*. Hence money wages must rise by 6%. For firms to continue to employ E_1 workers, prices must also rise by 6% so as to maintain the real wage at its existing level of w_1. For period 1, a second expectations-augmented Phillips curve ($EAPC(\pi^E = 3\%)$) is therefore relevant. Each time the expected rate of inflation changes, the $EAPC$ shifts. The absence of a long-run trade-off in Friedman's version of the competitive model is represented by the fact that the long-run Phillips Curve is vertical. It is vertical at $U = U_n$, the natural rate of unemployment.

Adjustment to an aggregate demand shock using the *IS/LM* model

How does an aggregate demand shock feed through to inflation and unemployment in the IS/LM model? We take the example of a consumption boom and assume that the central bank sticks to a constant growth rate of the money supply, $\overline{\gamma_M}$. The initial equilibrium of the economy is displayed in Fig. 3.15 by the points labelled A. The consumer boom, which we assume is a permanent change in behaviour, shifts the IS to the right to $IS(\bar{A}_1)$. The new medium-run equilibrium is at point Z. In the new medium-run equilibrium, the IS curve is at $IS(\bar{A}_1)$. Equilibrium employment and output are E_e, and y_e and the new equilibrium real interest rate is higher at r'_e. Hence in the IS/LM diagram, the new equilibrium is at the point Z.

A complication that arises concerns the IS/LM diagram itself since the IS curve is a function of the real interest rate and the LM curve of the nominal interest rate. This issue was dodged in Chapter 2 because we kept inflation to zero—the only situation in which real and nominal interest rates are the same. With inflation of π_0, the nominal interest rate will be π_0 above the real interest rate in both the new and old equilibrium. The most straightforward way of showing this on the diagram is to pull down the horizontal axis of the IS/LM diagram by the amount of (expected) inflation. Fig. 3.15 shows this: with an inflation rate of π_0 per year, the real interest rate in the medium-run equilibrium is r_e and the nominal interest rate is $i_e = r_e + \pi_0$. The nominal interest rate is shown in Fig. 3.15 using the dashed axes. To use the r/i version of the IS/LM diagram, it needs to be remembered that:

- The IS curve is defined in terms of r and behaves in the usual way.

- The LM curve is defined in terms of i; as usual, it shifts when the real money supply ($\overline{M^s}/P$) changes.

- Since the LM curve is defined in terms of i, the LM curve *shifts relative to* the IS curve whenever inflation changes: to the left when inflation falls and to the right when inflation rises. One way to see this is that the dashed horizontal axis shifts up when inflation falls and down when inflation rises and the LM moves with it.

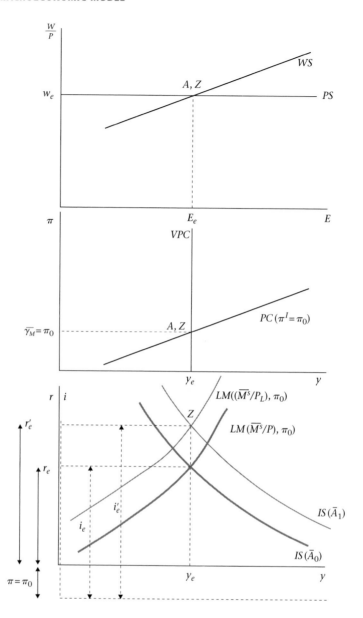

Figure 3.15 Permanent *IS* shock: new medium-run equilibrium at *Z*

- Hence the *LM* curve moves relative to the *IS* curve in response to a change in the real money supply and in response to a change in inflation. We therefore show the *LM* as $LM(\overline{M^s}/P, \pi)$.

   In our example, the growth rate of the money supply is unchanged throughout so the economy will be on the $PC(\pi^I = \pi_0)$ at point *Z* in the new equilibrium—just as it was in the original one. The new equilibrium is at *Z* in the *IS/LM* diagram: this means that the *LM* curve in the new equilibrium is shifted to the left as it must go through point *Z*. Since the inflation rate is π_0—exactly the same as it was in the initial equilibrium—the leftward shift in the *LM* implies that the real money supply is lower, with

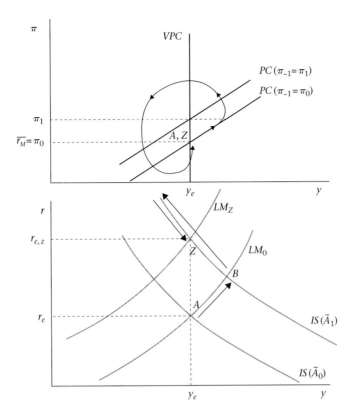

Figure 3.16 Sketch of the adjustment path to the new medium-run equilibrium at Z following a consumption boom

subscript L for 'low'. The real money supply is reduced during the adjustment because inflation rises above the growth rate of the money supply as output responds to the consumer boom.

The process of adjustment from A to Z is protracted and complicated to show. First, output and employment rise and the real interest rate is pushed up as the economy moves along the LM_0 curve to point B (see Fig. 3.16). This is the new short-run equilibrium. However, once wages and prices begin to adjust to the lower unemployment, inflation goes up to π_1 as we move up the Phillips curve, $PC(\pi^I = \pi_0)$. The LM curve shifts to the left because of the fall in the level of real money balances:

$$\pi > \gamma_M \Rightarrow \downarrow \frac{\overline{M^S}}{P}.$$

The next period, the Phillips curve shifts upward to reflect the fact that inflation has gone up.

So far output and employment have risen, which sparked off a rise in inflation. Given the constant monetary growth rate, aggregate demand was dampened as a consequence of the rise in the real interest rate. A lengthy process of adjustment to the new equilibrium is likely to ensue. The first phase during which output is higher than the equilibrium and inflation is rising is followed by a second phase during which output is below the equilibrium. Once output is below equilibrium, inflation begins to fall and the Phillips curve start to shift down. The economy is likely to follow a spiral-shaped adjustment path in the Phillips curve diagram as shown in Fig. 3.16. For as long as inflation remains above the growth rate of the money supply, output will tend to fall. But the high unemployment will dampen inflationary pressure and eventually the LM curve begins to shift to the right again and output starts to rise. The economy moves to the new equilibrium at point Z.

4 Labour Markets and Supply-Side Policies

Supply-side policies refer to those that shift the wage- or price-setting curves. Changes in unemployment benefits, minimum wages, union and employment protection legislation, child-care policy, and participation by the government in negotiations with unions and employers' associations may shift the *WS* curve. Changes in competition policy or in taxes may shift the *PS* curve. Taxation has effects on both the aggregate demand and supply sides of the economy: on the one hand it may be used to stabilize aggregate demand and on the other, it has supply-side implications. It has also been suggested that government expenditure programmes on training or education may be able to reduce equilibrium unemployment by raising productivity. We play down the role of efficiency wage setting in this chapter, not because we do not think it is important (see Chapter 2 and the appendix to Chapter 15), but because many labour market policy questions relate to a world of collective bargaining.

In the first section we explain how supply-side policies and labour market institutions affect the wage- or price-setting curve and, hence, equilibrium unemployment. The shift in equilibrium unemployment in turn implies a shift in the monetary rule in the Phillips diagram. We set out how output and inflation change in response to a supply-side shift and show the reaction of the central bank. In the face of a positive supply-side shift, the central bank lowers the interest rate since inflation falls below target; in the face of a deterioration on the supply-side, inflation goes up and prompts the central bank to raise the interest rate.

Section 2 focuses on factors that can shift the *WS* curve and the *PS* curve extending the analysis in section 6 of Chapter 2. These factors include the tax wedge, training provision, product market competition, industrial relations legislation, and agreements between unions and employers (that may also include the government) known as wage accords or incomes policies. Section 3 takes a closer look at the way in which the institutions of wage setting can affect equilibrium unemployment. We explain the logic of the so-called Calmfors–Driffill model, which proposes an inverse-U shaped relationship between the degree of centralization of wage setting and equilibrium unemployment, i.e. both highly decentralized and highly centralized wage-setting structures produce low unemployment.

In section 4, we explain the way in which a period of sustained unemployment due to weak aggregate demand can feed back to the supply side of the economy and result in a rise in equilibrium unemployment. This phenomenon is known as hysteresis. In the final section, we introduce the so-called flow approach to the labour market. In labour economics, job search theory has focused on the process by which the unemployed are matched with vacancies. We explain how the matching process can be represented in a downward-sloping relationship between the vacancy rate and the unemployment rate known as the Beveridge curve and show how this can be related to the *WS/PS* model to provide a richer analysis of equilibrium unemployment.

1 Supply-side structures, policies, and shocks

The charts in Chapter 1 show that unemployment rates differ widely across countries and that there are persistent trends in unemployment in some of them. This data suggests that we cannot rely on a model with a constant or time-invariant *ERU* but need to model how the *ERU* shifts about over time. In this chapter, we identify factors that can shift either the *WS* or the *PS* curve and therefore shift the equilibrium rate of unemployment.

Before looking at the likely causes of shifts in the *WS* and *PS* curves, we clarify the mechanics of their impact and the policy response. For brevity, we refer to any shift in the *WS* or *PS* curve as a supply-side shift or a supply-side shock. What is the implication of a supply-side shift for the medium-run equilibrium and how does the economy adjust following such a shift? In Fig. 4.1, we show the initial equilibrium at point A. Inflation is at its target level. Let us suppose the *WS* curve shifts down because union power is weakened by a change in legislation. There is a new medium-run equilibrium at Z with higher employment and with inflation at the original rate: the supply-side shift lowers the *ERU*. The assumption that the *PS* curve is flat means that the real wage in the new equilibrium is the same as it was originally. This is a rather striking result: lower union bargaining power means a lower *ERU* but an unchanged real wage. With a downward-sloping *PS* curve, the real wage is lower in the new equilibrium.

If the central bank had correctly anticipated the shock, it would have dropped the interest rate so as to boost aggregate demand and move the economy down the *IS* curve raising output to $y = y'_e$. The economy would jump straight from A to Z (see Fig. 4.1) and inflation would remain on target at π^T. With lags in response and in adjustment, this is unlikely. As an example of how adjustment occurs when there are lags in response and adjustment, assume that the central bank is using a monetary policy rule to target inflation (Fig. 4.1). The shift in the *WS* curve means that the vertical Phillips curve shifts to the right, to y'_e, which implies that the Phillips curve $PC(\pi^I = 4)$ shifts as well: it goes through the point marked Z. The Phillips curves associated with the new *ERU* are shown as grey lines. Following the shift in the *WS*, a gap opens up between the existing real wage, w_0 and point B' on the new *WS'* curve. The first thing to happen as a consequence is that inflation falls to 2% as shown by the new $PC(\pi^I = 4, y'_e)$: the economy goes from A to B. Inflation falls because at the current output level, in the face of the new situation in the labour market, workers are too weak to secure wage increases that would maintain the wage at w_0. Money wages rise by less than the previous period's inflation. Firms' costs therefore rise by less than in the past and they put their prices up by less. The fall in inflation triggers a reaction from the central bank: it cuts the interest rate. The Phillips curve facing the central bank is $PC(\pi^I = 2, y'_e)$. In the usual way, it chooses its preferred

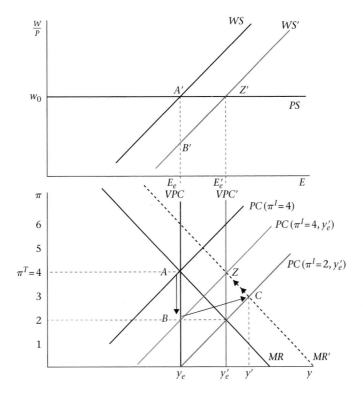

Figure 4.1 Downward shift of the *WS* curve: adjustment to the new equilibrium

position on this Phillips curve, say point C. This dictates the required cut in the interest rate to raise output to y'. The economy then adjusts from C to Z with the central bank adjusting the interest rate and the Phillips curve shifting until it gets to $PC(\pi^I = 4, y'_e)$.

The time profile of inflation is shown in Fig. 4.2. Inflation drops once wages and prices begin to adjust to the supply shift (presumably at the next wage round) and then it gradually returns to its initial level.[1]

For completeness, Fig. 4.3 shows the supply shock analysis in the same format as we have used for the inflation and aggregate demand shocks, i.e. with the *IS* diagram above the Phillips diagram. As we have just seen, a supply shock differs from the inflation and demand shocks because it shifts the *MR* schedule so that it goes through the point where inflation is at target and output at the new equilibrium: this is *MR'*.

In the *IS* diagram, we can see explicitly the cut in the interest rate from its initial level of r_S to r'. Once the economy is on the new monetary rule line, *MR'*, adjustment from C to the new equilibrium at Z takes place in the usual way. Note that the stabilizing interest rate is lower (at r'_S) in the new medium-run equilibrium. Since equilibrium output is higher as

---

[1] The adjustment process would be fairly similar in the case where the central bank fixes the growth rate of the money supply. As we have seen in Chapter 3, the main difference is that the fall in inflation triggers a rise in the real money supply, which in turn pushes down the interest rate and boosts demand and output.

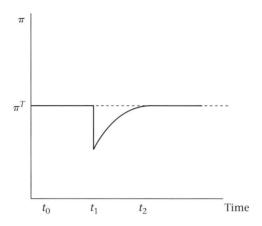

Figure 4.2 Sketch of the time path of inflation following a *WS* curve shift

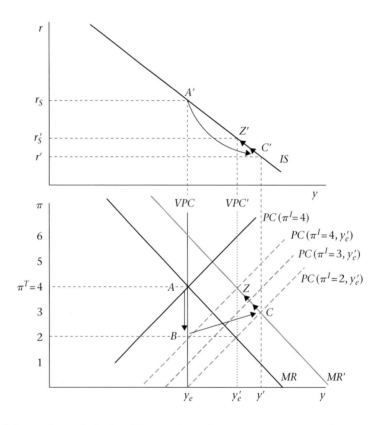

Figure 4.3 Aggregate supply shock and the monetary rule

a consequence of the supply-side shift, a lower real interest rate is required to provide the appropriate level of aggregate demand.

2 Factors that shift the *WS* and *PS* curves

The factors shifting the equilibrium rate of unemployment can be divided into:

- wage-push factors that shift the *WS* curve and
- price-push factors that shift the *PS* curve.

2.1 The tax wedge: how are *W* and *P* being measured?

Before providing examples of the wage and price-shift variables, one clarification is needed. To this point, we have used *W* as the money wage and *P* as the price level without worrying about their precise definition. Once income taxes, labour taxes such as social security contributions, and indirect taxes such as VAT are introduced, we have to be clear about what *W* and *P* measure and which measure we show on the axis in the labour market diagram. This is a matter of choosing a convention and we find it convenient to show the real consumption wage in the labour market diagram. This entails measuring *W* as the post-tax money wage paid to the employee and to measure P_c as the consumer price index, i.e. inclusive of indirect taxes.

$$P_c = P(1 + t_v).$$ (consumer price index)

This means that when we show $w = W/P_c$ on the axis of the labour market diagram, this is the real consumption wage—the concept relevant from the perspective of the utility of the worker.

By contrast, the real wage that is of relevance to the employer is the real product wage, which is the full cost of labour to firms—inclusive of income tax and non-wage labour costs such as social security contributions paid by employers and employees—divided by the price the firm gets for its product (i.e. excluding indirect taxes). This is called the producer price. The difference between the real consumption wage and the real product wage is called the tax wedge. Given the way we have defined the labour market diagram in terms of *W* and P_c, the wedge shows up as a price-push factor. Any increase in either direct or indirect taxation reduces the price-setting real wage and therefore shifts the *PS* curve downwards.

This is clear when we derive the *PS* curve including taxes. The wage element of costs for firms is the full cost of labour to firms—i.e. the gross wage paid to the worker (which includes the income tax and social security payments that have to be made by the worker) plus the employer's social security contributions. All direct taxes are summarized in the tax rate, t_d. This is shown in the pricing equation, where *P* is the producer price:

$$P = \frac{1}{1 - \mu} \cdot \frac{W^{\text{gross}}}{\lambda}$$ (price equation)

$$= \frac{1}{1 - \mu} \cdot \frac{W(1 + t_d)}{\lambda}.$$

In order to derive the price-setting real wage in terms of the real consumption wage, $\frac{W}{P_c}$, we rearrange the pricing equation and substitute $\frac{P_c}{1+t_v}$ for P to get:

$$P_c = \frac{(1+t_v)}{1-\mu} \cdot \frac{W(1+t_d)}{\lambda}.$$

The *PS*-equation including the tax wedge is:

$$w = \frac{W}{P_c} = \frac{\lambda(1-\mu)}{(1+t_d)(1+t_v)}. \qquad \text{(PS equation including tax wedge)}$$

Any fall in the wedge, for example, a fall in income tax, implies an upward shift in the *PS* curve, indicating that the real wage is higher at any level of employment since the tax take is smaller. The smaller wedge means that *WS* and *PS* curves cross at higher employment: there is a lower *ERU* because a higher real consumption wage on the *WS* curve is consistent with equilibrium for price setters (on the new higher *PS* curve). It is very important to note that what matters for shifting the *PS* curve and therefore for affecting equilibrium unemployment is the tax wedge as a whole: a rise in income tax or in indirect tax will push equilibrium unemployment up. There is nothing special about the effect of the so-called payroll taxes, i.e. the employer and employee social security contributions. Cross-country studies of unemployment in which many other determinants of unemployment are controlled for show rather consistent results for the estimated impact of the tax wedge on unemployment: a ten percentage point higher tax wedge is associated with a higher unemployment rate of between one and two percentage points.[2]

2.2 Price-push factors

We incorporate the tax wedge as one of the price-push factors and write the *PS* curve compactly as:

$$\frac{W}{P_c} = \lambda \cdot f(\mu, \mathbf{z}_p),$$

$$\text{(PS curve including price-push factors)}$$

where $\mathbf{z}_p$ is a set of price push variables including the tax wedge. The *PS* curve shifts up when there is a

- fall in the tax wedge, which is included in $\mathbf{z}_p$
- fall in the mark-up, μ, due, for example, to a change in competitive conditions
- rise in productivity, λ.

Other factors included in $\mathbf{z}_p$ may be regulations that increase the cost of employment, such as business registration and some employment regulations. However, such regulations do not necessarily have the effect of increasing price push and therefore raising the

---

[2] Baker et al. (2005) survey six studies, with estimates of the impact of a ten percentage point rise in the tax wedge on the unemployment rate that range from 0.91 to 2.08.

ERU. For example, although regulations enforcing health and safety standards impose costs on firms, they may have a compensating positive effect on productivity.

As we shall see in Chapter 18, in many empirical studies of unemployment, the real interest rate is included as a price-push factor. Most explanations centre on the impact of a higher real interest rate on the firm's investment decisions.[3] The idea is that a higher real interest rate depresses investment in physical capital stock, in worker training, retention, and recruitment. The precise way that this translates into a change in equilibrium employment is quite complicated because it depends, for example in the case of physical capital, on how substitutable labour and capital are in the production function. In our model, we ignore these complexities. It is therefore simplest to think of a rise in the real interest rate as reducing productivity, through its effect in discouraging investment in physical capital, in aspects of worker productivity and in the firm's customer base. In addition, a rise in the real interest rate pushes up the borrowing costs for firms who then cover these by pushing up the mark up.

2.3 Wage-push factors

We can write the *WS* equation:

$$\frac{W}{P_c} = b(E, \mathbf{z}_w) \qquad \qquad (WS \text{ curve})$$

where $\mathbf{z}_w$ is a set of wage push variables. The $\mathbf{z}_w$'s include institutional, policy, structural, and shock variables.

It is argued that the *WS* curve shifts down when:

- there is a fall in the level of unemployment benefits (or more precisely in the replacement ratio, which is the ratio of benefits to the average wage) or its duration because this shifts the balance toward accepting a job at a lower real wage at any given unemployment rate.

- unions are given less legal protection because this reduces the difference between the *WS* curve and the labour supply curve.

- unions are weaker, for example as measured by a lower proportion of trade union members amongst employees (lower trade union density) or when a lower proportion of employees are covered by collective bargaining agreements (lower collective bargaining coverage). In the appendix to this chapter there is a table showing trade union density and coverage for OECD countries from 1970–2000.

- unions agree to exercise bargaining restraint in the context, for example, of a wage accord because this lowers the real wage that is acceptable to unions at a given unemployment rate.

---

[3] See, for example, Phelps (1994), Rowthorn (1999).

2.3.1 Productivity increases

There is considerable debate about whether labour productivity, λ, should appear in the *WS* equation as well as in the *PS* equation, as follows:

$$\frac{W}{P_c} = \lambda b(E, \mathbf{z}_w).$$

To support including λ in the *WS* equation in a symmetrical way to its role in the *PS* equation, one may appeal to the stylized fact that productivity has been continuously rising but unemployment has not been continuously falling. If the *WS* equation takes this form, then a rise in productivity has no effect on the *ERU*: the wage aspirations of wage setters rise in line with productivity. We return to this debate in the appendix of Chapter 15 in the context of the discussion of efficiency wages.

An interesting empirical question arises when the model is put into a dynamic setting with productivity growth. One plausible scenario is that wage setters build the underlying growth in productivity into their wage-setting equation so that underlying productivity growth sets the baseline for wage setters' real wage claims. This would then be modified by the state of the labour market, i.e. by E and by the wage-push factors, $\mathbf{z}_w$. The question is what happens when trend productivity growth rises or falls? If wage setters are able to spot that the trend has changed then they will adjust their wage demands accordingly and the *ERU* is unchanged. If it takes time for the change in trend to make its way into wage setters' behaviour, then a slowdown in productivity growth will raise the *ERU* and a speed-up will lower the *ERU*. Effects of this kind appear to have been observed following the generalized slowdown in productivity growth in the advanced countries after 1970 and following the speed-up in productivity growth in the USA in the mid-1990s. To reflect the uncertainty about the precise role of productivity in the wage equation, we put λ inside the b function. This indicates that a rise or fall in productivity in the static context or a rise or fall in productivity growth in the dynamic one does not necessarily result in a shift of the *WS* curve exactly in line with that of the *PS* curve.

$$\frac{W}{P_c} = b(\lambda, E, \mathbf{z}_w).$$

(*WS* curve, including wage-push factors)

2.3.2 Training programmes

There are two channels through which increased government expenditure on training may lower equilibrium unemployment. First, if the training is effective, a more highly trained workforce will be characterized by higher productivity and this will shift the *PS* curve upwards. As discussed above, the rise in productivity may also shift the *WS* curve upwards.

Through a quite different mechanism, increased training may weaken the bargaining power of employees and operate to shift the *WS* curve downwards, helping to lower equilibrium unemployment. Whereas a shortage of skilled workers will tend to increase union bargaining power, the reverse will be the case if a shortage is reduced by higher levels of training. Programmes that enhance the skills of the unemployed (such as those in the 'Welfare-to-work' programme in the UK) can be interpreted in the same way—i.e.

if they improve the supply of workers able to actively compete in the labour market, the *WS* curve is shifted downward and equilibrium unemployment falls.

2.3.3 Wage accords, incomes policies, and industrial relations legislation

The idea of using a 'wage accord' or 'incomes policy' to reduce equilibrium unemployment derives from the possibility of introducing measures that lower the *WS* curve. As we shall see in the next section, differences in the institutional arrangements for wage setting in different economies (e.g. the degree to which wage setting is coordinated either by unions or by employers across the economy) are likely to generate differing degrees of wage restraint. In this section, we provide a more general argument that links wage restraint to government policy and industrial relations legislation.

At each level of employment, union negotiators have a choice as to how hard they push wage negotiations. The limits to this choice are set at the upper end by employers and at the lower end by individual union members. The ceiling for bargaining intensity can be referred to as the *WS*(ceiling): this is the real wage that unions can secure if they use their bargaining power to the full, i.e. if they use all the weapons at their disposal, including strikes. Changes in the environment in which unions operate such as changes in industrial relations legislation, the density of union membership, or the coverage of collective bargaining agreements may affect the weapons available to the unions and hence will shift the *WS*(ceiling). The position of the *WS*(ceiling) will also depend on the ability of firms to pay the wage and on their willingness to resist union demands. The employers will seek a minimum cost outcome by trading off the costs of a settlement against the costs of industrial action. Employer resistance to wage claims may well be strengthened by employers acting in concert in wage negotiations, drawing on such weapons as strategic lock-outs, where employers react to union strikes at key plants by locking workers out at other plants.

The floor to the real wage actually negotiated by the unions is set by the *WS*(floor), which is defined as the highest real wage that individual workers at local level will insist on, in the sense that they cannot be prevented by the union leadership from striking for it. Should the union leadership decide to operate on a *WS* curve below the *WS*(floor), we would expect to observe *unofficial* strike action as workers sought to negotiate higher wages at local level. The *WS*(floor) can be interpreted as a many-sided constraint covering minimally acceptable conditions of work such as the intensity or speed of work, as well as wages, hours of work, holidays, etc. Should any of these constraints be violated, then the workers would go on strike if this were necessary to rectify the shortfall in their minimum acceptable conditions of employment. In general, there will be a gap between the *WS*(ceiling) and *WS*(floor), which we define as the zone of bargaining discretion available to the unions between the constraints set by the employers and by their members. Bargaining discretion exists because individual workers or small groups of workers would generally be unable to gain as favourable a settlement as could the union for the industry as a whole (see Fig. 4.4).

The wage-setting curve along which negotiations actually take place, i.e. the *WS*, generally lies in the zone of bargaining discretion. This raises the obvious question of why should unions exercise any bargaining discretion, i.e. why does *WS* not coincide with *WS*(ceiling)? One rationale for such behaviour is union concern for the long-run future

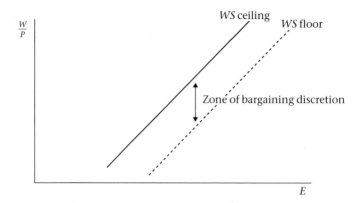

Figure 4.4 Zone of bargaining discretion between *WS* ceiling and *WS* floor

of the industry. The use of maximum bargaining intensity and the use of the associated weapons of industrial disruption might be thought likely to jeopardize investment plans in the industry.

A wage accord (or incomes policy) is a situation in which unions in their negotiations with employers agree to exercise bargaining discretion and shift the *WS* curve downwards within the zone of bargaining discretion. Such an accord may be part of a broader settlement in which the government agrees to undertake policy measures supported by the unions and or to give the unions an enhanced role in government economic policy making. An example in Europe is the 1982 Wassenaar Accord in the Netherlands between employers and unions, which was later endorsed by the government and which continues to affect wage setting. Unions offered wage restraint and more local flexibility in wage setting; employers agreed to a reduction in working hours. The unions agreed that reductions in working hours would not increase labour costs. Although the accord was bilateral between the unions and employers, the government agreed to deal with its fiscal problems (a burgeoning public sector deficit).[4] A second example is Ireland, where there have been a series of tripartite national wage agreements since 1987 and which continue to the present. As in the Dutch case, the phase of successful wage accords followed a period of unruly labour relations and unsatisfactory macroeconomic outcomes. In the 1980s, Ireland was experiencing rapid productivity growth and the accords were designed to ensure that real wage growth was not excessive. The government committed itself to respond to wage restraint with tax cuts and improved social benefits.[5] As we shall see in Chapter 18, both the Netherlands and Ireland succeeded in reducing unemployment very markedly in the 1990s. In each case, the wage accord appears to have played a part.

It is useful to note why it can be difficult to achieve agreement amongst unions on a wage accord. If there are many unions in the economy, the problem is that for each individual union there is a temptation to defect from any wage accord since it will then secure

---

[4] For further details see Nickell and van Ours (2000); for an earlier period, see Flanagan et al (1983). A broader discussion of the role of labour relations in explaining unemployment is to be found in Blanchard and Philippon (2004).

[5] For more details, see OECD, *Employment Outlook* (2004), ch. 3 and Honahan and Walsh (2002).

higher wages. However if all unions act this way, the wage accord collapses (the *WS* curve shifts upwards) and macroeconomic policy must be tightened to prevent inflation from rising. This problem has the structure of the famous prisoners' dilemma game: two prisoners implicated in the same crime are held in separate cells and cannot communicate. They are told that if both confess, they will each serve ten years; if one confesses and the other does not, the one that confesses goes free and the other serves twenty years whereas if neither confess, both get two years on a lesser charge. Each prisoner reasons as follows: if I confess and my partner does not, I go free; whereas if he, too, confesses, I get ten years. On the other hand, if I deny the charge but he confesses, I go down for twenty years; if he too denies, then we both get two years. Whether my partner confesses or not, I always get a shorter sentence by confessing: ten rather than twenty (if he confesses) or zero rather than two (if he doesn't confess). The implication—attributing the same reasoning to both prisoners—is that both confess and get ten years, whereas their joint utility maximizing strategy would be for both to deny, leaving each with a two-year sentence. The structure of this game is one in which there is a so-called *dominant strategy*, in the sense that one strategy ('confess') is preferred irrespective of the strategy chosen by the other party.

The parallel with the unions is that just like the prisoners, the temptation to defect (for the prisoner, by confessing whilst the other one denies; for the union, by breaking the wage accord whilst the others stick to it) makes agreement to the accord problematic. Yet in both cases, the failure to coordinate leaves the parties worse off. Economies characterized by highly centralized wage setting or where there is a single acknowledged leader union will find the achievement of a wage accord easier than economies in which there are a number of competing unions. We turn now to a model that connects wage restraint to the institutional structure of wage setting.

3 Unions, wage-setting arrangements, and the *ERU*

A standard argument is that greater union strength measured by the proportion of employees that belong to a union (union density) or by the proportion of employees whose wages are covered by union wage agreements (coverage) is a wage push factor that implies a higher *WS* curve and therefore raises the *ERU*. However, an influential article written by Lars Calmfors and John Driffill in the late 1980s[6] argued that there was a hump-shaped relationship between the degree of centralization of wage setting and the *ERU*. The Calmfors–Driffill model showed that a low *ERU* was consistent with either very decentralized wage setting or with very centralized wage setting; the worst institutional arrangement was a so-called intermediate level of wage setting. This is an interesting result because it highlights the possibility that union strength is not necessarily associated with an upward push in the *WS* curve. If union strength is associated with a particular structure of wage setting then it may, on the contrary, be associated with low unemployment. This argument provides a way of understanding the very low unemployment rates typical of a number of Nordic countries and Austria in the 1970s and 1980s, when it rose elsewhere.

---

[6] Calmfors and Driffill (1988).

The key insights of the Calmfors–Driffill model can be explained intuitively.[7] The model assumes that workers are unionized and compares three different contexts for wage setting: at firm level, at industry level and at the level of the economy as a whole.

- 'Firm level' or 'decentralized' means a situation in which there is a union specific to each firm that sets the wage in the firm.
- 'Industry level' or 'intermediate' means there is a union that sets the wage for all workers in an industry (e.g. the engineering industry union; the banking industry union).
- 'Economy-wide' or 'centralized' means there is a single union that sets the wage for all workers in the economy. As we shall see, wage setting does not have to be literally centralized for the economy-wide outcome to prevail: what matters is the extent to which wage setters take into account the economy-wide implications of their wage-setting decision. For this reason, the term 'coordinated' is often preferred to 'centralized'.[8]

In each case it is assumed that the union has the same utility function in which utility increases with employment and with the real wage. For simplicity, it is assumed that the wage is chosen by a monopoly union rather than by bargaining between the union and the employer (or the employers' association). The union unilaterally sets the wage and the employer chooses the level of employment.

There are two different forces for wage moderation—the first concerns the way in which the union expects employment to respond to a change in the wage and the second concerns the extent to which the union takes into account the impact of its decisions on the economy-wide price level. In relation to the first, as wage setting becomes more decentralized, the union becomes more concerned about the effect on the employment of its members if it increases the wage. It is worried that a wage increase in the firm will make the firm less competitive as compared with others. As a consequence the firm will decrease employment, which will have a negative impact on the utility of union members. This acts to limit the exercise of union power when wages are set by the union at firm level. By contrast, when wages are set by an industry union, the union will view the impact of its wage increase on the demand for industry output and hence on industry employment as limited. This is because the degree of substitutability between the products of different industries (e.g. between engineering equipment and textiles) is much less than between the products of different firms in the same industry (e.g. between the fork-lift trucks produced by firm A and firm B). Hence, the industry union will exercise less restraint and choose a higher wage than the firm-level union.

The second force for wage moderation is of a quite different kind. It arises from consideration of what are referred to as the general equilibrium effects of the wage increase. A union that is operating at the level of the firm takes as given the economy-wide price level and, when setting the money wage, assumes that this sets the real consumption wage for the workers in the firm (i.e. $\frac{W_i}{P}$, for firm i), which is what its members care about.

---

[7] A more formal version is set out in Chapter 15.

[8] For further discussion about how coordination in wage setting takes place see Soskice (1990).

However, if the union is setting the wage for all workers in the economy, the impact of its decision on the economy-wide price level cannot be ignored. The union will therefore recognize that any increase in the wage it sets will generate an increase in the price level as costs in the economy rise in line. The outcome will therefore be that the real consumption wage does not rise. Another way to put this is to say that when making its decision, the centralized union takes into account the fact that the economy will end up on the price-setting curve after wages and prices have been set. The centralized union realizes that it cannot achieve a real wage higher than that on the *PS* curve. In the simple case of a horizontal *PS* curve, the real wage is constant so when the centralized union picks its best point along the *PS* curve, it will choose to maximize employment. This implies that the centralized union chooses not to exercise its monopoly power in wage negotiations: its utility is maximized at the employment level where the labour supply curve cuts the *PS* curve. To relate this outcome to the previous section's discussion about the prisoners' dilemma game, in the case of a centralized union, it solves the coordination problem by having a single decision maker who is able to maximize the joint utility of the members.

To see the above argument diagramatically, we begin with the union indifference curves (see Fig. 4.5). These are best thought of as comprising two components: on the one hand workers and hence their unions are interested in maximizing the wage bill and this produces a downward-sloping indifference curve in the real wage-employment diagram. The second component is that there is a disutility of work so eventually the indifference curve slopes upward. The labour supply curve, E^S is derived by taking any real wage and finding the optimal amount of labour supplied so this goes through the minimum points of the indifference curves.

We now consider the case where unions are organized at industry level. As explained above, such unions believe that their wage decision will have little impact on employment since the degree of substitutability between the products of different industries

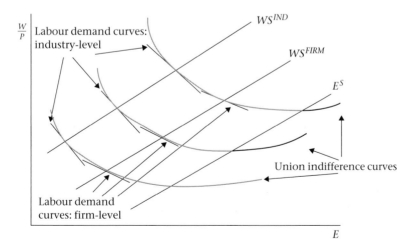

Figure 4.5 Deriving wage-setting curves under different institutional arrangements

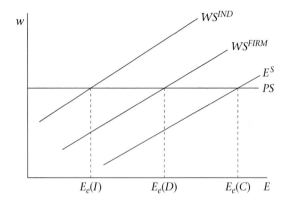

Figure 4.6 Equilibrium employment with centralized, industry-, and firm-level wage setting

is low. This is reflected in the rather steep industry-level labour demand curves. The industry-level union optimizes by choosing the highest indifference curve subject to the constraint of the labour demand curve. Three labour demand curves for different levels of aggregate demand in the economy are shown. By joining up the points of tangency, the wage-setting curve for the case of wage setting by industry-level unions is derived, WS^{IND} (see Fig. 4.5). As we move to a more decentralized context for wage setting, the union becomes more concerned about the impact of its wage decision on employment of its members: if it raises its wage, the firm will raise its price and demand will switch to other suppliers. The greater elasticity of demand produces flatter labour demand curves as shown in the diagram, with the consequence that the wage-setting curve for decentralized wage setting lies below that for industry-level wage setting, WS^{FIRM}.

To draw out the implications for equilibrium unemployment, we note that once wages are set, firms set prices. Returning to the level of the economy as a whole, we therefore have the *PS* curve as shown in Fig. 4.6. Equilibrium employment for the case of industry-level wage setting is shown by the intersection of the WS^{IND} and the *PS*. This is below that for the case of firm-level wage setting. As argued above, the centralized case brings in the second element in the Calmfors–Driffill story: the wage decision affects prices and as the coverage of wage setting increases, it becomes impossible for the union to ignore the consequences of its wage decision for the economy-wide price level and hence for the real consumption wage, which enters its utility function. Hence the centralized union uses the labour supply curve as its wage-setting curve, leading to equilibrium employment at $E_e(C)$.

We can see the implications for the *ERU* in Fig. 4.7: it is low in the case of centralized or decentralized wage setting and high when unions set wages at industry level. This is what produces the hump-shaped relationship between the centralization of wage setting and the *ERU*. In the appendix to this chapter, data on measures of centralization and coordination of wage setting are provided for OECD countries. In Chapter 18, we look at how different arrangements for wage setting have been measured and their role in accounting for differences across countries in unemployment patterns.

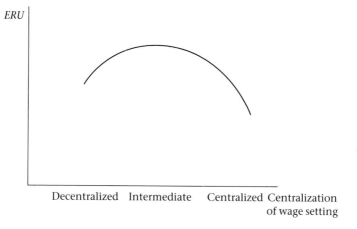

Figure 4.7 The hump-shaped relationship between unemployment and the centralization of wage setting

4 Introduction to hysteresis: actual *U* affects the *ERU*

We have seen that the equilibrium rate of unemployment is shifted by supply-side factors. The policy implication is twofold:

(1) aggregate demand shocks have a short-run effect on unemployment but no effect in the medium run.

(2) whilst aggregate demand policies have a role to play in stabilizing the economy around the *ERU*, they cannot influence its level.

However, it has been argued that if actual unemployment stays above equilibrium unemployment for an extended period, it could have a damaging effect on the supply side of the economy with the result that the *ERU* is raised. This is an example of so-called hysteresis, in which the equilibrium of the system depends on the history of the system. Often the term 'path dependence' is used to describe this phenomenon. In this section we provide examples of unemployment persistence stemming from mechanisms that work through the *WS* curve:

- the insider-outsider effect, where wages are set to benefit those in work, i.e. the insiders;

- the long-term/short-term unemployment effect, where the long-term unemployed (the outsiders) lose touch with the labour market and cease to influence wage setting.

We also explain a mechanism that operates via capacity scrapping and is represented by shifts in the *PS* curve. In Chapter 18, we look at the attempt to find empirical support for the role of hysteresis and persistence mechanisms in explaining European unemployment.[9]

---

[9] For a useful survey of the theoretical and empirical literature on hysteresis and unemployment, see Roed (1997).

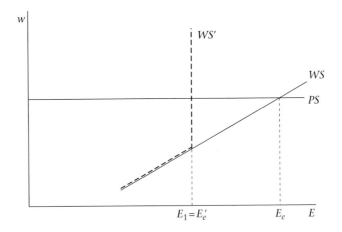

Figure 4.8 Hysteresis: the insider-outsider model

4.1 The insider-outsider effect[10]

We assume that the economy is initially at equilibrium employment, E_e in Fig. 4.8 and that there is a fall in aggregate demand that reduces employment to E_1. Our usual assumption is that the falling inflation at E_1 leads the central bank to cut the interest rate and boost aggregate demand so that the economy returns to $E = E_e$. If, however, the central bank is inactive and if the impact of falling inflation on aggregate demand, via the real balance effect on the demand for money (the keynes effect) or on consumption (the pigou effect), is weak then the economy may remain for some time at E_1. Two groups of workers may then be identified: the unemployed outsiders and the insiders who remain employed at E_1. They are in a strong bargaining position because, for example, their firm-specific skills mean that the firm cannot simply sack them and replace them with new workers. Insiders are presumed to be interested in maintaining their own employment and increasing their real wage; they attach no importance to the creation of employment for those currently unemployed.[11] The consequence is that the WS curve becomes vertical at E_1 as shown in Fig. 4.8. Any increase in aggregate demand will simply be reflected in a rise in the real wage until the $w^{WS} = w^{PS}$, after which, higher aggregate demand will produce rising inflation: equilibrium employment has fallen to $E_1 = E'_e$. This is a model of pure hysteresis in the sense that once unemployment has risen and insiders have emerged with wage-setting power, equilibrium unemployment goes up and remains at the new level. Although the rise in equilibrium unemployment originated with a fall in aggregate demand (that was not offset), only a supply-side change, which alters wage-setting arrangements can reduce equilibrium unemployment. The microeconomic working of the model is explained in more detail in Chapter 15.

---

[10] The original articles are: Lindbeck and Snower (1986) and Blanchard and Summers (1986).

[11] Note that implicitly in our usual discussions of wage setting, the utility function of workers (and unions) is based on a representative (or average) worker's preferences before they know whether they are employed or unemployed.

4.2 Long-term unemployment and unemployment persistence

An example of the interaction between aggregate demand and equilibrium unemployment focuses on the role of the long-term unemployed in the labour market.[12] The long-term unemployed are viewed as having in effect withdrawn from participation in the labour market because of a progressive loss of skills and erosion of psychological attachment to working life. They are therefore only poor substitutes for those in work and exert little competitive pressure in the labour market. The higher is the proportion of long-term unemployed in the overall pool of unemployment, the less impact will any given level of unemployment have on wage setting. If this is the case, then since a long period of high unemployment is likely to eventually push up the proportion of the long-term unemployed, equilibrium unemployment will rise. In the *WS/PS* diagram, the *WS* curve shifts upwards. This in turn weakens the self-equilibrating process through which high unemployment dampens wage inflation. The objective of reducing the scarring effects of unemployment lies behind 'welfare-to-work' programmes. The aim of such programmes is to reconnect unemployed workers with the labour market by using combinations of sticks (e.g. loss of benefits if active search is not undertaken) and carrots (e.g. grants for travel to job interviews, training for interviews).

To explain how the emergence of long-term unemployment can lead to a prolonged period of high unemployment, we take as an example the case of an economy initially in equilibrium with constant inflation at point *A* in Fig. 4.9. Let us assume that inflation is stable but high at point *A* and a newly elected government wishes to reduce inflation to π_L. This leads it to reduce aggregate demand to E_1 and to keep activity low until inflation has been reduced to π_L. However, with high unemployment at E_1, the share of long-term unemployment begins to rise: it rises to LTU_H, at which point it stabilizes. With a large pool of long-term unemployed, the *WS* curve shifts upward as explained above: this is $WS(LTU_H)$. As is clear from the diagram, disinflation is slowed down by the upward shift of the *WS* curve. If we assume that inflation is brought down to π_L then the government will want to move the economy back to E_e. However, because of the presence of higher share of long-term unemployed, equilbrium unemployment is now at E_2. But unlike the insider-outsider model, in this case, the economy will eventually return to equilibrium at *A*. The reason is that at point *D*, the share of long-term unemployed will begin to decline (since unemployment is lower than at E_1) and the $WS(LTU)$ curve will shift down.

Gradually, as employment recovers, the share of long-term unemployed will shrink and the economy will return to *A*. If the 'scarring' effect of long-term unemployment is very serious, specific policies targeted at reintegrating the long-term unemployed back into jobs may be necessary in order for the equilibrium at *A* to be attained. Once back at *A*, the government will have achieved its objective of reducing inflation but the process will be protracted if workers become disconnected from the labour force during the phase of high unemployment. The flatter *WS* curve (dashed) in the diagram shows the wage-setting curve when the long-term unemployment share is unchanging. As we have seen,

---

[12] Layard and Nickell (1986).

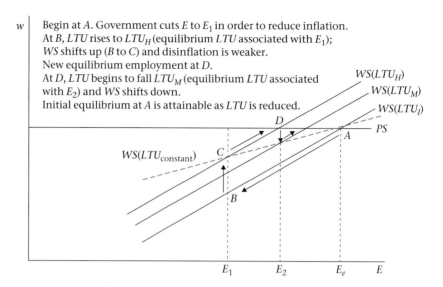

Begin at A. Government cuts E to E_1 in order to reduce inflation.
At B, LTU rises to LTU_H (equilibrium LTU associated with E_1);
WS shifts up (B to C) and disinflation is weaker.
New equilibrium employment at D.
At D, LTU begins to fall LTU_M (equilibrium LTU associated
with E_2) and WS shifts down.
Initial equilibrium at A is attainable as LTU is reduced.

Figure 4.9 Unemployment persistence: the role of long-term unemployment

beginning with an initially low share of long-term unemployment at B, it rises, stabilizing at the share denoted by LTU_H. It is the intersection of the dashed WS curve and the PS curve that fixes the 'long-run' equilibrium rate of unemployment: the shifting WS curve slows down the return to A and the economy will be observed at 'medium-run' constant inflation equilibria such as at point D.

It is also possible for persistence to operate through the price-setting curve in a way that is analytically similar to the long-term unemployment model. The intuition is as follows: depressed economic activity leads to the scrapping of capital stock.[13] When demand rises again, high rates of capacity utilization are encountered at higher unemployment rates than previously. It is plausible that firms increase their profit margins at very high rates of capacity utilization since they believe that pervasive shortage of capacity in the economy means it is safe to do so. Diagramatically this implies that the PS curve turns downwards as shown in Fig. 4.10. If we assume that the economy shifts initially from equilibrium at A to higher unemployment associated with E_1 perhaps as the result of the disinflation policy used in the previous example, then after a prolonged period of high unemployment and associated capital scrapping, the capital stock declines with the consequence that the downward-sloping part of the PS curve occurs at lower employment. When aggregate demand is subsequently increased, it is clear that equilibrium unemployment is higher: there is a new equilibrium with constant inflation at C. However, the economy will eventually return to the original equilibrium because high capacity utilization at C will stimulate investment. Eventually the economy will return to 'normal' capacity utilization at equilibrium unemployment.

[13] This follows Carlin and Soskice (1990), ch. 19.

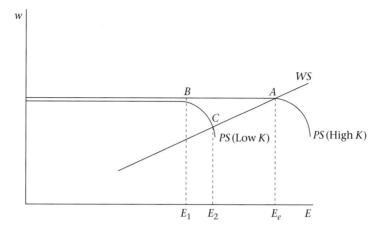

Figure 4.10 Unemployment persistence: the capacity scrapping effect

5 The Beveridge curve approach to unemployment

A quite different tradition of labour market analysis from the wage- and price-setting model focuses on the flows of people into and out of unemployment or employment. This is often referred to as the flow approach and belongs to part of labour economics known as job search theory. We explain the essence of this approach without getting into the technical details and show how it can be related to the *WS-PS* model. It is a useful additional tool when analysing unemployment as demonstrated in Chapter 18. In the job search tradition, unemployment is in equilibrium when flows into and out of unemployment are equal. With a constant labour force, labour market equilibrium in the flow approach means that hires, *H*, are equal to separations, *S*, from employment. The central idea is that workers and jobs are heterogeneous (a factor that has been neglected until now) with the consequence that an important aspect of how the labour market works is how well it achieves the matching of unemployed workers with unfilled job vacancies.

A simple version of the matching function can be explained as follows. It is assumed that U is the number of unemployed and V is the number of vacancies and α is the parameter that describes how efficient the matching process is in the economy. It is normally assumed that the matching function is characterized by constant returns to scale. We can therefore write the matching function as

$$H = \alpha \cdot m(U, V),$$

where a higher number of new hires is associated with higher matching efficiency ($\alpha > 0$). It is important to note that H and S are flows per period and that the period can be of any length as long as hires and separations are measured consistently. This describes how the unemployed are matched with the vacancies. Holding the matching efficiency and the number of vacancies constant, higher unemployment is associated with more matches since there are more applicants for each job. Similarly, holding unemployment constant, more vacancies are associated with more matches. If we assume that the flow of workers from employment to unemployment is $S = sE$ where s is the proportionate exit rate from employment, then the labour market will be in a flow equilibrium when the flow *into* unemployment, sE is equal to the flow *out of* unemployment into jobs, M:

$$sE = \alpha \cdot m(U, V).$$

Using the assumption that matching takes place under constant returns to scale and assuming for simplicity that the separation rate is an exogenous constant (i.e. that it does not depend on economic factors), we have:

$$s = \alpha \cdot m\left(\frac{U}{E}, \frac{V}{E}\right).$$

If we draw a diagram with the 'unemployment rate' ($u \equiv U/E$) on the horizontal axis and the vacancy rate ($v \equiv V/E$) on the vertical axis, the labour market equilibrium can be plotted as shown in Fig. 4.11. The vacancy/unemployment curve depicting labour market equilibrium in the flow model is called the Beveridge curve. The curve is downward sloping because at high unemployment, with a given matching technology, it will be necessary for vacancies to be low to deliver the constant number of matches required to balance the fixed separation rate, s. Conversely at low unemployment with fewer people looking for work, more vacancies are required to ensure that the number of those taking jobs is equal to the separation rate. Any decline in the efficiency of matching, α, will shift the curve to the right with the implication that flow equilibrium at a given unemployment rate will require a higher rate of vacancies in the economy.

But how does this approach to labour market equilibrium relate to the *WS-PS* model? To this point, vacancies have been ignored. However, once heterogeneity between workers and jobs is introduced, vacancies represent a measure of pressure in the labour market. Holding all the other determinants of the wage- and price-setting curves constant, for a

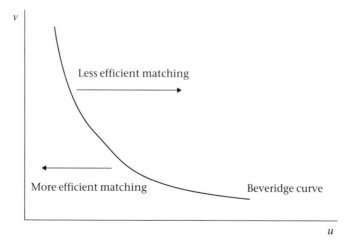

Figure 4.11 The Beveridge curve

given employment (or unemployment) rate, higher vacancies in the economy increase the wage workers can bargain for, or that employers need to set to attract good workers. The *WS* equation written in terms of employment is:

$$\frac{W}{P_c} = b(E, v, \mathbf{z}_w), \qquad \text{(WS curve)}$$

where v is the vacancy rate. The *WS* curve shifts up when the vacancy rate increases. As Fig. 4.12 shows, a higher rate of vacancies implies a lower equilibrium employment rate and hence higher equilibrium unemployment. In other words, there is a positive relationship between vacancies and equilibrium unemployment (at which *WS* and *PS* are equal). In the Beveridge curve diagram, we can now include the positively sloped line showing the wage- and price-setting equilibrium (Fig. 4.13). In the Beveridge curve diagram, full

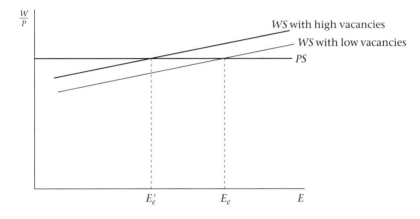

Figure 4.12 The *WS-PS* curve and vacancies

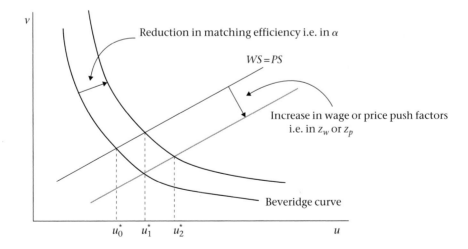

Figure 4.13 The Beveridge curve and the *WS-PS* equilibrium

equilibrium in the labour market is shown by the intersection of the Beveridge curve and the $WS = PS$ line. It is clear from the diagram that there will be higher unemployment if the ability of the economy to match workers to jobs worsens (an outward shift of the Beveridge curve). In this case, both unemployment and vacancies will be higher in the new equilibrium (at u_1^*). The adjustment of the economy to the new equilibrium can be explained as follows: if a deterioration in matching occurs, vacancies rise thereby pushing the WS curve upwards and raising inflationary pressure (as in Fig. 4.12). Equilibrium unemployment has gone up and aggregate demand will have to be reduced. The economy moves to the new equilibrium shown by u_1^* (in Fig. 4.13).

Alternatively, if there is a rise in wage (or price) push in the economy but the Beveridge curve remains unchanged, then the $WS = PS$ curve shifts to the right and equilibrium occurs at higher unemployment (at u_1^*) but with a lower vacancy rate. The intuition in the second case is that higher unemployment is associated with a lower vacancy rate (for matching reasons) and this somewhat offsets the effect of higher wage pressure, leaving equilibrium unemployment lower than would be the case if the vacancy rate did not fall. If equilibrium unemployment goes up with little change in the vacancy rate, this suggests that there has been a shift in both the WS/PS curves and in the Beveridge curve (as in the move from u_0^* to u_2^*).

By introducing the flow approach to the labour market, we have widened the set of factors that can account for changes in equilibrium unemployment. In addition to those that shift the WS or the PS curves, we now include features of the way the labour market brings workers and jobs together. Barriers to occupational and geographical mobility imply weaker matching and will shift the Beveridge curve outward; similarly policies to overcome these barriers by improving the efficiency of employment and training agencies or the operation of the housing market can have the opposite effect. Some forms of employment protection legislation may affect the willingness of employers to hire workers, weakening the matching process. Some factors will in principle shift both curves: for example, anything such as an increase in unemployment benefit duration, that weakens search intensity, shifts the Beveridge curve to the right and, as a wage-push factor, also shifts the WS upwards and hence the $WS = PS$ to the right. These effects are reinforcing, worsening equilibrium unemployment.

6 Conclusions

In this chapter, we have explored the implications for inflation and the ERU of shifts in the wage- and or price-setting curves. If the WS curve is pushed up or the PS curve is pushed down, the equilibrium rate of unemployment rises. The reverse—i.e. a fall in equilibrium unemployment—is the case for a downward shift in WS or an upward shift in PS. In the case of a negative supply shift, inflation goes up and the central bank will respond to this by raising the interest rate. Unemployment will be pushed above the new higher ERU in order to squeeze the higher inflation out of the economy. The central bank will then guide the economy along the new MR curve to the new higher ERU and inflation will return to its target rate.

Institutional and policy-related wage- and price-push factors have been identified. The price-setting curve shifts downwards when there is

- a rise in the tax wedge
- a rise in the mark-up (i.e. when monopoly power rises)
- a fall in productivity
- a rise in the real interest rate
- more employment regulation, to the extent that this is not offset by higher productivity or by an offsetting moderation of wage demands.

The wage-setting curve shifts upwards when

- there is a rise in the replacement ratio, i.e. when unemployment benefits become more generous in relation to the average wage
- unions are accorded more legal protection, e.g. in relation to the right to take industrial action or become more powerful as reflected in union density or in collective bargaining coverage
- unions exercise less wage restraint, e.g. as the consequence of the collapse of a wage accord
- there is a change in wage-setting structures toward an intermediate level of wage setting either away from a more decentralized structure or from a more coordinated one.

It is controversial as to whether a change in productivity (or in the trend of productivity growth) affects the equilibrium rate of unemployment. A slowdown in productivity growth (or a fall in productivity in a static context) will shift the *PS* curve downwards. Unless, and until, wage setters adjust their behaviour in line with this, the consequence will be a rise in the *ERU*. It has been argued that a prolonged period of high unemployment can lead to a deterioration in the effectiveness with which the unemployed compete for jobs, which in turn shifts the *WS* curve upwards. This is known as hysteresis.

We have seen how the flow approach to the labour market, with its emphasis on how unemployed workers and vacancies are matched adds a dimension to our understanding of the determinants of equilibrium unemployment. The Beveridge curve is downwards sloping in the unemployment/vacancy diagram and shows the flow equilibrium in the labour market. For a given exit rate from employment and given the institutions in the economy that facilitate the matching of the unemployed with vacancies, a high unemployment rate will be associated with a low vacancy rate and vice versa. The Beveridge curve will be shifted to the right if there are increased barriers to occupational or geographical mobility or if employment protection measures impair the matching process. We can combine the analysis of the impact on equilibrium unemployment of the factors that shift the *WS* and or the *PS* with those that shift the Beveridge curve.

■ **QUESTIONS**

Checklist questions

(1) What is a wage accord and why might it collapse?

(2) How should the central bank respond to the collapse of a wage accord? Show the path of real wages, inflation, and unemployment over time as the economy adjusts to this shock.

(3) Explain what is meant by the tax wedge. Does a change in the tax wedge affect inflation?

(4) Make a scatter-plot using the data on trade union membership density and collective bargaining wage coverage in the appendix Table 4.1. What does the plot show? Is there any change in the relationship over time? Can you detect any regional patterns?

(5) How might the observation that the productivity trend since 1820 has been upwards in Europe and that the trend of the unemployment rate has not been downward be reconciled with the *WS-PS* model?

(6) In section 2, the prisoners' dilemma game is explained. Construct an example to show how this game can be applied to a union wage accord.

(7) Explain how the *WS* curves and the labour supply curve are derived in Fig. 4.5.

(8) Why is equilibrium employment lower when wages are set at industry rather than at firm level? How would you expect this relationship to be affected—if at all—if the economy in question is open to international trade?

(9) Compare the role played by outsiders in the insider-outsider model with that played by the long-term unemployed in the unemployment persistence model.

(10) Why is the Beveridge curve downward sloping and why is the *WS* = *PS* curve upward sloping in the vacancy-unemployment diagram?

(11) How, if at all, would you expect the internet to affect the *WS*, *PS*, or the Beveridge curve?

Problems and questions for discussion

QUESTION A. Trace the effects on unemployment and inflation of a sudden and permanent rise in labour productivity due to a technological breakthrough.

QUESTION B. Through what mechanisms can hysteresis in unemployment operate? What are its consequences for the time-path of the unemployment rate following (*a*) a period of disinflation? (*b*) an investment boom?

QUESTION C. How may unemployment be affected by (*a*) barriers to regional mobility; (*b*) poor information about jobs; (*c*) stronger employment protection legislation?

QUESTION D. 'Unions and labour market regulation reflect the power of vested interests and create inefficiency.' 'Unions and labour market regulation are an efficient response to missing markets.' Investigate how economic theory can be used to support each of these lines of argument. Do you find either argument persuasive? [Suggested reading: Pissarides (2001), Agell (2002).]

QUESTION E. In 1998, Robert Solow reported on a study by McKinsey Global Institute, which analysed the economic performance of France and Germany in terms of employment and productivity in six industries: automobiles, housebuilding, telecommunications, retail trade, consumer banking, and computer software. Solow argues that the MGI report supports the following conclusion:

> The likelihood is that France and Germany have moved to high-unemployment regimes by sliding along their Beveridge curves, and not as victims of adverse shifts in their Beveridge curves. The implied weakness in job creation is most likely the result of excessive and anti-competitive product-market regulation, restrictive macroeconomic policy, especially monetary policy, and inadequate discipline from the capital markets.[14]

Can you interpret Solow's conclusion using the models developed in this chapter?

QUESTION F. Declines in union density are often attributed to structural change, globalization, and demographic changes. Why might this be so? What would you expect the macroeconomic impact to be? [Suggested reading: Checchi and Lucifora (2002), Lesch (2004).]

---

[14] Solow (1998).

■ **Appendix**

Table 4.1 Trade union density and collective bargaining wage coverage, 1970–2000 (%)

	Trade union density				Collective bargaining coverage		
	1970	1980	1990	2000	1980	1990	2000
Australia	44	48	40	25	80+	80+	80+
Austria	63	57	47	37	95+	95+	95+
Belgium	41	54	54	56	90+	90+	90+
Canada	32	35	33	28	37	38	32
Czech Republic	. .	. .	46	27	. .	. .	25+
Denmark	60	79	75	74	70+	70+	80+
Finland	51	69	72	76	90+	90+	90+
France	22	18	10	10	80+	90+	90+
Germany	32	35	31	25	80+	80+	68
Greece	. .	39	32	27	. .	. .	. .
Hungary	. .	. .	63	20	. .	. .	30+
Iceland	. .	75	88	84	. .	. .	. .
Ireland	53	57	51	38	. .	. .	. .
Italy	37	50	39	35	80+	80+	80+
Japan	35	31	25	22	25+	20+	15+
Korea	13	15	17	11	15+	20+	10+
Luxembourg	47	52	50	34	. .	. .	60+
Mexico	. .	. .	43	18	. .	. .	. .
Netherlands	37	35	25	23	70+	70+	80+
New Zealand	56	69	51	23	60+	60+	25+
Norway	57	58	59	54	70+	70+	70+
Poland	. .	. .	33	15	. .	. .	40+
Portugal	. .	61	32	24	70+	70+	80+
Slovak Republic	. .	. .	57	36	. .	. .	50+
Spain	. .	7	11	15	60+	70+	80+
Sweden	68	80	80	79	80+	80+	90+
Switzerland	29	31	24	18	50+	50+	40+
Turkey	. .	. .	27	33	. .	. .	. .
United Kingdom	45	51	39	31	70+	40+	30+
United States	27	22	15	13	26	18	14
OECD unweighted average	**42**	**47**	**42**	**34**	**67**	**66**	**60**
OECD weighted average	**34**	**32**	**27**	**21**	**45**	**38**	**35**

. . Data not available.
Notes: For detailed notes, see Table 3.3, OECD, *Employment Outlook* (2004).
Figures with a + sign represent lower-bound estimates.
For the purposes of calculating averages, the indicated value was increased by 2.5 percentage points.
Source: Table 3.3, OECD, *Employment Outlook* (2004).

Table 4.2 Measures of the centralization and coordination of wage setting in OECD countries, 1970s–1990s

	Centralization			Coordination		
	1970s	1980s	1990s	1970s	1980s	1990s
Australia	4	4	2	4	4.25	2
Austria	3	3	3	5	4.25	4
Belgium	3.75	3	3	3.75	4	4.25
Canada	1	1	1	2	1	1
Czech Republic	. .	. .	1	. .	. .	1
Denmark	5	3	2.5	5	3.5	3.5
Finland	5	4.5	5	5	4.5	5
France	2	2	2	2	2	2
Germany	3	3	3	4	4	4
Hungary	. .	. .	1	. .	. .	1
Ireland	4	1.75	4	4	1.75	4
Italy	2	2.75	2	2	2.75	3.5
Japan	1	1	1	4	4	4
Korea	1	1	1	1	1	1
Netherlands	3	3	3	3.5	4.25	4
New Zealand	3	3	1	4	4	1
Norway	4.5	4	4.5	4.5	4	4.5
Poland	. .	. .	1	. .	. .	1
Portugal	4.5	3	4	4.5	3	4
Slovak Republic	. .	. .	2	. .	. .	2
Spain	4.5	3.75	3	4.5	3.75	3
Sweden	5	3.75	3	4	3.25	3
Switzerland	3	3	2	4	4	4
United Kingdom	2	1	1	3.5	1	1
United States	1	1	1	1	1	1

. . Data not available.
Centralization:
1 = Company and plant level predominant.
2 = Combination of industry and company/plant level, with an important share of employees covered by company bargains.
3 = Industry level predominant.
4 = Predominantly industrial bargaining, but also recurrent central-level agreements.
5 = Central-level agreements of overriding importance.
Coordination:
1 = fragmented company/plant bargaining, little or no coordination by upper-level associations.
2 = fragmented industry and company-level bargaining, with little or no pattern setting.
3 = industry-level bargaining with irregular pattern setting and moderate coordination among major bargaining actors.
4 = (a) informal coordination of industry and firm-level bargaining by (multiple) peak associations.
   (b) coordinated bargaining by peak confederations, including government-sponsored negotiations (tripartite agreements, social pacts), or government imposition of wage schedules.
   (c) regular pattern setting coupled with high union concentration and/or bargaining coordination by large firms.
   (d) government wage arbitration.
5 = (a) informal coordination of industry-level bargaining by an encompassing union confederation.
   (b) coordinated bargaining by peak confederations or government imposition of a wage schedule/freeze, with a peace obligation.

Notes: For detailed notes, see Table 3.5, OECD, *Employment Outlook* (2004).

Source: Table 3.5, OECD, *Employment Outlook* (2004).

5 Monetary Policy

The aim of this chapter is to set out in more detail the way that monetary policy has been analysed in recent years. The main idea is that central bank behaviour can be thought about in terms of a 'reaction function' that the central bank uses to respond to shocks to the economy and steer it toward an explicit or implicit inflation target.

- The first task of the reaction function is to provide a 'nominal anchor' for the medium run, which is defined in terms of an inflation or price-level target. This pins down the medium-run inflation rate and to the extent that forward-looking expectations play a role, establishes a commitment to a low inflation environment.

- The second task of the reaction function is to provide guidance as to how the central bank's policy instrument, the interest rate, should be adjusted in response to different shocks so that the medium-run objective of stable inflation is met while minimizing output fluctuations.

We show explicitly how this broad structure for monetary policy can be formalized as an optimal monetary policy rule. By optimal monetary policy rule is meant that the monetary rule can be derived as the solution to the problem of the government or central bank optimizing with respect to the constraints it faces from the private sector of the economy.

Over the course of the past two decades, central banks in the OECD economies and in many transition and developing countries have shifted toward inflation-targeting regimes of this broad type—or have done so indirectly by fixing their exchange rate to a country where the central bank uses such a framework. Before setting out the details of an inflation-targeting regime, it is necessary to clarify why low inflation-targets have been adopted. We begin by asking two questions:

(1) What is wrong with inflation?

(2) What is the 'ideal' rate of inflation—is it zero, positive or negative? Negative inflation is a situation in which average prices are falling; this is known as deflation. We are led to ask as well, what is wrong with deflation? We shall see that the consensus view is that costs are minimized when inflation is kept low and stable.

In Chapters 2 and 3 the operation of monetary policy was discussed for an active, inflation-targeting central bank that uses the interest rate as its policy instrument and for a passive central bank that fixes the growth rate of the money supply. In section 2, we compare these two paradigms and investigate why modern central banks typically target the inflation rate using an interest rate rule rather than targeting the growth of the money supply. Section 3 sets out in detail the derivation of the central bank's monetary policy rule that was introduced in Chapter 3: as the *MR* curve in the Phillips diagram and the *MR* equation in the 3-equation model. Specifically, we shall see the role played by the following six key variables in central bank policy making:

(1) the central bank's inflation target

(2) the central bank's preferences

(3) the slope of the Phillips curve

(4) the interest sensitivity of aggregate demand (i.e. the slope of the *IS* curve)

(5) the equilibrium level of output

(6) the stabilizing interest rate.

Section 4 focuses on how an interest rate rule such as the famous Taylor Rule can be derived from the 3-equation model. Section 5 steps back from the mechanics of interest rate based inflation targeting and investigates the problems with using such rules in dealing with macroeconomic problems. In particular, the dangers posed by deflation are explored.

For the bulk of the chapter, we describe monetary policy making assuming it is in the hands of the central bank. However, in section 6 we look at why it might matter whether monetary policy decisions are actually made by the government and then implemented by the central bank or whether the central bank is independent of the government. Section 6 introduces the idea that if the government (or central bank) tries to achieve a target level of output above equilibrium—perhaps for politically motivated reasons—then the result will be that in equilibrium the inflation rate is higher than the target rate. This is called the inflation bias. We then show how inflation bias is related to the problem of central bank credibility and the time inconsistency of policy. To do this we need to introduce forward-looking inflation expectations. The delegation of monetary policy to an independent central bank is sometimes proposed as a method of reducing or eliminating the inflation bias. In this section, we explain that the debate about 'rules versus discretion' in the time-inconsistency literature uses a much narrower definition of 'rules' than the one adopted in our analysis of monetary policy. This can be a source of confusion in discussing how central banks behave.

In this chapter, we consider only a closed economy. The relationship between the exchange rate regime and monetary policy in the open economy is explained in Chapter 9 and we extend the analysis of monetary policy rules to the open economy in Chapter 11.

1 Inflation, disinflation, and deflation

In Chapter 3, we set out the *IS-PC-MR* model with the following features:

- In medium-run equilibrium, inflation is equal to the central bank's inflation-target if the central bank seeks to stabilize unemployment around the *ERU*. In the *IS/LM* version of the model, in the medium-run equilibrium, inflation is equal to the growth rate of the money supply set by the central bank.

• Because of delays in price and wage setting, inflation is persistent, which means that lagged inflation affects current inflation and there will be a trade-off between inflation and unemployment in the short run. The Phillips curves are therefore indexed by lagged inflation ($\pi^I = \pi_{-1}$) and shift whenever π_{-1} changes:

$$\pi = \pi^I + \alpha(y - y_e)$$
$$= \pi_{-1} + \alpha(y - y_e).$$

With Phillips curves of this form, the implication is that disinflation is costly: unemployment has to rise above the *ERU* for inflation to fall.

• With linear Phillips curves, the sacrifice ratio is constant and independent of the central bank's preferences. Although the time path of unemployment is affected by the choice between a policy for rapid disinflation (so-called 'cold turkey') and a more gradualist policy, the cumulative amount of unemployment required to achieve a given reduction in inflation does not depend on the degree of inflation aversion of the central bank. However, with non-linear Phillips curves, this is no longer the case: when, as seems empirically likely, the Phillips curves become flatter as unemployment rises, a 'cold turkey' policy of disinflation favoured by a more inflation-averse central bank entails a higher sacrifice ratio than does a 'gradualist' policy favoured by a less inflation-averse central bank.

In setting out the structure of the basic short- and medium-run model, we concentrated on the key results. It is now appropriate to investigate more deeply the presumption that the goal of a low, stable inflation rate is an appropriate one for policy makers to have. There seem to be obvious benefits of having a higher level of output—i.e. above the equilibrium level set by the intersection of the *WS* and *PS* curves and therefore closer to the competitive, full information market-clearing level. But what are the costs to the economy of the rising inflation that would ensue? As we have already seen, if inflation gets 'too high', bringing it down is likely to be costly. Finally, what problems arise when inflation is negative, i.e. when prices are falling?

1.1 Rising inflation

In an economy in which social groups—such as unions—wield economic power, a situation of rising inflation reflects inconsistent claims on output per head in the economy. If firms are able to adjust prices immediately after wages have been set, rising inflation reflects a situation in which workers' real wage aspirations are systematically frustrated: the real wage is typically on the *PS* curve, not on the *WS* curve. If there are lags in price setting as well as in wage setting, then the aspirations of neither workers nor firms are fully satisfied (the real wage lies between the *PS* and *WS* curves). This reflects distributional conflict as different social groups (wage setters/employees and price setters/employers) seek to protect their interests. Social tension rises as frustration mounts. As we shall see, inflationary episodes of this kind have typically been followed by painful periods of disinflation.

As we have seen in Chapter 3, for disinflation to be costless in the sense of not entailing a period of high unemployment, expectations of inflation must be formed using the Rational Expectations Hypothesis, the commitment of the government and central bank to a policy of low inflation at equilibrium unemployment has to be believed by the private sector and there must be no lags in the adjustment of wages and prices. For countries experiencing episodes of moderate inflation up to double digit rates per annum, these conditions do not appear to have been met. Lawrence Ball examines twenty-eight episodes of disinflation in nine OECD countries and finds that with only one exception, disinflation was contractionary, with sacrifice ratios ranging from 2.9 in Germany (i.e. for a one percentage point reduction in inflation, the increase in unemployment was 2.9 percentage points for a year) to 0.8 in the United Kingdom and France.[1]

1.2 Very high inflation and hyperinflation

Once inflation rates rise above 100% per annum, additional considerations come into play.[2] Between 1960 and 1996, there were more than 40 episodes in 25 different developing countries of such high inflation, which on average lasted for about 40 months. In addition, virtually all of the transition economies of Eastern Europe and the former Soviet Union experienced a bout of very high inflation as a consequence of price liberalization at the beginning of the transition in the early 1990s. Hyperinflation has traditionally been defined as referring to a situation in which inflation rates rise above 50% *per month*—this was more common in the first half of the twentieth century than either in earlier epochs or since. Situations of very high and hyperinflation are normally the result of governments being unable to finance their expenditure through normal means (borrowing or taxation) and they therefore resort to monetary financing. This is known as seignorage. The intimate connection between very high inflation and government deficits is explored in detail in Chapter 6 on fiscal policy after the concepts of the government deficit and debt have been elaborated. We examine there the scope for and limits to seignorage.

There is some evidence that the deterioration in the economic environment associated with very high inflation perhaps paradoxically can have the effect of creating the conditions for a relatively painless subsequent stabilization. Very high inflation is typically associated with very poor economic performance: investment, consumption, and output are all depressed. The length of wage contracts becomes very short and there is increasing recourse to the use of foreign currency for transactions. This means that the nominal rigidities that are one reason for costly disinflation virtually disappear. Achieving the credibility that is also required for the reform package to succeed is more elusive. It is fair to say that the way to achieve a successful, painless disinflation is not well understood. It requires that the *causes* of the unsustainable fiscal stance be addressed and that the central bank be prevented from financing the deficit through the creation of money but as is often the case in macroeconomics, this is easier said than done.

---

[1] Ball (1994).

[2] For a more detailed discussion of very high inflation, see Fischer, Sahay, and Végh (2002).

1.3 **Volatile inflation**

When inflation is high it also seems to be more volatile. Volatile inflation is costly because it creates uncertainty and undermines the informational content of prices. Unexpected changes in inflation imply changes in real variables in the economy: if money wages and pensions are indexed by past inflation and there is an unanticipated jump in inflation, real wages and pensions will drop. Equally, the real return on savings will fall because the nominal interest rate only incorporates expected inflation.

In an economy with technical progress, innovation takes place unevenly across sectors. In sectors with rapid innovation, prices will be falling relative to other sectors where technology is more stagnant. Volatile inflation masks the economically relevant changes in relative prices and therefore distorts resource allocation. In short, volatile inflation has real effects on the economy that are hard to avoid.

1.4 **Constant inflation—what level is optimal?**

Assuming that constant inflation is needed if expectations are to be fulfilled, we turn to the question of 'at what level'? In the model developed so far, this question has not been answered. We begin by noting that there are hypothetical circumstances under which the (constant) rate of inflation (i.e. high or low) should not matter much. Imagine that we move from a situation in which prices are rising at 3% per year to a rate of 10% per year. We assume that this change is announced well in advance and that the tax system is indexed to inflation so that all the tax thresholds are raised by 10% p.a. The same is assumed to be true of pensions and other benefits. The consequence of this change will be that all wages, benefits, and prices will now rise at 10% p.a. and the nominal interest rate will be 7% points higher. All real magnitudes in the economy remain unchanged. The economy moves from a constant inflation equilibrium with $\pi = 3\%$ p.a. to a constant inflation equilibrium with $\pi = 10\%$ p.a. The real interest rate and the levels of output and employment remain unchanged.

From our earlier analysis, we know that at the new equilibrium, the real money supply will be lower than initially. Why? At high inflation, people wish to hold lower money balances—they wish to economize on their holdings of money—so for equilibrium in the money market, the real money supply must be lower than in the initial low inflation equilibrium. Since

$$\frac{M^S}{P} = L(i, y)$$
$$= L(r + \pi^E, y),$$

at equilibrium output with low inflation, π_L, we have:

$$\left(\frac{M^S}{P}\right)_{high} = L((r_e + \pi_L), y_e)$$

and at equilibrium output with high inflation, π_H, we have:

$$\left(\frac{M^S}{P}\right)_{low} = L((r_e + \pi_H), y_e).$$

This highlights the fact that even in our simple example the shift from inflation of 3% to 10% p.a. is not quite as straightforward as it seems at first. After the move to 10% inflation, money wages, prices, the nominal money supply, and nominal output will rise by 10% each year. But at the time of the shift, there has to be an additional upward jump in the price level to bring down the real money supply (M^S/P) to its new lower equilibrium level ($(M^S/P)_{low}$) consistent with the demand for lower real money balances when inflation is higher.

What are the real costs of people economizing on money balances when inflation is high? These costs are sometimes referred to as 'shoe-leather' costs because of the wear and tear associated with more frequent trips to the bank or the cash machine. Other costs (so-called menu costs) arise because of the time and effort involved in changing price lists frequently in an inflationary environment. These costs are estimated to be quite low. We note here an apparent paradox: if the rate of inflation does not matter much, why should governments incur the costs of getting inflation down from a high and stable level to a low and stable one? One response is that it seems empirically to be the case that inflation is more volatile when it is higher and as noted above, volatile inflation brings additional costs. Another is that the initiation of disinflation policies frequently begins not simply with high but with high and rising inflation. In this case, since costs will be incurred in stabilizing inflation, it may be sensible for the government to go for low inflation as part of a package that seeks to establish its stability-oriented credentials.

Once we relax our assumption that indexation to inflation is widespread in the economy and that adjustment to higher inflation is instantaneous because all parties are fully informed and can change their prices and wages at low cost, it is clear that the costs of switching to a high inflation economy are likely to be more substantial. The continuous reduction in individuals' living standards between wage adjustments gives rise to anxiety. Distributional effects are also likely to occur: unanticipated inflation shifts wealth from creditors to debtors. It is also likely to make the elderly poorer since they rely on imperfectly indexed pensions and on the interest income from savings. Recognition of such costs is consistent with survey evidence that shows the general public is more averse to inflation than would be expected if the costs were really as low as they seem in the example of full information, complete indexation, and instantaneous adjustment.

Can we infer from this analysis that the optimal rate of inflation is zero or even negative? In thinking about the optimal inflation rate, we are led first of all to consider the following: the return on holding high-powered money (notes and coins) is zero so with any positive inflation rate, the real return turns negative. The negative real return leads people to waste effort economizing on their money holdings (shoe leather again) and this is inefficient given that it is virtually costless to produce high-powered money. If we follow the logic of this argument then with a positive real rate of interest, for the nominal interest rate to be zero, inflation would have to be negative (i.e. prices falling, which is called deflation). This was Milton Friedman's view of the optimal rate of inflation: the rate of deflation should equal the real rate of interest, leaving the nominal interest rate equal to zero.[3] Is deflation optimal?

---

[3] Friedman (1969).

1.5 Deflation

If inflation is negative (e.g. -2% p.a.), or equivalently there is a rate of deflation of 2% p.a., prices and wages will be 2% lower in a year's time than they are now. In a world of perfect information, there would only be benefits from this as we have already seen—shoe leather would be saved and the relative price changes associated with technical progress would be clearly revealed.

In spite of these arguments, there are two main reasons why deflation is not viewed as a good target by central banks. One relates to how economies work in 'normal times' and the other to the dangers of the economy getting stuck in a deflation trap caused by weakness in aggregate demand. The first reason relates to the apparent difficulty in cutting nominal wages.[4] If workers are particularly resistant to money wage cuts, then a positive rate of inflation creates the flexibility needed to achieve changes in *relative* wages. For example, if, due to a fall in demand for one kind of labour, a real wage cut is required it can be achieved with an inflation rate of, say, 2% p.a. with the money wage left unchanged in the sector where the real wage cut is necessary. This argument is referred to as inflation's role in 'oiling the wheels of the labour market'.

The second reason stems from the need for the central bank to maintain a defence against a deflation trap. A deflation trap can emerge when weak aggregate demand leads inflation to fall and eventually become negative. For this to happen, two things are necessary: (i) the automatic self-stabilizers that operate to boost aggregate demand when inflation is falling fail to operate sufficiently strongly and (ii) policy makers fail to stop prices falling. Attempts to use monetary policy to stimulate the economy result in the nominal interest rate falling. A nominal interest rate close to zero (as low as it can go) combined with deflation implies a positive real interest rate. This may be too high to stimulate private sector demand. Continued weak demand will fuel deflation and push the real interest rate up, which is exactly the wrong policy impulse. This will tend to weaken demand further and sustain the upward pressure on the real interest rate. Once deflation takes hold, it can feed on itself and unlike a process of rising inflation, it does not require the active cooperation of the central bank for the process to continue. The deflation trap is explored in more detail in section 4 and the recent Japanese experience with deflation is analysed in Chapter 17.

1.6 Summing up

The conclusion to this discussion is that policy makers should establish a nominal anchor for the economy that keeps inflation low and stable.[5] This raises a further question. Why do we observe economies with high, rising, and volatile inflation? We have already noted

---

[4] A famous study is Bewley (1999). A recent empirical study using high quality data confirms the existence of nominal wage rigidity: Lebow, Saks, and Wilson (2003).

[5] It is sometimes argued that a price-level target would be preferable to an inflation target since this would require the policy maker to make good policy misses in the past. This has some attraction in the context of deflation: e.g. following a couple of years of deflation, an inflation-targeting central bank may tighten policy too soon once prices begin to rise whereas a price-level targeter would be more relaxed as the price level moved back toward the target.

that governments may be tempted to take advantage of the short-run trade-off between inflation and unemployment. Since rising inflation reflects distributional conflict in the economy, one interpretation is that the political system is incapable of resolving these conflicts, which therefore come to be reflected in rising inflation. A variation on this theme is that the origin of situations of high and/or rising inflation lies with the financing of government spending. As we shall see in the next chapter when we discuss fiscal policy, there are situations in which the usual methods of financing government spending via taxation or borrowing are limited. Raising taxes may be politically unpopular and further borrowing may be prohibitively expensive because of the level of public debt that has already been built up. Under such circumstances, if the government is intent on raising its spending in response to pressure from politically important groups in the economy, it may have to get hold of the necessary resources by increasing the money supply. The use of money to finance government spending is called seignorage. We examine the scope for and limits to seignorage in the fiscal policy chapter, Chapter 6.

We highlight the asymmetry in the role of the central bank in situations of high and rising inflation as compared with situations of deflation. In the former, the active involvement of the central bank is required to keep the inflationary process going; in the latter, deflation can become self-sustaining. Many observers have argued that unlike inflationary problems, which often reflect unresolved social and political conflict and require painful and therefore politically unpopular solutions, deflation can be solved by the government generating demand through increased government spending or tax cuts financed by new money creation, which are popular. This suggests that it is bad policy (and bad luck) rather than politically expedient policy that leads to deflation traps.

2 Monetary policy paradigms

The purpose of this section is to provide an overview of the shift in monetary policy paradigm that has been discussed in a partial way and from different perspectives in earlier chapters.[6] Both paradigms take as given the inertia in inflation that produces the Phillips curves and both incorporate the *IS* curve. The first paradigm, which we shall call the money supply model or *LM* paradigm, is characterized by the following propositions:

(1) the ultimate determinant of the price level and rate of inflation is the money supply;

(2) the instrument of monetary policy is the money supply;

(3) the mechanism through which the economy adjusts to a new equilibrium with constant inflation following a shock is that embodied in the *IS/LM* model plus the inertia-augmented (or expectations-augmented) Phillips curve.

Let us examine how an *IS* shock is handled in this paradigm. We assume the economy begins at equilibrium unemployment with constant inflation equal to the growth rate of the money supply set by the central bank. For a positive *IS* shock, the impact of the rise in aggregate demand on output in the short run is dampened because the rise in income

---

[6] See also Allsopp and Vines (2000).

pushes up the demand for money. As portfolios are rebalanced, the interest rate rises. This is a movement along the *LM* to the north-east. The change in output and employment then feeds through to a rise in inflation, which given the fixed money supply growth rate triggers a leftward shift in the *LM* curve. This induces a further dampening of the initial stimulus. In this paradigm, monetary policy is passive (in the form of a fixed growth rate of the money supply) and the economy adjusts to the new equilibrium by following a protracted spiral-shaped path as lags in inflation interact with a shifting *LM* curve. The so-called 'Keynes effect' is doing the work of raising the interest rate: rising inflation relative to a fixed money supply growth reduces real money balances and leads to a portfolio adjustment with bonds being sold. Excess supply of bonds pushes bond prices down and the interest rate up. The higher real interest rate dampens interest-sensitive spending.

The second paradigm, which we shall call the interest rate reaction function or *MR* paradigm, is characterized as follows:

(1) the ultimate determinant of the price level and inflation is policy;

(2) the instrument of policy is the short-term nominal interest rate;

(3) the mechanism through which the economy adjusts to a new equilibrium with constant inflation following a shock is encapsulated in an interest rate rule.

We take the same example as above. For a positive *IS* shock, the central bank responds to the rise in inflation due to the increase in output: as a consequence it raises the interest rate. Output falls below the equilibrium and brings inflation down: the central bank adjusts the interest rate to guide the economy down the *MR* curve to achieve the inflation target at equilibrium output.

As far as monetary policy is concerned, the paradigm shift centres on two issues: the choice of monetary policy instrument and the choice of an active or a passive policy. From a stabilization perspective, it was clear a long time ago that to operate monetary policy in a passive fashion—be it with a fixed money supply or a fixed interest rate— was not necessarily optimal. William Poole provides a classic early treatment (1970) of the issue by looking first at how the relative importance of *LM* versus *IS* shocks affects the optimal choice of a money supply versus an interest rate instrument.[7] By drawing simple *IS/LM* diagrams, it is apparent that if the economy is characterized by *LM* shocks (e.g. in the demand for money), a fixed interest rate is better for output stability than a fixed money supply; the converse holds for *IS* shocks. The second contribution of Poole's paper is to show that an *active* monetary policy is normally superior to a *passive* one when the economy is characterized by shocks and by lags in adjustment. Poole's analysis is confined to the short run with prices fixed. The tenor of his arguments is even more persuasive when we move to the medium run and allow prices to adjust.

From the perspective of the second paradigm, it is not sensible for policy makers to leave the adjustment mechanism to work automatically via the Keynes effect as in the *LM* paradigm. As we have seen in Chapter 3 when setting out the analysis under a fixed monetary growth rate, the adjustment path to the new equilibrium following a distur-bance to the economy is protracted and complicated to explain. This is because of the interaction between inflation inertia and the portfolio adjustment process (the Keynes

---

[7] Poole (1970).

effect) through which changes in the real money supply affect the interest rate (e.g. *LM* shifts left as rising inflation relative to a fixed money supply growth cuts the real money supply). As we have seen, a further complication arises because of the impact of changes in the inflation rate on the demand for money (*LM* shifts right as the demand for money falls with rising inflation).

The complexities of explaining the dynamic path of adjustment is not simply a problem for those teaching macroeconomics or trying to learn about it but also reflects a problem facing policy makers. The spiral-shaped adjustment path could be short-circuited within the *LM* paradigm: having achieved a fall in inflation to the level desired (equal to the growth rate of the money supply) with unemployment above the *ERU*, the monetary authority could inject a one-off boost to the money supply to take the economy straight to the new equilibrium. However, this is an uneasy mixture of a passive monetary policy with occasional activism and could well be misinterpreted by the public as the inconsistent implementation of policy.

By contrast, in the second paradigm in the *IS-PC-MR* model, the monetary policy reaction function based on the use of the interest rate as instrument is an activist policy framework that is consistent with steering the economy toward equilibrium unemployment and providing a nominal anchor. Frequent adjustments have to be made to the interest rate in order to achieve the central bank's objective. This highlights the fact that it is quite consistent to think of the central bank as following a 'rule-based' approach to monetary policy, yet having to be very active. Fig. 17.14 in Chapter 17 illustrates the frequent interest rate adjustments made by central banks in the USA, the eurozone, and the UK since 1999.

It is crucial to see that it is the implementation of the policy rule itself that establishes the nominal anchor and thus ultimately determines the price level or the rate of inflation in this paradigm (depending on whether the target is the price level or the rate of inflation). The adjustment path is easy to explain and straightforward as we have seen in Chapter 3, since the central bank responds directly to shocks by changing the interest rate. The question of how to bring about the required change in the interest rate is then a technical problem for the central bank; whereas in the first paradigm, agents are faced with an economic problem of trying to figure out the impact of changes in inflation on portfolio choices and hence on the interest rate. These arguments form the central case for using the second paradigm. It is a better description of how monetary policy is conducted and it comes closer to how it should be conducted, given the objectives of the central bank. Milton Friedman, the most famous proponent of the use of the money supply as policy target by the central bank, has conceded that 'The use of the quantity of money as a target has not been a success.' He added: 'I'm not sure I would as of today push it as hard as I once did' (*Financial Times*, 7 June 2003).

3 The monetary policy rule in the 3-equation model

In Chapter 3, we developed a graphical method to predict how an inflation-targeting central bank that aims to minimize the fluctuations of output and inflation from its targets would respond to a variety of shocks. In this section, we pin down the role played by the following six key variables in central bank policy making:

(1) the central bank's inflation target, π^T
(2) the central bank's preferences, β
(3) the slope of the Phillips curve, α
(4) the interest sensitivity of aggregate demand (i.e. the slope of the *IS* curve), a
(5) the equilibrium level of output, y_e
(6) the stabilizing interest rate, r_S.

In order to make the discussion of monetary policy rules concrete, we shall use specific examples of the central bank's utility function, policy instrument, and constraints. However, the basic method for deriving a monetary policy rule will be the same if different variants are chosen. It involves the following steps:

(1) Define the central bank's utility function in terms of both output and inflation. This produces the policy maker's indifference curves in output-inflation space.
(2) Define the constraints faced by the policy maker: these are the Phillips curves, which are also shown in output-inflation space.
(3) Derive the optimal monetary rule in output-inflation space: this is the *monetary rule, MR* line. For a given Phillips curve that it faces, this shows the central bank's chosen combination of output and inflation. Roughly, the higher is inflation as determined by the Phillips curve the economy is on, the lower will the central bank set aggregate demand and hence output in order to reduce inflation. Hidden in this relationship is the policy instrument, r, that the central bank will use to secure the appropriate level of aggregate demand and hence output. We saw this graphically in Chapter 3: the central bank chooses the best point along the Phillips curve that it faces and in order to deliver the right level of aggregate demand, it must set the interest rate at the level shown by the *IS* curve.
(4) We can also derive the *interest rate rule*, which tells the central bank how to adjust the interest rate in response to current economic conditions.

3.1 The central bank's utility function

In Chapter 3, we introduced in an informal way the central bank's indifference curves representing the trade-off in its preferences between inflation and unemployment. We now explain how these can be derived more formally. We assume that the central bank has two concerns: the rate of inflation, π, and the level of output, y. Looking first at inflation and following the discussion in section 2, we assume that it has a target rate of inflation π^T and that it wants to minimize fluctuations around π^T. A simple way of writing this is to assume that it wants to minimize the loss function:

$$(\pi - \pi^T)^2.$$

Rather than having the central bank maximize a utility function, we have it minimize a loss function. A loss function is just like a utility function except that the higher the loss, the worse it is for the central bank (we use it rather than a utility function purely for convenience—by putting a minus sign in front of the expression above, the central bank will want to maximize it). This particular loss function has two implications. First, the central bank is as concerned to avoid inflation below its target as it is inflation above π^T. If $\pi^T = 2\%$ the loss from $\pi = 4\%$ is the same as the loss from $\pi = 0\%$. In both cases $(\pi - \pi^T)^2 = 4$. Second, it attaches increased importance to bringing inflation back to its target the further it is away from π^T; the loss from $\pi = 6\%$ is 16, compared to the loss of 4 from $\pi = 4\%$. The central bank's marginal disutility is increasing as the gap between inflation and the target grows.

We turn now to the central bank's second concern—about output and employment. We assume the central bank's target level of output is the equilibrium level y_e and it seeks to minimize the gap between y and y_e. At this point it is useful to draw attention to the fact that we have assumed that the equilibrium output level y_e is known, that the central bank's target output level is y_e, and that it is able to stick to this target. As we shall see in section 6, even if y_e is known, the central bank may target a higher level of output. Output (or employment) targets are likely to arise from the interplay of interest groups in the economy mediated by political institutions, and central banks may be unable or unwilling to go against these pressures at particular times (e.g. just before an election).

The central bank's loss as a result of output being different from its target of y_e is

$$(y - y_e)^2.$$

Note that this loss function again suggests a symmetrical attitude to positive and negative deviations—in this case, from the equilibrium level of output. The most straightforward way of thinking about this is that the central bank understands the model and realizes that inflation is only constant at $y = y_e$. If $y < y_e$ then this represents unnecessary unemployment that should be eliminated. If $y > y_e$, this is unsustainable and will require costly increases in unemployment to bring the associated inflation back down. Whenever the economy is disturbed, the central bank sees its task as steering the economy back to this constant-inflation output level.

If the two loss functions are added together, we have the central bank's objective function:

$$L = (y - y_e)^2 + \beta(\pi - \pi^T)^2, \qquad \text{(central bank loss function)}$$

where β is the relative weight attached to the loss from inflation. This is a critical parameter: a $\beta > 1$ will characterize a central bank that places less weight on deviations in employment from its target than on deviations in inflation, and vice versa. An inflation-averse central bank is characterized by a higher β; if the central bank cares only about inflation deviations and not at all about output deviations, $\beta = \infty$.

Let us first look at the geometry of the loss function in the Phillips curve diagram, on the assumption that $\beta = 1$. With $\beta = 1$, the weights on output and inflation deviations are the same, i.e. the central bank is equally concerned about inflation and output deviations from its targets.

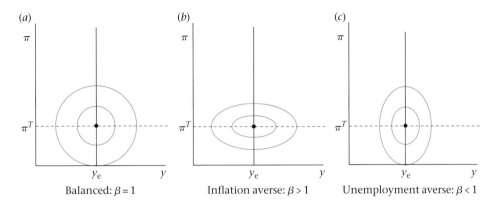

Figure 5.1 Central bank loss functions: utility declines with distance from the 'bull's eye'

The loss function is simple to draw: with $\beta = 1$, each indifference curve is a circle with (y_e, π^T) at its centre (see Fig. 5.1(a)). The loss declines as the circle gets smaller. When $\pi = \pi^T$ and $y = y_e$, the circle shrinks to a single point (called the 'bliss point') and the loss is at a minimum, which is zero. The diagram is easy to remember if you think of it as a target (as for archery) with the central bank's objective to get as close to the bull's eye as possible. With $\beta = 1$, the central bank is indifferent between inflation 1% above (or below) π^T and output 1% below (or above) y_e. They are on the same loss circle.

Only when $\beta = 1$, do we have indifference *circles*. If $\beta > 1$, the central bank is indifferent between (say) inflation 1% above (or below) π^T and output 2% above (or below) y_e. They are on the same loss curve. This makes the indifference curves ellipsoid as in Fig. 5.1(b). A central bank with less aversion to inflation ($\beta < 1$) will have ellipsoid indifference curves with a vertical rather than a horizontal orientation (Fig. 5.1(c)). In that case, the indifference curves are steep reflecting that the central bank is only willing to trade off a given fall in inflation for a smaller fall in output than in the other two cases. If the central bank cares only about inflation then $\beta = \infty$ and the loss ellipses become one dimensional along the line at $\pi = \pi^T$.[8]

3.2 The Phillips curve constraint

Next, we shall assume that the central bank can control the level of output via its ability to use monetary policy (by setting the interest rate) to control aggregate demand, y^D. However, it cannot control inflation directly—only indirectly via y. As we have already discussed, output affects inflation via the Phillips curve:

$$\pi = \pi_{-1} + \alpha.(y - y_e). \tag{5.1}$$

[8] The central bank's preferences can be presented in this simple way if we assume that the central bank's discount rate is infinite. This means that it only considers one period at a time when making its decision. In Chapter 3, we discussed informally the role that the central bank's discount rate can play when we compared a rapid disinflation policy that produces a large initial rise in unemployment ('cold turkey') with a gradualist policy.

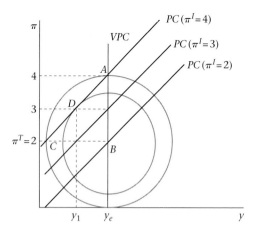

Figure 5.2 Loss circles and Phillips curves

This is shown in Fig. 5.2, where the upwards sloping lines are Phillips curves. For the moment for simplicity it is assumed that $\alpha = 1$, so that each Phillips curve has a slope of 45°. Each Phillips curve is labelled by lagged inflation. Assume that $\pi_{-1} = \pi^T = 2\%$ (remember that this PC must go through point B at which $y = y_e$ and $\pi = 2$). The central bank is in the happy position of being able to choose the bull's eye point B or (π^T, y_e) at which its loss is zero.

What happens if there has been a shock to inflation and it is not equal to the inflation target? Suppose, for example, that inflation is 4%. Given inflation inertia, this means that the central bank is faced with the constraint of the Phillips curve shown by $PC(\pi^I = 4)$ and can only choose between points along it. The bull's eye is no longer obtainable. The central bank faces a trade-off: if the central bank wants a level of output of $y = y_e$ next period, then it has to accept an inflation rate above its target, i.e. $\pi = 4 \neq \pi^T$ (i.e. point A). On the other hand, if it wishes to hit the inflation target next period, it must accept a much lower level of output next period (point C). Point A corresponds to a fully accommodating monetary policy in which the objective is purely to hit the output target ($\beta = 0$), and point C corresponds to a completely non-accommodating policy, in which the objective is purely to hit the inflation target ($\beta = \infty$).

In fact, as will be evident from Fig. 5.2, if the central bank is faced by $\pi^I = 4$, then given its preferences, it can do better (achieve a loss circle closer to B) than either point A or point C. It minimizes its loss function by choosing point D, where the $PC(\pi^I = 4)$ line is tangential to the indifference curve of the loss function closest to the bull's eye. Thus if $\pi^I = 4$ it will choose an output level y_1 which will in turn imply an inflation rate of 3%.

3.3 Deriving the monetary rule, *MR*

For simplicity, we use the form of the loss function in which $\beta = 1$ so that we have loss circles as in Fig. 5.2 above. This implies:

$$L = (y - y_e)^2 + (\pi - \pi^T)^2.$$

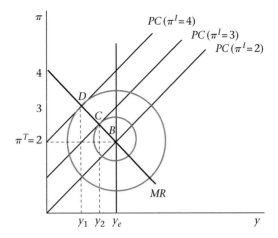

Figure 5.3 Deriving the *MR* line

And using the simplest version of the Phillips curve in which $\alpha = 1$ so that each *PC* has a $45°$ slope as in Fig. 5.2:

$$\pi = \pi_{-1} + y - y_e.$$

The geometry can be seen as follows: in Fig. 5.3, the points of tangency between successive Phillips curves and the loss circles show the level of output that the central bank needs to choose so as to minimize its loss at any given level of π_{-1}. Thus when $\pi_{-1} = 3$, its loss is minimized at C; or when $\pi_{-1} = 4$ at D. Joining these points (D, C, B) produces the *MR* line that we used in Chapter 3. We can see from Fig. 5.3 that a one unit rise in π_{-1} implies a half unit fall in y, for example an increase in π_{-1} from 3% to 4% implies a fall in y from y_2 to y_1.

We can derive the monetary rule explicitly as follows. By choosing y to minimize L we can derive the optimal value of y for each value of π_{-1}. Substituting the Phillips curve into L and minimizing with respect to y, we have:

$$\frac{\partial L}{\partial y} = 2(y - y_e) + 2(\pi_{-1} + (y - y_e) - \pi^T) = 0$$

$$= (y - y_e) + (\pi_{-1} + (y - y_e) - \pi^T) = 0.$$

Since $\pi = \pi_{-1} + y - y_e$,

$$\frac{\partial L}{\partial y} = (y - y_e) + (\pi - \pi^T) = 0$$

$$\implies (y - y_e) = -(\pi - \pi^T). \qquad \text{(MR equation)}$$

The monetary rule in the Phillips diagram shows the equilibrium for the central bank: it shows the equilibrium relationship between the inflation rate chosen indirectly and the level of output chosen directly by the central bank to maximize its utility (minimize its loss) given its preferences and the constraints it faces.

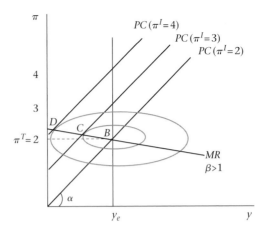

Figure 5.4 Inflation-averse government: flat *MR* line

Note: The angle marked α in the diagram is in fact the angle whose tangent is α. We adopt this convention throughout.

This shows the monetary rule as an inverse relation between π and y with a negative $45°$ slope (Fig. 5.3). Specifically, it shows that the central bank must reduce aggregate demand and output, y, below y_e so as to reduce π below π^T by the same percentage. Thus this could be thought of as monetary policy halfway between: (i) completely non-accommodating when the central bank cuts output sufficiently to bring inflation straight back to π^T at the cost of a sharp rise in unemployment; and (ii) a completely accommodating one, which leaves inflation (and output) unchanged. If the monetary rule was flat at π^T we would have a completely non-accommodating monetary policy; if it was vertical at y_e, we would have a completely accommodating monetary policy.

The monetary rule ends up exactly halfway between an accommodating and a non-accommodating policy because of two simplifying assumptions. By relaxing these, we learn what it is that determines the slope of the monetary rule. We shall see that the more inflation averse is the central bank (the flatter are the loss ellipses) and the more responsive are wages to employment (the steeper are the Phillips curves), the flatter is the *MR* line.

The degree of inflation aversion of the central bank is captured by β in the central bank loss function: $L = (y - y_e)^2 + \beta(\pi - \pi^T)^2$. If $\beta > 1$, the central bank attaches more importance to the inflation target than to the output target. This results in a flatter monetary rule as shown in Fig. 5.4. Given these preferences, any inflation shock that shifts the Phillips curve upward implies that the optimal position for the central bank will involve a more significant output reduction and hence a sharper cut in inflation along that Phillips curve than in the neutral case. Using the same reasoning, $\beta < 1$ implies that the monetary rule is steeper than the minus $45°$ line.

The second factor that determines the slope of the monetary rule is the responsiveness of inflation to output (i.e. the slope of the Phillips curve): $\pi - \pi_{-1} = \alpha(y - y_e)$. This factor was not discussed in Chapter 3. Thus far, we have assumed $\alpha = 1$. Intuitively if $\alpha > 1$ so the Phillips curves are steeper, any given cut in output has a greater effect in reducing inflation than when $\alpha = 1$. As we can see from Fig. 5.5, this makes the *MR* line flatter than

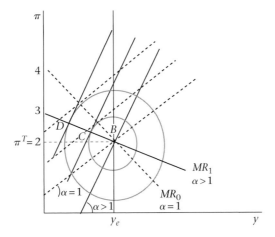

Figure 5.5 High responsiveness of inflation to output: flat *MR* line

in the case in which $\alpha = 1$: MR_0 is the old and MR_1 the new monetary rule line obtained by joining up the points D, C, and B.

By altering the slope of the Phillips curve, we also learn more about the monetary rule. Steeper Phillips curves make the *MR* line flatter: let us now compare the response of a central bank to a given rise in inflation in the case where the Phillips curves are steep with the case where they have a slope of one. Our intuition tells us that steeper Phillips curves make things easier for the central bank since a smaller rise in unemployment (fall in output) is required to achieve any desired fall in inflation. Let us show this in a diagram. In the left hand panel of Fig. 5.6 we compare two economies, one with flatter Phillips curves (dashed) and one with steeper ones. As we have already shown, the *MR* line is flatter for the economy with steeper Phillips curves: this is MR_1. Suppose there is a rise in inflation in each economy that shifts the Phillips curves up: each economy is at point B. We can see that a *smaller* cut in aggregate demand is optimal in the economy with the steeper Phillips curves (point D). This reflects our intuitive argument above.[9]

In the right hand panel, we compare two economies with identical supply sides but in which one has an inflation-averse central bank (the oval-shaped indifference ellipse) and show the central bank's reaction to inflation at point B. The more inflation-averse central bank always responds to this shock by cutting aggregate demand (and output) more (point D).

Having seen the role of the slope of the Phillips curve and of the central bank's preferences in the diagrams, we now derive the more general form of the central bank's monetary rule as follows. We also make explicit the timing structure in all of the equations. By choosing the interest rate in period zero, the central bank affects output and inflation in period 1. We assume it is only concerned with what happens in period 1. This is the reason that its loss function is defined in terms of y_1 and π_1. If we let β and α take any

---

[9] For those who are curious, with $\beta \geq 1$, the output cut in response to a given inflation shock is always less when $\alpha > 1$ as compared with $\alpha = 1$. For $\beta < 1$, the output cut is less as long as $\alpha > (1/\beta)^{\frac{1}{2}}$.

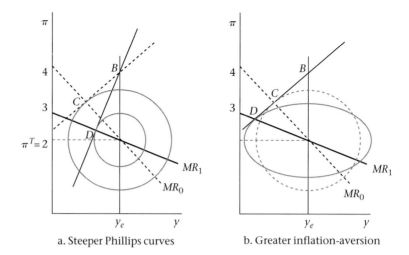

a. Steeper Phillips curves   b. Greater inflation-aversion

Figure 5.6 Comparing the response of the central bank in two cases: steeper Phillips curves and a more inflation-averse central bank

positive values, the central bank chooses y to minimize

$$L = (y_1 - y_e)^2 + \beta(\pi_1 - \pi^T)^2 \tag{5.2}$$

subject to

$$\pi_1 = \pi_0 + \alpha(y_1 - y_e). \tag{5.3}$$

By substituting (5.3) into (5.2) and differentiating with respect to y_1 (since this is the variable the central bank can control via its choice of the interest rate), we have:

$$\frac{\partial L}{\partial y_1} = (y_1 - y_e) + \alpha\beta(\pi_0 + \alpha(y_1 - y_e) - \pi^T) = 0. \tag{5.4}$$

Substituting equation (5.3) back into equation (5.4) gives:

$$(y_1 - y_e) = -\alpha\beta(\pi_1 - \pi^T). \qquad\text{(monetary rule, } MR)$$

Now it can be seen directly that the larger is α (i.e. the more responsive are wages to employment) or the larger is β (i.e. the more inflation averse is the central bank), the flatter will be the slope of the monetary rule. In the first case this is because any reduction in aggregate demand achieves a bigger cut in inflation, i.e. whatever its preferences, the central bank gets a 'bigger bang (i.e. fall in inflation) for its buck (i.e. fall in aggregate demand)'. In the second case, this is because, whatever the labour market it faces, a more inflation-averse central bank will wish to reduce inflation by more than a less 'hard-nosed' one.

3.4 Using the *IS-PC-MR* graphical model

By making explicit the determinants of the slope of the *MR* line, the role of each of the six key inputs to the deliberations of the central bank is now clear.

(1) the central bank's inflation target, π^T: this affects the position of the *MR* line;

(2) the central bank's preferences, β: this determines the shape of the loss ellipses and affects the slope of the *MR* line;

(3) the slope of the Phillips curve, α: this also affects the slope of the *MR* line;

(4) the interest sensitivity of aggregate demand, a: this determines the slope of the *IS* curve;

(5) the equilibrium level of output, y_e: this determines the position of the vertical Phillips curve and affects the position of the *MR* line;

(6) the stabilizing interest rate, r_S: the central bank adjusts the interest rate relative to r_S so it must always analyse whether this has shifted, e.g. as a result of a shift in the *IS* or due to a change in the equilibrium level of output, y_e.

On the basis of the more detailed discussion provided in this chapter, the *IS-PC-MR* graphical model can be used to analyse a wide variety of problems. In Chapters 3 and 4, the graphical analysis of inflation shocks, temporary and permanent aggregate demand shocks, and supply-side shocks is provided. In each case, the role of the six inputs to the central bank's decision can be analysed and experiments undertaken to evaluate the impact of variations in them.

We take one of those examples in order to clarify in the diagram each input to the central bank's decision and to highlight the role played by the lag in the effect of monetary policy on aggregate demand and output. The example shows that the central bank is engaged in a forecasting exercise: it must forecast next period's Phillips curve and next period's *IS* curve. We assume that the economy starts off with output at equilibrium and inflation at the target rate of 2% as shown in Fig. 5.7. We take a permanent positive aggregate demand shock such as improved buoyancy of consumer expectations: the *IS* moves to *IS'*. The consequence of output above y_e is that inflation will rise above target—in this case to 4%. This defines next period's Phillips curve ($PC(\pi^I = 4)$) along which the central bank must choose its preferred point: point *C*. The central bank forecasts that the *IS* curve is *IS'*, i.e. it judges that this is a permanent shock and by going vertically up to point *C'* in the *IS* diagram, it can work out that the appropriate interest rate to set is r'. As the Phillips curve shifts down with falling inflation, the central bank reduces the interest rate and the economy moves down the *MR* line to point *Z* and down the *IS'* curve to *Z'*.

This example highlights the role of the stabilizing real interest rate, r_S: following the shift in the *IS* curve, there is a new stabilizing interest rate and, in order to reduce inflation, the interest rate must be raised above the new r_S, i.e. to r'. To summarize, the rise in output builds a rise in inflation above target into the economy. Because of inflation inertia, this can only be eliminated by pushing output below and (unemployment above) the equilibrium. The graphical presentation emphasizes that the central bank raises the interest rate in response to the aggregate demand shock because it can work out the

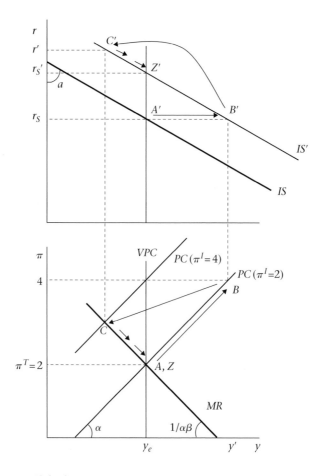

Figure 5.7 Permanent *IS* shock

consequences for inflation. The diagram highlights how the parameters a, α, and β affect the central bank's calculation of the required change in the interest rate.

The central bank is forward looking and takes all available information into account: its ability to control the economy is limited by the presence of inflation inertia i.e. lagged inflation in the Phillips curve and by the time lag for a change in the interest rate to take effect i.e. the lagged interest rate in the *IS* curve. In the *IS* equation it is the interest rate at time zero that affects output at time one: $y_1 - y_e = -a(r_0 - r_S)$. This is because it takes time for a change in the interest rate to feed through to consumption and investment decisions. In Fig. 5.7 in order to choose its optimal point C on the Phillips curve ($\pi^I = 4$), the central bank must set the interest rate now at r'. As is clear from the diagram, we have been working with this assumption throughout. However, it is interesting to see what happens if the central bank could affect output immediately, i.e. if $y_0 - y_e = -a(r_0 - r_S)$. In this case, as soon as the *IS* shock is diagnosed, the central bank would raise the interest rate to r_S'. The economy then goes directly from A' to Z' in the *IS* diagram and it remains at A in the Phillips diagram, i.e. points A and Z coincide. Since the aggregate demand shock is fully and immediately offset by the change in the interest rate, there is no chance for inflation to rise. This underlines the crucial role of lags and hence of forecasting for the central bank: the more timely and accurate are forecasts of shifts in aggregate demand (and of other kinds of shock), the greater is the chance that the central bank can offset them and limit their impact on inflation. Once inflation has been affected, the presence of inflation inertia means that the central bank must change the interest rate and get the economy onto the *MR* line in order to steer it back to the inflation target.

In addition to providing a framework for a systematic analysis of shocks to an individual economy and how aspects of the aggregate demand and supply-side structures affect central bank policy, the *IS-PC-MR* graphical model provides a useful way to investigate how a common currency area works, i.e. when different economies share a central bank. As an example, we can compare two economies with the same supply side (i.e. y_e and α are the same) and a common central bank (i.e. π^T and β are the same), but which differ in the interest sensitivity of expenditure (a is different) and which are both initially in equilibrium with constant inflation (with $r = r_S$). If both economies are subjected to the same shock to autonomous demand, we can analyse the consequences using the graphical 3-equation model (see Fig. 17.15).

As a second example, we could look at the implications for two economies in a currency union that are identical in all respects except for the responsiveness of inflation to changes in the level of output, e.g. one economy has a steep *WS* curve and therefore steep Phillips curves (high α) whereas the other has flat Phillips curves. If a common inflation shock affects both economies, how would the optimal response of a *national* central bank differ from that of a central bank that sets a common interest rate for both economies? Examples of this kind are discussed further in Chapter 17.

4 A Taylor Rule in the *IS-PC-MR* model

4.1 Interest rate rules

In the previous section, we looked at how the *IS* curve is used by the central bank to find out what interest rate to set once it has worked out its optimal output-inflation combination in the Phillips diagram, i.e. once it has located the best available position on the *MR* line. We now show how to derive an *interest rate rule*, which directly expresses the change in the interest rate in terms of the current state of the economy. We then show how it relates to the famous Taylor Rule.

We bring together the three equations:

$$\pi_1 = \pi_0 + \alpha(y_1 - y_e) \qquad \text{(Phillips curve)}$$
$$y_1 - y_e = -a(r_0 - r_S) \qquad \text{(IS)}$$
$$\pi_1 - \pi^T = -\frac{1}{\alpha\beta}(y_1 - y_e). \qquad \text{(MR)}$$

From these equations, we want to derive a formula for the interest rate, r_0 in terms of period zero observations of inflation and output in the economy. If we substitute for π_1

using the Phillips curve in the *MR*, we get

$$\pi_0 + \alpha(y_1 - y_e) - \pi^T = -\frac{1}{\alpha\beta}(y_1 - y_e)$$

$$\pi_0 - \pi^T = -\left(\alpha + \frac{1}{\alpha\beta}\right)(y_1 - y_e)$$

and if we now substitute for $(y_1 - y_e)$ using the *IS*, we get the interest-rate rule:

$$r_0 - r_S = \frac{1}{a\left(\alpha + \frac{1}{\alpha\beta}\right)}\left(\pi_0 - \pi^T\right). \qquad \text{(Interest rate rule)}$$

We can see that $\quad r_0 - r_S = 0.5\left(\pi_0 - \pi^T\right)$

if $a = \alpha = \beta = 1$.

Two things are immediately apparent: first, only the inflation and not the output devi-ation is present in the rule and second, all the parameters of the 3-equation model matter for the central bank's response to a rise in inflation. If each parameter is equal to one, the coefficient on the inflation deviation is one-half. If inflation is 1% point above the target, then the interest rate rule says that the real interest rate needs to be 0.5 percentage points higher. Since inflation is higher by 1% point, the nominal interest rate must be raised by $1 + 0.5$, i.e. by 1.5 percentage points in order to secure a rise in the *real* interest rate of 0.5 percentage points. For a given deviation of inflation from target, and in each case, comparing the situation with that in which $a = \alpha = \beta = 1$, we can see that

- a more inflation-averse central bank ($\beta > 1$) will raise the interest rate by more;
- when the *IS* is flatter ($a > 1$), the central bank will raise the interest rate by less;
- when the Phillips curve is steeper ($\alpha > 1$), the central bank will raise the interest rate by less.

Let us compare the interest rate rule that we have derived from the 3-equation model with the famous Taylor Rule,[10]

$$r_0 - r_S = 0.5.(\pi_0 - \pi^T) + 0.5.(y_0 - y_e), \qquad \text{(Taylor Rule)}$$

where π^T is the central bank's inflation target, y_e is the equilibrium level of output, and r_S is the 'stabilizing' interest rate, i.e. the real interest rate on the *IS* curve when output is at equilibrium. The Taylor Rule states that if output is 1% above equilibrium and inflation is at the target, the central bank should raise the interest rate by 0.5 percentage points relative to stabilizing interest rate. As above we interpret the difference between y and y_e as the percentage gap; this is the equivalent of defining y as the log of output. And if inflation is 1% point above the target and output is at equilibrium, then the Taylor rule says that the real interest rate needs to be 0.5 percentage points higher.

---

[10] Taylor (1993).

4.2 Interest rate rules and lags

The interest rate rule derived from the 3-equation model is similar to Taylor's rule, which he developed as an empirical description of how central banks behaved. However, it only requires the central bank to respond to inflation. At first sight, this seems paradoxical, given that the central bank cares about both inflation and output as demonstrated by its loss function (equation 5.2).

It turns out that to get an interest rate rule that is like the Taylor rule in which both the inflation and output deviations are present, we need to modify the 3-equation model to bring the lag structure closer to that of a real economy. In this section, we explain how this is done. However, for most purposes, the analysis of shocks and policy responses can be conducted with the simpler single lag model, which we keep as our core 3-equation *IS-PC-MR* model in the remainder of the book.

As before we assume that there is no observational time lag for the monetary authorities, i.e. the central bank can set the interest rate (r_0) as soon as it observes current data (π_0 and y_0). We continue to assume that the interest rate only has an effect on output next period, i.e. r_0 affects y_1. The *new assumption* about timing that is required is that it takes a year for output to affect inflation, i.e. the output level y_1 affects inflation a period later, π_2. This means that it is y_0 and not y_1 that is in the Phillips curve for π_1.[11] The 'double lag' timing assumptions match the view of the Bank of England (1999):

The empirical evidence is that on average it takes up to about one year in this and other industrial economies for the response to a monetary policy change to have its peak effect on demand and production, and that it takes up to a further year for these activity changes to have their fullest impact on the inflation rate.

The double lag structure is shown in Fig. 5.8 and emphasizes that a decision taken today by the central bank to react to a shock will only affect the inflation rate two periods later, i.e. π_2. When the economy is disturbed in the current period (period zero), the central bank looks ahead to the implications for inflation and sets the interest rate so as to determine y_1, which in turn determines the desired value of π_2. As the diagram illustrates, action by the central bank in the current period has no effect on output or inflation in the current period or on inflation in a year's time. Since the central bank can only choose y_1 and π_2 by its interest rate decision, its loss function is

$$L = (y_1 - y_e)^2 + \beta(\pi_2 - \pi^T)^2.$$

Given the double lag, the three equations are:

$$\pi_1 = \pi_0 + \alpha(y_0 - y_e) \qquad \text{(Phillips curve)}$$

$$y_1 - y_e = -a(r_0 - r_s) \qquad \text{(IS)}$$

$$\pi_2 - \pi^T = -\frac{1}{\alpha\beta}(y_1 - y_e). \qquad \text{(MR)}$$

---

[11] Three-equation models along these lines were developed by Svennson (1997) and Ball (1999b), and discussed in Romer (2001). See also Carlin and Soskice (2005).

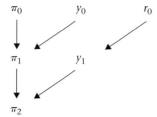

Figure 5.8 Lag structure in the *IS-PC-MR* model required to deliver a standard Taylor Rule

By repeating the same steps as above, we can derive the interest rate rule, which takes the form of a Taylor rule:

$$r_0 - r_S = \frac{1}{a\left(\alpha + \frac{1}{\alpha\beta}\right)}\left[\left(\pi_0 - \pi^T\right) + \alpha(y_0 - y_e)\right].$$

And $r_0 - r_S = 0.5(\pi_0 - \pi^T) + 0.5(y_0 - y_e)$

(Taylor rule in 3-equation (double lag) model)

if $a = \alpha = \beta = 1$.

We can also show how a Taylor Rule is derived geometrically from the *IS-PC-MR* model. This helps bring out the role that differences in economic structure (demand and supply sides) and in central bank preferences can have on the coefficients of Taylor Rules. In Fig. 5.9, the initial observation of output and inflation in period zero is shown by the large cross, ×. To work out what interest rate to set, the central bank notes that in the following period, inflation will rise to π_1 and output will still be at y_0 since a change in the interest rate can only affect y_1. The central bank therefore knows that the constraint it faces is the $PC(\pi_1)$ and it chooses its best position on it to deliver π_2. The best position on $PC(\pi_1)$ is shown by where the *MR* line crosses it. This means that output must be y_1 and therefore that the central bank sets r_0 in response to the initial information shown by point ×. This emphasizes that the central bank must forecast a further period ahead in the double lag model in order to locate the appropriate Phillips curve, and hence to determine its optimal interest rate choice for today: it chooses $r_0 \rightarrow y_1 \rightarrow \pi_2$. Once the economy is on the *MR* line, the central bank continues to adjust the interest rate to guide the economy along the *MR* back to equilibrium.

The remaining task is to give a geometric presentation of the double lag model and the associated Taylor Rule: $r_t - r_S = 0.5 \cdot (\pi_t - \pi^T) + 0.5 \cdot (y_t - y_e)$. Fig. 5.10 shows the example in Fig. 5.9 again. As shown in the left hand panel of Fig. 5.10, the two components of the Taylor Rule are shown by the vertical distances equal to $\alpha(y_0 - y_e)$ and $\pi_0 - \pi^T$, where α is the slope of the Phillips curve. If these are added together, we have the forecast of $\pi_1 - \pi^T$. Just one more step is needed to express this forecast in terms of $(r_0 - r_S)$ and therefore to deliver a Taylor Rule. As shown in the right hand panel of Fig. 5.10, the vertical distance $\pi_1 - \pi^T$ can also be expressed as $(\alpha + \gamma) \cdot a(r_0 - r_S)$, where α and $\gamma = \frac{1}{\alpha\beta}$ reflect the slopes of the Phillips curve and the monetary rule curve, respectively and a reflects the slope of

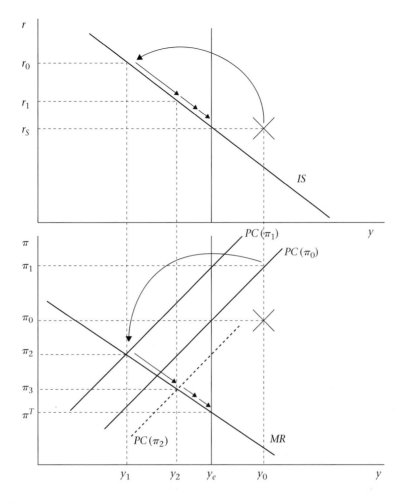

Figure 5.9 Taylor Rule example

the *IS* curve.[12] Thus, we have

$$(\alpha + \gamma) \cdot a(r_0 - r_S) = (\pi_0 - \pi^T) + \alpha(y_0 - y_e)$$

and by rearranging to write this in terms of the interest rate, we have a Taylor Rule:

$$r_0 - r_S = \frac{1}{(\alpha + \gamma)a} \left[\left(\pi_0 - \pi^T \right) + \alpha(y_0 - y_e) \right]$$
$$= 0.5 \cdot (\pi_0 - \pi^T) + 0.5 \cdot (y_0 - y_e)$$

if $\alpha = \gamma = a = 1$.

[12] Note that in the diagram, a, α, and γ refer to the angles shown and in the algebra to the gradients i.e. to the tangents of the relevant angles.

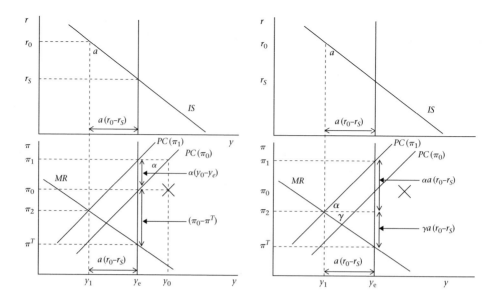

Figure 5.10 Deriving the Taylor Rule

One striking aspect of this discussion is that it helps to dispel a common confusion about Taylor Rules. It is often said that the relative weights on output and inflation in a Taylor Rule indicate the central bank's preferences for reducing inflation as compared to output deviations. However, we have already seen that in the single lag model, the interest rate rule only has the inflation deviation in it in spite of the fact that the loss function places weight on both inflation and output deviations: the degree of inflation aversion affects the size of the aggregate demand (and hence the interest rate) response of the central bank.

Once we modify the model to reflect the fact that a change in output takes a year to affect inflation (the double lag model), then both the inflation and output deviations appear in the interest rate rule and it resembles Taylor's Rule. The reason is that the current period output deviation serves as a means of *forecasting* future inflation to which the central bank will want to react now. The central bank's aversion to inflation affects its reaction to inflation and to the forecast of inflation contained in the output deviation term: it does *not* affect the relative weight on the inflation and output terms in the Taylor Rule. The relative weights on inflation and output in our Taylor Rule depend only on α, the slope of the Phillips curve, since the relative weights are used only to forecast next period's inflation.[13]

It is the slope of the Phillips curves (α) that affect the relative weight on inflation and output in the Taylor Rule. For $\alpha > 1$, the Phillips curves are steeper and the *MR* curve is flatter. There are two implications, which go in opposite directions. First, a more

[13] Bean (1998) derives the optimal Taylor rule in a model similar to the *IS-PC-MR* model. However in his model, the central bank's preferences do affect the Taylor Rule weights. This arises from his inclusion of lagged output in the *IS* equation: if the coefficient on lagged output is zero then the difference between the weight on inflation and on output in the Taylor rule only depends on the slope of the Phillips curve and not on preferences.

restrictive interest rate reaction is optimal to deal with any given increase in output because this will have a bigger effect on inflation than with $\alpha = 1$ (the *MR* curve is flatter). But on the other hand, a given rise in the interest rate will have a bigger negative effect on inflation. These two effects imply that with $\alpha > 1$, the balance between the coefficients changes: the coefficient on $(\pi_0 - \pi^T)$ goes down—so the central bank reacts less to an inflation shock whereas the coefficient on $(y_0 - y_e)$ goes up—the central bank reacts more to an output shock as compared with the equal weights in the Taylor rule.

We can see that Taylor's weights of 0.5 and 0.5 on the inflation and output deviations arise when the *IS* curve, the Phillips curves, and the *MR* curve all have a slope of one (or more precisely in the case of the *IS* and the *MR* of minus one). This implies that the appropriate coefficients on the Taylor rule form of the central bank's monetary rule will be different from $(0.5, 0.5)$ if economies differ in

- the inflation aversion of the central bank,
- the supply-side structure as reflected in the slope of the Phillips curve, or
- in the interest-sensitivity of aggregate demand.

5 Problems with using an interest rate rule

The central bank may sometimes be thwarted in its attempt to use an interest rate rule to stabilize the economy. One reason would be if investment or other components of aggregate demand fail to respond or to respond enough to the change in the interest rate. As we shall see in Chapter 7, empirical evidence for the impact of changes in the cost of capital (of which the interest rate is a key component) relative to the expected rate of return (measured for example by a change in Tobin's q) is rather weak. Another reason why the interest rate may fail to affect output in the desired manner arises from the fact that the interest rate that is relevant to investment decisions is the *long term real* interest rate. The central bank can affect the *short-term nominal* interest rate. As we know, the real and the nominal interest rates differ by the expected rate of inflation. It remains to explain how the short- and long-term interest rates are related. The relationship is referred to as the *term structure of interest rates*. The long-term interest rate refers to the interest rate now (i.e. at time t) on an n-year bond. We can express the long-term interest rate as follows:

$$i_t^n = 1/n \cdot [i_t^1 + i_{t+1|t}^1 + i_{t+2|t}^1 + \cdots + i_{t+n-1|t}^1] + \phi_{nt}. \tag{5.5}$$

In words, this means the long-term interest rate (say, the interest rate on twenty-year bonds) is equal to the average of the expected interest rate on one-year bonds for the next twenty years plus the term ϕ_{nt}, which is called the 'uncertainty premium'.

In tranquil times, we would expect the long-term interest rate to exceed the short-term rate by the uncertainty premium and we would expect short- and long-term interest rates to move in the same direction. Monetary policy will then have the desired effect. As a counter-example, consider the situation in which the central bank cuts the short-term interest rate to stimulate the economy because it fears a recession is imminent. If the financial markets believe that the underlying cause of the recessionary threat is likely to produce higher inflation in the long run, then markets will believe a higher long-run real interest rate will be necessary. Higher long-term interest rates are likely to dampen interest-sensitive spending at a time when the authorities are trying to stimulate the economy.

A third example of the limits to the use of monetary policy as a stabilization tool comes from the fact that the nominal interest rate cannot be negative. The reason for this— as we have seen—is that there is always the choice to hold cash with a zero nominal return. Zero places a floor on the cuts in the nominal interest rate that are available. Hence a problem can arise if the real interest rate required to stimulate activity in the economy were negative. In a very low inflation economy, there is therefore limited scope to use monetary policy to stimulate aggregate demand if the required real interest rate is negative, e.g. with an inflation target of 2%, the zero floor to the nominal interest rate means that real interest cannot be reduced below -2%. This is rather ironical— the successful implementation of a stability-oriented monetary policy along the lines outlined in this chapter may have the effect of producing an economy with low inflation in which the scope of monetary policy to stimulate the economy if it is hit by a negative shock is limited. We investigate the problem of a deflation trap below.

To summarize, the reasons that monetary policy can fail to have its desired effect on output include the following:

- investment is insensitive to the real interest rate;

- the long-run real interest rate does not move in line with changes in the short-term nominal interest rate;

- the central bank wishes to stimulate demand but the nominal interest rate is close to zero.

5.1 The deflation trap

The simplest way to see how a deflation trap may operate is to combine the fact that the nominal interest rate cannot be negative with the fact that the real rate of interest is approximately: $r = i - \pi^E$. Since $i \geq 0$, the minimum real rate of interest is $\min r = -\pi$. When inflation is positive, i.e. $\pi > 0$, this does not matter very much in general since the minimum r is negative. But when $\pi < 0$ the minimum real rate is positive. The problem that can arise is that the real rate needed to stabilize demand at y_e is less than the minimum feasible real rate, i.e. $r_s < \min r(\pi) = -\pi$. This condition is shown in Fig. 5.11 where the stabilizing real interest rate is below the minimum feasible rate of 1%. Given the depressed state of aggregate demand depicted by the position of the *IS* curve, if inflation has fallen to -1%, then it will be impossible to achieve the equilibrium level of output. The approach to monetary policy described in this chapter of using the nominal interest rate in order to set the real interest rate associated with aggregate demand at equilibrium output then ceases to work.

To see why, we assume the central bank sets the lowest real rate possible, namely $r = -\pi$, so that $y = y_0$ and the economy is at at point A. Since $y_0 < y_e$, the consequence is that inflation falls. That implies that the minimum real rate rises, further reducing output

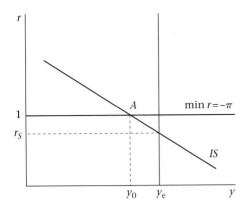

Figure 5.11 The zero floor to the nominal interest rate and the deflation trap

and hence increasing the speed at which inflation falls (in Fig. 5.11, the $\min r$ line shifts upward). The economy is thus caught in a vicious circle or a deflation trap.

It is clear from Fig. 5.11 that getting out of the deflation trap requires either

(1) a successful fiscal expansion or recovery of autonomous investment or consumption that shifts the IS curve to the right or

(2) the creation of more positive inflation expectations. If expected inflation becomes less negative, the $\min r$ line shifts down and the central bank can use the interest rate based monetary rule in the usual way to move the economy to the south-east along the IS curve.

However, the idea of escaping from the deflation trap by creating positive inflation expectations may not work in practice. Willem Buiter argues that this is 'spitting in the wind' because as the announcement has no implications for any current or future monetary policy instruments, it will not affect economic behaviour.[14] Another way to put this point is to say that the only way to create expectations of inflation in the future is to create expectations of future higher aggregate demand: if the authorities do not take measures to create the demand, it is no good hoping that people will expect higher inflation.

He stresses however, that assiduously pursuing a target of low but positive inflation may prevent the economy from getting into a deflation trap in the first place. Buiter argues that a helicopter drop of money of the kind that Milton Friedman discussed—but in a more practical form of, for example, issuing a cheque for every citizen financed by the issue of new high-powered money—would certainly raise aggregate demand as it would boost consumption spending (the IS curve would shift to the right). He points out however that independent central banks may be reluctant to do this since it is a combined fiscal and monetary policy measure (i.e. a fiscal transfer financed by new money creation). This points to the important role of coordinated fiscal and monetary policy in solving a deflation trap and to a largely unanticipated danger of creating independent central banks.

There is an additional channel through which a deflation trap can be sustained. Just as unanticipated inflation shifts wealth from creditors to debtors in the economy as the real

---

[14] See Buiter (2003).

value of debts is eroded, unanticipated deflation has the opposite effect. If asset prices in the economy (e.g. property prices) are falling as well as goods prices, then debtors in the economy will not only find that the real burden of their debt is rising (the debt is fixed in nominal terms but prices are falling) but also that the assets that they have used as security or collateral for the debt are shrinking in value. This so-called balance sheet channel may make investment less sensitive to changes in the real interest rate thereby steepening the *IS* curve and weakening the investment response even if positive inflation expectations could be generated. The situation is further complicated when deflation gets entrenched because bankruptcies weaken the balance sheets of banks, threatening the stability of the banking system. Alternatively, banks may continue to extend loans to failing firms so as to prevent the bad loans from showing up on their balance sheets: this may postpone but not prevent a banking crisis.

6 Credibility, time inconsistency, and rules versus discretion

6.1 Backward-looking Phillips curves and credibility

In the *IS-PC-MR* model, the Phillips curve is backward looking:

$$\pi = \pi_{-1} + \alpha.(y - y_e),$$

which means that current inflation is determined by lagged inflation (and the output gap). This is consistent with the evidence that disinflation is costly, i.e. that in order to reduce inflation, output must be reduced. Although the evidence on costly disinflation discussed in section 1 indicates that reducing inflation from moderate levels appears to require a sacrifice in terms of higher unemployment, it was noted in the discussion of hyperinflation that relatively painless disinflation has been observed under some conditions. The debate about how best to model the inflation process is a very lively one in macroeconomic research at present and is discussed in detail in Chapter 15. The key point to highlight here is that although the inertial or backward-looking Phillips curve matches the empirical evidence concerning inflation persistence, it has a major shortcoming. Because it rests on ad hoc assumptions–in particular about the inflation process–rather than being derived from an optimizing micro model of wage or price setters' behaviour, it does not allow a role for 'credibility' in the way monetary policy affects outcomes.

We can demonstrate the point using an example. In Fig. 5.12, we assume that the central bank's inflation target is 4% and the economy is initially at point *A* with high but stable inflation of 4% (on $PC(\pi^I = 4)$). The central bank now decides to reduce its inflation target to 2%, i.e. $\pi_1^T = 2\%$. With backward-looking Phillips curves, it is clear from Fig. 5.12 that disinflation will be costly and following the announced change in inflation target, unemployment first goes up (shown by point *B*). The economy then shifts only gradually to the new equilibrium at *Z* as the central bank implements the monetary rule. Whether or not the central bank's decision is announced and if so whether it is

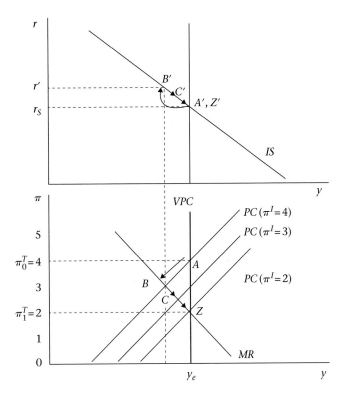

Figure 5.12 Central bank announces a new target: credibility and inertia

believed by the private sector makes no difference at all to the path of inflation. The inflation that is built into the system takes time (with higher unemployment) to work its way out. The inability of the model to take any account of the reaction of wage or price setters to *announced* changes in monetary policy is unsatisfactory. We could make a radically different assumption that incorporates rational expectations on the part of wage and price setters, credibility, and the absence of nominal rigidities. In this case, the announcement of a lower inflation target produces an immediate change in wage and price setting so as to produce wage and price increases based on expected inflation of 2% rather than on past inflation and the economy moves directly from *A* to *Z* without any increase in unemployment. However, this too is unsatisfactory as the evidence suggests that disinflation is indeed costly even when a lower inflation target is announced. As discussed in Chapter 15, recent developments in modelling the Phillips curve aim to provide a micro-optimizing based model that can produce both costly disinflation and a role for the credibility of monetary policy.

6.2 **Introducing inflation bias**

In the *IS-PC-MR* model to this point, medium-run equilibrium is characterized by inflation equal to the central bank's inflation target and output at equilibrium (i.e. determined by the intersection of the *WS* and *PS* curves). However, since we have seen that imperfect competition in product and labour markets implies that y_e is less than the competitive full-employment level, the government may have a higher target. We assume that the government can impose this target on the central bank. How do things change if the central bank's target is full-employment output, or more generally a level of output above y_e?

A starting point is to look at the central bank's new objective function. It now wants to minimize

$$L = (y - y^T)^2 + \beta(\pi - \pi^T)^2,$$ (5.6)

where $y^T > y_e$. This is subject as before to the Phillips curve,

$$\pi = \pi_{-1} + \alpha(y - y_e).$$ (5.7)

In Fig. 5.13 the new indifference curves are shown. The central bank's ideal point is now point A (where $y = y^T$ and $\pi = \pi^T$) rather than where $y = y_e$ and $\pi = \pi^T$ (i.e. point C). If we assume that $\alpha = \beta = 1$ (for simplicity), then each indifference circle has its centre at A. The whole set of loss circles have shifted to the right. Since nothing has changed on the supply side of the economy, the Phillips curves remain unchanged.

To work out the central bank's monetary rule, consider the level of output it chooses if $\pi^I = 2\%$ Fig. 5.13 shows the Phillips curve corresponding to $\pi^I = 2\%$. The tangency of $PC(2)$ with the indifference circle shows where the central bank's loss is minimized (point D). Since the central bank's monetary rule must also pass through A, it is the downward-sloping line *MR* in Fig. 5.13.

We can see immediately that the government's target, point A, does not lie on the Phillips curve for inertial inflation equal to the target rate of $\pi^T = 2\%$: the economy will only be in equilibrium with constant inflation at point B. This is where the monetary rule (*MR*) intersects the vertical Phillips curve at $y = y_e$. At point B, inflation is above the target: the target rate is 2% but inflation is 4%: this gap between the target rate of inflation and inflation in the equilibrium is called the inflation bias.

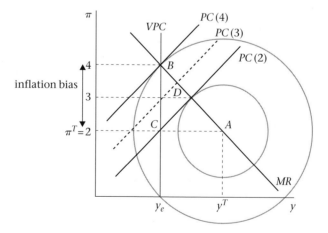

Figure 5.13 The inflation bias

We shall now pin down the source of the inflation bias and the determinants of its size. We begin by showing why the equilibrium is at point B. If inflation is initially at its target rate of 2%, the central bank chooses its preferred point on the $\pi^I = 2\%$ Phillips curve and the economy is at D. But with output above equilibrium, inflation goes up to 3% and the Phillips curve shifts up (see Fig. 5.13). The process of adjustment continues until point B: output is at the equilibrium and inflation does not change so the Phillips curve remains fixed. Neither central bank nor wage setters have any incentive to change their behaviour. The economy is in equilibrium. But neither inflation nor output are at the central bank's target levels (see Fig. 5.13).

We can derive the same result mathematically and pin down the determinants of the size of the inflation bias. Minimizing the central bank's loss function—equation (5.6)—subject to the Phillips curve—equation (5.7) implies

$$y - y^T + \alpha\beta(\pi_{-1} + \alpha(y - y_e) - \pi^T) = y - y^T + \alpha\beta(\pi - \pi^T)$$
$$= 0.$$

So the new monetary rule is:

$$y - y^T = -\alpha\beta(\pi - \pi^T). \tag{5.8}$$

This equation indeed goes through (π^T, y^T). Since equilibrium requires that $\pi_{-1} = \pi$ when $y = y_e$, we have

$$y_e = y^T - \alpha\beta(\pi_{-1} - \pi^T)$$
$$\Rightarrow \pi = \pi_{-1} = \pi^T + \underbrace{\frac{(y^T - y_e)}{\alpha\beta}}_{\text{inflation bias}}. \tag{inflation bias}$$

In equilibrium, inflation will exceed the target by $\frac{(y^T - y_e)}{\alpha\beta}$. This is called the inflation bias.[15] The significance of this result is that $\pi > \pi^T$ whenever $y^T > y_e$. The steeper is the central bank's monetary rule (i.e. the less inflation averse it is), the greater will be the inflation bias. A lower α also raises the inflation bias. A lower α implies that inflation is less responsive to changes in output. Therefore, any given reduction in inflation is more expensive in lost output; so, in cost-benefit terms for the central bank, it pays to allow a little more inflation and a little less output loss. As we shall see in the next subsection, the problem of inflation bias is usually discussed in conjunction with the problem of time inconsistency in which the central bank or the government announces one policy but has an incentive to do otherwise. For this kind of behaviour to arise, it is necessary to introduce forward-looking inflation expectations.

6.3 Time inconsistency and inflation bias

We can link the problem of inflation bias to problems of credibility and time inconsistency by adopting a forward-looking Phillips curve. The simplest assumption to

---

[15] For an early model of inflation bias with backward-looking inflation expectations, see Phelps (1967).

make is that inflation expectations are formed rationally and that there is no inflation inertia: i.e. $\pi^E = \pi + \varepsilon_t$, where ε_t is a random disturbance. The intuition is that wage setters know that whatever their expected rate of inflation, the condition for $\pi^E = \pi$ is that $y = y_e$. As we saw in Chapter 3, this is the so-called Lucas surprise supply equation, which we reproduce here:

$$y_t - y_e = \frac{1}{\alpha}\left(\pi_t - \pi_t^E\right)$$

$$y_t = y_e + \underbrace{\frac{1}{\alpha}\left(\pi_t - \pi_t^E\right)}_{\text{inflation surprise}} \qquad \text{(Lucas surprise supply equation)}$$

$$= y_e + \xi_t.$$

We continue to assume that the central bank chooses y (and hence π) *after* wage setters have chosen π^E. This defines the central bank as acting with *discretion*. Now, in order for wage setters to have correct inflation expectations, they must choose π^E such that it pays the central bank to choose $y = y_e$. That must be where the central bank's monetary rule cuts the $y = y_e$ vertical line, i.e. at point B in Fig. 5.13. Note that the positively sloped lines are now interpreted as Lucas supply equations rather than as Phillips curves. Inflation must be sufficiently high to remove the temptation of the central bank to raise output toward its target. With $\pi = 4\%$ and $y = y_e$, the temptation has been removed because any increase in output from B would put the central bank on a loss circle more distant from its bliss point A: wage and price setters rationally expect an inflation surprise of 2% over and above the target inflation rate of 2%.

The inflation bias presents a problem. As is clear from Fig. 5.13, the loss to the central bank at B is greater than the loss to the central bank at C since output is the same but inflation is higher at B. So the central bank would clearly be better off at C. Moreover, wage setters would be just as happy at C as at B, since employment and the real wage are the same in each case. What is to stop the central bank being at C? When wage and price setters are forward looking, the problem is called that of *time inconsistency*. Although the central bank claims to have an inflation target of π^T, if wage setters act on the basis of this target (2%), when it comes to act, the central bank does not choose the output level consistent with its target. In short, at point B there is no incentive for the central bank to cheat; whereas at point C, there is an incentive.

6.4 Solutions to the time-inconsistency problem

We have seen that the time-inconsistency problem arises under the following circumstances:

- the central bank or government has an over-ambitious output target (i.e. $y^T > y_e$)
- wage and price setters form their inflation expectations using rational expectations
- the central bank uses a rule-based reaction function but operates with discretion, i.e. chooses its desired level of aggregate demand after inflation expectations have been formed in the private sector.

There are three broad approaches to solving or mitigating the time-inconsistency problem manifested in inflation bias, which are referred to as replacing discretion by a rule; delegation; and reputation.

6.4.1 Replacing discretion by a rule: commitment

If the timing of the game between the central bank and private sector is changed so that the central bank cannot choose the rate of inflation after wage and price setters have formed their expectations, then the inflation bias disappears. This entails a structure through which the central bank is prevented from optimizing after the private sector has set wages and prices and is referred to as a policy of commitment rather than discretion. A contract that costs the chairman of the central bank his or her job if inflation deviates from the target is one possible method of enforcing this.

6.4.2 Delegation

The inflation bias is equal to $\frac{(y^T - y_e)}{\alpha\beta}$, and this may reflect a situation in which the *government* rather than the central bank controls monetary policy. The government could reduce the inflation bias by transferring control of monetary policy to a central bank with an output target closer to y_e and with more inflation aversion (higher β) than the government's. Since output in equilibrium is at $y = y_e$, inflation would be brought closer to the target and the government would be unambiguously better off if it delegates monetary policy to an independent central bank.

Fig. 5.14 illustrates the reduction in inflation bias through delegation of monetary policy to the central bank. The flatter sloped monetary rule is that of the central bank, MR_{CB}, and the more steeply sloped that of the government, MR_G. MR_G evidently implies a higher inflation bias with the equilibrium at point B. MR_{CB} on the other hand implies that equilibrium is at point A, with $\pi = 3\%$. Wage and price setters rationally expect a smaller inflation surprise when faced with an independent central bank than when faced by the government. The reduction in the inflation bias is due to the flatter slope of the central bank's MR line and to the fact that central bank's output target is closer to equilibrium output than is the government's.

For delegation to produce a *costless* move from high to low inflation, there must be no inflation inertia and expectations must be formed rationally. In this case, *if* wage setters believe that the policy maker's preferences have changed in the appropriate way, the economy will shift directly down the vertical Phillips curve at y_e from point B to the new equilibrium with $\pi = 3\%$ at point A.

One problem with this proposed solution is that if the government can delegate powers to the central bank, why can't it take them back when it wants to? It would pay the government to take back those powers at the moment that wage setters chose a low π^E corresponding to the loss function parameters of the central bank. For then the government would be tempted to opt for a level of output greater than y_e. This kind of reasoning is sometimes used to explain why governments have often found it necessary to make central banks constitutionally independent and why delegation is sometimes combined with commitment devices like the one discussed in 6.4.1.

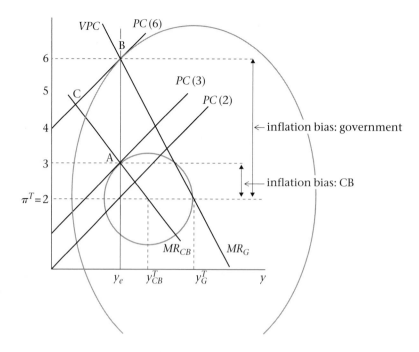

Figure 5.14 Inflation bias: central bank and government

6.4.3 Reputation

A third solution to the problem of inflation bias lies with the government or central bank building a reputation for being tough on inflation. Suppose that the government has delegated monetary policy to the central bank but wage setters remain unsure of just how independent the central bank is. They only know that there is a probability p that the central bank is independent and a probability $(1 - p)$ that it is a puppet of the government. The only way that they can find out is by observing the decisions taken by the central bank. If this is the case, how should the central bank behave? This problem can be analysed in detail using game theory. This is done in Chapter 16. Here we simply convey the flavour of the solution.

The situation is one in which the central bank interacts with wage setters more than once. Will a 'weak' central bank with an output target above the equilibrium find it rational to behave as if it were tough—i.e. with an output target closer to the equilibrium? If so, then we can say that it is possible to build a reputation for toughness as a method of solving the inflation bias problem. Let us begin with the case in which the interaction between the central bank and wage setters occurs twice: in period one, wage setters choose π_1^E with no knowledge of whether the central bank is weak or tough (but they know there is a probability of p that it is tough); the central bank then chooses output in period one, y_1 knowing π_1^E. In period two, the wage setters choose π_2^E knowing y_1; the central bank then chooses y_2 knowing π_2^E.

The result is that a weak central bank will choose to act like a tough one in the first period, which will establish a low expected inflation rate in the second period, thereby providing bigger gains from boosting output in the second period. The central bank gains because in the first period, the outcome is inflation at its target (no inflation bias) and output at the equilibrium (instead of the time inconsistency outcome of inflation above the target and output at equilibrium) whilst in the second period, it can gain by setting output above the equilibrium (i.e. by exploiting the short-run trade-off between inflation and unemployment by a surprise increase in inflation). As discussed in detail in Chapter 16, when the game is extended from two to many periods, the benefits to the central bank from behaving as if it were tough increase. This is because the situation in period one is repeated again and again until the last period. This type of model provides an explanation for the process by which a reputation for toughness can be built in the face of public scepticism.

6.5 Is $y^T > y_e$ a good model of central bank behaviour?

We have seen that the inflation bias problem is eliminated if the objective of the government or central bank is to stabilize the economy around the equilibrium level of output, y_e, i.e. when $y^T = y_e$ rather than $y^T > y_e$. This is the case both when inflation expectations are backward looking and when inflation expectations are rational. The central bank objective of $y^T = y_e$ is our benchmark model for monetary policy, introduced in Chapter 3. We are then led to ask whether the assumption that $y^T > y_e$ is a good way to think about central bank behaviour. It offers insights when the central bank is susceptible to pressure from a government, which in turn is tempted to run the economy at unemployment below the equilibrium. However, in many OECD economies, this is not the key problem for central banks, which in most cases are independent from government and are run by officials motivated by concern about their professional reputations. This point is summarized neatly by Peter Howitt:

The 'temptation' to raise the level of economic activity with some surprise inflation might exist if society were indeed locked into expectations. In reality, however, the temptation just doesn't arise, as practitioners of central banking have long maintained. Central bankers are keenly aware that although there are long and variable lags between monetary stimulus and any resulting rise in the level of economic activity, there are no lags at all between such stimulus and the currency depreciation and capital flight that will occur if the stimulus is taken by investors as a signal of future weakness in the currency. Because of this, there is no reason for believing that discretionary central banks have the inflationary bias that the game-theoretic [time-inconsistency] view attributes to them. . . .

[R]esponsible people entrusted with such important and delicate jobs as the management of a country's central bank are typically motivated by the desire to be seen as having done a good job, to have acquitted themselves well. They pursue this objective by doing everything possible to avoid major inflations, financial panics and runs on the currency, while carrying out the day to day job of making available the base money needed for the financial system to function.[16]

---

[16] Howitt (2001). Howitt refers to the useful paper by Mervyn King, then Deputy Governor of the Bank of England; from 2003, Governor of the Bank of England: King (1997). Another useful source is the short book of three lectures by Alan Blinder reflecting on how he used academic research when he was a Governor of the Federal Reserve Board: Blinder (1998).

6.6 **Rules and expectations versus discretion and learning**

We now return to the case in which there is no inflation bias and to our broader usage of the distinction between monetary rules and discretion. The broader usage is needed because the real-world examples of inflation-targeting central banks embody rule-based behaviour as summarized in a monetary reaction function, which nevertheless entails discretion in the time-inconsistency sense. We ask whether there are any gains from a framework of a clearly defined public monetary policy rule with an explicit inflation target as is the case for the Bank of England or the European Central Bank as compared with a framework of so-called 'constrained discretion' as characterizes the Federal Reserve of the USA. In practice, we observe a wide spectrum of arrangements for monetary policy amongst central banks. The USA under Alan Greenspan is the most famous case of a central bank operating constitutionally with discretion. Yet many articles have been written suggesting that the Fed has covertly been following an inflation-targeting rule.[17] This suggests that in practice there is not a sharp distinction amongst inflation-targeting regimes but rather some difference in emphasis on rules as compared with discretion.

It seems clear that there are gains from the operation of a widely understood and transparent process of monetary policy making. This suggests that providing information about the monetary policy reaction function is likely to be useful.[18] The main gain arises because economic agents are at least in part forward looking and will therefore anticipate the reaction of the central bank to a shock. If the reaction function is well understood, anticipation by the private sector may help to stabilize the economy's response to a shock.

For example, if we think of a negative aggregate demand shock, then the monetary policy reaction function indicates that interest rates will be lowered. The knowledge of this reaction will influence the expected future path of interest rates, which will help shift the long-term interest rate downwards—the rate relevant for interest-sensitive spending. Asset prices such as share prices or house prices may react rapidly to the expected path of interest rates and reinforce the efforts of the central bank to boost demand. In our example, the expectation of a lengthy period of low interest rates would tend to boost asset prices immediately (e.g. share prices and house prices). In turn as we shall see in Chapter 7, this raises Tobin's Q and permanent income and would therefore tend to raise investment and consumption, reinforcing the recovery of aggregate demand.

On the other hand, too great an emphasis on rules may take attention away from the benefits that can arise from a central bank that sees itself as actively learning about the economy and engaging in experiments—for example, to try to discover the equilibrium level of unemployment in an economy experiencing a burst of technological progress.

---

[17] For example, see the discussion in Mankiw (2002).

[18] Recent research suggests that adopting an inflation-targeting regime with an *explicit* inflation target improves macroeconomic performance in terms of both inflation and output stability by anchoring the public's inflation expectations to the central bank's objectives. For example, Orphanides and Williams (2005).

7 Conclusions

In this chapter, we have put the spotlight on monetary policy. The starting point was an examination of the phenomena of inflation, disinflation, and deflation, which was motivated by the question of why low and stable inflation is considered a desirable objective by policy makers. We examined the reasons behind episodes of rising inflation and the unsustainability of attempts to hold output above the equilibrium level. A falling general price level (deflation) is likely to bring dangers to macroeconomic stability.

We highlighted the difference between two monetary policy paradigms—the *LM* paradigm and the *MR* paradigm. In the *LM* paradigm, monetary policy is passive and the money supply growth rate determines the rate of inflation in the medium-run equilibrium. By contrast, in the *MR* paradigm, the central bank is active. It adjusts the interest rate so as to steer the economy back to target inflation at equilibrium output. The rate of inflation at medium-run equilibrium is therefore determined by policy. Since the nominal interest rate cannot be negative, monetary policy will become ineffective at very low or negative rates of inflation.

A systematic approach to monetary policy within the *MR* paradigm can be modelled by specifying the objectives of the central bank (or the government) and identifying the constraints it faces. The objective of the central bank is to minimize the extent to which the economy diverges from a target rate of inflation and from a target level of output. We have shown that

- when the output target is the equilibrium level of output, y_e, a monetary policy reaction function will enable the central bank to steer the economy to its inflation and output targets if the economy experiences an inflation, aggregate demand, or supply shock.

- The central bank will do this by adjusting the nominal interest rate so as to affect the real interest rate and the level of aggregate demand and output. The appropriate change in the real interest rate will depend on whether the stabilizing real interest rate has changed and on the interest sensitivity of aggregate demand (the slope of the *IS*), how inflation averse the central bank is, and the response of inflation to changes in unemployment (the slope of the Phillips curve).

- We have shown how to derive an interest rate rule from the 3-equation model. This takes the form of a Taylor Rule in which the central bank adjusts the interest rate in response to observed deviations of inflation from target and of output from equilibrium when the economy is characterized by a lag in the effect of the interest rate on output and a lag in the effect of a change in output on inflation. If output affects inflation in the same period, then the interest rate rule only has the inflation term in it. This highlights the fact that the coefficients on inflation and output in the Taylor rule are not the weights on inflation and output in the central bank's loss function.

- With a purely backward-looking Phillips curve, disinflation is always costly and that cost is not affected by the degree to which central bank announcements are believed.

- When the output target is above the equilibrium level of output, the central bank will not be able to achieve its inflation target in equilibrium. There will be an inflation bias.

We clarify the debate about rules versus discretion by explaining that the superiority of a rule that prevents the central bank from optimizing rests on the specification of the central bank's loss function. If the central bank targets a level of employment above the equilibrium, an inflation bias arises. When expectations are rational, this creates the time-inconsistency problem. By contrast, in our baseline case, which it is argued matches that of central banks in many countries, the objective is to stabilize the economy around equilibrium output, which eliminates the inflation bias. A fuller understanding by the public of the monetary reaction function can help to stabilize forward-looking expectations and facilitate the movement of asset prices consistent with the central bank's stabilization objectives.

■ QUESTIONS

Checklist questions

(1) 'If the economy has high but stable inflation, the government has much to lose and little to gain by reducing inflation to a low rate.' Explain and assess this statement.

(2) What are the advantages and disadvantages of an inflation rate of 3% as compared with one of 0% per annum? Would you advocate the replacement of the inflation target by a price level target?

(3) Explain what is meant by the central bank's loss function. How are the central bank's preferences reflected in the loss function? Use a numerical example and diagrams to explain how the central bank's preferences affect its reaction to a negative aggregate demand shock.

(4) How can the central bank diagnose what kind of shock has disturbed the economy?

(5) Compare the response of an inflation-targeting central bank to a permanent negative aggregate supply shock with that to a permanent negative aggregate demand shock.

(6) Suppose there are two regions of the country, in one of which the WS curve is quite steep and in the other, the WS is quite flat. Why might this be so? Compare the implications for inflation and unemployment of a common positive temporary aggregate demand shock. How should the central bank respond?

(7) If a central bank adopts an interest-rate based monetary policy rule like a Taylor Rule rather than a monetary growth rate rule, what would you expect to happen to the money supply?

(8) In implementing a Taylor-type interest rate rule, does the central bank need to know anything more than the coefficients in the rule, its inflation target, and current output and inflation?

(9) Write down the Taylor Rule in terms of the real interest rate. Holding the output gap constant, does a rise in inflation by x percentage points call for a rise in the *nominal* interest rate by more than, less than, or by just x percentage points? Explain.

(10) Under what circumstances will a central bank utilizing an interest rate based monetary rule to stabilize the economy fail in its objective of raising output?

(11) The central bank faces a short-run trade-off between inflation and unemployment (*a*) if inflation expectations are backward looking or (*b*) if inflation expectations are rational but are formed before the central bank chooses its optimal inflation-output pair. Explain each of these cases. What difference does it make whether (*a*) or (*b*) holds?

(12) Explain what is meant by the statement that a government that is determined to reduce inflation may have a problem in achieving this outcome because of a lack of credibility.

Problems and questions for discussion

QUESTION A. What are the incentives for a policy maker to exploit the short-run trade-off between unemployment and inflation? What are the consequences? Is this a good description of contemporary central bankers? Use official reports of a central bank of your choice to provide support for your argument.

QUESTION B. Consider a Central Bank that maximizes the following utility function:

$$Z = k(y - y_e) - (\pi - \pi^T)^2$$

where k is a positive constant. Its policy instrument is the growth rate of the money supply, γ_M. Assume that the inflation target is $\pi^T = 0$. Explain this utility function and compare it with the loss function used in the chapter. (Hint: focus on how the central bank's utility rises with output. Is this central bank 'overambitious'?) Now assume that the central bank sets the money supply growth rate after economic agents have incorporated their expectations about inflation into their decision making, and thus faces a Phillips curve:

$$\pi = \pi^E + \alpha(y - y_e).$$

(*a*) Assuming that agents have rational expectations, solve algebraically for the optimal inflation rate under discretion, i.e. find the inflation rate that the central bank will choose using its monetary policy instrument, γ_M. (Hint: maximize utility with respect to γ_M, having used the Phillips curve to substitute for y in the utility function; and used $\gamma_M = \pi$ to substitute for π.)

(*b*) Suppose that, before private sector inflation expectations were formed, the central bank could commit to a particular rate of inflation. What would that rate be? Discuss.

(*c*) Now return to the case of discretion, and suppose that we extend the model to cover two periods. In other words, the central bank now cares about the sum of its loss functions in each period, i.e.

$$\text{Total utility} = \left[k(y_1 - y_e) - \left(\pi_1 - \pi^T\right)^2 \right] + \left[k(y_2 - y_e) - \left(\pi_2 - \pi^T\right)^2 \right]$$

where the subscripts indicate the period.

Suppose also that in the first period, agents expect no inflation ($\pi^E = 0$), while when the second period arrives agents expect that inflation will be equal to the rate that actually occurs in the first period (i.e. expectations are adaptive, so $\pi_2^E = \pi_1$). What will be the equilibrium rates of output and inflation in each period? Discuss your findings.

QUESTION C. Is there a trade-off between stabilizing inflation and stabilizing the real side of the economy? Explain.

QUESTION D. Using Fig. 5.8 as a guide, draw the corresponding diagram to illustrate the lag structure in the standard version of the 3-equation model. Now assume that there is no lag between a change in the interest rate and its effect on output. Draw a diagram to illustrate this lag structure. Use all three figures to provide a concise summary of the role of lags in the operation of monetary policy. Go to the website of one of the central banks listed in the next question (or another one of your choice) and find out their view about the lags between a change in the interest rate and its effects on output and inflation. Do they identify the same factors as responsible for the lags?

QUESTION E. Select two out of the following central banks: Bank of England, Reserve Bank of New Zealand, Bank of Canada, and the Swedish Riksbank. Each of these central banks has adopted explicit 'inflation targeting'. For each of your chosen banks, find out how it explains what this means to the public. How does it communicate and explain its interest rate decisions to the public? Compare what each central bank did and how it explained its actions following the events of 11 September 2001.

6 **Fiscal Policy**

The government is responsible for fiscal policy. The macroeconomic roles of fiscal policy are:

- to provide *automatic stabilizers* that insulate the economy to some extent from shocks to aggregate demand. The stabilization provided by the automatic stabilizers is, however, largely a by-product of the structure of the tax and social security systems. These systems are typically designed to meet the government's income distribution and microeconomic goals rather than its macroeconomic objectives.

- to stabilize the level of output around the equilibrium rate by using *discretionary* changes in government expenditure and/or taxation.

- to plan the financing of government expenditure so as to maintain a sustainable burden of public debt in the economy.

We shall begin with the analysis of the short-run role of fiscal policy and examine how the macroeconomic effects of a change in government expenditure differ according to how the expenditure is financed. We shall compare the financing of government spending through taxation, borrowing from the public (i.e. issuing bonds) and borrowing from the central bank (i.e. new money creation). This discussion introduces the concept of the 'balanced budget multiplier'.

Once we have introduced the idea of the government's budget identity, we can use it to provide a framework to think more systematically about the role of the government in the economy. If the government borrows in order to finance its current year's expenditure, it is imposing an obligation on future taxpayers to pay the interest on the debt and eventually to repay the principal. This is why we extend the concept of the budget constraint to include explicitly its intertemporal component. This leads naturally to a consideration of what determines the 'solvency' of the government. What does it mean if the government's debt ratio is increasing? What factors determine whether this is sustainable—i.e. consistent with the solvency of the government?

The analysis of the sustainability of public debt brings us to the issue of fiscal policy rules. We shall investigate two sorts of fiscal policy rule. On the one hand it has been suggested that fiscal policy should be thought of in a similar way to monetary policy and that the contribution of fiscal policy to *stabilization* should be governed by a fiscal policy rule. On the other hand, concerns about *solvency* have led to the introduction by governments of a variety of fiscal rules. For example, the so-called Golden Rule says that only public investment and not public consumption should be financed by borrowing. The British government has introduced a fiscal rule like this. Other deficit and debt rules have been central to the Maastricht Rules for entry to EMU. How can such rules be fitted into the framework for analysing fiscal policy? Are they consistent with economic theory?

The interaction between fiscal and monetary policy is examined at several points in the chapter. We look explicitly at the connection between fiscal policy, monetary policy, and inflation. As we have seen in Chapter 5, a process of rising inflation requires that monetary policy accommodate this. Since rising inflation per se does not provide economic benefits, the roots of it must lie elsewhere. In this chapter we explore the role of *seignorage* in the link between government spending and inflation.

1 The automatic stabilizers

In the simple multiplier model, it is clear that introducing taxes that depend on the level of income reduces the size of the multiplier. Similarly, because unemployment benefit payments vary with the numbers unemployed, transfers increase as the level of output falls and this, too, reduces the size of the multiplier. The implication is that since the tax and benefit system is set up so that both taxes and transfers depend on the level of activity, they reduce the size of the multiplier and therefore dampen the impact on output of any exogenous change in private spending. In terms of the *IS/LM* model, recall that a smaller multiplier is reflected in a steeper *IS* curve that shifts less far horizontally in response to a change in exogenous expenditure (see Chapter 2). This is what is meant by the 'automatic stabilizer' role of the tax and social security system. A consequence of this feature of the fiscal structure is that the budget deficit rises when activity falls and declines when activity rises.

To interpret the significance of the budget deficit recorded at any particular time, it is necessary to know whether output is below, at, or above equilibrium. To assist policy makers, the cyclically adjusted budget deficit is calculated. This is the budget deficit that would prevail given existing taxes and spending commitments if the economy was operating at equilibrium output. Assuming we know equilibrium output, the concept of the cyclically adjusted deficit indicates whether fiscal policy is expansionary or contractionary. One practical problem with using the cyclically adjusted deficit as a measure of fiscal stance is in estimating the level of equilibrium output. Vivid examples of this problem show up when examining the origins of the large budget deficits that emerged especially in European economies in the 1970s and 1980s and in Japan in the 1990s.

Let us define the relationship between the different concepts of the fiscal balance as follows.

(primary) budget deficit ≡ cycl. adj. budget deficit + impact of aut. stabilizers

≡ discret. fiscal impulse + impact of aut. stabilizers

$$g(y_t) - t(y_t) \equiv [g(y_e) - t(y_e)] + a(y_e - y_t), \tag{6.1}$$

where a is a constant and the term $a(y_e - y_t)$ captures the impact on the budget deficit of the automatic stabilizers.[1] If current output, y_t, is below equilibrium output, y_e, the economy is in a recession. The automatic stabilizers will automatically help to stabilize the economy by raising government expenditure on transfers and depressing tax revenue $(a(y_e - y_t) > 0)$ thereby pushing up the actual deficit.

By definition, the impact on the budget deficit of the automatic stabilizers is zero when output is at its equilibrium level. A zero cyclically adjusted budget deficit implies zero *discretionary* fiscal impulse; a cyclically adjusted deficit implies an expansionary fiscal stance and a cyclically adjusted surplus implies a contractionary fiscal stance.

As we have just seen, an economy in recession with output below the equilibrium will tend to have a high actual deficit because the second term in the equation (6.1) is positive. If the cyclically adjusted deficit or surplus is zero then the actual deficit simply reflects the automatic stabilizers and will disappear once the economy returns to the equilibrium. In this case, fiscal policy is providing no additional discretionary stimulus to push the economy back toward the equilibrium (i.e. in *IS/LM* terminology, there is no rightward shift of the *IS* curve). Equally, if *discretionary* fiscal policy is used to stimulate the return of the economy to equilibrium (a rightward shift of *IS*), a cyclically adjusted deficit would be observed. In such a case, the government has to recognize that eventually it may have to take measures to reduce the increase in debt that will accompany the economy when it returns to equilibrium output. Such an opportunity would arise if, when the economy is above equilibrium output, the government tightened fiscal policy (say, by cutting government expenditure) so as to reinforce the monetary policy rule in guiding the economy back towards the equilibrium. We shall return to this issue when we analyse the medium-run problem of fiscal policy and public sector debt.

Before turning directly to discretionary fiscal policy, we briefly address the question of how much stabilization is done by the automatic stabilizers. For the tax schedule to act as an automatic stabilizer, it is necessary that the change in aggregate output leads to a change in disposable income and that this in turn leads to a change in consumption. As we shall see in more detail in Chapter 7, households at different positions in the income distribution tend to respond differently to such temporary changes in disposable income. In the pure permanent income hypothesis, temporary changes in income have no effect on consumption: by assumption it is only permanent income that affects consumption. If this is the case, then the automatic stabilizers are irrelevant. However, poorer households are more likely to be liquidity constrained than richer ones and they will therefore react more to temporary changes in their income. In order to estimate the effects of the automatic stabilizers, detailed information is needed not only on the operation of the tax system but also on the implications of changes in aggregate activity for households with different levels of income.

This question has been investigated recently for the USA.[2] The authors focus on the stabilization role of federal taxes and unemployment compensation. In the USA, Auerbach and Feenberg find that the tax system offsets about 8% and unemployment benefits

---

[1] Note that we are concerned here only with the budget deficit *excluding* interest payments on the outstanding government debt. As we shall see below, this is known as the *primary* budget deficit.

[2] See, for example, Auerbach and Feenberg (2000).

about 2% of any initial shock to GDP. This is rather modest and the effects will be greater in many European countries with higher taxation and more generous unemployment benefits.

2 Discretionary fiscal policy

In the *IS/LM* model presented in Chapter 2, government spending is normally assumed to be exogenous and taxation is usually modelled either as exogenous or as a function of the level of income. A change in government spending or taxation feeds through to aggregate demand via the multiplier process. To this point there has been no explicit consideration of how the increase in government spending is financed or, in other words, of the consequences of changes in the government deficit for the asset stocks (money and bonds) in the economy. We need to remedy these omissions here. We begin by introducing the concept of the government budget constraint and then proceed in two stages.

First, we assume that households and firms take the view that government bonds they hold comprise part of their wealth. From this viewpoint, bonds are a component of the financial assets of the personal sector of the economy. Assuming that bonds are wealth, we compare three different methods of financing an increase in government expenditure: taxation, bonds, and money. The concept of the balanced budget multiplier is introduced. This comparison shows that the method of financing an increase in government expenditure influences its impact on output.

Second, we investigate the logic of the claim that bonds are not wealth for the personal sector—this is the doctrine of 'Ricardian equivalence' in which the far-sighted household realizes that any bonds that are issued to finance extra government spending will have to be repaid by higher taxation later on. This suggests that there are circumstances under which tax and bond financed increases in government spending are indistinguishable. What are the implications for the way in which fiscal policy affects output (i.e. for the fiscal transmission mechanism) if bonds are not considered to be net wealth?

2.0.1 The government budget identity

Each period, the government must finance its expenditure plans and also pay interest on the government debt. Government debt is the stock of government bonds that have been sold to the private sector in the past. The government can use taxation, the sale of new bonds, or the printing of money to finance its expenditure. The sources of funds are on the right hand side of the identity and the uses of funds are on the left hand side. In *nominal* terms, the government's budget identity in each period is:

$$\underbrace{G}_{\text{govt. exp.}} + \underbrace{iB}_{\text{interest}} \equiv \underbrace{T}_{\text{tax revenue}} + \underbrace{\Delta B}_{\text{new bonds}} + \underbrace{\Delta H}_{\text{new money}}, \qquad \text{(government budget identity)}$$

where G is government expenditure on goods and services in nominal terms, i is the nominal interest rate, B is the outstanding stock of bonds and hence the value of the national debt at the beginning of the period, T is tax revenues measured net of transfers, ΔB is the value of the new bonds issued in the current period, and ΔH is the new high powered money printed by the government.

2.0.2 The fiscal policy transmission mechanism

The standard presentation of fiscal policy in the IS/LM model is shown by a shift in the IS curve: the expenditure multiplier comes into play to magnify the impact of the fiscal impulse. As the level of income rises, the demand for money is driven up, and, as a consequence, the interest rate rises and 'crowds out' some interest-sensitive spending by the private sector. In the short run, with no change in inflation or inflation expectations, the rise in the nominal interest rate is also a rise in the real interest rate. This is the fiscal policy transmission mechanism:

$$\uparrow g \rightarrow \uparrow y \rightarrow \uparrow \left(\frac{M}{P}\right)^{D} \rightarrow \uparrow r \rightarrow \downarrow I.$$

The IS curve shifts to the right; the economy moves north-east along the upward sloping LM curve. This is the simplest form of so-called financial crowding out. It occurs when prices are fixed—i.e. when there are no supply-side constraints on the expansion of activity. Output expands but because the increase in government spending is financed entirely by new bond issues, the interest rate is affected (see Fig. 6.1a). The rise in the interest rate means that the full multiplier effect of the rise in government spending does not

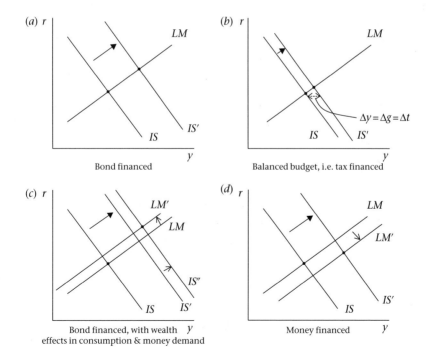

Figure 6.1 Different methods of financing an increase in government expenditure

occur: at the new short-run equilibrium, output is higher and its composition is different since there is a higher component of government expenditure and a lower component of investment than in the initial equilibrium. This kind of crowding out will obviously not occur if the interest rate is held constant, i.e. if the money supply is allowed to expand to meet the additional demand for money.

2.1 Tax finance and the balanced budget multiplier

Before we examine the implications of using taxation to finance government expenditure, we show that following a rise in government spending, although tax revenues rise because of the increase in output, the increase in taxation induced by the higher level of activity is insufficient to close the gap between expenditure and taxation. Suppose there is a proportional tax: $t = t_y y$. At the new equilibrium following the increase in government spending (if we assume for simplicity that the interest rate is constant), there will only be budget balance if

$$\Delta g = \Delta t$$
$$= t_y \Delta y$$
$$\implies \frac{\Delta y}{\Delta g} = \frac{1}{t_y}$$

i.e. if the multiplier effect of the change in g is $\frac{1}{t_y}$. But we know that the expenditure multiplier is equal to

$$\frac{\Delta y}{\Delta g} = \frac{1}{s_y + c_y t_y},$$

which is smaller than $\frac{1}{t_y}$. This implies that tax revenue at the new equilibrium level of output will be less than the increase in government spending. The reason is straightforward: the boost to income from higher government spending leads not only to higher tax revenues for the government but also to higher savings. This means that there is a *government budget deficit* at the new equilibrium: the increase in income to generate savings plus taxation (i.e. the so-called leakages) equal to the increase in government spending (i.e. the so-called injection) must be lower than the level of income at which extra taxation alone would be equal to the increase in government spending. Since there is a deficit, the government is borrowing to implement its spending plans. We return to the consequences of such borrowing below.

Now suppose that the government increases taxation by enough to finance the increased government spending so that there is no deficit at the new short-run equilibrium. What is the effect on the economy of a *fully* tax-financed expenditure programme? To see the answer to this question, it is simplest if we assume that the interest rate is fixed. Suppose that the government increases government spending and taxation revenue by exactly the same amount. The argument is transparent when taxation is exogenous— i.e. does not depend on the level of income. Consider first the impact on output of the change in g:

$$\Delta y = \Delta g + c_y \Delta g + c_y (c_y \Delta g) + \cdots \tag{6.2}$$

and second, the impact on output of the change in t:

$$\Delta y = -c_y \Delta t - c_y(c_y \Delta t) - \cdots \qquad (6.3)$$

Since by the assumption of tax finance, $\Delta g = \Delta t$, it is clear that the net effect of the balanced budget expenditure programme is

$$\Delta y = \Delta g = \Delta t$$

$$\text{i.e. } \frac{\Delta y}{\Delta g} = 1. \qquad \text{(balanced budget multiplier)}$$

The balanced budget multiplier result is a very important one: it does not depend on the assumption that taxes are exogenous. It hinges on the fact that the government spending on goods and services (Δg) generates extra output and income (6.2) whereas the increase in taxation *redistributes* spending power from taxpayers to those who provide the goods and services (6.3). If these two groups have the *same* marginal propensity to consume (as is assumed here, i.e. c_y is the same in (6.2) and (6.3)), then the balanced budget multiplier is equal to one. Why? Because aggregate consumption remains unchanged as a consequence of the redistribution of spending power. Hence the only impact on output comes from the first round effect of the government's purchases of goods and services.

The balanced budget multiplier result is important for practical policy purposes: a government that is unable or unwilling to use debt or money financing, can still raise the level of activity in the economy by engaging in a balanced budget expenditure programme. The size of the multiplier will be pulled down below one once the impact of the increased income on the demand for money and the interest rate are reintroduced (see Fig. 6.1*b*).[3] Of course, to the extent that the increase in output pushes it above the equilibrium level, the monetary policy rule will come into play to offset the expansionary impact of the balanced budget expansion.

2.2 Bond finance

In developing the short-run model, the possible effects on aggregate demand of the growing stock of bonds in the economy arising from a bond financed deficit have been ignored. As we have shown above, a rise in government spending will not induce sufficient extra tax revenue to wipe out the deficit. In other words, there will be a continuing requirement to sell bonds to cover the gap between expenditure and revenue. The stock of government bonds, i.e. the size of the national debt in the economy, will mount each year. For as long as the economy remains at the new level of output and maintains an unchanged monetary stance, the government will have to sell additional bonds to finance the deficit.

The implications of this depend on whether government bonds are considered by private sector agents to represent net wealth in the economy. For the moment, we assume

---

[3] But note that if the demand for money is a function of consumption or disposable income rather than of total income (we normally assume the latter in the *LM* curve), there will be no effect on the demand for money. Hence in such a case, the balanced budget multiplier remains equal to one even if the money supply is fixed. The reason is that disposable income and consumption are unchanged.

that government bonds are viewed by households as a form of wealth. If bonds are wealth, then changes in the stock of wealth will influence both consumption and the demand for money. This means that the government has to take into account the impact of these changes when setting both monetary and fiscal policy. A bond financed increase in expenditure will not only bring about a shift in the *IS* curve to the right (direct effect of the rise in spending) but will also lead to a further rightward shift in the *IS* as consumption rises with wealth.

In addition, the new bonds issued by the government will produce a portfolio effect in the demand for money. The demand for money contains financial wealth as an argument. At a given interest rate, higher wealth raises the demand for money and bonds in proportion so as to keep the portfolio balanced. The consequence of a bond financed expansion in government spending will be to raise the proportion of bonds to money in the economy—since, by assumption, the money supply remains constant. This will lead to an increase in the demand for money to restore portfolio balance. The *LM* curve will therefore shift to the left (see Fig. 6.1*c*).[4]

2.2.1 Are bonds net wealth? The Ricardian equivalence debate

Under special assumptions, a bond financed increase in government expenditure will have exactly the same effect on output as a tax financed one. If bonds are not considered as net wealth by households, then two implications follow. First, the consequences of changes in wealth as the government's debt rises disappear and second, the expansionary impact of the spending programme shrinks back to that of a balanced budget. These two effects are intimately connected: households do not view bonds as net wealth if they take into account the fact that taxes in the future will have to be raised to service the debt and to repay the principal on the debt. As noted earlier, this argument has a pedigree stretching back to the nineteenth-century classical economist David Ricardo and was revived in the 1970s by Robert Barro and is known as 'Ricardian Equivalence'.[5] The Ricardian equivalence result depends on the following assumptions:

- the absence of liquidity constraints on households, i.e. households are able to borrow against expected future income at the current interest rate;
- the interest rate and time horizon faced by households and the government are the same;
- households have children or heirs and incorporate the utility of their heirs in their consumption behaviour, i.e. households behave 'as if' they last forever.

After a clear statement of the nature of the assumptions required to deliver Ricardian equivalence, John Seater, in a survey in the *Journal of Economic Literature*, concludes:[6]

Finite horizons, non-altruistic or inoperative bequest motives, childless couples, liquidity constraints, and uncertainty can all lead to failure of Ricardian equivalence and it seems virtually

---

[4] The debate about such wealth effects is set out in more detail in Blinder and Solow (1973), a correction to that paper in Blinder and Solow (1976), and in Rau (1985).   [5] Barro (1974).
[6] Seater (1993: 155-6).

certain that some of these sources of non-equivalence are operative. It appears likely that the world is not Ricardian.

The consensus view appears to be that changes in fiscal policy are only partly offset by changes in private sector savings: the sources of 'non-equivalence' in the real world mean that Ricardian equivalence is not a good representation of macroeconomic behaviour.[7] We return to this debate in Chapter 7 because the Ricardian equivalence result is an extension of the intertemporal theory of consumption, i.e. the Permanent Income/Life-cycle Hypothesis.

2.3 **Money financed fiscal expansion**

The final method of financing an increase in expenditure is through an increase in the monetary base (i.e. ΔH in the government budget identity). In crude terms, the government sells bonds to the central bank and spends the newly printed money on its expenditure initiative. In a number of countries, this method of public finance has been ruled out by the constitution of the central bank. The reason for this has to do with the *medium-run* consequences of monetary financing. Monetary policy cannot both provide the nominal anchor for the economy as discussed in Chapter 5 and be used at will to finance government expenditure.

To see this, we can easily imagine a situation in which the request by the government for monetary financing of an expansion in spending is inconsistent with the central bank's monetary policy rule. Suppose that the economy is at equilibrium employment and that inflation is at its target rate. If the government increases its spending, this will trigger an increase in the interest rate as the central bank engages in open market sales of bonds. This withdraws liquidity from the economy and is the opposite move in monetary policy from that associated with a money-financed expansion. We shall return to the question of the monetary financing of government spending in the section after next, where we investigate seignorage.

In Fig. 6.1, the short-run effects of the different methods of financing an increase in government expenditure are illustrated.

3 **Deficits and debt**

In section 2, we introduced the concept of the government's budget identity, which shows the sources of the funds in any period to pay for the government's expenditure on consumption, transfers and investment, as well as paying the interest due on its stock of outstanding debt. But what determines the path of the government's debt over time? If the debt is rising, will it continue rising indefinitely?

To answer these questions, we need to move beyond the government's single period budget identity. We take the analysis in two steps—first, we exclude the possibility that

---

[7] For a recent study for OECD countries, see de Mello, Kongsrud, and Price (2004). A summary is provided in OECD, *Economic Outlook*, 76 (2004), ch. V.

the government can borrow from the central bank (i.e. that it can use the creation of high powered money to finance its deficit). We shall return to money financing in the next section. For now, the budget identity is as follows:

$$\underbrace{G}_{\text{govt. exp.}} + \underbrace{iB}_{\text{interest}} \equiv \underbrace{T}_{\text{tax revenue}} + \underbrace{\Delta B}_{\text{new bonds}}. \qquad \text{(government budget identity)}$$

We begin by distinguishing between the actual government deficit, which is the difference between total expenditure and revenue (i.e. actual deficit $\equiv G + iB - T$) and the primary deficit, which excludes the interest payments on the debt (i.e. primary deficit $\equiv G - T$). It is important to note that the stock of bonds in the economy (held by the public) is equal to the stock of government debt. By rearranging the budget identity, we can see that the actual deficit is equal to the change in the stock of government debt:

$$\Delta B \equiv (G - T) + iB \qquad (6.4)$$

change in debt $\equiv$ primary deficit + interest on outstanding debt

change in debt $\equiv$ actual deficit.

It is the government debt relative to national income that is of central concern. We therefore define the debt ratio as

$$\text{debt ratio} \equiv b = \frac{B}{Py},$$

where P is the price level and y is real national income, which means that $P.y$ is nominal national income. The next step is to rewrite the budget identity equation (government budget identity) by dividing through by Py. This gives us the actual deficit to GDP ratio ($\frac{\Delta B}{Py}$):

$$\frac{\text{actual deficit}}{\text{GDP}} = \frac{\Delta B}{Py} \equiv \frac{G - T}{Py} + \frac{iB}{Py}$$
$$\equiv d + ib, \qquad (6.5)$$

where the ratio of the primary deficit to national income is:

$$\frac{\text{primary deficit}}{\text{GDP}} = d \equiv \frac{G - T}{Py}.$$

In order to pin down the determinants of the growth in the debt to GDP ratio, i.e. Δb, we begin with the definition of b:

$$B \equiv bPy,$$

use the approximation that

$$\Delta B \approx Py\Delta b + by\Delta P + bP\Delta y$$

and divide each side by Py to give:

$$\frac{\Delta B}{Py} = \frac{b\Delta Py}{Py} + \frac{b\Delta yP}{Py} + \frac{\Delta bPy}{Py}$$
$$= b\pi + b\gamma_y + \Delta b,$$

where as usual, we write the growth rate of prices (i.e. the rate of inflation), $\frac{\Delta P}{P}$, as π and the growth rate of output as γ_y. Using $r = i - \pi$, we get the following expression for the change in the debt to GDP ratio:

$$\Delta b = d + (i - \pi - \gamma_y)b$$
$$= d + (r - \gamma_y)b. \tag{6.6}$$

This equation provides a powerful way of understanding the four key determinants of the growth of the debt to GDP ratio:

(1) the primary deficit ratio, d

(2) the real interest rate, r

(3) the growth of real GDP, γ_y

(4) the existing ratio of government debt to GDP, b.

As we shall see in the final section of the chapter, it also provides a framework for looking at the fiscal rules that governments have introduced or may consider introducing. To interpret the equation, let us consider two cases:

- Case 1. The real interest rate is above the growth rate (i.e. $r > \gamma_y$). The arithmetic of equation (6.6) says that in this case, the debt to GDP ratio will be rising unless d is negative, i.e. unless there is a primary budget surplus. The explanation is straightforward: with the real interest rate above the growth rate, the interest payments on the existing debt are rising faster than is GDP. Hence servicing the debt interest is pushing up the debt burden. The only way that this can be offset so that the debt ratio does not rise (i.e. for $\Delta b = 0$) is for the government to run a primary budget surplus.

- Case 2. The real interest rate is below the growth rate (i.e. $r < \gamma_y$). This case represents a benign scenario from the perspective of the government's finances. Since the growth of the economy is sufficient to reduce the impact of interest payments on the debt burden, some level of primary deficit is consistent with a constant ratio of debt to GDP. Indeed if the government were to run a primary surplus in this scenario, it would eventually end up with negative public debt. The public sector would own financial assets issued by the private sector.

A diagram helps to clarify the relationship between the primary deficit, the real interest rate, the growth rate, and the debt ratio and to highlight the difference between Case 1 and Case 2. We use a diagram with the debt to GDP ratio (b) on the horizontal axis and the growth of the debt to GDP ratio (Δb) on the vertical axis. The primary deficit, d, is the intercept term and the relationship between the real interest rate, and the growth rate determines the slope of the line showing the growth of the debt ratio. For any economy, in order to draw the appropriate 'phase line' (the name for the line showing Δb as a function of b), we need to know the current primary deficit, the real interest rate and the growth rate. The existing level of debt, b, at time t then tells us where we are on the phase line. Of course, unless the initial position of the economy is on the horizontal axis with $\Delta b = 0$, the debt ratio will have changed if we look at the economy at a later time.

Fig. 6.2 illustrates case 1: the real interest rate exceeds the growth rate. Fig. 6.2(a) shows an economy with a primary deficit. Once we know the existing level of debt, we can fix the economy's position on the phase line. But note that the economy will not remain stationary: it will be moving north-east along the phase line as shown by the arrows. When next observed, the debt ratio will be higher.

Fig. 6.2(b) shows an economy with exactly the same interest rate and growth rate as in Fig. 6.2(a) but with a primary surplus (hence the intercept is below the horizontal axis). Here we note the situation with three different initial debt ratios. If an economy happens to have an initial debt ratio shown by point A, its debt ratio will be falling (as shown by the arrows in the south-westerly direction). Why is this? This is because it is a situation in which the primary surplus is sufficiently large to offset the ($r > \gamma_y$) effect so that the debt ratio declines. If the debt ratio is as at point B, then the debt ratio will remain constant: the primary surplus (reducing the debt ratio) and the ($r > \gamma_y$) effect (raising it) exactly offset each other. But note that point B is not *stable*: a slight increase in the debt ratio triggers an ever-increasing debt ratio and a slight fall, a falling debt ratio. An appropriate primary surplus can hold the debt ratio constant but it cannot mitigate the underlying dynamics of the debt, which is determined by the relationship between r and γ_y. An economy with a debt ratio as at point C is characterized by an ever-increasing debt ratio.

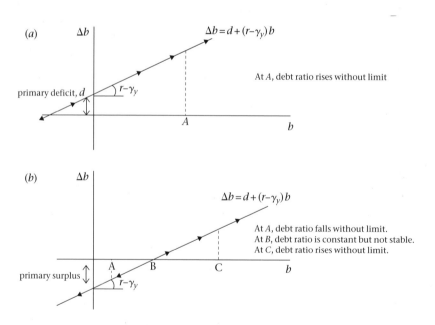

Figure 6.2 The government debt ratio. Case 1. Real interest rate exceeds the growth rate

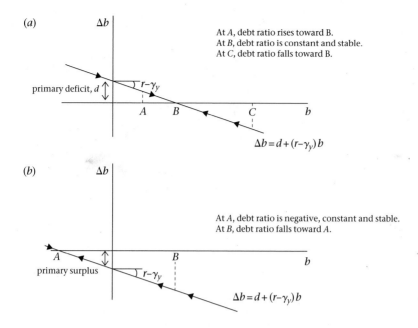

(a)

At A, debt ratio rises toward B.
At B, debt ratio is constant and stable.
At C, debt ratio falls toward B.

$\Delta b = d + (r - \gamma_y)\, b$

(b)

At A, debt ratio is negative, constant and stable.
At B, debt ratio falls toward A.

$\Delta b = d + (r - \gamma_y)\, b$

Figure 6.3 The government debt ratio. Case 2. Growth rate exceeds the real interest rate

Fig. 6.3 illustrates the case in which the growth rate exceeds the interest rate: the phase line has a negative slope. At point A in Fig. 6.3(a), the debt ratio is rising as shown by the arrows to the south-east. But what happens when we observe this economy some time later and the debt ratio has risen to the level shown by point B? As long as the primary deficit and interest and growth rates remain unchanged, the economy will remain at point B. Moreover, unlike point B in Fig. 6.2(b), this debt ratio is *stable*: a slight increase in the debt ratio will put the economy on to the segment with the north-westerly arrows taking it back to the equilibrium (and vice versa). How can we explain this? Let us compare point B in Fig. 6.2(b) with point B in Fig. 6.3(a). In Fig. 6.2(b), the fact that $r > \gamma_y$ means that when there is a small increase in the debt ratio, the interest burden of the debt reinforces the increase in the debt ratio. By contrast in Fig. 6.3(a), the fact that $r < \gamma_y$ means that the increase in the debt is dampened because output grows faster than the interest cost of the debt.

The lower panel of Fig. 6.3 shows the case where a primary surplus characterizes an economy in which the growth rate exceeds the real interest rate. As the diagram shows, such an economy will converge toward a negative debt ratio. The government will be a net holder of private sector financial assets.

We can use the debt diagram to explore some interesting examples. In the first example (Fig. 6.4(a)), the initial situation is one in which there is a primary deficit, the growth rate exceeds the real interest rate, and the debt ratio is declining (at time t, the economy is at point A); we assume the economy suddenly experiences a rise in the interest rate and/or a fall in the growth rate so that $r > \gamma_y$. What happens? The new phase line is shown by the upward-sloping line and the economy jumps from point A to point B. The debt

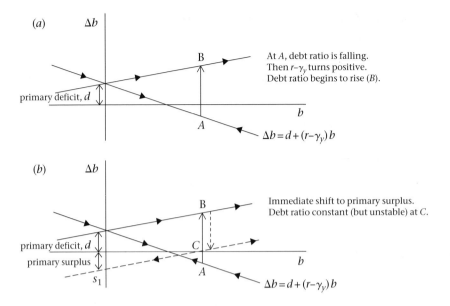

Figure 6.4 Switch from the situation where the growth rate is greater than the real interest rate to the growth rate less than the real interest rate

ratio begins to rise and will rise without limit unless the interest rate, growth rate, or the primary deficit changes.

In the second example (Fig. 6.4(b)), we follow the same economy but this time as soon as the switch in $r - \gamma_y$ occurs, the government immediately tightens fiscal policy so that the primary deficit is replaced by a primary surplus (s_1). This would require a dramatic cut in government spending and/or rise in taxation. If this could be done instantaneously, then the economy would move from point A to point C and the debt ratio would be constant (although unstable).

3.1 The costs of high and rising government debt

In the examples we have discussed, it is clear that the cost of high public debt differs according to whether the interest rate is higher or lower than the growth rate. If the growth rate is higher than the interest rate, then the economy is converging to a stable debt ratio—there is no problem with solvency. The problematic situation is one in which the real interest rate exceeds the growth rate. Although the latter has been typical of the advanced economies in the last twenty years, the former was characteristic of the previous twenty. Table 6.1 provides data for the USA and Germany. It is interesting to note that in the years when the growth rate exceeded the real interest rate, it was nevertheless the case that the real rate of return on capital remained above the growth rate. For the evolution of the debt ratio, it is the relationship between the real growth rate and real interest rate on government debt that matters. In the advanced countries, it is typically the case that

Table 6.1 Growth rates, real interest rates, and real rates of return

	USA			Germany		
	1960s & 1970s	1980s	1990s	1960s & 1970s	1980s	1990s
Growth rate (% p.a.)	3.7	3.2	3.1	3.5	1.4	1.8
Real interest rate (%)	0.9	5.4	4.5	2.7	4.5	4.2
Real profit rate (%)	10.0	7.8	8.6	14.1	8.9	10.3

Notes and sources: OECD, *Historical Statistics* (various years); the real profit rate is for the business sector and calculated for the USA from Bureau of Economic Analysis National Income and Product Accounts and for Germany from the Statistisches Bundesamt, Volkswirtschaftliche Gesamtrechnungen. Prior to 1995, Germany is West Germany.

the real interest rate on government bonds is risk free. This means that it is well below the real rate of return on fixed investment.[8]

As we have seen, with $r > \gamma_y$, a substantial primary surplus may be required to stop the debt ratio rising further and an even larger primary surplus is required to reduce the debt burden. This is likely to create problems for the economy for a number of reasons. Increasing the primary surplus either requires painful cuts in expenditure or politically unpopular increases in taxation. Because of their supply-side effects, increases in taxation are also likely to raise equilibrium unemployment (*PS* shifts down) and to make macro-economic management more difficult. A high level of debt that is rising without limit may trigger concerns that the government may default on its debt. If so, the government will face a higher interest rate on its borrowing to incorporate the premium for default risk. A higher interest rate will in turn feed back to worsen the debt burden as well as dampening investment. In addition, at some point, credit to the government may be cut off. To continue to finance its expenditure the government may resort to monetizing the debt as explained in the next section.

In explaining the mechanics of the debt dynamics, we have assumed that the interest rate and the growth rate are exogenous. However, we have now highlighted the potential feedback from the debt ratio to the interest rate. To see why this matters, let us consider the case of a government operating in the benign regime in which the growth rate exceeds the real interest rate. As we have seen, in this regime, a primary budget deficit is consistent with a stable debt ratio and a larger primary deficit is associated with a larger debt ratio. The higher is the debt ratio, the more vulnerable is the government in the event that the relationship between the growth rate and the real interest rate becomes adverse: it has to undertake a larger fiscal tightening in order to stem the rise in the debt ratio. This possibility may in turn lead to a rise in the risk premium and trigger such an adverse shift. This provides an argument for the government to be concerned about the size of the debt ratio even when there is no immediate threat of an ever-increasing debt ratio because the growth rate is above the real interest rate.

---

[8] As we shall see in Chapter 13, it is the relationship between the real growth rate and the real rate of return on fixed investment that is the focus of attention in discussions of so-called dynamic inefficiency.

The government's intertemporal budget identity can also be interpreted as its solvency constraint and as the requirement for the absence of a default risk on its debt. We begin with equation (6.6), we assume that there is positive government debt (i.e. $b > 0$), and focus on the conditions necessary for the debt ratio not to increase, i.e. for $\Delta b \leq 0$:

$$\text{Since } \Delta b = d + (r - \gamma_y).b,$$

this implies that for $\Delta b \leq 0$,

$$b \leq \frac{-d}{r - \gamma_y}$$

$$\text{i.e. debt/GDP} \leq \frac{\text{primary surplus/GDP}}{(r - \gamma_y)}.$$

In order to interpret the budget constraint in this way, we have to think of each variable in terms of its 'long-run' or 'permanent' value. The equation says that for long-run sustainability, with a given long-run real interest rate in excess of the expected long-run growth rate, there must be a long-run primary surplus if the debt ratio is to be constant. When interpreted in this way, as we shall see in the section on fiscal policy rules below, this equation provides a method for evaluating the sustainability of a fiscal policy programme.

3.2 The costs of fiscal consolidation: cold turkey versus gradualism

In the previous chapter on monetary policy, we discussed the choice facing a government that wishes to reduce the inflation rate. In the presence of lags in the adjustment of wages and prices and/or of inflation expectations, the government faces a trade-off between a rapid fall in inflation accompanied by a period of high unemployment and a more gradual fall in inflation accompanied by a longer period of adjustment but with a lower peak in unemployment. There is a similar trade-off when the government seeks to reduce the debt ratio. The term *fiscal consolidation* is frequently used to refer to the implementation of fiscal policy so as to achieve a sustainable debt ratio. The trade-off between a 'cold turkey' and a 'gradualist' strategy of fiscal consolidation is illustrated in Fig. 6.5.

The economy begins at point A in a situation with an unsustainable debt problem (note that the logic of the argument applies equally to a situation in which the existing debt ratio, although constant, is viewed as 'too high'). Let us suppose that the government wishes to reduce the debt to the level shown by point D. This will be consistent with a *lower* long-run primary surplus because once we achieve the lower debt ratio at D the primary surplus needed to offset the interest burden of the debt is lower. However, the government cannot relax fiscal policy immediately to the long-run primary surplus. If it did so, the debt would grow forever as shown by the arrows to the north-east along the original phase line. Instead, the government must tighten fiscal policy. One strategy would be to raise the primary surplus to s_1: the economy would go from point A to point B and move south-west toward point C. Once the desired debt ratio is reached, the fiscal stance can be shifted (i.e. relaxed) to the long-run position of s_2. This is a strategy for rapid debt reduction—the cost is the sharp tightening of policy initially.

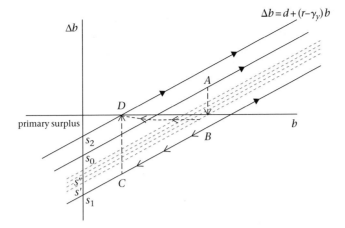

Figure 6.5 Comparison between 'cold turkey' and 'gradualist' strategies to reduce government debt

Note: Cold turkey: *A* to *B* to *C* to *D*—sharp rise in primary surplus to s_1; when debt falls to desired level (*C*), cut surplus to s_2
Gradualist: *A* to *D*—increase in primary surplus to s'; then gradual reduction to s_2.

Alternatively, the government could opt for a more gradual policy, raising the surplus by just enough to get the economy on to a south-westerly path (to s'). After a period of debt reduction, the government could once again adjust the surplus (to s'' and so on toward the long-run value). The process would continue until point *D* was reached. This is a gradualist policy and requires frequent readjustment of the fiscal stance to ease the economy toward the long-run sustainable position. Just as in the discussion of 'cold turkey' versus 'gradualism' in the disinflation strategy choice, the assessment of these alternatives depends on the preference function of the government.

3.3 Can fiscal consolidation be expansionary?

In the discussion of the costs of fiscal consolidation, it has been assumed so far that an increase in the primary budget surplus (i.e. a cut in government expenditure on transfers, consumption or investment and/or a rise in taxation) will have the short-run consequence of reducing the level of output and raising unemployment (because the *IS* curve shifts to the left). Arguments have been developed—partly in response to the experience of fiscal consolidation in the 1980s of a number of European countries—that a contractionary short-run effect may not necessarily occur. The standard prediction would be overturned if the fiscal consolidation has expansionary effects sufficiently strong to outweigh the standard contractionary ones.

Why might fiscal consolidation stimulate aggregate demand? If the economy is already in a state of so-called fiscal stress (an unsustainable fiscal position), then because of the risk premium the interest rate will be higher than it would be otherwise. In addition, in the expectation of some kind of crisis, households may have lowered their estimates of their wealth. A fiscal consolidation that was viewed by the public as credible may boost both investment and consumption by reducing the risk premium and restoring optimism about expected wealth.

Less dramatic arguments may also hold weight. If the government announces a fiscal consolidation plan that is based on cutting government consumption (e.g. the public sector wage bill) rather than cutting government investment or raising taxation, the public may believe that this signals a commitment to fiscal reform. This may lift households' expectations of lifetime wealth because they believe that taxes in the future will be lower. If wealth goes up, then for households that are not liquidity constrained and are therefore able to borrow against their expected future income, their consumption spending should rise. Cutting government expenditure will put downward pressure on the interest rate (over and above any effect from a reduction in the risk premium) and to the extent that the programme is believed to be an enduring one, expected future interest rates will be lower as well. As a result, investment will rise.

The idea that the *composition* rather than simply the size of the fiscal consolidation programme determines its short-run impact is an interesting one. Some empirical support for this is provided in the studies of European fiscal consolidation in the 1980s and 1990s.[9] The arguments centre on the expectational effects of the programmes: cutting government consumption is believed to be more costly in political terms than is either cutting government investment or raising taxes. Hence a government embarking on a consolidation programme based on reductions in consumption may more effectively signal its seriousness about fiscal reform and hence have a stronger effect on expectations in the private sector.

The insights from the imperfect competition macro model highlight the need to take account when analysing the impact of a fiscal consolidation programme of

- the supply-side impact of the consolidation policy,
- the stance of monetary policy, and
- other supply-side policies.

For example consolidation via higher taxes is likely to *raise* equilibrium unemployment (the *PS* curve is shifted downwards) and will lead to a monetary policy tightening under an inflation-targeting central bank. By contrast, a consolidation based on cuts in public sector pay or employment or in benefits is likely to *lower* equilibrium unemployment (the *WS* curve shifts downwards) and permits an easing of monetary policy.

An analysis of the details of fiscal consolidation programmes that were implemented in the 1980s and 1990s suggests that the impact of the programmes on output in the short run was influenced by the balance between expenditure cuts and tax increases in the programmes, the associated stance of monetary policy, and by wage accords. In particular, features of policy in countries observed to have expansionary fiscal consolidations were the following:

- expenditure-based consolidations,
- implementation of a devaluation of the exchange rate, and
- a wage accord at the same time as the consolidation.[10]

---

[9] See, for example, Alesina, Perotti, and Tavares (1998).

[10] See, for example, Alesina and Ardagna (1998). For a recent summary of the evidence, see Briotti (2004).

4 Monetizing the debt: seignorage and hyperinflation

If the government has high debt and wishes to continue to maintain or expand its expenditure, how can it do this if it cannot borrow more because the high risk of the government defaulting makes the public unwilling to lend and it is unwilling or unable to raise taxes? This leads us to consider the use of monetary financing of government expenditure.

In this section, we shall explore:

- the medium-run implications of the monetary financing of government expenditure;
- the connection between monetary financing, inflation, the inflation tax, and seignorage;
- the limits to how much seignorage can be collected and what may account for hyperinflation where inflation goes above the rate that would maximize the government's seignorage revenue.

To pursue these questions, we go back to the general form of the government's budget constraint in which the use of high powered money is an alternative source of finance to bonds:

$$\underbrace{G}_{\text{govt. exp.}} + \underbrace{iB}_{\text{int. payments}} \equiv \underbrace{T}_{\text{tax rev.}} + \underbrace{\Delta B}_{\text{new bonds}} + \underbrace{\Delta H}_{\text{new high-powered money}},$$

where H is high-powered money, and broad money, M, is: $M = \kappa.H$, where κ (kappa) is the banking (or monetary base) multiplier. (See the Appendix to Chapter 8 for the derivation of the banking (or monetary base) multiplier.) It is straightforward to modify the earlier analysis to include money finance:

$$\Delta B \equiv (G - T) + iB - \Delta H$$

and dividing through (as before) by nominal GDP, we have:

$$\frac{\Delta B}{Py} = \frac{G - T}{Py} + \frac{iB}{Py} - \frac{\Delta H}{Py}$$

$$= d + ib - \frac{\Delta H}{H} \cdot \frac{H}{Py} \tag{6.7}$$

$$= d + ib - \gamma_H h, \tag{6.8}$$

where γ_H is the growth rate of high powered money and h is the ratio of high powered money to nominal GDP ($\frac{H}{Py}$). Following the same steps as in section 3, we derive the expression for the change in the debt ratio:

$$\Delta b = d + (i - \pi - \gamma_y)b - \gamma_H h$$

$$= d + (r - \gamma_y)b - \gamma_H h. \tag{6.9}$$

We can see from equation (6.9) that the growth of the debt to GDP ratio will be reduced to the extent that the deficit is being financed by new money creation.

Let us look more closely at the term $\gamma_H \cdot h$. We know that when the economy is in medium-run equilibrium, the growth rate of the money supply is equal to the rate of inflation, and assuming the banking multiplier κ is constant, we have: $\gamma_M = \gamma_H = \pi$. Higher inflation will reduce the growth of the debt ratio—assuming that h remains constant. This has led to the use of the term *inflation tax* to refer to this method of financing government expenditure. It takes us to the closely related term *seignorage revenues*, which is used to refer to the amount of real expenditure the government is able to finance through its ability to create high powered money. Seignorage revenue is therefore,

$$
\begin{aligned}
S &= \frac{\Delta H}{P} \\
&= \frac{\Delta H}{H} \cdot \frac{H}{P} \\
&= \gamma_H \cdot \frac{H}{P}.
\end{aligned}
\tag{6.10}
$$

In medium-run equilibrium,
$$
S = \pi \cdot \frac{H}{P}.
\tag{6.11}
$$

As a proportion of real GDP, seignorage is

$$
\frac{S}{y} = \gamma_H \cdot h,
$$

which is the final term in the equation for the change in the debt ratio in equation (6.9).

The definition of seignorage suggests that the government can finance more of its expenditure through seignorage by raising the growth rate of the money supply and hence by raising inflation.[11] We have already seen in Chapter 5 that high and rising inflation imposes costs on the economy. We shall now see that there is a limit to the extent to which seignorage can be used as a source of revenue (and as a method of reducing the debt ratio). The limit arises because as inflation goes up, the public becomes less willing to hold money. Recall the condition for equilibrium in the money market:

$$
\text{money supply} = \text{money demand}
$$

$$
\left(\frac{M}{P}\right)^S = \left(\frac{M}{P}\right)^D
\tag{6.12}
$$

$$
= L(i, y)
\tag{6.13}
$$

$$
= L(r + \pi, y).
\tag{6.14}
$$

When the growth rate of the money supply and hence inflation are low, the demand for real money balances is high and when inflation is high, the demand for real money

---

[11] The relationship between average inflation, the growth rate of the money supply, seignorage revenue as a percentage of GDP, and the average budget deficit for high and low inflation countries is illustrated in Figure 1, Fischer, Sahay, and Végh (2002: 847).

balances is low: i.e. an increase in inflation *reduces* the demand for real money balances. If we now substitute the demand for money into the seignorage expression, we have:

$$S = \pi \cdot \frac{H}{P}$$
$$= \pi \cdot \frac{M}{P} \cdot \frac{1}{\kappa}. \tag{6.15}$$

Whilst higher money growth (and inflation) pushes up seignorage via the first term in equation (6.15) (π), it pushes it down via the second term ($\frac{M}{P} \cdot \frac{1}{\kappa}$). To use the tax analogy, pushing up the rate of taxation (in this case, π) has the effect of reducing the tax base (in this case, real money balances demanded, $\frac{M}{P}$, assuming κ is constant). Empirical studies suggest that the second effect begins to outweigh the first effect when inflation rates go higher than about 200% p.a.; this suggests that the maximum amount of revenue the government could raise this way would be about 10% of GDP.[12] These estimates indicate that governments typically curtail their use of seignorage not because they are near the maximum amount that can be collected but rather because the costs of higher inflation outweigh the benefits.

To complete the discussion of seignorage, we turn to the phenomenon of hyperinflation. Hyperinflation is usually defined as a situation in which the inflation rate is in excess of 50% *per month*. Our discussion so far does not answer the question of why inflation rates this high should occur. If very high inflation is driven by the government's need to finance its expenditure, why should inflation rise above the rate at which the maximum seignorage can be collected? One answer is that the seignorage equation holds in equilibrium. Hence if it takes time for people to adjust their demand for money to inflation (i.e. L reacts to π slowly), the government can always push up its revenue by raising the growth rate of the money supply fast enough. This mechanism lies behind a famous theory of hyperinflation developed by Phillip Cagan.[13]

5 Fiscal policy rules

In thinking about fiscal policy rules, a useful place to begin is with the government's intertemporal budget constraint and the associated solvency condition that we have set out in the earlier section.[14] To go from this to a rule for government policy, the first step is to recognize that a prudent fiscal policy is one in which the government is solvent based on long-run or 'permanent' values of the relevant variables. We shall then be able to examine how deviations from such permanent values due to (*a*) cyclical fluctuations and (*b*) structural changes to government expenditure (such as future government pension liabilities or long-term public investment programmes) can be handled by a fiscal rule.

Once the characteristics of this prudent fiscal policy rule (PFPR) are clear, it is possible to compare it with already existing fiscal policy rules. Widely discussed existing policy rules are the so-called Golden Rule introduced by the UK government, and the rules

---

[12] See, for example, the analysis in Fischer, Sahay, and Végh (2002).   [13] Cagan (1956).

[14] This discussion of fiscal rules relies heavily on the work of Willem Buiter. See for example Buiter (2001) and Buiter and Grafe (2004).

incorporated in the Stability and Growth Pact of the European Union. As we shall see, such existing fiscal policy rules are not necessarily consistent with the PFPR. This has potentially serious consequences for the countries in which the rules have been introduced—we set out examples of circumstances in which the application of existing policy rules are likely to have damaging effects. In the final subsection, we turn to the question: if existing fiscal policy rules are not consistent with prudent government behaviour, why have they been implemented? A common answer to this question refers to the tendency of governments to run 'excessive' budget deficits.

5.1 From budget constraint to prudent fiscal policy rule (PFPR)

It is useful to restate the government's budget constraint in terms of the change in the debt to GDP ratio focusing first on the role of the real interest rate (6.17) and then on the role of the nominal interest rate and the rate of inflation (6.19):

$$\Delta b = d + (r - \gamma_y)b \tag{6.16}$$
$$= (g/y - t/y) + (r - \gamma_y)b \tag{6.17}$$
$$\Delta b = d + (i - \pi - \gamma_y)b \tag{6.18}$$
$$= (d + ib) - (\pi + \gamma_y)b. \tag{6.19}$$

Given the pre-existing level of the debt ratio, b, the second form (6.19) highlights the fact that the debt ratio is raised by the actual deficit $(d + ib)$ and reduced by the growth of nominal GDP $((\pi + \gamma_y)b)$. The first form (6.17) highlights the fundamental determinants of the change in the debt ratio as the primary deficit (d) and the difference between the real interest rate and the real growth rate $((r - \gamma_y)b)$. It is also useful to write (6.19) in terms of the actual deficit:

$$\frac{\text{deficit}}{\text{GDP}} = (d + ib) = \Delta b + (\pi + \gamma_y)b. \tag{6.20}$$

Deriving a rule for prudent fiscal policy begins from the condition $\Delta b \leq 0$ for the debt ratio not to increase. This implies:

$$b \leq \frac{(t/y)^P - (g/y)^P}{r^P - \gamma_y^P}, \tag{6.21}$$

where the superscript P refers to the long-run or 'permanent' value. Let us assume that there is a given public expenditure programme that entails a long-run ratio of government expenditure to GDP, $(g/y)^P$. The question is how should this best be financed? For the debt ratio not to increase, rewriting (6.21) implies:

$$(t/y)^P \geq (g/y)^P + (r^P - \gamma_y^P).b.$$

A prudent fiscal rule is to set the share of tax in GDP at a constant level equal to the 'permanent' or long-run level required to satisfy the constraint:

$$\overline{(t/y)} = (t/y)^P \geq (g/y)^P + (r^P - \gamma_y^P)b. \qquad \text{(Prudent Fiscal Policy Rule)}$$

Substituting the PFPR into (6.17) implies that the debt ratio moves as follows:

$$\Delta b \leq (g/y - (g/y)^P) + [(r - r^P) - (\gamma_y - \gamma_y^P)]b. \tag{6.22}$$

Before going back to the rationale for picking a *constant* tax share as the basis of the rule, let us explain how it works. Sticking to the rule ensures solvency—although it relies on the government making public its forecasts about the real interest rate and growth rate and about expenditure programmes well into the future. The rule implies that if government expenditure is *temporarily* above its permanent level, borrowing should finance this—this entails a rise in the debt ratio and is consistent with the rule. This would be the case if there is a recession so that government transfers are higher than normal (i.e. the automatic stabilizers are working) and if the government uses discretionary fiscal policy to promote the return of the economy to equilibrium employment. It would also be the case if a major programme of exceptional government infrastructure investment is planned that would take government spending as a share of GDP above its long-run level for many years (or decades). An example of this might be the investment requirements associated with German unification. If the real interest rate is confidently known to be temporarily higher than its 'permanent' value or if growth is depressed relative to its long-run value, the rule says that the deficit can safely be allowed to widen (and the debt ratio to rise). Equally, the rule says that an expected rise in *permanent* government spending, for example, as a consequence of long-run government pension obligations must be funded by a rise in taxation.

5.2 How the PFPR deals with stabilization and structural problems

We shall look in turn in a little more detail at the stabilization and structural aspects of the government's fiscal policy.

5.2.1 Stabilization

What does the PFPR imply about the balance between the use of automatic stabilizers and discretionary fiscal policy? The rule implies that whilst the government's expenditure share can be expected to rise above its long-run level in cyclical downturns, this must be reversed in upswings. Averaged over the cycle, there is no case for a divergence between g/y and $(g/y)^P$. Assuming there is no other reason (such as structural policy discussed below) for a divergence between g/y and $(g/y)^P$, the implication is that the prudent cyclically adjusted primary budget deficit will depend on the pre-existing debt ratio and on the difference between the real interest rate and the growth rate (6.21). For example, if the existing debt ratio is 0.6 and the real interest rate exceeds the growth rate by 2.4%, then the PFPR says that the cyclically adjusted primary budget surplus should be at least 1.4% of GDP (since $0.6 \times 0.024 = 0.0144$). This counsels against the use of *discretionary* fiscal policy to the extent that there is no built-in mechanism for reversing it.

We can link this discussion with that in section 1 above. In introducing the concepts of the actual and the cyclically adjusted budget balance, the exercise was one of decomposing the observed budget deficit into the part due to the operation of the automatic stabilizers ($a(y_e - y_t)$) and the deficit that would characterize the economy when output was at the equilibrium. If, as has traditionally been the case, the automatic stabilizers are considered fixed by other *non-stabilization* policy objectives, then although they play a background stabilization role, the centre of attention is on the use of discretionary policy to stabilize output in the face of shocks. But another way of thinking about equation (6.1):

$$g(y_t) - t(y_t) \equiv [g(y_e) - t(y_e)] + a(y_e - y_t)$$

is as a rule for fiscal policy.[15] From this perspective, if the government's aim is to stabilize output at y_e with the budget in balance, it should calibrate the operation of the automatic stabilizers by choosing 'a' to achieve this objective. For example, if the government is having to use discretionary policy routinely in a cyclical context for stabilization, it could consider increasing the responsiveness of the automatic stabilizers by raising a.

Intuitively, the burden on fiscal policy to contribute to stabilization should depend on the role that monetary policy is playing. In the case where the national government does not have access to monetary policy, fiscal policy as a stabilization tool is potentially more important. This could be the case in a common currency area (and more generally under a fixed exchange rate regime) or when monetary policy is impotent (e.g. because the nominal interest rate is zero). We shall see below how the introduction of fiscal rules such as those in the EU's Stability and Growth Pact can interfere with the appropriate use of fiscal policy for stabilization.

5.2.2 Structural fiscal policy

Unlike monetary policy, fiscal policy relates not only to the cycle but to government expenditure programmes with effects lasting for decades. The government may wish to introduce (or may inherit) structural policies whose effects may not be 'permanent' despite extending over many business cycles. Other policies may be of indefinite duration, and should therefore be considered permanent. In the first category, one could think of a programme to renew the infrastructure of the economy (e.g. improving the railways after decades of neglect in the UK or communications infrastructure in East Germany in the wake of unification). According to the PFPR, since the current level of spending (as a share of GDP) is above its long-run level (i.e. $g/y > (g/y)^P$), a higher level of borrowing is called for to finance this. A different example is the case in which the government is committed to pay pensions into the indefinite future for its ageing population. This entails a higher level of permanent expenditure than is the case at present (i.e. $(g/y)^P > g/y$) and according to the PFPR, the tax share should be raised now to its higher long-run level. Alternatively, if the government does not wish to raise the tax share, the PFPR indicates that it should introduce changes in policy so as to reduce $(g/y)^P$ such as raising the retirement age or reducing the future retirement benefits (e.g. when the pension entitlement is defined as a proportion of final salary).

5.2.3 Why a constant share of taxation?

Why establish the PFPR rule in terms of a constant tax share? As we have seen, the rule has desirable properties in terms of allowing for stabilization over the cycle and

---

[15] Taylor (1997) discusses fiscal rules from this perspective.

in providing a clear method of analysing the financing of government investment or transfer programmes that have a structural rather than a cyclical time profile. An explicit rationale for a constant tax share is provided by applying to government a similar logic as applies to households in smoothing their consumption. If, as is usual, it is assumed that the distortions from raising taxes increase with the amount raised—i.e. there is an increasing marginal distortion cost—then, by analogy with the diminishing marginal utility of consumption, the optimal way for the government to behave is to smooth its tax revenue collection over time. Just as the rational household consumes a constant amount each period, smoothing consumption by borrowing and saving, the rational government taxes a constant amount each period and borrows and saves in response to temporary and/or unforeseen fluctuations in expenditure (due to the business cycle, wars, natural disasters, etc.).

5.3 Comparing existing fiscal rules with the PFPR

Existing fiscal rules tend to be expressed in terms of the *actual deficit* or the *cyclically adjusted deficit*. In order to compare the PFPR with existing rules, it is helpful to express the government budget constraint in the form (6.20):

$$\text{deficit/GDP} \; = \; (d + ib) = \Delta b + (\pi + \gamma_y)b.$$

We can then rewrite the PFPR (in terms of its implications for the deficit to GDP ratio) by substituting this into (6.22) and rearranging:

$$\text{deficit/GDP} \; \leq \; \left(g/y - (g/y)^P\right) + \left[(r - r^P) - (\gamma_y - \gamma_y^P)\right] b + (\pi + \gamma_y).b.$$

This form of the PFPR brings out the fact that a higher deficit ratio is compatible with solvency if the growth rate of nominal GDP (i.e. $\pi + \gamma_y$) is higher.

We are now in a position to compare this with existing rules. We shall not investigate the reasons for the adoption of the rules at this point.

5.3.1 Stability and Growth Pact (European Union)

The Stability and Growth Pact of the European Union contains two rules: that the budget deficit to GDP ratio must be less than 3% and the cyclically adjusted deficit ratio should be in balance or in surplus. We can write these as:

$$\text{deficit/GDP} \; \leq 0.03 \tag{6.23}$$

$$\text{cyclically adjusted deficit/GDP} \; \leq 0. \tag{6.24}$$

The first rule places a rigid limit on the deficit ratio and hence on the scope for fiscal stabilization. However, the PFPR indicates that there is no economic reason for the deficit limit to be a fixed number. If the rise in g/y above $(g/y)^P$ in a deep recession is sufficient to push the deficit ratio consistent with the PFPR above 3%, the 3% fiscal rule of the Stability and Growth Pact will prevent the appropriate stabilization. Appropriate stabilization will be prevented even if the rise in the deficit is entirely due to the working of the automatic stabilizers (i.e. even if the cyclically adjusted deficit is zero).

The second rule places a rigid limit on the extent to which fiscal policy can be used for structural purposes. As long as a government investment programme is worthwhile in the sense that the discounted present value of the expected social benefits exceeds the expected social costs, then consistent with the PFPR, current government spending may be above its permanent level ($g/y > (g/y)^P$), and the cyclically adjusted deficit will rise. This is forbidden by the second rule of the Stability and Growth Pact.

5.3.2 Golden Rule (e.g. UK)

The so-called Golden Rule of fiscal policy states that the cyclically adjusted deficit ratio must be no larger than is required to finance government investment spending (as a share of GDP):

$$\text{cyclically adjusted deficit/GDP} \leq \frac{\widetilde{g^I}}{y},$$

where the tilde symbol ($\sim$) indicates 'cyclically adjusted' and g^I is government investment spending. This rule is less restrictive than the Stability and Growth Pact for two reasons: first, since it only refers to the cyclically adjusted deficit ratio, it does not interfere with the operation of the automatic stabilizers, and second, it allows more scope for structural fiscal policy.

However the Golden Rule is not well designed if its objective is to keep the debt ratio low. It can condone borrowing to finance government investment programmes that a prudent fiscal policy would not and it can also forbid borrowing when it should be permitted. The logic behind the Golden Rule is that the salient difference between consumption and investment is that investment provides a rate of return in the future: since investment bears a return, this justifies borrowing to finance it. The problem with this argument is that it fails to distinguish between investment programmes that do and do not bring in a *cash* return to the government.

It is important to first make clear that the decision about whether the government should go ahead with an investment project depends on the comparison between the cost and the social rate of return on the project. The social rate of return can be decomposed into private returns and external returns; it can also be decomposed along a different dimension into cash returns and non-cash returns. The decision to undertake the project is independent of the question of how it should be financed. But once a project is approved, its characteristics in terms of the cash and non-cash components of the return become relevant to the issue of whether it should be financed by taxation or by borrowing. A project that will not bring cash returns is, from the perspective of prudent fiscal policy, equivalent to consumption spending by the government and should be financed by a rise in taxation. The PFPR only approves higher borrowing to finance the investment project if the cash rate of return (in real terms) is at least equal to the real interest rate.

5.4 The logic of existing rules

In trying to pin down and assess the arguments that have been used to support the introduction of the existing fiscal rules, it is helpful to separate the arguments that relate to a monetary union in which there are multiple fiscal authorities (and a single monetary authority) and those that relate to the standard situation of a single fiscal and single monetary authority.

5.4.1 Single fiscal authority and a single monetary authority

With a single fiscal and monetary authority, if the government seeks to maintain output above the equilibrium, it can, as we have seen, do so by using a balanced budget expansion. Nevertheless, the government may find it convenient to use deficit finance. If the risk of default increases through such a process, then the central bank may feel compelled to defuse this risk by monetizing the debt. The central bank relaxes monetary policy, this allows the government to pursue a fiscal policy that it could otherwise not finance. The revenue comes from 'seignorage' or the so-called inflation tax and has the effect of reducing the real value of the government's outstanding debt.

5.4.2 Multiple fiscal authorities and a single monetary authority

Behind the fiscal rules of the Maastricht Treaty and the Stability and Growth Pact of the European Union lies the concern that *cross-border externalities* may lead to fiscal irresponsibility. How could fiscal irresponsibility in one country 'contaminate' the other members of the common currency area? If one country increases its risk of default through running imprudent fiscal policies, the market would place a risk premium on its debt and eventually the country would find itself unable to borrow. Why is this of any concern to other countries? If the other countries were obliged to 'bail out' a member state facing default, then the higher risk premium would spread to them. But there is no clear reason why such a bail-out would be undertaken (or expected). The EU institutions themselves are forbidden by treaty from bailing out a member state.

It has also been suggested that an increase in the risk of default of one member country could lead via a 'contagion' effect to an increase in the risk premium in other members, even though there was no change in the fiscal sustainability position of the other countries. However, there seems to be little evidence that such contagion effects exist.

If the many countries in a currency union face a single inflation-targeting central bank, then by pursuing a fiscal policy that would raise its own inflation rate, a country will face a less harsh monetary response than it would do if its own central bank were using inflation targeting. Meanwhile the other members face a tighter monetary policy than they otherwise would because of the response by the union's central bank to the rise in union-wide inflation stemming from the single fiscal expansion. This is a 'cross-border' externality and in principle provides a rationale for placing constraints on national fiscal policy. But thought of more broadly, this argument is really about the need to coordinate fiscal and monetary policy in a monetary union, rather than to impose arbitrary fiscal rules. To see this, think of an alternative scenario.

Suppose there is a common negative demand shock to the union. The union's monetary policy rule will suggest a relaxation of monetary policy. But a relaxation of fiscal policy may also be needed (e.g. if the nominal interest rate is already very low). For any individual member, a relaxation of fiscal policy will (*a*) boost their deficit and heighten the risk of exceeding the permitted deficit and (*b*) will spread across the borders of other members, lessening the need for them to take such a fiscal action. This combination will lead to under-stabilization in the face of such a shock.

6 Conclusions

In this chapter, we have identified the role played by the automatic fiscal stabilizers in the economy. The presence of the automatic stabilizers dampens the impact on output of shocks to aggregate demand. Changes in the primary budget deficit can be decomposed into those due to

- the operation of the automatic stabilizers and
- the use of discretionary fiscal policy.

The cyclically adjusted budget deficit measures the discretionary fiscal impulse.

The short-run impact of fiscal policy depends on the contribution of taxation and expenditure and on how any expenditure increase is financed. It also depends on whether the change in fiscal stance is viewed as temporary or permanent. The concept of the balanced budget multiplier highlights the fact that a fully tax financed expansion can raise output. In the standard analysis, a bond financed increase in government expenditure raises output in the short run by more than does a tax financed expansion. However, if households' consumption behaviour is forward looking and based on their permanent income, there may be little difference between tax and bond financed expenditure programmes. Ricardian equivalence refers to the case where the two are identical because households take full account of the future tax obligations associated with the issue of new bonds.

From the definition of the government's budget constraint, the determinants of its solvency can be identified. The key determinants of solvency are

- the ratio of the primary deficit to GDP,
- the real interest rate,
- the real growth rate, and
- the existing debt ratio.

If the real interest rate exceeds the growth rate, a primary deficit is associated with an ever-increasing debt ratio. On the other hand, if the growth rate is above the real interest rate, a primary deficit is consistent with a constant and stable debt ratio. However, since a high debt ratio makes a government more vulnerable should the relationship between the interest rate and the growth rate turn adverse, a high debt ratio can itself push the interest rate up making an unstable debt path more likely. A government that finds itself on an unsustainable debt path faces unpleasant choices in stabilizing it. However, a fiscal consolidation programme is not necessarily contractionary: the composition of the programme appears to matter, along with the seriousness of the initial 'fiscal stress' and the complementary policies introduced.

If the government has access to high powered money creation by the central bank (seignorage), it can finance increased expenditure through the so-called inflation tax. The amount of seignorage raised depends on the inflation rate and the real demand for money. However, as inflation rises to high rates (about 200% per year), the demand for money declines by so much that total seignorage revenues fall. The costs of high and rising inflation are sufficiently high that inflation rates are normally kept well below this seignorage-maximizing level.

From the requirements for solvency of the government, a prudent fiscal policy rule can be derived. Such a rule can be expressed in terms of the constant tax share of GDP that ensures solvency. The rule allows for fiscal policy to be used for both stabilization and structural purposes. A constant tax share reduces distortions by smoothing, as the government saves or borrows in the face of unforeseen or temporary fluctuations in expenditure. The prudent fiscal policy rule requires transparency about the government's expenditure plans and its assumptions about the real interest rate and the growth rate. The PFPR provides a benchmark against which other fiscal rules introduced by governments can be evaluated.

■ QUESTIONS

Checklist questions

(1) What are the automatic stabilizers? How could the method of local government taxation affect the automatic stabilizers?

(2) Explain the logic of the balanced budget multiplier result. Investigate whether this result continues to hold if

   (a) the money supply is kept constant (rather than the interest rate);

   (b) there is a proportional income tax (rather than a lump sum tax).

(3) What is meant by the cyclically adjusted budget deficit? How can it be calculated? Why is it conceptually equivalent to the discretionary fiscal impulse? Is such a deficit sustainable?

(4) Assuming that households consider bonds to be net wealth, why does bond financing of government expenditure shift the *IS* curve further to the right than would otherwise be the case? Why does the *LM* curve shift to the left?

(5) What is meant by Ricardian equivalence? Does it imply that high public debt is no cause for concern? How would you test for its existence?

(6) Is the view that automatic stabilizers are effective consistent with the view that discretionary fiscal policy is not?

(7) Countries have traditionally borrowed to finance war expenditure. Is this justified by economic reasoning?

(8) Why is the *level* of the government debt ratio of any concern?

(9) Explain in words what is meant by the prudent fiscal policy rule. What is the main reason for 'tax smoothing'? Under this rule, how should a government react in the following scenarios:

    (*a*) defence spending is cut for the foreseeable future due to the end of the Cold War;

    (*b*) the government compensates farmers following a disease outbreak;

    (*c*) the Treasury releases a report forecasting that the cost of the tax-funded health service will treble within twenty years;

    (*d*) the government decides to contribute troops to a war that it expects to be over in a matter of weeks.

(10) 'The Golden Rule is attractive because although it has some drawbacks, it is superior to an arbitrary x% deficit rule on economic grounds and is easy to explain to the public and to monitor.' Assess this statement.

Problems and questions for discussion

QUESTION A. What role does seignorage play in creating and sustaining high inflation? Can you provide an explanation for why a rational government would allow high inflation? What about hyperinflation?

QUESTION B. Under what circumstances might policy makers wish to reduce the ratio of public debt to GDP? What factors should influence the policy adopted to achieve such a reduction.

QUESTION C. Should fiscal policy be delegated to an independent authority? If so, should it be the same body that sets monetary policy? Discuss.

QUESTION D. Begin with the scenario in Fig. 6.4(*a*). Following the shift to an explosive debt path, assume that the debt ratio has risen further before the government reacts. If its objective is to return the debt ratio to its initial level, explain using a diagram how it could achieve this by using fiscal policy.

QUESTION E. What light does the analysis of debt dynamics and the prudent fiscal policy rule throw on the question of the appropriateness of common fiscal targets for the transition countries that have just joined the EU and other members?

QUESTION F. A study by the credit rating agency Standard and Poors entitled 'In the end we are all debt: aging societies and sovereign ratings' published in 2005 stated: 'Notwithstanding the reform flurry of late, without further adjustment either to the current fiscal stance or to social security and health care costs, the general government debt-to-GDP ratios of France, Germany, and the U.S. will surpass the 200% of GDP mark by the middle of the current century, resulting in deficits that will be more akin to those currently associated with speculative-grade sovereigns [from the current rating of AAA to below BBB–]. Indeed, other factors being equal, sovereign ratings could begin to fall from their current levels early in the next decade.' Explain the logic of this prediction. Discuss the policy changes that are required.

PART TWO

Consumption, Investment, and Money

7 Consumption and Investment

The aim of this chapter is to look in more depth at two of the key components of the *IS* equation—consumption and investment behaviour. In the *IS* equation used so far, there is a simple linear Keynesian consumption function in which consumption depends on current income. More precisely, consumption is taken as having a constant positive component, which we have called 'autonomous consumption' and have assumed to be an exogenous constant up to now, and increases linearly with income with a marginal propensity to consume of less than one. The marginal propensity to consume provides the crucial ingredient of the multiplier process through which aggregate demand shocks or changes in government spending are transmitted to the level of output and employment in the short run. In the traditional model, the multiplier is greater than one so aggregate demand shocks are amplified. In introducing the investment function in Chapter 2, we used a linear function in which there is a positive 'autonomous' component combined with a negative dependence of investment on the real interest rate. We emphasized that changes in profit expectations or sentiment—sometimes referred to as 'animal spirits'—will shift the investment function by changing the autonomous component.

In this chapter, we show how consumption and investment functions can be derived from the analysis of the optimizing behaviour of households and firms. Examples of the former are consumption functions based on the permanent income hypothesis or the closely related life-cycle hypothesis. We shall see that there is a clear contrast between the predictions of the consumption function we have used up to now and a consumption function derived from a simple model of optimizing behaviour: in the Keynesian consumption function, current income determines consumption whereas in the simple permanent income hypothesis (PIH) consumption function, only 'permanent' income matters. To see where this difference comes from let us make some assumptions about how an individual or household behaves. It is usually assumed that people prefer a smooth pattern of consumption to one that jumps about from year to year. Let us also assume that they are very far-sighted and have clear vision in the sense that there is no uncertainty about their future prospects and that they are able to borrow on the same terms that they can lend. On the basis of this set of assumptions, the individual will be able to maximize her utility and enjoy a smooth flow of consumption over her life, which we can refer to as 'lifetime' or 'permanent' consumption. In the early years, she will typically borrow to sustain the lifetime consumption level. Later on, she will save so as to repay the early accumulation of debt and to fund the continuation of the lifetime consumption level after retirement. In addition to this broad pattern of borrowing, saving, and dissaving across the life cycle, the ability to borrow also means that any unexpected shocks to income will not affect consumption.

We explain how a consumption function based on the simple permanent income hypothesis can be derived and look at how well it matches reality. We shall see that it is necessary to relax some of the assumptions made to derive the simple PIH in order to account for the empirical behaviour of consumption expenditure: the importance of uncertainty about future income and the limited access that households have to financial markets in order to borrow is highlighted. Both factors mean that current income will play some role in explaining current consumption. This provides the basis for bringing together the conclusions on modelling consumption.

The second part of the chapter conducts a similar exercise for investment. The idea of a manager calculating the net present value of an investment project was introduced in Chapter 2. In this chapter, the determinants of investment are explored in more detail. We show how a commonly used investment function—the 'Q model'—can be derived in a world of perfect competition and how both the Q model and another commonly used model, the 'accelerator', can be seen as special cases of an imperfect competition investment function. When we look at how well such investment functions match reality, we find that limits on the ability of firms to borrow due to imperfections in the capital market are important—just as liquidity constraints are important for understanding consumption behaviour.

The chapter concludes by looking first at how incorporating forward-looking behaviour in the *IS* curve affects the way the *IS-PC-MR* model works. Secondly, it illustrates how some of the insights of the chapter can be used to interpret a real-world example and to provide predictions about the implications for consumption and investment behaviour of the 'New Economy' in the USA in the 1990s.

1 Consumption

1.1 Introducing intertemporal smoothing in consumption behaviour

In macroeconomics 'consumption' refers to spending by the household sector on durable and non-durable goods and on services. It does not include the purchase of new housing (which is part of 'investment') but includes the imputed services from housing. Spending on non-durable goods and on services comprises about 70% of UK consumption with the balance roughly evenly split between durables and housing. Consumer expenditure makes up about one-half of total final expenditure on goods and services in the economy. Its heavy weight in the aggregate economy suggests that it is important to understand the forces that lie behind changes in consumption. Interest in consumption behaviour has sharpened in recent years because of strong swings in consumer spending as a share of disposable income in a number of countries. In the UK and several Scandinavian countries there were pronounced boom-to-bust cycles in consumption in the 1980s and 1990s. The savings ratio in both the USA and the UK fell to historically low levels at the turn of the twenty-first century.

Consider first a consumption function with constant autonomous consumption (so $c_0 = \bar{c}$), as discussed in the standard IS/LM model presented in Chapter 2. We shall refer to this as a 'Keynesian consumption function':

$$c = \bar{c} + c_y(y - t). \qquad \text{(Keynesian consumption function)}$$

If we take autonomous consumption as given, we should expect two important things:

(1) aggregate consumption is volatile rather than smooth because any change in current income is reflected in a change in consumption in the Keynesian consumption function.

(2) there should be no difference between the effect on consumption of transitory changes in personal income and permanent changes. In the simple Keynesian consumption function, the change in consumption is predicted by the change in measured income irrespective of whether it is expected to be temporary or permanent.

But such predictions seem too extreme. They seem extreme for three reasons—the first has to do with the preferences of consumers, the second relates to the ability of people to look ahead and form a view about their future income prospects and the third hinges on the ability of people to borrow. Alternative views of consumption taking these factors into account were proposed in the so-called permanent income hypothesis (PIH) by Milton Friedman in 1957 and in the closely related life-cycle hypothesis (LCH) (by Franco Modigliani and Richard Brumberg in 1954). They suggested that consumption was a function not of measured income as in the Keynesian consumption function but of average or expected income or of the value of lifetime resources.

Another way to express this is to say that consumption depends on perceived ongoing wealth, not on the income of the moment. Think, for example, of a final year law student who has landed a training contract with a law firm and compare him with a final year philosophy student who has no clear plans for future employment. We assume that both students have the same current income (and existing debts) and are in all other respects identical. In particular, we assume that they have the same preferences. We would probably expect the law student to have a higher level of consumption than the philosophy student for two reasons. The law student will have a much clearer idea of his earnings over the years ahead and the law student is more likely to be able to borrow to sustain higher current consumption.

In both the PIH and the LCH, the emphasis was firstly on the use of saving and dissaving to even out the fluctuations in measured income in order to produce a much smoother flow of consumption and second, on the unresponsiveness of consumption to income changes that were perceived to be transitory. The LCH model starts from the insight that over most people's adult lives their incomes will follow a reasonably predictable pattern. When they are young they will be starting out in their jobs, be relatively unproductive because of their inexperience, and hence be able to command relatively low salaries. At some point in middle age most people reach their productivity and income peaks, which then decline slightly until they retire, at which point their incomes become much lower. Thus incomes rise from youth to middle age, then fall to very low levels in old age. But typically people's consumption is not expected to vary so dramatically (in contrast to prediction 1 above). People use their ability to borrow and save to *smooth* consumption. When they are young they borrow (say for mortgages or car loans) and pay off these debts as their income rises. When they are middle-aged, they save money which they then use to support themselves in retirement. This consumption smoothing is not predicted by the Keynesian consumption function.

The PIH also focuses on consumption smoothing, but has a slightly different kind of scenario in mind. Consider a recession, in which autonomous investment falls (we shall consider why this might happen below), leading to lower income. For example, some people might lose their jobs. The Keynesian consumption function predicts that consumption will fall as well as income, since they are related. But suppose that the recession is expected only to be temporary and that everyone expects to find new jobs quickly, which are as well paid as those before. Then it would seem undesirable to cut consumption dramatically only to raise it again a few weeks or months later. Why not, instead, just sustain consumption by borrowing a little while unemployed, then pay it back once a new job is found? What counts for how much we want to consume, according to the PIH, is not the income we earn at any one moment, but, rather, the average income we *expect* to be earning in any time period, because it is this *average* expected income that truly determines the resources we have available for consumption (since we have the possibility of saving and borrowing). This average income is referred to as 'permanent income'.

According to the PIH, then, if income falls in a recession, we would not necessarily expect consumption to fall along with it, unless people's expectations of ongoing future income have fallen as well. On the other hand, even if income does not change, if something happens to change people's expectations about future wages (say) we would expect consumption to change. In general terms, the discovery of any new information which leads to a changed assessment of permanent income can lead to a change in consumption:

$$\text{news} \longrightarrow \Delta\text{permanent income} \longrightarrow \Delta\text{consumption}.$$

In both the LCH and PIH consumption smoothing and average incomes rather than transitory incomes are important. Hereafter we shall focus on the simpler PIH model. The LCH produces qualitatively similar results.

We have already seen in the discussion of fiscal policy in Chapter 6 one important example of the difference the PIH model makes to macroeconomic policy: its predictions about the effect of running a budget deficit funded by bonds. In the standard analysis with a Keynesian consumption function, a deficit-funded increase in government spending has a bigger effect on output than does the same increase in spending financed by higher taxation (see Fig. 6.1 in Chapter 6). But the PIH model suggests that this may not be so. If the government sells bonds to fund its expenditure, these bonds will have to be paid back at some point. That means that one day taxes will have to be used to pay back these bonds. Now whether the taxes are raised today or in the future makes no difference to their effect on *permanent* income.[1] If they are raised in the future that just means that people

---

[1] There is a slight complication here if the debt is going to be paid back after the people alive today have died. We can get around this problem if we assume that the permanent income relates to an infinite stream of income to an infinitely-lived dynasty. For a discussion of how plausible this is, see Barro (1974) and Chapter 6.

need to save more today to pay off these debts later. In the extreme case, it may be that today's private savings would rise one-for-one with the budget deficit, so that it would make no difference to aggregate expenditure whether government spending is funded by taxes or by debt. As we have seen in Chapter 6, this claimed equivalence between debt funding and tax funding was first identified by David Ricardo, and is referred to as 'Ricardian equivalence'. If Ricardian equivalence holds, then the oft-proposed remedy for a recession that the government should cut taxes will simply not work—private savings will rise to exactly match the fall in government savings.

Ricardian equivalence is not predicted by the *IS* equation we have considered up to now, but we can incorporate it. If an economy exhibits Ricardian equivalence, then that simply means that any change in $(g - t)$ will be exactly matched by an equal and opposite change in c_0, i.e.

$$-\Delta c_0 = \Delta(g - t).$$ (Ricardian equivalence in *IS*)

We can also regard c_0 as encapsulating many other related issues here. For example, if the economy experiences some shock that changes future wage expectations, c_0 would be expected to change to reflect this. Suppose enormous oil reserves are discovered in a country. Then even before they are mined (i.e. even before incomes have actually risen), people's expected future wages will rise and hence their assessment of their permanent incomes have risen leading to higher consumption. In the *IS* equation, we can model this by saying that the discovery of the oil reserves leads to a rise in c_0 (which will, of course, have a multiplier effect similar to a rise in autonomous investment as discussed in Chapter 2).

Our message here is that one important difference between the simple Keynesian consumption function and the PIH consumption function is that the former assumes that there is a constant autonomous element of consumption, c_0, fixed, for example, by the minimum consumption required to survive with the consequence that the marginal propensity to consume is less than the average. By contrast, the PIH derives the consumption function from a microeconomic model of consumer behaviour: the prediction is that the average and marginal propensity to consume are equal and that the theory of consumption requires actual income to be decomposed into so-called permanent and transitory components.

1.2 Consumer preferences, income, and interest rates

1.2.1 Consumption and income: current, future, transitory, permanent

The basic ideas of the PIH can be explained using a two-period model. We assume that households live for two periods only and that they enter the world with no wealth and leave it with no wealth. First, we show how the idea that a smooth consumption pattern over the two periods is preferred is represented in household indifference curves. In Fig. 7.1(*a*) the indifference curves are shown: both consumption this period and next period contribute to utility so the household will prefer to be on an indifference curve further from the origin. The indifference curves are convex to the origin, which reflects the preference for smooth consumption over the lifetime. To see this, note that the household

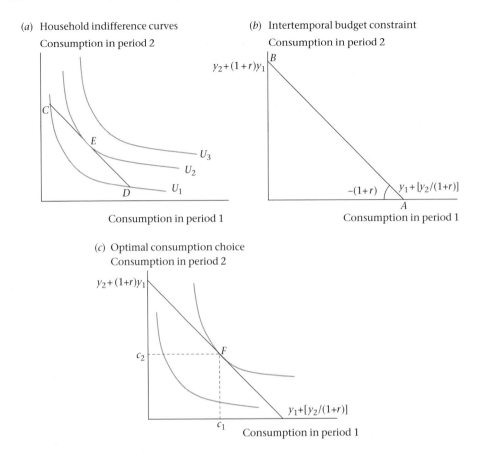

Figure 7.1 Consumption in a two-period model

is equally happy at points C and D on the indifference curve labelled U_1—since constant utility is delivered by the consumption combinations on any one indifference curve. At point D, the household has very high consumption in the first period and low consumption in the second; at C, it has the opposite. But note that at point E with a more balanced consumption pattern across the two periods, utility is higher—the household is on a higher indifference curve (U_2).

If we move now to Fig. 7.1(b), we can introduce the relationship between the household's income in each period, the choices for consumption available to it in each period and the real interest rate. The assumption that households enter and exit the world with no wealth allows us to concentrate on their labour income. Labour income in each period is y_1 and y_2 and consumption in each period is c_1 and c_2. The real interest rate is r. If wealth is zero at the start and the finish, the value today of lifetime consumption must be equal to the value today of lifetime income. If income in period two is not known, then y_2 is expected income. This is the intertemporal budget constraint:

$$c_1 + \frac{c_2}{1+r} = y_1 + \frac{y_2}{1+r}. \qquad (7.1)$$

present value of lifetime consumption $=$ present value of lifetime income

Fig. 7.1(*b*) shows the intertemporal budget constraint: point *A* shows how much consumption would be possible in period one if there was no consumption at all in period two. This is the present value of the entire lifetime income—i.e. the right hand side of the above expression. Point *B* shows the consumption that would be possible in period two if nothing was consumed in the first period. If $c_1 = 0$, then $c_2 = (1+r)y_1 + y_2$. The slope of the budget constraint is equal to $-(1+r)$ since any unit reduction in consumption in period one is transformed into $(1+r)$ units of consumption in period two.

The budget constraint shows all the combinations of consumption in the two periods that are available to the household. For the whole set to be available, without specifying the pattern of income in the two periods, it is assumed that the household is able to borrow against its future labour income. For example, if the interest rate is 4%, the budget constraint will be identical in the case in which y_1 is zero and y_2 is €102,000 as in the case in which y_1 and y_2 are each €50,000: $(0 + (102,000/1.04) = 98077 = 50,000 + (50,000/1.04))$.

Fig. 7.1(*c*) combines the indifference curves with the budget constraint. The household maximizes its utility by choosing a smooth pattern of consumption over the two periods at point *F*. Fig. 7.2(*a*) explores the implications of a rise in income in the first period only. A rise in period one income is depicted by an outward shift in the budget constraint. Why? Because higher consumption in the first period is now possible; similarly, more consumption in the second period is possible if the additional income is saved. The interest rate has not changed, so the budget constraint moves in a parallel fashion. The household will choose a higher level of consumption both now and in the second period. In our simple example, we can see that about half the rise in income will be consumed now and half next period.

What happens if the increase in income is in the second period rather than the first but it is known about at the outset? Once again, this will shift the budget constraint outwards and lead to a rise in current and future consumption of about the same amount. This underlines one implication of the PIH: the timing of changes in income does not make much difference to the impact on consumption. By contrast, the Keynesian consumption function would predict a rise in consumption in the first case but not in the second.

It is useful to note that if the indifference curves were symmetrical about the $45°$ line and the interest rate was zero, then consumption would go up in each period by half the increase in income, irrespective of the period in which it was received. Symmetric indifference curves reflect an equal *subjective* weight being placed on consumption in each period—i.e. neither impatience nor patience. A zero interest rate implies an equal *objective* weight is placed on each period in the sense that foregoing consumption in the first period is not rewarded by an increase in consumption in the second period over and above the foregone consumption.

We can take a third example: a rise in income in both period one and period two. Fig. 7.2(*b*) shows that consumption in each period will rise by the average increase in income. By contrast, the simple Keynesian consumption function would predict that consumption would rise less: in fact, it will rise by the same amount as in the case of a current period only rise in income. Whereas the PIH household satisfies its lifetime budget

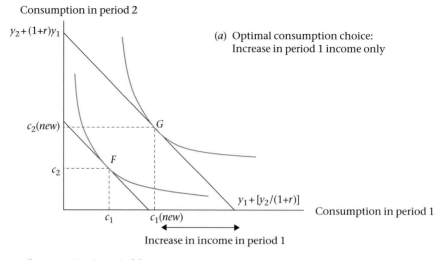

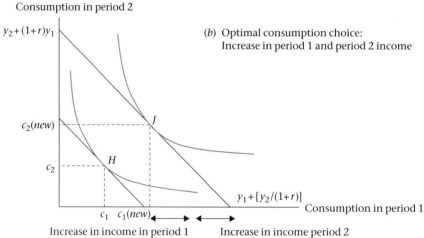

Figure 7.2 Consumption in a two-period model: the timing of income and consumption

constraint, the Keynesian household ends up with positive savings: this is a consequence of assuming a constant propensity to consume.

1.2.2 Consumption and interest rates

The two-period model is also useful in highlighting the role of a change in the interest rate on consumption. Since the slope of the budget constraint is $-(1 + r)$, it is clear that a change in the interest rate will be reflected in a change in the slope. The budget constraint will swivel in a clockwise direction about the existing income endowment point F in Fig. 7.3 because a higher interest rate reduces the present value of period two income bringing the budget constraint closer to the origin along the horizontal axis and raises the value in period two of period one income. If initially a household does no savings so that $c_1 = y_1$ and $c_2 = y_2$ as in Fig. 7.3, then the substitution effect (i.e. the effect

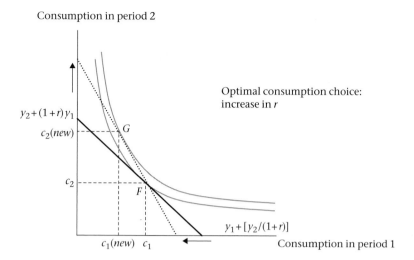

Consumption in period 2

Optimal consumption choice:
increase in r

$y_2 + (1+r)y_1$

$c_2(new)$ G

c_2 F

$y_1 + [y_2/(1+r)]$

$c_1(new)$ c_1 Consumption in period 1

Figure 7.3 Consumption in a two-period model: a rise in the interest rate

on consumption of the rise in the interest rate holding utility constant) will increase saving in the current period since the reward to saving has risen. The household moves from F to G.

What if the household initially borrows or saves? For a debtor household, the effect of a rise in the interest rate is negative, tending to lower consumption. For a creditor household, the effect of a rise in the interest rate is positive, tending to push consumption up. These are sometimes refused to as income or wealth effects. As we shall see, the aggregate consumption data indicates that changes in the interest rate have only a small effect on consumption: if anything, a rise tends to raise saving and reduce consumption. This will be the case unambiguously for debtor households in the simple two-period case and it will also be true of creditor households if the substitution effect outweighs the income effect.

A simple theory of consumption based on rational intertemporal optimizing behaviour (of which the permanent income/life-cycle model is an example) provides different predictions from the Keynesian consumption function. The main results discussed in the two-period case are summarized in Table 7.1. Note that once we extend the analysis beyond two periods, the effect of an increase in transitory income on consumption in the PIH model shrinks: intuitively, we can see that if it does not affect permanent income, then consumption will not change at all.

In the following two sections, we spell out in more detail the analytics of the intertemporal consumption function.[2] Once we move beyond two periods, more mathematics are needed. These sections (marked with a star) can be skipped by jumping to

---

[2] This analysis goes back to the pathbreaking contribution of the British economist Frank Ramsey, who died in 1930 at the age of 26. Keynes wrote in his obituary for Ramsey that Ramsey's 'A Mathematical Theory of Saving' was 'one of the most remarkable contributions to mathematical economics ever made, both in respect of the intrinsic importance and difficulty of its subject, the power and elegance of the technical methods employed,

Table 7.1 Comparison between PIH and simple Keynesian consumption functions

Impact on consumption this period of the following:	Simple PIH/LCH consumption function	Keynesian consumption function
↑ income (temporary)	↑ c_t by less than Δy_t	↑ $c_t = c_y \Delta y_t$
↑ income (permanent)	↑ $c_t = \Delta y_t = \Delta PI$	↑ $c_t = c_y \Delta y_t$
↑ income (permanent in later periods; information now)	↑ $c_t = \Delta y = \Delta PI$	no change
↑ predictable income	no change	↑ $c_t = c_y \Delta y_t$
↑ real interest rate	↓ c_t probably	no change

sections 1.5 and 1.6, where the key insights of the intertemporal model for the consumption function are explained. We then return to examine the empirical evidence on consumption behaviour.

1.3 *Modelling the Permanent Income Hypothesis

Consider a representative individual who faces no uncertainty (no shocks) and whose utility in any period t depends solely on her consumption in that period, c_t, and is given by

$$u(c_t) = \ln c_t.$$

We use a log form of utility here for two main reasons. The first reason is that it captures some important characteristics we would expect of preferences—namely that more consumption is preferred to less consumption (utility is increasing in consumption) and that the amount by which utility increases with consumption declines as consumption rises (diminishing marginal utility). The second reason is that, although other forms of utility function would exhibit increasing utility and diminishing marginal utility, the log form is very simple and tractable. Using logs here makes the maths easier for us without significantly changing the main results in which we are interested.

Suppose that our individual lives for T periods, and let us initially assume that real interest rates are zero and that she has no preference over when in her life she consumes (that is to say, she is not impatient). Her lifetime utility is therefore just the sum of her utility from consumption in each of those T periods:

$$U = \sum_{t=1}^{T} \ln c_t.$$

Next suppose that she is not allowed to die in debt nor to leave any bequests, so that the present value of her total lifetime consumption is equal to the sum of her initial wealth

and the clear purity of illumination with which the writer's mind is felt by the reader to play about its subject.'
Quoted in Newbery (1987).

(A_0) plus her total lifetime income:

$$\sum_{t=1}^{T} c_t = A_0 + \sum_{t=1}^{T} y_t.$$

Consider now the individual pondering whether she has allocated her consumption ideally across her lifetime. For her chosen consumption path to be ideal (in the sense of maximizing total lifetime utility), it needs to be the case that, for any period t, if she were to decrease consumption marginally in that period and increase it in the following period, that should have no effect on total lifetime utility.[3] Since the marginal utilities of consumption in period t and $t+1$ are $1/(c_t)$ and $1/(c_{t+1})$, the condition for an optimum is

$$\frac{1}{c_t} - \frac{1}{c_{t+1}} = 0$$

which can be rearranged to obtain

$$c_{t+1} = c_t = \text{ a constant.}$$

That is to say, our representative individual in this case consumes exactly the same in every period, regardless of when she receives her income. Her wages, y_t, might be very lumpy—say low when t is near zero or near T, but high in the middle years of her life. But that makes no difference to her consumption. She smooths her consumption because her preferences are characterized by diminishing marginal utility and because, implicitly, we have assumed that she is able to borrow against her expected future income.

1.4 *Adding interest rates and time preference

Suppose we now assume that our individual is impatient and that real interest rates are non-zero. Then our individual, who lives for T periods, has lifetime utility given by

$$U = \sum_{t=0}^{T} \frac{1}{(1+\rho)^t} \ln c_t$$

where ρ is her rate of time preference (a measure of her impatience).

We still assume that she is not allowed to die in debt nor to leave bequests, so that the present value of her total lifetime consumption is equal to the sum of her initial wealth (A_0) plus the present value of her lifetime labour income:

$$\sum_{t=0}^{T} \frac{1}{(1+r)^t} c_t = A_0 + \sum_{t=0}^{T} \frac{1}{(1+r)^t} y_t$$

assuming a constant real interest rate r.

---

[3] That it cannot increase utility should be obvious. The point about its not decreasing utility either is the usual one about the slope being zero at the maximum of a function.

Consider again the individual pondering whether she has allocated her consumption ideally across her lifetime. For her chosen consumption path to be ideal (in the sense of maximizing total lifetime utility), it needs to be the case that, for any period t, if she were to decrease consumption marginally in that period and increase it in the following period by $1 + r$ times the decrease in period t (she would have $1 + r$ times as much because of the interest from saving the income for the extra period), that should have no effect on total lifetime utility. Since the marginal utilities of consumption in t and $t+1$ are $1/((1 + \rho)^t c_t)$ and $1/((1 + \rho)^{t+1} c_{t+1})$ this condition for an optimum is

$$\frac{1}{(1 + \rho)^t c_t} - \frac{1 + r}{(1 + \rho)^{t+1} c_{t+1}} = 0$$

which can be rearranged to obtain

$$\frac{c_{t+1}}{c_t} = \frac{1 + r}{1 + \rho}.$$

By subtracting $c_t/c_t = 1$ from each side, this can also be written in terms of changes as

$$\frac{\Delta c}{c} = \frac{r - \rho}{1 + \rho}. \qquad \text{(discrete time Ramsey equation)}$$

1.5 The optimal consumption path

An individual allocating her consumption efficiently between periods will need to be indifferent as to whether she takes any unit of consumption in period t or period $t + 1$. A simple model of optimal consumption suggests that along the optimal consumption path

$$\frac{\Delta c}{c} = \frac{r - \rho}{1 + \rho}. \qquad \text{(discrete time Ramsey equation)}$$

The 'objective' rate of interest, r, is the increase in consumption that you get next period if you forgo one unit of consumption this period. The 'subjective' rate of time preference, ρ, is the extra that you would be prepared to pay now to bring forward a unit of consumption to the present period from the next period. Looking at this equation, it is obvious that in a special case, the change in consumption will be zero—i.e. the individual will choose to have a perfectly smooth level of consumption over their lifetime. This will be the case if the interest rate and the rate of time preference are equal. If both are equal to zero, this result is intuitively appealing: there is nothing to be gained objectively by 'waiting' and nothing to be lost 'subjectively'.

However, once there is the objective possibility of trading off present for future consumption and given the individual's subjective attitude to future consumption, it is not necessarily the case that consumption will be constant. For example, if the real interest rate exceeds the rate of time preference of an individual (i.e. $r > \rho$), then it is worthwhile for the individual to consume less at time t so as to consume more at time $t + 1$. In such a case, consumption at time t would be less than at time $t + 1$. We would find the opposite pattern in the case of a very impatient individual. It is worth noting that the assumption of diminishing marginal utility of consumption guarantees that there is some consumption each period.

From the Ramsey equation, it follows that consumption will be constant if the rate of interest is exactly equal to the rate of time preference. If the return to waiting and the degree of impatience exactly offset each other then the consumer is best satisfied with a constant level of consumption over their lifetime.[4] Lifetime resources are the key to consumption. The contrast with the simple Keynesian consumption function is stark. If the Keynesian consumption function is applied literally to an individual, it suggests that even if the person knew that they were going to inherit wealth or benefit from a rising income, it would not influence their current consumption.

But what does the Ramsey equation imply for current consumption? We assume that at time t the consumer has an amount of non-human wealth (this can be positive, e.g. assets such as money, financial assets, or a house, or negative such as a loan from the bank) and an estimate of the present value of their human wealth. The individual is assumed to be able to make a decision about their supply of labour over their lifetime in the light of information about the wage prevailing in the labour market. We will return to consider what happens if this is not a valid assumption: in an economy with involuntary unemployment, it will not be certain that a job will always be available at the going wage.

To calculate the present value of this annual flow of labour income, the prevailing interest rate must be used. For example, the present value of €50,000 that will be received in one year's time will be $50,000/(1 + r)$ which, if the interest rate is 5% amounts to just over €47,600; if the €50,000 was received in five years' time, then its present value would be $50,000/(1 + r)^5$ which is €36,176. This procedure needs to be applied to each year's expected labour income. It is also assumed that the rational individual will want to consume all of their lifetime wealth. This means that at time t, the present value of consumption over the remainder of the person's lifetime will be exactly equal to the present value of their non-human and human wealth at time t.

The path of consumption over the lifetime will then just depend on the individual's rate of time preference, ρ, and the present value of their wealth, Ψ_t :

$$c_t = \rho\Psi_t. \qquad \text{(Ramsey consumption function)}$$

More precisely, ρ is the subjective rate of time preference, and Ψ_t (called psi and pronounced 'sigh') is the sum of the value of non-human wealth (NHW) and the present value of human wealth (HW) (labour income over the remaining lifetime discounted at the interest rate r):

$$\Psi_t = NHW_t + PV_t(HW).$$

It is assumed that an individual can always borrow at the prevailing interest rate, r , in order to implement their lifetime consumption plan. We return later to consider what

---

[4] In terms of the simple two-period diagrams used earlier, the shape of the indifference curve has to be sufficiently asymmetrical to just offset the slope of the budget constraint in order that the tangency between the indifference curve and budget constraint lies on the 45° line. This will produce constant consumption in each period.

happens if this assumption is not correct. From this expression, it is clear that an impatient person will have a higher level of consumption in the current period than a patient one.

It is useful to write this expression in a slightly different way.

$$c_t = (r + \rho - r)\Psi_t$$
$$= \underbrace{r\Psi_t}_{\text{permanent income}} + (\rho - r)\Psi_t.$$

The term $r\Psi$ is known as 'permanent income' because it is the amount that can be consumed whilst leaving the value of wealth unchanged:

$$r\Psi_t = \text{permanent income.} \qquad \text{(definition of permanent income)}$$

We can now see how the Ramsey consumption function ties up with the Ramsey equation and with the PIH. If $\rho = r$ then consumption in the current and every subsequent period is equal to permanent income. This is in line with the Ramsey equation for $\rho = r$ since consumption is constant i.e. $\Delta c/c = 0$. But if $\rho \neq r$, the individual is either consuming now at a level above or below their 'permanent income' and hence consumption is either falling or rising. For example, if $\rho > r$ the rate of impatience is greater than the return from waiting. The consumption function tells us that if $\rho > r$ consumption this period is equal to permanent income plus an extra bit representing consumption out of wealth. The consequence for the path of consumption is clear: by shifting some consumption from the future to the current period, the individual will have a decline in consumption in the future. From the Ramsey equation, if $\rho > r$ then $\Delta c/c < 0$.

Of course the converse will be true in the case where the rate of time preference is less than the rate of interest. In this case, consumption will grow over time—the higher rate of interest makes it worthwhile to postpone some consumption now (i.e. to save more) and to benefit from growing consumption over the lifetime. This is a useful insight from the intertemporal model.

If we go back to the special case in which the real rate of interest is equal to the discount rate, i.e. $r = \rho$, we have the prediction of constant consumption over the lifetime. This is one rationalization for the simple PIH: consuming one's permanent income is consistent with intertemporal utility maximization if the interest rate and the rate of time preference coincide.

$$c_t = r\Psi_t \qquad \text{(PIH consumption function)}$$
$$= \text{permanent income.}$$

1.6 Consumption as a 'random walk'

As noted above, Friedman's basic idea in the permanent income hypothesis was that consumption was not driven by current income but rather by expected or average income. The initial empirically estimated consumption functions based on Friedman's approach used a backward-looking expectations hypothesis: permanent income was a weighted average of past income. But if the permanent income hypothesis is coupled with the rational expectations hypothesis as was done by Robert Hall, then we get a dramatically different story.[5] In every period the household incorporates into its consumption decision all of the information available about its permanent income, and its desired level of consumption is constant. Any change in government policy would therefore only lead to a change in consumption if it altered the individual's view about their permanent income. On this basis, apart from a random error, consumption next period would be expected to be just the same as consumption this period:

$$c_{t+1} = c_t + \epsilon_{t+1}.$$

A pattern like this in which the last period's value is the best prediction of what will be observed this period is called a random walk. The only thing that could produce a change in consumption in period $t+1$ would be the arrival of some information about ε_{t+1} that was not known in period t:

$$\text{news} \longrightarrow \Delta \text{permanent income} \longrightarrow \Delta \text{consumption}.$$

This interpretation of the permanent income hypothesis produced the strong empirical prediction that past values of consumption and income should provide no information additional to that incorporated in current consumption itself in helping to predict the path of consumption. This idea was rather shocking to macroeconomic modellers who had typically used a consumption function based on lagged values of income and consumption with which to forecast future consumption. We return to the empirical issues below. In the section that follows, Hall's result is derived. This can be omitted by going straight to section 1.7.

1.6.1 *The Hall (1978) result

Consider the following utility function:

$$u(c_t) = ac_t - \frac{b}{2}c_t^2,$$

where a and b are positive constants. There are two important things to note about this consumption function: first, that the coefficient on c^2 must be negative for consumption smoothing to be desirable and second, that we have switched from the log utility function to the quadratic one because for consumption to follow a random walk, quadratic utility is necessary.

Assume that, at $t = 0$, y_0 is known, but y_1 to y_T are random variables with mean $E(y_t)$. Because of the presence of uncertainty here, this time instead of simply maximizing her *actual* utility, the representative individual instead maximizes her *expected* lifetime utility as indicated by the presence of the expectations operator, E, which has the subscript zero to indicate that expectations are formed at time zero:

$$U = E_0 \left(\sum_{t=1}^{T} \frac{1}{(1+\rho)^t} \left(ac_t - \frac{b}{2}c_t^2 \right) \right).$$

[5] Hall (1978).

The lifetime resources constraint this time is given by

$$E_0 \left(\sum_{t=1}^{T} \frac{1}{(1+r)^t} c_t \right) = E_0 \left(A_0 + \sum_{t=1}^{T} \frac{1}{(1+r)^t} y_t \right).$$

By much the same argument as previously, our individual will only be at an optimum when, in any period, she would not change her expected utility by reducing her consumption in t a little and instead consume $(1+r)$ times as much in period $t+1$. In this case, the marginal utilities are $(a - bc_t)/(1+\rho)^t$ and $(a - bE(c_{t+1}))/(1+\rho)^{t+1}$, so the condition for an optimum is

$$\frac{(a - bc_t)}{(1+\rho)^t} - \frac{(a - bE(c_{t+1}))(1+r)}{(1+\rho)^{t+1}} = 0,$$

which may be rearranged to give:

$$E(c_{t+1}) = \frac{a}{b} \frac{(r - \rho)}{(1+\rho)} + c_t \frac{(1+\rho)}{(1+r)}.$$

From the definition of an expected value, this can be written equivalently as

$$c_{t+1} = \frac{a}{b} \frac{(r - \rho)}{(1+\rho)} + c_t \frac{(1+\rho)}{(1+r)} + \varepsilon_{t+1}$$

where $E(\varepsilon_{t+1}) = 0$. For the special case where the interest rate equals the rate of time preference, (i.e. $r = \rho$), this simplifies to

$$c_{t+1} = c_t + \varepsilon_{t+1}. \qquad \text{(the Hall result)}$$

This says that consumption follows a random walk, changing only subject to random shocks. We shall not do so here, but it is reasonably straightforward to show that, under these assumptions,

$$\varepsilon_{t+1} = E_{t+1}\bar{y} - E_t\bar{y}$$

where $\bar{y}$ is simply the expected value of average future income per period. Thus the Hall result says that consumption will only change between periods if expectations of future income change, and then the change in consumption will be equal to the change in future average income.

1.7 Empirical consumption functions

With the theoretical predictions in mind, we now turn to the empirical analysis of consumption. In developing the PIH, Friedman sought to reconcile the evidence about consumption from cross-sectional data with that from time-series macroeconomic data. The cross-sectional data supported the Keynesian consumption function with an intercept term and a marginal propensity to consume less than the average, whereas the time-series data suggested a rather constant consumption to income ratio in the long run, in

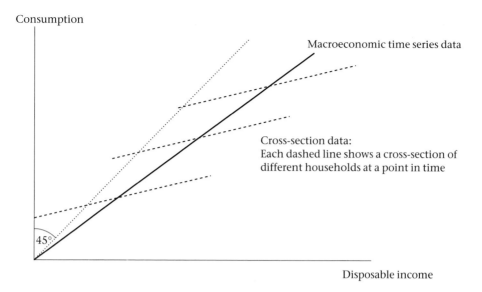

Figure 7.4 Friedman: reconciling cross-section and time-series data on consumption

line with the predictions of the PIH. Friedman's hypothesis was that the cross-sectional relationship included the effects of transitory income and that if the average relationship in successive cross-sections over time (and as average incomes rise) is used to measure the relationship between consumption and permanent income, the underlying relationship of a marginal propensity to consume higher in the long than the short run and equal to the average emerges (see Fig. 7.4).[6]

Nevertheless, puzzles remain in understanding consumption behaviour.[7] Two sorts of data have been used—aggregate macroeconomic data and microeconomic data from surveys of household expenditure.

1.7.1 Aggregate data

Problem 1: the excess sensitivity of consumption to current income. One strong prediction of the simple PIH model as discussed above is that changes in income that are predictable from past information should have no effect on current consumption (row 4 in Table 7.1). But there is by now a considerable body of work on aggregate consumption data that suggests this is wrong: it seems that consumption responds to a change in income (in the previous quarter) that could be predicted from the past pattern of income changes by 30–40% of the change. This empirical result is referred to as the 'excess sensitivity' of consumption because in terms of the simple PIH, consumption is excessively sensitive to predictable changes in income. This is an important result for economic

---

[6] For an explanation of the interaction between the theoretical and econometric modelling of consumption from Friedman onwards, see Meghir (2004).

[7] A good source for investigating this further is Deaton (1992). The article by Meghir (2004) is also very useful.

policy because it suggests that changes in income as a result, say, of tax changes can have a marked effect on consumption and hence on economic activity.

Problem 2: the excess smoothness of consumption in relation to 'news'. Second, closely related to the prediction by the simple PIH that predictable changes in income should have no effect on consumption, is the idea that news about a change in permanent income will lead to an immediate shift in consumption to the new level of permanent income. This is the case in rows 2 and 3 in Table 7.1 (change in permanent income or information now about a change in permanent income in the future). This appears not to be confirmed in the aggregate data: current consumption reacts much less to 'news' about changes in permanent income than the theory predicts. This result is referred to as the 'excess smoothness' of consumption because in terms of the simple PIH, consumption is too sluggish in responding to the 'news'.

Problem 3: borrowing and lending inadequate to achieve smoothing. Third, the simple PIH predicts that changes in assets (through lending or borrowing) will allow the required change in consumption associated with any change in permanent income to be implemented. But the analysis of aggregate data indicates that this is not the case. Households do not seem to engage in the extent of borrowing and lending that would be necessary to smooth changes in permanent income over the life cycle as the hypothesis suggests.

Problem 4: incomplete Ricardian equivalence. Fourth, the simple PIH predicts that if current government social security policies and pension commitments are unsustainable on the basis of current tax and contribution rates, far-sighted households will anticipate the higher future tax burden and the lower level of state provision of benefits for their retirement by increasing their current saving. (This is a case—in terms of the Table 7.1—of current information about lower future income.) This is a version of Ricardian equivalence, which we looked at in more detail in Chapter 6 when we considered fiscal policy and how it might affect economic activity. The evidence suggests that tax and social security policies are not completely 'undone' by the private sector adjusting their savings in this way although there appears to be some offsetting effect of this sort. That is to say, in *IS* terms, the evidence is that

$$0 < |-\Delta c_0| < |\Delta(g-t)|, \qquad \text{(incomplete Ricardian equivalence)}$$

where $|x|$ refers to the absolute value of x.

1.7.2 Microeconomic data

Microeconometric work shows that if *changes in preferences* over the life cycle (e.g. due to decisions about the timing and number of children) and the fact that consumption and labour supply decisions are made jointly are incorporated in the analysis, the PIH does provide a good description of the data.[8]

Such studies test a generalized version of the PIH using the so-called Euler equation approach. In the simple PIH, the Euler equation is the 'discrete time Ramsey equation', i.e. it is the intertemporal optimization condition. Testing the PIH using the Euler equation approach is attractive because by focusing on the marginal condition for optimization, it

---

[8] Prominent studies are Blundell, Browning, and Meghir (1994) and Attanasio and Weber (1995).

avoids the need to measure permanent income. The generalized Euler equation regresses the change in log consumption on the real interest rate, a measure of the trade-off between precautionary motives for saving (to which we return in the next section) and impatience, and a set of variables that measure changes in household composition, labour supply, etc. As in the Ramsey equation, a higher interest rate raises consumption *growth* and hence implies higher saving. Intuitively, when precautionary motives outweigh impatience, saving will also be higher and as noted above, the inclusion of demographic and labour supply variables reduces the impact of predictable changes in income growth on consumption.

1.8 Rational consumption and the *IS* equation

The previous section suggests:

- the simple Keynesian consumption function is quite at odds with some obvious characteristics of rational consumption behaviour;
- the simple PIH needs to be extended in order to be consistent with the evidence.

By introducing elements into a theory of intertemporal allocation that have been left out in the simple PIH, we can explain why aggregate consumption has some Keynesian elements. Two key omissions are

(1) uncertainty, which can give rise to savings for precautionary reasons and

(2) liquidity constraints, which prevent some households from borrowing as much as they would like to at the prevailing interest rate.

Both of these factors can help to explain 'excess sensitivity' of consumption to predictable income and 'excess smoothness' of consumption to new information about permanent income. Let us look first at precautionary saving and then at liquidity constraints.

1.8.1 Uncertainty and precautionary savings

In the simple PIH, the only motivation for saving is to build up a lump of assets with which to smooth consumption over the life cycle. In the early years of work, the household would save in order to repay the debt that was built up in the period during which consumption (= permanent income) was more than labour income and to supply the income for the retirement years when labour income has fallen to zero. But if there is uncertainty about future job opportunities or about health, for example, then the household may wish to put savings aside as insurance for future contingencies. In the face of uncertainty, households would tend to save more early in life than the PIH predicts. Instead of the average propensity to consume falling as income rises over the working life as in the simple PIH, the desire for precautionary savings leads to saving early on with result that consumption rises with income (not by more than income) early in the life cycle and the average propensity to consume rises later on. If saving for a rainy day is important, then the utility provided by having assets to tide the household over if need be outweighs the utility that would have come from higher consumption in the early years. In the two-period model, a household characterized by such prudent preferences wishes to save enough in period one to make the *expected* period two consumption greater than in period one.

1.8.2 Limits to borrowing: liquidity constraints

We can extend the simple two-period model to show that liquidity constrained households will have a very high marginal propensity to consume out of an increase in current income. In Fig. 7.5, the unconstrained household chooses to consume c_1^* in the first period and c_2^* in the second—i.e. at point A. Now suppose that consumption in period 1 is limited to current income, i.e. $c_1 \leqslant y_1$. The new budget constraint is shown by the heavy dashed line. The household maximizes utility and chooses point B—clearly, utility is lower than it was at A, in the unconstrained situation. First period consumption is lower and second period consumption is higher than at A. If the liquidity constraint is suddenly eased because of a rise in current period income, the household's budget constraint shifts to the right (dotted). The household now maximizes utility at point C. The entire increase in income is consumed in the current period. The presence of liquidity constraints sharply alters the predictions of the simple PIH.

An assumption made in the simple PIH that seems to fly in the face of reality is that households are able to borrow against their expected future labour income at the going interest rate. The kind of household that saves for precautionary reasons early in life might not want to borrow. But there may be others (e.g. students) with expectations of a profile of rising labour income that desire to consume more heavily early on than is possible with current income. Such households may find that they cannot find loans—a mortgage is different because that is secured by the value of the house. Such households are credit rationed as depicted in Fig. 7.5.

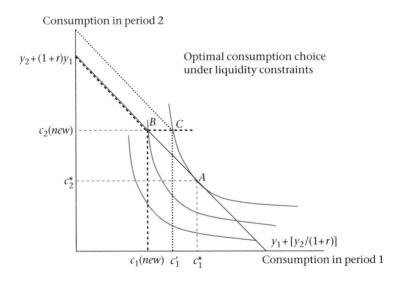

Figure 7.5 Consumption in a two-period model: liquidity constraints

An explanation for the refusal of banks to extend loans to households is provided by Joseph Stiglitz and Andrew Weiss's theory of credit rationing due to adverse selection.[9] The idea is based on the notion that different households present different risks of default-ing on loans but that the banks have no way of distinguishing between good and bad risks. If the bank puts up the interest rate to meet the cost of expected default, this will have the effect of attracting the high risk-high return households—those less likely to default will not be willing to take out a loan at the higher interest rate. The result is that banks ration loans at the going interest rate. If households are aware that credit rationing is likely so that they will not necessarily be able to borrow in the event of a rainy day, then this may motivate precautionary savings. But in this case, savings go towards a buffer of liquid assets to be drawn on in order to smooth consumption in case of a fall in labour income. If the buffer is exhausted, then consumption drops and will respond sensitively to any subsequent rise in labour income as we have seen in Fig. 7.5.

Another reason why individuals may face liquidity constraints is because of limits to what can be done to those who cannot pay their debts. Consider an entrepreneur who has a good idea and expects to be a millionaire in a year's time. According to the simple PIH, he will consume this year at the level of his permanent income; according to the Keynesian consumption function, he consumes only the autonomous level of c_0. For the simple PIH to hold, the entrepreneur is able to borrow in order to fund a very high level of consumption this year. Will a bank lend to him? If things go badly, he may go bankrupt, but it makes relatively little difference *how* bankrupt he goes. This means that his expected future utility is bounded on the downside, which would lead him to be overly optimistic in his borrowing decisions against future income because if he gets it wrong it makes little difference whether he is unable to pay back very high debts as opposed to merely high debts. This would lead to him overconsuming today, increasing his risk of default and increasing the bank's exposure to default. To counter this, banks limit the amount they are prepared to lend against future income growth, thereby reducing individuals' ability to smooth consumption and increasing the importance of current income.

Returning to the empirical evidence, a pragmatic approach is to take the view that whilst some proportion of households are not credit constrained and their consumption is well explained by their lifetime resources (along the lines suggested by the PIH), others are prevented from consuming according to a lifetime consumption plan because they are cut off from loans. For this group, predictable increases in income lead to increases in consumption (accounting for 'excess sensitivity' to predictable income and for 'excess smoothness' to news about permanent income). Any assets held are for precautionary rea-sons: Angus Deaton points out that many households in the USA have a very modest level of liquid assets that resemble more closely the buffer stock associated with precautionary saving than assets associated with a life-cycle motive for saving. Similarly research in the UK shows that the median household's holding of financial wealth (in banks, building societies, stocks and shares) is only €1,250.[10]

[9] Stiglitz and Weiss (1981). The concept of adverse selection is discussed further in Chapter 8.
[10] Banks and Tanner (1999).

1.9 Conclusions about consumption

In this section we have considered consumption in more detail than is offered in the consumption function incorporated in the *IS* equation. We have seen that:

(1) A systematic approach to the analysis of consumption requires a model of household or individual behaviour in which the assumptions about the nature of the capital market, uncertainty and preferences are set out.

(2) Empirical evidence casts doubt on how well actual consumption corresponds to that predicted by the simple PIH.

(3) This is to be expected given the nature of asymmetric information problems and consequent liquidity constraints faced in financial markets, the presence of precautionary motives for saving, as well as the interaction of labour supply, family formation, and consumption decisions.

In short, optimizing models of consumer behaviour provide a clear framework for analysing the determinants of consumption. They help clarify the empirical shortcomings of simple PIH models and the conceptual shortcoming of the Keynesian consumption function.

1.10 Appendix on consumption: estimating an aggregate consumption function

To conclude our discussion of consumption, it is instructive to take a look at an estimated aggregate consumption function. A good example to use is that estimated for the UK for data from 1956 to 1988.[11] The estimating equation incorporates many of the features discussed above that are necessary to augment the simple PIH. The model allows for some households to be credit constrained, for the effects of uncertainty, for an estimate of expected future income (estimated from a separate model), and for liquid assets (such as bank deposits) to have a different impact on consumption from illiquid assets (such as pension rights or housing).

The equation is:

$$
\Delta \ln c_t = \text{constant} + \underset{(0.12)}{0.51} (\ln y_t - \ln c_{t-1}) + \underset{(0.08)}{0.17} \Delta \ln y_t - \underset{(0.11)}{0.22} r
$$

$$
- \underset{(0.012)}{0.44} \Delta u_t - \underset{(0.070)}{0.20} ad_t + \underset{(0.042)}{0.066} \frac{LA_{t-1}}{y_t} + \underset{(0.0085)}{0.024} \frac{IA_{t-1}}{y_t}
$$

$$
+ \underset{(0.07)}{0.014} \left(\frac{\Delta y}{y} \right)^E + \text{'demographic and distributional effects'}
$$

$$
\bar{R}^2 = 0.950, \text{DW} = 1.93.
$$

The dependent variable is consumption (durable and non-durable) in real terms, y is real disposable income, r is the real interest rate, u is the unemployment rate, ad is the

---

[11] Muellbauer (1994).

absolute value of the gap between current income and its average over the past five years, *LA* is a measure of liquid assets and *IA* is a measure of illiquid assets (housing wealth, equities, and bonds) and $(\Delta y / y)^E$ is the expected growth of income. The standard errors of the coefficients are shown in brackets.

As Muellbauer explains, it is possible to extract information from this equation about the underlying model. Consumption reacts with a lag to changes in income (shown by the coefficient 0.51); changes in current income feed through to consumption and this can be interpreted as indicating the consumption share of households that are credit constrained $(0.17/0.51 = 0.33)$. The real interest rate has a negative effect on consumption. Uncertainty about future income is measured by the change in unemployment and by the deviation between current and average income and has a negative effect on consumption as the precautionary motive suggests. Higher wealth raises consumption but liquid assets have a much bigger impact than illiquid ones. Expected future income has a positive effect as would be expected with forward-looking PIH/LCH households. This example of an estimated aggregate consumption function shows the role of life-cycle, precautionary, and credit constraint factors:

$$c = c \left(\overset{+}{y}, \overset{-}{r}, \overset{-}{\Delta u}, \left(\frac{\overset{+}{\Delta y}}{y} \right)^E, \overset{+}{\Psi} \right).$$

It suggests that when using the *IS* equation, we need to be aware of the likely role of expected income growth, uncertainty, interest rate, and wealth effects in addition to that of current disposable income (and hence of liquidity constraints) already incorporated in the Keynesian consumption function. Since the interest rate effect seems to be negative, this will reinforce the negative interest rate effect on investment in the downward-sloping *IS* curve. Changes in expectations of income growth, in uncertainty (perhaps measured by changes in unemployment) and wealth effects will shift the *IS* curve.

2 Investment

By investment economists mean expenditure on man-made aids to production such as plant and machinery, dwellings and other buildings, and infrastructure such as roads. Investment is a flow concept that measures such expenditure over a period of time (such as a year). It is important to distinguish clearly between investment and the capital stock, which is the value of the stock of plant, machinery etc., and reflects investment spending over many previous periods.

Investment covers a diverse set of expenditures. One particularly important division of investment is into private and public sector expenditure, because the objectives of investment in these two areas are not necessarily the same. Similarly, about a fifth of all investment is in dwellings and the factors driving this are likely to differ somewhat from those determining investment in plant or machinery. Again, replacement investment may require a different explanation from investment aimed at expanding output.

Another interesting and important form of investment is stockbuilding. Stockbuilding (investment in inventories) may be negative as well as positive, and although not a particularly large item (only some 3% of fixed investment or 0.5% of GDP), it can be very volatile (as witnessed, for example, in the de-stocking and re-stocking in the USA in late 2001 and early 2002). However, although there is a diversity of forms of investment, in this section we concentrate on fixed capital formation by the business sector because different theories are needed for housing investment, government investment, and changes in inventories.

Investment plays a major role in macroeconomic fluctuations and it adds to the economy's productive capacity. Its role on the supply side is central to the theory of growth (Chapter 13). Here we concentrate on investment as a component of aggregate demand. In booms, investment tends to grow by more than GDP and in recessions, it tends to fall by more. But this is not always the case—for example in the recovery of the UK economy in the 1990s, investment grew by less than GDP.

The simple investment function in the *IS* equation presented in Chapter 2 contains two elements: $I = I(A, r)$ where A represents expectations of future profits such as Keynes's 'animal spirits' and r is the real rate of interest. A linear version of the investment function is: $I = A - br$, where A and b are positive constants. In this section, we follow the same strategy as for consumption by first asking if the aggregate investment function can be related to a model of rational microeconomic behaviour, second, seeing what we should do in the *IS* equation to allow for rational behaviour, and third, looking at the empirical evidence on investment behaviour.

2.1 Investment in the theory of the firm

We assume that firms aim to maximize profits, so they undertake investment projects if these offer a return that is higher than costs. The slight complication here is that the outlay on investment typically precedes the returns, which may be lumpy and spread over a number of years. The way to deal with this is to calculate the 'Present Value' (V) of the expected flow of profits Π, where $\Pi_1, \Pi_2, \ldots$ is the flow of profits in period 1, etc.. Suppose that interest rates are 10%. Then if I save €100 today I will have €110 in a year's time $(100 \cdot (1 + 10\%))$. Expressed the other way around, we could say that €110 in a year's time has the same value as €100 today. More generally, if interest rates are constant at r, the value of X in n years' time is the same as that of $X/(1 + r)^n$ today. We can calculate the present value of our stream of expected profits, Π, from an investment project by:

$$V = \frac{\Pi_1}{(1 + r_1)} + \frac{\Pi_2}{(1 + r_1)(1 + r_2)} + \cdots = \sum_{t=1}^{T} \frac{\Pi_t}{R_t}$$

where $R_t = (1 + r_1)(1 + r_2) \ldots (1 + r_t)$, for the general case where the interest rate can vary over time.

If the cost of the machine is greater than the present value of the flow of profits from the machine, then it would be more profitable not to buy the machine but instead put the money in the bank or in bonds. Similarly, if the money to purchase the machine is being borrowed, then if the cost of the machine is greater than the present value, buying the machine will be unprofitable. On the other hand, if the present value is greater than the cost, then this investment is profitable, and a profit-maximizing firm will go ahead with it.

The simple present value analysis suggests that two important components drive investment. If expected future profitability rises, then expected net returns Π will rise and we would think that more investment projects will become viable, other things being equal, so we would expect more investment to take place. In the investment function in the IS, $(I = A - br)$, this would be captured by the A term increasing, shifting the investment schedule (and the IS curve) to the right. On the other hand, if real interest rates rise then the present value of all investment projects falls, and we would expect investment to fall as we move left up the investment schedule (and in a north-westerly direction along the IS curve).

One complication arises immediately—because we cannot see into the future and investment decisions are inextricably connected with forecasting a flow of *future* profits, uncertainty is bound to play a central role. Sentiment about *future* real interest rates is as important in determining the viability of an investment as is the current real interest rate.

In the next section, we set out a simple model of investment. Our aim is to explain how two commonly used models of investment—the 'Q model' and the 'accelerator model'—fit into a more general analysis of how a rational firm makes its investment decisions. The Q model is a very neat theory that can be derived from profit-maximizing behaviour: we shall see that it predicts that investment will be positive when the marginal return from installing a unit of extra capital stock exceeds its cost and that the amount of investment will depend on the marginal cost of actually making adjustments to the size of the capital stock. Its other virtue is that the theory can be connected to observable variables and tested against data. However, it has not proved an unqualified success in empirical testing.

By contrast, the accelerator model is very crude: it is based on the idea that changes in demand for output determine investment. Although crude and ad hoc, accelerator-type effects have frequently been found in empirical testing. This suggests that we should not simply throw it away, but try to understand why the accelerator may cast light on actual investment behaviour. We begin by working through some theory so as to explain which assumptions produce which kind of investment function. We shall see that imperfect competition in the product market is required to derive an investment function from microfoundations that has an accelerator component.

2.2 A simple model of investment

Net investment[12] is equal to the change in the capital stock, K:

$$I_t = K_t - K_{t-1}. \tag{7.2}$$

---

[12] Note that aggregate demand depends on gross rather than net investment; gross investment includes investment to offset capital consumption, which depends on the capital stock and rates of obsolescence.

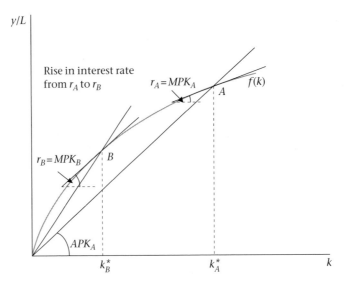

Figure 7.6 Optimal capital stock: a rise in the real interest rate

Suppose there is a desired capital stock at any moment of time, K_t^*. Because of costs of adjusting from the existing to the desired capital stock, a simple assumption is that investment makes up each period some proportion, $\alpha < 1$, of the difference between the two:

$$I_t = \alpha \left(K_t^* - K_{t-1} \right). \tag{7.3}$$

The next question is to ask what determines the desired capital stock. If the production function linking capital and labour to output, $y = F(K, L)$ is concave (diminishing returns to capital), the desired capital to labour ratio declines as the rate of interest rises. If we assume the production function has constant returns to scale we can use the production function in so-called intensive form. We divide each side of the production function by L and write it as follows: $y/L = F(K/L, 1) = f(k)$, where $k \equiv K/L$.[13] The production function is shown in Fig. 7.6. The slope of the production function is the marginal product of capital and we know that a profit-maximizing firm will choose the capital stock such that the marginal product of capital is equal to the real interest rate: $MPK = f'(k) = r$, which is assumed to be set, for example, by the central bank. An increase in r implies a lower desired capital stock as shown by point B. The slope of the line from the origin to the production function is the output/capital ratio: moving from point A to point B is associated with a rise in the marginal (MPK) and average product of capital (APK).

---

[13] Note that we define y as the level of output in this chapter in line with the chapters on the short- to medium-run model: in the growth models of Chapter 13 where the intensive production function is introduced, y is defined as output per worker.

This can be written

$$\left(\frac{K_t}{y_t}\right)^* = v(r_t)$$

$$\Rightarrow K_t^* = v(r_t)y_t \tag{7.4}$$

where v is the capital to output ratio and $v'(r) < 0$, as we have seen in Fig. 7.6. If the level of output y is not fully known at the time investment decisions are made, then it is plausible to assume that $K_t^* = v(r_t)y_t^E$, where y^E is the expected level of output. Putting the last two equations together, we have:

$$I_t = \alpha \left(K_t^* - K_{t-1}\right)$$

$$= \alpha \left[v(r_t)y_t^E - K_{t-1}\right]. \tag{7.5}$$

This illustrates how investment is a function of the rate of interest via its role in determining the desired capital stock. The assumption that only a proportion of the gap between the current and the desired capital stock can be made up in one period completes the investment function.

If we make two more assumptions, then we can see how to derive the simple accelerator equation from this model. In particular, we have to assume that $\alpha = 1$, so that investment, I, fully makes up the difference between K^* and K each period. The second assumption is that the capital output ratio is constant, so $v(r_t) = \bar{v}$. With these two assumptions we have

$$I_t = K_t^* - K_{t-1}^*$$

$$= \bar{v}\left[y_t^E - y_{t-1}^E\right]. \qquad \text{(accelerator investment function)}$$

This is the accelerator relationship: investment in period t is completely determined by the constant capital output ratio and by the expected growth in output.

2.3 A more general approach to the investment function

A more general approach to a model of investment based on microfoundations starts from asking what is the profit stream derived from some particular level of the capital stock, K, where K was bought in period $t = 0$. To simplify matters, we shall suppose that employment does not enter the picture—that output is produced simply using capital stock so that $y = f(K)$ and also, initially, that there is no depreciation. In looking at the profit stream derived from K, we are not yet concerned with the cost of buying the capital goods, K. In any one period t, the profit from K is

$$Pf(K), \tag{7.6}$$

where P is the price level at which $y = f(K)$ is sold, and which is assumed not to change over time. The simplification about only capital being used in production does not affect the reasoning and means that we do not have to subtract labour costs from the firm's revenue. For simplicity, we assume that the interest rate remains constant over time. In order to calculate the present value of the stream of profits, starting from $t = 0$, each period's profit is discounted by the real rate of interest, $(1 + r)^{t+1}$, so that the discounted present value is:

$$V_0 = \frac{1}{(1+r)}Pf(K) + \frac{1}{(1+r)^2}Pf(K) + \frac{1}{(1+r)^3}Pf(K) + \dots$$
$$= \frac{Pf(K)}{r}. \tag{7.7}$$

We can develop different theories of investment by applying a number of different assumptions to this general result that the present value of the profit stream generated by K is $(Pf(K))/r$. Each theory presupposes that the firm chooses the level of investment to maximize the present value of its profits after having paid for the investment. If the cost of the investment is $C(I)$, the firm chooses I to maximize $V_0 - C(I) = [Pf(K)/r] - C(I)$, subject to the definition $I_t = K_t - K_{t-1}$.

That is, the firm chooses I to maximize

$$\frac{Pf(I + K_{-1})}{r} - C(I).$$

The character of the investment function that can be derived from this maximization problem depends on the assumptions that are made. Three assumptions are of particular importance:

(1) The distinction between perfect and imperfect competition in the product market. We shall assume, first of all, that there is perfect competition. This implies that the firm can sell any increase in output at the market price; hence investment has no effect on the price and P can therefore be taken as constant.

(2) The presence or absence of adjustment costs. This relates to the cost of investment, $C(I)$. There are said to be no adjustment costs if the cost of investment is simply $P_I I$, where P_I is the unit price of a machine, and if P_I is independent of the amount of investment undertaken in a period.

(3) The efficiency or otherwise of the capital market. If the firm can raise as many funds as it wishes at the market rate of interest, the market is operating efficiently, and the formula $Pf(K)/r$ is correct. In such a capital market, the firm faces no credit rationing and the cost of external finance for investment is simply the market rate of interest.

2.3.1 Perfect competition, no adjustment costs, and an efficient capital market

In this case, P is taken as constant and since there are no adjustment costs, the only cost of investment is the cost of purchasing the capital goods themselves: $C(I) = P_I I$. The net profit to the firm is equal to V_0 less the cost of investment, $P_I I$, so in period $t = 0$, the firm chooses investment, I, to maximize:

$$\frac{Pf(I + K_{-1})}{r} - P_I I$$

$$\Rightarrow \frac{Pf'(K)}{r} - P_I = 0$$

$$\Rightarrow \frac{Pf'(K)}{rP_I} = 1,$$

where

$$\frac{Pf'(K)}{rP_I} \equiv q. \qquad \text{(definition of marginal } q)$$

This expression tells us that firms always invest, to ensure that q (usually referred to as 'marginal q') is always equal to one, where q is the ratio of the return to the marginal unit of capital in any one period of time to the cost of capital during that period. The numerator of q, $Pf'(K)$, is the marginal return the firm gets. This is the marginal value product of capital, or the price at which the firm sells its output times the extra output from a marginal unit of capital. The denominator of q, rP_I, is the cost of the capital during that period (or the 'user cost of capital'), which in this simple cases is $P_I r$: the interest lost from having P_I—the market value of this marginal unit of capital—being used as capital rather than invested in a financial asset.

But this profit maximization condition still does not tell us how much investment should take place. Let us call K^* the optimal level of the capital stock. If we know the functional form of $f(K)$, the formula

$$q(K^*) = \frac{Pf'(K^*)}{rP_I} = 1$$

enables us to find K^* explicitly. The condition that $q = 1$ implies that

$$f'(K^*) = rP_I/P.$$

To find K^* explicitly, let us take the example of a specific production function: $y = f(K) = K^{1/2}$. Thus

$$f'(K^*) = 0.5(K^*)^{-1/2} = rP_I/P.$$

So

$$K^* = 1/\left(2rP_I/P\right)^2.$$

Now to see how much should be invested, we have investment, I:

$$I = K^* - K_{-1}$$

$$= 1/\left(2rP_I/P\right)^2 - K_{-1}. \qquad (7.8)$$

More generally,

$$I = I(\bar{r}, \bar{P_I}, \overset{+}{P}),$$

where the signs above the variables indicate the direction of the effect of a change in the variable on investment, holding all other variables constant. This gives us a key result for the investment function in the *IS* curve, namely an increase in r implies a decline in investment, and vice versa.

2.3.2 Perfect competition, an efficient capital market, depreciation and adjustment costs: Tobin's Q model of investment

The cost of adjusting the capital stock (over and above the cost of purchasing the new capital goods ($P_I I$)) can be thought of as including the costs of training workers to operate the new equipment and the disruption to current production caused by installing and testing new equipment. The assumption that the cost of adjusting the capital stock increases more than proportionately with the amount of investment is crucial for the result. A simple model of adjustment costs is $(a/2)P_I I^2$. We therefore have the cost of investment as follows:

$$C(I) = P_I I + (a/2)P_I I^2. \tag{7.9}$$

In addition, we now assume that K depreciates by δ each period so that $I_t = K_t - (1 - \delta) K_{t-1}$. To make the analysis easier, we assume the production function is linear, so that $y = f_K K$, where f_K is the constant marginal productivity of capital. We shall see—perhaps surprisingly—that by including quadratic adjustment costs a very neat investment function emerges. The firm chooses I to maximize [14]

$$\frac{Pf_K K}{1+r} + \frac{Pf_K K(1-\delta)}{(1+r)^2} + \cdots - P_I I - (a/2)P_I I^2 = \frac{Pf_K(I + (1-\delta)K_{-1})}{r+\delta} - P_I I - (a/2)P_I I^2 \tag{7.12}$$

which implies

$$\frac{Pf_K}{r+\delta} - P_I - aP_I I = 0$$

$$\Rightarrow \frac{Pf_K'}{r+\delta} = P_I(1 + a.I)$$

$$\Rightarrow I = \frac{1}{a}\left[\frac{Pf_K'}{P_I(r+\delta)} - 1\right]. \tag{7.13}$$

Using the definition of 'marginal q' introduced above now including depreciation, we have:

$$I = \frac{1}{a}[q - 1]. \qquad \text{(Tobin's } Q \text{ model)}$$

This is a very neat formula. It says that if $q > 1$, so that the capital stock is too low, investment will take place to reduce this gap, and that the extent to which it is reduced in

[14] To get this result, use the fact that the sum of the infinite series $1 + x + x^2 + \ldots$ is $1/(1 - x)$; and rewrite

$$\frac{1}{(1+r)} + \frac{(1-\delta)}{(1+r)^2} + \frac{(1-\delta)^2}{(1+r)^3} + \ldots = \frac{1}{(1+r)}\left[1 + \frac{(1-\delta)}{(1+r)} + \frac{(1-\delta)^2}{(1+r)^2} + \ldots\right] \tag{7.10}$$

The RHS term is then

$$\frac{1}{(1+r)}\left[\frac{1}{1 - \frac{(1-\delta)}{(1+r)}}\right] = \frac{1}{(1+r)}\left[\frac{1}{\frac{r+\delta}{1+r}}\right] = \frac{1}{r+\delta}. \tag{7.11}$$

any one period of time depends on *a*, the marginal cost of adjusting the capital stock. The bigger is *a*, the less investment will make up the gap immediately, and the more spread out the process will be.

Each of the factors that can influence investment are considered in turn:

- *Adjustment costs.* We have assumed a simple form of adjustment costs: in general, the only requirement for deriving the *q* model is that adjustment costs be convex—i.e. the cost of adjustment increases more than in proportion to the amount of investment. The higher are the adjustment costs (*a*), the smaller is investment. There is a slower adjustment of the capital stock to its desired level. We return to discuss this assumption about adjustment costs below.
- *Value of the marginal product of capital.* Any technological progress or a technology shock will shift the production function and alter the value of the marginal product of capital. Similarly, if we introduce uncertainty about the future, then it is clear that expectations about future marginal productivity will enter the equation. A higher expected price for output will boost expected revenue and raise investment.
- *Price of capital goods.* A change in the price of capital goods (P_I) relative to the general price level (*P*) through, for example, the introduction of an investment subsidy by the government would change the level of investment. A subsidy lowers the user cost of capital and therefore boosts investment; a tax does the opposite.
- *Real interest rate.* A rise in the real interest rate increases the opportunity cost of investment in physical capital. From an initial position of equilibrium, a rise in the interest rate means that the desired capital stock is lower than the actual capital stock and disinvestment will occur.
- *Depreciation rate.* This is normally assumed to be a constant although faster technical progress in the future will mean reduced profits from investing now.

Tobin's *Q* investment function is derived from a model of microeconomic optimization behaviour (plus an ad hoc adjustment cost function). Investment is a negative function of the real rate of interest just as in the simple investment function that we used in the *IS* equation, $I = I(A, r)$. The thrust of Tobin's *Q* model is that given the adjustment costs, *q* is a *sufficient* determinant of investment. All the relevant expectational factors that shift the investment function and hence the *IS* curve by changing *A* are captured by the forward-looking variable *q*. We shall return below to the question of how one might test how important *q* actually is in influencing investment.

At this point it is useful to note that we can use financial market valuations as a way of measuring *q*. As we have seen, *q* is the expected value of the profit stream generated by an increase in the capital stock divided by the cost of the additional capital goods. The market value of the firm is equal to the value of its shares plus its net debt. If we call this *MV*, then we can think of ΔMV as the financial market's valuation of the profit stream from a small change in the firm's capital stock. In other words:

$$\frac{\Delta MV}{\text{purchase price of additional capital goods}} = q.$$

We can now define 'average q' or Q as follows:

$$Q = \frac{MV}{\text{replacement cost of firm's entire capital stock}} \qquad \text{(definition of average } q\text{: Q)}$$

where the replacement cost is the cost of replacing the entire capital stock at current prices of capital goods.

Although average and marginal q are not in general the same, they are related to each other and because average q can be measured by using stock market valuations of companies, the Q model of investment can be tested. We return to this below. But first, it is useful to relax the assumption of perfect competition in our basic model.

2.3.3 Imperfect competition, efficient capital markets, and no adjustment costs

We now use the same approach to go in a rather different direction. In particular, we wish to explore how a shift from a perfectly competitive product market to one of imperfect competition affects the investment function. Under imperfect competition the price of the firm's product is not fixed exogenously: firms set prices so as to maximize their profits and the price that they set will depend on the expected level of demand that they face. Imperfectly competitive firms face downward-sloping demand curves. We assume now that the firm operates under conditions of monopolistic competition and faces the demand curve

$$y_i = P_i^{-\eta}(A/n) \qquad (7.14)$$

where A is aggregate demand, η is the elasticity of demand and there are n sectors. Furthermore, to keep things simple, we shall assume that $y = f(K) = K$. In other words, we are assuming that the marginal (and average) product of capital is constant and equal to one. It is not necessary to make this assumption but in order to focus on the difference that imperfect competition makes, we want to simplify the rest of the story.

Now consider the discounted present value expression for firm i:

$$V_0 = \frac{P_i f(K)}{(r+\delta)}.$$

Under imperfect competition, an increase in the capital stock, K, is no longer consistent with a constant price of output, P_i. Rather, an increase in the capital stock, which implies an increase in the firm's output means either that P_i falls or alternatively that aggregate demand, A/n, has risen (or is expected to rise). Let us see the consequences.

The firm chooses investment to maximize:

$$\frac{P_i f(K)}{r+\delta} - P_I.I$$

so the condition for profit maximization is

$$\frac{1}{r+\delta}\frac{\partial [P_i f(K)]}{\partial I} - P_I = 0. \qquad (7.15)$$

We now need to incorporate the imperfectly competitive setting by substituting for the firm's price, P_i in the maximization condition, using the expression for the demand curve:

$$y_i = P_i^{-\eta}(A/n)$$
$$\Rightarrow P_i = y_i^{-\frac{1}{\eta}}(A/n)^{\frac{1}{\eta}} \tag{7.16}$$

We proceed in two steps, concentrating first on $\partial\left[P_i f(K)\right]/\partial I$:

$$\frac{\partial\left[P_i f(K)\right]}{\partial I} = \frac{\partial}{\partial I}\left[y_i^{-\frac{1}{\eta}}(A/n)^{\frac{1}{\eta}}K\right]$$
$$= \frac{\partial}{\partial I}\left[K^{-\frac{1}{\eta}}(A/n)^{\frac{1}{\eta}}K\right]$$
$$= \frac{\partial\left[K^{1-\frac{1}{\eta}}(A/n)^{\frac{1}{\eta}}\right]}{\partial I}. \tag{7.17}$$

Hence, starting from equation (7.15), we have:

$$\frac{1}{r+\delta}\cdot\frac{\partial\left[P_i f(K)\right]}{\partial I} - P_I = \frac{(A/n)^{\frac{1}{\eta}}}{r+\delta}\cdot\frac{\eta-1}{\eta}K^{-\frac{1}{\eta}} - P_I = 0$$
$$\Rightarrow K^* = \left[\frac{(\eta-1)}{\eta(r+\delta)P_I}\right]^{\eta}\cdot\frac{A}{n} \tag{7.18}$$

Linking this condition for the optimal capital stock, K^*, with the investment definition and bearing in mind there are no costs of adjustment, we have:

$$I = K^* - (1-\delta)K^*_{-1}$$
$$= n^{-1}\left[\frac{(\eta-1)}{\eta(r+\delta)P_I}\right]^{\eta}\cdot[A - (1-\delta)A_{-1}] \tag{7.19}$$

Investment is a function of the expected change in demand. If the rate of interest is constant, then this is the accelerator formula. This helps to explain where the accelerator investment function comes from. An investment function with an accelerator component *cannot* be derived from microfoundations in a perfectly competitive model with constant returns to scale where firms can sell as much as they like at the market price but it arises naturally in a setting of imperfect competition where the investment decision is intimately connected with demand expectations.

2.4 **Data and testing**

2.4.1 **Puzzles**

Empirical studies of aggregate investment have frequently found:

• a substantial role for a 'scale' term (output or cash flow or both).

• a modest role for capital costs (measured by Q or its components including the real interest rate).

A comprehensive survey of empirical studies of investment concluded:[15] 'It appears to this author that on balance the response of investment to price variables tends to be small and unimportant relative to quantity variables.'

The puzzle of understanding the determinants of investment has not been completely solved but a number of recent developments provide some pointers toward explaining:

- why relative costs may be important for investment behaviour but difficult to measure in aggregate data and

- why a scale effect (such as output or cash flow) is important for investment although it is omitted from the 'marginal-q' investment function. The presence of an output growth term is quite consistent with a model of investment under imperfect competition. The role of cash flow suggests that capital market imperfections are important.

2.4.2 Cost of capital: marginal and average Q and taxation

As we have already seen, there is a way to test the theory that investment depends on q because we can link the numerator of marginal q to a change in the market value of the firm when the capital stock is increased and the denominator to the replacement cost of the new capital goods. We can measure average q:

$$Q = \frac{MV}{\text{replacement cost of firm's entire capital stock}} = \frac{MV}{P_I K},$$

where MV is the market value of the firm and $P_I K$ is the replacement cost of the firm's existing capital stock, K_t, valued at the current prices of capital goods, P_I.

In line with Keynes's stress on the role of expectations as a determinant of investment, Tobin argued in favour of Q in the investment function because it represented a way of measuring the expectational influences on future profitability reflected in the stock market valuation of the firm. Keynes wrote:[16]

daily evaluations of the Stock Exchange ... inevitably exert a decisive influence on the rate of current investment. For there is no sense in building up a new enterprise at a cost greater than that at which a similar existing enterprise can be purchased; whilst there is an inducement to spend on a new project what may seem an extravagant sum, if it can be floated off on the Stock Exchange at an immediate profit.

Q can only be measured easily for firms that are listed on liquid stock exchanges since the share price provides a readily available measure of the market value of the firm. But it is unlikely that the firms quoted on the stock exchange operate under the perfectly competitive and frictionless conditions necessary for marginal and average q to be equal. Even if the marginal-q investment function is a good model, measured Q might not be very successful in an empirical investment function because of the influence on share prices

---

[15] Chirinko (1993).　　[16] Keynes (1936: 151) quoted in Chirinko (1993: 1888).

of factors that are not related to the fundamental value of the firm. As discussed further in Chapter 8 well-documented phenomena of fads and speculative bubbles influence share prices. A recent study using US micro data (over 1,000 firms from 1982 to 1999) shows that a Q model of investment can be successfully estimated when analysts' forecasts of a firm's earnings are used instead of stock market price to measure its fundamental value.[17]

Another empirical research strategy has pursued the argument that clearer evidence of capital cost effects may be revealed after a change in taxation that affects the cost of capital. A number of studies have pursued this approach by looking at specific episodes of tax reforms and have uncovered more substantial cost of capital effects on investment than have been found in aggregate data.[18] In addition to its value as a device for trying to pin down the role of capital costs in general for investment behaviour, the analysis of the impact of taxes on investment is an important substantive issue in macroeconomic policy analysis. The return to the investor from installing new capital equipment or structures is affected by taxation in a number of different ways: first, corporate profits are taxed under the corporation tax system; second, after profits have been distributed to owners as dividends, they are subject to income tax (if the recipient is liable to income tax); and third, owners who realize capital gains by selling shares are subject to capital gains tax. Working in the opposite direction—to reduce the cost of capital—are so-called capital allowances that allow some investment expenditures to be set against current profits and thus reduce taxation. Evidence from OECD countries suggests that the tax/subsidy system has the overall effect of raising the cost of capital.[19]

2.4.3 The lumpiness of investment and the assumption of smooth adjustment costs

In the search for a more satisfactory understanding of investment, empirical researchers have looked very closely at the pattern of investment in individual firms and plants. They found something extremely interesting and quite at odds with the stylized picture of investment with the kind of adjustment costs discussed above. As emphasized in the discussion of adjustment costs, the cost of adjusting the capital stock was assumed to *increase* more than proportionately with the size of the investment: the cost was a function of the square of investment (i.e. the adjustment costs were quadratic). This led to a smooth adjustment process because big changes in the capital stock incurred big adjustment costs. But when economists looked at very detailed microeconomic data for very large numbers of plants, they found that contrary to the idea of a smooth investment flow, investment was in fact very lumpy.[20]

One study that used data from 360,000 plants in the USA found that nearly one-fifth of aggregate investment in one year took place in 100 of the plants (whereas only about 10% of production took place in the top 100 producers). Equally striking was their finding in a sample of 12,000 plants for which they had investment data for seventeen years, that for the median establishment nearly 40% of all of its investment over the period took place in one episode (a burst of investment in one or two adjacent years). These results point toward very large, infrequent adjustments of the capital stock—quite the opposite

---

[17] Bond and Cummins (2001). [18] See, for example, Cummins, Hassett, and Hubbard (1994).
[19] See, for example, Bond and Jenkinson (1996).
[20] The following discussion draws on the survey chapter on 'Investment' by Caballero (1999).

of smooth, incremental adjustment. Large, infrequent bursts of investment would be expected if there is a fixed cost to undertaking investment. This may be one reason for the empirical difficulties with fitting an investment function such as the marginal-q one based on quadratic adjustment costs. If there is a large fixed cost of investment, then a given value of marginal-q can be associated both with zero investment and with a large amount of investment because only when the gap between the firm's actual capital stock and its desired capital stock has become sufficiently large is the fixed cost of investment offset and investment triggered. Although aggregate series for investment are relatively smooth, evidence is beginning to build up to support the view that a model that incorporates lumpy adjustment fits the aggregate data better than one in which smooth adjustment is assumed. One part of the story that may help to reconcile the lumpy micro and smoother aggregate investment data is the introduction of the entry of new firms (with new capital stock) and the exit of firms (scrapping of capital stock) into the model.

2.4.4 Cash flow, profits, and credit constraints

Empirical investment equations typically include both a measure of the cost of capital such as Q and a measure of cash flow and/or output. The cash flow variable is normally both more significant and more important in accounting for investment than the cost of capital variable. As we have seen, there is no room in the marginal-q investment function for any variable other than q. It is difficult to reconcile the importance of cash flow for investment with the marginal-q theory. The reason is that forward-looking firms should take into account any credit constraints that they face: these should already be incorporated into q, with the consequence that any additional cash flow variable should add no explanatory power.

The importance of cash flow variables in estimated investment equations is reminiscent of the importance of current and lagged income variables in estimated consumption functions. In the consumption function, current income was shown to matter because there are households with small or zero assets who are denied access to credit and hence are liquidity constrained. This factor was relevant to the presence of the so-called excess sensitivity of consumption to predictable changes in income. Similarly, the presence of cash flow terms in estimated investment functions strongly suggests that there are firms that do not have access to frictionless capital markets. In other words if there are firms that cannot borrow as much as they would like or cannot sell as much equity as they would like in order to finance their investment plans, then investment will be limited by their internal funds.

This is sometimes referred to as the excess sensitivity of investment to internal funds. For firms like this, cash flow would be expected to be an important determinant of investment. The reason why firms may be rationed in their access to debt (e.g. bank loans) or equity finance is explored in Chapter 8 when we look at credit market imperfections in the context of the monetary policy transmission mechanism.

The presence of liquidity or credit constraints has been found in many studies of investment using disaggregated data for a number of different countries.[21] Although there are

---

[21] See, for example, Chirinko (1993).

still lively debates about econometric methodology, the weight of evidence seems to suggest that for a substantial proportion of firms, it is not appropriate to model investment decisions as if these firms had access to a perfect capital market. For such firms investment is sensitive to the amount of internal funds that are available. Internal funds are in turn highly responsive to current profits—the more so because interest payments are fixed and firms are reluctant to cut dividends.

An example of the results obtained from UK microeconomic data is the following. A study using UK company data for the period 1975–86 found that company investment was significantly influenced by Q and by liquidity constraints.[22] The impact of Q was found to be very small: a 10% rise in the stock market value of a company was associated with an immediate rise in the investment rate of only 2.5%. Cash flow was very important. The sample period was divided into two and it was found that the impact of Q was lower and the impact of cash flow higher in the first part of the sample during which the UK economy was in a deep recession. This is consistent with the idea of liquidity constraints biting especially hard in a recession. Another study uses a completely different econometric methodology on macroeconomic data for UK fixed investment in manufacturing for 1968–90 and finds similar results.[23] Investment is found to depend on Q, output and on the debt structure of firms (which captures the imperfections in the capital market).

2.4.5 High hurdle rates for investment: the option value of waiting

A widely discussed hypothesis that may account for some of the puzzles in investment behaviour relates to the role of uncertainty.[24] The following three features are common to many investment decisions:

(1) Investment entails a sunk cost, i.e. not only may there be a large fixed cost of investment as discussed in the earlier section but the cost may be sunk, i.e. not recoverable in the event of the project becoming unprofitable.

(2) There is pervasive uncertainty in the economic environment and information arrives gradually as time passes.

(3) The decision involves not only whether to go ahead with the project but also when to do so.

Under these circumstances, there is a value to waiting to undertake an investment project since with the passing of time and the arrival of more information, the costs of delay (lost profits from the project) may be outweighed by more secure information on the balance between the costs including those sunk in the project and the benefits of undertaking it. The upshot of such considerations is that an expected rate of return considerably higher than the cost of capital will be required to trigger investment. Dixit gives examples to show that including the so-called option value of waiting can double the hurdle rate for an investment project to proceed. It will be optimal to wait longer (i.e. there is a higher hurdle rate)

---

[22] Blundell et al. (1992).   [23] Cuthbertson and Gasparro (1993).
[24] This discussion draws on Dixit (1992). See also Pindyck (1991).

- when the future is less heavily discounted
- when there is more uncertainty about earnings.

Imperfect competition plays a central role in this model of investment. If the investment opportunity is available to all firms, i.e. there is a perfectly competitive market with free entry, then the option value of waiting disappears. As Dixit puts it:

In the simple example, the opportunity to invest was assigned to just one firm. But if it is available to any of several firms, then waiting is no longer feasible. The option to wait will expire because some competitor will seize the opportunity. Then some firm will invest as soon as the expected present value crosses zero. (1992: 118)

The model provides a link to the discussion of hysteresis in Chapter 4. It gives an explanation as to why sunk costs whether in skilled workers or in fixed investment, make firms on the one hand reluctant to abandon projects and on the other hand more cautious to embark on new ones. Hence the effects of a recession can persist for a lengthy period as such effects play out and will vary across economies as a consequence of differences in

- the importance of firm-specific skills
- hiring and firing regulations
- the specificity of sunk costs.

2.5 Conclusions about investment

Investment remains a tricky subject for economists. Much progress has been made by using the discipline of modelling a rational profit maximizing firm as the starting point for the empirical analysis of investment. We have seen that the cost of capital and the expected growth of output are determinants of investment in the general imperfect competition case. In addition, once capital market imperfections are introduced, cash flow will play a role. The use of Q to provide a direct measure of forward-looking expected profitability has proved empirically significant but the role of capital costs captured by Q in explaining investment is often small. Liquidity constraints seem to be important at least for some proportion of firms so that a cash flow term has to be included in empirical investment functions. The more detailed examination of investment suggests that the investment function would take the form:

$$I = I(\overset{+}{A}, \overset{-}{r}, \overset{+}{CF}) \qquad \text{(investment function)}$$

where A measures the expectational factors including the expected growth of output that influence the profits expected to be generated by the investment, r is the real rate of interest, and CF is a measure of the cash flow of the firm. Current cash flow is a function of the current sales and therefore output of the firm, so we can write:

$$I = I(\overset{+}{A}, \overset{-}{r}, \overset{+}{y})$$
$$= A - b_0 r + b_1 y.$$

In practice the degree of moral hazard, the nature of liquidity constraints, and their impact on cash flow are hard to quantify. Expectations will not always be accurately measured by the market value of the firm: the stock market will not always reflect the 'fundamentals'. However, these insights should allow us to take note of how policy decisions, structural changes, or economic shocks may affect the investment function that we use in the *IS* equation. The expectations component of *Q* is included in the *A* term (along with the expected growth of output): these factors will shift the *IS* curve. The sensitivity of investment to the cost of capital is captured by the coefficient on *r* and the direct effect of current output on investment (e.g. for firms that are liquidity constrained) will be reflected in the multiplier: both of these will affect the slope of the *IS* curve.

3 Conclusions on consumption and investment

To conclude this chapter, we sketch how the working of the *IS-PC-MR* model is affected by incorporating forward-looking behaviour into the analysis of aggregate demand. This is followed by a discussion of how the more detailed examination of the determinants of consumption and investment behaviour in this chapter can be used to explore the debate at the turn of the twenty-first century in the USA about the so-called New Economy.

3.1 A forward-looking *IS* curve and the *IS-PC-MR* model

In Chapter 15 we look at how the behaviour of the *IS-PC-MR* model is affected if

- households are assumed to make their consumption decisions on the basis of their expected future income;
- households work out the effect on future output and hence on their current demand of the consequences of shocks for the actions of the central bank; and
- the central bank takes account of the effect of future output on current demand in the *IS* curve.

We can sketch the intuition here and leave the details for Chapter 15. Suppose there is an inflation shock. Households can forecast that a positive inflation shock now will lead the central bank to instigate a sequence of increased (though declining) interest rates over future periods until equilibrium is again restored. Hence households immediately dampen demand by more than the impact of an increased short-term interest rate so as to smooth the effect of the future higher interest rates on their consumption path. As we have seen in this chapter, with forward-looking households, current demand is a function, not just of the lagged real short-term interest rate, but of all (expected) future real short-term interest rates. Thus household demand immediately contracts in response to the full course of expected future real interest rates. This means in turn that the central bank—so long as it works through the implications of forward-looking household behaviour—needs to raise interest rates by less than it otherwise would to achieve the desired reduction in inflation. The anticipatory behaviour of households and the central bank are reinforcing, so that output falls and interest rates rise less than in our previous examples (with the traditional *IS* curve). With an ordinary *IS* curve, households do not take into account the future pattern of deflation the central bank will impose in the event of a shock of this kind. Therefore the central bank has to impose a bigger recession. In short, the presence of forward-looking households reduces the fluctuations in the economy in response to shocks when the behaviour of the central bank is well understood and predictable.

3.2 An example: a 'New Economy'?

In this section we shall explore a real-world example to illustrate how the insights of this chapter in coordination with the *IS*/*LM* or 3-equation model can be used to interpret a real world example, namely the behaviour of the US economy in the late 1990s. Suppose that a new discovery is made or a new development occurs that leads everyone to believe that productivity growth rates in the future are going to be higher (for example, suppose the development of the internet leads to higher productivity). Since future productivity levels are now going to be higher than previously expected, future wages, also, would be expected to be higher. Since people expect higher future wages, their assessment of their permanent incomes has increased, and so they will consume more (even if their current incomes have not yet risen). This higher consumption is captured in the *IS* equation as an increase in c_0, which, being an autonomous component of expenditure, leads (through the multiplier effect) to a shift right of the *IS* curve, and thus to an increase in output.

However, because autonomous consumption has risen but income has not risen yet (it is expectations of future income that have risen, not present income itself), that means that consumer debt levels must have risen also (i.e. the difference between what is consumed and this period's income). Expressed in terms of net savings rather than the change in debts, we can say that savings $(y - c)$ will fall. If we have an open economy, the rise in output will lead to a rise in imports, and thus to a reduction in net exports (and therefore to an increase in the trade deficit). We therefore have a number of predictions of what will happen if expected future productivity growth rises:

(1) Consumption will rise.

(2) Output will rise.

(3) Net savings will fall (i.e. debts will rise).

(4) Net exports will fall (i.e. the trade deficit will rise).

In the mid to late 1990s, features (1) to (4) were indeed displayed by the US economy following the widespread belief that the USA had entered a 'new economy' phase in which higher, internet-related, productivity growth was possible. Our augmented *IS* equation offers us insights into that internet-related boom. One interesting feature to note relates to the 'sustainability' of the debt levels. Financial newspaper comment articles often speculate over whether debt levels in a boom are 'sustainable', with the implication being that if they are not sustainable that is dangerous. In our New Economy example, the expected level of debts would not be sustainable if that proportion of income were borrowed each period forever. However, our agents are not expecting to continue to borrow this proportion. Once the productivity rises occur and wages rise, debt levels would be expected to fall by themselves. To be sure, these debt levels are unsustainable—but then again no one is expecting to sustain them.

However, suppose now that, at some point, agents decided that, in fact, the increase in productivity growth was not going to be as high as they had expected. Then debt levels would no longer be sustainable because the wage rises are no longer expected to enable agents to pay off their debts. If that were the case we would expect consumption plans to be revised downwards, output to fall, net savings to rise, and the trade deficit to fall. However, in 2001 when the US economy slowed, it did not exhibit these features. Consumption continued to grow strongly and personal debts rose. This suggests that the end of the New Economy boom is not to be explained as a loss of confidence by wage earners in the productivity yield of the internet, or else it suggests that consumers take some time to 'catch up' in understanding that future productivity growth will not be as high as expected, and that when they do catch up there will be further contraction as c_0 falls. In either case, a different explanation is needed for what happened in 2001.

To understand the behaviour of the economy in 2001, we shall consider investment, for it was investment that fell significantly and dragged the US economy into recession. Why did that happen? One possibility is that companies obtain information about future productivity growth earlier than consumers, and that it takes some time for the price signals arising from investment decisions to filter through to consumption behaviour (perhaps because of the adjustment cost issues that were relevant in determining investment behaviour). On that interpretation, 'A' in the investment function was shifted up in the 1990s because of higher future profit expectations arising from the internet, driving up investment. In 2000 this sentiment was reversed, as reflected in the dramatic falls in technology stocks towards the end of that year. Investment accordingly contracted. In that case we should expect consumption to follow suit eventually, as market signals filter through to rational consumers—perhaps leading to a classic 'double dip' recession as typically observed in the case of US slowdowns.

On the other hand, another possibility is that future productivity will be higher, but investors have realized that the fruits of higher productivity will be taken in the form of higher wages and lower margins. This would lead to a fall in the mark-up, μ, in our basic model, and hence in the medium-run to higher output, but when investors realize this it also leads to a fall back in 'A' and a shift left in the investment schedule, but this time without any corresponding fall in c_0 to follow. In that case the recession of 2001 would not be expected to be followed by a double dip since consumption plans do not need to be adjusted.

A third possibility relates to cash flow constraints. Because of the asymmetric information problems discussed further in Chapter 8, loans may be a less effective form of finance than equity for risky ventures like internet start-ups. If that is so, and the falls in the technology sector of stock markets meant that it was hard to raise equity for internet start-ups, investment in the internet may have become depressed through cash flow constraints. Investment may then stay low until stock market sentiment recovers (which may have little to do with the underlying fundamentals of future productivity and profitability of internet ventures).

One last possibility is that something happened in 2000 or 2001 that changed the assessment of future real interest rates. If future real interest rates were expected to be higher, then investment would become less profitable, even if future productivity levels will be higher as expected. One possibility here is that it came to be believed that there is a significant risk of prices starting to fall rapidly. In that scenario, given that the minimum level of nominal interest rates is zero (because cash offers a nominal interest rate of zero), the real interest rate would become very high, and many otherwise profitable investment projects would no longer be viable. How to explain the New Economy boom and subsequent contraction remains an open question, to which we shall return in more detail in Chapter 17. But the discussion here illustrates how we can use the more detailed study of consumption and investment to improve our understanding of contemporary situations.

■ QUESTIONS

Checklist questions

(1) What is the relationship between the marginal and average propensity to consume in the standard Keynesian consumption function? In the permanent income hypothesis?

(2) Provide concise explanations in words for the results summarized in Table 7.1.

(3) Use the Discrete Time Ramsey equation and the Ramsey consumption function and explain what happens to the growth of consumption and to current consumption under the following circumstances:
   (*a*) a rise in the rate of interest;
   (*b*) the individual becomes more impatient;
   (*c*) the individual unexpectedly inherits a house.

(4) What is precautionary saving? What assumptions are needed for precautionary savings to arise? Does precautionary saving resolve some empirical puzzles in consumption behaviour?

(5) What is meant by the term 'random walk'? Under what conditions will consumption follow such behaviour?

(6) What is meant by the expression 'excess sensitivity' of consumption? How do the assumptions of the simple PIH have to be amended to account for this finding?

(7) Explain what is meant by the 'excess smoothness' of consumption and why it may characterize behaviour.

(8) Why may households not be able to borrow against the value of their future income?

(9) This question relates to the consumption function presented in section 1.10. Suggest why the real interest rate may have a negative effect on consumption. Use an *IS* diagram to represent the consumption function and discuss how consumption and hence the *IS* curve responds (*ceteris paribus*) to,

 (*a*) a higher proportion of creditors in the economy;

 (*b*) an easing of liquidity constraints (e.g. because of more competition in the credit sector);

 (*c*) more uncertainty about future income growth;

 (*d*) lower overall wealth (e.g. due to the bursting of a housing price bubble).

(10) Using the simple investment function: $I = A - br$ explain what happens to the *IS* curve if

 (*a*) profitability in the future is expected to be lower;

 (*b*) the real interest rate falls;

 (*c*) the future real interest rate is expected to fall.

(11) What assumptions are required in order to derive the accelerator investment function? Why does investment take place according to this model?

(12) How does the introduction of adjustment costs and imperfect competition alter the modelling of investment?

(13) What is the difference between q and Q? Under what assumptions is investment solely a function of q? Do empirical Q based investment models fail because these assumptions are invalid or because Q is a poor measure of q?

(14) Compare the investment function of Chapter 2 ($I = A - br$) with the investment function in section 2.5 ($I = A - b_0 r + b_1 y$). Why is the additional output term in the equation? How would the following affect the *IS* curve (*ceteris paribus*):

 (*a*) increased sales;

 (*b*) a change in competition law that will allow firms to exploit more economies of scale opportunities in the future;

 (*c*) a fall in corporation tax;

 (*d*) a fall in the interest rate;

 (*e*) higher interest sensitivity of investment;

 (*f*) higher output sensitivity of investment.

Problems and questions for discussion

QUESTION A. Aggregate consumption varies less than GDP and aggregate investment varies more. Can you reconcile these observations with the assumption that consumption and investment decisions are taken by rational, forward-looking agents?

QUESTION B. Explain how you would expect a boom in asset prices to affect the macroeconomy.

QUESTION C. There is widespread concern in the OECD economies about the inadequacy of (*a*) public pension arrangements and/or (*b*) private savings to provide adequately for retirement. Is this observation consistent with the models of consumption presented in this chapter?

QUESTION D. Examine how well the theories of investment presented in the chapter account for the fact that aggregate investment is procyclical.

QUESTION E. The US economy went into recession in March 2001 and, in response, the government introduced a tax rebate programme which amounted to cheques of $300 or $600 in value being sent to about two-thirds of US households. The aim was to mitigate the recession. What would the consumption theories discussed in this chapter predict to be the outcome? [To find out what actually happened, see Johnson, Parker, and Souleles (2004).]

8 | Money and Finance

What is the role of money and finance in macroeconomics? In short- and medium-run macroeconomics, we ask where the questions about money and finance fit into the *IS-PC-MR* model or the *IS/LM* model. The answer is that they matter for the aggregate demand rather than for the supply side of the economy. We have already seen that the modelling of central bank behaviour is the key difference between the two models. Money and finance also fit into the analysis of the *IS* relation, which is common to both models. This chapter deals in turn with the implications of money and finance for the *IS* and then for the monetary rule/*LM*.

On the *IS* side, an understanding of the variety of assets that are used as stores of wealth by households is useful for the analysis of consumption behaviour. We have seen that liquidity constraints play a role in both consumption and investment behaviour. Firms and households do not generally have access to perfect capital markets: they cannot borrow as much as they would like at the same interest rate at which they could lend. For firms, this has the effect of making *external finance* whether it be borrowing (debt finance) or raising finance by selling equity more expensive than *internal finance*. Some firms may be entirely reliant on internal funds—i.e. they can only undertake investment spending if they have sufficient cash flow. To explain why households and firms can face liquidity constraints, we need to look at why banks and other financial institutions exist and how information problems lead to credit rationing. In the modelling of investment, the role of profit expectations was highlighted. In the Q theory, for example, investment responds to any difference between the market valuation of the firm (as measured by the value of its shares listed on the stock market) and the replacement cost of its capital stock. This raises the question of how shares are valued.

Turning to the monetary rule in the *IS-PC-MR* model and to the *LM* in the *IS/LM* model, we have already discussed many relevant issues in Chapters 2, 3, and 5. However, there remain a few questions to tidy up and these are dealt with here. In particular, we set out the logic of the argument of those who view central banks as setting the monetary base (as assumed in the definition of the *LM*) and those who view central banks as setting the interest rate. The mechanics of the monetary base multiplier are set out and the practical steps by which the central bank actually sets the interest rate are explained, using as an example the procedures of the Bank of England. We also discuss the demand for money, why it may be volatile and why that matters.

We begin the chapter with a discussion of different assets and their characteristics. This takes us to a brief description of key institutions: banks, the central bank, and the stock market. This is followed by a section on information problems and their significance for the role of money and finance in macroeconomics. This entails looking at the role of firms and how information problems affect their ability to finance investment. The fourth section discusses money supply and money demand. The chapter concludes by bringing the *IS* and *MR* related discussions together to discuss the transmission of monetary policy to the real economy and the role played by finance in the propagation of macroeconomic shocks. This incorporates the more realistic features of firms, banks and other institutions developed in this chapter.

1 Assets

We begin by clarifying the characteristics of the different assets in the economy, who holds them and why. When shocks to the economy or changes in policy affect the value of an asset, we need to know what kind of agent holds the asset in order to be able to predict the likely implications for economic activity. Will consumption or investment be affected—or the demand for money? Assets differ in liquidity, return, and risk characteristics and in the direct utility that they may provide. Compare for example money, equities, and housing. Money is liquid and provides utility because it allows transactions to be undertaken with ease but it provides no return. Its nominal value is fixed but its value in real terms will be reduced by inflation. By contrast, a bond cannot be used for transactions but pays interest; the nominal value of a bond changes with a change in the interest rate. Equities have intermediate liquidity (there are transactions costs involved in trading them), they offer no guaranted return but offer an expected return with a degree of risk. Risk lovers may derive utility from holding equities but otherwise they provide no direct utility. Housing is relatively illiquid. It provides direct utility for owner-occupiers. It provides no guaranteed return. Table 8.1 has a summary of the definitions, characteristics (liquidity, risk, and return) and likely holders of different kinds of assets.

1.1 Money

In a decentralized economy with many different kinds of goods, money serves the purpose of allowing transactions to occur without requiring the 'double coincidence of wants'. The availability of money as a *medium of exchange* means that, say, the electric pump manufacturer can hire workers who want to work in order to purchase groceries and consumer durables—not electric pumps. The central role of money in facilitating transactions can explain why people are willing to hold money in its narrowest form such as notes and coins or cheque accounts even though in terms of return it is dominated by other safe assets that pay interest such as a term account. In other words, the difference between narrow money and the term account is liquidity, which measures the ease with which money can be used for transactions. Whilst cheque accounts sometimes pay interest, it is at a very low rate. Other safe assets pay higher interest rates but they offer less liquidity. Periods of notice are required to withdraw money from high interest accounts and it is often necessary to keep a minimum balance in such an account, reducing the flexibility with which it can be used for transactions.

Table 8.1 Main asset types

Asset	Definition	Characteristics	Asset of whom?	Liability of whom?
M0, H	High powered money, monetary base. Currency in circulation + commercial bank reserves at CB.	Liquid, capital-safe (nominal), nil return.	HH, F	CB
M1, M2	Narrow money. Currency in circulation + deposits in current accounts.	Liquid, capital-safe (nominal), interest.	HH, F	B
M3, M4	Broad money. Narrow money + deposits in savings accounts with restricted & unrestricted access + in non-bank financial institutions.	Less liquid, capital-safe (nominal), higher interest.	HH, F	B, nbfi
Bonds (government)	Pays fixed nominal payments at stated intervals.	Less liquid, value varies with i, default risk, interest.	HH, F, B, nbfi	Government
Bonds (company)	Same as government bond.	Less liquid, value varies with i, higher default risk, interest.	HH, B, nbfi	F
Equity, shares	Pays unspecified dividend.	Less liquid, value varies with firm profits, risky.	HH, nbfi	F
Housing		Illiquid; housing services to owner occupier.	HH	
Pensions	Pays benefit in retirement.	Illiquid.	HH	Government, F, nbfi

Key: HH = household; F = firm; B = commercial bank; CB = central bank; nbfi = non-bank financial institution.

Money has a second role as a *store of value*. This enables people to engage in trades that are separated in time. If a journalist is paid for writing an article in boxes of tomatoes, she will need to eat those tomatoes quickly before they rot. In contrast, if she is paid in money then she can wait for years before turning the product of her work into consumption. That gives her more flexibility over her trading choices.

The third important role of money is as a *unit of account*. In a barter economy if we can find a double coincidence of wants we may be able to discover that our one goat is worth two bags of apples, and that a chicken can buy a haircut. But that does not tell us how many apples a chicken is worth, or the relative prices of goats and haircuts. Money allows us to compare the value of all goods and services in terms of a common standard—the unit of account. This is very valuable as it provides us with important information about the relative value of tasks—for example, whether it is more profitable for the journalist to write articles or to be an accountant.

Each of the functions of money enables specialization and promotes efficiency. Money cuts down enormously on the time spent obtaining information about the relative costs and profitability of different ventures, and on finding people with whom one can trade. Quite apart from technological progress (such as scientific discoveries or engineering advances), improvements in the efficiency of the payments system through money is a potential source of economic growth. At its simplest, fewer resources are tied up in making the payments system operate; more importantly, better functioning money may boost growth by reducing the frictions associated with assessing the profitability of investment projects. Similarly, anything that undermines the functions of money will diminish economic output. The most notorious example of this is inflation, which particularly undermines the store of wealth function of money and (if it is volatile, as high rates of inflation usually are) the ability to use money as a unit of account or in extreme circumstances even as a medium of exchange. Managing money so as to maintain confidence that it will serve its functions effectively is potentially of great value in terms of real output.[1]

1.2 Bonds

A bond promises to pay a series of fixed payments at fixed dates. Since the payments are fixed, the market value of the bond can be worked out by discounting the stream of payments at the current interest rate. Any change in the interest rate will change the present value of the stream of payments and therefore change the market value of the bond. There are three potential sources of riskiness in holding a bond:

(1) A change in the interest rate will change the market value of the bond if it is sold before it matures.

(2) Unexpected inflation will erode the value of the bond, shifting wealth from the creditor to the debtor; the reverse holds for unexpected deflation.

(3) The issuer of the bond can default on it—e.g. if a company goes bankrupt it may be unable to pay back its creditors, including bondholders. If the government's fiscal policy is inconsistent with ensuring its solvency (see Chapter 6), then there is a risk of default by the government on the bonds outstanding. The consequences for macroeconomic behaviour of variations across countries in default risk on government bonds is discussed in Chapter 9.

There are two main types of government bonds—zero coupon bonds and coupon-bearing bonds. A zero coupon bond only pays a fixed sum at maturity, where the maturity is usually quite short—e.g. three months. A coupon-bearing bond pays a fixed amount regularly (e.g. every year) until maturity (e.g. five years or thirty years) and then pays a final coupon and the face value of the bond. In addition, as noted in the discussion of real and nominal interest rates in Chapter 3, in some countries index-linked bonds have been issued. Another historically important class of government bonds is 'consols'. These are infinite term (no maturity date) and pay a fixed nominal annual interest payment.

Although in advanced countries there is seldom a default risk on government bonds, company bonds have a positive default risk—if the company goes bankrupt then the creditors including bondholders may get little or nothing. So-called 'junk' bonds became popular in the 1980s. They offered high interest rates but there was also a high risk of default because the companies that issued them borrowed so heavily.

---

[1] For an interesting discussion of barter, money, and trust, see the two short chapters (4 and 5) in Seabright (2004).

1.3 Equity

Equity or shares represent a step further along the riskiness profile: by purchasing an equity stake in a company, the shareholder is promised nothing specific as a return. The shareholder gains or loses according to the fortunes of the company. If the shares are in a publicly quoted company in an economy with a liquid stock exchange, buying and selling shares incurs transactions costs similar to those associated with bond trading. But if the equity is in a private company or the stock exchange is poorly developed, it may be very difficult to liquidate one's stake. This helps to explain why the sale of new equity is virtually non-existent as a method of financing investment in countries with poor legal enforcement of shareholders' rights.[2]

Company law establishes a 'pecking order' in which claims are met when a company goes bankrupt: wages and taxes are paid first out of any resources of the company, then creditors are paid, beginning with bank loans and followed by bondholders. Equity owners are last. Equally, in the good times, the fixed commitments to workers, the tax authorities, and creditors are settled and unless the firm has a profit-sharing scheme with its workers, only equity owners benefit from the profits.

1.4 Illiquid assets

In many European countries, housing wealth represents over half of all household net wealth. The impact of changes in the interest rate on housing prices depends greatly on the institutional characteristics of the housing market. The UK is at one extreme and continental countries like Germany are at the other extreme. Owner-occupied housing is more common in the UK and house prices are more responsive to interest rate changes in the UK than in Germany because the interest rate on most British mortgages is the current interest rate. In Germany, fixed interest rate mortgages are the norm. Other factors that increase the sensitivity of house prices to changes in the interest rate in the UK are high ratios of loans to the value of the house, a small market rented sector, and relatively low transactions costs for buying and selling houses.

Pension arrangements vary greatly across countries. In some countries, private pension funds predominate. Households save for their retirement by making contributions to a fund that consists of bonds and equities. Such pension rights constitute wealth but they are an illiquid asset. Changes in the interest rate and in share prices change the value of this wealth. By contrast in countries with so-called 'unfunded' or 'pay-as-you-go' pension systems, a pension fund in the form of a stock of assets specific to an individual is not built up. Rather the pension system (government backed) promises to pay a pension on retirement out of current social security contributions and taxation (e.g. a fixed proportion of the final salary). If pension rights are in the latter form, then wealth to income ratios in the country are much lower and there may be a much smaller effect of a change in the interest rate on behaviour via its impact on wealth. In a pay-as-you-go scheme, pensioners benefit in retirement from past productivity growth as reflected in the level of their final salary; in a funded scheme, a pensioner's income depends on capital gains (or losses) on the accumulated fund.

---

[2] For an interesting discussion and empirical evidence from 49 countries, see La Porta et al. (1997).

Such cross-country institutional differences have been much debated in the context of the operation of the European Monetary Union. For example, it has been shown that in its early years, the European Central Bank (ECB) behaved in a very similar fashion to the US Fed in responding to changes in forecast inflation with interest rate adjustments. It is argued that 'the interest rate decisions of the ECB are remarkably close to what the Fed would have done, had it been faced with Euro area data.'[3] Meanwhile there is a widespread view that the ECB has acted too cautiously. These two observations could be reconciled if it is the case that for institutional reasons (e.g. in housing and pension arrangements) changes in the interest rate have a weaker effect on output in the eurozone than in the USA.

2 Institutions

In this section, a simple description is provided of key financial and monetary institutions in the economy. Readers who are already familiar with these should skip to the next section.

2.1 Commercial banking and finance

Modern commercial banks evolved from safehouses that simply looked after valuables for wealthy people. Consider the stylized balance sheet of the owner of a safehouse that looks after gold (Table 8.2). Let us suppose this safehouse is looking after 100 gold coins for someone and that one gold coin is worth 1 euro.

The gold coins in the vaults of the safehouse are an asset for the owner and the owner promises to repay the depositor €100. This promise represents a liability and is called a deposit note. Over time, it became acceptable for deposit notes to be used in transactions as a substitute for physical gold—i.e. they were accepted as money and are referred to as customary money. Since the gold stored in their vaults was only rarely withdrawn, the owners of safehouses realized that they could make money by lending some of it out and charging interest on the loans. Their balance sheet might then look more like Table 8.3.

Note that the loans extended are assets of the safehouse, because they represent promises by the borrowers to make payments. Once deposit notes were widely accepted as a means of payment, gold was only rarely withdrawn and the owner of the safehouse could afford to have more deposit notes on his gold than he has gold itself. In the situation

Table 8.2 Balance sheet of a safehouse

Liabilities	€	Assets	€
Deposit Notes	100	Gold Coins	100
Total	100	Total	100

---

[3] Giavazzi and Favero (2003: 107).

Table 8.3 Balance sheet of a more sophisticated safehouse

Liabilities	€	Assets	€
Deposit Notes	1,000	Gold Coins	100
		Loans	900
Total	1,000	Total	1,000

Table 8.4 A bank balance sheet

Liabilities	€	Assets	€
Deposits	1,000	Cash	100
		Loans	900
Total	1,000	Total	1,000

above, he has gold covering only 10% of the potential claim on it. We shall assume that experience has shown that this is a prudent amount to hold, in the sense that it is sufficient to meet the day-to-day demands for the actual withdrawal of gold. The safehouse owner would make a higher profit if he could lend out more money, but he runs the risk of not having enough gold to meet obligations actually called in (he may not be sufficiently liquid). Banks that are too greedy, or have bad judgement, or even are occasionally just unlucky, and as a consequence end up facing calls on their funds that they cannot meet, experience what is called bank failure, as we shall explain in more detail below. Thus bankers face a trade-off between profitability and liquidity.

Deposit notes accepted as payment are a form of financial instrument. Such notes were increasingly accepted and came to be called bank notes. Instead of directly transferring deposit notes, in modern banks cheques are used to transfer bank deposits from purchaser to seller. We turn now to an example of deposit creation.

We assume as in Table 8.4 that instead of gold coins, we have cash that is made up of notes and coins. We could also include 'operational balances', which are deposits at the central bank that can be converted into cash on demand. (We return to the origin of the central bank shortly.) Similarly, instead of deposit notes, we now have bank deposits. As above, the proportion of cash held is only 10% of deposits. This is called the 'reserve to deposit ratio' (rd), and the practice of holding less cash than claims on it is known as *fractional reserve banking*. By lending out multiples of the cash held, banks create money in a process referred to as deposit creation.

Suppose there is only one bank in the economy, a prudent reserve asset ratio of 10% and that an additional €100 is deposited. Now suppose the bank made an extra €90 of loans and these are withdrawn in cash (Table 8.5).

When these loans are spent and assuming those receiving payments deposit the cash, the banks are again in a position of surplus reserves, which allows for further loans to be made (i.e. cash rises to 200 and deposits to 1,190 so the reserve deposit ratio is 16.8%).

Table 8.5 A bank balance sheet with loan withdrawn in cash

Liabilities	€	Assets	€
Deposits	1,100	Cash	110
		Loans	990
Total	1,100	Total	1,100

New rd = (110 cash)/(1100 deposits) = 10%

Table 8.6 A bank balance sheet with extra loans

Liabilities	€	Assets	€
Deposits	2,000	Cash	200
		Loans	1,800
Total	2,000	Total	2,000

New rd = (200 cash)/(2,000 deposits) = 10%

The money supply (cash + deposits held outside the banking system) has risen as a result of the loan. The process of expansion of the money supply continues until deposits have risen to 2000 (Table 8.6).

To generalize from this example, recall that $rd \equiv R/D$, where R is reserves and D is deposits. If banks stick rigidly to the minimum prudent reserve ratio so that so rd is a constant, then the *deposit creation multiplier* is given by $\Delta D/\Delta R = 1/rd$, which, in our example, is 10. In practice, some cash drain from the bank can be expected i.e. as the money supply expands some part of the increase will be held outside banks as cash, so the deposit creation multiplier will tend to be smaller than this. It may also be the case that there is not unlimited demand for loans, again reducing the multiplier. This example illustrates that the vast majority of the money supply in the economy will not be held as cash. It is held in bank accounts and arises through the deposit creation process. Thus to understand the money supply in detail we need to understand why banks exist and what factors determine how much they lend.

2.1.1 Financial intermediation

A bank is a form of financial intermediary—i.e. it is an institution that stands between savers and borrowers. But, of course, using this middleman is not free. So why do savers not simply lend directly to borrowers? The reason is that financial intermediaries serve a number of important functions:

(1) Aggregation—typical savings quantities (e.g. regular savings by households) are much smaller than typical loan requirements (e.g. for lumpy investment projects).

(2) Maturity transformation—agents want to save for a short time, but borrow for a long time.

(3) Specialization and economies of scale—particularly in information gathering. We shall see the importance of information later in this section.

(4) Risk pooling—some borrowers will default, which might bankrupt individuals. Larger institutions can withstand a certain proportion of defaulting, and hence offer little or no risk to savers.

Banks are part of a wider financial sector that also includes pension funds, finance houses, insurance companies, and building societies. Functions of the financial system include payments, savings, credit (loans), insurance, advice, and consultancy. A typical financial system includes a number of different financial markets, such as a capital market (including the stock exchange and the bond market); money markets (including a discount house market, the interbank market, a market for certificates of deposit, a finance house market, a local authority market, an intercompany market, and a domestic currency commercial paper market); and a foreign exchange market.

For macroeconomics it is probably most important to understand the function of financial intermediation in *information gathering* and *risk transformation*. Banks have important advantages over other institutions (such as a bond market) in transforming risk. Banks can offer simpler and less expensive *ex ante* risk pooling. Since it is in the nature of banks to deal with risk, information about the riskiness of projects is an important factor in determining bank lending policies. Problems to do with information play a crucial role in determining bank behaviour. Understanding such information problems is necessary to see how bank crises can arise and how changes in the money supply feed through, via changes in lending and borrowing behaviour, to changes in output. When there is risk, differences between the information possessed by the borrowers and the lenders can be very significant, as we shall see.

2.2 The central bank

As we have discussed above, the proper functioning of money is extremely valuable in terms of promoting economic efficiency. To ensure that it can perform its functions effectively there are two main tasks:

(1) The supply of money must be regulated so that it is sufficiently scarce that money can serve as a store of value, yet sufficiently abundant that there is enough of it to service all the desired transactions.

(2) The banking system must be sufficiently robust and stable that economic agents can have confidence that their customary money holdings in bank accounts (i.e. the vast majority of the money supply) could actually be used if required, whilst yet maintaining proper incentives for lending to go to viable and plausible projects, rather than wildly risky ones.

A great deal is wrapped up in the first statement. As we shall see in more detail in section 4, whatever instrument the central bank uses must have the effect of limiting the growth of the monetary base, H. The second point to make is that there is a tension between the role of ensuring sufficient base money so as to avert financial crises and the role of establishing the nominal anchor. Central banks can therefore be seen as performing a difficult balancing act between preventing financial collapse on the one hand and inflation on the other.

The main practical functions of a typical central bank include:

(1) Banker to the government and the commercial banks.

(2) Conduct of monetary policy. Sometimes this is simply the operational dimension, such as the setting of interest rates to try to achieve a target for inflation set by the government. Sometimes it also includes determining the *objective* of monetary policy.

(3) Supervision of the financial system. Sometimes this is separated from the central bank. For example, in the UK, it is now conducted by the Financial Services Authority (FSA).

(4) Note issuer.

(5) Manager of the 'exchange equalization account'—i.e. the country's stock of gold and foreign currencies, mainly used for intervention in the foreign exchange markets.

Central banks are normally charged with the task of maintaining a stable and efficient monetary and financial framework. This entails aiming to maintain the integrity and value of the currency and in practice, as discussed in Chapter 5, it often means pursuing price stability (or an inflation target) through setting the interest rate. The central bank may also attempt to achieve its targets by seeking to influence expectations through statements made by the bank and members of the monetary policy committee and by foreign exchange intervention. An example of how the central bank is able to set the interest rate is provided in section 4 below.

Central banks also aim to maintain the stability of the financial system in a number of other ways: for example, by monitoring developments in the financial system and the links between individual institutions and between financial markets; by analysing the state of the economy; by close cooperation with financial supervisors both domestically and internationally; and by promoting sound financial infrastructure including efficient payment and settlement arrangements. Central banks may also be charged with promoting the development of a financial system that offers opportunities for firms of all sizes to have access to capital on terms that give adequate protection to investors. In extreme circumstances, central banks typically provide (or assist in arranging) last resort financial support where this is needed to avoid systemic damage.

2.3 The stock market

A stock market is where shares (titles on a proportion of a company) are traded. Shares in a company entitle the holder to a proportion of the votes in general meetings of the company to decide who has operational (day-to-day) control of the company—for example, who is the chief executive, and who sits on the board of directors. Shares also attract dividends, which are payments (in nominal terms) per share held. For most shareholders (i.e. those who do not intend to exercise operational control at any point) dividends are the ultimate financial justification for holding shares. They are the yield. However, shares can be sold, resulting in a capital gain or loss (depending on whether they are sold at a higher or lower price than they are bought).

Shares in companies take a number of different forms: those of large publicly listed companies are freely traded, are available to any member of the public to buy and sell, and are included in stock market indices like the Financial Times Stock Exchange (FTSE) indices or the Dow Jones Industrial averages. But shares are also held in companies that make 'private offerings' (as compared with the 'public offerings' on the stock market) to individuals or syndicates. Large private companies are often family businesses (even quite big ones, like the British retailer Littlewoods or the German automotive and consumer goods producer Bosch) in which members of families hold shares that are not quoted publicly. Such companies do not float on the stock market.

A typical stock market involves trades in shares by large numbers of individuals and by a relatively small number of large institutions (such as banks, pension funds, investment houses, or national governments). This setting of a few large players and many small players gives rise to many complicated dynamics. For example, stock markets often involve 'big players'—i.e. controllers of a large institution (e.g. someone who manages a major pension fund)—whose moves are watched closely and followed by other players. For example, if certain big pension funds are selling the shares of a company, other traders may interpret that as a sign that the pension fund managers know something bad about the company (perhaps their analysis suggests that its profits will be low), so they in turn sell those shares. In addition there are the 'market makers' who stand ready to buy or sell shares of particular companies on behalf of other financial institutions or their own clients. The decisions of market makers can have a significant impact on the behaviour of the market, and can significantly affect the prices of particular shares, or even of the market as a whole.

Trading in stock markets takes place within a settlement window. Typically, there is a two-week cycle. People buying shares between Friday of one week, and the Thursday thirteen days later, must pay their debts on the Friday, the fourteenth day. Similarly, if shares are sold in this window, they must be given over to the purchaser on that Friday. This window makes complex trading strategies possible. For example, traders can 'go long'—that is to say, they can purchase shares early in the trading window with money they do not have. Then, later, they can sell those shares and use the money from the later sale to pay off their earlier debts. Such a strategy can work well if shares are rising in price, since prices two weeks later might be higher. Similarly, traders can go short—they can sell shares they do not yet possess, and buy these shares later in the trading window so that they can surrender the certificates when required.

The combination of the presence of market makers and the possibility of going long or short creates very complex dynamics in stock markets. Market makers may think that others will follow them in buying if they go long. Because many traders are trying to buy, this itself bids up prices and the market makers can make large profits just by exercising their market power. When behaviour of this kind dominates, there can be so-called bull markets in which stock prices rise in a manner that may be unconnected with any fundamental features of the profitability or prospects of companies. Alternatively, if market makers believe that others will follow them in selling if they go short, prices can fall dramatically and a 'bear' market may ensue.

Such behaviour may give rise to 'financial bubbles'—situations in which stock prices are driven up or down simply through complicated herding behaviour on the part of market makers and those who follow them. Such bubbles can have important macroeconomic consequences. Much household wealth is held in the form of shares (often indirectly, through claims on pension funds), and as we have seen in Chapter 7 people's assessment of their wealth is very important for planning consumption. Similarly, the ability of firms to raise finance through offering their shares to float on the stock market is obviously highly dependent on whether the market as a whole is going up or down. If the market is falling, for example, companies may find it hard to raise equity, and since for certain kinds of projects equity may be a superior form of finance to loans, that may mean overinvestment during bull market bubbles and underinvestment during bear market bubbles.

There is not universal agreement among economists about the role of bubbles in explaining movements of stock market prices. An alternative account is the 'efficient markets hypothesis'. According to this theory, share prices simply reflect the best information available to traders at the time. Rising markets arise when the best information suggests that future profits are going to be higher than previously expected.[4] Falling markets arise when either the positive news behind the rising market ceases to be believed, or when some previously unanticipated bad news appears.

If the efficient markets hypothesis is correct, then stock market swings are not irrational, and do not need to be regulated, or managed, or compensated for by macroeconomic policy. On the other hand, if the idea of financial bubbles is correct, stock market booms or crashes can inflate or depress consumption and investment for reasons that do not reflect 'real' changes in the economy (in terms of innovations or future profit opportunities), and that might create an opportunity for fiscal or monetary policy to regulate demand so as to compensate for the irrational swings in the economy induced by financial bubbles.

3 Information problems

3.1 Problems of asymmetric information

We begin with the question of why might households not be happy to deposit money in banks, and what are the consequences? Households will not be prepared to lend money to banks if they think there is too much risk of their not being able to get their money out when they claim it—i.e. if there is a significant risk of the bank failing. If households worry about bank failure, they may not be prepared to lend, even at relatively high interest rates. Since banks facilitate lending through the gains from financial intermediation, if

---

[4] For example, in the late 1990s it was believed that the internet and related information and communications technologies were going to lead to higher future productivity growth in the USA—a 'New Economy'—and were associated with a rapidly rising stock market. However, as Ofek and Richardson (2002) show, it is extremely hard to explain the internet boom as rational.

households will not save in banks, there will be a fall in lending to businesses and hence a fall in investment. In this way, perceived risk to the soundness of banks can lead to a fall in output.

Next we ask why might banks not be prepared to lend money to firms, and what are the consequences? Banks may not lend money to firms if they believe that there is a substantial risk of firms going bankrupt and being unable to pay back the loans, or if they feel unable to believe firms' projections of returns (consider a case of lending to a company that has previously been involved in a corruption scandal like that of WorldCom in 2002, in which reported profits were exaggerated). A reduction in bank lending for these reasons would lead to a reduction in investment and hence output.

In each of these situations there are important macroeconomic effects arising from differences in information between lenders and borrowers. At its crudest, 'asymmetric information' means that one person knows something that someone else does not know. We shall speak of a situation involving asymmetric information, when it involves transactions in which at least one of the parties to the transaction knows something relevant to optimal decision making that is not known by the other party.

It is simplest to illustrate the idea with a few examples:

(1) How healthy are you? You are likely to know this better than someone trying to sell you health insurance.

(2) Was the stereo for sale at the second-hand shop stolen? The shopkeeper is likely to be able to guess this better than you can.

(3) Should I sell all my shares in a corporation because the company is about to go bankrupt? The corporation's chief accountant knows this better than I do. So suppose a chief accountant offered to sell you a million shares in his company at just below the current market price—would you buy them?

Situations involving asymmetric information raise a number of different problems.[5] Two of the most important in banking and financial services are those of adverse selection and moral hazard. In section 3.2, we set out a model that shows how asymmetric information problems can influence macroeconomic outcomes.

3.1.1 Adverse selection

Adverse selection is the name given to a problem that can occur in situations where the information asymmetry arises *before* the transaction. For example, the people who most want health insurance are those most likely to be unhealthy. If the sellers of health insurance cannot distinguish between the healthy and the unhealthy, the consequence is that the market price of health insurance is likely to be geared around the likelihood of an unhealthy person falling ill, and hence premiums will be higher. Therefore healthy people may not be able to get health insurance at a reasonable price, even though if the insurance company knew they were healthy there would be a mutually beneficial

---

[5] The Nobel prize was awarded in 2001 to the three economists who pioneered the analysis of markets with asymmetric information: George Akerlof, Michael Spence, and Joseph Stiglitz. For more details see: www.nobel.se/economics/laureates/2001/. Two of the classic articles most relevant to this discussion are Akerlof (1970) and Stiglitz and Weiss (1981).

insurance contract. A classic example of this phenomenon is the second-hand car market, the market for 'lemons'. Why is a car for sale if there is nothing wrong with it?

3.1.2 Moral hazard

Moral hazard is the name given to a problem that can arise in situations where the information asymmetry arises *after* the transaction. For example, once you have insured your car against theft, you may not take much trouble to lock it or to park it in a safe place. Therefore insurance companies will offer theft insurance on the assumption that you will not bother to take care of your car, making the insurance more expensive. This will make insurance 'too expensive' so some people will not insure their cars against theft, even though there would be a mutually beneficial insurance contract if they could promise to lock their cars.

3.1.3 Asymmetric information in finance

These issues can become important in a number of financial contexts. One important example is where firms issue shares (i.e. equity or stocks) but investors cannot distinguish between low risk, high profit firms and high risk, low profit firms. Suppose there was a market in which both types of firms tried to issue shares. The most an investor would be prepared to pay would be the average expected return. But then good firms will not issue shares because the price investors will pay will be less than such shares are worth. Hence this market for new issues of shares will be dominated by bad firms. This argument may help to explain two interesting facts about financial markets, namely that shares are not the most important source of *external* financing for firms, and that issuing marketable debt and equity securities is not the primary way in which businesses finance their operations.

Adverse selection and moral hazard are also clearly important problems in bank lending. Adverse selection in loans arises because the people who most want loans are likely to be those who are irresponsible, or sick, or have bad luck, or whatever it is that might make them a bad risk to lend to. Similarly, once money has been lent to someone, there is often relatively little the bank can do to prevent that person from spending that money on extravagant short-term consumption and later declaring himself bankrupt, thereby giving rise to a moral hazard problem.

Such asymmetric information problems may mean that households and firms face liquidity constraints—that is to say, they are not able to borrow as much as they would like to, even in circumstances where they would be expected, on average, to pay the money back with interest. The presence of liquidity constraints is important in explaining consumption and investment behaviour, as we have seen in Chapter 7. Subsection 3.2 below provides a formal model to show how information problems can lead to credit constraints.

3.1.4 Solving asymmetric information problems

The simplest solution is to remove the asymmetric information. For example, in financial markets, people supplying funds would have full details about borrowers. How should this be done? The most direct option would appear to be using private rating agencies (e.g. Standard & Poor's). But there is a problem here of so-called free-riding. For example, suppose Investor A buys information about company X, and on the basis of that information buys shares in X. Investors B, C, D, etc. (i.e. pretty much everyone else) do not buy information, but instead just follow Investor A, free-riding on his purchase of information. But then A will not make any special profit by buying the information. So no one will buy information.

In such situations, bank loans have an advantage over other forms of financing. Banks can form personal relationships with clients and engage in non-tradeable loans (rather than tradeable equity or bonds), which makes it worthwhile for the bank to find out information about clients. This is another important reason why banks exist.

Apart from using personal relationships, there are two other main possible solutions to this problem. First, the government could provide information itself. Alternatively, there could be government regulation to encourage honest revelation (e.g. rules insisting that firms disclose information about themselves and publish accounts in standard forms). The regulatory option is common. This partially explains why the financial system is among the most heavily regulated sectors of the economy. Banks around the world face many regulatory restrictions, including disclosure rules; restrictions on entry; restrictions on assets and activities; deposit insurance; limits on competition; restrictions on interest rates; and reserve requirements. Much banking regulation is what is called prudential— that is to say, it is geared towards preventing banks being imprudent in their lending. This regulation is supposed to prevent bank runs and panics.

3.1.5 Bank runs and panics

A 'banking panic' arises when throughout the banking system, bank debt holders suddenly demand that banks convert their debt claims into cash (at par—i.e. one-for-one with the deposits) to such an extent that banks suspend convertibility of deposits into cash. As a consequence of the deposit creation process discussed earlier, deposits in banks are much greater than the cash held by banks. This means that any bank will be unable to pay out to everyone if all its depositors try to withdraw their funds at once.

The classic scenario involving banking panics is the USA during the early 1930s.[6] During the Great Depression, about 20% of US banks failed. To get a sense of the scale of what occurred, and what difference regulation is believed to have made, note that in the 1920s there were about 600 bank failures per year. Then, between 1930 and 1933 there were about 2,000 failures per year. When mergers and liquidations are also taken into consideration, of the 25,000 US commercial banks in operation at the peak of business in mid-1929, there were only 15,000 left by mid-1933. Since most of the money supply takes the form of bank deposits, as we have seen, this scale of bank failure also resulted in a dramatic one-third reduction in the money supply over the period.[7]

In the banking literature there are two main sets of models to explain banking crises. The first class are called 'random withdrawal risk' or 'coordination problem' models.

---

[6] However, one should not get the idea that this was a problem specific to that time or place. There were many serious banking panics in the UK in the past (e.g. in the 1820s), and there were severe banking panics in Argentina in 2002. There were also other US banking crises in 1819, 1837, 1857, 1873, 1884, 1893, 1907, and in the 1980s, but these were all less severe than that of the early 1930s.

[7] The crisis led to the establishment of the Federal Deposit Insurance Corporation (FDIC) in 1934. The FDIC is a compulsory insurance policy on bank deposits, and guarantees that the first $100,000 of deposits will be returned. Between 1934 and 1981 on average there were fewer than 15 bank failures per year.

These note that the underlying function of banks is to provide insurance against (liquidity) risk. This means that banks facilitate profitable but illiquid investment. Hence many of a bank's assets (its loans) are relatively illiquid and cannot be converted into cash on demand, while its liabilities (the deposits in it) are very liquid, and banks pay out cash on demand in order of who turns up. If there is a panic trigger it can create a self-fulfilling belief that banks will fail. The argument is simple: because the depositor at the front of the queue will certainly get back all his funds while there simply might not be enough cash in the bank to pay the depositor at the back of the queue (even if the bank is essentially sound), there is an incentive to be the first to withdraw if there is a danger that everyone might withdraw.[8] In this model bank runs and panics are problems (arising perhaps from irrational 'animal spirits') that may be overcome by deposit insurance, pro rata service, and coordinated action.

The second class of model stresses the asymmetric information issues we have just been considering, particularly moral hazard. This time the moral hazard problem applies to the bank manager, rather than to the entrepreneurs. Bank depositors may find it difficult to tell how hard bank managers work at checking the loans they make. The risk that depositors may withdraw their funds acts as a discipline on the bank manager, in two senses. First, if depositors become suspicious that the bank manager has unidentified bad loans on his books, they may withdraw their funds. The bank manager therefore has an incentive to keep the quality of loans well identified. Secondly, if the bank becomes bankrupt there will be a close investigation of all its dealings, so there is the risk that any impropriety by the bank manager might then be identified. Since he has the risk of this happening at any time (almost randomly, if the banking panic is irrational), he has an incentive always to maintain high quality loans and best practice. Thus in this model, the possibility of bank failures is, in some sense, a 'Good Thing'—a sort of discipline by the market that keeps bank managers honest.

Which of these effects dominates is, of course, important in determining what sort of banking regulation is best. Furthermore, it makes a difference whether the proper conduct of monetary policy should be geared towards preventing or avoiding banking panics (which might be the case on the first interpretation of banking panics), or, instead, should sometimes allow them to happen or even encourage them (as might be implied by the second class of model). Both types of approach have been taken by central banks in the past. The response of the Japanese central bank to the crises of the 1990s was to avoid banking failures. The approach of the US Federal Reserve in the early 1930s was passive or even encouraging, as witnessed by the famous suggestion that the US banking crisis of the early 1930s was good because it would 'purge the rottenness out of the system'.[9] Although the Japanese approach avoids a sharp collapse, there may nevertheless be macroeconomic

---

[8] This argument is less straightforward than it may look at first sight, however, since why would a sound bank not be able to borrow cash from other banks to cover the panic-driven withdrawals? Is it perhaps a situation in which every bank in the country is under threat? Perhaps then, as we shall see, there is an important role for a 'central bank' that can issue unlimited amounts of cash as a 'lender of last resort'.

[9] Andrew Mellon, the US Secretary of the Treasury at the time, urged the market to 'liquidate labour, liquidate stocks, liquidate the farmers, and liquidate real estate . . . It will purge the rottenness out of the system.' (Quoted in *The Economist*, 28 Sept.–4 Oct. 2002.)

consequences with persistent uncertainty about bank solvency a possible cause of stagnant investment.

3.2 *A model of asymmetric information and credit constraints

One particular model of asymmetric information in finance (originally due to Robert Townsend[10]) has received much attention over the years in explaining how credit constraints at the individual level can influence outcomes at the level of the macroeconomy. It provides a mechanism through which financial institutions may induce or amplify shocks to the economy. The model has two basic ingredients based on observations of how banks finance projects. Let us consider for the moment an entrepreneur who has developed a new and promising production technology that will generate a positive return at some future date.

- The first ingredient of the model is the claim that in general the return on the investment project is uncertain *ex ante* to the entrepreneur and to any potential investors who may be interested in investing in it. Once the project is completed, the investors will suffer an information asymmetry as compared to the entrepreneur since they will not be in a position to observe directly the extent to which the project was successful. For example, the entrepreneur may very well choose *ex post* to misreport her profits in order to deprive the investors of their expected return thus keeping more of the pie for herself. Of course the investors would have anticipated this possibility and would demand to write an *ex ante* contract that delivers the right incentives and protects their share of the investment. However, in order for this contract to be implementable investors will need to be able to verify the return to the project after its completion.

- The second ingredient of this type of model is therefore the assumption that such *ex post* verification is costly: if it were not costly, there would be no information asymmetry. Once we combine the uncertain returns with a costly verification procedure such as an audit of the project we are led to a model that emphasizes how external finance and collateral play a role in the way the economy responds to shocks. Moreover the economy will suffer from a degree of inefficiency as compared with one that does not face this kind of information asymmetry.

Let us now present a stylized version of such a model. Our economy consists of a number of entrepreneurs and banks. An entrepreneur in this context is simply an individual who has created the blueprints for a new production technology. A bank is simply an institution that possesses a large amount of funds that it would like to invest so as to derive a return that is as large as possible. In addition each entrepreneur has a particular level of wealth w, where $w > 0$, which she is prepared to invest in her own project and which we assume to be the same for all entrepreneurs. Each entrepreneur is different however in the sense that each has access to blueprints of different qualities. *Ex ante*, each entrepreneur knows that on average projects will generate a return of 1 but is uncertain about the return to her particular project. In fact it is common knowledge that the return to a project is a

---

[10] Townsend (1979).

random variable x where x is uniformly distributed on the interval $[0, 2]$. To say that x is uniformly distributed on the interval $[0, 2]$ means that there is an equal probability that x will have any value between 0 and 2. The expected value is therefore halfway along the interval, i.e. equal to one. In order to initiate a project however, an entrepreneur needs to purchase machinery and raw materials which cost 1 unit of output.[11] Thus, it is easy to see that although all entrepreneurs are required to invest the same amount of resources in their projects some will be lucky while others will be less lucky. Those entrepreneurs who succeed can double their investment while those who fail will lose everything. In between these two extremes, entrepreneurs can be more or less successful.

Not all entrepreneurs have initial wealth levels $w > 1$ that would allow them to pursue their projects on their own without the need for financing from the banks. Those entrepreneurs with initial wealth levels $w < 1$ will need to obtain a loan of value $1 - w$ from the banks in order to start their project. We assume that banks have sufficient funds to finance every request they receive, even though as we shall see it is not optimal for them to do so. In addition banks have the possibility to invest abroad in which case they will receive a return of q which is a known fixed constant (the vagaries of exchange rate changes are assumed away). If a bank decides to make funds available to the entrepreneur, it will commit those funds and expect to receive a certain amount of the return obtained by the entrepreneur once the outcome of the project is realized. Of course the entrepreneur may lie about the return and claim that it was much lower than it was in fact. This would allow the entrepreneur to keep more resources for herself but the bank would undoubtedly make losses on its investment. We assume however that after the project return is realized a bank can pay a cost c and verify the claim made by the entrepreneur. On the basis of this, the bank will want to write a contract that ensures that the entrepreneur has no incentive to misreport her realized return.

Of course, designing the right contract is not trivial and this literature has explored in depth how to find the optimal mechanism. It turns out that for our stylized example it suffices to consider a *debt contract* in which the entrepreneur promises to pay a return d if and only if the realized return x exceeds d. The contract also stipulates that whenever the entrepreneur claims that she cannot pay back the promised return d, the bank will automatically pay the verification cost c and audit the entrepreneur. If the entrepreneur is found to be misreporting the truth then the bank seizes all available returns. One can show that this contract is optimal in the sense that the entrepreneur will never lie about her returns. Of course the bank will still have to audit in the case where the entrepreneur is unsuccessful in order to guarantee the correct incentives for the entrepreneur who is successful but might otherwise be tempted to lie.

Let us now try and determine equilibrium behaviour in this model. First let us assume that banks are perfectly competitive in the sense that the expected return to an agreement to lend an amount of $1 - w$ is the same in expectation whether the bank invests in the entrepreneur's project or takes the same amount of money overseas and invests there with a guaranteed return q. The bank expects to receive d if the entrepreneur is successful (i.e. when $x \geq d$) and $x - c$ if $x < d$, the entrepreneur reports failure and the bank has to pay costly auditing fees. Thus the unconditional expected return to a bank that writes a

---

[11] Note that we are ignoring nominal prices here and all quantities are measured in units of the output good for simplicity.

debt contract as specified above is given by:

$$E[R_{Bank}] = E[x - c | x < d] \Pr(x < d) + E[d | x \geq d] \Pr(x \geq d).$$

Since x is uniformly distributed on $[0, 2]$, it is intuitively reasonable that the probability of $x < d$ is $d/2$ and conversely that the probability of $x \geq d$ is $(2 - d)/2$. Moreover, we know that the expectation of a constant is just the constant (i.e. $E[d | x \geq d] = d$) and that the expected value in the interval $[0, d]$, i.e. $E[x | x < d]$ is $d/2$. Hence we can rewrite the unconditional expected return to the bank as

$$E[R_{Bank}] = \frac{d^2}{4} + d\left(\frac{2 - d}{2}\right) - c\frac{d}{2}.$$

In equilibrium the expected return to the bank lending money to the entrepreneur must equal that of the bank that invests abroad, $E[R_{Bank}] = q(1 - w)$. Let us denote by $\tilde{C}(d) = cd/2$ the expected verification costs of the bank and move it to the left hand side. We can now rewrite the expression above as

$$E[R_{Bank}] + \tilde{C}(d) = d - \frac{d^2}{4} = q(1 - w) + \tilde{C}(d). \tag{8.1}$$

The optimal debt contract will have d^* chosen by solving the equation above.

We can see how it is chosen from Fig. 8.1. On the horizontal axis is the amount of debt, d, and on the vertical, the expected return to the bank, $E[R]$. The curved line represents the left hand side of equation 8.1 (i.e. $d - \frac{d^2}{4}$, so the maximum is at $d = 2$). We display the linear right hand side (i.e. $q(1 - w) + \tilde{C}(d)$) of this equation for two levels of wealth of the entrepreneur: $w = 0$ and for some positive $w < 1$. The slope of the line is $c/2$.

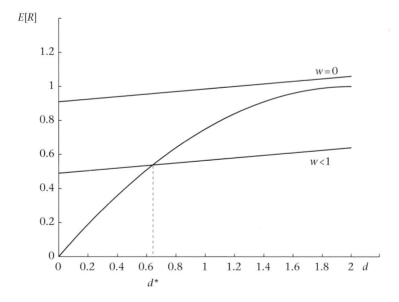

Figure 8.1 Finding the optimal debt contract for competitive banks

Where the curved and the straight line intersect determines the amount the bank will lend, i.e. the optimal debt contract, d^*. We can easily see that if the entrepreneur has more initial wealth the line will be lower down so the equilibrium level of debt will be lower, since the entrepreneur does not need to rely on the bank for financing. However, we can also see in this picture that if $w = 0$ there is no equilibrium in the model. This is because there is no level of debt that the bank would wish to contract over that would make it profitable for the bank to finance the entrepreneur, rather than to take its money and invest it abroad. This happens when

- the investment opportunities abroad for the bank are very good: $q \uparrow$;
- the initial wealth levels of the entrepreneur are low: $w \downarrow$;
- the bank's expected verification costs are high: $c \uparrow$;
- the expected return to the entrepreneur's project is low. Notice from Fig. 8.1 that the highest point on the curved line occurs at 1 for $d = 2$, which we noted earlier to be the expected return for the project. Intuitively if this is low, it becomes less likely for the two curves to intersect and thus for an equilibrium to exist.

However, obtaining the equilibrium value of d^* is only part of the story, for all along we have assumed that the entrepreneur is willing to enter the contract to obtain finance from the bank and proceed to implement her production blueprint for the new technology. Let us now assume that the entrepreneur also has the possibility to take her initial wealth and simply put it in a savings account in the bank. If she does so the bank will use this money to invest abroad and will pay her a return equal to qw. Clearly we need to find out when it is profitable for the entrepreneur to do this. In order to evaluate this condition let us repeat the previous analysis from the viewpoint of the entrepreneur. The entrepreneur expects to receive $x - d$ if she is successful (i.e. when $x \geq d$) and 0 when she reports failure. She gets zero either because she was totally unsuccessful and the investment did not lead to any strictly positive returns or because she attempted to mislead the bank, which investigated the business and confiscated any positive returns that may have existed. Thus the unconditional expected return to an entrepreneur who enters a debt contract with $d = d^*$ is given by:

$$E[R_{Entrepreneur}] = 0 + E[x - d^* | x \geq d^*] \Pr(x \geq d^*).$$

In order to evaluate this equation we first have to determine the conditional expectation on the right hand side. [12] This produces the result:

$$E[R_{Entrepreneur}] = 1 - d^* \left(1 - \frac{d^*}{4}\right). \tag{8.2}$$

For the entrepreneur to be willing to undertake the investment and implement the blueprint she must expect to receive a return that is at least as large as that from putting

---

[12] $Ex|x \geq d^*$ is the expected value of x, where x is uniformly distributed between d^* and 2, i.e. the average of d^* and 2, or $(2+d^*)/2$. So $E[x-d^*|x \geq d^*] = (2+d^*)/2 - d^* = 1 - d^*/2$. $\Pr(x \geq d^*)$ is $(2-d^*)/2 = 1 - d^*/2$. Hence $E[R_{Entrepreneur}] = (1 - d^*/2)^2 = (1 - d^*(1 - d^*/4)$.

the money in a savings account. Thus in order for the optimal debt contract d^* to be implemented the entrepreneur requires that

$$E[R_{Entrepreneur}] = 1 - d^* \left(1 - \frac{d^*}{4}\right) \geq qw. \tag{8.3}$$

If we now add equation 8.3 to equation 8.1, evaluating both at the equilibrium debt contract d^* we obtain

$$1 \geq q + \tilde{C}(d^*).$$

Let us now compare this outcome with that in an efficient economy in which there are no information problems—i.e. without credit constraints or costly state verification. In an efficient economy where unconstrained borrowing is possible, the entrepreneur will implement her blueprints as long as her expected return is greater than the return to savings from investment abroad, that is as long as $1 \geq q$. In our economy however the investment is only possible if the return to a project covers both the opportunity cost from investing abroad and the bank's expected verification costs. Moreover, we can see from Fig. 8.1 that the optimal contract d^* is decreasing in the initial wealth levels. This implies that there is a certain wealth level w^* such that for all $w \leq w^*$, $q + \tilde{C}(d^*) \geq 1$, which means that entrepreneurs with low levels of initial wealth will not be able to implement their projects. Essentially, they would have to borrow more than the amount the financial markets see as feasible. Projects that would be undertaken in an efficient economy are ruled out because of the information problems.

3.2.1 Summing up

This type of model suggests a number of channels by which financial markets can induce or promote volatility at the level of the macroeconomy. If entrepreneurs who are not able to implement their projects become unemployed as a consequence and the projects that are not implemented would have contributed in any significant amount to aggregate output, we see how in the presence of credit constraints, previously unimportant factors such as initial wealth levels and opportunities abroad become significant. The initial wealth level may represent shares owned by the entrepreneur or a house or even land that can be used as collateral for the loan. A loss of value in any of these will negatively affect the entrepreneur's ability to borrow and hence reduce output and employment in the aggregate.

4 Money supply and demand

4.1 Money supply

The simplest possible assumption was made about the money supply in Chapter 2: namely that the central bank fixes the supply of money. Any changes in money supply are brought about by the central bank buying or selling bonds in open market operations.

The chain of events is:

$$\underset{\text{monetary base}}{H} \quad \rightarrow \quad \underset{\text{money supply}}{M} \quad \rightarrow \quad \underset{\text{interest rate}}{i}.$$

In practice, the causality may be reversed: the high powered money stock is the outcome of the decision of the central bank to set a particular rate of interest:

$$\underset{\text{interest rate}}{i} \quad \rightarrow \quad \underset{\text{money demand}}{L} \quad \rightarrow \quad \underset{\text{money supply}}{M} \quad \rightarrow \quad \underset{\text{monetary base}}{H}.$$

We look now at these two contrasting descriptions of central bank behaviour.

4.1.1 Does the central bank set *H* or set *i*?

Textbook presentations of the *IS/LM* model rely on monetary policy operating through the so-called monetary base multiplier that connects H, the base money that is assumed to be under the control of the central bank, and M, the money supply in the hands of the public. It is then the interaction of the money supply thus determined with the demand for money that fixes the interest rate:

$$H \rightarrow M \rightarrow i.$$

This representation of central bank behaviour and of the money supply became established in the teaching of macroeconomics with Hicks's original version of the *IS/LM* model.[13] The longevity of the model in the face of efforts of monetary economists[14] to show that central banks do not behave in this way and have not done so for more than a century in some cases reflects the analytical power of the *IS/LM* framework and the failure of a good substitute framework to emerge. However, as we have seen in Chapters 3 and 5, the *MR* paradigm provides such an alternative, embedding the 'central bank sets the interest rate' in a model of an inflation-targeting central bank using a monetary policy reaction function.

The traditional *LM* view ($H \rightarrow M \rightarrow i$) has three components:

- Step 1. The central bank sets the volume of the monetary base, H, through open market operations. The choice of H is usually assumed to be an exogenous one—i.e. not as a response to feedback from other economic variables.

- Step 2. The money stock or money supply is then determined by the behaviour of the private sector—households, firms, and banks. The monetary base multiplier is the link from H to M and depends on the desired cash to deposit ratio on the part of households and firms and the desired reserve ratio on the part of commercial banks. The monetary base (or banking) multiplier, κ (called kappa) is

$$\kappa = \frac{1 + cd}{cd + rd}$$

---

[13] Hicks (1937).

[14] One of the most notable opponents of the *LM* view is Victoria Chick, e.g. Chick (1977) and (1992). The following draws on Goodhart (2002).

so that

$$M = \kappa.H,$$

where cd is the cash to deposit ratio and rd is the reserve to deposit ratio of commercial banks. For a more detailed explanation of the mechanics of the monetary base multiplier, see the Appendix.

- Step 3. Given that the level of the money supply, M, is fixed through steps 1 and 2, the level of the short-term interest rate is the outcome of the interaction between M and the demand for money (L).

We now contrast this with the view that the central bank sets the interest rate ($i \rightarrow L \rightarrow M \rightarrow H$).

- Step 1. The central bank uses its reaction function to set the interest rate—i.e. it actively responds to economic developments that threaten the nominal anchor.

- Step 2. Given the short-term interest rate, the private sector responds by determining the volume of borrowing it wants from the commercial banking system.

- Step 3. The commercial banks respond to the credit demands on them by adjusting their own relative interest rates, marketable assets (e.g. government bonds), and their borrowing from other banks so as to meet the demand. This determines the money stock (M) and its breakdown into different kinds of deposits. Given the required reserve ratio, this fixes the demand of the commercial banks for bank reserves.

- Step 4. In order to maintain the short-term interest rate at the level established by the reaction function in Step 1, the central bank has to use open market operations to satisfy the commercial banks' demand for reserves established in Step 3. The changes in high powered money used for the open market operations fixes H. The mechanics of how the interest rate is set by the central bank is set out below.

4.1.2 How does the central bank set the interest rate?

In practical terms, central banks do not literally *set* the interest rates used by high-street banks in their dealings with households and firms. The institutional arrangements differ across central banks. We shall use the example of the Bank of England. They have an explanation on their website of how they set the interest rate and the following discussion is a summary of this.[15] The Bank of England's explanation begins:

Central banks have a variety of techniques for influencing interest rates but they are all designed, in one way or another, to affect the cost of money to the banking system. In general this is done by keeping the banking system short of money and then lending the banks the money they need at an interest rate which the central bank decides.

The central bank's ability to influence interest rates in the economy rests with the fact that it has a monopoly in the supply of the monetary base (cash). Commercial

---

[15] www.bankofengland.co.uk/factmpol.pdf. For an explanation of how the Federal Reserve sets the interest rate, see 'Setting the interest rate', FRBSF Economic Letter Number 2002-30, 11 Oct. 2002.

banks are interested in making profits through extending loans to the private sector. They want to minimize the amount of cash that they hold, but on the other hand they must have enough cash to be able to meet the demands of their depositors seeking to withdraw funds. The Bank of England is banker to the commercial banking system in the UK, which means that the transactions between commercial banks are finally settled between their accounts at the Bank of England. The commercial banks have to maintain positive balances at the Bank of England at the end of each day. The three key players are the central bank, the government, and the commercial banks: the commercial banks' funds at the Bank are the outcome of their transactions with the Bank and their transactions with the government (since the transactions between banks can only redistribute funds between them and cannot offset an overall shortage of funds at the Bank of England).

We begin with the situation in which the Bank of England is not trying to bring about a change in the interest rate—i.e. how does it conduct its activities to maintain the interest rate unchanged at the desired level? Each morning a Bank of England official makes a forecast of the cash shortage that will occur during the day. One element of this is calculating the likely pattern of tax payments. The Bank will also know that a certain amount of its short-term lending to the banking system will be due to be repaid by commercial banks during the day. This lending is now conducted through repos (repurchase agreements): the commercial bank hands over an eligible asset (such as a Treasury Bill) to the Bank of England and agrees to repurchase it fourteen days later at a price that implies it is paying the base rate on this borrowing. In order to finance its 'repurchases', the banks will need to borrow again from the Bank and if the interest rate is to be kept constant, the Bank will refinance the subsequent round of 'repos' at the same rate.

Suppose that another event that the Bank expects to take place during the day is that a British company with an account at a UK commercial bank will pay a large tax cheque to the tax authority, the Inland Revenue, say of £100 million. At this point, the banking system moves into a negative balance vis-à-vis the Bank of England because it transfers money to the government's account. As we have noted, this must be resolved by the end of the day. To get hold of the cash, the commercial bank will sell some of its assets—e.g. Treasury Bills. This will tend to reduce the price of such bills and push up the interest rate. If the Bank of England is to prevent this change in the interest rate, the Bank must make a correspondingly larger number of repurchase agreements.

We now move to the situation where the Bank of England wants to raise the interest rate—e.g. the monthly meeting of the Bank's monetary policy committee takes the decision to put the interest rate up. It will now undertake the refinancing arrangements by charging a higher interest rate on the 'repos'. In other words, it is in 'setting the interest rate for these operations that the Bank influences the general level of interest rates across the economy'. The Bank of England's announcement of a rise in the interest rate is quickly transmitted through the banking system. The result will be a fall in the demand for loans by the commercial banking system: credit will become tighter.

In a world of increasing financial sophistication, in order for the central bank to be able to control the interest rate, it is crucial that its announcements are credible. By credible we mean that the markets believe the policy will be maintained consistently until its objectives are met. Peter Howitt explains the importance of credibility in relation to the Bank of Canada's interest rate instrument the 'operating band' like this:[16]

Without supportive expectations, however, a central bank has only limited scope for controlling the level of aggregate expenditures. If no one thought that interest rates beyond the overnight rate would be affected by the Bank's tightening, there would be little effect on the longer-term interest rates that influence spending decisions in the economy. Nor would there be any point in the Bank trying to intervene directly in longer-term asset markets with the hope of affecting those rates through open market operations without supportive expectations, because financial markets have grown too large in relation to the Bank's balance sheet. Thus to produce a major effect the Bank must make people believe that the tightening it induces by raising the operating band will continue until it does have an effect. In other words, the 'announcement effect' of monetary policy is becoming more and more the primary channel through which the central bank can control aggregate spending.

4.1.3 Monetary targeting: failures and successes

Two conditions must hold for a policy of monetary targeting to be successful in its objective of controlling inflation:

- First, the relationship between inflation and the targeted monetary aggregate must be reliable and
- second, the central bank must be able to control the chosen monetary aggregate.

Problems can arise at both points: although the central bank can control high powered money or a narrow money aggregate, its relationship to inflation is often weak, undermining the role of the target in shaping inflation expectations. In the UK, it was argued that whenever the monetary authority attempted to control a particular monetary aggregate as its target, there would be a response by the financial system in the form of the emergence of close substitutes or near-moneys that would lie outside the target and therefore serve to undermine it.[17] Shifts in the demand for money (often referred to as velocity instability) will sever the connection between the targeted money supply aggregate and inflation, making monetary targeting ineffective. These problems undermined monetary targeting in the USA, Canada, and the UK. More detail is provided in the next section about the UK case.

By contrast, monetary targeting is viewed as a success in securing low inflation in Germany and Switzerland following its adoption in 1974. However, analysis of the Bundesbank's monetary policy suggests that it did not adopt a rigid policy of targeting the growth of monetary aggregates. Indeed its behaviour seems to be well captured by a Taylor-type monetary policy rule.[18] The Bundesbank was successful in using the language of monetary targeting to communicate to the public the orientation of monetary policy toward long-run stability of inflation at a low rate.[19]

---

[16] Howitt (2001).　　[17] For details, see Goodhart (1989).

[18] Clarida and Gertler (1997). Working paper version: www.nber.org/papers/w5581.pdf.

[19] Mishkin (1999).

4.2 Money demand

The standard money demand function used in Chapter 2 reflects both money as a medium of exchange as reflected in the transactions motive for holding money and money as a store of value as reflected in the asset or speculative motive. To provide a simple way of thinking about the demand for money, we looked at the transactions demand and the asset/speculative demand separately. Putting them together produced the demand for money function:

$$\frac{M^D}{P} = L(\overset{+}{y}, \overset{-}{i}) = \underbrace{\left(\bar{l} - l_i i\right)}_{\text{asset/speculative demand}} + \underbrace{\left(\frac{1}{v_T} \cdot y\right)}_{\text{transactions demand}}.$$

We focused attention on the impact of the transactions velocity, v_T, on the interest sensitivity of the asset demand for money, l_i and on the role of expectations in financial markets that can drive shifts in the speculative demand ($\bar{l}$).

In this section, we deepen the analysis of the demand for money by looking at models of interest sensitivity using inventory and portfolio models. We then return to the issue of the instability of the demand for money function.

4.2.1 Interest sensitivity of demand for money: inventory and portfolio models

It is quite straightforward to incorporate in the demand for money function a more sophisticated approach to the transactions motive in which the balances held are a function not only of the level of income but also of the rate of interest. This is important because it provides an explanation for the demand for *narrow* money as a function of both income and the interest rate. Early examples are the so-called inventory models. The idea was a simple one: households would receive wages periodically (e.g. once a month) and would choose their level of narrow money balances to allow for a smooth expenditure path by trading off

- *the transactions costs* involved in switching between bonds or interest-bearing but illiquid 'near money' such as term deposits and narrow money (cash and cheque account deposits) and

- *the opportunity cost* of holding narrow money, as measured by the interest rate.

Models of the demand for narrow money that emerge from more recent utility maximizing models in which households gain utility from both consumption and from holding money, or in which money is assumed to be necessary in order to purchase consumption goods, are similar to the earlier inventory models.

In addition to the role of the interest rate in explaining the level of money balances held for transactions purposes, it will influence the role of money in an individual's portfolio of assets. From a 'store of value' or wealth perspective, it is obvious that the narrowest definitions of money (coins and notes) and cheque accounts (included in the narrow money aggregate) are strictly dominated by savings and term accounts (included in broad money)—i.e. by capital safe assets that pay interest (refer to Table 8.1). The portfolio analysis cannot explain the demand for narrow money but it may be important in explaining the demand for broad money aggregates that include savings and term

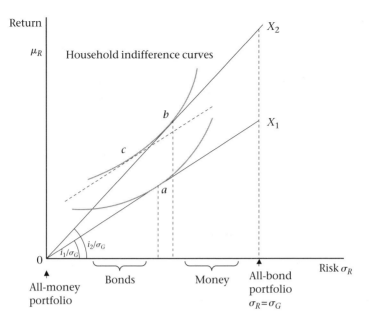

Figure 8.2 Tobin's model of portfolio allocation

accounts. The demand for broad money will depend on how households allocate their wealth between assets with different risk and return profiles.

James Tobin's theory of portfolio choice addresses this decision problem. Fig. 8.2 can be used to illustrate the theory. We consider the choice between holding money (savings or term account) and bonds. The model can, however, be extended easily to analyse the choice between a wider range of assets including equities. The vertical axis represents the expected return from the portfolio and the horizontal axis the risk associated with the portfolio. The investor is uncertain about the capital gain or loss, G, associated with investing €1 in bonds. Such capital gains or losses result from either falls or rises in interest rates in the future. She has a probability distribution for G that has a mean of zero. The return on the portfolio depends on the interest rate on bonds, on G, and on the proportion A_2 of the portfolio that is held in bonds ($A_1 + A_2 = 1$), where A_1 is the proportion held in cash and A_2 the proportion held in bonds:

$$R = A_2 \cdot (i + G),$$

where R is the return on the portfolio. The expected return on the portfolio is

$$E(R) = \mu_R = A_2 \cdot i$$

since the expected value of the capital gain is zero. Tobin measured the risk of the portfolio by the standard deviation of the return on the portfolio, σ_R. A portfolio is risky when there is a high probability of large deviations (i.e. capital gains and losses) from the expected return, μ_R. The risk of the portfolio, σ_R, depends on the proportion of the portfolio in bonds and on the standard deviation of the capital gains, σ_G.

Thus, in Fig. 8.2 it is possible to represent the opportunity locus facing the investor as a straight line showing the cost in terms of greater risk associated with attaining a higher expected return. The opportunity locus is $\mu_R = (i/\sigma_G) \cdot \sigma_R$ and has a slope equal to the interest rate divided by σ_G. An all-money portfolio is represented by the origin since the expected return and risk are both zero. An all-bond portfolio ($A_2 = 1$) will occur when the risk on the portfolio is equal to σ_G. Fig. 8.2 shows the opportunity locus associated with an interest rate of i_1 as OX_1. In the same diagram the indifference curves of households are drawn. These will be positively sloped since risk-averse house-holds will be indifferent between some combination of low mean and variance (i.e. low return and low risk) and high mean and variance (high return and high risk). In the diagram, the indifference curves are concave upwards: as the riskiness of the portfolio increases, the individual requires a higher and higher increase in the return to take on additional risk.

With the interest rate at i_1 and the lower indifference curve, the portfolio represented by point a is chosen. A higher interest rate swivels OX_1 to OX_2: the familiar income and substitution effects come into play. The income effect is the move $a \rightarrow b$ and the substitu-tion effect is the move $b \rightarrow c$. While the income effect may lead to a reduction in the proportion of the portfolio held in bonds, the substitution effect increases bondholdings since the return associated with a given variance has increased. It is normally assumed that the substitution effect outweighs the income effect to ensure an inverse relationship between the interest rate and the demand for money. Tobin's model of portfolio selection provides a micro-based explanation for the inverse relationship between the interest rate and the demand for money at the level of the household.

4.2.2 Speculative demand for money

Tobin's analysis is based on the idea that uncertainty about how interest rates and thus capital values will move makes holding bonds risky. Keynes introduced a different argu-ment, which is that the general market sentiment about future interest rates need not be that they would most likely stay as they are at present. If the general belief is that interest rates would fall (perhaps they were high relative to normal levels), then people would also believe that bond prices would rise. Accordingly their demand for money would be lower as the overall return on bonds (interest plus capital gain) would be less. In terms of Tobin's diagram, the return locus, OX, would swivel upwards and the demand for money would probably be lower than if the expectation was for no change in interest rates. Conversely, a generally expected rise in interest rates (implying capital losses on bonds) would mean a higher demand for money—in Keynes's terminology, there would be a speculative demand to hold money in order to invest in bonds later after the fall in their prices.

The net result of Keynes's argument is that the expected interest rate enters into the function determining the demand for money. This is extremely important in the context of the central bank's conduct of monetary policy. Suppose a hike in the short-term interest rate is seen as a sign of the government's determination to squeeze out inflation. If the bond market now believes that interest rates over the medium term will be higher than previously anticipated, then they will expect a fall in bond prices as bondholders switch to higher yielding short-term assets in order to protect themselves from such capital losses.

They will unload their bonds now. Bond prices fall and the long-term interest rate moves up. This underlines the decisive importance of expectations in the behaviour of financial markets and thus the conduct of monetary policy. Movements in the short-term interest rate can be very powerful if they move the general state of expectations in the appropriate direction. Of course, reactions can be perverse. A sharp cut in the short-term interest rate during a recession can, if mishandled, lead to the view that the central bank has new information implying the recession is worse than expected—even as bond prices rise, equity prices could fall as investors expect lower profits and dividends, and the beneficial impact of the interest rate cut would be neutralized.

4.2.3 Empirical demand for money functions

The demand for money is one of the most intensively studied aggregate economic relationships. For a number of advanced countries, very long data series are available, allowing estimation to run from some time in the nineteenth century to the end of the twentieth century. A recent study for the UK,[20] estimates the demand for broad money from 1878 to 1993. The model is set up as a long-run specification similar to one discussed above: the demand for real money balances is a function of the level of real income (a so-called scale variable) and a measure of the opportunity cost of holding money. It is assumed that there are various kinds of transactions costs associated with adjusting real balances to their desired long-run level. It is therefore necessary to model the 'equilibrium correction mechanism' through which the adjustment toward the long-run level takes place.

In estimating the demand for money function, one central problem is to decide what money is and how to handle changes in its definition over time. Since money is a social institution invented by humans to overcome the problems and costs of organizing barter arrangements, it is to be expected that innovations will occur and that 'money' will therefore change. This problem is linked to the frequently discussed issue of the instability of the demand for money.

This insight suggests that to model the demand for money over a long historical period, it is necessary to allow for changes in the way that money is defined and to allow for innovation and for changes in the institutional set-up (e.g. changes in regulation that affect how non-bank financial institutions operate). Moreover, a model estimated over one time period cannot be expected to predict well with more recent data if these factors are not taken into account. The work of Ericsson et al. illustrates these issues. They begin with a model that appears to perform well for nearly a century from 1878 to 1975 and then look to see if it is consistent with the new data for the 1976–93 period. The first model includes dummy variables to take account of shifts in the demand for broad money in each world war and those associated with the credit control regulations operating from 1971 to 1975 in the UK. When the eighteen new years are added to the data set, the demand for money equation performs poorly: the short-term interest rate is no longer significant and neither is the equilibrium correction term (representing the short-run adjustment process). The authors argue that such a mechanistic approach to modelling the demand for money will not work—it is necessary to recognize that changes

---

[20] Ericsson, Hendry, and Prestwich (1998).

in the economic environment in the most recent two decades require changes in the model.

First, the definition of broad money changes in the late 1980s and this implies a change in the opportunity cost of holding money. Specifically, the new definition includes building society deposits, which are interest bearing, with the consequence that there is a sharp reduction in the opportunity cost of holding money. Second, financial innovation and deregulation were dramatic in the 1980s and 1990s—with the introduction of interest-bearing current accounts, credit cards, debit cards, and cash machines. They 'changed the role of money as an asset in portfolios, as a source of liquidity, and as the main component of the transactions medium'.[21] In the UK, there were also wide-ranging changes in the regulatory environment—initially, as market mechanisms played a larger role in determining rates of return on assets and later as non-bank financial institutions were allowed to transform themselves into banks. To take one example, when interest-bearing current accounts were permitted, the opportunity cost of holding narrow money went down and demand went up.

The model is modified to take account of these issues: a different measure of the interest rate is used so as to incorporate the change in the opportunity cost, and the deregulation dummy is used for the period in the 1980s (1986-9) in addition to the earlier period (1971-5). When this is done, the estimated model is satisfactory and comparable to the earlier model estimated up to 1975.[22] But what are the policy implications that can be drawn from this exercise? The first point is that in terms of forecasting the demand for money, the use of a model that fits well may be poor at forecasting if the relevant changes in the economic structure in the forecast period are not known *ex ante*. The authors of this study point out that the effect of each world war on the demand for money appears to be the same—so at least with hindsight, we can say that using the estimate from the first would have predicted the effect of the second. Unfortunately, we still do not know if this information would be useful in predicting the effect of a third world war.

The second issue is what we can learn about the direction of causality between money and prices. In the early 1980s, there was a large increase in the real money supply: the big question is whether this was due to

- the money supply being allowed to rise in line with an increase in the *demand* for money (e.g. because of the portfolio shifts associated with financial innovation as discussed above) with the stance of monetary policy unchanged or

- to a change to a looser monetary policy, which would show up in higher inflation in the future.

If it was due to higher demand for money, then this can be thought of as a leftward shift in the *LM* curve. The authorities would have had to accommodate this by allowing

---

[21] Ericsson, Hendry, and Prestwich (1998), 305.

[22] For a clear and interesting discussion of the issues surrounding the econometric identification of the demand function, see ibid. 317–18.

the money supply to rise in line with the increased demand if output was to remain unchanged. Alternatively, if there is a stable demand for money function, then observing higher money balances would suggest the cause was a rise in the money *supply,* which would, in turn, lead to a change in the price level in the long run. The *LM* curve would shift to the right, raising aggregate demand and prices through the Phillips curve mechanism. The model estimated by Ericsson et al. including their modifications for the changes in economic structure after 1975 suggests that for the UK the former is the correct interpretation for the early 1980s.

We can conclude this discussion by noting that innovations in the payments process and changes in the regulatory environment will affect the demand for money. This will make difficult the use of the money supply as the instrument of monetary policy. Monetary targeting in the UK was notably unsuccessful in the 1980s when the structural changes discussed above were occurring. Under such circumstances, monetary authorities will tend to rely on changing the interest rate as their preferred method of influencing the level of activity in the economy.

5 Monetary transmission mechanisms and the role of finance in propagating shocks

The 'monetary transmission mechanism' is the term used to refer to the channels through which a change in monetary policy (i.e. a change in interest rates, a change in the monetary base, or a change in the money supply) influences economic activity. At the beginning of the chain is a policy decision by the monetary authority to either tighten or loosen monetary conditions. At the end of the chain that makes up the monetary transmission mechanism is the impact of a change in aggregate demand on output.

Here we set out the main channels by which changes in monetary policy feed through to changes in aggregate demand and to output in the short run. This provides a richer background to the analysis of monetary policy in Chapters 2, 3, and 5. The aim is to show how the considerations introduced in this chapter together with those introduced in Chapter 7 influence the transmission of monetary policy. We can also reinterpret the channels explained below to show the role the financial sector can play in propagating shocks from the private sector through the economy. Because of information problems, capital markets are far from perfect with the result that the economy is characterized both by credit rationing and equity rationing: not only is external finance from banks or from the sale of equity more expensive than internal finance but it may not be available at all. This highlights the role of balance sheet effects, which are especially important for small and medium sized firms. A characteristic of balance sheet effects is that the impact on the losers can easily outweigh that on the winners. If firms go bankrupt as a consequence of deflation or unexpected disinflation, this can affect aggregate demand in addition to the traditional interest rate channel. The irreversibility of bankruptcy is one reason that balance sheet effects help to explain why shocks are amplified and why the effects persist.

Traditional effects

A higher nominal interest rate leads to a higher real interest rate, which in turn leads to lower investment, lower purchases of residential housing (mortgages), lower expenditure on consumer durables (e.g. loans for TV sets or cars), and to lower output.

$$\uparrow i \rightarrow \uparrow r \rightarrow \downarrow I \rightarrow \downarrow y.$$

As discussed, the short-term money market rates will quickly follow the official rate and banks will announce changes in their base interest rates for lending (e.g. overdraft rates). Competition amongst banks and building societies will lead to similar changes in mortgage lending rates and in the rates for savings.

But the transmission mechanism requires that the change in the short-term nominal rate also affects the long-term real rate, which is relevant for investment. As noted in Chapter 5, there is no absolutely rigid connection between changes in the short-term and long-term interest rates. The long-term interest rate depends on the current short-term rate and the expected future short-term rates: this makes it clear that the impact of a change in the short-term rate depends crucially on how the central bank is expected to behave later on. One possible scenario is that a rise in the official interest rate is interpreted by the markets as successfully calming the economy and preventing it from 'overheating'. In this case, it might be thought that the official rate would be reduced in the medium run. If this belief is held widely and strongly in the financial markets, then the rise in the short-term rate could be associated with a *fall* not a rise in the long-term rate. Although this reaction cannot be ruled out, it is probably more often the case that the financial markets believe that tighter monetary conditions will need to be maintained until spending, output, and employment respond—this suggests a longer horizon for tighter monetary conditions and therefore a rise in the short-term rate will be followed by a rise in the long-term rate. Investment and output will fall.

Tobin's Q

Recall that $Q = \frac{\text{Market value of firm}}{\text{Replacement cost of capital}}$. A fall in the long-term interest rate will be accompanied by a rise in the price of bonds with a longer maturity. The value of other financial assets such as equities will also rise because any given expected income stream is discounted at a lower rate, which raises its value. This boosts Q and investment rises.

$$\downarrow i \rightarrow \uparrow P_{\text{assets}} \rightarrow \uparrow Q \rightarrow \uparrow I \rightarrow \uparrow y$$

As we have seen in Chapter 7, if Q is high, the market value of firms as reflected in their stock market valuation is high relative to the replacement cost of capital. This implies that new plant and equipment is relatively cheap. Hence we would expect investment spending to rise because firms can buy a lot of investment goods with only a relatively small issue of new shares.

As we have seen in this chapter, swings in the stock market may not be driven by fundamental determinants of firm value. Such financial bubbles will affect market valuation and hence Q. This can produce phases of over- or underinvestment, with both short- to medium-run effects on output, employment and inflation as well as longer-run effects on capital accumulation and growth.

Wealth

Higher share prices boost the financial wealth of households, so their lifetime resources are higher. The life-cycle hypothesis or permanent income hypothesis would predict that they consume more.

$$\downarrow i \rightarrow \uparrow P_{assets} \rightarrow \uparrow \text{wealth} \rightarrow \uparrow c \rightarrow \uparrow y.$$

Household liquidity effects

If households are liquidity constrained, then a relaxation of monetary policy or a boom in asset prices can release the constraint.

$$\downarrow \quad i \rightarrow \uparrow P_{assets} \rightarrow \uparrow \text{value of financial assets} \rightarrow$$
$$\downarrow \quad \text{likelihood of financial distress} \rightarrow$$
$$\uparrow \quad \text{consumer durable and housing expenditure} \rightarrow \uparrow y$$

Balance sheet

If borrowers become less wealthy they have less to lose by taking risks, so adverse selection problems become greater and lending will decrease.

$$\uparrow \quad i \rightarrow \downarrow P_{assets} \rightarrow \uparrow \text{moral hazard, adverse selection} \rightarrow$$
$$\downarrow \quad \text{bank loans} \rightarrow \downarrow I \rightarrow \downarrow y$$

Cash flow

Lower interest rates lead to lower interest payments and thus higher cash flow. Increased liquidity makes it easier to know whether a borrower will be able to pay back her loans.

$$\downarrow \quad i \rightarrow \uparrow \text{cash flow} \rightarrow \downarrow \text{moral hazard, adverse selection} \rightarrow$$
$$\uparrow \quad \text{bank loans} \rightarrow \uparrow I \rightarrow \uparrow y$$

Unanticipated change in the price level

Debt payments are often fixed in nominal terms, so an unanticipated rise in the price level reduces firms' liabilities (the real value of their nominal debt) but does not reduce the real value of the firms' assets. Hence their net worth increases and moral hazard falls. If monetary easing leads to an *unanticipated* rise in the price level, this mechanism predicts a rise in investment.

$$P > P^E \rightarrow \downarrow \text{moral hazard, adverse selection} \rightarrow \uparrow \text{bank loans} \rightarrow \uparrow I \rightarrow \uparrow y$$

Exchange rate effect

A higher interest rate relative to the world interest rate leads to an appreciation of the exchange rate (a fall in e, where it is defined as domestic currency units per foreign currency unit), which makes imports cheaper and exports more expensive and hence leads to lower net exports. This mechanism is discussed at length in Chapter 9.

$$\uparrow i \rightarrow \downarrow e \rightarrow \downarrow (x - m) \rightarrow \downarrow y$$

6 Conclusions

In this chapter, we have shown how a deeper investigation of money and finance allows us to use the 3-equation model with more subtlety. On the *IS* side, we have examined the characteristics of the different assets that households can choose as means of holding their wealth. We have seen that institutional features of the financial system interact with other features of the economy such as the pension system and housing market to influence how changes in monetary policy are transmitted to consumption and investment decisions. In addition, it is possible that the way financial institutions work can be a source of disturbances to the real economy. For example, speculative bubbles may emerge in the stock market and produce waves of excessive optimism or pessimism that influence investment decisions.

We have seen how information problems help to explain

- the existence of financial institutions such as banks,
- the need for government regulation of the financial system, and
- why households and firms may face liquidity constraints.

On the monetary side, the traditional *LM* view assumes the central bank controls the monetary base and the interest rate is the outcome of the interaction of money supply and demand. By contrast, the *MR* view assumes the opposite chain of causality with the central bank setting the interest rate; given the demand for money, the monetary base adjusts as required. The demand for money will be affected by financial innovation and by changes in the regulatory environment. There has been a shift in practice away from monetary policy based on money-supply targeting (and in economic analysis from the *IS/LM* model) toward using the interest rate as the instrument of monetary policy in the context of an inflation target (and toward the 3-equation model with the *MR*).

■ QUESTIONS

Checklist questions

(1) Imagine you are running a safehouse in the early nineteenth century. Assume there are 2,000 gold coins deposited with you and that you have issued these people with deposit notes. You have lent 1,800 gold coins.

    (*a*) Apart from lending money, what is the essential service that you provide?

    (*b*) What determines how much money you lend?

(c) Why will people rarely withdraw their gold?

(d) What is your implicit reserve asset ratio?

(e) If an additional 200 gold coins are deposited, how many additional deposits will you create?

(f) Why may the calculation you made in (e) not be entirely accurate?

(g) In a neighbouring village, a banker was unable to meet calls on his funds and he went bankrupt. You decide to increase your reserve asset ratio to 20%. Why is it a bad idea to call in loans you have already made in order to meet the higher ratio?

(h) An additional 1,000 coins are deposited by people from the neighbouring village. How many gold coins will you hold in cash and how many loans will you want to make if you decide to adjust to the more cautious reserve asset ratio?

(2) What is meant by 'internal' finance for investment and why may it be cheaper than 'external' finance?

(3) Distinguish between adverse selection and moral hazard. Illustrate with examples. How have the concepts of asymmetric information and moral hazard affected our understanding of macroeconomics?

(4) Why is the financial system heavily regulated?

(5) Compare the two broad explanations of bank runs. In particular, what is the underlying difference in the assumption about bank depositors' behaviour in the two approaches? What do you see as the main problems with these assumptions about their behaviour?

(6) What is a bull market? What is a bear market? How can the presence of 'market makers' explain their existence?

(7) What is the 'money multiplier'? What determines its size? What leverage does this give the central bank over the money supply?

(8) Why might the cash/deposit ratio and the reserve asset ratio be decreasing functions of the rate of interest? How does an interest-sensitive money supply affect the *LM* curve? Illustrate using an example, comparing the new *LM* with the standard *LM*.

(9) In what ways did British experience in the early 1980s illustrate the problems with monetary targeting?

Problems and questions for discussion

QUESTION A. How does the presence of asymmetric information affect macroeconomic outcomes?

QUESTION B. In the early 1990s in Russia, barter was widespread and there were billions of US dollars circulating. Why was the rouble not fulfilling its function as money? What costs did this impose on the Russian economy? [Reading: see the chapters by Seabright (2004) referred to in the chapter and references therein.]

QUESTION C. 'Inflation targeting is a success but money supply targeting was a failure in the UK. Money supply targeting as a method of achieving low inflation was a success in Germany.' Do you agree with these claims? What might account for these differences?

QUESTION D. In Japan, the price of real estate dropped dramatically in the late 1980s. Many Japanese firms have long-term relationships with a so-called main bank. How would you expect a deterioration of the balance sheets of Japanese firms and of their main banks to affect investment? Would you expect smaller or larger firms to be most affected?

■ APPENDIX: THE MONETARY BASE MULTIPLIER

In this appendix, we provide an explanation of the monetary base multiplier as it works in the traditional *LM* view. In this view, money is created through the operation of the monetary base multiplier. Suppose the central bank puts more cash in the economy (it prints the notes and buys bonds in open market operations). The public holds only, say, one-third of this as cash and deposits the rest in commercial banks to maintain their cash to deposit ratio of 0.5. The banks lodge say 10% in the central bank to maintain their desired reserve ratio and extend loans to the public with the rest. Eventually this process of credit creation will raise the money supply by 2.5 times the original injection of cash by the central bank.

We can see how this works as follows. If the initial injection was €100, the initial increase in the money supply is €100. Given the public's *cd* of 0.5, then they will hold on to one-third of the cash and place two-thirds of it on deposit in a commercial bank (€66.7). The rise in deposits in the commercial bank means that it will increase its reserves at the central bank by €6.67. This leaves it free to extend loans to the public using the extra €60 in cash. Thus €60 end up in the hands of the public (e.g. firms or households borrow from the bank) and the money supply has increased by another €60. This process continues until the public's cash to deposit ratio is stable at one-half and the commercial banks' reserve ratio is stable at 10%. It is easy to see that the new cash in the economy will end up partly in the hands of the public and partly as reserves of the commercial banks. Because cash/deposits = 0.5 and reserves/deposits = 0.1, (cash + reserves)/deposits = 0.6. In our example, deposits will have increased by 100 ÷ 0.6 = 166.7. Cash in the hands of the public will be 0.5 × 166.7 = 83.3. Hence the money supply, which is equal to the cash held by the public and their deposits with banks, will have increased by €250 implying a monetary base multiplier of 2.5.

The increase in the money supply of €250 (since $\kappa = \frac{(1+cd)}{(cd+rd)}$) can be thought of as being made up of the 100 units of currency or so-called *outside money* created by the central bank and 150 units of *inside money* created by the commercial banking system. What are these 150 units of inside money? This is the total amount of new loans extended by the commercial banks. The asset side of the commercial banks' balance sheet shows €16.66 of new assets in the form of cash reserves and €150 loans to the public. This adds up to €166.7 which is exactly equal to the increase in the banks' deposits i.e. their liabilities.

It is worth noting that both the cash to deposit ratio and the reserve ratio are likely to be sensitive to the rate of interest. In the former case, portfolio considerations may play a part in the decision to hold cash or deposit and in the latter, commercial banks will alter their reserve holding dependent on the rate of interest.

This can be incorporated into the *LM* as follows: the *LM* is defined for a given stock of high powered money. Comparing the *LM* curve with and without an interest-sensitive supply of money, a given rise in the interest rate will be associated with a higher level of income than is the case for the standard *LM*: i.e. *LM* will be flatter. The *LM* is normally positively sloped because at a higher interest rate there is a lower demand for money and hence for a given supply of money, a higher level of income is necessary to drive up the transactions demand sufficiently to clear the money market. With an interest-sensitive money supply, this effect is reinforced—the higher interest rate not only reduces the demand for money but also increases the supply, which implies an even higher level of income is needed for money market equilibrium. Now consider a tightening of monetary policy by the central bank: the high powered money stock is reduced. For a given *IS* curve, there will be a smaller effect on the interest rate and hence on activity of a given change in the monetary base because as the interest rate is pushed up, the money supply expands partially offsetting the initial reduction of the monetary base.

PART THREE

The Open Economy

9 The Open Economy in the Short Run

In the analysis of macroeconomics to this point in the book, we have assumed a completely closed economy. Even for an economy the size of the USA, this is only a first approximation: exports constitute about 10% of GDP. This is also the case for some other large economies like Brazil, India, and Japan. With an export share of above 25% of GDP, China is far more integrated in international trade than Japan or India. In Europe, the British and German economies have export sectors of about 25% of GDP. In smaller countries, such as the Netherlands or Belgium, exports amount to more than 50% of GDP. In small economies with high levels of processing and re-export of imported goods such as Ireland or Singapore, the export share can exceed 100%. In Asia, Taiwan, Thailand, and South Korea have export shares of between 40 and 50%.

Moreover, the financial markets of advanced and emerging economies are integrated into global markets. Hence we have to understand how to deal with both exports and imports and with the integration of domestic and international financial markets. Happily, understanding the closed economy takes us a large part of the way to being able to analyse economies that are plugged into the world economy. The focus in most of this chapter is on the small open economy: this is one that is assumed to be too small to influence the level of world output or the world interest rate. Conditions in the rest of the world are taken as given.

Few economists would think of analysing a region of a country as a closed economy itself. It is too obvious in the case of a region within a country that its financial market is integrated into the national one. It is also evident that much of what is produced in a region is exported from the region, and much of what is consumed is imported from outside the region. Yet the open region is not identical to the open economy for two reasons. First, unlike the open economy, there may be considerable labour mobility between different regions in the same economy. In fact we make the assumption in what follows that there is no labour mobility between open economies.[1] Second, the region has no control over monetary policy, and the region usually has only limited (or no) say in fiscal policy. Both monetary and fiscal policy are the prerogative of the national not the regional government. In the case of an open economy, the national government or government and central bank (in the case of an independent central bank) can decide on monetary and fiscal policy.

---

[1] Economic migration is an important feature of the modern world as can be seen from the football pages of any newspaper. However it is unlikely to be strongly affected by relatively short-term changes in domestic economic conditions. Moreover economic analysis becomes impossible when too many variables are treated as endogenous. We therefore treat national populations as given in what follows.

Table 9.1 Types of open economy

Type of open economy	Fiscal policy	Monetary and exchange rate policy	Labour market mobility
National economy not in a monetary union	No institutional constraints	Control over monetary and exchange rate policy	No mobility across national boundaries
National economy in a monetary union	Monetary union may impose (weak) institutional constraints	No control over monetary and exchange rate policy	Limited mobility across national boundaries
Region in an economy	National economy imposes (strong) institutional constraints	No control over monetary and exchange rate policy	Mobility across regions

There is an exception to the control by the national government (or central bank) of monetary policy. This is when a group of economies share a common currency, and hence a common monetary policy, like the member countries of EMU, the European Economic and Monetary Union. For a member of a common currency area, the national government has no control over monetary policy, including the exchange rate. As in the standard open economy case and in contrast to the regional case, the national government does control fiscal policy (subject to any rules of the monetary union). Table 9.1 provides a summary of the differences between the three main types of open economy.

The fundamental concepts developed for the closed economy remain at the core of the macro analysis of the open economy and, once the treatment of the standard small open economy has been completed, it will be quite easy to extend the analysis to the case of a region and to that of an economy within a monetary union. Thus the extra effort needed for open economy analysis will have a large payback in terms of our ability to analyse real world situations.

This chapter is about the economy in the short run, that is to say, when prices and wages are given. The following issues are addressed:

- How is output determination in the short run affected by trade and financial openness?
- What determines the trade balance and why does it matter?
- What is the real exchange rate and how does it affect output and trade?
- How do fixed and flexible exchange rate regimes work?

The chapter is organized in the following way. Section 1 deals with the consequences of opening the goods market and section 2 with the opening of the financial market. The groundwork for the short-run open economy model is to be found in those two sections. Before putting them together, a short section highlights how fixed and flexible exchange rate systems operate. Section 4 pins down the balance of payments concepts that are needed for open economy macro. In section 5, the Mundell–Fleming model is put together and used to analyse fiscal, monetary, and exchange rate policy in the short run.

The way the economy adjusts to a new short-run equilibrium depends on how exchange rate expectations are formed. One important case is where forward-looking expectations and sticky prices lead to exchange rate overshooting. After section 5, the way is open to go on to the analysis of the medium run in Chapter 10. Section 6 shows what happens when we relax three of the key assumptions made in this chapter: that there is perfect international capital mobility, that the home economy is small, and that international financial assets are perfect substitutes. In Chapter 10, the short-run Mundell–Fleming model is extended to analyse what happens to equilibrium employment and inflation in the open economy. Chapter 11 puts the model to work by analysing different kinds of shocks and alternative policy responses.

1 Opening the goods market

In this section, we take the following steps:

(1) extend the analysis of goods market equilibrium by including exports and imports. This allows us to define the open economy *IS* curve, the *ISXM* curve.

(2) show how by running a current account surplus or deficit an open economy increases or decreases its wealth.

(3) explore the extent of integration of goods markets internationally and how firms set prices in the open economy. This leads to a discussion of relative price and relative cost definitions of the real exchange rate.

(4) analyse the volume and terms of trade effects of an exchange rate change (the Marshall–Lerner condition).

(5) incorporate the real exchange rate in the *ISXM* curve.

Both the purchase of goods and services from abroad (imports) and the sale of home-produced output abroad (exports) influence the level of output in the economy in the short run. Holding all else constant, imports of goods depress domestic output because demand for home production goes down and conversely, exports raise domestic output as foreign orders boost demand for home production. We shall modify the goods market equilibrium condition to take account of this.

The extension of the model to include imports and exports raises a second issue. At the economy's short-run equilibrium level of output, there may be a trade deficit, trade balance, or surplus. If there is a trade surplus, exports exceed imports with the result that the home economy is increasing its wealth.[2] The trade surplus can be used to buy foreign assets or to increase the official foreign exchange reserves in the home country's central bank. If there is a trade deficit, the home country is purchasing more from abroad than its receipts from the sale of exports. In order to pay for the imports in excess of exports, the home country has to borrow from abroad or run down its foreign exchange reserves: its wealth is declining. So tracking the trade balance is important because of its implications

---

[2] We ignore the receipt of net interest payments for the moment.

for the country's wealth. As we shall see, such changes in wealth may eventually affect the terms on which the country can borrow, the exchange rate or the level of aggregate demand through wealth effects on consumption. The trade balance will therefore be monitored throughout the analysis of the open economy.

1.1 Goods market equilibrium

Recall the goods market equilibrium condition from Chapter 2:

$$y^D = y, \qquad \text{(goods market equilibrium)}$$

where y is output and y^D is aggregate demand. Aggregate demand in turn depends in the closed economy on planned expenditure on consumption and investment by the private sector and planned government spending:

$$y^D \equiv c(y, t, r, \text{wealth}) + I(r, A) + g, \qquad \text{(planned expenditure, closed economy)}$$

where c is consumption, I is planned investment, g is government spending, and t is taxation, all in real terms.

Trade in goods has two effects. First, the demand for the home economy's output is boosted by demand from abroad, in the form of exports, x. Second, it is dampened by goods imported from abroad, m, which substitute for domestic output. Domestic absorption, Abs, is defined as total spending by home agents on consumption, investment, and government purchases *irrespective* of the origin of the goods or services:

$$Abs \equiv c + I + g. \qquad \text{(domestic absorption)}$$

To calculate *domestic* spending on *home* produced goods and services, it is necessary to subtract spending on imports, m, and to add foreign demand for exports, x, to determine *total* demand for *home* produced goods and services, y^D. So if the French government plans to increase its expenditure by purchasing Italian-made metro carriages, this shows up as a rise in domestic absorption ($\uparrow g$) and a rise in imports ($\uparrow m$) of the same size. These two items cancel out and planned expenditure on home produced goods and services does not change. More generally,

$$
\begin{aligned}
y^D &\equiv (c + I + g) - m + x \\
&\equiv Abs + (x - m) \\
&\equiv Abs + BT, \qquad \text{(planned expenditure, open economy)}
\end{aligned}
$$

where the trade balance, BT, is

$$BT \equiv x - m. \qquad \text{(trade balance)}$$

The term net exports is used interchangeably with trade balance. In our French example, although planned expenditure does not change, the trade balance deteriorates due to the rise in imports.

We turn now to the determinants of exports and imports (and hence of the balance of trade). Let us assume for simplicity that exports are exogenous and fixed, and that imports depend only on the level of domestic output or income. Hence

$$x = \bar{x}$$

and

$$m = m_y y,$$

where m_y is a constant and is called the marginal propensity to import.

Therefore the balance of trade is

$$BT \equiv x - m$$
$$\equiv \bar{x} - m_y y$$

and the level of income at which trade is balanced, i.e. $BT = 0$, y_{BT}, is

$$y_{BT} = \frac{1}{m_y}\bar{x}.$$

The level of output y_{BT} tells us nothing about the actual level of output, only the level of output at which the balance of trade is zero.

There are four different ways of expressing the goods market equilibrium condition, each of which provides a different insight. To simplify, let consumption be a simple linear function of *disposable* income and let investment and government spending be exogenous. There is a linear tax function: $t = t_y y$ so we have $c = c_0 + c_y(y - t_y y)$. The goods market equilibrium condition becomes

$$y = Abs + BT \qquad\qquad \text{(goods market equilibrium No. 1)}$$
$$= c_0 + c_y(y - t_y y) + I + g + \bar{x} - m_y y,$$

where $I = I(r)$ and for the moment, we assume that the real interest rate is constant and equal to $\bar{r}$. Collecting the terms in y on the left hand side and rearranging gives the goods market equilibrium condition in the form: output is equal to the multiplier times the exogenous components of demand. Thus

$$y = \frac{1}{s_y + c_y t_y + m_y}\,(c_0 + I + g + \bar{x}), \qquad \text{(goods market equilibrium No. 2)}$$

where s_y is the marginal propensity to save ($s_y = 1 - c_y$). As compared with the closed economy, the multiplier, $\frac{1}{s_y + c_y t_y + m_y}$ is lower because of the marginal propensity to import, m_y.

It is useful to think about the goods market equilibrium condition in a third way. If we multiply the left hand side of the goods market equilibrium condition by the denominator of the multiplier, we have:

$$\underbrace{(s_y + c_y t_y + m_y) \cdot y}_{\text{planned leakages}} = \underbrace{c_0 + I + g + \bar{x}}_{\text{planned injections}}. \qquad \text{(goods market equilibrium No. 3)}$$

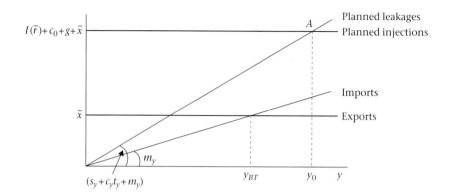

Figure 9.1 Equilibrium output (planned injections = planned leakages); balanced trade output

This shows that the goods market will be in equilibrium when the planned leakages of demand from the flow of income in the economy through savings, taxation and imports are equal to the planned injections of demand in the economy in the form of autonomous consumption, investment, government expenditure, and exports.

We can also rearrange the trade balance equation:

$$m_y y = \bar{x}$$

and show both the goods market equilibrium and the trade balance in the same diagram (see Fig. 9.1). Balanced trade output is shown by y_{BT}—the level of output at which exports are equal to imports. The goods market equilibrium condition is shown: planned leakages are equal to planned injections at point A—i.e. at an output level of y_0. At this level of output, it is clear from the comparison of imports with exports that there is a trade deficit.

Holding constant the marginal propensity to import and the exogenous level of exports as shown in Fig. 9.1, trade balance would require a reduction in the short-run equilibrium level of output to y_{BT}. This could be achieved either by a reduction in size of the multiplier (through a rise in the tax rate or by a drop in the marginal propensity to consume), which steepens the planned leakages line, or by a fall in one of the exogenous components of domestic demand (a downward shift in the planned injections line).

We can now use this model to examine the implications for output and the trade balance of, for example, an exogenous change in exports. Since a rise in exports raises the level of equilibrium output, which in turn raises imports, it is not immediately obvious what the trade balance will be in the new short-run equilibrium. However, the answer is clear from Fig. 9.2. In response to an exogenous increase in exports, balanced trade output rises by more than actual output. The consequence is that from an initial position of balanced trade, there is a trade surplus at the new equilibrium level of output. The reason that a rise in exports leads to a trade surplus is that the new equilibrium level of output will occur when additional leakages equal to the increase in exports have been generated by a rise in income. Since savings and taxation are leakages in addition to imports, the equilibrium level of output must be below the new balanced trade level. We have shown this using a simple model, but the key insight carries over to more complicated ones and will be a recurrent theme in the analysis of the open economy.

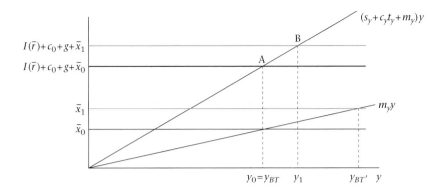

Figure 9.2 A rise in exports improves the trade balance

In Fig. 9.2, the economy is initially at goods market equilibrium at point A with an output level of y_0. Since exports and imports are equal at this output level, there is trade balance: the y_{BT} line goes through point A. Then there is a rise in the level of exports to $\bar{x}_1$. Leakages are equal to injections at point B. The new level of output is y_1. At this level of output, exports exceed imports (note the rightward shift of y_{BT}) and B is therefore a position of trade surplus.

1.2 Sector financial balances

Another useful way of manipulating the goods market equilibrium condition is to write it in terms of sectoral savings and investment balances. Three sector balances are of interest: the private sector financial balance (private savings net of its investment), the government sector financial balance (taxation net of government expenditure), and the trade balance (net investment abroad). *Ceteris paribus*, a trade surplus means that stocks of foreign assets are increasing in the home economy. This measures the increase in the holdings of foreign wealth in the home economy and is therefore referred to as net investment abroad. We rearrange the leakages and injections equation to separate out taxation and show the sector financial balances:[3]

$$\underbrace{(s_y y^{disp} - c_0 - I)}_{\text{private sector financial balance}} + \underbrace{(t_y y - g)}_{\text{government financial balance}} = \underbrace{\bar{x} - m_y y}_{\text{net inv abroad}},$$

(goods market equilibrium No. 4)

where y^{disp} is disposable income, $y^{disp} = (1 - t_y)y$.

This expression is a very useful one because it highlights the flow equilibrium in the economy. One sector, for example, the private sector, can only run a financial deficit

---

[3] A step-by-step derivation is shown below: in the first line, we multiply through by y, shift imports to the right hand side and the domestic components of demand to the left hand side. In the second line, we add and subtract $s_y t_y y$ and in the third line, we use the fact that $s_y + c_y = 1$.

$$s_y y + c_y t_y y - c_0 - I - g = \bar{x} - m_y y$$
$$s_y (y - t_y y) + s_y t_y y + c_y t_y y - c_0 - I - g = \bar{x} - m_y y$$
$$(s_y y^{disp} - c_0 - I) + (t_y y - g) = \bar{x} - m_y y$$

(investing more than it is saving) if another sector (the government or foreign trade sector) runs a surplus. Whenever the goods market is in equilibrium, private savings net of investment (the private sector's financial balance) plus the government budget surplus (the government's financial balance) is equal to the trade surplus. Dramatic swings in the financial balances in the United States over the course of the 1990s and into the 2000s are shown in Fig. 17.16 in Chapter 17: in the early 1990s the current account was virtually in balance and the large government deficit was matched by a large private sector surplus. The government was in effect borrowing from the private sector. By 2003, the current account recorded a deficit of nearly 6% of GDP and the private sector was in balance. This time the large government deficit meant that the government was, in effect, borrowing from abroad. As we shall see in Chapter 17, this way of presenting the state of the goods market provides a useful insight into macroeconomic developments.

1.3 Real and nominal exchange rates

What affects our demand for foreign goods and services and the demand of foreign residents for our tradeable products? Tradeables are the goods and services that can potentially be bought or sold across international borders. One obvious influence on the demand for tradeables is 'relative prices'. If our goods are relatively expensive, then demand from foreigners will be reduced and home residents will tend to buy imported goods. In order to compare prices across countries, we need to convert them to a common currency, i.e. we want a measure of 'price competitiveness':

$$\theta \equiv \frac{\text{price of foreign goods expressed in home currency}}{\text{price of home goods}}$$

$$\equiv \frac{P^* e}{P}, \qquad \text{(price competitiveness, real exchange rate)}$$

where P^* is the foreign price level, P is the home price level and e is the nominal exchange rate measured as the number of home currency units per unit of foreign currency:

$$e \equiv \frac{\text{no. units of home currency}}{\text{one unit of foreign currency}}. \qquad \text{(nominal exchange rate)}$$

Another name for θ is the *real exchange rate* because it measures the rate at which domestic and foreign *goods* exchange for each other. Consider a Mars bar, which costs 30 pence in the UK and assume that the UK's exchange rate is 0.6 (£/€). If the price of a Mars bar is €0.50 in Germany, then the real exchange rate is equal to one (since $\theta = \frac{0.5 \times 0.6}{0.3} = 1$). If the price of a Mars bar goes up to €0.55 in Germany but is still 30 pence in the UK (and there is no change in the nominal exchange rate), then the real exchange rate is now 1.1: the price of a Mars bar in the UK is low relative to that in Germany. On observing a shift in the UK's real exchange rate from 1 to 1.1, we would say that price competitiveness in the UK had risen and that the UK's real exchange rate had depreciated.

Defining the nominal exchange rate of the home country as the units of home currency per unit of foreign currency is only a convention. The opposite convention is used as well. The choice of convention differs by country and even across different economics books

Table 9.2 Defining the level and movements in the nominal exchange rate

Home curr.	For. curr.	Home's nom. exch. rate	Depreciation/ Devaluation	Appreciation/ Revaluation
€	$	$e \equiv \frac{€}{$}$	$\uparrow e \equiv \uparrow \left(\frac{€}{$}\right)$	$\downarrow e \equiv \downarrow \left(\frac{€}{$}\right)$

and articles. If the home country is a eurozone country (say, Italy) and the foreign country is the USA, then according to the above definition, Italy's nominal exchange rate is $e \equiv \frac{€}{$}$ or euros per dollar and an increase in e means that one dollar purchases more euros, which implies that the dollar has become relatively more valuable and the euro less valuable. It is said that the euro has *depreciated* against the dollar. Similarly, a decrease in e is an appreciation of the euro (see Table 9.2).[4]

1.4 Price setting in the open economy

After defining the real exchange rate, we look next at how prices are set in the open economy. Given that companies normally operate under imperfect competition and thus face a downward-sloping demand curve, we will assume that firms set home prices on the basis of home costs. But when it comes to foreign markets, two alternative pricing rules are suggested:

- the first—home-cost pricing—is that firms set export prices in the same way as for goods sold at home, i.e. based on domestic costs;

- the second—world pricing—is that firms set export prices based on the prices of similar products produced abroad.

Imagine that there is an increase in costs in the home country but not abroad (and assume that the nominal exchange rate remains unchanged).

- Under the first pricing hypothesis, the prices of home's exports would go up relative to the price of the output of firms abroad. This would reduce home country competitiveness and represent a real appreciation for the home country.

- Under the second, home producers would not change their export prices because prices charged by firms abroad have not changed. In this case, there is no change in the price competitiveness of exports. But we would expect this to have an impact on the ability of firms to compete internationally. If the costs of home firms rise relative to their competitors but prices are unchanged, then the profit margins of home firms are squeezed. This means that home firms will be at a relative disadvantage in their access

---

[4] It should be clear that discussion of 'a rise in the exchange rate' or of the exchange rate being 'high' or 'low' only makes sense when it is clear which convention is being used. In order to minimize confusion, it is safest to avoid using the terms 'rise' or 'fall' or 'high' or 'low' in relation to the exchange rate. It is better to stick to the terms 'appreciation' or 'depreciation' or, when referring to discrete changes in the exchange rate, to the terms 'devaluation' or 'revaluation'.

to internal finance to fund future investment, marketing, research and development, or after-sales service. Although price competitiveness is maintained, 'non-price competitiveness' will be reduced. This means that in this case a definition of competitiveness and the real exchange rate based on relative *costs* rather than relative *prices* is appropriate.

One commonly used measure of competitiveness is called relative unit labour costs or RULC and is defined as follows:

$$\text{RULC} \equiv \frac{\text{foreign unit labour costs expressed in home currency}}{\text{home unit labour costs}}$$

$$\equiv \frac{ULC^* e}{ULC}. \qquad \text{(cost competitiveness; real exchange rate)}$$

A rise in RULC indicates a rise in foreign costs relative to home's, i.e. an improvement in home's competitiveness. A rise in RULC is a real depreciation and a fall in RULC is a real appreciation.[5]

1.5 Evidence on international integration of goods markets

The two pricing rules can be compared to the so-called Law of One Price (LOP) and to the hypothesis of purchasing power parity. According to the Law of One Price, the common currency price of a traded good is identical in different countries. For any good, j, that is traded,

$$P_j = P_j^* e. \qquad \text{(Law of One Price)}$$

The logic of the LOP is straightforward: international trade should have the effect of equalizing prices for the same good in different countries since profits can be made by transporting a good from a location where the price is low and selling it where the price is high. If the LOP holds for all goods *and* the same basket of goods is consumed in different countries, then this basket of goods will have the same common currency price anywhere in the world. This is referred to as Absolute Purchasing Power Parity: if for all goods j in a basket of goods that is common to consumers in both countries,

$$P_j = P_j^* e \text{ for all goods } j$$
$$P = P^* e$$
$$\implies \theta = 1.$$

(absolute purchasing power parity)

The hypothesis of Absolute Purchasing Power Parity implies that the real exchange rate is always equal to one. If we add the assumption of perfect competition, then since under perfect competition, price is equal to marginal cost, marginal costs will be equalized in

---

[5] Just as is the case with the price-based measure of the real exchange rate, conventions vary. Sometimes RULC is defined with home costs in the numerator, in which case a rise in RULC is a deterioration of home's competitiveness and hence a real appreciation.

all countries and there will be no supernormal profits. Hence, unlike the world pricing hypothesis discussed above, where costs can differ across countries and profit margins can expand and contract, in a world of absolute PPP and perfect competition, neither price *nor* cost competitiveness can vary.

There is a great deal of empirical evidence that neither the LOP nor absolute PPP are true. Transport costs and barriers to international trade will interfere with the LOP and the presence of non-traded goods and services in the consumption bundle and differences in consumer tastes across countries will prevent the absolute purchasing power parity hypothesis from holding. However, transport costs and trade barriers are not big enough to explain the deviations from LOP that are observed. Nor is the role of non-traded goods able to account for the failure of absolute PPP to hold. In evaluating the accumulated evidence, Obstfeld argues that '[a]pparently consumer markets for tradables are just about as segmented internationally as consumer markets for nontradables'.[6]

In fact, a central part of the explanation rests on the pervasiveness of imperfect competition in international markets. Most tradeables—both goods and services—are differentiated products and producers pursue pricing strategies to maximize their long-run profits. This entails, for example, taking account of the impact on customers of frequent changes in price (e.g. in response to changes in the nominal exchange rate) and setting different prices in different markets to take advantage of differences in the elasticity of demand. An extensive survey of pricing strategies is provided by Goldberg and Knetter.[7] They report evidence of the widespread use of so-called pricing to market and of the incomplete pass-through of exchange rate changes into prices: 'world pricing' incorporates both these effects.

It seems that firms pursue pricing strategies that lie between the two alternatives of home-cost based and world pricing presented above. Fortunately the main results of the macro model do not depend on which of these simple pricing hypotheses is used: the way that shocks and policy responses are transmitted varies but the qualitative results are similar. Results are only very different if a model of highly integrated perfectly competitive markets without nominal rigidities or inertia is adopted (LOP plus perfect competition as the microeconomic hypothesis; purchasing power parity as the macro hypothesis).

To see the difference in macro implications between the 'segmented' and 'integrated' views of international goods markets, consider the implications of a change in the nominal exchange rate under the different pricing rules. Suppose there is a depreciation of home's nominal exchange rate.

- Under home-cost based pricing, the domestic currency price of exports is unchanged and the price in foreign currency falls. There is a rise in home's competitiveness and the real exchange rate depreciates in line with the nominal exchange rate.

- Under world pricing, the price in foreign currency terms is kept constant (i.e. in line with the price prevailing in the export market). Hence there is no change in relative prices so price competitiveness remains unchanged. However, because of the nominal depreciation, the price of exports in terms of home currency has risen. This raises the

---

[6] Obstfeld (2001). [7] Goldberg and Knetter (1997).

profit margins of home firms relative to their competitors and home's cost competitiveness has improved.

- By contrast, under the LOP and absolute PPP, the integrated goods market means that the depreciation will be immediately offset by a rise in the price of home's goods so as to bring common currency prices back into equality. The nominal exchange rate changes, but the real exchange rate quickly reverts to unity through arbitrage (buying cheap, selling dear) in the goods market.[8]

Yet one of the big facts that has emerged since the era of floating exchange rates began in 1973 is that the fluctuations in nominal exchange rates have been accompanied by fluctuations in real exchange rates. To quote Obstfeld's evaluation of the evidence: 'Real exchange rate variability tends to be almost a perfect reflection of nominal rate variability, with changes in the two rates highly correlated and independent movements in price levels playing a minor, if any, role' (2001: 12). So an appropriate model should accommodate this fact. Either the home-cost or world pricing rule would do but we shall stick to the home-cost based pricing rule because it conveniently allows us to use the real exchange rate defined in terms of price competitiveness. The assumption that prices are set by home costs implies that the price level of home-produced goods sold at home and in the export market is the same and that the price in home currency of imports is set by the price in the rest of the world (i.e. by costs in those economies).[9] Hence we have:

$$P_x = P = \frac{1}{1-\mu} \cdot \text{unit cost} \qquad \text{(export price)}$$

$$P_m = P^* e, \qquad \text{(import price)}$$

where μ is the mark-up.

1.6 Exports and imports: volume and price effects

In the home market, home goods with price P compete with imports (in home currency terms) with price $P^* e$. The relative price is therefore our measure of competitiveness, $\theta \equiv \frac{P^* e}{P}$. In export markets, home produced goods (exports) with price P compete with world goods priced (in home currency terms) at $P^* e$. Once again, the relative price is our measure of competitiveness, θ. We can now pin down export and import functions to reflect the role of competitiveness. For exports, our share of world output will depend on

---

[8] There is a weaker form of purchasing parity that requires the *ratio* of the common currency prices of home and foreign goods to remain constant. This is so-called relative purchasing power parity and requires:

$$P = \frac{P^* e}{k}$$
$$\Rightarrow \theta = k,$$

where k is a constant. In this case too, a change in e requires a change in P so as to keep the *ratio* of home to foreign prices (in the home currency) constant.

[9] After summarizing the evidence, Obstfeld (2001: 22) states: 'These relationships are consistent with a model in which domestic marginal cost (consisting mainly of wages) is sticky in domestic-currency terms, and export prices are set as a (perhaps somewhat variable) markup over marginal cost.'

θ; for imports, the marginal propensity to import, m_y, will depend on θ. A rise in θ will raise the volume of goods exported and depress the volume of goods imported at any level of home income.

The nominal value of exports in home currency terms, X, is equal to the price index of exports times the volume. The volume of exports can be expressed as a share of world output, where the share function σ (sigma) depends positively on competitiveness and y^* is world output:

$$X = P_x x_{\text{volume}} \qquad \text{(exports in nominal terms)}$$

$$= P_x \times \underbrace{\sigma\left(\frac{P^*e}{P}\right)}_{\text{home's share}} \times \underbrace{y^*}_{\text{world output}}.$$

To get the export function in real terms, we divide each side by the domestic price level, P:

$$x = \sigma\left(\frac{P^*e}{P}\right) \times y^*$$

$$= \sigma(\theta) \times y^*. \qquad \text{(export function)}$$

The value of imports M in home currency terms is the price index, $P_m = P^*e$ times the volume of imports, m_{volume}. In turn, the volume depends on the marginal propensity to import, which will be a negative function of competitiveness, and on the level of domestic output.

$$M = P_m \times m_{\text{volume}} \qquad \text{(imports in nominal terms)}$$

$$= P_m \times \underbrace{m_y(\theta)}_{\text{marginal propensity to import}} \times \underbrace{y}_{\text{home output}}.$$

To derive the import function in real terms, we divide each side by P.

$$m = \frac{P_m}{P} \times m_y(\theta) \times y$$

$$= \frac{P^*e}{P} \times m_y(\theta) \times y$$

$$= \theta \times m_y(\theta) \times y. \qquad \text{(import function)}$$

This means that the balance of trade is:

$$BT = \sigma(\theta) \times y^* - \theta \times m_y(\theta) \times y \qquad \text{(balance of trade)}$$

$$= x(\theta, y^*) - \theta \times m(\theta, y).$$

We can now return to one of the questions set out at the beginning of the chapter:

- What determines the trade balance?

First, we want to know how a change in θ affects the trade balance, holding the level of output constant.[10] We discuss the *full* consequences of a change in θ for the trade balance (i.e. once output has adjusted) in the next subsection.

It is not obvious from the expression for the balance of trade what the effect of a change in the real exchange rate on the trade balance is. The reason is that there are two effects—one is the volume effect and the second is the relative price, or terms of trade, effect. The volume effect is the effect on the volume of exports and of imports due to a change in θ. This is unambiguous: a rise in θ boosts the volume of exports ($\sigma(\theta)$ rises as home takes a larger share of world output) and reduces the volume of imports ($m_y(\theta)$ falls as home's marginal propensity to import falls). But a rise in θ will raise the relative price of a given volume of imports.

Another way of expressing the 'relative price effect' of a change in θ is to use the concept of the terms of trade. The terms of trade is defined as the price of exports divided by the price of imports:

$$\frac{P_x}{P_m} = \frac{P}{P^*e} = \frac{1}{\theta}, \qquad \text{(terms of trade)}$$

where an increase in $\frac{P_x}{P_m}$ is an improvement in the terms of trade because a greater volume of imports can be bought for a given volume of exports. Conversely, an increase in θ means a rise in the price of imports relative to exports: it is a deterioration in the terms of trade.[11] For a given volume of imports, this will produce a decline in the trade balance.

In summary, given the way that import and export prices have been defined, a rise in θ (the converse holds for a fall in θ) for the home economy is a

- rise in price competitiveness
- depreciation of the real exchange rate
- deterioration in the terms of trade
- rise in the real cost of imports.

The outcome of a change in the real exchange rate for the trade balance is therefore ambiguous. As long as the volume effects are sufficiently strong so as to outweigh the countervailing terms of trade effect, then a real depreciation (a rise in θ)—i.e. an improvement in home's price competitiveness—will lead to an improvement in the trade balance. This result is reflected in the famous Marshall–Lerner condition, which states that as long as the sum of the price elasticity of demand for exports and the price elasticity of demand for imports exceeds one, a depreciation will improve the balance of trade. The simplicity of the Marshall–Lerner condition depends on the assumption that goods are in perfectly elastic supply (i.e. the price does not change as output increases)[12] and that we begin in

---

[10] We focus here on the partial derivative: $\partial BT / \partial \theta$.

[11] Our baseline pricing hypothesis is consistent with the evidence that a nominal depreciation is associated with a deterioration of home's terms of trade: Obstfeld and Rogoff (2000*b*).

[12] It should be noted that the pricing assumptions that have been made imply that neither export nor import prices are affected by changes in the volume sold (within the range of variation considered). This is the traditional assumption made in the proof of the simple Marshall–Lerner condition that supply elasticities are infinite. (There are many ways to prove the Marshall–Lerner condition—one is shown in the appendix to this chapter.)

trade balance, but the crucial insight of comparing the volume with the terms of trade effects is a general one.

A numerical example illustrates how the Marshall–Lerner condition works. For example, suppose the home economy begins in trade balance with exports equal to imports, which are equal to 100. The elasticity of demand for exports is 0.75 and for imports is 0.50. Consider the implications of a 1% rise in competitiveness arising for example from a rise of 1% in foreign relative to domestic prices:

- export volume rises by 0.75 to 100.75;
- import volume falls by 0.50 to 99.50;
- the real price of imports rises by 1%, pushing the import bill up to 100.495 (since $1.01 \times 99.5 = 100.495$).
- In this case, the balance of trade improves because $BT = 100.75 - 100.495 = 0.255$.

If, on the other hand, export demand elasticity was considerably lower at just 0.25, export volume would only rise by 0.25 to 100.25. Everything else stays the same so the balance of trade actually deteriorates ($BT = 100.25 - 100.495 = -0.245$).

The elasticities used in the example are more 'pessimistic' than the consensus estimates from empirical studies. Dornbusch reports estimates for the absolute value of the price elasticity of demand for exports of 1.06 in Germany, 1.31 in the USA, and 1.68 in Japan and for imports of 0.50 in Germany, 0.97 in Japan, and 1.35 in the USA.[13] The requirement that the sum of the price elasticities of demand is greater than one is easily met for each of these countries. More generally, Dornbusch concludes that '[a]fter 50 years of research on this topic, the finding is sturdily in support of the effectiveness of the price mechanism'. So from now on, we shall assume that there is a positive relationship between the real exchange rate, θ, and the trade balance, given the level of output. This implies that if the price level at home and abroad is constant, there is a positive relationship between the nominal exchange rate, e, and the trade balance. In other words, a depreciation of home's currency is *ceteris paribus* associated with an improvement in the trade balance.

However, empirical studies often find that the trade balance actually deteriorates following a depreciation, only to improve some months later. This empirical pattern is called the J curve since the trade balance traces out (the bottom half of) a J over time in the aftermath of a depreciation. The trade balance can worsen in the short run, for two reasons.

(1) The short-run price elasticity of demand for exports and imports is much lower (approximately one-half) its long-run value. This means that the volume response to the devaluation is initially weak.

(2) To the extent that exports are invoiced in domestic currency, the dollar value of exports falls immediately, while imports invoiced in foreign currency remain unchanged in dollar terms. In home currency terms, export receipts are unchanged while the import bill rises immediately. Hence the trade balance worsens.

---

[13] Dornbusch (1996).

1.7 Output and trade balance in the short run

The condition for goods market equilibrium in the open economy can be enriched by the new import and export functions in which imports and exports depend on the real exchange rate.

$$y = y^D,$$

where

$$y^D = \underbrace{c(y) + I(r) + g}_{Abs} + \underbrace{x(\theta, y^*) - \theta m(\theta, y)}_{BT}.$$

In summary, aggregate demand for domestic output is:

$$y^D = f(y, r, \theta, y^*),$$

where

- the marginal propensity to spend on domestic output lies between zero and one. Hence, we have: $0 < \frac{\partial y^D}{\partial y} < 1$;
- investment is negatively related to the real interest rate. Hence, $\frac{\partial y^D}{\partial r} < 0$;
- a rise in θ i.e. a depreciation of the real exchange rate or a rise in world output, y^*, boosts the trade balance. Hence, $\frac{\partial y^D}{\partial \theta} > 0$ and $\frac{\partial y^D}{\partial y^*} > 0$.

The role of government spending and taxation are basically unchanged from the closed economy and are not shown explicitly above. The only extra point to note is that government spending on imports does not add to the aggregate demand for domestic output.

We can now define the open economy version of the *IS* curve: the *ISXM* is the goods market equilibrium condition and represents the combinations of the interest rate and output at which domestic output is equal to the planned expenditure on domestically produced goods and services. The equation for the *ISXM* curve is:

$$y = \frac{1}{s_y + c_y t_y + \theta m_y(\theta)} \left(c_0 + I(r) + g + \sigma(\theta) \cdot y^* \right). \qquad \text{(open economy } ISXM\text{)}$$

The difference between the closed economy *IS* curve and the open economy *ISXM* curve is highlighted by answers to the following questions.

(1) Why is the *ISXM* steeper than the *IS* curve? The reason is that the size of the multiplier is reduced in the open economy because the marginal propensity to import is positive. There is an additional source of leakage of demand away from home produced goods: as income rises, not only do taxation and savings rise, but so does the level of imports.

(2) How does the *ISXM* curve shift with a change in the real exchange rate? A rise in θ is a depreciation of home's real exchange rate (i.e. an improvement in home's price competitiveness). Since we assume that the Marshall–Lerner condition holds, this boosts

the trade balance and aggregate demand. For any interest rate, goods market equilibrium will therefore occur at a higher level of output. A rise in θ shifts the $ISXM$ to the right and a fall in θ shifts it to the left.

(3) How does the $ISXM$ curve shift with a change in world output, y^*? A rise in world output *ceteris paribus* raises the demand for exports from the home country. Therefore for any interest rate, goods market equilibrium will occur at a higher level of output: a rise in y^* shifts the $ISXM$ to the right and a fall in y^* shifts it to the left.

The trade balance is:

$$BT = x - m \qquad \text{(trade balance)}$$
$$= \sigma(\theta)y^* - \theta m_y(\theta)y$$

and we can therefore write the level of output at which trade is balanced, y_{BT} as:

$$y_{BT} = h(\theta, y^*). \qquad (y_{BT} \text{ line})$$

To the right of y_{BT} there is a trade deficit and to the left there is a trade surplus. A rise in price competitiveness increases the level of output at which trade is balanced and a higher level of world demand has the same effect: in each case the y_{BT} line shifts to the right in the $ISXM$ diagram.

Earlier (in Fig. 9.2) we looked at the consequences for the level of output and for the trade balance of a change in exogenous exports. We can now look at what happens to output and the trade balance when there is an exchange rate change or a change in world output. Consider an exchange rate depreciation. The economy begins in goods market equilibrium and with balanced trade at A in Fig. 9.3. With fixed prices, the depreciation improves price competitiveness and on the usual assumption that the Marshall–Lerner condition holds, will raise net exports. This is the 'partial' effect of a change in θ on net exports discussed earlier. Since net exports increase, the result will be the same: output will rise by less than the new balanced trade level of output and there will be a trade surplus at the new goods market equilibrium (point B).

This is shown in Fig. 9.3. The $ISXM$ curve shifts to the right and so does the y_{BT} line. We assume that the interest rate remains unchanged. The rise in net exports due to the rise

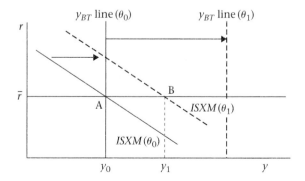

Figure 9.3 Real depreciation ($\uparrow \theta$): impact on output and the trade balance

in θ raises aggregate demand (y^D), which pushes up output and income until a new goods market equilibrium is established. The new goods market equilibrium is established when the higher savings, taxation, and imports induced by the rise in net exports is equal to the net injection of demand (*ISXM* shifts to *ISXM*(θ_1) and output rises from y_0 to y_1 in Fig. 9.3). The level of income at which trade is balanced will be at the level at which the increased imports generated by the higher incomes is equal to the change in net exports. Trade balance would therefore occur at a higher level of output than the new goods market equilibrium (y_{BT} line (θ_1)). Output is to the left of the new y_{BT} line and there is therefore a trade surplus at *B*.

2 Opening financial markets

By the late 1980s values traded in international markets for financial assets far exceeded the value of international trade in goods and services. It is trade in international financial markets that dominates the foreign exchange market. To understand the essential aspects of international financial markets, it is useful to make some simplifying assumptions.

- F1. There is *perfect international capital mobility*. This means that, for example, home residents can buy or sell foreign bonds with the fixed nominal world interest rate, i^*, in unlimited quantities at low transactions cost.

- F2. The home country is assumed to be *small* in the sense that its behaviour cannot affect the world interest rate.

- F3. Just as in the simple *IS/LM* model, we assume there are just *two assets* that households can hold—bonds and money. But now they can hold foreign or home bonds. We assume that they hold only home money.

- F4. There is *perfect substitutability* between foreign and home bonds. This assumption means that that there is no risk premium on foreign bonds. If the riskiness of foreign and home bonds is identical, then the only relevant difference between home and foreign bonds is the expected return on them. Two issues lie behind this assumption. The first is whether governments differ in their default risk—i.e. in the likelihood that bonds will not be honoured. The second is whether investors care about the composition of their asset portfolio. By assuming perfect substitutability, we are ruling out differences in the riskiness of bonds and assuming that investors do not care about the balance between home and foreign bonds in their portfolio.

Once we have a working model based on these assumptions, we return in section 6 of this chapter to discuss their empirical plausibility and what happens in the model when they are relaxed.

2.1 Uncovered interest parity condition

Given that home residents have the opportunity to hold foreign bonds in their portfolio, we need to consider what will influence their choice. In a well-functioning capital market it is impossible for there to be a different expected return on assets with the same risk. Assuming that there is no difference in risk between the bonds issued by the two governments, two factors will affect the expected return on home as compared with foreign bonds:

- any difference in interest rates and
- a view about the likely development of the exchange rate.

Take an example using government one-year bonds. Assume that government authorities (i.e. the government or the central bank) can set the interest rate and that the interest rate in the UK is 6.5% and in the USA is 4%. This means that by holding UK rather than US bonds, the investor gets an additional interest return of 2.5%. In the context of highly integrated international capital markets, such a situation offers an opportunity for investors to make profits by switching from US to UK bonds. In order to buy UK bonds, pounds are needed so there will be a surge in the demand for pounds. This will lead to an immediate *appreciation* of the pound.

The expectation that the exchange rate adjusts immediately, stems from empirical observation. In a survey of foreign exchange dealers in the UK, they were asked: 'How fast do you think the market can assimilate the new information when the following economic announcements from the major developed economies differ from their market expectations?'[14] For an unexpected interest rate announcement, more than two-thirds of the traders said 'less than 10 seconds' with most of the rest saying less than one minute. According to this survey, speedy reaction is most common for news about interest rates, which also has a bigger impact on foreign exchange markets than announcements about inflation, unemployment, the trade deficit, the money supply, or GNP.

Now let us ask what expectations about a *change* in the exchange rate investors would need to have in order *not* to want to switch between dollars and pounds despite the interest rate difference of 2.5%. The answer is simple: investors would need to believe that the pound would *depreciate* by 2.5% over the period for which the interest differential is expected to persist. Then the 2.5% gain in terms of higher interest on pound (sterling) bonds would be wiped out by the expected loss from the depreciation of the pound. For the expected return on pound and dollar bonds to be equalized as they must in a well-functioning capital market, the expected capital loss from holding the pound bonds for one year because of a depreciation of the pound exchange rate has to be equal to the interest rate gain. This is the uncovered interest parity condition (*UIP*).

The condition that the interest rate differential in favour of bonds denominated in currency A must be equal to the expected exchange rate depreciation of currency A over the period for which the interest differential is expected to persist is called the uncovered interest parity condition and can be stated as follows:

$$\underbrace{i - i^*}_{\text{interest gain (loss)}} = \underbrace{\frac{e_{t+1}^E - e_t}{e_t}}_{\text{expected depreciation (appreciation)}}, \qquad \text{(uncovered interest parity)}$$

[14] Cheung, Chinn, and Marsh (2000: 30).

where i is the home and i^* the foreign interest rate, e is the nominal exchange rate of the home country and e^E is the expected exchange rate.[15]

It is useful to take the example a step further. Assume that initially interest rates are 4% in both the USA and the UK and investors expect no change in the exchange rate. Thus we start in equilibrium: the *UIP* condition holds because there is no difference in interest return and no expected change in the exchange rate so the exchange rate adjusted return is equal for dollar and pound bonds. The UK government then raises the interest rate to 6.5%. Now suppose investors have a fairly clear idea about two things. First, that the interest differential will last for one year and second, that whatever happens to the exchange rate in the short run—and they know it must change since the current situation is unsustainable—it will eventually come back to the current level. In other words investors think the exchange rate is at its 'correct' long-run level. Investors bid up the value of the pound by buying pounds in order to purchase the attractive high interest pound bonds. The pound will appreciate instantaneously by 2.5%. Why? Because an appreciation of 2.5% is exactly what is required to establish equilibrium. The pound is now expected to depreciate by 2.5% (back to its unchanged long-run expected value) over the course of the year during which the interest advantage of UK pounds is 2.5%.

To summarize, we can work out how much the exchange rate will appreciate immediately because we know that trading in the financial market will ensure that all opportunities to make a profit are exhausted. This means that the interest rate gain from holding UK bonds must be offset by the expected loss from the depreciation of the pound exchange rate over the period for which the interest difference prevails. What happens is that when any interest rate differential is opened up, there is a jump in the exchange rate just sufficient to eliminate the interest rate gains. Then over the period for which the interest differential on the bonds is expected to remain, the exchange rate appreciation gradually unwinds and the exchange rate returns to its expected or 'correct' long-run value. An important distinguishing characteristic of financial markets (as compared with goods and labour markets) is that jumps in prices are commonly observed.

---

[15] To derive the UIP condition, we begin with the arbitrage equation below. Assume that Home is the UK and the USA is foreign. If you begin with $1, then the left hand side says: this is the return after one year from converting the $1 to pounds at the start of the year using the current or spot exchange rate e_t and buying sterling bonds. The right hand side says: this is the return after one year from using the $1 to buy dollar bonds, which are converted at the end of the period to pounds at the forward exchange rate that prevails today, F, i.e. the contract to buy the pounds in one period's time is purchased today. This 'covers' the investor for exchange rate uncertainity. Arbitrage will ensure that the left and right hand sides are equal.

$$e_t(1+i) = (1+i^*)F.$$

The arbitrage condition is called the covered interest parity condition. To turn this into the *UIP* condition, we replace the forward rate at time t with the unknown expected rate at $t+1$ leaving the investor 'uncovered' in relation to exchange risk. In addition, we use the approximation that $\frac{1+i}{1+i^*} \approx 1+i-i^*$ and simplify as follows:

$$1+i-i^*-1 = \frac{e_{t+1}^E - e_t}{e_t} \Rightarrow i-i^* = \frac{e_{t+1}^E - e_t}{e_t}.$$

Working through a numerical example helps to clarify this important relationship. Consider one-year government bonds. Initially, interest rates in the two countries are identical and the nominal exchange rate is 0.650 pounds per dollar. Then suppose that the interest rate in the UK is raised to 6.5% and is expected to stay above the US interest rate for one year. This means that there is a 2.5% ($6.5 - 4 = 2.5\%$) gain from holding pound rather than dollar bonds. As stated above, for the expected return on pound and dollar bonds to be equalized, it must be the case that the expected capital loss from holding the pound bonds for one year because of a depreciation of the pound exchange rate is equal to the interest rate gain. Thus to work out the exchange rate, e_t, that will deliver an expected exchange rate loss of 2.5%, we need to have a view about the exchange rate that will prevail in one year's time. On our assumption that the exchange rate was originally at, and will return to its 'correct' long-run value, this is simply the exchange rate at time t_0 when interest rates were equal at 4%. Then the expected depreciation of the exchange rate between time 1 and time 2 must equal the interest rate differential:

$$\frac{e_2^E - e_1}{e_1} = \frac{0.650 - e_1}{e_1} = 2.5\%$$

Therefore $e_1 \approx 0\ 635$.

This means that on the announcement of the rise in the UK interest rate, the pound exchange rate immediately *appreciates* from a rate of 0.650 to 0.635. Over the course of the year from t_1 to t_2 the pound *depreciates* back to the original level of 0.650. Table 9.3 shows the data for each period.

The paths of the nominal exchange rate and the interest rate are shown in Fig. 9.4.

2.2 Using the *UIP* condition

The *UIP* condition is very useful because it provides a direct link from a change in monetary policy (which changes the nominal interest rate) to a change in the exchange rate. Fig. 9.5 shows the *UIP* condition in a diagram with the interest rate on the vertical axis and the nominal exchange rate on the horizontal axis. The first point defined in the diagram is *A*, an equilibrium characterized by the home interest rate equalling the world interest rate ($i = i^*$) and fulfilled exchange rate expectations ($e_0 = e_0^E$).

To fix another point on this *UIP* curve, consider a rise in the home interest rate to i_1 that is expected to prevail for one year. Assuming that the expected exchange rate remains fixed at e_0^E, then since the interest rate is now above the world interest rate, there must be

Table 9.3 Uncovered interest parity: an example

	Time $= t_0$	Time $= t_1$	Time $= t_2$
i^{UK}	4	6.5	4
i^{US}	4	4	4
e	0.650	0.635	0.650

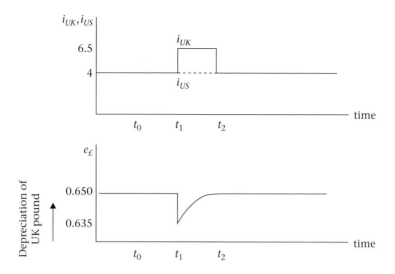

Figure 9.4 Paths of UK interest rate and UK pound exchange rate: the interest rate on UK bonds exceeds that on US bonds for 1 period

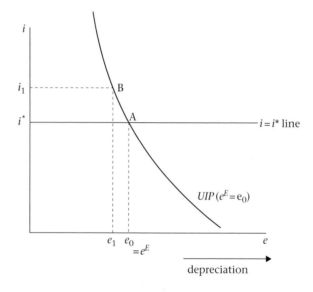

Figure 9.5 The uncovered interest parity condition

a change in the actual exchange rate. According to the *UIP* condition, the exchange rate will appreciate immediately (jump) to e_1 so that its expected depreciation over the year is equal to the interest rate differential. This requirement fixes point *B* and defines the *UIP* curve.[16]

---

[16] Note that if you draw the UIP curve accurately, it will be steeper than shown in Fig. 9.5. We magnify the scale on the horizontal axis to allow for easier viewing of exchange rate changes.

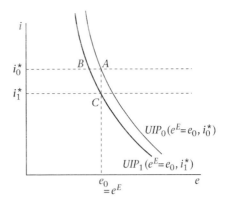

Figure 9.6 The uncovered interest parity
condition: fall in the world interest rate

The key features of the *UIP* diagram are:

- each *UIP* curve must go through the point (e^E, i^*)
- for a given world interest rate, any change in the expected exchange rate shifts the *UIP* curve
- for a given expected exchange rate, any change in the world interest rate shifts the *UIP* curve.

To illustrate how the *UIP* curve works, suppose there is a fall in world interest rates. What is the implication for the home country's exchange rate assuming that there is no change in the home interest rate? To answer this question, assume no change in the expected exchange rate. The shift in the *UIP* curve from UIP_0 to UIP_1 due to the fall in the world interest rate is shown in Fig. 9.6. The economy is initially at point A on UIP_0. With the expected exchange rate equal to e_0^E and with the home interest rate now above the world interest rate of i_1^*, arbitrage in the financial market will lead to an immediate appreciation of the exchange rate as shown by point B on the new *UIP* curve, UIP_1; a fall in the world interest rate will lead to an immediate appreciation of the home currency. The diagram also helps to illustrate that there will be no exchange rate change if the central bank in the home country shifts the interest rate down so that it is equal to the new lower world interest rate: the economy then shifts from A to C.

A final exercise is the analysis of a change in sentiment in the foreign exchange market. If traders suddenly change their view about the likely exchange rate in a year's time, the *UIP* curve will shift. If a depreciated exchange rate is expected, the *UIP* curve will shift to the right. With the home and world interest rates equal, such a change in sentiment will have the effect of leading to an immediate depreciation of the exchange rate to its new expected value. This illustrates that expectations about future developments are incorporated into today's exchange rate. If the government is to prevent an immediate depreciation, it must raise the interest rate as shown by the new *UIP* condition to compensate holders of home bonds for the expected depreciation. The sooner traders expect an exchange rate change to occur, the higher the home interest rate will have to go to keep the current exchange rate unchanged. This is especially relevant in the case in which a country has a fixed exchange rate and where doubts emerge about the 'credibility' of the exchange rate peg.

3 Fixed and flexible exchange rate regimes

In an open economy, it is useful to think about two polar exchange rate regimes. At one extreme is the case of a freely floating, fully flexible exchange rate where neither the government nor central bank intervenes in the foreign exchange market to influence the price at which one currency trades with another. The exchange rate is then determined by supply and demand for the currency relative to other currencies. At the other extreme is the case of fixed exchange rates where the government sets a rate (a so-called peg) at which it will buy or sell foreign exchange as necessary in order to keep the 'price' fixed. These sales or purchases of foreign exchange by the central bank are called official intervention and we denote them by ΔR, where R stands for the central bank's foreign exchange reserves. The purchase by the home central bank of foreign exchange is $\Delta R > 0$ and the sale of foreign exchange is $\Delta R < 0$. In a flexible exchange rate regime, there is no official intervention ($\Delta R = 0$).

Fig. 9.7 shows the foreign exchange market: the home exchange rate is on the vertical axis and the quantity of foreign exchange is on the horizontal axis. The supply and demand curves for foreign exchange are shown. As e depreciates ($\uparrow e$), the foreign currency becomes more valuable and the supply of foreign exchange rises. Similarly, the demand for foreign exchange is downward sloping. Initially the market is in equilibrium with an exchange rate of e_0. Suppose there is a rightward shift in the supply of foreign exchange (e.g. as a consequence of a rise in the domestic interest rate relative to the world interest rate). Since home bonds are now more attractive than foreign ones at the given exchange rate, there is an excess supply of foreign exchange. Under a flexible exchange rate regime,

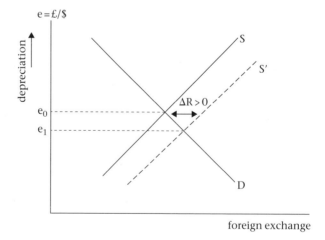

Figure 9.7 The foreign exchange market

the exchange rate would appreciate to e_1 and there would be no official intervention, i.e. $\Delta R = 0$. Under a fixed exchange rate with a peg set at e_0, the central bank will have to intervene in the market to absorb the excess supply of foreign exchange in order to keep the exchange rate fixed. Hence home's official foreign exchange reserves will rise by ΔR (see Fig. 9.7).

Under flexible exchange rates, the uncovered interest parity condition shows how arbitrage in the international financial market will lead to changes in the exchange rate in response to a change in:

- home's interest rate assuming that exchange rate expectations and the world interest rate remain unchanged,

- the world interest rate assuming that exchange rate expectations and the home interest rate remain unchanged and

- exchange rate expectations if interest rates at home and abroad remain unchanged.

In a fixed exchange rate regime, the government requires that the central bank actively intervenes in the foreign exchange market in order to keep the exchange rate constant. As the interest parity condition makes clear, if the expected depreciation or appreciation of the exchange rate is zero (as in a fixed exchange rate regime), then the home interest rate must always be equal to the world interest rate.

Fig. 9.8 shows the comparison between the flexible exchange rate regime and the fixed exchange rate regime when there is an exogenous fall in the demand for money. In the upper panel (flexible exchange rates), the fall in the demand for money lowers the home interest rate (A to B). The *UIP* condition in the left hand panel shows that this leads to an immediate depreciation of the home exchange rate (A' to B'). By contrast in the fixed exchange rate case (lower panel), the fall in the demand for money puts downward pressure on the interest rate and the incipient collapse in the demand for pounds requires the central bank to intervene in the foreign exchange market to buy pounds. It uses foreign exchange reserves to do this ($\Delta R < 0$) and the result is a decline in the money supply to match the new lower demand for money (from A to B). The interest rate and exchange rate remain unchanged (at A'). As the economy is affected by domestic or foreign shocks, the domestic money supply moves around in order to keep $e = e^E = $ *exchange rate peg* and $i = i^*$.

It is important to bear in mind that the home money demand function is the same as in the closed economy. The difference that opening the economy makes is that it creates a connection between the home interest rate, the world interest rate (and hence money demand and supply in the rest of the world), and the exchange rate. The money supply is under the control of the domestic authorities in the flexible exchange rate economy but not in the fixed exchange rate economy because official intervention to stabilize the exchange rate (ΔR) endogenizes the money supply.

It is useful to set in context the link between the change in official reserves and the money supply by summarizing the ways in which the money supply can increase.

- We introduced the simplest case in the closed economy (Chapter 2). This is where the central bank engages in an open market operation in which it uses newly printed money to purchase bonds from the public. This has the effect of increasing the stock of

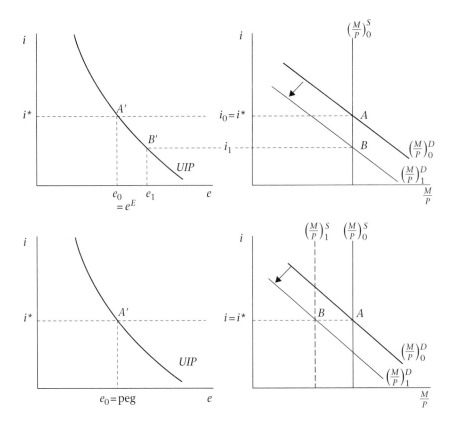

Figure 9.8 Fall in the demand for money: consequences under flexible (top panel) and fixed (bottom panel) exchange rates

high powered money and reducing the stock of bonds in the hands of the public. The central bank's assets rise by the increase in bonds and its liabilities rise exactly in line with the increase in high powered money (*LM* shift only).

- The second case is where the government has a budget deficit that it has to finance, i.e. government expenditure exceeds its tax revenues. It could sell more bonds *to the public* to finance its deficit (*IS* shift only) with no implications for the money supply but it could also sell the bonds *to the central bank* in exchange for newly printed money (*IS* and *LM* shift). The central bank ends up with more bonds (assets) and a matching rise in liabilities.

- The third way in which the money supply can rise is if the central bank intervenes in the foreign exchange market and buys foreign exchange with newly printed money. The central bank's assets rise (by the increase in foreign exchange reserves) as do its liabilities (*LM* shift only). This highlights the fact that any change in the central bank's assets (its holdings of bonds or of foreign exchange reserves) will have a counterpart in a change in its liabilities, i.e. the money supply in the hands of the public (see the balance sheet in Table 9.4).

Table 9.4 Central bank balance sheet in the open economy

Assets	Liabilities
Government bonds + foreign exchange reserves	High-powered money in hands of public
$B + R$	H

4 Trade balance and balance of payments

Before putting together a model of how output and the balance of trade are determined in the short run, the open economy accounting concepts are clarified. The transactions between the home country and the rest of the world are recorded in the balance of payments. The balance of payments account is divided into the current account and the capital account.[17]

The **current account**

- consists of the trade balance plus net interest and profit receipts. Net interest and profit receipts arise from earnings from foreign assets (e.g. bonds, equities) owned by residents of the home country less payments of interest and profit to foreigners who own home country assets.

The **capital account**

- records changes in the stock of various types of foreign assets owned by home residents and home assets owned by overseas residents and changes in official foreign exchange reserves of the central bank.

To understand the balance of payments accounts, it is useful to separate the private and official parts of the capital account.

$$BP \equiv \left(\underbrace{(X - M)}_{\text{trade balance}} + \text{net interest receipts} \right) + \underbrace{(\text{capital inflows-capital outflows})}_{\text{capital account}}$$

$$\underbrace{\phantom{(X - M) + \text{net interest receipts}}}_{\text{current account}}$$

$$\equiv (BT + INT) + (F - \Delta R) \equiv 0,$$

---

[17] With the publication of the IMF's *Balance of Payments Manual* fifth edition in 1993, the official terminology changed. The main change was to reclassify some transfers from the current account into the redesignated 'capital and financial' account. We shall continue to use the more familiar standard terminology since we are only concerned with the most basic decomposition of the balance of payments account. The IMF's *Balance of Payments Manual* fifth edition (1993) is available from www.imf.org/external/np/sta/bop/BOPman.pdf.

where BT is the balance of trade and INT is net receipts of factor income from abroad. F records private net capital inflows and $-\Delta R$ records the net decline in official foreign exchange reserves.

If we rearrange the balance of payments equilibrium by putting the increase in foreign exchange reserves on the left hand side, we have:

$$\Delta R = (BT + INT) + F.$$

If there is a current account surplus, there will be no change in official reserves if the net private capital outflow is equal to the current account surplus. The net capital outflow (i.e. $F < 0$) reflects the *acquisition* by the home country of foreign assets. In the opposite situation of a current account deficit (i.e. a situation in which domestic savings is less than domestic investment) for there to be no change in official reserves, there must be a net capital inflow (i.e. $F > 0$). Home is borrowing from abroad and thereby acquiring a foreign liability.[18]

It should now be clear that official foreign exchange reserves will rise ($\Delta R > 0$) when a current account surplus exceeds the net private capital outflow. Similarly, official reserves will fall when a current account deficit is not fully financed by a private capital inflow. Under flexible exchange rates, the nominal exchange rate moves to secure balance of payments equilibrium without the need for official intervention.

There are two questions about the balance of payments that we need to answer:

(1) Why is the balance of payments equal to zero?

(2) Does it matter if the current account or trade balance is in surplus or deficit? If the balance of payments is always zero, how can there be a balance of payments crisis?

4.1 Why is the balance of payments equal to zero?

The balance of payments identity requires that

$$BP \equiv (BT + INT) + (F - \Delta R) \equiv 0.$$

We begin by considering the export of mobile phones from Sweden to New Zealand and ask how this transaction will show up in the Swedish balance of payments statistics. Sweden is the home country in this example. The export of mobile phones will be registered as a positive item in the current account (i.e. $BT > 0$). For the identity to hold and assuming for simplicity that net interest payments are zero, there are three different ways in which the Swedish balance of payments could record this transaction:

• (i) an exactly equal value of imports from New Zealand to Sweden takes place. In this case, the current account balances and the capital account (private and official) is zero.

[18] At first sight it may seem paradoxical that a negative F in the balance of payments represent the acquisition by home of foreign assets. This is explained by the fact that the balance of payments records the sources and uses of foreign exchange: the purchase of foreign assets is a use of foreign exchange and therefore has a negative value in the balance of payments accounts.

- (ii) an exactly equal capital outflow from Sweden to New Zealand takes place ($F < 0$). The kronor are used to purchase New Zealand assets. In this case, the current account is in surplus, the private capital account is in deficit and there is no change in official reserves.

- (iii) an official intervention in the foreign exchange market—e.g. the Swedish Central Bank sells kronor and buys New Zealand dollars ($\Delta R > 0$). In this case, there is a current account surplus and a capital account deficit that takes the form of a rise in foreign exchange reserves.

One of these three alternatives (or some suitable mixture) must take place. Why? The answer is that the Swedish exports have to be paid for in kronor so through some means or other, the kronor have to be found. After all, the world is a closed system. The balance of payments is the method by which records of international transactions are kept. In practice, the records are incomplete, with the result that an entry for errors and omissions has to be added to make the balance of payments sum to zero.

To tie up the loose ends, let us take one further example. What happens if the current account is in balance, there is no official intervention and there is a private capital outflow from Sweden. For example, suppose a Swedish firm is setting up a mobile phone subsidiary in New Zealand. This is a long-term flow of capital from Sweden to New Zealand as the Swedes buy assets (e.g. land and a factory) (i.e. $F < 0$). In order to buy the New Zealand assets, the Swedish firm needs NZ dollars. Since the current account is in balance and there is no official intervention, the Swedish firm would have to borrow New Zealand dollars in order to engage in the investment in New Zealand. Borrowing NZ dollars means that there is capital inflow on Sweden's capital account (the NZ dollars) (i.e. $F > 0$). This matches the capital outflow and the balance of payments is equal to zero.

4.2 Do current account imbalances matter?

Turning to the second question, does it matter from an economic perspective if there is a current account or trade deficit or surplus in the economy? To answer this question, it is necessary to recall that any non-zero current account reflects a change in the country's wealth. If the home country has a current account surplus then this means that it is lending abroad—if it has a current account deficit, then it is borrowing from abroad (refer back to sections 1.2 and 4.1). If there is a trade deficit, then the domestic private and public sector savings are inadequate to finance private and government investment. The home country must therefore borrow from abroad. Since this borrowing will have to be repaid (with interest) in the future, the trade deficit represents a decline in the home country's wealth. A trade deficit will imply a current account deficit unless the home country receives a sufficient net inflow of interest and profit receipts on the foreign assets that it owns.

A decline in wealth sounds like a bad thing—but this is not always the case. When a student goes into debt to finance their university studies, their financial wealth falls. The wisdom of this move depends on the extent to which the university education increases the student's human capital and improves their earning capacity. Similarly, if the home country's trade deficit reflects a high level of investment in profitable projects in the home economy, then the possibility of borrowing from abroad is a method of increasing the wealth of the home country in the future. Provided the investments in the home economy bear fruit, its exports rise and it is able to repay its international debts. A good example of this is the Norwegian economy in the 1970s: it had persistent current account deficits as it borrowed abroad to develop its oil reserves. Equally, for a country that does not have very profitable investment opportunities at home, it makes sense that domestic savings are used for net investment abroad. The purchase of foreign assets that the current account surplus represents may provide a higher return than would higher investment at home. High saving economies in Asia such as Singapore provide examples here.

If all economic agents act rationally weighing up the relative returns from different investment opportunities, then a current account imbalance simply reflects the differences in preferences and in investment opportunities across countries. However, a persistent current account deficit is not necessarily benign. A current account deficit may not reflect higher investment at home in response to especially attractive investment opportunities—rather, it may reflect low savings because of high private or government consumption or it may reflect investment in wasteful projects. A persistent or excessive current account deficit may become increasingly difficult to finance. In practice this means that under flexible exchange rates, there may be a depreciation of the exchange rate. Under fixed exchange rates, if private counterparties cannot be found to finance the deficit, the central bank will be obliged to sell foreign exchange reserves in order to maintain the exchange rate. It may clamp down on the access of home residents to foreign exchange, thereby keeping them from engaging in the purchase of foreign bonds. If so, the assumed perfect international capital mobility breaks down—i.e. it becomes difficult for home residents to lend at the world interest rate. In circumstances such as these, the government and central bank will be obliged to change domestic policy so as to reduce the current account deficit.

Since a current account deficit implies a running down of the home country's wealth (an increase in its foreign liabilities) whereas a surplus represents an accumulation of wealth, there is an essential asymmetry between the two. Foreigners may stop lending to the home economy: they cannot stop the home economy from lending abroad. In Chapter 17, the causes and consequences of the emergence of a large current account deficit in the USA in the early 2000s are analysed.

4.3 What is a balance of payments crisis?

If the balance of payments must sum to zero, what is a balance of payments crisis? Similarly, why is there reference to a balance of payments 'deficit' or 'surplus' if the balance of payments is always in balance? The explanation lies in an unfortunately sloppy use of terms. Balance of payments surplus, deficit, or crisis refer to the state of the current account plus the capital account *excluding official intervention* —i.e. to $(BT + INT) + F$ in our terminology. Thus a balance of payments surplus arises when the sum of the current account and net capital inflows is positive. This means that official reserves are rising: since $BT \equiv 0$ and $(BT + INT) + (F) > 0$, this implies that $\Delta R > 0$. Conversely a deficit means that the private capital inflows are inadequate to finance the current account deficit with the result that official reserves are falling. The possibility of a crisis should now be clear. If a balance of payments deficit persists, the central bank may eventually run out of reserves. A potential crisis of this kind will lead to a change in government policy (e.g. the introduction of contractionary policies to stem imports; a devaluation of the exchange rate to boost net exports) and possibly ultimately to intervention by the IMF.

5 The Mundell–Fleming model for the short run

The elements are now ready to be combined to provide a useful model, which shows the impact of policy and of domestic and foreign shocks on output and the balance of trade in the short run. We make the following assumptions:

- MF1. Prices and wages are fixed. Hence inflation and expected inflation are zero and the real and nominal interest rates are equal. (This allows us to use an IS/LM diagram with the nominal interest rate on the vertical axis).

- MF2. The home economy is small. This means the home economy cannot affect the world interest rate or world output.

- MF3. Perfect capital mobility and perfect asset substitutability. Residents of the home economy can buy and sell bonds of the foreign country (with the interest rate i^*) in unlimited amounts at low transactions costs. There is no difference in risk between the bonds. This implies that uncovered interest parity holds.

The Mundell–Fleming model consists of four elements:

(1) the open economy version of the goods market equilibrium condition for the home economy summarized in the $ISXM$ curve

(2) the money market equilibrium condition for the home economy summarized in the LM curve

(3) the financial market arbitrage or uncovered interest parity condition summarized in the UIP curve and

(4) the condition for financial integration when expectations are fulfilled in the foreign exchange market, summarized in the $i = i^*$ line.

Short-run equilibrium is when the goods market is in equilibrium and where the exchange rate is not expected to change. This means that the economy must lie on the $i = i^*$ line because as the UIP condition requires, only when home and world interest rates are equal is the expected exchange rate equal to the actual exchange rate.

The model can be used to analyse policy choices by the home government and also the implications of a change in economic conditions emanating from the rest of the world—e.g. a change in the world interest rate or a change in world aggregate demand—or from the domestic economy—e.g. a consumption boom or a slump in investment. We draw together the results for different disturbances under different exchange rate regimes, leaving the task of working through the details of each case as an exercise for the reader.

5.1 The Mundell–Fleming model and monetary policy

5.1.1 Fixed exchange rates

As we have seen above, when the exchange rate peg has to be maintained, the home economy loses control of its money supply so any attempt by the home economy to use monetary policy is bound to be ineffective. Let us take the example of an expansionary monetary policy. The central bank engages in an open market operation that consists of the purchase of home bonds in exchange for newly printed money. The *LM* curve shifts to the right (Fig. 9.9).

What is the new short-run equilibrium? Since the exchange rate is fixed, equilibrium in the international financial market summarized in the *UIP* condition dictates that the interest rate must be equal to the world interest rate. Hence the new equilibrium must be at *A*: monetary policy has no effect. This is because the purchase of home bonds by the central bank bids up their price and pushes the interest rate downwards, making pound bonds unattractive. But the central bank is committed to maintaining the exchange rate so it must use foreign exchange reserves to purchase pounds and prevent the exchange rate from depreciating. This decline in the monetary base exactly offsets the initial injection of new high powered money. The *LM* curve shifts left again back to its initial position.

5.1.2 Flexible exchange rates

With flexible exchange rates, the exchange rate can adjust to any discrepancy between the domestic and the world interest rate generated by a change in home monetary policy. An expansionary monetary policy will push down the home interest rate. This will make pound bonds unattractive and lead to a depreciation of the exchange rate. The depreciation will boost net exports of the home economy and push up the level of output. As output rises the demand for money will rise and the home interest rate will return to the world level. Monetary policy can therefore affect output and the trade balance.

The new short-run equilibrium must lie on the $i = i^*$ line with the exchange rate equal to the expected exchange rate and the interest rate equal to the world interest rate. Given the new *LM* curve, this means that the new equilibrium will be at point *Z* in Fig. 9.10. Hence the *ISXM* curve must shift to the right and intersect both the *LM'* and $i = i^*$ line

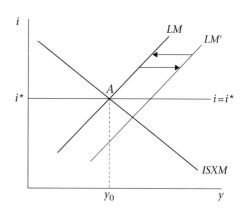

Figure 9.9 Expansionary monetary policy: fixed exchange rates

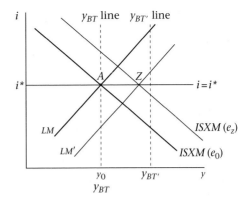

Figure 9.10 Expansionary monetary policy: flexible exchange rates

at Z. The rightward shift in the *ISXM* curve will be brought about by the depreciation of the exchange rate. We also know that the exchange rate depreciation shifts the y_{BT} line to the right. There will be a trade surplus at the new short-run equilibrium because the depreciation will have increased output by more than the increase in domestic absorption (refer back to section 1.1 above).

But how does the economy adjust from the initial equilibrium of A to the new equilibrium of Z and what role is played by the *UIP* condition? In Fig. 9.11, we draw the initial *UIP* condition in the left panel. Remember that this is drawn for a given expected exchange rate, e^E and shows what will happen to the nominal exchange rate if the interest rate deviates from the world rate. The process of adjustment to the new equilibrium depends on how exchange rate expectations are formed. Assume that agents update their exchange rate expectations using a form of adaptive expectations so that if the exchange rate depreciates from e_0 to e_1, then we shall assume that the new expected exchange rate is equal to to e_1. After looking at the adjustment process, we consider what happens if we assume rational expectations instead.

- Step 1. The rightward shift of the *LM* curve leads to a fall in the domestic interest rate and output rises $(A \rightarrow B)$ in the *ISXM*/*LM* diagram.

- Step 2. The fall in the interest rate implies via the *UIP* condition that there is an immediate depreciation of the exchange rate to e_1 in order that the expected appreciation from B' back to A' would offset the expected interest loss from holding pound rather than dollar bonds. The depreciation occurs because home residents sell pounds and buy dollars with which to purchase the higher interest dollar bonds.

- Step 3. The depreciation of the exchange rate leads to a rightward shift of the *ISXM* curve to *ISXM*(e_1) which raises output further $(B \rightarrow C)$ in the *ISXM* diagram. This leaves the home interest rate below the world interest rate.

- Step 4. Because of the depreciation of the exchange rate, the expected exchange rate changes according to the adaptive expectations rule. The new *UIP* curve crosses the $i = i^*$ line where the expected exchange rate equals e_1 (see Fig. 9.11). Given that the

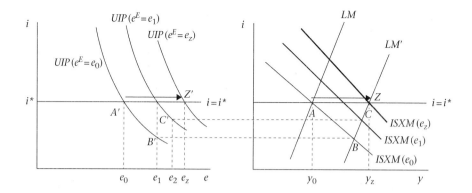

Figure 9.11 Expansionary monetary policy: adjustment under flexible exchange rates
(a) Slow adjustment of exchange rate expectations (adaptive expectations) and slow adjustment of output and employment: A to B to $C \ldots$ to Z.
(b) Immediate adjustment of exchange rate expectations to the new short-run equilibrium (rational expectations) and rapid adjustment of output: A to Z.

expected exchange rate is now e_1 the actual exchange rate will depreciate further to e_2 and the economy will move to C' in the *UIP* diagram.

- Step 5. This is simply a repetition of step 3: the depreciation to e_2 shifts the *ISXM* further to the right.

Once the home interest rate is equal to the world interest rate again, there will be no further adjustment: the economy is at the new stable short-run equilibrium at Z.

We could take a radically different assumption about expectations. Suppose that all agents understand the model of the economy and can figure out the exchange rate that is consistent with the new short-run equilibrium at Z. To do this they must figure out the extent of depreciation required to shift the *ISXM* curve sufficiently far to the right that it intersects the new *LM'* at $i = i^*$. This means that they expect the nominal exchange rate to be $e^E = e_Z$ as soon as the new monetary policy is announced. This implies that the *UIP* curve jumps from UIP_0 to UIP_Z immediately (see Fig. 9.11). *If* the goods market adjusts equally rapidly, then the *ISXM* curve also jumps immediately to $ISXM(e_Z)$ and the economy moves straight to the new short-run equilibrium at Z. With so-called rational exchange rate expectations and rapid adjustment in the goods market, we observe the shift from A to Z.

It is very important to note that the new short-run equilibrium exchange rate, e_Z, is *not* equal to e_1. The move *along* the initial *UIP* curve from A' to B' is solely a consequence of the arbitrage condition in the *financial* market given the fall in home's interest rate. The *shift of* the *UIP* curve from $UIP(e^E = e_0)$ to $UIP(e^E = e_Z)$ reflects completely different economic forces: this reflects the change in e that is required in the *goods* market to increase net exports and shift the *ISXM* from $ISXM(e_0)$ to $ISXM(e_Z)$. There is therefore no reason why the depreciation from e_0 to e_1 implied by financial arbitrage is the same as the depreciation from e_0 to e_Z required for the new goods market equilibrium.

5.1.3 Introduction to exchange rate overshooting: example of contractionary monetary policy

Exchange rate overshooting occurs when agents have rational expectations and there is sluggish adjustment in the goods market.[19] In contrast to the two scenarios in the previous section, this does not make either of the problematic assumptions; agents do not repeatedly use an erroneous forecasting rule (adaptive expectations) nor does the goods market adjust instantaneously.

As it happens, there is plenty of evidence that changes in the real exchange rate take a long time to feed through.[20] In the case of a contractionary monetary policy, the *ISXM* curve will therefore shift only slowly to the left in response to the real appreciation. Let us suppose that expectations in the foreign exchange market react in a forward-looking way to the monetary contraction, which means that the expected exchange rate jumps to the new equilibrium rate, e_z and the new *UIP* curve is UIP_z in Fig.9.12. If output only adjusts sluggishly to the monetary contraction, then the economy moves up the $ISXM(e_0)$ to point *B*. With the home interest rate above the world interest rate, the nominal exchange rate must therefore appreciate *further* than e_z. As shown in Fig. 9.12, the exchange rate jumps to e_1. The extra appreciation beyond that associated with the new short-run equilibrium is referred to as 'exchange rate overshooting'. As the *ISXM* shifts gradually to the left in response to the appreciation, the economy moves down the UIP_z curve from B' to Z'. Since sluggish adjustment in the goods market is well documented, exchange rate overshooting is believed to be a factor lying behind the volatility of the exchange rate. Exchange rate overshooting is a worrying phenomenon since volatility

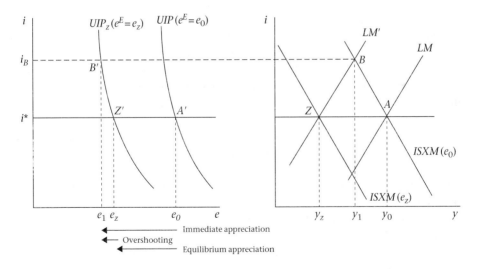

Figure 9.12 Contractionary monetary policy: an example of exchange rate overshooting

[19] The initial model of overshooting was developed by Rudiger Dornbusch (1976). For a very readable introduction to the Dornbusch model, see Rogoff (2002).

[20] For example, Carlin et al. (2001) report that the full effect on export market share of a change in the real exchange rate (measured by cost competitiveness) takes five to six years to feed through.

in the real exchange rate caused by this can lead to the misallocation of resources, for example, away from the tradeables sector to the non-tradeables sector in the economy. Production units in the export sector may be closed prematurely and new investment may take place in response to exchange rate signals that do not reflect fundamental economic conditions.

5.1.4 *An explicit model of overshooting

A simple model of overshooting is useful to see exactly how participants in the exchange markets calculate the amount by which the exchange rate has to appreciate and hence the size of the overshooting that will occur. This assumes, of course, that foreign exchange market participants use rational expectations to determine the future values of the exchange rate. Before looking at overshooting, imagine that everything adjusts immediately. We can do this using Fig. 9.12. We take the simple Mundell–Fleming case of a cut in the money supply under flexible exchange rates, say from M to $(1 - \theta)M$. This is the equivalent of the inward shift in the LM curve in Fig. 9.12 from LM to LM'. A definition of equilibrium is a stable exchange rate, so that in the short-run equilibrium at the end of the process, $\log e_1^E = \log e$. This will be at Z' in the UIP diagram, where the final UIP schedule is UIP_z given by $i = i^* + \log e_1^E - \log e = i^*$ or $i = i^* + \log e_z - \log e_z = i^*$, although we do not yet know the value of e_z. Using the UIP condition expressed in terms of the log of the exchange rate simplifies the calculations below. We also use explicit forms for the LM and the $ISXM$ equations in order to be able to calculate the extent of overshooting.

But it is not difficult to find out the value of e_z. The new equilibrium level of output (y_z) must be where the LM' curve cuts the $i = i^*$ line, at Z in the $ISLM$ diagram. LM' is given by $i^* = \lambda y_z - \mu(1 - \theta)M$ at Z. Since in the new equilibrium, the new $ISXM(e_z)$ curve is $y_z = A - ai^* + \log e_z$, we can substitute this into LM' to get

$$i^* = \lambda y_z - \mu(1 - \theta)M = \lambda(A - ai^* + \log e_z) - \mu(1 - \theta)M.$$

We now compare this with the old equilibrium before the cut in the money supply

$$i^* = \lambda(A - ai^* + \log e_0) - \mu M$$

and we can see

$$\lambda(\log e_z - \log e_0) = -\mu\theta M$$

implying an appreciation between the old and new equilibrium of $-\frac{\mu\theta}{\lambda}M$, that is:

$$\log e_z - \log e_0 = -\frac{\mu\theta}{\lambda}M \ \Rightarrow \ \log e_z = \log e_0 - \frac{\mu\theta}{\lambda}M.$$

This immediate adjustment of e to its new equilibrium level is a consequence of the assumption that the IS/LM system adjusts immediately.

What if it does not? Dornbusch developed his model of overshooting in a medium- rather than a short-run context, i.e. he assumed that the objective of governments in reducing the money supply was to lower the price level. And he asked: if it takes time before the decline in output as a consequence of the increase in the interest rate leads to the desired fall in the price level, what is the implication for exchange rate behaviour? Since we have not yet introduced price changes and inflation in the open economy, we shall show the extent of overshooting in a short-run model. The logic of the model is exactly the same as in Dornbusch's medium-run example. We simply assume that the economy remains at B in Fig. 9.12 for a period of time before the fall in exports and rise in imports have taken place that shift the $ISXM$ curve from $ISXM(e_0)$ to $ISXM(e_z)$. We shall assume in fact that the economy stays at B for 3 periods with the interest rate at i_B. If exchange market participants know this to be the case, how will this affect their view of the path of the exchange rate? (In the introduction to overshooting above, the implicit assumption was that the economy remains at B for just one period.)

Thus exchange market participants know that $i = i_B$ in periods 1, 2, and 3; and that in period 4, $i = i^*$ and $\log e_4 = \log e_z = \log e_0 - \frac{\mu\theta}{\lambda}M$. They also know that the UIP has to apply each period. So they reason

$$i_1 = i_B = i^* + \log e_2^E - \log e_1$$
$$i_2 = i_B = i^* + \log e_3^E - \log e_2^E$$
$$i_3 = i_B = i^* + \log e_4^E - \log e_3^E$$
$$i_{4+n} = i^* \quad n \geq 0$$
$$\&\ \log e_4^E = \log e_z = \log e_0 - \frac{\mu\theta}{\lambda}M.$$

Now the question is: how much should e change immediately, between periods 0 and 1, on receipt of the news about the cut in the money supply?

Mathematically this is straightforward. We add the first three equations together to get

$$3(i_B - i^*) = \log e_4^E - \log e_1$$

and then substitute in the fifth equation to get

$$3(i_B - i^*) = \log e_4^E - \log e_1 = \log e_0 - \frac{\mu\theta}{\lambda}M - \log e_1$$

or

$$\log e_1 = \log e_0 - \left[\frac{\mu\theta}{\lambda}M + 3(i_B - i^*)\right].$$

In other words there is an immediate appreciation equal to the equilibrium appreciation, $-\frac{\mu\theta}{\lambda}M$, *plus* the additional overshooting appreciation, $-3(i_B - i^*)$.

So what precisely is going on? In period 1, market participants expect a depreciation of $(i_B - i^*)$ to balance the $(i_B - i^*)$ interest rate gain; similarly in period 2 they expect a further depreciation of $(i_B - i^*)$; and a further depreciation of $(i_B - i^*)$ in period 3. Thus, whatever the value of $\log e_1$, they expect the exchange rate to have depreciated cumulatively by $3(i_B - i^*)$ by period 4: that is, $\log e_4^E = \log e_1 + 3(i_B - i^*)$.

At the same time, market participants have worked out that the exchange rate in period 4 must have appreciated by $-\frac{\mu\theta}{\lambda}M$ over the exchange rate in period 0: $\log e_4^E = \log e_0 - \frac{\mu\theta}{\lambda}M$. For both statements to be true there must be an immediate appreciation of the currency by $\left[\frac{\mu\theta}{\lambda}M + 3(i_B - i^*)\right]$ in period 1. Thus, if i is going to be above i^* by $(i_B - i^*)$ for 3 periods, requiring the currency depreciates by $i_B - i^*$ in each of those 3 periods, and if it is going to end up with an *appreciation* of $-\frac{\mu\theta}{\lambda}M$ above the initial exchange rate in period 0, then it has to appreciate by enough in period 1 (by $\left[\frac{\mu\theta}{\lambda}M + 3(i_B - i^*)\right]$) to be able to depreciate by $i_B - i^*$ for each of 3 periods and still have appreciated by $-\frac{\mu\theta}{\lambda}M$ over period 0. This extra appreciation is the phenomenon of overshooting. This extended example highlights that the size of the overshooting will depend on the length of the period expected before the economy adjusts to the new short-run equilibrium. Exactly the same principle is at work in the case Dornbusch focused on, which was adjustment to a medium-run equilibrium.

5.1.5 Discrete changes in the peg: the fixed exchange rate equilibrium of monetary policy

The use of monetary policy—either by changing the money supply or by directly changing the interest rate—cannot affect the level of output in the fixed exchange rate economy. However, the government or central bank has the option of making a discrete change in the exchange rate peg. In order to reduce output, the authorities need to announce a new peg for the exchange rate: they must revalue the exchange rate and intervene at a lower value of $e \equiv \frac{\text{home curr.}}{\text{foreign curr.}}$. With a revaluation of the exchange rate, the *ISXM* curve shifts to the left. This in turn pulls the interest rate below the world rate and induces an incipient capital outflow. To maintain the new peg, the central bank sells foreign exchange ($\Delta R < 0$). As the monetary base shrinks, the *LM* curve shifts to the left. The process continues until the new short-run equilibrium at lower output (with $i = i^*$) is reached.

It is important to note that if a government changes the exchange rate peg repeatedly, this is likely to give rise to speculation about future moves, with the consequence that the government will have to change the interest rate in order to hold the announced peg. A fixed exchange rate system cannot survive with the existing peg intact if an atmosphere of exchange rate speculation develops. Thus there are limits to the extent to which changes in the exchange rate can be made and a fixed rate system maintained.

5.2 The Mundell–Fleming model and fiscal policy

The same logic is used to analyse an *ISXM* shift as a consequence of a change in fiscal policy.

5.2.1 Fixed exchange rates

Whereas the expansionary monetary policy was completely ineffective under fixed exchange rates, a fiscal expansion in an open economy with fixed exchange rates, is very effective in raising output. The reason is that the increase in the demand for money that follows from the fiscal expansion leads to an increase in the money supply in order to keep the interest rate equal to the world interest rate.

As before, we look first at the new equilibrium and then at the adjustment path. The initial policy change is shown in Fig. 9.13 by the rightward shift of the *ISXM* from *ISXM*(g_0)

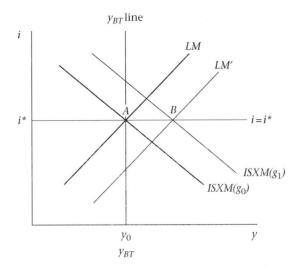

Figure 9.13 Expansionary fiscal policy: fixed exchange rate

to $ISXM(g_1)$. Since the new short-run equilibrium must lie on the $i = i^*$ line, it must be at the higher output level of B. This means that the LM curve must shift from LM to LM'. The y_{BT} line does not move because the real exchange rate remains unchanged—so at the new short-run equilibrium there is a trade deficit (imports have increased).

The adjustment process centres on the impact of the upward pressure on the home interest rate due to the fiscal expansion. This upward pressure on the interest rate creates excess demand for pounds in the foreign exchange market. In order to keep the exchange rate fixed, the central bank will have to use newly printed money to purchase foreign currency. The foreign exchange reserves rise ($\Delta R > 0$) with the result that the domestic money supply expands. This shifts the LM curve to LM'. The intervention by the central bank re-equilibrates the foreign exchange market. Simultaneously the rise in money supply in the home economy (via the increase in the monetary base as reserves rise in line with the increase in demand), maintains the interest rate at the world rate.

5.2.2 Flexible exchange rates

The intuition here is that under flexible exchange rates an expansionary fiscal policy will lead to a counteracting depressive effect because the increase in the domestic interest rate will lead to an appreciation of the home currency, which will weaken net exports.

To find the new short-run equilibrium, we know that the ISXM shifts initially to the right to $ISXM(g_1, e_0)$ and that in the new equilibrium the economy must be on the $i = i^*$ line. It is therefore clear that the appreciation of the exchange rate must be sufficient to shift the ISXM to the left to $ISXM(g_1, e_z)$, which intersects the $i = i^*$ line at A (see Fig. 9.14). The level of output at the new short-run equilibrium (Z) is exactly the same as it was originally. But there is a higher level of government expenditure and a lower level of net exports: the increased government spending has 'crowded out' some net exports. This is confirmed by the fact that the y_{BT} line shifts to the left to a new equilibrium: a less

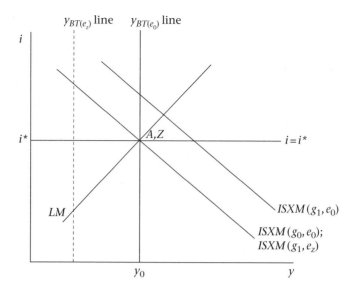

Figure 9.14 Expansionary fiscal policy: flexible exchange rate

competitive exchange rate implies that trade balance will occur at a lower output level. There is therefore a trade deficit at the new short-run equilibrium.

The process of adjustment to the new equilibrium can be analysed using the same steps as were introduced in the analysis of the expansionary monetary policy and is left as an exercise for the reader. Adjustment will look somewhat different in each of the expectations scenarios: backward looking, rational with rapid adjustment of output, and forward looking with slow adjustment of output (i.e. overshooting).

6 Extensions

In the model of the small open economy the aim was to provide analytical clarity by using benchmark cases. Specifically we have developed a model of

- a small open economy
- in a world of perfect capital markets and
- perfect asset substitutability.

The assumptions about financial integration (perfect capital mobility and perfect asset substitutability) establish hard corners on the so-called inconsistency triangle or open economy trilemma. Only two of the following three can be maintained simultaneously:

(1) open capital market

(2) fixed exchange rate

(3) monetary policy oriented to domestic goals.

With perfect international capital mobility, either (*a*) the exchange rate has to be fixed—with the implication that monetary policy cannot pursue domestic objectives or (*b*) monetary policy is used to pursue domestic objectives—with the implication that the exchange rate as a target has to be given up. Because the extent of internationalization of capital markets has been increasing in recent decades, it has been suggested that countries are increasingly forced into the two corners—either by adopting a hard exchange rate peg or by adopting a free float. This is the so-called 'bipolar' view of exchange rate regimes.[21]

We shall explore what happens to the short-run behaviour of the economy when the three assumptions of perfect capital mobility, smallness, and perfect asset substitutability are relaxed, but first the evidence in relation to international financial integration is discussed.

6.1 Evidence on financial integration

Under the assumption of perfect international capital mobility, changes in the nominal exchange rate are caused by developments affecting the capital account. In principle, any current account imbalance can be financed through the capital account at the world interest rate. This is summarized in the *UIP* condition. This feature of the small open economy model raises two questions: how significant are current account imbalances and how good is the *UIP* condition in practice in accounting for exchange rate changes? Research in this field is in an intense phase and new findings are likely to emerge over the coming years. Yet the answers to both questions suggest that the assumptions made to date in this chapter are open to challenge.

A feature that continues to distinguish countries from regions is that the current account imbalances that are observed for countries are much smaller than they are for regions within countries. In other words, there is a tight connection between domestic savings and investment at the national level but very little connection when we look at the subnational level. Limited spatial correlation is exactly what would be expected if the capital market was doing its job of allocating savings to the most productive investment projects—irrespective of where the savings were generated. The high correlation between national savings and investment rates was first documented by Feldstein and Horioka.[22] Feldstein and Horioka found a correlation between the share of investment in GDP and savings in GDP of 0.89 for the period 1960–74; a more recent study has found a correlation of 0.6 for OECD countries between 1990 and 1997 (which rises to 0.76 if Korea is included).[23] Thus even in the 1990s, national borders appear to matter for access to capital. It has been argued recently that national borders are of diminishing importance within the European Union.[24]

The *UIP* condition predicts that if the home interest rate is above the world interest rate, the exchange rate is expected to depreciate. However, a large number of empirical studies have shown that the interest rate differential between two currencies is not a good predictor of changes in the exchange rate. For periods of up to one year, the predicted

[21] For a good introduction, see Fischer (2001).   [22] Feldstein and Horioka (1980).
[23] Obstfeld and Rogoff (2000*a*: 175).   [24] Blanchard and Giavazzi (2002).

change in the exchange rate often has the wrong sign. Studies using longer periods, have found results more in line with the predictions of *UIP* but interest differentials are still able only to predict a small proportion of exchange rate variation.[25]

6.2 Imperfect capital mobility

If there is perfect international capital mobility residents of country A can buy or sell bonds denominated in the currency of country B with the international interest rate i^* with low transactions costs and in unlimited quantities. There are two main reasons why this assumption may be unwarranted. First, a country may deliberately implement a policy that aims to limit capital mobility. Such a policy is referred to as one of capital controls. Second, information problems and the limited development of financial institutions in the economy may prevent domestic residents from having free access to international capital markets. Capital controls have been used by countries both to restrict inflows of foreign capital and to restrict outflows. Large flows of foreign exchange are implicated in currency crises. Because of this a country may seek to reduce its vulnerability to a *future* currency crisis by restricting capital inflows now: the foreign exchange can then no longer suddenly be withdrawn and precipitate a crisis. A policy of preventing capital outflows is frequently a futile attempt to contain a currency crisis that is already in motion, although the effectiveness of capital controls in mitigating crises has recently resurfaced as a contested policy tool.[26]

We shall look at two examples of how constraints on capital mobility affect the operation of macroeconomic policy.

• Example 1. Monetary policy under fixed exchange rates.

The attraction of capital controls for a country operating with a fixed exchange rate is that it means that monetary policy can have an effect on output. As we have seen, under fixed exchange rates and perfect capital mobility, an expansionary monetary policy does not get off the ground. Financial integration under perfect capital mobility and fixed exchange rates requires the home and world interest rates to be equal. If the government is able to control the access of agents holding domestic currency (pounds) to the foreign exchange market, then the arbitrage mechanism in the *UIP* condition cannot function smoothly. To the extent that those holding pounds cannot purchase dollars so as to shift into the now more attractive dollar bonds, the central bank is able to keep the domestic interest rate below the world interest rate. Monetary policy is therefore effective in raising output under fixed exchange rates. Since the private incentives for evading the capital controls are very strong, the government is unlikely to be able to prevent completely a leakage of reserves. This loss of reserves will ultimately place a limit on the use of this policy.

Note that in the opposite case, where the government uses capital controls in conjunction with a tightening of monetary policy it is seeking to prevent an inflow of foreign exchange reserves that would offset its objective of raising the interest rate. Whilst private

---

[25] A recent study that includes a survey of previous results is Chinn and Meredith (2002).

[26] For example, see Kaplan and Rodrik (2001).

incentives to evade these controls are the same as in the previous case, the government has more freedom of manoeuvre because the accretion of foreign exchange reserves is not as immediately problematic as the running down of reserves. We have noted this asymmetry earlier. Indeed if the central bank is able to insulate the economy from the effects of an increase in foreign exchange reserves, the ability to use monetary policy under fixed exchange rates increases. In the analysis so far, we have assumed that a change in foreign exchange reserves has a direct impact on the domestic money supply since foreign exchange reserves form part of the monetary base. This direct connection can be broken if 'sterilization' is possible. We discuss the meaning of and scope for sterilization below.

• Example 2. Monetary policy under flexible exchange rates.

In our model of the small open economy with perfect capital mobility, monetary policy is highly effective in changing the level of output. As we saw in section 5.1.2, full flexibility of the exchange rate has the effect of preventing the government from choosing the domestic interest rate in the new short-run equilibrium: although there is full monetary policy autonomy its effects on the economy are entirely through the so-called *exchange rate channel*.

If capital mobility is less than perfect then financial integration will not require that the economy be on the $i = i^*$ line. Being on the $i = i^*$ line means that a trade deficit or surplus is offset by a capital inflow or outflow financed at the constant world interest rate i.e. there is a perfectly elastic supply of capital at the world interest rate. By contrast, if capital mobility is imperfect, then there is no automatic financing of a current account deficit or automatic lending of a current account surplus at the world interest rate. Instead, the size of the required capital inflow or outflow will affect the interest rate consistent with short-run equilibrium. For example, a larger trade deficit implies not only a larger accumulation of debt but also a less favourable rate of interest. Recall the balance of payments identity:

$$BP \equiv (BT + INT) + (F - \Delta R) \equiv 0.$$

We are looking at the flexible exchange rate economy so there is no official intervention and therefore $\Delta R = 0$ and for simplicity, we ignore net interest receipts (i.e. we assume that $INT = 0$). For balance of payments equilibrium, we require:

$$BP \equiv BT(\theta, y) + F(i) = 0,$$

where $F(i)$ is private net capital inflow and is a positive function of i. The BP line in Fig. 9.15 replaces the horizontal $i = i^*$ line under imperfect capital mobility. The BP line is upward-sloping in the interest rate-output diagram and is drawn for a given level of the real exchange rate. At a low level of output such as y_L, BT is high (since imports are depressed). Thus for balance of payments equilibrium, the net capital inflow must be low, and only a low interest rate, i_L, will be required to finance it. Conversely, at a high level of output, a weak trade balance has to be offset with a net capital inflow, which requires a high interest rate, i_H. Note that since we are interested in rather small deviations from perfect capital mobility, we shall assume that the BP line is flatter than the LM. The BP

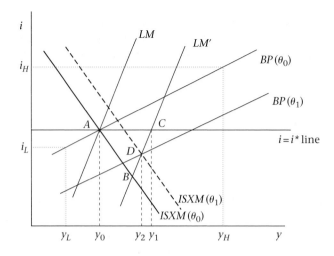

Figure 9.15 Imperfect capital mobility and flexible exchange rates: a monetary expansion

line shifts with a change in the real exchange rate. If at y_L, the real exchange is θ_1 (i.e. competitiveness is higher) instead of θ_0, then BT will be higher and balance of payments equilibrium will require a smaller net capital inflow and hence a lower interest rate than i_L. Hence the BP line for θ_1 lies below that for θ_0.

We turn now to examine how an expansionary monetary policy would work under imperfect capital mobility. With an expansionary monetary policy, the LM moves to LM'. This leads to a lower interest rate and an expansion of output. The current account deteriorates and the exchange rate depreciates. With perfect capital mobility, the exchange rate changes because of disequilibrium in the asset (bond) market; under imperfect capital mobility, it is the flow disequilibrium arising from the trade imbalance that leads to exchange rate changes. Under *perfect capital mobility*, the new short-run equilibrium is at point C with a trade surplus (the surplus is lent at the international interest rate i^*). Under *imperfect capital mobility*, the trade surplus entails a capital account outflow (net investment abroad) that will attract a lower interest rate than i^*. This is shown by point D.

At point D, since the domestic interest rate is below i^*, output is increased above its initial level (y_0) through two channels:

- (i) the *interest rate channel*, which leads to a movement along the $ISXM$ and
- (ii) the *exchange rate channel* (due to the depreciation), which shifts the $ISXM$. The economy must be on the LM' curve: hence the new $BP(\theta)$ curve will go through point D.

We have the result that the new short-run equilibrium will lie between that of the closed economy (B) and the small open economy with perfect capital mobility (C).

To summarize, capital immobility has implications for the efficacy of monetary policy. Under fixed exchange rates, some role for monetary policy in influencing the level of output in the short run is reinstated. Under flexible exchange rates, an additional channel for monetary policy to influence the level of output is introduced: instead of having its effect entirely through the exchange rate, monetary policy also affects domestic demand directly because the home interest rate can diverge from the world interest rate in the short-run equilibrium.

6.3 The large open economy

All the analysis in this chapter has assumed that the home economy is unable to influence the world interest rate. Together with the perfect capital mobility and perfect asset substitutability assumptions, this allowed us to specify the response of the economy to domestic policy changes and external shocks using the Mundell–Fleming model.

The simplest way of modelling a large open economy is to have a world comprising just two economies. Whenever one of these economies changes fiscal or monetary policy, it will have an effect on the other—and hence, on outcomes for 'the world'. In Chapter 12 we develop a simple two-country extension of the small open economy model. Here we provide an intuitive explanation of how monetary and fiscal policy affect the outcome for a large open economy.

As our large country, say the eurozone, loosens monetary policy, this will lower its interest rate relative to the other country, say the USA. As a consequence of perfect capital mobility, the exchange rate of the eurozone will depreciate. By virtue of its size, the fall in the eurozone's interest rate will pull down the world interest rate, i^*. The new short-run equilibrium for the eurozone will be at a point such as D in the left hand panel of Fig. 9.16: on the new LM' curve, with the world interest rate at $i^{*\prime}$ and with the $ISXM$ shifted to $ISXM(\theta_1)$ by the depreciation.

The impact on output of a monetary expansion under flexible exchange rates in a large open economy differs in two respects from that of the small open economy. First, there are now two channels through which output is raised: the *exchange rate channel* and the *interest rate channel*. The second difference is that the rise in output will be somewhat

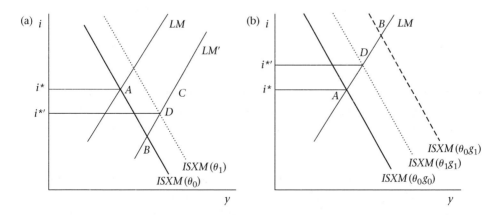

Figure 9.16 Flexible exchange rate large open economy
(a) Expansionary monetary policy (b) Expansionary fiscal policy

less than in the small open economy case. The large open economy ends up at point D between that of the closed economy (B) and the small open economy (C).

In the small open economy with flexible exchange rates, fiscal policy is completely ineffective in changing the level of output and employment because the exchange rate moves to completely offset the impact of fiscal policy on aggregate demand. However, in a large open economy, this will not be the case. Instead, the economy will end up on the original LM curve at a point such as D in the right hand panel of Fig. 9.16: the world interest rate rises and the exchange rate of the eurozone appreciates. Both the interest rate and exchange rate channels are working to reduce the expansionary impact of the higher government spending but their combined effect does not fully offset the expansionary impulse. Just as in the case of a monetary expansion, the behaviour of the large open economy lies between that of the closed economy (B) and of the small open economy (A), which is an intuitively appealing result.

6.4 Perfect asset substitutability and the risk premium

Another key assumption that we made was that home and foreign bonds were perfect substitutes. This means that only the expected return on bonds influences the choice between them, and that agents are indifferent about the composition of their portfolio. Since the expected return is identical on foreign and home bonds and there is no difference in riskiness, even risk-averse investors are quite happy to put all their eggs in the one basket. Once the possibility of different degrees of risk between the bonds arises, then risk-averse investors will prefer a more balanced portfolio. It is necessary to amend the uncovered interest parity condition so that it is the 'risk-adjusted expected return' that is equalized through arbitrage:

$$i_t = i_t^* + \frac{e_{t+1}^E - e_t}{e_t} + \rho_t, \qquad \text{(risk-adjusted } UIP \text{ condition)}$$

where ρ (rho) is the risk premium. Specifically if the home currency is the euro, then the interest rate on euro bonds will be equal to the interest rate on dollar bonds plus the expected depreciation of the euro plus any additional risk premium that is required to compensate the investor in euros.

There are two ways of explaining the risk premium. First, there may be a difference in the default risk on the two bonds—for example, it is plausible that investors would require a positive risk premium to hold Russian bonds as compared with euro bonds because of the greater likelihood that the Russian government would default on its obligations to honour the bonds. Second if investors are concerned about unexpected fluctuations in the exchange rate, a balanced portfolio would be preferred.

We look at two examples of why the existence of risk premiums can matter for macroeconomic outcomes:

- an increase in risk that occurs with a change of government and
- the deliberate attempt by the central bank to use changes in portfolio composition as a tool of monetary policy.

6.5 Unplanned increase in risk

Let us suppose that a new government is elected and is considered more likely to default on its debt. In terms of our earlier diagram, the *UIP* curve shifts upwards. To see why, note that on the assumptions we have made, the expected exchange rate remains fixed, as does the world interest rate: all that changes is the emergence of a risk premium. The risk adjusted *UIP* condition tells us that the domestic interest rate must now be equal to $i^* + \rho$ for the exchange rate to remain at its expected value.

In a fixed exchange rate regime, if the government is to maintain the exchange rate peg, it will have to *raise* the interest rate to ensure that the expected return on home bonds *including the risk premium* is equal to the world interest rate. As the risk premium emerges, people will want to switch out of home bonds. To do so, they must sell domestic currency in order to buy foreign bonds. Hence, in order to hold the peg, the central bank must intervene to buy home currency. This loss of reserves leads to a leftward shift in the *LM* and the interest rate rises. The outcome is therefore a recession for the home economy. In Fig.9.17, the new short-run equilibrium is shown by point Z_{FIX} in each panel.

Under a flexible exchange rate regime, we look first at the immediate impact of the upward shift in the *UIP* curve. The lower risk adjusted interest return on home bonds as compared to foreign bonds (i.e. $i - \rho < i^*$) produces a depreciation: a move from *A* to *B* in the left hand diagram. Following through the standard logic, the depreciation leads to a rightward shift in the *ISXM*. The new short-run equilibrium is established at point Z_{FLEX} at which point the home interest rate exceeds the world interest rate by the risk premium. This produces the perhaps surprising result that a rise in the risk premium boosts output in the home economy. However, this result should be treated with scepticism: growing concern about the creditworthiness of the government may lead to an increase in the demand for money and hence a leftward shift in the *LM*, which would reverse the depreciation and induce a recession. Alternatively, speculation may mount about likely future depreciation of the exchange rate, which could spark a currency crisis: if the expected

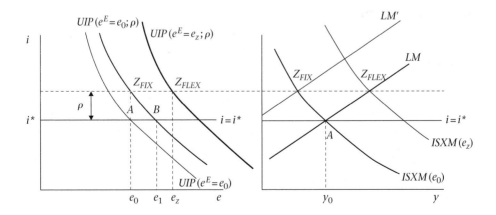

Figure 9.17 Risk premium: short-run implications under fixed and flexible exchange rates
Z_{FIX} is the new equilibrium under fixed exchange rates
Z_{FLEX} is the new equilibrium under the flexible exchange rates

exchange rate depreciates sharply, the *UIP* curve shifts to the right and the government would have to raise the interest rate further to prevent the exchange rate from collapsing.

6.6 Sterilized intervention by the central bank

Although there is considerable scepticism amongst economists as to whether central banks are able to engage successfully in sterilized intervention in the foreign exchange market for any length of time, it is important to understand the principle. Without using the term, we have only considered 'non-sterilized' foreign exchange market interventions to this point. To explain what this means, we take the case of a contractionary monetary policy in a fixed exchange rate regime. We have seen that this is fruitless when capital markets are perfect since the reduction in the monetary base due to the initial open market sale of bonds is exactly offset by the rise in monetary base due to the rise in official foreign exchange reserves as the central bank intervenes to hold the exchange rate constant when investors seek to switch to home-currency denominated bonds. In principle, however, the central bank can neutralize the impact of the rise in foreign reserves on the money supply by matching its acquisition of foreign assets ($\uparrow R$) with a sale of government bonds ($\downarrow B$). In the central bank balance sheet (Table 9.5), sterilization means that the rise in R is offset by a fall in B; since H does not change, there is no change in the money supply.

The reason why this is so difficult to achieve is that when the central bank sells the bonds, the price will tend to fall and the interest rate to rise: this is just what the central bank does not want because it will elicit a further capital inflow. In theory there is a way around this if the sales of bonds have a sufficient effect in raising the risk premium and therefore in influencing the public's desired portfolio. If the central bank sells more bonds, the public has to hold a higher proportion of the outstanding total stock of bonds: the central bank will hold fewer and the public will hold more. If the public care about the composition of their portfolio, then they will require additional compensation in the form of a risk premium for holding home bonds. Hence the central bank is able to raise the risk premium and therefore hold the exchange rate unchanged. This is consistent with the risk adjusted *UIP* condition because the domestic interest rate is above the world interest rate by exactly the amount of the risk premium; the expected depreciation of the exchange rate is zero so the peg is maintained. The aim of the sterilization is thus to drain liquidity in a way that does not make home bonds more attractive. Manipulating the risk premium is in principle a way of doing this. To the extent that sterilized intervention of this kind is possible, the central bank is able to use the interest rate and the exchange rate as independent instruments.

Under flexible exchange rates, because as we have seen there is no official intervention, the issue of 'sterilized intervention' does not arise. However suppose that the central bank

Table 9.5 Central bank balance sheet

Assets	Liabilities
Government bonds + foreign exchange reserves	High-powered money in hands of public
$B + R$	H

chooses to intervene in the foreign exchange market in an ostensibly flexible exchange rate regime. There is substantial empirical evidence that central banks in countries that declare that they have a freely floating exchange rate engage in considerable intervention activities.[27] This type of exchange rate regime has no announced exchange rate target or peg that the government is standing ready to defend (as in the fixed exchange rate case). We are therefore investigating how the government could try to influence the exchange rate through intervention. Take the case where the government is trying to dampen activity in the economy but it does not want an appreciation of the exchange rate (as would occur under a flexible rate regime if monetary policy was tightened): the aim is to raise the home interest rate but prevent an immediate appreciation of the currency (as dictated by the *UIP* condition). Why might the government want to do this? One possible explanation is that the government is concerned not only about the *level* of output but also about the structure of the economy. It may then seek to dampen interest-sensitive expenditure rather than tradeables activity. The central bank would have to intervene in the foreign exchange market in exactly the manner described for the fixed exchange rate case—selling home bonds to mop up the liquidity from the excess supply of foreign currency. This will only work if portfolio composition matters to investors and the risk premium on home bonds rises.

These examples provide an illustration of the mechanics of an exchange rate regime that lies somewhere between fixed and flexible. If policy can be used to manipulate the risk premium, then the interest rate can diverge from the world interest rate even when the exchange rate is at its expected value. Once again, it should be noted that in the case in which the government is seeking to run a looser monetary policy but prevent a depreciation, the use of the sterilization policy will be limited by the available foreign exchange reserves. It must be stressed that risk premiums could only account for the kinds of deviation from the uncovered interest parity condition that are observed empirically if these vary dramatically over time and in the manner that has been assumed. However, attempts to explain such premiums empirically via portfolio-balance effects have been unsuccessful. Hence the notion that sterilization can be used systematically through changing the risk premiums as described in this section should be treated with yet more scepticism.

7 Conclusions

In this chapter, many of the tools required for open economy analysis have been introduced.

- The concepts of the nominal and real exchange rate and the terms of trade have been explained.
- The *IS/LM* model has been extended to include exports and imports and international financial markets.

---

[27] Calvo and Reinhart (2002).

- The international financial arbitrage condition—uncovered interest parity (*UIP*)—provided a vital link from the interest rate to the exchange rate.
- The Mundell–Fleming model puts the *ISXM/LM* model together with the *UIP* condition to enable us to conduct macroeconomic analysis of policy changes and changes in private spending emanating from home or abroad. A summary of the model in equation form is provided in the Appendix.

In the short run with prices and wages given, what happens in response to a policy change or a change in private spending behaviour depends on

- what happens to the home interest rate relative to the foreign interest rate.

In turn, the implications of that discrepancy depend on

- the exchange rate regime

  — if exchange rates are fixed, then the domestic money supply will automatically change to offset any excess demand or supply for money

  — if exchange rates are flexible, then the exchange rate will appreciate or depreciate in response to the interest rate differential and this will affect net exports and aggregate demand

- how exchange rate expectations are formed.

We have set out the implications of relaxing the Mundell–Fleming assumptions of smallness, perfect capital mobility, and perfect asset substitutability. In a large open economy with perfect capital mobility and in a small open economy with imperfect capital mobility, an interest rate channel is opened up through which monetary policy can operate. By relaxing the assumption of perfect asset substitutability, we are able to investigate how unintended changes in the risk premium affect the economy. We can also show how the central bank may attempt to influence the way monetary policy operates in the open economy by manipulating the risk premium. Under fixed exchange rates, this is one way that sterilized intervention could, in principle, work.

We are now ready to move on to analyse inflation and unemployment in the open economy. In Chapter 10, we complement the Mundell–Fleming model of the short run with explicit consideration of what happens in the medium run once we allow prices and wages to respond in the wake of output and exchange rate changes.

■ **QUESTIONS**

Checklist questions

(1) What is the difference between the real and the nominal exchange rate? Give an example to explain this to a non-economist. Is an improvement in the terms of trade the same as an improvement in price competitiveness? Is an increase in the real cost of imports an improvement or a deterioration in the terms of trade?

(2) Explain two ways of measuring the real exchange rate. How well correlated would you expect them to be, and why?

(3) Explain the sense in which an improvement in price competitiveness might be considered a 'good thing' for the economy. Might it also be considered a 'bad thing'?

(4) Is the behaviour of the volume of exports a satisfactory measure of a country's competitiveness?

(5) Construct a numerical example to show how the Marshall–Lerner condition works. Why might its predictions not hold in the very short run?

(6) Explain what is meant by the passage in italics in the statement that the Marshall–Lerner condition relates to the impact on the trade balance of a change in the real exchange rate, *holding the level of output constant.* Apart from the price elasticity of demand what extra information do you need to work out the effect on the trade balance of a change in the exchange rate?

(7) A small open economy has a government budget surplus and a trade deficit. Explain whether there is a private sector surplus, deficit, or balance. Examine the consequences in the short run for output, the trade balance, and the budget balance of a sudden fall in private consumption in this economy under (*a*) fixed exchange rates, (*b*) flexible exchange rates.

(8) What would it mean to describe an economy as a 'small, open economy with imperfect capital mobility'; a 'large, open economy with perfect capital mobility'?

(9) In an open economy, home residents can hold home or foreign bonds in their portfolio. What assumption allows us to write the demand for money in the open economy in the same way as in the closed economy, i.e. as a function of domestic output and the home nominal interest rate?

(10) What is meant by arbitrage in international financial markets? Give a numerical example to explain the concepts of the covered and uncovered interest parity conditions.

(11) What assumptions must be made for the uncovered interest parity condition to hold? Explain what you would expect to happen to the domestic interest rate and the exchange rate in a small open economy following a rise in the demand for money, making clear the role of the *UIP* condition in this chain of events.

(12) Suppose that there is less than perfect capital mobility. Explain why in the interest rate-output diagram the $i = i^*$ line is replaced by the balance of payments equilibrium condition: $BT(\theta, y) + F(i) = 0$. Why does this '*BP*' curve in the interest rate-output diagram shift with a change in θ?

(13) 'Devaluation cannot affect the trade deficit because the latter must equal the difference between investment and saving, and neither of these magnitudes is affected by the exchange rate.' What is wrong with this argument in the context of an open economy with sticky prices?

(14) Explain the concept of exchange rate overshooting and develop two different examples using private sector shocks—in one of which the equilibrium adjustment

of the exchange rate is an appreciation and in the other, the equilibrium adjustment is a depreciation.

Problems and questions for discussion

QUESTION A. Assume that wages, prices, and the exchange rate are fixed. (*a*) Will a fall in the budget deficit due to a cut in government spending always improve the trade balance? Explain your answer. (*b*) What is the impact on output and the trade balance of a balanced budget increase in government spending? (For simplicity, consider a lump-sum tax.) Does the change in output differ from that in a closed economy following a balanced budget increase in government spending—if so, in what way? In the open economy case, what happens to private savings net of investment? Summarize what has happened to the sector financial balances.

QUESTION B. Find out what happened to the nominal interest rate set by the Federal Reserve in the USA and by the ECB in the eurozone, and to the $-euro exchange rate following 11 September 2001 (to the end of 2001) [plot the data]. See the resources below for sources of data and discussion. The relevant interest rates are the Federal Funds Rate (US) and the minimum bid rate in the main refinancing operations (ECB). Is this behaviour consistent with the predictions of the *UIP* condition?
[Resources: **www.bankofengland.co.uk/mfsd/rates/daily2001.xls** (this excel spreadsheet of daily rates is useful if you want to draw a graph;)
www.economist.com/markets/Currency/graphs.cfm or www.x-rates.com
www.imf.org/external/pubs/ft/weo/2001/03/pdf/chapter2.pdf (for commentary on exchange rate developments, see in particular, box 2.4);
www.ecb.int/stats/monetary/rates/html/index.en.html#data or
https://stats.ecb.int/stats/ download/weas01_02/weas01_02/weas01_02.pdf (for ECB official interest rate: this is the Main Refinancing Rate. The series splits in June 2000—this simply relates to the switch from fixed to variable rate tenders and is a technicality that you don't need to worry about;) **www.federalreserve.gov/fomc/ fundsrate.htm** (for US Federal Reserve official interest rate).]

QUESTION C. Use the Mundell–Fleming model and assume perfect capital mobility. Suppose there is a fall in the world interest rate. (*a*) Does this have an expansionary or contractionary impact on output in a small open economy? (*b*) Does the trade balance improve or deteriorate? Explain your answer. Look at both fixed and flexible exchange rate regimes.

QUESTION D. Consider two economies: the home country is Norway (currency is the Krone), and the foreign country is the USA. State the uncovered interest parity condition, assuming that the default risk is identical between the two countries. For each of the scenarios discussed below, assume that initially the US and Norwegian interest rates are identical and that the US interest rate remains unchanged throughout.

Scenario 1. The Norwegian interest rate is expected to remain above the US rate for one year. What relationship between the interest rate differential and change in the Krone exchange rate would be observed on average during the year?

Scenario 2. At the beginning of the year, the Norwegian government introduces a permanent increase in government spending. By the end of the year, the Norwegian and

US interest rates are identical. Provide an account of the adjustment of the Norwegian economy during the year. What relationship between the interest rate differential and change in the Krone exchange rate would be observed on average during the year? You may assume that wages and prices do not adjust within the year.

What light do your findings throw on the question of whether the *UIP* condition predicts exchange rate changes?

QUESTION E. A new government is elected and as a consequence the country is considered to be less risky. (*a*) Explain what is meant by 'less risky'? (*b*) Would you expect this to have a positive or negative impact on output in the short run in a fixed exchange rate economy and a flexible exchange rate economy? You may assume that the economy is a small open one with perfect capital mobility. (*c*) Now assume you are engaged in a discussion about your results in an international economics consultancy. Assess the plausibility of your results and explain how you could introduce additional considerations into the model to enhance their plausibility.

■ APPENDIX

The Marshall–Lerner condition: a proof

Assume that trade is initially balanced and that the prices of exports and imports do not change in response to the volume sold. Since $BT = \sigma(\theta)y^* - \theta m_y(\theta)y$, the change in the trade balance in response to a change in competitiveness is

$$
\begin{aligned}
\frac{dBT}{d\theta} &= \sigma'(\theta)y^* - \theta m_y'(\theta)y - m_y y \\
&= \sigma y^* \frac{\sigma'(\theta)}{\sigma} - \theta m_y'(\theta)y - m_y y.
\end{aligned}
$$

But by assumption, $BT = 0$, i.e. $\sigma(\theta)y^* = \theta m_y(\theta)y$, and therefore

$$
\frac{dBT}{d\theta} = \theta m_y y \frac{\sigma'(\theta)}{\sigma} - \theta m_y'(\theta)y - m_y y.
$$

Dividing through by $m_y y$,

$$
\frac{1}{m_y y} \cdot \frac{dBT}{d\theta} = \frac{\theta\sigma'(\theta)}{\sigma} - \frac{\theta m_y'(\theta)}{m_y} - 1.
$$

Since $m_y y > 0$, $\frac{dBT}{d\theta} > 0$ if and only if

$$
\frac{\theta\sigma'(\theta)}{\sigma} - \frac{\theta m_y'(\theta)}{m_y} > 1.
$$

Now, $\frac{\theta\sigma'(\theta)}{\sigma}$ is *minus* the elasticity of demand for exports, since θ is the inverse of the real price of exports. Similarly, $\frac{\theta m_y'(\theta)}{m_y}$ is the elasticity of demand for imports. The Marshall–Lerner condition for an improvement in the balance of trade to follow from a rise in competitiveness is that the sum of the absolute values of the demand elasticities is greater than one; i.e.

$$
\left| \frac{\theta\sigma'(\theta)}{\sigma} \right| + \left| \frac{\theta m_y'(\theta)}{m_y} \right| > 1.
$$

The Mundell–Fleming model: a pocket version

This way of working with the Mundell–Fleming model is developed in Chapter 12. First the *ISXM* schedule is written

$$y = ag - bi + cB(e)$$

where B is the balance of trade and a, b, and c are positive constants. We can use i rather than r because we assume inflation is zero. B depends positively on the exchange rate (we assume that the Marshall–Lerner condition holds) and for simplicity we assume $B(e) = e$. We write the net changes from the initial to the new short-run equilibrium, e.g. from y_0 to y_2, as $\triangle y = y_2 - y_0$, etc. So we can write this as

$$\triangle y = a\triangle g - b\triangle i + c\triangle e.$$

Next the *LM* schedule is $i = \lambda y - \mu M$ or in difference terms

$$\Delta i = \lambda\Delta y - \mu\Delta M$$

where Greek letters are chosen to represent the constants in the *LM* equation so as to make it easy to see how the parameters of the *ISXM* and of the *LM* come into play. To focus on the essentials, let us assume that $a = c = 1$. We then have:

$\Delta y = \Delta g - b\Delta i + \Delta e$

$\Delta i = \lambda\Delta y - \mu(\Delta M^H + \Delta M^I)$ where ΔM^I is the inflow of money.

Flexible exchange rates $\Rightarrow \Delta M^I = 0$

Fixed exchange rates $\Rightarrow \Delta e = 0$

$\Delta i = 0$ under both regimes.

Results:

(i) Flex, $\Delta g > 0$, $\Delta M^H = 0$:

$\Rightarrow \Delta y = \Delta g + \Delta e$

& $\lambda\Delta y = 0$

$\Rightarrow \Delta y = 0$ & $\Delta e = -\Delta g$.

(ii) Fix, $\Delta g > 0$, $\Delta M^H = 0$:

$\Rightarrow \Delta y = \Delta g$

& $\lambda\Delta y = \mu\Delta M^I$.

(iii) Flex, $\Delta g = 0$, $\Delta M^H > 0$:

$\Rightarrow \Delta y = \Delta e$

& $\Delta y = (\mu/\lambda)\Delta M^H$.

(iv) Fix, $\Delta g = 0$, $\Delta M^H > 0$:

$\Rightarrow \Delta y = 0 \rightarrow (\Delta M^H + \Delta M^I) = 0$

$\Rightarrow \Delta M^H = -\Delta M^I$.

10 Inflation and Unemployment in the Open Economy

This chapter brings together the supply side of the economy with the demand side and the trade balance to provide a model for analysing the open economy. It builds on the imperfect competition model of the supply side developed in Chapters 1 to 3 and on the Mundell–Fleming short-run model of the open economy developed in Chapter 9. The model can be used to answer the following questions:

- What determines the level of output and employment in the short run?
- What factors influence the rate of unemployment and output level that can be sustained in the medium run without problems of inflation?
- Why might a medium-run position of stable inflation but trade imbalance be unsustainable in the long run?

In this chapter, we explore a key difference between an open and a closed economy. In the closed economy, there is a unique unemployment rate consistent with constant inflation. By contrast, in an open economy, there is a range of unemployment rates consistent with the absence of inflationary pressure. Whereas a fiscal expansion in a closed economy that is initially at equilibrium unemployment raises output in the short run, it leads to higher inflation and the only medium-run equilibrium is back at the initial level of unemployment: the economy goes through a phase of output above equilibrium, of higher inflation and then of output below equilibrium as inflation is squeezed out of the system. In the new medium-run equilibrium, inflation and unemployment are back at their initial levels and the real interest rate is higher. As we shall see, the medium-run outcome of a fiscal expansion for a small open economy is a higher level of output with stable inflation at its initial level—under both fixed and floating exchange rate regimes. This possibility may make expansionary fiscal policy as a means of cutting unemployment attractive to policy makers and we shall see that understanding the difference between open and closed economies in this respect is helpful in understanding important policy questions such as the rationale for imposing fiscal rules on members of the eurozone. The reason why open economies behave differently from closed ones lies with the impact of changes in the real exchange rate on real wages and hence on the equilibrium in the labour market.

The wage-setting curve in the open economy is just the same as in the closed economy: as employment rises, the wage-setting real wage rises. In the closed economy, the price-setting real wage is constant (or downward sloping). Hence there is just one level of employment at which wage- and price-setting real wages are equal: this fixes the unique equilibrium rate of unemployment (*ERU*), or *NAIRU* (non-accelerating inflation rate of unemployment), as it is often called in empirical studies. But in the open economy, the price setting real wage is a function of the real exchange rate: it will shift up and down as the real exchange rate changes. The simplest way to think of this is that when the real exchange rate depreciates, the real cost of imports goes up and this reduces the price-setting real wage. We shall see that a fiscal expansion produces a real appreciation and therefore an upwards shift in the price-setting real wage curve: equilibrium unemployment therefore declines. The flexibility of the real exchange rate and hence of the real cost of imports means that the price-setting real wage can be equal to the wage-setting real wage over a range of unemployment rates. It is intuitively plausible that the more closed is the economy, the narrower the range of equilibrium unemployment rates: in the closed economy there is a unique *ERU*.

Since there is a range of constant inflation unemployment rates in the open economy, can macroeconomic policy makers choose any desired unemployment rate by using fiscal policy to alter the level of aggregate demand? Policy makers in the open economy are likely to be constrained by the consequences of their actions for the external balance. If the economy is running either a persistent current account surplus or deficit, there are a number of mechanisms that may come into play at some stage to push the economy toward current account balance. These pressures arise because the surplus or deficit represents a change in the economy's wealth position. A change in wealth can affect private sector expenditure and access to international capital markets. Equally, a persistent deficit or surplus may affect exchange rate expectations. In the long run it is likely that the current account position will place a constraint on the unemployment rate that can be sustained. However, to the extent that the constraint comes from the operation of the foreign exchange market, it is likely to have less effect on a member country of a common currency area such as the eurozone.

This chapter begins by asking how wages and prices react in the open economy following the move to a new short-run equilibrium. We then integrate the supply side more systematically into open economy analysis. A new core diagram that is used from this point onwards in the book is introduced. The diagram has the real exchange rate and output on the axes. Section 3 is short—it simply shows how to translate the aggregate demand side and trade balance analysis from Chapter 9 into the new diagram. In the fourth section, the demand and supply sides are put together to create the open economy model. The differences between the short-run, medium-run (i.e. constant inflation) and long-run (i.e. current account balance) equilibria are examined. The chapter concludes with a discussion of the reasons why in the longer run, the economy may be constrained to an unemployment rate close to current account balance.

1 Inflation and unemployment in the open economy

In what ways do we need to alter the analysis of the supply side in the closed economy to make it fit the open economy? First, let us recall the closed economy model. Medium-run

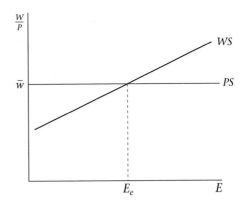

Figure 10.1 Equilibrium employment in the closed economy

equilibrium in the closed economy is characterized by constant inflation: the rate of unemployment at which inflation is constant is referred to as the 'equilibrium' rate, the *ERU* (or *NAIRU*). For illustrative purposes it is simplest to assume constant labour productivity, λ, and a constant mark-up. Given the wage-setting curve and the price-setting curve, there is a single employment level (and associated unemployment rate) at which the expected real wage set by wage setters is equal to the real wage that is implied by price-setting behaviour. Equilibrium employment, E_e, is shown in Fig. 10.1.

At E_e for a given expected inflation rate, money wages will rise in line with expected inflation to deliver the real wage $\overline{w}$ and prices will rise in line with money wages to keep the profit margin unchanged. Thus inflation will remain equal to its expected rate: there is constant inflation at E_e. At any other employment level, the wage-setting real wage will be either higher than the price-setting real wage (when employment is higher than E_e) or lower than the price-setting real wage (when employment is lower than E_e). There will be upward pressure on inflation in the first case and downward pressure in the second case. Inflation will be constant only when employment is at E_e because only here are the expectations of both wage and price setters fulfilled. There is no pressure on inflation. This is the medium-run equilibrium.

As discussed in Chapter 3, the labour market must be in equilibrium for inflation to be constant. The rate of inflation at the medium-run constant inflation equilibrium is determined by monetary policy. We discussed two different monetary policy regimes: in one, the medium-run inflation rate was set by the growth rate of the money supply and in the other it was set by the inflation target of the central bank.

When we turn to the open economy, we pose three familiar questions:

(1) What determines the unemployment rate at which inflation is constant?

(2) What determines the constant rate of inflation at a medium-run equilibrium?

(3) How does inflation behave when the economy is not at a constant inflation equilibrium?

We shall answer these questions in this chapter. In the introductory section, we provide the answers and an intuitive explanation for them. The detail is provided in the rest of the chapter.

- What determines the unemployment rate at which inflation is constant?

The answer to this question in the open economy takes the same general form as in the closed economy: when wage and price setters are in equilibrium, inflation is constant. Once again, we are looking for the intersection between the *WS* and the *PS* curves. These curves are determined by the supply-side features of the labour and product markets. However, the first new twist in the open economy is that the *PS* curve and hence the actual real wage is affected by the real cost of imports and therefore by the real exchange rate. A real appreciation means that the real cost of imports is lower. This raises real wages and means that we can have a constant inflation equilibrium at lower unemployment. The second new twist is that a fiscal expansion and, more generally, an *IS* shock, can shift the economy to a new constant inflation equilibrium.

- What determines the constant rate of inflation at a medium-run equilibrium?

Just as in the closed economy it is the monetary policy regime that establishes how the medium-run inflation rate is determined. In a *flexible* exchange rate economy in a medium-run equilibrium, inflation will be constant at the growth rate of the money supply set by the central bank or at the central bank's inflation target if it is using a monetary policy rule such as a Taylor rule. In a *fixed* exchange rate economy, inflation will be constant at the 'world' inflation rate. In turn, 'world' inflation will be set by the growth rate of the money supply as fixed by the central bank in the economy to which the home economy's exchange rate is pegged or at that central bank's inflation target.

- How does inflation behave when the economy is not at a constant inflation equilibrium?

In the closed economy, the short-run Phillips curve captures the response of inflation when the economy is away from the medium-run equilibrium: unemployment below the *ERU* means rising inflation and vice versa. In the open economy, when we think about the consequences for inflation of any disturbance to the economy, we have to take into account not only what has happened to unemployment, i.e. the Phillips curve mechanism, but also what has happened to the real wage as a consequence of any change in the exchange rate.

To explore these three questions further, we shall take as a starting point an example familiar from Chapter 9: a fiscal expansion. We shall begin with the economy in a medium-run equilibrium with constant inflation and then implement a fiscal expansion. After noting the new short-run equilibrium, we ask how prices and wages will move once they are allowed to adjust. We shall see that wages and prices not only react to changes in the level of output (as in the closed economy) following changes to fiscal or monetary policy but also to any change in the real exchange rate that has occurred. This is because a change in the real exchange rate affects real wages and therefore disturbs the equilibrium in the labour market. As we work through the chapter, we shall see that although a fiscal expansion takes the economy to a new medium-run equilibrium with constant inflation, a monetary expansion does not. Just as in the closed economy, a change in monetary policy has only a short-run effect in the open economy.

1.1 Example 1. Fiscal expansion with fixed exchange rates: what happens to inflation?

Let us begin by assuming that the small open economy is at equilibrium employment at E_0 with a real wage of w_0 (see Fig. 10.2). We assume that inflation in the rest of the world is 3%. The home economy begins with 3% inflation as well and we assume that the exchange rate is fixed. The real exchange rate, $\theta = \frac{P^* e}{P}$, is therefore constant: e is fixed and P^* and P are growing at the same rate of 3%. Suppose there is a rise in aggregate demand as the result of a fiscal expansion. As usual, higher demand boosts output in the home economy and employment increases to E_2. This is the new *short-run* equilibrium in the Mundell–Fleming model (point C).

The question is what will happen to wages and prices when we allow them to adjust. Since employment has risen, wage setters will require a higher expected real wage (WS is positively sloped). Hence money wages rise by more than 3%, i.e. inflation goes up. The unit costs of home firms therefore increase. According to our usual assumption about pricing behaviour, home firms raise their prices to reflect these higher costs (so home prices will rise in line with wages, i.e. at a rate above 3%). This in turn pushes up consumer price inflation. Since this is an open economy, home consumers buy both imported goods and home produced goods. The price of imported goods has only risen by 3%, the consumer price index does not rise by as much as does the price index of home produced

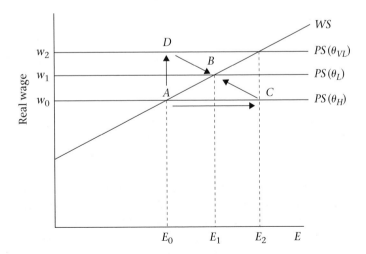

Figure 10.2 Equilibrium employment in the open economy at low A and high B employment
Fiscal expansion: A to C to B (fixed exchange rates); A to D to B (flexible exchange rates)

goods. This has a very important consequence. The rise in consumer prices wipes out some but not all of the rise in money wages: hence the real wage increases and the *PS* curve shifts up a bit.

The change in relative prices has implications for *aggregate demand* as well. As home prices are pushed up relative to world prices, the home economy loses competitiveness (the real exchange rate appreciates) and output and employment fall below E_2. The economy moves north-west from C as shown by the arrow. It will come to rest at point B. When we allow prices and wages to adjust following a fiscal expansion under fixed exchange rates, there is a burst of inflation above 3% and then the economy comes to rest at a medium-run equilibrium at a point such as B: with employment and real wages higher than initially and with inflation constant and equal to world inflation. Since home producers have protected their profit margins throughout, the wage-setting real wage and the price-setting real wage are equal at the new higher level of employment. We have therefore found a second equilibrium employment level at E_1.[1]

The sequence of events is summarized in Table 10.1.

If real wages are higher and real profits are the same, where have the extra resources come from at the new employment level to pay for the higher real wages? The answer is that the new resources have come from abroad. The terms of trade for the home economy $(\frac{P_x}{P_m} = \frac{1}{\theta})$ have improved because the price of goods exported ($P_x = P$) has risen relative to the price of goods imported ($P_m = P^*e$) so the volume of imported goods that can be obtained by selling a given volume of exports has increased. The *PS* curve that intersects the *WS* curve at E_1 is associated with a lower value of θ and is labelled $PS(\theta_L)$.

The possibility that the terms of trade can change in an open economy provides an indication that the open and closed economies can work in somewhat different ways. In the closed economy, there is a unique equilibrium rate of unemployment (*ERU*). In an open economy, if the terms of trade can change, then the total amount of resources available to domestic wage and price setters is no longer fixed. This means that there is no longer a unique unemployment equilibrium: a range of unemployment rates is consistent

Table 10.1 Fiscal expansion under fixed exchange rates

1st New short-run equil. at C	$\uparrow g \rightarrow \uparrow y \rightarrow \uparrow E \Longrightarrow$
	$\Delta E > 0$ and $\Delta w = 0$
2nd Wages & prices adjust	$\uparrow E \rightarrow \uparrow W \rightarrow \uparrow P$ rel. to $P^* \rightarrow \uparrow w$ and $\downarrow \theta \rightarrow \downarrow y \rightarrow \downarrow E$
3rd New medium-run equil. at B	π constant, w higher, θ lower, E higher

---

[1] To see why employment will not shrink right back to its initial level of E_0, remember that government spending is higher (due to the expansionary fiscal policy). That means that for the economy to return to point A so there is no change in output, the real exchange rate would have to appreciate in order to reduce net exports by the full amount of the increase in government spending (i.e. $\Delta g = -\Delta(x - m)$). But if the real exchange rate at point A has *appreciated* relative to its initial level, then the real cost of imports will be *lower* (since $P_m/P = P^*e/P = \theta$, which has fallen) and real wages will therefore be *higher* than they were initially. If so, the labour market will not be in equilibrium since the real wage will be above the wage-setting real wage (i.e. $w > w^{WS} = w_0$ at E_0). As we shall see in the next example, this would take us to point D.

with the absence of inflationary pressure and fiscal policy can have a medium-run effect on output and employment.[2]

1.2 Example 2. Fiscal expansion with flexible exchange rates: what happens to inflation?

We shall see that this feature of the open economy does not depend on the exchange rate regime in place. If inflation expectations are rational and there are no nominal rigidities the economy moves directly from point A to point B in Fig. 10.2. To see how the economy goes from A to B when exchange rates are flexible but there is nominal stickiness, we follow the same steps as for Example 1: beginning with the move to the Mundell–Fleming equilibrium (no wage or price adjustment) and then allowing wages and prices to respond. From Chapter 9 we know that a fiscal expansion under flexible exchange rates has no effect on output since in the new short-run (Mundell-Fleming) equilibrium, net exports are lower by exactly the increase in government expenditure i.e. there is complete crowding out of net exports by the higher government spending. In Fig. 10.2, the economy goes from point A to point D. This takes place because of the appreciation of the exchange rate in response to the higher domestic interest rate via the *UIP* condition. Now let us look at the consequences for prices and wages when the economy is at the new short-run equilibrium. Output is at its initial level (the composition has changed) and there has been an appreciation of the real exchange rate (e has fallen (appreciated) and P and P^* are unchanged; hence $\theta = P^*e/P$ has fallen). Competitiveness has fallen to the very low level, θ_{VL}.

Will inflation remain constant? To answer this, we ask whether wage and price setters are in equilibrium? An appreciation of the real exchange rate means that the real cost of imports has gone down ($P_m/P = P^*e/P = \theta$, which has fallen) and therefore real wages have gone up. Looking at Fig. 10.2, with employment at E_0 in the new short-run equilibrium, the real wage is above w_0, at w_2 (point D). Clearly, wage setters are not on the *WS* curve. The result will be lower money wage settlements (i.e. below the going rate of inflation of 3%). Home producers will reduce their prices in line with their falling costs. But since the prices of imported goods continue to rise at 3%, whilst money wages have risen by less than 3%, real wages fall. Since prices of home produced goods have risen by less than the prices of world goods, the result will be an improvement in competitiveness. This will raise net exports with the result that output and employment will begin to rise. The economy moves south-east from point D and comes to rest at point B. We can summarize as in Table 10.2.

We shall set out the details in the rest of the chapter. Here we note that although the short-run effect of fiscal policy is very different depending on whether the exchange rate is fixed or flexible, the medium-run outcome is identical.

---

[2] Of course, not all countries can improve their terms of trade at the same time. We investigate the implications of this when we relax the 'small country' assumption in Chapter 12, which focuses on interdependent economies.

Table 10.2 Fiscal expansion under flexible exchange rates

1st New short-run equil. at D	$\uparrow g \rightarrow \downarrow \theta \rightarrow \downarrow (x-m) \Longrightarrow$
	$\Delta E = 0$ and $\Delta w > 0$
2nd Wages & prices adjust	$\uparrow w \rightarrow \downarrow W \rightarrow \downarrow P$ rel. to $P^* \rightarrow \uparrow \theta \rightarrow \uparrow y \rightarrow \uparrow E$
3rd New medium-run equil. at B	Same as Table 10.1.

1.3 Summing up

We have seen that when we move from the short to the medium run, and allow wages and prices to adjust, the open economy behaves somewhat differently from the closed economy. Changes in the real exchange rate affect not only aggregate demand but also real wages. This has two consequences: first, it means that instead of wages and prices responding only to shifts in *employment* from the initial constant inflation equilibrium, they also respond to changes in the *real wage* that occur as a consequence of any change in the real exchange rate. We saw this clearly in Example 2 when the fiscal expansion led to a nominal appreciation and therefore raised real wages in the short run. Second, it means that following an expansionary fiscal policy the response of wages and prices ensures that the economy ends up at a new medium-run equilibrium with higher output: the medium-run equilibrium is the same irrespective of whether exchange rates are fixed or flexible.

Why do we have a new constant inflation equilibrium at lower unemployment following a fiscal boost in the open but not the closed economy? The answer is that in the closed economy, *WS* and *PS* intersect at a unique level of employment: this is the unique *ERU*. By contrast, in the open economy, the price-setting real wage is an inverse function of the real exchange rate: changes in the real cost of imports affect real wages. Hence following a fiscal expansion, a new constant inflation equilibrium is feasible: a real appreciation implies that higher real wages and lower real import costs are consistent with equilibrium for price setters and wage setters at lower unemployment.

2 Supply side in the open economy

2.1 Wage and price setting in the open economy

In this section, we provide a systematic treatment of why there is a range of medium-run equilibrium unemployment rates in the open economy. To define this range we need to set out the details of wage and price setting in the open economy. We stick to the cost-plus pricing rule for home produced goods sold at home and exported:

$$P = P_x = \frac{1}{1-\mu} \cdot \text{unit cost} \qquad \text{(cost-plus pricing)}$$

where μ is the mark-up.

In the open economy, it is necessary to be more careful about what is meant by real wages. The reason is that we can no longer talk about a single price level. The price level that is relevant in the assessment by workers of the real value of money wages is the money wage in terms of consumer prices (i.e. $\frac{W}{P_c}$, where P_c is the consumer price index). The consumer price index includes the prices of final consumer goods that are imported. By contrast, the real wage that is relevant as a cost to firms is the money wage in terms of the product price, P. The core open economy model can be best understood if we make a simplification: we assume that it is only final consumer goods that are imported into the economy. In Chapter 11, when we want to investigate external supply shocks such as oil shocks, we introduce the role of imported materials.

To define the consumer price index P_c it is assumed that consumers purchase a bundle of goods. Those which are imported have a price of P^*e and those which are home produced have a price of P. The share of the consumption bundle that is imported we will call ϕ, ϕ (pronounced 'phi') for 'foreign'.[3] The consumer price index is:

$$P_c = (1 - \phi)P + \phi P^*e \qquad \text{(consumer price index)}$$

where we use the fact that $P_m = P^*e$. Whenever we use the term 'real wage' or w we mean the real wage in terms of consumer prices:

$$w = \frac{W}{P_c}. \qquad \text{(real wage)}$$

The next step is to set out wage- and price-setting behaviour in the open economy and then to look at the implications for the wage- and price-setting curves.

2.1.1 Wage setting

Wage-setting behaviour is the same as in the closed economy. The only modification is to make explicit the role of the consumer price index:

$$W = P_c \cdot b(E). \qquad \text{(wage equation)}$$

The wage-setting curve is defined by

$$\frac{W}{P_c} = b(E)$$
$$w^{WS} = b(E) \qquad \text{(wage-setting real wage)}$$

where a rise in employment is associated with a rise in the wage-setting real wage.

2.1.2 Price setting

As discussed above, we use a cost plus pricing rule for the open economy. In the absence of any imported materials, price setting in the open economy is the same as in the closed economy, i.e. prices are set as a mark-up on unit labour costs:

$$P = P_x = \frac{1}{1 - \mu} \cdot \frac{W}{\lambda}, \qquad \text{(price equation)}$$

[3] ϕ is equal to $\frac{m_y}{c_y}$.

where P is the price of home goods sold at home and in export markets and λ is the level of labour productivity. To work with the wage- and price-setting curves, both must use the same definition of the real wage. This means that we need to express the price-setting real wage in terms of the consumer price index, i.e. $\frac{W}{P_c}$.

The first step is to substitute the price equation into the equation for the consumer price, P_c.

$$P_c = (1 - \phi)P + \phi P^* e$$
$$= (1 - \phi)\left[\frac{1}{1 - \mu}\frac{W}{\lambda}\right] + \phi P^* e.$$

In order to find the expression for the price-setting real wage, we now divide each side by $P = \frac{1}{1-\mu} \cdot \frac{W}{\lambda}$. This is shown in line (10.1). Then we use the definitions of the real wage, $w = \frac{W}{P_c}$ and of the real exchange rate, $\theta = \frac{P^* e}{P}$ to simplify the equation (10.2). In the third line, we rearrange the equation so that the real wage is in the numerator (10.3).

$$\frac{P_c(1 - \mu)\lambda}{W} = (1 - \phi) + \frac{\phi P^* e}{P} \tag{10.1}$$

$$\frac{(1 - \mu)\lambda}{w} = (1 - \phi) + \phi\theta \tag{10.2}$$

$$\frac{w}{(1 - \mu)\lambda} = \frac{1}{(1 - \phi) + \phi\theta}. \tag{10.3}$$

In the final step, we rearrange the equation so that the price-setting real wage is on the left hand side:

$$w^{PS} = \frac{\lambda(1 - \mu)}{1 + \phi(\theta - 1)} \qquad \text{(price-setting real wage, open)}$$

$$= F(\theta), \tag{10.4}$$

where the inverse relationship between θ and w^{PS} can be denoted by $F'(\theta) < 0$.

We can see from this that the price-setting real wage in the open economy is equal to the closed economy price-setting real wage (i.e. $\lambda(1 - \mu)$) modified by the real exchange rate, θ. If there are no imported goods the weight of imports in the consumer price index is zero (i.e. $\phi = 0$) and so it is easy to see that the price-setting real wage is indeed equal to its closed economy value,

$$w^{PS} = \lambda(1 - \mu). \qquad \text{(price-setting real wage, closed)}$$

The price-setting behaviour of firms means that the wage measured in terms of domestic output is fixed in exactly the same way and at the same level as in the closed economy. But workers choose to spend some of their wages on imported goods. The higher the price of imports, the fewer the bundles of domestic output plus imported goods (in proportions $(1 - \phi)$ and ϕ) they can afford. So the real wage is reduced. Given the world price of imports, P^*, the price to consumers varies with the exchange rate. See Fig. 10.3 for a comparison between the closed and open economy price-setting curves.

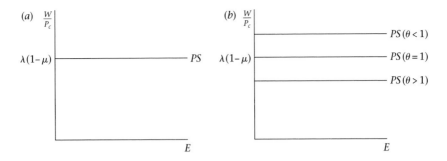

Figure 10.3 Price-setting curves in closed and open economies.
(a) Closed economy, (b) Open economy

This highlights that the most important feature of the price-setting real wage in the open economy is that it is inversely related to the real exchange rate, θ:

- a rise in θ raises the real cost of imported goods and therefore reduces the price-setting real wage.

2.2 Medium-run equilibrium

If we now bring together the wage-setting and price-setting curves, we can see that since θ can vary, there is a range of unemployment rates at which wage and price setters are in equilibrium in the sense that wage setters are on the *WS* curve and price setters are on the $PS(\theta)$ curve. Another way of putting this is to say that the claims on output per head of wage earners and firms are consistent with the available output per head across a range of rates of unemployment. When wage and price setters are in equilibrium—i.e. their claims are consistent with the level of output per head available, then inflationary pressures are absent. Just as in the closed economy, we refer to any unemployment rate (and the associated level of output and employment) at which wage and price setters are in equilibrium as an equilibrium rate of unemployment (*ERU*). It may also be referred to as a competing claims equilibrium.

In the closed economy, the claims for real wages per head and profits per head are equal to output per head only at a single unemployment rate: the *WS* curve and the *PS* curve intersect at a unique unemployment rate. In the open economy, there is a range of equilibrium rates of unemployment. In the top panel of Fig. 10.4, equilibrium rates of unemployment at *A* and at *B* are shown. At *A*, unemployment is relatively high and as a consequence, the labour market position of workers is rather weak. This means that the wage-setting real wage is relatively low. For an equilibrium rate of unemployment, the price-setting real wage must also be at this relatively low level. With a fixed real profit margin per worker, the price-setting real wage will be relatively low when the real cost of imports in the basket of goods consumed is relatively high. The price-setting real wage associated with high import costs is shown by $PS(\theta_H)$.

When unemployment is much lower at point *B*, the tight labour market situation implies a higher wage-setting real wage. For an equilibrium rate of unemployment, the

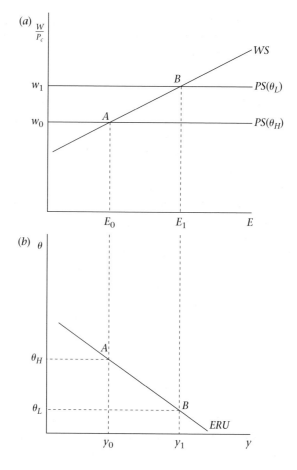

Figure 10.4 Equilibrium rate of unemployment curve (*ERU*).
(a) *WS* and *PS* curves (b) *ERU* curve

Note: As θ increases, the real cost of imports increases

price-setting real wage must therefore also be higher. For this to be possible with the claim of real profits per worker unchanged, the real cost of imported goods in the basket of goods consumed must be relatively low. This is indicated by the price-setting real wage curve labelled $PS(\theta_L)$.

2.2.1 Equilibrium rate of unemployment (*ERU*) curve

It turns out to be very useful when analysing the open economy to work with a diagram with the real exchange rate and output on the axes. This is because changes in the nominal or real exchange rate are frequently the focus of attention. We can easily map the range of equilibrium unemployment rates from the wage- and price-setting diagram to (θ, y) space. We show the equation for the equilibrium rate of unemployment or *ERU* curve in the appendix.

To derive the equilibrium rate of unemployment curve in the θy–diagram (bottom panel of Fig. 10.4), we start by asking the question: how can a low level of unemployment and the associated high level of output be sustained without inflationary pressure? As we have just seen, a low rate of unemployment implies that wage bargainers will only be satisfied by a high real wage. For this to be an equilibrium, the price-setting real wage must be at the same high level. This requires that the real cost of imported goods is sufficiently low. At point B in the top panel of Fig. 10.4 there is a high value of employment—and therefore a high level of output. This means that for equilibrium in the labour market, we have to have a low value of θ so that import costs are low (see point B in the bottom panel). A low value of $\theta = \frac{P^*e}{P}$ means that the world price level and hence the price of imported goods (P^*e) is low relative to the price of home goods and hence of exports (P). With low import costs, real wages can be high without affecting the real value of profits. Living standards are boosted because imports are cheap. This gives point B at the combination of a low value of θ and a high level of output.

Exactly the same logic lies behind the location of point A. When unemployment is high and output is depressed, workers are in a weak position in the labour market and there is a low wage-setting real wage. For the price-setting real wage to be at this low level as is required for supply-side equilibrium, the cost of imported goods must be high. At point A there will be a combination of low output and high import costs, i.e. high θ. Hence the equilibrium rate of unemployment (ERU) curve in the θy–diagram is downward sloping (bottom panel of Fig. 10.4). It is important to keep firmly in mind that the ERU curve represents equilibrium in the *labour market*: in the next section, we shall derive a *positively* sloped relationship between θ and y from the *aggregate demand* side.

The ERU curve is defined as the combinations of the real exchange rate and output at which the wage-setting real wage is equal to the price-setting real wage. At any point on the ERU curve, the real exchange rate, θ, is constant and inflation is constant.

2.2.2 Slope of the *ERU* curve

A glance at Fig. 10.4 suggests that the steepness of the ERU curve will be important in fixing the range of output and employment levels consistent with stable inflation. If the ERU curve was vertical, then there would be a unique equilibrium unemployment rate—a very steep ERU curve would display only a narrow range of unemployment equilibria. A steep ERU curve means that a very large change in the real exchange rate is required to bring about the change in the real cost of imports that is necessary to allow the wage- and price-setting real wage to be equal at a higher level of employment. This could be because the import propensity is very small so that a very big change in relative prices is needed to alter the real cost of imports in the consumption bundle.

It could also be because the wage-setting real wage is very steep, i.e. real wages are very sensitive to a change in unemployment. In such a case, a given fall in unemployment leads to a very big rise in the wage-setting real wage and hence for a given import propensity, requires a large cut in the real cost of imports (fall in θ) to allow the necessary rise in the price-setting real wage.

By contrast, a flat *ERU* curve would indicate a wide range of medium-run equilibria. In this case, a high import share would mean that only a small fall in θ would be required for supply-side equilibrium at lower unemployment. Equally, if real wages are rather insensitive to employment, then a given fall in unemployment will be associated with only a modest rise in the wage-setting real wage along the *WS* curve and therefore only a small fall in θ is needed to ensure equilibrium at lower unemployment. (Details for sketching the *ERU* curve are shown in the appendix to this chapter. For simplicity we show the *ERU* curve as linear.)

To summarize:

(1) If the economy is closed so that there are no imports (i.e. $\phi = 0$), there is a unique equilibrium level of output and hence a unique equilibrium unemployment rate. This will define a vertical *ERU* curve.

(2) As the share of imports rises, the *ERU* curve becomes flatter. More open economies have flatter *ERU* curves.

(3) If the wage-setting curve is flatter (i.e. real wages are less sensitive to employment), this will make the *ERU* curve flatter. Economies in which labour market institutions make the wage-setting real wage more insensitive to changes in unemployment have flatter *ERU* curves.

2.2.3 Off the *ERU* curve, the real exchange rate is rising or falling

Every point *on* the *ERU* curve is a point at which the wage- and price-setting curves intersect: inflation is constant and so is the real exchange rate. However, since we cannot normally assume that the economy adjusts to any disturbance by moving immediately to a new equilibrium, it is important to know what it means to be *off* the *ERU* curve. We assume that prices adjust more rapidly than do wages so that the economy is always on the price-setting curve (i.e. $w = w^{PS}$) but not necessarily on the wage-setting curve. We assume that world inflation is constant and that in a medium-run equilibrium, home and world inflation are equal.

Let us consider a situation shown in Fig. 10.5 in which the employment level is E_1. Throughout this discussion, we hold the level of employment constant at E_1 so as to focus entirely on wage and price adjustment. We begin with the economy off the *ERU* curve at point B' with the real exchange rate equal to θ_H. This means that the economy is on the $PS(\theta_H)$ in the upper panel and that the real wage is equal to w_0.

As is clear from the top panel, when the economy is on the *PS* curve, $PS(\theta_H)$, the real wage is below the wage-setting real wage at this employment level. There will therefore be upward pressure on inflation. At point B' with low unemployment, we know that given the expected price level, P_c, wages will be set according to the wage-setting equation to deliver the higher expected real wage shown by the *WS* curve (i.e. at point B). When producers set their prices immediately after wages, the price level rises since the rise in wages increases unit costs. Although nothing has happened to the prices of imported goods, the rise in home prices means that the consumer price level is above the price level expected when wages were set. This means that at points above the *ERU* curve (like point B'), $w = w^{PS} < w^{WS}$ with the consequence that $P_c > P_c^E$.

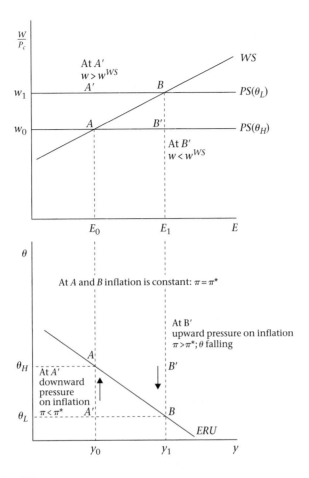

Figure 10.5 Off the *ERU* curve

According to the wage-setting equation, a higher than expected price level will result in higher money wages. Since by assumption, nothing has happened to the price of imported goods, the consumer price index will rise, but not by as much as money wages. As a result, the real wage rises and the real cost of imports falls: the *PS* curve shifts up and θ falls. This can be summed up by saying that at points above the *ERU* like point B', home inflation is above world inflation. The higher domestic wage and price inflation depresses home's competitiveness and raises home's real wages.

At point B, the wage- and price-setting real wages are equal and $P_c = P_c^E$. In the θy-diagram, the real exchange rate appreciates as home prices rise relative to foreign prices and price competitiveness falls to θ_L. At B, the economy is once more on the *ERU* curve. Inflationary pressures have disappeared.

A parallel argument tells us that at a point such as A' where the economy is below the *ERU* curve (lower panel) and the real wage is above the wage-setting real wage (i.e. $w = w^{PS} > w^{WS}$) at point A' in the upper panel, then $P_c < P_c^E$. Home wage and price inflation will therefore be below world inflation, the real wage will fall, θ will rise (the real cost of imports will rise), and the economy will move back to the *ERU* curve at point *A* with a real exchange rate of θ_H.

These results can be summarized as follows:

- On the *ERU* curve, inflation is constant.

- At points above the *ERU* curve, the real wage is *below* the *WS* curve so there is upward pressure on inflation. Wages are too low to satisfy wage setters at this level of employment. Home inflation is above world inflation. Hence θ is falling and real wages are rising.

- At points below the *ERU* curve, the real wage is *above* the *WS* curve so there is downward pressure on inflation. Wages are too high for wage-setting equilibrium given the low level of employment. Home inflation is below world inflation. Hence θ is rising and real wages are falling.

3 Demand side and trade balance

In section 1, we saw how changes in the real exchange rate induced by wage and price adjustment fed back to affect aggregate demand and therefore output and employment. The task here is to show how to translate the key features of goods and financial market equilibrium and of trade balance into the new θy–diagram. Since a rise in competitiveness boosts net exports (assuming as usual that the Marshall–Lerner condition holds), we shall derive a positively sloped line to represent goods market equilibrium: a real depreciation is associated with a new goods market equilibrium at higher output. This step prepares the ground for section 4 in which the supply side, the demand side, and the trade balance are brought together to form the open economy model. We shall see that using the θy–diagram greatly clarifies open economy analysis. As usual we assume that the Marshall–Lerner condition holds so that a rise in price competitiveness (a real exchange rate depreciation) boosts the trade balance (holding the level of output constant).

Goods market equilibrium is summarized by:

$$
\begin{aligned}
y = y^D \\
= c + I(r) + g + (x - m) \\
= c + I(r) + g + \sigma(\theta)y^* - \theta m_y(\theta)y
\end{aligned}
$$

and

$$
r = r^*.
$$

Note that we assume that the home *real* interest rate is equal to the exogenous world *real* interest rate. In effect, we are assuming that the Mundell–Fleming adjustment process, discussed in detail in Chapter 9, has brought the economy to a short-run equilibrium. For now the focus is on the medium run. Fig. 10.6 shows the construction of the *AD* curve in the θy–diagram.

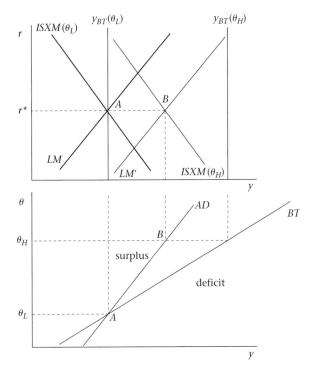

Figure 10.6 Short-run equilibrium (goods & money market): *AD* curve; and trade equilibrium: *BT* curve

The AD curve shows the combinations of the real exchange rate, θ, and level of output, y, at which the goods market is in equilibrium with the real interest rate equal to the world real interest rate.

It is positively sloped because of the assumption that the Marshall–Lerner condition holds: high competitiveness (high θ) raises aggregate demand and output must therefore be high for goods market equilibrium. The move from *A* to *B* can be thought of as coming about in two different ways: either we have a fixed exchange rate economy and the government devalues (i.e. it changes the peg). This causes a rightward shift in the *IS* curve first, which raises the interest rate and induces a capital inflow, which in turn causes the *LM* to shift to the right. The economy is then at point *B*. The alternative is to think of a flexible exchange rate world in which the government first loosens monetary policy: *LM* shifts to the right, which lowers the interest rate. This causes a depreciation, which in turn causes the *ISXM* to shift to the right taking the economy to point *B*.

We can also easily show the trade balance condition in the θy–diagram.

The BT curve shows the combinations of the real exchange rate, θ, and the level of output, y, at which trade is balanced: x = m.

An increased level of price competitiveness (higher θ) raises exports (assuming the Marshall–Lerner condition holds) and requires a higher level of output to drive up the demand for imports and deliver trade balance. Hence the *BT* curve is positively sloped. To the left of the *BT* curve there is a trade surplus and to the right there is a trade deficit.

The *BT* curve is flatter than the *AD* curve. The underlying reason for this result was explained in detail in Fig. 9.3 when we asked what the outcome for the balance of trade would be if there was a depreciation of the real exchange rate. The answer was that there would be a trade surplus: this is shown by point *B* in Fig. 10.6. The intuition is that from an initial equilibrium at point *A* at which trade is balanced, a given increase in θ implies a new goods market equilibrium at point *B*, where the level of output is lower than would be consistent with trade balance. This is because there are leakages in the form of savings and taxation (in addition to imports). This leaves the economy in goods market equilibrium at a level of output below the level that would generate imports equal to the new higher level of exports.

A sense of the usefulness of the new θy–diagram is conveyed by the following exercise.[4] Think of a government that has two targets for economic policy—high output and external balance, as defined by trade balance. The government has two instruments of economic policy—the nominal exchange rate and fiscal policy. There are two relationships linking the targets and the instruments: the *ISXM* equilibrium (with $r = r^*$) summarized in the *AD* curve and the balance of trade curve, *BT*.

Suppose that the country suffers from high unemployment and a trade deficit: this is shown by point *A* in Fig. 10.7. What should be done by a government that seeks to attain a level of output of y_1 and trade balance?

If the government devalues the exchange rate from e_0 to e_2, then the economy moves from point *A* to point *B*. θ rises from θ_0 to θ_2 in Fig. 10.7. The devaluation boosts aggregate demand and this is shown by a move along the *AD* curve. Output rises to y_2 because of the expansionary effect of the devaluation. But although output is higher and trade is balanced at point *B*, this level of output is higher than the government's target of y_1. It must therefore use its other policy instrument (fiscal policy) in combination with a smaller

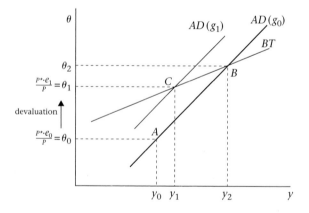

Figure 10.7 Use of a devaluation (or looser monetary policy) and fiscal policy to achieve target output level, y_1, and trade balance

---

[4] This analysis is very similar to the original 'Salter–Swan' diagram. In the next section, we integrate the supply side, which is ignored here and in the Salter–Swan analysis by virtue of the assumption of fixed wages and prices.

devaluation (to e_1) to adjust the level of output to y_1. This leaves the economy at point C with the desired output level and with balanced trade. In this example, contractionary fiscal policy is combined with a devaluation.

In this example, we have used a discrete change in the exchange rate as the policy instrument in a fixed exchange rate regime. As we have seen in Chapter 9, under flexible exchange rates, the government can use monetary policy to achieve the same result: an increase in the money supply shifts the LM to the right reducing the interest rate below the world interest rate; this leads to a depreciation, which in turn raises output via a rightward shift in the $ISXM$. The economy ends up in a new short-run equilibrium with higher output and a higher level of θ. In other words, we can reinterpret the shift along the AD curve in this example in the context of flexible exchange rates as the consequence of a loosening of monetary policy. We therefore ask how the government can use its two instruments of monetary and fiscal policy to achieve its two objectives of trade balance and target output.

The example shows that it will generally be necessary to use two instruments in order to achieve the government's two targets of 'internal' and 'external' balance. But is position C really a position of internal balance? What does the level of the real exchange rate at C imply for the real wage? Is this real wage compatible with wage-setting behaviour in the economy? These questions signal that we must bring the aggregate supply and the demand sides of the economy together with the trade balance condition in order to fully assess the characteristics of a point such as C with target unemployment and balanced trade. We do this in the next section by putting together the open economy model.

4 The open economy model

The basic model for analysis in the small open economy consists of

- the demand side represented by the AD curve. On the AD curve, the goods market is in equilibrium and $r = r^*$.
- the supply side represented by the ERU curve. On the ERU curve inflation is constant.
- the balance of trade equilibrium represented by the BT curve.

In the short run, when the economy is in goods market equilibrium it will be on an AD curve. For a given nominal exchange rate and a given price level, the level of output is fixed by the AD curve. This is not necessarily a medium-run equilibrium.

For medium-run equilibrium, the economy must also be on an ERU curve. Only on the ERU curve are the wage- and price-setting real wages equal and the labour market in equilibrium. In the medium run, therefore, the economy will be on an AD curve and on the ERU curve.

Only by chance will the medium-run equilibrium also be characterized by trade balance. Long-run equilibrium is at a position on the ERU curve and at current account balance. As we have seen in Chapter 9, when the current account is balanced, the country's wealth is constant. To make the exposition as simple as possible, we ignore the

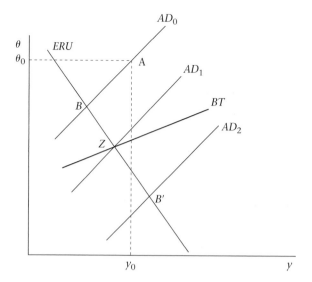

Figure 10.8 Short-run, medium-run, and long-run equilibria in the open economy

difference between the trade balance and the current account. This allows us to define the long-run equilibrium as the intersection of the *ERU* curve and the *BT* curve.

As discussed in Chapter 9, in the long run, there may be pressures that tend to ensure that there is current account balance in the economy. Such pressures can arise from private sector changes in aggregate demand through the wealth effects on consumption expenditure associated with a trade surplus (home wealth is rising) or a trade deficit (home wealth is falling). Equally, pressure may mount in the foreign exchange market and force the government to change its policy.

The difference between short-, medium-, and long-run equilibria in the basic model is illustrated by the example in Fig. 10.8. Let us compare the characteristics of points *A*, *B*, *B'*, and *Z*.

- Short-run equilibrium at point *A*—the economy is on the aggregate demand curve AD_0 but not on either the *ERU* or *BT* curves. At point *A*, the level of output is y_0, the real exchange rate is equal to θ_0 and the economy is above the *ERU* curve. This means that the prevailing real wage is below the real wage that wage setters can expect at the relatively low unemployment rate associated with y_0. Workers are in a rather strong position in the labour market and the money wage that is set will rise relative to the expected price level. Home prices will rise relative to foreign prices. Home inflation is above world inflation. Assuming that the nominal exchange rate is constant, this depresses price competitiveness and the economy moves along the *AD* curve toward point *B*. Output falls because of the lower export demand generated by the fall in competitiveness.

- Medium-run equilibria such as at points *B* and *B'*—the economy is on *ERU* and *AD* and *AD'* respectively but not on *BT*. Inflation is constant at points *B* and *B'* because each is on the *ERU* curve. There is a trade surplus at point *B* because it is to the left of the *BT* curve and a trade deficit at point B' because it is to the right of the BT curve. The economy can remain at points like B and B' with stable inflation. However, in the longer run, pressures may emerge as a consequence of the external position that tend to push the economy away from B or B' toward point Z.

• Long-run equilibrium at point Z—on AD, ERU, and BT. At point Z, labour market equilibrium coincides with the balanced trade level of output. This is likely to be a sustainable long-run position for the economy.

Having put together the open economy model, we can now re-examine the situation described in Fig. 10.7 above: recall that the government used its two policy instruments of a change in the nominal exchange rate (either as the result of a discrete change in the peg under fixed exchange rates or due to a loosening of monetary policy under flexible rates) and an adjustment of fiscal policy to achieve its two targets, the desired output level of y_1 and trade balance. We asked the following questions: Is position C really a position of internal balance? What does the level of the real exchange rate at C imply for the real wage? Is this real wage compatible with wage-setting behaviour in the economy? These questions can be summarized by asking whether point C is on the ERU curve. If so, then the economy can remain there without problems of inflation. Since trade is balanced at C, it would also represent a long-run equilibrium. However, if the ERU curve lies below point C as shown in Fig. 10.9, then C is not a medium-run equilibrium: the real wage is below the wage-setting real wage and the economy will experience upward pressure on inflation: inflation will rise above world inflation. The ERU curve represents a third constraint on the economy and the government will not be able to achieve its output target of y_1 with balanced trade through the use of just two instruments. It will have to use supply-side policy to shift the ERU curve so that it intersects the BT curve at point C. We investigate the use of supply-side policy more closely in Chapter 11. Failing this, the government will have to accept a more modest output target and trim aggregate demand accordingly (see point D in Fig. 10.9).

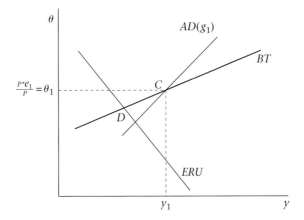

Figure 10.9 Point C at target output and trade balance is not a medium-run equilibrium

4.1 Inflation in the open economy

In this section, we bring together the determinants of inflation in the open economy. We have already noted how inflation rises or falls when the economy is off the *ERU* curve. We shall now examine how the inflation rate is pinned down when the economy is in a medium-run equilibrium—i.e. when it is on an *ERU* curve with constant inflation. At any medium-run equilibrium—i.e. at a point on the *ERU* curve—the real exchange rate is constant. In the next section, we examine the factors that might eventually cause the economy to move from such a medium-run equilibrium.

If $\theta = \frac{P^* e}{P}$ is constant, this implies that home inflation is equal to world inflation plus the depreciation of home's nominal exchange rate:

$$\frac{\Delta P}{P} = \frac{\Delta P^*}{P^*} + \frac{\Delta e}{e}.$$

Alternatively, we can use π to refer to the rate of inflation and write:

$$\pi = \pi^* + \frac{\Delta e}{e}.$$

The intuition is that competitiveness remains constant as long as home and abroad's prices are rising at the same rate in a common currency. But what determines the rate of home inflation? The answer depends on whether exchange rates are fixed or floating.

- *Under fixed exchange rates*, the nominal exchange rate is fixed by assumption, i.e. $\frac{\Delta e}{e} = 0$ so for the real exchange rate to be constant as in the equation above, home inflation must be equal to world inflation:

$$\pi = [\pi^*].$$

Since home is a small country, its inflation rate is determined by world inflation. The square brackets are used to indicate an exogenous variable.

But this leaves open the question of how equilibrium in the home money market is achieved. For equilibrium in the home money market, the demand for money must be equal to the supply. Let us look first at the demand for money. The demand for money is a function of the level of output and the nominal interest rate. In a medium-run equilibrium, the level of output is fixed at y_e. The nominal interest rate is equal to the real interest rate plus expected inflation ($i \approx r + \pi^E$),[5] and in a medium-run equilibrium inflation is at its expected rate. With inflation at the world rate and with the home real interest rate equal to the world rate ($r = r^*$), we can write the equation for equilibrium in the home money market as follows:

$$\left(\frac{M}{P}\right)^S = \left(\frac{M}{P}\right)^D$$
$$= L(y_e, i)$$
$$= L(y_e, r + \pi^E)$$
$$= L(y_e, r^* + \pi^*).$$

---

[5] We assume in what follows that the approximation holds.

- For equilibrium in the home money market the real money supply, $\frac{M}{P}$, must be constant since all the determinants of the demand for money are fixed. We know that $\pi = [\pi^*]$. Hence the money supply must grow at the exogenously given world rate of inflation in order to keep the money supply constant:

$$\frac{\Delta M}{M} = \pi = [\pi^*].$$ \hfill (fixed exchange rates)

Another way of putting this result is that the growth rate of the money supply is endogenous in the fixed exchange rate economy—in Chapter 9, we saw that the money supply was endogenous in the short run in the fixed rate economy; here we see that it is endogenous in the medium run as well. Thus as long as foreign inflation remains constant and the exchange rate is fixed, home inflation is constant at the foreign rate in medium-run equilibrium. We assume constant world inflation.

- *Under flexible exchange rates*, in medium-run equilibrium, it is also the case that the real exchange rate, θ, is constant. Hence

$$\pi = \pi^* + \frac{\Delta e}{e}.$$

At a medium-run equilibrium, we have:

$$\left(\frac{M}{P}\right)^S = \left(\frac{M}{P}\right)^D$$
$$= L(y_e, r^* + \pi).$$

At the medium-run output level, inflation is constant at its expected rate. This implies that the home money supply must grow at the rate of home inflation. We assume that the growth rate of the home money supply is exogenous: this determines the rate of home inflation. (Alternatively if the home country is targeting inflation, then $\pi = [\pi^T]$ and the home money supply adjusts to come into line with the inflation target.)

$$\left[\frac{\Delta M}{M}\right] = \pi.$$

But what does this imply for the nominal exchange rate? Since both home and world inflation are now determined exogenously, the real exchange rate will only be constant if any discrepancy between home and world inflation is offset by a constant rate of change of the nominal exchange rate:

$$\frac{\Delta e}{e} = [\pi] - [\pi^*].$$

If home inflation is below world inflation, then the exchange rate must be constantly appreciating to keep the real exchange rate constant. Conversely, if home inflation is above world inflation, there will be a constant depreciation of home's exchange rate to keep the real exchange rate constant. This implies that the nominal exchange rate is endogenous in the medium run, just as it is in the short run under flexible exchange rates.

4.2 Summing up

In the open economy, there is a range of output and employment levels consistent with constant home inflation in the medium run. The economy can be at any point on the *ERU* curve with constant inflation equal to the growth rate of the home money supply—this is set by world inflation in the fixed exchange rate economy and by the home central bank in the flexible exchange rate economy. In Chapter 11, we shall take examples of shocks and policy changes and examine how the economy reacts both in the short and in the medium run. The key lesson from this section is that whatever the shock, the inflation rate in the medium run will return to its initial rate once adjustment is complete. The medium-run inflation rate only changes if there is a change in world inflation in a fixed exchange rate economy or a change in the inflation target (or money supply growth rate) in the flexible rate economy.

5 Long-run equilibrium

In the open economy, the economy is on an *AD* curve in the short run and on the *ERU* curve in the medium run. Experience suggests that economies can remain for considerable periods at a medium-run equilibrium on the *ERU* curve but with a current account imbalance. We look here at forces that might eventually lead the economy back to the long-run equilibrium on the *BT* curve.

A country at a position such as *A* in Fig. 10.10 is in medium-run equilibrium with constant inflation but has a current account surplus. As explained in Chapter 9, the counterpart to the current account surplus is a capital account deficit: country *A* is lending to the

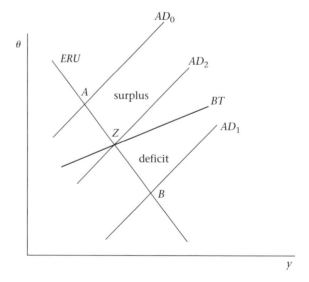

Figure 10.10 Long-run equilibrium in the open economy: on the *BT* and *ERU* curves

rest of the world at the world interest rate. It is acquiring foreign assets. The increase in the stock of foreign assets owned by the home country as it runs a trade surplus generates a stream of interest receipts to the home country that add to the current account surplus.

By contrast, the country at B has a trade deficit and is borrowing from abroad to finance this. Country B is therefore acquiring foreign liabilities: its foreign debt is rising every year that it runs a trade deficit. It must pay interest on the accumulated debt. This means that even if the trade deficit remains constant, the current account deficit worsens as interest payments mount up.

A number of questions arise. Since wealth is changing when the economy is at A or B, will the economy eventually shift to Z (i.e. why might the AD curve shift to AD_2)?

- Are there automatic forces in the economy that tend to push the economy to the long-run equilibrium at Z through the adjustment of aggregate demand?

- Are there market forces that exert pressure on the government to adjust macroeconomic policy so as to shift the economy to the long-run equilibrium?

- Are there political pressures from home or abroad on the government to adjust policy?

We first examine these three mechanisms that might push the economy toward the long-run equilibrium (where the ERU and BT curves intersect). At this stage, we assume that exchange rate expectations are stable—i.e. that they are not affected by the external position. In a second step, we look at how the economy may shift toward the long-run equilibrium as a consequence of the impact of the external position on exchange rate expectations.

5.1 Mechanisms with stable exchange rate expectations

5.1.1 Wealth effects

One automatic mechanism that might produce a shift to long-run equilibrium is the operation of wealth effects. As noted in Chapter 9, home consumers may incorporate the changes in national wealth into their consumption decisions. It is obvious that a country cannot run down its wealth indefinitely: far-sighted consumers in the deficit country, B, may take the view that the deficit does not reflect a programme of investment in the home economy that will bear fruit in the longer term. They may believe that belt tightening will eventually be required in the home economy to service and repay the foreign debt. As a result, they may adjust downward their estimate of permanent income and implement the associated cut in consumption spending. For a country such as country A with a trade surplus, the opposite considerations may lead to a rise in the assessment of permanent income and hence consumption may increase. To the extent that these reactions occur, the AD curve will shift toward the long-run equilibrium. These forces alone are unlikely to be powerful enough to guarantee long-run equilibrium.

5.1.2 Market pressure

Throughout the analysis of the open economy in this chapter, we have made the assumption of perfect international capital mobility. Countries can borrow indefinitely at the international interest rate. But a country with a persistent trade deficit faces a build-up of its foreign debt. As noted above, it is possible that the deficit arises from the country taking advantage of especially favourable investment opportunities at home by borrowing from abroad. If so, then the investments will eventually bear fruit and directly or indirectly improve the country's export base allowing it to move from trade deficit to trade surplus and repay its debt. Norway provides an illustration of this pattern: there were substantial current account deficits averaging nearly 5% of GDP from the mid-1970s and into the 1980s as the domestic oil industry was developed, which were followed by surpluses in the 1990s.

If the sentiment in international financial markets is that the trade deficit reflects high home consumption or wasteful investment, then funds will cease to be available to country *B* at the world interest rate. Private expenditure will tend to be dampened by the change in credit conditions. In addition, the government may implement a tightening of aggregate demand policy to reduce the trade deficit.

5.1.3 **Political pressure**

The economic pressures on deficit countries to adjust are typically stronger than those on surplus countries. If wealth effects on consumption are weak, then a country is able to run a trade surplus for a lengthy period of time. This suggests there may be an asymmetry between deficit countries like *B* and surplus countries like *A*. Unless the investment opportunities abroad are particularly profitable, the wisdom of running a persistent surplus is questionable. This may lead to political pressure from within the country for the government to boost activity and operate at a lower unemployment rate. Surplus countries can also come under political pressure at the international level to adjust their policies (e.g. the USA exerted pressure on the Japanese authorities during the 1980s).

5.2 **Unstable exchange rate expectations**

In the open economy model, we have assumed that the exchange rate remains at its expected level. But even under fixed exchange rates, a country with a persistent trade deficit may find it difficult to defend the exchange rate peg indefinitely. As discussed in Chapter 9, if private counterparties are not willing to purchase the home currency and finance the deficit, then the home country's central bank will have to sell foreign exchange reserves. There is a limit to the extent to which this is possible because foreign exchange reserves are limited and borrowing to supplement them may be difficult. Once exchange market operators begin to speculate on a devaluation, the central bank may be forced to combine interest rate rises to try to hold the exchange rate peg with intervention in the foreign exchange market. Eventually, the government may be forced to tighten fiscal policy to move the economy toward the long-run equilibrium. Policy combinations are examined in more detail in Chapter 11.

Under flexible exchange rates, the stability of a medium-run equilibrium is an open question. There is no consensus about the sustainability of a medium-run equilibrium because the process by which exchange rate expectations are formed is not well understood.

The aim of this section is to show that if we take a very different expectations hypothesis from the standard one in the basic model, then the results can change dramatically. For

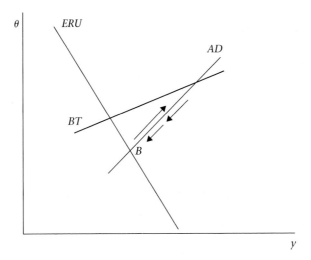

Figure 10.11 Medium-run equilibrium at B (trade deficit) is disturbed by an exchange rate depreciation

example, let us suppose that the exchange rate is expected to adjust immediately to deliver a real exchange rate consistent with trade balance, i.e.

$$e_t = e_t^E \text{ if and only if } BT = 0.$$

This implies that if there is a trade deficit, the exchange rate is expected to depreciate and if there is a trade surplus, the exchange rate is expected to appreciate.

In Fig. 10.11, the economy is at the medium-run equilibrium at point B with a trade deficit and constant inflation. The stability of this position depends on the assumption in the basic model that the expected exchange rate remains unchanged. Under the new balanced trade expectations hypothesis, this expected exchange rate is not sustainable in the long run. A depreciation of the exchange rate will be expected. The depreciation leads to a movement along the AD curve toward the north-east as price competitiveness improves.[6] But we know that when the economy is above the ERU curve, domestic inflationary pressures will emerge.

---

[6] To be precise, the economy will move in a north-easterly direction but to the left of the AD curve. The reason is that the expected depreciation of the real exchange rate implies that home's real interest rate must be above the world real interest rate. A higher real interest rate implies lower output than shown by the AD curve since the AD curve is drawn assuming $r = r^*$. The financial arbitrage condition with perfect capital mobility (UIP condition) is translated into real terms by substituting the definitions for the home and world real interest rates into the UIP condition and using the fact that

$$\left(\frac{\Delta\theta}{\theta}\right)^E = \left(\frac{\Delta P^*}{P^*}\right)^E + \left(\frac{\Delta e}{e}\right)^E - \left(\frac{\Delta P}{P}\right)^E.$$

This implies:

$$r - r^* = \left(\frac{\Delta\theta}{\theta}\right)^E$$

i.e. an expected depreciation of the real exchange rate implies that the home real interest rate is above the world real interest rate.

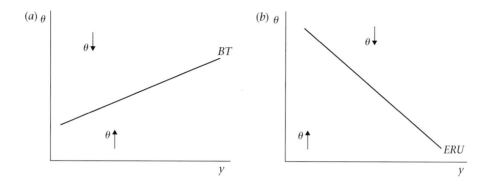

Figure 10.12 Interaction of foreign exchange market and labour market: unique constant inflation equilibrium if exchange rate expectations are oriented to trade balance
(a) Pressure on e and hence on θ
(b) Pressure on inflation and hence on θ

The two sources of inflationary pressure are easy to see: on the one hand, output and employment have increased, so the wage-setting real wage is higher and money wage increases will follow; on the other hand, the exchange rate depreciation has increased the real cost of imports and cut real wages. Money wages will increase in response to this too. Hence there will be a 'tug-of-war' going on as the economy is pulled toward the *BT* line by nominal exchange rate depreciation ($\theta \uparrow$) and pulled back toward the *ERU* curve ($\theta \downarrow$) by domestic wage and price inflation. The consequence will be rising inflation.

Figure 10.12 shows two panels. In the first one, the pressures emanating from the foreign exchange market that drive the economy toward balanced trade via nominal exchange rate depreciation or appreciation are shown. In the second one, the pressures emanating from the supply side through wage and price setting that drive the economy toward the *ERU* curve via wage and price inflation (above or below world inflation) are shown.

Under the 'balanced trade exchange rate expectations' hypothesis, the *BT* curve becomes the *full exchange market equilibrium condition*.

Under this condition, and assuming that inflation expectations are formed adaptively (i.e. $\pi^E = \pi_{-1}$) then on the *BT* curve, the nominal exchange rate will be changing to maintain the real exchange rate consistent with trade balance, given lagged inflation:

$$\frac{\Delta e}{e} = \pi_{-1} - \pi^*.$$

On the *ERU* curve, home inflation will be such that the real exchange rate is consistent with wage- and price-setting equilibrium, given the lagged change in the exchange rate:

$$\pi = \left(\frac{\Delta e}{e}\right)_{-1} + \pi^*.$$

The consequence is that between the *BT* and *ERU* curves there will be rising inflation (in zone III) and falling inflation (in zone IV) as shown in Fig. 10.13. By contrast, in zone II pressures from the foreign exchange market and from the labour market are both pushing

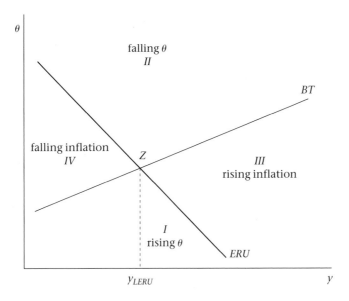

Figure 10.13 Unique constant inflation equilibrium if exchange rate expectations are oriented to trade balance

the real exchange rate in the same direction (falling price competitiveness) and in zone I (rising competitiveness). We can therefore conclude that the only stable position is where the *BT* curve intersects the *ERU* curve. Only at point *Z* in Fig. 10.13 are (i) exchange rate expectations consistent with balanced trade fulfilled and (ii) the inflation expectations of wage and price setters fulfilled. There is a unique long-run equilibrium rate of unemployment, *LERU*. The attempt by the authorities to maintain a level of activity higher than y_{LERU} will require an ever-increasing growth of the money supply to fuel the rising inflation. Ever-increasing inflation will eventually lead the government to implement a restrictive fiscal policy and shift the economy to the lower level of employment that is consistent with exchange rate expectations and with price- and wage-setting behaviour in the long run.

6 Conclusions

The open economy model set out in this chapter provides the tools for analysing a rich variety of disturbances to the economy from the demand and supply sides and coming from home and abroad. It enables us to diagnose the nature of the disturbances and to identify the role of economic policy in responding to them. This is the task of Chapter 11.

The key results of the open economy model are the following:

- There is a range of unemployment rates at which inflation is constant and at which the economy can remain in the medium run.
- There is an inverse relationship between the real exchange rate and the medium-run level of output and employment illustrated by the *ERU* curve.

- The range of medium-run equilibria is wider in a more open economy; in a completely closed economy, there is a unique constant inflation equilibrium.
- The range of medium-run equilibria is wider, the less responsive is the wage-setting real wage to changes in unemployment.
- At a medium-run equilibrium the rate of inflation is determined by world inflation in a fixed exchange rate economy and by home's monetary policy in a flexible exchange rate economy.
- Following a disturbance to a medium-run equilibrium, there will be upward or downward pressure on inflation depending on what has happened to employment and the real wage.
- Starting from a medium-run equilibrium, an expansionary fiscal policy leads to a new medium-run equilibrium at a higher level of output whereas an expansionary monetary policy or a devaluation leads only to a short-run rise in output. We shall return to this result in Chapter 11.
- In the long run, wealth effects or market pressures, including exchange rate instability, may push the economy toward the long-run equilibrium with current account balance.
- Any external or supply-side change that shifts the *BT* curve or the *ERU* curve leads to a change in the long-run sustainable unemployment rate.

In Chapter 11, we shall put the basic open economy model to work. We look at aggregate demand shocks and at the use of aggregate demand and exchange rate policies to respond to them. Demand shocks can be caused by changes in private sector behaviour in the home economy or they can come from abroad. We shall look at supply-side shocks (e.g. changes in the exercise of bargaining power by unions or changes in product market competition) and at supply-side policies (e.g. supply-side fiscal measures, labour and product market regulation). Foreign trade shocks and external supply shocks, such as oil or commodity price shocks, are also examined. In each case, the implications for the *AD* curve, the *ERU* curve, and the *BT* curve and hence for output, inflation, and the external balance are investigated.

■ QUESTIONS

Checklist questions

(1) Compare the adjustment to medium-run equilibrium after a fiscal contraction of a fixed and flexible exchange rate economy. What happens in the short run and during the adjustment to the medium run? Compare your results with the closed economy case.

(2) What is the difference between the wage-setting real wage curve in the open and closed economies; what is the difference between the price-setting real wage curve in the open and closed economies?

(3) Explain why there is a range of constant-inflation unemployment rates in an open economy. What determines how broad this range is? What effect do the following have on the slope of the *ERU* curve?

    (*a*) a change in tastes: domestic consumers now prefer more foreign goods;

    (*b*) new employment protection legislation makes real wages less sensitive to the level of unemployment;

    (*c*) the country relaxes restrictions on foreign trade.

(4) Assume that there are two identical small open economies except that in one of them, buoyant expectations have resulted in a higher level of consumption. Compare the economies in terms of employment, real wages, trade balance, and inflation.

(5) Compare the characteristics of the medium-run equilibrium (e.g. inflation rate) in an economy with fixed exchange rates before and after a rise in the world inflation rate. Do the same for flexible exchange rates, assuming that the world inflation rate and the domestic inflation rate were initially equal.

(6) Compare the impact on inflation of an increase in union militancy in a closed economy with that in a fixed exchange rate open economy. How do the medium-run equilibria compare?

(7) Is the response of real wages to a contractionary fiscal policy the same as to a contractionary monetary policy in a flexible exchange rate open economy? Explain.

(8) Why is the *AD* curve in the θy–diagram flatter in the presence of imperfect capital mobility? Why does it coincide with the *BT* curve when there is zero capital mobility?

(9) Under a floating exchange rate regime, suppose that the exchange rate is expected to adjust immediately to deliver a real exchange rate consistent with trade balance. Is there still a range of unemployment rates at which inflation is constant?

Problems and questions for discussion

QUESTION A. 'A fiscal expansion leads to a new medium-run equilibrium with higher output in an open economy but a monetary expansion does not.' Do you agree? Does your answer depend on the exchange rate regime?

QUESTION B. An economy with a fixed exchange rate is in a deep recession and has a substantial current account deficit. Would you advise devaluation?

QUESTION C. Identify the consequences in the medium run of a fall in the world interest rate under fixed and flexible exchange rates. Compare your results with those obtained using the Mundell–Fleming model (QUESTION C in Chapter 9).

QUESTION D. Begin with an economy at a medium-run equilibrium with a trade deficit. Assume that there is a flexible exchange rate regime and that exchange rate expectations are initially stable.

(1) Why is the current account deficit increasing?

(2) What may push the economy toward long-run equilibrium and why?

(3) Assume now that there is a change in the way expectations are formed in the foreign exchange market so that a trade deficit leads to the widespread expectation of depreciation. Why might the reasoning of forex market participants change in this way? What are the likely effects and how should the government respond?

■ APPENDIX: SKETCHING THE *ERU* CURVE

If we express the wage-setting real wage equation in terms of output and use a simple linear form, then

$$w^{WS} = \alpha y,$$

where α is a positive constant. The price-setting real wage is

$$w^{PS} = \frac{\lambda(1 - \mu)}{1 + \phi(\theta - 1)}.$$

In equilibrium, $w^{WS} = w^{PS}$. Hence if we substitute the equations for the wage- and price-setting real wage and rearrange to get the level of output on the left hand side, we have:

$$w^{WS} = w^{PS}$$
$$\alpha y = \frac{\lambda(1 - \mu)}{1 + \phi(\theta - 1)}$$
$$y = \frac{1}{\alpha} \frac{\lambda(1 - \mu)}{1 + \phi(\theta - 1)}, \qquad \text{(ERU curve)}$$

which is an equation for competing claims equilibrium in terms of y and θ.

The negative relation between θ and y that we have discussed in developing the *ERU* curve is clearly reflected in the equation. We can also see the role of the share of imports (ϕ) and of the sensitivity of real wages to output (or employment) in wage setting (α) in determining the shape of the *ERU* curve.

The easiest way to see these characteristics is to sketch the *ERU* curve. First, assume that $\theta = 0$. This gives an intercept on the y axis of

$$y = \frac{1}{\alpha} \frac{\lambda(1 - \mu)}{1 - \phi}.$$

Now consider what happens when θ becomes very large. As $\theta \to \infty$, the denominator of the equation for the *ERU* becomes very large and $y \to 0$. Hence the *ERU* curve is asymptotic to the vertical axis. Fig. 10.14 shows the *ERU* curve.

We examine what happens to the *ERU* curve as the import share changes. As we have already noted, if $\phi = 0, y = \frac{1}{\alpha}\lambda(1 - \mu)$ and this is simply the closed economy unique equilibrium output level (Fig. 10.15). We have also seen before that in the open economy if $\theta = 1$, the output level on the *ERU* curve will be at the closed economy equilibrium level: i.e. if $\theta = 1$,

$$y = \frac{1}{\alpha}\lambda(1 - \mu).$$

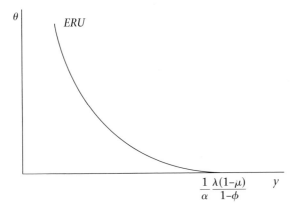

Figure 10.14 The *ERU* curve

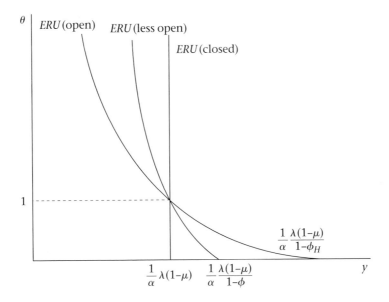

Figure 10.15 *ERU* curves in open, less open, and closed economies

This gives us a point on the open economy *ERU* curve. To find a second point, we look for the intercept with the y axis, i.e. when $\theta = 0$. If there is a low share of imports, ϕ, then at $\theta = 0$, $y = \frac{1}{\alpha} \frac{\lambda(1-\mu)}{1-\phi}$ which will be to the right of but quite close to $y = \frac{1}{\alpha}\lambda(1 - \mu)$ (see Fig. 10.15). Hence the *ERU* curve for an open economy that has only a small share of imports is steep.

If we now take the case of a very open economy with a high share of imports, ϕ, the point at which the *ERU* curve intersects the y axis will be much further to the right than in the previous case (see Fig. 10.15). And we know that at $\theta = 1$, the *ERU* curve will go through the same point as in the previous case: $y = \alpha\lambda(1 - \mu)$. The three contrasting cases are shown in Fig. 10.15.

We have already discussed the intuition behind the effect of an increased sensitivity of the wage-setting real wage to employment in steepening the *ERU* curve. To see this diagramatically, it is easy to

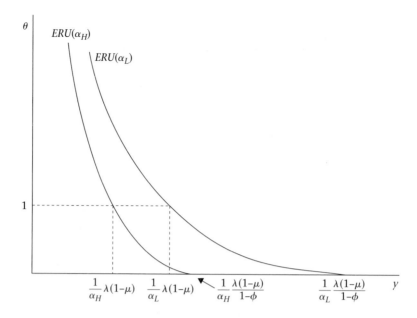

Figure 10.16 *ERU* curves reflect the sensitivity of real wages to employment

see that an increase in α from α_L to α_H shifts to the left the intercept with the y axis: $y = \frac{1}{\alpha} \frac{\lambda(1-\mu)}{1-\phi}$. We now look at what happens when $\theta = 1$. With α_L, the output level on the *ERU* curve is $y = \frac{1}{\alpha_L}\lambda(1 - \mu)$. With a highly employment-sensitive *WS* curve, $y = \frac{1}{\alpha_H}\lambda(1 - \mu)$. Because $\frac{1}{1-\phi} > 1$, the leftward shift of the *ERU* curve in the case of the high level of α is greater when $\theta = 0$ than when $\theta = 1$. Hence, a higher level of α means a steeper *ERU* curve (see Fig. 10.16).

11 Shocks and Policy Responses in the Open Economy

In this chapter, the open economy model developed in Chapters 9 and 10 is put to work to examine government policy instruments and to analyse shocks that may disturb the economy. The term 'shocks' is used to describe a disturbance to the economy that is unanticipated. Firms and households are likely to be forward looking and, at least to some extent, are able to incorporate anticipated changes in their economic environment into their behaviour. It is the different kinds of unanticipated changes in the economic environment on which we focus in this chapter. We use the model to analyse

- aggregate demand shocks,
- supply shocks, and
- external shocks.

In each case, it is necessary to diagnose the implications of the disturbance for the private sector and for policy makers—does it shift the *AD* curve, is it a shift along the *AD* curve, does it shift the *BT* curve or the *ERU* curve? Some shocks are relatively simple to analyse in the sense that they have an impact on only one of the three relationships in the model. Others are more complex—for example, shifting more than one relationship.

The importance of the correct diagnosis of the type of shock is demonstrated by the experience of the advanced countries in the 1970s. In 1973 and again in 1979, the world price of oil increased sharply. The immediate consequence of the first oil shock was a fall in aggregate demand in the oil-importing OECD countries. Policy makers responded by treating it as an aggregate demand shock—one that shifted the aggregate demand curve to the left. Yet the attempt to offset the impact of the shock on employment through fiscal expansion and loosening monetary policy was accompanied by rapid deterioration in the trade balance and rising inflation. A number of European countries experienced inflation rates rising well into double digits at a time of rising unemployment. The second oil shock in 1979 was met by quite a different policy response. By then it was clearer to policy makers that the rise in the price of oil was an external *supply* shock, which had the effect of shifting the *AD*, *BT*, and *ERU* curves in an adverse direction.

This chapter begins with an introductory section that looks at fiscal, monetary, and supply-side policy in the open economy. This ties together the Mundell–Fleming analysis (from Chapter 9) with the medium- and long-run analysis in Chapter 10. This is followed by an examination of four different kinds of shocks: domestic aggregate demand shocks, domestic supply shocks, foreign trade shocks, and external supply shocks. In each case, we ask what the implication of such a shock is for the short-run, the medium-run, and the long-run equilibrium. This helps us to analyse what would happen after each kind of shock if the government did not react to it at all. We can then ask whether there are appropriate tools available to the government with which to offset such a shock or to mitigate its effects on the economy. Section 5 brings together the implications of fluctuations in aggregate demand and of supply-side policy measures for the behaviour of real wages. Section 6 applies the lessons of the chapter to the analysis of how a currency union operates and the advantages and disadvantages of membership. In the final section, section 7, we show how to interpret a monetary policy reaction function in the open economy and how the way the economy adjusts to a demand shock differs under an inflation-targeting regime from a regime of floating exchange rates with a constant growth rate of the money supply.

1 Fiscal, monetary, exchange rate, and supply-side policies

The open economy model is very useful for analysing the impact on the economy of policy changes at home and abroad as well as the impact of shifts in private sector behaviour. The key components of the model set out in Chapter 10 are:

- the AD curve. This shows the combinations of the real exchange rate θ and level of output y at which the goods market is in equilibrium and the real interest rate is equal to the world real interest rate.

- the ERU curve. This is defined as the combinations of the real exchange rate and output at which the wage-setting real wage is equal to the price-setting real wage. At any point on the ERU curve, inflation is constant.

- the BT curve. This shows the combinations of the real exchange rate θ and the level of output y at which trade is balanced: $x = m$.

1.1 Timing assumptions

This is an appropriate point at which to spell out the assumptions that are being made about the speed of adjustment of different macroeconomic variables in the open economy.

- **The short run.** In the short run, the goods market equilibrium is established and arbitrage in financial markets ensures that the home real interest rate is equal to the world real interest rate. In the short run, we observe changes in the nominal interest rate, the nominal exchange rate, output, and employment.[1] The end of the short-run adjustment is marked by the attainment of the short-run equilibrium on the AD curve. In the short run, it is assumed that wage and price setters do not change wages or prices.

---

[1] By virtue of any change in the exchange rate, the consumer price index changes. Although this will influence the short-run equilibrium in the money market, this effect is normally ignored.

- **The medium run.** The medium run begins when wage and price setters start to respond to two things:

(a) to any change in the level of activity (output, employment) in the economy that has occurred in the short run and

(b) to any change in the real wage that has been brought about by a change in the nominal (and hence the real) exchange rate in the short run.

- Wage setting is assumed to happen periodically and price setters are assumed to adjust their prices rapidly in the wake of wage changes. This means that the actual real wage in the economy is always equal to the price-setting real wage.[2] The end of the medium run is marked by the attainment of the medium-run equilibrium with the economy at the intersection of the *AD* curve and the *ERU* curve, and hence with constant inflation.

- **The long run.** In the long run, the presence of a current account surplus or deficit may produce shifts in the *AD* curve (as consumers react to the changes in wealth implied, or the government adjusts fiscal policy in response to market or political pressures). The presence of a persistent surplus or deficit may lead to a change in the way exchange rate expectations are formed, with the consequence that there is constant inflation only at the intersection of the *ERU* and *BT* curves as discussed in Chapter 10. This in turn may lead the government to adjust fiscal policy to shift the economy to the long-run equilibrium.

In this section, we concentrate on three key results from the open economy model:

- a change in *fiscal* policy *shifts* the aggregate demand curve, which implies there is a new medium-run equilibrium for the economy at a different level of output and real exchange rate. In the absence of government intervention, the economy moves from the new short-run equilibrium to the new constant-inflation rate of unemployment. Since the short-run equilibrium is different under fixed and flexible exchange rates, the adjustment path to the new medium-run equilibrium differs under fixed and flexible exchange rates. In particular, the impact on inflation—whether there is a temporary rise or a temporary fall in inflation—depends on the exchange rate regime.

- a change in *monetary* policy under flexible exchange rates or a change in the *exchange rate peg* in a 'fixed' exchange rate system is a shift *along* the aggregate demand curve and therefore does not lead to a new medium-run equilibrium. The levels of output and unemployment change only in the short run. A temporary rise in inflation in the case of a devaluation/expansionary monetary policy or a temporary fall in inflation in the case of a revaluation/contractionary monetary policy leads the economy back to the original medium-run equilibrium.

- a change in *supply-side* policy is a shift in the *ERU* curve (under both fixed and flexible exchange rates). This changes both the medium and the long-run equilibrium.

---

[2] This is obviously a simplification—if price setting is sluggish in the wake of cost increases, then the real wage will lie between the wage-setting real wage and the price-setting real wage (i.e. between the *WS* curve and the *PS* curve).

We are not concerned here with why the government might want to use fiscal or monetary/exchange rate policy or supply-side policy—we come to that when we look at the different kinds of shocks that may affect the economy. For now, the aim is simply to pin down the effects of different policies. This is easiest to understand if we begin in full equilibrium at the intersection of the *AD*, *BT*, and *ERU* curves. Our standard assumption is that world inflation is constant and that under fixed exchange rates home sets the inflation rate in the medium-run equilibrium at a rate equal to world inflation.

1.2 Fiscal policy

We focus first on the implications for aggregate demand of a change in fiscal policy: we examine the supply-side aspects of some kinds of fiscal policy later on when we look at supply-side policy. Suppose the economy is at point *A* at full equilibrium in Fig. 11.1. The government undertakes an expansionary fiscal policy. The aggregate demand curve then shifts to the right. (A fiscal contraction will produce an exactly symmetrical set of results.)

1.2.1 New medium-run equilibrium

A fiscal expansion implies a rightward shift of the *AD* curve. This leads to a new medium-run equilibrium at point *B*. At the new medium-run equilibrium,

- output is higher and unemployment lower,
- θ is lower (i.e. a real appreciation), and the real wage is higher,
- there is a trade deficit, and
- inflation is constant.

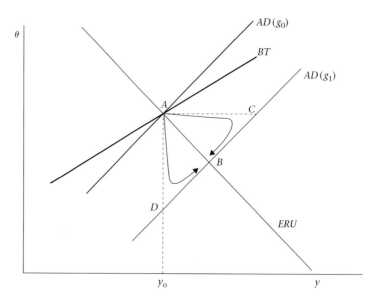

Figure 11.1 Fiscal policy shifts the *AD* curve: new medium-run equilibrium at *B* and comparison with Mundell–Fleming predictions

This example was discussed at the beginning of Chapter 10, where we used the labour market diagram to discuss the implications of a fiscal expansion. The adjustment path from A to B depends on the exchange rate regime.

1.2.2 Under fixed exchange rates

As we saw in Chapter 10, under fixed exchange rates, output in the economy expands with the real exchange rate constant. In the Mundell–Fleming model expansionary fiscal policy has the full multiplier effect on output because in the new short-run equilibrium, the interest rate remains unchanged at the world rate. In Fig. 11.1, this is the move from A to C. But in the medium run, after output and employment in the economy have expanded, wages and prices will begin to respond. At a position above the *ERU* curve (see Fig. 11.1), the existing real wage lies *below* the wage-setting real wage at the new higher level of activity (see Fig. 10.2). The reason is that the *WS* curve is upward sloping: as employment rises, so does the real wage that wage setters can expect when money wages are set. As a consequence, at the next occasion on which wages are set, wages rise relative to expected inflation. From the pricing equation ($P = \frac{1}{1-\mu} \cdot \frac{W}{\lambda}$), we know that when money wages rise, prices will be put up by home firms in proportion to the labour cost increase in order to keep the mark-up, μ, constant. Two things follow from this.

- First, from the definition of the consumer price index ($P_c = (1 - \phi)P + \phi P^* e$), it follows that consumer prices rise in the wake of the home price rise. However, the consumer price index will not rise by as much as does the price level of home produced output because nothing has happened to the rate of inflation for imported goods. This implies that the real wage, (W/P_c), has increased.

- Second, because home inflation has risen and nothing has happened to world inflation, price competitiveness $\left(\theta = \frac{P^* e}{P}\right)$ has fallen. Another way of looking at this is that, in terms of the goods that the home economy exports, imports have become cheaper, i.e. the *real* cost of imports has declined.

The economy therefore moves in a south-westerly direction down the $AD(g_1)$ curve. This is the mirror image of the north-westerly movement in the labour market diagram in Fig. 10.2. The home economy experiences a temporary rise in inflation relative to world inflation. Once the economy is at point B, real wages, the real exchange rate and inflation are constant. An example is provided in the appendix to this chapter to show in detail using Phillips curves how inflation changes as the economy moves from one medium-run equilibrium with constant inflation to another one following an expansionary fiscal policy. The time paths of real wages and inflation are sketched in Fig. 11.2. The policy change occurs at time t_0 after which follows the short-run adjustment: nothing happens to inflation or real wages. Time t_1 marks the beginning of the medium-run period during which wages and prices respond. Time t_2 marks the end of the medium-run adjustment—i.e. the attainment of a new medium-run equilibrium.

1.2.3 Under flexible exchange rates

In the Mundell–Fleming model, the increase in output stimulated by a fiscal expansion is wiped out in the short run by the exchange rate appreciation induced by the fact

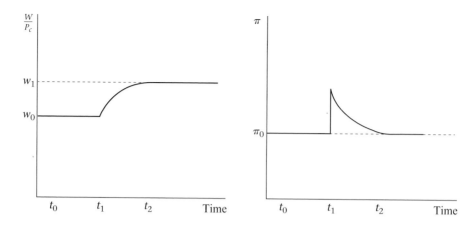

Figure 11.2 Adjustment of real wages and inflation: fiscal expansion under fixed exchange rates

that the home nominal interest rate is temporarily higher than the world rate. In the medium run, however, there is higher output at the new equilibrium. As we saw in Chapter 10, the initial nominal exchange rate appreciation to point D (the Mundell–Fleming short-run equilibrium) in Fig. 11.1 implies that price competitiveness has fallen and real wages have risen. Real wages have risen because the nominal appreciation cuts the price (in domestic currency terms) of imported final goods in the consumption bundle (i.e. $\downarrow e \Rightarrow \downarrow P_c \Rightarrow \uparrow \frac{W}{P_c}$). The upward jump in the real wage is shown at time t_0—i.e. it happens in the short run. In the medium run, wage setters will react to this. With real wages at y_0 *above* the level associated with wage-setting equilibrium, money wages will fall relative to the expected price level (refer back to Fig. 10.3). Since this reduces labour costs for firms, home prices are reduced by price setters in line with the fall in nominal wages. Nothing has happened to world inflation so the consumer price index falls by less than the fall in the price level of home goods. The consequence is that real wages do fall. Since home inflation has fallen below world inflation, price competitiveness rises (the real exchange rate depreciates). The improvement in competitiveness boosts net exports and the economy moves in a north-easterly direction along the $AD(g_1)$ curve toward the new medium-run equilibrium at Z (this mirrors the south-easterly move from point D in Fig. 10.3). The home economy experiences a temporary fall in inflation relative to world inflation. The fall in real wages and drop in inflation from the beginning of the medium run (from t_1) are shown in Fig.11.3. Once adjustment is complete (at time t_2), the real wage is higher than initially and inflation is back at its initial level.

1.2.4 Summing up

Following an expansionary fiscal policy,

- under fixed exchange rates, adjustment to the new medium-run equilibrium is via rising output and a temporary increase in inflation (relative to world inflation), which weakens competitiveness and dampens the expansion.

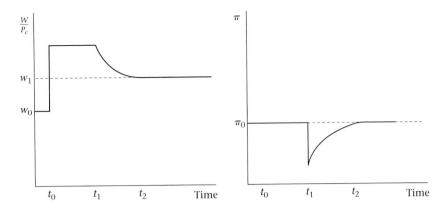

Figure 11.3 Adjustment of real wages and inflation: fiscal expansion under flexible exchange rates

- under flexible rates, adjustment is via an initial exchange rate appreciation that offsets the effect of the expansionary fiscal policy on output. This is followed by a temporary fall in inflation (relative to world inflation), which boosts competitiveness and raises output.

1.3 Monetary and exchange rate policy

In a flexible exchange rate economy with perfect capital mobility, monetary policy works through its effects on the nominal exchange rate. As we saw in Chapter 9, a change in monetary policy alters the home interest rate relative to the world interest rate and this leads to a change in the nominal exchange rate. In the new short-run equilibrium, the nominal interest rate is once more equal to the world interest rate and there is a different level of the nominal exchange rate.

We can recall from Chapter 9 that in a fixed exchange rate regime monetary policy is ineffectual even in the short run. The requirement to keep the nominal exchange rate fixed means that any change in domestic monetary policy is wiped out by offsetting changes in the monetary base before it gets off the ground. Therefore the analogue to monetary policy in a fixed exchange rate regime is the possibility that the exchange rate peg can be changed. A devaluation mimics an expansionary monetary policy: the right-ward shift in the *ISXM* raises the domestic interest rate and induces a capital inflow, which shifts the *LM* to the right. Similarly, a revaluation mimics a contractionary monetary policy by inducing a capital outflow.

We now look more closely at the short- and medium-run consequences of changes in monetary policy (under flexible exchange rates) and a one-off change in the exchange rate peg under fixed exchange rates. Under flexible exchange rates, monetary policy is very effective in raising output in the Mundell–Fleming model. Monetary expansion has a strong impact because of the boost to aggregate demand due to the exchange rate depreciation induced by the temporary fall in the interest rate below the world rate. If we turn to the medium run, then we know that a change in monetary policy under flexible exchange rates cannot shift the medium-run equilibrium: in Fig.11.4 the *AD* curve and

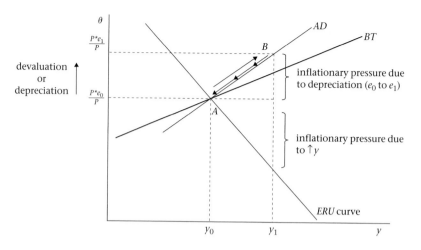

Figure 11.4 Monetary/exchange rate policy is a shift along the *AD* curve: medium-run equilibrium remains unchanged at *A*

the *ERU* curve remain fixed so the medium-run equilibrium remains at point *A*. Exactly the same analysis applies in the case in which there is a discrete change in the exchange rate under a 'fixed' rate system (from e_0 to e_1—see Fig. 11.4).

Following a loosening of domestic monetary policy or a nominal devaluation, net exports and output expand to y_1: the short-run Mundell–Fleming equilibrium is at point *B*. However, in the medium run, with the economy at point *B*, we must consider the implications for the supply side of the economy. The real depreciation of the exchange rate implies a lower real wage. This is because the rise in the price of imports, i.e. $P_m (= P^*e)$, due to the exchange rate depreciation from e_0 to e_1, implies a deterioration in the terms of trade for the home economy. Since the price of exports has not changed, a rise in the price of imports turns the terms of trade against the home economy. This cuts real wages because workers consume both imported and home produced goods. The higher price of imports feeds directly into the consumer price index and cuts the real wage.

In the medium run, wage setters will react to the *rise* in employment and the *fall* in the real wage. Since output has increased in the short run from y_0 to y_1, there are two sources of pressure pushing money wages up: the fall in unemployment means a higher wage-setting real wage and the depreciation means that the actual real wage has fallen. The result will be a rise in money wages relative to expected prices followed by an increase in the prices of home produced goods relative to world prices. After the initial depreciation, the nominal exchange rate remains fixed so that there are no further changes in import prices. As a consequence, the consumer price index rises by less than money wages: real wages rise and price competitiveness falls. This pattern is familiar: the economy is *above* the *ERU* curve and, as we have seen before, this results in a temporary burst of inflation (above world inflation) until the real wage has risen to a level equal to the wage-setting real wage. The rise in home relative to world inflation eats away at the initial rise in competitiveness due to the depreciation/devaluation and the economy moves back to point *A* (see Fig. 11.4).

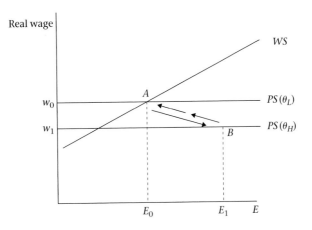

Figure 11.5 Monetary policy expansion under flexible exchange rates: inflation erodes short-run effect on employment

Table 11.1 Monetary expansion under flexible exchange rates

1st New short-run equil. at B	$\downarrow i \longrightarrow \uparrow e \rightarrow \uparrow \theta \rightarrow \uparrow (x-m) \Longrightarrow$
	$\Delta E > 0$ and $\Delta w < 0$
2nd W and P adjust to change in E & w	$\uparrow E$ and $\downarrow w \longrightarrow \uparrow W \rightarrow \uparrow P$ rel. to $P^* \rightarrow \downarrow \theta \rightarrow \downarrow y \rightarrow \downarrow E$
3rd Medium-run equil. at A	π, w, θ, E back to initial levels

It is a good idea to see how the adjustment process is represented in the labour market diagram. This is shown in Fig. 11.5 and the steps are summarized in Table 11.1.

Why does the economy end up back at its initial level of employment? Monetary policy raised output because it caused a real depreciation of the exchange rate and raised net exports and therefore aggregate demand. But a real depreciation cuts real wages and we know that the labour market is only in equilibrium at the initial level of employment (E_0) when the real wage is w_0. Therefore a burst of domestic wage and price inflation above world inflation will drive the economy back to its initial position at A. Monetary policy has only a short-run impact on output and employment in the open economy: there is a burst of inflation above world inflation and above the inflation target. In the new medium-run equilibrium, inflation is once again equal to its initial level. The time paths of the real wage and inflation are shown in Fig. 11.6 .

1.3.1 Summing up

Following an expansionary monetary policy or a devaluation, output and employment expand due to the effect of the rise in competitiveness on net exports. But this is only a temporary effect: since the devaluation has its effect by raising the real cost of imports, once wages and prices respond to this, there will be a bout of domestic wage and price inflation in excess of world inflation. The higher inflation will reverse the boost to competitiveness and the cut in real wages and the economy will return to its original position.

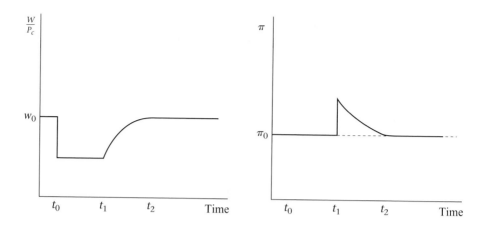

Figure 11.6 Adjustment of real wages and inflation: looser monetary policy under flexible exchange rates, or devaluation

1.4 Supply-side policy

To analyse supply-side policies, we have to focus our attention on the *ERU* curve. Supply-side policies are those that shift the *ERU* curve—either by shifting the wage-setting curve (*WS*) or by shifting the price-setting curve (*PS*(θ)). In Chapters 2 and 4 the determinants of the wage- and price-setting curves were introduced. Here we apply that discussion to the open economy.

It is useful to separate out the factors that shift the *WS* curve from those that shift the *PS*(θ) curve. We can recall from Chapter 4 that when we introduce taxes into the supply side of the model, it is necessary to be careful in defining both the money wage and the price level. We stick to the principle that the real wage shown on the vertical axis of the *WS–PS* diagram is the real wage relevant to wage setters. This is the real consumption wage defined as the 'take home' wage deflated by the consumer price index:

$$w = \frac{W}{P_c} = \frac{\text{wage net of income tax and social security}}{\text{consumer price index including VAT}}. \qquad \text{(real consumption wage)}$$

1.4.1 Policies that shift the wage-setting curve

The wage-setting curve shows the real take home wage at each level of employment that workers believe they have negotiated. As discussed in Chapter 2, the wage-setting curve lies above the competitive labour supply curve either because of the presence of unions or because of efficiency wage considerations. At each level of employment, wage setters set the money wage to secure this real wage, assuming that a specific price level will prevail over the course of the wage contract.

$$W = P_c^E \cdot b(E). \qquad \text{(wage equation)}$$

The wage-setting curve is therefore:

$$w^{WS} = \frac{W}{P_c^E} = b(E). \qquad \text{(wage-setting real wage)}$$

Any policy that affects the wage-setting decision will shift the *WS* curve. Policies discussed in Chapter 4 include changes in the worker's outside option such as changes in unemployment benefit, labour legislation, or the negotiation by the government of a wages accord with unions and employers' associations.

The *WS* curve shifts down

- if there is a fall in unemployment benefits (or more precisely in the replacement ratio, which is the ratio of benefits to the average wage),
- if unions are given less legal protection or become weaker as union density or coverage declines,
- if unions agree to exercise bargaining restraint—in the context, for example, of a wages accord.

1.4.2 Policies that shift the price-setting curve for a given real exchange rate

We turn now to the policies that shift the $PS(\theta)$ curve. The price-setting curve shows the outcome for real consumption wages of the decisions of the price setters in the economy. Price setters set their prices in order to secure the mark-up μ, given the unit labour costs that they face. We saw in the closed economy that the price-setting curve will shift up if there is a

- reduction in the tax wedge
- reduction in the mark-up, due, for example, to a change in competitive conditions
- fall in the real interest rate
- rise in efficiency, such as a change in the level or the trend of labour productivity growth. Note that this is likely to be incorporated eventually into workers' beliefs—in which case, the *WS* curve will shift as well (see the discussion in Chapter 4).

In the open economy, the $PS(\theta)$ curve shifts up—showing that real take home wages in the economy consistent with price-setting behaviour are higher—in response to any of these changes. We also know that in the open economy, the price-setting curve shifts as a consequence of changes in the real exchange rate. Since the *ERU* curve is drawn in real exchange rate—output space, although a change in θ shifts the price-setting curve, it does not shift the *ERU* curve. If the price-setting curve shifts for *any other reason*, this implies a shift in the *ERU* curve.

Looking at each of these factors in turn, in the open economy, changes in the pressure of product market competition can arise from trade liberalization policies. A good example for European countries is the reduction of tariff barriers to trade between members of the European Economic Community, which began in 1957 with the Treaty of Rome. This was followed in the late 1980s with an initiative to remove non-tariff barriers to trade so as to increase product market competition in the internal market of the European Union. There is some evidence to suggest that monopoly power has fallen in the EU following the so-called '1992' Single Market measures.[3] An increase in product market competition is likely not only to shift the *PS* curve upwards but also shift the *WS* curve downwards.

---

[3] See, for example, Allen, Gasiorek, and Smith (1998).

More pressure in the product market has the effect of dampening union bargaining power. However, since both of these effects (an upward shift in the $PS(\theta)$ curve and a downward shift in the WS curve) shift the ERU curve in the same direction, we simplify here by considering competition effects under 'price setting' only.

The analysis of taxes is very similar to that in the closed economy. The only extra consideration is the tax treatment of exports and imports. Exports are exempt from value added tax. The logic of this arrangement is that indirect taxes should be 'destination based' in order that cross-country differences in tax rates do not distort competition in the domestic market for final goods. This principle means that imports attract the VAT rate of the importing country. In the derivation of the price-setting real wage that is set out in detail in the appendix to this chapter, these factors are taken into account.

The impact of a change in productivity (or in the rate of productivity growth in a dynamic context) on equilibrium employment depends on its effects on the wage-setting and price-setting curves. If we abstract from productivity growth, and examine the impact of a policy that raises the level of productivity, the most obvious effect is to shift the price-setting real wage upward.[4] More output per head is available for real wages at each level of employment. Education and training policies may have the effect of raising efficiency.

By recalling the derivation of the ERU curve (Chapter 10, section 1), it is clear that any policy that shifts the wage-setting curve or shifts the $PS(\theta)$ curve implies a shift in the ERU curve. A downward shift in the WS curve implies *ceteris paribus* a rightward shift in the ERU curve. An upward shift in the $PS(\theta)$ curve implies *ceteris paribus* a rightward shift in the ERU curve. We take an example of a supply-side policy that shifts the WS curve and another that shifts the $PS(\theta)$ curve.

1.4.3 Example: wage accord

In Fig. 11.7, the WS curve shifts down. This could be for any of the reasons listed above. In this example, we assume that it shifts because of the negotiation of a wages accord by the government. The conclusion of an agreement through which unions agree to exercise bargaining restraint implies a rightward shift in the ERU curve, as explained above.

What are the implications for the economy? Consider an initial position of medium-run equilibrium. Then shift the WS curve down. This reflects the fact that at the existing employment level, wage setters will set a lower nominal wage to secure the lower expected real wage. At an unchanged level of the real exchange rate (i.e. an unchanged real cost of imports) and with a given profit margin, this implies that lower unemployment will be compatible with medium-run equilibrium. At lower unemployment the wage claims of wage setters will be boosted sufficiently so as to restore equality between the price-setting real wage (given θ and μ) and the wage-setting real wage. The shift in the wage-setting curve from WS to WS' implies a shift in the ERU curve to ERU' (see Fig. 11.7). To derive the new ERU curve from the WS/PS diagram, note that at point A with $\theta = \theta_0$, $WS = PS(\theta_0)$ at an employment level of E_0. This is reflected in a point on ERU of (y_0, θ_0). We can also

---

[4] Higher productivity may also have the effect of shifting the wage-setting curve upwards—in which case, there would be no effect on equilibrium unemployment. This certainly seems a sensible assumption for the long run. In the short to medium run, however, wage claims may not adjust rapidly to unexpected shifts in productivity.

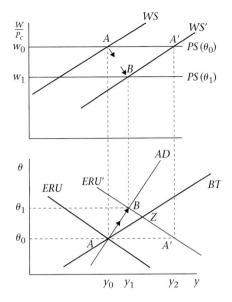

Figure 11.7 Supply-side policy: *WS* shifts down. Step 1 Derive the new *ERU* curve. Step 2. Examine adjustment to the new medium-run equilibrium at *B*

see that $WS' = PS(\theta_0)$ at employment level E_2, i.e. at point A'. This is reflected in a point on ERU' of (y_2, θ_0).

Nothing happens in the short run because wages and prices are assumed to be given. The new medium-run equilibrium for the economy is at point B with lower unemployment and higher price competitiveness. The economy adjusts gradually from A to B in the following way: at A following the shift in the WS curve, the existing real wage, w_0, is above the new wage-setting real wage on the WS' curve. Money wages fall, home prices fall in line—but because nothing has happened to the prices of imported goods, the consumer price index falls by less than does the price of home output. Hence, the real wage falls and because domestic prices have fallen relative to world prices, price competitiveness rises. The rise in θ boosts net export demand and the economy moves along the AD curve in a north-easterly direction from A toward B. In the top panel of Fig. 11.7, the $PS(\theta)$ curve shifts down as θ rises: the economy moves from A to B. We observe falling real wages and rising employment in the economy on the path to the new medium-run equilibrium. There is a trade surplus at the new equilibrium.

The implication of the downward shift in the WS curve for the long run is that the economy's long-run equilibrium is at lower unemployment and a higher level of price competitiveness (see point Z in Fig. 11.7). The adjustment of inflation and real wages over time to the new medium-run equilibrium is shown in Fig. 11.8.

1.4.4 Example: supply-side fiscal policy—cut in income tax

What is the consequence of a supply-side policy that shifts the *ERU* curve through its effects on the $PS(\theta)$ curve? In Fig. 11.9, the *ERU* curve shifts to the right as a consequence of a fall in tax rates. To show this, begin at point A in each panel. In the WS/PS diagram, at the initial equilibrium, we are on the $PS(\theta_0, t_0)$. This is reflected in the point (y_0, θ_0) on the *ERU* curve. Now there is a fall in the tax rate to t_1. This has the effect of shifting

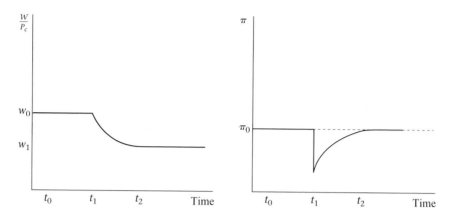

Figure 11.8 Adjustment of real wages and inflation: wage accord

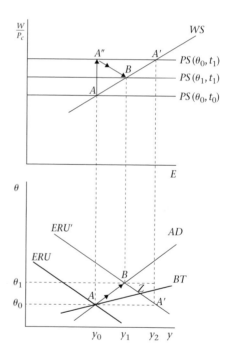

Figure 11.9 Supply-side policy. Tax cut means $PS(\theta)$ shifts up. Step 1 Derive the new ERU curve. Step 2 Examine adjustment to the new medium-run equilibrium at B

the $PS(\theta)$ curve up to $PS(\theta_0, t_1)$, which intersects the WS curve at point A'. This is in turn reflected in the point (y_2, θ_0) which defines the new ERU' curve (point A').

In order to focus entirely on the supply-side implications of the tax fall, we assume that the impact on aggregate demand of the tax cut is fully offset by an appropriate decrease in government spending. Hence, the AD curve remains fixed. The new medium-run equilibrium is at point B with lower unemployment and higher price competitiveness. The new long-run equilibrium is at point Z at lower unemployment. In the new medium-run equilibrium, real profits are unchanged but both real wages and real import costs are higher—real taxes per worker are lower.

The economy adjusts to the new medium-run equilibrium as follows. The economy begins at point A on the $PS(\theta_0, t_0)$ curve. The cut in tax rates (e.g. income tax) raises the real consumption wage. This is shown by point A'' on the new $PS(\theta_0, t_1)$ curve. Note that nothing has happened to the real exchange rate—the upward shift in the $PS(\theta)$ curve is entirely due to the cut in the tax rate. The real wage is above the wage-setting real wage (compare A'' with A) and the economy is *below* the ERU' curve. Given the expected price level, this leads to a fall in money wages when wages are next set. Lower money wages reduces unit labour costs and firms lower their prices in line. There is no change in import costs so the consumer price level falls by less than the price of home goods. Hence real wages begin to fall. Price competitiveness rises. The economy moves along the path from A'' to point B in the $WS-PS$ diagram; and from point A to point B in the θy-diagram.

The message from this example is that tax changes can be used as a supply-side measure. Moreover, when they are introduced into the economy for other reasons, the impact on the supply side should be taken into account.

2 Aggregate demand shocks

A shift in autonomous consumption or investment or a change in the world interest rate or in world trade leads to a shift of the AD curve. In this section, we look at such pure shifts in the AD curve.[5] Changes in world trade also shift the AD curve, but they shift the BT curve as well and such external trade shocks are analysed below. In the analysis of fiscal policy we have looked in some detail at how the economy adjusts in the short- and medium-run to a shift in the AD curve. It is not necessary to repeat that analysis here. We can summarize the results as follows. We use the example of a negative aggregate demand shock, i.e. a fall in autonomous consumption or investment (see Fig. 11.10).[6]

Under *flexible exchange rates*, a negative aggregate demand shock

- leads in the *short run* to an exchange rate depreciation. Output stays unchanged in the short run (point D). This happens because the effect on output of the fall in aggregate demand is completely offset by the depreciation induced by the fall in the interest rate.

- Because the depreciation cuts real wages, this is followed by a phase in which domestic inflation is higher than world inflation, which worsens competitiveness and leads to a fall in output (the economy moves to point B).

Under *fixed exchange rates*, a negative aggregate demand shock

- leads in the *short run* to a fall in output (point C).

- The fall in output is followed by a phase in which domestic inflation is below world inflation (the economy moves to point B).

---

[5] Under flexible exchange rates, a change in the world interest rate also leads, in the short run, to a shift along the new AD curve. The simplest way to see this is to run through the Mundell–Fleming analysis (as in Chapter 9) for this case.

[6] Note that a monetary shock such as a shift in the demand for money function that shifts the LM entails a move along the AD curve.

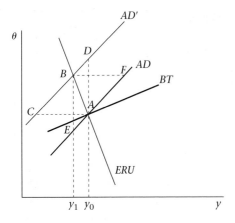

Figure 11.10 Negative aggregate demand shock

Under both flexible and fixed exchange rates, the new medium-run equilibrium is the same (*B*). Output and employment are lower, price competitiveness is higher and the real wage is lower, and there is an improvement in the trade balance. Inflation is constant at its original level.

If there is no policy intervention, then the economy will adjust first to the short-run equilibrium. If there is still no policy intervention, then over time, the economy will move to the new medium-run equilibrium. The question that arises is how the government can respond to a shock of this kind.

In the *closed* economy, the focus of attention in the wake of an aggregate demand shock is the speed with which the automatic mechanisms will push the economy back to the unique equilibrium unemployment rate. In the event of a negative demand shock, the government may intervene with expansionary fiscal policy or it may loosen monetary policy by cutting the interest rate so as to speed up the return of the economy to the equilibrium unemployment rate. The rationale for intervention is to minimize the costs associated with unemployment above the equilibrium rate. Slow adjustment and therefore high costs would occur if the downward adjustment of wages and prices is very slow. This would be exacerbated if, for example, there is a weak interest rate response to the rise in real money balances or if the response of investment to a fall in the interest rate is weak.

In the *open* economy, the situation is different because an aggregate demand shock leads to a new medium-run constant inflation equilibrium. Remember that in the open economy, the unique equilibrium unemployment rate has been replaced by the downward-sloping *ERU* curve. Following a shift in the *AD* curve, the economy can remain at point *B* in the case of a negative demand shock (see the left panel of Fig. 11.10). There are no automatic forces in the medium run leading to a shift back to the initial equilibrium. The government may be reluctant to wait for the possible impact of wealth effects on consumption to kick in in the long run and push the economy back to the long-run equilibrium or for the aggregate demand shock to be reversed in another way. In the meantime, the economy suffers the costs of lower output and higher unemployment. We examine the options available to the government, looking first at fiscal and then at monetary policy.

If the government can identify the shock as an aggregate demand shock and can react to it in the short run, then the obvious policy tool to use is an offsetting fiscal policy to shift the *AD* curve back to the right. Adjustment would occur via point *F* under fixed exchange rates and point *E* under flexible rates. However, there are problems that arise with using fiscal policy to offset shocks in this way. In the case of a negative shock, the government needs to use expansionary fiscal policy. As we have seen in Chapter 6, if the government already has a high debt to GDP ratio, it may be reluctant to implement a deficit-financed increase in government spending to offset a negative shock. Cutting taxes to offset a temporary negative shock also increases the budget deficit. In addition, it may be difficult to reverse the policy when the shock has disappeared. The third option of a balanced budget expansion, i.e. an increase in government expenditure matched by higher taxation, is attractive because it does not increase the government's deficit. But as we have seen, a change in direct or indirect taxation is likely to have supply-side effects: a rise in taxation would tend to shift the *ERU* curve to the left. This may make the government cautious in using changes in taxes to stabilize the economy.

When we turn to a possible monetary policy response to the negative demand shock, we see that a loosening of monetary policy (or a devaluation in a fixed exchange rate economy) can raise the level of activity to y_0: this would mean a move from point *B* to point *D* (see Fig. 11.10). Point *D* is not a medium-run equilibrium, however, and eventually the economy will return to point *B* as a consequence of domestic wage- and price-setting responses.

3 Domestic supply shocks

Examples of domestic supply shocks are changes in union behaviour, changes in product market competition, the emergence of coordinated wage-setting behaviour, or a change in 'efficiency', such as a change in the trend of productivity growth. The analysis is exactly the same as the analysis of the implementation of a supply-side policy discussed earlier. A domestic supply-side shock shifts the wage- or price-setting curve and therefore shifts the *ERU* curve.

To take an example, we assume that a wages accord collapses unexpectedly. This is an example of a domestic cost shock. The collapse of the accord implies a leftward shift in the *ERU* curve. The new medium-run equilibrium for the economy is at higher unemployment and lower price competitiveness. If there is no government intervention, the economy adjusts gradually to the new medium-run equilibrium through a burst of domestic wage and price inflation. It is the falling competitiveness that weakens net exports and depresses output. There is a trade deficit at the new medium-run equilibrium. The economy moves from point *A* to point *B* in Fig.11.11.

It is clear that only a supply-side improvement can offset the effects of this shock: a shift back of the *ERU* curve, through policies that either shift the wage-setting curve down or price-setting curve (for a given level of the real exchange rate) up, is necessary to re-establish the medium- and long-run equilibria at their initial levels. The use of fiscal or monetary/exchange rate policy under these circumstances can provide only

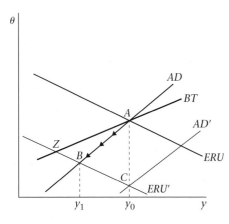

Figure 11.11 A domestic supply-side shock

a partial or temporary solution. For example, using expansionary fiscal policy to boost the level of employment would worsen the trade deficit (point C). Using a relaxation of monetary policy or a devaluation would lead in the short run to a boost in employment and an improvement in the trade deficit. Suppose that the exchange rate depreciation/devaluation restored the initial level of output and real exchange rate (i.e. to point A). This provides a solution to the domestic cost shock but it is only temporary. The depreciation cuts the real wage and leaves the economy *above* the new ERU curve. Hence, in subsequent rounds of wage setting, money wages will rise relative to expected prices and a gradual process of erosion of the impact on competitiveness of the devaluation will ensue from A back to B.

4 External trade and supply shocks

4.1 External trade shocks

An external trade shock is defined as an unanticipated shift in the AD curve *and* the BT curve. For a given level of the real exchange rate, the volume of net exports changes. There are three main reasons why this can happen.

(1) The level of world trade may change. This is a change in y^*. This could arise from a boom or a slump in an important region of the world.

(2) For a given level of world trade and at a given real exchange rate and level of home output, the home country's share of world trade may change. This is a change in σ which reflects the home country's share of world exports in the export function, or a change in the marginal propensity to import, m_y, in the import function. This could be because of a change in tastes in the world economy. Consumers may shift their preferences away from the style or type of goods produced in the home economy toward those produced elsewhere. In discussions of the economics of a single currency area, the example is often given of a two-country world in which tastes change in favour of the

products of one of the countries. For example, preferences shift from beer to wine, benefiting French net exports to the detriment of German net exports. This is an example of an external trade shock. Another example is where there is a change in the non-price attributes of the products of one country. For example, suppose that at a given price, the quality of Czech-made cars suddenly increases. This represents a positive external trade shock for the Czech Republic and a negative shock for its competitors in the auto industry.

(3) The world price of a key imported raw material may change. This is a change in the terms of trade at the world level between manufactures and raw materials, where τ (tau) $= P^*_{rm}/P^*_{manuf}$, where P^*_{rm} is the world price index of raw materials and P^*_{manuf} is the world price index of manufactures. An example of an increase in τ is a rise in the world price of oil. A rise in the price of oil relative to manufactures means that for the home country, which is assumed to import raw materials and export manufactures, a higher volume of exports must be sold to purchase a given volume of imports. This represents a negative external trade shock for the home country and is a deterioration in its terms of trade. As we will see in the next section, a raw materials price shock is not only an external trade shock but also a supply shock because it shifts the *ERU* curve.

The analysis of the impact of an external trade shock is straightforward. It will shift the *AD* curve and the *BT* curve in the same direction. The horizontal shift of the *BT* curve will be greater than that of the *AD* curve for the same reason that the *AD* curve is steeper than the *BT* curve (refer back to section 2 in Chapter 10). A simple way of seeing this is that if we look at the initial output level, y_0, at which the *AD* curve and the *BT* curve intersect (see point A in Fig. 11.12) then the new *AD* curve, *AD'*, and the new *BT* curve, *BT'*, will intersect at y_0 (at point A'). This is because the exchange rate depreciation that would leave output unchanged in the face of the exogenous fall in net exports must reverse the fall in net exports, and hence it must leave the trade balance unchanged.

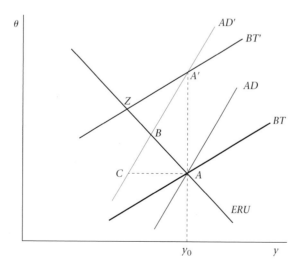

Figure 11.12 A negative external trade shock

Let us now examine the implications of the external trade shock. As an example, we consider a negative trade shock. As is clear from Fig.11.12, the new medium-run equilibrium is at point *B* with higher unemployment, a lower real wage, higher real import costs, and a trade *deficit*. The intuition behind this outcome is that the trade shock depresses activity through the usual goods market equilibrium channel. At higher unemployment, the wage-setting real wage is lower. For price- and wage-setting equilibrium, the price-setting real wage must also be lower and this corresponds to a higher real cost of imports.

The *short-run* impact of the trade shock depends on the exchange rate regime. Under fixed exchange rates, output and employment contract and the economy moves to point *C* before the wage- and price-setting process sets in train the adjustment from point *C* to the medium-run equilibrium at *B*. In a floating rate system, a depreciation will occur in the short run and the economy will move to point *A'* before the adjustment down the *AD'* curve takes place. The possibility of changing the exchange rate can reduce the output cost of the adjustment to point *B* but with the consequence that there is a bout of rising wages and prices in the home economy relative to the rest of the world.

The difference between the impact of an external trade shock and a pure aggregate demand shock is that the *BT* curve moves in the case of an external trade shock. This has two consequences: first, points *C* and *B* are positions of trade surplus if there is a pure aggregate demand shock and of trade deficit if there is an external trade shock. Second, in the case of an external trade shock, the long-run equilibrium of the economy shifts (from *A* to *Z*).

4.2 External supply shocks

An external supply shock is defined as an unanticipated change in the world terms of trade between manufactures and raw materials: a change in the world price of oil is a good example. As noted in the previous section, this type of shock combines the effects of an external trade shock with a supply-side impact on the price-setting real wage curve. The consequence is that there is a shift in the *AD* curve, in the *BT* curve, and in the *ERU* curve: all curves shift in the same direction.

To see why the *ERU* curve shifts, we need to look closely at what is meant by a change in the world price of oil. If we say that the world price of oil rises, this means that it rises relative to the world price of manufactured goods, where $\tau = P^*_{\text{rm}}/P^*_{\text{manuf}}$. In other words, we are talking about a change in *relative* prices, or to put it another way, a change in the *real* price of oil. The price-setting curve is defined for a given real exchange rate, θ. Now suppose that the world price of oil rises. For a given θ, a rise in the price of an essential input like oil raises costs for firms in the home economy so if firms are to protect their profit margins, then real wages must be lower. Hence the price-setting real wage curve shifts downward when the world price of oil rises (see Fig. 11.13). This implies a leftward shift in the *ERU* curve. The derivation of the price-setting curve incorporating imported materials is presented in a footnote.[7]

---

[7] It is simplest to assume that there is no mark-up on imported materials. Assume the only imports are of raw materials. Then

$$P_c = P + v\tau P^* e$$

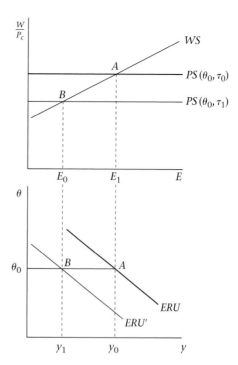

Figure 11.13 A negative external supply shock: increase in the oil price shifts *ERU* curve left

We can now analyse the full impact of an exogenous and permanent change in the world price of an essential commodity such as oil. We take the case of a rise in the price of oil. For simplicity, we assume that the home country only imports oil—it does not import final goods. This changes nothing essential and allows for a more direct examination of the issue at hand. We can investigate the three effects:

(1) the impact on aggregate demand

(2) the impact on the trade balance

(3) the impact on price and wage setting and hence on the *ERU* curve.

We have already examined the first two effects in the analysis of an external trade shock in Fig. 11.12: there is a downward shock to net exports because the increase in the cost of the essential imported raw material absorbs a higher proportion of home income at a given real exchange rate. This shifts the *AD* curve and the *BT* curve to the left.[8]

where $P = \frac{W}{(1-\mu)\lambda}$ is the price index of value added and v is unit materials requirement. This implies a price-setting real wage:

$$w^{PS} = \frac{(1-\mu)\lambda}{1 + v\tau\theta}.$$

Any rise in τ reduces the price-setting real wage. Note that any fall in unit materials requirement through increased energy efficiency, for example, would tend to offset this.

[8] Since the oil price shock is a 'world' phenomenon, there will be a fall in world aggregate demand and world output, y^*, as all exporters of manufactures suffer from the supply shock. This assumes—realistically—that the exporters of raw materials, who have experienced an increase in their wealth, are unable to increase their expenditure sufficiently to compensate. This would reinforce the leftward shifts in the *AD* and *BT* curves.

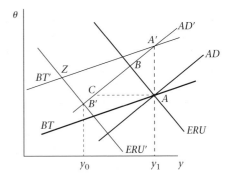

Figure 11.14 External supply shock

We turn to the consequences of the shift in the *ERU* curve. The first observation is that the inflationary consequences of the commodity price rise are clear. Following the external supply shock, the initial equilibrium point *A* is *above* the new *ERU* curve. This means that at y_0, the real wage is below the wage-setting real wage. The reason is that the costs of home firms have gone up and higher domestic prices cut the real consumption wage. There will be upward pressure on inflation.

In terms of the assessment of the adjustment paths under fixed and flexible exchange rates, it is clear that as compared with a pure external trade shock, the costs of the adjustment via exchange rate depreciation (higher inflation via point *A'* in Fig. 11.14) go up relative to the costs of adjustment with a fixed exchange rate. This is clearly illustrated by reference to the two oil shocks in the 1970s. In response to the first oil shock in 1973, many countries focused on the aggregate demand consequences and sought to offset them via expansionary fiscal and monetary policies. If we look at the consequences of an accommodating monetary policy, this allowed the exchange rate to depreciate (to *A'*). The consequence was the onset of so-called stagflation: rising unemployment and rising inflation (as the economy eventually adjusted from *A'* to *B'* with unemployment rising and a burst of inflation).

When the second oil shock struck in 1979, the nature of the shock was better understood and many countries attempted to use tight monetary policy to prevent exchange depreciation and hence prevent a big upsurge in inflation. In terms of Fig. 11.14, this allows adjustment from *A* to *C* to *B'*. Some countries were able to negotiate wages accords to shift the wage-setting curve downward and hence offset (at least partially) the leftward shift of the *ERU* curve.

5 Real wages in open and closed economies

There are two different questions to address:

(1) what happens to real wages over the business cycle—i.e. in response to changes in the level of aggregate demand?

(2) what happens to real wages when there is a supply-side change such as a shift in the wage-setting curve?

The contrast between the open and the closed economy is interesting. In the closed economy if the price-setting curve is flat as we normally assume and if prices are adjusted immediately to any change in costs, then the economy would always be on the price-setting curve and real wages would not vary over the cycle. Real wages would be acyclical. A rise in aggregate demand from an initial equilibrium would boost money wages: if the rise in costs is fully incorporated in prices, the real wage will revert to its initial level (on the PS curve). However, if it takes time for firms to mark their prices up in response to the higher costs, real wages will rise temporarily. The real wage will be above the PS curve until full adjustment had occurred and there would be some evidence of procyclical real wages. The key result is that in equilibrium, real wages are determined by the price-setting real wage. Thus if the PS curve happened to be downward sloping, then real wages would be countercyclical. Inertia in the adjustment of prices to changes in wages would be needed to overturn this prediction.

In the closed economy, the response of real wages to fluctuations in aggregate demand depends on:

- the slope of the WS curve
- the slope of the PS curve
- inertia in wage and price setting.

By contrast in the open economy, what happens to real wages when output fluctuates depends on the exchange rate regime and on the nature of the shock, as well as on the lags in wage and price setting and the slope of the PS curve. As we have already seen, in the open economy procyclical real wages in the medium run are likely to be observed following an IS shock (e.g. consumption, investment, government spending, taxation) as the economy settles at a new medium-run equilibrium on the ERU curve. The economy moves up the WS curve in the event of a positive shock and down in the event of a negative shock. Fig. 11.15 illustrates: the rise in employment from E_0 to E_1 to E_2 is associated with a rise in real wages from w_0 to w_1 to w_2.

Of course, if activity fluctuates because of changes in monetary policy or shifts in the money demand function (so-called LM shocks) then the economy will move *along* the AD curve. A loosening of monetary policy (associated with a depreciation) will lead to a rise in output and a rise in competitiveness (θ). This entails a fall in the real wage. Thus with fluctuations coming from LM shifts, real wages will move countercyclically. Unlike the fluctuations associated with IS shifts, movements along the AD curve will only be observed in the short run.

In the closed economy with a flat PS curve, supply-side policies that shift only the wage-setting curve have no effect on the medium-run real wage. Fig. 11.16 illustrates this by taking the case of a downward shift in the WS curve. This could have been the result of a labour market reform that weakened union bargaining power or it could have been due to the negotiation of a social pact. Either way if the WS curve shifts down, the equilibrium unemployment rate falls but real wages remain unchanged at the new ERU at point B. Equilibrium employment rises because of the reduction in *wage pressure* and not because of a reduction in real wages.

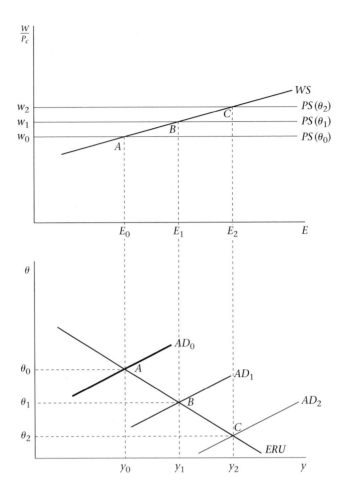

Figure 11.15 Procyclical real wages in the open economy

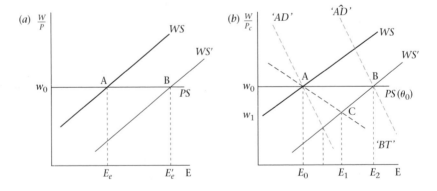

Figure 11.16 Supply-side policy and real wages: comparing the closed and open economies
(a) Closed economy (b) Open economy

How does a downward shift in the *WS* curve affect real wages in the open economy? The *AD* curve and the *BT* curve are shown in the real wage/employment diagram and labelled as '*AD*' and '*BT*' respectively. In an open economy, a similar result can be achieved to that in the closed economy if the downward shift in the *WS* curve is accompanied by an expansionary fiscal policy so that the *AD* curve moves to the right to *ÂD*. Higher employment would be achieved without any fall in actual real wages. But unlike the closed economy, this is not sustainable in the *long run* in the open economy. At *B*, there is a trade deficit. The real wage has to fall to w_1 to eliminate the deficit, and this requires a trimming back of the employment gain (point *C*). Exchange rate depreciation plus a tightening of fiscal policy will achieve this. The fundamental point is that in an open economy, a rise in employment can only be sustained in the long run by a fall in real wages, even if such a fall is not required to make production profitable (i.e. even when the *PS* curve is flat). The fall in real wages is necessary to raise competitiveness and secure a satisfactory external account.

6 Introduction to the economics of currency unions

The question of whether a country should hold on to its separate currency or join a currency union raises many issues. A major one is whether the loss of the exchange rate represents the loss of a useful policy instrument. We can tackle this question with the framework developed in this chapter. Specifically, we ask whether in the face of an aggregate demand, external trade, or supply shock the exchange rate is a useful policy instrument. If a change in the nominal exchange rate is the 'best response' to a shock that may hit the economy, then giving up that instrument has a cost, which must be weighed up against the benefits of a currency union. The benefits are typically viewed as being of the following kind:

- on the microeconomic side, from the elimination of transactions costs associated with changing currencies. The assumption is that the creation of a single currency area would help to reduce the segmentation of national goods markets (see Chapter 9). This would boost product market competition, which may raise the incentive to innovate and therefore enhance the growth rate. Models of endogenous growth in which competition can raise growth are discussed in Chapter 14. A second channel for microeconomic benefits lies with the assumption that a reduction in exchange rate uncertainty would reduce the misallocation and duplication of investment facilities in different locations. This produces a static benefit as resources are saved and a dynamic benefit if investment rises as a consequence.

- on the macroeconomic side, a common currency area may provide a benefit in establishing inflation credibility if the national authorities find that difficult to establish themselves. This clearly raises the question of the quality of monetary policy management in the currency union as compared with the country. There is no reason why in principle quality should be higher in one than in the other. The issue of inflation credibility was introduced in Chapter 3 and is investigated in detail in Chapter 5.

We turn now to the often cited macroeconomic cost of membership of a single currency area: the loss of the exchange rate. From our analysis of the different kinds of shocks that can affect an economy and of the role of different policies that can be used to respond to them, it is possible to draw together a set of circumstances in which the availability of a change in the nominal exchange rate can be a valuable tool. Three reasons why it can be useful are:

(1) It can have a substantial and immediate impact on competitiveness.

(2) If the new short-run equilibrium achieved by a devaluation is not a medium-run equilibrium (e.g. it is *above* the *ERU* curve), the beneficial effects on employment and competitiveness can nevertheless last for several years.

(3) If the new short-run equilibrium achieved by a devaluation is a medium-run equilibrium (i.e. on the *ERU* curve) then devaluation allows the economy to get to the medium-run equilibrium faster and at lower cost than would be the case if domestic wage and price adjustments are relied on. More generally, whenever a change in the real exchange rate is required—because of a structural change or a shock—the availability of the nominal exchange rate can help achieve this at lower cost to the extent that there is inertia in nominal wages and prices.

In the classic analysis of the optimal currency area (OCA), Robert Mundell focused on what we have labelled a negative external trade shock. Tastes in consumption shift so that at a given real exchange rate net exports of the home economy decline. In the case of a negative external trade shock, we have argued that the correct policy response is not to use fiscal policy to offset the shock since this widens the external imbalance. Under these circumstances, devaluation (or depreciation) has something to commend it as an interim measure. Devaluation helps to mitigate the impact of the external trade shock on output and on the trade balance. However as we have also seen, it only provides a temporary solution since the devaluation takes the economy above the *ERU* curve by cutting real wages. The benefits to competitiveness will be eroded in subsequent wage- and price-setting rounds. In the face of a *temporary* external trade shock devaluation is a useful shock absorber. However if the external trade shock signifies a more serious underlying problem for the economy such as a shift in tastes away from the goods that the home economy specializes in, then devaluation may divert the attention of both private and public sector actors from the source of the problem in the supply side of the economy.

The discussion in the OCA literature that compares the use of a nominal exchange rate change with a change in wages can also be clarified. In the extreme case of *real* wage flexibility, the *WS* curve is vertical and an external trade shock implies a new medium-run equilibrium at unchanged output but with lower real wages. In this case, the debate about the use of devaluation hinges only on the presence of *nominal* wage and price rigidity. If nominal wages and prices adjust immediately, then the exchange rate regime is irrelevant: the economy moves immediately from the initial equilibrium at A to the new medium-run equilibrium at C' in Fig. 11.17. If nominal wages and prices are sticky, then a nominal exchange rate change will insulate the economy—in output terms—from an external trade shock more effectively than is possible under a common currency.

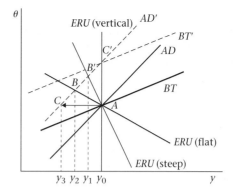

Figure 11.17 Assessing the role of devaluation

With very sticky wages and prices, the economy would have to go to C before adjusting eventually to C' through a period of inflation below world inflation.

We can draw a second lesson by combining the analysis of shifts in the *ERU* curve with the analysis of the role of exchange rate changes. A supply-side policy that shifts the *ERU* curve to the right allows the economy to move to a medium-run position with lower unemployment. However as noted above, the adjustment process may be very slow as wages and prices fall relative to world prices over successive rounds of wage setting. If the government has the possibility of devaluing the exchange rate, a rapid shift to the new medium-run equilibrium is possible. The possibility of delivering quick results for employment may make it easier to gain approval for the supply-side policy (e.g. a wages accord). The combination of wage accord and devaluation to accompany policies of fiscal consolidation was implemented by a number of European countries in the 1980s (see Chapter 6 for further details). This policy combination is not available inside a currency union.

To summarize, if an economy is characterized by the complete absence of nominal stickiness of wages and prices, the exchange rate regime is irrelevant and there is no cost to the loss of the exchange rate instrument. If there is nominal stickiness, in the sense that money wages and prices respond slowly to changes in the level of activity, and if the *WS* curve is relatively steep, there is a cost associated with the loss of the nominal exchange rate as a method of adjusting the real exchange rate rapidly (compare the flat with the steep *ERU* in Fig. 11.17). Hence, unless it is believed that membership of a common currency area would reduce the likelihood of external trade shocks or alter the economy's nominal inertia or real wage flexibility, such an economy might wish to retain the exchange rate instrument unless the other benefits of membership were sufficiently high.

7 Monetary rules in the open economy

In this section we see how to model an inflation-targeting central bank in the open economy. We focus on the flexible exchange rate case since under fixed exchange rates, the economy has no independent monetary policy. Under flexible exchange rates, the contrast is between monetary policy using a money supply target (LM) as in our treatment of the open economy up to this point and a monetary rule (MR).

To make the discussion concrete, we concentrate in this section on an aggregate demand shock such as an exogenous positive boom in domestic investment. Since the nature of the monetary policy regime does not affect the supply side, we know that the medium-run equilibrium will be the same whether monetary policy is MR or LM based. Just as we have emphasized when comparing fixed and flexible exchange rates, it is only the adjustment path that is affected by the monetary policy regime. We quickly run through the consequences of a positive aggregate demand shock under an LM based monetary policy:

(1) The new Mundell–Fleming equilibrium is at an unchanged output level with the boost to domestic aggregate demand completely offset by a contraction in net exports due to the exchange rate appreciation.

(2) However, this is not a medium-run equilibrium because the appreciation raises real wages, which, with output unchanged, leads to a drop in inflation relative to world inflation. Home's competitiveness improves and the economy adjusts to higher output. The new medium-run equilibrium is at higher output and a higher real exchange rate (i.e. lower θ) than initially.

Two key points emerge from this summary. The nominal exchange rate plays a role in the short run only and adjustment from the short- to the medium-run equilibrium takes place through wage and price adjustment. Another way to put this is that in the short run, the real exchange rate adjusts entirely because of nominal exchange rate changes whereas in the medium run, the real exchange rate adjusts entirely because of changes in wages and prices. The model therefore produces big swings in the real exchange rate as the economy reacts to shocks; followed by slower changes in θ driven by wage and price adjustment. This is the outcome of a passive monetary policy.

Intuitively, it would seem that an inflation-targeting monetary policy can avoid the tendency for the real exchange rate to overshoot in the way described. We assume the central bank's inflation target is the world rate of inflation, π^*, and inflation is assumed to be defined as usual in terms of consumer price inflation. The central bank's interest rate rule (see Chapter 5) tells it to respond by raising the interest rate in response to either a deviation of inflation from target or of output from equilibrium. Following a positive aggregate demand shock,

(1) output rises. Assuming that nothing happens to inflation in the short run, the central bank does nothing and since the interest rate is therefore unchanged at the world interest rate, the economy moves to the new short-run equilibrium with a constant real exchange rate (point B in Fig. 11.18). (Indeed, this is the short-run Mundell–Fleming equilibrium under *fixed* exchange rates.)

(2) To steer the economy back to equilibrium at the inflation target, the central bank must work out the consequences of the shock for future inflation: it must get the economy onto the appropriate MR line. Given that there is a new medium-run equilibrium, the MR line will intersect target inflation and the new equilibrium output level: this is MR_1. To work out its preferred position on MR_1, the central bank needs to work out the Phillips curve for period 2, which we call the $PC(\pi_1)$ for short: since the Phillips curve will go

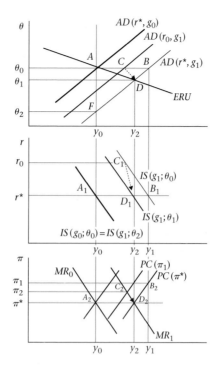

Figure 11.18 *MR* adjustment to increased government spending, with inflation and exchange rate inertia

through the point D_2, inflation will rise to π_1 (point B_2), we can identify the $PC(\pi_1)$. The central bank's preferred position on MR_1 is therefore point C_2.

(3) To get the economy onto MR_1, the central bank raises the interest rate above the world interest rate to r_0. To this point nothing has happened to the exchange rate or to inflation, so the new IS curve is $IS(g_1, \theta_0)$ and the new AD curve is $AD(r_0, g_1)$.

(4) From points C, C_1, and C_2, the economy adjusts to D, D_1, and D_2 through the following simultaneously operating mechanisms:

(a) Since output is below the new equilibrium throughout this stage, inflation will be falling in each period.

(b) Although it is falling, inflation is above world inflation and competitiveness is falling. This has two effects: it shifts the IS curve down and it raises real wages, which reinforces the process of falling inflation.

(c) With the home interest rate above the world interest rate, the nominal exchange rate appreciates.[9] This reinforces the downward shift of the IS. As the economy

---

[9] We remind the reader of the reason for this with inertial exchange rate expectations $e_{t+1}^E = e_{t-1}$. Remember that from the *UIP* condition, $i_t - i^* = \log e_{t+1}^E - \log e_t$. With the slight fudge that $\pi^E = \pi^* = \pi^{*E}$, we can write this as

$$r_t - r^* = \log e_{t+1}^E - \log e_t$$

Think of this as the equation which determines e_t. If $r > r^*$, then the exchange market will only be in equilibrium if it is expected that the home currency will depreciate and wipe out the interest rate advantage of holding home's currency. So whatever determines market expectations e_{t+1}^E of e_{t+1}, e_t must adjust (up or down) so that $\log e_t$ is below $\log e_{t+1}^E$ by $r - r^*$. If expectations are inertia based, so $e_{t+1}^E = e_{t-1}$ that means $\log e_t$ will have fallen relative

approaches the new equilibrium along the *MR*, the extent to which home's interest rate exceeds the world interest rate diminishes and each successive appreciation is smaller. Thus the *AD* curve shifts gradually to the right.

The economy adjusts to the new medium-run equilibrium along the *MR* curve: this is the fundamental difference as compared to adjustment under an *LM* based monetary regime, where adjustment from the short-run Mundell–Fleming equilibrium (point *F*) to the medium-run equilibrium takes place along the *AD* curve through wage and price adjustment only.

In the explanation of the *MR* based adjustment, two assumptions have been made. We have assumed that inflation is characterized by inertia, just as in the closed economy. Less plausibly, we have assumed that exchange rate expectations are formed in a backward-looking way, i.e. that the exchange rate expected for next period is last period's actual exchange rate. With this assumption, the *UIP* curve shifts steadily to the left as the interest rate is adjusted by the central bank. As we discussed in Chapter 9, this has the unfortunate implication that in each period when exchange market operators expect a depreciation, there is in fact an appreciation. If we switch to the assumption of rational exchange rate expectations, the foreign exchange market can work out the real exchange rate at the new equilibrium (θ_1). In this case, instead of the economy moving first to point *B*, the rapid adjustment of the exchange rate takes the economy straight to point *D*, the new equilibrium. If the exchange rate adjusts immediately, the real wage rises to its new equilibrium level so the increase in output does not spark off any rise in inflation.[10] Without a rise in inflation above the target and with output at the new equilibrium, y_2, there are no signals to the central bank to change the interest rate. This is an interesting result: even with inertia in the inflation process, if there are rational expectations in the foreign exchange market, the economy moves directly to the new medium-run equilibrium. This is because the change in the foreign exchange rate is an alternative to wage and price movements.

7.1 Central bank does not know the equilibrium has changed

In this case, the central bank does not have a theory about the equilibrium of the economy. Suppose it believes the equilibrium is initially $y_0 = y_{e0}$. It infers that the equilibrium level of output has increased if it observes π below π_{-1} with $y_0 = y_{e0}$. Since $\pi = \pi_{-1} + \alpha(y - y_e)$, the central bank can work out the new value of y_e if $y = y_{e0}$. It

---

to $\log e_{t-1} = \log e^E_{t+1}$. Hence e_t will have to appreciate. Thus it follows, with the assumption that $e^E_{t+1} = e_{t-1}$, that e will be continuously appreciating while $r_t > r^*$, thus $d \log e < 0$.

[10] There is only one θ, y combination at which $r = r^*$; that is d where $y = y_e = y_2$ and $\theta = \theta_e = \theta_1$. This is because being at D is a necessary condition for being at D_2 in πy-space; and it is only at D_2 that the central bank will want $r = r^*$. D is not a sufficient condition for D_2: we also require $\pi = \pi^*$. Now in period $t = 0$, $\pi = \pi^*$. Start at A, before g has increased. Then the rationally expected exchange rate as soon as g has increased is the nominal exchange rate which takes the economy immediately to θ_1. If $\theta = \theta_1$, and if $r = r^*$, the relevant *AD* schedule is $AD(g_1, r^*)$ which goes through the *ERU* at $\theta = \theta_1$. Since $\pi = \pi^*$, we are at D_2 so that the central bank will indeed set $r = r^*$. Since $\theta_0 = P^* e_0 / P$, and since neither P^* nor P change in the immediate move to D, the new nominal exchange rate needed to bring about this shift is $\theta_1 = P^* e_1 / P$; so $e_1 = e_0 \theta_1 / \theta_0$. At D it is indeed true that $e^E = e_1$, since $r = r^*$.

does this as follows: it observes $\pi = \pi_1 < \pi_{-1}$ with $y = y_{e0}$. Hence it infers that the new equilibrium, y_1^e is given by

$$y_{e1} - y_{e0} = \alpha^{-1}(\pi_{-1} - \pi_1).$$

In other words, the central bank knows that the correct short-run Phillips curve must go through the correct vertical Phillips curve at π_{-1}. The correct Phillips curve must also go through the observation π_1, y_0. The correct Phillips curve is then derived by joining up these two points. The new equilibrium output level is then given by the output level at which $\pi = \pi_{-1}$.

If this argument is correct, the central bank can immediately infer from any new data what the new level of equilibrium output, y_e, is. It therefore behaves no differently from the central bank that does have a model of the economy. Of course, this is to take no account of measurement errors and random fluctuations in the economy. The central bank might think, for instance, that the output increase does not imply an increase in equilibrium output but simply represents a one-off demand shock. However, it is interpreted as being accompanied by a measurement error in the rate of inflation, hence explaining why inflation is unexpectedly low. In that case, if the central bank was sure of its analysis, it would raise interest rates according to the pre-existing MR after making some assumption about what the 'true' inflation rate was.

7.2 Summing up

Adjustment to a shock in a flexible exchange rate open economy is different when monetary policy is operated with a monetary rule from when there is a monetary growth target. With inflation inertia, but rational exchange rate expectations, the economy will move directly to the new medium-run equilibrium when the monetary rule is in place. The real exchange rate overshooting characteristic of adjustment with a money supply target disappears. When exchange rate expectations also exhibit inertia, the new medium-run equilibrium is approached along the MR line. In the case of a positive aggregate demand shock with the (nominal and real) exchange rate appreciating and inflation falling gradually back to the target level.

8 Conclusions

In this chapter the open economy model has been used to examine the impact on the economy of a series of different kinds of policies and shocks. Fiscal policy, monetary/exchange rate policy, and supply-side policy have been investigated. The analysis has been applied to the question of how real wages move over the cycle and to the costs of joining a common currency area.

- Aggregate demand shocks that shift the AD curve and therefore the medium-run equilibrium are changes in autonomous consumption and investment. The short-run effects of an aggregate demand shock can be best offset by using fiscal policy.

- Changes in monetary policy in a flexible exchange rate regime or discrete changes in the exchange rate peg in a fixed rate system lead to a shift along the *AD* curve and therefore do not change the medium-run equilibrium.

- Supply shocks and supply-side policies are defined as those that shift either the wage-setting curve, the price-setting curve (for a given real exchange rate) or both. In the open economy, a supply shock or policy is one that shifts the *ERU* curve and hence shifts the medium- and long-run equilibrium rate of unemployment.

- External trade shocks are defined as those that change the level of net exports for a given real exchange rate. Such shocks shift the *AD* and the *BT* curves and therefore change the short-, medium-, and long-run equilibria.

- External supply shocks such as a change in the world price of an essential commodity shift all three of the *AD*, *BT*, and *ERU* curves.

- The model predicts that there will not be a fixed relationship between real wages and employment e.g. procyclical or countercyclical real wages in the open economy. The pattern will depend on the nature of the shock (e.g. *IS* shock, *LM* shock, or supply-side shock).

- The costs of giving up the nominal exchange rate by joining a common currency area depend on the nature of the shocks the economy is likely to encounter, its structural characteristics (e.g. the lags in wage and price setting and the responsiveness of the wage-setting real wage to changes in unemployment) and the availability of complementary policies (e.g. fiscal policy, supply-side policies).

- The open economy model was extended by showing how an inflation-targeting central bank in a flexible exchange rate small open economy responds to an aggregate demand shock. The major difference that characterizes the inflation-targeting regime from the money supply-targeting one is that the central bank adjusts the interest rate so as to keep the economy close to the constant-inflation *ERU* line by prompting appropriate changes in the nominal exchange rate. The economy adjusts to the new medium-run equilibrium along the *MR* line. Required changes in the real exchange rate are therefore achieved without the larger than necessary swings in the nominal rate characteristic of a floating regime with an *LM*-based monetary policy. With rational exchange rate expectations, the monetary targeting regime shifts immediately to the new medium-run equilibrium even in the presence of inflation inertia.

■ **QUESTIONS**

Checklist questions

(1) An open economy experiences an unexpected fall in domestic aggregate demand. Compare the policy responses available to the authorities if the economy is (*a*) outside a currency union and (*b*) inside a currency union.

(2) Consider a fixed exchange rate economy operating at medium-run equilibrium with a trade deficit.

(*a*) Why is the combination of a wages accord and a devaluation particularly useful to a policy maker if it wishes to restore trade balance?

(*b*) How would the economy adjust if the wages accord was not accompanied by a devaluation?

(*c*) What would happen if only the devaluation was successfully implemented (e.g. the wages accord collapsed)?

(*d*) What is the alternative for a policy maker to restore trade balance if it cannot devalue (e.g. it is in a monetary union with its major trading partners) or negotiate a wages accord (e.g. relations with trade unions are bad)?

(3) What is the difference between an external trade shock and an aggregate demand shock? Provide two examples of each and clarify the difference by exploring the implications for output, the trade balance, and for the policy responses that are most appropriate.

(4) In a floating exchange rate economy, what policy combination can a government use to bring about a move along the *ERU* curve without letting wages and prices adjust? Assuming the policy maker can get this right, why might it prove particularly useful?

(5) What is meant by the 'world terms of trade between manufactures and raw materials'? Explain how a change in them will be reflected in the '*AD*', '*BT*', and '*ERU*' curves.

(6) Can involvement in a war abroad help a country to recover from a recession? How is your answer affected if the war has a major effect on world energy prices?

(7) Why is the combination of tight monetary policy and wage accords a better response to an adverse external supply shock than expansionary fiscal and monetary policies? Explain by comparing the process of adjustment to the new medium-run equilibrium.

(8) Consider a small economy that joins a currency union with its major trading partners. In θy–space show the effect of increased product market competition, increased investment, and an improved productivity trend and give the main reasons why these beneficial aspects may be expected to occur.

(9) Is the nominal exchange rate more valuable as a policy instrument to an economy with real wages that are highly sensitive to unemployment than to an economy with less sensitive real wages? Is it more valuable to an economy with a high propensity to import than to one with a lower propensity to import? Explain why.

(10) Explain why a government might find it desirable to give control of monetary policy to 'unelected central bankers' or to 'foreigners'.

(11) Does international capital mobility undermine the ability of a central bank to control inflation in a country with floating exchange rates?

(12) Consider a small open economy with a fixed exchange rate and imperfectly competitive markets for output and labour. There is nominal stickiness of prices and wages, but only in the short run. Trace the effects on output and the trade balance of

a reduction in income tax. What constraints limit the ability of the government of a country with a fixed exchange rate to maintain a high level of real income through the use of fiscal policy? How would you expect such constraints to operate in practice?

Problems and questions for discussion

QUESTION A. In an open economy with a flexible exchange rate, the government wishes to see an unemployment rate of 5% of the labour force, but has been advised that the current 10% is the equilibrium rate. Under what circumstances are there feasible policies which would enable the government to achieve its unemployment objective without compromising its inflation record? What might such policies consist of? Why might the government be reluctant to introduce them?

QUESTION B. Consider a small open economy. There is perfect capital mobility and a flexible exchange rate. The initial position of the economy is one of constant inflation and trade balance. Four years later, unemployment is observed to be markedly lower (a rate of 4% as compared with 6%). Inflation is constant. Two hypotheses about what has happened in the intervening period are discussed:

(1) The economy experienced a positive aggregage demand shock.
(2) Supply-side reforms to the labour market and welfare system were implemented.

Explain the logic of each of these hypotheses. Suggest the patterns in the data that would be consistent with each hypothesis.

QUESTION C. Consider a common currency area (CCA). Does the absence of pressure from the foreign exchange market and the fact that inflation is set by the central bank of the CCA mean that a member country can achieve any desired unemployment rate without having to worry about problems of inflation or trade balance? What are the consequences for the operation of the CCA? Explain your answer.

QUESTION D. In January 2001, Milton Friedman said that although the high inflation of the 1970s followed the decision of oil producers to cut production, similar behaviour by the oil producers now would not be followed by high inflation because 'central bankers behave differently'. Provide an explanation of this statement. Does this mean that we should not be concerned about oil price rises? Explain your answer.

QUESTION E. 'It is possible to distinguish an aggregate demand shock from an aggregate supply shock by looking at whether the subsequent changes in output and inflation are positively or negatively correlated.' Do you agree with this statement? You may answer this by referring to a model of the closed economy or the open economy or both.

QUESTION F. Concern about the burden of government debt has led many countries to introduce policies to try to reduce it. How would changes in government expenditure and/or taxation help achieve this policy objective and which is likely to be more effective in the longer run? Would a floating exchange rate make the task easier or more difficult? Would you recommend other policies?

■ APPENDIX: OPEN ECONOMY INFLATION AND SHORT-RUN PHILLIPS CURVES: AN EXAMPLE

It may be useful to work through an example to show in detail how inflation changes as the economy moves from one medium-run equilibrium to another—for example, in the aftermath of an aggregate demand shock. This illustrates how the Phillips curve analysis operates in the open economy. As an example, let us take the case under fixed exchange rates in which the government decides to use a fiscal expansion to push the economy to lower unemployment. The diagrammatic analysis is less messy if we assume that expected inflation in the economy is equal to world inflation throughout. An assumption of inertial or adaptive expectations could just as easily be used but this diverts attention from the shifts in the Phillips curve caused by changes in the real exchange rate.

The example is developed using the θy–diagram, the wage-setting and price-setting diagram, and the Phillips curve diagram (Fig. 11.19). The economy begins at point A with output of y_0 and unemployment of U_0. The government undertakes a fiscal expansion to take the economy to point Z at lower

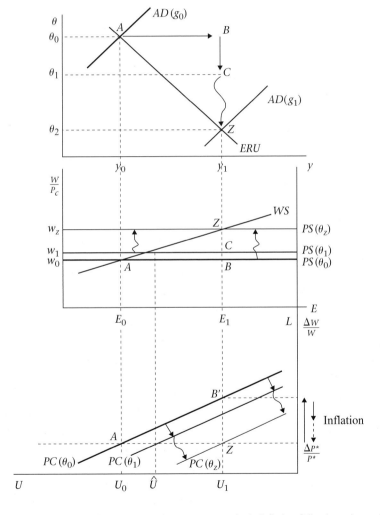

Figure 11.19 Phillips curves in the open economy: temporary rise in inflation following a loosening of fiscal policy under fixed exchange rates

unemployment. From our analysis of the medium-run model, we know that there is a new medium-run equilibrium at Z at which inflation will be constant. Since this is a fixed exchange rate economy, the inflation rate at Z is equal to world inflation—just as it was at A. But what happens to inflation along the path from A to Z?

In this example, we assume:

$$\left(\frac{\triangle P}{P}\right)^E = \frac{\triangle P^*}{P^*} \quad \text{and} \quad \frac{\triangle e}{e} = 0.$$

At point A, home wage and price inflation are equal to world inflation. The government increases spending from g_0 to g_1. The AD curve shifts to the right. In the short run, the rise in aggregate demand drives up output and employment through the usual multiplier process (point B in the top panel).

We now turn to the medium run. The key equations are the following:

$$W = P_c^E b(E) \qquad \text{(wage equation)}$$
$$P = P_x = \frac{1}{1-\mu}\frac{W}{\lambda} \qquad \text{(price equation)}$$
$$P_c = (1-\phi)P + \phi P^* e \qquad \text{(consumer price index)}$$
$$w = \frac{W}{P_c} \qquad \text{(real wage)}$$
$$\theta = \frac{P^* e}{P}. \qquad \text{(real exchange rate)}$$

With a higher level of employment, E_1, we can see from the wage- and price-setting diagram that the wage-setting real wage at E_1 is well above the existing real wage of w_0 (in the middle panel, compare point B on the price-setting curve $PS(\theta_0)$ with point Z). The increase in money wages that this gives rise to can be read off from the Phillips curve diagram: the Phillips curve that is relevant to point B is the one defined by expected inflation of $\left(\frac{\triangle P}{P}\right)^E = \frac{\triangle P^*}{P^*}$ and the equilibrium unemployment rate of U_0 (where the WS curve intersects the $PS(\theta_0)$ curve). Money wage inflation goes up to the level shown by point B' in the Phillips curve diagram (bottom panel). Home firms will immediately mark up their prices by the same percentage. From the price-setting equation, we know that price inflation of home produced goods and services will equal the rate at which unit labour costs have increased.

As we have seen before, the crucial point is that consumer prices do not rise by as much as domestic producer prices. The reason is that consumer price inflation depends on world inflation (the rate at which the prices of imported final goods rise), domestic price inflation, and on ϕ, the weight of foreign goods in the consumption bundle. Nothing has happened to world inflation and ϕ is constant. Hence, consumer prices rise by less than the prices of home produced goods (i.e. $\frac{\triangle W}{W} = \frac{\triangle P}{P} > \frac{\triangle P_c}{P_c} > \frac{\triangle P^*}{P^*}$) which implies that the real wage $\left(\frac{W}{P_c}\right)$ increases and price competitiveness (θ) decreases. In Fig. 11.19, the real wage rises from w_0 to w_1 and θ falls from θ_0 to θ_1. The economy is now at point C. The upward shift of the price-setting curve is shown in the central panel: this means that the equilibrium rate of unemployment has decreased to $\widehat{U}$. A new Phillips curve must therefore be drawn: it is indexed by the level of θ (i.e. $PC(\theta_1)$) and shows that in the following period, money wages will rise by less than in the previous period. The reason is straightforward: the real wage has risen closer to the value of the wage-setting real wage at U_1. Thus there is less discrepancy between the real wage that workers anticipate and the wage they actually receive, which in turn means that wage inflation has to exceed expected inflation by a smaller percentage.

In subsequent periods, wages and prices increase according to the above pattern (i.e. $\frac{\triangle W}{W} = \frac{\triangle P}{P} > \frac{\triangle P_c}{P_c} > \frac{\triangle P^*}{P^*} \Rightarrow \downarrow \theta$ and $\uparrow w$) until the real wage is equal to w_z and the real exchange rate is equal to θ_z. The economy will then be at the new medium run equilibrium at point Z. At point Z, $\frac{\triangle W}{W} = \frac{\triangle P}{P} = \frac{\triangle P_c}{P_c} = \frac{\triangle P^*}{P^*}$ and there is constant inflation at the lower unemployment rate, U_1. The real wage and the real exchange rate remain constant at the values w_z, θ_z.

▨ APPENDIX: THE PRICE-SETTING CURVE IN THE OPEN ECONOMY WITH TAXES

The wage element of costs for firms is the full cost of labour to firms—i.e. the gross wage paid to the worker (which includes the income tax and social security payments that have to be made by the worker) plus the employer's social security contributions. All of these direct taxes are summarized in the tax rate, t_d. This is shown in the pricing equation:

$$P = P_x = \frac{1}{1 - \mu} \frac{W^{gross}}{\lambda} \qquad \text{(price equation)}$$

$$= \frac{1}{1 - \mu} \frac{W(1 + t_d)}{\lambda}.$$

In order to derive the price-setting real wage, it is necessary to note that we must express the price-setting real wage in terms of the real consumption wage, $\frac{W}{P_c}$. We use the definition of the consumer price index as before, but include value added tax at the rate t_v. The home country's VAT is levied on imported final goods.

$$P_c = [(1 - \phi)P + \phi P^* e](1 + t_v). \qquad \text{(consumer price index)}$$

After some tedious algebraic manipulation, which is shown in the footnote, we derive the expression for the price-setting real wage in the open economy including tax variables:[11]

$$w^{PS} = \frac{\lambda(1 - \mu)}{(1 + t_d)(1 + t_v)[1 + \phi(\theta - 1)]}. \qquad \text{(price-setting real wage, open)}$$

Although this expression looks complex, it is not difficult to interpret. It is simply the usual open economy price-setting real wage adjusted for the so-called tax wedge. Any increase in either direct or indirect taxation reduces the price-setting real wage and therefore shifts the $PS(\theta)$ curve downwards.

---

[11] Divide P_c by P

$$\frac{P_c(1 - \mu)\lambda}{W(1 + t_d)} = \left[(1 - \phi) + \phi \frac{P^* e}{P}\right](1 + t_v)$$

therefore

$$\frac{W(1 + t_d)}{P_c(1 - \mu)\lambda} = \frac{1}{\left[(1 - \phi) + \phi \frac{P^* e}{P}\right](1 + t_v)}$$

$$\frac{W}{P_c} = \frac{\lambda(1 - \mu)}{(1 + t_d)(1 + t_v)[(1 - \phi) + \phi\theta]}$$

$$= \frac{\lambda(1 - \mu)}{(1 + t_d)(1 + t_v)[1 + \phi(\theta - 1)]}.$$

12 Interdependent Economies

In the analysis of the open economy to this point, we have normally assumed that the economy in question is so small that its economic behaviour has no ramifications beyond its own borders. At the end of Chapter 9, we took a first look at interdependence and at how policy choices in one large economy spill over to affect another. In this chapter we make a systematic examination of how open economies interact with each other. There are two main goals. The first is to develop tools to analyse the interactions between the major economic blocs in the world—e.g. between the USA and the eurozone or between the USA and Japan. The second is to understand better the internal workings of the eurozone.

We begin the chapter in section 1 by setting out a way of modelling macroeconomic interdependence using a world that consists of two large economies (or blocs), for example the USA and the eurozone. Spillovers can be positive or negative: one country acting in its own interest may produce unintended benefits or costs for another country. We introduce two forms of spillover that can take place in the short run: a locomotive effect (a positive demand spillover), where expansion in one economy produces expansion in the other, and a beggar-thy-neighbour effect (negative spillover), where expansion in one economy induces contraction in the other. When the adjustment of wages and prices is sluggish, short-run effects such as these can create tension between the blocs. This raises the question of whether there are benefits from the international coordination of policy. The next step—explored in section 2—is to go beyond the short run to examine how endogenous wage and price adjustments alter the short-run spillover effects.

Section 3 brings together the short- and medium-run analysis and sets out both a diagrammatic and algebraic method of working through different cases. In section 4, we focus specifically on the analysis of the eurozone economy, showing

- how to derive the constraints on the eurozone as a whole,
- the role of the European Central Bank (ECB) in responding to symmetric shocks and
- how the eurozone economy behaves when there are differences between countries or asymmetric shocks.

The logic of a eurozone fiscal policy rule that is imposed on its members is outlined in section 2 in the context of the discussion of spillovers. In section 4 its consequences for macroeconomic adjustment are examined. By setting out a simple model, we shall see that even if the supply side of the economy of a member country is exactly the same as that of the other members, it may get stuck with high unemployment if private sector aggregate demand is very weak and if it is constrained from using fiscal policy because of a fiscal rule such as the Stability and Growth Pact. We also examine the use of supply-side policies in the context of EMU.

1 The 2-Bloc Model

In this section, we examine the interrelations between two major trading blocs in a world of perfect capital mobility. We set out a systematic way of analysing interdependence in both the short and medium run under different exchange rate arrangements. This formalizes and extends the sketch at the end of Chapter 9: the short-run implications of fiscal and monetary policy changes in a large open economy lie between those for the closed economy and for the small open economy. We shall maintain our assumption that global capital markets are highly integrated (the *UIP* condition holds), whereas goods markets are segmented because of imperfect competition and differentiated products. We refer to the two countries as 'Home' and 'Foreign'—Home's variables are shown as x and Foreign's as x^*. Before setting out the model, we explain the main economic issues that arise:

(1) the nature of the spillovers between economies may be positive or negative.
    Examples of each are the 'locomotive' and 'beggar-thy-neighbour' effects.

(2) spillovers can lead to a prisoner's dilemma game between economies.

(3) the logic of policy coordination.

The key results relating to the spillover of policy actions between countries are the following:
In the short run,

• there is a positive aggregate demand spillover often referred to as a *locomotive effect* (i.e. $\Delta y > 0$ and $\Delta y^* > 0$) of a Home expansionary fiscal policy under flexible exchange rates. Unlike the small open economy in which Home's output returns to its original level following a fiscal expansion, the exchange rate appreciation is less in the interdependence case with the result that Home's output is higher ($\Delta y > 0$). The reason Foreign's output also rises is due to the depreciation of its exchange rate when Home's appreciates: this boosts Foreign's net exports and output rises ($\Delta y^* > 0$). A Home expansionary monetary policy under fixed exchange rates also has a locomotive effect: the world money supply rises and pushes down the world interest rate so output expands in both Home and Foreign. To the extent that exports respond positively to higher output in the other country, the locomotive effects are reinforced.

• there is a negative spillover referred to as a *beggar-thy-neighbour effect* (i.e. $\Delta y > 0$ and $\Delta y^* < 0$) of a Home expansionary monetary policy under flexible exchange rates. Home's monetary expansion produces a depreciation for it and hence an appreciation for the foreign country, which depresses its net exports and output. Likewise a Home fiscal expansion under fixed exchange rates is contractionary for Foreign: the world interest rate is pushed up and this depresses output abroad.

In the medium run, i.e. after wages and prices at Home and abroad have adjusted,

- short-run monetary policy effects disappear: Home and Foreign return to their initial equilibrium levels of output.

- in the medium run, the effects of a Home fiscal expansion are independent of the exchange rate regime. The outcome is $\Delta y > 0$ and $\Delta y^* < 0$. In the new medium-run equilibrium, inflation in both economies is constant but output is higher in Home. Home's fiscal expansion therefore has a beggar-thy-neighbour effect.

- Thus, the *locomotive effect* of a Home fiscal expansion under flexible exchange rates is reversed in the medium run, so that in the new equilibrium: $\Delta y > 0$ and $\Delta y^* < 0$. The short-run locomotive effect for Foreign comes from the exchange rate depreciation but this pushes Foreign outside its *ERU* curve and inflation goes up once wages and prices respond. As its competitiveness declines, it returns to the *ERU* at lower output than its initial equilibrium, because the world interest rate is higher. Conversely, the Home economy reinforces its output gain as falling inflation boosts competitiveness.

- The *beggar-thy-neighbour effect* of a Home fiscal expansion under fixed exchange rates prevails i.e. $\Delta y > 0$ and $\Delta y^* < 0$ but is attenuated in the medium run. The reason is that output in Foreign falls in the short run at a given real exchange rate (because of the rise in the world interest rate); this leaves Foreign inside its *ERU* with falling inflation and the resulting rise in competitiveness for Foreign offsets some of the initial output fall.

The mechanisms at work are exactly those that have been used in the small open economy model. In section 2, we shall see that a simple extension of the θy–diagram allows the medium-run results for the 2-bloc case to be easily visualized. An algebraic method of deriving the results is also provided.

Once we accept the logic of the beggar-thy-neighbour phenomenon, i.e. that a country can use a policy to improve its economic outcomes at the expense of another country, this opens the way for *mutually* damaging policies when *both* countries pursue their own interests in this way. In turn, this sets the context for discussions of policy coordination.

1.1 Spillovers and the case for policy coordination

To draw policy implications from the phenomenon of spillovers and to discuss the case for policy coordination, it is useful to take an example. This entails looking at what happens when both Home and Foreign independently choose a policy that is in each country's own best interest but that results in a worse outcome for both than would have occurred had the two countries coordinated their policy choices.

Suppose that Home and Foreign are identical economies with a floating exchange rate and that the initial position of the 'world' is that each country is outside its *ERU* curve with the result that inflation in both countries, and hence in the world, is rising. This could be the outcome, for example, of a common external supply shock such as a rise in world oil prices. Now, suppose that each country wishes to reduce inflation but at minimum cost in terms of the associated rise in unemployment: if they simultaneously implement the appropriate monetary contraction, each will return to a stable inflation equilibrium with higher unemployment and with an unchanged exchange rate. We shall go through the details in section 3. However, if Home implements a more restrictive monetary policy than Foreign, it will benefit from stronger disinflation since exchange rate appreciation will reinforce the downward pressure on inflation coming from the reduction in output. Conversely, Foreign is harmed by Home's unilateral action because the implied depreciation of Foreign's exchange rate will exacerbate Foreign's inflation. Hence, by the same logic, Foreign has an incentive also to implement an overly restrictive monetary policy. We know that the exchange rate of both economies cannot appreciate and the net result of the more restrictive monetary policies implemented by both is an unnecessary and costly rise in the world interest rate and reduction in world output.

This problem has the structure of a so-called prisoners' dilemma game, which was introduced in Chapter 4. There are two policy options for each player— in this case, each country: either to implement a restrictive monetary policy or a very restrictive one. Each country considers the outcome (pay-off) that it will get in the event that the other country chooses either the restrictive or very restrictive policy. For Home, if Foreign were to choose the restrictive policy then Home would get a higher pay-off by choosing the very restrictive policy. If Foreign were to choose 'very restrictive', then again, Home is better off choosing the very restrictive option. Exactly the same logic applies to Foreign's decision-making process. Since both players do better—independent of the choice of the other—if they implement the very restrictive policy, this is what they will choose. In the language of game theory, this is the unique Nash equilibrium: only by both playing 'very restrictive', does neither have an incentive to change their strategy, i.e. to 'cheat'.

However, we know that if both countries implement the very restrictive policy, this produces a worse outcome for both than were they both to choose the less restrictive one. The essence of the problem is that unless they can come to a binding agreement not to renege, each will be tempted to tighten policy further (choosing 'very restrictive') since by doing so, they gain. This example demonstrates the way that interdependence can produce suboptimal outcomes for the world economy and shows where the motivation for the international coordination of policy comes from. However, it also highlights the problems associated with policy coordination. Policy coordination often refers to agreements made by leaders of countries at international summit meetings. We have seen that a binding agreement is needed in order for the solution that maximizes the utility of both parties, to be achieved. The beauty of the prisoners' dilemma game is that it pins down the difficulty of sustaining the joint utility maximizing solution even when both parties are identical, the strategies available are simple and known to both parties, and there are no other disturbances. It is likely to be very much more difficult to implement policy coordination in a turbulent world economy with non-identical economies and with uncertainty about how policy actions translate into outcomes.

Given the difficulty in securing binding agreements between countries in the example discussed, it is interesting to interpret the creation of exchange rate arrangements as a way of establishing a longer-term form of policy coordination. As we have noted, the locking of exchange rates is a kind of policy coordination. This rules out beggar-thy-neighbour policies that operate via changes in the exchange rate in the case discussed of a 'competitive disinflation' via a restrictive monetary policy or in the opposite case of a 'competitive depreciation' via an expansionary monetary policy. One of the arguments used in support of the formation of the Bretton Woods fixed exchange rate system was to reduce the likelihood of the occurence of the damaging competitive devaluations that took place in the inter-war period and that unleashed a wave of protectionism (with its additional economic costs). The formation of the ERM in 1979 was motivated in part by the analysis of the damaging effects of using the exchange rate to achieve competitive disinflation. In a parallel fashion, one set of arguments in favour of the creation of the eurozone was that in order to protect the benefits from trade integration achieved in the European Union (spurred by the Single Market Programme), the temptation for countries to engage in competitive depreciations should be removed.

1.2 Interdependence in the short run: extending the Mundell–Fleming model

In this subsection, we show

- how to extend the short-run analysis of the small open economy in the 2-bloc model;
- the origin of spillover effects such as locomotive and beggar-thy-neighbour effects;
- how a sufficiently strong income feedback effect can outweigh the beggar-thy-neighbour effect;
- how spillovers give rise to arguments for policy coordination.

In the short run, prices and wages are given in both economies. We simplify further by assuming that inflation in both is zero, which means that the nominal and real interest rates are equal and we can draw the IS/LM diagram with the nominal interest rate on the vertical axis. To analyse interdependence, we place the UIP diagram, representing the integrated capital market, between the IS/LM diagrams for Foreign and Home (Fig. 12.1).

To establish the starting point for the analysis, the diagram is drawn with the same interest rate in both economies, $i_0 = i_0^*$. This guarantees that there will be no change in the exchange rate, if we assume that the expected exchange rate is equal to the pre-existing exchange rate. This reflects the uncovered interest parity condition, in which the

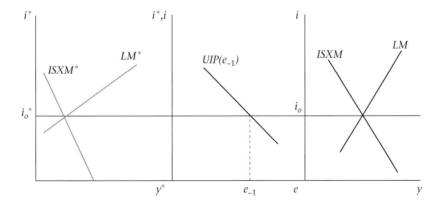

Figure 12.1 The 2-bloc model diagram

expected percentage depreciation of the nominal exchange rate between the Home and the Foreign country must be equal to the excess of the domestic rate of interest above the foreign rate:

$$\underbrace{i - i^*}_{\text{interest gain (loss)}} = \underbrace{\frac{e^E_{t+1} - e_t}{e_t} \approx \log e^E_{t+1} - \log e_t = \log e_{t-1} - \log e_t.}_{\text{expected depreciation (appreciation)}}$$

(uncovered interest parity)

In all the diagrams, e referes to $\log e$. The exchange rate will remain unchanged when the two interest rates are equal. We can now ask the Mundell–Fleming questions: what happens as we change monetary and fiscal policy? As noted in the introduction, the nature of the spillovers from policy in Home to outcomes in Foreign in the short run depends on the exchange rate regime.

1.2.1 Flexible exchange rates

We look first at policy changes in the Home country, while both fiscal and monetary policy in the Foreign country are held constant.

Fiscal policy: Home expansion

Our intuition suggests that under flexible exchange rates, the spillover from Home's fiscal expansion results from the fact that the appreciation of the exchange rate for Home, due to the upward pressure on the interest rate, entails a depreciation for Foreign and that this will boost its output. In the small open economy case, a Home fiscal expansion has no short-run effect on output at Home because the exchange rate appreciates sufficiently to fully offset the expansionary fiscal impulse. In analytical terms, since LM is fixed and i^* is exogenous for the small open economy, the only possible new short-run equilibrium (with $i = i^*$) is with output back at its original level. In the 2-bloc model, there is no longer an exogenous world interest rate.

The analysis is shown in the diagram (Fig. 12.2). We begin with the right-hand Home quadrant. The initial position is (i_0, y_0) at the intersection of $ISXM$ and LM. We assume

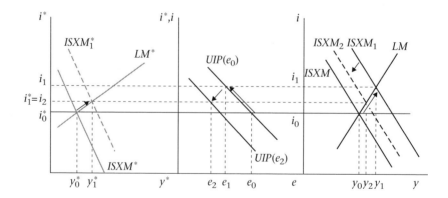

Figure 12.2 Locomotive effect of a fiscal expansion in home: flexible exchange rates

the initial Foreign equilibrium is at (i_0^*, y_0^*) where $ISXM^*$ cuts LM^* with $i_0^* = i_0$. The foreign exchange market is in equilibrium with $e_1^E = e_0$. Now government expenditure is increased in Home, which pushes the $ISXM$ curve to $ISXM_1$. The Home economy moves up the LM curve (see the upwards-sloping arrow), pushing up the interest rate to i_1 and output to y_1. Nothing has so far happened in Foreign. The rise in the interest rate implies that $i = i_1 > i^* = i_0^*$; and this triggers an appreciation of e from e_0 to e_1. Foreign is now affected. This is because $e^* = -e$: remember that the 'e's are in logarithmic form. Hence Home's appreciation is an equiproportionate depreciation for Foreign.

The exchange rate impacts on each country's exports. The appreciation in Home lowers Home exports, and this is manifested in a backwards shift of $ISXM$, from $ISXM_1$ to, say, $ISXM_2$. This pulls down i. By contrast, Foreign's depreciation raises Foreign's exports, pushing $ISXM^*$ up, say, to $ISXM_1^*$. And this pushes up i^*. So long as $i > i^*$, e will go on appreciating and e^* depreciating; this in turn means that Home exports and $ISXM$ will go on falling (moving leftwards) and Foreign exports and $ISXM^*$ will go on rising; thus so long as $i > i^*$ there is an automatic process pushing i down and i^* up until the two equalize. At that point e stops appreciating (e^* depreciating), and $ISXM$ and $ISXM^*$ stop moving; a new equilibrium has been reached. For simplicity as we have drawn it, i^* rises to i_2^* and this is equal to the new value of i, namely i_2. In any case, in principle, as $ISXM^*$ moving up raises i^* and $ISXM$ moving down lowers i, at some point the two interest rates will equalize, and there will be no further pressure on e to go on appreciating (or for e^* to go on depreciating).

The new equilibrium exchange rate is e_2. We have explained the adjustment process using backward-looking exchange rate expectations but the new short-run equilibrium will be reached instantly if exchange market operators know the model and output adjusts fast. In this case, the exchange rate jumps immediately to e_2 and the common interest rate to $i_2 = i_2^*$. In the short run, both economies benefit in terms of higher output from Home's fiscal expansion: higher government spending at Home crowds out net exports, which provides demand for Foreign. The higher world interest rate entails some crowding out of investment spending in both economies but higher government spending outweighs the effect of this on output at Home and higher net exports outweighs this in Foreign.

Some simple mathematics

It is useful to show this result (and others) analytically. To simplify the algebra, we use linear functions and focus on the net changes from the initial to the new short-run equilibrium. First the $ISXM$ schedule is written

$$y = ag - bi + cB(e)$$

where B is the balance of trade and a, b, and c are positive constants. B depends positively on the exchange rate (we assume that the Marshall–Lerner condition holds) and for simplicity we assume $B(e) = e$. We write the net changes from the initial to the new short-run equilibrium, e.g. from y_0 to y_2, as $\Delta y = y_2 - y_0$, etc. So we can write this as

$$\triangle y = a\Delta g - b\Delta i + c\Delta e.$$

Next the *LM* schedule is $i = \lambda y - \mu M$ or in difference terms

$$\Delta i = \lambda \Delta y - \mu \Delta M,$$

where Greek letters are chosen to represent the constants in the *LM* equation so as to make it easy to see how the parameters of the *ISXM* and of the *LM* come into play. For Foreign we have

$$\Delta y^* = a\Delta g^* - b\Delta i^* - c\Delta e,$$

where we again simplify by assuming that Foreign's trade balance is $B^*(e) = -e$. And

$$\Delta i^* = \lambda \Delta y^* - \mu \Delta M^*.$$

Also, for convenience it is assumed that the schedules in both blocs have the same parameters.

Now bear in mind that a Home fiscal expansion in a flexible exchange rate system implies $\Delta M = \Delta M^* = \Delta G^* = 0$. In addition, $\Delta i = \Delta i^*$. This is true for all policy changes with perfect capital mobility and with the assumption that in the new short-run equilibrium, $e^E = e$. In other words, even if interest rates diverge during the adjustment process, they must eventually be the same if the exchange rate is to be stabilized. Next, these assumptions are plugged into the four equations. We get for Home,

$$\Delta y = a\Delta g - b\lambda \Delta y + c\Delta e.$$

Note that $\Delta i^* = \lambda \Delta y^* = \Delta i = \lambda \Delta y$, so $\Delta y = \Delta y^*$. Hence from the two Foreign equations

$$\Delta y = -b\lambda \Delta y - c\Delta e.$$

Adding these two equations together

$$2\Delta y = a\Delta g - 2b\lambda \Delta y$$
$$\Rightarrow \Delta y = \frac{a}{2(1 + b\lambda)}\Delta g = \Delta y^*.$$

This expression gives us a clearer focus on comparative results:

- As we have seen, by comparison with the small open economy case, $\Delta y > 0$ since i^* rises, and thus exchange rate appreciation with $i > i^*$ does not force i back all the way to its original value implying $\Delta y = 0$.

- The comparison with the closed economy is also interesting: in the closed economy, i simply stays at i_1 in Fig. 12.2—there is no pressure from the exchange market to push it down again. The equations are simply $\Delta y = a\Delta g - b\Delta i$ and $\Delta i = \lambda \Delta y$, so $\Delta y = \frac{a}{(1+b\lambda)}\Delta g$. In the 2-bloc case the appreciation of the exchange rate leads to the decline of i from i_1 to i_2 (but not i_0 as in the small economy case). Thus the deflationary effect of the exchange rate is obviously greater on y than in the closed economy case. So $\Delta y = \frac{a}{2(1+b\lambda)}\Delta g$ instead of $\Delta y = \frac{a}{(1+b\lambda)}\Delta g$ in the closed economy.

We can also use this approach to work out the effect of fiscal policy on the interest rate and the exchange rate. Since $\Delta i = \lambda \Delta y$ it follows that

$$\Delta i = \lambda \Delta y = \frac{a\lambda}{2(1+b\lambda)}\Delta g.$$

Note that this is an increase of i exactly half that of the increase in the closed economy where $\Delta i = \frac{a\lambda}{(1+b\lambda)}\Delta g$. These results confirm the informal argument at the end of Chapter 9, where we claimed that the results for the large open economy (the 2-bloc model is the simplest way of analysing this) were in between those for the small open economy and the closed economy. Substituting the previous two equations into $\Delta y = a\Delta g - b\lambda \Delta y + c\Delta e$ implies

$$\Delta e = -\frac{ab\lambda}{c(1+b\lambda)}\Delta g.$$

Monetary policy with flexible exchange rates: Home expansion

Home increases the money supply. Remember in the small open economy case there is an initial increase in output from y_0 to y_1 as Home moves down the $ISXM$ with the fall in i. In addition $i < i^*$, so e rises (depreciates) and this continues—pushing up exports and hence pushing $ISXM$ rightwards—until i has returned to i^*. Hence by contrast to the fiscal expansion in the small economy, monetary policy is highly effective in stimulating output. But what happens in the 2-bloc case?

As can be seen in the right hand panel of Fig. 12.3, we start at $i_0 = i_0^*$ and y_0 at the intersection of $ISXM$ and LM. LM then moves down to LM_1 representing the increase in Home money supply: i falls to i_1 and y is pushed up to y_1. Since $i = i_1$ is now below $i^* = i_0^*$, the exchange rate depreciates, e rising from e_0 to e_1.

As long as $i < i^*$, e will continue to depreciate and Foreign's exchange rate to appreciate, pushing $ISXM$ rightwards and $ISXM^*$ leftwards. As $ISXM$ moves rightwards up LM_1, i rises and as $ISXM^*$ moves leftwards down LM^*, i^* falls. At some point the rising i meets the falling i^*. Assume this takes place when $ISXM$ has risen to $ISXM_1$ and when $ISXM^*$ has fallen to $ISXM_1^*$; this is shown in Fig. 12.3. Thus the result of monetary expansion in

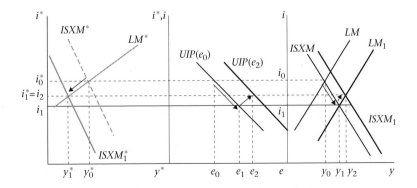

Figure 12.3 Beggar-thy-neighbour effect of a home monetary expansion: flexible exchange rates

Home is that Home output increases from y_0 to y_2 while Foreign output falls from y_0^* to y_1^*. The mechanism is that monetary expansion in Home leads to a depreciation of e and an appreciation of Foreign's exchange rate.

By modifying the equations to fit this case (i.e. by putting $\Delta g = 0$ and $\Delta M^* = 0$), we can show: (i) Output increases in Home, $\Delta y > 0$, and declines in Foreign, $\Delta y^* < 0$. (ii) Total output increases, $\Delta y + \Delta y^* > 0$. (iii) The interest rate falls, $\Delta i = \Delta i^* < 0$. And (iv) Home's exchange rate depreciates and Foreign's appreciates, $\Delta e > 0$.

In short, what happens is that the looser monetary policy in Home pulls down the interest rate; the world interest rate is the average result of monetary policy in the two blocs; so since foreign monetary policy does not change, the world interest rate falls by roughly half the initial fall in i. Since the world interest rate falls, total world output, $y + y^*$, increases. But since Home initiated the interest rate fall, which meant that the Home exchange rate depreciates and Foreign appreciates, the $ISXM^*$ schedule must shift leftwards down the LM^* curve; and since the LM^* curve is upwards sloping, y^* must fall (see Fig. 12.3) even though the decline in the world interest rate softens the fall. This case is otherwise referred to as that of 'competitive depreciation': the fixed exchange rate equivalent is a discrete devaluation, i.e. 'competitive devaluation'. This is the classic beggar-thy-neighbour policy where Home's welfare gain from higher output relies on the output loss in Foreign.

1.2.2 Fixed exchange rates

Fiscal policy: Home expansion

In the small open economy case a fiscal expansion is highly effective since the interest rate remains unchanged and therefore there are full multiplier effects. Note that, although the domestic money supply remains unchanged, foreign funds enter as soon as i rises above i^* thus augmenting M, pushing the LM curve rightwards and pushing i back down again to i^*. Thus fiscal expansion is more effective in the small open economy than in the closed economy where the LM curve remains fixed: in that case the IS curve moves up the LM curve and part of the fiscal boost is blunted by the rising rate of interest.

The 2-bloc model is in between these two cases. World money supply, $M + M^*$, is constant. The Home expansion of fiscal policy initially pushes i above i^*, and this leads to an inflow of foreign money: the consequence is a move right of the Home LM curve and a move left of the Foreign LM^* curve; thus i is partially pushed down by the inflow of money, but the reduction in Foreign money supply pushes up i^* so that i does not fall fully back to its original level. In short, fiscal policy (in one country) is more effective than in the closed economy case because there is a transfer of world money to Home—as in the small open economy model; but less effective than in the small open economy model because that transfer is large enough to raise the foreign interest rate i^*. We can follow through what happens in Fig. 12.4.

We start at the intersection of $ISXM$ and LM in Home and $ISXM^*$ and LM^* in Foreign. A Home fiscal expansion pushes the $ISXM$ curve rightwards towards $ISXM_1$. As i rises above i^*, Foreign funds purchase the Home currency shifting LM towards LM_1—damping the rise in i—and LM^* towards LM_1^*, pushing up i^*. Thus equilibrium is reached in Home at the intersection of $ISXM_1$ and LM_1 with $i = i_1 = i^* = i_1^*$ and $y = y_1$; and in Foreign at the intersection of $ISXM_1^*$ and LM_1^* with $y^* = y_1^*$. Home's fiscal expansion raises the

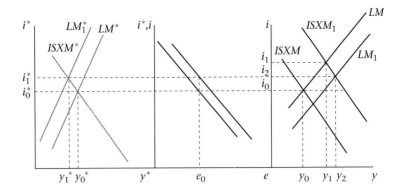

Figure 12.4 Home fiscal expansion: fixed exchange rates

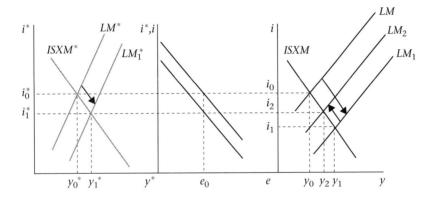

Figure 12.5 Home monetary expansion: fixed exchange rates

world interest rate and therefore imposes a cut in output on Foreign. To work out the result using the equations, we need to put $\Delta e = 0$, $\Delta g^* = 0$ and $\Delta M + \Delta M^* = 0$: the world money supply is constant.

Monetary policy: Home expansion

By contrast with the small open economy case where monetary expansion under fixed exchange rates has no effect on output, in the 2-bloc model output expands equally in both countries. Another way of putting this is to say that it makes no difference whether the expansion of the money supply takes place in Home or Foreign. The intuition is the same as pouring water into one end or the other of a trough—all that happens is that the water level rises everywhere until the surface is again flat; in this case, the extra money spreads itself around the world until interest rates are equalized at a new common lower level. In Fig. 12.5, we start as before at the intersections of *ISXM* and *LM* and of *ISXM** and *LM**. The money supply increases by ΔM and this pushes *LM* down to LM_1, implying a cut in the interest rate to i_1 from $i = i_0^* = i_0$. (The *ISXM* curve does not shift.) Given that $i_1 < i^* = i_0^*$, and that there is no exchange rate risk ($e^E = e_0$) investors immediately transfer funds out of Home into Foreign to get the high rate of interest. Thus LM now shifts up reflecting this loss of reserves at the same time as LM^* moves down as these funds augment M^*. This process stops as soon as interest rates are equalized again with $i_2 = i_2^*$ or where LM_2 intersects $ISXM$ and LM_1^* intersects $ISXM^*$. Output expands equally in both economies: at Home from y_0 to y_2 and in Foreign from y_0^* to y_1^*. Checking the results using the equations proceeds as in the other cases: here $\Delta g = 0$ and we assume that $\Delta i = \Delta i^*$.

1.3 Adding the income feedback effect

To this point, spillovers between economies have occurred only through changes in the interest rate and exchange rate. We have not taken account of the possibility that a change in Foreign income boosts Home aggregate demand via increased Home exports and vice versa. In the small economy analysis of Chapter 9, it was assumed that Home policies had no effect on Foreign income, so that there were no feedback effects from Foreign as a result of Home policies. On the other hand, we did include world output (y^*) as a determinant of exports. In the 2-bloc model, it is the case that an expansion of output in Home will raise demand in Foreign since Home's imports rise with income and constitute Foreign's exports. How are the results for the 2-bloc model modified or amplified by income feedback effects? In the four cases so far, the changes in y and y^* have been:

(1) flexible exchange rate/ fiscal expansion, $\Delta y, \Delta y^* > 0$;

(2) flexible exchange rate/monetary expansion, $\Delta y > 0, \Delta y^* < 0$;

(3) fixed exchange rate/fiscal expansion, $\Delta y > 0, \Delta y^* < 0$;

(4) fixed exchange rate/monetary expansion, $\Delta y, \Delta y^* > 0$.

In cases (1) and (4), where we have locomotive effects in play in the sense that the effects on output are positive in both blocs, further positive linkages between Home and Foreign output will reinforce those positive effects. What is more interesting is that the positive income feedback effect—if sufficiently strong—can alter the beggar-thy-neighbour predictions of (2) and (3).

To illustrate this, we take case (3), a fiscal expansion under fixed exchange rates. The key modification in the equations is to add a term in Δy^* to the $ISXM$ equation and in Δy to the $ISXM^*$ equation. We therefore have the two $ISXM$ and the two LM equations. First, the $ISXM$ equations for Home and Foreign:

$$\Delta y = a\Delta g - b\Delta i + d\Delta y^*$$
$$\Delta y^* = -b\Delta i + d\Delta y$$

and the LM equations are:

$$\Delta i = \lambda\Delta y - \mu\Delta M$$
$$\Delta i = \lambda\Delta y^* - \mu\Delta M^*$$

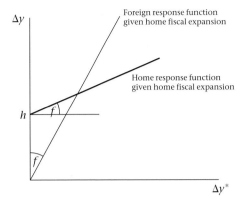

Figure 12.6 Locomotion effects: home fiscal expansion: fixed exchange rate

where $\Delta M + \Delta M^* = 0$. The LM equations imply that $\Delta i = \frac{\lambda}{2}\Delta y + \frac{\lambda}{2}\Delta y^*$, so we have the two reduced form aggregate demand equations:

$$\Delta y = \frac{a}{1 + \frac{b\lambda}{2}}\Delta g + \frac{d - \frac{b\lambda}{2}}{1 + \frac{b\lambda}{2}}\Delta y^*$$

$$\Delta y^* = \frac{d - \frac{b\lambda}{2}}{1 + \frac{b\lambda}{2}}\Delta y.$$

This is illustrated in Fig. 12.6.

The angle f is $\frac{d - \frac{b\lambda}{2}}{1 + \frac{b\lambda}{2}}$ and the distance h is $\frac{a}{1 + \frac{b\lambda}{2}}\Delta g$. Thus the shallower upwards-sloping line is the aggregate demand equation for Δy and the steeper that for Δy^*. The equilibrium is where they intersect. As the two lines have been drawn both Δy and Δy^* are positive. As can be seen from the formula for f, the slope of these lines depends on the sign of $d - \frac{b\lambda}{2}$. To get both Δy and Δy^* positive, requires $d > \frac{b\lambda}{2}$. There is a simple interpretation of this condition: it is that the positive income effect of y^* on y, namely d, outweighs the negative effect of y^* via i on y, namely $\frac{b\lambda}{2}$.

In the previous subsections without the income feedback effect, $d = 0$ so evidently $d - \frac{b\lambda}{2} < 0$. In that case the intersection of the two aggregate demand lines is in the top left quadrant with $\Delta y > 0$ and $\Delta y^* < 0$. In the balancing case of $d = \frac{b\lambda}{2}$, so that the Δy^* aggregate demand line is vertical and the Δy line is horizontal, the intersection of the two lines is on the vertical axis with $\Delta y > 0$ and $\Delta y^* = 0$. In this case, f is zero.

2 International spillovers in the medium run

We now turn to analyse what happens when wages and prices are allowed to adjust. In the medium run, i.e. after wages and prices have adjusted:

- The effects of monetary policy actions disappear: Home and Foreign return to their initial equilibrium levels of output.

- In the medium run, the effects of a Home fiscal expansion are independent of the exchange rate regime: the outcome is $\Delta y > 0$ and $\Delta y^* < 0$.[1]

- Thus, the *locomotive effect* of a Home fiscal expansion under flexible exchange rates is reversed in the medium run. The short-run locomotive effect for Foreign comes from the exchange rate depreciation but this pushes it outside its *ERU* curve and inflation goes up. As its competitiveness declines, it returns to the *ERU* curve at lower output than its initial equilibrium, because the world interest rate is higher. Conversely, the Home economy reinforces its output gain as falling inflation boosts competitiveness.

- The *beggar-thy-neighbour effect* of a Home fiscal expansion under fixed exchange rates prevails but is attenuated in the medium run. The reason is that output in Foreign falls in the short run at a given real exchange rate (because of the rise in the world interest rate); this leaves Foreign inside its *ERU* curve with falling inflation and the resulting rise in competitiveness for Foreign offsets some of the initial output fall.

This set of results highlights the fact that *fiscal* imbalances are a potential source of international tension in the medium run that is assumed away in the small open economy case.

What about the long-run implications? Fiscal imbalances are associated with wealth transfers between the blocs with a current account deficit associated with fiscal expansion in one economy and vice versa for the other economy. In the small open economy, we saw that a medium-run equilibrium with falling or rising wealth could persist for a long period. Eventually, the accumulated foreign debt associated with the country running a persistent current account surplus triggers a decline in private sector demand and a reduction in the current account imbalance. This happens via wealth effects or via a more contractionary fiscal stance—directly, as a consequence of concern about solvency or indirectly, as a consequence of inflation generated by exchange rate depreciation as foreign exchange markets anticipate the recourse to a burst of inflation as a means of reducing the debt. In the 2-bloc model, there is also no automatic mechanism for restoring long-run equilibrium. The analysis of interdependence helps to explain the political difficulty of unwinding accumulated international imbalances. For example, under flexible exchange rates, as we have seen, a fiscal contraction in the deficit country has the short-run effect of reducing output in Foreign as well: Home's exchange rate depreciates and Foreign's appreciates. This will be reinforced by any income feedback effects.

2.1 Basic diagram for medium-run analysis in 2-bloc model

The basic diagram we use to analyse the medium run is a development of the *ERU* diagram of Chapters 10 and 11. In effect the Home *ERU* diagram is the north-east quadrant, with y on the right horizontal and θ on the rising vertical axes (for simplicity, all the variables are measured in logs). The Foreign *ERU* diagram occupies the south-west quadrant,

---

[1] If both countries are using a monetary rule (under flexible exchange rates) then the adjustment to the medium-run equilibrium will be different (just as we have seen in Chapter 11 in the small open economy context). With rational exchange rate expectations and rapid output adjustment, the economies will go straight to the medium-run equilibrium. With more realistic assumptions, the adjustment path to the medium-run equilibrium under a monetary rule regime in both countries is likely to look more like that under fixed exchange rates: either way, there is no locomotive effect.

with $-\theta$ on the left horizontal axis and y^* on the falling vertical axis. In equilibrium with constant inflation, as we saw in Chapter 10, a country has to be on its *ERU*. In the small open economy case, it is assumed that a country can alter its competitiveness, θ, in relation to the rest of the world—the country is small enough that the rest of the world does not notice. In the 2-bloc model, as we have seen, a change in Home's real or nominal exchange rate is an equal and opposite change in Foreign's exchange rate. In 'world' equilibrium, both Home and Foreign must be on their respective *ERU*s, and in addition the level of competitiveness of the two blocs must be consistent: this constraint was ignored in the small open economy and is shown in Fig. 12.7.

As can be seen, the Home *ERU* is in the north-east quadrant and the Foreign *ERU* in the south-west. The constraint that a rise in Home's real exchange rate is a fall in Foreign's is shown by the line in the north-west quadrant. It has a slope of 45° indicating that a one-unit increase in Home's competitiveness implies a one-unit reduction in Foreign's and vice versa. We can put together the three conditions that each bloc is on its *ERU* and that the competitiveness of each bloc is consistent with that of the other to work out what combinations of y and y^* are equilibrium combinations for the 2-economy world as a whole. We call the set of equilibrium combinations of y and y^* the World *ERU*, or *ERU_W*. Two sets of equilibrium combinations of y and y^* are derived explicitly in the diagram. If we begin with a low level of output in Home, y_L; to be on Home's *ERU* implies a high level of competitiveness θ_H (low y means high unemployment, which means a low real wage and hence a high level of competitiveness); θ_H means in turn that competitiveness in Foreign is low, which in turn implies that equilibrium output in Foreign is high (high y^* means low unemployment, which entails a high real wage and hence a low level of competitiveness). Thus the first equilibrium combination is (y_L, y_H^*), which can be found by tracing the dashed line through the four quadrants of the diagram. By following exactly the same procedure, starting with y_H, we get the combination (y_H, y_L^*).

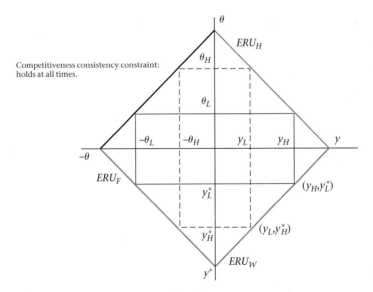

Figure 12.7 Deriving the world *ERU* curve

We defined equilibrium in earlier chapters in terms of constant inflation rates, and it will be useful to show that the ERU_W represents constant *world* inflation, see Fig. 12.8. We make the following assumptions:

$$\pi^W = .5\pi + .5\pi^* = .5\frac{\dot{W}}{W} + .5\frac{\dot{W}^*}{W^*},$$

where π^W is world inflation, π and π^* are Home and Foreign inflation, and $\frac{\dot{W}}{W}$ and $\frac{\dot{W}^*}{W^*}$ are nominal wage inflation in Home and Foreign. This follows from assuming labour productivity is constant in Home and Foreign. Next

$$\frac{\dot{W}}{W} \lesseqgtr \pi_{-1} \text{ as } (y, \theta) \text{ is } \begin{matrix} \text{inside} \\ \text{on} \\ \text{outside} \end{matrix} \quad ERU_H$$

and

$$\frac{\dot{W}^*}{W^*} \lesseqgtr \pi^*_{-1} \text{ as } (y^*, -\theta) \text{ is } \begin{matrix} \text{inside} \\ \text{on} \\ \text{outside} \end{matrix} \quad ERU_F.$$

To understand why world inflation is constant when the world economy is on ERU_W, the simplest case to take is when an equilibrium output combination, such as (y_L, y^*_H),

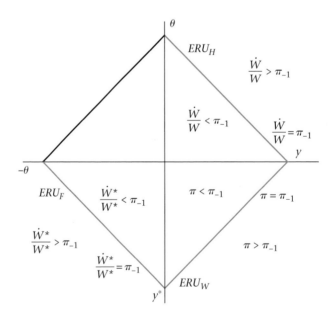

Figure 12.8 Stable inflation along the ERU_W

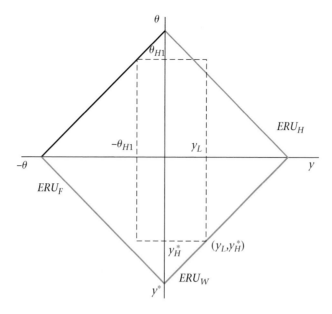

Figure 12.9 Stable world inflation: home inflation rising and foreign inflation falling

goes with both Home and Foreign being on their respective ERUs. The argument is then straightforward: since $\pi^W = .5\frac{\dot{W}}{W} + .5\frac{\dot{W}^*}{W^*}$ and since (y_L, θ_H) and $(y_H^*, -\theta_H)$ are both on their respective ERUs, this implies that $\frac{\dot{W}}{W} = \pi_{-1}$ and $\frac{\dot{W}^*}{W^*} = \pi_{-1}^*$. Inflation remains constant in each economy so it will remain constant in the world economy.

Inflation can be constant in the world even if (y_L, θ_H) and $(y_H^*, -\theta_H)$ are not on their respective ERUs, as long as the world economy is on the world ERU. We see this in Fig. 12.9.

In the example (y_L, y_H^*) are an equilibrium combination, i.e. on the ERU_W, but neither (y_L, θ_{H1}) nor $(y_H^*, -\theta_{H1})$ are on their individual ERUs. However ERU_W still implies constant inflation as long as the rising inflation in Home exactly offsets the falling inflation in Foreign. This will be the case as long as a technical assumption is met: that is, that the Home Phillips curve $\frac{\dot{W}}{W} = \pi_{-1} + k$ where k is the orthogonal distance of (y, θ) from ERU_H and with an equivalent condition holding for Foreign. We state without proving—it should be visually evident—that if (y, y^*) is an equilibrium combination, then (y, θ) and $(y^*, -\theta)$ are equidistant from their respective ERUs, with $(y^*, -\theta)$ inside its ERU and (y, θ) outside its ERU (or vice versa). If these conditions hold, $\pi^W = .5\frac{\dot{W}}{W} + .5\frac{\dot{W}^*}{W^*}$, $\frac{\dot{W}}{W} = \pi_{-1} + k$, and $\frac{\dot{W}^*}{W^*} = \pi_{-1}^* - k$. Hence as long as an output combination is on ERU_W, the world inflation rate will be constant with rising inflation in one economy balanced by falling inflation in the other.

2.2 Aggregate demand

We next introduce Home and Foreign aggregate demand curves. These operate similarly to the AD curves in Chapter 10 (see section 3). However there is one important difference.

In Chapters 10 and 11, the *AD* curve is drawn for a given world interest rate since the world interest rate is exogenous to the small economy. The consequence was that exogenous shifts in the world interest rate shifted the *AD* curve. In the 2-bloc model our assumption of integrated capital markets means as usual that $i = i^*$ throughout; but by contrast with the small economy case, monetary and fiscal policy change *both i* and *i**. Each aggregate demand schedule is drawn for a single value of $i = i^*$. But when the actual level of aggregate demand changes (either because of monetary or fiscal policy, or because of changing inflation) then $i = i^*$ will change and we move to a new *AD* curve. We shall show how this takes place below for the different cases of fixed and floating exchange rates and monetary and fiscal policy.

2.3 Excess world demand

As a preliminary, we show what happens if aggregate demand in the two blocs creates an overall inflationary situation, i.e. that (y, y^*) lies outside the ERU_W line. In Fig. 12.10, the *AD* and *AD** lines are respectively the Home and Foreign aggregate demand schedules. We assume that the two economies have identical parameters, including for the money supply and government expenditure. In addition $\theta = -\theta$.

Home is at point *b* and Foreign at point *b**. It can be seen that the outcome of these *AD* curves is that (y, y^*) is outside ERU_W, and (y, θ) and $(y^*, -\theta)$ are outside their respective *ERU* schedules by equal amounts—so that domestic inflationary pressures are the same in both blocs. We also assume exchange rates are fixed. From the diagram, it is clear that with the levels of government expenditure in each country fixing the *AD* curves as

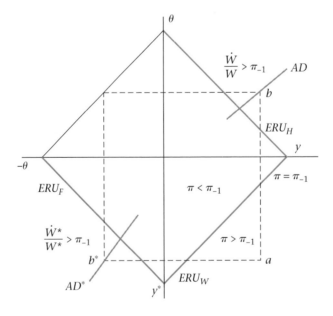

Figure 12.10 Excess world aggregate demand

shown, an equilibrium on the countries' and the world *ERU* is impossible. The outcome will therefore be rising inflation in both countries and rising world inflation, as shown by point *a* outside the world *ERU*.

This can be interpreted as another example of the impact of spillovers: each country seeks to achieve a new constant inflation medium-run equilibrium at lower unemployment by raising government spending. If the other country remains passive, Home achieves this outcome (this was always the assumption in the small open economy analysis). However, since both countries reason in the same way, both choose the high level of government spending, with the consequence that world inflation rises. The world interest rate will then rise, shifting the *AD* curves in a restrictive direction in each country: each will return to lower output but at the cost of a period of higher inflation. The problem of a fiscal policy spillover of this kind in the eurozone where exchange rates are irrevocably fixed is one motivation for the presence of a fiscal policy rule within a monetary union. We return in section 4 to discuss the Stability and Growth Pact of the eurozone.

The adjustment path back to the constant inflation equilibrium is shown in Fig. 12.11: the system begins at *a* in the south-east quadrant and at *b* and b^* in the north-east and south-west quadrants, with $y^* = y_0^* = y = y_0$. We call the initial interest rate i_0, so that y_0 is on $AD(i_0)$ and y_0^* is on $AD^*(i_0)$. At *a*, inflation is rising with the result that the real money supply is reduced in both blocs at a uniform rate. Thus in terms of the $ISXM/LM$ diagram, the interest rate is being pushed up and the *AD* curves shift in a deflationary direction to reflect this. Note that exactly the same process is happening in both blocs so no money needs to flow between them. Since the exchange rate is fixed, and inflation is the same in both blocs, the real exchange rate remains unchanged. Thus the rise in the

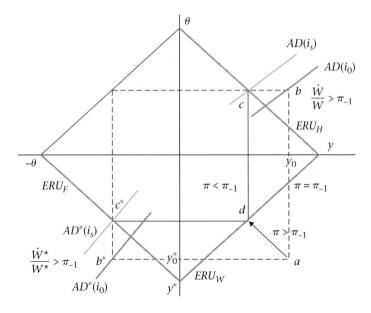

Figure 12.11 Excess world demand: adjustment via rising interest rates

real interest rate reduces y and y^* equiproportionately so that in the south-east quadrant, we move up the 45° line from a towards d. Correspondingly there is a horizontal shift in Home's quadrant, as y falls while θ remains constant and a vertical shift in the Foreign quadrant as y^* falls with its real exchange rate constant. This process goes on until $y = y^*$ and Home and Foreign reach symmetric equilibrium values at c and c^*. The interest rate is labelled i_S to indicate that this is the stabilizing interest rate associated with world output at equilibrium at point d. In section 3, we work through each of the cases of fiscal and monetary policy under fixed and floating exchange rates.

3 Interdependence in the short and medium run: a simple model

In this section we look at where economies end up in the medium run in the case of expansionary fiscal and monetary policies under both fixed and flexible exchange rate regimes. In each of these four cases, we assume that there has been a Home expansion while monetary and fiscal policies in Foreign remain unchanged. Diagrams are provided in the Appendix for each case in addition to an explanation of the process of adjustment from the short- to the medium-run equilibrium.

Each case can be described by three equations for Home: IS, LM, and ERU, and the corresponding three for Foreign, IS^*, LM^*, and ERU^*. These equations are all in first difference form, so that, instead of writing IS as $y = g - ai + \theta$, it is written $\Delta y = \Delta g - a\Delta i + \Delta\theta$; LM becomes $\Delta i = \lambda\Delta y - \mu(\Delta M - \Delta P)$; and ERU is $\Delta y = -\Delta\theta$. Correspondingly, IS^* is $\Delta y^* = \Delta g^* - a\Delta i^* - \Delta\theta$, LM^* is $\Delta i^* = \lambda\Delta y^* - \mu(\Delta M^* - \Delta P^*)$ and ERU^* is $\Delta y^* = \Delta\theta$.

As well as these six equations we also have the uncovered interest parity condition for short-run equilibrium in the foreign exchange market, $i - i^* = e^E - e$. We assume in addition that $e^E = e$, so that $i = i^*$, and hence in our LM and IS equations, we can impose the condition that $\Delta i = \Delta i^*$. Finally, we need to remember the definition $\theta \equiv \frac{P^* e}{P}$, so that $\Delta\theta = \Delta e + \Delta P^* - \Delta P$ (remember the variables are in logs). Next, we look at the conditions which define fixed and flexible exchange rate regimes.

Fixed exchange rate regime This is defined first by $\Delta e = 0$: the nominal exchange rate does not change. But there is also the requirement that the world money supply is given and the money supply in each economy is endogenous: $\Delta M + \Delta M^* = \Delta\overline{M}$. Thus under this regime we have nine equations, our original six plus $\Delta\theta = \Delta e + \Delta P^* - \Delta P$, and in addition $\Delta e = 0$ and $\Delta M + \Delta M^* = \Delta\overline{M}$. And there are nine unknowns: Δy, Δy^*, Δi, $\Delta\theta$, ΔP, ΔP^*, Δe, ΔM and ΔM^*. $\Delta\overline{M}$, Δg, Δg^* are exogenous.

Flexible exchange rate regime Here by contrast the money supply in each country is given, so that ΔM is given, as is ΔM^*. In this case there are seven equations, our original six plus $\Delta\theta = \Delta e + \Delta P^* - \Delta P$, and seven unknowns, Δy, Δy^*, Δi, $\Delta\theta$, ΔP, ΔP^* and Δe, with ΔM, ΔM^*, Δg and Δg^* exogenous.

We assume in what follows that expected inflation in the medium-run equilibrium is zero, so that we do not need to distinguish between nominal and real interest rates.

3.1 Monetary expansion under fixed exchange rates

In this case we assume $\Delta g = \Delta g^* = 0$. Wherever monetary expansion comes from, i.e. from Home or from Foreign, it implies an equivalent expansion of the world money supply, so $\Delta \overline{M} > 0$. Thus our equations are:

$$\Delta y = -a\Delta i + \Delta\theta \tag{IS}$$
$$\Delta y^* = -a\Delta i - \Delta\theta \tag{IS*}$$
$$\Delta i = \lambda\Delta y - \mu(\Delta M - \Delta P) \tag{LM}$$
$$\Delta i = \lambda\Delta y^* - \mu(\Delta M^* - \Delta P^*) \tag{LM*}$$
$$\Delta y = -\Delta\theta \tag{ERU}$$
$$\Delta y^* = \Delta\theta \tag{ERU*}$$
$$\Delta\theta = \Delta P^* - \Delta P$$

It can be seen at once from the *ERU* equations that $\Delta y + \Delta y^* = 0$. This is the fundamental condition for medium-run equilibrium— we have to be on the world *ERU*, ERU^W, so if output in one economy rises it has to fall equivalently in the other. This is another way of saying that the world economy has a unique equilibrium rate of world output for constant world inflation. And each country needs to be on its *ERU* for stable domestic inflation.

This means that world demand is constant and since $\Delta\theta$ has no effect on *world* demand, the change in world demand is $-2a\Delta i$ (from adding the two *IS* curves together). So $\Delta i = 0$. If $\Delta i = 0$, $\Delta y = \Delta\theta$ from the *IS* curve but $\Delta y = -\Delta\theta$ from the *ERU*. Hence $\Delta y = \Delta\theta = -\Delta\theta = 0$. And the same is true for Foreign: $\Delta y^* = -\Delta\theta = 0$. Moreover if $\Delta\theta = 0$, that implies under fixed exchange rates that $\Delta P^* = \Delta P$. Finally from the *LM* curve $\Delta M = \Delta P$ since $\Delta i = \Delta y = 0$, and from LM^*, $\Delta M^* = \Delta P^*$. So $\Delta M = \Delta M^*$. Since $\Delta M + \Delta M^* = \Delta \overline{M}$, $\Delta M = \Delta M^* = \Delta \overline{M}/2$.

In short, monetary expansion under fixed exchange rates has no real effects in either economy. All that happens is that prices rise equiproportionally to the increase in the money supply in each country, and that is half the world increase in the money supply.

3.2 Monetary expansion under flexible exchange rates

Here again and for the same reasons $\Delta y = \Delta y^* = \Delta\theta = \Delta i = 0$. There are no real effects in either Home or Foreign. From LM^*, since $\Delta M^* = 0$, that implies that $\Delta P^* = 0$. And from LM, $\Delta P = \Delta M > 0$. Thus the rise in the money supply, confined under flexible exchange rates to Home, implies that P rises equiproportionally to M. Finally, this means that the nominal exchange rate has to depreciate, $\Delta e > 0$, to maintain a constant real exchange rate, $\Delta \theta = \Delta e + \Delta P^* - \Delta P = \Delta e - \Delta P = 0$, so that $\Delta e = \Delta P$.

3.3 Fiscal expansion under fixed exchange rates

In this and the next case we assume there is an expansion in government spending in Home, but not in Foreign: $\Delta g > 0$ and $\Delta g^* = 0$. We shall see that the result under both exchange rate regimes is a rise in Home's output and an equal fall in Foreign's. The short-run beggar-thy-neighbour effect under fixed exchange rates is somewhat attenuated in the medium run. To see the logic of the medium-run result, we apply the simple model set out above.

As always $\Delta y + \Delta y^* = 0$ (adding *ERU* and *ERU** together). Since world output must remain unchanged, and since $\Delta \theta$ has no net effect on world demand, i must increase to offset the increase in demand caused by Δg. Hence, adding *IS* and *IS** together, we have $\Delta g = 2a\Delta i$, so that

$$\Delta i = \Delta g / 2a.$$

It follows (substituting this into *IS*, and using the *ERU* requirement that $\Delta \theta = -\Delta y$,) that

$$\Delta y = \Delta g - \Delta g / 2 - \Delta y = \Delta g / 4 = -\Delta y^* = -\Delta \theta.$$

What happens to prices? This is a little more complicated. First since $\Delta \theta = \Delta P^* - \Delta P = -\Delta g / 4$, we know that $\Delta P - \Delta P^* = \Delta g / 4$. This says that the rise in y caused by the rise in g requires an appreciation of the real exchange rate for Home to stay on its *ERU*, and this in turn requires P to rise relative to P^*. But by how much do P and P^* have to rise?

Here *LM* and *LM** come into play. Since i has risen (in both countries) by $\Delta g / 2a$, the real demand for money needs to rise equally in both countries relative to its supply. Thus

$$\frac{\Delta g}{2a} = \lambda \frac{\Delta g}{4} - \mu(\Delta M - \Delta P)$$

$$\frac{\Delta g}{2a} = -\lambda \frac{\Delta g}{4} - \mu(\Delta M^* - \Delta P^*).$$

Since the world nominal money supply is constant, as is the world transactions demand for money, $\lambda \frac{\Delta g}{4} + \left(-\lambda \frac{\Delta g}{4}\right) = 0$, it can be seen that by adding *LM* and *LM** together that world prices have to rise by $\Delta P + \Delta P^* = \Delta g / a\mu$. Together with $\Delta P - \Delta P^* = \Delta g / 4$, $\Delta P = \frac{\Delta g}{2}\left(\frac{1}{a\mu} + \frac{1}{4}\right)$, and $\Delta P^* = \Delta g\left(\frac{1}{a\mu} - \frac{1}{4}\right)$.

Subtracting *LM** from *LM*, it is clear that the real money supply in Home has to rise relative to that in Foreign for the net real demand for money to rise equally in both countries:

$$(\Delta M - \Delta P) = (\Delta M^* - \Delta P^*) + \frac{\lambda \Delta g}{2\mu}.$$

Since $\Delta P > \Delta P^*$, this implies that money has to flow from Foreign to Home, both to allow the money supply to increase in Home relative to Foreign and to compensate the reduction of the relative real money supply in Home caused by $\Delta P > \Delta P^*$. From the last equation, $(\Delta M - \Delta M^*) = (\Delta P - \Delta P^*) + \frac{\lambda \Delta g}{2\mu}$. Since $\Delta P - \Delta P^* = \Delta g / 4$, and $\Delta M + \Delta M^* = \Delta \overline{M} = 0$,

$$(\Delta M - \Delta M^*) = 2\Delta M = \frac{\Delta g}{4} + \frac{\lambda \Delta g}{2\mu} \Rightarrow \Delta M = \frac{\Delta g}{4}\left(\frac{1}{2} + \frac{\lambda}{\mu}\right) = -\Delta M^*.$$

The intuition is as follows: world aggregate demand increases by Δg, but there is no increase in world supply in equilibrium ($\Delta y + \Delta y^* = 0$). Hence i has to rise; but with no increase in the world demand for money since $\Delta y + \Delta y^* = 0$, the world real money supply has to fall so that there is an increase in money demand *relative* to supply in order to push up the interest rate, i. But the nominal world money supply is constant, so world prices have to rise (pushed up by the gap between world demand and supply) until i rises sufficiently to eliminate the increase in world demand. At the same time, since the increase in demand is in Home, y rises and y^* falls, necessitating a real appreciation and hence requiring (with fixed exchange rates) that P rises relative to P^*. The rise in y and the fall in y^* also implies that Home's real money supply needs to rise by more than Foreign's since the net real demand for money must rise by the same amount in both countries. This is aggravated by $\Delta P > \Delta P^*$. Thus the world nominal money supply has to flow from Foreign to Home to bring about an appropriate relative increase in Home's real money supply.

3.4 Fiscal expansion under flexible exchange rates

The outcome for the real variables is identical to the fiscal expansion under fixed exchange rates, i.e. Home's output is higher and Foreign's is lower in the new medium-run equilibrium. Indeed the second paragraph of the previous section applies unchanged to this case, with $\Delta y = \Delta g / 4 = -\Delta y^* = -\Delta \theta$ and $\Delta i = \Delta g / 2a$.

However, now money cannot flow between Home and Foreign ($\Delta M = \Delta M^* = 0$), so the full burden of ensuring that the real money supplies in Home and Foreign rise appropriately falls on P and P^* respectively. Thus ΔP and ΔP^* follow directly from LM and LM^*. Substituting for Δi and Δy in LM gives $\Delta g / 2a = \lambda \Delta g / 4 + \mu \Delta P$ or

$$\Delta P = \frac{\Delta g}{2\mu}\left(\frac{1}{a} - \frac{\lambda}{2}\right)$$

$$\Delta P^* = \frac{\Delta g}{2\mu}\left(\frac{1}{a} + \frac{\lambda}{2}\right)$$

where the bottom equation comes from LM^*. It may seem surprising at first that P falls in Home where g has increased. But what has happened in this case is that the short-run response of the exchange rate to the rise in g is an appreciation: this pushes Home inside ERU and Foreign outside ERU^*. Hence in the medium term P falls relative to P^*.

We know that $\Delta \theta = \Delta e + \Delta P^* - \Delta P = -\Delta g / 4$. From the two equations above $\Delta P^* - \Delta P = \lambda \Delta g / 2\mu$. So

$$\Delta e + \frac{\lambda \Delta g}{2\mu} = -\frac{\Delta g}{4} \Rightarrow \Delta e = -\frac{\Delta g}{2}\left(\frac{1}{2} + \frac{\lambda}{\mu}\right).$$

Thus in order to get the necessary real appreciation of the exchange rate to allow for y to rise, e has to appreciate by $\Delta\theta$ plus the real depreciation caused by the relative price movements of $\lambda\Delta g/2\mu$.

3.5 Conclusion on medium-run outcomes

In the medium run, the exchange rate regime has *no* effect on real outcomes in contrast to the short run. Expansionary fiscal policy in Home always increases y and reduces y^*, with consequent reduction of θ (real appreciation for Home) and increase in i; and monetary policy has no medium-run real effects. In the Appendix, we set out how adjustment from the short- to the medium-run equilibrium takes place.

4 EMU: a common currency area

In developing the analysis of the European Economic and Monetary Union (EMU), we assume, first, that EMU is composed of a large number of small economies: each economy will be assumed to have no influence on the EMU inflation rate or output level. The important point here is that, if we neglect the rest of the world, we can think of EMU as a large closed economy, and each of the member states as its sectors or regions. It then has a unique aggregate employment rate at which inflation is stable. Thus although individual members have little effect (if they are small) on EMU aggregates, joint excessive aggregate demand can cause system-wide inflation and thus cause the ECB to raise interest rates. For this reason, there is a Stability Pact which constrains the fiscal policies of individual member states: otherwise (it is argued) they might be tempted to use expansionary fiscal policies without internalizing the aggregate inflationary cost. A primary motivation of this section is to see under what circumstances individual member states can achieve satisfactory employment outcomes, given the absence of individual monetary control and the presence of a constraint on fiscal policy such as a Stability Pact.

4.1 Constraints on the aggregate EMU economy

As we have seen in Chapter 10 there is no unique unemployment or output rate in a small open economy. Such an economy can undertake a fiscal expansion and then—through a burst of inflation above the world inflation rate—experience an appreciation of its real exchange rate that increases its real wage in line with the increase in the wage-setting real wage.

What if all economies were to try and do this simultaneously? Evidently this is not possible since all economies would be unable to appreciate their real exchange rates against each other. How precisely does this work?

We shall call the log of the price level in economy i, P_i. Let us simplify the pricing process in this economy so that P_i is just set equal to the log of the unit labour cost, $W_i - \lambda_i$, i.e.

$$P_i = W_i - \lambda_i.$$

Next assume that a consumer in each economy consumes the same bundle of goods, in which each good is symmetric; each good is produced in a different economy (the ith good is produced in economy i); and each good sells for the same price throughout EMU. Thus the consumer price index can be written:

$$P = \sum N^{-1} P_i = \sum N^{-1}(W_i - \lambda_i),$$

where P is the log of the CPI and there are N economies. For convenience we can write $\overline{W} - \overline{\lambda}$ as the average unit labour cost for EMU.

We can now rewrite the above equation to get the *aggregate* real wage implied by the price-setting relationship (or PS curve) for EMU as a whole:

$$\overline{W} - P = \overline{\lambda}.$$

Its also useful to express this in terms of competitiveness, θ. First call the log of the real exchange rate (or competitiveness) of economy i, θ_i. Second remember that e is fixed (for all time) for the EMU economies; it will be simplest to set $e = 0$ and then forget about it. Competitiveness for the individual economy is measured by the aggregate price level relative to the price of its good, so

$$\theta_i \equiv P - P_i.$$

This provides a straightforward way of deriving the *aggregate* value of θ implied by price-setting behaviour:

$$\theta = \sum N^{-1} \theta_i = P - \sum N^{-1} P_i = 0.$$

Thus we can either say that price-setting implies that $\theta = 0$ or $\overline{W} - P = \overline{\lambda}$. It is not difficult to see that each implies the other. We reintroduce the WS schedule for each individual economy, and assume here that they are the same:

$$W_i - P = \sigma + \beta y_i$$

or in aggregate

$$\overline{W} - P = \sigma + \beta \sum N^{-1} y_i \equiv \sigma + \beta \overline{y}$$

where $\overline{y} \equiv \sum N^{-1} y_i$ is the average rate of output.

We can now derive the equilibrium $\overline{y}$ in one of two identical ways—via the real wage or via the real exchange rate. The familiar way is via the real wage (the WS and PS curves). These are then

$$WS : \overline{W} - P = \sigma + \beta \overline{y}$$
$$PS : \overline{W} - P = \overline{\lambda}$$

$$\Rightarrow y_e = \frac{\overline{\lambda} - \sigma}{\beta}.$$

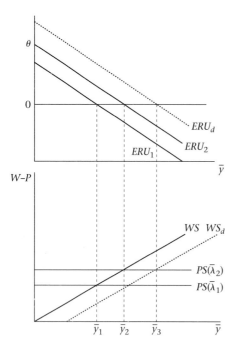

Figure 12.12 Deriving *ERU*s from the *WS* and *PS* diagram

This reproduces for the aggregate EMU economy the standard results for the closed economy: equilibrium output will be higher the lower (more restrained) are σ and β, and the larger is $\bar{\lambda}$.

But we can also get the same result for the aggregate economy via competitiveness:

$$WS: \quad -(\overline{W} - P) = -(\sigma + \beta\bar{y}) \Rightarrow$$
$$-\left(\sum N^{-1}P_i - P\right) = \theta = \bar{\lambda} - \sigma - \beta\bar{y}$$
$$PS: \quad \theta = \sum N^{-1}\theta_i = P - \sum N^{-1}P_i = 0.$$

Hence, putting the *WS* condition $\theta = \bar{\lambda} - \sigma - \beta\bar{y}$ together with the *PS* condition $\theta = 0$, we get $\bar{y}_e = \frac{\bar{\lambda}-\sigma}{\beta}$.

In Fig. 12.12, the bottom diagram is the familiar *WS-PS* intersection diagram. All the variables are averages. Thus the intersection of the $PS(\bar{\lambda}_1)$ schedule and the *WS* schedule shows the equilibrium level of average output in EMU consistent with stable inflation, $\bar{y}_1$. In the top diagram this same equilibrium is represented by the intersection of ERU_1 and the $\theta = 0$ horizontal line. An increase in labour productivity from $\bar{\lambda}_1$ to $\bar{\lambda}_2$ pushes up the *PS* schedule in the standard way in the bottom diagram so that the new equilibrium is at $\bar{y}_2$. And in the top diagram this new equilibrium is represented by the intersection of ERU_2 and the $\theta = 0$ horizontal line at $\bar{y}_2$. Note that the equilibrium value of θ is unaltered by the increase in labour productivity.

We also introduce at this stage a second possible reason why equilibrium EMU-wide output may change. Wage determination in most of the EMU member states is dominated by collective bargaining; and in addition the bargaining is quite coordinated at the national level. Thus one possibility may be that bargainers can moderate wage-bargaining

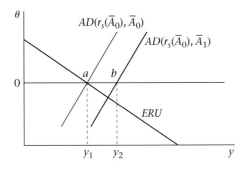

Figure 12.13 Expansion of EMU-wide AD

pressure at any given level of income. As we have seen in Chapter 4, a simple way of characterizing this moderation is by a downwards shift in the WS schedule, to WS_d, implying an increase in y_e to $\bar{y}_3$. This is reflected in the top diagram by a rightwards shift in ERU to ERU_d and a corresponding increase in equilibrium EMU-wide output to $\bar{y}_3$.

What are the implications for aggregate demand? In Fig. 12.13, the AD schedules are again aggregate schedules. The aggregate demand curve consistent with EMU-wide equilibrium is given by $AD(r_S(\bar{A}_0), \bar{A}_0)$, where $\bar{A}_0$ is the initial average level of autonomous demand across the EMU member states. $r_S(\bar{A}_0)$ is the interest rate that ensures that $AD(r_S(\bar{A}_0), \bar{A}_0)$ cuts ERU with $\theta = 0$. The stronger the aggregate autonomous domestic demand, $\bar{A}$, the higher will $r_S(\bar{A})$ have to be. As a reminder, $y = \bar{A} - ar + \theta$, so $y_e = \bar{A}_0 - ar_S(\bar{A}_0)$, with $\theta = 0$.

We now assume that $\bar{A}$ increases to $\bar{A}_1$ while interest rates do not change, $r = r_S(\bar{A}_0)$. Thus the aggregate demand schedule shifts to $AD(r_S(\bar{A}_0), \bar{A}_1)$. Note that by definition, for the 'world' as a whole, θ is always 0: in aggregate, the real exchange rate must be unity and its log must be zero. Thus EMU moves from a to b.

What happens at b depends on monetary policy. So we shall now introduce the first of three critical policy instruments in EMU: the monetary policy of the European Central Bank (ECB).

4.2 ECB and monetary policy: symmetric shocks

By joining the single European currency, individual economies lose any control over their money supply and their nominal exchange rate. The monetary response function of the ECB has never been clearly stated. However, for analytical purposes, we shall assume that it uses a monetary reaction function in which it seeks to stabilize the eurozone economy around the inflation target. As emphasized in Chapter 5, for the ECB to achieve its inflation target, it must seek to minimize the deviation of inflation from target and of output from equilibrium. If it seeks to achieve an output target *above* equilibrium, there will be an inflation bias, i.e. inflation at equilibrium unemployment will be above the inflation target. Having noted this, we shall assume that the ECB's output target is equilibrium output.

In response to system-wide shocks, the ECB will then respond in exactly the same way was set out in Chapters 3 and 5 for the closed economy. As long as the shock—be it an aggregate demand, inflation, or supply-side shock—affects all the eurozone economies in the same way then each member state will be guided back to equilibrium through the actions of the ECB. This analysis assumes as well that each economy responds in an identical way to the ECB's interest rate changes. As set out in detail in Chapter 5, the key parameters in an optimal Taylor-type rule that are assumed identical across member countries if this analysis is applied to the eurozone members are: the interest-sensitivity of aggregate demand, the slope of the Phillips curve, and the lag structure of output and inflation responses.

4.3 Asymmetric shocks

Given monetary policy as expressed in a central bank reaction function, all economies adjust to a symmetric equilibrium if they behave identically. What happens if they do not? We look at two types of disturbances that are relevant in the context of EMU. In both cases, we shall assume initially that $\theta_i = 0$ and $\bar{A}_i = \bar{A}$ for all i. And in both cases we assume that the eurozone as a whole remains in equilibrium. If we assume for simplicity that the inflation target is zero, this requires that $\pi = \sum \pi_i/N = 0$ and that $\sum \bar{A}_i/N = \bar{A}$, with $y_e = \bar{A} - ar_s(\bar{A})$; note that in any case $\sum \theta_i/N = 0$—the sum of the logs of relative real exchange rates is zero by definition.

4.3.1 Differences in θ_i and real exchange rate changes induced by differential inflation

We assume that the identical *AD* schedule goes through the equilibrium point *a* in Fig. 12.14 where $\theta = 0$ intersects the *ERU*. However, different economies now have different values of θ. A simple assumption is that there are two evenly sized groups of member states, in the first of which $\theta = \theta_1 > 0$, and in the second $\theta = \theta_2 = -\theta_1$.

The situation is shown in Fig. 12.14, where the first group of economies (group 1) is at point *x* with $\theta_1 > 0$ and the second group is at point *z* with $\theta_2 = -\theta_1 < 0$. Note that because the eurozone as a whole is in equilibrium (i.e. in the language of the previous section, the eurozone economy is on the 'world' *ERU* curve, shown by point *a*, the ECB

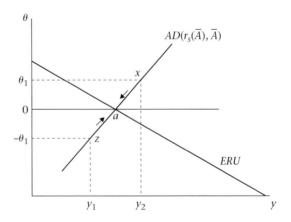

Figure 12.14 Differences in real exchange rates and real exchange rate adjustment

does nothing. There is nonetheless an automatic response mechanism since the group 1 economies at x are characterized by rising inflation and therefore an appreciating real exchange rate with the result that they move down the AD curve to the south-west as net exports shrink. At x, $\Delta P_1 \equiv \pi_1 > 0$ (assume that $\pi^E = 0$) so $\Delta \theta_1 = -\pi_1 < 0$. This process continues until the group 1 economies return to equilibrium at a. The exact inverse process takes place in the group 2 economies. There inflation falls, the real exchange rate depreciates, and aggregate demand increases until these economies move back to equilibrium.

This illustrates a fundamental point about economies in a single currency area. Differential rates of inflation are the way in which the adjustment of the real exchange rate is brought about. Even if the nominal exchange rate is inexorably fixed, the real exchange rate is not: inflation allows required adjustments to come about. That this is not fully understood in the relevant policy circles is illustrated by an episode that occurred in 2002 when the EU Commission attempted to bring Ireland to account for its high rate of inflation. In fact Ireland was in the process of using a high inflation rate to appreciate its real exchange rate and hence to squeeze out inflationary pressures as the Irish economy returned to equilibrium. This example shows that if disequilibrium reflects an overvalued or an undervalued real exchange rate it will be corrected eventually by relative inflation movements. However, it is as well to note that the presence of asymmetries in the inflation/disinflation process may impair smooth adjustment. Specifically, the group 2 economies at z may already have low inflation and there may be greater downward than upward stickiness of inflation.

4.3.2 Asymmetric aggregate demand shocks ($\bar{A}_i$)

We now examine the case of asymmetric demand shocks (Fig. 12.15). The system as a whole is assumed to be in equilibrium: $\theta = 0$ and aggregate output is at a. Both groups of economies are assumed to be on their *ERU* curves. Note therefore that the two possible modes of adjustment discussed above cannot operate: ECB monetary policy remains set at $r = r_S(\bar{A})$, since system-wide aggregate demand is consistent with equilibrium; and the

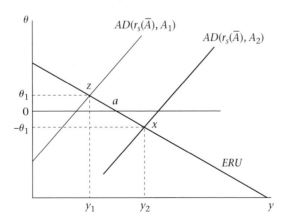

Figure 12.15 Differences in aggregate demand schedules

automatic mechanism of real exchange rate adjustment via differential inflation is also ruled out since both groups are on their respective *ERU*s, implying that inflation rates of both groups remain the same and we assume they are at the ECB's target rate.

Group 1 economies at point x have no particular reason to want to adjust: they have high output and employment, together with stable inflation at the EMU-wide level. It may be that they are running current account deficits (—indeed they are in our simple model since the current account balance is equal to θ and $\theta_1 < 0$), but that puts no direct pressure on the member states in this group to adjust since they do not face pressure from the foreign exchange market.

But group 2 economies at point z would like to adjust since they have low output and employment. There are in principle two types of policies they might use, supply-side and fiscal. It is important to note, however, that these economies are not in their current position as a result of supply-side failure. In this model, the structure of the supply side is captured by an economy's *ERU* and the *ERU*s of all the member states are identical in this example. Thus an EMU economy without supply-side problems (or unprepared or unable to use structural policies)—and unprepared or unable to use fiscal policy—is literally stuck if its exogenous demand $\bar{A}_i$ is too low. Such economies will remain at point z. We look in turn at the constraints on the use of fiscal and of supply-side policies.

4.4 Fiscal policy under EMU: the Stability Pact constraint

The Stability and Growth Pact of EMU requires that member states do not run a public sector deficit greater than 3% of GDP. States that break the conditions of the SGP may be financially penalized by the Council of Finance Ministers of the EU. We analyse the use of fiscal policy by individual economies on the assumption that the SGP is binding, although as is widely known several economies have broken the SGP conditions (France, Germany, Italy, and Portugal) without being penalized. The problems with the design of the SGP from the perspective of a prudent fiscal policy rule that ensures long-run fiscal sustainability are set out in Chapter 6. Here we are concerned with a different question, namely the consequences of the adoption of the SGP for macroeconomic outcomes in the eurozone. In section 1 of this chapter, we set out the basic logic underlying the adoption of a rule to restrain the use of fiscal policy in a common currency area: each country acting independently sees a gain from a fiscal expansion that permits lower unemployment with constant inflation (as is the case for a small open economy) yet the medium-run outcome is one of unchanged unemployment with a higher real interest rate and a period of inflation.

Before asking what impact the SGP has in constraining economies, it is convenient to assume that all economies in the eurozone are following some type of public sector deficit (PSD) strategy. A simple way of modelling this is to assume that each economy aims to keep its deficit at some target percentage, and to simplify the analysis we assume that the target is for the primary deficit, i.e. excluding interest payments. The deficit ratio, $D/y \equiv (g - ty)/y$, where the variables are written in natural numbers, and where it is assumed that government revenue can be summarized as ty. Hence the PSD strategy of keeping the ratio at some fixed percentage, δ, implies that $D/y \equiv (g - ty)/y = \delta$, or $g - ty = \delta y$ or $g = (\delta + t)y$. Reverting to logs $g = k + y$, where $k \equiv \log(\delta + t)$.

The requirement that the deficit be less than or equal to 3% of GDP can be written in natural numbers as $D/y \leq 0.03$. A simple assumption is that the deficit is the difference between government expenditure (g) and tax revenue from a constant proportional tax rate (t): thus $(g_i - ty_i)/y_i \leq 0.03$, or $g_i \leq (t + 0.03)y_i$ where t will be taken as uniform across member states for convenience. With g_i and y_i now being logs as in the rest of the chapter, the SGP constraint is

$$\text{SGP: } g_i \leq \log(t + 0.03) + y_i = k^{SP} + y_i,$$

where, given t, $k^{SP} = \max_{\delta} \log(t + \delta)$ allowed by the SGP.

Let us imagine a slightly different set-up from that of the last subsection. First, we shall define A now as the non-interest-sensitive component of *private* exogenous demand; thus total *private* exogenous demand is $A - ar$. Until now we have simplified by assuming that the coefficient on g is unity. We now write $y_i = A_i - ar + \phi g_i + \theta_i$ where ϕ is the elasticity of aggregate demand with respect to government expenditure.[2] Thus total exogenous demand is $A - ar + \phi g$. We still look at the situation of an asymmetric demand shock, and concern ourselves with an economy, i, with A_i below average, where average A is written as $\bar{A}$. In terms of the previous section, this is a group 2 economy. But we now assume our economy is small enough to have no impact on the average. In terms of the AD for the ith economy assuming the SGP binds so that $g_i = k^{SP} + y_i$:

$$y_i = A_i + \phi g_i - ar_S + \theta_i$$
$$= A_i + \phi(k_i + y_i) - ar_S + \theta_i.$$

We know that for the average,

$$\bar{y} = \bar{A} + \phi(\bar{k} + \bar{y}) - ar_S$$

with r_S defined by

$$y_e = \bar{A} + \phi(\bar{k} + \bar{y}) - ar_S.$$

So a convenient way of looking at aggregate demand in the ith economy is in terms of how it deviates from the average:

$$y_i - y_e = (A_i - \bar{A}) + \phi(k_i - \bar{k}) + \phi(y_i - y_e) + \theta_i$$
$$= \frac{(A_i - \bar{A}) + \phi(k_i - \bar{k})}{1 - \phi} + \frac{\theta_i}{1 - \phi}.$$

If we define $-[(A_i - \bar{A}) + \phi(k_i - \bar{k})] \equiv X_i$, we can rewrite the AD_i equation as:

$$\theta_i = X_i(\bar{A}, A_i, \bar{k}, k_i) + (1 - \phi)(y_i - y_e)$$
$$= X_i + (1 - \phi)(y_i - y_e).$$

---

[2] Suppose that the model is linear in natural numbers, $y = A + g$, where g is real government expenditure. Then $\Delta y/y = (\Delta g/g).(g/y)$, or $\Delta \log y = (g/y).\Delta \log g$; integrating, $\log y = \kappa + (g/y) \log g$; hence $0 \leq \phi = g/y \leq 1$, in this model.

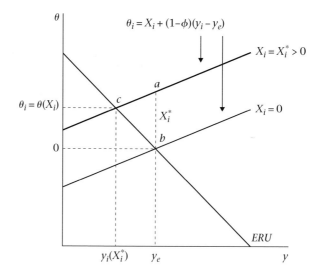

Figure 12.16 Constant public sector deficit ratio strategies

We show this in the standard θy–diagram (Fig. 12.16). X_i is a measure of the additional exogenous demand needed to make $y_i = y_e$, given $\bar{A}, A_i, \bar{k}$ and k_i. Thus if $X_i = 0$, no additional demand is needed, which means that the AD function $\theta_i = (1 - \phi)(y_i - y_e)$ goes through the point ($\theta_i = 0, y_i = y_e$), so that relative inflation movements will eventually generate $y_i = y_e$. But $X_i = X_i^* > 0$ implies that an extra X_i^* of exogenous demand is required, where X_i^* is measured by the vertical distance between a and b in Fig. 12.16.

For given $\bar{A}, A_i$, and $\bar{k}$, the SGP requirement that $k_i \leq k^{SP} \equiv \log(t + 0.03)$ shows the lowest possible X_i: this is shown in Fig. 12.17. Initially $k_i < k^{SP}$ and the economy is at point c. If there is then an increase in the deficit that is allowed, this reduces the additional private demand required to take the economy to higher equilibrium output. For example, an increase in the deficit ratio being targeted to 3%, i.e. a move to k^{SP}, implies a move graphically from c to d; this entails in turn a fall in θ_i and an increase in equilibrium output to y_{i2}.

We can draw the following conclusions:

(1) The punchline is that the SGP puts a limit on the use of fiscal policy to make good deflationary demand shocks. The condition for country i attaining equilibrium output, y_e, while respecting the SGP constraint is that $A_i + k^{SP} \geq \bar{A} + \bar{k}$. Thus if A_i is too weak; or if $\bar{A}$ is too strong; or $\bar{k}$ is too close to k^{SP}, then country i will be unable to use fiscal policy to close the gap with equilibrium output at y_e. In that case, neither fiscal nor monetary policy is available to country i. Given the difficulties of introducing supply-side changes, that may be a sobering conclusion—in particular, since in this example, economy i is assumed to be as efficient as the other economies in terms of its ERU.

(2) But it may be that fiscal policy is not terribly effective. In the context here that is equivalent to saying that ϕ is small. Clearly if $\phi = 0$, fiscal policy can have no effect.

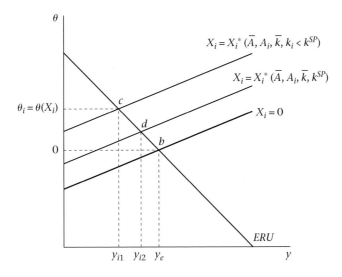

Figure 12.17 Impact of the Stability and Growth Pact: economy i is stuck at $y < y_e$

(3) Even if we are concerned that the SGP may be too constraining, it is nevertheless important to realize that loosening it may give many economies an incentive to use fiscal policy to expand output and employment. This is because (apart from the SGP constraint) the standard constraints on fiscal expansion (external to the government) no longer exist: these are short-term financial markets and the foreign exchange market. For countries in the eurozone, short-term interest rates are determined by the ECB, and the country's nominal exchange rate no longer exists. Let us now set out what would happen if all member states raised their k simultaneously in response to an easing of the SGP. The real rate of interest is determined by the requirement that $\bar{y} = y_e$ or $y_e = \bar{A} + \phi(k + y_e) - ar_S$. Hence $\phi dk = adr_S$. The interest-sensitive component of private demand, $-ar_S$, has to fall by exactly the amount by which government expenditure has increased. There is no increase in output.

(4) Finally, from a policy perspective, if fiscal policy is a useful anticyclical device and if the current SGP does not enable it to be used effectively, there is a case for increasing k for economies in difficulty while limiting $\bar{k}$ for the average economy. But whether or not it would be possible for Ecofin to monitor and enforce such an arrangement is quite unclear.

4.5 Supply-side policies

In this section we see how supply-side policies can influence an economy in the eurozone. As discussed in Chapter 4 and Chapter 11, supply-side or structural policies are those that shift the *PS* and/or *WS* schedules, and which therefore in this context shift the *ERU*. In particular we ask what are the consequences for macroeconomic equilibrium of three types of supply-side policy: a wage accord (or incomes policy), policies that stimulate labour productivity, and policies that increase product market competition. In each case, the macroeconomic consequences of the policies follow from their impact on the *ERU* of the economy concerned. As in the last section we look at a member country, *i*, which is so small that it has no impact on the eurozone economy as a whole.

We assume here that there is a single monopoly union in the *i*th economy. We start by showing non-rigorously how a wage accord can alter equilibrium output and employment. Our concept of equilibrium output requires that the economy is on its *ERU*; in the case we explore here we assume the initial *ERU* of the economy to be ERU^*. Thus, the economy's initial output, y_i^*, is at a^*, the intersection of ERU^* and *AD* in Fig. 12.18.

4.5.1 Wage accord

A wage accord shifts downwards the bargained real wage or *WS* schedule. As a reminder, the *WS* schedule in economy *i* is given by

$$w_i = W_i - P = \sigma + \beta y_i,$$

where w_i is the real wage in economy *i*, W_i the nominal wage. *P* is the eurozone price level, which is the consumer price level in each eurozone economy (since workers buy goods produced in each of the eurozone economies). All variables are in logs. A wage accord is represented by a decrease in either or both of the constants, σ and β.

The next step is to translate this into *ERU* terms. The *PS* schedule is defined by

$$P_i = \mu_i + W_i - \lambda_i,$$

where μ_i is the log of the profit mark-up on unit labour costs, and reflects the competitiveness of the product market. As usual labour productivity is represented by λ. Since the real exchange rate is $\theta_i \equiv P - P_i$, it is easy to see how σ and β enter the *ERU*, since we can write the *ERU* as

$$\theta_i = \lambda_i - \mu_i - \sigma - \beta y_i.$$

Thus far in this chapter the (common) *ERU* has been written $\theta = \alpha - y$; so we shall assume that ERU^* is characterized by $\alpha = \lambda - \mu - \sigma$, with $\lambda_i = \lambda$ and $\mu_i = \mu$ for all *i*; and $\beta = 1$. Thus if the wage accord takes the form of a reduction in σ, ERU_1 is defined by $\theta_i = \alpha - \Delta\sigma - y_i$, with $\Delta\sigma < 0$, so that ERU_1 shifts outwards in a parallel manner. This can be seen in Fig. 12.18 as the shift from ERU^* to ERU_1. What effect does this have on y_i^*? Since the *AD* is assumed not to shift this implies a move up along the *AD* from a^* to a, and y_i is given by the intersection of *AD* with ERU_1.

In Fig. 12.18, *ERU* shifts up vertically by $\rho \equiv -\Delta\sigma$—we can think of ρ (rho) as standing for restraint. Since *y* increases by $\rho/2$, *y* only increases by half the outward shift of *ERU*. Note that before the shift of *ERU*, ERU^* is defined by

$$\theta_i = \alpha - y_i$$

and after by

$$\theta_i = \alpha - \Delta\sigma - y_i.$$

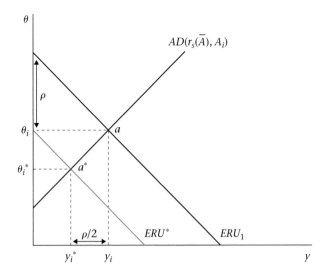

Figure 12.18 Wage accord: new medium-run equilibrium

Throughout, the *AD* schedule is constant:

$$y_i = A_i - ar + \theta_i.$$

Before the wage accord, y_i is given by

$$y_i = A_i - ar + \theta_i = A_i - ar + \alpha - y_i$$
$$y_i = \frac{A_i}{2} - \frac{ar}{2} + \frac{\alpha}{2} = y_i^{\text{pre}}.$$

After, using the same reasoning,

$$y_i^{\text{post}} = \frac{A_i}{2} - \frac{ar}{2} + \frac{\alpha}{2} - \frac{\Delta\sigma}{2}$$

so that

$$y_i^{\text{post}} - y_i^{\text{pre}} = \frac{\rho}{2}.$$

The implication is that there has to be an increase in aggregate demand shifting the *AD* outwards if y_i is to increase by more than $\rho/2$.

4.5.2 Structural policies to improve labour productivity

Policies that improve labour productivity have an identical effect on the *ERU* as does a wage accord embodying a reduction in σ. This can be seen by rewriting the *ERU*

$$\theta_i = \lambda_i - \mu_i - \sigma - \beta y_i.$$

Thus an improvement in labour productivity also leads to a parallel outwards shift in the *ERU* curve and a move up the *AD* schedule to the north-east.

4.5.3 Structural policies to improve product market competition

Policies to improve product market competition can operate in various ways. A standard effect of such policies is in one form or another to increase the elasticity of product demand that firms face. Reverting from logs to non-log values of the variables for a moment: if the demand curve facing the firm in economy i is $y_i = p_i^{-\eta}A$, the goal of competition policy can be thought of as increasing the elasticity of demand, η, where $p_i \equiv (P_i/P)$.

We need first to show how μ is related to η. This is set out in detail in Chapter 15. Briefly here, we assume that there is a monopoly that maximizes profits $p_i y_i - w_i.(y_i/\lambda) \equiv p_i.[p_i^{-\eta}.A] - w_i.(p_i^{-\eta}.A/\lambda)$, where $w_i \equiv W_i/P$. Since A is just a constant, the firm chooses p_i to maximize $p_i^{1-\eta} - w_i.p_i^{-\eta}/\lambda$, and this implies $p_i = \frac{\eta}{\eta-1}(w_i/\lambda)$. Now reverting back to logs and remembering that in logs $p_i \equiv P_i - P$ and $w_i \equiv W_i - P$, we have:

$$P_i = \log \frac{\eta}{\eta - 1} + W_i - \lambda_i$$

$$\Rightarrow \mu \equiv \log \frac{\eta}{\eta - 1}.$$

It is easy to see that an increase in η leads to a decline in the log mark-up μ: when, say, $\eta = 2$, $\frac{\eta}{\eta-1} = 2$; an increase in η from 2 to 3 implies a decline in $\frac{\eta}{\eta-1}$ to 1.5.

Since the *ERU* is $\theta_i = \lambda_i - \mu_i - \sigma - \beta y_i$, the first effect of competition policy is to shift the *ERU* outwards by reducing μ_i. But there is a second effect, this time in reducing the monopoly power of the union. This is more complex, but the intuition is straightforward. η is also the elasticity of the derived demand for labour schedule. Hence an increase in η implies that there is a greater loss in employment for any given rise in the real wage. This will reduce the real wage demanded at any given level of employment, thus shifting down the *WS* schedule. (The details are set out in Chapter 15.) Thus there is a secondary effect shifting the *ERU* outwards via a decline in σ.

4.5.4 Supply-side policies, aggregate demand, and the SGP constraint

We saw above that if aggregate demand remains unchanged then y only increases by 50% of the outward shift in the *ERU*. The reason that output increases only by a fraction of the amount made possible by the supply-side reform is that output rises because the supply-side reform improves the competitiveness of economy i and the slope of the *AD* curve reflects how this is translated into higher net exports and output. The geometry is illustrated in Fig. 12.19: if the *ERU* shifts up by $\rho\%$, then since $y = A - ar + \theta$, the effect is to increase y by the full $\rho\%$ (note that bb^* is equal to a^*b and both to ρ); however, this would mean that y is outside the new *ERU* at point b^*. In the new medium-run equilibrium at point a, the increase in y is $\rho/2$.

This assumes that g_i is held constant. What would happen if the ith economy was following a constant public sector deficit ratio policy? As we shall see in Fig. 12.20, the rise in output boosts tax revenue and under a constant PSD policy, allows the government to increase government expenditure, with the result that the rise in output in the new medium-run equilibrium is greater than $\rho/2$.

In Fig. 12.20, the *AD* schedule assumes that $g_i = k_i + y_i$ and is labelled $AD(r_S(\bar{A}), A_i, k_i)$. As we saw earlier, this has a flatter slope, namely $1 - \phi$, than the *AD* schedule with g_i

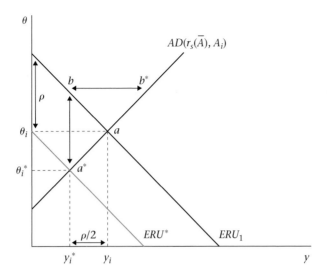

Figure 12.19 Wage accord with a stable AD curve

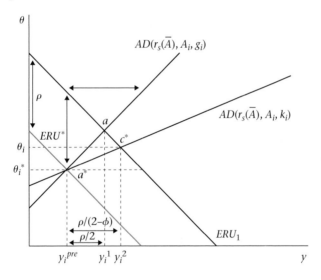

Figure 12.20 Wage accord combined with a public sector deficit ratio policy

fixed (labelled $AD(r_S(\bar{A}), A_i, g_i)$), with a slope of 1. How much more does y_i rise than in the fixed g_i case? As shown in the footnote, the effect of switching government expenditure regimes is to increase y_i by $\rho/(2 - \phi)$ instead of $\rho/2$: the medium-run equilibrium is at point c^*.[3]

---

[3] Before the wage accord, we have:

$$\theta_i^{\text{pre}} = X_i + (1 - \phi).(y_i^{\text{pre}} - ye)$$
$$\theta_i^{\text{pre}} = y_e - y_i^{\text{pre}}$$

5 Conclusions

Important new insights emerge when the macroeconomic model is extended to account for the interdependence of economies. The key results of this chapter are the following.

- The short-run analysis reveals the operation of two kinds of spillover: the 'locomotive' and the 'beggar-thy-neighbour' effects. In the short run locomotive effects occur—in the sense that output rises in Foreign as well as in Home—following either a fiscal expansion by Home under flexible exchange rates or a monetary expansion by Home under fixed exchange rates. By contrast, Foreign's output shrinks in the face of a Home fiscal expansion under fixed exchange rates or a Home monetary expansion under flexible rates. Since Home's gain is at the expense of Foreign's loss, this is referred to as a 'beggar-thy-neighbour' effect.

- In the medium run, the short-run effects of monetary policy on output disappear. The medium-run effects of fiscal policy are independent of the exchange rate regime: the outcome is that a Home fiscal expansion raises its output but that of Foreign declines as a consequence of the rise in the world interest rate that characterizes the new medium-run equilibrium. The medium-run effect of a unilateral Home fiscal expansion is therefore always 'beggar-thy-neighbour'.

- Efforts at the international coordination of macroeconomic policy stem from the existence of incentives for economies to pursue beggar-thy-neighbour policies. However, the prisoners' dilemma structure of the problem underlines the problems in trying to build credible international cooperation agreements.

- The roots of the logic of the Stability and Growth Pact of the eurozone can be traced to the prisoners' dilemma in fiscal policy. With the external discipline of the money market and the foreign exchange market absent for individual member countries in the eurozone, the temptation to seek to reduce unemployment by a fiscal expansion is a potential problem: if all members reason the same way, the result is a higher union interest rate and a phase of higher inflation that is costly to eliminate. However, as it has been designed, the SGP can pose an obstacle to the achievement of higher activity by a member country simply as a consequence of inadequate private sector aggregate demand

so that

$$y_e - y_i^{\text{pre}} = \frac{X_i}{(2 - \phi)}.$$

Likewise after the outward shift of *ERU* by ρ:

$$\theta_i^{\text{post}} = X_i + (1 - \phi).(y_i^{\text{post}} - y_e)$$
$$\theta_i^{\text{post}} = y_e - y_i^{\text{post}}$$

so that

$$y_e - y_i^{\text{post}} = \frac{X_i}{(2 - \phi)}$$

Hence

$$y_i^{\text{post}} - y_i^{\text{pre}} = \frac{\rho}{(2 - \phi)}.$$

in that country. We have seen that this problem can arise even if the supply side of all member countries is identical. For an economy constrained by the SGP, a country-specific supply-side policy such as a wage accord, an increase in productivity or in product market competition allows for a rise in activity. Since this will also relax the SGP constraint, a combination of supply-side reform and fiscal easing will produce a larger boost in output than a supply-side reform alone.

- By modelling the eurozone as a group of small economies (sectors or regions), we have shown the determinants of equilibrium unemployment for the eurozone as a whole and how it may be altered by, for example, EMU-wide wage restraint. The response of the ECB to common shocks is straightforward to analyse using the closed economy model when the member economies are modelled as symmetric across all the relevant dimensions.

- We have shown the role played by inflation differences between member states as the means for them to adjust their real exchange rates in response to asymmetric shocks or structural differences that require changes in the real exchange rate.

■ PROBLEMS

QUESTION A. In the case of fixed prices the *ISXM* and *LM* equations for two economies are

$$\Delta y = a\Delta g - b\Delta i + \Delta e \tag{12.1}$$

$$\Delta y^* = \alpha\Delta g^* - \beta\Delta i^* - \Delta e \tag{12.2}$$

$$\Delta i = l\Delta y - m\Delta M \tag{12.3}$$

$$\Delta i^* = \lambda\Delta y^* - \mu\Delta M^* \tag{12.4}$$

We assume in these questions that the coefficients may differ across the two economies. There is perfect capital mobility, and we assume that $e^E = e$ throughout.

(i) If exchange rates are fixed and the home money supply is increased by $\Delta\bar{M}$: (*a*) How much will y and y^* increase? (*b*) Why is this different from the Mundell–Fleming result for a small economy?

(ii) If exchange rates are flexible and g is increased by $\Delta\bar{g}$: (*a*) By how much will y and y^* increase? (*b*) Why is this different from the Mundell–Fleming result for a small economy?

QUESTION B. Using the same model as in A above, assume fixed exchange rates. What are the values of Δy and Δy^* if the money supply is increased in one country by the same amount as it reduced in the other? Explain the mechanisms that bring about your result.

QUESTION C. Now take the case of flexible prices. The equations for the two economies are:

$$\Delta y = a\Delta g - b\Delta i + \Delta\theta \tag{12.5}$$

$$\Delta y^* = \alpha\Delta g^* - \beta\Delta i^* - \Delta\theta \tag{12.6}$$

$$\Delta i = l\Delta y - m(\Delta M - \Delta P) \tag{12.7}$$

$$\Delta i^* = \lambda \Delta y^* - \mu(\Delta M^* - \Delta P^*) \tag{12.8}$$

$$\Delta y = -\Delta \theta \tag{12.9}$$

$$\Delta y^* = \Delta \theta \tag{12.10}$$

$$\Delta \theta \equiv \Delta e + \Delta P^* - \Delta P \tag{12.11}$$

$$\Delta i = \Delta i^*. \tag{12.12}$$

(i) If there is a fixed exchange rate regime, find the values of Δy and Δy^* when g is increased by $\Delta \bar{g}$. (ii) If there is a flexible exchange rate regime, find the values of Δy and Δy^* when the Home money supply is increased by $\Delta \bar{M}$.

QUESTION D. Using the same model as in C above, find the values of Δy and Δy^* if the money supply is increased in one country by the same amount as it reduced in the other, (*a*) assuming fixed exchange rates, and (*b*) assuming flexible exchange rates. Explain the mechanisms that bring about your results.

■ **APPENDIX**

Short to medium run: how adjustment occurs

In the short run as we have already seen in our extension of the Mundell–Fleming model, the exchange rate regime matters. So what does the overall pattern of adjustment look like? Some readers may find it useful to see the patterns of adjustment shown geometrically in our two-country *ERU/AD* diamond diagram.

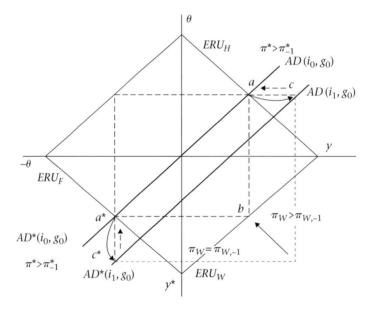

Figure 12.21 Adjustment in the medium run: monetary expansion under fixed exchange rates

Monetary policy under fixed exchange rates

The economies start at (a, a^*) in Fig. 12.21. As we saw in the short-run analysis, monetary expansion in Home implies a fall in i and hence a downward (expansionary) shift of both AD and AD^*. θ remains unchanged in the short run, so both y and y^* increase to c and c^* respectively.

In the medium run, the economies end up back at a and a^* with i back up at its original level. This comes about because Home and Foreign are both outside their respective ERU curves so that P and P^* are both increasing. This reduces the real money supplies in both economies until i has been pushed back up to its original level. The movement back is shown by the arrows in the diagram.

Monetary expansion under flexible exchange rates

With flexible exchange rates, Home starts at a and Foreign at a^* (in Fig. 12.22). The short-run effect of monetary expansion is a depreciation of the exchange rate accompanied by a fall in i. The fall in i shifts the AD and AD^* schedules downwards (i falls from i_0 to i_1) and the depreciation moves Home up the new AD schedule to c corresponding to the rise in θ (implying an increase in demand and hence y). For Foreign, the depreciation implies a loss of competitiveness and a worsening of the trade balance and hence a decline in demand and in output: Foreign moves to c^*. These movements are shown by the straight arrows in the diagram.

In the medium run, Home is outside ERU_H so P is rising, while Foreign is inside ERU_F so P^* is falling. This causes the real money supply in Home to contract and in Foreign to rise pushing up i (relative to i^*), hence implying an appreciation of the exchange rate. This process continues until i has risen back to i_0 and the appreciation of the exchange rate has brought θ back down to its original level. This is the move back to a and a^* along the dashed arrow.

Fiscal expansion under fixed exchange rates

In the short-run, $\Delta g > 0$ implies that AD increases by Δg from g_0 to g_1 (Fig. 12.23). At the same time i rises from i_0 to i_1, but not so as to eliminate the positive effect of Δg on Home's output level. Thus AD

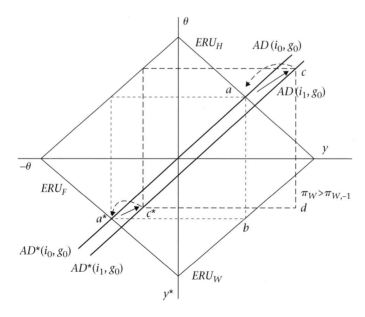

Figure 12.22 Adjustment in the medium run: monetary expansion under flexible exchange rates

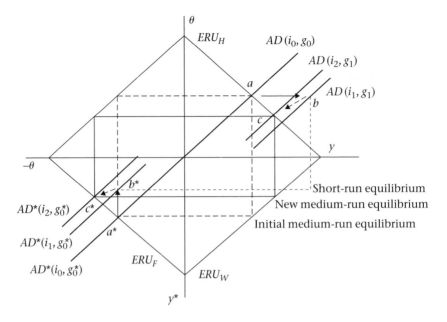

Figure 12.23 Adjustment in the medium run: fiscal expansion under a fixed exchange rate

shifts downwards to the right to $AD(i_1, g_1)$. Since the exchange rate is fixed, and prices do not change in the short run, θ remains unchanged: hence Home moves horizontally from the initial equilibrium at a to b on $AD(i_1, g_1)$. This horizontal move is shown by the continuous arrow in the top right hand quadrant.

Foreign's AD^* shifts up in the short run since i has increased to i_1 without any change in g^* from $AD^*(i_0, g_0^*)$ to $AD^*(i_1, g_0^*)$. Since θ does not change in the short run, Foreign moves vertically up (y^* falls) from a^* to b^* as shown by the continuous vertical arrow in the bottom left hand quadrant.

In the medium run, prices are free to move. Since Foreign is inside ERU_F, P^* falls; and since Home is outside ERU_H, P rises. Given a fixed nominal exchange rate, the real exchange rate appreciates, $\Delta\theta = \Delta P^* - \Delta P < 0$. Holding $i = i_1$ constant, this pushes Home down the $AD(i_1, g_1)$ curve towards ERU_H and Foreign down the $AD^*(i_1, g_0^*)$ curve to ERU^*. Thus y is falling and y^* rising.

But in addition there are net inflationary pressures as a result of y having risen in the short run by more than y^* has fallen, as illustrated by the fact that the short-run equilibrium is outside the world ERU_W (see Fig. 12.23). This pushes aggregate prices up, cutting the world real money supply and hence pushing i up from i_1 to i_2 in the medium run. This implies that AD shifts back up to $AD(i_2, g_1)$ and AD^* shifts up to $AD^*(i_2, g_0^*)$. Thus y^* rises from b^* to c^* and y falls from b to c. At (c, c^*) Home, Foreign, and the world economy are in medium-run equilibrium, with y having increased by the amount that y^* has fallen, with a corresponding appreciation of the real exchange rate to damp down inflationary pressures in Home and prevent deflationary pressures in Foreign. And i has risen to eliminate the net increase in world demand that would otherwise have come from $\Delta g > 0$.

Fiscal expansion with flexible exchange rates

In this case, Home increases g by Δg, while Foreign does not change its fiscal policy (and there is no change in M or M^*). The short-run analysis then implies that the real money supply changes in neither Home nor Foreign, so given $i = i^*$ in the short-run equilibrium, $\Delta i = \lambda\Delta y = \lambda\Delta y^*$ from LM and LM^*, so that $\Delta y = \Delta y^* > 0$. Since the negative impact on y and y^* of the rise in i is the same, and since y rises because of Δg, the real exchange rate must appreciate sufficiently to ensure $\Delta y = \Delta y^*$. Intuitively, y is pushed up by g; this pushes up i relative to i^* and hence e appreciates, moderating the rise in y while

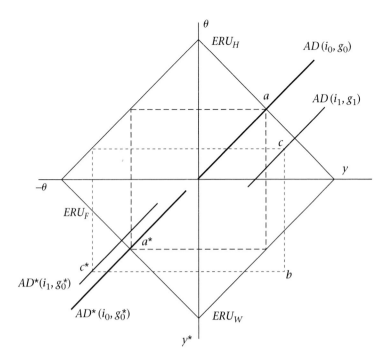

Figure 12.24 Adjustment in the medium run: fiscal expansion under flexible exchange rates

directly increasing y^*; this process continues until $i = i^*$ and $y = y^*$. This is shown in Fig. 12.24 where Home and Foreign move from (a, a^*) to (c, c^*) respectively.

Note that the AD schedule for Home has increased and that for Foreign has decreased; but the depreciation has been sufficient to ensure that y^* rises by the same amount as y. Also, for the transition to the medium-run analysis, note that c is inside ERU_H and c^* outside ERU_F.[4]

Before seeing how we get to the new medium-run equilibrium from these short-run positions, let us see where the medium-run position will be. First, we note that both economies must be on their $ERUs$. This implies that (whether or not y and y^* change) $\Delta y = -\Delta y^*$ starting from the symmetric equilibrium. In turn the ERU equations $y = \alpha - \theta$ and $y^* = \alpha + \theta$ imply that $\Delta y = -\Delta \theta$ and $\Delta y^* = \Delta \theta$. Finally it is evident that the Home AD schedule containing Δg but with the same i as Foreign must be to the right of the symmetric AD schedule and the Foreign AD schedule to the left of it. This is shown in Fig. 12.25 in which Home is at point d and Foreign is at point d^*.

---

[4] The algebra is as follows: the short-run change uses only the IS and LM equations for Home and Foreign:

$$\Delta y = \Delta g - a\Delta i + \Delta \theta$$
$$\Delta y^* = -a\Delta i - \Delta \theta$$
$$\Delta i = \lambda \Delta y$$
$$\Delta i^* = \Delta i = \lambda \Delta y^*.$$

We can see directly from the two LM equations (remember there is no change in the real money supply in either country in the short run) that Δy must be equal to Δy^*. Using $\Delta y = \Delta y^*$ and $\Delta i = \lambda \Delta y$ and adding the two IS curves together, we get $2\Delta y = \Delta g - 2a\lambda \Delta y$ so that the short-run increase in y is $\frac{\Delta g}{2(1+a\lambda)}$. Hence $\Delta i = \lambda \frac{\Delta g}{2(1+a\lambda)}$. Finally to find $\Delta \theta$, subtract the two IS curves to get $\Delta \theta = -\Delta g/2$.

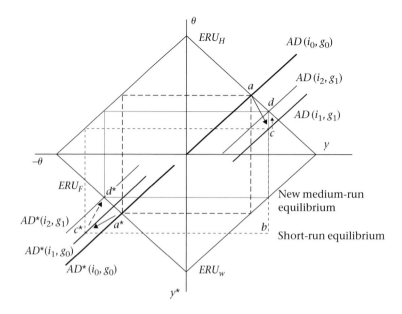

Figure 12.25 Fiscal expansion under flexible exchange rates: short- and medium-run adjustment

The move from the short-run equilibrium to the medium-run one can be seen in Fig. 12.25: in the short run, Home goes from a to c, and Foreign from a^* to c^*. And in medium run, Home goes from c to d and Foreign from c^* to d^*. At (c, c^*), there are inflationary pressures ($\Delta y + \Delta y^* > 0$), so i is being pushed up since the real money supply is on average contracting. And this pushes AD and AD^* left and upwards. In addition, since P^* is rising and P is falling, θ is rising. This process continues until Foreign hits ERU_F at d^* and Home hits ERU_H at d.

PART FOUR

Growth

13 Exogenous Growth Theory

Long-run economic growth determines how living standards change. The theory of economic growth and the questions it addresses were introduced in Chapter 1. The aim of this chapter and the following one is to follow up the material presented there by showing in more detail how theory can be used to shed light on the process of growth. Simple empirical regularities of the type presented in Chapter 1 help provide a general framework within which to develop models of growth. Modelling economic growth can prove challenging even at an introductory level. A greater use of mathematical techniques is required to explain the mechanics of growth models than is the case in the rest of the macroeconomics presented in this book. However, we provide intuitive and diagrammatic explanations before presenting the mathematical derivation of the results. More detailed technical explanation on a number of aspects of growth theory is provided in the appendix to this chapter.

This chapter introduces exogenous growth theory. We begin our exploration with the most widely known paradigm: the Solow–Swan model. The model was formulated independently in 1956 by Robert Solow at MIT in Cambridge Massachusetts and by Trevor Swan at the Australian National University in Canberra. Almost half a century old, it is still a powerful starting point for understanding economic growth. Once the ingredients of the model are combined, we can derive equations that pin down the role of capital, savings, population growth, and technological progress in determining the equilibrium levels of output per worker in the economy. Two of the key concepts in growth theory are those of the steady state or balanced growth path and of the so-called transitional dynamics, i.e. what happens when steady state growth is disturbed.

In this chapter, we set out the Solow–Swan model and see how well its predictions match up with the first five of the stylized facts of growth that were presented in Chapter 1.

(1) Large discrepancies between both levels and growth rates of per capita income persist across countries and across time.

(2) In the long run economies exhibit a *balanced growth path*, that is output per capita and capital per capita grow at roughly constant positive growth rates over time.

(3) The real rate of return to capital is approximately constant over the long run, while real wages grow at a rate close to that of output per head. From (2) and (3) it follows that the ratio of capital to output shows no trend over time and the shares of capital and labour in total income stay roughly constant.

(4) High investment rates in both physical capital and formal education are closely related to high living standards.

(5) Low population growth is associated with high living standards.

In growth models, the long run is characterized as one of *steady state growth* or equivalently as a *balanced growth path* in which output and employment grow at constant proportional rates and in which net saving (and investment) is a constant share of output. As we shall see, in the Solow–Swan growth model without technological progress, output and employment grow at the *same* rate in the steady state, which implies that the *level* of output per worker remains constant. In this case, the growth rate of output per capita is zero in the steady state. A rise in the savings (and investment) share of output shifts the economy to a new steady state characterized by higher output per worker: as the economy moves from the old to the new steady state, output per worker is rising. Thus the main finding of the Solow–Swan growth model is that in the absence of technological progress, economic growth, in the sense of the *growth* in output per worker, is only a transitional process. To account for the steady growth in output per capita (and living standards) that has occurred over recent centuries, it is therefore necessary to introduce technological progress to the Solow–Swan model.

Before setting out the Solow–Swan model, we introduce the concept of the growth rate itself and how it is measured. Section 2 explains how the Solow–Swan model works and what is meant by a steady state equilibrium in this model. The determinants of the characteristics of the steady state are discussed and we show how the economy moves from one steady state to another when there is a change in the savings rate or in the rate of population growth. In section 2, there is no technological progress. This is introduced in sections 3 and 4: in section 3, Solow's method of quantifying the role of technological progress in growth is explained. This is known as (Solow) growth accounting. In section 4 we add technological progress to the basic Solow–Swan model and show how with this modification, there is constant growth in output per worker when the economy is on its balanced growth path. We compare the predictions of the Solow–Swan model with the stylized facts of growth set out in Chapter 1. A key characteristic of the Solow–Swan model is that technological progress is introduced as an *exogenous* force. This means it is modelled as the steady improvement in the technology available to the economy where these improvements are not the outcome of economic forces. Alternatives to the assumption of exogenous technological progress in models of growth are the subject of Chapter 14.

Section 5 returns to the question of what determines income disparities across countries and investigates the reasons why income per worker may or may not converge across different economies. Key concepts in the discussion of income disparities are those of absolute (or unconditional) and conditional convergence. The hypothesis of absolute convergence is that countries with lower levels of output per worker grow faster than those with higher levels, and therefore converge to the same living standards. If this hypothesis is applied to the economies of the world, the data presented in Chapter 1 and shown again in Fig. 13.1 clearly demonstrate that it is not supported. For there to be convergence, there would be a clear negative relationship between the initial level of income per capita in 1960 and growth from 1960 to 2000, with the initially poor

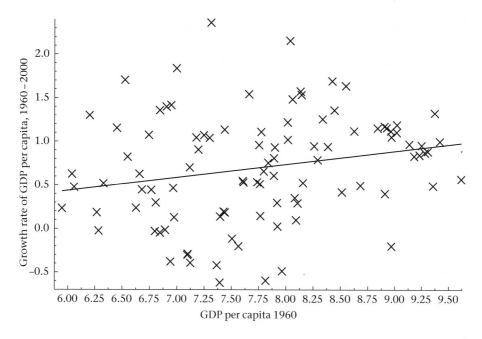

Figure 13.1 Is there cross-country convergence? Scatter plot of growth rates of GDP per capita between 1960 and 2000 against the initial log of the level of GDP per capita
Source: PWT 6.1

countries having high growth (i.e. located in the top left hand corner) whilst the initially rich countries would tend to be in the bottom right corner. The scatter plot does not show this pattern.

A much weaker notion of convergence is labelled conditional convergence. The hypothesis of conditional convergence highlights the fact that countries would not be expected to converge to the same living standards unless they are similar in important respects, such as having the same savings rate. As we shall see, in the Solow–Swan model, a lower savings rate is associated with a lower level of per capita income in the steady state. If we were to compare two otherwise identical economies, one with a high and the other with a low savings rate, then the hypothesis of conditional convergence says only that controlling for the differences in saving rates, the country that is further from its steady state will grow faster than the one that is closer. This means that poor countries will not catch up and achieve the living standards of the rich unless the poor country is able to change the determinants of its steady state. In this section we bridge the gap between theory and empirical analysis by introducing the basic elements of econometric estimation that allows us to test the convergence hypotheses with real data. We shall see that some of the empirical discrepancies that arise when we try to apply the Solow–Swan model to the real world can be explained if human capital is included (in addition to physical capital).

Section 6 focuses on the question of how to evaluate social welfare in the context of economic growth. This provides a basic framework for designing economic policy. Our exploration of exogenous growth theory concludes with Section 7, with some extensions of the basic framework of the Solow–Swan model.

Although the Solow–Swan model provides the foundation for growth theory, there has been much work on developing models in which the growth of living standards is endogenous, rather than the result of 'exogenous technical progress'. A number of different models of endogenous growth are explored in Chapter 14.

1 Growth and the growth rate

Before introducing the growth models, aspects of the mathematical concept of the rate of growth used in growth theory are set out. This section can be either be read and absorbed first or it can be skimmed and referred back to as the concepts and techniques arise in the explanation of the growth models.

Notation used in growth theory. Throughout this chapter we use the so-called dot notation $\dot{Y}$, to refer to the rate of change of key variables.[1] 'Y dot' is the rate of change of output and is closely related to the familiar concept of the change in output between period t and period $t+1$, $Y_{t+1} - Y_t$, which is often abbreviated as ΔY. $\dot{Y}$ stands for the continuous time equivalent of ΔY and is defined as the time derivative of Y, that is dY/dt. To summarize:

$$\Delta Y \equiv Y_{t+1} - Y_t \qquad \text{(rate of change, discrete time)}$$
$$\dot{Y} \equiv dY/dt. \qquad \text{(rate of change, continuous time)}$$

In previous chapters, we have typically used discrete time. Does it matter whether we work in continuous time or discrete time? Generally speaking in growth theory it is easier and requires less cumbersome notation to derive the results in continuous time.[2] The *(proportional) rate of growth* is defined in discrete time as

$$\gamma_Y = \frac{Y_{t+1} - Y_t}{Y_t} = \frac{\Delta Y}{Y} \qquad \text{(growth rate, discrete time)}$$

and in continuous time as

$$g_Y = \frac{\dot{Y}}{Y} = \frac{dY/dt}{Y}. \qquad \text{(growth rate, continuous time)}$$

In each case, the growth rate, e.g. 0.02, is multiplied by 100 to produce a *percentage* growth rate.

---

[1] Note that throughout the discussion of growth, it is output in real terms that is relevant. Contrary to our usual convention of using lower case letters to denote real, and upper case letters to denote nominal quantities, in the growth chapters, Y is real output. We use y to denote output per capita, $y \equiv Y/L$.

[2] From a mathematical point of view we could prove all our results in discrete time as well, and the equations we have derived in continuous time would hold as approximations to the discrete time results.

Calculating growth rates. As this chapter is about economic growth it is crucial to understand the concept of a growth rate and how to measure it using data. The simplest notion of a growth rate is the percentage change in GDP between periods (quarters or years) as defined above. For example US GDP in the year 2000 was $8, 987 billion and it was $8, 627 billion in the year 1999 (both measured in 1995 prices). Hence the US economy grew by 4.2% between 1999 and 2000.

Once we move beyond growth rates over very short periods, it is necessary to calculate the so-called compound growth rate. Economists interested in growth often focus on average annual growth rates over lengthy periods of time. We take an example and compare three methods.

- First, we calculate the average growth rate in Chinese GDP per capita between 1988 and 1998 using a 'long average' method: $1/10 \cdot (\frac{Y_{98} - Y_{88}}{Y_{88}}) \cdot 100 = 7.16\%$ p.a.

- Second, we calculate the annual growth rate each year of the decade and take the average: the answer is 5.7% p.a.

- Third, we calculate the annual compound growth rate using a formula: AGR (annual percentage growth rate) = $(\exp(1/10 \cdot \log(Y_{98}/Y_{88})) - 1) \cdot 100 = 5.6\%$ p.a. Note that it is the ln function on the calculator or spreadsheet that must be used since this is the natural logarithm function; although we use log in the text, this always refers to the natural logarithm.

The 'long average' method is incorrect because it ignores compounding: it overstates the growth rate because it neglects the fact that the base for growth is continuously rising.[3] The average of the annual growth rates will be a reasonable approximation to the compound growth rate for low growth rates but loses accuracy as the growth rate rises. The comparison between the average of the annual growth rates and the compound growth rate is exactly the same as between simple interest (compounded annually) and compound interest (compounded continuously). The AGR is the equivalent of the APR for interest rates (the annual percentage rate of interest reported on credit card bills, for example). We need to explain some more concepts before we return to show where the formula for the annual compound growth rate (AGR) comes from.

1.1 Growth rates, exponential and log functions

To see that the growth of GDP in discrete time, γ_Y, is the same as the growth rate in continuous time, g_Y, when the time period is short enough, let us start from the proportional growth of GDP between two periods in time given by, t and $t + \Delta t$, where Δt is small. When we make this interval smaller and smaller, we say that we are taking the limit as Δt

---

[3] To see why the first method is incorrect, apply the 7.16% annual growth rate to the base year GDP per capita of $1,816 and then for each subsequent year. The result is a level of GDP p.c. in 1998 far higher than that recorded ($3,117).

tends to zero:

$$\lim_{\Delta t \to 0} \gamma_Y = \lim_{\Delta t \to 0} \left\{ \frac{Y_{t+\Delta t} - Y_t}{\Delta t} \cdot \frac{1}{Y_t} \right\}$$

$$= \frac{dY}{dt} \frac{1}{Y} = \frac{\dot{Y}}{Y} = g_Y.$$

We express the proportional growth expression per unit of time and then the rules of calculus tell us that if we make this period of time very small the first term in the brackets is nothing other than the definition of the derivative of output with respect to time, $\dot{Y}$. g_Y is known as the instantaneous growth rate. Thus when we quote $g_Y = 0.02$, this means that the growth rate of GDP during the period of interest is 2%.

It is very useful to see that the growth rate can be expressed in several equivalent ways:

$$g_Y = \frac{\dot{Y}}{Y} = \frac{dY/dt}{Y} = \frac{d \log Y}{dt}. \qquad \text{(equivalent expressions, growth rate)}$$

In order to see that the last equality holds we can use the chain rule of calculus and the fact that the derivative of the log of a variable, Y, is $\frac{1}{Y}$, i.e. $\frac{d \log Y}{dY} = \frac{1}{Y}$:

$$\frac{d \log Y}{dt} = \frac{d \log Y}{dY} \frac{dY}{dt} = \frac{dY/dt}{Y}.$$

We now explore further what economists mean when they say that 'output grows exponentially'. Let us start with the previous example where for some economy $g_Y = 0.02$. In this case, if we know the level of output initially, Y_0, and the growth rate, then the level of output at time t comes from the equation $Y_t = Y_0 \exp(g_Y \cdot t)$, where exp is the exponential function and the growth rate g_Y is assumed to be constant. This equation can also be written as $Y_t = Y_0 e^{gt}$, where g is used instead of g_Y to simplify the notation. How do we know that this equation describes the evolution of output for our economy that grows at rate $g_Y = 0.02$? It is easier to see this if we do the proof in 'reverse'. That is, let us start from the equation:

$$Y_t = Y_0 \exp(g_Y \cdot t),$$

where Y_0 stands for the initial value of output. Taking logs of both the left and the right side of this we obtain:

$$\log Y_t = \log Y_0 + g_Y \cdot t \qquad (13.1)$$

If we now take derivatives with respect to time of this expression we obtain

$$\frac{d \log Y_t}{dt} = \frac{d \log Y_0}{dt} + g_Y$$

$$= g_Y.$$

The initial value of output is of course fixed at all future values and hence $\frac{d \log Y_0}{dt} = 0$. Thus we have shown that $g_Y = d \log Y/dt$, as expected.

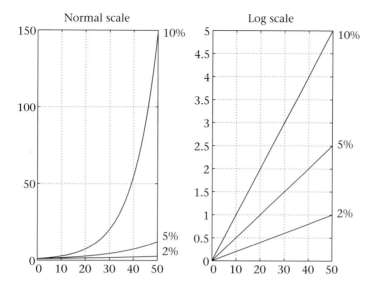

Figure 13.2 Simulation of exponential growth on a normal and logarithmic scale

An understanding of the relationship between exponential growth and logs is very useful for any analysis of growth.[4] As the plots in the left hand panel of Fig. 13.2 show, once we have the initial value for GDP, Y_0, and the growth rate, we can read off the level of output at any subsequent date. Growth paths for GDP are shown for a 2%, 5%, and 10% growth rate. We also note that the equation for $\log Y_t$ is linear (equation 13.1), with the slope of the line equal to the growth rate. The growth paths for GDP are shown in the right hand panel using the log scale: the growth paths are straight lines.

A second reason for understanding the relationship between logs and growth rates is that this relationship lies behind some very useful rules for handling growth rates. The following rules are used frequently:

(1) If $Y = X^\alpha$ then $\log Y = \alpha \log X$. This is useful because it allows us to go from levels to growth rates. For example, if we begin with the widely used production function, the Cobb–Douglas,

$$Y = K^\alpha L^{1-\alpha}, \qquad\qquad \text{(Cobb–Douglas production function)}$$

where $0 < \alpha < 1$, and first take logs:

$$\log Y = \alpha \log K + (1 - \alpha) \log L,$$

---

[4] For a concise and insightful discussion of the exponential and logarithmic functions, see Chapter 9 in Pemberton and Rau (2001).

then differentiate with respect to time and use the fact that $\frac{d \log Y}{dt} = \frac{\dot{Y}}{Y}$ we get:

$$\frac{d \log Y}{dt} = \alpha \frac{d \log K}{dt} + (1 - \alpha) \frac{d \log L}{dt}$$

$$\frac{\dot{Y}}{Y} = \alpha \frac{\dot{K}}{K} + (1 - \alpha) \frac{\dot{L}}{L}.$$

We can see from this that the growth rate of output is a weighted average of the growth rates of capital and labour inputs.

(2) The growth rate of the ratio of two variables is equal to the difference between the two growth rates: $g_{\frac{X}{Y}} = g_X - g_Y$. This rule is used often. For example, it says that the growth rate of output per worker ($\frac{Y}{L}$) is equal to the growth rate of output ($\frac{Y}{Y}$) minus the growth rate of workers ($\frac{\dot{L}}{L}$). To show this, the same technique is used as for (1): $\log(\frac{X}{Y}) = \log X - \log Y$ and $\frac{d \log(\frac{X}{Y})}{dt} = \frac{d \log X}{dt} - \frac{d \log Y}{dt}$; hence $g_{\frac{X}{Y}} = g_X - g_Y$.

(3) The growth rate of the product of two variables is equal to the sum of their growth rates: $g_{XY} = g_X + g_Y$. This follows the same logic as for 2.

1.2 Useful definitions for growth theory

In growth models in continuous time, the concept of the growth rate is $g_Y = \frac{\dot{Y}}{Y} = \frac{d \log Y}{dt}$, which we can express also using $Y_t = Y_0 \exp(g_Y \cdot t)$ and equivalently as $\log Y_t = \log Y_0 + g_Y \cdot t$. As noted above, the growth rate g_Y is the *instantaneous* growth rate and may be calculated from data as follows:

$$\log Y_t = \log Y_0 + g_Y \cdot t$$

$$g_Y \cdot t = \log Y_t - \log Y_0$$

$$g_Y = \frac{1}{t}(\log Y_t - \log Y_0), \qquad \text{(log difference method)}$$

where t is the number of years, Y_0 is the base year level of output, and Y_t the final year level. g_Y is multiplied by 100 to get the percentage growth rate. This is often referred to as the 'log difference' method of calculating the growth rate. When referring to the growth of output, economists often mean the annual growth rate (the discrete time concept), rather than the instantaneous growth rate (the continuous time concept). Similarly, when discussing interest rates, it is the annual percentage rate (APR) rather than the instantaneous rate that is typically reported. The annual percentage growth rate (or annual compound growth rate as it is sometimes called) is $(\exp g_Y - 1)$ expressed as a percentage and this is the formula for calculating the compound growth rate provided above:

$$AGR = (\exp g_Y - 1) \cdot 100$$

$$= \left[\exp \left(\frac{1}{t}(\log Y_t - \log Y_0) \right) - 1 \right] \cdot 100.$$

The relationship between the different concepts of the growth rate is clarified by noting that when we consider growth for one year, the familiar proportional rate of growth is G (multiplied by 100):

$$Y_1 = Y_0(1 + G)$$
$$G = \frac{Y_1 - Y_0}{Y_0} = \frac{\Delta Y}{Y}.$$

Extending to many periods, we have

$$Y_t = Y_0(1 + G)^t$$
$$\log \frac{Y_t}{Y_0} = t \log(1 + G)$$
$$\exp\left(\frac{1}{t}(\log Y_t - \log Y_o)\right) = 1 + G$$
$$G = \exp\left(\frac{1}{t}(\log Y_t - \log Y_o)\right) - 1$$
$$= \exp g_y - 1.$$

This illustrates that the AGR is the multi-period analogue to the one-period proportional growth rate.

1.3 Summary

- When using data to measure economic growth, the average of the annual percentage growth rates is a close approximation to the true annual (compound) percentage growth rate (AGR) when the growth rate is low (less than 5% p.a.). In the earlier example of Chinese growth, the average of the annual percentage growth rates is 5.58% p.a.; and the AGR is 5.55% p.a.

- Taking the difference between the natural logarithms of output at the start of the period and the end of the period and dividing by the length of the period gives the instantaneous growth rate, g_Y. When multiplied by 100, this is the percentage growth rate in continuous time. To get the AGR, we use the fact that AGR $= (\exp g_Y - 1) \cdot 100$. This is the percentage growth rate in discrete time. When referring to data, economists normally use discrete time concepts and therefore refer to the AGR; however growth theory is normally expressed in continuous time, with reference to g_Y. When growth rates are low, these are close to each other. In the example of Chinese growth, the AGR $= 5.55\%$ p.a. and $g_y \cdot 100 = 5.40\%$ p.a.

- Growth theory makes heavy use of the following equivalent expressions for the (instantaneous) growth rate: $g_Y = \frac{\dot{Y}}{Y} = \frac{dY/dt}{Y} = \frac{d \log Y}{dt}$; $Y_t = Y_0 \exp(g_Y \cdot t)$ and $\log Y_t = \log Y_0 + g_Y \cdot t$.

- Frequent use is made of the procedure of 'taking logs and differentiating' to go from expressions in levels to growth rates, and of the rules $g_{\frac{X}{Y}} = g_X - g_Y$ and $g_{XY} = g_X + g_Y$.

2 The Solow–Swan model

We begin with the formal model of economic growth developed both by Robert Solow and Trevor Swan in 1956. Deceptively simple, it has stood the test of time as one of the most robust pieces of economic modelling. It has long been the starting point for many explorations, both theoretical and empirical, into the nature of economic growth. It is important to become acquainted with the assumptions underlying the model; among other things, this allows us to judge whether the Solow–Swan model is applicable or not in a particular situation.

A notion of what is meant by capital and in particular the aggregate capital stock is a key part of the Solow–Swan model. In a way, it is close to the everyday use of the word capital and it includes things like cars and computers. But one needs a more precise understanding of the concept in order to apply it to growth models.

- Capital is *productive* but it does not need to be productive all the time. An aeroplane that has been temporarily taken out of service because of low demand for air travel, for example, still counts as part of the capital stock of the economy. Importantly, inventories of raw materials, intermediate and finished goods are also part of the capital stock of the economy.

- Capital is itself created from existing resources in the economy so agents face a trade-off between consuming some resources today or transforming them into capital, which will potentially produce more resources tomorrow. The process of transforming current resources into capital and away from current consumption is called *investment*.

- Capital *earns a return*, or equivalently, it is assumed that capital can be rented at the real rate R.

- Capital also *depreciates*, which means it becomes less and less productive as time progresses and it will eventually become obsolete. This is a very intuitive aspect of capital and it reflects the important notion that the computer in use today will not be very useful in several years from now: its components are bound to fail and ongoing technological progress means it will not be able to run the latest software. It is assumed that capital depreciates at the constant rate, δ. The real interest rate is equal to the rental rate, R, minus the depreciation rate: $r = R - \delta$. Since the depreciation rate is normally assumed to be constant, the real rate of return and the real interest rate move together.

- A conceptually more tricky property, which we can ascribe to capital is that it is a *rival good*. This means that the usage of one unit of capital by an individual necessarily means that no one else can use it. As we shall see in Chapter 14, there are goods that do not have this property and that play an important role in models of economic growth. Most important amongst non-rival goods for growth theory are ideas: once calculus has been discovered anyone who has learned the appropriate methods will be able to use it productively without interfering with the use of it by others.

Next we need to be more specific about what the aggregate capital stock of an economy is. If you doubt that one can aggregate apples and pears, you may be sceptical about aggregating all the different types of capital in an economy. This type of scepticism sparked off a classic debate between economists in the 1950s and 1960s. This debate, known as the 'Cambridge Controversy' involved Joan Robinson[5] in Cambridge, England, and Robert Solow and Paul Samuelson in Cambridge, Massachusetts. Robinson argued that models relying on the assumption that capital can be measured and also aggregated are most likely to be invalid. As most contemporary economists would acknowledge, one has to be very careful when extrapolating from one-good models to the multi-product markets of the real economy because only under very special circumstances is aggregation mathematically warranted. Solow's response to this argument was to show that the main insights of the theory are robust to more realistic and complicated representations of technology.

Keeping in mind these reservations, we can now provide an exposition of growth in a one-good economy. There are two key elements to the model:

- the production function, i.e. how the inputs of capital and labour are transformed into output;
- how the labour and capital inputs change over time.

2.1 The production function

We begin with production in such a one-good economy. The single good can be consumed or it can be invested, i.e. used as a capital input, so as to produce more goods next period. Labour is also used in production, which takes place according to the *production function* $Y = F(K, L)$, where the production function is smooth and where the marginal products of capital and labour are positive and diminishing. All variables are in real terms. It is important to note here that the production function relates flows of output to flows of capital services and flows of labour services.

In growth models, we do not normally have to worry about the difference between employment and the labour force so we use L to refer to the labour input in the production function. As sketched in the introductory discussion of growth theory in Chapter 1, the assumption of diminishing returns to capital plays a central role in defining the difference between models of exogenous and endogenous growth. Additionally we shall assume that the production function exhibits *constant returns to scale* (CRS). This is most easily visualized as the generalization of the idea that duplicating production facilities doubles output. More generally, it means that if both inputs are increased by the same factor, output rises by that factor as well, i.e. $F(\theta K, \theta L) = \theta F(K, L)$, where θ is a positive constant. The constant returns to scale assumption is very convenient because it allows us to define output and capital in *intensive form* (i.e. in per worker terms) as $y = Y/L$ and $k = K/L$. A refresher on the concepts of returns to scale and returns to a factor is provided in the appendix to this chapter.

We can rewrite the production function in intensive form as:

$$y = \frac{Y}{L} = \frac{1}{L} F(K, L) = F(\frac{K}{L}, \frac{L}{L}) = F(k, 1) = f(k).$$

(production function in intensive form)

5 Robinson (1953–4).

Other features of the production function play a key role in the Solow–Swan model. In particular, the constant returns to scale assumption implies that average and marginal returns to each factor depend only on the factor ratio, i.e. on K/L. It then follows from the assumption of diminishing returns to each factor that the average product of capital, APK, and marginal product of capital, MPK, are decreasing functions of K/L (and the average product of labour, APL, and marginal product of labour, MPL, are increasing functions of K/L). We have:

$$APK = f(k)/k \text{ and } APL = f(k);$$

and

$$MPK = f'(k) \text{ and } MPL = f(k) - f'(k)k.$$

The derivation of the expression for MPL is shown in the appendix. For the results of the Solow–Swan model to hold, the production function must be 'well-behaved' so as to ensure that there is a unique steady-state equilibrium in the growth model and that it is unique. The additional assumptions needed can be found in the appendix.

In practice it is often convenient to work with a specific representation of the production function that has all these properties. Such a function is the Cobb–Douglas production function given by

$$Y = K^\alpha L^{1-\alpha} \tag{13.2}$$

$$\frac{Y}{L} = \frac{K^\alpha}{L} \frac{L}{L^\alpha} \tag{13.3}$$

$$y = k^\alpha, \tag{13.4}$$

where we divide through by L to get it in intensive form. Using the Cobb–Douglas production function as an example, many of the properties of the production function are derived in the appendix.

2.2 How labour and capital inputs change over time

We shall assume that the labour force grows at a constant positive exponential growth rate n. If we work in continuous time it is natural to define this growth rate as:

$$n = \frac{\dot{L}}{L} = \frac{dL/dt}{L}, \qquad \text{(growth rate of labour input: exogenous)}$$

which implies that the labour force grows exponentially and for any initial level L_0, at some point t in the future the level of the labour force is $L_t = L_0 \exp(nt)$.

By contrast with this assumption about labour force growth, the growth of the capital stock depends on economic factors. We assume that we are dealing with a closed economy, which means that no borrowing from abroad is possible and hence savings are equal to investment. In addition, the economy has a constant exogenously given savings rate s out of current income. Together, these imply that

$$I = sF(K, L). \tag{13.5}$$

where I is gross investment. To see how the capital stock changes, i.e. dK/dt (or $\dot{K}$), we need to deduct depreciation from gross investment, i.e.

$$\dot{K} = I - \delta K,$$

where δ is the rate at which capital depreciates. Next, we incorporate the condition that savings is equal to investment:

$$\dot{K} = I - \delta K = sF(K,L) - \delta K. \tag{13.6}$$

By dividing through by K, we have

$$g_K = \frac{\dot{K}}{K} = s\frac{Y}{K} - \delta = s \cdot APK - \delta \qquad \text{(growth rate of capital)}$$

which says that the growth of the capital stock depends on the APK and is therefore a declining function of the capital–labour ratio (k).

2.3 Steady state or balanced growth

If we take a constant growth rate of the labour force, n, then when the capital stock is growing at the same rate, i.e. when

$$g_K = n$$

the capital–labour ratio will be constant. This is called the steady-state capital–labour ratio k^*. Note that g_K, n and k^* are shown in Fig. 13.4. Hence, steady-state growth requires

$$s\frac{Y}{K} - \delta = n$$

which implies:

$$v^* = \frac{K^*}{Y^*} = \frac{k^*}{y^*} = \frac{s}{n+\delta} \qquad \text{(steady-state capital–output ratio: Domar's formula)}$$

Domar's formula is useful because it provides an explicit expression for the steady-state capital–output ratio, which does not depend on the particular form of the production function. We can summarize the results of the Solow–Swan growth model so far :

- in steady-state growth, output and capital grow at the same rate as the exogenously given growth rate of the labour force. There is no growth in output per capita in the steady state.

- the capital–output ratio in the steady state is higher, the higher is the savings rate and the lower are the labour force growth rate and depreciation.

There is a second way of characterizing the steady-state growth path, where we use the intensive form of the production function. We now divide both sides of equation 13.6 by L to rewrite the expression per unit of labour and we obtain:

$$\frac{\dot{K}}{L} = sf(k) - \delta k. \tag{13.7}$$

In order to rewrite our equation in terms of k only, we note that

$$\frac{\dot{k}}{k} = \frac{\dot{K}}{K} - \frac{\dot{L}}{L}$$

and multiplying each side by K/L and simplifying gives

$$\dot{k} = \frac{\dot{K}}{L} - kn$$

so $\frac{\dot{K}}{L} = \dot{k} + kn$. Substituting this expression in equation 13.7 and rearranging, we obtain the *Fundamental Solow Equation of Motion,* which describes how capital per worker varies over time:

$$\dot{k} = sf(k) - (\delta + n)k. \tag{13.8}$$

It is worth exploring in some detail what equation 13.8 tells us. The first term shows the extent to which investment is adding to the capital stock per worker. The second term shows the amount of investment needed to offset depreciation (δk) and to equip additions to the labour force at existing levels of capital per head (nk). Note that if there were no savings in the economy ($s = 0$) then $\dot{k} = -(\delta + n)k$, that is, capital per head would be falling under the pressures of

(1) an increasing population, $n > 0$;

(2) capital depreciation, $\delta > 0$.

If $sf(k) > (\delta + n)k$, capital per worker increases because investment per head is greater than the reduction in capital per head due to an increasing population and depreciation. If on the other hand $sf(k) < (\delta + n)k$, capital per worker decreases because investment per head is smaller than the reduction in capital per head due to an increasing population and depreciation.

We present this result in a standard Solow diagram (Figure 13.3) by plotting the two parts of the right hand side of equation 13.8. Since s is a fraction, the shape of the $sf(k)$ curve is given by the properties of the production function. As δ and n are constant the second term is a line from the origin with a slope of $\delta + n$. The difference between the two curves at any level of k determines $\dot{k}$.

The point where the two curves intersect is given by the level of capital per worker (k^*) where $sf(k^*) = (\delta + n)k^*$. At this point $\dot{k} = 0$ and $\dot{y} = 0$, which means that the level of capital per worker and output per worker are constant. As we have noted above, this defines a *steady state* in the Solow–Swan model: at k^* both K, and L grow at the same constant rate n. In Fig. 13.3, the steady-state level of output per head (y^*) and of consumption per head (c^*) are shown. We can easily see that the steady-state level of output per head is given by

$$y^* = f(k^*) \qquad \text{(steady-state output per head)}$$

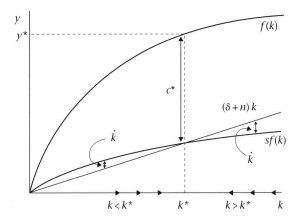

Figure 13.3 Standard Solow diagram (without technological progress)

while the steady-state level of consumption per head is also a constant and is a fraction of steady state income. It is given by

$$c^* = f(k^*) - sf(k^*) = (1-s)f(k^*). \qquad \text{(steady-state consumption per head)}$$

To complete the description of the model, there is one loose end to tie up: what is the growth rate of output, i.e. $g_Y = \dot{Y}/Y$? We already know from the Domar formula that in the steady state, output grows at the same rate as does capital and labour. We can also derive a general expression for the growth of output, which is useful.

Let us now differentiate the production function, $Y = F(K, L)$, with respect to time and obtain (using the chain rule):

$$\dot{Y} = F_K \dot{K} + F_L \dot{L}, \qquad (13.9)$$

where $F_K = \frac{\partial F(K,L)}{\partial K}$ and $F_L = \frac{\partial F(K,L)}{\partial L}$. We divide both sides by Y in order to obtain the growth rate of output on the left hand side:

$$g_Y = \frac{F_K \dot{K}}{Y} + \frac{F_L \dot{L}}{Y}. \qquad (13.10)$$

Next, in order to express the right hand side in terms of growth rates, we multiply and divide each component by the appropriate factor from the production function:

$$g_Y = \frac{F_K K}{Y} g_K + \frac{F_L L}{Y} g_L,$$

which, with a constant growth rate of labour, n, can be written as:

$$g_Y = \sigma_K g_K + \sigma_L n \qquad \text{(growth rate of output)}$$

where $\sigma_K = \frac{F_K K}{Y}$ and $\sigma_L = \frac{F_L L}{Y}$. In the appendix, it is shown that $\sigma_K + \sigma_L = 1$ (by Euler's Theorem). We now have an expression for the growth of output as the weighted average of the growth rates of capital, and of labour input. In a competitive economy, the weights are the factor shares of capital and labour. To see this, we note that since F_K is the marginal product of capital and under competitive conditions, this is equal to R the real rental rate of capital, $(RK)/Y$ is capital's share and similarly, $(wL)/Y$ is labour's share. Fig. 13.4 illustrates the steady state equilibrium at k^*, along with the growth rates of output, capital and labour. The $g_K = s\frac{Y}{K} - \delta$ curve is downward sloping because as we have already seen, the APK is a decreasing function of the capital–labour ratio. This is just a reflection of the properties of the production function (constant returns to scale and diminishing returns to each factor). The alternative Solow diagram (as in Fig. 13.4) is very useful for analysing the growth of output, whereas the standard diagram (Fig. 13.3) is useful for analysing the growth of output per capita.

Before looking in more detail at the behaviour of the model out of equilibrium, i.e. when the capital–labour ratio is not at its steady-state value, k^*, let us review the extent to which the model in its present form delivers what we aimed for, i.e. a model of economic growth in the sense of the growth in per capita output. To do this, we concentrate on the steady state, since this defines the path of the economy when it is in equilibrium. It is apparent that although we have made substantial progress in understanding the role of capital in the economy, we still do not have an explanation of economic growth in the steady state.

- In the model so far, the steady state is characterized by a constant level of output per worker, y^*, or in other words, by $\dot{y} = 0$. In the steady state, population and capital grow at the same rate, which ensures that capital per worker remains constant at k^* and output per worker at y^*.

- The intuition for this result should be clear by now: diminishing returns to capital (represented by the curvature of $f(k)$) ensure that extra units of capital per worker produce less and less; at the same time depreciation does not diminish. Eventually all savings will be deployed to replace the existing capital. This is the point at which the $sf(k^*)$ function cuts the $(\delta + n)k$ line in Fig. 13.3, the point at which the economy will be in equilibrium with $\dot{k} = 0$.

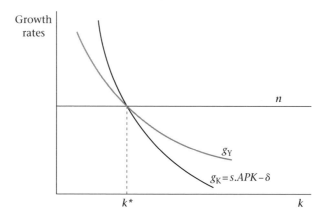

Figure 13.4 Alternative Solow diagram (without technological progress): $g_Y = \sigma_K g_K + \sigma_L n$

This seems to be a rather unsatisfactory response to the challenge of modelling the persistent growth of per capita output and we shall see in section 4 that to produce steady-state growth in output per worker the Solow–Swan model must be extended by introducing technological progress.

2.4 Transitional dynamics: what happens out of equilibrium?

Although simple, the Solow–Swan model is still surprisingly rich when it comes to adjustment to equilibrium and convergence to the steady state. We have mentioned already (and illustrated in Fig. 13.3) that if the capital–labour ratio is below the steady-state value, capital intensity will increase and vice versa if the capital–labour ratio is above k^*. The economy will continue to adjust until $k = k^*$. To focus specifically on the 'out-of-equilibrium' adjustment, it is useful to present the model in a slightly different way. Let us now return to equation 13.8 and consider $g_k = \dot{k}/k$, the growth rate of capital per worker. First divide equation 13.8 by k to obtain:

$$g_k = \frac{sf(k)}{k} - (\delta + n) \tag{13.11}$$

$$= s \cdot APK - (\delta + n). \tag{13.12}$$

We plot the two components of the right hand side of this expression in Fig. 13.5. Clearly $\delta + n$ is a positive constant and hence can be represented by a horizontal line. As we have noted above, since $f(k)/k$ (output per unit capital) is the *average product of capital* it falls as k increases. In the steady state equilibrium, when $k = k^*$, $sf(k^*)/k^* = \delta + n$. Thus the growth rate of capital per worker is given by the vertical difference between the curves.

At low k, the average product of capital ($f(k)/k$) is high and with a constant savings rate, this produces high gross investment relative to the existing capital and hence a rapid increase in the capital stock, since the amount of investment required to keep the

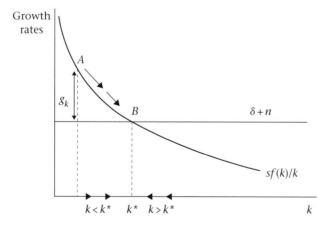

Figure 13.5 Transitional dynamics in the Solow–Swan model

capital stock constant is fixed by the depreciation factor δ. Given the growth of the labour force, n, capital stock per worker also grows. The economy moves from A to B in Fig. 13.5. Similarly, for high k, capital stock per worker will decline.

Ultimately however, the transition path of *output* per worker is of more interest than is that of *capital* per worker. The growth rate of output per worker is defined in the usual fashion as $g_y = \dot{y}/y$. Following the same procedure that we used for working out the growth rate of output, we have:

$$g_y = \frac{MPK}{APK} g_k = \sigma_K g_k, \qquad \text{(growth rate of output per head)}$$

where with competitive markets, σ_K is capital's share of output and is positive and less than one. In the steady state, the equation still holds because $g_y = g_k = 0$.

2.4.1 Policy experiment 1: a rise in the savings rate

Let us now consider the following policy experiment: at time t_1, there is an exogenous rise in the savings rate. In Fig. 13.6 we trace the impact of this shock and show how k and y adjust as the economy moves to a new steady state. In the first panel this is represented by an upward shift in the $sf(k)$ curve corresponding to the increase of s to s'. The economy slowly adjusts from the old steady state k^* to the new steady state k^{**} where capital per worker is higher than at t_0. The transition dynamics are better illustrated in the second panel where we can inspect growth rates directly. Immediately after the exogenous shock occurs at t_1, the growth rate of capital per worker jumps up from zero at point A to B.

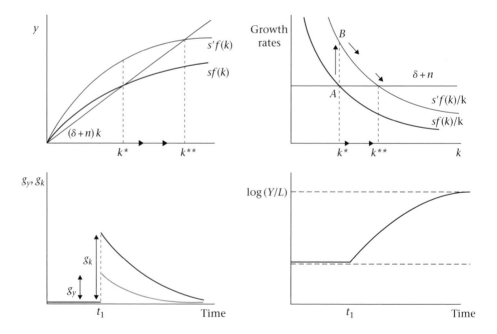

Figure 13.6 Policy experiment 1: an exogenous increase in the savings rate, $s' > s$

As the economy slowly converges to the new capital per worker long-run steady state k^{**}, the growth rate g_k (and hence g_y too) falls to zero. In the last two panels we show the time trajectories of capital per worker and of $\log Y/L$ before and after time t_1. As we have already noted, in this model we only observe positive growth rates in the per worker variables if the economy experiences a parameter shift. Once the system returns to its steady state we are back on the balanced growth path with zero growth of output per capita, i.e. with output, capital, and labour all growing at the same rate.

The explanation for what at first may seem to be a surprising result lies once again in the assumption of diminishing returns to capital accumulation. This means that the initial rise in the growth rate of the capital stock does *not* bring a proportionate increase in output. Thus along with the rise in capital per worker and productivity, there is a rise in the capital–output ratio. This means that the faster capital stock growth generated by the higher savings rate fades away as depreciation eventually swallows up all the additional investment effort.

2.4.2 Policy experiment 2: a rise in the population growth rate

To make sure the mechanics of this model are clear, consider another experiment where the population growth rate suddenly and permanently goes up due to an exogenous change in fertility. In Fig. 13.7, the impact of this shock on the system is traced and we show how k and y adjust to the new steady state. In the first panel this is represented graphically by a counter-clockwise rotation of the line corresponding to the increase of n

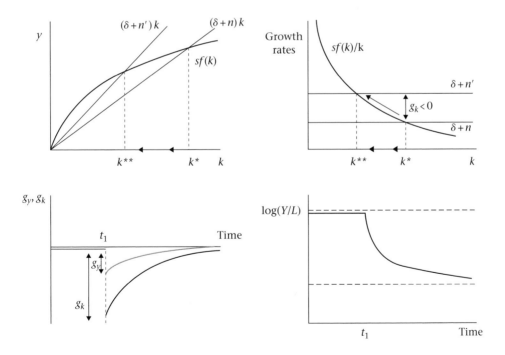

Figure 13.7 Policy experiment 2: an exogenous increase in fertility, $n' > n$

to n'. The economy slowly adjusts from the old steady state k^* to the new steady state k^{**} where capital per worker and output per worker is *lower* than at t_1.

The reason is that the level of investment (given an unchanged savings and investment share) is insufficient to equip—at the existing level of capital intensity—the larger numbers now entering the labour force. Capital intensity therefore declines until the investment required to maintain it constant is just equal to the actual investment level. As before, the transitional dynamics are better illustrated in the second panel where growth rates in per capita terms can be inspected directly. We note that immediately after the exogenous shock occurs at t_1 the growth rate of capital per worker is negative. As the economy slowly converges to the new long-run steady-state level of capital per worker k^{**}, the growth rate g_k (and hence g_y too) returns to zero. In the lower panels we show the time trajectories of the growth rate of output and capital per worker and of log Y/L before and after time t_1. Once the system returns to equilibrium, we are in a new steady state with a lower level of output per capita.

But what happens to the growth rate of *output* in this economy? To see this, it is better to use the alternative Solow diagram as shown in Fig. 13.8 and to note that a change in population growth rate shifts the g_Y curve so that it goes through the intersection of the new population growth line, n' and the unchanged g_K curve. When the population growth rate rises, output growth also *rises* as shown in the move from point A to point B. However, since output growth does not rise by as much as population growth, the growth of output *per head declines* as shown in Fig. 13.7. In general, to work out what happens to output growth and the growth of the capital stock, the alternative Solow diagram should be used.

These experiments leave open the question of what generates the type of sustained growth rates we have documented in Chapter 1 for many of the world's economies over recent centuries. The model so far can only account for this by either

(1) the presence of very long adjustment periods as the economy transits from one steady state to another or

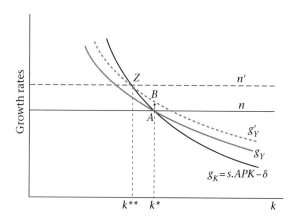

Figure 13.8 Policy experiment 2: an exogenous increase in fertility, $n' > n$ — implications for output growth

(2) the presence of repeated shocks, e.g. a steadily rising savings share or a steadily falling population growth rate.

As we shall see, more consistent with the stylized facts is a modification of the model that allows steady-state growth in output per capita by introducing technological progress.

3 Solow growth accounting: measuring the impact of technology

In the next section the standard Solow–Swan model is extended by including technological progress explicitly. Parallel with extending his model of growth to include technological progress, Solow (and others) developed a technique for measuring the empirical counterpart of technological progress. The idea was to account for the contribution to the growth of output made by the growth of factor inputs (capital and labour) and to associate any growth unaccounted for with 'technological progress'. Solow referred to this residual as total factor productivity growth. Total factor productivity growth captures the impact of intangible aspects of human progress that allow both labour and capital to increase their productivity. Thinking of the period 1990 to 2000, what has made the US economy more productive was not simply the fact that firms have invested and bought computers, but rather that the information revolution has allowed new machines based on computer technology to be more productive and workers who use computers to be more efficient.

Solow's method of calculating total factor productivity growth is known as (*Solow*) *growth accounting*. To see how this works we can start from a production function defined in terms of capital, labour, and an index of the level of technological progress given by A, which is a function of time:

$$\dot{Y} = F_K \dot{K} + F_L \dot{L} + F_A \dot{A}, \tag{13.13}$$

where F_K is $\frac{\partial F(K,L,A)}{\partial K}$, F_L is $\frac{\partial F(K,L,A)}{\partial L}$, and F_A is $\frac{\partial F(K,L,A)}{\partial A}$. Applying exactly the same technique as used above in deriving the expression for the growth rate of output, we obtain:

$$g_Y = \frac{F_K K}{Y} g_K + \frac{F_L L}{Y} g_L + \frac{F_A A}{Y} g_A. \tag{13.14}$$

The growth of output is equal to a function of the growth rates of capital, labour, and the technology factor. Just as we have seen before, it is possible to simplify this further if we make further assumptions about the market environment. This will enable it to be used to get an estimate of the contribution of 'technological progress' from data. We assume that labour and capital are traded in competitive markets and are paid their respective marginal products. This means that the marginal product of labour, $F_L = w$, where w is the real wage, and that the marginal product of capital, $F_K = R$, where R is the rental cost of capital in the economy. Additionally, we define the *Solow residual* by $SR = \frac{F_A A}{Y} g_A$.

We can now rewrite the expression above as:

$$g_Y = \frac{RK}{Y} g_K + \frac{wL}{Y} g_L + SR. \tag{13.15}$$

Since $\sigma_K = (RK)/Y$ corresponds to the share of total income spent by the economy on payments to capital, while $\sigma_L = (wL)/Y$ corresponds to the share of total income spent by the economy on payments to labour, we have a compact expression for the Solow residual as

$$SR = g_Y - \sigma_K g_K - \sigma_L g_L. \quad \text{(total factor productivity (TFP) growth: the Solow residual)}$$

The Solow residual is the difference between output growth and a weighted sum of factor input growths with weights given by the factor shares, i.e. it is the growth that is not attributed to the growth of either labour or capital inputs. If we accept the market assumptions we have used to derive the formula above we now have an expression that can be used to estimate the Solow residual (i.e. TFP growth) from actual macroeconomic data. When the production function is constant returns to scale, the sum of the labour and capital shares is one and we can simplify the previous equation to

$$\text{TFP growth} = SR = g_Y - \sigma_K g_K - (1 - \sigma_K) g_L.$$

In empirical analysis, it is often illuminating to work in per capita terms and we can rearrange this equation as follows:

$$\text{TFP growth} = (g_Y - g_L) - \sigma_K g_K + \sigma_K g_L$$
$$= g_y - \sigma_K g_k,$$

where $y \equiv Y/L$ and $k \equiv K/L$. We can also turn the equation around and decompose the growth of productivity into the contribution from the growth of capital intensity and the contribution of TFP growth:

$$g_y = \sigma_K g_k + \text{TFP growth}.$$

Growth-accounting exercises may also seek to separately identify the contribution to the growth of output per worker from improvements in labour quality, e.g. as measured by increased average years of education. This will lead to a further component in the above equation:

$$g_y = \sigma_K g_k + (1 - \sigma_K)q + \text{TFP growth},$$

where q is the growth rate of the quality of labour inputs (per worker). This is weighted by labour's share in output, $1 - \sigma_K$.

In Table 13.1 we present an analysis of growth accounting as reported by the Bureau of Labor Statistics in the United States. It is interesting to note that according to growth accounting, the so-called New Economy phase of US growth in the late 1990s is associated

Table 13.1 Solow growth accounting for the United States, 1948–2001, % p.a.

	1948–2001	1948–1973	1974–1995	1996–2001
Total GDP Growth	2.5	3.3	1.5	2.5
– due to capital	0.9	0.9	0.7	1.2
– due to labour	0.2	0.2	0.2	0.4
Solow residual	1.3	2.1	0.6	0.9

Source: Bureau of Labor Statistics

with a higher contribution from factor input growth, especially capital, *and* faster TFP growth. TFP growth in the late 1990s is, however, not as fast as in the 1950s and 1960s. In Chapter 17, we report on how growth accounting has been used to try to uncover the role of information and communications technology (ICT)-producing and ICT-using sectors in the US economy in the late 1990s.

Over the years economists have come up with many objections to Solow's attempt to use a simple accounting identity to measure technological progress.[6] We look at one of these, the presence of imperfect competition, in the appendix. Much research is being conducted to find better ways of measuring technological progress by including finer concepts of the factors of production. It remains undisputed however, that technological progress is an important driving force behind output growth and we now incorporate it into the model of exogenous economic growth.

4 Technological progress in the Solow–Swan model

We are now in a position to introduce technological progress explicitly into the Solow–Swan model. In the growth model without technological progress, output and employment grow at the same rate in the steady state; however, empirical data suggests that the steady state is characterized by output growth faster than labour growth so that output per worker grows at a relatively constant rate. Consistent with the notion of steady-state growth, capital and output grow at the same proportional rate, so the capital–output ratio remains broadly constant. In fact it turns out that in general only one modification of the production function delivers the result of steady-state growth with positive per capita growth: this is called the Harrod-neutral form of technological progress. The Harrod-neutral specification implies that the effect of technological progress on output is channelled into production through labour. Technological progress takes effect by increasing the productivity of existing labour on a given capital stock. The Solow–Swan model is often criticized for assuming that new technology arrives in the economy 'like manna from heaven'. Probably a better way to think about the model is to see the task as one of understanding how 'the path of aggregate output adjusts to the rate

---

[6] For a wide-ranging, recent, and critical assessment, see Lipsey and Carlaw (2004).

of population growth and the rate of technological progress, whatever they happen to be and for however long they persist'.[7] The Solow–Swan model provides neither a theory of what determines population growth nor one that determines the rate of technological progress.

It helps to clarify what is special about Harrod-neutral technological progress by contrasting it with two alternatives. There are different ways of modifying the production function so as to take into account the technology variable (which we call A_t) in addition to capital and labour:

(1) 'Hicks-neutral' or *factor*-augmenting technological progress: $Y = A_t F(K, L)$ where the technology variable affects the productivity of capital and labour;

(2) 'Solow-neutral' or *capital*-augmenting technological progress: $Y = F(A_t K, L)$;

(3) 'Harrod-neutral' or *labour*-augmenting technological progress: $Y = F(K, A_t L)$.

In each case, A_t grows at a constant exogenously given growth rate g_A and can be thought of as something like world technological know-how and hence is not determined by any one economy. A feature of the Cobb–Douglas production function is that the three different types of technological progress are identical as shown in the appendix.

The fact that Harrod-neutral technical progress enhances the productivity of labour means that the Fundamental Solow Equation is easily modified to include it. First we introduce the concept of labour measured in efficiency units: in the production function $Y = F(K, AL)$, the term AL is *labour measured in efficiency units*. To measure labour in efficiency units means that the amount of labour L is magnified by the technology factor, A. Although it turns out to be very convenient to work with labour in efficiency units, it is essential to remember that it is output or consumption per unit of natural labour that matters for economic welfare. It is therefore necessary to be able to go back to natural labour units as the issue at hand demands. We now define

$$\hat{y} = \frac{Y}{AL} \qquad \text{(output per efficiency unit of labour)}$$

and

$$\hat{k} = \frac{K}{AL} \qquad \text{(capital per efficiency unit of labour)}$$

where hats refer to variables measured in efficiency units of labour.

We repeat the same steps as before but with the added complication of technological progress—this also serves to reinforce the mechanics of the basic growth model. We divide the production function by AL, to obtain

$$\hat{y} = \frac{Y}{AL} = \frac{1}{AL} F(K, AL) = F(\hat{k}, 1) = f(\hat{k}).$$

Just as before the resource constraint (i.e. the requirement that savings is equal to investment) is given by $sY = \frac{dK}{dt} + \delta K$. We can now express it in efficiency units by dividing

[7] Solow (2000: 98).

by AL:

$$s\hat{y} = \frac{\dot{K}}{AL} + \delta\hat{k} = \frac{K}{AL}\frac{\dot{K}}{K} + \delta\hat{k} = \hat{k}g_K + \delta\hat{k}.$$

From the definition of $\hat{k}$, we can express capital as $K = \hat{k}AL$ and using the properties of growth rates discussed in section 1, we have $g_K = g_{\hat{k}} + g_A + g_L$. Parallel to the assumption that the growth of population is constant at rate n, it is assumed that the rate of technological progress is constant at rate x, where 'x' suggests 'exogenous'. We therefore use x to refer to the exogenous rate of Harrod-neutral, i.e. labour-augmenting, technological progress.

Hence, using the same techniques for rearranging the equation as before, we have the Fundamental Solow Equation with technological progress:

$$\dot{\hat{k}} = sf(\hat{k}) - \hat{k}(\delta + x + n) \text{ or}$$

$$g_{\hat{k}} = \frac{sf(\hat{k})}{\hat{k}} - (\delta + x + n). \qquad \text{(Fundamental Solow Equation; with tech. progress)}$$

We note first that Domar's formula for the steady-state capital–output ratio (when $g_{\hat{k}} = 0$) is:

$$v^* = \frac{\hat{k}^*}{\hat{y}^*} = \frac{s}{\delta + x + n}. \qquad \text{(Domar's formula)}$$

We can represent the Fundamental Solow Equation in a Solow diagram (Fig. 13.9), which is very similar to the one without technological progress. Net investment in physical capital takes place ($\dot{\hat{k}} > 0$) when the curve representing $sf(\hat{k})$ is above $\hat{k}(\delta + x + n)$, which corresponds to the case where the amount of savings outweighs the amount of capital:

- required to replace the capital lost due to depreciation ($\delta\hat{k}$),
- required to gainfully employ the additional labour force due to population growth ($n\hat{k}$) and
- made profitable by the increased productivity of the existing labour force as a result of technological progress ($x\hat{k}$).

Given the technical assumptions about the shape of the production function specified at the beginning of this chapter, we know that only one point exists (corresponding to the capital level $\hat{k}^*$), such that the two curves intersect. That point corresponds to our notion of equilibrium where $\dot{\hat{k}} = 0$ and our economy has reached its long-run steady state.

4.1 Steady state/balanced growth path properties

Let us focus on the steady-state values of the variables of this system and their balanced growth paths and see to what extent they correspond to the stylized facts summarized in

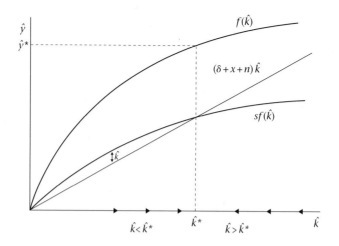

Figure 13.9 Standard Solow diagram in the model with technological progress

the introduction. First we note that the long-run steady state of the economy is given by the pair $(\hat{k}^*, \hat{y}^*)$. Since these represent equilibrium values, we know that $g_{\hat{k}^*} = g_{\hat{y}^*} = 0$. But we can express $g_{\hat{y}^*} = g_y - x$. Hence $g_y = x$ in equilibrium and by the same argument $g_k = x$. Thus in the steady state, output per worker and capital per worker grow at the same rate, given by the exogenous rate of technological progress:

$$x = g_y = g_k.$$

If we take the Cobb–Douglas production function with technological progress such that $\hat{y} = \hat{k}^\alpha$, it is possible to solve for the steady state values of $\hat{k}^*$ and $\hat{y}^*$ explicitly. The equilibrium property $\dot{\hat{k}} = 0$ implies $s(\hat{k}^*)^\alpha = \hat{k}^*(\delta + x + n)$, where we can rearrange for $\hat{k}^*$ and obtain the steady-state value of capital and output per efficiency unit of labour (after substituting for the optimal value of capital in the production function):

$$\hat{k}^* = \left(\frac{s}{\delta + x + n}\right)^{\frac{1}{1-\alpha}} \tag{13.16}$$

$$\hat{y}^* = \left(\frac{s}{\delta + x + n}\right)^{\frac{\alpha}{1-\alpha}} \tag{13.17}$$

Furthermore, we can use this last expression to solve for the steady-state value of output per worker:

$$y^* = A_t \left(\frac{s}{\delta + x + n}\right)^{\frac{\alpha}{1-\alpha}}. \tag{13.18}$$

This tells us that at time t after the economy has reached its long-run steady-state growth path, output per head is:

(1) increasing in the level of technological development A_t at time t;

(2) increasing in the savings rate of the economy, s;

(3) decreasing in the rate of population growth, n;

(4) decreasing in the depreciation rate, δ.

Consistent with our intuition, this shows that economies that save more, have lower fertility, and are advanced technologically will be richer. But note that whilst higher savings and lower population growth mean a higher level of living standards, only faster technological progress (higher x) can raise the *growth rate* of living standards.

One of the stylized facts of growth is the tendency for factor shares to remain fairly constant over time. We cannot test this against the predictions of the Solow–Swan model if we use the Cobb–Douglas production function because the shares are constant by assumption in that case. The share of capital is given by the parameter α and that of labour, by $1 - \alpha$. However, we can show that even for an arbitrary production function that satisfies our initial assumptions, the model with labour augmenting technological progress also implies constant shares. This offers another perspective on the logic of growth accounting. To see that this is so, we use the homogeneity property of the production function (see the appendix) to rewrite it as:

$$Y = F(K, AL) = KF\left(1, \frac{AL}{K}\right) = Kf\left(\frac{AL}{K}\right).$$ (13.19)

The marginal product of labour is given by the derivative of the production function Y with respect to labour L, and at the steady state, it is

$$MPL = \frac{d\left[Kf\left(\frac{AL}{K}\right)\right]}{dL} = Kf'\left(\frac{AL}{K}\right)\frac{A}{K} = Af'\left(\frac{1}{\hat{k}^*}\right) = w,$$ (13.20)

where w is the real wage, assuming a competitive labour market. The share of labour is defined as $\sigma_L = \frac{wL}{Y}$, that is the total income paid out as wages to the workforce expressed as a proportion of GDP. We know that at the steady state $\hat{y}^* = Y/(AL)$ and we derive the share of labour as:

$$\sigma_L = \frac{Af'\left(\frac{1}{\hat{k}^*}\right)L}{Y} = \frac{f'\left(\frac{1}{\hat{k}^*}\right)}{\hat{y}^*} = \text{constant.}$$

We have now shown that the share of labour is constant under the assumption of labour augmenting technological progress. This implies that real wages grow at the same rate as labour productivity, i.e. at the rate x.

By a similar argument we can show that under the same assumptions the return to capital is also constant. If we think of the return to capital as the ratio of profits (Π) to the stock of capital, we can further decompose this as the product between the share of profits (profits/total income) times the output–capital ratio

$$\frac{\Pi}{K} \equiv \frac{\Pi}{Y}\frac{Y}{K}.$$

We have already seen that both of these are constant at the steady state, hence the return to capital is also constant.

4.2 Policy experiment 3: a rise in the rate of technological progress

Let us now consider the following policy experiment: at time t_0 an exogenously determined increase in the rate of technological progress occurs. A historical example might be the transition to a more humanistic and secular society that occurred in Western Europe during the Renaissance and which stimulated creative geniuses to invest their effort in exploring the natural world free of theological constraints and prejudice. Alternatively this could be the result of a sustained government programme to subsidize research or support technological start-ups.

In Fig. 13.10 we trace the impact of this shock on the system and show how $\hat{k}$ and $\hat{y}$ adjust to the new steady state; we also see how the growth of output responds. In the first panel this is represented graphically by a steepening in the line corresponding to $(\delta + x + n)\hat{k}$ as x increases to x'. The economy slowly adjusts from the old steady state $\hat{k}^*$ to the new steady state $\hat{k}^{**}$, where capital per worker in efficiency units is *lower* than at t_0. The transition dynamics are also illustrated in the second panel where we can inspect growth rates directly. Immediately after the exogenous shock occurs at t_0, the growth rate of capital in efficiency units of labour jumps down as a result of the higher growth rate of technological progress. At first sight, the adjustment dynamics and new equilibrium appear counter-intuitive: faster technological progress reduces $\hat{y}$. To understand what is going on, we must consider the economics of the transition to the new steady state and see how a lower $\hat{y}^*$ and $\hat{k}^*$ are nevertheless associated with a higher level of output *per worker* at every point from t_0 onwards and with higher growth of y and k in the new steady state.

The reason for the decline in the amount of capital to labour measured in efficiency units (i.e. $g_{\hat{k}} < 0$) is that given the savings rate, there is initially insufficient investment

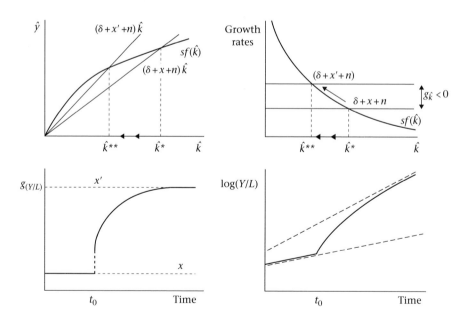

Figure 13.10 Policy experiment 3: an exogenous acceleration in the rate of technological progress

to take advantage of the faster rate of technological progress. Adjustment continues until the capital–output ratio has declined sufficiently such that the growth rate of the capital stock is increased to the now faster growth of the labour force measured in terms of efficiency units. This is shown in the second panel in Fig. 13.10 as $g_{\hat{k}}$ rises back to zero.

In the lower panels we show the time trajectories of the growth rate of output per worker and of log Y/L before and after time t_0. We know that in the steady state the growth rate of output per worker equals that of technological progress, which is now higher. The lower left panel shows how the growth rate of output per worker jumps up initially and then slowly adjusts upwards to reflect the new (and higher) rate of technological progress. In the lower right panel, the rate of technological progress gives the slope of the log of output per worker. Thus output per worker adjusts so as to increase at an increased rate, which reflects the higher rate of technological progress. Once the system attains a steady state the economy is on a new balanced growth path, which is steeper.

Just as in the case of the model without technical progress, it is useful to use the alternative Solow diagram when the focus is on the implications for growth per se of a change in the rate of technological progress. The only modifications required to the diagram are that capital is measured per efficiency unit on the horizontal axis and the growth of the labour force is measured in efficiency units, which means that the horizontal line shows $x + n$. Just as before, output growth is a weighted average of capital growth and of the labour force (but now measured in efficiency units):

$$g_Y = \sigma_K g_K + (1 - \sigma_K)(g_A + g_L) = \sigma_K g_K + (1 - \sigma_K)(x + n).$$

We can see from Fig. 13.11 that when the rate of technical progress goes up, output growth in the economy jumps up (point A to point B); it continues to rise until it reaches the new higher growth rate in the new steady state. In the new steady state at point Z, we can see that $g_Y = x' + n$ so the growth rate of output per head is $g_y = x' + n - n = x'$.

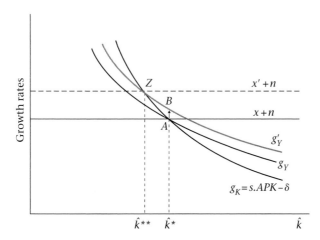

Figure 13.11 Policy experiment 3: an exogenous acceleration in the rate of technological progress—implications for output growth

4.3 **Technological progress and growth accounting**

In the previous section, we explained how growth accounting can be used to make an estimate from data of the contribution to growth that is not accounted for by the growth of factor inputs. This is called total factor productivity growth and is often referred to as the contribution of 'technological progress' to growth.[8] As we have seen, the growth accounting relationship can be written as follows:

$$g_y = \sigma_K g_k + \text{TFP growth},$$

where the growth in output per capita is attributed to capital deepening and 'technological progress'. We now compare this with the analysis of technological progress and growth in the Solow–Swan model. Once the Solow–Swan model is extended to include Harrod-neutral technological progress, we have seen that the steady state is characterized by

$$g_y = g_k = x, \qquad \text{(Solow–Swan model with tech. progress)}$$

where x is the rate of exogenous, Harrod-neutral technical progress. Substituting this in the growth accounting equation, gives

$$\text{TFP growth} = (1 - \sigma_K)x,$$

and

$$g_y = \sigma_K g_k + (1 - \sigma_K)x, \qquad \text{(growth accounting)}$$

which suggests that exogenous technological progress accounts for only a proportion $(1 - \sigma_K)$ of the growth in per capita output. However, we know that there would have been no growth in per capita output without the exogenous technological progress. This puzzle arises because growth accounting assigns the growth in output per capita to both technological progress and to the increase in capital intensity stimulated by the faster technological progress. So it is true in the Solow–Swan model that growth in output per capita is ultimately caused only by technological progress but growth accounting gives credit to the growth in the capital stock induced by the technological progress.[9]

5 **Economic convergence**

One additional prediction can be made using the Solow–Swan model that is controversial and is not confirmed by empirical results. According to the model if the level of capital is low (i.e. below the steady-state equilibrium level k^*) the growth rate will be high. This suggests that we should observe poor countries growing at much faster rates than rich ones. But as shown in Fig. 13.1 and discussed in Chapter 1, over the past century there

---

[8] It also includes other unobservable sources of growth as well as measurement errors but we shall ignore them in this discussion.

[9] For a more detailed discussion of this, see Barro and Sala-i-Martin (2004: 457–60).

are many examples of poor countries (e.g. Chad, Tanzania) that have not grown at all or have experienced negative growth rates. It is interesting to note that Solow did not think of his growth model as providing a model for explaining cross-country growth performance—rather, he believed it was a way of thinking about the growth dynamics of a single economy. Nevertheless, the model has been widely used for cross-country comparisons. In this section the theoretical background to the concepts of conditional and unconditional convergence is presented along with empirical findings and the mechanics of measuring convergence.

The *hypothesis of unconditional convergence* states that countries with lower initial levels of capital and output will grow faster and catch up with those countries that start off with higher levels. We illustrate this in Fig. 13.12 for two countries A and B, where A is poorer than B. Country A grows faster as it converges to the new steady state. It is clear from Fig. 13.12 that the reason the poorer country grows faster is that the average product of capital ($APK = \frac{f(\hat{k})}{\hat{k}}$) is higher at lower initial levels of capital per worker (and all the other parameters of the model are identical for each country).

To see this mathematically let us return to the fundamental Solow equation:

$$g_{\hat{k}} = \frac{sf(\hat{k})}{\hat{k}} - (\delta + x + n) \tag{13.21}$$

and ask how different levels of capital impact on the growth rate. We take the derivative of this expression with respect to capital:

$$\frac{dg_{\hat{k}}}{d\hat{k}} = \frac{\hat{k}sf'(\hat{k}) - sf(\hat{k})}{\hat{k}^2} = \frac{s[\hat{k}f'(\hat{k}) - f(\hat{k})]}{\hat{k}^2} \tag{13.22}$$

which we rearrange and divide by $\hat{k}$ to obtain

$$\frac{dg_{\hat{k}}}{d\hat{k}} = \frac{s\left[f'(\hat{k}) - \frac{f(\hat{k})}{\hat{k}}\right]}{\hat{k}} = \frac{s}{\hat{k}}(MPK - APK) < 0. \tag{13.23}$$

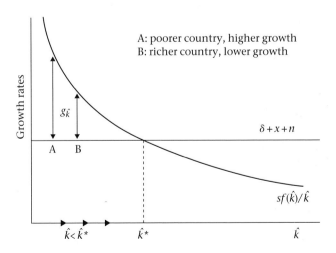

Figure 13.12 Unconditional convergence in the Solow model with technological progress

This says that the growth rate of the capital–labour ratio declines as capital intensity rises. It is a function of the properties of the production function (discussed further in the appendix): diminishing returns to capital means that $MPK < APK$. This expression confirms the hypothesis of unconditional convergence since it implies that poor countries with low capital levels will tend to grow faster.

So far it has been assumed that all countries modelled have identical parameters and have instantaneous access to new technology as it arrives at the rate x. Thus implicitly all countries have access to the same technology, have similar demographic characteristics, and their populations are homogeneous enough to have similar attitudes towards work and savings. Given the large diversity along these dimension of countries in the world, it is unsurprising that Fig. 13.1 shows that there is no such convergence among the world's economies.

But let us now investigate what happens if we restrict our attention to economies that intuitively ought to be similar to each other such as the set of OECD countries or the fifty states of the USA. First let us look at the US states. In Fig. 13.13 we show the distribution of real gross state product (GSP) per worker across the Unites States. We immediately see substantial heterogeneity in GSP levels in 2001, thus even within a developed country like the United States we can observe substantial differences across regions. Low levels of GSP seem to be more common across the Northern United States and the Midwest, while the States on both coasts seem to have higher levels of productivity. But this visual analysis is inherently limited since although it tells us that the United States experiences heterogeneous levels of productivity today, it does not tell us whether the different regions have been converging or not.

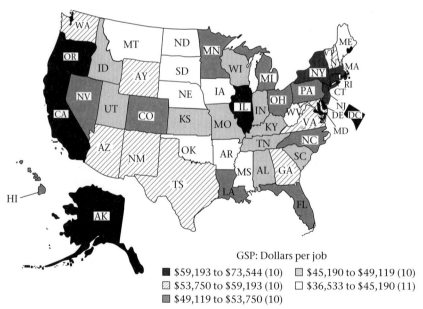

Figure 13.13 Distribution of real GSP per worker across the United States in 2001
Source: Bureau of Economic Analysis.

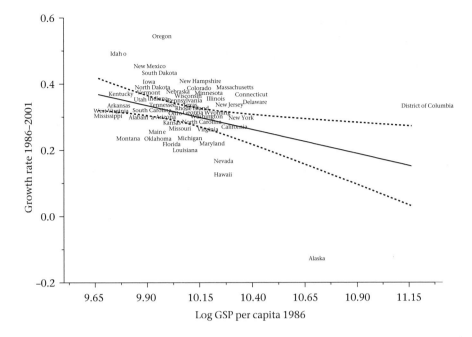

Figure 13.14 Growth Convergence in the USA: growth rate of GSP per capita 1986–2001 vs. level of GSP per capita 1986

Note: The dotted lines correspond to 95% confidence bands.

Sources: Bureau of Economic Analysis, US Census Bureau.

Thus for a more precise analysis we first construct a real GSP per capita series for the period 1986 and 2001. Each point of the graph, Fig. 13.14, corresponds to one state and shows its average growth rate in GSP per capita over the period 1986 to 2001 and the logarithm of its level of GSP per capita in 1986. We also plot the corresponding linear regression line (we discuss in the next section how to construct such a line), which corresponds to a linear trend fitted according to the Least Squares method through the data points. If the convergence hypothesis is correct we would expect this line to be downward sloping, that is we would expect low levels of GSP per capita in 1986 to be associated with a higher growth rate over this period. It seems that this prediction is indeed met for the case of the fifty US states over this period.

Nevertheless, we might worry that this result is not as crisp as we may want it to be. For a start, some states such as Alaska and DC appear to be outliers. Our method of Least Squares tries to fit a straight line through all the data points and as such it gives equal weight to each data point. We exclude Alaska and DC from the sample and plot the same figure for the remaining states. This graph is shown in Fig. 13.15.

This figure paints a more heterogeneous picture of the relationship between GSP growth between 1986 and 2001 and levels in 1986. Moreover, the fitted Least Squares regression now has a smaller negative slope and the relationship looks very weak. This opens up the question of how to measure this relationship precisely and perform statistical inference that would allow us to test for the significance of such a relationship. We address this

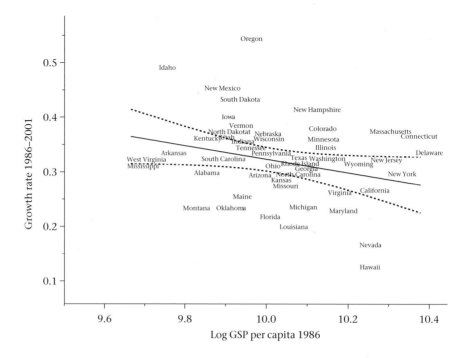

Figure 13.15 Growth convergence in the USA: growth rate of GSP per capita 1986–2001 vs. level of GSP per capita 1986: excluding outliers.

Note: Alaska and DC are excluded as outliers. The dotted lines correspond to 95% confidence bands

issue in the next section where we present the corresponding econometric estimation results.[10]

Let us now perform the same analysis for countries of the OECD for the period 1970–2002. The corresponding graph is shown in Fig. 13.16. Once again we see that a linear relationship exists between the growth rate of GDP per capita and some 'initial' level of GDP per capita. Moreover, this relationship is clearly negative. That is, the lower the starting level of GDP per capita was, the higher we would expect the growth rate to have been over the subsequent decades.

So far our analysis suggests that the concept of unconditional convergence does not hold for the world as a whole but does hold for some suitably chosen subset of economies that share similar characteristics. This suggests that there is no unique steady-state equilibrium to which all economies converge but rather that they may each converge to an equilibrium that is determined by their individual characteristics such as technology, tastes, savings rates, and more broadly social, legal, and cultural institutions. If however, these steady states are determined by relatively similar factors, as is clearly the case for the states of the USA or for the countries of the OECD, then their steady states will be relatively close together. Hence as a first approximation we can think of this subset of economies as unconditionally converging to the same steady state.

---

[10] For a long-run analysis of convergence across US states from 1880–2000, see Barro and Sala-i-Martin (2004), chapter 11.

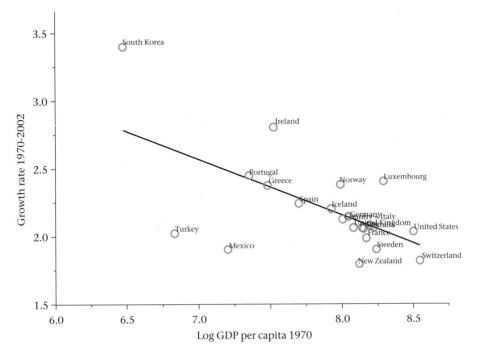

Figure 13.16 Growth convergence for the OECD, 1970–2002

Source: OECD.

These results suggest a second, weaker notion of convergence, namely *conditional convergence*, where each economy converges to its own steady state. The steady state in each case is characterized by the model parameters such as savings rates, population growth, or access to technology that may differ between countries. Does this suggest that poor economies will grow faster than rich ones? The logic of the analysis suggests a poor country will only grow faster than a rich one if it is further from its steady state than the rich one is from its steady state. This is illustrated in Fig. 13.17 where we consider a poor country (A) with lower output per capita that is in every other respect identical to the rich country (B) except that it has a lower savings rate. The diagram illustrates how it is possible for the rich country to experience higher growth of per capita output: the reason is that B is further from its steady state than is A so transitional growth in B is higher. Once country A and country B are at their steady state, then each will grow at the same rate, i.e. at $g_y = x$ and the poor country will never catch up to the rich one. It is also clear that should the savings rate of the poor country increase to equal that of the rich one, then the poor country's steady state coincides with that of the rich and its growth would be faster: it would begin to catch up and eventually it would converge to the same balanced growth path as the rich country. When trying to understand why poor countries remain poor, this result throws the burden on explaining why the poor country's steady state is different from the rich country's and how it might be changed. In our example, this amounts to asking why A's savings rate is lower than B's.

To see this more formally, let us return once more to the fundamental Solow equation (13.21). We solve for the savings rate at the steady state (by setting $g_{\hat{k}} = 0$) to get

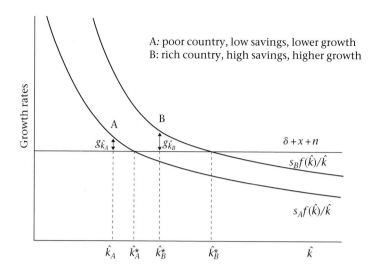

Figure 13.17 Conditional convergence in the Solow model: different growth rates due to different savings rates

$s^* = [(\delta + x + n)\hat{k}^*]/f(\hat{k}^*)$. Now we can substitute this in equation 13.21 and rearrange to obtain:

$$g_{\hat{k}} = (\delta + x + n)\left(\frac{APK}{APK^*} - 1\right). \tag{13.24}$$

This equation tells us that the growth rate will be higher, the higher is the *APK* compared to *APK** (i.e. at the steady state). It will only be zero if the two coincide. Thus, it only tells us that countries will grow faster the further they are from their own steady state, but it makes no prediction that poor countries will grow faster than rich ones.

5.1 Measuring the speed of convergence, *b*

We now consider how the speed of convergence can be measured. This is very important for both econometric estimation of economic growth models and for determining whether steady-state characteristics or transitional dynamics are more important: if convergence is very fast then intuitively it seems more important to look at steady states, while if convergence is very slow it seems more important to look at the transitional dynamics.

In the appendix we show that the growth rate of output per capita in efficiency units in the Solow–Swan model can be approximated by:

$$g_{\hat{y}} = -b(\log \hat{y} - \log \hat{y}^*), \tag{13.25}$$

where $\hat{y}^*$ is the (constant) steady state level of output per efficiency unit of labour in the economy and the speed of convergence coefficient *b* is given by

$$b = (1 - \sigma_K)(\delta + x + n). \qquad \text{(speed of convergence; Solow model)}$$

With the Cobb–Douglas production function, σ_K is constant and equal to α. The interpretation of this parameter b is that the gap between current output per worker in efficiency units and the steady-state value of output per worker in efficiency units disappears at constant rate b. Sometimes this convergence speed is expressed as the half-life of the gap, i.e. the time it takes for half the (numerical) gap between the current and steady-state values to disappear. For example if we were to observe a value $b = 0.05$, this means that 5% of the gap between current and steady-state income levels per worker in efficiency units disappears in one year. This suggests solving for t in the equation $\exp(-bt) = 0.5$, where b is the estimated value of b. To do so, we can simply take logs of both sides and solve for t, which gives:

$$\exp(-bt) = 0.5$$
$$\Rightarrow \log bt = \log 2$$
$$\Rightarrow t_{\text{Half-life}} = \frac{\log 2}{b} \cong \frac{0.6931}{b}.$$

For $b = 0.05$, this implies a half-life of approximately $\frac{0.6931}{0.05} = 14$ years.

It is important to understand the intuition behind the formula for $b = (1-\alpha)(\delta+x+n)$ and the reason why some parameters are included.

- Role of α: The parameter α is equal to the ratio of the *MPK* to *APK* and this ratio is less than one for concave production functions (diminishing returns to capital).

  (1) If α is high (approaching one) then there is little difference between the marginal and average product, hence the production function exhibits only weakly diminishing returns to capital.

  (2) If α is low (approaching zero) then the marginal product is much smaller than the average product, which implies a strong curvature of the production function, i.e. strongly diminishing marginal returns to capital.

  (3) In the formula for b, a higher α means slower convergence and we can now link this with the presence of weakly diminishing returns.

- Role of x and n: Higher values of x and n (or δ) imply faster convergence. If x or n is high, then holding everything else constant, this raises the *APK* near the steady state, which raises the speed of convergence (the experiment requires that the economy be the same distance from the steady state in each case).

- No role for the savings rate s.[11]

What values of b would be reasonable to plug into the formula to calculate the rate of convergence predicted by the model? For the US economy, the following values are deemed reasonable: $\delta = 0.03$, $x = 0.02$, and $n = 0.01$. For α, the value $1/3$, which is the approximate value of the share of capital in the economy, is used. Substituting these values in the expression above produces $b = 0.04$, i.e. a speed of convergence of 4% p.a.

---

[11] There is no simple intuitive explanation for the savings rate having no effect on the speed of convergence. It arises from the fact that the savings rate is constant. In a more complicated model such as the Ramsey model discussed in section 7.1 in which the savings rate can change, the result no longer holds.

which means a half-life of 17 years, i.e. that transitions between steady states are relatively short. Does this correspond to the facts? To answer this question we need to learn how to estimate the speed of convergence from data.

5.2 Estimating the speed of convergence from data

We address this in two steps: first by taking the case where we have a group of countries for which tastes (the savings rate), technology (the rate of technological progress), and demographic parameters (population growth) are considered sufficiently similar for the countries to share a common steady state. This leads to a test for absolute convergence. In the second step, the possibility that countries differ in their steady states is allowed, with the result that the test is for the weaker concept of conditional convergence.

To find the convergence parameter, b, for a set of countries with similar taste, technology, and demographic parameters, we begin by substituting for $\log \hat{y} = \log y - \log A$ in equation 13.25 so as to move to measures of output per capita and obtain

$$\frac{d(\log y - \log A)}{dt} = -b(\log y - \log A - \log y^* + \log A). \tag{13.26}$$

This holds for all countries in our sample. We can now choose one comparator country, say the USA and naturally the same expression will also hold for the USA and we are assuming a common steady state so that $y^* = y_{US}^*$:

$$\frac{d(\log y_{US} - \log A)}{dt} = -b(\log y_{US} - \log A - \log y^* + \log A). \tag{13.27}$$

We can now subtract equation 13.26 from 13.27, which gives:

$$\frac{d(\log y_{US} - \log y)}{dt} = -b(\log y_{US} - \log y). \tag{13.28}$$

The expression $(\log y_{US} - \log y)$ is the proportional difference between output per worker in the USA and output per worker in the country in question and is called the *common technology gap* (G_A):

$$G_A = \log y_{US} - \log y = \log \left(\frac{y_{US}}{y} \right). \tag{13.29}$$

We can now rewrite equation 13.28 using this expression to obtain the result that

$$\dot{G}_A = -bG_A, \tag{13.30}$$

which means that according to the Solow–Swan model with technological progress, the gap between economies with identical technology, tastes, and demographics declines exponentially with exponential coefficient b.

The value of b can be estimated using data for a panel of countries, where GDP per capita is observed at two dates $t = 0$ and $t = T$. As shown in the Appendix, equation 13.30 can be used to obtain an estimating equation of the following type:

$$\log y_T - \log y_0 = a - b \log y_0 + \epsilon \tag{13.31}$$

Table 13.2 Growth convergence regressions

	OECD countries	US states including AK, DC	US states excluding AK, DC
Intercept	5.4500*	1.7713*	1.5601*
	(0.8561)	(0.5302)	(0.6380)
Slope ($\tilde{b}$)	−0.4118*	−0.1451*	−0.1237
	(0.1083)	(0.0527)	(0.0637)
R^2	0.376	0.1338	0.0743

* indicates significance at the 5% level
Note: Standard errors are shown in brackets.

Let us now use this estimating equation and apply it to empirical data in order to estimate the slope of the relationship between the rate of economic growth over a certain period and the level of GDP at the beginning of the period of analysis. This allows us to quantify the concept of economic convergence for a given subset of economies and to perform statistical inference on the estimated magnitude. Thus, we will be able to present precise evidence on the strength of this relationship beyond that given in Figs. 13.14–16. We will be able to say more than simply that the observed relationship seems to be negative. Econometrics allows us to estimate the slope of the fitted line and to verify whether it is significantly different from zero.

But let us first look at the estimation results before proceeding with the interpretation. We estimate equation 13.31 for two samples: in each case, the dependent variable is the log difference between output per capita at the start and the end of the period. The first sample is given by the OECD countries, while the second corresponds to the fifty US states. The estimation results are summarized in Table 13.2. Each column of the table shows the estimated value of the parameters a and b from the estimating equation 13.31 above. Here the row labelled intercept corresponds to the estimated value of a while the row labelled slope corresponds to the estimated value of b, which we call $\tilde{b}$ (called b tilde) to refer to the econometric estimate of the parameter b from our regression analysis. If our model holds we expect $\tilde{a}$ to be positive, while $\tilde{b}$ to be negative. We shall have to divide $\tilde{b}$ by the number of years in the sample (T) to find the estimated annual convergence rate. Under each estimated value we also report the standard error corresponding to our estimated value. This is a measure of the estimated precision with which the corresponding parameter value was obtained. Moreover, we indicate by (*) whether the t-statistic corresponding to each value suggests that our estimate is significantly different from zero at the 5% confidence level.[12]

[12] Two statistics are reported in the table that provide information about the model: the t-statistic and the R^2 coefficient. The t-statistic is a measure of statistical significance and is defined as $t = \hat{\beta}/\sqrt{Var(\hat{\beta})}$ where $\hat{\beta}$ is the estimated coefficient and $Var(\hat{\beta})$ is its variance. In our case it can be calculated by dividing the row corresponding to the value of the estimated parameter by the row with the standard error of the same parameter. Econometric theory tells us that t is a random variable that is distributed according to the t-distribution for which the Gaussian distribution is often a good approximation. Values of the t-distribution are tabulated in statistical tables but as a rule of thumb if the absolute value of the t-statistic is greater than 2 we say that the parameter is statistically

Let us first look at the column for OECD countries. The slope is -0.4118 and statistically different from zero at the 5% confidence level. This corresponds to an annual convergence rate of 1.3% per year (i.e. $0.4118/32$ years $\times$ 100). Using the formula we have previously derived we can compute the half-life to be about 53 years (i.e. $0.6931/.013$). If we now consider convergence for the US states, the estimate of b is -0.1451 which seems to suggest a convergence rate of only 0.97%, which corresponds to a half-life of 71 years. As we discussed before, the technicalities of Least Squares Estimation place equal weight on all observations and thus the results are influenced by the presence of outliers. Alaska has limited industry (except for oil extraction) and DC is not even a state which make them less convincing candidates for our convergence club. If we now exclude these from our estimation our results suggest an estimated value of b of -0.1237 and a corresponding t-statistic that suggests that it is not statistically different from zero at the 5% confidence level. This implies that we do not have enough statistical evidence to distinguish this from an estimated value of the coefficient equal to zero. This means that we only have limited statistical evidence to even support the claim the US states actually converged over the period since 1986.

Moreover, if we look at the value of the R^2 coefficients on these regressions we seem to explain little of the observed variation in growth rates by regressing on the log-level of GSP per capita in 1986. This suggests that there is a lot of unobserved heterogeneity for which we do not account in our equation. Hence, we should be careful when applying these simple concepts of growth convergence since even economies that may seem a priori homogeneous enough to have very similar steady states may in fact be converging to different ones. In their longer-run analysis of convergence across 47 US states, Barro and Sala-i-Martin (2004) find a significant convergence rate of 1.7% over the period from 1880 to 2000 (with a high R-squared of 0.92) but they too find that there is no significant convergence in the final two decades of their sample, the 1980s and 1990s.

We now broaden the exercise to include countries that differ in their steady states—differences that could arise from the determinants of the steady state: the savings rate, population growth, rate of technological progress, or depreciation rate. The usual assumption is that depreciation (δ) and the rate of technological progress (x) are constant across countries—depreciation because there is no particular reason to think this should vary greatly and x because this represents the advancement of the world's technological frontier and is not specific to a country. The model makes the 'heroic' assumption that new technology is instantly diffused across countries. We consider how this assumption can be modified so that we can discuss how new technology is diffused across countries in section 5.4. Since we are considering *conditional* convergence, the growth rate will be a function of the determinants of the steady state. The estimating equation for conditional convergence was derived in Mankiw, Romer, and Weil (1992) (MRW):[13]

$$\log y_T - \log y_0 = a - b \log y_0 + b \frac{\alpha}{1-\alpha} \log s - b \frac{\alpha}{1-\alpha} \log(n + x + \delta) + \epsilon,$$

significantly different from zero at the 5% level. This means that we are at least 95% sure that the parameter we have measured does not have a true value of zero. The R^2 coefficient is a very simple measure of the goodness of fit of the estimated equation. Thus the closer it is to 1 the better we expect our model to fit the data. It is however only a very rough and approximate measure and its magnitude should not be taken too seriously.

[13] For a recent critique of MRW, see Dowrick and Rogers (2002).

where the growth of output per capita is regressed on the initial level of output and the determinants of the steady state.

The empirical data suggests that $\tilde{b}$ is about 2% per annum in the sample of OECD countries (it is much slower still in the samples that include poorer countries outside the OECD). If $\tilde{b} = 0.02$, this gives a half-life of 35 years and the economy will only be three-quarters of the way to the steady state after 70 years. Let us now compare this estimated speed of convergence from the data with the value of b that we calculated above by plugging values for $\alpha = 1/3, \delta = 0.03, x = 0.02$ and $n = 0.01$ into the formula for the speed of convergence from the Solow–Swan model: i.e. $b = (1 - \alpha)(\delta + x + n)$. This gives $b = 0.04$, which means a half-life of 17 years. This comparison suggests that something has gone wrong with our a priori calculation.

In order to reconcile the formula with the regression estimate, the focus of attention is on the role of capital in the convergence equation. If the capital share was closer to 0.7, the value of $b = (1 - \alpha)(\delta + x + n) = 0.3 \times 0.06 = 0.018$ comes down to the value estimated from the cross-country data. But where does the additional capital come from? So far we have only used a *narrow* definition of capital, which focused on physical capital. In order to obtain a capital share coefficient that is closer to the required one in order to square the model with the empirical findings, we have to focus on a *broad definition* of capital, which includes *human capital* as well.

5.3 Human capital

We have seen that if the concept of capital is broadened to include human capital, the model will fit the empirical reality better. National income accounts tell us how much *raw* capital and labour we have in the economy, so it must be that the additional input to production comes from factors that affect productivity but have not so far been included in our model. One possibility is *education*, the idea being that more education increases the marginal product of labour for all given levels of raw physical capital and labour. In Table 13.3 we present selected data on educational achievement in different countries across the globe. It shows the percentage of people aged 25 or over who have reached a certain education level as their final completed education before permanently committing themselves to the labour force in both 1960 and 2000.[14]

Browsing through the data one is led to contemplate the possibility that education is linked to economic performance. Are we surprised to find that the United States as the world's richest economy has only 1% of its population without schooling and the average number of years spent in some form of education is 12.25 for most Americans, while in Sudan, one of the world's poorest economies, over 60% of the population has no schooling and on average its people have less than two years of formal education? Similarly, other rich economies such as Japan, the UK, or Sweden have a very low percentage of their respective populations without education (0%, 2.9%, and 2.0% respectively), high secondary and post-secondary attendance, and their workers spent around ten years on average in some form of education. It is perhaps not surprising that countries that have performed well in terms of growth such as Botswana or China have improved their educational standing significantly since the 1960s. The percentage of the population without

---

[14] The data comes from the Barro–Lee data set (Barro and Lee 2003), www.cid.harvard.edu/ciddata /Appendix%20Data%20Tables.xls.

Table 13.3 Completed educational attainment of total population over 25 years of age in percentages

Country	Year	No Schooling	Primary	Secondary	Post-secondary	Average (yrs)
Argentina	1960	12.0	73.4	11.6	3.0	4.99
	2000	5.8	49.6	24.9	19.7	8.49
Iraq	1960	97.8	0.6	0.9	0.7	0.21
	2000	40.1	33.7	17.7	8.6	4.34
Israel	1960	19.1	43.1	27.9	9.9	6.99
	2000	13.7	24.6	33.2	28.6	9.23
Sudan	1960	90.4	8.9	0.7	0.0	0.29
	2000	64.1	24.5	9.5	2.0	1.91
Botswana	1960	71.4	25.4	3.0	0.3	1.46
	2000	28.8	46.5	20.8	3.9	5.35
Japan	1960	2.9	59.9	30.9	6.3	6.87
	2000	0.0	28.1	47.9	24.0	9.72
China	1975	52.0	25.5	21.5	1.0	3.40
	2000	20.9	40.7	35.7	2.7	5.74
USA	1960	2.3	37.4	43.8	16.5	8.66
	2000	1.0	9.3	39.6	50.1	12.25
UK	1960	2.0	71.7	24.5	1.8	7.67
	2000	2.9	38.9	39.1	19.1	9.35
Sweden	1960	0.6	58.0	33.9	7.5	7.65
	2000	2.0	17.7	57.2	23.1	11.36
Hungary	1960	3.7	86.4	6.5	3.4	6.65
	2000	2.0	51.3	34.7	12.0	8.81
Australia	1960	0.0	36.6	50.4	13.0	9.43
	2000	2.2	24.4	43.6	29.8	10.57

Source: Barro and Lee (2003).

any schooling went down from 71.4% to 28.8% in Botswana and from 52% to 20.9% in China. Similarly the average number of years spent in educational and secondary and post-secondary participation have all increased as well. Hungary, one of the East European transition countries that is performing well, has educational indicators that are close to those of other developed economies. A cautionary note is called for at this point since all that the data suggests is that there is a correlation between living standards and levels of education: it says nothing about causality. Just as plausible as the idea that more education raises living standards is that higher living standards and growth in a country lead to more expenditure on education.[15]

Setting the causality issue to one side, we turn to the task of augmenting the Solow–Swan model by including human capital. In this context we can think of education as a

[15] For a recent discussion of causality in both directions, see Bils and Klenow (2000).

proxy for *human capital*. Other components of human capital might include the health of the workforce and the quality of education. Once we have decided how to measure human capital the next question is how to incorporate it in the production function. Growth models do this in two main ways: one is to treat human capital as analogous to physical capital, in the sense that it is accumulated like physical capital and measured in units of output (i.e. $\dot{H} = s_h Y - \delta H$ is parallel to $\dot{K} = s_k Y - \delta K$; s_h is the share of output devoted to human capital accumulation and s_k is the share devoted to physical capital accumulation). The augmented Cobb–Douglas production function is:

$$Y = K^\alpha H^\beta (AL)^{1-\alpha-\beta},$$

where $\alpha, \beta < 1$ and $\alpha + \beta < 1$.

The second approach, associated with Robert Lucas, treats the accumulation of human capital differently from that of physical capital. In this case, it is assumed that the accumulation of human capital depends on the time devoted to it as well as on the returns to studying. In Chapter 14, we shall see how the Lucas approach leads to a model of endogenous growth, where the growth rate in the steady state is driven by human capital accumulation.

Here we use the first formulation, which broadens the concept of capital within the original Solow–Swan model. Following the same steps as in section 4.1, we solve for the steady-state level of output per head in the augmented Solow–Swan model. This allows us to derive the analogous equation to equation (13.18), which is reproduced below:

$$y^* = A_t \left(\frac{s}{\delta + x + n} \right)^{\frac{\alpha}{1-\alpha}}.$$

With human capital included, we have

$$y^* = A_t \left(\frac{s_k}{\delta + x + n} \right)^{\frac{\alpha}{1-\alpha-\beta}} \left(\frac{s_h}{\delta + x + n} \right)^{\frac{\beta}{1-\alpha-\beta}}.$$

This equation tells us that rich countries have the following characteristics:

(1) high savings/investment rates in physical and human capital and low population growth rates;

(2) access to advances in technology (otherwise, they will not have access to A_t).

Mankiw, Romer, and Weil (MRW) estimate the augmented Solow–Swan model on data for GDP per capita in 1985 for a sample of 98 countries. They find that the model accounts much better for the variation in GDP per capita across countries than does the model without human capital. Moreover, they find that the implied values of α and β are each about 0.3. This means that the elasticity with respect to output is about the same for each of physical capital, human capital, and labour. The implication is that the share of physical plus human capital is 0.6, which delivers a convergence rate, $b = (1 - \alpha - \beta)(\delta + x + n) = 0.4 \times 0.06 = 0.024$.

When MRW re-estimate the convergence equation including investment in human capital as a determinant of the steady state as follows:

$$\log y_T - \log y_0 = a - b \log y_0 + b \frac{\alpha}{1 - \alpha - \beta} \log s_k + b \frac{\beta}{1 - \alpha - \beta} \log s_h$$
$$- b \frac{\alpha + \beta}{1 - \alpha - \beta} \log(n + x + \delta) + \epsilon,$$

they find strong evidence for conditional convergence, with the convergence rate close to that predicted by the augmented Solow–Swan model (i.e. about 0.02). The inclusion of human capital has the effect of raising the convergence rate to between 1.4 and 1.8 per cent per annum for samples that include poor countries. The MRW results suggest that in the long run when the transitional dynamics have played themselves out, the growth rate of GDP per capita is common across countries and equal to the rate of exogenous technical progress. However, to the extent that countries differ in their underlying parameters, the balanced growth paths will be parallel. There will be a distribution of levels of GDP per capita across countries on their balanced growth paths, according to the determinants of the different steady states, but in the long run countries will grow at the same rate.

The result of augmenting the Solow–Swan model by including human capital provides a way of narrowing the gap between theory and empirical analysis. We take up the debate about how best to model growth in the context of models of endogenous and Schumpeterian growth in Chapter 14 but first, we introduce the process of technology transfer as a different mechanism for convergence that can be compared with the standard one in the Solow–Swan model.

5.4 Human capital, technology transfer, and convergence

The idea that we shall discuss in this section is that education speeds up technological innovation. This suggests

- that human capital may play a quite different role in growth from that in the Solow–Swan model augmented with human capital and

- that convergence can take place through technology diffusion and not just via rising capital intensity as in the Solow–Swan model.

In particular, we relax the assumption that new technology is available instantaneously in all countries. Rather, new technology diffuses from the frontier to lagging countries and the level of education of workers in lagging countries affects the speed with which it is introduced and hence the rate of growth in living standards during the phase of catch-up.

In an influential article published in 1966, two US economists, Richard Nelson and Edmund Phelps used the example of the impact of education on the diffusion of new agricultural techniques to farmers within the USA to illustrate the microeconomics of this process.[16] Farmers with a relatively high level of education tended to adopt innovations

---

[16] Nelson and Phelps (1966).

earlier than those with little education. A plausible explanation for this is that the better educated farmers were able to understand and assess the information on new varieties of grain and livestock that was available from magazines, the Department of Agriculture, commercial seed companies, and the like. The less well-educated farmers who were not as good at assessing new techniques and products waited until their success had been demonstrated before adopting them. The return to more educated farmers from early adoption of new products and processes is higher than for the less educated ones.

This insight can be integrated with the Solow–Swan model in the following way. Technological progress now consists of two components: the first is the rate of exogenous technical progress, x, and the second is the rate at which frontier technology is absorbed. This depends on the level of human capital and the gap between existing technology and that at the frontier: $f(h_i) \cdot \left(\frac{\overline{A}}{A_i}\right)$ where $f(h_i)$ is a positive function of the average level of education (e.g. years of schooling per worker) in country i, $\overline{A}$ is the level of technology at the frontier and A_i, the level in country i. In empirical studies, $\overline{A}$ and A_i are measured by estimates of TFP in the initial year of the data series.

In the Solow–Swan model, we have

$$\frac{\dot{A}}{A} = x,$$

where x is exogenous. In the Nelson–Phelps model, we have technology in the frontier country growing at the rate x and in the catching-up countries growing at a rate that depends on the gap to the frontier and on the level of education:

$$\dot{\overline{A}}/\overline{A} = x \text{ and } \frac{\dot{A}_i}{A_i} = f(h_i) \cdot \left(\frac{\overline{A}}{A_i}\right).$$

If we take a country inside the frontier with positive human capital such that $f(h_i) \cdot \left(\frac{\overline{A}}{A_i}\right) > x$, then the country will have faster productivity growth than the frontier and will be catching up through technology diffusion. As its technology gets closer to the frontier, the gap term shrinks and so does country i's growth rate. In the steady state, country i will be growing at the same rate as the frontier, i.e. $\frac{\dot{A}_i}{A_i} = x$, which implies that any remaining gap to the frontier is accounted for by the level of human capital in country i. To put it another way, country i's level of technology in the steady state will be higher (closer to the frontier), the higher is the level of human capital. The first empirical study to test for this mechanism in a country cross-section framework used growth rates for 78 countries over a 20-year period and found that the interactive term was statistically significant.[17] In the context of the Nelson and Phelps theory, this can be interpreted as saying that the return to adopting new technology is raised by a higher level of education in the country. We shall return to models of technology transfer in Chapter 14.

---

[17] Benhabib and Spiegel (1994). The effect has been confirmed in more recent work by Dowrick and Rogers (2002).

6 Welfare and the Golden Rule

So far in this chapter there has been little mention of welfare. Economic agents derive utility from consumption and it is therefore interesting to ask whether consumption per head is maximized in the steady state in the Solow–Swan model. Although the savings rate in this simple model is exogenous and hence independent of the decisions of individual agents, imagine for now that the policy maker is able to determine the savings rate.

The simplest way to see which savings rate the policy maker would choose so as to maximize consumption per head is in the standard Solow diagram (Fig. 13.18). Consumption per head is shown by the distance between savings per head and the production function (output per head). We ignore technical progress to make the discussion as staightforward as possible and note that the extension to the case with technological progess does not introduce any new features. In the steady-state equilibrium, the savings rate, $sf(k)$, and the $(\delta + n)k$ line must cross. The policy maker takes the production function and n and δ as given and therefore needs to find the level of k^* at which the slope of the production function is equal to $(\delta + n)$. The savings rate that makes the $sf(k^*)$ curve cross the $(\delta + n)k$ line at this level of k^* is the so-called Golden Rule savings rate. The labels k_G^* and s_G indicate the Golden Rule values.

To show this algebraically, we take the following steps. Since we know that at the steady state, $\dot{k} = 0$, which implies $sf(k^*) = (\delta + n)k^*$, it is straightforward to find consumption at the steady state:

$$c^* = (1 - s)f(k^*) = f(k^*) - sf(k^*) = f(k^*) - (\delta + n)k^*. \tag{13.32}$$

If the government chooses s so as to maximize consumption in the expression above, this is mathematically equivalent to choosing k^* so as to maximize the same expression, since

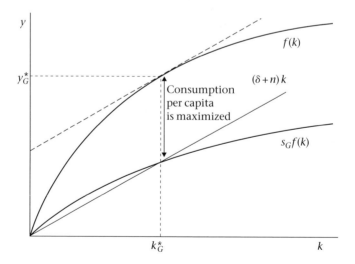

Figure 13.18 The Golden Rule savings rate

we have shown how to derive an expression for c^* that depends only on k^*. The first order condition for this maximization is given by:

$$f'(k^*) = \delta + n, \qquad (13.33)$$

and we can invert this function (ϕ is the inverse function) to obtain an expression for $k_G = \phi(\delta + n)$, where k_G stands for the *Golden Rule* level of capital intensity, that is the capital/labour ratio that maximizes welfare in the economy. We can now calculate from the steady-state condition the Golden Rule savings rate, which is given by:

$$s_G = \frac{(\delta + n)k_G}{f(k_G)}. \qquad (13.34)$$

A government that has to adopt a policy affecting the savings rate thus has to consider whether or not s (the current savings rate of the economy) is smaller or larger than s_G (the Golden Rule savings rate) if it aims to maximize the welfare of the workers in the economy. Fig. 13.19 compares the path for consumption per capita following a rise in the savings ratio from s—in economy 1 such that the new savings rate, $s' > s_G$ and in economy 2, such that the new savings rate $s'' < s_G$. This shows that consumption per head drops in both economies initially but it ends up higher in economy 2 where the new savings rate is below the Golden Rule.

If $s > s_G$ the economy is accumulating too much capital at the expense of current consumption. This is what economists mean when they say that an economy is *dynamically inefficient*. The inefficiency arises because the government could lower the savings rate to the level suggested by the Golden Rule and everyone in the economy will be made better off. With $s' > s_G$, the current generation is worse off (higher savings and lower consumption) and so are all future generations since their consumption is lower than it need be. If on the other hand $s < s_G$ then the government may want to increase the savings rate in order to increase future consumption. This will make the economy richer in the long run and households will be able to enjoy higher living standards at a later stage. However, increasing the savings rate today will require households to consume less today (see Fig. 13.19). There is a trade-off between the interests of the current and

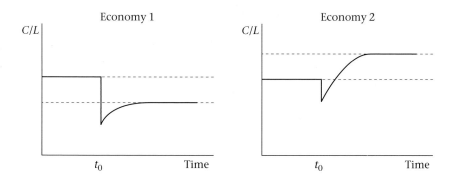

Figure 13.19 Policy experiment 1: rise in the savings rate

Note: Economy 1. New savings rate above s_G. Economy 2. New savings rate below s_G.

future generations. Whether the government chooses to raise the savings rate therefore depends on the relative weight it places on consumption today against consumption tomorrow. Since the benefits of higher economic growth and the higher living standards in the future might not materialize for a generation or two, whether this is even feasible depends on the politics of economic decisions.

7 *Extensions

The aim of this section is to give a flavour of some of the ways in which the Solow–Swan model can be extended. First, it is extended to incorporate the endogenous determination of savings: this is called the Ramsey model and relates to the analysis of consumption in Chapter 7. This involves a more mathematically complex framework of analysis and is usually explored in more specialized books on economic growth and more advanced graduate level courses.[18] We show that the basic insights of the Solow–Swan model remain unchanged once we relax the assumption of constant savings. The second extension shows how the model may be extended so as to include taxation. The focus here is on the intuition behind these extensions and the results are presented in a discursive way.

7.1 Endogenous savings

The assumption of a constant savings rate plays an important part in the Solow–Swan model: in order to derive the Fundamental Solow Equation (equation 13.8), we start off from the resource constraint, which states that total output in the economy is divided between consumption and investment ($Y = C + I$). Now if savings are constant and the agents in our economy can either save their income or consume it, it is trivial to see that investment will also be a constant proportion of total income. Although a constant savings rate greatly simplifies the mathematics of the Solow–Swan model it may seem unrealistic. We have allowed for different savings rates in different economies, as a way to explain why some economies are richer than others. But we have not opened up the question of what determines the savings rate. The process whereby we take account of how the savings rate affects economic growth while keeping in mind that economic performance affects the savings rate itself, is what economists refer to as the process of *endogenizing the savings rate.*

   The ideas underlying this section are those of the optimal consumption behaviour of rational agents, which we introduced in Chapter 7 when we discussed aggregate consumption. The idea is that the individual or household chooses the path of per capita consumption so as to maximize their discounted utility into the future. There is no uncertainty and hence the agent can choose the optimal consumption path given the capital accumulation constraint of the economy. Solow suggests that the natural interpretation of this is that the agent is a peasant household with consumption and production taking

---

[18] A good (and standard) starting point to explore the more advanced literature on economic growth is Barro and Sala-I-Martin (2004).

place within it; individuals die but the family goes on forever.[19] It is interesting to note that the same model can be interpreted either as a way of thinking about how a well-meaning social planner would allocate resources or as a description of how a market economy functions. The market economy is highly stylized and all market imperfections and institutions are swept away.

For simplicity, we initially ignore technological progress and labour force growth. Solving for the first order conditions of this optimization problem will reveal an intertemporal optimality condition (called an Euler equation) that tells us how to balance consumption today against savings and hence consumption tomorrow. For more detail, see the appendix. Specifically, the household equates the rate of return to saving, r, to the rate of return from consumption, which consists of two elements: (i) the rate of time preference, $\rho > 0$, which indicates that deferring consumption is costly and (ii) the rate of decrease of the marginal utility of consumption due to rising per capita consumption (which reflects the intertemporal elasticity of substitution). As we have already seen in Chapter 7, when $r = \rho$, households want consumption to be constant, i.e. $\dot{c}/c = 0$. If we make the simplifying assumption that the intertemporal elasticity of substitution is equal to one,[20] then the Euler equation produces the following:

$$\frac{\dot{c}}{c} = r - \rho. \tag{13.35}$$

It can be used in conjunction with the Solow equation of motion we have previously discussed. We can then solve for the equilibrium of the economy as the consumption, capital pair such that $\dot{c} = 0$ and $\dot{k} = 0$. The mechanics of this are discussed in the appendix, but let us review the main results of this extension to the Solow–Swan model. Once population growth and technological progress are brought back into the model along with endogenous savings, we find that

(1) the rate of economic growth (output per capita) in the steady state depends only on the rate of technological progress. Endogenizing savings does not affect the central feature of the Solow–Swan model that growth is exogenous.

(2) the level of output per capita depends on consumption behaviour (just as in the standard Solow–Swan model).

(3) on the steady-state growth path, the share of savings/investment is constant and using a Cobb–Douglas production function, it can be shown that higher population growth and technological progress raise the savings rate in the steady state and a higher discount rate reduces it.[21] This is intuitively plausible.

(4) at equilibrium the optimal savings behaviour does not necessarily maximize consumption per capita (this is largely due to impatience as the agents want to consume more at the expense of future generations). For a steady-state growth path,

---

[19] Solow's discussion of how endogenizing savings affects the Solow model is clear and interesting. See chapter 7, Solow (2000).

[20] This will be the case if the utility function is $U(c) = \log c$.

[21] Deriving this result is relatively difficult and is presented in appendix 2C, pp. 135–7, Barro and Sala-i-Martin (2004).

the optimal savings rate, s^*, is less than the share of capital in output, α. This is sometimes referred to as the 'modified Golden Rule'.

There are several reasons why this model (originally due to the British economist Frank Ramsey) has become the standard workhorse of macroeconomic modelling. The first is that it is more general and allows for more extensions than the Solow–Swan model. For example, we could now introduce shocks in technology or in preferences, and explore economic performance in an uncertain environment more closely related to the real world. The real business cycle approach follows this direction in the attempt to develop a unified model of cycles and long-run growth. In addition, it avoids the aggregation problems discussed in the introduction to this chapter. If the model has complicated technology or more than one asset, then the equation $I = sY$ (the resource constraint in the Solow–Swan model) loses its simplicity, because it is not obvious how I and Y should be defined in such a model. The Ramsey model also allows for the analysis of how the savings rate changes on the transition from one steady state to another. This has the consequence that the preference parameters—the rate of time preference and the intertemporal elasticity of substitution—affect the speed of convergence. However, as far as understanding the basic facts of growth the simpler Solow–Swan model leads to the same predictions.

7.2 Economic policy: government and taxation

In this section we investigate how to introduce in the Solow–Swan model a very stylized idea of a government with the ability to tax the consumers in the economy. First we shall assume that the money collected in taxation by the government is used for exogenous purposes, which do not explicitly affect decision making in the economy. An example would be the French government collecting taxes in order to send peacekeepers abroad to a small isolated nation in the aftermath of a civil war. As long the economic impact of the peacekeepers on the French economy is minimal, the French intervention abroad will not affect capital accumulation at home. By including government spending in the model, this implies that the resources of the economy will have to divided each period between consumption, savings, and the amount spent to finance government spending. If there is a proportional income tax,τ, then the budget constraint is given by $f(k_t) = y_t = c_t + s_t + \tau y_t$ and we can derive the Fundamental Solow Equation for this case.

We know that net capital accumulates according to $\dot{K}_t = I_t - \delta K_t$ from section 1. Furthermore, if all savings are used for capital investment, then $I_t = S_t = (1 - \tau)Y_t - C_t$. Hence,

$$\dot{K}_t = (1 - \tau)sY_t - \delta K_t$$

and we divide both sides by $A_t L_t$ and rearrange the equation to obtain the Fundamental Solow Equation of Motion with government spending:

$$\hat{k}_t = (1 - \tau)sf(\hat{k}) - \hat{k}(\delta + x + n). \tag{13.36}$$

We solve for the equilibrium level of capital per worker in efficiency units and of output per worker for the Cobb–Douglas production function:

$$\hat{k} = \left(\frac{s(1 - \tau)}{\delta + x + n} \right)^{\frac{1}{1-\alpha}}, \tag{13.37}$$

$$y^* = A_t \left(\frac{s(1 - \tau)}{\delta + x + n} \right)^{\frac{\alpha}{1-\alpha}}. \tag{13.38}$$

Notice that for any given values of s, x, and n, an increase in τ implies a reduction in output per capita in the steady state. In just the same way as a rise in the savings rate produces a transitory rise in the growth rate as the economy moves onto the new growth path at higher output per capita, a cut in the tax rate will produce the same effect. The validity of this result depends on the assumption that none of the other parameters of the model changes with taxation. One reason why government policy might affect the model through different channels than the straightforward income effect modelled above has to do with the degree to which consumers are long-sighted. If we endogenize savings in the way introduced in the Ramsey model, we must assume that consumers are forward looking and anticipate correctly the future taxes they will have to pay. Thus, if the consumers are convinced that a tax reduction today will imply higher taxes in the future, since the government will have to repay its debt, they might anticipate the future increase in taxes by increasing savings today. This is an example of so-called Ricardian equivalence and is discussed in more depth in Chapter 6 and 7. This will offset any attempts to stimulate (temporary) economic growth through a cut in taxes.

8 Conclusions

The Solow–Swan model provides a powerful platform from which to begin the study of economic growth. The basic model without technological progress shows the limits to capital accumulation as the engine of growth, as diminishing returns to capital eventually kick in.

The key results of the model without technological progress are:

- Steady-state growth is characterized by a constant capital–output ratio and constant wage and profit shares in GDP.

- There is no growth of per capita GDP.

- A rise in the savings/investment rate or a fall in the population growth rate leads to a period during which GDP per capita grows as a consequence of the increasing capital intensity of production, but growth eventually dies out because of the role of diminishing returns to capital.

- The *level* of output per capita in the steady state is higher, the higher is the savings/investment share, and the lower, the rate of population growth. The model identifies these as the determinants of whether a country is rich or poor.

- A poor country otherwise identical to a rich one except that it has low savings (or high population growth) will catch up to the rich one if it is able to raise the savings rate (lower the population growth rate) to equal that of the rich country. This is known as 'absolute convergence'. Catching up takes place through a phase of rising capital intensity in the poor country.

- As long as the steady-state characteristics of the poor country are different from those of the rich country, the poor country will converge to its own steady state: it will not catch up with the rich one. If the rich and the poor country are both away from steady-state growth, the poor country will only grow faster than the rich one if it is initially further from its own steady state. This is known as 'conditional convergence'.

- If the government is able to keep raising the savings/investment rate (e.g. in a planned economy), there will come a point at which this reduces welfare in the economy, where this is measured by the steady-state level of consumption per head. The savings rate that maximizes consumption per head is known as the Golden Rule rate.

The Solow–Swan model must be modified if it is to be consistent with the stylized fact of steady growth in per capita GDP. This is accomplished by including Harrod-neutral technological progress in the model: i.e. it is assumed that the productivity of labour is enhanced by improvements in technology on the existing capital stock that take place at a constant exogenously given rate. This modification allows for balanced growth with rising GDP per capita. The model predicts

- conditional convergence in levels of GDP per capita if countries differ in the characteristics that pin down the steady state and

- absolute convergence if the determinants of the steady state are identical across countries.

- In the long run, the model predicts convergence of growth rates of living standards across countries to the rate, x, of exogenous technical progress.

When the Solow–Swan model with exogenous technological progress is tested using cross-country growth data, an inconsistency emerges. An estimate of the speed of convergence can be made in two ways: either by plugging *ex ante* reasonable values into the formula for b, the speed of convergence, or by estimating b econometrically from data. The data suggests that convergence to the steady-state path is much slower than expected by the a priori calculation. By augmenting the Solow–Swan model with the inclusion of *human* as well as physical capital as a factor of production, the inconsistency is reduced. Combined human and physical capital has the effect of increasing the share of broad capital in output and hence in weakening diminishing returns to 'capital'. This is consistent with the slower estimated speed of convergence and provides an account of the pattern of cross-country growth in terms of conditional convergence.

By introducing the idea that education speeds up technology transfer, we have shown an alternative mechanism through which poor countries may catch up. Even if the technology frontier grows at the exogenous rate x, if we relax the Solow–Swan assumption that access to new technology is universal,

- countries can catch up by adopting frontier technologies if their level of education is sufficient.

- The fastest catch-up is predicted in countries that are a long way behind the frontier but have a high level of education.

This is one reason why economists predicted that some former planned economies would experience rapid catch-up growth after the fall of communism at the beginning of the 1990s. However, they underestimated how difficult it would be to create the institutions that are necessary for the effective functioning of catch-up in a market economy.[22]

In spite of the many insights it provides, the Solow–Swan model remains silent on the fundamental question of what lies behind the steady rise in living standards observed for many countries over the past few centuries. This puzzle has fuelled the search for models of endogenous growth which will be addressed in the next chapter. In the next chapter we shall also delve deeper into more recent work on the economics of growth. This allows us to investigate how institutions ranging from entrepreneurial firms to the patent system, from the extent of competition in the product market to the financial system may influence growth and catch-up.

■ QUESTIONS

(1) In the Solow–Swan model explain what is meant by a steady state when population is constant and there is no technological progress. Extend the concept to the case in which the population is growing at a constant rate and in which there is a constant rate of technical progress.

(2) What do empirical measurements of Solow's residual tell us about the role of technological progress in economic growth? What are their shortcomings in capturing the role of technology?

(3) Information technology is an important contributor to economic growth in modern economies. Discuss how you would measure the impact of information technology on economic growth.

(4) Assume that at time zero there is a rich country and a poor country. You are in a Solow world without technical progress. When the countries are observed at a later date, there is no difference in the standard of living between the two countries. Is this consistent with (*a*) absolute convergence; (*b*) conditional convergence? Specify your assumptions about technology, demography, tastes, and policy.

(5) Can shocks to technology explain macroeconomic volatility?

(6) 'Technology remains the dominant engine of growth, with human capital investment in second place' (Robert Solow, Nobel Prize Lecture, 1987). Do you agree? Explain your reasoning.

---

[22] Gerard Roland's book (2000) provides a framework for analysing the role of missing institutions in explaining why transition in many countries was more painful than expected (e.g. ch. 8). For a fascinating analysis of how reform worked in China, see Qian (2003).

(7) If the savings rate falls permanently, what happens to welfare measured as per capita consumption in the Solow–Swan model?

(8) Use the analytical tools acquired in this chapter to analyse the introduction of a welfare system financed through taxation on the long-run performance of the economy. Does it matter whether lump-sum or proportional taxes are raised?

Problems and questions for discussion

QUESTION A. In the Solow model, assume the economy is initially in a steady state in which there is no growth of output per capita. At time t there is a sudden fall in the growth rate of the population and it remains at the new lower growth rate. Describe what happens to output growth and to the growth of living standards in the economy and why. Now assume there is labour augmenting technical progress: how does that affect the growth of the economy in response to a fall in the population growth rate?

QUESTION B. Consider an economy which experiences civil war. How will this affect the short-run performance of the economy? Describe the steady state to which the economy returns after the end of the civil war. Are there any long-run effects of civil war that may affect the economy many years after the civil war ended? (Hint: Discuss the effect of civil war on human capital.) [Background reading: For the long-run effects of civil wars see Ghobarah, Huth, and Russett (2003).]

QUESTION C. In an economy characterized by a Cobb–Douglas production function and exogenous labour-augmenting technical progress, labour's share of income is 70% and the depreciation rate is 3% per annum. The economy is in a steady state with GDP growth at 4% per year and with a capital–output ratio of 2. Find the saving rate and the marginal product of capital. At time t the saving rate in this economy increases to a new constant level, with the outcome that the economy converges to the Golden Rule steady state. What is the new savings rate, capital–output ratio, and marginal product of capital? Use diagrams with time on the horizontal axis to sketch the path of the capital–output ratio, the marginal product of labour, and of consumption per effective unit of labour.

QUESTION D. Use the models discussed in this chapter to explore the possible implications for growth in output and in output per capita in Australia of the data presented in Fig. 13.20.[23] Using the right hand scale, the chart shows the trend in the fertility rate (the average number of children born to a woman in her lifetime). Measured against the left scale are shown (a) the rate at which girls stay on to the final year

---

[23] We are grateful to Steve Dowrick for generously providing this data. The sources for the data are: Participation: Reserve Bank of Australia, 'Australian Economic Statistics 1964-96'; Australian Bureau of Statistics, 'Labour Force (prelim) 1997-2001' Fertility: Australian Bureau of Statistics, 'Births, Australia' (Cat. no. 3301.0). School Retention: Collins, Kenway, and McLeod (2000).

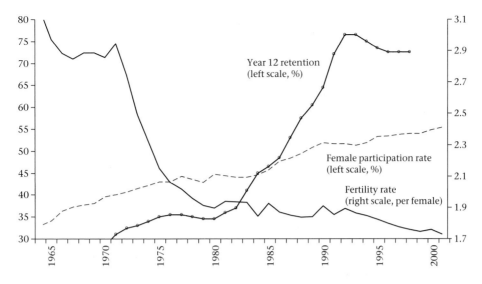

Figure 13.20 Fertility, education, and female labour force participation: Australia

(year 12) of secondary education and (*b*) the female participation rate in the labour force.

Table 13.4 GDP per capita by region in the Czech Republic and Austria, 1995 and 2002 (EU average = 100)

Czech Republic	1995	2002	Austria	1995	2002
Prague	129	153	Vienna	184	173
Strední Cechy	54	55	Kärnten	107	100
Jihozápad	67	61	Steiermark	105	103
Severozápad	67	64	Oberösterreich	118	113
Severovýchod	60	57	Salzburg	144	134
Jihovýchod	63	60	Tirol	132	124
Strední Morava	59	52	Vorarlberg	131	126
Moravskoslezko	66	57			

Source: Eurostat website.

QUESTION E. The data in the Table 13.4 show the GDP per capita relative to the EU25 average adjusted for purchasing power parity for the regions of the Czech Republic and Austria for 1995 and 2002. The EU25 average is set equal to 100 in each year. Note that the same purchasing power parity is used for all the regions within a country. Provide a concise description of the data presented in Table 13.4. Show how the concepts of absolute and conditional convergence can be used to discuss the evolution of living standards in these two countries.

▓ APPENDIX

The aim of this appendix is to present an introduction to some of the most commonly used concepts and techniques in the analysis of economic growth.

Properties of production functions

Production functions are central to the theory of economic growth since they provide a mathematical representation of the process of transforming inputs to production such as labour power or physical capital into goods and services. We have previously defined a production function to be $Y = F(K, L, A)$, where K, L, and A denote capital, labour, and technology respectively. In general we treat production functions like a black box, in the sense that we leave unspecified the exact process through which inputs to production are transformed into outputs. In order to make progress however, it is often useful to impose a number of assumptions on the structure of the production functions. These assumptions give rise to various properties that will be addressed below. We shall provide more concrete examples of these properties by looking at the most commonly used production function in economic growth theory, namely the Cobb–Douglas production function.

It is necessary to impose some technical assumptions on the production function, which are summarized as follows:

(1) $f(0) = 0$, which means that inputs are essential for production;

(2) f is concave with $f'(k) > 0$, which means that output per head rises as the capital to labour ratio rises and $f''(k) < 0$, which means that the increment to output per head from a rise in the capital–labour ratio falls as k rises (diminishing returns). We note that the marginal product of capital can be written in different ways:

$$f'(k) \equiv F_K(K, L) \equiv MPK, \tag{13.39}$$

and that the concavity of the production function imposes diminishing returns to capital in the economy.

(3) the so-called 'Inada conditions':
   (a) $\lim_{k \to 0} f'(k) = \infty$,
   (b) $\lim_{k \to \infty} f'(k) = 0$. The importance of the Inada conditions from the perspective of understanding the economics of the Solow–Swan model is that they ensure that a steady state exists for all values of s, x, n, and δ. Whereas the other features of the production function ensure that there is at most one steady state and that it is stable, the Inada conditions rule out endogenous growth by ensuring there is at least one steady state. This will become clearer once the mechanics of endogenous growth are explained in Chapter 14.[24]

Returns to scale and returns to a factor

The difference between returns to scale and returns to a factor can often seem confusing, even though the underlying concepts are easily distinguishable. In a nutshell, returns to scale refers to the effect on output of increasing or decreasing *all factors* of production, while returns to a factor refers to the impact on output of changing only *one factor* while keeping all other factors constant. Let us now explore these ideas in detail.

---

[24] Rather than assuming the Inada conditions hold, an alternative strategy would be to assume that a steady state exists for the range of the parameters being considered. This would allow the use of a production function in which at, say, a very high savings rate there is endogenous growth, or at a very low one there is 'immiseration'.

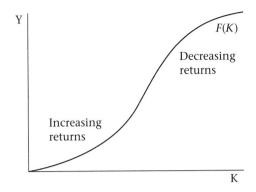

Figure 13.21 Production function exhibiting both convexities and concavities

Returns to scale captures the effect of the size of a plant, industry, or economy on its productive capacity. Thus, the question to be answered is whether doubling the size of the productive unit will increase or decrease production and by what proportion. Consider the example of a manager of a software company who has to evaluate the impact of doubling all the inputs to production (this involves both new office space and equipment as well as programmers). Will the firm be able to produce more than twice as many computer programs per year, less than twice as many, or will production increase exactly by a factor or two? It seems likely that production of new software will at least increase by a factor of two and possibly even more. To illustrate let us assume that programmers work independently with each using one office and one computer to produce one computer program a year. Now if we double the number of offices, computers, and programmers we should expect that the number of programs produced during the year by this firm will also double. This case is referred to as a case of *constant return to scale* (CRS).

Will production ever increase by a factor greater than two? It seems plausible that the firm may use its workers not to develop software individually but rather to work jointly on a big project, where each worker produces only a component of the big program (say an operating system). When assembled the operating system may well bring the firm much more revenue than the sum of the small programs that would have been developed by each programmer individually. This is a case of synergy in production, which we refer to by saying that production exhibits *increasing return to scale* (IRS).

Do we have any reason to believe that production might increase but only by a factor less than two? One story would be that as the scale of production increases various inefficiencies arise that prevent the firm from exploiting its full potential. One suggestion in our example would be that as the firm gets bigger and bigger it becomes impossible for real talent to shine through the hierarchy and as a result brilliant ideas are never put into practice. Thus, if as a result of doubling its size the firm is only able to produce less than twice the output, we refer to this as a situation of *decreasing returns to scale* (DRS). Although a theoretical possibility they often seem less plausible in reality.

It is important to realize that one type of returns to scale does not have to apply to the entire range of the production function. It is possible for a production function to exhibit increasing returns to scale when it is small, constant returns to scale when it has achieved a medium size, and decreasing returns to scale when it is very large. A production function (for only one input: $Y = F(K)$) displaying increasing returns at low levels of output and decreasing returns at high levels is illustrated in Fig. 13.21.

Returns to scale and homogeneity

From a mathematical point of view the concept of returns to scale is closely related to that of the *degree of homogeneity* of a function. Consider for example an arbitrary function $g(x_1, x_2, \ldots, x_n)$, and let us

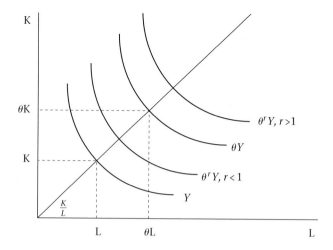

Figure 13.22 Isoquants illustrating the returns to scale property

multiply each of the arguments of the function by some non-zero constant θ. This function is said to be homogeneous of degree r if,

$$g(\theta x_1, \theta x_2, \ldots, \theta x_n) = \theta^r g(x_1, x_2, \ldots, x_n). \tag{13.40}$$

If g were a production function, then the case $r = 1$ corresponds to the constant returns to scale, $r > 1$ to increasing returns to scale, and $r < 1$ to decreasing returns to scale. If we have only two factors of production (which we also label K and L) we can use *isoquants* to represent the related concepts of homogeneity and returns to scale. Isoquants are loci of point in (K, L) space that correspond to the same level of output. Clearly if capital and labour are substitutable, at least to some extent, there exist many combinations of capital and labour that result in the same level of output. In Fig. 13.22 we show the impact of increasing both capital and labour by a factor of θ. The locus of Y points shifts outwards and depending on the degree of homogeneity r of the function it will be either to the left or to the right of θy points. If they exactly coincide we have constant returns to scale.

Example. A commonly used example of a constant returns to scale production function in this chapter is the Cobb–Douglas production function with $Y(K, L) = K^\alpha L^{1-\alpha}$, where

$$Y(\theta K, \theta L) = (\theta K)^\alpha (\theta L)^{1-\alpha} = \theta^{(\alpha+1-\alpha)} K^\alpha L^{1-\alpha} = \theta Y(K, L).$$

Diminishing returns to capital

The other very important concept in this chapter is that of *diminishing returns to capital*. The concept of returns to a factor refers to the impact on output of varying one single factor while keeping all the other ones constant. It reflects the idea that as we add more and more of one factor of production while keeping everything else unchanged the additional units will become less and less productive at the margin. For example hiring more and more labour while keeping the amount of capital constant will produce overcrowding and eventually the marginal worker employed will not produce anything as there will not be enough physical capital in the plant for the worker to use and thus be productively employed. Similarly if the software company in our earlier example increases the number of computers, while keeping the number of programmers constant, it seems plausible that although one programmer might use more than one computer in her office to write or test software, eventually there will be plenty of unused computers lying around not being put to any productive use.

From a mathematical point of view this corresponds to the notion of *concavity* of the production function. A function is concave if the tangent to that function at any point lies above the graph of the function. This is illustrated in Fig. 13.23 for some production function, $Y = F(K, L)$, where we keep L constant and only vary K; this is indicated by writing the production function as $Y = F(K; L)$. It is easy to see that as we increase capital it becomes less and less productive at the margin and the production function takes the usual concave shape.

Example. If we now look again at the Cobb–Douglas function we can easily show that it exhibits diminishing returns to its factors (capital and labour). The marginal products are given by the first order derivatives with respect to each factor. In order to show *diminishing* marginal returns to each factor we further take the second derivatives;

$$Y_{KK} = \alpha(\alpha - 1)\frac{Y}{K^2} \tag{13.41}$$

$$Y_{LL} = \alpha(\alpha - 1)\frac{Y}{L^2} \tag{13.42}$$

Since $\alpha \in [0, 1]$, we have $Y_{KK} < 0$ and $Y_{LL} < 0$, hence Y exhibits diminishing marginal returns to both factors. It can be shown that decreasing or constant returns to scale imply diminishing marginal products, while increasing returns to scale may or may not imply diminishing returns to a factor.

Intensive form production functions

Even the simplest production functions generate three data points, one for capital, one for labour, and one for output. As it is often quite cumbersome and not particularly informative to attempt to visualize or manipulate information in many dimensions, we often apply a very useful trick of expressing the factors of production as ratios of each other. The most commonly used example occurs when we focus on the role played by capital in the neoclassical growth model and consequently use as an argument the capital per worker ratio $k = K/L$. In the model augmented with technological progress we use $\hat{k} = K/(AL)$. In both cases we refer to 'capital in intensive form' and the production function $y = f(k)$ or $\hat{y} = f(\hat{k})$ as the *intensive form* production function. The intensive form production function rests on the assumption of constant returns to scale: $\frac{Y}{L} = \frac{F(K,L)}{L} = F(K/L, 1)$; hence $y = f(k)$, where $f(k) = F(k, 1)$. One useful property to remember is that the slope of the intensive form production function equals the marginal

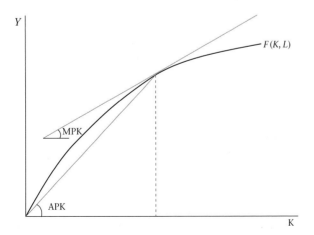

Figure 13.23 A typical concave production function with diminishing returns to capital

product of capital, $MPK = F_K(K, L) = f_k$, which can be shown to hold using the chain rule:

$$F_K(K, L) = \frac{dF(K, L)}{dK} = \frac{d(Lf(k))}{dK} = Lf_k\left(\frac{dk}{dK}\right) = Lf_k\left(\frac{k}{L}\right) = f_k(k). \tag{13.43}$$

Euler's Theorem. Euler's Theorem is often used in deriving basic results in growth theory and makes use of the idea of homogeneity. It states that a function $g(x_1, x_2, \ldots, x_n)$ is homogeneous of degree r if the following holds:

$$x_1 \frac{\partial g}{\partial x_1} + \ldots + x_n \frac{\partial g}{\partial x_n} = r\, g(x_1, x_2, \ldots, x_n) \tag{13.44}$$

that is, the sum over the marginal effect of each argument (e.g. $\frac{\partial g}{\partial x_i}$) times the value of the argument (x_i) is proportional to the value of the function, with a proportionality coefficient equal to the degree of homogeneity. In the case of a production function this has a very natural economic interpretation: the sum over the marginal product of each factor times the amount of the factor is proportional to total output. In the case of constant returns to scale, the degree of homogeneity is one ($r = 1$), so it holds with equality.

Example. For a CRS production function we have:

$$Y = F_K K + F_L L,$$

where we can now divide both sides by L and obtain $y = f_k k + f_L$, which means that the average product of labour equals the marginal product of capital times capital per worker plus the marginal product of labour.

Incorporating technological progress

In its most general form the production function that incorporates some concept of technological progress is written as $Y = F(K, L, A)$. It is often useful to make a more precise assumption about the way in which technological progress enters this utility function and we have already introduced three distinct possibilities that have been considered in the literature:

(1) 'Hicks-neutral' or *factor*-augmenting technological progress: $Y = AF(K, L)$;

(2) 'Solow-neutral' or *capital*-augmenting technological progress: $Y = F(AK, L)$;

(3) 'Harrod-neutral' or *labour*-augmenting technological progress: $Y = F(K, AL)$.

Example. For the Cobb–Douglas production function the three specifications are identical. Let us see that this is indeed the case. It is easy to see that for the Cobb–Douglas case $Y = A_1 F(K, L) = F(A_2 K, L) = F(K, A_3 L)$ implies that $A_1 K^\alpha L^{1-\alpha} = A_2^\alpha K^\alpha L^{1-\alpha} = A_3^{1-\alpha} K^\alpha L^{1-\alpha}$. Hence, if we let $A = A_3 = A_1^{1/(1-\alpha)} = A_2^{\alpha/(1-\alpha)}$, then the three specifications of the Cobb–Douglas production function are indeed identical.

Growth accounting and imperfect competition

Solow used the technique of growth accounting to estimate total factor productivity growth (the Solow residual) over long periods of time and found a strong correlation between the residual and the rate of economic growth. But how robust is this explanation to the assumption of perfect competition? We have argued extensively in this book that firms operate in an imperfectly competitive environment and use mark-up pricing in the goods market. Here, we derive a simple extension of the Solow residual that takes into account imperfect competition in the goods market.[25]

Let us assume that the production function is characterized by increasing returns to scale:

$$Y = AK^\alpha L^\beta,$$

[25] We are grateful to Nicholas Oulton for this derivation.

where $\alpha + \beta > 1$.

The growth rate of TFP is given by

$$g_A = g_Y - \alpha g_K - \beta g_L$$

and we ask the question as to the error we will make if we estimate this by the usual Solow residual (i.e. assuming perfect competition):

$$SR_{pc} = g_Y - [1 - (wL/Y)]g_K - (wL/Y)g_L.$$

With increasing returns to scale, we must assume imperfect competition where the firm equates the wage to the marginal revenue product of labour:

$$w = (MR/P) \cdot \beta Y/L.$$

If we assume monopolistic competition, we have

$$MR = MC \text{ and } P = AC, \text{ hence } MR/P = MC/AC = 1/(\alpha + \beta)$$

(since AC/MC is the degree of returns to scale). So the Solow residual is

$$SR_{ipc} = g_Y - [\alpha/(\alpha + \beta)]g_K - [\beta/(\alpha + \beta)]g_L.$$

Hence, we have $SR_{pc} > SR_{ipc}$: the Solow residual exaggerates the true rate of technological progress, g_A.

Taylor's Theorem. Taylor's Theorem provides a method to deal with non-linear functions within close proximity of the steady state. The underlying intuition is that as long as we are only interested in the behaviour of our model when the economy is not too far off its long-run steady state, we can approximate a highly non-linear function to an arbitrary degree of accuracy by a polynomial with terms of increasing order. In most applications it is not necessary to add many terms of higher orders to our polynomial and indeed the first two or three terms will often be sufficient to derive a reasonable degree of accuracy. If a first order approximation is deemed sufficient for the task at hand, that is we approximate a non-linear function by a straight line tangent to the original function at the steady state: this is called *linearizing* the function. We shall use this Theorem to approximate a particular function, the non-linear savings part of the Fundamental Solow Equation of motion $sk^{\alpha-1}$ (rewritten using the growth rate formula derived in equation 13.11 for a Cobb–Douglas production function). We illustrate in Fig. 13.24 how Taylor's theorem is applied to approximate this expression using polynomials of increasing order around an arbitrary steady state k^*.

The original function we are planning to approximate is highly non-linear for $\alpha = 0.3$. The first suggestion is to fit a polynomial of order zero, i.e. a constant function. We can see from the figure that this would be a poor approximation since it does not resemble the original function at all. However, it is still accurate if we actually are at the steady state. Then we attempt to fit a first order polynomial, i.e. a linear function. We notice that this is already a reasonably good approximation for values very close to the steady state k^*, but is only a poor approximation for values remote from the steady state. To obtain even better approximations for the non-linear function we expand the original function using a second order and fifth order polynomial around the steady state. Fig. 13.24 clearly shows how increasing orders allow us to get closer and closer to the original function. Of course the gains in accuracy have to be balanced against the losses in analytical simplicity and computational time.

But let us now see how to implement this mathematically. Taylor's theorem states that any function $f(x)$ that is continuous and has at least n derivatives in an interval close to the point x^*, may be approximated at a point sufficiently close to x^* using the following formula:

$$f(x^* + \delta x) \cong f(x^*) + \left.\frac{df(x)}{dx}\right|_{x^*} (\delta x) + \left.\frac{d^2f(x)}{dx^2}\right|_{x^*} \frac{(\delta x)^2}{2!} + \cdots + \left.\frac{d^nf(x)}{dx^n}\right|_{x^*} \frac{(\delta x)^n}{n!}. \tag{13.45}$$

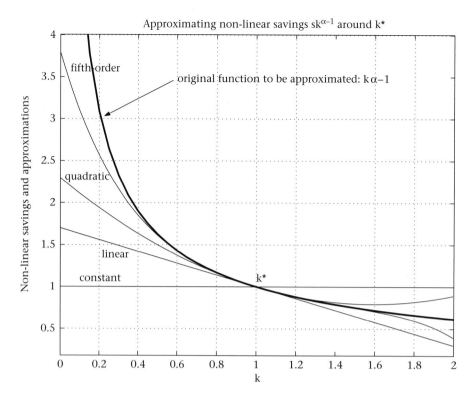

Figure 13.24 Numerical illustration of progressive Taylor approximations of the non-linear savings part of the Fundamental Solow Equation of Motion around the steady state k^*

This formula looks complicated at first glance but it can be explained as follows. All it says is that if we are interested in approximating the value of the function $f(x)$ at a point close to x^* given by $x^* + \delta x$, we can do this by a polynomial in the distance of the point of interest from the point x^*. The coefficients of this polynomial are given by the derivatives of the original function evaluated at x^* and rescaled by the factorial of the order of the respective term. Thus essentially we can say that we are approximating the function $f(x)$ at some point y close to x^* by a polynomial of the following form: $f(y) \cong c_0 + c_1 y + c_2 y^2 + c_3 y^3 + \cdots + c_n y^n$.

Convergence and log-linear approximation. Even simple dynamic models often present analytical challenges due to inherent non-linearities in the equations of interest. It has become increasingly common to use computers to simulate transitional dynamics, especially in situations where the implied equations are well beyond human intuition. If however we search for an analytical presentation we have to approximate the equations of our system close to the steady state. This procedure is called *log-linearization*.[26] As long as we are only interested in small deviations from the steady state log-linearization can be quite rewarding. We shall illustrate this method by deriving the equation for the convergence speed of an economy.

We start from the Fundamental Solow Equation and use a Cobb–Douglas specification for the production function:

$$\dot{\hat{k}}_t = s\hat{k}^\alpha - \hat{k}(\delta + x + n) \tag{13.46}$$

[26] For more technical details and much more advanced and general treatment see Campbell (1994).

we can divide this expression by $\hat{k}$ and obtain

$$\left(\frac{1}{\hat{k}} \frac{d\hat{k}}{dt} = \right) \quad \frac{d \log \hat{k}}{dt} = s\hat{k}^{\alpha-1} - (\delta + x + n). \tag{13.47}$$

We define $\hat{k}^*$ such that $s(\hat{k}^*)^{\alpha-1} - (\delta + x + n) = 0$. We now use a Taylor approximation (see previous section) to linearize the non-linear savings part of the Fundamental Solow Equation $s\hat{k}^{\alpha-1}$ around the steady state $\hat{k}^*$ and obtain

$$s\hat{k}^{\alpha-1} \cong s(\hat{k}^*)^{\alpha-1} + \left. \frac{ds\hat{k}^{\alpha-1}}{d \log \hat{k}} \right|_{\hat{k}^*} (\log \hat{k} - \log \hat{k}^*),$$

for all $\hat{k}$ near $\hat{k}^*$. Further substitutions result in:

$$\begin{aligned} s\hat{k}^{\alpha-1} &\cong s(\hat{k}^*)^{\alpha-1} + \left. \frac{ds\hat{k}^{\alpha-1}}{d\hat{k}} \cdot \frac{d\hat{k}}{d \log \hat{k}} \right|_{\hat{k}^*} (\log \hat{k} - \log \hat{k}^*) \\ &= (\delta + x + n) + (\alpha - 1)(s\hat{k}^{\alpha-2} \cdot \hat{k}) \Big|_{\hat{k}^*} (\log \hat{k} - \log \hat{k}^*) \\ &= (\delta + x + n) + (\alpha - 1)s(\hat{k}^*)^{\alpha-1} (\log \hat{k} - \log \hat{k}^*) \\ &= (\delta + x + n) + (\alpha - 1)(\delta + x + n)(\log \hat{k} - \log \hat{k}^*), \end{aligned}$$

which we can replace in the Taylor approximation and collect terms to obtain:

$$\frac{d \log \hat{k}}{dt} = \underbrace{-(1 - \alpha)(\delta + x + n)}_{b} (\log \hat{k} - \log \hat{k}^*). \tag{13.48}$$

Since $\hat{y} = \hat{k}^\alpha$ we can multiply by α and obtain the equation for the growth rate of output as:

$$g_{\hat{y}} = -b(\log \hat{y} - \log \hat{y}^*), \tag{13.49}$$

where $\hat{y}^*$ is the (constant) steady state of the economy and the convergence speed coefficient b is given by $b = -(1 - \alpha)(\delta + x + n)$.

In section 5.2 we derive equation 13.30, which tells us that the output gap evolves as an exponential decay function with parameter b:

$$\dot{G}_A = -bG_A,$$

where $G_A = \log y_{US} - \log y$. We can use this fact to derive an estimating equation that can be used in empirical work to consistently estimate the speed of convergence from data on GDP. If equation 13.30 holds between $t = 0$ and T we can integrate it:

$$\frac{1}{G} \frac{dG}{dt} = -b \quad \Rightarrow \quad \int_{G_0}^{G_T} \frac{1}{G} dG = \int_0^T -b dt$$

$$[\log G]_{G_0}^{G_T} = [-b]_0^T \quad \Rightarrow \quad \log G_T - \log G_0 = -bT$$

$$G_T = G_0 \exp(-bT).$$

We can now subtract G_0 from both sides in order to eliminate the need for a comparison country and focus on the data for each country.

$$G_T - G_0 = G_0[\exp(-bT) - 1],$$

which we can rewrite in terms of output per capita as:

$$\log y_T - \log y_0 = \text{constant} + [\exp(-bT) - 1]\log y_0. \tag{13.50}$$

We can approximate the term involving b on the right hand side if we remember that $[\exp(-bT) - 1]/T \simeq (1 - bT - 1)/T = -b$. Thus we can divide both sides by T which (after adding the usual stochastic error term) gives us an estimating equation that relates the average growth rate of GDP per capita between two periods to the initial log in GDP per capita with unknown coefficient b. This equation can then be estimated for similar countries using an appropriate estimator, e.g. by OLS regression.

Optimization. The theory of optimization is a particularly well-developed and complete branch of mathematics[27] that deals with finding maxima or minima of various functions given certain constraints. In economics it is very often used to find the optimum quantities of various variables of the economy (such as capital or labour) that maximize social welfare. The methods can be extended to deal with multi-period problems, interacting agents, and multiple constraints. Additionally it works for both continuous time and discrete time systems.

Our aim in this section is to derive the equations of motion for the Ramsey model, an extension of the standard Solow–Swan model, where consumers choose optimally each period how much to save out of their current income. Thus, we relax the assumption of constant savings by allowing rational consumers to endogenize their consumption choice.

In order to do so the consumers will need to optimize an *objective function*, that is they need to have some goal for which they will need to maximize. One simple assumption is that consumers derive utility in each period from current consumption, given by $U(c_t)$. The objective function for the consumers is thus the discounted sum of utilities from consumption in all periods. A consumer has to decide how much to consume today, by taking into account how her choice today will affect the options available to her in the future and hence how much she will be able to consume tomorrow. This is true since we can intuitively see that more consumption today implies less savings tomorrow and less capital investment, which translates into a lower output per capita tomorrow and hence a lower ability to consume tomorrow. Choices we make today always affect the choices that are available to us in the future and it is only reasonable that we take this into account when making economic decisions. However, consumption in the future does not equal consumption today. For a start consumption today provides us with immediate gratification, while consumption in the future is only anticipated consumption and human impatience prevents us from valuing it equally from the point of view of today. What this implies is that the proper way to think of a rational agent's lifetime utility is as a discounted sum of individual utilities derived in the different periods. The rational agent will aim to maximize $\sum_{t=0}^{t=\infty} \beta^t U(c_t)$ subject to the technological and resource constraints, where β is the psychological discount parameter between today and tomorrow. We shall use the conceptual framework of the social planner we discussed in section 7.1 to write down the maximization problem as:

$$Max \sum_{t=0}^{t=\infty} \beta^t U(c_t)$$

$$s.t. \quad c_t + s_t = f(k_t)$$

$$k_{t+1} - k_t = i_t - (1 - \delta)k_t,$$

where the social planner maximizes the discounted intertemporal sum of utilities from current period consumption for the representative agent, subject to the resource constraint, which states that the agent

[27] A useful book in this context is Venkataraman (2002).

has to divide her total disposable income $f(k_t)$ between consumption c_t and savings s_t and the capital accumulation constraint which states that net investment has to equal gross investment given by i_t minus the amount of capital lost on depreciation $(1 - \delta)k_t$. Notice that we are here ignoring both population growth and technological progress. This is for mathematical simplicity in order to allow us to focus on the task at hand. Of course as these are only constants of the model they will not affect the optimization process itself.

Substituting the first constraint into the second we obtain

$$c_t + k_{t+1} = f(k_t) + (1 - \delta)k_t$$

which can be rewritten as

$$c_t = f(k_t) + (1 - \delta)k_t - k_{t+1}.$$

We can now substitute this expression into the objective function to obtain an unconstrained optimization problem which is much easier to solve:

$$Max_{k_{t+1}} \sum_{t=0}^{t=\infty} \beta^t U(f(k_t) + (1 - \delta)k_t - k_{t+1}). \tag{13.51}$$

Since at any time t the social planner knows current production and the current level of capital, all that remains to be done is to determine the optimal level of capital in the next period, i.e. k_{t+1}, for all periods. In order to obtain the first order condition for this problem we will need to notice that we only have two adjacent terms of the summation which involve the variable k_{t+1}:

$$\ldots + \beta^t U(f(k_t) + (1 - \delta)k_t - k_{t+1}) + \beta^{t+1} U(f(k_{t+1}) + (1 - \delta)k_{t+1} - k_{t+2}) + \cdots$$

Hence after taking the derivative with respect to k_{t+1} of these terms, the first order condition is given by:

$$-\beta^t U'(f(k_t) + (1 - \delta)k_t - k_{t+1}) +$$
$$+\beta^{t+1} U'(f(k_{t+1}) + (1 - \delta)k_{t+1} - k_{t+2})[f'(k_t) + (1 - \delta)] = 0.$$

This is what economists refer to as the *Euler Condition*. It is a very important result because together with the *transversality condition*[28] it tells us everything we need to know about the model. It is a mathematical condition that links the optimal capital level between yesterday, today, and tomorrow and can be used iteratively to derive the capital level at each point in time.[29] Notice that the Euler Condition above can also be written in terms of consumption as:

$$-\beta^t U'(c_t) + \beta^{t+1} U'(c_{t+1})[r_t + 1] = 0, \tag{13.52}$$

where we have used the fact that with competitive factor markets $f'(k_t) = r_t + \delta$. We can rearrange this to obtain

$$\frac{U'(c_t)}{U'(c_{t+1})} = \beta(1 + r_t). \tag{13.53}$$

---

[28] The transversality condition is a technical condition that describes the asymptotic behaviour of the model and is discussed in detail in more advanced mathematical treatments of dynamic optimization.

[29] For more details on how to actually implement this solution method see Ljungqvist and Sargent (2004), chs. 2–3.

It may however be useful to return to the continuous time framework we have used in most of this chapter. To do so we will need to assume a special form of the utility function, $U(c_t) = \log c_t$. Using this specification we can now rewrite the Euler condition as:

$$\frac{c_{t+1}}{c_t} = \beta(1 + r_t),\qquad(13.54)$$

and after taking logs of both sides we obtain

$$\log c_{t+1} - \log c_t = \log \beta + \log(1 + r_t).\qquad(13.55)$$

To simplify this expression even further we shall make two approximations. First we shall assume that β the psychological discount parameter can be rewritten as $\beta = 1/(1 + \rho)$, where $\rho > 0$ is the rate of time preference and hence $\log \beta = -\log(1 + \rho) \cong -\rho$ and similarly, $\log(1 + r_t) \cong r_t$. Hence,

$$\log c_{t+1} - \log c_t \cong r_t - \rho.\qquad(13.56)$$

We have already seen that the left hand side of this expression can be thought of as a rate of change and thus expressed in continuous time as:

$$\frac{\dot{c}_t}{c_t} \cong r_t - \rho.\qquad(13.57)$$

The Ramsey model reduces to the following two dynamical equations:

$$\frac{\dot{c}_t}{c_t} = f'(k_t) - \delta - \rho\qquad(13.58)$$

$$\dot{k}_t = f(k_t) - c_t - \delta k_t.\qquad(13.59)$$

We could perform the same steps as above but take into account population growth and technological progress.[30] There are many ways to solve the model from here whereby we can determine the equilibrium levels of capital, consumption, and output per worker as well as the behaviour of the economy on and off the equilibrium path. As we have already noted although this gets rid of the criticism that the consumers in the economy do not act as rational utility maximizers when choosing how much to save, the results of the Ramsey model still predict monotonic convergence to the steady state. The dynamics of convergence to the steady state however is more complicated since it now involves the parameters of the utility function in addition to those of the production function.[31]

Optimal control interpretation. When solving dynamic models like the Ramsey model which involve a substantial component of intertemporal optimization, economists often use the language of *optimal control*, which is a branch of engineering. The idea behind optimal control is a set of mathematical procedures that allow us to 'control' how a system evolves over time, given certain constraining factors and a set of actions we can take at each point in time in order to achieve some stated objective. A useful illustration is that of landing a rocket on the moon given the technology available to us and the laws of physics. The engineer has to design an optimal strategy that would guarantee the success of the mission. We can think of the rocket in motion as the system of interest. This system is characterized by a set of *state variables* and a set of *control variables*. State variables are variables of the system that describe how the system behaves at any point in time and that can be altered through the control variables. State variables would be things like the position or velocity of the system. In the Ramsey model capital is the state variable. Control variables are variables that can be freely chosen at any point in time in order to modify the behaviour of the system. In the rocket case these include the power output of the propulsion system

---

[30] See Barro and Sala-I-Martin (2004), chs. 2 for the solution.
[31] Transitional dynamics is introduced in section 2.6 of Barro and Sala-i-Martin (2004).

or whether or not the landing gear is operational. In the Ramsey model consumption is the control variable as at any point in time the social planner can freely choose how much of current disposable income should be devoted to consumption and how much to savings. There are different widely used methods to solve this type of problem. One particularly neat approach is given by *dynamic programming*, which has now become a basic tool of much theoretical macroeconomics.[32]

[32] Still the best (but challenging) economics textbook on the subject is Stokey, Lucas, and Prescott (1989). A good starting point for the continuous time analysis is Chiang (2000).

14 Endogenous and Schumpeterian Growth

In the previous chapter, we have seen how the Solow–Swan model augmented with technological progress explains a great deal of what we are interested in when we study economic growth. Together, the steady-state analysis, transition dynamics, and the associated concepts of convergence provide a way of interpreting many of the observed features of the growth of economies. We obtained some insight into the role of capital formation as the mechanism by which a society accumulates wealth and how the presence of diminishing returns to factor accumulation imposes a limit on the extent to which changes in policy or institutions can affect growth in the long-run. For the Solow–Swan model, changes in the rate of growth of output per capita in the long-run steady state come from changes in the rate of exogenous technological progress. Endogenous growth theory proposes a number of mechanisms that could overcome diminishing returns to capital and thereby open up the possibility that changes in policy or in preferences can affect the growth rate in the long-run steady state. The characteristic that changes in policy or preferences can alter the long-run growth rate of output per capita is what distinguishes a model of endogenous from one of exogenous growth.

Fig. 14.1 illustrates several growth paths, a number of which are already familiar. The path ABC shows an economy on one steady-state growth path throughout the period. The path ABDE shows a Solow–Swan-type economy subjected to a shock such as a rise in the savings/investment rate at time t_0. This produces a transition path (B to D) during which growth is faster; following the transition, the economy is on a new higher level steady-state growth path with growth at the original rate (the new path is parallel to the old one). The path ABGH shows a Solow–Swan-type economy that experiences an exogenous rise in the rate of technological progress at time t_0. Following the transition, the output per capita in the economy grows forever at a faster rate. Finally, the path ABF cannot be explained within the Solow–Swan model. This shows the case of an economy in which the growth rate rises immediately and forever at t_0. We shall see how a model of endogenous growth produces this outcome as the consequence, for example, of a rise in the savings/investment rate. For now, it is interesting to note that when analysing data, it is likely to be difficult to distinguish between the new steady-state path of the endogenous growth economy (ABF) and the transition path of the Solow–Swan economy subjected to the same shock (ABD), unless the transition to the new steady-state path for the Solow–Swan economy is very quick.

In the first part of this chapter, we explain the mechanics of switching from exogenous to endogenous growth and then explore three different channels—knowledge spillovers from the accumulation of physical capital, investment in human capital, and in research

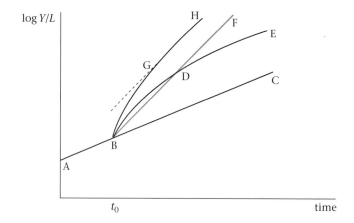

Figure 14.1 Growth paths with exogenous and endogenous growth

and development—that might drive endogenous growth. Although such models have the attraction of providing hypotheses to suggest which economic factors may lie behind the continuous growth in living standards, they are less convincing in accounting for features of the world such as the patterns of convergence that are observed amongst some groups of economies.

In the second part of the chapter, we introduce the Schumpeterian approach to endogenous growth. A simple version of the Aghion–Howitt model of Schumpeterian growth is set out, which characterizes innovation as a process of creative destruction as it was described by Joseph Schumpeter. This approach emphasizes the role of imperfect competition in sustaining the innovation process. The model can be extended to include not only the determinants of the pace of innovation at the world technology frontier but also of the rate of growth of countries who may be able to catch up through a process of technology transfer, which was introduced in Chapter 13. The distinction between technology transfer through imitation and the creation of new blueprints that advance the frontier opens up the possibility that different kinds of policies or institutions may raise growth for countries that are catching up, as compared with those that are at the frontier.

1 Endogenous growth theory

1.1 The *AK* model

The *AK* model is the prototype model of endogenous growth.[1] Once diminishing returns to capital are no longer present, we can represent the production function by

$$Y_t = AK_t, \tag{14.1}$$

---

[1] The treatment in this section and the next one was influenced by section 1.4 of Aghion and Howitt (1998), ch. 1.

where A is a constant that reflects the level of technology in the economy and does *not* vary with time. For the moment, we ignore labour. As usual, we assume a constant savings rate, s.

Let us now return to the capital accumulation equation:

$$\dot{K} = sY - \delta K = sAK - \delta K$$
$$= K(sA - \delta) \tag{14.2}$$
$$\frac{\dot{K}}{K} = sA - \delta. \qquad (AK \text{ model})$$

Contrast this with the equivalent expression in the Solow–Swan model:

$$\dot{K} = sF(K, L) - \delta K,$$

or in the case of the Cobb–Douglas production function:

$$\dot{K} = sK^{\alpha}L^{1-\alpha} - \delta K.$$

With the neoclassical production function, it is not possible to write an expression for $\frac{\dot{K}}{K}$ as a function of the exogenous variables:

$$\frac{\dot{K}}{K} = \frac{sL^{1-\alpha}}{K^{1-\alpha}} - \delta, \qquad (\text{Solow–Swan model})$$

which, when written like this, shows clearly that as the capital stock expands, its growth rate declines. This is just another way of saying that returns to capital are not constant and that raising the savings rate does not raise the growth rate of the capital stock permanently. By contrast, in the new AK-type production function, it is easy to see that a higher savings rate raises the growth rate of the capital stock and of output permanently.

It is important to note that the exponent on capital in the AK production function has to be exactly equal to one to produce endogenous growth. If it is marginally less than one, the model reverts to exogenous growth, albeit with very slow convergence and if it is marginally greater than one, growth is 'explosive', not constant. This means that output becomes infinite in finite time. The properties of the AK model are shown in Fig. 14.2. The linearity of the production function is apparent; as is the permanent effect on growth of a change in the savings rate.

The main results of the AK model are:

(1) The AK model allows for growth in output at a rate determined by $sA - \delta$.

(2) Higher savings s, a higher *level of technology*, A, and lower depreciation positively affect the growth rate of output.

(3) The model does not exhibit convergence since countries starting with different initial values for capital will continue to diverge at a rate prescribed by g_K. There are also no transitional dynamics: the growth rate jumps instantaneously whenever there is a change in parameter value.

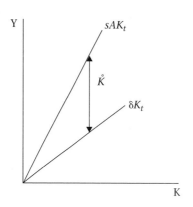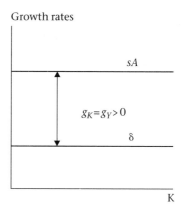

Figure 14.2 The *AK* model

The *AK* model is not a complete model because the *assumption* of constant returns to capital produces the result: it leaves unexplained why there are no diminishing returns to capital. However, it highlights the key component required of any model of endogenous growth: there must be constant returns to the factor (or factors) that can be accumulated. We shall see in the following sections how this is achieved in different ways by knowledge spillovers to capital accumulation, by the accumulation of human capital, and by research and development activity.

1.2 Knowledge spillovers and growth models

Our first complete model of endogenous economic growth was originally published in 1962 by Marvin Frankel.[2] He begins by considering the relative merits of the Cobb–Douglas as a neoclassical production function and an *AK*-type production function. He finds the neoclassical production function inadequate in the growth context:

[T]his approach leads to the unhappy consequence that growth in productivity takes place independently of growth in the capital stock. . . . This adaptation of the Cobb–Douglas function to a growth setting entails, in a sense, the sacrifice of a satisfactory explanation of growth itself.

On the other hand, he finds the *AK*-type production function useful for modelling growth at the aggregate level but unconvincing when applied to individual firms:

Economists have found such models attractive because of the emphasis they give to capital accumulation as an 'engine of growth'—an emphasis with deep roots in economic thought—and because of their pragmatically satisfying results. . . . Unfortunately the [*AK*] production function has nothing interesting to say about resource allocation or income distribution.

Frankel's contribution is to find a way of 'reconciling the two production functions so that the desirable properties of each, but none of the limitations, are retained'. The idea

---

[2] Frankel (1962). It was later developed with endogenous savings by Paul Romer in 1986.

is ingenious: the economy is populated by many firms, each of which is characterized by a Cobb–Douglas production function:

$$Y_i = K_i^\alpha (AL_i)^{1-\alpha},$$

where instead of A being an exogenous productivity factor as in the Solow–Swan model, it is modelled as the *outcome* of aggregate capital accumulation in the economy. Notice that knowledge enters the production function through labour, hence representing the idea that knowledge in the economy translates into skill at the micro level of the firm and thereby augments labour productivity. This is an example of the phenomenon known as 'learning by doing', which takes place through the accumulation of capital.[3] Thus, we have at the level of the firm

$$A_i = A_0 K^\eta$$

where η is a positive constant. It is assumed that each firm's knowledge is a public good in the sense that it is available to all other firms in the economy at zero cost. We can therefore aggregate across all firms to get an expression for economy-wide knowledge, A:

$$A = A_0 K^\eta,$$

where K is the aggregate capital across all firms in the economy. As we have seen, each firm takes A as given. However, the production function for the economy as a whole is:

$$Y = K^\alpha (AL)^{1-\alpha} = K^\alpha (A_0 K^\eta L)^{1-\alpha} = A_0^{1-\alpha} K^{\eta(1-\alpha)+\alpha} L^{1-\alpha}.$$

The features of the firm's and the economy's production function are as follows:

(1) for the firm, there are constant returns to scale and diminishing returns to capital, since A is constant for the firm.

(2) for the economy, there are increasing returns to scale ($\eta(1-\alpha) + \alpha + 1 - \alpha > 1$).

(3) The size of the knowledge spillovers from capital accumulation, η, will determine whether returns to aggregate capital accumulation are constant ($\eta = 1$), increasing ($\eta > 1$) or diminishing ($\eta < 1$).

It is immediately clear that if we take the special case of $\eta = 1$, where knowledge rises directly in proportion to capital,

$$Y = A_0^{1-\alpha} K L^{1-\alpha}.$$

In other words if there are constant returns to capital accumulation in terms of the accumulation of knowledge, then the aggregate economy is described by the AK model. This provides an explanation for endogenous growth (if $\eta = 1$) that is consistent with the presence of a neoclassical production function for the firm.

---

[3] The famous model of learning by doing was published by Kenneth Arrow, also in 1962.

Moreover, there are interesting insights from the knowledge spillovers model that go beyond its role in providing a microeconomic based story for the possibility of endogenous growth.

- First, it makes clear that a model of endogenous technological progress does not necessarily entail endogenous growth. If $\eta < 1$, then the economy grows at a rate independent of the savings/investment rate (unlike the AK model) but its output per capita does grow (unlike the Solow–Swan model). To see this, we take the production function: $Y = A_0^{1-\alpha} K^{\eta(1-\alpha)+\alpha} L^{1-\alpha}$ and look for a common exponential growth rate for output and capital. This requires us to take logs and differentiate with respect to time to get:

$$g_Y = [(\eta(1 - \alpha) + \alpha)]g_K + (1 - \alpha)n$$

and then set $g_Y = g_K$, to get

$$g_Y = g_K = \frac{(1 - \alpha)n}{1 - \eta + \eta\alpha - \alpha} = \frac{(1 - \alpha)n}{(1 - \alpha)(1 - \eta)} = \frac{n}{(1 - \eta)}.$$

The growth rate of output *per capita* in the steady state is $g_Y - n = \frac{n}{(1-\eta)} - n$ and therefore

$$g_y = \frac{\eta}{1 - \eta}n.$$

This contrasts both with the Solow–Swan model without technological progress, where $g_y = 0$ and the model with technological progress, where $g_y = x$, where x is exogenous. In our new model, growth of per capita output is due entirely to technological progress but this is now endogenous, in the sense that it arises from knowledge spillovers associated with capital accumulation. However, a higher savings/investment share does *not* raise the growth rate. This will only be the case when $\eta = 1$ i.e. in the AK case. The model also implies that faster population growth leads to faster growth of living standards, which is not a result that accords with the stylized facts of growth. The three cases are contrasted in Fig. 14.3.

- Second, the knowledge spillovers model raises an interesting policy issue. Since decision makers at the level of the firm take no account of the impact of their investment decisions on knowledge available throughout the economy, there is a difference between the optimal amount of investment from the perspective of firms and from the perspective of the economy as a whole. A social planner looking from the perspective of the economy as a whole takes into account the externalities that arise from capital accumulation. In this context the actions taken by a firm may not be *Pareto optimal* from the social point of view. This means that there are actions available that would make everyone better off without harming anyone. The reason they are not chosen is because firms fail to recognize an aspect of the decision process that is only properly internalized in the decision once we adopt the perspective of the social planner. In order to see to what extent this matters consider the problem of how much to invest in capital from the perspective of both the individual firm and the social planner. As we have seen in the analysis of investment behaviour in Chapter 7, firms pay a price given by the real interest rate for

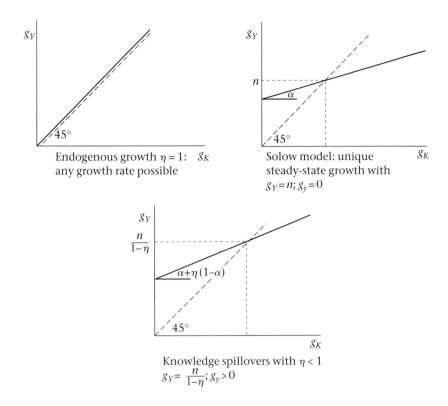

Figure 14.3 Knowledge spillovers lead to endogenous growth ($\eta = 1$) or exogenous growth ($\eta < 1$). Comparison with Solow

capital services and choose the optimal level of capital K_{it}^* they wish to implement such that it maximizes their profits. This means equating the marginal revenue product from installing an extra unit of capital with the real interest rate. From the social planner's perspective, the optimal capital stock will be chosen where the social marginal revenue product is equal to the real interest rate. So it all boils down to the difference between the private and social marginal revenue: the presence of externalities from capital accumulation means that $MRP_K > MRP_{K_i}$ and hence that the social planner will choose a higher level of capital stock than will characterize the decentralized economy. This provides a rationale for the government to introduce subsidies for investment.

1.3 Human capital accumulation

At a superficial level, models introducing human capital can provide yet another mechanism by which returns to capital stay constant as the economy accumulates more and more units of capital. Yet on a more fundamental level, by modelling human capital economists respond to the increasing realization that it matters for the long-run economic performance of an economy. This realization is driven not only by the correlations at the macro level of the kind discussed in Chapter 13 but also by the observations at firm level made by managers of successful businesses that enterprises that have highly skilled employees, diverse and meritocratic hiring policies, and a supportive corporate culture tend to outperform their competitors.

For investment in human capital to provide a means for avoiding diminishing returns to 'capital', an equation of the following form for the accumulation of human capital is needed:

$$\dot{h}_t = ch_t(1 - u_t), \tag{14.3}$$

as developed by Robert Lucas.[4] The amount of human capital per person available to the economy is h_t, the fraction of labour hours spent in education in order to learn new skills that can be used in production is $1 - u_t$, and c is a scaling parameter. Note that for this model to produce endogenous growth, the exponent on the stock of human capital must be exactly one. In other words, human capital accumulation is linear in the h—human capital grows in proportion to the existing stock. In the Solow–Swan model devoting more resources to capital accumulation via a higher savings rate raises the level of output per head but not the growth rate. The result is exactly the same in the MRW extension of the Solow model when the share of resources devoted to human capital accumulation is increased. In each case, diminishing returns to accumulation prevent a permanent growth effect from occurring. By contrast in the Lucas model, devoting more labour to human capital accumulation (as compared with production) raises the growth rate of human capital permanently and hence the rate of growth of per capita output.

The intuition behind the plausibility of constant returns is that there is a strong kind of dynamic feedback from education. It is certainly the case that some kinds of learning open the way for further learning without leading to diminishing returns. Whether this feedback is strong enough to merit the assumption of linearity remains an open question. The intensive production function corresponding to this model will then be given by:

$$y_t = Ak_t^\alpha (u_t h_t)^{1-\alpha}, \tag{14.4}$$

$$y_t = \underbrace{Au_t^{1-\alpha}}\ \underbrace{k_t^\alpha h_t^{1-\alpha}} = \Lambda \kappa_t. \tag{14.5}$$

If we can assume that u_t is constant, that is that for the economy as a whole the fraction of labour hours dedicated to work stays constant, we can simply rewrite the production function in the standard AK form by redefining $\Lambda = Au^{1-\alpha}$ for all time periods and $\kappa_t = k_t^\alpha h_t^{1-\alpha}$, which we can interpret to be a broad measure of capital for the economy, that includes both physical and human capital. This confirms that with the human capital accumulation equation in the above form, the model is one of endogenous growth: more time spent studying raises the growth rate permanently. We can say more about the implications of this model using the techniques used in Chapter 13. From the accumulation equation for human capital we can write the growth rate of human capital as

$$g_h = \frac{\dot{h}}{h} = c(1 - u), \tag{14.6}$$

---

[4] Lucas (1988).

which is constant under the assumption that u_t is constant. Let us now look at the 'Solow equation' for this model. This equation will of course be very similar to that of the standard Solow–Swan model with a constant exogenously given savings rate, except that we are using a different production function:

$$\dot{k}_t = s[Ak_t^\alpha(u_t h_t)^{1-\alpha}] - (\delta + n)k_t. \tag{14.7}$$

We can divide by k_t and rewrite this equation in terms of the growth rate for capital per worker and rearrange to obtain:

$$g_k = \Lambda\left(\frac{k}{h}\right)^{\alpha-1} - (\delta + n). \tag{14.8}$$

This expression provides another slant on the endogenous growth property of the Lucas model: it tells us that if a steady-state exists where capital per worker grows at a constant rate it is necessary for the ratio k/h to be constant. Of course this is only the case if both k and h grow by the same rate in the long-run. But we already know what the growth rate of human capital g_h is from equation 14.6.

To sum up, the Lucas model provides a mechanism for endogenous growth based on a broad measure of capital and a coherent economic story as to why the growth rate of output per worker is increasing in the time spent investing in education by learning skills that can be used productively later on. However, for endogenous growth to emerge, the strong assumption of constant returns to human capital accumulation (h) must hold.

Lucas's growth model has a further interesting contribution to make. He argues that human capital has an external effect as well, i.e. for a given level of my own human capital, the higher is the level in the economy, the higher will be my productivity. This notion of spillovers from human capital accumulation is sometimes discussed in terms of the concept of 'social capital' and refers not only to information flows and the sharing of ideas but also to the role of reciprocity and norms of behaviour.[5] This adds a term $\overline{h}^\varphi$ to the production function ($y_t = Ak_t^\alpha(u_t h_t)^{1-\alpha}\overline{h}^\varphi$): the bar indicates that for each agent in the economy, the level of economy-wide human capital is taken as constant (φ is called phi). The exponent $\varphi < 1$ measures the size of the spillover. The presence of this external effect is quite separate from the endogenous growth dimension of the model (as we have seen, endogenous growth depends on the linearity of the human capital accumulation process). It introduces the same potential role for government policy as was the case in the knowledge spillovers model: to the extent that the social return to human capital accumulation is greater than the individual one ($0 < \varphi < 1$), there is a case for subsidies to education.

1.4 Research and development

This section provides an introduction to the role of ideas and technological innovation as the engine of economic growth. The approach to technological progress in the Solow–Swan model places the process outside the realm of economic forces. There are two aspects

---

[5] As discussed, for example, in Putnam (2000).

to this: on the one hand, improvements in productivity appear like manna from heaven at no resource cost and on the other hand, access to the new technology is universal so it has the character of a public good that is not excludable. Both aspects are challenged in the growth models that put R&D at the centre of attention.

The Economist once called innovation 'the industrial religion of the twentieth century'. The inventors that push forward the boundaries of human knowledge through the discovery of new materials or goods represent only one part of the driving force behind technological progress. Innovation works through entrepreneurs who implement these discoveries and bring them successfully to the market. R&D is about innovation and firms dedicate billions of dollars to it. Naturally, as economists, we ask the question what difference does it make to the long-run performance of an economy?

The notion that innovation as the outcome of purposeful economic activity is ultimately the engine of economic growth can be traced back to the work of Joseph Schumpeter, an Austrian economist working at Harvard, writing in the first half of the twentieth century. Schumpeter identifies the entrepreneur as the key agent in innovation and distinguishes five major forms:[6]

- developing a new route by which existing factors of production are channelled into the production process;
- developing a new product or improving the quality of an existing product;
- developing a completely new production process for an existing product;
- introducing a completely new market, where there previously was none;
- changing the industrial landscape of an industry or economy through reorganization (vertical or horizontal mergers) that improve productive efficiency.

But the entrepreneur is a rather different creature from the benevolent social planner. The social planner is the fictitious agent we have used to investigate whether the actions of decentralized agents in the economy acting in their own interests produce the socially optimal outcome, i.e. the one the social planner would choose. While the social planner is motivated purely by the welfare of society, the entrepreneur is driven by profits. Thus, innovation can only happen if entrepreneurs can at least for a limited period of time earn profits in the market place. In order to understand why a framework of imperfect competition is both possible and necessary in order to facilitate the process of innovation we turn our attention to the nature of *ideas*.

In some sense, ideas are both the input and the output of innovation. R&D takes existing ideas from the pool of human knowledge, from calculus to physics and biology, and translates them into blueprints for new computers or drugs. As Schumpeter noticed however, innovation does not only generate new products, it may also lead to better products (the Pentium 4 is not a new product but rather an improvement upon the Pentium 3), or new markets (the entrepreneur who successfully introduced commercial photocopiers or home delivery of pizzas created a completely new market). The ideas that form the output of the innovation process however are different from many of the other goods we

---

[6] Schumpeter (1934; 1961 edition: 66).

encounter in everyday life and economists refer to them as possessing the properties of *non-rivalry* and *excludability*.

Non-rivalry refers to the use of an existing idea at zero marginal cost. Leibniz invented calculus in 1674 and since then everyone who has invested the effort in learning how to differentiate can perform this task without imposing any additional cost on anyone else. Of course not all goods are non-rivalrous, and it is the rivalrous nature of most natural resources that lies behind much human conflict. Most goods you encounter in everyday life are both excludable and rivalrous. If I cook dinner tonight, my use of these additional food resources comes at a marginal cost and I can prevent you (in most circumstances anyway) from eating my dinner. If I use calculus on the other hand, my use of the mathematical theory does not come at a marginal cost, nor does it prevent you from using the same mathematical methods.

But the ideas that result from innovation are different from other ideas. Economists often envisage them as blueprints, that is directions that can be put to productive use. Innovation results in blueprints on how to build the latest plane or what ingredients to put in the latest AIDS medicine. Of course once a blueprint becomes available, anyone who understands it can start to use it and market their own products based on it. This explains why we have generic drug companies that produce drugs that are chemically identical to their most famous branded cousins. Hence ideas in the context of innovation are non-rivalrous. However, they are excludable, since a firm can obtain a patent that will prevent other firms from using its blueprint for a given number of years.

The excludability property of ideas in the process of innovation naturally leads to an imperfect market structure in the market for blueprints. Patents allow firms to earn supernormal profits for a limited period of time and these profits can be used to finance R&D. Pharmaceutical companies invest billions of dollars in developing new drugs and without the protection of patents they would never be able to recover their costs. If drugs were marketed at marginal cost (think of how low the marginal cost of producing one pill is) they would soon go out of business and all innovation would stop. Thus above marginal cost pricing in the market for ideas is entailed by the intrinsic properties of ideas as blueprints and has to be guaranteed through an adequate legal system that protects the returns to innovation through patents.

To incorporate these notions into a simple growth model, we begin with a production function over capital and labour, but with a twist: we distinguish between workers who are employed in production and those employed in research. This is a very natural generalization of the standard Solow–Swan framework to an economic environment with more than one sector. We denote by L_t^Y the total number of workers employed in the final goods market. These are the workers that use the blueprints in conjunction with physical capital and raw labour to produce final goods. We also denote by L_t^R the number of workers employed in R&D. These are the researchers who increase the stock of knowledge in the economy through innovation. They create blueprints that will be later on be used in production by workers in the final goods sector.

We use a Cobb–Douglas production function for final goods:

$$Y_t = K_t^\alpha (A_t L_t^Y)^{1-\alpha}, \tag{14.9}$$

where A_t now stands for ideas, which is not an exogenous constant, but is rather an integral component of the model. Total labour in the economy at time t is given by $L_t = L_t^Y + L_t^R$, that is, the sum of the labour employed in the manufacturing sector producing the final output and the labour employed in the research sector producing intermediate blueprints. Total labour grows at a constant rate n and labour involved in R&D grows at the rate, n^R.

But what can we say about the accumulation equation for ideas? One general specification is:

$$\dot{A}_t = cA_t^\eta L_t^R, \tag{14.10}$$

which says that ideas accumulate proportionally to the number of workers L_t^R employed in R&D and proportional to the current stock of ideas A_t, for some constant of proportionality c. Let us try and think through the importance of the parameter η for the accumulation equation.

(1) From the earlier models, we know that if $\eta = 1$, there are constant returns to the accumulation of ideas and this will be a source of endogenous growth. This version of the model is often referred to as the Romer model.[7]

(2) For $0 < \eta < 1$, past knowledge exerts a positive externality on future innovation.

(3) For $\eta = 0$, the stock of ideas rises by an amount determined by the number of people involved in research (i.e. by cL_t^R).

(4) For $\eta < 0$, there is a negative externality of current knowledge on the accumulation of future knowledge. It seems rather unlikely that the more we know the more difficult it will be to innovate.

(5) For $\eta > 1$, there are increasing returns to knowledge. This corresponds to the case where the more we know the more accelerated the innovation process will be.

It is clear that we obtain completely different results depending on what assumptions about η are made in our analysis. There are two assumptions that have commonly been made in the literature: $\eta = 1$ and $0 < \eta < 1$. Let us first assume that $\eta = 1$. In this case the accumulation equation for ideas is simply given by

$$\dot{A}_t = cA_t L_t^R, \tag{14.11}$$

where we can now divide both sides by A_t to obtain the growth rate of ideas

$$g_A = cL_t^R. \tag{14.12}$$

But we have already seen when we discussed the Solow–Swan model with exogenous technological progress that this production function implies that the growth rate of output will equal the growth rate of ideas. This means that under the assumption that $\eta = 1$, the economy grows faster the more people are employed in the research sector. This may

---

[7] This is an outline of the model developed by Paul Romer (1990).

seem rather implausible especially if we also assume that L_t^R grows, in which case growth in the labour force employed in R&D leads to explosive growth in output.

As argued by Charles Jones, the unpalatable implications of the Romer model in terms of the scale effect can be eliminated by replacing the assumption that $\eta = 1$ with the assumption that $0 < \eta < 1$.[8] In this case the growth rate of ideas will be given by

$$g_A = cA_t^{\eta-1}L_t^R. \tag{14.13}$$

If a balanced growth path exists at the equilibrium it implies that $g_Y = g_K = g_A$, but in order for g_A to be constant at the equilibrium we need the ratio $L_t^R/(A_t)^{1-\eta}$ to be constant. This implies that $n^R = g_{A^{1-\eta}}$, that is, the labour force involved in innovation, grows at the same rate as $A^{1-\eta}$. We also know that this implies

$$n^R = (1 - \eta)g_A. \tag{14.14}$$

If we make the additional assumption that the proportion of workers employed across the R&D sector and the manufacturing sector stays constant, it will follow that $n^R = n$, which is an exogenously given constant depending on fertility and immigration policy. Substituting in the above equation and rearranging we obtain

$$g_Y = g_A = \frac{n}{1 - \eta}. \tag{14.15}$$

Economic growth in the Romer model as modified by Jones is therefore driven by population growth, n, and the extent to which the fertility of ideas profits from the already existing knowledge base in the economy, η. In terms of the effect of the research sector, it is the growth rate of the research sector that matters in this version (unlike in Romer's) and not its absolute scale. We shall return to this issue in the discussion of Schumpeterian growth.

This result is reminiscent of the one we derived from the knowledge spillovers model. When we allow for the endogenous generation of technical progress (in this case, through research and development activity; in the previous case, through unintended learning spillovers from capital accumulation) but stop short of making the linearity assumption required for endogenous growth, we find that there is a unique steady-state growth rate in the economy. As long as population growth is positive, growth in per capita GDP takes place and its speed depends on the strength of the returns to the accumulation of ideas.

Much of the interest in a model of growth based on the role of ideas lies with how the structure of a market economy can lead to the allocation of resources to the production of blueprints, i.e. how do we account for employment in the research sector of the economy? This is what interested Schumpeter and we investigate it in the following section.

---

[8] Jones (1995). See also the overview by Jones (2005), available at http://elsa.berkeley.edu/~chad/handbook200.pdf.

2 Schumpeterian growth models

Schumpeter's concept of creative destruction captures the dual nature of technological progress: in terms of 'creation', entrepreneurs introduce new products or processes in the hope that they will enjoy temporary monopoly profits as they capture markets. In doing so, they make old technologies or products obsolete—this is the 'destruction' referred to by Schumpeter. The idea of modelling innovation as 'vertical' in the sense that it takes the form of a quality improvement rather than 'horizontal' (the introduction of a new variety of good) allows Schumpeter's basic insight that new goods or techniques push out old ones to be formalized in an endogenous growth model. The most famous such model based on quality-improving innovations is due to Philippe Aghion and Peter Howitt.[9] In this section, we shall set out a simple version of the Aghion–Howitt model and explain how it provides the basis for a rich array of investigations into aspects of growth and development.

The motivation for innovators is to make a temporary monopoly profit by stealing a march on other producers. As noted in the discussion of the excludability property of innovations, this requires that the innovation (or new combination, in Schumpeter's words) cannot immediately be copied by an imitator. Formal patents are one method of protecting the temporary monopoly profits of the entrepreneur, trade secrets are another, and being the first mover into a market is a third.

Before introducing Aghion and Howitt's simplified version of their model of Schumpeterian growth, we can provide a link between the Solow–Swan model of growth with exogenous technological progress and a Schumpeterian model. In the Solow–Swan model, we can compare different steady-state growth paths for different rates of exogenous technological progress, x. As we have seen in Chapter 13, given the savings rate, population growth rate, and depreciation in the economy, a higher rate of technical progress implies a lower level of capital per efficiency unit of labour on the steady-state growth path (see Figures 13.10 and 13.11). This allows us to derive a downward-sloping relationship between the level of capital per efficiency unit of labour, $\hat{k}$, and x, the rate of technological progress, which in turn defines the growth rate of output per capita in the steady-state. This downward-sloping line is shown in Fig. 14.4 and labelled the 'Solow–Swan steady-state relationship'.

Next, a Schumpeterian element is introduced by modelling the determinants of x, the rate of technological progress, as a function of innovative activities:

$$x = \lambda \sigma q$$

where λ is the probability that each unit spent on R&D yields a successful innovation, σ is the extent to which each innovation raises the productivity parameter, and q is R&D intensity. Attention then turns to the economic determinants of q, each of which is taken to be exogenous by the entrepreneur. R&D intensity, q, is a function of the discounted

---

[9] For a comprehensive treatment, see Aghion and Howitt (1998). For a shorter and more accessible presentation, see Aghion and Howitt (2005).

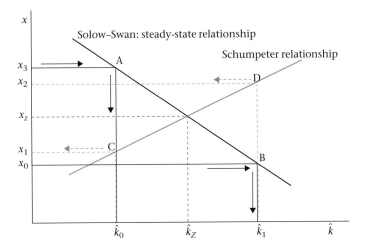

Figure 14.4 Endogenous determination of x, the rate of technological progress

value of expected returns and will depend positively on λ and σ, negatively on r the real interest rate, positively on $\hat{k}$, capital per efficiency unit, which can be thought of as an indicator of the size of potential markets for innovators, and on institutional features of the economy such as the extent of product market competition and how well the property rights on new innovations are protected from imitation:

$$q = q(\lambda, \sigma, r, \hat{k}, \text{competition, protection of property rights of innovators,} \ldots).$$

Since the rate of technological progress, x, depends on q, which in turn, depends on $\hat{k}$, we have a second relationship between x and $\hat{k}$. This positively sloped relationship is labelled the 'Schumpeter relationship' in Fig. 14.4. On the steady-state growth path, the economy is characterized by a growth rate of x_z.

We now consider two policy experiments—first, an increase in the savings ratio and second, an improvement in the returns to innovation due to a rise in λ or σ. If there is an increase in the saving rate in the economy, this shifts the Solow–Swan line outwards. This pushes up capital per efficiency unit (as in the standard Solow–Swan model with exogenous technological progress), which in turn prompts more R&D activity via the innovation (i.e. Schumpeter) equation. The economy moves to a new steady-state growth path fixed by a point to the north-east of point Z at point B in Fig. 14.5. In contrast to the Solow–Swan model, this means that higher saving produces a permanently higher growth rate. It is interesting to note as well that to the extent there is a causal link of this kind from capital per efficiency unit to R&D and via R&D to growth as suggested by the Schumpeter relationship, a regression framework such as the one used by Mankiw–Romer–Weil discussed in Chapter 13 will overestimate the direct contribution of capital to growth by ignoring the fact that part of its contribution is via the R&D that it stimulates.

In the second experiment, we assume that R&D becomes more fruitful. This shifts the Schumpeter line upwards. As a result, R&D intensity rises, which raises the rate of technological progress and the economy adjusts to a new steady-state growth equilibrium

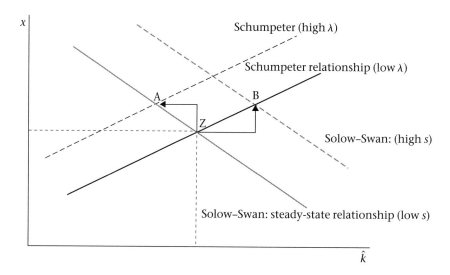

Figure 14.5 Policy experiments and endogenous growth: rise in savings; rise in productivity of R&D

to the north-west of point Z at point A. Similarly, better protection of innovation from imitators through, for example, more effective enforcement of property rights, shifts the Schumpeter line upwards and raises the steady-state growth rate. Conversely, the Schumpeter line is shifted down by a higher interest rate as this depresses the present value of expected profits from the innovation. By reducing the entrepreneur's expected profits, increased product market competition is predicted to have the same depressing effect on innovation and steady-state growth.

To move from a broad framework for discussing Schumpeterian growth to one in which the process of creative destruction itself is modelled requires specifying in more detail how innovation takes place. The fundamental relationship that we need to introduce is a so-called research arbitrage condition in which the marginal cost of R&D is equated to the expected marginal benefit. In order to show how to derive the arbitrage condition in a way that can be easily grasped, Aghion and Howitt provide a stripped-down version of their basic model. In this simplified model, there is no capital. There are two goods in the economy: final goods and intermediate goods. Innovation only takes place in the intermediate goods sector. The final good, Y, is produced using the intermediate good only (i.e. no labour is used in the production of the final good) and as quality improvements in intermediate goods take place, this raises the output of final goods. The production function for final goods is therefore written as:

$$Y = Am^\alpha$$

where m is the intermediate good and α is a constant less than one. A is the productivity parameter and in this model, it reflects the quality of the intermediate good. Any quality improvement of the intermediate good due to innovation will raise A. The key assumption necessary for the model of endogenous *technical progress* to produce endogenous *growth* is that each innovation raises the quality of the intermediate good from A to γA,

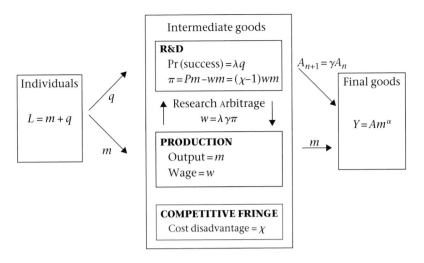

Figure 14.6 Schematic illustration of the Aghion–Howitt model of Schumpeterian growth

where $\gamma > 1$ and n is the nth innovation:

$$A_{n+1} = \gamma A_n.$$

This is where the 'constant returns' assumption that we have seen to be necessary to deliver endogenous growth appears in this model.[10]

The production function for the *intermediate good* is very simple: one unit of labour produces one unit of m. This means that m also measures the amount of labour used in the production of the intermediate good so the total labour force is split between the production of the intermediate good and R&D activity directed toward improving its quality:

$$L = m + q,$$

where q is the amount of labour devoted to R&D. It is assumed that the market for the final good is perfectly competitive. But in the intermediate goods sector, anyone who innovates has a monopoly for one period before the quality improvement is imitated by the other producers. Fig. 14.6 provides a schematic illustration of how the different elements of the model fit together.

Each individual in this economy lives for just one period and aims to maximize their consumption at the end of the period. The decision they face is how to maximize their consumption by making a choice between on the one hand, working in the intermediate goods sector and receiving a wage of w and, on the other hand, engaging in R&D in the hope of innovating and making monopoly profits. The return from engaging in R&D depends on the probability of success and it is assumed that the investment of q

---

[10] As Solow points out, if the effect of innovation on output takes a different form such as $A_{n+1} = A_n + \gamma$ instead of $A_{n+1} = A_n \gamma$, where n is the nth innovation, then growth will not be endogenous (Solow 2000: 177).

units of labour in R&D leads to a quality improvement with probability λq. Although a successful innovator has a monopoly in the production of the higher quality intermediate good, there is a so-called competitive fringe of producers who can produce the lower quality version of the good. The presence of the competitive fringe limits the price the innovator can charge. The unit cost of the competitive fringe is higher because they have not innovated and they can produce good m at a cost of χ (pronounced 'ki') units of labour, where $\chi > 1$ as compared to the one unit of labour required by the firm that has innovated. If the cost disadvantage of the competitive fringe is very large, i.e. $\chi \geq \frac{1}{\alpha}$, then the monopolist is able to charge the monopoly price and the extent of competition plays no role. In order to rule this out, it is assumed that $\chi < \frac{1}{\alpha}$. In this case, the maximum price that the innovator can charge is χw: at this price, the competitive fringe will not produce the intermediate good because they prefer to receive the wage, w. The profit for a successful innovator is equal to total revenue minus total cost and is higher, the higher is χ:

$$\pi = Pm - wm$$
$$= (\chi - 1)wm.$$

The two key equations are for the clearing of the labour market and the research arbitrage condition. Labour market clearing is, as we have seen:

$$L = m + q.$$

We now have all the ingredients for the research arbitrage condition:

$$w = \lambda\gamma\pi$$
$$= \lambda\gamma(\chi - 1)wm.$$

Substituting for m using the labour market-clearing equation gives:

$$\frac{1}{\lambda\gamma(\chi - 1)} = L - q$$
$$\Rightarrow q = L - \frac{1}{\lambda\gamma(\chi - 1)}.$$

This determines the amount of labour devoted to R&D in the steady-state. The growth of productivity in the steady-state will be equal to

$$x = \lambda q(\gamma - 1).$$

In words, productivity will grow according to the incremental size of the innovation, i.e. $\gamma - 1$, the amount of resources devoted to R&D, q, and the probability that R&D delivers an innovation, λ. By substituting the steady-state equation for q, we can see the set of determinants of the growth rate:

$$g_y = x = \lambda(\gamma - 1)[L - \frac{1}{\lambda\gamma(\chi - 1)}].$$

Growth in output per capita in this economy is permanently higher, the higher is the probability that R&D delivers an innovation (λ), the bigger is the incremental size of the innovation, γ, the larger is the size of the labour force, L, and the larger is χ. The role of the first two factors is clear.

However, the idea that a larger labour force per se or a larger number of R&D workers can increase the rate of growth forever does not accord with the facts: the fivefold increase in the number of R&D workers in the USA since the 1950s has not been accompanied by a change in the rate of productivity growth. Aghion and Howitt show how their model of Schumpeterian growth can be modified to eliminate this so-called scale effect whilst retaining the feature of endogenous growth. First of all they extend the simple model to allow for the existence of many varieties of the intermediate good. They then argue that the number of varieties proliferates as the economy grows and that in steady-state growth, extra R&D input is dissipated by being spread across all varieties so that there is no relationship in the steady-state between the size of the labour force and the growth of productivity. This produces a modified equation for steady-state growth:

$$g_y = f[\lambda, (\gamma - 1), (\chi - 1)]$$

in which the size of the labour force plays no role but in which the other determinants remain in place.[11] Policies that impinge on the research arbitrage equation so as to increase the share of resources devoted to R&D will raise the growth rate in this model.

It is interesting to contrast this way of eliminating a scale effect with the approach proposed by Charles Jones and discussed in section 1.4 above. Jones modifies Romer's model of R&D based endogenous growth: specifically, if past knowledge exerts a positive externality on future innovation but returns to R&D are not constant (i.e. $0 < \eta < 1$ where η is the exponent on the existing stock of blueprints in the accumulation equation for ideas: $\dot{A}_t = cA_t^\eta L_t^R$), then the growth of output per worker in the steady state will be:

$$g_y = \frac{n}{1 - \eta},$$

where n is the population growth rate. This means that the growth rate of living standards depends ultimately on the growth rate of R&D workers, which in turn depends on the population growth rate, n, which is exogenously given. In other words, Jones's approach entails reverting from endogenous ($\eta = 1$) to exogenous growth.

Aghion and Howitt provide some evidence from the USA for the post-war period to suggest that the data is more consistent with the prediction of their endogenous growth model that productivity growth should track the ratio of R&D expenditure to GDP (q in the model) than with the prediction from Jones's model that productivity growth should track the growth rate of R&D workers (n).

Finally, we turn to the role of χ in the Schumpeterian model. The higher is χ, the higher is the cost disadvantage of the non-innovating competitive fringe in the intermediate goods sector and as we have seen, this raises the profits for an innovator and hence is associated with a higher growth rate. χ can be interpreted as an inverse measure of

---

[11] This is explained in more detail in Aghion and Howitt (forthcoming 2005), section 5.

product market competition in the intermediate goods sector: in a more competitive economy, χ will be closer to one and the monopoly profits available to a successful innovator are lower. This captures Schumpeter's insight that stronger product market competition may blunt the incentive for innovation. However, Schumpeter also stressed the pro-innovation role of the competitive struggle to be the first to innovate. We turn next to providing an introduction to the debate about the role competition plays in innovation.

2.1 Product market competition and Schumpeterian growth

A broadly held view is that there was a causal connection between the absence of competitive forces in the communist economies and their limited ability to develop innovative products and processes. A notable exception where both innovation and competition were present was in the space race with the USA in which the Soviet Union made substantial innovations. Yet the simple model set out in the previous section predicts that a more competitive product market is associated with less innovation and lower growth.

A modelling framework has recently emerged that reconciles the basic Schumpeterian mechanism of creative destruction with our intuition that competition is good for growth but that too much competition can dampen innovation.[12] It is assumed that there is a leading edge technology in each sector at a global level. The economy we are concerned with is divided up into three different kinds of sectors according to whether the sector begins the period with technology at the frontier, one step behind or two steps behind. Innovation is always 'step-by-step', which means that a firm can only upgrade its technology by one step as a result of innovation activity: there is no leap-frogging. Just as was the case in the simple Schumpeterian model, it is assumed that in each sector there is a competitive fringe of firms that can produce the intermediate good at a higher cost by the factor $\chi > 1$. The other key assumption about the competitive fringe is that in all except frontier sectors it is assumed to be able to keep up with the prevailing quality level. So if in a one-step-behind sector, a firm innovates, this increases its productivity by γ and the productivity of the fringe also increases by γ. The innovator simply benefits from its cost advantage (because $\chi > 1$). By contrast, in a frontier sector, if a firm innovates, its productivity rises by γ but that of the fringe does not. The model assumes that the global technology frontier moves as follows:

$$\overline{A}_t = \gamma \overline{A}_{t-1}$$

where $\overline{A}$ is the frontier level of productivity and $\gamma > 1$. After firms have had the chance to innovate, the quality of the intermediate good produced by the competitive fringe rises with that of the sector if innovation has occurred (i.e. by γ), but can be no higher than $\overline{A}_{t-1}$.

Let us look at how competition affects innovation for firms in the different kinds of sectors. It is assumed that technology spillovers in the economy mean that it is not possible for sectors to stay more than two steps behind the frontier. This means that

---

[12] This work is based on Aghion et al. (2001). It is presented in Aghion and Howitt (forthcoming 2005), section 4.

there is no incentive for firms in two-step-behind sectors to engage in innovation since they will automatically upgrade their technology by the maximum possible of one step during the period. All attention is therefore focused on the one-step-behind and frontier sectors. If we take the one-step-behind sectors first, this is equivalent to the situation we discussed above: the returns to innovation will be higher, the higher is χ because weaker competition from the competitive fringe (higher costs) allows the innovator to charge a higher price and therefore make higher profits as a result of innovating.

But what of sectors at the frontier? At the frontier, an innovator not only produces at lower cost than the competitive fringe but also improves quality relative to the competitive fringe by the factor γ. In the frontier sector, an innovator stands to gain from innovation in quite a different way as compared with the one-step-behind case. In particular, as long as the advantage from innovation is large enough, the innovator in the frontier sector can establish a temporary monopoly in the sector and charge the monopoly price.[13] An increase in competition, i.e. a fall in χ, reduces the profits of a firm that does not innovate and by widening the gap between pre- and post-innovation profits, enhances the incentive to innovate so as to escape the competition. This option is not available in the one-step-behind sectors because the competitive fringe is always (potentially) viable there, which prevents an innovator from charging the monopoly price. In the presence of a competitive fringe, less competition stimulates innovation by raising the price the innovator can set.

To summarize, the impact of a change in product market competition on innovation and growth is ambiguous.

- For frontier sectors, the 'escape competition' effect dominates because more competition makes more attractive the carrot of monopoly pricing that would follow a successful innovation.

- For sectors inside the technology frontier, there is no chance to escape the competitive fringe and under such circumstances, more competition dampens innovation by lowering the successful innovator's mark-up.

There is interesting empirical support for the existence of both these effects in an analysis of the patenting activities of British firms. Aghion et al. (2005) use firm-level data from the UK on patents as a measure of innovation and on the price-cost margin as an inverse measure of the extent of competition in the product market.[14] When this relationship is plotted using a quadratic estimator (which allows for a non-linear relationship), the outcome is as shown in Fig. 14.7. The data suggest that the relationship is inverse-U, i.e. at low levels of competition, increased competition is associated with more innovation, whereas at high levels of competition, increased competition dampens innovation. This suggests that at low levels of competition, the 'escape competition' effect prevails,

---

[13] In the model set out in Aghion and Howitt (2005), this requires that $\frac{1}{\alpha} < \gamma\chi$. This possibility is ruled out for the one-step-behind sectors by the assumption that the cost disadvantage of the fringe is not too great ($\chi < \frac{1}{\alpha}$) and that there is a competitive fringe that can produce the same quality good whether or not a firm innovates.

[14] Aghion et al. (2005). Data kindly provided by Nick Bloom.

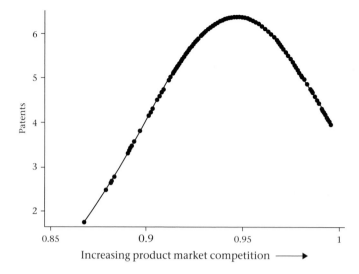

Figure 14.7 The relationship between innovation and competition: UK firms

whereas in a very competitive environment, the traditional Schumpeterian effect of an inverse relationship between competition and innovation dominates.

In general it is difficult to test the relationship between competition and innovation in a market economy because on the one hand it is hard to control for the fact that firms face very different innovation opportunities, and on the other hand those opportunities will lead to entry as new firms seek to take advantage of them. This in turn will alter the competitive environment. The end of the planning era in the former communist economies of Central and Eastern Europe and the former Soviet Union offers a unique opportunity to capture how competition affects innovation. With the removal of planning and the liberalization of markets, all firms face innovation opportunities and before an equilibrium in market structure emerges, there is the chance of observing how different competitive conditions are related to innovation and growth. Using firm-level data for over 3,000 firms in twenty-five transition economies, an inverse-U relationship is found (Fig. 14.8), which suggests that intense rivalry generates more growth at firm level.[15]

2.2 Convergence clubs and technology transfer

One of the notable features of the endogenous growth models introduced in the first part of this chapter is that they do not predict the convergence of growth rates across countries. Yet as we have seen in Chapter 13, at least for a set of countries, the presence of conditional convergence has been found in the data: this means that although the steady-state level of income per capita may differ across countries in the long run (according to the determinants of the steady state), countries grow at the same rate in the long-run. This long-run rate of growth is exogenous in the Solow–Swan model. In Chapter 13 we introduced the idea that convergence could take place through technology transfer

---

[15] Carlin, Schaffer, and Seabright (2004).

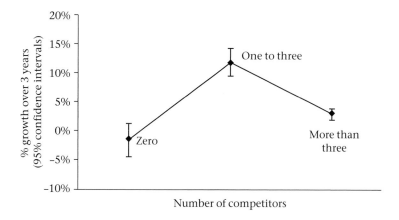

Figure 14.8 Average sales growth by number of competitors (3,288 firms in 25 transition economies)

as well as through capital accumulation. As we shall see, in the Schumpeterian model, convergence takes place through technology transfer and the same framework is used to explain the pace of technology transfer and the pace of innovation at the frontier.

An extension of the Schumpeterian model to a multi-country setting allows for the prediction that growth rates converge to be consistent with the presence of endogenous growth. The basic intuition stems from the idea of technological spillovers occuring across countries—i.e. by innovating, a country with a level of technology inside the world frontier can move up to the frontier level. The point is that innovation is not just associated with the pushing out of the global technology frontier but also with the ability of countries that are inside the frontier to adopt leading edge technologies. As long as there is innovation in a particular country, its economy in the long run will be characterized by productivity at a constant ratio of the frontier level: this means that in the long run, growth is the same as the rate at which the technology frontier is advancing. An economy with no innovation does not converge to the growth rate of the frontier. The same sort of factors are identified as determinants of innovation inside the frontier as of innovation at the frontier: e.g. property rights protection and the macroeconomic environment (the real interest rate).

A simple version of the model works in the following way. It is assumed that the world is characterized by many countries, in each of which there are many sectors producing intermediate goods. There is a technology leader in each sector. To make the model as simple as possible, it is assumed that a successful innovation takes the productivity level right up to that of the frontier. Hence the average productivity level in any country depends on the probability that innovation occurs; when it does not, productivity remains at the pre-existing level of the country. The productivity equation is therefore:

$$A_t = \mu \overline{A}_t + (1 - \mu)A_{t-1}$$

where μ is the probability of innovation, A_t is the average productivity in the country at time t, and $\overline{A}_t$ is the leading edge level of productivity. When there is a higher probability of innovation in the country, more sectors are at the frontier since they will have innovated recently. Hence average productivity is closer to the world frontier. In this model, the hypothesis that backwardness is an advantage is captured by the fact that whenever innovation takes place in a sector, it takes productivity up to the level of the frontier. Hence, the bigger the gap to the frontier, the larger is the size of an innovation and, hence, the larger is the impact on growth. It is assumed that the frontier level of productivity grows at the rate $x = \mu\sigma$ so that

$$\overline{A}_t = \overline{A}_{t-1}(1 + x).$$

By dividing the first expression by $\overline{A}_t$ and rearranging, we get

$$\frac{A_t}{\overline{A}_t} = \mu + (1 - \mu)\frac{A_{t-1}}{\overline{A}_{t-1}(1 + x)}$$

$$a_t = \mu + \frac{(1 - \mu)}{(1 + x)}a_{t-1},$$

where $a_t = \frac{A_t}{\overline{A}_t}$. In the long run, $a_t = a_{t-1}$, with the result that the economy converges to a fixed

$$a_t^* = \mu\frac{(1 + x)}{(\mu + x)}$$

if the probability of innovation, μ, is positive and to $a_t^* = 0$ if $\mu = 0$. In the latter case, output per capita does not grow at all and the economy stagnates. A world comprising a set of economies in which innovation occurs (i.e. $\mu > 0$) and a set with such poor institutions that innovation does not take place (i.e. $\mu = 0$) would be characterized by two so-called convergence clubs. In one club, countries would be converging to the same growth rate of living standards and in the latter, they would not participate in growth: living standards would therefore diverge between the two groups. In a fully specified model,[16] μ is the outcome of a research arbitrage condition in the same way as we have discussed above, i.e. according to the trade-off between the expected benefits and costs of engaging in innovation activities. This is the way in which the policy determinants of innovation feed through to pin down whether a country belongs to the convergence club or whether it will stagnate.

To summarize, growth in a lagging country will be higher

- the higher is the probability of innovation there. Such innovation takes the level of productivity up to the world frontier. This probability is higher the more favourable are the institutional conditions in the country for innovation. We return to the question of what these are in the next section.

- the bigger the size of the average innovation. This depends on the gap between the country and the frontier—a larger gap raises the size of the average innovation.

- the faster the growth of the international productivity frontier, which will depend on the factors that promote innovation.

---

[16]   See, for example, section 3 of Aghion and Howitt (forthcoming 2005).

- Any country in which innovation to take advantage of frontier technology exists will eventually converge to the same growth rate as the frontier; a country unable to innovate will not grow at all. The model therefore predicts the existence of convergence clubs in growth rates.

2.3 Appropriate institutions and economic growth

The Schumpeterian growth model can be enriched further by incorporating the insights of the Russian-born economic historian Alexander Gerschenkron, who taught at Harvard from 1948. Gerschenkron analysed the development of the follower countries of Germany, Russia, France, Italy, Austria, and Bulgaria. He argued that the late-comers to industrialization were able to grow more rapidly than the initiators by making use of different institutions. He brought together three arguments, two of which have already been introduced in the previous section:

- the first is that countries inside the technology frontier can catch up by investing resources in innovation,
- the second, is that catching up is easier, the larger is the gap to the frontier, and
- the third is that *different* institutions are conducive to catch-up as compared with innovation at the frontier and that institutional innovation is promoted by the 'tension between the promise of economic development as achieved elsewhere, and the reality of stagnancy. Such a tension motivates institutional innovation and promotes locally appropriate substitution for the absent preconditions of growth.'[17]

To sketch how Gerschenkron's analysis can be brought into the Schumpeterian growth framework, it is useful to introduce the distinction between 'imitation' and 'innovation'. Imitation refers to the process of adopting leading edge innovations in the 'backward' country and 'innovation' refers to the frontier. We have already encountered this distinction in the discussion of frontier, one-step-behind and two-steps-behind sectors above. Indeed, we have seen that the same 'institution' is predicted to have a different effect on innovation depending on whether the sector is on the technology frontier or is one step behind: more intense product market competition boosts innovation for frontier sectors but depresses it for one-step-behind sectors. Some of the countries that experienced the most impressive bursts of catch-up growth in the second half of the twentieth century such as Japan and Korea were characterized by policies that shielded industry from international competition combined with incentives to encourage firms to increase their share of export markets: firms in sectors at the frontier should be confronted with intense competition but protection should be afforded to those catching up. The logic of the argument set out in section 2.1 is that as a sector gets close to the world technology frontier, the importance of intense product market competition increases. One way to test this empirically is to use growth rate data from a large number of countries, for which the 'distance to frontier' can be gauged by the ratio of their GDP per capita to that in the USA at the outset of the period and to find a proxy for the extent of product market competition. Acemoglu, Aghion, and Zilibotti use a measure of a country's openness to

[17] Fishlow (1987). Gerschenkron's most famous statement of his argument is Gerschenkron (1962).

trade as a proxy for the extent of competition. They find that for countries that are a great distance from the frontier, openness does not affect their growth. However, it becomes of increasing importance, the closer a country gets to the frontier.[18]

To this point, backwardness has been an advantage in the sense that as long as the institutions in a particular country are conducive to R&D broadly interpreted to include imitation, catch-up is easier the larger is the gap to the frontier. However, if it is the case that the resources required for undertaking R&D depend on the ability of entrepreneurs to borrow to finance it, backwardness can hamper catch-up. As discussed in Chapter 8, the ability to borrow will be reduced by lower initial wealth (i.e. by backwardness itself) and by weaker institutions (e.g. by weak enforcement of the rights of creditors, which will make banks less willing to extend loans). This consideration implies that there will be a positive interaction between the level of financial development of a country and its level of backwardness. It also highlights how some forms of state intervention including the role of central planning in the industrialization of the Soviet Union and China, and of institutional development such as the emergence of the German universal banks, the Grossbanken, in the nineteenth century and of the integrated financial and industrial groups of East Asia (keiretsu and chaebols, for example) have been associated with rapid catch-up by mitigating the problems of limited access to finance for imitation.

In an empirical study using industry performance data and measures of the financial structure in countries, Carlin and Mayer find evidence that financial institutions play a different role in growth for countries at different stages of development.[19] In lower GDP per capita countries, a *more* concentrated banking system is positively related with growth in bank-dependent industries. By contrast, in the advanced countries, *less* concentrated banking systems and greater transparency of accounting information are associated with higher growth and R&D in industries that are dependent on equity finance. In terms of the distinction between imitation and innovation, it is likely that innovation is more important in equity-dependent industries and imitation in bank-dependent ones.

The distinction between imitation and innovation activities can be captured by writing the productivity equation for the intermediate goods sector as:

$$A_t = \underset{\text{imitation}}{\eta \overline{A}_{t-1}} + \underset{\text{innovation}}{\gamma A_{t-1}} \, ,$$

where productivity growth via imitation is captured by the first term (since this raises productivity by making use of the pre-existing technology frontier) and via innovation by the second term (since this raises productivity at the local level by the factor $\gamma > 1$). This expression brings together the two processes discussed separately before, i.e. the pure *imitation* process where $A_t = \mu \overline{A}_t + (1 - \mu)A_{t-1}$ where μ was the probability of imitation occuring and the pure *innovation* process where $A_t = \gamma A_{t-1}$. As before, we assume that the frontier progresses at the rate x so that

$$\overline{A}_t = \overline{A}_{t-1}(1 + x)$$

and as before define $a_t = \frac{A_t}{\overline{A}_t}$, which gives

$$a_t = \frac{1}{1 + x}(\eta + \gamma a_{t-1}).$$

[18] Acemoglu, Aghion, and Zilibotti (2002).   [19] Carlin and Mayer (2003).

This says that when the economy is far below the frontier so that a_{t-1} is close to zero, the distance to frontier depends mainly on imitation (η), whereas when the economy is close to the frontier so that a_{t-1} is close to one, the relative importance of innovation (γ) increases.

It is then clear that if the institutions that foster imitation differ from those that foster innovation, institutional change will be necessary as the economy approaches the frontier. As we have seen, one example of the sensitivity of institutions to the level of economic development is the hypothesis that stronger product market competition is more important close to the frontier. It has also been argued that whereas secondary education is important for imitation, tertiary education is essential for innovation, which takes on greater importance when countries come close to the frontier. In Chapter 13 we discussed the argument that education speeds up technology diffusion and noted the evidence that the interaction between the level of education and the technology gap is a significant determinant of the pace at which lagging countries catch up to the frontier. This insight is taken one step further if it can be established that some types of education are the key to pushing the technology frontier outwards and others to catching up. Some preliminary empirical evidence in support of this hypothesis comes from panel data on TFP growth in nineteen OECD countries for the period 1960–2000: a higher fraction of the population with tertiary education has a stronger effect in raising growth, the lower is the distance of the country from the technology frontier.[20]

The literature on varieties of capitalism suggests that there are complementarities between financial, labour market, and training/education institutions, which need to be respected if economies are to perform effectively. Moreover there are different patterns of complementarities across the OECD economies. Liberal market economies, such as the USA or the UK, work well with education institutions that produce general skills, with deregulated labour markets that promote job mobility and with financial markets that force firms to take rapid advantage of new profitable opportunities and allow for high-risk radical innovation. By contrast, coordinated market economies (e.g. Germany, Sweden, and the Netherlands) produce a labour force with vocational and company-specific skills, in which employees have representation within firms, there are well-developed welfare states to make such specific investments safer, and a financial system that provides 'patient' capital to companies. The comparative advantage of these economies is in incremental innovation and in the production of high quality goods and services, which require well-trained and experienced workers.[21]

3 Conclusions

In spite of the rich insights it provides, the Solow–Swan model remains silent on the fundamental question of what lies behind the steady rise in living standards observed for many countries over the past few centuries. This puzzle fuels the search for models of

---

[20] Vandenbussche, Aghion, and Meghir (2004).
[21] For an exposition of the varieties of capitalism hypothesis, see Hall and Soskice (2001).

endogenous growth. A number of plausible candidate mechanisms have been put forward that could prevent diminishing returns to capital from setting in and hence open up the possibility of endogenous growth:

- unintended knowledge spillovers to the economy as a whole as a consequence of capital accumulation,
- productivity growth through human capital accumulation, and
- the generation of new higher productivity blueprints through R&D activity.

In each case, in contrast to the Solow–Swan model, a policy or institutional change leads to *permanently* higher per capita GDP growth. In the case of knowledge spillovers, this follows a rise in the savings/investment share; in the case of human capital, it follows an increase in the proportion of time spent studying; and in the case of R&D, it follows an increase in the number of people working in the R&D sector. The special assumption of linearity in the accumulation process that is needed to produce endogenous growth remains controversial. However, even if knowledge spillovers, human capital accumulation, or R&D do not behave in the way required to produce endogenous growth, these processes enrich our understanding of growth. First, their presence can account for long-run growth in per capita GDP even when the growth rate is exogenous. Second, they bring to the fore the likely existence of a wedge between private and social returns to these activities, which provides a rationale for subsidies, e.g. for education or R&D.

Although models of endogenous growth succeed in finding a role for economic policy as a determinant of the long-run growth of living standards, they fail key empirical tests. In particular, their predictions of non-convergence do not accord with the empirical findings of cross-country convergence of growth rates. In the past decade much progress has been made in developing micro-based models of endogenous growth in the Schumpeterian tradition. One such development shows how it is possible to reconcile the presence of endogenous growth with predictions of convergence: a multi-country model is used in which the pace at which the frontier technology moves is determined endogenously and countries inside the frontier are able to catch up by investing in R&D. By broadening the concept of R&D to include the investments required to acquire and implement existing frontier technologies, the Schumpeterian model provides a unified framework for pinning down the determinants of innovative activity in the form of a so-called research arbitrage equation. It also accounts for the existence of convergence clubs: countries that do not innovate will not experience growing living standards, whereas countries that are able to benefit from technology transfer will move toward the frontier by growing faster than frontier countries. In the long-run, their growth rate will be the same as the rate at which the frontier is advancing.

The research arbitrage equation shows that resources devoted to innovation will be greater when the rewards are higher and when there is stronger protection from appropriation of innovators' temporary monopoly profits. Stable macroeconomic conditions, which reduce the real interest rate, and institutions that establish the rule of law are conducive to innovation and hence to growth. The role of some institutions is more subtle: more intense product market competition fosters innovation under some circumstances but hinders it under others. More broadly, once the distinction is drawn between imitation of frontier technology and innovation at the frontier, it is likely that some institutions will be most suited for fostering catch-up whilst others will be necessary for the development of new blueprints.

■ QUESTIONS

Checklist questions

(1) Does accepting that new technology is deliberately produced, and that a larger or smaller share of GDP may be devoted to it, imply that the long-run growth rate is endogenously determined?

(2) What is the distinction between exogenous and endogenous growth models? Does endogenous growth require a different definition of the steady-state of the economy than the one we used in the Solow–Swan model?

(3) We have seen how the *AK* model serves as the prototype for endogenous growth models and how changes to the Solow–Swan modelling framework can lead to endogenous growth (e.g. knowledge spillovers). Starting from the Solow–Swan model described in the previous chapter, can you think of any additional assumptions (not already covered in this chapter) that can produce a model with endogenous growth?

(4) Given that knowledge is an international commodity, would you expect its impact to be the same in all countries?

(5) Choose three models covered in this chapter and contrast the mechanisms through which they may explain cross-country heterogeneity in long-run economic performance.

(6) Consider the data in Fig. 14.9 from a recent UNICEF Report (April 2005), which shows the distribution of children of primary school age who are not attending school in different regions of the world. Choose one of the models introduced in this chapter and explain how you would expect the distribution of per-capita GDP and long-run economic growth rate to vary by region of the world.

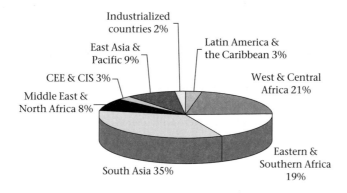

Figure 14.9 Percentage of primary school age children not attending school, by region, 2001

(7) Does unemployment matter for economic growth?

(8) Can R&D models of endogenous economic growth explain regional differences in long-run economic performance? Can geography affect knowledge spillovers?

(9) Can the European colonization of Africa and Latin America help explain heterogeneity in the long-run economic performance of the developing world? (Hint: Think of the effect of institutions e.g. property rights, on economic growth.)

(10) 'Monopoly profits are necessary to provide an incentive for innovation'; 'Competition in the product market is a spur to innovation.' Are these two statements contradictory? Explain using the Schumpeterian growth model.

(11) By December 2004, the World Health Organization reported that in Africa 8% of 15–45-year-olds with AIDS who needed antiretroviral therapy were receiving it. Should pharmaceutical companies be allowed to enforce patents for AIDS drugs? (The data is reported in WHO (2005). '3 by 5' Progress Report: **www.who.int/3by5/progressreport05/en/**.)

(12) Anti-globalization activists argue that economies need to be localized and empower small local investors in order to promote human welfare in the long run. (See for example, Korten (2001).) Do you agree? Use the Schumpeterian models introduced in this chapter to argue for or against this statement.

Problems and questions for discussion

QUESTION A. Consider the model of economic growth with spillovers introduced in section 1.2 of this chapter. Explain why we need to have many firms with an identical production function. Do you find the functional form of the firms' production function realistic? Explain. Do you find the functional form of the economy-wide production function realistic? Explain. Assume that the economy with $\eta = 1$ experiences an unexpected increase in A to $\tilde{A}$. Describe its effect. Can this model explain cross-country heterogeneity? Does this model imply unconditional or conditional convergence?

QUESTION B. In many countries rural to urban migration is a significant phenomenon. Table 14.1 shows the growth of the urban population over the past half-century in China.

Consider the effect of rural to urban migration on the model of R&D introduced in section 1.4 of this chapter. You may wish to make the strong simplifying assumptions that the economy consists of two sectors, rural and urban, which manufacture goods and ideas respectively. Furthermore, assume that the migration is driven by higher wages. Initially wages in both the rural and urban sectors are the same, but as the economy expands wages in the urban sector increase while those in the rural sector remain unchanged. Describe the long-run growth path of this economy.

QUESTION C. 'In rural Western Kenya, the Ministry of Agriculture recommends the use of hybrid seeds and fertilizer to increase maize yields. This recommendation is based on evidence from experimental farms that fertilizer substantially increases yield. In 2000, however, according to a survey we conducted in a random sample of farmers, just 45%

Table 14.1 Urban population growth in China

Year	% urban population
1952	12.5
1977	17.3
1990	26.4
1999	30.9

Source: China statistical yearbook, 1999.

of farmers had ever used fertilizer, and just 15% had used fertilizer in the year before.' (Duflo, Kremer, and Robinson (2005).)

Using the concepts discussed in this chapter (e.g. learning spillovers, social capital, financial development) describe your intuitions of why so few people use fertilizer even though it has a clear potential to improve economic prosperity. What are the implications of this outcome for the prospect of long-run economic growth? Can you think of policy tools to alleviate this problem?

QUESTION D. Consider the following quotation from Kremer (2004).

Malaria, tuberculosis, and the strains of HIV common in Africa kill 5 million people each year, almost all of them in low-income countries. Effective vaccines against these diseases are desperately needed. Yet there is a striking dearth of research and development (R&D) on vaccines and treatments for diseases primarily affecting poor countries. Of the 1,233 drugs licensed worldwide between 1975 and 1997, only 13 were for tropical diseases, and only 4 of those were specifically developed by commercial pharmaceutical firms to treat tropical diseases in humans. Half of all global health R&D in 1992 was undertaken by private industry, but of that, less than 5 percent was spent on diseases specific to poor countries.

Consider the Schumpeterian growth model and take health as exogenous to the model. Discuss the effect of the lack of advanced healthcare on the growth prospects of a low-income economy. Now endogenize health by assuming that it is possible for at least part of the R&D effort of this country to be focused on health. How will this change the discussion above? Can the government help through regulation or institutional change? Evaluate the importance of technological transfers from abroad for these low-income economies.

PART FIVE

Micro-Foundations and Political Economy

15 New Keynesian Microfoundations

In the twentieth century macroeconomics was frequently the scene of fierce debates between advocates of fundamentally different perspectives and methodologies. In the current period, although differences remain, the middle ground of consensus is far broader. There is agreement that a satisfactory macroeconomic model should allow for wage and price rigidities, should be based on optimizing behaviour by micro agents, and that individual behaviour should satisfy rational expectations. To summarize, the features that characterize mainstream models used for macro policy analysis are:

- imperfectly flexible wages and prices associated with imperfections in labour and/or product markets;
- rational intertemporal optimizing behaviour of all agents;
- rational expectations.

The aim of this chapter is to set out a unified framework to show where the mainstream New Keynesian macro model with microfoundations comes from. In most of this book, we have used a stripped down macro model of this kind: we have chosen to prioritize the ability of the model to better match the stylized facts over the desirability of satisfying the requirements for fully rational and optimizing behaviour. Although for the most part, the implications of the model that we have used in the book are in line with those of a microfounded New Keynesian model, we highlight in this chapter some important cases where this is not so. We also show that the New Keynesian model is still under construction—important issues remain unresolved.

Keynesian economics developed in the 1930s as a reaction to the inability of the neo-classical economics of the inter-war period to explain the Great Depression in which unemployment in the UK and in other countries remained above 20% for several years. Such unemployment was clearly involuntary. The neoclassical orthodoxy held that, with perfectly competitive labour and product markets, flexible prices and wages would act as market-clearing mechanisms and would eliminate involuntary unemployment: it argued that the consistent application of competitive micro foundations had no other conclusion. Keynes took issue with this view in his 1936 *General Theory*, arguing that even with competitive markets and flexible prices, there could be involuntary unemployment in equilibrium. Keynes went to some lengths in the *General Theory* to base his microfoundations on perfect competition, which makes somewhat ironical the recent use of the term 'New Keynesian' to refer to models that generally incorporate imperfectly competitive microfoundations.

While the *General Theory* has had an enormous subsequent impact on macroeconomic analysis, its major force has been on the need to understand aggregate demand as the key factor in the short and medium run in driving output and employment away from equilibrium. In two important ways, the *General Theory* has been less successful: first, Keynes's position that aggregate demand could determine *equilibrium* output and employment and thus explain persistent involuntary unemployment is now taken less seriously. As has been the position in this book, equilibrium output and employment are today seen largely as supply side phenomena determined by the structural characteristics of product and labour markets—although multiple equilibria and hysteresis mechanisms provide routes through which aggregate demand can influence the medium-run equilibrium, and a range of constant inflation equilibria characterize the open economy. Second, Keynes's microfoundations of competitive markets with flexible prices and wages are not seen as adequate even to explain why aggregate demand should keep output away from equilibrium in the short run.

On the contrary, it is now widely accepted that if there are perfectly competitive product and labour markets with price flexibility, and if there is complete information and rational expectations, output and employment will never deviate from equilibrium. We shall refer to this as the neoclassical benchmark model (NCBM). The limitation of the NCBM is not a theoretical one: given its assumptions, it is fully coherent. Its problem is that it fails to predict some of the most important empirical facts about macroeconomic behaviour. What are these stylized facts?

(1) First and foremost, output and employment appear to deviate from their equilibrium values for considerable periods of time. It is useful to decompose this fundamental empirical problem into three parts:

- The initial impact of an increase in aggregate demand is on output and employment not on prices and wages (as should happen with competitive markets).

- An initial demand shock may be amplified by subsequent changes in consumption and possibly investment as incomes change.

- Inflation only responds slowly to disequilibrium situations: it displays 'inertia'. This is what we have so far captured in the inertial or backward looking Phillips curve in the basic New Keynesian model.

(2) In addition, there are two stylized facts about the character of equilibrium:

- Some part of equilibrium unemployment is involuntary.

- There may be multiple equilibrium output and employment rates.

The challenge in constructing a New Keynesian macro model has been to see whether it is possible to account for these facts while maintaining the assumption that individual agents behave and form their beliefs rationally. Central to meeting this challenge has been the view that prices and wages are set by firms (and perhaps also by unions) rather than resulting from a Walrasian process of market clearing through flexible prices and wages. The dominant New Keynesian approach has been that price-setting firms, and perhaps wage-setting unions, are assumed to operate under conditions of imperfect competition, for example as differentiated monopolists. This explains why output and employment rather than prices respond to changes in aggregate demand. Additional assumptions are introduced that generate slow adjustment of prices and wages. Thus the key assumption of the neoclassical benchmark model, that there is perfect competition and perfectly flexible prices and wages, is rejected. However, the issue of how best to explain precisely why prices and wages adjust slowly in response to disequilibrium and how inertial inflation is produced remains controversial. We set out two much debated approaches: the New Keynesian Phillips curve and the Sticky Information Phillips curve. The assumption of imperfectly competitive markets also provides microfoundations for the existence of involuntary unemployment. The mainstream New Keynesian model incorporating an interest-rate based monetary policy rule provides the framework for policy making in central banks and governments in many countries.

It is now accepted that macro models should be anchored in microfoundations with optimizing agents who have rational expectations and hence that such models should be immune to the Lucas critique (i.e. it should be presumed that private agents take into account the future response of policy makers when choosing their actions). This methodology characterizes microfounded New Keynesian models. It is however due to the contributions of economists coming from the neoclassical rather than the 'Keynesian' tradition. The seminal article about rational expectations by John Muth was published in 1961. Muth stated concisely what he meant by rational expectations:

In order to explain fairly simply how expectations are formed, we advance the hypothesis that they are essentially the same as the predictions of the relevant economic theory. In particular, the hypothesis asserts that the economy generally does not waste information, and that expectations depend specifically on the structure of the entire system.[1]

This innovation in the modelling of expectations was followed by a set of papers by Robert Lucas, Finn Kydland, and Edward Prescott, amongst others, who applied it to macroeconomic questions.[2] We have discussed the ideas of policy credibility and the Lucas critique in Chapters 3 and 5 and we return to them later in this chapter as we build up the microfoundations of a New Keynesian model based on rational expectations.

In addition to contributing the analysis of rational expectations and policy credibility to mainstream macroeconomics, these economists have established the foundations of a research programme that has sought to match the empirical facts of macroeconomic behaviour by building models of macroeconomic fluctuations as *equilibrium phenomena*. A fundamental feature of this approach is that agents are always able to optimize: for example, in a business cycle trough, employees choose to supply less labour. A feature common to models in the Lucas tradition is that the intertemporal elasticity of labour supply plays an important role in propagating shocks.[3] This means that consumers freely choose between leisure and consumption each period and will respond to shocks by raising or lowering their supply of labour. By comparison, in the New Keynesian approach, business cycles are normally characterized as fluctuations about the equilibrium and are therefore modelled as *disequilibrium phenomena*.

---

[1] Muth (1961: 315).   [2] Lucas (1972); Kydland and Prescott (1977).
[3] Landmark articles include the following: Kydland and Prescott (1982); Long and Plosser (1983).

In real business cycle (RBC) models it is technology shocks that drive business cycles. These models represent a view of business cycles that is quite distinct from the mainstream New Keynesian one: whereas cyclical behaviour is traditionally thought of as representing an inefficient phenomenon—overheating in the boom and underutilization of resources in the trough—the RBC presumption is that cycles reflect the optimizing decisions of agents to increase and decrease their supply of labour in response to technology shocks, which alter their opportunities to produce. Despite differences of emphasis as to the origin of the disturbances to the economy and the way shocks are propagated, the RBC tradition has influenced the mainstream in two ways: first, in highlighting the importance of modelling how the equilibrium level of output is determined. Although New Keynesian models are concerned with persistent departures from equilibrium due to fluctuations in aggregate demand, they also analyse supply shocks and incorporate the determinants of the evolution of the equilibrium level of output and employment.

Second, RBC economists have developed a new method of theoretical and empirical investigation known as Dynamic Stochastic General Equilibrium modelling (DSGE). Since real business cycles relate to fluctuations of the equilibrium level of output, such models provide a natural way of integrating growth and business cycle analysis. They introduce uncertainty in the form of random shocks in the production function. These are highly stylized general equilibrium models that are complex and have to be solved by numerical methods. The procedure is to use microeconomic evidence from other studies to provide estimates for the underlying technology and preference parameters. Using these values for the parameters, the model is then calibrated and can be used to provide predictions about the key variables in the model and how they co-vary, which are compared with macroeconomic data from the economy. Since the microeconomic foundations are well specified, such models are suitable for conducting welfare analysis.

In the two decades since these early DSGE models were developed, the methodology has been used increasingly broadly and New Keynesian features have been introduced to them. The methodology has proved useful in a range of settings and is now applied in central banks to complement more traditional econometric modelling techniques. For example, the Bank of England has developed a new macro model (NMM) that incorporates many of the principles of DSGE modelling. As compared with its existing model, the NMM is more theoretically coherent but unlike the DSGE models used in academic settings, the Bank of England's uses pragmatic modifications to better match the dynamics in the data. This relates both to the incorporation of inertia in behaviour in the NMM and to a less complete specification of the nature of shocks than is the case in academic DSGE models.[4] It remains to be seen how the NMM will be used in practice by the Bank of England's Monetary Policy Committee.

The most fundamental contribution of the Lucas tradition in macroeconomics has been to emphasize the requirement for macroeconomic models to have well-specified foundations in microeconomic behaviour. As the discussion about the Bank of England's new model makes clear, this is easier to achieve in academic models than those on which policy makers must rely.

---

[4] For a clear and accessible discussion of the Bank of England's models, see Pagan (2003).

In the remainder of this chapter, we pull together the microfoundations for a New Keynesian macroeconomic model. As noted above, we begin by providing a neoclassical benchmark model with which the New Keynesian model is compared. Section 1 sets out a summary of the argument developed in the rest of the chapter.

1 Summary of the argument

The characteristics of the New Keynesian model that we have used in the earlier chapters of the book are as follows:

(1) There is involuntary unemployment in equilibrium.

(2) Supply-side features of the economy determine equilibrium unemployment.

(3) Aggregate demand shocks can shift output in the economy away from equilibrium: this means that it is output and employment rather than wages and prices that respond initially to such shocks.

(4) Aggregate demand shocks may be amplified through the operation of the multiplier, i.e. consumption responds to changes in output. Other channels through which amplification can occur are set out in Chapter 7. Aggregate demand shocks may also be dampened in the New Keynesian model to the extent that the proportion of households able to lend and borrow is large enough and they rationally anticipate the response of the central bank to aggregate demand shocks.

(5) The inertia of inflation allows the disequilibrium—i.e. output either above or below equilibrium—to persist.

(6) The central bank is forward looking and guides the economy back to equilibrium by using a reaction function to change the interest rate in response to inflation, aggregate demand, and supply shocks.

(7) Multiple equilibria may exist because of variations in labour productivity or in the elasticity of demand at high and low output.

(8) The persistence of output away from equilibrium may itself affect the supply side, and hence equilibrium unemployment. This is known as hysteresis.

(9) The introduction of considerations that affect workers' utility other than consumption and leisure, such as fairness, may lead to the existence of a range of equilibrium employment rates.

In earlier chapters elements of microeconomic behaviour were introduced—for example, models of consumption and investment behaviour based on rational behaviour of households and firms were set out in Chapter 7, where we also sketched how the microfounded models would affect the *IS* curve. We also developed an optimizing model of central bank behaviour as the basis for the central bank's reaction function. Similarly, we sketched the role of optimizing behaviour by wage setters as the basis for the *WS* curve and of price setters for the *PS* curve. The task of this chapter is to integrate the microeconomic components into a New Keynesian model. This section summarizes the arguments that lie behind the nine characteristics listed above and they are discussed in detail in the remainder of the chapter. This introductory summary may be skipped by those who prefer to go straight to the equations. Alternatively, those who prefer words may read this section and skip the rest of the chapter.

It is useful to begin with a benchmark model in which markets are complete and competitive against which the New Keynesian assumptions are then compared. We call this the neoclassical benchmark model: NCBM. The first step is to model the two key decisions of households: to supply labour and to consume. Households are modelled as making consumption and labour supply decisions so as to maximize their intertemporal utility. They are assumed to derive utility from consumption and from leisure, subject to a budget constraint. The budget constraint specifies that consumption plus saving in a given period are equal to income from employment and interest income on their pre-existing wealth. The household takes as given the wealth it has accumulated in the past, the interest rate and the prices it faces in the markets for labour and goods, i.e. the real wage. This enables us to derive optimal consumption and labour supply behaviour over time, given the basic parameters of the model. Before proceeding further we use this approach to show how a simple real business cycle model can be constructed, in which employment decisions are optimizing choices by households in the face of technology and preference shocks.

In the NCBM we introduce a simplification to allow the optimal consumption and labour supply decisions to be treated separately. A commonly used specific form of the consumption function is chosen and the utility maximization problem is solved, treating labour income as given. This leads to the result of the consumption-smoothing model (also shown in Chapter 7), i.e. households choose to keep consumption constant over time when the real interest rate is equal to the discount rate. If the interest rate exceeds the discount rate then lower consumption is chosen this period than the next since it is worthwhile to postpone consumption and enjoy higher consumption in the future.

The labour supply curve is derived from the same household utility maximization problem, but to allow for a tractable labour supply curve, the consumption decision is simplified. Labour supply is a positive function of the wage—reflecting the disutility of work. In the NCBM production takes place under perfect competition with the result that the real wage is equal to the marginal product of labour. The simplification of constant labour productivity is made throughout the chapter, and this implies that the labour demand curve, which is also the average and marginal product of labour curve, is horizontal and equal to labour productivity. By combining the production sector with household labour supply, the equilibrium in the labour market is determined. This pins down the unique market-clearing level of employment and the real wage, which can be directly compared with the equilibrium under imperfect competition.

The modelling of household behaviour brings out a second point of comparison with the New Keynesian model: the role of consumption-smoothing in the *IS* curve. Throughout this chapter we follow the common practice—adopted for convenience in New Keynesian models—of omitting investment from the *IS* curve. This allows us to concentrate on how the inclusion of consumption smoothing affects the model. The microfoundations of investment behaviour are set out in Chapter 7. The *IS* refers to goods market equilibrium, where demand comprises consumption and a second exogenous component, which includes government expenditure. The consumption-smoothing model says that consumption this period is equal to consumption next period plus a component that depends negatively on the real interest rate (holding the discount rate constant). As we have seen, the second component drops out when the interest rate is equal to the discount rate. The presence of consumption-smoothing means that the *IS* curve includes the expected future values of output and exogenous demand. This is called the forward-looking *IS* curve: it is integral to the NCBM and we shall see that if it is brought into the New Keynesian model, it introduces a mechanism through which business cycles are dampened.

However, in the NCBM, aggregate demand and hence the *IS* play a very limited role: because markets clear instantly and there are no imperfections, the economy is always at equilibrium output. The role of the *IS* curve is to fix the real interest rate. Given equilibrium output, a fall in exogenous demand implies that higher consumption expenditure must be 'crowded in' to bring demand up to equilibrium output and this requires a lower real interest rate. The way that this happens is through the effect on the real money supply of changes in the price level brought about by excess demand. In our example of a fall in aggregate demand, the price level falls and according to the *IS* curve, this requires a lower real interest rate to compensate for the fall in demand. A fall in the price level raises the real money supply and this lowers the interest rate.

To complete the description of the NCBM, it is necessary to discuss inflation and the monetary rule. With output always at equilibrium, there are no short-run Phillips curves: only the vertical Phillips curve is relevant. The monetary rule is therefore very simple: the optimizing central bank simply has to set inflation equal to its target. The NCBM is summarized in a horizontal *IS* curve at the stabilizing interest rate, by a vertical Phillips curve at the unique equilibrium unemployment rate and by a horizontal *MR* curve at target inflation (see Fig. 15.3). In section 2, we set out the equations that deliver these results.

Having set up this benchmark model, it is then possible to bring in the modifications that are required to deliver the New Keynesian model. We introduce product and labour market imperfections in the simplest way in the form of a monopoly producer and a monopoly union. As usual firms maximize profits and it is assumed that the union maximizes the utility of its members, which is modelled in exactly the same way as that of households above. The economy is modelled as comprising a number of sectors, each of which produces a differentiated product. What happens is that the union in a particular sector chooses the wage and then the firm chooses the price. However, since the firm's choice of its relative price affects employment in the sector and employment (as well as the wage) enters the union's utility function, the union must take into account how the price is set when making its wage decision. The outcome of firm and union behaviour once all sectors have set wages and prices is a price-setting curve below the average (= marginal) product of labour curve (which is the NCBM equivalent of the price-setting curve in the New Keynesian model) and a wage-setting curve above the neoclassical labour supply curve: hence equilibrium employment is lower than in the NCBM and if we take the real wage at equilibrium employment in the New Keynesian model, there are households that would be willing to supply labour at the equilibrium real wage. Hence there is *involuntary unemployment in equilibrium*. This is result number 1.

The gap between the equilibrium employment rate in the New Keynesian model and the NCBM depends on two key parameters, which are defined as real wage pushfulness and real wage rigidity. We use the term *real wage pushfulness* to refer to the disparity between the wage- and price-setting curves at the labour market-clearing (or 'natural') unemployment rate. This disparity reflects the factors that push the price-setting curve below the marginal product of labour curve and the wage-setting curve above the labour supply curve. It is increased by a less competitive product market for two reasons: most straightforwardly, a higher mark-up by firms reduces the price-determined real wage. On the other hand, the lower elasticity of demand that lies behind the higher mark-up leads unions to set a higher wage since the perceived impact on employment of a given wage increase is lower. This behaviour pushes the wage-setting real wage up. The upward shift of the wage-setting curve and the downward shift of the price-setting curve result in lower equilibrium employment. In our simple model, there is a monopoly union so it is not possible to increase union power. However, in a richer model with union bargaining, real wage pushfulness would also increase with union bargaining power. *Real wage rigidity* is the slope of the wage-setting curve and is a function of the disutility of work parameter. The interesting result is that it is the interaction of this feature of individual behaviour (the disutility of work) and imperfect competition that has the effect of widening the gap between equilibrium employment in the New Keynesian model and the NCBM when the disutility of work is higher. This is result number 2: *Supply-side features of the economy determine equilibrium unemployment.*

The New Keynesian feature that it is output rather than prices that respond first to aggregate demand shocks requires the presence of imperfect competition in the product market. It is useful to show first that with perfect competition, there will be no response in output to a change in aggregate demand when prices are held fixed. Profit maximization under perfect competition requires that price be equal to marginal cost. If prices and wages are held constant and there is a fall in demand, firms will not alter output since neither price nor marginal cost has changed. (Of course this highlights the oddity of the assumption that prices cannot fall to clear the market in a situation of perfect competition.) However, once we move to imperfect competition, hold prices fixed, and take a fall in aggregate demand as an example, then a profit-maximizing firm will cut its output in line with the fall in demand. At this level of output, its behaviour is optimal given the fixed price: higher output could not be sold (so marginal revenue would be zero) and lower output would entail the loss of profits on the marginal unit sold. This is result number 3: *Aggregate demand shocks shift output in the economy away from equilibrium. This means that it is output and employment rather than wages and prices that respond initially to such shocks.*

We turn now to the question of the magnitude of the effect of a change in exogenous aggregate demand on output. We have just seen that in the NCBM, the effect is zero. In the New Keynesian model, there are three possible outcomes of a negative aggregate demand shock: output could fall one-for-one with the fall in demand or it could fall by more or by less.

- When it falls one-for-one with a fall in exogenous aggregate demand this is consistent with consumption-smoothing—i.e. consumption is not a function of current income so it does not change when aggregate demand and income does.

- When it falls by more, the demand shock is amplified and this is associated with the traditional multiplier process. In order for the multiplier to appear in a model with consumption-smoothing, it is necessary to assume that some proportion of households are prevented from optimally smoothing their consumption because they are unable to borrow and they do not have accumulated assets. We explored this in detail in Chapter 7.

- When it falls by less, the demand shock is dampened. This is the case with the forward-looking *IS* curve introduced above, in which output this period depends on expected output next period. The way this works in the New Keynesian model is that when a shock has occurred, forward-looking households anticipate that the central bank will intervene to stabilize the economy by cutting the interest rate. Since a lower interest rate means that households prefer higher current relative to future consumption, they will respond to the negative demand shock by raising current consumption and this will help to dampen the impact of the shock on output. The central bank, in turn, anticipates this behaviour by households and does not cut the interest rate by as much as it otherwise would. The outcome is that cycles are more muted as the forward-looking behaviour of households and the central bank reinforce each other.

This is result number 4: *Aggregate demand shocks are amplified through the operation of the multiplier, i.e. consumption responds to changes in output. Aggregate demand shocks may also be dampened in the New Keynesian model to the extent that the proportion of households able to lend and borrow is large enough and they rationally anticipate the response of the central bank to aggregate demand shocks.*

The New Keynesian model seeks to provide microfoundations for the sluggish response of wages and prices to disequilibrium. In the stripped-down New Keynesian model used in the bulk of this book inflation inertia is simply assumed in the Phillips curve: inflation depends on last period's inflation plus a function of the output gap. A major challenge to New Keynesian macroeconomics is to find a proper analysis of the Phillips curve based on rational expectations and optimizing behaviour. The relevance of this problem is clear when we consider that the ad hoc inertial Phillips curve predicts identical behaviour for the economy in the face of (*a*) an inflation shock and (*b*) an announced change in the inflation target. In an economy with forward-looking agents, we would expect that the degree of credibility of the central bank would influence the difference between the predicted path of the economy following (*a*) or (*b*).

There have been two recent attempts to fill this gap: the New Keynesian Phillips Curve (NKPC) and the Sticky Information Phillips Curve (SIPC). Unlike the backward-looking or inertial Phillips curve, both incorporate fully rational agents with forward-looking behaviour. In both models therefore, the credibility of central bank announcements affects the behaviour of the economy.

In the NKPC, the Phillips curve is derived from a model of price setting known as the Calvo model, where it is assumed that firms cannot adjust their price at will—rather, only a random percentage of firms can set their price each period. Knowing this, when they get the chance to set their price, firms take account of expected future changes in the output gap since these would alter their desired price. This produces the so-called NKPC, in which inflation this period is equal to a function of the current output gap and expected future inflation. There is no role for last period's inflation, despite sticky prices. The NKPC provides a microfounded Phillips curve based on rational expectations and solves the credibility problem: an announced reduction in the inflation target will produce an immediate reduction in inflation and no change in output whereas an inflation shock will produce a one-period deviation of output from equilibrium. An announced lowering of the inflation target does not affect the output gap and simply reduces expected future inflation: the result is an immediate reduction in inflation and no change in output. In response to an inflation shock, on the other hand, only the proportion of firms that can change their prices this period are able to respond optimally—the rest can only adjust their output. The result is a fall in output below equilibrium. The following period the economy is back at equilibrium because the cost shock has gone and the inflation outcome the previous period has no lasting effect on either group of firms. So whilst the NKPC has the merit of being able to distinguish between announced changes in the inflation target and inflation shocks and hence is able to take into account the credibility of the central bank it is a poor model of the empirical inflation process since it can only account for a one-period deviation of inflation from target: prices are sticky but inflation is not persistent.

The second model replaces the assumption that prices are sticky by the assumption that information is sticky in the sense that information about a change in monetary policy, for example, diffuses slowly through the economy. This produces a Phillips curve in which inflation this period is equal to a function of the current output gap and the expectation formed last period of this period's inflation target. As in the NKPC all firms have rational expectations. Because it is the absence of information that prevails here, the SIPC predicts both that central bank credibility affects the response of the economy to a change in the inflation target and also that the adjustment back to equilibrium will be associated with inflation persistence. A proportion of firms have full information and the rest are uninformed—but all have rational expectations. If we assume that the central bank shifts to a lower inflation target but only the informed firms are aware of this, then what happens is that the fully informed ones adjust their prices in line with the new target but the rest do not. This leaves inflation 'too high' with the implication that the central bank sets the interest rate so that output is below equilibrium. Depending on the speed of information diffusion, the economy adjusts either next period or over a number of periods to the new equilibrium with inflation at target and output at equilibrium.

The SIPC is better able than the NKPC to match the stylized facts about inflation inertia but a question mark remains over the source of inflation stickiness: why does it not pay firms to be better informed and what is the sense in which firms operating in the context of central banks with monetary rules are inadequately informed? Both the NKPC and the SIPC produce result 5 on the basis of microfoundations and rational expectation although question marks remain over how satisfactory an account is provided of the origin of inflation persistence. Result 5: *The inertia of inflation allows the disequilibrium— i.e. output either above or below equilibrium—to persist.* When combined with the SIPC or NKPC, the monetary policy rule of the optimizing central bank as set out in Chapter 5, produces result 6: *The central bank guides the economy back to equilibrium by using a reaction function to change the interest rate in response to inflation, aggregate demand and supply shocks.*

The final three results relate to the possibility that equilibrium unemployment is not unique. Two simple examples are given to provide result 7: *multiple equilibria may exist because of variations in labour productivity or in the elasticity of demand at high and low output.* In the first, it is simply assumed that at low aggregate output productivity is low and when output is high productivity is high. If this is the case, then given a positively sloped wage-setting curve, there will be one equilibrium at low activity where the (low) wage-setting real wage is equal to the (low) price-setting wage and a second equilibrium at high activity where the (high) wage-setting real wage is equal to the (high) price-setting wage. If this situation prevails, then an economy could get stuck in the low activity equilibrium since small fluctuations in aggregate demand will be insufficient to shift the economy to the high employment equilibrium. A parallel result emerges if the elasticity of demand varies with the level of activity. Potential entrants are less likely to enter a market when activity is low. They will find entry attractive when activity is high and customers are finding it hard to find suppliers because incumbent firms have full order books. This suggests that the elasticity of demand is low at low activity and vice versa and indicates that the *PS* curve is upward sloping (if labour productivity is constant). However, it is also plausible that competition with existing suppliers is intense when activity is low and vice versa, which would suggest the opposite pattern for profit margins and hence for the slope of the *PS* curve. Greater sensitivity to entry produces an upward-sloping *PS* whereas if behaviour is more sensitive to the competitive threat of incumbents, then the *PS* will be downward sloping. The possibility of multiple equilibria arises only in the former case.

An idea that has attracted considerable interest in macroeconomics is that there is an interaction between the actual employment level and equilibrium employment. We have already encountered this idea in Chapter 4, where we saw that a negative aggregate demand shock that leads to prolonged unemployment and raises long-term unemployment can reduce the effectiveness of the unemployed in holding down wage pressure. The consequence is a rise in equilibrium unemployment—i.e. the demand shock produces deterioration on the supply side of the economy. In this chapter we develop further the model focusing on the behaviour of insiders and outsiders in the labour market introduced in Chapter 4. In this model, the union cares only about its members who are currently employed: the result is that when a negative aggregate demand shock occurs and employment falls, membership declines and the *WS* curve becomes vertical at the current employment level. Equilibrium employment has therefore declined and will not respond to a reversal of the demand shock. The economy gets stuck at higher unemployment. This is result 8: *The persistence of output away from equilibrium may itself affect the supply side, and hence equilibrium unemployment. This is known as hysteresis.*

Finally, we introduce fairness considerations to the usual assumption that workers derive utility from consumption and from leisure. The basis of the fairness argument is that when workers are getting at least as high a wage as comparable groups, their only concern is to maximize their real income but if they are getting a lower wage then their utility level is reduced. This introduces a kink into the indifference curves when they cross the *PS* curve. The consequence is that the wage-setting curve becomes flat over a range of employment levels. In this range, the extent of which depends on how much workers need to be compensated as a result of fairness considerations, the *WS* coincides with the *PS* curve, which implies that inflation is constant. Hence we have result 9: *the introduction of considerations that affect workers' utility other than consumption and leisure, such as fairness, may lead to a range of equilibrium employment rates.*

2 The neoclassical benchmark model (NCBM)

We set out in this section a very simple model with perfect competition and perfect information. What is distinctive about the NCBM is the assumption that product and labour markets are perfectly competitive and clear instantaneously with perfectly flexible wages and prices.

2.1 Preliminary: household utility maximization

Throughout this chapter the rational behaviour of households is important for two reasons: households decide how much labour to supply and how much to consume each period. The first decision is central to the analysis of labour markets and the second to the derivation of the *IS* curve. We start by setting out a general model in which households choose consumption and employment each period to maximize their utility function intertemporally. We then show how to get simpler (but similar results) by using one model for choosing consumption intertemporally and another for choosing employment each period.

In the more general model the household at t maximizes

$$U_t \equiv \sum_{i=0}^{\infty} u(c_{t+i}, e_{t+i}) = [u(c_t) - v(e_t)] + \frac{1}{1+\rho}[u(c_{t+1}) - v(e_{t+1})] + \cdots \quad (15.1)$$

where $u(c_t)$ is utility from consumption, $v(e_t)$ is disutility from work, and ρ is the discount rate. This is subject to the budget constraint each period

$$c_t = y_t + r_{t-1}\Psi_t - (\Psi_{t+1} - \Psi_t), \text{where} \quad (15.2)$$

$$y_t = w_t e_t \quad (15.3)$$

and Ψ_t is household wealth at the start of t. It is assumed that the household receives interest $r_{t-1}\Psi_t$ on Ψ_t at the end of $t-1$, so that it counts as income in t. $(\Psi_{t+1} - \Psi_t)$ is the savings the household makes in t, and therefore c_t is total income, earned plus unearned, $w_t e_t + r_{t-1}\Psi_t$, less savings $(\Psi_{t+1} - \Psi_t)$.

To maximize U_t it is simplest to substitute the budget constraint into U_t

$$U_t = [u(w_t e_t + r_{t-1}\Psi_t - (\Psi_{t+1} - \Psi_t)) - v(e_t)]$$
$$+ \frac{1}{1+\rho}[u(w_{t+1}e_{t+1} + r_t\Psi_{t+1} - (\Psi_{t+2} - \Psi_{t+1})) - v(e_{t+1})] + \cdots \quad (15.4)$$

At t, the following variables are given to the household: Ψ_t (the accumulated result of savings decisions in the past), and w_{t+i} and r_{t-1+i} which are market prices. As can be seen the household has to choose optimal values of current and future employment levels, $e_t, e_{t+1,...}$ and wealth in all future periods, $\Psi_{t+1}, \Psi_{t+2},..$ (instead of $e_t, e_{t+1,...}$ and $c_t, c_{t+1}, ...$).

We begin with the decision about current employment: e_t just comes into the first square bracket so the first order condition is

$$w_t u_c(c_t) = v_e(e_t) \tag{15.5}$$

and future employment levels are likewise given by $w_{t+i} u_c(c_{t+i}) = v_e(e_{t+i})$, where $u_c \equiv \frac{\partial u}{\partial c}$ and $v_e \equiv \frac{\partial v}{\partial e}$. These equations state that employment should be increased in any period until the marginal disutility of employment $v_e(e_t)$ is equal to marginal utility of consumption provided by w_t.

Turning to the choice of next period's wealth, Ψ_{t+1}, a marginal rise in Ψ_{t+1} comes out of current consumption and increases next period's consumption by $(1 + r_t)$. Thus the household will optimize such that:

$$u_c(c_t) = \frac{1}{1 + \rho}(1 + r_t)u_c(c_{t+1}). \tag{15.6}$$

Future consumption levels are similarly given by $u_c(c_{t+i}) = \frac{1}{1+\rho}(1 + r_{t+i})u_c(c_{t+1+i})$. These are the classical consumption-smoothing equations. Since the first order conditions entail optimization across periods, they are examples of Euler equations.

In the rest of this chapter we will frequently put $u(c)$ and $v(e)$ into the following explicit functional forms. Economists working on consumer behaviour frequently use the following utility function,[5]

$$u(c) = \frac{c^{1-\theta}}{1 - \theta} \tag{15.8}$$

where $\theta > 0$ and which yields quite simple results and implies that

$$u_c(c) = c^{-\theta}. \tag{15.9}$$

And for $v(e)$[6]

$$v(e) = \frac{\phi e^\sigma}{\sigma}. \tag{15.10}$$

2.1.1 A note on the real business cycle approach

What is common to Keynesian approaches is that employment changes are seen as caused by changes in aggregate demand. Real Business Cycle (RBC) models aim to explain employment fluctuations as the consequence of optimal household responses

---

[5] The utility function is the Constant Relative Risk Aversion function, with a relative risk aversion of θ, which is independent of the level of consumption:

$$RRA \equiv -c\frac{u_{cc}(c)}{u_c(c)} = \theta c\frac{c^{-\theta-1}}{c^{-\theta}} = \theta \tag{15.7}$$

[6] This was introduced in Blanchard and Kiyotaki (1987).

to technology or preference shocks, rather than as consequences of changes in aggregate demand. At the same time RBC theorists want to be able to show that employment and output movements are positively correlated.

Using the two explicit forms for $u(c)$ and $v(e)$ from above, we first construct a simple Real Business Cycle (RBC) model, in which the household maximizes

$$U = \left(\frac{c_0^{1-\theta}}{1-\theta} - \phi\frac{e_0^{\sigma}}{\sigma} \right) + \frac{1}{1+\rho} \left(\frac{c_1^{1-\theta}}{1-\theta} - \phi\frac{e_1^{\sigma}}{\sigma} \right) + \cdots$$

subject to

$$c_t = w_t e_t + r_{t-1}\Psi_t - (\Psi_{t+1} - \Psi_t).$$

When this is substituted into the utility function, we get

$$U = \left(\frac{(w_0 e_0 + r_{-1}\Psi_0 - (\Psi_1 - \Psi_0))^{1-\theta}}{1-\theta} - \phi\frac{e_0^{\sigma}}{\sigma} \right)$$
$$+ \frac{1}{1+\rho} \left(\frac{(w_1 e_1 + r_0\Psi_1 - (\Psi_2 - \Psi_1))^{1-\theta}}{1-\theta} - \phi\frac{e_1^{\sigma}}{\sigma} \right) + \cdots$$

From this optimization, we can derive the following first order conditions:

$$\frac{\partial U}{\partial e_0} = 0 \Rightarrow w_0 c_0^{-\theta} = \phi e_0^{\sigma-1} \tag{15.11}$$

$$\frac{\partial U}{\partial \Psi_1} = 0 \Rightarrow c_0^{-\theta} = \frac{1+r_0}{1+\rho}c_1^{-\theta} \tag{15.12}$$

$$\frac{\partial U}{\partial e_1} = 0 \Rightarrow w_1 c_1^{-\theta} = \phi e_1^{\sigma-1} \tag{15.13}$$

$$\frac{\partial U}{\partial \Psi_2} = 0 \Rightarrow c_1^{-\theta} = \frac{1+r_1}{1+\rho}c_2^{-\theta} \tag{15.14}$$

and so on for $c_2, c_3, \ldots$ and $e_2, e_3, \ldots$ If equation (15.13) is substituted into equation (15.12) and (15.12) into (15.11), this implies:

$$w_0 \left(\frac{1+r_0}{1+\rho} \right) \frac{\phi}{w_1}e_1^{\sigma-1} = \phi e_0^{\sigma-1}$$

or

$$\log e_0 = \log e_1 + \frac{1}{\sigma-1} \left[\log \frac{w_0}{w_1} + (r_0 - \rho) \right].$$

This is an 'employment smoothing' equation: lifetime utility maximization says that it makes sense to keep employment at the same level over time. As can be seen there are two reasons why it may pay to work harder (or less hard) in the present relative to the future. Let's look at why employment might decline:

(i) $w_0 < w_1$. This is a classic example of a short-run negative productivity shock, which is at once translated into a fall in the real wage. In this case households choose to work less. Note too that output falls, both because employment has declined and because of the negative productivity shock: $\Delta \log y_0 = \Delta \log e_0 + \Delta \log \lambda_0$, (where λ is labour productivity). Hence output and employment are positively correlated, and the decline in employment is an optimizing response to a technology shock.

(ii) $r_0 < \rho$. A decline in r can come about for several reasons, including a fall in capital productivity or a change in preferences for exogenous demand including government expenditure. Given the possibility of lending and borrowing, it now makes more sense to work less hard in the current period and harder next period, borrowing from next period to cover current consumption. Again output and employment are correlated (because $\Delta \log y_0 = \Delta \log e_0$ with constant productivity), and again the decline in employment is an optimizing response—this time to a preference shock.

As we noted in the introductory section of this chapter, RBC models that stress technology shocks and their propagation through equilibrium cycles (operating via the intertemporal substitution of labour) have not performed particularly well empirically. Nominal rigidities and imperfections in markets have been introduced in many later RBC-type models. Given the limitations of space and the emphasis of this book on the role of aggregate demand in generating business cycle fluctuations and equally, on the role of monetary policy in affecting the level of activity in the short to medium run, we do not take further the RBC approach.

2.2 Simplifying household optimization

We can simplify household optimization by working with two separate models. The first will be used when we are dealing with consumption decisions and the second with employment decisions.

2.2.1 A simple household intertemporal consumption model

In this simple model the household no longer makes labour supply decisions. Instead it treats income as given and maximizes $U_t = u(c_t) + \frac{1}{1+\rho}u(c_{t+1}) + \cdots$. The household now maximizes

$$U_t = \frac{c_t^{1-\theta}}{1-\theta} + \frac{1}{1+\rho}\frac{c_{t+1}^{1-\theta}}{1-\theta} + \cdots \tag{15.15}$$

subject to

$$c_t = y_t + r_{t-1}\Psi_t - (\Psi_{t+1} - \Psi_t). \tag{15.16}$$

The first order condition as before $u_c(c_t) = \frac{1}{1+\rho}(1+r_t)u_c(c_{t+1})$, which now has the simple form

$$c_t^{-\theta} = c_{t+1}^{-\theta}\frac{1}{1+\rho}(1+r_t), \tag{15.17}$$

which implies in logs

$$\log c_t = \log c_{t+1} - \frac{1}{\theta} \log \frac{(1 + r_t)}{1 + \rho} = \log c_{t+1} + \frac{1}{\theta} \log(1 + \rho) - \frac{1}{\theta} \log(1 + r_t) \quad (15.18)$$

or using the first order approximation $\log(1 + x) \approx x$

$$\log c_t = \log c_{t+1} - \frac{1}{\theta}(r_t - \rho). \quad (15.19)$$

Thus in the consumption-smoothing model, as we have seen in Chapter 7, consumption remains constant over time when the real interest rate and discount rate are equal: c_t is equal to c_{t+1} when $r_t = \rho$. The interpretation is straightforward: if $r_t > \rho$, there is an incentive to save today to get a higher income tomorrow which is not outweighed by the rate at which future utility is discounted, hence $\log c_t < \log c_{t+1}$. It is also useful to note a 1% increase in r_t implies a $\frac{1}{\theta}$% fall in c_t. We will use this equation in the *IS* subsection below.

2.2.2 A simple household employment choice model

Now we develop a simple model of household labour supply decisions. Starting as before from the utility function $U_t \equiv [u(c_t) - v(e_t)] + \frac{1}{1+\rho}[u(c_{t+1}) - v(e_{t+1})] + \cdots$, we can simplify and assume

$$u(c) = c \quad (15.20)$$

and

$$v(e) = \frac{\phi e^2}{2}. \quad (15.21)$$

(It is assumed that $\phi > 1$; this guarantees subsequently an equilibrium with the equilibrium employment rate $e_e < 1$.) So households maximize:

$$U_t = \left(c_t - \frac{\phi e_t^2}{2}\right) + \frac{1}{1+\rho}\left(c_{t+1} - \frac{\phi e_{t+1}^2}{2}\right) + \cdots \quad (15.22)$$

subject to

$$c_t = w_t e_t + r_{t-1}\Psi_t - (\Psi_{t+1} - \Psi_t). \quad (15.23)$$

Substituting the budget constraint into the utility function implies

$$U_t = \left(w_t e_t + r_{t-1}\Psi_t - (\Psi_{t+1} - \Psi_t) - \frac{\phi e_t^2}{2}\right)$$
$$+ \frac{1}{1+\rho}\left(w_{t+1}e_{t+1} + r_t\Psi_{t+1} - (\Psi_{t+2} - \Psi_{t+1}) - \frac{\phi e_{t+1}^2}{2}\right) + \cdots \quad (15.24)$$

The maximization over e is simple since we can take each period separately: for example e_t only appears in the terms $w_t e_t$ and $-\frac{\phi e_t^2}{2}$ in the first bracket. Thus the household chooses e_t to maximize $w_t e_t - \frac{\phi e_t^2}{2}$, which implies

$$e_t = \phi^{-1} w_t. \tag{15.25}$$

Likewise, $e_{t+1} = \phi^{-1} w_{t+1}$, and so on. As we shall see in the next section, this equation is the labour supply schedule E^S. It says that if the real wage is w, the amount of labour a household will choose to supply will be $\phi^{-1} w$.

What are the implications for consumer behaviour? In fact this model is not a sensible one to use to examine consumption behaviour over time if borrowing and lending are permitted. This can be seen by maximizing over Ψ_{t+1}: we get $\frac{\partial U_t}{\partial \Psi_{t+1}} = -1 + \frac{(1+r_t)}{1+\rho}$; this says, save everything if $r_t > \rho$ and consume everything if $r_t < \rho$. However, this is hardly useful advice. So we shall use this model primarily for employment decisions; and only look at implications for consumption when saving and borrowing are not permitted.

Using the general form of $v(e)$

For future reference we will make use of the more general form of $v(e)$ introduced in equation (15.10). This is

$$v(e) = \frac{\phi e^\sigma}{\sigma}. \tag{15.26}$$

Thus now in each period (in this simple no-borrowing, no-lending model) the household maximizes

$$we - \frac{\phi e^\sigma}{\sigma}. \tag{15.27}$$

This implies the first order condition:

$$w = \phi e^{\sigma - 1}. \tag{15.28}$$

In fact we shall normally work in log-linear forms, so that

$$\log w = \log \phi + (\sigma - 1) \log e. \tag{15.29}$$

This shows the amount of labour the household will choose to supply or the E^S schedule, $\log e^S = \frac{1}{\sigma-1} \log \phi^{-1} + \frac{1}{\sigma-1} \log w$.

2.3 Output and employment equilibrium: the labour market diagram

We commence with the labour market diagram shown in Fig. 15.1. In this chapter it will often be clearer to discuss the labour market diagram with e, employment, on the horizontal axis rather than the level of output, y.

The upward-sloping line in Fig. 15.1 is the individual labour supply function, E^S. We have seen in the last subsection that this is given by $e_t = \phi^{-1} w_t$. It is also useful to see the

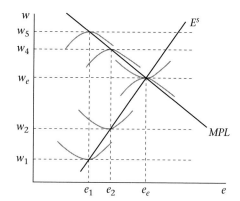

Figure 15.1 Labour supply and demand

derivation of the E^S curve geometrically using indifference curves. From the last section the indifference curve corresponding to a utility level $\bar{u}$ is given by $we - \frac{\phi e^2}{2} = \bar{u}$, omitting the t subscripts. These are the U-shaped indifference curves: the higher an indifference curve the higher the level of utility since holding e (hours of employment) constant, an increase in w, the hourly real wage, increases utility. To see why the indifference curves are U-shaped, we totally differentiate $we - \frac{\phi e^2}{2} = \bar{u}$, to get $edw + wde - \phi ede = 0$ or $\frac{dw}{de} = \frac{\phi e - w}{e}$. Thus we can first see that the slope of the indifference curve is zero when $\phi e = w$, i.e. when we are on the E^S curve; when $\phi e > w$, we are to the right of the E^S curve and the indifference curve is then upward sloping; finally when $\phi e < w$, we are to the left of the E^S curve and the indifference curve is then downward sloping.

Because the labour market is perfectly competitive, workers can choose to supply as many hours of work as they wish at the given real wage. Since they maximize utility, the choice of e is at the highest utility level possible given the real wage; hence it will be where the bottom of an indifference curve is just touching the horizontal line representing a given real wage. The E^S schedule traces out the choice of e corresponding to increasing values of w. We assume that E^S is increasing with w, that is that a higher real wage leads workers to choose to supply more labour (at some stage of course the amount of labour supplied stops rising since the worker's hours per day are limited, but we assume here that this point is not reached).

The downward-sloping line in Fig. 15.1, is the marginal product of labour, MPL. Under perfect competition firms produce up to the point at which the price P at which they can sell a unit of output is equal to the cost of labour needed to produce it, namely Wde/dy where W is the nominal hourly cost of labour and de/dy is the number of hours needed to produce one more unit of output. $P = Wde/dy$ (price equals marginal cost) implies $w \equiv W/P = dy/de$ (the real wage equals MPL). The MPL is measured on the vertical axis together with w, and declining marginal productivity implies that dy/de falls as e increases. For future reference, note that if labour productivity is constant, as assumed in much of the rest of this chapter and in the book, the MPL is flat.

At any given real wage the profits a firm makes are lower than the maximum possible at that real wage when employment is above or below the employment level which equates MPL to w. Hence we can draw iso-profit curves (the equivalent of indifference curves for firms) showing increasing profits as w falls and at any given w, these are tangential to the horizontal line representing that real wage (see Fig. 15.1).

The equilibrium is where the MPL and the E^S cross, i.e. at (w_e, e_e). At w_e workers will choose to supply exactly the amount of employment that employers will choose to demand. This leads to two important contrasts with New Keynesian macro results:

(1) At this equilibrium, unemployment is entirely voluntary. All workers are supplying the amount of labour they choose to supply at the existing real wage w_e. We show in section 3 how the introduction of imperfections in labour and product markets can account for involuntary unemployment in equilibrium.

(2) As can be seen, the equilibrium is unique. We discuss in section 7 the possibility that there are multiple equilibria in the economy. Again this is associated with the role of imperfections in labour and product markets.

We conclude this subsection by making the argument here easier to relate to the New Keynesian model of subsequent sections, and especially the next section (3) on employment equilibrium. First, the MPL schedule needs to be compared with the w^{PS} schedule under imperfect competition. Write the MPL schedule in terms of the price level, $P = W(de/dy)$. Assume the productivity of labour is constant and equal to unity so that $de/dy = 1$. Hence $P = W$. In the subsequent New Keynesian sections we will work with a multi-sectoral model, in which the price level in sector i is P_i and the wage level W_i. The relative price level in i is $p_i \equiv P_i/P$, and the sectoral real wage is $w_i \equiv W_i/P$, with P the aggregate price level. In the New Keynesian model, price setters set p_i in the relation to w_i as a result of profit maximization—so that typically $p_i = (1 + \mu)w_i$ where μ can be interpreted as a mark-up. This is then the sectoral w^{PS} schedule. In the NCBM marginal cost pricing implies $p_i = w_i$, and we shall compare this with the sectoral w^{PS} schedule under imperfect competition.

To express the E^S schedule in a way we shall be able to compare to the w^{WS} schedule under imperfect competition, we use the form $v(e_i) = \phi e_i^\sigma / \sigma$, implying as it does $w_i = \phi e_i^{\sigma-1}$.

Taking logs and aggregating the sectoral MPL schedules we get

$$\log p \equiv N^{-1} \sum \log p_i = N^{-1} \sum \log w_i \equiv \log MPL. \tag{15.30}$$

Doing the same to the E^S schedules

$$\log w^S \equiv N^{-1} \sum \log w_i = \log \phi + (\sigma - 1).N^{-1} \sum \log e_i \equiv \log \phi + (\sigma - 1) \log e, \tag{15.31}$$

where the superscript, S, highlights the fact that this is the labour supply equation. Since the average of relative prices must be equal to one (and its log equal to zero), $\log p = 0$. Equilibrium employment is defined by $w^{PS} = w^{WS}$, which in the perfectly competitive case is $\log MPL = \log w^S$:

$$0 = \log MPL = \log w^S = \log \phi + (\sigma - 1) \log e_e$$

$$\Rightarrow \log e_e = \frac{1}{\sigma - 1} \log \phi^{-1}. \tag{15.32}$$

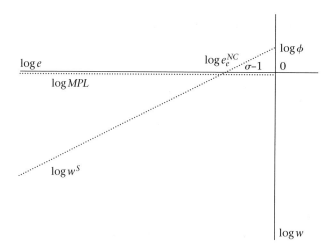

Figure 15.2 Equilibrium employment under perfect competition

This is shown in Fig. 15.2. Note that the employment rate increases to a maximum of 1 in natural numbers when $\log e = 0$ and the real wage increases to a maximum of 1 in natural numbers, since labour productivity is assumed to be 1. Here the $\log MPL$ schedule is equal to zero since labour productivity is 1 and there is no profit mark-up and it is shown as the horizontal dashed line coincident with the horizontal axis. The $\log w^S$ schedule (the labour supply curve) is upward sloping with constant term of $\log \phi$ and slope of $\sigma - 1$. The equilibrium employment rate $\log e_e^{NC}$ is given by the intersection of $\log w^S$ and $\log MPL$. As can be seen $\log e_e^{NC} < 0$. In natural numbers, the employment rate, $e_e^{NC} < 1$ since $\phi > 1$, i.e. because there is a disutility of labour.

2.4 The *IS* curve

From our simple consumption-smoothing model above, consumption is negatively related to the interest rate:

$$\log c_t = \log c_{t+1} - \frac{1}{\theta}(r_t - \rho).$$
(15.33)

In line with other microfounded models, investment is ignored here (a discussion of micro based models of investment can be found in Chapter 7). The *IS* curve states that aggregate demand $\log y$ is equal to $\omega_c \log c + \omega_a \log a$, where a is non-consumption demand, for example government expenditure; ω_i is the elasticity of y with respect to i. Hence the *IS* curve can be written

$$
\begin{aligned}
\log y_t &= \omega_c \log c_t + \omega_a \log a_t \\
&= \omega_a \log a_t + \omega_c \log c_{t+1} - \frac{\omega_c}{\theta}(r_t - \rho) \\
&= \omega_a \log a_t + (\log y_{t+1} - \omega_a \log a_{t+1}) - \frac{\omega_c}{\theta}(r_t - \rho).
\end{aligned}
$$
(15.34)

Since future variables have to be forecast at t, the *IS* curve is

$$\log y_t = \omega_a \log a_t + E_t(\log y_{t+1} - \omega_a \log a_{t+1}) - \frac{\omega_c}{\theta}(r_t - \rho). \qquad (15.35)$$

It will prove convenient to express this relationship in terms of excess demand, x, where

$$\log x_t \equiv \log y_t - \log y_e \qquad (15.36)$$

and as usual, y_e is the equilibrium level of output, i.e. corresponding to the employment rate, e_e. Going back to the terminology introduced in Chapter 3, the so-called stabilizing rate of interest at t, $r_{S,t}$, is defined as the real rate of interest which equates aggregate demand at t to equilibrium output:

$$\log y_e = \omega_a \log a_t + E_t(\log y_e - \omega_a \log a_{t+1}) - \frac{\omega_c}{\theta}(r_{S,t} - \rho). \qquad (15.37)$$

Subtracting this equation from the y_t form of the *IS* curve above gives the excess demand form of the *IS* curve as

$$\log x_t = E_t \log x_{t+1} - \frac{\omega_c}{\theta}(r_t - r_{S,t}). \qquad (15.38)$$

Thus far these equations are common to the NCBM and a New Keynesian model, in which there is consumption-smoothing. In the NCBM with full information, perfect price flexibility and rational expectations, a key result is that

$$\log x_t = E_t \log x_{t+1} = 0, \qquad (15.39)$$

in other words the economy is always in equilibrium. In the NCBM an increase in aggregate demand cannot cause an increase in output or employment. This follows directly from the analysis of the labour market in which it was shown that with rational expectations, workers will always supply $e = e_e$ and firms produce $y = y_e$. We shall see shortly how aggregate demand is brought into line with the equilibrium level of output fixed by the supply side. It has an important implication for the *IS* curve in the NCBM. Substituting $\log x_t = E_t \log x_{t+1} = 0$ into the *IS* curve, $\log x_t = E_t \log x_{t+1} - \frac{\omega_c}{\theta}(r_t - r_S)$, implies that in the NCBM, the *IS* curve reduces to the horizontal line

$$r_t = r_S. \qquad (15.40)$$

This is shown in Fig. 15.3. This reflects the fact that in the NCBM, aggregate demand is irrelevant for the level of output and employment: it simply determines the real interest rate. Hence, for the given equilibrium level of output, higher aggregate demand, for example from government expenditure, implies a higher real interest rate since the higher real interest rate is required to crowd out private consumption expenditure so as to allow government expenditure to rise.

To show how aggregate demand is brought immediately into line with equilibrium output, it is necessary to include the money market in the model. We assume that the government has a zero inflation target. This requires it to hold the nominal money supply constant. We now show that perfectly flexible prices and rational expectations ensure that $r_t = r_{S,t}$ and this ensures that $\log x_t = E_t \log x_{t+1} = 0$. Rational expectations imply that $E_t \log x_{t+1} = 0$. So $\log x_t = -\frac{1}{\theta}(r_t - r_{S,t})$. If say $\log x_t > 0$, perfect price flexibility implies that P rises. The rise in P operates to push r_t up to $r_{S,t}$. This mechanism operates through the demand and supply of money, the *LM* curve equation.

Throughout much of this book the *LM* curve has had a rather shadowy existence because we have assumed the monetary authorities can set the real interest rate at whatever level they wish. As we have noted elsewhere, this does not 'do away with' the *LM* curve. Rather, it means that in order to deliver their chosen real rate of interest, the authorities have to ensure the real money supply supports the real demand for money at that rate. The price flexibility mechanism in the NCBM requires that we refer to the components of the *LM* curve, since the rise in P affects the interest rate by reducing the real demand for money.

The *LM* curve is given by

$$\frac{\overline{M}}{P_t} = L(i_t, y_t) = L(r_t + \pi_t^E, y_t), \tag{15.41}$$

where L is the real demand for money, $i_t = r_t + \pi_t^E$ is the nominal interest rate, and $\frac{\overline{M}}{P_t}$ the real supply of money. The current nominal money supply is known to be, say, $\overline{M}$. With a zero inflation target, expected inflation is zero and the real and nominal interest rates are identical. This makes the discussion less clumsy but does not change the logic.

Now we can see the mechanism through which perfect price flexibility keeps $\log x_t = 0$. If $\log x_t > 0$, then the price level P rises immediately to keep the labour market in equilibrium: firms on their marginal product curve and households on their labour supply curve. As P rises and hence $\frac{\overline{M}}{P_t}$ falls, the excess demand for money pushes the interest rate up. As r rises $\log x_t$ falls. Both the rise in r and the fall in $\log x$ reduce the demand for money. Suppose that r has not risen yet to $r_{S,t}$ (at which point $\log x_t = 0$), then it is still true that $\log x > 0$. But if $\log x > 0$, then P must rise further. This process continues until $r = r_S$, and $\log x = 0$. If there is perfect price flexibility then this process happens in principle infinitely fast. Hence the flexibility of the price level keeps the labour market in equilibrium and ensures that excess aggregate demand is eliminated.

2.5 The Phillips curve and the *MR*

What determines the rate of inflation? As we have assumed before, we assume the monetary authorities want to minimize the loss function:

$$x_t^2 + \beta(\pi_t - \pi^T)^2. \tag{15.42}$$

Since $x_t = 0$ anyway in the NCBM, the authorities need merely to set $\pi_t = \pi^T$. The existence of perfect price flexibility means that there is no 'short-run' Phillips curve in the NCBM since there is no excess demand x_t. However, it is still true that $\pi_t = \pi^E$ and this defines the vertical long-run Phillips curve in the NCBM. Since the Phillips curve is

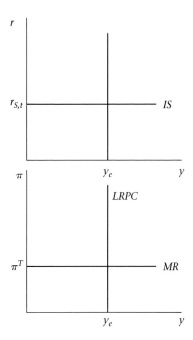

Figure 15.3 *IS*, *MR* and *LRPC* curves in the *NCBM*

vertical, the authorities do not face a trade-off between x and $\pi - \pi^T$. Instead they simply choose the inflation rate, and that choice is $\pi_t = \pi^T$. Thus in the NCBM, we have a vertical Phillips curve at $y = y_e$ and a horizontal monetary rule line, *MR*, at $\pi = \pi^T$. This is shown in Fig. 15.3.

A final question is: how do the authorities set $\pi = \pi^T$ if they no longer control the interest rate r, since $r = r_S$? We return to the *LM* curve. In equilibrium $r = r_S$ and $y = y_e$ and hence the *LM* curve must be

$$\frac{\overline{M}_t}{P_t} = L(r_{S,t} + \pi_t^E, y_e) \tag{15.43}$$

and since it is known that $\pi_t = \pi^T$, rational expectations imply that $\pi^E = \pi^T$. Suppose that $r_{S,t} = r_{S,t+1}$ and $\pi_t^T = \pi_{t+1}^T$ so that $\pi_t^E = \pi_{t+1}^E$. This implies that the real money supply is constant ($m_t = m_{t+1}$), which implies $\frac{P_{t+1}}{P_t} = \frac{\overline{M}_{t+1}}{\overline{M}_t}$; in other words the rate of inflation is equal to the growth rate of the nominal money supply. Thus in the NCBM the monetary authority can control the rate of inflation costlessly via the growth of the nominal money supply.

Finally, in addition to points 1 and 2 above, we can note the following further points of difference with the New Keynesian model. In the NCBM,

(1) demand shifts change prices and not output;

(2) demand shifts are not amplified: there is 100% crowding out of '*IS*' shocks via the real interest rate;

(3) inflation is always equal to target inflation.

3 Equilibrium output and involuntary unemployment

In this section we show how, if we move from competitive to imperfect product and labour markets, equilibrium output and employment may be associated with the presence of involuntary unemployment. We assume first that there are N symmetric sectors in the economy, each sector producing a differentiated product. The demand for output, y_i, and employment (labour productivity is unity), e_i, is given by a constant elasticity demand function

$$y_i = e_i = p_i^{-\eta} A/N,$$

where η is the elasticity of demand and A is aggregate demand. Note that since p_i is the relative price of good i, demand for i is A/N when $p_i = 1$.

There are a number of different models of price-setting and wage-setting behaviour under one form or another of imperfect competition that we can draw on. A common approach assumes a monopoly producer in each sector (differentiated products à la Dixit–Stiglitz) and sometimes in addition a monopoly union (Blanchard–Kiyotaki). This fits well with the microfoundations of the Phillips curve, which will occupy section 6. Since the rest of the chapter makes use of the union wage-setting model, we have put the derivation and analysis of the efficiency wage model of wage setting in the appendix so as to improve the flow of the argument.

3.1 The monopoly producer, monopoly union model

In this model, the union chooses the money wage in sector i, W_i, and the producer then chooses the price level P_i. However, since the union is interested in $w_i = W_i/P$ the union actually chooses w_i, just as the producer chooses p_i; (there is no difference in the final result, but it is simpler to use w_i and/or p_i as the direct instrument). Even though the union chooses w_i and the firm chooses p_i given w_i, the union needs to know what p_i the firm will set for any given w_i. So we start with the firm choosing p_i given w_i.[7]

The firm maximizes its profits:

$$\Pi = p_i y_i - w_i e_i$$

subject to the demand curve $y_i = e_i = p_i^{-\eta} A/N$, so that $\Pi = p_i^{1-\eta} A/N - w_i p_i^{-\eta} A/N$. Hence

$$\frac{\partial \Pi}{\partial p_i} = (1 - \eta)p_i^{-\eta} A/N + \eta w_i(p_i^{-\eta} A/N)/p_i = 0$$

$$\Rightarrow p_i = \frac{\eta}{\eta - 1} w_i. \tag{15.44}$$

This is the firm's price-setting curve.

We assume the union maximizes the utility of the representative employee in sector i, as in the Blanchard–Kiyotaki model $U_i = w_i e_i - \phi e_i^\sigma /\sigma$, which was introduced in the

---

[7] This is the way to derive a subgame perfect equilibrium in the game between union and firm. This concept is explained in Chapter 16.

previous section, 2.1.2.[8] The employee puts a positive weight on consumption $c = w_i e_i$ and leisure $-\phi e_i^\sigma / \sigma$. Whereas in 2.1.2. the leisure component was $-\phi e_i^2 / 2$, more generality is assumed here by replacing 2 with σ; (we could equally have done this in the NCBM). Substituting the employment demand function $e_i = p_i^{-\eta} A/N$ with $p_i = \frac{\eta}{\eta-1} w_i$ into U_i, the union chooses w_i to maximize $U_i = w_i^{1-\eta} \left(\frac{\eta}{\eta-1} \right)^{-\eta} A/N - \phi \left(w_i^{-\eta} \left(\frac{\eta}{\eta-1} \right)^{-\eta} A/N \right)^\sigma / \sigma$; defining $k \equiv \left(\frac{\eta}{\eta-1} \right)^{-\eta} A/N$ for convenience

$$\frac{\partial U_i}{\partial w_i} = (1-\eta) w_i^{-\eta} k + \eta \phi (w_i^{-\eta} k)^{\sigma-1} . w_i^{-\eta} k / w_i = 0$$

$$\Rightarrow w_i = \frac{\eta \phi}{\eta - 1} e_i^{\sigma-1} \tag{15.45}$$

remembering that $e_i = w_i^{-\eta} k$. This is the ith union's wage-setting curve.

Putting the price- and wage-setting curves in log-linear form:

$$\log p_i = \log \left(\frac{\eta}{\eta - 1} \right) + \log w_i \tag{15.46}$$

$$\log w_i = \log \left(\frac{\phi \eta}{\eta - 1} \right) + (\sigma - 1) \log e_i. \tag{15.47}$$

To find the equilibrium for the economy as a whole, we first take the averages of $\log p_i$, $\log w_i$, and $\log e_i$. Remember from the NCBM that $\log e \equiv N^{-1} \sum \log e_i$, and likewise $\log p \equiv N^{-1} \sum \log p_i$, and $\log w \equiv N^{-1} \sum \log w_i$. Hence

$$\log p = \log \left(\frac{\eta}{\eta - 1} \right) + \log w \tag{15.48}$$

$$\log w = \log \left(\frac{\phi \eta}{\eta - 1} \right) + (\sigma - 1) \log e. \tag{15.49}$$

By definition

$$\log p = 0$$

since the average relative price must be equal to unity. And therefore

$$\log w^{PS} = -\log \left(\frac{\eta}{\eta - 1} \right) = \log \left(\frac{\eta - 1}{\eta} \right) \tag{15.50}$$

$$\log w^{WS} = \log \left(\frac{\phi \eta}{\eta - 1} \right) + (\sigma - 1) \log e. \tag{15.51}$$

---

[8] We neglect to add profits to income on the grounds that the effect is too small if portfolios are widely spread.

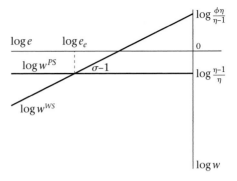

Figure 15.4 Equilibrium employment with imperfect competition

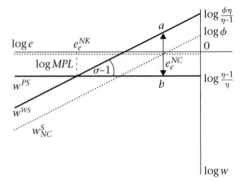

Figure 15.5 Equilibrium employment: real wage pushfulness and real wage rigidity

The $\log w^{PS}$ and $\log w^{WS}$ schedules are illustrated in Fig. 15.4. Equilibrium employment, e_e^{NK}, is given by the intersection of the $\log w^{PS}$ and $\log w^{WS}$ schedules as can be seen. Hence

$$\log w^{PS} = \log w^{WS}$$

$$\log w_e = \log \left(\frac{\eta - 1}{\eta} \right)$$

$$\log e_e = \frac{1}{\sigma - 1} \log \left[\phi^{-1} \left(\frac{\eta - 1}{\eta} \right)^2 \right]$$

$$= -\frac{1}{\sigma - 1} \log \left[\phi \left(\frac{\eta}{\eta - 1} \right)^2 \right]. \tag{15.52}$$

We can now compare equilibrium employment in this imperfect competition New Keynesian model (equation 15.52) with equilibrium employment in the NCBM (equation 15.32). In Fig. 15.5 we have suppressed the logs in front of w^{WS}, e_e, etc. to make the diagram more readable.

The NCBM equilibrium employment, $\log e_e^{NC}$, is given as before in section 2.3 by the intersection of $\log MPL$ and $\log w_{NC}^S$ and e_e^{NC} represents zero involuntary equilibrium unemployment, since e_e^{NC} is the unique equilibrium employment rate chosen by households. By contrast at e_e^{NK}, with $\log w = \log \frac{\eta-1}{\eta}$, households would have liked to have chosen employment at the intersection of w_{NC}^S (which shows employment choices at each level of w) and the w^{PS} line.

Comparing equilibrium employment between the NCBM and the New Keynesian model, we have

$$\log e_e^{NC} = -\frac{1}{\sigma - 1} \log \phi \tag{15.53}$$

$$\log e_e^{NK} = -\frac{1}{\sigma - 1} \log \left[\phi \left(\frac{\eta}{\eta - 1} \right)^2 \right], \tag{15.54}$$

which implies

$$\log e_e^{NK} - \log e_e^{NC} = -\frac{1}{\sigma - 1} \log \left(\frac{\eta}{\eta - 1} \right)^2. \tag{15.55}$$

As can be seen from Fig. 15.5 and the above equation, $\log e_e^{NK}$ increases relative to the competitive benchmark NCBM $\log e_e^{NC}$ if $\left(\frac{\eta}{\eta - 1} \right)^2$ and/or $1/(\sigma - 1)$ increases. These two terms are thus of great importance in understanding the involuntary component in equilibrium unemployment. We shall refer to the first as *real wage pushfulness* and to the second as *real wage rigidity*:

$$Real\ wage\ pushfulness \equiv \log \left(\frac{\eta}{\eta - 1} \right)^2 \tag{15.56}$$

$$Real\ wage\ rigidity \equiv 1/(\sigma - 1) \tag{15.57}$$

$$\log e_e^{NK} - \log e_e^{NC} = -Real\ wage\ rigidity \times Real\ wage\ pushfulness. \tag{15.58}$$

In the diagram above, real wage rigidity is just the inverse of the slope of the w^{WS} schedule and real wage pushfulness is the vertical distance between a and b. As we shall see below, real wage rigidity plays a critical role in retarding the adjustment of the economy back to equilibrium in the face of a shock.

3.2 Extensions

3.2.1 Elasticity of demand

In the simple model set out in this section, the determinant of real wage pushfulness is the elasticity of demand. A fall in the elasticity of demand increases pushfulness through two mechanisms: the market power of firms over consumers increases and of unions over firms increases. The first is represented visually by a downward shift of the *PS* curve and the second by the upward shift of the *WS*. The distance a to b increases, widening the gap between equilibrium in the NCBM and the now lower employment in the New Keynesian model.

3.2.2 Bertrand competition rather than monopoly

For simplicity we assume there are two firms in each sector. There are no fixed costs of production, labour is the only factor of production, and labour productivity is equal to one for each firm. Bertrand competition assumes that each firm sets a price and they both set their prices at the same moment so that neither can respond to the other. In any sector, both firms produce the same product: thus if firm A sets a lower price than B (assuming the goods are genuinely identical) A will get the whole market demand. We shall see that the only 'Nash equilibrium' is where both firms in sector i set the same price, namely $P_i = W_i$, i.e. price is set equal to marginal cost. To see this, suppose this was not the case and firm A set a price above W_i, say $W_i + k$; it would then pay B to set a price marginally below $W_i + k$; but that could not be a Nash equilibrium, since it would then pay A to set a still slightly lower price in order to take the entire market. But nor would either firm set a price below W_i since that would mean a price below marginal cost and would result in a loss. Hence both set $P_i = W_i$.

If there is Bertrand competition in the product market instead of monopoly pricing, there are no super-normal profits so the pricing equation is

$$p_i = w_i, \tag{15.59}$$

which implies that $\log w^{PS} = 0$, instead of $\log w^{PS} = \log\left(\frac{\eta-1}{\eta}\right)$ as above in the monopoly producer case. If we now equate $\log w^{PS} = \log w^{WS}$, we have equilibrium employment with a monopoly union and Bertrand competition in the product market:

$$\log e_e^{NK} = -\frac{1}{\sigma-1}\log\left[\phi\left(\frac{\eta}{\eta-1}\right)\right]. \qquad \text{(Bertrand competition)}$$

This compares with equilibrium employment with a monopoly union and monopoly in the product market

$$\log e_e^{NK} = -\frac{1}{\sigma-1}\log\left[\phi\left(\frac{\eta}{\eta-1}\right)^2\right] \qquad \text{(monopoly producer)}$$

and with the NCBM in which there are no market imperfections in either the labour or product market:

$$\log e_e^{NC} = -\frac{1}{\sigma-1}\log\phi. \qquad \text{(NCBM)}$$

This comparison shows that equilibrium employment is reduced by the presence of the imperfection in the labour market (i.e. the monopoly union) and again by monopoly in the product market (as compared with Bertrand competition). The shift from monopoly to Bertrand competition reduces real wage pushfulness by the factor $\frac{\eta}{\eta-1}$.

3.2.3 Replacement rates

Real wage pushfulness and hence the gap between equilibrium unemployment in the New Keynesian model and in the NCBM is increased by the presence of unemployment benefits. We assume that households receive b per hour for hours for which they are able to claim unemployment benefit. Dropping the subscript i, the utility function is now:

$$U = we + (1-e)b - \frac{\phi e^\sigma}{\sigma}, \tag{15.60}$$

which is maximized with respect to w subject to $e = w^{-\eta}\left(\frac{A}{N}\right)$, i.e.

$$U = w^{1-\eta}A/N + (1 - w^{-\eta}A/N)b - \frac{\phi}{\sigma}\left(w^{-\eta}A/N\right)^{\sigma}.$$

This implies that

$$\frac{\partial U}{\partial w} = (1 - \eta)(w^{-\eta}A/N) + b\eta\frac{(w^{-\eta}A/N)}{w} + \eta\phi(w^{-\eta}A/N)^{\sigma-1}\frac{(w^{-\eta}A/N)}{w} = 0.$$

Dividing through by $(w^{-\eta}A/N)$, multiplying by w and using $e = w^{-\eta}\left(\frac{A}{N}\right)$ we get

$$(1 - \eta)w + b\eta + \eta\phi e^{\sigma-1} = 0$$

so that

$$w^{WS} = \frac{b\eta}{\eta - 1} + \phi\frac{\eta}{\eta - 1}e^{\sigma-1}.$$

With Bertrand pricing,

$$w^{PS} = 1 = w^{WS} = \frac{b\eta}{\eta - 1} + \phi\frac{\eta}{\eta - 1}e^{\sigma-1}$$

and therefore

$$e_e^{NK} = \left[\frac{1}{\phi}\left(\frac{\eta - 1}{\eta} - b\right)\right]^{\frac{1}{\sigma-1}}.$$

Therefore $b > 0$ implies a reduction in e_e^{NK}. Since $e_e^{NC} = \left(\frac{1}{\phi}\right)^{\frac{1}{\sigma-1}}$,

$$\log e_e^{NK} - \log e_e^{NC} = \frac{1}{\sigma - 1}\log\left(\frac{\eta - 1}{\eta} - b\right)$$

$$= -\frac{1}{\sigma - 1}\log\left(\frac{\eta}{\eta(1 - b) - 1}\right). \qquad (15.61)$$

The presence of unemployment benefits does not alter real wage rigidity, which remains equal to $\frac{1}{\sigma-1}$ but increases real wage pushfulness, as can be seen by comparing the above expression with the equation labelled (Bertrand competition).

3.2.4 Coordinated wage-bargaining

Calmfors–Driffill

In Chapter 4, we set out a simple version of the famous Calmfors–Driffill model[9] that predicts that economies with either highly centralized or highly decentralized wage-setting structures have low equilibrium unemployment, whereas those with 'intermediate' or industry-level wage setting have high equilibrium unemployment. Here we show how the result can be derived from the micro model that we have been using in this chapter.

---

[9] Calmfors and Driffill (1988).

The analysis focuses on the role of the number of sectors, N, for each of which there is a union wage setter and on the elasticity of demand for sectoral output, η. It is assumed that N and η are independent. To simplify the algebra, we assume that $\sigma = 2$. The union in sector i maximizes

$$U_i = w_i e_i - \phi \frac{e_i^2}{2} \text{ with respect to } w_i \text{ subject to } e_i = w_i^{-\eta}(y/N), \tag{15.62}$$

where y is aggregate demand. This implies

$$(1 - \eta)w_i^{-\eta}(A/N) + w_i^{1-\eta}\frac{1}{N}\frac{\partial y}{\partial w_i} + \phi\eta(w_i^{-\eta}(A/N))\frac{w_i^{-\eta}}{w_i}(A/N)$$

$$- \phi(w_i^{-\eta}(A/N))w_i^{-\eta}\frac{1}{N}\frac{\partial y}{\partial w_i} = 0.$$

We simplify this by dividing through by $(w_i^{-\eta}(y/N))$ and defining $\epsilon_{yw_i} \equiv \frac{w_i}{y}\frac{\partial y}{\partial w_i}$:

$$(1 - \eta) + \epsilon_{yw_i} + \phi\eta\frac{e_i}{w_i} - \phi\frac{e_i}{w_i}\epsilon_{yw_i} = 0$$

$$w_i(\eta - 1 - \epsilon_{yw_i}) = [\phi(\eta - \epsilon_{yw_i})]e_i,$$

$$\therefore w_i = \frac{[\phi(\eta - \epsilon_{yw_i})]}{[\eta - 1 - \epsilon_{yw_i}]}e_i. \tag{15.63}$$

In order to evaluate the responsiveness of output to wages in sector i, ϵ_{yw_i}, we need to bring in the Central Bank's monetary policy rule (Chapter 5). We write this as:

$$\pi - \pi^T = -\gamma(y - y_e) \tag{15.64}$$

and

$$\therefore y = -\frac{\pi}{\gamma} + K, \text{ where } K = y_e + \frac{\pi^T}{\gamma}. \tag{15.65}$$

Returning to ϵ_{yw_i}, we have

$$\epsilon_{yw_i} = \frac{w_i}{y}\frac{\partial y}{\partial w_i} = \frac{\partial \log y}{\partial \log w_i} = -\frac{1}{\gamma}\frac{\partial \log \pi}{\partial \log w_i} = -\frac{1}{\gamma}\frac{\partial(\log P - \log P_{-1})}{\partial \log w_i} = -\frac{1}{\gamma}\frac{\partial \log P}{\partial \log w_i}.$$

We can show[10] that $\frac{\partial \log P}{\partial \log w_i} = \frac{1}{N-1}$ and therefore

$$\epsilon_{yw_i} = -\frac{1}{\gamma}\cdot\frac{1}{N-1}.$$

[10] Since $\frac{\partial \log P}{\partial \log w_i} = \frac{\partial \log P}{\partial(\log W_i - \log P)} = 1/\left(\frac{\partial \log W_i}{\partial \log P} - 1\right)$ and $\frac{\partial \log P}{\partial \log W_i} = \frac{\partial N^{-1}\Sigma \log P_i}{\partial \log W_i} = 1/N$, we have

$$\frac{\partial \log P}{\partial \log w_i} = \frac{1}{N-1}.$$

Hence,

$$w_i = \frac{\phi\left(\eta + \gamma^{-1} \cdot \frac{1}{N-1}\right)}{\eta - 1 + \gamma^{-1} \cdot \frac{1}{N-1}} \cdot e_i$$

and remembering that $\gamma = 1/\alpha\beta$ (from Chapter 5), we have with Bertrand pricing,

$$e_e(N, \eta) = \frac{\eta - 1 + (\alpha\beta)/(N-1)}{\phi(\eta + \alpha\beta/(N-1))}. \tag{15.66}$$

If we assume that $\alpha = 1 = \beta$ (i.e. the slope of the Phillips curve is equal to one and the weight in inflation in the central bank's loss function is equal to one), we have

$$e_e(N, \eta) = \phi^{-1}\left[\frac{\eta - 1 + \frac{1}{N-1}}{\eta + \frac{1}{N-1}}\right]. \tag{15.67}$$

As the number of sectors, N, increases, equilibrium employment falls and as the elasticity of demand increases, equilibrium employment rises. The 'number of sectors' effect captures the extent to which wage setters internalize the impact of the wage they set on the economy-wide price level, taking account of the behaviour of the central bank: this is reflected in the term ϵ_{yw_i}. The 'elasticity of demand' effect captures the effect on product demand at sectoral level of a rise in the wage and hence of sectoral prices.

The simplest way of relating this result (equation 15.67) to the Calmfors–Driffill hump-shaped relationship is to assume that the elasticity of demand remains fairly constant as the number of sectors rises initially. This produces the result that as we go from wage setting taking place in a centralized way with one sector only, i.e. $N = 1$ and increase the number of sectors, the equilibrium employment rate falls. However once there are many sectors, the elasticity of demand will begin to rise as the number of sectors increases further. The elasticity effect will eventually outweigh the 'number of sectors' effect and equilibrium employment will rise as decentralization increases (see Fig. 15.6).

Coordinated wage bargaining and central bank preferences

A rather surprising result that comes from this model is that with a limited number of sectors and therefore relatively coordinated wage bargaining, the higher the weight on inflation in the central bank's utility function, the higher is the equilibrium employment

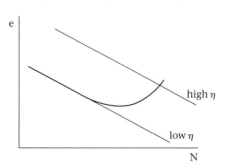

Figure 15.6 Equilibrium employment: the Calmfors–Driffill result

rate in the economy.[11] This is paradoxical: one might after all have expected that the higher the weight that the central bank attached to *employment*, the higher would be the equilibrium employment rate. To see this result all we need to do is to look again at the equation (15.66):

$$e_e(N, \eta) = \frac{\eta - 1 + (\alpha\beta)/(N-1)}{\phi(\eta + \alpha\beta/(N-1))}.$$

The preference of the central bank for low inflation relative to employment is given in this equation by β. Hence, holding η and N constant, an increase in β leads to an increase in e_e. (Suppose $\eta = 4$ and $x = 1$ then an increase of 1 in x implies that $\frac{\eta-1+x}{\eta+x}$ is now $5/6$ whereas before the increase it was $4/5$.) But the effect of an increase in β is weighted by $1/(N-1)$ so the smaller is N (i.e. the greater the coordination of wage bargaining), the bigger will be the increase in e_e as a result of an increase in β. The result hinges on the reasoning of the union: when N is small, the union knows that its wage decision will affect economy-wide inflation and, in turn, this will elicit a contractionary response from the central bank: thus the more inflation averse is the central bank, the more restrained will be the union and hence, the higher will be equilibrium employment.

4 Disequilibrium (1): demand shocks and output response

The last section showed how imperfect competition could explain involuntary unemployment in equilibrium. The next three sections attempt to explain why there can be—perhaps prolonged—periods of disequilibrium. Again imperfectly competitive product and labour markets are central to the explanation. The basic framework of analysis will be the 3-equation model, as in the rest of the book; but here the focus is on the micro behaviour of firms and households, as well as that of the government.

Disequilibrium is caused by shocks. We shall concentrate throughout on the case of an adverse demand shock. Fundamental to the analysis is the slow adjustment of inflation to disequilibrium. In sections 4 and 5 this slow adjustment is taken as given. In this section we see that imperfect competition is necessary for the adverse demand shock to be reflected in a reduction in output. In the next section, we ask under what conditions an initial demand shock is amplified (the multiplier) or dampened (the forward-looking *IS* curve). And in section 6, competing explanations for the slow adjustment of inflation are set out (the New Keynesian Phillips curve and the Sticky Information Phillips curve). Each of the three sections respond to empirical observations: that a demand shock generates a change in output before prices change (section 4); that the demand shock is often amplified via household behaviour (section 5); and that inflation only adjusts relatively slowly in response to equilibrium (section 6).

Why then is market structure necessary to explain the output response to a demand shock? In the NCBM, an increase in aggregate demand is immediately eliminated by an

---

[11] The full model showing this result is set out in Soskice and Iversen (2000).

appropriate automatic increase in prices. Moreover output and employment remain at their equilibrium levels. This does not accord with empirical evidence. An increase in aggregate demand normally leads first to an increase in output and employment and only subsequently to price increases.[12]

We show in this section:

First, that a necessary condition for output to increase in response to an increase in aggregate demand without a prior rise in prices is the absence of perfect competition.

Second, that, if firms are operating under conditions of imperfect competition, output will increase under a range of conditions, even if prices are fixed.

(Note that the underlying assumption of this and the next section is that prices are fixed or at any rate that inflation adjusts slowly to disequilibrium. It is not being argued that imperfect competition by itself sustains disequilibrium: with imperfect competition, fully flexible wages and prices imply continuous equilibrium as much as with perfect competition.)

4.1 Output under perfect competition and fixed prices

The first proposition is that under perfect competition and constant prices an increase in demand has no effect on output. In Fig. 15.7 the same basic assumptions are made about sectors and sectoral demand functions as in the last section. There are N sectors and the ith sectoral demand function is $p_i^{-\eta}(A/N)$. But now we assume that each sector is perfectly competitive. There are M firms in each sector, where M is a very large number. Assume output is distributed equally among the firms (y_0 per firm), and that aggregate demand is initially A_0. The sectoral relative price level is P_i^0/P. Hence $y_0 = (P_i^0/P)^{-\eta}(A_0/MN)$. Since we start in equilibrium, $P_i^0 = MC = W_i^0/MPL(y_0)$, where W_i^0 is the initial money wage in sector i. Note that at y_0 each firm maximizes profits since higher ouput implies $MC > P_i^0$ and lower output $MC < P_i^0$.

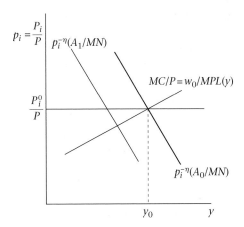

Figure 15.7 Perfect competition and output responses

[12] For example, Christiano, Eichenbaum, and Evans (2005).

Now there is an adverse demand shock: aggregate demand falls from A_0 to A_1 and the demand curve shifts inwards. By assumption, P_i^0 and W_i^0 remain fixed (and assume this is true in all sectors so that P does not change). Thus neither relative price nor the real MC curve have shifted. Hence the individual firm has no incentive to cut output below y_0. If it did so, price would be greater than marginal cost so that it would pay to expand output. Thus, absent prior price increases, output remains fixed under perfect competition in the face of adverse demand shocks.

4.2 Output under imperfect competition and fixed prices

To resolve this problem we need to move to imperfect competition (see Fig. 15.8). We now adopt the assumptions of the last section: the ith firm has a monopoly for the good it produces. It is initially in equilibrium with marginal revenue equal to marginal cost, i.e. $MR_0 = MC/P$, with a profit-maximizing relative price of P_i^0/P. There is then an adverse demand shock and aggregate demand falls from A_0 to A_1. As above we assume that P_i^0/P remains constant as does the MC/P schedule. What happens to profit-maximizing output?

In the new situation with reduced demand, but with the relative price fixed at P_i^0/P, the maximum quantity of goods that the ith firm can sell is y_1. At that relative price consumers will not be prepared to buy more. Moreover, it will always pay the firm to sell at least y_1, since the marginal real profit on the last good sold will be the distance between P_i^0/P and the real MC curve.

Thus it will pay the firm to reduce its output by the full amount of the reduction in demand at constant relative prices under the assumptions we have made. (In fact if the demand curves are downward-sloping, and the real MC curve is not too downwards sloping, this result is generally true.) One final point is that the usual downward-sloping marginal revenue curve for the A_1 demand curve has no meaning if prices are fixed. Instead the correct marginal revenue curve is now the fixed price for $y < y_1$; the marginal revenue for the firm is P_i^0. But above y_1 the firm can sell nothing, so the marginal revenue drops at once to zero. Hence the correct marginal revenue schedule is the inverted dotted L line, MR_1.

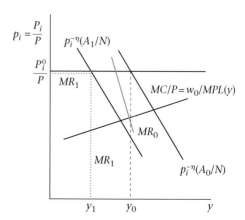

Figure 15.8 Adverse demand shock with imperfect competition and fixed prices

5 Disequilibrium (2): Amplification and the dampening of demand shocks

Following the last section, the assumption of perfect price and wage flexibility is dropped in both this and the next section; and it is assumed that a change in aggregate demand translates directly into a corresponding change in output. As we have seen in the last section this requires some degree of imperfect competition: here that will be a background assumption, while it will be the focus of interest in section 6. This section asks the question: given an adverse exogenous demand shock, is its effect on aggregate demand one-for-one ($dy = dA$) or amplified ($dy > dA$) or dampened ($dy < dA$), where y is aggregate demand and A is exogenous demand?

One of the best known of Keynesian arguments is the multiplier effect. The effect on aggregate demand of an initial change in exogenous demand will be increased by the multiplier. In its standard form, if $y = cy + A$, where y is output, c the propensity to consume, with $0 < c < 1$, and A exogenous demand, $\Delta y = \Delta A/(1 - c)$, where $1/(1 - c) > 1$ is the multiplier. Thus the effect of an adverse demand shock is *amplified* by the multiplier. This argument, transposed into deviations from income ($x \equiv y - y_e$), is developed in section 5.2.

The multiplier effect has no place in the NCBM for two reasons. First, the economy is always in equilibrium as a result of wage and price flexibility (an assumption dropped in New Keynesian economics). Moreover, the theory of the consumption function set out in the NCBM argues against the existence of a multiplier effect. If a household can spread consumption over long periods of time via saving and borrowing, then average consumption should depend on lifetime earnings, consumption should normally be constant to maximize utility, and changes in consumption should reflect interest rate movements relative to its subjective discount rate. This can be seen by the consumption-smoothing equation (15.19) in section 2, $\log c_t = \log c_{t+1} - \frac{1}{\theta}(r_t - \rho)$. This approach as we noted goes back to Friedman's Permanent Income Hypothesis. Under the assumptions of perfect foresight and costless lending and borrowing, adverse exogenous demand shocks only affect consumption to the extent that they change estimates of lifetime income.

Moving to the New Keynesian world, we ask how the optimizing intertemporal consumption analysis is incorporated. We take as given the New Keynesian assumption that in the face of an aggregate demand shock, a change in the real interest rate by the central bank cannot have an immediate effect on aggregate demand so as to offset the shock before output is affected. Hence the shock will affect aggregate demand but will it be amplified or dampened? The PIH approach makes perfectly good sense in a New Keynesian world in which inflation adjusts slowly, and in which there can be disequilibrium between demand and equilibrium output. In such a world the consumption smoothing approach implies the absence of amplification. But if consumption is constant in the face of a fall in A there is no dampening either.

Starting from a similar logic more recent work on the so-called 'Forward looking *IS* curve'[13] suggests an additional dampening effect. They argue as follows: given the lagged

---

[13] McCallum and Nelson (1999). Also, see Clarida et al. (1999) and Woodford (2003).

effect of interest rates (as discussed in Chapter 5) the consumption function can be written

$$\log c_t = \log c_{t+1} - \frac{1}{\theta}(r_{t-1} - \rho).$$ (15.68)

Households can predict that the central bank will react to an adverse demand shock by reducing current interest rates, r_t. Hence c_{t+1}^E is increased and hence c_t will be increased. Thus the adverse shock is dampened.

Assuming perfect foresight and rational expectations, and starting from the simple model (2.1.1) developed in the NCBM section, which of these effects dominates depends on the ability of households to spread consumption via savings and borrowing.

5.1 Dampening: the forward-looking *IS* curve

In this subsection, we show how households may dampen the impact of adverse demand shocks. This arises via consumption smoothing and rational expectations. Households can work out that the central bank will respond over time with low interest rates in order to return the economy to equilibrium. Hence there will be higher expenditure in the future and it therefore pays households to increase expenditure now.

In what follows we basically use the the model in 2.1.1 with complete borrowing and lending and perfect foresight. However, in order to compare the dampening argument with the amplification (multiplier) argument it will be simpler not to work in logs: this implies that the results in what follows are only approximately true if the assumptions of the model in 2.1.1 hold.

Consumption behaviour with complete borrowing and lending and perfect foresight is given by $c_t = c_{t+1} - \theta^{-1}(r_t - \rho)$. From $y_t = c_t + A_t$, $c_t = y_t - A_t$. Similarly, $c_{t+1} = y_{t+1} - A_{t+1}$. Hence, returning to the consumption-smoothing equation,

$$y_t - A_t = y_{t+1} - A_{t+1} - \theta^{-1}(r_t - \rho).$$ (15.69)

As before it is simplest to express the argument in terms of excess demand, $x \equiv y - y_e$. To do this define $r_{S,t}$ by

$$y_e - A_t = y_e - A_{t+1} - \theta^{-1}(r_{S,t} - \rho)$$ (15.70)

and subtract equation (15.70) from (15.69):

$$x_t = x_{t+1} - a(r_t - r_{S,t}),$$ (15.71)

where $a \equiv 1/\theta$. This is the forward-looking *IS* curve, since current excess demand depends on next period's excess demand via consumption smoothing.

We use the double lag structure of the monetary policy chapter. Thus we rewrite the previous equation as:

$$x_t = x_{t+1} - a(r_{t-1} - r_{S,t}).$$ (15.72)

To be clear about periods, assume the current period is $t = 0$.

$$x_0 = x_1 - a(r_{-1} - r_{S,0}).$$ (15.73)

And, at $t = 0$, A increases from A_0 to $\hat{A}_0$. Define $\Delta A = \hat{A}_0 - A_0$. We can relate ΔA to a corresponding change in r_S from $r_{S,0}$ to $\hat{r}_{S,0}$: before A_0 increases

$$y_e - A_0 = y_e - A_1 - a r_{S,0}$$

and after A_0 increases to $\hat{A}_0$

$$y_e - \hat{A}_0 = y_e - A_1 - a\hat{r}_{S,0}$$

so that

$$\Delta A = \hat{A}_0 - A_0 = a(\hat{r}_{S,0} - r_{S,0}) = a\Delta r_S.$$

Now, taking changes on both sides of equation (15.73), we have:

$$\Delta x_0 = \Delta x_1 + a\Delta r_{S,0} = \Delta x_1 + \Delta A.$$ (15.74)

The impact effect of ΔA is thus simply $\Delta x_0 = \Delta A$. The dampening effect comes as a result of the simultaneous $\Delta x_1 > 0$, if households believe that x_1 rises as a result of the adverse shock, ΔA. Here is why rational households should expect x_1 to increase: if, in $t = 0, x_0 < 0$ that implies via the period 1 Phillips curve (i.e. $\pi_1 = \pi^T + \alpha x_0$) that $\pi_1 < \pi^T$. So the Central Bank will reduce r_0 to ensure that $x_1 > 0$ in order to return π to its target value π^T. This means that x_1 will increase, thus increasing x_0 because of consumption smoothing.

The question is, how do households at time 0 work out, using rational expectations, the effect of ΔA on Δx_1? x_1 is given by the intersection of the monetary rule line, MR, and the Phillips curve for π_2, (PC_2). We shall assume in this section that the Phillips curve is backward looking, so $\pi_2 = \pi_1 + \alpha x_1$. Since π_1 is unknown, households can use the period 1 Phillips curve, $\pi_1 = \pi^T + \alpha x_0$ to express π_1 in terms of x_0. For simplicity assume $\pi^T = 0$. Then $\pi_1 = \alpha x_0$ and therefore

$$PC: \pi_2 = \pi_1 + \alpha x_1 = \alpha x_0 + \alpha x_1$$

As usual we write the monetary policy rule, MR, as

$$MR: \pi_2 = -\gamma x_1$$

so eliminating π_2

$$-(\alpha + \gamma)x_1 = \alpha x_0.$$

Now take changes on both sides

$$-(\alpha + \gamma)\Delta x_1 = \alpha \Delta x_0$$

and using $\Delta x_0 = \Delta x_1 + \Delta A$

$$-(\alpha + \gamma)\Delta x_1 = \alpha(\Delta x_1 + \Delta A)$$

$$\Delta x_1 = -\frac{\alpha}{2\alpha + \gamma}\Delta A.$$

Finally, again using $\Delta x_0 = \Delta x_1 + \Delta A$, we can see the full effect of ΔA on Δx_0:

$$\Delta x_0 = \Delta x_1 + \Delta A = -\frac{\alpha}{2\alpha + \gamma}\Delta A + \Delta A$$

$$= \Delta A. \left(1 - \frac{\alpha}{2\alpha + \gamma}\right) = \Delta A. \left(\frac{\alpha + \gamma}{2\alpha + \gamma}\right).$$

Since

$$0 < \left(\frac{\alpha + \gamma}{2\alpha + \gamma}\right) < 1$$

the effect of ΔA on Δx_0 is dampened:

$$\Delta A < 0 \;\Rightarrow\; 0 > \Delta x_0 = \Delta A. \left(\frac{\alpha + \gamma}{2\alpha + \gamma}\right) > \Delta A. \tag{15.75}$$

It may also be useful to look at this process geometrically. In Fig. 15.9, we first note what happens if the consumption function takes the form $\hat{x}_0 = -a(r_{-1} - r_S)$, i.e. without consumption smoothing. The inflation and output gap terms for this case have hats. Thus, we have $\hat{x}_0 = \Delta A < 0$. So $\hat{\pi}_1 = \pi^T + \alpha\hat{x}_0 = \pi^T + \alpha\Delta A$. And $\hat{x}_1$ is given by the intersection of MR and the $\hat{\pi}_2$ Phillips curve that goes through $\hat{\pi}_1 = \pi^T + \alpha\Delta A$ on the vertical $x = 0$ line. We now introduce consumption smoothing. x_1 is determined at the intersection of MR and the π_2 Phillips curve. From above, the latter is $\pi_2 = \pi^T + \alpha\Delta A + 2\alpha x_1$, and this is shown in the diagram by the dashed line passing through the same point on the vertical Phillips curve but with a slope twice as steep as the $\hat{\pi}_2$ Phillips curve. Since $x_0 = x_1 + \Delta A$, x_0 must be ΔA less than x_1, as shown in the diagram. Hence, it is clear that following the shock, the initial output gap is smaller (in absolute terms) than without consumption smoothing, so that dampening has occurred.

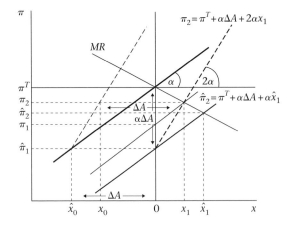

Figure 15.9 The forward-looking *IS* curve and the dampening of a demand shock

5.2 Amplification: liquidity constrained consumption and the multiplier

In a traditional Keynesian world, by contrast, demand shocks are amplified via the multiplier. The amplification of a demand shock via the multiplier operates through consumption: a cut in exogenous demand cuts output and income and this leads to a reduction in consumption, thus further depressing demand. There are therefore two elements to the mechanism:

(1) A cut in demand cuts output and income. This applied as much to the last subsection; and in the last section, we demonstrated that this required inflexible prices and wages in the short run and imperfect competition.

(2) A cut in income cuts consumption expenditure. There is considerable empirical evidence (see Chapter 7) that this mechanism is an important one—even if the size of the multiplier may not be all that great. The questions are: how is this consistent with the rationality of micro actors? And—given that the multiplier effect does not operate in the NCBM—what assumptions of the NCBM do we need to drop?

That there is a problem for household rationality is evident from the model in 2.1.1. If households can save and borrow, and if they have perfect foresight, then they will engage in consumption smoothing as implied by $c_t = c_{t+1} - \frac{1}{\theta}(r_{t-1} - \rho)$; in which case, as the last subsection showed, the dampening argument operates. Thus the simplest way of motivating the multiplier is to assume that some proportion of households ω has neither assets nor borrowing capacity, and to simplify, that they do not save. It is then rational for them to consume all their income; and unconstrained borrowing and lending are the assumptions of the NCBM that we drop.

Assume all incomes are equal, and that initially there is no change in A_0: then the total consumption of the constrained households is ωy, and the consumption of the unconstrained households is $(1 - \omega)c$, so that

$$y_0 = \omega y_0 + (1 - \omega)c_0 + A_0$$

Hence

$$c_0 = y_0 - A_0/(1 - \omega)$$
$$c_1 = y_1 - A_1/(1 - \omega).$$

Since the consumption of the unconstrained (smoothing) households is

$$c_0 = c_1 - a(r_{-1} - \rho)$$

we have

$$y_0 - A_0/(1 - \omega) = y_1 - A_1/(1 - \omega) - a(r_{-1} - \rho)$$

and as before

$$y_e - A_0/(1 - \omega) = y_e - A_1/(1 - \omega) - a(r_S - \rho)$$

so that

$$x_0 = x_1 - a(r_{-1} - r_S).$$

Thus far we have assumed no change in A_0. Now assume A_0 falls to $\hat{A}_0$, so that as before $\Delta A = \hat{A}_0 - A_0$. As we did in the dampening case, we can again relate ΔA to Δr_S, by using $\Delta A = \hat{A}_0 - A_0 = a(\hat{r}_{S,0} - r_{S,0}) = a\Delta r_S$:

$$y_e - \hat{A}_0/(1 - \omega) = y_e - A_1/(1 - \omega) - a(\hat{r}_S - \rho)$$

to get

$$\Delta A/(1 - \omega) = a\Delta r_S.$$

Now take changes on both sides of $x_0 = x_1 - a(r_{-1} - r_S)$ and

$$\Delta x_0 = \Delta x_1 + \Delta A/(1 - \omega). \tag{15.76}$$

This equation enables us to look at the impact effect of a change in A under two assumptions. The first assumes that x_1 is constant. This is the assumption that the borrowing-saving households do not take into account the effect on x_1 via monetary policy explored in the previous subsection, 5.1. The result is the standard Keynesian multiplier

$$\Delta x_1 = 0 \quad \Rightarrow \quad \Delta x_0 = \Delta A/(1 - \omega), \tag{15.77}$$

where the multiplier is $1/(1 - \omega).1/(1 - \omega)$, which is greater than one, since $0 < \omega < 1$. Hence

$$\Delta A < 0 \quad \Rightarrow \quad 0 > \Delta A > \Delta x_0 = \Delta A/(1 - \omega). \tag{15.78}$$

5.3 Comparing dampening and amplification

The second assumption is the contrary one, that the effect on x_1 via monetary policy is taken into account: this will enable us to compare the amplifying and the dampening effects together. Just as before, to work out Δx_1 through rational expectations, we use the Phillips curve and the central bank's monetary rule to find Δx_1 in terms of Δx_0:

$$-(\alpha + \gamma)\Delta x_1 = \alpha \Delta x_0.$$

Now

$$\Delta x_0 = \Delta x_1 + \Delta A/(1 - \omega)$$

so that

$$\Delta x_1 = -\frac{\alpha}{2\alpha + \gamma}\frac{\Delta A}{1 - \omega}.$$

Note the dampening: Δx_1 has the opposite sign to ΔA. And hence

$$\Delta x_0 = \frac{\Delta A}{(1 - \omega)} \left(\frac{\alpha + \gamma}{2\alpha + \gamma} \right). \tag{15.79}$$

The critical question is now whether or not $(\alpha + \gamma)/(2\alpha + \gamma)(1 - \omega) \gtreqless 1$. If $(\alpha + \gamma)/(2\alpha + \gamma)(1 - \omega) > 1$, then the net effect is amplifying; if < 1, the net effect is dampening; and if $= 1$, it is neutral. The condition is straightforward:

$$\left(\frac{\alpha + \gamma}{2\alpha + \gamma} \right) / (1 - \omega) \gtreqless 1 \Leftrightarrow \omega \gtreqless \frac{\alpha}{2\alpha + \gamma} = \frac{1}{2 + \gamma/\alpha}. \tag{15.80}$$

Since $1/(2 + \gamma/\alpha) < 0.5$, a sufficient condition for amplification is that $\omega \geq 0.5$. Any flattening of the MR curve (with slope $\gamma = \frac{1}{\alpha\beta}$) reduces amplification. An increase in β reduces amplification because β measures the inflation aversion of the central bank: for a given fall in π_1, the central bank will increase x_1 substantially. So the initial fall in A will be considerably dampened by an increase in x_1 if β is high. Similarly if α is high, the Phillips curves are steep so again the MR is flat. For the same reason as above, the central bank will react strongly to the initial fall in A and dampening will be enhanced.

5.4 Summary

This section has provided two quite different New Keynesian perspectives on the impact effect of exogenous demand shocks on aggregate demand. The standard multiplier approach, based on some degree of liquidity constraint on households, implies an amplification of the exogenous demand shock. The forward-looking IS curve, allowing borrowing, implies dampening as rational households take account of the expansionary impact of endogenous monetary policy on future consumption and hence via consumption smoothing on present consumption.

In 5.3 these two approaches were put together to get an idea of the net impact of exogenous demand change on aggregate demand. An increase in α, the slope of the Phillips curve, implies an increase in relative dampening: the reason for this is that the main effect of an increase in α is its initial effect of translating x_0 into a fall in inflation of $\pi_1 - \pi^T = \alpha \Delta x_0$. The bigger the initial decline in inflation the larger will be the increase in x_1 as a result of monetary policy trying to raise π_2 back to π^T. And the larger the increase in x_1, the bigger (i.e. closer to zero) will be x_0. So x_0 is more dampened. A decrease in β reduces dampening: this is because the looser is monetary policy the less will be the rise in x_1 (the monetary authorities being less concerned to return π promptly to π^T). And, finally, the bigger is the weight of credit-constrained households, ω, the greater the multiplier effects. As we discussed in Chapter 7, an alternative route to produce amplification in a model in which investment as well as consumption is modelled is the presence of financing constraints on firms, which implies that for some proportion of firms, their ability to implement investment plans depends on cash flow and hence on current activity.

6 Disequilibrium (3): Sustained disequilibrium and microfoundations of Phillips curves

The analysis of sustained disequilibrium, with rational expectations and maximizing agents, is the centrepiece of the New Keynesian approach. Focusing the analysis so far on an adverse demand shock, a necessary condition for the shock to translate into below equilibrium output is that wages and prices are not perfectly flexible; and a second necessary condition, given imperfect wage and price flexibility, is some form of monopoly or oligopolistic competition (section 4). In an appendix, we set out the menu cost theory of price (or wage stickiness), which shows why a small cost of adjusting prices or wages may in the context of imperfect competition entail large macroeconomic effects.

What is still missing however is a model of wage and price stickiness, grounded in rational expectations, maximizing agents and imperfect competition, which shows how wages and prices adjust over time to disequilibrium: in other words a proper micro-founded analysis of the Phillips curve in which π^E is based on rational expectations. Thus far in the book the *IS-PC-MR* model has been based on maximizing behaviour by the monetary authorities as embodied in the *MR*, and—introduced in section 5.1—maximizing behaviour by households in the *IS*. But we have assumed throughout that, either for some unexplained reason there is inflation inertia so that the Phillips curve takes the form $\pi = \pi^I + \alpha x$, with $\pi^I = \pi_{-1}$, or what amounts to the same thing in practice $\pi = \pi^E + \alpha x$ with $\pi^E = \pi_{-1}$. The justification for doing this is empirical: inflation inertia, $\pi = \pi_{-1} + \alpha x$ fits the data well.

There are two components required for proper microfoundations for the Phillips curve. First, we need to show how decisions made by individual price setters imply $\pi = \pi^E + \alpha x$, where we take expected inflation as given. This is done in the first subsection. Second, we need to develop a rational expectations based theory of π^E. This is pursued in the following subsections in which we set out two proposed approaches: the New Keynesian Phillips curve based on sticky prices and the Sticky Information Phillips curve.

6.1 The microfoundations of the inertial Phillips curve: $\pi = \pi_{-1} + \alpha x$

We can provide microfoundations for the Phillips curve, $\pi = \pi_{-1} + \alpha x$ as follows. From section 3 and equation (15.47)

$$\log w_i = \log \left(\frac{\phi \eta}{\eta - 1} \right) + (\sigma - 1) \log e_i$$

and assuming Bertrand pricing to simplify the exposition:

$$\log p_i = \log w_i$$

we have

$$\log p_i = \log \left(\frac{\phi \eta}{\eta - 1} \right) + (\sigma - 1) \log e_i.$$

In equilibrium:

$$0 = \log\left(\frac{\phi\eta}{\eta-1}\right) + (\sigma-1)\log e_e$$

and therefore

$$\log p_i = (\sigma-1)[\log e_i - \log e_e]$$

and if labour productivity is constant, we can switch from employment to output:

$$\log p_i = (\sigma-1)[\log y_i - \log y_e],$$

which implies

$$\log P_i = \log P + (\sigma-1)[\log y_i - \log y_e].$$

In setting P_i, the ith firm has to make an assumption about $\log P^E$, i.e.

$$\log P_i = \log P^E + (\sigma-1)[\log y_i - \log y_e]. \tag{15.81}$$

Summing over N sectors, we have

$$N^{-1}\sum \log P_i = \log P^E + (\sigma-1)\left[N^{-1}\sum \log y_i - \log y_e\right]$$
$$\therefore \log P = \log P^E + (\sigma-1)[\log y - \log y_e]$$
$$\log P - \log P_{-1} = \log P^E - \log P_{-1} + (\sigma-1)[\log y - \log y_e],$$

which implies

$$\pi = \pi^E + (\sigma-1)\log x. \tag{15.82}$$

Hence, the steeper is the wage-setting curve (i.e. the greater is $\sigma - 1$) or equivalently, the lower is real wage rigidity (since RWR$\equiv 1/(\sigma - 1)$) the greater will be the effect of disequilibrium on inflation. To this point, therefore, the Phillips curve has microfoundations. So, in analysing sustained disequilibrium resulting, for example, from an exogenous demand shock, where we have got to amounts to this: section 4 explains why a negative demand shock translates into $x < 0$. Section 5 sets out the arguments for how an exogenous demand shock is amplified or dampened to produce the *net* demand shock and hence x. Given x, $\pi = \pi_{-1} + \alpha x$ shows how disequilibrium gradually reduces the inflation rate. In the knowledge of this, the monetary authorities choose how to modify x through the use of the monetary rule. However, we have so far simply assumed that $\pi^E = \pi_{-1}$. There are two problems with this: first as we said above, the model lacks forward-looking microfoundations on the part of wage and price setters. Second, the credibility of the monetary authorities has no role in the speed with which the economy returns to equilibrium.

This point is clarified if we compare two situations: one in which the economy is affected by an inflation shock and the other in which the central bank announces a lower inflation target. With the inertial Phillips curve, the economy responds to each event in the same way: the central bank raises the interest rate in order that $x < 0$ and the economy adjusts down the MR to equilibrium. However, if the central bank has credibility, we would expect there to be a difference in the response of the economy to the two situations: with a credible central bank, an announced reduction in the inflation target would lead price and wage setters to adjust their expectations of inflation downwards and the central bank would be able to achieve the reduction in inflation to target at a smaller output cost than would a central bank that lacked credibility. For credibility to matter, price and wage setters must be forward looking. Putting these two points together: the inability of the model to take account of the reaction of price setters to the credibility (or not) of monetary policy is unsatisfactory; and the way to take such reactions into account is to base the Phillips curve on explicit forward-looking behaviour by price setters.

Recent developments in modelling the Phillips curve aim to provide a micro-optimization based model that can both allow sustained disequilibrium and a role for the credibility of monetary policy. We examine first the so-called New Keynesian Phillips curve (NKPC), which has been widely adopted in the literature (e.g. Clarida et al. 1999). It is based on a model of staggered price setting developed by Calvo.[14] We then look at an alternative approach based on sticky information.

6.2 The New Keynesian Phillips curve (NKPC)

The standard derivation of the NKPC is somewhat lengthy.[15] By cutting some corners, however, there is a much simpler derivation that makes the intuition behind the NKPC clear.

6.2.1 Deriving the NKPC

Calvo assumes that a random percentage, δ, of firms get to set their price in the current period. If $\log P_t$ is the log of the aggregate price level in t, and $\log P_t^*$ the log of the price set in t by those firms who can do so

$$\log P_t = \delta \log P_t^* + (1 - \delta) \log P_{t-1} \qquad (15.83)$$

since $(1 - \delta)$ of firms still charge the same price as in the last period.

This can be rewritten (since $\pi_t \equiv \log P_t - \log P_{t-1}$, $\pi_t^* \equiv \log P_t^* - \log P_{t-1}$)

$$\pi_t = \delta \pi_t^*. \qquad (15.84)$$

What inflation rate will the firms that can reset their prices in t choose? Given imperfect competition they will want to raise their relative price if $\log x > 0$ and reduce it if $\log x < 0$. Thus (if they knew they could also reset their price next period as well) they would choose $\pi_t^* = \pi_t + \alpha \log x_t$. However the price they set now has to last until they get a chance to reset their price. There is a $(1 - \delta)$ chance they will be unable to reset their price in $t + 1$, a $(1 - \delta)^2$ chance in $t + 2$, and so on. In addition they care less about the future because of the discount factor $\psi < 1$. Thus they attach a value of 1 to having the right price in the

---

[14] Calvo (1983).   [15] For example, Clarida et al. (1999).

current period, $(1 - \delta)\psi$ to having the right price in $t + 1$, $(1 - \delta)^2\psi^2$ in $t + 2$, etc. So their chosen π_t^* has to be the correct rate for the current period plus the correct rate for $t + 1$ weighted by $(1 - \delta)\psi$ plus the correct rate for $t + 2$ weighted by $(1 - \delta)^2\psi^2$, and so on. Hence:

$$\pi_t^* = [(\pi_t + \alpha \log x_t) + (1 - \delta)\psi(E_t\pi_{t+1} + \alpha E_t \log x_{t+1})$$
$$+ (1 - \delta)^2\psi^2(E_t\pi_{t+2} + \alpha E_t \log x_{t+2}) + \cdots]$$

and $\pi_t = \delta\pi_t^*$ implies

$$\pi_t = \delta[(\pi_t + \alpha \log x_t) + (1 - \delta)\psi(E_t\pi_{t+1} + \alpha E_t \log x_{t+1})$$
$$+ (1 - \delta)^2\psi^2(E_t\pi_{t+2} + \alpha E_t \log x_{t+2}) + \cdots].$$

Next we take the expectation of price setters at t about the same relation in $t + 1$, multiply both sides through by $(1 - \delta)\psi$:

$$(1 - \delta)\psi E_t\pi_{t+1} = \delta[(1 - \delta)\psi(E_t\pi_{t+1} + \alpha E_t \log x_{t+1})$$
$$+ (1 - \delta)^2\psi^2(E_t\pi_{t+2} + \alpha E_t \log x_{t+2}) + \cdots]$$

and subtract this from the previous equation to get

$$\text{NKPC: } \pi_t = \frac{\alpha\delta}{1 - \delta} \log x_t + \psi E_t\pi_{t+1}. \tag{15.85}$$

This is the NKPC. Note first that the expected inflation term relates not to the expected value of current inflation but to next period's inflation. Second in the standard inertial Phillips curve, the coefficient on $\log x$ is $\alpha \equiv \sigma - 1$. Here it is $\alpha\delta/(1 - \delta)$. If $\delta = 0.5$, the impact of $\log x$ on π is the same in the NKPC as in the standard Phillips curve. If $\delta < 0.5$, then the impact of $\log x$ on π is muted by the fact that a limited number of firms can adjust their price each period. As δ goes to 1, prices become more and more flexible: $\delta = 1$ corresponds to perfect flexibility and there is immediate adjustment since $\log x$ must go to zero if inflation is to be non-infinite.

6.2.2 Deriving $E_t\pi_{t+1}$

Dropping the expectations operators for convenience, price setters know the following NKPC equations:

$$\pi_{t+i} = \frac{\alpha\delta}{1 - \delta} \log x_{t+i} + \psi\pi_{t+i+1} \quad \forall i > 0$$

and the following MR equation

$$\pi_{t+i} = -\gamma \log x_{t+i}$$

if we assume that $\pi^T = 0$.

So in each period $t + i$ we can eliminate $\log x_{t+i}$ in the NKPC and MR pair of equations for $t + i$. This implies

$$\pi_{t+i} = \frac{\psi\gamma(1-\delta)}{\alpha\delta + \gamma(1-\delta)}\pi_{t+i+1}$$

where

$$0 < \beta \equiv \frac{\psi\gamma(1-\delta)}{\alpha\delta + \gamma(1-\delta)} < 1$$

which means that either $\pi_{t+i} = 0, \forall i > 0$ or $\pi_{t+i} \to \infty$ as $i \to \infty$. If we rule out this second possibility then

$$E_t\pi_{t+i} = 0 \ \forall i > 0. \tag{15.86}$$

The implication of this is that the disequilibrium only lasts one period: this is because (assuming there is a one-period lag before interest rates have any effect) $\log x_0 < 0$ as a result of the adverse shock, and therefore $\pi_0 = (\alpha\delta/1 - \delta)\log x_0 + \psi\pi_1$. In fact since $E_0\pi_1 = 0$, $\pi_0 = (\alpha\delta/1 - \delta)\log x_0 < 0$. But in period 1, $\log x_1 = 0 = \pi_1 = \pi_2$. And the same is true in all future periods.

6.2.3 Critique of the NKPC

The NKPC offers an elegant solution to the problems posed by the standard inertial Phillips curve. The NKPC is a forward-looking Phillips curve derived from microfoundations with rational expectations. Moreover it can take into account the credibility of the central bank to use its monetary rule: any change in the inflation target next period will be immediately reflected in current expectations about next period's inflation rate.

However, it fails signally to predict a sustained disequilibrium, because it does not predict inflation inertia. Instead, the disequilibrium lasts one period. Then inflation returns to the target level and output returns to equilibrium. The only way in which a sustained disequilibrium is allowed in the NKPC model is through the incorporation of an auto-correlated error in the original shock, an ad hoc procedure which goes quite against the elegance of the model.

6.3 The Sticky Information Phillips curve (SIPC)

The NKPC brings back rational expectations into the inflationary process, but it throws out the baby (the empirical fact of inflation inertia) with the bathwater of non-rationality. An important recent development by Mankiw and Reis argues that this is a consequence of basing the microeconomics on sticky prices.[16] Instead they argue that many price setters only have delayed awareness of up-to-date information about monetary policy. Mankiw and Reis call the Phillips curve based on this assumption the Sticky Information Phillips curve (SIPC).

[16] Mankiw and Reis (2002).

In the Mankiw–Reis formulation, the SIPC is somewhat complex mathematically. This results in part from the assumption that monetary policy is based on the growth of the money supply rather than the interest-rate based monetary rule, and in part from the assumption that a given proportion δ of price setters acquire up-to-date information each period. We develop instead a simple model using the interest rate based monetary rule and assuming that, while the proportion δ of price setters acquire up-to-date information each period, the remaining $(1 - \delta)$ receive that information one period later.

6.3.1 Deriving the SIPC

We leave aside for a moment the question of just what information is only acquired by the proportion δ of price setters each period. Remember that whether a firm has full or only limited information, all firms use rational expectations. So everyone knows that

$$\pi_t = \delta \pi_t^{FI} + (1 - \delta)\pi_t^{LI}. \tag{15.87}$$

As in the previous section, when a firm sets its price it will want to raise its relative price when $\log x > 0$ and vice versa. Expressed in terms of inflation, those with full information will choose the inflation rate $\pi_t^{FI} = \pi_t + \alpha \log x_t$ since they are assumed to know or be able to work out π_t and $\log x_t$. And those with limited information will set $\pi_t^{LI} = E_{t-1}(\pi_t + \alpha \log x_t)$. Hence, all parties know the equation:

$$\pi_t = \delta(\pi_t + \alpha \log x_t) + (1 - \delta)(E_{t-1}\pi_t + \alpha E_{t-1} \log x_t)$$
$$= \frac{\alpha\delta}{1 - \delta} \log x_t + E_{t-1}\pi_t + \alpha E_{t-1} \log x_t.$$

Of course those with limited information will not necessarily know π_t and $\log x_t$. However, using rational expectations they can deduce

$$E_{t-1}\pi_t = \frac{\alpha\delta}{1 - \delta}E_{t-1} \log x_t + E_{t-1}\pi_t + \alpha E_{t-1} \log x_t$$
$$\implies E_{t-1} \log x_t = 0.$$

This means that the SIPC takes the form:

$$\pi_t = \frac{\alpha\delta}{1 - \delta} \log x_t + E_{t-1}\pi_t. \tag{15.88}$$

We need to highlight the critical difference with the NKPC. In the NKPC $\pi_t = (\alpha\delta/1 - \delta) \log x_t + \psi E_t\pi_{t+1}$. In the SIPC, the $E_t\pi_{t+1}$ term is replaced by $E_{t-1}\pi_t$. In other words, if wage and price setters are rational in an NKPC world it is difficult to see how inflation inertia can come about, since $E_t\pi_{t+1}$ depends on expectations at t about *future* inflation. But in an SIPC world the most up to date information that $(1 - \delta)$ per cent of firms may have in forming their views about π_t at $t - 1$, ie $E_{t-1}\pi_t$, may plausibly include past factors that influence π_{t-1}.

6.3.2 Deriving $E_{t-1}\pi_t$

To find out $E_{t-1}\pi_t$ those with limited information now simply have to use the MR, namely $\pi_t = \pi_t^T - \gamma \log x_t$. This implies with rational expectations

$$E_{t-1}\pi_t = E_{t-1}\pi_t^T - \gamma E_{t-1}\log x_t = E_{t-1}\pi_t^T$$

since $E_{t-1}\log x_t = 0$. (The only qualification to this is that those with limited information may not know the up-to-date value of γ; we assume this is not the case.)

Going back to the earlier equation for π_t, this can now be simply rewritten as the Sticky Information Phillips curve

$$\pi_t = E_{t-1}\pi_t^T + \frac{\alpha\delta}{1-\delta}\log x_t \tag{15.89}$$

and together with the MR

$$\pi_t = \pi_t^T - \gamma \log x_t \tag{15.90}$$

these two equations determine π_t and $\log x_t$.

An example of limited information: the inflation target

A simple case is where those with limited information do not know that π^T has been lowered in period t. Assume in $t-1$ the economy was in a full information equilibrium with $\pi_{t-1} = \pi_{t-1}^T$ at point A. Assume also that $E_{t-1}\pi_t^T = \pi_{t-1}^T$. Then the SIPC in period t goes through $\log x = 0$ and $\pi = \pi_{t-1}^T$, as is shown in Fig. 15.10. The new MR goes through $\log x = 0$ and $\pi = \pi_t^T$. Thus the economy starts off at $\log x_{t-1} = 0$ and $\pi_{t-1} = \pi_{t-1}^T$. At t, $\log x$ becomes negative and π falls some of the way between π_{t-1}^T and π_t^T. Finally in $t+1$, the economy moves to its new equilibrium at point C with $\log x_{t+1} = 0$ and $\pi_{t+1} = \pi_t^T$ (assuming this remains the new target).

Two consequences should be noted. First, disinflation is costly in this approach. This contrasts with the NKPC approach. But note that an adverse demand shock is also immediately reversed unless there is an informational lag. Second, once those with limited information have understood the inflation target has fallen they immediately adjust their behaviour. Thus by contrast with the backwards-looking Phillips curve, central bank credibility matters here.

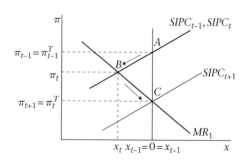

Figure 15.10 The Sticky Information Phillips curve: change in inflation target

6.3.3 A better comparison between the SIPC and the NKPC

It is not really appropriate to compare the SIPC with a one-period delay in information assimilation to the NKPC, because the NKPC assumes there is a distribution over time in the ability of firms to reset their prices. The appropriate comparison entails allowing information to diffuse more slowly in the SIPC. When we allow for more than a one-period lag in information assimilation this has the effect of slowing down the adjustment of the economy back to equilibrium, with the result that it is better able to predict the phenomenon of inflation persistence or inertia.

To illustrate this we now assume that the share δ_1 of firms acquire immediate knowledge of the reduction in π^T, δ_2 after one period, δ_3 after two periods and all firms after four periods.

In period 1 the SIPC is

$$\pi_1 = \pi_0^T + \frac{\alpha\delta_1}{1 - \delta_1} \log x_1.$$

That is, the share δ_1 believe that $\pi^T = \pi_1^T$ and have changed their price appropriately, while $(1 - \delta_1)$ still believe it is $\pi^T = \pi_0^T$.

In period 2 the SIPC is

$$\pi_2 = \pi_0^T + \frac{\alpha\delta_2}{1 - \delta_2} \log x_2$$

since δ_2 now have full information and $(1 - \delta_2)$ still believe that $\pi^T = \pi_0^T$. Likewise in period 3

$$\pi_3 = \pi_0^T + \frac{\alpha\delta_3}{1 - \delta_3} \log x_3$$

and only in period 4 when there is full information is the SIPC ($\pi_4 = \pi_1^T$, $\log x_4 = 0$). Thus in each period the SIPC gets steeper reflecting the increasing proportion of those with full information. This is shown in Fig. 15.11.

After π^T has risen from π_0^T to π_1^T, the *MR* curve is derived from the minimization of $(\log x)^2 + \beta(\pi - \pi_1^T)^2$, subject to the SIPC $\pi = \pi_0^T + (\alpha\delta/1 - \delta) \log x$ for $0 < \delta < 1$. Hence the *MR* curve is

$$\pi - \pi_1^T = -\frac{1 - \delta}{\alpha\beta\delta} \log x \qquad (15.91)$$

so as δ increases, the *MR* curve becomes flatter. This is also shown in Fig. 15.11. Hence we get a closer approximation to inflation inertia in the SIPC approach.

6.3.4 Critique of the SIPC

The SIPC performs better than the NKPC in important respects. Critically it explains inflation persistence and hence sustained disequilibrium more plausibly than the NKPC, without invoking ad hoc assumptions. At the same time it allows central bank credibility a role in reducing the costliness of adjustment, and it meets the requirements of rational

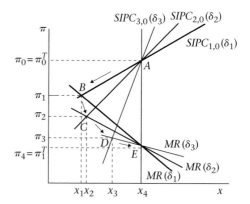

Figure 15.11 SIPC: information diffusion over several periods

behaviour and expectations. What is less clear is the nature of informational deficiencies. Here there are two points. First, we might like to know whether firms invest in information: it would be attractive at any rate to know why some firms have access to better information than others if not via some form of expenditure; but if so, why some firms and not others? But second, and perhaps more important, what are the informational deficiencies? If they concern the targets of the monetary authorities, we might expect most firms to gain full information sooner or later. So if targets seldom change the SIPC approach might not have enough bite to explain the continuing persistence of inflation inertia.

7 Multiple equilibria

In the remaining three sections of the chapter we turn to some very different ideas. In each section the assumption that there is a unique equilibrium rate of output, y_e, is dropped: in this section two models with more than one (exogenous) equilibrium are developed. In section 8, we ask whether aggregate demand can itself shift the equilibrium (hysteresis). And in section 9, moving away from the underlying assumption that households and their unions are interested solely in consumption and leisure, it is shown how concern for fairness may generate multiple equilibria.

Work on multiple equilibria has not reached a stage in which any particular models have become standard. We shall therefore set out in this section a simplistic model that illustrates the main ideas behind multiple equilibria. Before deriving the model mathematically with multiple sectors it may be useful to set it out in terms of PS and WS schedules, as shown in Fig. 15.12.

In Fig. 15.12, we have the usual upward sloping wage-setting curve. However, the price setting curve is quite different. As before we assume that $P = W/\lambda$ where λ is labour productivity. A new assumption, however, is made about labour productivity: when levels of economic activity are high economy-wide, there is a high level of productivity, when they are low, low productivity: specifically, when the economy-wide level of employment is above e_M labour productivity λ_H is high; when the economy-wide level of employment

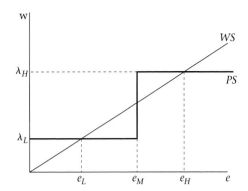

Figure 15.12 Multiple employment equilibria: different levels of productivity

is below e_M labour productivity λ_L is low. In that part of the price-setting curve above e_M the real wage implied by price setting is given by $P = W/\lambda_H \Rightarrow W/P = \lambda_H$. In that part of the price-setting curve below e_M the real wage implied by price setting is given by $P = W/\lambda_L \Rightarrow W/P = \lambda_L$. Thus the price-setting real wage curve has three segments as shown. There is a large literature attempting to explain procyclical labour productivity.[17]

In the standard diagram, the *WS* curve intersects the *PS* curve once, which fixes the unique equilibrium. In Fig. 15.12, there are three intersections, at e_L, e_M, and e_H.

7.1 **Microeconomics**

In this subsection, we show how the results above can be derived from a microeconomic basis using an approach similar to that in section 3.

The firm maximizes

$$\Pi = p_i y_i - w_i e_i$$

subject to the demand curve $y_i = p_i^{-\eta} A/N$, and $\lambda(e)e_i y_i$, so that $\Pi = p_i^{1-\eta} A/N - w_i \lambda(e)^{-1} p_i^{-\eta} A/N$. Hence

$$\frac{\partial \Pi}{\partial p_i} = (1 - \eta)p_i^{-\eta} A/N + \eta w_i \lambda(e)^{-1}(p_i^{-\eta} A/N)/p_i = 0$$

$$\Rightarrow p_i = \frac{\eta}{\lambda(e)(\eta - 1)} w_i. \tag{15.92}$$

This is the firm's price-setting curve.

Taking logs of both sides, taking averages and noting that $N^{-1} \sum \log p_i = 0$, enables us to derive the $\log w^{PS}$ schedules:

$$N^{-1} \sum \log w_i = \log w^{PS}(e) = \log \frac{\lambda(e)(\eta - 1)}{\eta}$$

[17] For a recent overview of competing theoretical and empirical explanations, see Wen (2004). Wen argues in favour of an explanation based on the cost of adjusting labour.

where

$$\log w^{PS}(e > e_M) = \log \frac{\lambda_H(\eta - 1)}{\eta}$$

$$\log w^{PS}(e < e_M) = \log \frac{\lambda_L(\eta - 1)}{\eta}.$$

The ith union as before maximizes

$$w_i e_i - (\phi/\sigma) e_i^\sigma \tag{15.93}$$

subject to $y_i = (P_i/P)^{-\eta} A/N$. Labour productivity is λ, but λ depends on aggregate employment e: $\lambda = \lambda_H$ when $e > e^*$, $\lambda = \lambda_L$ when $e \leq e^*$. We can rewrite the demand curve as $\lambda(e).e_i = \left(\frac{W_i}{P}.\lambda(e)^{-1}\right)^{-\eta} A/N$ or

$$e_i = w_i^{-\eta} \lambda(e)^{\eta-1}(A/N). \tag{15.94}$$

In maximizing (15.93) subject to (15.94), the individual union takes $\lambda(e)$ as given, since λ depends on *aggregate* employment over which the union has no control (if N is large enough).

Substituting (15.94) into (15.93), the union has to maximize

$$w_i^{1-\eta}\lambda(e)^{\eta-1}(A/N) - \phi(w_i^{-\eta}\lambda(e)^{\eta-1}(A/N))^\sigma,$$

which implies for a maximum (in fact, just as before):

$$w_i = \frac{\eta \cdot \phi}{\eta - 1} e_i^{\sigma-1}$$

so that the wage-setting real wage schedule, w^{WS}, becomes

$$\log w^{WS} = \log \frac{\eta \cdot \phi}{\eta - 1} + (\sigma - 1)\log e.$$

Therefore there are two equilibrium values of e at which $\log w^{WS} = \log w^{PS}$:

$$\log e_e^H = \frac{1}{\sigma - 1} \log \frac{\lambda_H}{\phi}\left(\frac{\eta - 1}{\eta}\right)^2 \tag{15.95}$$

$$\log e_e^L = \frac{1}{\sigma - 1} \log \frac{\lambda_L}{\phi}\left(\frac{\eta - 1}{\eta}\right)^2 \tag{15.96}$$

and these are shown in Fig. 15.13.

7.2 Multiple equilibria and shifting demand elasticities: a sketch

There are many reasons for multiple equilibria in macro models. We give one further example. Like the productivity example this one also assumes that a key parameter that

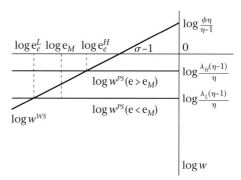

Figure 15.13 Multiple employment equilibria: exogenous differences in aggregate productivity at different employment rates

enters the price-setting equation is influenced by the level of aggregate economic activity. As before with monopolistic pricing, $w^{PS} = [(\eta - 1)/\eta]\lambda$. In the last subsection it was assumed that $\lambda = \lambda(e)$. Here we assume that $\eta = \eta(y)$ while $\lambda = 1$. Hence

$$w^{PS} = \frac{\eta(y) - 1}{\eta(y)}. \tag{15.97}$$

Why should the elasticity of demand vary with aggregate economic activity?[18] There are two main reasons: first, the threat of entry of new competitors (and thus the medium-term elasticity of demand) is likely to be low when economic activity is low. This means that firms already in the market may feel less worried about higher mark-ups on costs in a period of low activity. By contrast, high economic activity is a good time to enter a market as customers may be finding it hard to find suppliers. Second (and this works in the opposite direction on profit margins), competition with existing suppliers is likely to be high when economic activity is low; customers can shop around. High economic activity reduces competition between suppliers, since businesses have full order books.

These two effects go in opposite directions, and they may perfectly cancel each other out. If they do the assumption that η is constant is sensible. If businesses are more sensitive to the threat of entry than to internal competition, then η may be procyclical: margins will be higher when activity is low than when activity is high, and the w^{PS} schedule will be upwards sloping. If businesses are more sensitive to internal competition than to the threat of entry, then η will be countercyclical: margins will be lower when activity is low than when activity is high, and the w^{PS} schedule will be downward sloping. In the latter case it is not difficult to see that there will only be one equilibrium: the w^{PS} schedule is declining and the w^{WS} schedule is increasing. We focus here on the sensitivity to entry case, in which the w^{PS} schedule is rising. Clearly, this could be associated with no equilibria at all (i.e. if it is always above w^{WS}—however, this is pretty unlikely if w^{WS} becomes steep at full employment), a unique equilibrium or multiple equilibria, which is the case considered here. Suppose there is some level of aggregate economic activity (proxied by the aggregate employment rate) at which the likelihood of entry starts to rise. Up to that point incumbent businesses have been able to maintain a high profit margin (low η) so that w^{PS} is low. From then on incumbents perceive a flatter demand curve (high η) if they

---

[18] For a survey of the theory and evidence, see Rotemberg and Woodford (1999).

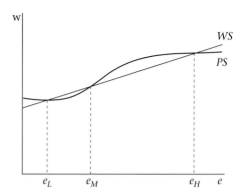

Figure 15.14 Multiple employment equilibria: elasticity of demand varies with aggregate activity

raise profit margins, as that would invite new entry. Thus w^{PS} rises to take account of the increased risk of entry. Imagine in consequence that the w^{PS} schedule can be drawn as in Fig. 15.14.

7.3 Choice of equilibria, coordinated aggregate demand, and monetary policy

The main purpose of this section has been to show how, with imperfect competition, it is possible to have more than one equilibrium level of output and employment. From a Keynesian perspective this possibility is interesting because the equilibrium that is chosen depends on aggregate demand. In the general context of the focus of the book on monetary rules as central to macro policy making, it is worth asking briefly whether this causes problems for monetary policy.

Before looking directly at monetary policy, we might ask what the Phillips curve diagram looks like if there is more than one equilibrium level of output or employment. The answer is straightforward, but may be a bit surprising at first. As shown in Fig. 15.15 there are three long-run vertical Phillips curves corresponding to the three equilibrium levels of employment: if we are actually at any of the three, the rate of inflation will be constant since $w^{WS} = w^{PS}$ at each of those employment rates.

For each expected rate of inflation there is a single expectations augmented Phillips curve: the surprise is the shape they take. We have drawn two here, corresponding to $\pi^E = \pi^1$ and $\pi^E = \pi^T$. Note that they go through each vertical Phillips curve at the same level of inflation as that expected: so, for example, the $\pi^E = \pi^1$ curve goes through the three long-run vertical Phillips curves at π^1. We also know that π is falling to the left of e_L, rising to the right of e_H, rising between e_L and e_M, and falling between e_M and e_H. This explains the shape of the short-run expectations Phillips curves: when inflation is rising the curve has to be above its expected value and vice versa.

Assume now that it is common knowledge across both households and the central bank that there are two equilibrium levels of output and employment, $y_e^H = e_e^H$ and $y_e^L = e_e^L$. Then the question is whether those equilibria are supportable by aggregate demand. This is a pertinent question since if households coordinate their beliefs on y_e^L and if they engage

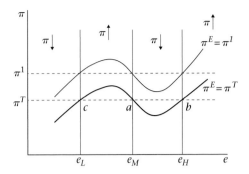

Figure 15.15 Phillips curves: multiple equilibrium employment rates

in consumption smoothing, their consumption will be based on permanent income of y_e^L. It is reasonable to assume that the central bank will prefer y_e^H to y_e^L; (although of course that requires an addition to the standard loss function that the central bank has so far been assumed to take as its objective). Say that r^* is the real interest rate that the central bank would need to impose to achieve y_e^H given that households coordinated on y_e^L. Then the central bank would only be able to impose y_e^H if $r^* \geq \bar{r}$ where $\bar{r}$ is the minimum feasible real interest rate set by the zero nominal interest rate bound (see Chapter 5). But it is not implausible that $r^* < \bar{r}$. In that case, the only equilibrium would be one in which the central bank coordinated on y_e^L.

The central bank might of course have a theory about the determinants of the common belief of households as to the correct equilibrium output. For instance the central bank might believe that if it set $r = \bar{r}$, so that $y > y_e^L$, that might switch the belief set of households to y_e^H. But we are now in an area in which little work has been done. Another possibility is that the central bank believes that y_e^L is the unique equilibrium. As can be seen from the Phillips curve diagram, increases in output above y_e^L would reinforce the central bank's believe, unless that increase pushed output above y_e^M—for then inflation would start to fall. In any case, this is a rich field for research if an accepted theory of multiple equilibria can be developed.

8 Hysteresis

In this section we examine the argument that there is a unique employment and output equilibrium at any one point in time, but that it is a function of the history of unemployment.[19] In Chapter 4, we introduced a number of different mechanisms through which persistence or hysteresis could operate. For example, when unemployment increases, some workers remain unemployed for longer than others and may progressively lose skills—certainly employers have no incentive to continue to train workers who are

---

[19] Early models of unemployment persistence include that of Blanchard and Summers, who argue that a negative productivity shock leads to some insiders being fired, which raises the bargaining power of the remaining insiders. Hence the WS curve is pushed up and equilibrium unemployment rises. Blanchard and Summers (1986).

unemployed. If they find it very hard to find jobs they may in consequence drop out of the labour market. Suppose employers set efficiency wages[20] by reference to the likelihood of getting another job within a given period of time; then, as unemployed workers drop out of the labour market, so the probability will rise that someone who is currently employed will get a new job quickly if they become unemployed—there is less competition around for jobs. That will cause employers to raise wages at the current level of employment: the w^{WS} schedule will shift up, and the equilibrium rate of employment will in consequence decline.

On this argument, a decline in aggregate demand will reduce the equilibrium rate of employment. Conversely an increase in aggregate demand may bring back these discouraged workers into the labour market so that they actively seek jobs and increase competitition for employment.

We look in this section at another reason for hysteresis, the so-called insider-outsider model. This is potentially a dangerous model for the economy, since unlike the argument above, it may only work in a downward direction. Declines in demand may reduce equilibrium employment; increased demand may not increase equilibrium employment, producing a ratcheting downwards effect.

In both this and the next section (Fairness and a Range of Equilibria), it is simpler to use a linear model of product and labour markets than the log linear model used so far. We set this out in 8.1 with the union utility function $U_i = w_i e_i$ in sector i; in this and the next section two different modifications of the utility function are made but the rest of the model is unchanged. It is shown in what follows that with $U_i = w_i e_i$, the model has the standard properties of a unique equilibrium independent of the history of aggregate demand.

8.1 Linear model of product and labour markets

The product demand curve in the ith sector is now

$$y_i = A/N - \eta(p_i - 1). \tag{15.98}$$

(Note that this sums to $\sum_{i}^{N} y_i = A$.) We shall assume Bertrand pricing (i.e. each of two or more producers in each sector sets price equal to marginal cost), and that labour productivity is unity. Hence in each sector

$$p_i = w_i$$

and the demand curve for labour in sector i is

$$e_i = A/N - \eta(w_i - 1).$$

There is a union in each sector, and the ith union maximizes

$$U_i = w_i e_i$$

[20] See the appendix to this chapter for the analysis of efficiency wage setting by firms.

subject to labour demand. Choosing w_i to maximize $U_i = w_i.(A/N - \eta(w_i - 1))$ implies

$$w_i = \eta^{-1} e_i.$$

In equilibrium as before

$$p_i = 1 \ \Rightarrow \ w^{PS} = 1.$$

The w^{WS} curve is

$$w^{WS} = \eta^{-1} e.$$

So

$$w^{PS} = 1 = w^{WS} = \eta^{-1} e \ \Rightarrow \ e_e = \eta. \tag{15.99}$$

8.2 The insider-outsider model

In this model[21], the union is concerned only about its currently employed members: for example union policy may be dictated by those who are employed; or the union may be formed by those who are employed; or it may be that firms negotiate with those who are employed. Suppose current employment in i is e_{i0}. Hence—assuming as before that the union chooses w_i—it will never choose a combination (w_i, e_i) in which $e_i > e_{i0}$ over a combination (w_i^*, e_{i0}) in which $w_i^* > w_i$. Only if $e_i < e_{i0}$ will it maximize $w_i e_i$. Thus the union maximizes

$$\begin{aligned} U_i &= w_i e_i \quad e_i < e_{i0} \\ &= w_i \quad e_i \geq e_{i0}. \end{aligned}$$

If we assume that the rest of the model is as in 8.1, the union will set wages as follows

$$\begin{aligned} w_i &= \eta^{-1} e_i & e_i \leq e_{i0} \\ &= \overline{w}_i \geq \eta^{-1} e_{i0} & e_i \geq e_{i0}. \end{aligned}$$

As can be seen in Fig. 15.16, $\overline{w}_i$ is given by intersection of the vertical line $e_i = e_{i0}$ and the labour demand curve $e_i = A/N - \eta(\overline{w}_i - 1)$. Thus $\overline{w}_i$ is defined by $e_{i0} = A/N - \eta(\overline{w}_i - 1)$. $\overline{w}_i = w_{i0} = \eta^{-1} e_{i0}$ when $A = A_0$ and $\overline{w}_i = w_{i1}$ is implicitly defined by $e_{i0} = A_1/N - \eta(w_{i1} - 1)$. And $\overline{w}_i = 1$ when $A = A_2$.

Now imagine the economy is initially in equilibrium at $(1, e_e)$, with $A = A_e$. There is then an adverse demand shock which reduces A to A_0. Each sector i then moves to (w_{i0}, e_{i0}). This is not an equilibrium since $w^{PS} = 1 > w_{i0}$. Suppose there is a positive shock to demand to take it to A_2. Then, the ith union is only interested in raising w_i rather than allowing employment to increase above e_{i0}. So instead of moving up $w^{WS} = \eta^{-1} e$, the economy moves vertically up $w^{WS}(e_0)$. Thus $(1, e_{i0})$ is the new equilibrium in the economy: any attempt to expand demand further leads to $w^{WS}(e_0) > w^{PS}$.

---

[21] See Blanchard and Summers (1986) and Lindbeck and Snower (1986).

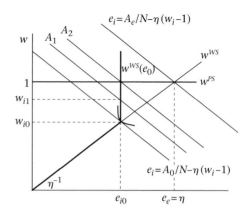

Figure 15.16 The insider-outsider model

So in this insider-outsider model, there is a ratchet effect on equilibrium employment. A decline in aggregate demand pulls down equilibrium employment; but a subsequent increase does not restore the original level.

9 Fairness and a range of equilibria

A rather different approach to multiple equilibria stems from introducing the concept of 'fairness' into employee utility functions. In discussing microfoundations of macroeconomics we have been careful to follow what most economists take as one of the touchstones of rationality, that individuals are concerned about their real incomes—and what can be bought with them—and the amount of leisure that they have. But there is strong evidence both from psychological research and from day-to-day observation of how people behave, that most of us attach a high importance to being treated 'fairly'. And, while all may be fair in love and war, that is seldom true of the workplace. Common observation suggests that many, perhaps most, employees become concerned, even angered, if they see that they are being treated less well than other similar employees—either in the same firm or elsewhere. Specifically, that they are more concerned to avoid being paid less than a similar group of workers elsewhere than to be paid a corresponding amount more than them. The 'injustice' of doing worse is of more consequence than the pleasure of doing better than a group of similar workers. In the appendix, we present the efficiency wage model of wage setting in which considerations of fairness provide the motivation for one class of such models. A brief summary is also provided there of the empirical evidence on the role of fairness considerations in wage setting.

In a paper by V. Bhaskar (1990) it is shown how this type of behaviour can lead to a range of equilibria. We set out a simple version of the argument in this section.[22]

---

[22] The literature on a range of equilibria and the role of fairness has been developed further for example by Ian McDonald (e.g. McDonald 1995 and Steiner Holden (e.g. Holden and Driscoll 2004). For further papers, including empirical application to Australia, see: www.economics.unimelb.edu.au/staffprofile/imcdonald/equilibria.htm.

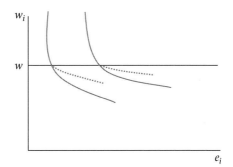

Figure 15.17 Worker indifference curves with fairness considerations

9.1 The Bhaskar fairness model

Now we use the model of 8.1 to set out the Bhaskar argument. It requires one modification to the utility function. We assume now that unions maximize

$$U_i = w_i.e_i \qquad\qquad \text{if } w_i \geq w$$
$$U_i = w_i.e_i + \delta(w_i - w) \quad \text{if } w_i < w,$$

where δ is a positive constant. The critical second term that is added to the utility function, $\delta(w_i - w)$, is the fairness term. In particular, in line with the discussion above, this says: when workers are getting at least as high a wage as comparable groups, their only concern is to maximize their real income. But if they getting a lower wage, i.e. if $w_i < w$, then their utility level is reduced by $\delta(w_i - w)$. Typical shapes of the indifference curves are shown in Fig. 15.17. The continuous indifference curves assume there is no fairness term. That is correct above the w horizontal line. But when $w_i < w$, below the horizontal line, the indifference curve now switches to the dotted line. This is because compensation is needed to make up for the psychological cost of the unfairness.

We assume that all sectors except the ith behave identically. Then since $P = W$, the real wage $w = 1$ and is shown in Fig. 15.18 as the w^{PS} schedule. The slope of each indifference curve therefore changes as the curve cuts the w^{PS} horizontal line. Each indifference curve has a steeper slope above the line than it has below the line.

The ith union chooses the point on each demand curve to reach the highest indifference curve. Up to now that has been straightforward: it is where the demand curve is tangent to the highest indifference curve. Where demand is very low, as at A_0/N, then there is no problem about this formula since for low enough demand the demand curve will be tangential to the 'fairness' part of the indifference curve, i.e. the part where considerations of fairness are included—at f. Equally, when demand is very high as at A_4/N, the demand curve will be tangential to the 'non-fairness' section of the indifference curve at g.

But as demand is progressively increased above A_0/N, it eventually reaches a point such as a when demand is A_1/n. At a, the demand curve is still tangential to the fairness part of the indifference curve (ic_1) but because $w_i = w = 1$, the indifference curve is at a kink at the point. The slope of the indifference curve is equal to the demand curve below the w^{PS} line, but is greater than that of the demand curve above it. It can however be clearly seen that the choice of $w_1 = w = 1$ maximizes the union's utility. Since the wage-setting

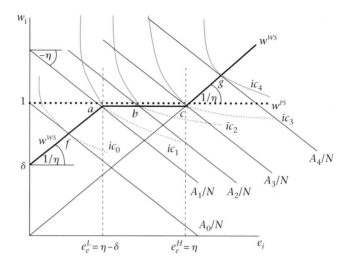

Figure 15.18 Fairness in the utility function: a range of employment equilibria

real wage is the same as the price-setting real wage at a, this is an equilibrium for the economy.

As demand increases, for instance to A_2/N, $w_i = w = 1$ remains the optimum wage for the union, even though as can be seen at b the demand curve is tangential to neither sector of the indifference curve (ic_2) which just touches the demand curve: the fairness (lower) part of the indifference curve has a flatter slope than the demand curve, and the non-fairness (upper) part has a higher slope. But b is also an equilibrium of the economy since here too the bargained real wage is equal to the price-set real wage.

Continue increasing demand until $A/N = A_3/N$. At this point, c, the new demand curve is tangential to the upper part of the indifference curve, but not the lower flatter part. Here again we are in equilibrium. In fact we are in equilibrium at all the points between a, which marks the start of the range of employment equilibria and c, which marks the end.

The w^{WS} curve therefore has three segments. The upper and lower segments are not equilibria, but each point on the horizontal segment is. An interesting question is therefore: what is the length of the range of equilibria, the highest equilibrium employment rate and the lowest?

To answer this question we need to derive the three-segment w^{WS} schedule mathematically. The union maximizes $U_i = w_i e_i + \delta(w_i - w)$ subject to $e_i = A/N - \eta(w_i - 1)$, the labour demand equation, when $w_i < w$ and it maximizes $U_i = w_i e_i$ subject to $e_i = A/N - \eta(w_i - 1)$ when $w_i > w$. It is simplest to solve this in three stages.

First, we can work out immediately the segment above $w = 1$. In this segment δ is not relevant so we have the same problem as in 8.1 (the simple basic model). As we saw there, in this segment the WS schedule is

$$w_i = \frac{e_i}{\eta} \text{ when } w_i > w = 1.$$

The second segment we derive is that to the left below $w = 1$. The maximization condition here is

$$\frac{dU_i}{dw_i} = (A/N - \eta(w_i - 1)) - \eta w_i + \delta = e_i - \eta w_i + \delta = 0$$

which implies for the lower part of the *WS* schedule:

$$w_i = e_i/\eta + \delta \text{ when } w_i < w = 1.$$

We now turn to the horizontal segment. The upper and lower points of this range of equilibria can now be easily worked out. The upper point is the limiting lowest point on the right upwards-sloping segment, when $w_i = w = 1$. Hence,

$$1 = e_i/\eta \Rightarrow e_H^e = \eta.$$

The lower point is the limiting highest point on the left upwards-sloping segment, when $w_i = w = 1$. Hence,

$$1 = e_i/\eta + \delta \Rightarrow e_L^e = \eta - \delta.$$

Thus we have the simple and intuitive result that the range of employment equilibria runs from $e_L^e = \eta - \delta$ to $e_H^e = \eta$; that the range is equal to δ; and that the highest point on the range, $e_H^e = \eta$, is equal to the unique equilibrium employment rate in the basic model. So in this fairness model, the authorities can increase aggregate demand between A_1 and A_3 without increasing the rate of inflation or to put it another way, policy activism is needed to achieve the high rather than the low end of the range if the economy is affected by a negative demand shock.

10 Conclusions

Section 1 sets out an integrated summary of the argument. We do not repeat that here. These concluding remarks are what we see as the most significant results of the New Keynesian approach. The analysis in this chapter offers an interpretation of why we might expect cyclical fluctuations to be more restrained than in the past. Two institutional developments are relevant: the increased access of households to credit and the emergence of forward-looking central banks. As we have seen, there will be a mutually reinforcing dampening of cycles due to the behaviour of forward-looking consumers with access to credit and of a forward-looking central bank. The expectation that the central bank will actively stabilize the economy induces stabilizing behaviour by households. However, two caveats are in order. Reasons why this may be too optimistic a view for countries in a monetary union such as the eurozone are discussed in Chapter 12. Secondly, the neglect of investment in many New Keynesian models diverts attention away from bubble phenomena, which may be fuelled in more highly developed financial markets.

The idea that markets will not automatically produce the stabilizing interest rate, for example, because of information failures (discussed further in Chapter 8), means there is a role for macroeconomic policy. The role played by a forward-looking optimizing central bank in coordinating private sector expectations is quite consistent with Keynes's diagnosis of why macroeconomic policy is needed. The second theme of the chapter also echoes Keynes's analysis: once the New Keynesian microfoundations are put into place the relevance of fluctuations in aggregate demand as a source of fluctuations in and persistence of unemployment gains considerably in importance. Fluctuations in demand can drive business cycles, adjustment back to equilibrium may be protracted, and multiple equilibria due to entry behaviour, hysteresis, or to fairness considerations mean that the economy can get stuck with high unemployment without associated falling inflation.

Finally we might ask: are there fundamental differences with the neoclassical RBC approach or only minor ones? Here the answer is: it all depends. The only formal differences between the New Keynesian approach and RBC theory are the New Keynesian assumptions of imperfect competition and wage and price stickiness. Otherwise the structure of the models is in principle similar. Even the emphasis of RBC models on productivity shocks can be carried into New Keynesian models. But in terms of practical policy making the two approaches are far apart. RBC theory, by assuming perfect competition and modelling cycles as equilibrium phenomena implies continuous optimality, which rules out a stabilization role for macroeconomic policy.

■ **PROBLEMS**

QUESTION A. Assume households live for two periods, periods 0 and 1. Their utility is given by:

$$U = c_0 - \frac{b}{2}c_0^2 - \frac{\phi}{2}e_0^2 + \frac{1}{1+\rho}\left(c_1 - \frac{b}{2}c_1^2 - \frac{\phi}{2}e_1^2\right).$$

In period 0, they can choose to save S_0, and this increases their income in period 1 by $(1+r)S_0$. The real wage in period i is w_i.

(a) Assume $w_0 = w_1 = 1$ and $r = \rho$. (i) Find c_0, c_1, e_0, e_1. (ii) Show that $S_0 = 0$. Why? (iii) Find $\frac{\partial c_0}{\partial a}, \frac{\partial c_1}{\partial b}, \frac{\partial e_1}{\partial \phi}, \frac{\partial c_0}{\partial \phi}$ and explain the signs.

(b) Now let $w_i = \lambda_i$, where λ_i is (exogenously given) labour productivity in period i. Assume $\lambda_0 = \lambda > 1$ and $\lambda_1 = 1$; (so we can think of there being a one-period labour productivity shock in period 1). If $r = \rho$, how does this affect consumption and employment in both periods and the level of savings in period 1.

(c) What if $\lambda_1 = \lambda$ and $\lambda_0 = 1$? (Assume that both λs are known in advance.)

(d) Assume $w_0 = w_1 = 1$ and $(1+r)/(1+\rho) = \beta$. Find c_0, c_1, e_0, e_1. What is the sign of S_0 if (i) $\beta > 1$ and (ii) $\beta < 1$?

QUESTION B. In each industry, i, the utility function of a worker is $w_i e_i$. All workers in i are in the ith union and the union maximizes $w_i e_i$. The union sets a monopoly wage, w_i, in the ith industry whose demand curve is given by $y_i = A/n - (b/2)p_i$, where A is aggregate demand and n is the number of identical industries.

(i) There is Bertrand competition in the industry so that $p_i = w_i/\lambda$ where λ is labour productivity. (So $e_i \lambda = y_i$.) Derive the ith union's wage bargaining curve showing the wage it will set as a function of employment in the ith industry.

(ii) Still assuming Bertrand competition, what is the equilibrium employment rate in the economy? How does it change if λ increases?

(iii) Assume $\lambda = 1$. And now assume there is a monopoly producer in each industry, as well as a monopoly union: derive the union's wage bargaining curve and the equilibrium employment rate.

QUESTION C. In the 3-equation model, x_t is excess demand in period t, r is the rate of interest, r_S is the rate of interest which implies $x = 0$, and the target inflation rate is zero. The economy is described by

$$x_t = -(r_{t-1} - r_S)$$
$$\pi_t = \pi_{t-1} + x_t$$
$$\pi_t = -x_t.$$

In period $t = -1$, $\pi_{-1} = 0$, $x_{-1} = 0$ and $r_{-1} = r_S$. Assume $r_S = 0$.

(i) Assume $\pi_0 = 2$ (inflation shock). Find the values of π, x and r_{-1} in periods $t = 1, \ldots, 5$. Explain the economic intuition behind your derivations.

(ii) Now assume that $\pi_0 = 0$ and that there is an aggregate demand shock in $t = 0$, reflected in an increase in r_S from $r_S = 0$ to $r_{S,0} = 2$. (*a*) Explain why a demand shock increases r_S. (*b*) Find the values of π, x and r_{-1} in periods $t = 1, \ldots, 5$. Again explain the economic intuition behind your derivations.

QUESTION D. Now assume a forward-looking *IS* curve, $x_t = x_{t+1} - (r_{t-1} - r_S)$, as well as the Phillips curve and *MR* used in question C. Assume that $r_{-1} = r_S = 0$, so that

$$x_0 = x_1.$$

Now assume an inflation shock in period 0,

$$\pi_0 = 2 + x_0.$$

We also have

$$\pi_1 = \pi_0 + x_1$$

and

$$\pi_1 = -x_1.$$

Households can work out, once they know the 2% inflation shock in $t = 0$, that the CB will raise r_0 and hence reduce x_1. Work out the exact effect of this on x_0 and explain the intuition behind your derivation.

■ APPENDIX: EFFICIENCY WAGES

We now consider a quite different way of setting wages: it is assumed that *firms* set the wages of their employees or potential employees. If a firm is in a position to set wages, why should it want to set a wage above the minimum at which it can hire labour from the market? The answer is that for many firms wage setting (and reward setting more generally) is a key instrument in maintaining a well-qualified and cooperative workforce. Management textbooks refer to the problems of motivation, retention, and recruitment. When wages are set by employers to address these problems, this is often referred to as efficiency wage setting. The firm chooses the wage that is *efficient* in terms of its contribution to solving the firm's problems. Before we look in detail at how this is done, we shall initially consider how efficiency wage setting differs from what we have done before.

To this point, we have had a price-setting equation that was derived from profit-maximizing behaviour by *firms* and a wage-setting equation derived from the utility-maximizing behaviour of *unions*. But with efficiency wages we assume that firms set *both* prices and wages. This works in the following way: the firm maximizes profits with respect both to the price and to the wage. As before, 'the price' is the relative price ($p_i = P_i/P$) and 'the wage' is the real wage ($w_i = W_i/P$), i.e. the money wage in the sector relative to the average price level in the economy. The first order condition that results from maximizing with respect to the price level (holding the wage constant) is the *price-setting equation*. The first order condition that results from maximizing with respect to the wage (holding the price level constant) is the *wage-setting equation*.

With both monopoly pricing and Bertrand pricing, the price-setting equations that emerge from the dual maximization procedure (maximizing with respect to both the relative price and the real wage) are identical to the price-setting equations derived above. The relative price the firm charges p_i is proportional to the real wage in the firm (or sector), w_i. In the case of sectoral monopoly pricing, the price-setting equation is $p_i = \eta/(\eta - 1)w_i/\lambda$ in firm (or sector) i. With Bertrand pricing, the price-setting equation is simply $p_i = w_i/\lambda$. Both remain true in the context of the efficiency wage model.

The difference between a monopoly union and efficiency wage setting by the firm appears in the wage setting equation. To this point, union-based wage setting implied a wage-setting equation of the form $w_i = F(e_i)$: namely, the sectoral real wage is a function of the employment rate in the sector. However, when firms set an efficiency wage, they are not so much interested in the real wage they set for their employees as with how the wage they set compares with average wages for employees elsewhere in the economy. The reason is that it is the relative wage w_i/w that is more relevant for motivation, recruitment, and retention. How high the relative wage needs to be to secure the goals of motivation, recruitment, and retention depends very much on the state of the overall labour market. If the overall employment rate e is very high, then w_i/w will need to be high; for with low unemployment, it will be easy for workers to leave and find jobs elsewhere if they think they can earn more. But if the labour market is depressed (low e) then firms will feel secure that they will not lose workers and will be able to recruit the workers they want with lower relative wages. Thus at least in the simple models that we shall develop, the efficiency wage-setting equations have the form $w_i/w = F(e)$.

This difference in the form of the wage-setting equation when we move from union to firm wage setting has an important implication for the equilibrium employment rate, but not for the equilibrium real wage. As before, the equilibrium real wage remains fully determined by the price setting equation. For example, assume we have monopolistic price-setting in each sector so

$$p_i = \frac{\eta}{\eta - 1} \frac{w_i}{\lambda}.$$

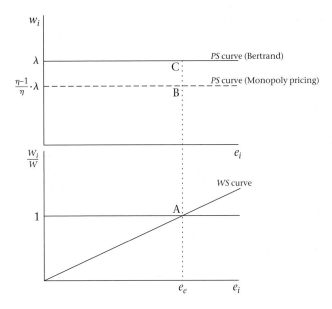

Figure 15.19 Efficiency wage setting

Irrespective of how wage setting works, equilibrium requires that relative prices are equal to 1, i.e.

$$p_i = 1 = \frac{\eta}{\eta - 1} \frac{w_i}{\lambda} \lambda, \text{ which implies } w_i = w = \frac{\eta - 1}{\eta}.$$

In other words, irrespective of how wage setting takes place, the price-setting equation determines the equilibrium real wage. This is shown in Fig. 15.19: where price-setting curves under Bertrand and monopoly pricing are shown.

We turn now to the equilibrium employment rate. With *union* wage setting $w_i = F(e_i)$, so in equilibrium

$$w_i = w = \frac{\eta - 1}{\eta} = F(e_i) = F(e).$$

If $F(e) = \alpha e$,

then as we have seen

$$e_e = \frac{w}{\alpha} = \frac{\lambda}{\alpha} \frac{\eta - 1}{\eta}.$$

This means that if the equilibrium real wage rate changes value, the equilibrium employment rate will also change.

But with *efficiency* wage setting this is no longer true: the wage-setting equation now takes the form

$$w_i/w = F(e).$$

Equilibrium requires that relative wages are equal to 1—if that was not the case, the wage level in each firm would be above or below the average level. Hence, $w_i/w = 1 = F(e)$. For convenience, let us assume that

$$F(e) = \alpha w_i/w.$$

Then in equilibrium

$$e_e = \frac{1}{\alpha}.$$

This means that changes in the parameters of the price-setting equation have no effect on the equilibrium employment rate. In other words, in the efficiency wage model, the equilibrium employment rate is fixed purely by the wage-setting curve. The real wage is fixed (as it is in the monopoly union model) by the price-setting curve. In Fig. 15.19, the lower panel shows the wage-setting equation with w_i/w on the vertical axis. The equilibrium employment rate is shown by the intersection of the $w_i/w = 1$ line with the WS curve. Equilibrium in the economy is at A in the lower panel and at B in the upper panel in the case of monopoly pricing; at C in the case of Bertrand pricing.

By introducing efficiency wage setting, one solution is provided to the productivity puzzle discussed in Chapter 4. Under efficiency wage setting, only the WS curve is relevant to the determination of equilibrium employment. A change in productivity has no effect on the WS curve and hence, in this model, on equilibrium employment. However, the real wage shifts proportionately with productivity.

- In the efficiency wage model, productivity growth affects real wages but not equilibrium employment.

Efficiency wages and motivation

Now let us turn to a direct analysis of efficiency wage setting. In this subsection we assume that efficiency wage setting is combined with monopoly price setting. In each of the three cases—motivation, retention, and recruitment—the basic structure of the firm's problem is similar. The firm has to choose the price level p_i and the wage level w_i to maximize profits

$$\pi_i = p_i y_i - w_i e_i. \tag{15.100}$$

This is subject to two constraints: first, as before, there is a 'competition' or market structure constraint that depends on the price-setting model we are using. In the case of the monopoly firm, this is the product demand curve

$$y_i = p_i^{-\eta} A. \tag{15.101}$$

To this point, the second constraint faced by the firm was the production function constraint, $e_i = y_i/\lambda$, where λ is labour productivity. We then substituted this constraint in the profit objective to get

$$\pi_i = p_i y_i - w_i y_i/\lambda.$$

Once motivation, recruitment, and retention are introduced, things are not so simple because the worker's productivity can no longer be considered fixed.

We begin with motivation. A worker's productivity now depends on how motivated the employee is to work hard and effectively, or as it is sometimes expressed, to exert effort. For simplicity, we assume that the output of the worker, labour productivity, is equal to his or her motivation. What determines λ now? The assumption made in much of the efficiency wage literature is that it depends on the wage the employee is getting in the firm compared to what he or she would be likely to get elsewhere, i.e. on w_i/w, where w is the average wage elsewhere. It also depends on the state of the labour market and how long it would take to find a job outside: this can be summarized by the economy-wide employment rate e. The higher is w_i/w, the more satisfied the employee will be with the current firm; and the lower is e—the poorer the state of the external labour market—also the more satisfied the employee. The assumption then is that $\lambda_i = \lambda(w_i/w, e)$; and that an increase in w_i/w has a positive effect on λ_i and an increase in e has a negative effect on λ_i.

Why should employees respond in this way? There are two explanations for this effect that are commonly given.

Akerlof's gift exchange. One is a psychological explanation, described by Akerlof as a *gift exchange*.[23] In essence this amounts to the employee saying to herself: this firm treats me well since my wage is above the level other firms would pay me; so I will respond in kind by working hard.

Shapiro–Stiglitz's shirking model. The second explanation is based on purely rational behaviour, and it relies on uncertainty—or, to be more precise, on the inability of the firm to monitor how hard its employees are working all the time.[24] If it knew which workers were shirking then it could instantaneously dismiss them, and—absent hiring and firing costs—getting workers to work hard at the market wage would then be no problem for the firm. Assume the firm gets information from time to time about how hard individual employees are working. The firm reasons as follows: if an employee is caught shirking, the employee gets sacked. To make shirking (and the sack) unattractive, the firm needs to pay employees above what they could expect to get elsewhere. What they could get elsewhere depends on the outside wage w and on the probability that they would find employment e, thus on w_i relative to *we*. If the employee thinks she is very unlikely to be observed shirking then w_i will need to be high relative to *we* to give her the appropriate incentive to work hard; if she thinks it is likely she will be observed then w_i can be lower in relative terms.

In any case, for both theories, the new constraint is

$$y_i = e_i \lambda(w_i/w, e). \tag{15.102}$$

The firm has to maximize (15.100) subject to (15.101) and to (15.102). It works out the price-setting equation by differentiating with respect to p_i holding w_i constant. And it works out the wage-setting equation by differentiating with respect to w_i holding p_i constant. Substituting first (15.102) and then (15.101) into (15.100) gives:

$$\begin{aligned}
\pi_i &\equiv p_i y_i - w_i e_i \\
&= p_i y_i - \frac{w_i}{\lambda(\frac{w_i}{w}, e)} y_i \\
&= p_i^{1-\eta} A - \frac{w_i}{\lambda(\frac{w_i}{w}, e)} p_i^{-\eta} A.
\end{aligned} \tag{15.103}$$

Deriving the price-setting equation. To derive the price-setting equation we differentiate (15.103) by p_i holding w_i constant. Note that w and e are exogenous to the firm's decision making. This implies

$$(1-\eta) p_i^{-\eta} A + \eta \frac{w_i}{\lambda(\frac{w_i}{w}, e)} p_i^{-\eta-1} A = 0$$

$$\implies p_i = \frac{\eta}{\eta-1} \cdot \frac{w_i}{\lambda(\frac{w_i}{w}, e)}, \tag{15.104}$$

which is precisely the original formula for the monopoly price-setting equation ($p_i = \eta/(\eta-1).w_i/\lambda$) except of course that λ is no longer exogenous.

Deriving the wage-setting equation. To derive the wage-setting equation we differentiate (15.103):

$$\pi_i = p_i^{1-\eta} A - \frac{w_i}{\lambda(\frac{w_i}{w}, e)} p_i^{-\eta} A$$

with respect to w_i holding p_i constant. If p_i is held constant it is easy to see that maximizing π_i is equivalent to minimizing

$$\frac{w_i}{\lambda(\frac{w_i}{w}, e)}.$$

[23] Akerlof (1982).   [24] Shapiro and Stiglitz (1984).

So let us do this:

$$\frac{\partial\left(\frac{w_i}{\lambda(\frac{w_i}{w},e)}\right)}{\partial w_i} = \frac{1}{\lambda} - \frac{w_i}{\lambda^2}\frac{\partial\lambda(\frac{w_i}{w},e)}{\partial(w_i/w)}\frac{1}{w} = 0$$

$$\Rightarrow \quad \frac{w_i/w}{\lambda}\frac{\partial\lambda}{\partial w_i/w} = 1$$

$$\Longrightarrow \quad \frac{\partial\log\lambda}{\partial\log(w_i/w)} = 1. \tag{15.105}$$

This condition was originally derived by Solow, and says that the elasticity of effort with respect to relative wages must be equal to 1. The intuition is very simple: we want to minimize unit labour costs w_i/λ; we therefore want to go on increasing w_i until a 1% increase in wages increases λ by 1%. If the increase in wages increases λ by more, unit labour costs will fall, so it should pay to go on increasing wages; if λ rises by less, wages are too high.

However, equation (15.105) does not look much like the wage-setting equations we have developed so far. To convert it into an equation linking w_i/w to e, we need to specify a functional form for $\lambda(w_i/w, e)$. A very simple form is

$$\lambda = \exp\beta(e)(w_i/w) \quad\Rightarrow\quad \log\lambda = \beta(e)(w_i/w). \tag{15.106}$$

What form might $\beta(e)$ have? An increase in e, cet. par., decreases effort. Hence $\beta'(e) < 0$. A possible form is therefore $1/(\phi e)$. This means

$$\log\lambda = \frac{1}{\phi e}(w_i/w)$$

$$\Longrightarrow \quad \frac{\partial\log\lambda}{\partial\log(w_i/w)} = 1$$

$$\frac{1}{\phi e}\frac{\partial(w_i/w)}{\partial\log(w_i/w)} = \frac{1}{\phi e}w_i/w = 1$$

$$\Longrightarrow \quad w_i/w = \phi e. \tag{15.107}$$

So with *efficiency* wage setting, the wage-setting and price-setting equations for the firm are:

$$w_i/w = \phi e \tag{15.108}$$

$$p_i = \frac{\eta}{\eta - 1}\frac{w_i}{\lambda(\frac{w_i}{w}, e)}. \tag{15.109}$$

This illustrates clearly the difference between the implications of union wage setting and efficiency wage setting for the equilibrium employment rate (at least with the simple examples we have used). The corresponding equations for *union* wage setting and monopoly price setting are

$$w_i = \frac{\alpha\eta}{\eta - 1}e_i \tag{15.110}$$

$$p_i = \frac{\eta}{\eta - 1}\frac{w_i}{\lambda}. \tag{15.111}$$

In the efficiency wage case, the wage-setting equation determines the equilibrium employment rate by itself: the equilibrium conditions are that $w_i = w$ and that $p_i = 1$. w_i must equal w if each sector behaves identically, since w is the average real wage. And since p_i is the relative price of sector i it must be equal to one in equilibrium if all sectors behave identically. Equation (15.108) then implies that $e_e = 1/\phi$, so that the equilibrium employment rate is determined just by the wage-setting equation. The monopoly price-setting equation then uses the equilibrium employment rate result to determine the level of the real wage from:

$$1 = \frac{\eta}{\eta - 1} \frac{w}{\lambda(1, 1/\phi)};$$

that is,

$$w = \frac{\eta - 1}{\eta} \lambda.$$

By contrast, in the union wage-setting case the monopoly price-setting equation alone determines the real wage

$$w = \frac{\eta - 1}{\eta} \lambda;$$

then, substituting that result into the wage-setting equation, the equilibrium employment rate is determined as

$$e_e = \left(\frac{\eta}{\eta - 1} \right)^2 \frac{\alpha}{\lambda}.$$

Efficiency wages and retention

We have dealt at length with the motivation case. The other two cases can now be explained much more quickly, and they are indeed closely related phenomena. We start with the retention case and define the quit rate from the firm as q. Thus $q.e_i$ employees leave the firm each period (assuming no one is sacked). The firm wants to maintain output at some particular level, y_i, and therefore employment at $e_i = y_i/\lambda$. To do so requires $q.e_i$ new recruits. Assume for the time being that $q.e_i$ recruits can be hired from the market at whatever the wage the firm offers. In the recruiting case that we consider shortly, we shall see that this assumption will be dropped. Although there is no problem hiring new recruits, there is a cost to doing so. The cost is that the experienced employees who quit have firm-specific skills; new recruits will have to acquire the skills, and the firm will have to pay for this. Since by definition firm-specific skills are only of value in a particular firm, it is the firm and not the worker who will pay the training cost.

We assume the cost of training each new recruit is t. Since qe_i new recruits are required to replace the employees who have quit, the cost to the firm of doing so is tqe_i. If the firm has to hire trainers, paying them w_i, then t will be proportional to w_i, say $t = w_i\tau$. The total cost of training, given q is then $w_i\tau qe_i$. The firm therefore has an incentive to reduce q. As discussed above, we assume that q depends positively on w_i/w and negatively on the economy-wide employment rate e, say $q = q(w_i/w, e)$. Thus the total wage bill is

$$w_i e_i + w_i \tau q(w_i/w, e)e_i = w_i(1 + \tau q(w_i/w, e))e_i$$

and the firm maximizes profits of

$$\pi_i = p_i y_i - w_i(1 + \tau q(w_i/w, e))e_i$$
$$= p_i^{1-\eta} A - w_i(1 + \tau q(w_i/w, e))p_i^{-\eta} A. \tag{15.112}$$

Differentiating with respect to p_i holding w_i constant implies (on exactly the same lines as before) that the price-setting equation is

$$p_i = \frac{\eta}{\eta - 1} w_i(1 + \tau q(w_i/w, e)), \tag{15.113}$$

where $w_i(1 + \tau q(w_i/w, e))$ is the unit cost of labour including the training of new recruits. As before to derive the wage equation we differentiate (15.112) with respect to w_i holding p_i constant. It is easy to see from the right hand side of (15.112) that this is the same as minimizing the unit cost of labour $w_i(1 + \tau.q(w_i/w, e))$ with respect to w_i. Differentiating this term with respect to w_i gives

$$1 + \tau q(w_i/w, e) + w_i \tau \frac{\partial q(w_i/w, e)}{\partial w_i} = 0. \tag{15.114}$$

To turn this equation into a recognizable wage-setting equation, we need to give $q(w_i/w, e)$ a functional form. A simple one is

$$q(w_i/w, e) = \bar{q} - \alpha \frac{w_i}{w.e}, \tag{15.115}$$

where $\bar{q}$ is the underlying quit rate in the economy. This says that a rise in w_i relative to $w.e$ (think of the latter as the expected value of the wage if an employee leaves the firm) reduces the quit rate q by a constant amount α. Substituting (15.115) into (15.114) produces:

$$1 + \tau\bar{q} - \tau\alpha \frac{w_i}{w.e} - \tau\alpha \frac{w_i}{we} = 0$$

$$\implies \frac{w_i}{w.e} = \frac{1 + \tau\bar{q}}{2\tau\alpha}$$

$$\implies \frac{w_i}{w} = \left(\frac{1 + \tau\bar{q}}{2\tau\alpha}\right) e. \tag{15.116}$$

This has the properties we want:

(1) The higher is the employment rate in the economy, the higher w_i/w has to be.

(2) The higher is $\bar{q}$ (the underlying quit rate), the higher is w_i/w.

(3) The higher is α (the sensitivity of the quit rate to $w_i/(w.e)$), the lower is w_i/w.

Efficiency wages and recruitment

To this point we have assumed that the firm can recruit as many new employees as it wants at the firm's wage. But recruitment is normally a difficult process, in which the firm has to compete against other firms to get the new hires it wants. A realistic assumption is that the proportion of its vacancies that it can fill depends positively on the relative wage it offers and negatively on the state of the labour market. The number of vacancies the firm will have will be equal to its quit rate times its employment, $V = qe_i$. Let h be the percentage of vacancies filled by new hires, H, so $H = hV = hqe_i$. So we assume that $h = h(w_i/w, e)$. Assume now for simplicity that the quit rate q is constant. We are now in a world in which the firm may not choose to fill all its vacancies—it simply may cost too much in terms of a high relative wage to do so. The counterpart to this will be a cost the firm must bear as a result of unfilled vacancies. We need to assume that this cost is substantial—otherwise the firm would not worry about unfilled vacancies. The failure to meet orders may indeed lead to a range of potential damages, including loss of reputation, the transfer of customers to other firms, as well as straightforward loss of profit. We shall call this cost cw_i: it is likely to be proportional to the wage if the firm has to use employees to make up for the damage it has incurred. And we assume that $c > 1$ to indicate that the firm would gain on the margin from hiring extra labour.

We are now in a position to look at the cost of an average unit of labour, given the probability that an employee may quit and the possibility that the position may not be filled:

$$w_i[1 - q + h(w_i/w, e)q] + w_i c[q - qh(w_i/w, e)]. \tag{15.117}$$

In the first term $[1 - q + h(w_i/w, e)q]$ is the percentage of desired jobs e_i filled, namely the proportion of those who don't quit $(1 - q)$ and the proportion of those who do quit who are replaced by new recruits (hq). Thus the first term is the cost of actual employment. The second term is the cost (per worker) of unfilled vacancies—the proportion of those who quit who are not covered by new recruits ($q - qh$)—multiplied by the cost of an unfilled vacancy, $w_i c$.

This time we dispense with deriving the price-setting equation—it should be clear enough how to do so in this case—and work out the wage-setting equation by differentiating (15.117) with respect to w_i. This gives:

$$1 - q + hq + c[q - hq] + w_i q(1 - c)\frac{\partial h(w_i/w, e)}{\partial w_i} = 0. \tag{15.118}$$

Again a functional form is needed for h, and we assume simply that

$$h = \bar{h} + \alpha \frac{w_i}{w.e}. \tag{15.119}$$

Substituting in (15.118) gives

$$\frac{w_i}{w} = \left(\frac{1 + q(c - 1)(1 - \bar{h})}{2q(c - 1)\alpha} \right) e. \tag{15.120}$$

Both the intuitive and the formal similarity between the recruitment and retention cases is clear. We can summarize the properties of the wage-setting curve in the recruitment case as follows:

(1) The higher is the employment rate in the economy, the higher w_i/w has to be.

(2) The lower is $\bar{h}$ (the underlying hiring rate) the higher is w_i/w.

(3) The higher is α (the sensitivity of the hiring rate to $w_i/(we)$, the lower will be w_i/w.

Efficiency wages—what is the evidence?

Attempts have been made to test Shapiro and Stiglitz's shirking explanation for the existence of efficiency wages. Whilst some supportive evidence has been found, the use of surveys of firms to ask managers directly about the relationship between effort and wages has produced greater support for the role of fairness considerations as emphasized by Akerlof. An example of the first type of study is by Alan Krueger, who makes use of the implication of the shirking model that the monitoring of workers and efficiency wages are substitute mechanisms for eliciting effort from workers.[25] Krueger compares wages in fast-food shops that are franchises and company owned. The idea is that managers in franchises have stronger incentives to monitor than do managers in company-owned shops because the agency problem is greater in the company-owned outlet. The consequence of the difference in ownership structure for firms producing identical products is that it would be predicted on Shapiro–Stiglitz grounds that wages would be lower in franchises. The company-owned shops would need to make greater use of wages as an incentive mechanism because of the weaker monitoring of workers by managers. Krueger found some but not overwhelming evidence to support this hypothesis and he was not able to exclude other explanations for the modest wage gap reported.

Although the Shapiro–Stiglitz model is appealing, its empirical relevance has been questioned. Recent studies using survey evidence and laboratory experiments have suggested that questions of fairness play a role in wage setting in the way proposed by Akerlof's version of efficiency wages. For a survey of the experimental evidence, see the survey by Gächter and Fehr.[26] Respondents to survey questions[27] say that wages are not cut in a recession because it will lead to lower effort by workers and that this effect is stronger when workers take the view that they are being paid less than the 'fair' wage. Comparisons of wages with workers elsewhere seem to be important in affecting what is perceived by workers as fair. Campbell and Kamlani (1997) also report support for explanations that

[25] Krueger (1991).   [26] Gächter and Fehr (2001).
[27] For example, Campbell and Kamlani (1997). Also Bewley (1999).

focus on the effect of wages on retention: 'firms fear the loss of firm-specific human capital when experienced workers quit almost as much as they fear the cost of hiring and training replacements' (p. 785). Agell and Lundborg (2003) examine the same question using survey evidence from Swedish firms during a period of prolonged recession with low inflation. They find that wage cuts almost never occurred and that workers became, if anything, more concerned about relative wages. Consistent with efficiency wage theories, they also found that unemployment raises effort and reduces substandard performance.

■ APPENDIX: MENU-COST PRICING THEORIES

In the presentation of the NKPC in section 6, the focus was on deriving a Phillips curve from a model of price setting with rational agents using Calvo's model in which a randomly selected proportion of firms can reset their price each period. Calvo's model is related to the so-called menu cost models of price setting. In the menu-cost approach, the focus is on pinning down the macroeconomic implications when firms face a small cost to adjusting their price. What Calvo does is to model the firm as facing an adjustment cost in terms of what happens if there is a discrepancy between the actual price and the optimal price. By specifying the cost of not resetting prices this way and combining it with the random 'staggering' assumption, the NKPC is derived. In this section, we show how a menu-cost model can explain why price (or wage) adjustments are infrequent. Unfortunately the menu-cost model does not translate directly into a Phillips curve. It is therefore difficult to integrate it into a macro model and for this reason, we concentrate on the Calvo model in the main text.

The menu cost approach is designed to explain why price adjustments may be infrequent. It gets its name from the fact that restaurants tend only to change prices on menus at intervals, reflecting in part the cost of printing new menus. Its name implies that the cost of changing prices may not in fact be very great: so it asks the question—can small costs of changing prices account for the slow adjustment of prices and prolonged departures of employment from equilibrium?

Before seeing what may be at the core of an answer to this question, we shall set out in a very simple model the basic mechanics. And we adopt a slightly different approach to much of the menu-cost literature[28] by asking why unions do not set wages continuously instead of why firms do not change prices. The reason for looking at wage setting is that the cost of changing wages is more evident than that of changing prices—a bargaining process has to be entered into, which takes time and resources. We use a simpler union utility function and employment demand curve than in earlier sections because we can get neater and more comprehensible solutions.

The ith union maximizes $U_i = w_i e_i$, and it faces a linear demand curve

$$e_i = m - \eta w_i + \eta \tag{15.121}$$

where m is now the real money supply, w_i is the real wage in sector i, and we are no longer working in logs. As before we assume Bertrand pricing and labour productivity of 1. Suppose m changes, will it pay the union to renegotiate or not? We assume the cost of a renegotiation is C. Since unions in each sector face identical conditions it is plausible that either it will pay all unions not to renegotiate or the reverse. Is it an equilibrium for all unions to keep their wage fixed (or at least under what conditions is that the case)? This is asking the question: is the strategy of fixed wages a so-called Nash equilibrium? The method for proving this is simple. We ask: if all other unions are keeping their wages fixed, does it pay me to alter mine? If the answer is no, and since all unions are in identical circumstances, it means that it does not pay any union to alter their wage. To check whether this is so we have first to find out the utility my union gets if it follows all the other unions and keeps its wage fixed (say it gets U_{fix}); then find out its utility if it chooses the optimal wage in the new circumstances (say U_{flex}); and finally see under what conditions $C \geq U_{flex} - U_{fix}$. Note that it will always get at least as much utility from choosing its optimal wage. If we start off from equilibrium, U_{flex} must equal U_{fix} at equilibrium, with $U_{flex} \geq U_{fix}$ outside equilibrium

---

[28] The key original papers on menu costs are Akerlof and Yellen (1985) and Mankiw (1985).

and the question is whether the greater utility from flexible wages compensates the cost of bargaining, which is measured by C.

We begin with U_{fix}. Since all unions are setting the same real wage ($w_i = W_i/P$), and since $W_i = P_i$ from Bertrand pricing, we have $w_i = W_i/P = P_i/P = w = 1$. Using this in equation (15.121) implies that $e_i = m$. Hence:

$$U_{fix} = w_i e_i = m. \tag{15.122}$$

Next, we look at U_{flex}. The ith union chooses w_i to maximize $w_i e_i$ subject to equation (15.121). This yields

$$\frac{\partial w_i e_i(w_i)}{\partial w_i} = \frac{\partial w_i(m - \eta w_i + \eta)}{\partial w_i}$$

$$\Rightarrow m - 2\eta w_i + \eta = 0$$

$$\Rightarrow w_i = \frac{m + \eta}{2\eta}. \tag{15.123}$$

So $w_i e_i = \left(\frac{m+\eta}{2\eta}\right)(m - \eta w_i + \eta) = \left(\frac{m+\eta}{2\eta}\right)\left(m - \eta\left(\frac{m+\eta}{2\eta}\right) + \eta\right) = \left(\frac{m+\eta}{2\eta}\right)\left(\frac{m+\eta}{2}\right) = \eta^{-1}\left(\frac{m+\eta}{2}\right)^2$ i.e.

$$U_{flex} = \eta^{-1}\left(\frac{m+\eta}{2}\right)^2. \tag{15.124}$$

The condition for keeping wages fixed is therefore

$$C \geq \eta^{-1}\left(\frac{m+\eta}{2}\right)^2 - m. \tag{15.125}$$

We can now ask how large does a shift in aggregate demand, as measured by m in this model, have to be to cause wages to be reset? In Fig. 15.20, $U_{fix} = m$ is the $45°$ line and $U_{flex} = (m+\eta)^2/4\eta$ is the quadratic. As we have shown above, when m is at its equilibrium value of η,

$$U_{flex} = (2\eta)^2/4\eta = \eta = m = U_{fix}.$$

We can also show that the slope of U_{flex} is equal to that of U_{fix} when $m = \eta$:

$$\frac{\partial (m+\eta)^2/4\eta}{\partial m} = \frac{m+\eta}{2\eta} = 1 \text{ when } m = \eta. \tag{15.126}$$

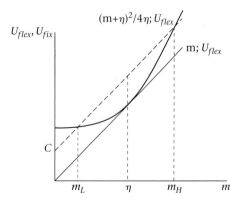

Figure 15.20 'Menu' costs and wage stickiness

Thus as can be seen in Fig. 15.20, the quadratic $U_{flex} = \eta/4$ when $m = 0$, touches m when $m = \eta$ and then rises again. In fact $(U_{flex} - U_{fix})$, the gain in utility from resetting wages, is symmetric either side of $m = \eta$. For example, when $m = 0$, $(U_{flex} - U_{fix}) = \eta/4$; and this is also the case when $m = 2\eta$: $(m + \eta)^2/4\eta - m = (3\eta)^2/4\eta - 2\eta = 9\eta/4 - 8\eta/4 = \eta/4$.

Now we can find graphically the values of m at which wages are reset: $(U_{flex} - U_{fix})$ is simply the vertical distance between U_{flex} and U_{fix}. Using the 45° line which starts from C on the vertical axis, we can then see that there are two values of m, m_L and m_H, at which $C = (U_{flex} - U_{fix})$. Since $(U_{flex} - U_{fix})$ is symmetric either side of $m = \eta$, $\eta - m_L = m_H - \eta$. Clearly, as C falls—just shift the C line down towards the m line—m_L rises towards η and m_H falls towards η. And of course when $C = 0$, we can see that any change in m away from η will lead to wages being reset. So, not surprisingly, a rise in the cost of wage setting implies that wages only get reset for larger fluctuations in m.

The menu cost approach has the advantage that it takes explicitly into account maximization behaviour by firms or (as here) unions. But there are two main problems with it. The first problem is the following. The longer the union expects a decline in aggregate demand to last, the more rapidly it should reset wages. This is because the cost of resetting wages, C, is a one-off cost, while $(U_{flex} - U_{fix})$ is the profit loss which continues as long as m remains at its new value. Thus we should really be comparing C with $\left(\eta^{-1}(m + \eta/2)^2 - m\right)T$ where T is the length of time m is expected to be at its new value (leaving aside discounting). Consider

$$\frac{C}{T(m)} = \left(\eta^{-1}\left(\frac{m + \eta}{2}\right)^2 - m\right).$$

If $T \geq T(m)$, it pays to reset wages at once. If $T < T(m)$, then wages and prices remain unchanged. These calculations assume that m will return to η at the end of T. Thus the theory can explain reasonably well why a monetary policy such as

$$m_t = \eta + \varepsilon_t \text{ with } \varepsilon_t \text{ i.i.d}, \ E\varepsilon = 0 \text{ uniformly in } [m_L.m_H], \ T = 1$$

would be associated with fixed wages and prices.

The second problem is related to the first. If monetary policy is more complex, for instance a stable growth over time

$$m_t - m_{t-1} = \gamma_m$$

then it becomes considerably more complex to work out the implications for wage and price developments. In consequence, the menu-cost approach is a sort of limbo theory: many economists believe it captures reality and explains why profit-maximizing firms or utility-maximizing unions do not change wages and prices continuously. However; no simple formulations have developed from it that translate into Phillips curves and hence tractable macro models.

16 | Political Economy

One theme in this book is that macroeconomics must be built on microeconomic foundations. That premiss requires that we look at the behaviour of individual actors. We have spent time analysing how households, unions, and firms take decisions. But relatively little space has been devoted to analysing the decision making of the government. Despite the great importance of government policy decisions in this book—in fiscal, monetary, and supply-side policy—we have either simply looked at the *consequences* of different policy choices in terms of economic outcomes, or (notably in the chapter on monetary policy) assumed that the government or central bank is maximizing a utility function in which it seeks to keep output and inflation as close to their respective targets as possible. For much of that chapter, we assumed that the government's target for output was equilibrium output and that it wanted a low rate of inflation: such a government's behaviour is consistent with a sustainable equilibrium (i.e. stable inflation with expectations fulfilled). Toward the end of the monetary policy chapter, we raised the question of what would happen if the government had an output target above equilibrium. This leads to the problem of time inconsistency in monetary policy in which such a government suggests that it can deliver inflation at target with output above the equilibrium, which is impossible. The outcome is output at equilibrium with inflation above target, i.e. an inflation bias. The contrast between an overambitious government and one that aims to keep inflation close to target with output close to equilibrium helps to explain some changes in institutional arrangements that have been introduced in recent years such as independent central banks.

To pursue these issues further requires a theory of government in the same way that we have a theory of the firm or of union behaviour. Ideally we need to get inside the black box of government. This involves understanding voting behaviour, political parties, coalition building, and so on. An important literature has developed in economics over the last twenty years, which is usually referred to as *political economy* and which seeks to model political behaviour. It would be a great exaggeration to claim that a coherent theory of government and politics now exists but some important steps have been made. In this chapter we shall set out some of those that are most relevant to macroeconomics.

In one important way, the study of political decision making is different from decision making by households and firms. In political decision making just as in consumption behaviour or labour supply decisions, we start from the assumption that the actor is maximizing an objective function. Thus households maximize a utility function, and in setting prices, hiring labour, or making investment decisions, firms maximize profits. But there is a key difference: in general, in doing so, households assume that they do not need to take account of the reaction of other agents to their own actions: the assumption on which this is based is that they are small enough to take external conditions as given. Political actors, however, nearly always have to take into account the reactions of other actors (voters, political opponents, wage setters, etc.). Political actors behave *strategically*. This means that game theory becomes a central tool of analysis.

Political economy is a rapidly expanding field, with major implications for macroeconomics and in order to understand the political economy literature some understanding of the basic methods of modern game theory is necessary. This chapter is organized so as to provide an introduction to political economy by selecting a number of the most important applications to macroeconomics. In doing so, we explain some of the key concepts used in game theory.[1]

Although political economy does not yet provide a coherent model of politics or government, it has produced a large number of useful and suggestive models of political behaviour. In this chapter we set out some of the models most relevant to the themes of this book. They cover four areas:

(1) Monetary and fiscal policy when governments have an output target greater than y_e. This provides a deeper analysis of the problem of time inconsistency introduced in Chapter 5.

(2) The analysis of the interaction between the government or central bank and wage setters, where wage setters do not know whether the monetary policy maker is 'tough', with an output target equal to y_e, or 'weak', with a higher target level of activity. This introduces the analysis of games with incomplete information, in particular signalling games.

(3) Voting behaviour and government policy. This both introduces the idea of the 'political business cycle' and addresses the question of how voting behaviour could affect the tax rate set by the government.

(4) Interdependence in policy making between two governments. This develops the analysis introduced in Chapter 12 when we moved away from the assumption of a small open economy to consider the interaction between policy makers in two economies.

The chapter begins by showing how the problem of time inconsistency can be represented in a game between the government and wage setters, where the government is known to have a target level of output higher than the equilibrium, i.e. $y^T > y_e$. Rational behaviour on the part of wage setters and the government leads to the outcome of an inflation bias. However, we shall see that, once we allow for the possibility that the interaction between the government and wage setters takes place repeatedly, it is possible that wage setters are able to discipline the government and ensure that the government sets output at equilibrium. We shall therefore see the conditions under which an overambitious government has an incentive to behave as if its target is $y^T = y_e$.

---

[1] Readers who have done a course in game theory will note that extensive form games and subgame perfection are introduced in this chapter before normal form games and Nash equilibrium.

An institutional solution to the problem of time inconsistency is for the government to hand over decision making in monetary policy to an independent central bank with $y^T = y_e$. But what if the government keeps control of fiscal policy? This leads us to look in section 2 at a game between an overambitious government ($y^T > y_e$) with control over fiscal policy and a central bank that controls monetary policy and sets $y^T = y_e$.

In section 3, a different issue is raised by the possibility that wage setters are unsure as to whether the central bank really is tough (with $y^T = y_e$) or not (with $y^T > y_e$). This problem with incomplete information can be analysed as a signalling game and the focus of attention is on pinning down the circumstances under which a weak central bank has the incentive to pursue a so-called pooling strategy and behave as if it were tough.

Section 4 looks at the effect of voting on government behaviour. Three models are presented: first, what happens if there are left and right partisan candidates in an election, where the left candidate is known to favour an employment target above equilibrium and the right below equilibrium? Second, can non-partisan but power-hungry candidates use the electoral process opportunistically? For example, it is sometimes suggested that incumbent governments will deliberately boost the economy before an election in order to raise their chances of re-election. Thirdly, can voting theory tell us anything about the tax rates that voters will successfully be able to impose on a government?

The final section of the chapter deals with the interdependence in policy making between two governments: i.e. the game in this case is between two governments. As we saw in Chapter 12, if both governments place a positive value on higher output but a negative one on higher government spending (because it raises their budget deficit), the interdependence in levels of output between the two that arises from trade means that both gain from higher government expenditure by the other. We sketched out how this game might be resolved in a simple way in Chapter 12. In this chapter we show how game theory can help us understand a range of different ways in which the interaction between two rational governments can be resolved.

The treatment of game theory in this chapter is limited and selective, but it can be followed without prior knowledge. By centring our discussion on two economic examples that we have explored extensively already (time inconsistency and interdependence) and for which the economic intuition has been provided, it is possible to introduce a number of key game theory concepts and methods in a way that is relatively easily absorbed. When game theory is taught, it usually begins with *simultaneous* move games such as the famous Prisoners' Dilemma game (discussed in Chapter 4). However, in this chapter we begin with the monetary policy example in which the government and wage setters are the players in the game. In this game, the players move *sequentially*. Later on in the chapter, we encounter problems in which the players move simultaneously. The examples show how reformulating familiar economic problems in terms of game theory can provide for a more systematic and satisfying analysis. Readers who want a fuller introduction to the use of game theory in economics may want to read Robert Gibbons's excellent book *Game Theory for Applied Economics*.[2]

---

[2] Gibbons (1992).

1 Monetary policy and time inconsistency: the problem of overambitious governments

1.1 Time inconsistency in a game tree

We begin with the time-inconsistency problem. This was introduced in Chapter 5, but not in an explicitly game-theoretic form. It may be useful for the reader to revise sections 6.1 and 6.2 of the monetary policy chapter before continuing. By taking a problem that we have analysed extensively already, the introduction to game-theoretic methods is made easier. The key contribution of game theory methods is to impose a clear discipline on the rationality of decision making by agents at all stages. Here we analyse the problem as a game that is played over time in the sense that the players move sequentially. When a game is analysed as being played over time it is called a game in extensive form. To bring out the strategic aspects, we put the problem in a simplified form in this chapter. We simplify greatly by assuming that the government has only two levels of output it can choose: either y_e, equilibrium output, or y^T, the government's target output, where we assume that the target is above the equilibrium level. This is what defines the government as 'overambitious'. Similarly wage setters, WS, can only choose two expected rates of inflation: 2% and 4%. The relevant game tree is shown in Fig. 16.1.

We assume wage setters (WS) have the first move and can choose just one of two expected rates of inflation, $\pi^E = 2\%$ or 4%. In the knowledge of what WS has chosen, the government (G) has the second move and can choose either $y = y_e$ or $y = y^T > y_e$. These possibilities are shown in the diagram.

For readers who are unfamiliar with extensive-form games, the diagram is read as follows: the square boxes indicate which player, WS or G, makes a move when the game gets to that box. For future reference the boxes are usually called *decision nodes*. The game starts at the top box or decision node, with WS having the first move. The two lines going down from the WS box indicate the two choices open to WS, $\pi^E = 4\%$ or $\pi^E = 2\%$. If WS chooses $\pi^E = 4\%$, the game moves down the left hand line to the left hand G decision

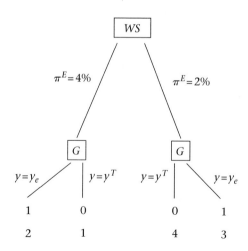

Figure 16.1 Time inconsistency in monetary policy: $y^T > y_e$

node. G now moves and can choose either $y = y_e$ or $y = y^T > y_e$, as shown by the two lines coming down from the left hand decision node. If WS chooses $\pi^E = 2\%$, the game moves down the right hand line to the right hand G decision node. G now moves and can again choose either $y = y_e$ or $y = y^T > y_e$, as shown by the two lines coming down from the right hand decision node. After G has moved the game ends. As can be seen there are four possible pairs of choices $(2\%, y_e)$, $(2\%, y^T)$, $(4\%, y_e)$, and $(4\%, y^T)$. The pay-offs to the two players are shown underneath each of the four final moves by the government, with the pay-off to wage setters shown above that to the government.

For simplicity, it is assumed that the wage setters are interested only in whether π is equal to π^E or not. If it is, their pay-off is 1; if not, their pay-off is zero. We use a simple Phillips curve: $\pi = \pi^E + y - y_e$. As usual, inflation is as expected, only when output is at equilibrium: $\pi = \pi^E$ when $y = y_e$. Thus WS gets a pay-off of 1 from the combinations $(2\%, y_e)$ and $(4\%, y_e)$ since both imply $\pi = \pi^E$. And WS gets a pay-off of 0 from $(2\%, y^T)$ and $(4\%, y^T)$ since $\pi > \pi^E$ in both these cases.

We now turn to the pay-offs of the government. The pay-off to G stems from its order of preferences over the four possible outcomes. The order of preferences from best to worst is $(\pi^E = 2\%, y = y^T)$, $(\pi^E = 2\%, y = y_e)$, $(\pi^E = 4\%, y = y_e)$, $(\pi^E = 4\%, y = y^T)$. Reflecting this order of preferences we assume the pay-offs to G are 4, 3, 2, and 1 respectively. To understand these preferences remember first, from the Phillips curve $\pi = \pi^E + y - y_e$, that $\pi = \pi^E$ when $y = y_e$; assume that when $y = y^T$ instead of y_e that adds a percentage point to π, i.e. $\pi = \pi^E + y^T - y_e = \pi^E + 1$. This implies that the inflation rate in the four outcomes is 3% (when $\pi^E = 2\%$ and $y = y^T$), 2% (when $\pi^E = 2\%$ and $y = y_e$), 4% (when $\pi^E = 4\%$ and $y = y_e$), and 5% (when $\pi^E = 4\%$ and $y = y^T$). Now, the key assumption about G's preferences is that when inflation is low, G attaches little importance to a slightly higher rate of inflation: therefore it will be prepared to set $y = y^T$ even if the cost is 3% rather than 2% inflation. Hence G prefers $(\pi^E = 2\%, \pi = 3\%, y = y^T)$ to $(\pi^E = 2\%, \pi = 2\%, y = y_e)$. But when inflation is high, G is much more concerned about raising the rate of inflation further. Hence G prefers $(\pi^E = 4\%, \pi = 4\%, y = y_e)$ to $(\pi^E = 4\%, \pi = 5\%, y = y^T)$.

How is the game solved? We begin by showing how the government would like the game to work out and then demonstrate why this is not a solution. Clearly it is in the government's interest for WS to set $\pi^E = 2\%$ since then G gets a pay-off of 3 or 4; by contrast, if WS sets $\pi^E = 4\%$, G gets a pay-off of 1 or 2. So we might imagine a crafty government saying to the wage setters before the wage setters have moved: 'If you choose $\pi^E = 2\%$, we guarantee that we will choose y_e. This is in our interest because we end up with a pay-off of 3. And it is in your interest because you end up with $\pi^E = \pi$ or a pay-off of 1, which is the best result for you.'

Should the wage setters believe this promise? The answer is no, as we have already seen in Chapter 5. By setting out the game in its extensive form, we shall now see the same logic at work and also see more generally why the game format is useful for analysing whether promises are credible or not. In this case, the government's promise is not a credible one, at least if the wage setters believe the government is rational. Rational behaviour here means the following: when it comes to the government's turn to move, the government will make the choice that maximizes its pay-off at that point. To see why the promise is not credible using the tools of the extensive game, we begin by supposing the wage setters choose $\pi^E = 2\%$. Then the government finds itself in the right hand decision node or box. If it chooses $y = y_e$, its pay-off is 3; but if it chooses $y = y^T$ its pay-off is 4. Hence the government—if it is rational—will choose $y = y^T$. Thus the G's promise to choose $y = y_e$ if WS chooses $\pi^E = 2\%$ is not credible if WS believes G is rational.

Given that G's promise is not credible, what should wage setters do? If they are rational (and they believe G is rational), they will see that choosing $\pi^E = 2\%$ implies G will choose $y = y^T$, so that their pay-off from $\pi^E = 2\%$ is 0. What if they choose $\pi^E = 4\%$? As can be seen from the diagram, G will then choose $y = y_e$, since G's pay-off from $y = y_e$ is 2 while its pay-off from $y = y^T$ is 1 if $\pi^E = 4\%$. So wage setters can guarantee that G will choose $y = y_e$—giving them a pay-off of 1—if they choose $\pi^E = 4\%$. Hence if rational wage setters believe the government is rational, they will set $\pi^E = 4\%$, and G will set $y = y_e$. (This is of course exactly the same argument put into more explicit game theory form that we have already made in Chapter 5 when showing how wage setters would behave with rational expectations.)

The government's problem is that it cannot credibly commit itself to a level of output in advance of wage setters deciding their inflation expectations. If it could, there would be no problem. It would commit itself to $y = y_e$ if $\pi^E = 2\%$. Wage setters would then be prepared to set $\pi^E = 2\%$ and, by the definition of a credible (or binding) commitment, the government would then set $y = y_e$. (In the example here, WS is indifferent between $\pi^E = 2\%$ and $\pi^E = 4\%$ in the case of a binding commitment because we have assumed that all that matters to them is that inflation expectations are fulfilled (and hence that $y = y_e$); in practice we might plausibly assume that WS has at least a slight preference for the lower rate of inflation and would thus choose 2%). Note that if we follow this suggestion and substitute a pay-off to WS of 1.5 (instead of 1) for the outcome of $\pi^E = 2\%, y = y_e$ this does not affect the time-inconsistency outcome in the absence of a binding commitment.

Time-inconsistency problems are frequently encountered in economics and probably in real life more generally as well. We can take another example to illustrate. Suppose that entrepreneur A makes an investment in machinery with a zero second hand value that can only be used profitably with worker B's particular skills. In that case the profits are 10 and A will undertake the investment if he can split the profits with B so that both get 5—we assume that both are better off with 5 than without the investment. But once A has made the investment, B is in a strong bargaining position to get, say, 8 since A can do nothing else with the machinery. However, if A only gets 2, let us assume that that does not cover the costs of the investment. Hence B has a problem of time inconsistency. Unless she can commit in advance not to bargain 8 after the investment has been made, A will not make the investment and B will be worse off. In the commercial world it may be possible for A and B to write a contract stating that both A and B will receive 5 from the transaction, but such contracts may be difficult to enforce legally. For instance B may not work fully cooperatively unless she receives 8, but this may be difficult to prove in court. In any case, with government choice of monetary policy, contracts would usually be meaningless. Given an inability to precommit, time inconsistency can be a major problem.

1.1.1 Summing up

By working backwards through the game tree, it is clear that if WS chooses $\pi^E = 2\%$ the government will choose $y = y^T > y_e$. Only if the wage setters choose $\pi^E = 4\%$ can they be sure that the government will set $y = y_e$. We have therefore shown that the government cannot commit credibly to an inflation target of 2%. We shall look at how the government can solve its problem (revisiting some of the ideas discussed in Chapter 5) after introducing a little more game theory.

1.2 Introducing some game theory

The way our simple extensive form game was solved was by the method of *backward induction*. It is applicable to extensive games with a finite number of moves. It means that you start with decision nodes (the boxes in our game) at which, whatever choice is made, the game ends. These are the two G boxes. For each of these decision nodes (which are often called *terminal* decision nodes), the optimal choice of the player at that point will be evident: the player at a terminal decision node can see the pay-offs of each choice. Thus at the left hand terminal decision mode, G chooses $y = y_e$ because the pay-off of 2 is greater than the pay-off to the other choice $y = y^T$ of 1. It is customary, if we are using an extensive game diagram to show how the game is solved, to represent this choice by a thicker line—here by a thicker dashed line, as can be seen in Fig. 16.2 on the $y = y_e$ choice line from the left hand terminal decision node of G. Now follow the same procedure for all the other terminal decision nodes: in our case that is simply the right hand G node, where G's choice of $y = y^T$ is preferred to $y = y_e$. Again this choice is marked by a dashed line.

Having done this for all the terminal decision nodes, we move back up the game to the penultimate decision nodes. There is only one in our game, WS's initial decision node. What will be the pay-off from each choice at this decision node? This is easy to calculate because we know what G's move will be for each of WS's possible decisions. Visually, the pay-off to each of WS's choices is seen by going down the relevant dashed line to the pay-offs at the end of it. Thus if WS chooses $\pi^E = 4\%$, the pay-off—of 1—is seen by going down the dashed line $y = y_e$. So WS will choose $\pi^E = 4\%$ over $\pi^E = 2\%$ since the pay-off to WS of the latter is 0. So now draw a dashed line on the $\pi^E = 4\%$ choice line. The game

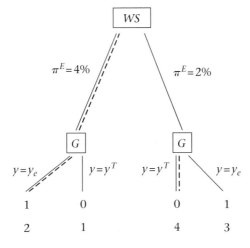

Figure 16.2 Backward induction

is now solved: the solution moves down the dashed lines from the start of the game until its end. This path, $\pi^E = 4\%$ then $y = y_e$, is called the *equilibrium path* of the game. By examining the pairs of pay-offs, it is obvious that this is not the outcome that maximizes the joint utility of *WS* and *G*: with $y = y_e$ and $\pi^E = 2\%$, the government is better off and the wage setters no worse off. But the game tree demonstrates why such an outcome will not be observed in this game.

Game theory goes a little bit further in explaining exactly why it is rational for *WS* and *G* to behave in the way they do. It uses the concept of a *subgame perfect equilibrium* (SGPE). A subgame, at least in the absence of uncertainty as we are assuming here, is the game which starts at a decision node. In our game there are three subgames, starting from each of the three decision nodes. Thus the game itself is also classified as a subgame.

The notion of an SGPE basically means that a player behaves rationally at each of that player's decision points (irrespective of whether they are on the equilibrium path). To define an SGPE we need the concept of a player's strategy. A strategy is the choice a player will make at each of its decision nodes. We will put a strategy in curly brackets {}. Since *WS* has only one decision node it has only the two possible strategies $\{\pi^E = 4\%\}$ and $\{\pi^E = 2\%\}$. It is more complicated for *G* since *G* has two decision nodes, each following from a different choice of *WS*: thus a *G*-strategy will take the following form {if $\pi^E = 4\%$, then $y = y^T$, and if $\pi^E = 2\%$, then $y = y_e$}. Evidently there are four possible *G* strategies. The *equilibrium* or *chosen* strategy of *WS* is of course $\{\pi^E = 4\%\}$, and that of *G* {if $\pi^E = 4\%$, then $y = y_e$, and if $\pi^E = 2\%$, then $y = y^T$}.

The requirement of an SGPE is that, for all the subgames (or decision nodes, if there is no uncertainty) in a game, the player whose turn it is to move at the start of the subgame must have a rational strategy from then on given (if necessary) the other player's chosen strategy from then on.[3] In our game it is far more simple. At the two subgames which start with *G* decision nodes, no subsequent strategies have to be taken into account in the rational choice since they are terminal nodes. At the subgame (the whole game) which starts at *WS*'s decision node, *WS* has to take account of *G*'s chosen strategy from then on. Thus the dashed lines in Fig. 16.2 capture exactly the idea of SGP strategies, and the method of backward induction (in a game of this sort) guarantees an SGPE. The critical point of an SGPE is that both players are rational whenever it is their turn to move; and this includes assuming that the other player will behave similarly, i.e. also rationally, at subsequent moves.

In a game that is finite (i.e. in which there is a fixed number of moves) and in which there is no uncertainty, solving the game using the method of backward induction implies that the solution is an SGPE. If an equilibrium is an SGPE, it rules out non-credible commitments or promises (or indeed threats): that is its critical importance in game theory and the reason it is so useful in understanding why time-inconsistency problems may arise between fully rational players.

---

[3] We can put this more formally and generally. Let σ_A and σ_B be the strategies of players *A* and *B*. A strategy states what the player will do at the start of each subgame at which the player has the move. And let $\sigma_A(i)$, $\sigma_B(i)$ be the strategies of *A* and *B* respectively at the start of the *i*th subgame. Then σ_A and σ_B are a SGPE strategy pair if and only if at each subgame *i* at which *A* has the initial move, $\sigma_A(i)$ is *A*'s optimal strategy for subgame *i* given $\sigma_B(i)$; and vice versa at each subgame *i* at which *B* has the initial move.

1.2.1 **Summing up**

The game tree provides a graphical way of presenting an extensive form game and backward induction can be used to identify a subgame perfect equilibrium strategy. Using this technique, we see why, in the game between the government and the wage setters, the outcome that maximizes their joint utility is not observed.

1.3 Using game theory methods to look at solutions to the time-inconsistency problem

There are three broad solutions to the time-inconsistency problem of monetary policy. All three involve altering the nature of the game. The first is, in one form or another, to change the objective function of policy makers: the most common way of doing this is via *delegation* of powers to an independent central bank, which is required to promote low inflation. The approach corresponds to changing the objective function of those responsible for monetary policy (in the model presented here, this entails that the output target changes from $y^T > y_e$ to $y^T = y_e$, or alternatively changing G's pay-offs in Fig. 16.1 so that, if $\pi^E = 2\%$, G's pay-off from y_e is 4 and from y^T is 3). This is discussed in Chapter 5 on monetary policy and in a more institutional setting in Chapter 8. We follow up this solution in section 2 when we ask what happens if the government delegates monetary policy to an independent central bank but keeps control of fiscal policy.

The second approach is to consider what happens when the game between wage setters and an overambitious government is repeated over an indefinite number of periods. If the government knows that wage setters will 'punish' it by choosing a high expected inflation rate after G has set a high rate of output, it will pay the government to set output at the equilibrium level each period under certain conditions. The idea is that it will indeed pay the G to behave toughly if it can persuade wage setters to punish it unless it behaves in the same way as a tough government would behave. We shall elucidate the conditions under which this outcome will occur.

The third approach presupposes that wage setters do not know if the government or central bank (*CB*) has a 'tough' or an 'accommodating' objective function. It may then pay the *CB* to build a *reputation* for being tough (i.e. persuading wage setters it is tough) by playing tough—whether it is actually tough or actually accommodating (this solution was sketched in section 6.2 of Chapter 5). This of course requires that the *CB* and wage setters play more than one round of the game. We shall see what happens in a two-round game in which wage setters start each round by choosing π^E and the *CB* then sets y. In the first round, wage setters have no idea whether the *CB* is tough or accommodating since the *CB* has done nothing; but at the start of the second round the wage setters can make an assessment since they have seen what value of y the *CB* set in round one. This approach with incomplete information is the subject of section 3.

1.4 Multiperiod games: endogenous enforcement and punishment

We recall the one-period complete information game where wage setters know the government is weak and has an output target above the equilibrium. As we have seen, the outcome in the one-period game is the time inconsistent one with the consequence of inflation bias. Now we turn to examine what happens when this game is repeated. Can the wage setter 'enforce' good behaviour on the government? Up to this point, we have argued that if *WS knows* that the government is 'weak', we cannot escape from the time-inconsistency problem: there will be an inflation bias. This is certainly true if the game lasts one period (or in fact a predetermined finite number of periods). But it may be possible for the wage setter to enforce good behaviour on the government—and for the government to benefit by escaping from time inconsistency—so long as the interaction between *WS* and *G* carries on infinitely and *G* values future outcomes enough. We could equally well imagine this game being played between *WS* and a central bank, where the central bank is known by the wage setter to be weak.

Imagine that at the start of each period, *WS* sets π^E equal either to π_L or to π_H; and then *G* sets y equal to either y_e or $y^T > y_e$. *G*'s utility function is the present value of the discounted sum of the utility flow that *G* gets in each period t (which is $u(\pi_t, y_t)$), where the discount factor is δ. We can write *G*'s utility as:

$$U_G = u(\pi_0, y_0) + \delta u(\pi_1, y_1) + \delta^2 u(\pi_2, y_2) + \cdots \tag{16.1}$$

Similarly, *WS*'s utility function is the discounted sum of the utility flow *WS* gets each period t from the combination π_t and y_t. Before analysing the repeated game, we recall in Fig. 16.3 the one-period game between *WS* and *G*: this is the same as we have analysed before with one modification. We now set *WS*'s payoff from playing $\pi^E = \pi_L$ at 1.5 (rather than 1), i.e. *WS* strictly prefers an outcome of equilibrium output and low inflation to one of equilibrium output and high inflation. As is clear from running through the backward induction exercise again, this has no effect on the outcome in the one-period game: time inconsistency prevails.

Assume now that the extensive game in Fig. 16.3 is repeated indefinitely. As we shall see, the time-inconsistency problem can now be dealt with by *WS* being prepared to set π^E equal to π_L each period so long as *G* continues to set y equal to y_e. But if *G* ever sets y equal to y^T, *WS* will always set $\pi^E = \pi_H$ subsequently. So *WS* now has an interest in cooperating with *G* so that—if *G* continues to cooperate—the moves are (π_L, y_e) each period.

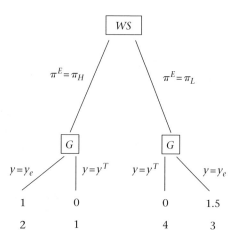

Figure 16.3 Time inconsistency in the one-period game

At the start of each period t it is useful to define two possible 'histories' of moves in each previous period of the game—i.e. from 0 to $t-1$. In the first, G has cooperated in each period by setting $y = y_e$. Call this type of history GC (standing for G has always cooperated so far). In the second, G has at least once set $y = y^T$. And call this type of history GD (for G has defected from the agreement on at least one occasion). WS has the following strategy:

- $WS(a)$: If the history at the start of period t is GC, set $\pi_t^E = \pi_L$. In other words if G has cooperated so far then continue cooperating by setting a low expected rate of inflation in the current period.
- $WS(b)$: If the history at the start of period t is GD, set $\pi_t^E = \pi_H$, i.e. if ever G fails to keep its side of the bargain, then punish G by setting $\pi_t^E = \pi_H$. As can be seen, this involves punishing G in each future period, since once G sets y^T the history of the game is always GD.

G has the following strategy:

- $G(a)$: If GC, set $y_t = y_e$, i.e. if G has cooperated continuously, then it should maintain the cooperation rather than defect and be permanently punished for doing so.
- $G(b)$: If GD, set $y_t = y_e$ if $\pi_t^E = \pi_H$, and set $y_t = y^T$ if $\pi_t^E = \pi_L$. What this says is that, given G is now being punished every period, G should just do whatever maximizes its one-period pay-off.

Are these strategies a game-theoretic equilibrium? The appropriate equilibrium concept here is that of a subgame perfect equilibrium (SGPE), since the game is in extensive form with complete information. This requires us to show that each player's strategy is optimal in each subgame given the future strategy of the other player. Fortunately, we only have a limited number of subgames to consider because all past histories divide into one of two groups GC and GD.

So consider WS's strategy first. There are two subgames to consider. (i) If the history of game is GD, WS knows that if it sets $\pi_t^E = \pi_L$ then G will respond with $y_t = y^T$ as can be seen from $G(b)$; if WS sets $\pi_t^E = \pi_H$, G will respond with $y_t = y_e$. Clearly WS does best by choosing getting a pay-off of 1 rather than 0. Hence $WS(b)$ is optimal for WS given GD. (ii) If the subgame starts with GC, WS knows that whatever move it makes G will set $y_t = y_e$. In which case it is optimal to choose $\pi_t^E = \pi_L$ since that gives WS a pay-off of 1.5 in the current period against a pay-off of 1 if it chooses $\pi_t^E = \pi_H$. Thus WS's strategy is optimal given G's strategy.

Now consider G's strategy: There are four possible subgames: (i) GD and $\pi_t^E = \pi_L$. G knows that WS will set $\pi_t^E = \pi_H$ in each future period, so what G does now has no repercussions beyond the current period. Hence $y_t = y^T$ is optimal. (ii) GD and $\pi_t^E = \pi_H$. Again G knows that WS will set $\pi_t^E = \pi_H$ in each future period, so what G does now has no repercussions beyond the current period. Hence $y_t = y_e$ is optimal. (iii) GC and $\pi_t^E = \pi_H$ (which WS will only choose by accident). G optimises by setting $y_t = y_e$. (iv) GC and $\pi_t^E = \pi_L$. The pay-off to continued cooperation, i.e. $y_t = y_e$, is the present value of 3 in the current and each future period (since the outcome will be $\pi_t^E = \pi_L$ and $y_t = y_e$ in this and all subsequent periods), which is equal to $3/(1 - \delta)$:

$$U_G(y_e) = u_G(\pi_L, y_e)[1 + \delta + \delta^2 + \cdots] = u_G(\pi_L, y_e)/(1 - \delta) = 3/(1 - \delta) \qquad (16.2)$$

The pay-off from defection, i.e. $y_t = y^T$, is 4 in the current period, but since every subsequent history will be GD, in each future period the outcome will be (π_H, y_e) with a per period pay-off of 2. Hence the pay-off from defection is $4 + 2\delta/(1 - \delta)$:

$$U_G(y^T) = u_G(\pi_L, y^T) + u_G(\pi_H, y_e) \cdot [\delta + \delta^2 + \delta^3 + \ldots] = 4 + 2\delta/(1 - \delta). \qquad (16.3)$$

Thus it pays to cooperate so long as

$$3/(1 - \delta) > 4 + 2\delta/(1 - \delta) \Rightarrow \delta > 1/2. \qquad (16.4)$$

Hence it will pay the government to maintain y_e unless the discount factor is very low.

1.4.1 Summing up

Although in the one-period game between the overambitious government and the wage setter, an inflation bias results, this can be overcome if the game is repeated indefinitely. In particular, the wage setter can induce the government to set output at equilibrium in response to inflation expectations set low by the wage setter by threatening that any defection by the government will be punished in all subsequent periods by the wage setter playing $\pi_t^E = \pi_H$. We have shown that G and WS's strategies of (π_L^E, y_e) are subgame perfect if there is sufficient weight on future periods, in our example, this required the discount factor to be $\delta > 1/2$.

2 Fiscal and monetary policy conflicts

We have assumed so far in this chapter that the government has been using monetary policy to choose output or employment in order to control the rate of inflation. Reducing the time-inconsistency problem has been analysed in terms, *inter alia*, of delegating authority for monetary policy to agents with a stronger commitment to inflation fighting than the government. But what if the government retains control of fiscal authority? Could not the government simply use fiscal policy to counter whatever measures the central bank were to take to control monetary policy? Since it is difficult to imagine government being prepared to relinquish control of fiscal policy, what consequences might this have?

The answer depends critically on the timing of the setting of monetary and fiscal policy. The simplest example of monetary–fiscal conflict is where the fiscal authority (say G) is interested solely in a target output or employment level so it seeks to minimize the deviation of output from its target:

$$L_G = (y - y^T)^2, \qquad (16.5)$$

where L_G is the government's loss function—it is minimizing a loss function rather than maximizing a utility function. And the monetary authority (CB) is concerned to minimize the deviation of inflation from its target of zero inflation:

$$L_{CB} = \pi^2. \tag{16.6}$$

As usual the Phillips curve is:

$$\pi = \pi^E + y - y_e. \tag{16.7}$$

In addition in this game we need to specify the instruments of the fiscal and monetary authorities. We assume that G uses a fiscal instrument f, which raises aggregate demand y, and CB uses the rate of interest r, which lowers it. A simple model of aggregate demand is

$$y = f - r. \tag{16.8}$$

Finally, wage setters choose π^E rationally. In terms of the order of moves, WS always moves first. We can then consider two main possibilities: G moves second followed by CB, or vice versa. Both games are solved by backward induction to arrive at an SGPE.

2.1 Sequence 1: *CB* follows *G*

Using backward induction, we consider first the CB's choice of r. Bear in mind that WS and G have already moved, so that CB knows π^E and f before choosing r to minimize its loss function:

$$\pi^2 = (\pi^E + y - y_e)^2 = (\pi^E + f - r - y_e)^2$$
$$\Rightarrow r = \pi^E + f - y_e. \tag{16.9}$$

Note that this implies for all values of f, that $\pi = \pi^E + f - r - y_e = 0$. Hence $\pi^E = 0$ and

$$r = f - y_e. \tag{16.10}$$

Now G has to choose f to minimize $(y - y^T)^2$. However it is not difficult to see that there is nothing G can do using f to change y:

$$(y - y^T)^2 = (f - r - y^T)^2 = (f - (f - y_e) - y^T)^2 = (y_e - y^T)^2. \tag{16.11}$$

Since the CB moves last it simply raises r by whatever is necessary to keep $y = y_e$.

This is an almost classical picture of monetary–fiscal interaction: the government can set fiscal policy as it likes, but this leads the CB to raise r to ensure that y remains equal to y_e and thus that π remains equal to zero. As we have written G's objective function, G is indifferent as to the level of f it chooses. We could however augment G's objectives by adding a target level of government expenditure

$$L_G = (y - y^T)^2 + (f - f^T)^2. \tag{16.12}$$

The government will choose $f = f^T$ to minimize L_G.

2.2 Sequence 2: *G* follows *CB*

If, however, *G* moves after *CB*, then the tables are turned. Again using backward induction, *G* minimizes $(y - y^T)^2 = (f - r - y^T)^2$, given r. This implies

$$f = r + y^T. \tag{16.13}$$

In other words, *G* will now always set fiscal policy so as to ensure $y = y^T$. *CB* can do nothing about this: it minimizes $\pi^2 = (\pi^E + y - y_e)^2 = (\pi^E + f - r - y_e)^2$ in the knowledge that $f = r + y^T$. Hence it minimizes $\pi^2 = (\pi^E + (r + y^T) - r - y_e)^2 = (\pi^E + y^T - y_e)^2$. But the choice of r has no effect; whatever r is chosen *G* simply raises f to offset any impact an increased r might have on y and hence π.

In this particularly simple case, $\pi^E = \infty$ for the following reason: from the above, $\pi = \pi^E + y^T - y_e$. Hence $E\pi = \pi^E + y^T - y_e > \pi^E$ if $y^T > y_e$. But $E\pi = \pi^E$ if π^E is finite; so only $\pi^E = \infty$ makes $E\pi = \pi^E = \pi^E + y^T - y_e$.

We can make π^E finite by changing *G*'s objective function so that the government, too, has some inflation aversion, β, as indicated by the inclusion of the term $\beta\pi^2$ in its loss function. We therefore assume that *G* minimizes

$$L_G = (y - y^T)^2 + \beta\pi^2 = (f - r - y^T)^2 + \beta \cdot (\pi^E + f - r - y_e)^2 \tag{16.14}$$

which implies

$$(f - r - y^T) + \beta \cdot (\pi^E + f - r - y_e) = 0$$

$$\Rightarrow f = r + \frac{y^T - \beta\pi^E + \beta y_e}{1 + \beta}. \tag{16.15}$$

Now, π^E has to be chosen such that $y = y_e$ and given that $f = r + y$, π^E has to satisfy the following:

$$y_e = \frac{y^T - \beta\pi^E + \beta y_e}{1 + \beta} \Rightarrow \pi^E = \beta^{-1} \cdot (y^T - y_e). \tag{16.16}$$

We can therefore see that with this more realistic government objective function, the inflation bias is finite: $\pi = \pi^E = \beta^{-1} \cdot (y^T - y_e)$. But the government is now constrained to set $y = y_e$, although it can trump whatever the central bank does with the interest rate.

2.3 Summing up

A first conclusion is that if the government is to create an independent central bank with full powers over monetary policy, the government can always sabotage its objectives if it moves after the central bank. Does this mean that the timing of moves should be built into the grant of independence to a central bank? This is unnecessary, since it is fairly clear in practice that central banks can move much faster in changing the interest rate than governments can in changing the fiscal stance. Governments have long-drawn-out budgetary processes to go through, which normally take place to an annual timetable.

Central banks can usually move quickly within a month or less. So a more measured view is that independence of the central bank will be sufficient to impose a low rate of inflation, even though the government maintains control of fiscal policy. It is also important to note that the game analysed here made the assumption crucial to the time inconsistency results that the government's target is a level of output above the equilibrium. As we have argued in Chapter 6, the requirement to remain solvent (i.e. to set fiscal policy so as to meet the constraint of the intertemporal budget constraint) may well enter the government's utility function. Both the pure monetary policy games and the fiscal–monetary interaction games that we have analysed entail that either the central bank or the government sets objectives that are inconsistent with a target inflation outcome. We return in section 4 to how such behaviour can be rationalized as a consequence of the pressure of voters on politicians seeking reelection.

3 *Reputation: Introduction to games of incomplete information

Games of incomplete or asymmetric information are amongst the most important for political science and economics. In particular, the games of interest are where one actor lacks knowledge about the preferences or type of another actor, and where the latter can send a signal to the former that contains information (perhaps misleading) about her preferences or her type. These are called signalling games. For instance is a Central Bank tough or weak on inflation? Note that the 'type' of *CB* is simply embodied in the strength of its preference for low inflation relative to employment—so we can either talk about the type of a player or that player's preferences. In the *CB* game, the uncertainty for the wage setter, *WS*, is over the form of the *CB*'s objective function and hence its pay-offs from different outcomes of the game.

The way that a signalling game works is easiest to explain using what has become a classic example, the so-called 'beer-quiche' game. We explain that game first and then return to apply the insights to the central bank game. We begin by setting out the simple signalling game (beer-quiche) and show how it is played. This allows us to introduce the key concepts. We shall then go back and look at the principles behind the equilibrium solution(s) to the game.

Suppose there are two actors. The first actor may be one of two types (tough (T), weak (W)). The second actor knows only the probability, p, that the first actor is tough. The game consists of 3 moves (although the first is really a modelling trick[4]).

- Move 1. In the first move 'nature' chooses the type of the first actor, on a purely random basis—tough with probability p, weak with probability $1 - p$. The use of 'nature' is just a device to get the game going and to indicate that the choice is exogenous to the actors in the model. The second actor does not know which type has been chosen, only that there has been a p chance that the type is tough.

---

[4] Actually the trick earned John Harsanyi the Nobel Prize! Harsanyi (1967–8).

• Move 2. The first actor has a choice between two actions, and the second actor is informed of this choice. This choice can be seen as sending a signal or message to the second actor; in consequence, the first actor is sometimes called the Sender and the second actor the Receiver. The signal may be designed either to reveal the Sender's type: for instance, a tough Sender might make a choice that revealed she was tough. Or it may be designed to hide her type, by sending the same choice as the other type would send; thus a weak Sender might send the same message as a tough sender, thus engaging in mimicking.

• Move 3. The receiver then reacts to the message and chooses between two actions. The game then ends.

3.1 The beer-quiche game

We start with a simple and famous game due to Cho and Kreps,[5] the beer-quiche game. You are either a 'tough' (T) or a 'wimp' (W). You go into a bar in which drinkers are sitting waiting to pick a fight with a wimp, while wanting to avoid fighting a tough. We shall refer to the drinkers as the public or P, and treat P as though he were a single actor. You can choose whether to order a beer or a quiche. What you order is observed by the public. Toughs prefer beer, wimps prefer quiches. Neither toughs nor wimps want to fight. A useful way of drawing the extensive game is in Fig. 16.4.

Nature (N) moves first (shown at the centre of the diagram), and chooses T with probability p and W with probability $1 - p$. This is not observed by the public who only knows that there is a p chance that the orderer is tough. We then move to either T's move or W's. They can choose to order b (beer) or q (a quiche). The order for beer or quiche is observed by P, the public; but P does not know whether the order was made by a tough or by a wimp who is mimicking a tough.

Suppose beer b was ordered. Then if the new entrant is T, the game moves from T's decision node left to a P decision node (top left). If the new entrant is W, the game moves from W's decision node left to a P decision node (bottom left). P knows only either that he is at one of the two P decision nodes on the left. Now we need to introduce a bit more

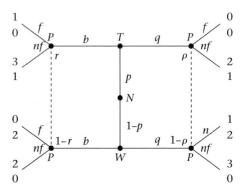

Figure 16.4 The beer-quiche game

[5] Cho and Kreps (1987).

game theory terminology: when a player (P in this case) has a move but does not know which of two (or possibly more) decision nodes he is at, those two decision nodes are said to constitute an *information set*. An information set is shown on an extensive game diagram as a long-dashed line linking the relevant decision nodes. In this case, since beer was ordered, P is at the left information set. By definition, if a player has the move—and it is part of the rules of the game that the player always knows if he does or does not have the move at any particular moment of the game—the player always knows which information set he is at; but, of course, if the information set has more than one decision node he does not know which decision node he is at. So, if q was signalled, P finds himself in the right hand information set, without knowing whether he is at the top or bottom decision node. At each information set, the public then chooses either to fight (f), or not to fight (nf). The game ends with the top pay-off being that of the sender (T or W), and the bottom pay-off that of the public.

One final point needs to be made before we see what strategies the players might use. A player at an information set is not given any information about which decision node he is at. That doesn't mean that he can't make more or less sensible guesses. Indeed, we shall see that in this type of game, the player at an information set has to do his best to work out the probability that he is at one decision node rather than the other. Working out the probabilities of where one is in an information set is central to playing these games. Let us write r for the (subjective) probability that P will assign to being at the top decision node in the left information set and hence $1 - r$ as the probability of being at the bottom left decision node. And correspondingly ρ and $1 - \rho$ as the probabilities of being at the top and bottom decision nodes respectively of the right information set. Remember that P does not know these probabilities in advance but has to work them out. ρ and r can be seen in Fig. 16.4.

The term *information set* was coined to describe these situations where a player with the move has more than one decision node. But it can also be used to describe the situation where a player with the move has just one decision node—it is then usually called a *singleton information set*. With this wider definition, the set of a player's information sets is the set of points in a game where the player has the move: the player knows exactly where he is in the game if he is at a singleton information set, otherwise he knows the information set he is at but not at which of the decision nodes linked by dashed lines he is at.

3.1.1 Possible solutions: pooling and separating equilibria

We examine two sorts of possible solutions. The first are pooling or mimicking equilibria. The obvious possibility here is that it will pay wimps to pretend they are tough by ordering a beer rather than a quiche. It seems a reasonable idea for them to do this in the sense that they would like to avoid a fight—of course, there is a trade-off involved because they would prefer to have quiche than beer. However, if it does not have the desired effect of avoiding a fight, the wimps will not pursue this strategy. Game theory provides the tools for systematically analysing the different elements that enter the decision-making process. Let us see whether the wimps mimicking the behaviour of the toughs is consistent with rational behaviour of all concerned. To examine the pooling equilibrium, we assume that both toughs and wimps order beer and ask whether the public will react in such a way as to have made this a rational choice by the wimps.

3.1.2 Pooling: wimps and toughs both order beer

It will pay wimps to order beer, despite their preference for quiche, if the public does not fight beer drinkers and does fight quiche eaters. This can be seen from the pay-offs: W gets 2 from drinking beer and not fighting but only 1 from eating quiche and fighting. It would obviously not pay a wimp to order beer if the public didn't fight quiche eaters—since the wimp prefers quiche, and/or if the public *did* fight beer drinkers—in which case, it would also pay the wimp to order quiche since he would have to fight whatever he ordered. Thus the full set of strategies of the players in this potential equilibrium is as follows: both senders order beer; and the public fights quiche eaters but does not fight beer drinkers. It is called a pooling equilibrium because both types take the same action, i.e. both toughs and wimps act tough by ordering beer.

So we need to check under what conditions it would be rational for P not to fight beer drinkers but to fight quiche eaters. The critical point to remember in working through whether a solution is an equilibrium or not is that each actor works out whether his or her strategy is rational on the assumption that the other actors stick to their strategies. In other words we assume that it is common knowledge to all the actors that the new entrant (i.e. the person who enters the bar) is pooling on beer, and then ask—if so, is it rational for P to behave in such a way that it pays both T and W to order beer?

Thus P needs to ask himself: given that both toughs and wimps order beer, should I fight or not? Since P knows everyone orders beer, P can easily calculate that the probability, r, that the person who has ordered beer is a tough is the same as the probability in general that someone is a tough, namely p. And the probability that someone who has ordered beer is a wimp is the same as the probability in general that someone is a wimp, namely $1 - p$. In other words the signal 'beer' gives no additional information to P about the sender's type than the knowledge that there is a p probability that a tough has entered the bar. Thus the public's expected pay-off from *not* fighting a beer-drinker is:

$$p \cdot \text{pay-off from not fighting a beer-drinking } T \text{ (1)}$$
$$+ (1 - p) \cdot \text{pay-off from not fighting a beer-drinking } W \text{ (0)} = p.$$

The public's expected pay-off from fighting a beer drinker is:

$$p \cdot \text{pay-off from fighting a beer-drinking } T \text{ (0)}$$
$$+ (1 - p) \cdot \text{pay-off from fighting a beer-drinking } W \text{ (2)} = 2 \cdot (1 - p).$$

Therefore it pays P not to fight a beer-signalling sender if $p > 2 \cdot (1 - p)$ or $p > 2/3$. The intuition here is straightforward: the greater the likelihood p that the signaller is T, the less it pays P to fight.

What about fighting a quiche eater? Now the public is in a more difficult position, because if everyone sticks to the pooling strategy there should be *no* quiche eaters. This leads to a very important question in pooling equilibria. How is the public to interpret so-called *off-equilibrium behaviour?* For the public to decide what it would do in response to off-equilibrium behaviour, it has to assign some probability—call it ρ—to whether it is a wimp or a tough who is behaving in this way. But since it is irrational for either a wimp or a tough to order a quiche in the pooling equilibrium, it is simply unclear how P assigns a probability.

Let us assume (at this stage) that there is no rational ground for assigning one probability rather than another, and ask instead what ρ would have to be for it to be rational for the public to fight a quiche eater. The public's expected pay-off from fighting a quiche eater is:

$$\rho \cdot \text{pay-off from fighting a quiche-eating } T\ (0)$$
$$+ (1 - \rho) \cdot \text{pay-off from fighting a quiche-eating } W\ (2) = 2 \cdot (1 - \rho).$$

Against this, the public's expected pay-off from not fighting a quiche eater is:

$$\rho \cdot \text{pay-off from not fighting a quiche-eating } T\ (1)$$
$$+ (1 - \rho) \cdot \text{pay-off from not fighting a quiche-eating } W\ (0) = \rho.$$

Therefore the public will fight a quiche eater if $2 \cdot (1 - \rho) > \rho$ or $\rho < 2/3$.

Thus so long as $p > 2/3$ and so long as the public assigns a probability on quiche eaters being tough of $\rho < 2/3$, it will pay the public not to fight beer drinkers and to fight quiche eaters. Hence it will certainly pay a tough to order beer: it's what the tough prefers and he does not have to fight. And it will also pay the wimp to order beer because avoiding fighting is worth more to the wimp than having to drink beer rather than eat quiche: a pay-off of 2 against a pay-off from eating quiche and having to fight of 1. This pooling equilibrium is shown in Fig. 16.5.

The long-dashed lines show the choices that actors make at each decision point or information set they reach. Thus T and W both choose b; at P's subsequent information set (after b) it chooses nf: note that it has to make the same choice at each decision node in its information set since it cannot distinguish between the individual decision nodes. If either T or W were (against their strategies) to choose q, P chooses f at the subsequent information set. In each information set, we have also put in the probabilities assigned by the actor who moves at that information set to the different decision nodes in the

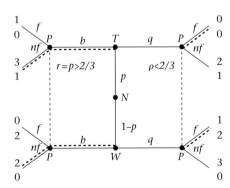

Figure 16.5 The beer-quiche game: pooling on beer

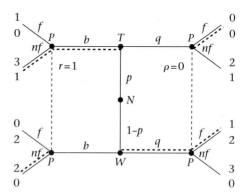

Figure 16.6 The beer-quiche game: a separating equilibrium?

information set, whether or not the information set is on the equilibrium path. Although we have not yet looked at the formal criteria for rational behaviour in this sort of game, but it is pretty clear that this pooling equilibrium will satisfy them.

3.1.3 Separating equilibrium: toughs order beer, wimps order quiches?

Now let us look at a different potential equilibrium, which we shall see does not stand up to the requirement of rational behaviour. Here are the strategies: if tough, order beer; if wimp, order quiche; public: if beer is ordered, don't fight; if quiche is ordered, fight; assign probability $r = 1$ to a beer orderer being a tough; assign probability $\rho = 1$ to a quiche orderer being a wimp.

This is known as a (potential) separating equilibrium because the different types of actors choose different actions. The sender's choice signals to P whether the sender is a T or a W. Thus the signal 'separates' the two types. This can be seen in Fig. 16.6. But this isn't an actual equilibrium because rational players won't use it. We can see why as follows. If P receives the signal b, P must assign a probability $r = 1$ to the sender being a tough and to being at P's top left decision node. If P receives the signal q, P must assign a probability $1 - \rho = 1$ to the sender being a wimp and to being at P's bottom right decision node. Thus if q is signalled, P knows the sender is a wimp and therefore fights, with a pay-off of 2 as opposed to 0 from not fighting. But the wimp would then be irrational to signal q since W's pay-off is then 1: if W signalled b, P would assume that the sender was a T, would therefore not fight, so W's pay-off would be 2 from ordering beer.

3.1.4 Summing up

In games of incomplete information, two different kinds of sets of strategies arise: 'pooling', in which both types take the same action, e.g. act tough, and 'separating', in which the types act differently, e.g toughs act tough and wimps act in a wimp-like fashion. Using the diagram, it is possible to examine each possibility to see if rational players would pursue it. When we come to apply these insights to a game between the central bank and wage setters, we shall be especially interested in the pooling equilibrium in which wimps mimic the behaviour of toughs. This occurs when the probability of a type being tough is high enough. As we shall see in the central bank case, if wage setters believe that the probability of it being tough is high enough, they don't need to worry about weak central banks since the weak central bank will behave as though it is tough.

3.1.5 Perfect Bayesian Equilibrium: conditions for equilibrium strategies in signalling games

We have already informally been through the conditions for the strategies in a signalling game to be an equilibrium. Here we define and discuss the conditions that need to be satisfied. Up to now we have used the concept of an SGPE to set out the conditions for a set of strategies to be an equilibrium set or 'equilibrium' strategies. But SGPE can only fully solve games in the absence of uncertainty about where players are in the game, that is when all information sets have only one decision node. This is because an SGPE only checks on the rational behaviour of players *if* their move starts off a subgame. But subgames *only* start from singleton information sets. So SGPE is not generally very useful in discussing the rationality of a player (such as *P*) whose move never starts a subgame. As we shall see, a Perfect Bayesian Equilibrium (PBE) follows the basic intuition of an SGPE—namely each player must behave rationally at each point in the game where he has a move. But an SGPE has to be augmented to deal with the fact that the player may not know which decision point he is at when it is his move. The PBE explains how to take this uncertainty into account.

There are essentially three conditions for a Perfect Bayesian Equilibrium:

(1) At each (non-singleton) information set, the player with the move must assign probabilities to being at the different decision nodes at that information set. These probabilities are assumed to be common knowledge to all the players.

Thus in the simple game above, there are two information sets with more than one decision node. *P* has to therefore assign values to *r* and to ρ. These values are then common knowledge: that is, the sender knows them, *P* knows that the sender knows them, the sender knows that *P* knows that the sender knows them, etc.

(2) Given these probabilities, whenever a player has the move, that player must move rationally. Specifically, the player's strategy from then on must be optimal given the subsequent strategies of the other player(s). In effect, this is the extension to non-singleton information sets of the SGPE requirement that players should behave rationally whenever they have the move at the start of each subgame or singleton information set. In terms of the beer-quiche game *P* has to choose rationally *f* and *nf* at each of his two information sets, given his probability assignments of *r* and ρ; and the sender *T* or *W* has to choose rationally between *b* and *q* given the knowledge of *P*'s strategy. *P* does not have to take account of the sender's subsequent strategy when he moves since the sender does not have any subsequent moves.

(3) The probabilities have to be chosen rationally as far as possible given the strategies of the players. In the beer-quiche game (and the games of incomplete information in the rest of the chapter) this means: use your common sense in assigning probabilities. Here's how this works in the beer-quiche game: take *P*'s assignment of *r*. If we are in a pooling equilibrium on beer, the sender's strategy to signal beer says nothing about the sender's type; so *P* should assign a probability $r = p$. If by contrast we are in a separating equilibrium with *T* signalling beer, then *P* should assign a probability of $r = 1$ that the sender is *T*. But if there is a pooling equilibrium on beer, then *P* has nothing to go on in assigning ρ. That is the point of 'as far as possible' in condition (3).

Another way of writing (3) is: 'Whenever possible use Bayes's rule in assigning possibilities.' Indeed this is why the equilibrium is called a Perfect *Bayesian* Equilibrium. As we have just said, Bayes's rule basically involves using your common sense. Readers who want to know more should consult an elementary probability textbook. An important element in Bayes's rule is updating prior probabilities on the receipt of new information. In a pooling equilibrium, the signal gives no new information about the sender's type, so $r = p$. But a separating equilibrium tells the receiver the sender's type: so in the separating equilibrium with T signalling beer, the receipt by P of the signal 'beer' should lead P to update the prior probability p that the sender is T to the posterior probability $r = 1$.

3.1.6 Pooling on q: a perverse PBE and the Intuitive Criterion

Plausible though these three conditions may seem, it turns out that some equilibria that satisfy (1) to (3) are far from convincing. The problem always concerns assigning probabilities to decision nodes in off-equilibrium information sets—information sets that the game won't reach if the players play rationally. Consider the pooling equilibrium in which both toughs and wimps order quiches. This is shown in Fig. 16.7.

In this equilibrium, both toughs and wimps order quiche; P therefore assigns a probability $\rho = p$ to a quiche orderer being tough; it follows that P will rationally not fight a quiche orderer. But there is nothing in the history of the game to tell the public what probability it should assign to a beer orderer being a tough. If the public assigns a probability less than $2/3$ to that event, then it pays P to fight a beer orderer. Now come back to the rationality of toughs and wimps ordering quiches. It clearly pays a wimp to do so (quiche without a fight) rather than ordering beer (beer and a fight). Moreover, as can be seen from the figure, it pays a tough to do so too: the tough gets 2 from the 'quiche, no fight' option, and only 1 from the 'beer, fight' alternative.

Hence the three criteria for a Perfect Bayesian Equilibrium are clearly satisfied:

(1) ρ and r are both assigned by P and their values are common knowledge: $\rho = p$ and $r < 2/3$.

(2) Given these probabilities, it is rational for P not to fight if quiche is ordered but to fight if the order is for beer. And knowing P's strategy, it is rational for either T or W to order quiche.

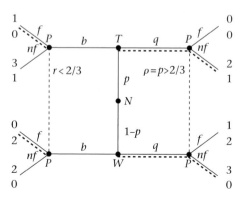

Figure 16.7 Pooling on q: a perverse equilibrium and the Intuitive Criterion

(3) P correctly assigns a probability of $\rho = p$ given that the sender's strategy is to pool on ordering quiche; and since P has no rational reason to constrain his choice of r he can consistently assign $r < 2/3$.

On the other hand the result is absurd. It rests on P assigning a relatively high probability to a beer orderer being a wimp, *viz.* $1 - r > 1/3$. Simply using the assumptions of the model there is no way of explaining why any rational tough or wimp should order beer. So the public's assignment of a high probability to a wimp doing so is perfectly consistent with the history of the game. We might nonetheless ask whether it is more rational for the wimp or the tough to do so—even though it isn't rational for either. Cho and Kreps (1987) developed the Intuitive Criterion to decide. What they said was: if (say) the wimp would always worsen his pay-off whatever the public did if he ordered beer compared to the pay-off given the equilibrium strategy of the public from ordering quiche, then the public should assign a zero probability to the wimp ordering beer—unless the same was also true of the tough. As can be seen in the figure, the tough will do better ordering beer if the public does not fight (3) than ordering quiche without a fight (2). But the wimp does worse ordering beer whether the public fights (0) or not (2) than ordering quiche without a fight (3). Therefore on the Intuitive Criterion, the public should assign *zero* probability to the wimp ordering beer. In that case the quiche pooling equilibrium collapses.

3.1.7 **Summing up**

The equilibrium concept in a game with incomplete information that parallels the subgame perfect equilibrium (SGPE) in the complete information game is the Perfect Bayesian Equilibrium (PBE). The three conditions for a PBE are supplemented by the so-called Intuitive Criterion to rule out implausible pooling equilibria (in the beer-quiche game, the implausible pooling equilibrium is for both toughs and wimps to order quiche).

3.2 **A simple central bank reputation signalling game**[6]

We now develop a simple game between the central bank and wage setters along similar lines to the beer-quiche game. Wage setters (WS) do not know whether the central bank (CB) is Tough (T) or Weak (W), only that there is a probability of p that CB is T and $1 - p$ that CB is W. In the simple signalling game presented in this subsection, the moves are as follows:

(1) Nature (N) moves first and chooses the type of CB, so that CB knows whether it is T or W but WS does not.

(2) CB (knowing whether it is T or W) then moves by choosing either a High (H) or Low (L) level of output in period 1. Of course T may choose a different level of output to W. (We assume that WS has already moved at the start of period 1, but we will only model WS's choice of expected inflation in period 1 in the more sophisticated model of the next subsection.) H or L in effect gives a signal that WS then takes into account in choosing expected inflation at the start of period 2.

---

[6] The original version of the games in this and the next subsection is in Vickers (1986).

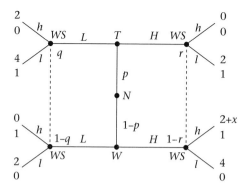

Figure 16.8 A simple CB signalling game

(3) *WS* chooses expected inflation in period 2 as either high (*h*) or low (*l*), knowing and using the signal given by *CB* in its choice of output in period 1.

These moves are shown in Fig. 16.8. The pay-offs to *WS* are straightforward. We assume that a tough central bank, *T*, will always choose output in period 2 to engineer low inflation; so that *WS* gets a pay-off of 1 from choosing *l* and zero from choosing *h* if the *CB* is in fact *T*; likewise, 1 from *h* and 0 from *l* if *CB* is *W*. *T* gets a highest pay-off of 4 when *T* chooses *L* in period 1 thus guaranteeing low inflation in period 1, and *WS* chooses *l* at the start of period 2 thus enabling *T* to choose the appropriate level of output to ensure low inflation in period 2. Note that we don't explicitly model the central bank's choice of output in period 2 in this simple version of the signalling game, but this will be done in the next subsection. Likewise *T* gets 2 with *L* and *h*; or with *H* and *l*; and 0 with *H* and *h*. The weak central bank, *W*, gets 4 with *H* and *l* (the best of all worlds for *W*); 2 with *L* and *l*; and 0 with *L* and *h*. We will assume that *W* gets $2 + x$ from *H* and *h*, where *x* may be positive, negative, or zero. This will indeed turn out to be of importance: and we explain the significance and sign of *x* below. We shall now look at the possible pooling or separating equilibria in this model.

3.2.1 Pooling on *L*: i.e. both weak and tough central banks signal low output

The critical thing to remember in evaluating equilibria, is that it is common knowledge to all the players which equilibrium is being played. What we have to do is then to test if the purported equilibrium is indeed a *PBE*. We first work out, for non-singleton information sets, what probabilities *WS* and *CB* should assign to the different nodes using Bayesian reasoning and given the purported equilibrium strategies. And we then test that the moves implied by the strategies are rational at each information set of the two players.

In this case, that is relatively easy: the only information sets that have more than one decision node (i.e. are non-singleton) are when *WS* has the move after *CB*'s signal. There are two such information sets: the one that follows a low output *L* signal and the one that follows a high output *H* signal.

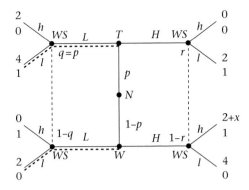

Figure 16.9 CB signalling game: pooling on L

Consider the information set of WS after L has been signalled. The pooling equilibrium is shown in Fig. 16.9. Given that we are in a pooling equilibrium on L, WS knows that CB will always choose L whether CB is T or W. So WS has no more information on CB other than its knowledge that there is a p chance that CB is T and a $1 - p$ chance that CB is W. So in the pooling equilibrium on L, we can replace q by p.

The other non-singleton information set is the information set of WS after H has been signalled. Here, WS has nothing direct to go on since the WS was not expecting the signal H in this equilibrium. Assume for the moment then that WS can only say that r is between 0 and 1.

Now look at the rationality of moves given these probability assignments. If WS receives the signal L, it can be seen that the expected pay-off to WS from choosing h is $p \cdot 0 + (1 - p) \cdot 1 = 1 - p$, and the expected pay-off to choosing l is $p + (1 - p) \cdot 0 = p$. Therefore WS chooses h if $p < 1/2$ and l if $p > 1/2$. This accords with common sense. WS will choose l if the likelihood of the central bank being tough, T, is high relative to that of of it being weak, W, and vice versa.

Will it pay T to choose L? If $p > 1/2$, the answer is clearly yes: for then the WS will choose l and T's pay-off will be 4. Note that whatever WS were to choose if CB signalled H, T would get at the most 2 (if WS chose l). Therefore T will certainly play L in this equilibrium. What about the weak central bank, W? W gets 2 from signalling L if $p > 1/2$. What does W get from signalling H? This depends on WS's assignment of r. Simply using Bayesian probability does not help WS here as we have noted above. But we can use the Intuitive Criterion we discussed above. WS can reason as follows: T gets 4 from L; the best T can get from H is 2; therefore it could never be rational for T to signal H; therefore by the Intuitive Criterion, WS should assign $r = 0$. This implies that if H is signalled in this equilibrium, WS will infer that CB is W and will then choose h. The value of x is then critical: if $x < 0$, W will signal L; if $x > 0$, W will signal H; if $x = 0$, W is indifferent.

It may be plausible to assume $x < 0$. This would be the case if we thought of period 1 as short relative to the rest of the game. The reasoning behind this is as follows: in period 1, W has the possibility of creating a reputation for being tough. If W does not take that opportunity, W will be (correctly) classified as weak by WS for however long WS believes that CB has not changed its type; and this may be for a long period of time. Hence the

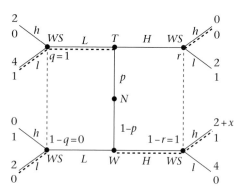

Figure 16.10 CB simple signalling game: a separating equilibrium?

pay-off from a short burst of H in period 1 with WS unclear whether CB is W or T and a much longer period dominated by high inflation expectations from WS will be low compared to L, l. Thus pooling on low output, L, is indeed a Perfect Bayesian Equilibrium if $x < 0$, if $p > 1/2$ and if we use the Intuitive Criterion to assign a zero probability to T signalling H.

3.2.2 Other equilibria

Under what circumstances can there be a separating equilibrium with tough and weak central banks revealing their types by behaving differently? Fig. 16.10 shows a potential separating equilibrium (T plays L, W plays H). By repeating the steps above, it is only an equilibrium for $x > 0$. Finally, we can use the Intuitive Criterion to rule out pooling on H as an equilibrium if $p > 1/2$.

3.2.3 Summing up

The signalling game can be applied to the interaction between the central bank and wage setters in a situation in which the type of the central bank is not known. It clarifies the conditions under which a pooling equilibrium will occur in which a weak central bank mimics a tough one. An important issue that emerges relates to the weight on current and future periods, which is modelled in the simple signalling game by the role of x, i.e. whether x is positive or negative. This suggests the next step of moving to an explicit two-period setting for the game.

3.3 Explicit two-period central bank reputation signalling game

Now we turn to a more sophisticated version of this simple signalling game. The key assumption is that at the start of the game, the wage setters only know that there is a probability p that the central bank is independent (tough) and a probability of $1 - p$ that it is the puppet of the government (weak). The key question that we wish to answer is whether a secretly weak central bank has an incentive to build a reputation as a tough one? In other words, under what conditions does it pay a weak CB to mimic the behaviour of a tough one? Thus in this game we will only look at the possibility of a pooling equilibrium.

Assume the weak *CB* maximizes:

$$U_W = \left(y_1 - \frac{\beta}{2}\pi_1^2\right) + \delta\left(y_2 - \frac{\beta}{2}\pi_2^2\right) \tag{16.17}$$

where $\left(y_1 - (\beta/2)\pi_1^2\right)$ is the pay-off from the first period and $\left(y_2 - (\beta/2)\pi_2^2\right)$ for the second, with a time-discount factor of δ. The subscript W refers to 'weak' and for simplicity, we assume the inflation target is zero so the government derives utility from higher output and from inflation being as close to zero as possible. As discussed in Chapter 5, β represents the inflation aversion of the government or central bank. The pay-off says that the weak *CB* has a simple trade off between output, which it wants *as much of as possible*, and inflation, which it would like to be as close to zero as possible.

The tough *CB* by contrast maximizes

$$U_T = -\pi_1^2 - \delta\pi_2^2 \tag{16.18}$$

which reflects that its only concern is with any deviation of inflation from zero. We assume that the inflation aversion of the tough government is infinity, which implies that it always sets inflation equal to zero. In the language of Chapter 5, the tough central bank is completely non-accommodating. In each period the *CB* faces the Phillips curve constraint

$$\pi_t = \pi_t^E + y_t - y_e. \tag{16.19}$$

The timing of moves and the information each player has at its decision node is as follows.

(1) *WS* chooses π_1^E with no knowledge of whether the actual central bank is tough or weak, but does know that there is a probability p of the *CB* being tough.

(2) *CB* chooses y_1, knowing π_1^E.

(3) *WS* chooses π_2^E, knowing y_1.

(4) *CB* chooses y_2, knowing π_2^E.

What is interesting for us is to investigate the conditions under which a pooling equilibrium exists in this two-period game. We shall then go on to show that there is a stronger incentive to pool the more periods there are in the game. As we have emphasized, a critical assumption made in game theory when we are looking at a particular equilibrium is that both players are convinced that that is the equilibrium being played—it is common knowledge between them. Thus in this case both *WS* and *CB* believe it is a pooling equilibrium with both types playing the strategy of the tough central bank. If *CB* is tough, its strategy is very simple. The best it can do is to ensure that $\pi_1 = \pi_2 = 0$—it cannot achieve a higher utility than that. Therefore it will always choose y_1 and y_2 to make $\pi_1 = \pi_2 = 0$. This can always be achieved since $\pi_t = \pi_t^E + y_t - y_e$, so $\pi_t = 0 \Rightarrow y_t = y_e - \pi_t^E$.

What does a weak *CB* do? In period 1, its strategy is very simple. To be mistaken for a strong *CB* it must set $\pi_1 = 0$, and therefore set $y_1 = y_e - \pi_1^E$—any other rate of inflation in period 1 would at once betray its type as weak.

But period 2 is the last period and its move is the last move. Therefore it pays the weak *CB* in period 2 to choose whatever level of output maximizes $\delta\left(y_2 - (\beta/2)\pi_2^2\right)$ subject to the Phillips curve constraint that $\pi_2 = \pi_2^E + y_2 - y_e$. That is the weak *CB* maximizes

$$\delta\left(y_2 - \frac{\beta}{2}(\pi_2^E + y_2 - y_e)^2\right),\tag{16.20}$$

which implies

$$y_2^W = \beta^{-1} + y_e - \pi_2^E.\tag{16.21}$$

Now we need to find out what inflation expectations *WS* forms in the two periods. In period 1 the answer is straightforward. Since *WS knows* there is a pooling equilibrium, it also knows that whether *CB* is weak or tough $\pi_1 = 0$. Hence

$$\pi_1^E = 0.\tag{16.22}$$

WS has therefore gained no information about *CB*'s type from period 1 since both types set $\pi_1 = 0$. In period 2, *WS* knows that a tough *CB* will set $\pi_2^T = 0$. *WS* also knows that a weak *CB* will set $y_2^W = \beta^{-1} + y_e - \pi_2^E$; since $\pi_2^W = \pi_2^E + y_2^W - y_e$, $\pi_2^W = \pi_2^E + \beta^{-1} + y_e - \pi_2^E - y_e = \beta^{-1}$. And *WS* also knows no more than that there is a p probability *CB* is tough and $1 - p$ probability that *CB* is weak. Hence

$$\pi_2^E = p \cdot \pi_2^T + (1 - p) \cdot \pi_2^W = (1 - p) \cdot \beta^{-1}.\tag{16.23}$$

Thus *WS* chooses $\pi_1^E = 0$; both a weak and a tough *CB* choose $\pi_1 = 0$; *WS* then chooses $\pi_2^E = (1 - p) \cdot \beta^{-1}$; and a tough *CB* chooses $\pi_2 = 0$, while a weak *CB* chooses $\pi_2 = \beta^{-1}$.

Is it in fact rational for a weak *CB* to play according to this pooling equilibrium? The answer is yes, so long as it does not pay the weak *CB* to defect in the first period. That is, it might take advantage of *WS* setting $\pi_1^E = 0$ to go for a higher y_1 and thus choose $\pi_1^W > 0$. To check whether it would pay a weak *CB* to defect from the pooling equilibrium in this way (so it wouldn't hold up as an equilibrium), we need to see if it would increase the value of the weak *CB*'s objective function to do so.

First, we need to calculate the value to the weak *CB* of behaving according to the pooling equilibrium. Recall the weak *CB*'s objective function:

$$U_W = y_1 - \frac{\beta}{2}\pi_1^2 + \delta\left(y_2^W - \frac{\beta}{2}\left(\pi_2^W\right)^2\right).\tag{16.24}$$

First, $y_1 = y_e - \pi_1^E = y_e$ since $\pi_1^E = \pi_1 = 0$. It follows that the first period's pay-off is simply y_e. Next, $y_2^W = \beta^{-1} + y_e - \pi_2^E$ (see above) $= \beta^{-1} + y_e - (1 - p) \cdot \beta^{-1} = y_e + p/\beta$. Finally, $\pi_2^W = 1/\beta$. Putting these together gives

$$U_W = y_e + \delta\left(y_e + \frac{p}{\beta} - \frac{\beta}{2}\left(\frac{1}{\beta}\right)^2\right) = y_e \cdot (1 + \delta) + \delta\left(\frac{p}{\beta} - \frac{1}{2\beta}\right).\tag{16.25}$$

This is the pay-off to a weak *CB* that mimics a tough *CB* in period 1.

What is the pay-off if the weak CB defects in period 1? We need at this point to ask how WS interprets the CB choosing $\pi_1 > 0$. This is an off-equilibrium move, not predicted by the pooling equilibrium. This requires us to specify WS's off-equilibrium beliefs. The most natural interpretation is for WS to assume that if the CB sets $\pi_1 > 0$, the CB is more likely to be weak than tough. And indeed we can use the Intuitive Criterion to rule out the possibility that a tough CB would choose $\pi_1 > 0$: the Intuitive Criterion says that if an off-equilibrium move leads to a lower pay-off for the type making the move than the equilibrium pay-off, *however* other players respond to the move, then we can assign a zero probability to that type making the move (at least if the same is not true of the other or another type). This is quite clearly applicable in this situation. On the equilibrium path, the tough CB can guarantee a maximum possible pay-off of zero by setting $\pi_1 = \pi_2 = 0$: remember that $U_T = -\pi_1^2 - \delta\pi_2^2$; and that in this game the central bank can always set whatever level of π_i by choosing the appropriate level of y_i. Thus setting $\pi_1 > 0$ necessarily implies a lower pay-off for the tough CB. Hence WS will assign a probability of 1 that a CB setting $\pi_1 > 0$ is weak.

In period 1, the weak CB who defects will choose π_1^W to maximize its objective function since whatever π is chosen above 0 will imply to the wage setter that the central bank is weak. Since whatever it does has no impact on period 2 (other than telling WS that it is weak), the CB has simply to maximize $\left(y_1 - \beta/2 \cdot \pi_1^2\right) = \left(y_1 - \beta/2 \cdot \left(\pi_1^E + y_1 - y_e\right)^2\right)$. This implies $y_1^W = \beta^{-1} + y_e - \pi_1^E = \beta^{-1} + y_e$. (Note that π_1^E is still 0, since WS chose π_1^E in the belief that both types of CB would choose $\pi_1 = 0$.) This implies in turn that $\pi_1^W = \beta^{-1}$.

In period 2, the weak CB again does as well as possible and this, as we have seen, involved choosing $y_2^W = \beta^{-1} + y_e - \pi_2^E$. But now WS knows in period 2 that the CB is weak; hence $\pi_2^E = \pi_2^W = 1/\beta$, so that $y_2^W = \beta^{-1} + y_e - \pi_2^E = \beta^{-1} + y_e - \beta^{-1} = y_e$.

Putting these results together, we can work out the pay-off to a weak CB from defecting as:

$$U_W^D = \beta^{-1} + y_e - \frac{\beta}{2}\left(\beta^{-1}\right)^2 + \delta\left(y_e - \frac{\beta}{2}\left(\beta^{-1}\right)^2\right) = y_e \cdot (1 + \delta) + \frac{1}{2\beta}(1 - \delta). \quad (16.26)$$

It pays not to defect if $U_W > U_W^D$, or

$$\frac{\delta}{\beta} \cdot \left(p - \frac{1}{2}\right) > \frac{1}{2\beta}(1 - \delta) \Rightarrow 2\delta p > 1. \quad (16.27)$$

This is then the condition for a pooling equilibrium. Obviously the gain to a weak CB from pooling in the first period is that $\pi_1^E = 0$; that is a gain whether or not the weak CB defects. The formula tells us the gain from pooling rather than defecting: the intuition here is that with pooling (and not defecting) you gain in the second period because π_2^E will be relatively low and therefore you can get a bigger output gain in the second period. So the more you value the second period (the bigger is δ), the greater will be your gain from pooling rather than defecting in the first period; and the bigger is p the lower will π_2^E be because the wage setter will think it the more likely that the central bank is tough, and hence the larger will be the second period gain from pooling rather than defecting. Note the parallels between the condition for a pooling equilibrium here and in the simple signalling game.

So far we have looked at a two-period game. We have already seen that the closer to 1 is δ, the discount factor on the second period, the less likely the weak CB will be to defect in the first period. The intuition is: the more important the future is to a weak CB, the more it will pay such a CB not to defect, but to build up its reputation. A natural way to think about this is to assume that the CB is in existence for many periods: e.g. imagine a central banker is in office for six years. So we build an N-period model, and this will confirm our intuition that the longer is the future, the more it pays the weak CB to continue engaging in reputation building by continuing a pooling strategy across periods.

As we have seen with the pooling solution to the two-period game, the weak CB gets the result ($y = y_e$ and $\pi = 0$) in the first period, and gains in addition in the second period by being able to set $y_2 > y_e$, because π_2^E is set by WS when all they know is that there is a p probability that the CB is strong and $1 - p$ that it is weak. We shall call this second period benefit ω.

Games between central banks and wage setters typically take place over many periods, rather than just one or two. The real benefit to a weak CB from mimicking a strong one can be seen when the incomplete information game takes place over many periods. Intuitively, it pays the weak CB to go on mimicking until the penultimate period. For then the weak CB will get $y = y_e$ and $\pi = 0$ in each of the pooling periods, and the additional benefit ω in the last period. Thus the CB's pay-off is

$$U_W = y_e + \delta y_e + \delta^2 y_e + \cdots + \delta^N y_e + \delta^{N+1}\omega. \tag{16.28}$$

If the CB stops mimicking at any point, from then on WS knows the CB is weak. Hence in each subsequent period it will always set $\pi^E = \beta^{-1}$. From then on, the CB loses $-1/2\beta$ each period as a result of π being β^{-1}. Thus suppose, without WS knowing whether the CB is weak or strong, it knows that there will be a pooling equilibrium for only two periods, the pay-off to a weak CB would be

$$U_W = y_e + \delta y_e + \delta^2\omega + \delta^3(y_e - 1/2\beta) + \cdots + \delta^{N+1}(y_e - 1/2\beta). \tag{16.29}$$

Evidently, comparing the last two equations, the cost of giving up pooling early is a string of inflation rates, $\delta^3/2\beta + \cdots + \delta^{N+1}/2\beta$, higher than the weak CB would like. Thus the real benefit of building a reputation via pooling comes not in the two-period context but over the longer term.

3.3.1 Summing up

By extending the central bank signalling game to many periods, the insight from the simple signalling game is confirmed: when more weight is put on the future, the weak central bank is more likely to pool on the low inflation strategy of the tough central bank. This analysis also highlights the parallels with the *repeated complete* information game. In the complete information game, the game must be repeated indefinitely for the time-inconsistent outcome to be avoided. As we have seen, in the incomplete information game as soon as the weak central bank reveals its type by ceasing to mimic the tough central bank, the inflation bias returns.

4 Voters

4.1 The political business cycle: opportunistic politicians and elections[7]

A major problem in democratic theory is that it may be difficult to judge the competence of the politicians who stand for election. Given that we generally have incomplete information about the 'types' of politicians (e.g. their competence) before they become politicians, there are various ways in which we might (or not) discover their competence level. It is possible that they might show it directly in for example public debates (on television or in the legislature, such as the House of Representatives or the House of Commons). If we believe such evidence measures political competence, then there is no problem. However, it is unclear how easy it is to provide evidence of the 'competence to govern'.

A second possibility is that the political system selects for competence (or lack of it). That is to say, although her competence is private information to the new entrant to the political arena, the costs and rewards of the political system are such that it would only pay someone with high competence to enter. In technical terms, this is an example of adverse selection—although it isn't adverse in this case. However, unless an awful lot of politicians are hiding their lights under a bushel, this doesn't seem likely either.

A third possibility is that parties have access to information on types even though voters do not, and the institutions of party choice of candidates ensure competence. Although parties may constrain and control candidates once selected, some scepticism is nevertheless warranted.

Here we consider an alternative, namely that politicians *signal* their competence. This is different from direct revelation in that in principle both a competent and incompetent politician can send the same signal (as in the beer-quiche game). We assume that the only way in which a signal can be sent is via the measures that an *incumbent* politician can take. This turns out to be a crucial assumption in what follows so we highlight it here—only by being in government, is a politician able to signal competence; opposition politicians cannot do so.

The model we use is a simplified version of Persson and Tabellini's. It uses a model of competence and elections to discuss four observations that arise either from the empirical voting literature or from macroeconomic theory:

(1) How challengers behave matters a lot less than how incumbents do ('the opposition doesn't win the election, the government loses it'). In the model, this is because only incumbents can send signals.

(2) Why should rational voters vote retrospectively, i.e. using information from past actions? The answer, according to the model, is that voters are using the signals that retrospective data gives them to predict the future competence and hence performance of candidates.

---

[7] This section is based on a model of Persson and Tabellini (1990).

(3) Why should voters vote about what is happening just before the election and not over the whole time period of office? In the model, this is because only the most recently elected incumbent can be re-elected so only performance that reflects the actions of an incumbent standing for re-election (i.e. recent performance) matters. We shall see how the timing assumptions of the model deliver this.

(4) Why do governments generate GDP growth just before elections (this phenomenon is known as the 'political business cycle'), if rational voters know this will simply lead to inflation afterwards? According to the model, the answer is that it may pay *competent* incumbents to do so if they can signal their competence in this way, *and* if it does *not* pay *incompetent* incumbents to mimic them. We shall see why this is the case below using a signalling game.

4.1.1 The model

Assume there are two candidate teams at the forthcoming election, the government or incumbent (G) and the opposition or challenger. Each candidate team has two members, who remain in the team for two periods; each period a new member joins the team and the older surviving member leaves. In fact we will only be interested in the government team—as hinted at already, it will be assumed that only incumbent politicians can send signals about their competence—so we will just talk in terms of the government team G. The competence of a member who joins G in period t is written μ_t. The competence of G in t is written c_t and is the sum of the competences of the two members: hence

$$c_t = \mu_t + \mu_{t-1} \tag{16.30}$$

where μ_t is the competence of the member who joined G in the current period and will remain to the next period $t+1$, and μ_{t-1} is the competence of the member who joined in the previous period and will leave at the end of t. This is shown in Fig. 16.11.

Periods at which an individual joins the government are shown on the horizontal axis. The competence of governments at different periods is shown on the vertical axis. μ_0 is the competence of the individual who joins a government at 0. He contributes to the competence first of the government at 0, c_0, and then to the competence of the government next period t_1, c_1. Each bold line represents a government at time 0, 1, 2, etc.,

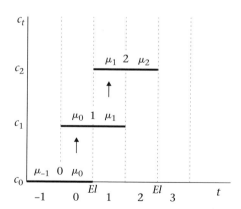

Figure 16.11 Government competence in different periods

the period of the government being the number in the middle of the relevant bold line; the bold line shows that it is composed of two individuals from the current and the previous period. For example c_1 is measured as follows: add together the two μs on the bold line labelled 1. Assume now that the same government is in office in each of these periods. The government at t_0 has one member (with competence μ_0—we identify members simply by their competence level from now on) who has joined in t_0 and will stay in the government in period t_1. This is shown by the vertical arrow moving μ_0 up from the period 0 government to the period 1 government (joining the member with competence μ_1).

The next assumption is that there are elections every two periods. This is also shown in the diagram with elections (El) at the end of t_0 (or indifferently at the start of t_1) and the end of t_2. One implication of this is that the government elected at $El0$ remains in office in periods 1 and 2. Thus the government elected in $El0$ has competence $c_1 = \mu_0 + \mu_1$ in its first period of office t_1 and $c_2 = \mu_1 + \mu_2$ in its second and last period t_2 (unless it is re-elected at $El2$).

Observation (1): 'governments lose elections, oppositions do not win them' In the model, the most important question is what information voters at $El0$ can gather about the competence of the government they then elect for periods 1 and 2. We assume that before the politician with competence μ_t has been in a government team, nothing is known about μ_t. Voters can therefore only learn about competence from performance in office. The opposition team at $El0$ is uninteresting to voters because nothing can be learnt about their future competence from their past performance if elected as the next government. It is the model's assumption that only incumbents can signal competence that produces observation (1).

Next we make some specific assumptions about μ_t: μ_t is a random variable drawn from a distribution independent of t with two values: μ_L (or low competence) with probability $1 - \rho$ and μ_H (high competence) with probability ρ. Thus μ_t is independent of μ_{t-i}. This means that the competence of any politician is independent of that of the other politicians in the party. In addition it is assumed that the expected value of μ_t is zero:

$$E\mu_t = \rho\mu_H + (1 - \rho)\mu_L = 0. \tag{16.31}$$

Note that this implies that $\mu_H > 0$ and $\mu_L < 0$.

Observations (2) and (3): 'retrospective voting' and 'only recent performance matters' These assumptions dramatically simplify the argument. We go back to the diagram and look at the voter at the election at the end of t_0 and assume the voter to be rational. Therefore all she is interested in—in assessing the competence of the incumbent government (which has been in office in periods -1 and 0 and perhaps earlier)—is what that will enable her to predict about the future performance of the current government (assuming it is re-elected). She can find out nothing about the competence level of μ_1 or μ_2 since they have not been in government yet. The only member of any future team about whom she can find out anything by the election at the end of period 0 is μ_0. μ_0 is the only politician whose performance is observable before the election and who will be in government after the election if the incumbent government is re-elected.

Rational voters vote retrospectively because the behaviour of the government before the election supplies the *only available information* on competence after the election. And rational voters (according to this model) are interested only in *recent* performance because that and only that gives a guide to the more recently arrived members of the government team who will still be around in period 1.

The underlying assumption of the model is that μ_0 or the current government team cannot directly reveal its competence, but it can send a signal from which the voter may be able to infer μ_0's competence level. However, and this is what makes it into an interesting signalling game, the government is technically capable of sending this signal whether μ_0 is μ_H or μ_L. Thus there may be either a separating or a pooling equilibrium (or both) in the game. If there is a separating equilibrium it will pay a competent μ_0 to send the appropriate signal but not an incompetent μ_0. In that case the voter will know if μ_0 is competent or not; if μ_0 is competent, the voter can predict the expected value of the government if re-elected, namely

$$Ec_1 = \mu_0 + E\mu_1 = \mu_H + E\mu_1 = \mu_H. \tag{16.32}$$

Since the voter has no basis for assigning a competence prediction to the opposition, she will vote to re-elect the incumbent. We shall show shortly exactly why the voter prefers a competent government. If (continuing with this separating equilibrium) μ_0 signals incompetence, the voter votes for the opposition. This is because $Ec_1 = \mu_L$ if the incompetent incumbent is elected as against $Ec_1 = 0$ if the voter votes for the opposition. However, if there is a pooling equilibrium it will pay the incompetent μ_0 to mimic the competent μ_0; hence the voter will have no basis to distinguish between the government and opposition and will therefore vote randomly.

In order to provide an insight into observation (4), i.e. the tendency for governments to expand output before an election, it is necessary to set out how the economy is assumed to work: the Persson–Tabellini model introduces the crucial assumption that a competent government is able to reduce equilibrium unemployment.

The economy
Persson–Tabellini add two assumptions to those we have made in models up to this point. First, as noted above, they assume that the competence of the government has economic effects: specifically, competence adds to the supply potential of the economy so that it is $y_e + c$. This is an interesting and strong assumption: competent governments are able to lower the equilibrium unemployment rate. For example, a competent government may be able to pursue effective policies in areas such as education and training, competition policy, technology transfer, and labour market regulation, which improve the supply side of the economy. A range of such policies is discussed in Chapter 4. Thus the Phillips curve becomes

$$\pi_t = \pi_t^E + y_t - (y_e + c_t). \tag{16.33}$$

In short, competence allows a higher level of output without adding to inflation. In particular note that for t_1,

$$\pi_1 = \pi_1^E + y_1 - (y_e + \mu_0). \tag{16.34}$$

Second, Persson and Tabellini make a critical although economically reasonable timing assumption, that while y_t is observable in t, π_t is not observable until the next period. So, while voters at $El0$ know y_0 they will only get to know π_0 after the election in period 1. If voters could observe π_0 as well as y_0 before $El0$ they could work out μ_0 since $\pi_0 = \pi_0^E + y_0 - (y_e + \mu_0)$ and it is assumed they know π_0^E. It is central to the model that voters can only infer competence μ_0 *indirectly* by observing the level of output, y_0; they have no way of inferring competence directly. We shall see below that the value of y_0 will be treated by voters as a signal of competence. However, because they can't observe π_0, voters do not know whether a high y_0 comes from:

- high competence i.e. the ability of the government to raise equilibrium output itself ($\mu_0 = \mu^H > 0$), or
- from the behaviour of a low competence incumbent ($\mu_0 = \mu^L < 0$), who pushes output above the equilibrium because it tries to signal that it is competent. In this case, higher inflation will be the consequence of the pre-election boom.

Voters

We now turn to voters. In terms of their *goals*, they are strictly forward looking. We assume that voters prefer higher output and prefer inflation close to zero. Specifically, in each period, they would like as high a value as possible of

$$by_t - \pi_t^2/2, \tag{16.35}$$

where b reflects the weight they place on output relative to inflation. If they have infinite lives and a discount factor of δ, they maximize $\sum_1^\infty \delta^t (by_t - \pi_t^2/2)$. However, for the reasons we have given, voters cannot predict competence apart from in t_1. (Remember that $c_2 = \mu_1 + \mu_2$, so that the voter at $El0$ has no basis for assessing μ_1 or μ_2.) Thus the rational voter is only concerned with choosing a government that will produce the highest value of

$$by_1 - \pi_1^2/2. \tag{16.36}$$

Candidates

As we have already seen, the opposition is completely passive in this game ('governments lose elections, oppositions don't win them'). We only need to consider the government, which chooses y_0 in period 0 and, if it wins the election $El0$, y_1 in period 1. The government is assumed to maximize:

$$(by_0 - \pi_0^2/2) + \delta(by_1 - \pi_1^2/2) + P_I \tag{16.37}$$

where

$$P_I = P \tag{16.38}$$

if the incumbent wins and

$$P_I = 0 \tag{16.39}$$

if the incumbent loses. P is the utility that accrues from being in power. To understand the government's utility function, it is necessary to understand the key idea in the game that it is costly for an incompetent incumbent (*I-inc*) to mimic a competent incumbent (*C-inc*) by choosing a high y_0 since this entails a high inflation rate π_0, from which the incumbent loses. Remember that the difference between the competent and incompetent incumbent lies in the ability of the competent incumbent to raise equilibrium output, i.e. to raise output without raising inflation. In other words, the candidates are not just power hungry ($P > 0$), but are also concerned about policy outcomes—even if those policy outcomes are *not* known until after the election. This assumption may appear questionable but it (or some such assumption) is critical for the model.

4.1.2 Separating equilibrium

A competent incumbent, *C-inc*, signals μ_H by choosing a high output level, y^s (where *s* stands for 'superior'). *If* there is a separating equilibrium—we'll assume there is and test for it later—the implication is that it does *not* pay an incompetent incumbent, *I-inc*, to mimic this. This is because mimicking y^s would force *I-inc* to accept too a high rate of inflation. To see this, it is important to remember two things: that only the competent incumbent is able to reduce equilibrium unemployment and that voters voting at the end of t only observe y_t, they do not observe π_t. The problem for the competent incumbent is that an incompetent one could mimic the level of output the competent one would optimally set: in order to prevent this, the competent one has to set a higher level of output in order that it becomes suboptimal for the incompetent one to mimic this because it would produce inflation that was too high (given *I-inc's* preferences).

The outcome in a separating equilibrium is that *I-inc* chooses the optimal level of output for its type, y_0, and accepts that it will lose the election. Note that if there is a separating equilibrium *and* it is the only equilibrium, it means that observing a rise in output before elections (a so-called political business cycle) is a reflection of a well-functioning political system: competent governments are able to reduce equilibrium unemployment and voters are able to identify this competence and ensure they are elected. To follow through the argument, it is now necessary to calculate both the benefits of winning for *C-inc* and *I-inc*, and also the costs of choosing y^s to signal competence, which enables *C-inc* and *I-inc* (if it mimics *C-inc*) to win the election.

The gains from winning for *C-inc* and *I-inc*
In period 1 the government will set an optimal policy for itself since it has no need to signal anything. Note that what happens in period 1 has no effect on the election at

the end of period 2, since performance in period 1 says nothing about the competence of μ_2 and μ_3, the participants in the post EI2 government (see Fig. 16.11). The relevant maximand for the government in period 1 is simply $by_1 - \pi_1^2/2$, which it maximizes subject to $y_1 = y_e + c_1^I + \pi_1 - \pi_1^E$, where c_1^I is the competence of the period zero incumbent government in period 1 and I stands for incumbent, so $c_1^I = \mu_0^I + \mu_1^I$. The period zero government knows μ_0^I but not μ_1^I (since that depends on the competence of the member of the leadership group who joins in period 1); hence $Ec_1^I = E\mu_1^I + \mu_0^I = \mu_0^I$.

To get the first order condition, we substitute the constraint into the maximand and differentiate with respect to π_1, which results in $\pi_1 = b$. This is true whether we have a competent or incompetent incumbent. Since any government will set $\pi_1 = b$, it follows that everyone knows that this is the case so that $\pi_1^E = b$ and hence

$$y_1 = y_e + \mu_0^I + \pi_1 - \pi_1^E = y_e + \mu_0^I + b - b = y_e + \mu_0^I.$$

The value of winning is therefore $\delta(b(y_e + \mu_0^I) - b^2/2) + P$.

The net value of winning, however, is the difference between this and what would have happened if the opposition had won. In that case $P = 0$, $y_1 = y_e$, (since $E\mu^O = 0$, where the superscript O denotes the opposition) and $\pi_1 = b$ for the same reasons as above. So if the opposition had won, the pay-off to the defeated government is $\delta(by_e - b^2/2)$. Hence, the net value of winning is

$$W(\mu_0^I) = \delta(b(y_e + \mu_0^I) - b^2/2) + P - \delta(by_e - b^2/2) = \delta b\mu_0^I + P. \qquad (16.40)$$

The cost of signalling

We define $C(y, \mu_0^I)$ as the signalling cost of setting $y_0 = y$, given μ_0^I. Thus it pays a competent incumbent, *C-inc*, to signal y^s if

$$W(\mu_H^I) = \delta b\mu_H^I + P > C(y^s, \mu_H^I).$$

But the additional condition that is required for voters to accept this as a credible signal is that the signaller of y^s is indeed competent: namely it must *not* pay the incompetent incumbent, *I-inc*, to mimic it. Hence, it must also be the case that the cost for *I-inc* of signalling y^s is greater than the value of winning the election, i.e.

$$C(y^s, \mu_L^I) > W(\mu_L^I) = \delta b\mu_L^I + P.$$

How is $C(y, \mu^I)$ calculated? The costs to the incumbent of signalling are borne in the current period 0, before the election. As we have seen, the incumbent is interested in economic performance in both periods 0 and 1. Leaving aside signalling, it would set $\pi_0 = b$ optimally; but as we noted above an effective signal may require a higher value of π_0. $C(y, \mu_0^I)$ is the pay-off in period 0 to an incumbent from choosing its optimal level of y_0, less the period 0 pay-off to an incumbent from choosing a suboptimal level of output. In other words, $C(y, \mu_0^I)$ is the reduction in the period 0 pay-off from signalling as opposed to adopting the optimal policy. The *optimal* pay-off from period 0 for an incumbent (i.e. with no signal) is $b(y_e + \mu_0^I + b - \pi_0^E) - b^2/2$, since optimal $\pi_0 = b$. The (lower) pay-off from sending an arbitrary signal y^s (we'll work out y^s later) is $by^s - \pi(y^s, \mu_0^I)^2/2$, where $\pi(y^s, \mu_0^I)$ is the value of π_0 required by μ_0^I to attain a signal y^s.

So:

$$C(y^s, \mu_0^I) = b(y_e + \mu_0^I + b - \pi_0^E) - b^2/2 - (by^s - \pi(y^s, \mu_0^I)^2/2). \tag{16.41}$$

Since $y^s = y_e + \mu_0^I + \pi(y^s, \mu_0^I) - \pi_0^E$, this implies

$$\begin{aligned}
C(y^s, \mu_0^I) &= b(y_e + \mu_0^I + b - \pi_0^E) - b^2/2 - (b(y_e + \mu_0^I + \pi(y^s, \mu_0^I) - \pi_0^E) - \pi(y^s, \mu_0^I)^2/2) \\
&= b^2/2 - b\pi(y^s, \mu_0^I) + \pi(y^s, \mu_0^I)^2/2 \\
&= (\pi(y^s, \mu_0^I) - b)^2/2. \tag{16.42}
\end{aligned}$$

As can be seen, the signalling cost depends on how high the π_0 implied by an incumbent signalling y^s is above b, but we can express it more usefully than this.

First since $\pi(y^s, \mu_0^I) = \pi_0^E + y^s - y_e - \mu_0^I$, we substitute into the above expression to get:

$$C(y^s, \mu_0^I) = 0.5(\pi_0^E + y^s - y_e - \mu_0^I - b)^2.$$

Second, we need to evaluate π_0^E and to do this, we assume that wage setters use rational expectations. They do not know whether μ_0^I is competent or incompetent, but they know that a separating equilibrium strategy is being played with the voters. Hence there is a

- ρ probability that $\mu_0^I = \mu_H$, which implies that $\pi(y^s, \mu_H) = \pi_0^E + y^s - y_e - \mu_H$; and a
- $1 - \rho$ probability that $\mu_0^I = \mu_L$, who will therefore set an optimal y_0 implying $\pi_0 = b$. In other words, the μ_H incumbent has to set the level of π_0 necessary to signal y^s (whatever that may be—see below), while the μ_L incumbent sets the optimal level of π_0 since it does not pay μ_L to mimic μ_H in this separating equilibrium.

Hence with a separating equilibrium,

$$\begin{aligned}
\pi_0^E &= (1 - \rho)b + \rho\pi(y^s, \mu_H) = (1 - \rho)b + \rho(\pi_0^E + y^s - y_e - \mu_H) \\
&= b + \frac{\rho}{1 - \rho}(y^s - y_e - \mu_H). \tag{16.43}
\end{aligned}$$

Now we can derive the cost of signalling for $\mu_0 = \mu_H$:

$$\begin{aligned}
C(y^s, \mu_H) &= 0.5(\pi_0^E + y^s - y_e - \mu_H - b)^2 \\
&= 0.5\left(b + \frac{\rho}{1 - \rho}(y^s - y_e - \mu_H) + y^s - y_e - \mu_H - b\right)^2 \\
&= \frac{0.5}{(1 - \rho)^2}(y^s - y_e - \mu_H)^2. \tag{16.44}
\end{aligned}$$

The cost of signalling for $\mu_0 = \mu_L$ can be derived analogously:

$$\begin{aligned}
C(y^s, \mu_L) &= 0.5(\pi_0^E + y^s - y_e - \mu_L - b)^2 \\
&= \frac{0.5}{(1 - \rho)^2} \cdot (y^s - y_e)^2. \tag{16.45}
\end{aligned}$$

Now that we have worked out the benefits from winning for μ_H and for μ_L and likewise their respective signalling costs we can see whether there is a separating equilibrium in which μ_H sets $y_0 = y^s$ and μ_L sets y_0 so as to minimize $C(y^s, \mu_L)$, i.e. μ_L sets $y_0 = y_e$. Remember that there are two conditions for a separating equilibrium. First, that the gain from winning for μ_H is greater than or equal to the cost of signalling,

$$W(\mu_H) = \beta b \mu_H + P \geqslant C(y^s, \mu_H) = \frac{0.5}{(1-\rho)^2} \left(y^s - y_e - \mu_H\right)^2 \qquad (16.46)$$

and second that the gain from winning for μ_L is less than the cost of signalling,

$$W(\mu_L) = \delta b \mu_L + P < C(y^s, \mu_L) = \frac{0.5}{(1-\rho)^2} (y^s - y_e)^2. \qquad (16.47)$$

We examine the first condition in Fig. 16.12. The benefit to μ_H from winning is the horizontal line $W(\mu_H)$. The cost of signalling is the quadratic function $C(y^s, \mu_H)$ which is equal to zero when $y^s = y_e + \mu_H$, i.e. when there is no signalling. Clearly if y^s is any output level between $y_e + \mu_H$ and y^* the first condition will be satisfied: it will pay μ_H to signal—at least so long as the second condition is also satisfied.

To map out the second condition we superimpose $W(\mu_L)$ and $C(y^s, \mu_L)$ on Fig. 16.12. This is shown in Fig. 16.13. Note that $C(y^s, \mu_L)$ and $C(y^s, \mu_H)$ are identical quadratics, except that the cost of signalling is zero for μ_H when $y^s = y_e + \mu_H$ and for μ_L when $y^s = y_e$. In Fig. 16.13 we can see that it will only pay μ_L to signal if the signal is less than y^s. For only then will the gain from winning outweigh the cost of signalling. Hence μ_H will signal y^s. This is the lowest—thus cheapest—signal that μ_H can make *and* which it will just not pay μ_L to copy. Thus μ_H will signal y^s and μ_L will set $y_0 = y_e$.

Fig. 16.13 highlights the fact that a separating equilibrium must exist in this model. It is guaranteed by the fact that the benefits from winning for the incompetent incumbent are lower than for the competent (i.e. $W(\mu_L) < W(\mu_H)$) and that the costs of signalling are always higher for the incompetent (i.e. $C(y^s, \mu_L)$ is always greater than $C(y^s, \mu_H)$). This is an optimistic result as to the effectiveness of the democratic system. It implies

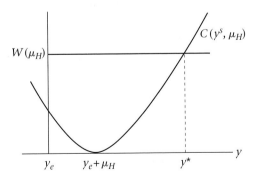

Figure 16.12 *C-inc's* benefit from winning and signalling cost

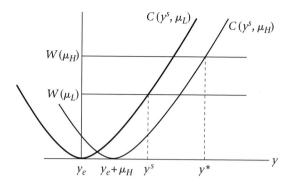

Figure 16.13 *C-inc* and *I-inc* election winning benefit and signalling cost

that (at least if one is prepared to accept the assumptions of the model), a separating equilibrium always exists that enables a competent incumbent to make himself known to the voters and hence to get elected. However, this is not necessarily the only equilibrium.

4.1.3 Pooling equilibrium

Is there a pooling equilibrium in which it pays an incompetent incumbent to mimic a competent one? If so, then both *C-inc* and *I-inc* set the same y_0. Hence the voter cannot distinguish the competence of μ_0 from the choice of y_0, and so will vote randomly for the opposition or for the government. If *C-inc* knows he cannot signal competence it pays him to choose the y_0 that is optimal for him and to accept that *I-inc* will copy it.

C-inc's **behaviour**

C-inc will choose optimal values in period 0 and therefore incur no signalling costs. μ_H maximizes

$$by_0 - \pi_0^2/2 \tag{16.48}$$

subject to the Phillips curve constraint

$$\pi_0 = \pi_0^E + y_0 - (y_e + \mu_0) \tag{16.49}$$

which implies

$$\pi_0^H = b \tag{16.50}$$

and from the Phillips curve

$$y_0^H = \pi_0^H - \pi_0^E + y_e + \mu_H = b - \pi_0^E + y_e + \mu_H. \tag{16.51}$$

I-inc's behaviour

I-inc simply copies *C-inc's* choice of $y_0 = y_0^H$. Hence

$$y_0 = y_0^P = b - \pi_0^E + y_e + \mu_H, \tag{16.52}$$

where y^P is the common or 'pooling' output level. Does it pay *I-inc* to pool, as opposed to setting an optimal y_0? To work this out, we need to find the pooling value of y_0, which we call y_0^P, and then ask whether the cost to *I-inc* of mimicking y_0^P together with 0.5 probability that that gives *I-inc* of being re-elected outweighs the pay-off of setting the optimal y_0 for *I-inc* and abandoning the possibility of re-election.

Testing the pooling equilibrium

We saw earlier that the signalling cost of y_0^P for μ_L is

$$C(y_0^P, \mu_L) = 0.5 \cdot (\pi(y_0^P, \mu_L) - b)^2, \tag{16.53}$$

where b is *I-inc's* optimal π_0 and $\pi(y_0^P, \mu_L)$ is the inflation rate implied by μ_L mimicking *C-inc*—setting $y_0 = y_0^P$. We need to evaluate $\pi(y_0^P, \mu_L)$:

$$\pi(y_0^P, \mu_L) = y_0^P + \pi_0^E - y_e - \mu_L = b - \pi_0^E + y_e + \mu_H + \pi_0^E - y_e - \mu_L = b + \mu_H - \mu_L. \tag{16.54}$$

Note that $\pi(y_0^P, \mu_L)$ will increase as μ_H increases; this is because the higher is μ_H the higher will *C-inc* set y_0^P optimally; and therefore the higher will $\pi(y_0^P, \mu_L)$ be if μ_L mimics μ_H. Hence

$$C(y_0^P, \mu_L) = 0.5 \cdot (\mu_H - \mu_L)^2 \tag{16.55}$$

so that the mimicking cost is higher the more competent is *C-inc* and higher the less competent is *I-inc*. So it will pay *I-inc* to mimic *C-inc* and only if

$$0.5W(\mu_L) > 0.5 \cdot (\mu_H - \mu_L)^2 \Rightarrow \delta b \mu_L + P > (\mu_H - \mu_L)^2. \tag{16.56}$$

Thus as long as the competence gap between *C-inc* and *I-inc* is not too great, there will be a pooling equilibrium. This result is not as reassuring as the separating equilibrium, but at least it implies that incompetent incumbents will not mimic incumbents who are significantly more competent.

4.1.4 Summing up

The Persson–Tabellini model of the political business cycle centres on the limited information available to voters as to the competence of the government. They have no information at all about the competence of the opposition, so elections are decided on the basis of how the voters interpret the actions taken by the incumbent government. Moreover, there is a fixed pattern of turnover of politicians in the incumbent party assumed in the model, so only the most recent actions of the government carry any information relevant to its future competence. Only a competent government is able to reduce equilibrium unemployment but an incompetent one could have the incentive to choose high output before an election in an attempt to signal competence. The model indicates that a separating equilibrium always exists but that if the gap between competent and incompetent incumbents is not too great, there may also be a pooling equilibrium in which it pays an incompetent government to set output high, i.e. to behave in the same way as a competent one.

4.2 Partisan parties, voting, and economic policy

Now we turn away from opportunistic politicians with different levels of competence to politicians with opposing partisan preferences. The analysis typically focuses on left versus right political parties and governments. There is a large literature on the effect of partisanship on macroeconomic outcomes. The broad question is whether left governments are more likely to produce relatively higher inflation and employment than right governments. The leading initial contributor was Douglas Hibbs[8] who argued within an old Keynesian perspective that this was indeed the case. In the original Keynesian tradition, there was no unique equilibrium in the labour market. Stable inflation was believed to be consistent with any rate of employment, although the higher the rate of employment, the higher the rate of inflation. In the policy language of the time, there was a lasting trade-off between employment and inflation; the 'long-run Phillips curve' was not vertical (as in Phillips's original curve shown in Chapter 3). Hence left governments would be associated with permanently higher inflation and employment than right governments. More recent approaches[9] have begun from the premiss that such a trade-off cannot exist (i.e. that the long-run Phillips curve is vertical). We examine first Hibbs's model and then Alesina's more recent approach.

Hibbs's model (with a non-vertical Phillips curve)

In our simple version of Hibbs's model, the left party, if in government, maximizes

$$\theta_L e - \pi^2/2,$$

where e is the employment rate and π is inflation. We report this model in terms of employment rather than output because this is closer to the spirit of the original debate. The right party, if in government, maximizes

$$\theta_R e - \pi^2/2,$$

where critically of course

$$\theta_L > \theta_R,$$

i.e. the left government attaches more importance to employment (relative to inflation) than the right government.

An indifference curve with this type of maximand is upwards sloping. To see this, consider the indifference curve at utility level $\bar{U} = \theta_i e - \pi^2/2$. To stay at the same level of

[8] Hibbs (1977).   [9] Alesina (1987).

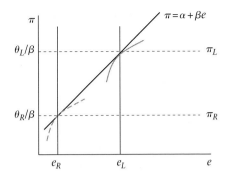

Figure 16.14 Hibbs's partisanship model

utility an increase in e must evidently be counterbalanced by an increase in π (whatever the value of θ_i—so long as $\theta_i > 0$). Formally, the slope can be derived by differentiating the indifference curve totally: $d\bar{U} = \theta_i de - \pi \cdot d\pi = 0 \rightarrow d\pi/de = \theta_i/\pi > 0$. Note that a movement to the south-east increases utility.

In the old Keynesian model, the Phillips curve is not dependent on the expected rate of inflation, and both left and right governments accept that it takes the form

$$\pi = \alpha + \beta e.$$

Since the slope of the Phillips curve is constant and equal to β, the optimal position for the left government is where the slope of an L (for left government) indifference curve is equal to β, so $d\pi/de = \theta_L/\pi_L = \beta \Rightarrow \pi_L = \theta_L/\beta$. And likewise $\pi_R = \theta_R/\beta$. This is illustrated in Fig. 16.14: thus $\pi_R = \theta_R/\beta < \pi_L = \theta_L/\beta$. Using the Phillips curve we can see that this implies

$$e_L = (\pi_L - \alpha)/\beta = ((\theta_L/\beta) - \alpha)/\beta > e_R = (\pi_R - \alpha)/\beta = ((\theta_R/\beta) - \alpha)/\beta.$$

So, in Hibbs's model, left governments will choose higher employment and higher inflation rates than right governments.

Modern macroeconomics no longer accepts an inflation–employment trade-off if wage setters have rational expectations. Assuming that governments and their advisers are aware of this, we should no longer expect left-wing governments to be associated with more expansionary and inflationary policies than right-wing governments. The evidence however suggests that some such effect is visible. What might explain it? The other major contributor to this literature is Alesina. We shall explain Alesina's highly ingenious argument, which assumes rational expectations by wage setters and full knowledge of the model by government.

Alesina's model (with a vertical Phillips curve, rational expectations of wage setters and full knowledge of the model by the government)

A term of government lasts two periods, 1 and 2. There is an election at the end of period 0. If the left-wing party wins it maximizes

$$U_L = \theta_L e_1 - \pi_1^2/2 + \theta_L e_2 - \pi_2^2/2$$

in the two periods in office. If a right-wing party does, it maximizes

$$U_R = \theta_R e_1 - \pi_1^2/2 + \theta_R e_2 - \pi_2^2/2.$$

As in Hibbs, the left is assumed to be relatively favourable to employment with $\theta_L > \theta_R$. (The utility functions here are simply a two-period version of the functions used above. We assume for simplicity that there are no discounting effects.) The electorate is assumed to have full information about the parties and their objectives, so nothing an incumbent might do in period 0 will have an effect on the outcome of the election or on what happens subsequently.

The key difference as compared with Hibbs is that the government faces (and knows it faces) a Phillips curve in which there is no long-run trade-off between employment and inflation. The government, whether left or right, faces the same constraints in periods 1 and 2:

$$\pi_t = \pi_t^E + e_t - e_e.$$

A consequence of the government's utility function is that, although it will choose different employment rates depending on the expected rate of inflation, it will end up with the same inflation rate in both periods. In fact, as we shall now show for the left government, it will end up with $\pi = \theta_L$ in both periods, and the right government will end up with $\pi = \theta_R$.

Substituting the Phillips curve constraint into the left government's utility function, we have

$$U_L = \theta_L \left(\pi_1^L - \pi_1^E + e_e \right) - \left(\pi_1^L \right)^2/2 + \theta_L \left(\pi_2^L - \pi_2^E + e_e \right) - \left(\pi_2^L \right)^2/2.$$

Differentiating by π_1^L (the left government's inflation rate in period 1), gives

$$\theta_L - \pi_1^L = 0 \Rightarrow \pi_1^L = \theta_L$$

and differentiating by π_2^L implies

$$\pi_2^L = \theta_L.$$

In Fig. 16.15, the continuous indifference curves are those of the left government and the dashed ones are those of the right. For purely illustrative purposes Fig. 16.15 shows what levels of employment will be chosen by L and R respectively when π^E is first equal to θ_L and then equal to θ_R. Note that if wage setters choose the correct expected inflation rate for the government in office, employment is at the equilibrium rate for both governments.

The difference between the two periods relates to the choice of employment not inflation. The only—but crucial—difference between the constraints in the two periods concerns π_1^E and π_2^E. Indeed this is what drives the Alesina model: wage setters—this is Alesina's critical assumption—do *not* know when they choose π_1^E which party will win the election. Thus there is electoral uncertainty when they choose π_1^E but they do of course

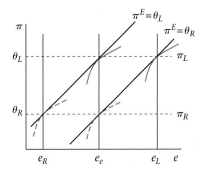

Figure 16.15 The Alesina model with full knowledge

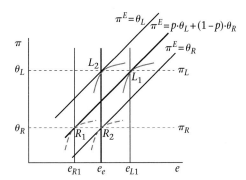

Figure 16.16 The Alesina model with electoral uncertainty

know which party has won when they choose π_2^E. Thus in period 2, since wage setters know whether the government is L or R, they will set π_2^E correctly. As shown in Fig. 16.16, the economy will be at L_2 with L in power and R_2 with R in power.

The critical question is therefore what is the value of π_1^E? Let us assume that wage setters believe there is a probability p that L will win. Then wage setters set:

$$\pi_1^E = p \cdot \pi_1^L + (1-p) \cdot \pi_1^R = p \cdot \theta_L + (1-p) \cdot \theta_R.$$

Since $\theta_L > \theta_R$, $\theta_L > \pi_1^E = p \cdot \theta_L + (1-p) \cdot \theta_R > \theta_R$. Fig. 16.16, sets this out. As can be seen, there is a unique equilibrium employment rate e_e. In the second period of office, both a left government and a right government will choose $e_2 = e_e$, since wage setters will correctly set π_2^E equal to θ_L and θ_R respectively. The two chosen positions in Fig. 16.16 are L_2 for L and R_2 for R: as above, the L indifference curves are continuous and the R indifference curves dashed.

In the first period, however, when wage setters have set π_1^E before the election results are known, this means that the Phillips curve is as shown in Fig. 16.16 and it overestimates inflation if R wins and underestimates it if L wins. As can be seen in the figure, L gains by this procedure: it moves temporarily to a higher utility indifference curve (at L_1) with employment $e_1^L > e_e$. R loses, moving temporarily to a lower utility indifference curve (at R_1) with employment $e_1^R < e_e$.

4.2.1 Summing up

In the Hibbs's model, the assumption that there is a permanent trade-off between unemployment and inflation lies behind the prediction of the model that left governments choose higher employment and inflation rates than do right governments.

In the Alesina model, which uses the now-standard assumption that there is no lasting trade-off between inflation and unemployment, the result is that we should *not* associate permanently higher employment with left governments or permanently lower employment with right governments. That would be to deny the existence of a unique equilibrium employment rate, which both colours of government have to respect. Instead deviations from equilibrium will be *temporary*, at the start of periods of office and due to the inability of wage setters to predict inflation exactly because inflation expectations are set before the outcome of the election is known. There is a temporary effect by which employment is boosted in the first period after an election of a left government and reduced in the first period after an election of a right government.

4.3 Voting: the Meltzer–Richard model and the choice of tax rates

Thus far we have seen how voting may affect macroeconomic outcomes:

- before an election in the opportunistic incumbent model and
- after the election in the partisan government model.

We now turn to a quite different and more fundamental role of voting. A democracy can be thought of as a redistribution struggle between voters. If a majority of voters in a democracy can decide laws, then why should it not pass a law redistributing money from the rich minority to the less well-off majority? This is the basic idea behind a famous model of how taxes might be set in a democracy. A simple set-up is where there is a uniform rate of income tax, t, the proceeds of which are used to give every voter a flat rate benefit, b. Thus if y_i is the gross income of the ith voter and if $i = 1, \ldots, N$

$$b = \left(t \sum_{i=1}^{N} y_i \right) / N$$

and disposable income (or consumption) for the ith voter is

$$c_i = y_i(1 - t) + b.$$

Evidently low income voters will want a high tax rate since they will pay little themselves and get more back in the form of b. For exactly opposite reasons high income voters will want low tax rates.

4.3.1 Downs's median voter result

To go further we need to specify how elections are organized. A famous result[10] relates to a common form of election, the plurality or first-past-the-post system. This is the normal

---

[10] Downs (1957).

method of organizing elections in both the UK and the USA: the candidate with the most votes wins. Such a system is sometimes called a majoritarian system. We shall restrict ourselves to two candidates or parties, A and B, whose only goal is winning the election. Each party has a platform, which in our case consists solely of a proposed tax rate t_A or t_B. We assume that the party that gets the most votes and is therefore elected is committed to implementing its proposed tax rate and distributing the proceeds equally across all the voters. We also assume that there are no abstentions.

First, we look at voter preferences on taxes. We can order the voters according to their pretax income levels, from low to high, and let us write the order as $y_1, y_2, ..., y_N$ where y_1 is the lowest and y_N the highest pretax income. We shall also assume that there is one voter, whom we call the *median* voter, y_m, such that there are as many voters with lower incomes than y_m as there are voters with higher incomes than y_m. We make a critical assumption (but one that is hardly implausible) that the higher the income of a voter, the lower the tax rate the voter ideally wants. So (say) the median voter wants a tax rate of t_m, voter i wants a tax rate of t_i, and $t_1 \geq t_2 \geq ... \geq t_{m-1} \geq t_m \geq t_{m+1} \geq ... \geq t_{N-1} \geq t_N$.

Downs's rather remarkable theorem says that, assuming both parties are solely interested in maximizing their chances of winning the election, if we can order the preferences of voters in this one-dimensional manner, and if (one final assumption) a voter always votes for the party with the proposed tax rate closest to that voter's preferred tax rate—so-called sincere voting—then both parties will propose the tax rate preferred by the median voter t_m and each will have a 50% chance of winning.

Why? The answer is very simple: if A proposes a tax rate above t_m, B can win by proposing a tax rate of t_m. B will get all the votes with incomes above that of the median voter and the median voter's vote as well, while A only gets the votes of the voters with incomes below that of the median voter. Hence B wins. The converse holds if B proposes a tax rate below t_m.

In fact, we can think of this voting game as a simultaneous move game between the two parties, so that the equilibrium must be a Nash equilibrium. $(t_A = t_m, t_B = t_m)$ is a Nash equilibrium: if the other party proposes t_m it doesn't pay you to propose anything different. In the next subsection, we explain the concept of a Nash equilibrium—this can be skipped by those familiar with the concept.

4.3.2 The Nash equilibrium

Until now the games we have been considering have all involved players moving in sequence, so that only one player moves at a time. These games can be represented diagrammatically in game tree form as we have done. This way of representing them is called extensive form. Some games however which we will come across in the next section assume that players move simultaneously—so that any one player does not know what moves the other players have made until after she has moved. In fact, the players do not literally need to move simultaneously: all that is necessary is that they do not know what moves the other players are making. A common feature of these games is that players have just one move. They are often referred to as one-shot games. Of course, we can have games in which players move simultaneously period after period, but we do not consider them here.

Suppose there are two players, A and B, in a one-shot game. Player A has to choose a value of a out of a set of possible values of a and likewise B a value of b. We shall call the set of all possible or feasible values of a, P_A, and of b, P_B. The set of possible values of a may be finite e.g. from the set $(a_1, a_2, a_3, \ldots)$ or infinite e.g. from the interval $[\underline{a}, \bar{a}]$ where very often $\underline{a} = -\infty$ and and $\bar{a} = \infty$. Associated with each possible pair of moves are the pay-offs to each player. Thus if A played a_i and B played b_j, the pay-off or utility which A got could be defined as $U_A(a_i, b_j)$ and that for B, $U_B(a_i, b_j)$.

What moves should A and B play, given that they can't get together to agree—at least not to make a binding agreement on what they should both do? A necessary condition if both A and B are rational[11] is that the pair of moves should be a Nash equilibrium. This simply means that A's choice of move, say a^* should produce the highest pay-off for A given B's choice of move b^*, and vice versa. This can be simply put as

$$U_A(a^*, b^*) \geq U_A(a, b^*) \,\forall a \in P_A$$
$$U_B(a^*, b^*) \geq U_A(a^*, b) \,\forall b \in P_B.$$

The first line says: given B has played b^*, the pay-off to A from a^*, $U_A(a^*, b^*)$, must be greater than or equal to the pay-off to A from any value of a in the feasible set P_A; the notation $\forall a \in P_A$ means just 'for all a in P_A'. And the same must also be true of B.

How can we work out what the Nash equilibrium is in a game? If each player has a (small) finite number of moves, this could be done by simply going through all the possible combinations of moves and checking if a particular combination is a Nash equilibrium. The games we will encounter in the following sections will not be like that because P_A and P_B (or their analogues) will all be intervals in the real line, for example $[0, 1]$ in the case of political platforms, and $[0, \infty]$ in the case of choices of government expenditure. Finding the Nash equilibrium will then either require common sense—as in the political platform case, or the following method, which we illustrate by taking the Cournot–Nash duopoly model as an example, since it may already be familiar to readers.

The two duopolists are A and B, and they each simultaneously and independently choose quantities of output, a and b respectively, where $a \in P_A$ where P_A is $[0, \infty)$ and P_B is $[0, \infty)$. The pay-offs to A and B are their profits; we assume for simplicity that their costs are zero, so A's profits are $\pi_A \equiv p \cdot a$ and B's profits are $\pi_B \equiv p \cdot b$. The common price level is determined by the industry demand curve $q = k - p$, where k is a constant, and the total quantity of output, which is $q = a + b$:

$$q = a + b = k - p$$
$$\text{or } p = k - (a + b).$$

Hence A's pay-off is $\pi_A(a, b) = p \cdot a = (k - a - b) \cdot a$ and B's is $\pi_B(a, b) = p \cdot b = (k - a - b) \cdot b$.

---

[11] And it is 'common knowledge' to both of them that they are rational—i.e. A knows B is rational, A knows B knows A is rational etc.

The procedure for finding (a^*, b^*), the Nash equilibrium, is now simple. First, find, for any b, the level of a that maximizes A's pay-off:

$$\frac{\partial \pi_A (a, b)}{\partial a} = (k - a - b) - a = 0$$

$$\Rightarrow k - 2a - b = 0$$

$$\Rightarrow a = \frac{k - b}{2}.$$

When we do the same for B, we get $b = (k - a)/2$. Since $a = (k - b)/2$ shows the profit-maximizing value of a for any value of b; and $b = (k - a)/2$ shows the profit-maximizing value of b for any value of a, we simply solve these two equations, which implies

$$a^* = b^* = \frac{k}{3}.$$

Thus in the Cournot–Nash duopoly model, the Nash equilibrium is $a^* = b^* = \frac{k}{3}$.

4.3.3 The Meltzer–Richard result

Using the Downs model and still assuming that the government will set a constant proportional tax rate t, Meltzer–Richard[12] argue that the preferences of the median voter will be decisive. What tax rate t_m will the median voter prefer? If we assume that the gross income of voters is unaffected by the tax rate—i.e. there are no disincentive effects—then there is a rather surprising result: the median voter will either want a tax rate of one or zero. We show this result first as it captures rather dramatically the basic insights of the model. But we shall then need to bring in disincentive effects of higher taxes to produce more realistic results.

We need next to find the tax rate, t_m, that the median voter, m, prefers. m will choose t_m to maximize c_m, where the median voter's income is equal to her post tax income ($y_m(1 - t)$) plus the tax rate times the average income of the rest of the voters, since this will be her share of the redistributed income ($b = t \left(\sum y_j / N\right)$):

$$c_m = y_m(1 - t) + b = y_m(1 - t) + t \cdot \left(\sum y_j / N\right) = y_m(1 - t) + t\bar{y} = y_m + t \cdot (\bar{y} - y_m).$$

Thus m will prefer as high a tax rate as possible if $\bar{y} > y_m$ and as low as possible if $\bar{y} < y_m$. This is because m loses $t \cdot y_m$ via taxation and gains $t \cdot \bar{y}$ via the flat rate benefit. So if median income is below average income, m will want $t_m = 1$ and if median income is above average income m will want $t_m = 0$. Since all standard distributions of income are left-skewed more people have incomes below the average than above it: hence $y_m < \bar{y}$ and m prefers $t_m = 1$!

The Meltzer–Richard result with disincentive effects. This result is somewhat implausible because it ignores the incentive effects of higher taxation: if taxes are too high, people will not work as hard and take more leisure instead. How should this be modelled? We assume that voters work less if the tax rate is high. Specifically we assume the ith voter has an

---

[12] Meltzer and Richard (1981).

hourly productivity of λ_i, etc. and this is equal to the hourly gross wage, w_i (via marginal productivity in a competitive labour market). The ith voter maximizes the utility function

$$U_i = w_i e_i (1 - t) + b - \alpha e_i^2 / 2,$$

where e_i is the number of hours that i works, t is the uniform tax rate and b the uniform benefit. Net disposable income or consumption is $w_i e_i (1 - t) + b$ and $\alpha e_i^2 / 2$ stands for the cost of leisure. Given t and b, how many hours will i work? i maximizes the utility function with respect to e_i and this implies that

$$e_i = w_i (1 - t) / \alpha = \lambda_i (1 - t) / \alpha,$$

which implies that i works harder the higher is the hourly wage, and the lower is the tax rate and the value of leisure. We are interested in the median voter's choice of t. The median voter chooses hours $e_m = \lambda_m (1 - t) / \alpha$. So m's preferred tax rate is found by substituting for this optimal value of e_m in the utility function

$$U_m = \lambda_m \left(\lambda_m (1 - t) / \alpha \right) (1 - t) + b - \alpha \left(\lambda_m (1 - t) / \alpha \right)^2 / 2 = \left(\lambda_m^2 (1 - t)^2 / 2\alpha \right) + b,$$

where

$$b = t \cdot \left(\sum \lambda_i e_i \right) / N = t \cdot \left(\sum \left(\frac{\lambda_i^2 . (1 - t)}{\alpha} \right) \right) / N = t \cdot (1 - t) \bar{\lambda}^2 / \alpha,$$

with $\bar{\lambda}^2$ defined as $\sum \lambda_i^2 / N$. So $\bar{\lambda}^2$ is the average level of squared productivity. The above equation can be expressed more simply as:

$$U_m = \left(\lambda_m^2 (1 - t)^2 / 2\alpha \right) + t \cdot (1 - t) \bar{\lambda}^2 / \alpha.$$

We now maximize U_m with respect to t

$$\frac{\partial U_m}{\partial t} = -\frac{\lambda_m^2}{\alpha} (1 - t) + (1 - t) \bar{\lambda}^2 / \alpha - t \bar{\lambda}^2 / \alpha = 0$$

$$\Rightarrow \frac{\lambda_m^2}{\bar{\lambda}^2} = \frac{1 - 2t}{1 - t}.$$

The critical variable is $\lambda_m^2 / \bar{\lambda}^2$, the ratio of m's squared productivity (or wage) and the average level of squared productivity. We shall call this ratio r_m. Since $r_m = \frac{1 - 2t}{1 - t}$, it follows that $t_m = \frac{1 - r_m}{2 - r_m}$. If this ratio is unity or above, the median voter's earning capacity is the same as that of the average voter, we would not expect the median voter would want any taxes; that can indeed be seen to be the case, $t_m = 0$. By contrast, if $r_m = 0$, $t_m = 1/2$, which is the maximum possible value of t_m (since t_m increases as r_m declines).

4.3.4 Summing up

Once we allow for the disincentive effects of taxation, the Meltzer–Richard result is far less dramatic. In the particular specification of disincentive effects adopted here, the maximum tax rate the median voter would choose to impose is 0.5, but that is only in the case in which the median voter has an exceptionally low level of earning capacity. But the general implication is an interesting one: the more skewed the income distribution towards the top end, the lower will be the *relative* earning capacity of the median voter (i.e. relative to the average) and therefore the *higher* the democratically chosen tax rate.

5 Games between interdependent economies

As the final section in this chapter, we turn to games between governments. In the model of interdependent economies in Chapter 12, we showed how strategic considerations can enter into the way macroeconomic policy is made. This strategic interaction is set out more fully as a game in this chapter. There are two governments, Home (H) and Foreign (F). We shall assume that both want increases in output (y or y^* respectively); but neither want to increase their own government expenditure (G or G^*) to achieve increased output—since that would worsen their public sector deficit. A simple utility function that expresses this is

$$U_H = \log y - \alpha G$$

and

$$U_F = \log y^* - \alpha G^*$$

for H and F respectively.

How does the interdependence of the two economies come in? As we saw in Chapter 12, it simplifies the models of interdependence if we assume that monetary policy is accommodating so that we do not need to consider the interest rate. The aggregate demand equations linking G and G^* with y and y^* are then given by

$$y = aG + cy^*$$

and

$$y^* = aG^* + cy,$$

where $0 < c < 1$. Thus

$$y = \frac{a}{1 - c^2} G + \frac{ac}{1 - c^2} G^* = \beta G + c\beta G^*$$

and

$$y^* = \frac{a}{1 - c^2} G^* + \frac{ac}{1 - c^2} G = \beta G^* + c\beta G$$

where $\beta \equiv \frac{a}{1-c^2}$. We focus on H, although the argument applies equally to F. As can be seen from the above equation for y, H's output can increase either as a result of an increase in G or in G^*. Clearly H will prefer the second channel; and conversely for F.

This implies that H and F are playing a game against each other, both wanting the other to increase government expenditure. To analyse this game, the key questions are

(1) whether or not the two countries can negotiate a binding agreement between themselves or not; and

(2) if not, what is the order of the moves—either H can choose G and then F can follow knowing the value of G set by H (or vice versa), or both H and F move simultaneously. We examine these possibilities in turn.

5.1 No binding agreement possible: H moves first

This is a two-stage game: first H moves and chooses G; then F moves and chooses G^* in the knowledge of G. In this case, H is the 'leader'. This was a situation analysed by the German economist von Stackelberg for duopolists, and is often referred to as the Stackelberg leader case. To analyse the game, we need to apply backward induction. H needs to ask: what value of G^* will F choose for each possible value of G; this produces a 'best-response' function by F to whatever may be H's choice of G. This best-response function is of the form $G^* = BR^F(G)$: it enables H to know what F will do for any given choice of G by H. We begin by working out the foreign government's best response function, $G^* = BR^F(G)$.

F wants to maximize $U_F = \log y^* - \alpha G^*$. From the aggregate demand models linking the two economies, we know that $y^* = \beta G^* + c\beta G$. Hence F maximizes $U_F = \log(\beta G^* + c\beta G) - \alpha G^*$. To find the best response of F to G, we simply find the value of G^* that maximizes U_F with respect to G^*, holding G constant.

$$\frac{\partial U_F}{\partial G^*} = \frac{\partial \log(\beta G^* + c\beta G)}{\partial G^*} - \alpha = 0$$
$$\Rightarrow \frac{\beta}{\beta G^* + c\beta G} = \alpha$$
$$\Rightarrow G^* = 1/\alpha - cG.$$

This result is shown in Fig. 16.17. This shows that F's indifference curves (U_{F1} and U_{F2}) increase as G increases. To see F's best response to, say, G_1 draw a vertical line up from G_1. F has to be somewhere on that vertical line (since $G = G_1$) and the best value of G_1 is where the highest F indifference curve just touches the vertical line, implying $G^* = G_1^*$. On the same basis, it can be seen that if H increases G to G_2, this implies that F will set G_2^*; thus an increase in G makes F better off. In addition this shows that as G rises F will choose to do less to boost y_F through G^*—in other words, F will free ride on H's higher levels of G.

Given that this will be F's response to whatever choice H makes of G, and that H can work this out, what value of G should H choose? H knows that it can only in effect choose a point on F's BR function. In other words H is constrained by $G^* = 1/\alpha - cG$. This is shown in Fig. 16.18. In the diagram we show home's indifference curves. These increase as G^* rises since a higher G^* is better for H. H has to choose a point on foreign's best

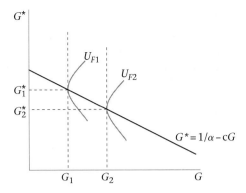

Figure 16.17 Foreign's best response function

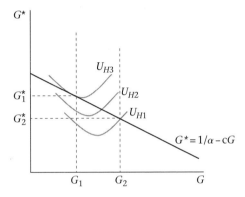

Figure 16.18 H as Stackelberg leader

response function. To maximize its utility, home will therefore choose that point on F's best response function that gets it to its highest indifference curve. Home does this by choosing G_1, which then guarantees H a utility level of U_{H3}—the indifference curve corresponding to U_{H3} just touches F's best response function. Before going through the algebra of the Stackelberg leader case, we look at the case in which both F and H move simultaneously.

5.2 No binding agreement possible: H and F move simultaneously

This case can be analysed as a Nash equilibrium. If both H and F move simultaneously, and if they each know that they are moving simultaneously, they each need reassurance that their move is optimal given the move by the other. That means they need to choose the moves corresponding to where their best response functions cross. This is shown in Fig. 16.19.

In Fig. 16.19, H's best response function is the downwards-sloping line, $G = 1/\alpha - cG^*$. It is constructed in just the same way as F's best response function. For each value of G^*, the best response by home is the G that enables H to get onto the highest possible indifference curve. Thus each H indifference curve sits on H's best response function with a zero slope.

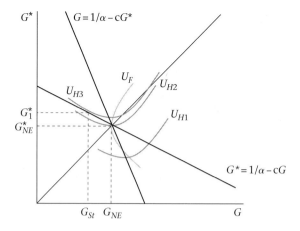

Figure 16.19 Nash equilibrium with simultaneous moves

The Nash equilibrium is where the two best response functions cut. As can be seen, if F sets $G^* = G^*_{NE}$, the best response by H is G_{NE}. And vice versa for F: if H sets $G = G_{NE}$, the best response by F is G^*_{NE}.

Let us now compare the Nash equilibrium with the Stackelberg equilibrium when H moves first. As we can see, the level of home's output is higher in the Stackelberg case ($G_{St} < G_{NE}$) and hence, home's utility is higher in that case. This shows that H has first mover advantage. By choosing a lower value of G, H forces F to select a higher value of G^*, thus to some extent free riding on F. It can be seen that H attains a higher indifference curve as a result of this first mover advantage. To show this algebraically is straightforward.[13]

5.3 Binding agreements

Is it possible for *both* sides to do better? In Fig. 16.20, the area indicated PS is the set of points with utility higher than U_{H2} for H and U_F for F. Thus each point in PS implies a

---

[13] To derive the Nash equilibrium, find the values of G^* and G that satisfy both best response functions, namely $G^* = 1/\alpha - cG$ and $G = 1/\alpha - cG^*$. Since these two functions are symmetric, G and G^* will be the same in equilibrium. Hence we need simply solve $G = 1/\alpha - cG$, implying

$$G_{NE} = G^*_{NE} = \frac{1}{\alpha}\frac{1}{1+c}.$$

To derive the Stackelberg equilibrium, H needs to choose G to maximize U_H subject to $G^* = 1/\alpha - cG$. Since $U_H = \log y - \alpha G$, and $y = \beta G + c\beta G^*$, we can write H's utility function as $U_H = \log(\beta G + c\beta G^*) - \alpha G$. And since the maximization is subject to $G^* = 1/\alpha - cG$, we can substitute that into U_H to get $U_H = \log(\beta G + c\beta[1/\alpha - cG]) - \alpha G = \log(\beta(1 - c^2)G + c\beta/\alpha) - \alpha G$. Hence

$$\frac{\partial U_H}{\partial G} = \frac{\beta(1 - c^2)}{\beta(1 - c^2)G + c\beta/\alpha} - \alpha = 0$$

This implies

$$G_{St} = \frac{1}{\alpha}\frac{1}{1+c}\left(\frac{1 - c - c^2}{1 - c}\right) = G_{NE} \cdot \left(\frac{1 - c - c^2}{1 - c}\right) < G_{NE}.$$

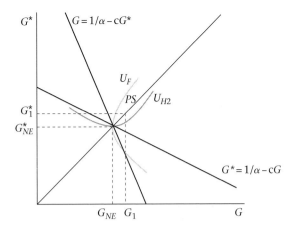

Figure 16.20 Optimizing through binding agreements

higher utility for both H and F. If H and F can reach a binding agreement that neither will move, they could agree to be at a combination such as G_1 and G_1^* which leaves them both better off than at the Nash equilibrium. The agreement needs to be binding, however, since it would pay each country to reduce their own government expenditure.

This is the type of reasoning that leads to formalized international agreements, such as binding treaties or membership of international institutional arrangements such as European Monetary Union, which imposes rules on members. But, as EMU has itself shown, binding rules on national governments are difficult to enforce, especially if there is any ambiguity about the rules that are being enforced. International agreements remain difficult in the area of macroeconomics.

5.3.1 Summing up

In this example of interdependence between two governments, setting it up as a game highlights the way a free-rider problem affects the outcome. There is a clear advantage to the government who is able to move first. If both move simultaneously then they do worse than they could do if a binding agreement were possible. This highlights the temptation that each has to cheat on any agreement and hence the difficulty with negotiating such arrangements. It also shows the attraction to both countries of developing binding treaty agreements.

6 Conclusions

This chapter has sought to develop a series of models with three purposes in mind:

(1) To give some idea of what a diverse and interesting field political economy is, while at the same time emphasizing how much space there is for further development. It is still in its infancy, but many regard it as one of the most exciting and promising new areas of economics, and in particular of macroeconomics.

(2) To explain a number of the key game theory techniques that are needed to navigate this new field. We have not done this systematically; but the reader who has persevered through the chapter will have a reasonable grasp of many of the important tools that are needed to go further.

(3) To set out a number of models that enable the reader to pursue in greater depth some key issues discussed in other chapters. This is especially the case for monetary policy.

■ **PROBLEMS**

QUESTION A. In the game shown in Fig. 16.21, wage setters move first and choose the expected rate of inflation. Then the government moves and chooses the actual rate of inflation. The wage setters' pay-off is listed first followed by the government's. There is complete information. (i) Find the subgame perfect equilibrium solution to this game. (ii) Why would the government like to be able to commit to a strategy before the wage setters had moved? What strategy would the government commit to?

QUESTION B. Each period the government (G) chooses fiscal policy and the central bank (CB) chooses monetary policy. The choices are made simultaneously (without knowing the other's choice). Fiscal policy can be expansionary (E) or neutral (N). Monetary policy can be Tight (T) or accommodating (A). The per period utility, U_G, to G from E is 2 if monetary policy is T and 5 if monetary policy is A. The per period utility to G from N is 0 if T and 4 if A. The per period utility to CB, U_{CB}, from T is 2 if E and 5 if N. And it is -5 from A if E and 4 from A if N.

The present value of G's per period utilities at $t = 0$ is $V_G = \sum_{t=0}^{\infty} \beta^t U_G(t)$, and the present value of CB's per period utilities at $t = 0$ is $V_{CB} = \sum_{t=0}^{\infty} \beta^t U_{CB}(t)$. $U_I(t)$ is the per period utility of $I = CB, G$ in period t.

(i) If this game is played once only (say in $t = 0$), what will be the Nash equilibrium choices of G and CB? (ii) What if it is played 10 times? (iii) Suppose it is played indefinitely: assume G's strategy is 'If either you or I ever played T or E in the past, I will always play E from now on,' and CB's strategy is 'If either you or I ever played T or E in

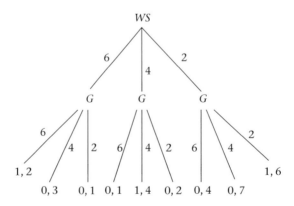

Figure 16.21 Game for Question A

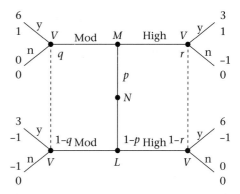

Figure 16.22 Game for Question C

the past, I will always play T from now on,' for what values of β are these strategies a subgame perfect equilibrium?

QUESTION C. In the signalling game shown in Fig. 16.22, a voter has to choose whether to vote Labour or not. If she does, Labour wins the election, if not it loses. She is middle class and is unsure whether the Labour leader will set moderate taxes on the middle classes if elected—favouring the middle classes (type M leader); or whether the Labour leader will set high taxes on the middle classes—favouring low income groups (type L leader). The leader can send a signal 'moderate taxes' or 'high taxes'. Both types of leader, L and M, want to get elected; but neither leader likes to send a signal which will upset his supporters in the party—so M doesn't want to send the signal 'high' and L doesn't want to send the signal 'mod'.

Specifically the voter gets a pay-off of 1 if she elects an M type, and −1 if she elects an L type. If she votes against the Labour candidate she gets a pay-off of 0. Both types of leader get a pay-off of 0 if they lose, and 6 if they win, after having signalled their preferred policy, and −1 if they lose, and 3 if they win, after having signalled the policy to which they are opposed.

The voter, V, knows that there is a priori a probability p that the Labour leader is M.

(i) Show that there are no separating equilibria. (ii) For what values of p and r is there a pooling equilibrium on Mod? (iii) Use the Intuitive Criterion to justify a particular value of r. (iv) Could there be a pooling equilibrium on High? Can you use the Intuitive Criterion to rule it out?

QUESTION D. As in Question B the government sets fiscal policy and the central bank sets monetary policy. This time fiscal policy can be any positive number, $f \geq 0$; where a higher value of f is more expansionary. And monetary policy can be any positive number, $m \geq 0$, where a higher value of m is a tighter monetary policy. G's utility function is now

$$U_G = f - f^2 - 0.5(m - mf). \tag{16.57}$$

This says that G gains up to a point from a more expansionary fiscal policy for any given level of m. The tighter is monetary policy, the worse off is G, but the higher is the rate of return on fiscal policy (to compensate for the tighter monetary policy). CB's utility function is now

$$U_{CB} = m - m^2 - 0.5(f - fm) \tag{16.58}$$

and this can be rationalized in a similar way.

  (i) Assume G and CB choose f and m simultaneously, what are the Nash equilibrium values of f and m?

 (ii) Now assume that G chooses f first and then CB chooses m in the knowledge of G's choice of f. Find the subgame perfect equilibrium strategies of G and CB. Is it an advantage or disadvantage for G to be the first mover?

(iii) Suppose that G and CB could make a binding agreement that they would both stick to a common value of $f = m$, what value would they agree on?

(iv) You should be able to show that f is highest in the answer to (i) and lowest in the answer to (iii). Can you illustrate your answers on a graph with f on the vertical and m on the horizontal axis?

PART SIX

Applications

17 Performance and Policy in Europe, the USA, and Japan

An important motivation for writing this book is to present an integrated model of short- and medium-run macroeconomics that would be useful for analysing economic policy and performance. The purpose of this chapter is to show how this can be done. In particular, this chapter:

(1) shows that the graphical presentation of macro models developed in this book is useful for analysing a wide range of performance and policy episodes in contemporary economies.

(2) provides an account of some key features of what has happened in the advanced economies in recent decades.

(3) identifies major policy changes and their economic effects.

During this period a broad consensus has emerged amongst many policy makers and observers in the OECD countries as to the appropriate framework for the conduct of monetary and fiscal policy. Whilst disagreements remain, it is nevertheless the case that common ground is firmer than in many earlier epochs. The consensus rests on the view that in the long run, monetary policy does not affect the real economy. The consequence is that monetary policy makers should aim to ensure the stability of inflation at a low rate, guarding against the dangers posed both by inflation and deflation. Moreover, by actively changing the interest rate, the central bank should help steer the economy toward the stable inflation equilibrium in the face of short-run disturbances.

In terms of fiscal policy, the consensus centres on the requirement for government to design its fiscal management system to ensure long-run fiscal sustainability whilst allowing for short-run stabilization and the achievement of the government's structural objectives. Chapters 5 and 6 set out these features in detail. Although there is broad consensus in the theoretical literature about monetary and fiscal policy, one debate relevant to the analysis of recent economic performance concerns the extent to which 'excessively tight' macroeconomic policy may have been responsible for European sluggishness. This argument rests on the existence of so-called hysteresis mechanisms through which aggregate demand policies are thought to affect the supply side of the economy (as described in Chapter 4 and modelled in more detail in Chapter 15). We return to this issue in the next chapter where we address the question of supply-side policy, institutions, and economic reform in the context of the debate about the determinants of medium-run unemployment performance.

In this chapter we take four episodes as our focus. We begin at the outset of the 1990s with the shock to Germany, Europe's largest economy, of unification. In the period before unification, Germany played a pivotal role in monetary policy across Western Europe as the key currency country in the European Exchange Rate mechanism (ERM). As a consequence German unification had macroeconomic ramifications well beyond its borders. The ERM collapsed and the EU spent the rest of the decade with macro policy dominated by the requirements for the creation of the European Monetary Union (EMU). We look at how one prominent country—the UK—that dropped out of the ERM and did not enter EMU fared in that decade.

In section 2, we address the macroeconomics of monetary union. The ECB is beginning to establish a track record as a monetary policy maker and its behaviour can be analysed. Since the ECB has responsibility for responding to *common* shocks hitting the EU, we also need to analyse the responses of members to country-specific disturbances. This in turn leads to the question of whether Union level rules for fiscal behaviour are justified.

In section 3, the performance of the US economy since 1990 is examined. The 1990s were a benign decade for the US monetary authority, the Federal Reserve Board. Unlike Europe, which was confronted by a major macroeconomic shock and then the upheavals associated with large-scale institutional reform, the Fed had a single leader and the absence of any external shocks. During the Clinton presidency, fiscal consolidation was undertaken, leaving the economy in a stable macroeconomic condition. The return in the mid-1990s of reasonable rates of productivity growth to the US economy after an absence of some twenty years provided the economy with a positive supply shock and a lengthy boom followed. We look at the character of the boom and of the subsequent 'bust' at the turn of the new century.

Section 4 addresses the malaise of the Japanese economy in the last fifteen years. After decades of impressive performance, the Japanese economy entered a prolonged slump in 1992, from which it had not emerged by 2004. From 1992, growth averaged only 1% p.a.: one-quarter its rate from the mid-1970s. Inflation fell during the first half of the 1990s and was followed by deflation in the second half. We use the tools developed in this book to illuminate the role of macroeconomic policy in the stagnation.

1 German unification, the collapse of ERM, and its aftermath

1.1 Background: the ERM and Germany's role in it

As we shall see later in the chapter, the 1990s was a benign decade for macroeconomic policy makers in the United States. This was far from the case in Europe. The most dramatic event was the unification between West and East Germany in 1989. This event was important for two main reasons: West Germany was Europe's largest economy and it played a key role during the 1980s in Europe's monetary policy making. West Germany's role in European monetary policy was due to the operation of the Exchange Rate Mechanism (ERM) of the European Monetary System: most West European countries had effectively given up domestic monetary policy autonomy by joining the ERM, which was to lead by the end of the 1990s to the formation of a single currency zone. To explain the impact of unification on ERM member countries other than Germany, it is therefore necessary to explain briefly how ERM worked and why countries joined it. This background is also essential for the analysis of EMU in section 2. We shall see that the 3-equation model provides a helpful framework for distinguishing between the so-called credibility and discipline explanations for the role of ERM membership in European disinflation. We then move to the open economy model to pin down the way in which a decision to fix the exchange rate can enable disinflation.

The primary motivation for the establishment of the ERM in 1979 by a number of West European countries was to create exchange rate stability because fluctuating exchange rates were believed to be damaging to the creation of a more integrated and competitive European market. Although the European Exchange Rate Mechanism was formally established as a so-called symmetric system with no country playing the dominant role in monetary policy, it evolved into a de facto asymmetric system in which Germany (West Germany at the time) was the key currency country.[1] The German Bundesbank emerged as the dominant monetary policy maker. This was the result of a set of interlocking characteristics:

(1) the German central bank's long-standing reputation for keeping inflation low, which promised gains for other countries in terms of anti-inflation credibility.

(2) the benefits to other countries from 'tying their hands' in terms of monetary policy by 'handing over' responsibility for it to the Bundesbank.

(3) the common interest of the non-German ERM countries in disinflation as their primary policy objective.

Thus although the main motivation for establishing more orderly exchange rate arrangements stemmed from concerns about the detrimental effect of exchange rate fluctuations on trade and investment decisions, the eventual shape of the ERM with the Bundesbank's de facto central role, was the outcome of macroeconomic imperatives in the member countries. Specifically, these countries sought to achieve low and stable inflation and were sceptical about achieving this under a regime of autonomous monetary policy (i.e. with floating exchange rates).

The German central bank, the Bundesbank, had a long-standing reputation for maintaining low inflation. Many of the other countries had spent the 1970s struggling to reduce inflation and believed that by tying their exchange rate to the Deutschmark they would promote falling inflation. Two routes through which this could happen were identified. The first is often referred to as the 'credibility' hypothesis. By fixing the exchange rate to the Deutschmark (DM), it was hoped to directly affect the inflation expectations of domestic wage and price setters. In theory, this would allow a painless reduction in inflation as the short-run Phillips curve shifts down to reflect a lower expected rate of inflation.

---

[1] For an accessible account, see various editions of Paul de Grauwe's book *Economics of Monetary Integration*; later called *Economics of Monetary Union* (de Grauwe 2003).

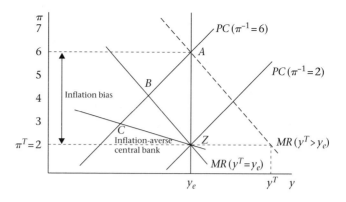

Figure 17.1 Credibility vs. discipline effects with a monetary rule

Before looking at why ERM membership may have been attractive to a country with an inflation problem, let us use the 3-equation analysis from Chapter 5 to consider how disinflation could be achieved in a single closed economy. In Fig. 17.1, we can think of the high inflation economy as initially at point A, with an inflation bias of 4%, i.e. inflation is constant at 6%, which is 4% above the target rate of 2%. The reason for the inflation bias is clear: the output target is above the equilibrium, which means that the constant inflation equilibrium with the lowest rate of inflation is where the government's indifference curve is tangential to a short-run Phillips curve with output at y_e (inflation bias is discussed in detail in Chapter 5). We can see in the diagram how, in theory, a costless reduction in inflation could occur:

- If the objectives of the central bank could be changed such that $y^T = y_e$, then the monetary rule line shifts to the left and intersects $\pi = \pi^T$ and $y = y_e$ at Z as shown.
- If the change in monetary arrangements has an immediate effect on wage and price setters and there is no inertia in wage or price setting, then the Phillips curve jumps down to go through point Z.

This would leave unemployment unchanged (since output remains at y_e) and inflation would drop immediately to the target rate of 2%. This is the case of a 'costless disinflation', which *in theory* could be brought about by a change in institutional arrangements, such as making the central bank independent of the government.

However, if there is inflation inertia, then although the monetary rule shifts to left, the economy is initially stuck with being on the Phillips curve, $PC(\pi_{-1} = 6)$. Disinflation is therefore costly: unemployment must rise in order for inflation to fall. Disinflation takes place along the MR line from point B to point Z. If the change in monetary policy arrangements such as making the central bank independent of the government has the effect of changing the *preferences* of the monetary policy maker by increasing the loss associated with inflation being above target, then the new MR is not only shifted to the left but becomes flatter as shown. Disinflation is faster but 'more painful' because output falls further (initially to point C) and unemployment rises by more on the adjustment path to the inflation target.

If a change in institutional arrangements produces a costless disinflation or a reduction in the cost of disinflation, the term 'credibility' is often applied: the institutional change is credible and this credibility is reflected in the adjustment of the behaviour of private sector agents. The 'credibility' hypothesis is contrasted with the 'discipline' hypothesis: in the latter case, a change in institutional arrangements is viewed as necessary in order for disinflation to be possible. However, there is no presumption that the behaviour of private sector agents changes so there is no claim that the costs of disinflation are affected.

Although the shift to a fixed exchange rate regime such as the entry of countries to the ERM is often discussed in much the same terms as for a closed economy, the analysis needs to be modified in some respects. As we shall see, the ERM was not a system of completely fixed exchange rates, but it is useful to assume fixed rates so as to highlight the new elements introduced in the open economy. In particular, there is obviously no *MR* curve for the country once it has adopted a fixed exchange rate: it does not have an independent monetary policy any longer. So how does disinflation take place? In the absence of inflation inertia, a completely credible switch to a fixed exchange rate would result in a drop in the inflation rate to equal that of the country setting monetary policy—in the ERM case, West Germany. By adopting a fixed exchange rate, the country is adopting the German inflation rate as its target. As usual, eliminating frictions in the economy makes the analysis quite simple: there is a costless drop in inflation to the German inflation rate.

To see how disinflation occurs within a fixed exchange rate arrangement in the presence of inflation inertia, we take the case where the nominal exchange rate is credibly fixed but where the behaviour of wage and price setters does not immediately adjust to an inflation rate equal to that in the key currency country. A plausible initial scenario is of a country operating with flexible exchange rates with constant inflation above π^*; it is in a medium-run equilibrium with a constant real exchange rate so the nominal exchange rate is depreciating at a constant rate: $\Delta e / e = \pi - \pi^*$. If the nominal exchange rate is now fixed against important trading partners, then higher domestic inflation will weaken competitiveness (with $\pi > \pi^*$ and a fixed nominal exchange rate, e, $\Delta \theta < 0$). The economy will move south-west down the *AD* curve and output and employment will fall as shown in Fig. 17.2. This will drive inflation down for two reasons: unemployment is rising, which weakens wage setters in the labour market and real wages are rising because of the real appreciation, which reduces the money wage increase workers can secure at any given unemployment rate. Once inflation is below π^*, competitiveness will begin to improve and the economy will move back toward the *ERU* curve. Eventually, the economy will be back at point A, but with inflation equal to π^*. Disinflation has been achieved but at the cost of a period of high unemployment.

Let us now compare the options facing a high inflation open economy: it could attempt to achieve disinflation by retaining monetary control itself through adopting a flexible exchange rate and implementing an inflation-targeting regime. By analogy with the closed economy, the adoption of an effective inflation-targeting regime may entail institutional change such as central bank independence. Alternatively the high inflation country could decide to tie its exchange rate to a country with the desired inflation rate. The latter option may be attractive if the government has doubts about its ability—even with the use of institutional change—to successfully alter the objectives of monetary

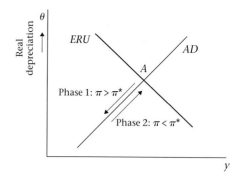

Figure 17.2 'Competitive disinflation' following the shift to ERM

policy. In terms of the model, this means to shift and possibly also alter the slope of the *MR* line. It may also believe that there is more chance of affecting private sector inflation expectations by ceding monetary policy to a body outside the country. On the other hand, even if the fixed exchange rate did not prove to be a magic bullet in terms of shifting inertial inflation, high inflation countries may see merit in 'tying their hands' by handing over monetary policy. Blame for the costs could be shifted to those external arrangements and this could lessen the political pressure on the government to weaken its anti-inflation resolve.

With this background, we return to the ERM. It is important to note that monetary policy was not literally 'handed over' to the Bundesbank: this would only have been the case if the high inflation countries had moved into a currency union with Germany and adopted the DM as their currency. In this context it is useful to recall the assumptions that need to be made for the adoption of a fixed exchange rate to remove all domestic control of monetary policy (see Chapter 9): the economy must be small, there must be perfect capital mobility, and home and foreign government bonds must be perfect substitutes. As the uncovered interest parity condition makes clear, when international capital mobility is perfect, it is impossible to run a different monetary policy whilst retaining a credible peg: if $e_t = e_{t+1}^E$ then assuming the bonds from each country are of equal risk, $i = i^*$. In the context of the Single European Market programme, capital market controls were lifted in Europe and capital mobility increased: the assumption of perfect international capital mobility becomes more applicable in the late 1980s. Applying the *UIP* condition to the context of the ERM, any attempt to hold the interest rate below that of Germany would lead either to a loss of reserves by the central bank (since the money supply is endogenous under fixed exchange rates) or to a devaluation. Although the ERM operated with exchange rate bands, for most countries these were quite narrow and allowed a fluctuation around the 'central bilateral rate' of only ±2.5%. Hence, members had to

- fall into line with German monetary policy, or
- seek an exchange rate realignment within the system, or
- leave it.

The lack of credibility of the new exchange rate arrangements in the financial markets meant that central banks in ERM countries frequently had to raise the domestic interest rate so as to prevent the exchange rate from moving outside the agreed exchange rate

Table 17.1 Exchange rate realignments and inflation differentials: France in the ERM

	1979–1983	1984–1987
Number of realignments: Franc v. DM	4	2
Average size (A)	7.1	4.5
Average cumulated price differential cf. Germany (B)	6.7	8.3
Degree of offsetting (A/B × 100)	105.4	54.5

Source: Emerson (1992), table 2.4, p. 42.

band. As we shall see, the ERM was a much looser arrangement than the textbook 'fixed exchange rate' case and in its early years, many realignments of exchange rates took place.

In fact there were three phases of operation of the ERM, with the disciplining effect attaining greater importance over time. To see how to use Fig. 17.2, we take the French economy as an example. As Table 17.1 shows, from 1979 to 1983 the average change in the nominal exchange rate was as great as the accumulated price differential vis-à-vis Germany. As such, there was no clear real appreciation in France in the first period, which means that disinflation pressure was largely absent. However, between 1984 and 1987, nominal exchange rate changes were clearly less than would compensate for the inflation differential: θ fell (a real appreciation) thereby imposing falling output and rising unemployment, which triggered disinflation (the French economy moved south-west along the *AD* curve in Fig. 17.2). In the final phase up to 1992, no changes in the nominal exchange rate occurred and by 1991, France had lower inflation than Germany. Disinflation had been achieved.[2]

To explore the question of whether ERM membership reduced the cost of disinflation, one approach is to calculate the sacrifice ratios (the cost in terms of unemployment of reducing inflation, see Chapter 3).[3] We can do this for the periods of disinflation in the mid-1970s and in the first half of the 1980s. The results suggest that ERM membership did not cut the unemployment cost of reducing inflation—either as compared with the earlier period or as compared with countries outside the ERM. This is shown in Table 17.2, where sacrifice ratios are presented for a number of European countries inside and outside the ERM. A comparison of France and the UK is striking: sacrifice ratios are similar in France and the UK in each period and in both cases, they *increase* in the 1980s. ERM membership may have helped France to achieve disinflation but it did not reduce the cost. Discipline, rather than credibility, seems to be the explanation for the role of the ERM in European

[2] For an analysis of the French disinflation strategy, see Blanchard and Muet (1993).

[3] In Table 17.2, the sacrifice ratio (SR) is defined as the cumulative amount of unemployment in percentage points in excess of the estimated ERU divided by the fall in inflation in percentage points over the period. For example, an SR of 2 would arise if unemployment is 1% point above the ERU for two years and inflation is 1% lower after two years; or if unemployment is 2% above the ERU for one year to achieve a reduction of inflation by 1%.

Table 17.2 Sacrifice ratios for ERM and non-ERM countries in the 1970s and 1980s

	Inflation change 1974–8	Inflation change 1980–6	Sacrifice ratio 1970s	Sacrifice ratio 1980s
ERM group				
Germany	−4.3	−5.6	2.0	2.0
France	−4.4	−11.0	0.6	2.2
Netherlands	−5.5	−6.5	0.6	2.3
Denmark	−5.1	−8.6	2.0	1.1
Non-ERM group				
UK	−9.4	−13.2	0.7	2.1
Finland	−9.1	−8.7	0.6	0.9
Austria	−5.9	−4.6	0.1	0.5

Source: Calculated from IMF data and from OECD estimates of ERUs.

disinflation. It is interesting to note that Germany—the monetary policy maker in the ERM—has the same sacrifice ratio in each period.[4]

To summarize, it is because the member countries of the ERM had the common goal of reducing inflation during the 1980s (refer back to Fig. 1.3 in Chapter 1 to see what had happened to inflation in the 1970s) that the ERM operated as an asymmetric exchange rate system with the Bundesbank as the monetary policy maker. The Bundesbank set monetary policy for the members by consent.[5]

1.2 German unification

During the so-called 'hard' phase of the ERM, when countries committed themselves to *not* realigning their exchange rates, the unanticipated shock of German reunification occurred. The background to the existence of two German economies in the 1980s can be sketched very briefly. At the end of the Second World War, the defeated German economy was divided into four zones of military occupation. The three western zones became the Federal Republic of Germany in 1949 and the Russian zone became the German Democratic Republic. The East German economy shifted from a war economy footing to a centrally planned economy. In West Germany the ownership of productive assets reverted to private owners and the economy was reintegrated into the western world trading system. Between 1949 when the two economies were separated and 1961, 2.7 million

---

[4] Egebo and Englander survey the evidence and conclude that there are no clear credibility effects associated with ERM membership: Egebo and Englander (1992). Similar conclusions about the limited response of the labour market to announced changes in monetary policy are found for the switch to base money targeting under Volcker at the Federal Reserve in the USA and the Thatcher government's medium-term financial strategy, both of which were introduced in 1979. For the former, see Blanchard (1984) and for the latter, see Buiter and Miller (1981).

[5] For an influential early article about the discipline and credibility effects of ERM membership, see Giavazzi and Pagano (1988).

people left East for West Germany. The magnitude of the migration led the East German government to create a physical separation of the two countries by building the Berlin Wall in 1961.[6]

Before the Second World War, living standards in the two parts of Germany were very similar. In 1989 when the Wall came down, it emerged that the average East German real wage was one-third that of West Germany and average labour productivity in exporting industries was one-sixth that in the west. German Economic and Monetary Union in 1990 amounted to the absorption of the smaller poor region of East Germany (16 million inhabitants) into the larger rich one of the West (62 million). East Germany's GDP was only 7% that of the west. Monetary union meant that East Germany abandoned its currency, the Ostmark, in favour of the DM. This took place at an exchange rate of 1 DM=1 OM—we shall return to the implications of the design of the monetary union below.

The full 'Economic and Monetary Union' entailed the transfer to East Germany of all West German economic and legal institutions. This has had far-reaching implications for the transition from a planned to a market economy in East Germany as compared with its eastern neighbours. It was assumed by the politicians and other policy makers in West Germany that generous fiscal transfers from the west combined with the immediate effectiveness of legal and institutional infrastructure transferred from West Germany would drive a very rapid process of catch-up for East Germany. Using the Solow–Swan model, rapid catch-up is predicted if, by virtue of unification, East Germany acquires the same steady-state characteristics as West Germany and the speed of convergence is fast: i.e. there are sharply diminishing returns to the accumulation of human and physical capital. As we shall see, the smooth transition to a higher balanced growth path as predicted by the Solow–Swan model on these assumptions, did not take place.

West German government support took the form of:

- direct subsidies to firms for restructuring and breaking up the giant enterprises of the planned economy,

- subsidies for investment in East Germany,

- investment in public infrastructure projects to modernize the communications, transport, power, and water supply systems and raise the rate of return to private investment,

- subsidies to the social security system to provide pensions in line with West German pension provisions and to pay unemployment benefits.

Meanwhile in East Germany, the economy collapsed. By 1991, GDP in East Germany was at two-thirds of its 1989 level, industrial output was at one-third of the 1989 level, and unemployment had gone from roughly zero to a rate of 30%. This was a worse depression than ever previously observed in an industrialized economy. By comparison, in the Great Depression between 1928 and 1933 industrial output in Germany fell by 40% and in the USA by 35%. The peculiarity of the East German case is that in spite of the catastrophic

---

[6] For excellent background material and analysis of German unification, see Sinn and Sinn (1994). This is a source for data reported; see also Carlin and Soskice (1997).

collapse of its economy, living standards were sustained by transfers from the west. To put this into national accounting terms, domestic absorption in East Germany was far higher than its output. There was a huge trade deficit amounting to some 75% of East German GDP and transfers from West to East Germany amounted to 50% of East German GDP in 1991.

Why did the economy collapse? The main reasons are:

- productivity, especially in the tradeables sector, was revealed to be extremely poor (in extreme cases output was unsaleable at a price close to zero),
- wage costs had to be paid in DM at the exchange rate of 1 : 1 at unification, and
- wages in DM went *up* after unification, compounding the massive loss of competitiveness of East German producers.

In summary, real wages in terms of the price of export goods quadrupled—a real exchange rate appreciation of 400%. Although the 1 : 1 exchange rate at unification has often been blamed for East Germany's loss of competitiveness, the force of this argument is weakened by the fact that wages went *up* after unification: given that the initial exchange rate created a disequilibrium that required a fall in wages, it is clear that something other than the initial parity must have been at work to push wages in the opposite direction. The unification optimists believed that productivity convergence would happen very fast; the political opportunists found this prediction convenient and promised East Germans that they would only gain from unification. The powerful West German unions sought to eliminate competition from cheap eastern production by agreeing to the rapid convergence of East to West German wages and the West German employers' associations did not oppose this.[7] The persistence of the loss of competitiveness for East Germany can therefore be traced to political and institutional reasons rather than the 'technical' decision about the exchange rate parity.

1.3 West German policy response

We turn from the story of what happened in East Germany to the consequences for the West German economy and indirectly for the rest of Western Europe. We can use Fig. 17.3 to present a stylized picture of the starting position of West Germany in 1989: West Germany was characterized by a current account surplus and stable and low inflation at a position such as *A* in Fig. 17.3. As we have seen above, the Bundesbank was pivotal in changing interest rates for the ERM member countries: to analyse West Germany, we need to use the 'large economy' model in which the *AD* curve is a function of the German interest rate. The unification shock to West Germany takes the form of a positive aggregate demand shock so the *AD* curve shifts to the right as shown—initially the interest rate remained unchanged. Much of the massive increase in spending in East Germany by consumers, firms, and government spills back to West Germany. For West Germany, the new medium-run equilibrium is at point *B*, at higher output and employment, a current account deficit, and at lower competitiveness. A real appreciation is required to permit constant inflation at lower unemployment. Two adjustment paths are shown in

---

[7] Sinn and Sinn (1994), chapter 5.

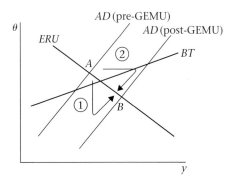

Figure 17.3 West Germany: adjusting to German unification

the diagram: the one labelled path 1 entails a nominal appreciation and as a result the new equilibrium is approached from below the *ERU* curve. The nominal appreciation raises real wages and removes the inflationary pressure associated with the tighter labour market. The second path, labelled 2, shows the fixed exchange rate adjustment, where the real appreciation occurs via a period of higher inflation than in West Germany's trading partners.

West Germany was situated in a fixed exchange rate arrangement with its largest trading partners and, as noted above, the ERM had entered its 'hard' phase with members determined not to realign. As a consequence path 1 was not taken: if it had been, the macroeconomic development of Western Europe in the 1990s might have been very different. To see why, consider the consequences of path 2: higher aggregate demand in West Germany drives output and employment up and brings with it inflationary pressure (the economy is above the *ERU* curve). There is also some evidence that the *ERU* curve shifted to the left at this time because West German workers were unwilling to accept the higher taxes imposed on them as the 'reunification surcharge'.[8] As we have seen in Chapter 4, a rise in taxation shifts the *ERU* to the left and exacerbates the inflationary pressure. A rise in inflation occurred and led the Bundesbank to intervene according to its monetary policy rule and raise the interest rate. This dampened the boom in West Germany (*AD* shifts left, because West Germany sets the 'world' interest rate for the ERM countries as well as other European countries that targeted the DM). This had important consequences for the rest of the ERM, to which we return in the next subsection.

If exchange rate realignment had been permitted, then West Germany could have adjusted to the shock via a nominal appreciation of the DM: this would have dampened inflationary pressure as adjustment to the new medium-run equilibrium would have taken place from below the *ERU* curve (path 1). Why was exchange rate realignment ruled out? It seems that the other ERM member countries were unwilling to countenance a revaluation of the DM within the ERM: this would have implied a devaluation of their currencies against the DM. Having incurred heavy unemployment costs in acquiring a reputation for 'anti-inflation credibility' via a fixed exchange rate, the view in a number of European central banks and governments was that hard-won reputations would be at stake if a realignment occurred.

[8] Carlin and Soskice 1997.

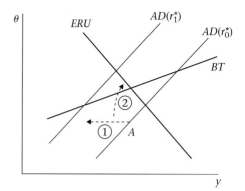

Figure 17.4 'Rest'-ERM countries and the Bundesbank after GEMU

1.4 The collapse of the ERM

For a typical non-German ERM country, the initial position in 1989 can be shown in Fig. 17.4. The country is in the phase of disinflation (see point A in Fig. 17.4) with falling inflation and with unemployment above the medium-run equilibrium. When the Bundesbank raised the interest rate, the other ERM countries had to follow suit in order to keep their exchange rates within the narrow bands. The rise in the interest rate is shown in Fig. 17.4 as a leftward shift of the AD curve since each non-German ERM country takes the German interest rate as given. This drove output down and raised unemployment further (path 1), which was politically unpopular.

The position in which the countries in the ERM (apart from Germany) found themselves lies behind one explanation for the collapse of the ERM in 1992. It is obvious from the diagram that an exchange rate depreciation (path 2) for a so-called rest-ERM country would improve its performance relative to path 1. A depreciation would effect a swift improvement in competitiveness, which would stem the rise in unemployment. Given that the initial position for these economies was below the ERU curve (the outcome of the painful period of disinflation), there was scope for this to be non-inflationary. Since a depreciation—even if not approved of *ex ante* by a rest-ERM government—appears beneficial *ex post*, this is viewed as one source of speculation in the foreign exchange market in 1992 against some of the ERM member currencies. If sentiment in the market takes the view that a government would not be unhappy *ex post* with a depreciation, a speculative attack can be successful. This is a case of speculation driven by self-fulfilling expectations.[9]

An explanation along these lines has been used to account for the successful attacks on the pound sterling, the Italian lire, and the Spanish peseta in 1992. One country that successfully defended its parity in the face of attack was France—confirming the depth of the French resolve not to take refuge in devaluation.

This analysis suggests that the fixed exchange rate arrangement of the ERM was successful whilst the members shared a common policy goal: the achievement of low inflation. However, the asymmetric shock of German unification meant that the interests of the members diverged and failure to agree on how the costs of adjustment should be shared undermined the exchange rate system. As noted earlier, the speculative attacks on the

[9] For an interesting discussion of this issue see: Eichengreen and Wyplosz (1993); also, Artis and Lewis (1993).

rest-ERM currencies were facilitated by the abolition of controls on capital flows. This took place in the context of the change in policy and institutional arrangements associated with the implementation of the Single European Market Programme (the so-called 1992 programme launched in 1986).

A puzzling feature surrounding the collapse of the ERM is the timing of the speculative attacks. One hypothesis is that the piece of news that sparked off the self-fulfilling attacks was the Danish vote against the Maastricht referendum endorsing Danish membership of the proposed common currency area. The idea is that this vote meant that the political costs associated with an exchange rate change in one of the countries was now lower because the No vote signalled increased uncertainty about the euro-project. Hence governments would be somewhat less concerned about an exchange rate change. It can be argued that this opened the way for a speculative attack.

1.5 The UK economy after the ERM

The exit of the pound sterling from the ERM was one of the most spectacular episodes in the wave of speculation surrounding the ERM in the autumn of 1992. Before turning to the ERM period, it is useful to sketch briefly the UK's experience with a variety of monetary policy regimes. Fig. 17.5 shows the different monetary regimes in operation in the UK since the early 1970s.

In the 1970s, monetary policy was largely accommodating and 'incomes policy' rather than monetary policy was viewed as the instrument to deal with the high inflation following the first oil shock in 1973. In 1979 Margaret Thatcher became Prime Minister and her government introduced an anti-inflationary monetary policy referred to as the Medium-Term Financial Strategy, which focused on targeting the growth of the money supply.

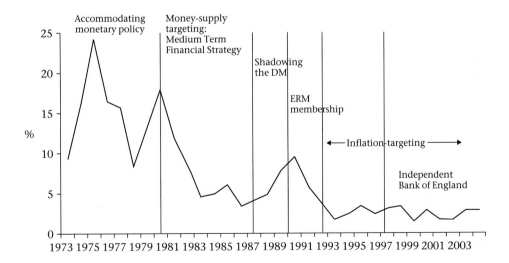

Figure 17.5 Retail Price Inflation under different monetary regimes in the UK
Source: ONS; Bank of England.

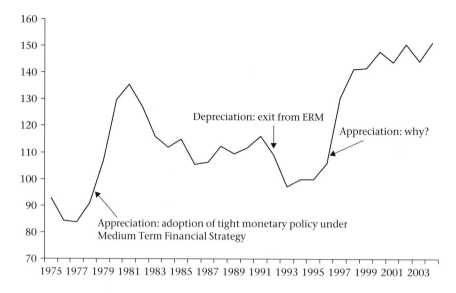

Figure 17.6 The real exchange rate in the UK, 1975–2003 (relative unit labour costs in manufacturing: rise is a real appreciation)
Source: ONS, IMF, OECD.

The decline in inflation was triggered by a sharp appreciation of the pound sterling in 1980. Many economists viewed the exchange rate appreciation as a case of exchange rate overshooting (see Chapter 9 for an explanation of the mechanics of overshooting): the combination of rapid reaction in the foreign exchange market to the tightening of monetary policy combined with sluggish adjustment of wages, prices, and output on the real side resulted in a nominal and real appreciation much larger than expected (see Fig. 17.6).

As a consequence, unemployment shot up as shown in Fig. 17.7. As discussed in Chapter 8, money supply targeting was regarded as a failure in the UK because of the unpredictable behaviour of money aggregates especially at a time of financial sector innovation and deregulation. This led to the adoption of an exchange rate target in a period in which the Deutschmark was shadowed, and then to official ERM membership in 1990.

The exit of the pound sterling from the ERM was very costly for the Conservative government in political terms but provided a well-timed boost to the British economy. The UK had laboured under a very uncompetitive exchange rate since it entered the ERM in 1990. The exit from the ERM amounted to a sharp depreciation of the effective nominal exchange rate. As can be seen in Fig. 17.6, the improvement in competitiveness was maintained in real terms, which means that the impact of the depreciation was not rapidly eroded by inflationary wage claims. There are a number of reasons for the muted response of inflation at this time, which are consistent with the macro model:

(1) Unemployment continued to rise for two years (1992 and 1993) after the bottom of the early 1990s recession.

(2) The major changes to the supply side in the UK set in motion in the 1980s gradually fed through and began to exert an anti-inflationary effect. The supply-side reforms comprised measures to reduce union bargaining power (union membership fell

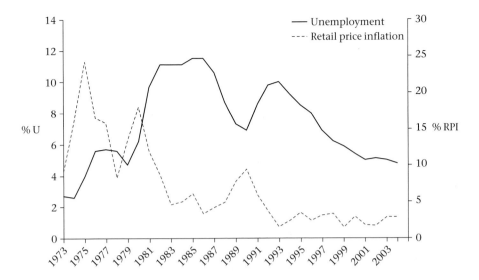

Figure 17.7 UK: inflation and unemployment, 1973–2003
Source: ONS.

from 51% in 1980 to 39% in 1990; the coverage of union wage agreements fell from 70% to 40% in the same period; days lost in strikes per 1,000 employees in all industries tumbled from 523 in 1980 to 80 in 1989); and the generosity of unemployment benefits was reduced (the replacement ratio fell from 56% to 42%).[10] Given that the organization of wage setting in the UK in the pre-reform period was generally acknowledged to be very uncooperative and to produce a high union mark-up, the effect of both labour market and benefit reforms was likely to have shifted the wage-setting curve downwards.

(3) World prices of commodities were falling, which helped offset the effect of the depreciation on the domestic currency price level in the UK.

As we have seen in the model, a depreciation shifts the economy rapidly along an *AD* curve to the north-east and if at the same time the *ERU* curve drifts to the right as a consequence of the feeding through of supply-side reforms,[11] the economy benefits from a period of non-inflationary growth. For the UK, it can be said that the timing of the collapse of the ERM was fortuitous.

The second half of the 1990s through to the early years of the new century saw the most successful period of macroeconomic performance for the UK in the post-war era. The most striking feature was the decline in unemployment in the face of low inflation (see Fig. 17.7). The argument that supply-side reform in the context of a sensible framework for macroeconomic policy accounts for the sustained fall in unemployment without

[10] OECD *Employment Outlook* (2004), table 3.3; Strike data from *Employment Gazette*, March 1983; December 1991.

[11] For a useful description of the supply-side reforms and an evaluation of their impact, see Card and Freeman (2004).

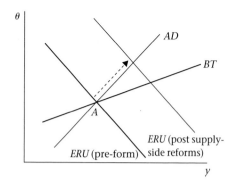

Figure 17.8 UK from 1997: supply-side reforms hypothesis
Source: ONS.

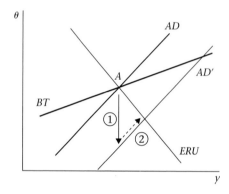

Figure 17.9 UK from 1997: aggregate demand shift hypothesis

rising inflation from 1997 can be illustrated in Fig. 17.8. The economy begins in 1996–7 at a point like *A* with trade balance and inflation at about the level of its trading partners. Assuming that the *ERU* shifts to the right due to the supply-side reforms, the economy will experience falling unemployment and inflation below its competitors as shown. Note that according to this hypothesis, the channel for the supply-side reforms to drive up output is through their impact on the real exchange rate and net exports. The current account improves steadily.

However, it is obvious from the data in Fig. 17.6 that there is a problem with this as the sole explanation because of the behaviour of the real exchange rate. From 1997, there was a large real appreciation, driven by an appreciation of the *nominal* exchange rate. Yet according to the pure supply-side reform story, the real exchange rate should be depreciating. To illustrate this point, let us consider a completely different hypothesis to account for falling unemployment and modest inflation. For the sake of this example, suppose that the supply side remains unchanged but there is a boom in aggregate demand (e.g. a consumption boom). In a floating exchange rate regime, this would lead to a nominal appreciation (path 1) in Fig. 17.9 followed by adjustment along the new *AD* curve with low inflation (path 2). The economy ends up with lower unemployment, a real exchange rate appreciation, and a weaker external balance.

As the diagrams show, both scenarios are consistent with the combination of falling unemployment and low inflation. Yet they imply very different outcomes for real wages, the real exchange rate, and for the trade balance. In the first scenario, real wages decline, the real exchange rate depreciates, and the trade balance improves. In the second one, real wages rise, the real exchange rate appreciates, and the trade balance deteriorates.

Do either of these stylized pictures fit the UK's experience? As we have seen, the first corresponds poorly with the behaviour of the nominal and real exchange rate. The second entails a real appreciation but ignores the supply-side reforms and rests on the effect of an exogenous aggregate demand boom producing a nominal appreciation via a rise in the domestic interest rate (as in the small open economy Mundell–Fleming model). In addition, as we have already noted in relation to the first hypothesis, the idea that output growth was driven by rising competitiveness (path 2 in Fig. 17.9) is at odds with the facts. For most of the period, UK inflation was slightly above that of its trading partners—where the inflation rate was also on a declining trend. But there is some truth in the notion that consumer behaviour was an important part of the post-1997 growth phase. One trigger for a consumption boom was windfall gains to consumers due to changes in the financial sector (e.g. demutualization of building societies); as the stock market and real estate boom took hold this probably led consumers to view their wealth as higher and to reduce savings. As the consumption boom slackened, public expenditure took over in maintaining the growth of demand. The Labour government was able to consolidate the public finances during a period of robust private sector growth in its first term, which gave it the scope, within its fiscal rules (see Chapter 6) to introduce major public expenditure programmes in its second term from 2001.

Lying behind Fig. 17.9 is the small open economy model in which an appreciation following a positive '*IS* shock' such as a consumption boom is caused by a rise in the domestic interest rate relative to the world interest rate. However from 1997, the UK had an inflation-targeting regime, with the Bank of England using a Taylor-type Rule to adjust the interest rate. It raised the interest rate in 1997 but it is unlikely that this can account fully for the appreciation of the nominal exchange rate. As we have stressed throughout our discussion of the open economy, economic explanations of exchange rate movements are poor. One further change to the UK economy that is relevant to nominal exchange rate behaviour in the period from the mid-1990s is the emergence of export strength in knowledge-based services such as banking, finance, consulting, and other business services.[12] This helps to explain the limited deterioration of the current account balance in the face of the large real appreciation. Such a shift in export capability (a rise in net exports at a given real exchange rate) is represented in the model by a rightward shift of the *BT* curve and may help to account for the nominal appreciation. If we combine the aggregate demand, supply-side, and *BT* shifts as in Fig. 17.10, we have the elements for a systematic consideration of the driving forces behind the evolution of the British economy since the mid-1990s.

[12] For an interesting analysis of the changing structure of the UK balance of payments (in an international perspective), see Rowthorn and Coutts (2004).

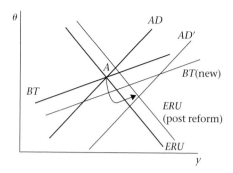

Figure 17.10 UK from 1997: synthetic hypothesis

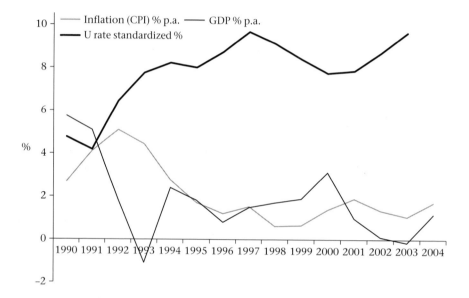

Figure 17.11 Germany: growth, unemployment, and inflation 1990–2004
Source: OECD.

1.6 **Longer-term effects on Germany**

The drama of German unification was analysed for West and East Germany separately. But how did the German economy as an entity look as the 1990s proceeded? For Germany, the unification boom was rapidly replaced by a sharp recession in 1993. In the decade from 1994, the economy grew slowly at around 1.4% p.a. The eurozone as a whole grew at 2.1% p.a. The recession was partly the outcome of the natural unwinding of the extraordinary boost to demand in 1990 and partly the result of the tightening of monetary policy discussed earlier. Unemployment remained stubbornly high throughout the decade and inflation after peaking in 1992 at 5% fell to close to zero by 1998 (Fig. 17.11). The nominal exchange rate appreciated by about 20% from 1991 to 1995 (as other trading partners previously in the ERM experienced depreciations); there was little movement in the second half of the decade.

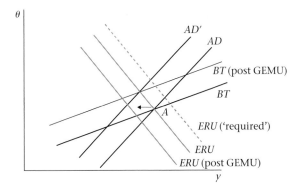

Figure 17.12 Unified Germany, 1990s

For the German economy as a whole, unification represented a negative external trade shock: the export capability of the eastern part was extremely low given the real wage that emerged as part of the political settlement. Hence the economy had a new region with a huge external deficit. In Fig. 17.12, this is shown by the leftward shift in both the *AD* and *BT* curves. Moreover, the low capital stock per East German worker implies a negative productivity shock for the German economy as a whole. To the extent that wage claims were not moderated in the light of this, the *ERU* curve shifts left. This was exacerbated by the additional taxes associated with unification—which at least in the short term were resisted by West German workers. The widening federal government deficit associated with unification is likely also to have produced a downward revision by consumers of their wealth: as the decade proceeded, the vision of East Germany as a profitable 'investment project' receded. This is probably part of the explanation for depressed consumption expenditure in Germany. When considered together, these consequences of unification amount to a negative external supply-side shock for Germany—and provide a marked contrast with the fortunes of the UK over the same period.

In contrast to some early predictions, a rapid productivity catch-up to bring the supply side of East Germany up to a level comparable with the west has not taken place. In the face of a negative external supply-side shock, in order for unemployment to decline in a sustainable way, the *ERU* curve must be shifted to the right (as shown by the 'required' *ERU* curve in Fig. 17.12). In other words, supply-side improvements are required to enable Germany to overcome the legacy of unification. Germany needs a real depreciation vis-à-vis its main trading partners, many of whom are inside the eurozone. Real wages must be cut relative to productivity to bring about a real depreciation. It may be more difficult to achieve a real depreciation when a nominal depreciation is not available to use in conjunction with any supply-side reform. An additional difficulty is that although lower inflation in Germany is required to achieve a real depreciation, lower German inflation inside the eurozone implies a *higher* real interest rate in Germany than in the other members. A higher real interest rate will dampen investment and other interest-sensitive spending, depressing the overall level of activity. We shall return to the problems of achieving the required wage restraint within a monetary union in the next section.

However, a balanced diagnosis of the current weakness of the German economy requires attention also to be drawn to the persistently depressed state of *domestic* aggregate demand. Relative to other eurozone economies net exports have performed well in

Table 17.3 Contributions of domestic demand and the external balance to GDP growth, eurozone 1995–2005

% p.a.	Real GDP	Domestic demand	External balance
Eurozone	2.0	1.8	0.2
Germany	1.3	0.6	0.7
France	2.2	2.4	−0.2
Italy	1.5	1.9	−0.4
Spain	3.2	3.7	−0.6

Source: Oxford Economic Forecasting.

Germany, suggesting that there has been some turnaround in the impact of unification on exporting capacity. As Table 17.3 illustrates, Germany's low growth as compared with other eurozone economies is associated with a strong contribution of net exports and an extremely weak contribution of domestic demand. With its specialization in capital goods and vehicles, Germany has benefited from the strong growth in demand for machinery and equipment from China. It has also utilized the opportunities to enhance export competitiveness that have come from outsourcing activities to the low cost transition economies in central Europe. This is discussed further in Chapter 18. Consumption, investment, and the public sector have made a very limited contribution to demand. The weakness of investment is a worrying indicator that even the relative strength of the export sector may be vulnerable. In terms of Fig. 17.12 some reversal of the leftward shifts of the *BT* and *ERU* curves appear to have taken place; meanwhile the *AD* curve has shifted further left, leaving the economy with a substantial external surplus. Weak growth is reflected in the deterioration in the public sector financial balance and the rise in the private sector financial balance as well as the external surplus (see Fig. 17.13). As set out in Chapter 2, the relationship between the financial balances can be seen by rearranging the goods market equilibrium condition.

$$(s_y y^{disp} - I(r) - c_0) + (t_y y - g) = x - m_y y \qquad \text{(goods market equilibrium condition)}$$

The series for the private sector financial balance in Fig. 17.13 is constructed using the accounting identity equivalent of this equation.[13] The pattern of the financial balances in the 2000s in Germany is reminiscent of the pattern in Japan at the outset of its long period of stagnation (see Fig. 17.24).

1.7 Summing up

We used the macro model to examine the nature of the German unification shock and to explore its consequences for Germany—East, West, and unified—and for other countries in the ERM system. Although the initial impact of the shock was a positive aggregate

---

[13] The private sector financial balance includes the statistical discrepancy. Note also that the current account is shown rather than the trade balance.

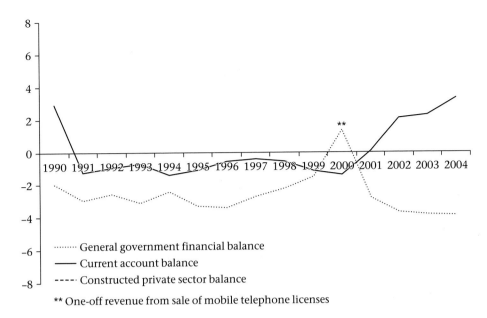

Figure 17.13 Germany financial balances, 1990–2004, % GDP
Source: OECD.

demand shock for West Germany, the deeper negative supply-side consequences only became apparent in later years and were exacerbated by the conditions agreed at unification between unions, employers associations, and government for the rapid convergence of East to West German wage levels irrespective of productivity developments. We emphasized the importance of the ERM in providing an external anchor for members seeking to reduce inflation. This helps to explain their reluctance to participate in an orderly realignment of exchange rates in the aftermath of unification. Such a realignment may have prevented the sharp tightening of monetary policy by the Bundesbank and the subsequent collapse of the ERM. As we have seen, some countries benefited from the monetary easing that accompanied their exit from the ERM. The UK economy recovered and in this context, a new macroeconomic policy framework was developed, which culminated in the independence of the Bank of England in 1997.

Over the past decade the performance of the German and British economies contrast sharply.

The British economy:

• reaped the benefits of earlier supply-side reforms
• benefited from the depreciation associated with ERM exit
• introduced a stable macroeconomic policy framework
• experienced strong consumption demand and timely fiscal consolidation
• benefited from a favourable improvement in the terms of trade, which helped contain inflationary pressures.

The German economy:

- suffered from the unfavourable supply-side shock associated with German unification
- lost the ability to use monetary policy by joining EMU
- experienced weak consumption demand.

2 Macroeconomic policy within EMU

Formally, Economic and Monetary Union began in 1999 when the exchange rates were irrevocably fixed between the members. However, it came into full effect with twelve members when the euro was introduced and national currencies removed on 1 January 2002. This represents a unique and untested structure for the conduct of macroeconomic policy in modern times: there is one independent central bank, twelve politically independent fiscal authorities, and twelve labour markets. In this section, we use the macro model to look at the part played by the single central bank, the national fiscal policy makers, and national labour markets in the operation of the monetary union and the performance of its members.

2.1 What kind of monetary policy maker is the European Central Bank?

The ECB was established as a monetary policy maker independent of governments: it was to set its own target (target independence) and choose its policy instrument(s) (instrument independence). The two key influences over its constitution were, on the one hand, the legacy of its predecessor as monetary policy maker for Europe, the German Bundesbank, and on the other, the prevailing mainstream consensus amongst economists as to how monetary policy should be conducted. The Bundesbank was constitutionally required to maintain a stable price level and had always placed weight on developments in the monetary aggregates (measures of the money supply) as a guide to how monetary policy should be adjusted. The consensus view amongst economists is captured in the idea of the central bank using a Taylor-type Rule to actively adjust the interest rate so as to steer the economy toward an inflation target (refer back to Chapter 3 and Chapter 5 for details of the Taylor Rule and to Chapter 8 for monetary targeting).

The ECB set itself an inflation target *zone* of 0 to 2% and defined its monetary policy strategy as having 'two pillars', where the pillars are the inflation rate and the growth rate of monetary aggregates. By contrast, the newly independent Bank of England was given its *symmetric* inflation target by the government (initially 2.5%; lowered to 2% at the end of 2003) and describes its strategy as that of 'inflation targeting'. The contrasting experience of West Germany and the UK with earlier episodes of targeting monetary aggregates is reflected in these differences (see Chapter 8 for further discussion). Under the ECB's initial set-up, there was no presumption that it would act if inflation fell below 2% and, given the dangers of deflation (discussed in Chapter 5 and below in relation to Japan), this is a worrying aspect of the policy design. In 2003, the ECB clarified its

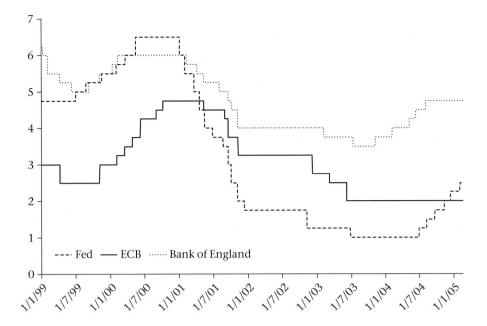

Figure 17.14 Official interest rates: US Federal Reserve, ECB, and Bank of England
Source: Bank of England, ECB, US Federal Reserve Board

definition of price stability to state that it 'aims to maintain inflation rates below but close to 2% over the medium term'.[14] Although this reduces the asymmetry, it does not remove it. The experience of the Bank of England also suggests that it may have been wiser for the ECB to have had a somewhat higher inflation target initially and then to lower it.

From the analysis by economists over its early years of operation, it appears that the ECB is indeed operating a Taylor-type monetary policy rule. One empirical study suggests that on the basis of the analysis of data up to the end of 2002, the ECB's decisions on the interest rate are well predicted using a Taylor Rule in which the weights on inflation and the output gap are the same as the ones that characterize the decisions of the US Federal Reserve.[15] These weights predict better than do those that were characteristic of the Bundesbank.[16] Yet the ECB has been widely criticized as reacting sluggishly to the slowdown in the European economy in 2001. Fig. 17.14 displays the official interest rates set by the US Federal Reserve, the ECB, and the Bank of England.

There are several ways of reconciling the fact that the ECB's decisions seem to match those that the Fed would have taken faced with the same data and the perception that the ECB's decisions have been 'too little, too late'. If the ECB uses the same Monetary

---

[14] European Central Bank (2004: 51).   [15] For example, Giavazzi and Favero (2003).
[16] The weights estimated for the Fed by Giavazzi and Favero are 1.10 on the inflation term and 0.79 on the output gap; for the Bundesbank, 1.95 on the inflation term and 0.30 on the output gap. The rule is expressed in terms of the nominal interest rate and therefore the comparison is with weights of 1.5 and 0.5 respectively in Taylor's original estimates for the Fed.

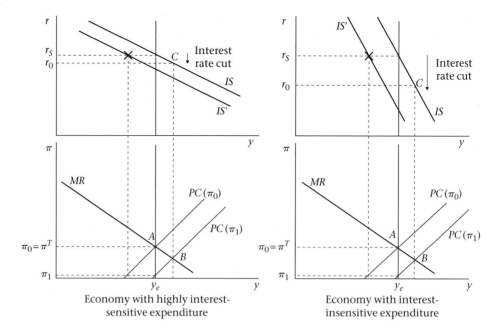

Figure 17.15 Interest rate decisions following an *IS* shock

Policy Rule as the Federal Reserve, it will produce the appropriate stabilizing effect for the EMU economy only if the EMU economy responds to it in the same way as does the US economy to the Fed's decisions. As we have seen in Chapter 5, the coefficients in the 'optimal' Taylor-type rule for an economy depend on

- the slope of the Phillips curve,
- the slope of the *IS* curve, and
- the weight on inflation in the central bank's preference function.

Even if the weights on inflation and output in the loss function of two central banks are identical, if one economy has a flatter Phillips curve (greater real wage rigidity) and a steeper *IS* curve (less sensitivity of aggregate demand to the real interest rate) then its Taylor Rule should place less weight on output deviations relative to inflation deviations and a higher weight on both than in the economy with steeper Phillips curves and more interest-sensitive expenditure.

As an illustration, we compare two economies identical in all respects except in the interest sensitivity of expenditure (Fig. 17.15). Both economies are subjected to the same negative temporary *IS* shock—e.g. as the result of a loss of confidence due to a terrorist attack (*IS* shifts to *IS'*). Each central bank observes a fall in output as shown by the large × and works out the optimal interest rate response. This is the cut in the interest rate that will raise output to the level associated with point *B* in the lower panel. As the diagram makes clear, the supply side of the two economies is identical and so is the utility function of the two central banks. Hence the lower panel for each economy is identical. But in response to the same 'signal' of lower output, the central bank in the economy (on the right) with the less interest-sensitive expenditure should implement a larger cut in the interest rate. If it implements the same interest rate cut as the other economy, it will delay the return of the economy to equilibrium output. The situation is worse if private sector agents are more affected by the pessimism associated with the shock than by the action and rhetoric of the central bank and/or if they doubt the effectiveness with which the central bank will respond to shocks. This may turn a temporary *IS* shock into a longer-lasting one and therefore require larger interest rate cuts since the stabilizing interest rate (r_S) will also have fallen.

In addition to substantive concerns about the ECB's reaction function, the analysis of monetary policy in Chapter 5 suggests that the ECB should:

- have a clearly stated symmetric inflation target or target range. This may help to stabilize private sector expectations and put in place a firmer bulwark against the possibility of deflation.
- operate with greater transparency. A clearer understanding by the public of how decisions are made would come with the publication of minutes of the Governing Council meetings and of the ECB's forward-looking forecasts for inflation and other variables. As we have seen in Chapter 7, the interaction between forward-looking private sector agents and a forward-looking central bank can be stabilizing but this useful feedback mechanism is neutralized if the behaviour of the central bank is poorly explained and poorly understood.

2.2 Member country adjustments within EMU

In Chapter 11, we showed how to analyse whether a country would suffer from giving up the nominal exchange rate as a policy instrument. The same tools help us to examine what happens at the individual country level when it becomes a member of a common currency area like the eurozone. The issue is how the absence of the exchange rate instrument (or equivalently, of domestic monetary policy autonomy) affects the adjustment of the economy to a country-specific shock or to an underlying structural change that is not common across the member countries of the currency union.

2.2.1 Country-specific aggregate demand shocks

We recall from Chapter 11 that the effect on output of a temporary negative aggregate demand shock would be fully offset under a flexible exchange rate regime via a depreciation. However, an inflation-targeting central bank is unlikely to allow full offsetting because of the consequences for future inflation (by cutting real wages, the depreciation takes the economy above the *ERU* line and therefore entails a rise—albeit temporary—in inflation). Nevertheless, to the extent that some depreciation takes place in response to the shock, the impact on output will be less harsh than in an economy in a currency union.

Clearly depreciation is not an option in the face of a country-specific shock inside the eurozone. Irrespective of the exchange rate/monetary policy regime, the automatic fiscal stabilizers will operate to cushion the impact on the economy of the aggregate demand shock—unless they are prevented from working by a fiscal rule. In addition, the government may use discretionary fiscal policy to offset the shock. We have seen in Chapter 6 that to ensure fiscal prudence over the longer run, a government using fiscal policy for stabilization must ensure that the measures are reversed when cyclical conditions improve. This may cause greater political difficulties than does the use of monetary/exchange rate responses to temporary fluctuations.

2.2.2 Real exchange rate adjustment

A major issue that arises within a common currency area is how required changes in the real exchange rate between members can be brought about. Italy's performance provides a useful example. The weakness of Italy's export performance over the past decade is reflected in the data in Table 17.3. Moreover since 2000, there has been a 20% deterioration in Italy's competitiveness as measured by relative unit labour costs, which would be expected to produce a further weakening of net exports. In the past, Italy traditionally relied on periodic depreciations of the nominal exchange rate to restore its competitive position. Within EMU, this is not possible.

We have already encountered the case of Germany, which as a consequence of unification experienced a negative external trade shock. Italy's problems may reflect a more gradual erosion of its competitive strength generated by the emergence of new sources of supply of manufactures in Europe (as the transition economies have restructured their production sectors and upgraded the quality of their exports) and Asia. To restore output and employment, it is necessary for there to be a real depreciation of the exchange rate. For this to be sustainable, the *ERU* curve has to shift to the right, i.e. supply-side changes must be implemented. As discussed in Chapter 4, there are a range of policy measures that can shift the *ERU* curve: e.g. labour and product market reforms, social security reforms, a wage accord. The shift in the *ERU* is required irrespective of the exchange rate regime: however, when a change in the nominal exchange rate is not available, all the adjustment must take place through domestic wage and price inflation lower than elsewhere in the union. When currency union inflation rates are already low, this is likely to be both difficult and potentially hazardous as deflation may set in.

The opposite situation can also arise within the eurozone. Suppose that a country in the eurozone experiences a positive external trade shock. Ireland would be a good candidate. In this case, the economy needs to move to a new medium-run equilibrium at lower unemployment and with a real appreciation: higher real wages are consistent with trade balance. To achieve this adjustment without a nominal appreciation, there needs to be a period with Irish inflation above that of the rest of the union. As shown in Fig. 17.16, path 1 involving a nominal appreciation is not available to Ireland within EMU. Path 2 entails a period with higher inflation than the eurozone average. Countries that require such a real appreciation should not be subject to criticism within the union because of the rise in inflation: this is the only way that real exchange rate adjustment can occur. Once again, the situation is likely to be complicated by the fact that a rise in Irish inflation will reduce the real interest rate and may well fuel a domestic aggregate demand boom; a tightening of domestic fiscal policy would be appropriate to help stabilize this.

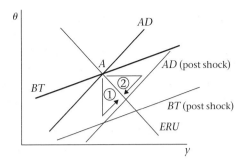

Figure 17.16 Adjustment to a positive trade shock inside (2) and outside (1) EMU

2.3 Does EMU need fiscal rules?

Since the flexible national use of fiscal policy for stabilization takes on greater importance for countries that belong to a currency union, why are there fiscal rules for EMU members? In Chapter 6, we set out the arguments for countries at the *national* level managing their fiscal policy according to the principles of the prudent fiscal policy rule. To make the case for fiscal rules at the *supranational* level of EMU, it is necessary to argue

- that membership of a common currency area reduces the constraints on the use of national fiscal policy to achieve lower medium-run unemployment and

- reduces the incentives for countries to adopt fiscal rules that ensure the solvency of the government, and

- that there are spillovers from national fiscal profligacy to the union as a whole.

The fiscal policy prisoners' dilemma in a currency union. As we have seen, for a small open economy, a fiscal expansion allows the economy to move to a medium-run equilibrium at lower unemployment with stable inflation (at the target rate) because the terms of trade can be shifted in its favour. External constraints from the reaction of the money market and the foreign exchange market provide a check on this behaviour for an economy operating under either fixed or flexible exchange rates. However, with such external discipline absent for individual member countries in the eurozone, the temptation to seek to reduce unemployment by a fiscal expansion is a potential problem. If all members reason the same way, the result is a higher interest rate for the monetary union and a phase of higher inflation that is costly to eliminate since for the currency union as a whole (thinking of it as a closed economy), equilibrium unemployment is unique. The roots of the logic of the Stability and Growth Pact of the eurozone may lie in this prisoners' dilemma in fiscal policy. A more detailed analysis of the prisoners' dilemma in this context is provided in section 4 of Chapter 12.

'Bail out' for a government in a currency union. If a country is unable to finance its expenditure (i.e. pay for its current expenditure and service its existing outstanding debt) either by raising taxation or by selling more bonds, it is said to face a debt crisis. What are the consequences? It must either default on its debts, receive transfers from other countries, or reduce the value of the debt by monetizing it through inflation. The use of a rise in inflation to generate seignorage revenue is explained in Chapter 6. Applying these arguments to EMU countries, a member facing a debt crisis could default, be 'bailed out' by other

members, or secure the help of the ECB to relax monetary policy and allow inflation to rise. Since each of these alternatives potentially entails spillovers to other eurozone members, there is a prima-facie argument for the existence of fiscal rules.

Spillovers from national fiscal profligacy. Externalities include the contagion effect that might flow to other financial markets in the eurozone if one country defaulted or was in danger of defaulting. Although the markets may price in the additional risk solely to the country concerned, there is a danger that this would spill over to other members, raising the risk premium and therefore the cost of borrowing for all eurozone countries. Such a spillover would be more likely if it was thought that there would be a bail-out of the fiscally irresponsible government. A 'bail-out' via transfers from other members would impose a direct cost on them; a rise in union inflation if ECB behaviour was affected would impose an indirect cost via the increase in inflation. As noted in Chapter 6, there is a vigorous debate as to the plausibility and likely size of such effects. In addition to the question of whether externalities exist is the issue of whether the incentives for fiscal prudence are affected by membership of a currency union. As noted above, for a country outside a currency union, fiscal profligacy can prompt speculation in the foreign exchange market against the currency. This potential punishment may be an effective external control on government behaviour that is removed on entry to a common currency area.

The benchmark of the prudent fiscal policy rule allows fiscal policy to play a role in stabilization (the full effects of the automatic stabilizers are allowed to work plus discretionary fiscal policy is available for use in the event of a country-specific demand shock). Moreover, it provides a framework for evaluating whether structural government expenditure problems can be safely addressed by allowing borrowing to increase or whether taxation has to rise. As noted in Chapter 6, the fiscal rules in the EU's SGP are not necessarily consistent with the PFPR. By limiting government deficits to 3%, the SGP may limit the role of the automatic stabilizers. The consequence is that fiscal policy can become procyclical. The failure of the large eurozone economies to meet the 3% limit in the early years of EMU highlights the dangers of a poorly designed policy. By failing to penalize these countries, the credibility of the policy framework is undermined; on the other hand, had penalties been imposed, an even stronger procyclical impulse may have occurred.

The second component of the SGP, that the cyclically adjusted deficit to GDP ratio be less than or equal to zero, imposes an arbitrary constraint on the appropriate method of dealing with structural problems, such as situations in which a cumulative shortfall in expenditure on public infrastructure needs to be made good. Equally, the rule is unnecessary for solvency in the case of economies with low debt to GDP ratios and in which the growth rate exceeds the real interest rate (refer back to Chapter 6 for the details on debt dynamics). Such a rule may therefore prevent some of the accession economies which are catching up and therefore have growth rates in excess of the real interest rate from setting an optimal fiscal policy.

2.4 Summing up

Europe has introduced a highly experimental framework for macroeconomic policy making. One success of the framework has been revealed by the episode of the depreciation of the dollar in 2004–5. In previous decades a depreciation of the dollar led to upward pressure on the Deutschmark and to exchange rate tensions between European economies. The single currency prevents this. However, evaluating the framework through the lens of the macro model has revealed many pitfalls in its design and implementation. The ECB's goals and choice of instruments lack the clarity of the inflation-targeting framework established around the same time for the Bank of England. The ECB has failed to convey its intention of robustly stabilizing the European economy. As we shall see, this contrasts with the behaviour of the US Federal Reserve. The attempt to mitigate the legitimate problem of a prisoners' dilemma in fiscal policy in member states by imposing fiscal rules has backfired as the rules were poorly designed and have proved impossible to implement in the context of a weak European economy. Finally, too little attention appears to have been given to the problems that arise from the need for real exchange rates to change between member countries.

3 USA: the new economy boom and its aftermath

The decade of the 1990s was a good one for the US economy. The economy displayed both increased dynamism and less instability than was true of earlier post-war decades. Table 17.4 shows the key economic indicators for each post-war decade. The improvement in performance in the 1990s as compared with the 1970s and 1980s is clear in terms of inflation and unemployment. Looking at GDP growth, the variability of growth as measured by the standard deviation is lower than in any of the previous post-war decades. This led some observers to claim at the end of the 1990s that successful management of US macroeconomic policy had resulted in the end of business cycles. The second major phenomenon from the mid-1990s was the revival in the growth of productivity driven by information and communications technology (ICT). The two combined—the 'end of cycles' and 'new technology boom'—were referred to as the 'New Economy'. The recession in 2001 and the sharp rise in unemployment thereafter suggest that the claim that cycles have been eliminated was too hasty.

3.1 The benign 1990s

As compared with the dramatic developments in Europe with the fall of communism, the reunification of Germany, and the creation of an experimental macroeconomic policy framework in the European Monetary Union, the 1990s was a decade free of major external or domestic shocks for the US economy. Unlike the 1970s and 1980s in which there were major swings in world commodity and energy prices, these prices were rather stable and on average price shocks were downwards rather than upwards.

Macroeconomic policy was also characterized by the absence of major policy mistakes. Monetary policy was in the hands of the activist Federal Reserve under the Chairmanship of Alan Greenspan. Continuity was the hallmark of the period: the Fed seemed to be following an implicit inflation-targeting policy with the objective of stabilizing growth

Table 17.4 US economic performance by decade: 1950s–1990s

	1950s	1960s	1970s	1980s	1990s
GDP growth, ave.	4.2	4.4	3.3	3.0	3.0
Standard deviation	*3.9*	*2.1*	*2.8*	*2.7*	*1.6*
Productivity growth, ave.	2.8	2.8	2.1	1.5	2.1
Standard deviation	*4.3*	*4.2*	*4.3*	*2.9*	*2.6*
Unemployment, ave.	4.5	4.8	6.2	7.3	5.8
Standard deviation	*1.3*	*1.1*	*1.2*	*1.5*	*1.0*
Inflation, ave.	2.1	2.3	7.1	5.7	3.0
Standard deviation	*2.4*	*1.5*	*2.7*	*3.5*	*1.1*

Note: Productivity growth is for the non-farm business sector.
Source: Mankiw (2002).

expectations as well as keeping inflation low and stable. In an overview of monetary policy in the 1990s, Greg Mankiw (2002) concluded by noting that:

- the period was a benign one for the Fed in the sense that shocks, especially bad ones, were largely absent;
- such a period makes the policy maker look good;
- the strength of the dollar made the Fed's job easier by dampening inflationary pressure.

Fiscal policy was relieved of active stabilization duties during this decade. The Clinton administration took advantage of the favourable circumstances of buoyant private sector demand to undertake a serious fiscal consolidation. The cyclically adjusted (i.e. structural) government balance went from a deficit of 4.5% in 1990 to a surplus of 0.9% in 2000 and the ratio of gross government debt to GDP peaked at 76% in 1993 and had fallen to 59% by 2000.[17] Clinton advisors argued that a determined fiscal consolidation would not be contractionary and could even be expansionary (see Chapter 6 for the details of the logic of so-called expansionary fiscal consolidations). Clinton's Secretary of the Treasury Robert Rubin argued that the fiscal consolidation was a crucial condition for the boom in the second half of the 1990s:[18]

I have no doubt that the 1993 [deficit reduction] program and the eight years of a policy of fiscal discipline were key and indispensable in a virtuous cycle of deficit reduction promoting growth which further reduced the deficit, which then in turn further increased growth and so on back and forth, and that this policy was thus key and indispensable in generating the economic and fiscal developments of the Clinton years. . . . I think a lasting legacy of this administration will be

---

[17] OECD *Economic Outlook* (December 2003), Annex table 29.
[18] Rubin (2002:132–3). In his comment on the same paper (p. 124), Ronald Reagan's chief economic adviser, Martin Feldstein, has a more cynical interpretation: 'Although it is tempting to think of these budget surpluses as a deliberate policy of national debt reduction, I think the reality is simply that Republicans in Congress blocked spending increases . . . while President Clinton blocked Republican initiatives to cut taxes'.

the successful experiment of promoting economic recovery and sustained growth through fiscal discipline rather than through fiscal expansion . . .

3.2 New technology boom

The US economy experienced a positive supply-side shock associated with the introduction and diffusion of new technology from the mid-1990s. The evidence suggests that the USA was unique amongst the advanced economies in relation to the new technology shock in two important respects:

(1) the bulk of the key innovations in the ICT sector took place in the USA, and

(2) diffusion of the innovations across the economy occurred more rapidly there than elsewhere. Table 17.5 shows how the contribution of ICT to the acceleration of productivity growth from 1995 can be quantified.[19]

From the growth-accounting calculations in Table 17.5, we can see that ICT makes a contribution to productivity growth via capital deepening—i.e. in the form of higher levels of computer hardware, software, and other communications equipment per worker. This contribution more than doubles to account for nearly 1% per annum growth of productivity after 1995. Note that the contribution of 'other types of capital' and of 'labour quality' is unchanged in the post-1995 period. The row 'total factor productivity growth' shows the contribution to labour productivity growth that cannot be attributed to either

Table 17.5 Estimates of the role of new technology in the post-1995 US productivity revival: annual percentage rates of change

	1973–95	1995–2002
Labour productivity	1.4	2.6
Contributions from:		
A. Capital deepening, of which	0.7	1.2
ICT capital	0.4	0.9
other types of capital	0.3	0.3
B. Labour quality	0.3	0.3
C. Total factor productivity, of which	0.4	1.1
ICT producing industries	0.3	0.7
other industries	0.1	0.4

Source: Gordon (2004) (from table 3). Gordon updates the estimates by Oliner and Sichel (2000).

[19] This table uses the growth-accounting methodology explained in Chapter 13. Note that the estimated effect of ICT capital assumes the investment was productive. The collapse of the boom revealed that this was not always the case with the resulting excess capacity of ICT capital.

capital deepening or to changes in labour quality. This increased sharply because of technological progress by ICT producers and elsewhere in the economy, which reflects the diffusion of the new technologies.

In Chapters 13 and 14, we examined the way the economy adjusts to a faster rate of technical progress in the Solow-swan growth model. In this section, we focus on the implications of a faster rate of technical progress for macroeconomic policy, from a short- to medium-run perspective. In Chapter 4 and again in Chapter 15 in the section on wage and price setting, we raised the question of what a rise in productivity means for equilibrium employment. It was argued there that eventually changes in productivity (or in productivity growth) will be incorporated into wage-setting behaviour with the result that in the long-run equilibrium unemployment is unaffected. However, it may take some years for a change in trend productivity growth to be distinguishable from a purely cyclical effect or from a transitory productivity shock, and incorporated into wage-setting behaviour. During this time, equilibrium employment rises because the *PS* curve shifts up relative to the *WS* curve.

Fig. 17.17 illustrates how an inflation-targeting central bank responds to a supply-side shock, where we show the supply shock by the rise in equilibrium output from y_e to y'_e. The first indication of the productivity shock is a fall in inflation: faster productivity growth means a lower growth of unit costs and hence of prices (A to B). The central

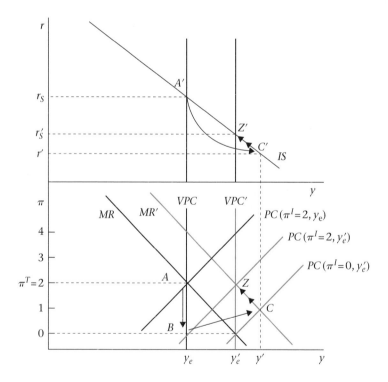

Figure 17.17 Positive supply shock: the US technology boom

bank can deduce from this signal that a possible cause is a positive supply-side shock. Its optimal response is a cut in the interest rate to r' as shown (points C and C'). Each period, the central bank must examine the data to check that it is consistent with a permanent supply-side improvement and to see whether wage behaviour has begun to incorporate the productivity growth improvement. If inflation behaves in line with this hypothesis, the central bank will use its monetary rule to guide the economy along the new MR curve (MR') back to target inflation at the lower equilibrium unemployment rate (point Z). It is unlikely that the reduction in equilibrium unemployment will last indefinitely, however, since we would expect real wage growth expectations eventually to adjust to the new faster growth rate of productivity. In terms of the simple model, this means that eventually, the WS curve shifts up in line with the initial shift in the PS, returning equilibrium employment to its original level.

In the *Economic Report of the President* 2000 (written by the Chairman of the Council of Economic Advisers), it is noted that[20]

the new higher trend growth rate of productivity since 1995 could have temporarily lowered the NAIRU, because it can take many years for firms and workers to recognize this favorable development and incorporate it into their wage-setting process. In the meantime, the productivity surprise can stabilize inflation of unit labor costs and prices even at unemployment rates below the previous NAIRU.

The Report suggests that a one-percentage-point positive surprise in productivity growth has the effect of lowering the equilibrium rate of unemployment by one and a quarter percentage points.

3.3 Imbalances, twin deficits, and the decline of the dollar

The counterpart of the fiscal consolidation undertaken by the Clinton administration during the 1990s was a dramatic swing in the private sector's financial balance from a surplus of 5% of GDP in 1991–2 to a deficit of 6% in the year 2000 (Fig. 17.18). A major driver of the deterioration in the private sector balance over the 1990s was a change in household savings behaviour, which was about 7% of disposable income in the early 1990s but only 1.7% in 2001 (comparing the two recession years). As the discussion of savings behaviour in Chapter 7 makes clear, the influence of the technology boom on the evaluation by households of their lifetime wealth may have played a role. The return to financial balance of the private sector by 2003 is mainly due to an unusually large increase in retained profits (i.e. business sector savings) and a decline in business sector investment in this period: the household savings ratio has remained unchanged at about 2% of disposable income.

The analysis of US performance in the 1990s to this point has largely ignored the openness of the economy. But in the early 2000s, the US economy saw the emergence of a very large current account deficit as shown in Fig.17.18. Indeed the US economy has been characterized by the so-called twin deficits with the private sector in financial balance and a large government deficit financed by borrowing from abroad. During the

---

[20] US Government (2000).

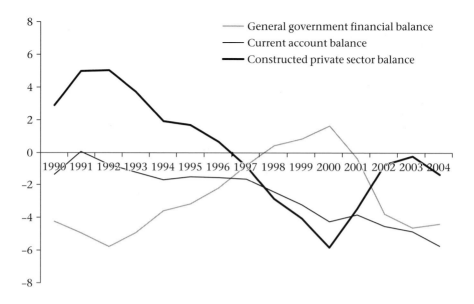

Figure 17.18 US financial balances, 1990–2004, % GDP
Source: OECD.

1990s, the deterioration in the current account partly reflected strong private investment in the USA and partly the collapse of household savings—i.e. it was financing private investment and consumption in the USA. Since 2000, it is mainly financing government borrowing. In the short run, the implementation of a very expansionary fiscal policy in 2002 and 2003 provided a strongly countercyclical boost, which reinforced the aggressive loosening of monetary policy begun in 2001 (see Fig. 17.14). This helped the economy to return to strong growth as shown in Fig. 17.19. This contrasts with the much tighter fiscal policy stance in the eurozone. Table 17.6 shows that the discretionary fiscal boost provided by the US government in the four years from 2000 was 5.6% of GDP as compared with a boost of 0.3% of GDP provided by eurozone governments. Many economists believe that US fiscal policy has been irresponsibly expansionary in this period. Eurozone governments have been criticized for breaking the rules of the Stability and Growth Pact, but as we can see, the fiscal impulse was actually very small.

Taking account of the open economy aspects, the trajectory of the US economy over the 1990s can be shown in Fig. 17.20. The economy began in approximate current account balance in 1990 and with stable inflation. By 2000, equilibrium unemployment was lower (shown in the diagram in terms of higher output); there was little change in the real exchange rate over the period and there was a substantial current account deficit at the end. The shift in the *AD* curve was driven in this period by strong private sector consumption and investment expenditure; the *ERU* shifted to the right as a consequence of the positive supply shock associated with the technology boom. The weakening of private sector demand in 2000–1 was offset to a large extent by countercyclical monetary and fiscal policy as discussed above.

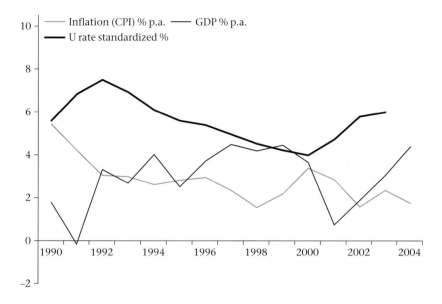

Figure 17.19 USA: growth, unemployment, and inflation, 1990–2004
Source: OECD.

Table 17.6 Discretionary fiscal policy in the USA and the eurozone, 2000–2003: change in the cyclically adjusted (structural) deficit (% GDP)

	US	Eurozone
2000–01	1.4	0.5
2001–02	3.2	0.1
2002–03	0.9	−0.4
2003–04	0.1	0.1

Note: +ve means an increase in the structural deficit, i.e. a positive fiscal impulse.
Source: OECD *Economic Outlook* (December 2004), tables.

It has been widely argued that the US current account deficit is not sustainable.[21] A particularly clear way of characterizing the problem for the USA is that the trade deficit (i.e. goods and services) is about the same size as the current account deficit. For example, in 2003, the current account deficit was 4.8% of GDP and the trade deficit including transfers such as the remittances of immigrant workers was 5.1%. To see why this is important, it is useful to draw a parallel with the debt dynamics of the public sector as explained in Chapter 6. We saw there that *if* the real interest rate exceeds the growth

[21] For a short, clear summary, see Quiggin (2004). For a more extensive analysis, see Obstfeld and Rogoff (2004). For an early discussion of imbalances in the USA, see Godley and Izurieta (2001).

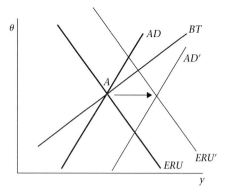

Figure 17.20 The 1990s in the USA

rate, the debt ratio will only be constant if there is a primary budget surplus. The actual budget balance can be in deficit reflecting the interest payments on the debt but the primary balance must be in surplus. Transferring this analysis to external borrowing, the analogue of the primary balance is the trade balance including transfers and of the actual budget balance is the current account balance, which includes net interest flows. Just as a primary budget deficit is inconsistent with stabilizing the government debt ratio and the actual deficit, a trade deficit is inconsistent with stabilizing the ratio of external debt to GDP and holding the current account deficit constant. The logic of debt dynamics means that the US trade deficit must be radically reduced in order to stabilize the current account deficit and the external debt ratio.[22]

From Fig. 17.20 it is clear that a reduction in the trade deficit requires some combination of the following:

- a reduction in aggregate demand that shifts the *AD* curve to the left (from *AD'*) through increases in private savings and a return of the public sector to surplus;

- a real depreciation of the dollar, which would produce a shift to the north-east along the *AD'* curve;

- a positive external trade shock that would shift the *BT* curve to the right.

As the diagram makes clear, for a sustainable reduction of the deficit, a depreciation would have to be accompanied by a tightening of aggregate demand to take the economy to a position on the *ERU'* curve closer to the intersection with the *BT* curve. Because of the size of the US economy, a deficit of 5–6% of its GDP entails a rapid build-up of foreign ownership of US assets. A consequence of the small size of the tradeable sector in relation to the US economy as a whole is that a large real depreciation is required to bring about the required deficit reduction. Obstfeld and Rogoff provide an illustrative scenario

[22] The external position of the USA is complicated because it has huge overseas assets, which earn a higher return than its even larger overseas liabilities. This means that it was actually receiving 0.3% of GDP in net property income in 2003 despite having net overseas liabilities of some 25% of GDP. This makes the relationship between the trade deficit, the growth rate, and the real interest rate more complex than the analysis for the public sector in Chapter 6. Nevertheless the conclusion that the US trade deficit must be radically reduced to ensure overseas debt converges to a sustainable ratio to GDP still holds good.

to suggest that a rapid reduction of the current account by 4% of GDP could entail a real depreciation of as much as 40%.

Although the dollar depreciated in 2003–4 by over 30% against the euro, the corresponding trade-weighted depreciation was much less—around 13%. The explanation lies in the behaviour of governments and central banks in Asia. Japan intervened heavily to prevent the appreciation of the yen and the Chinese currency has remained fixed against the dollar, with the Chinese also building up large official reserves of dollars. This example highlights the difficulties with achieving orderly changes in real exchange rates. We saw in the discussion of EMU the difficulties that arise when real exchange rate changes are required within a currency union; this example brings out the difficulties that exist when nominal exchange rate changes are possible. It is unclear how appropriate changes in the nominal exchange rate can be brought about and whether international cooperation between governments can play a role. The difficulties of international policy coordination are discussed in Chapter 12. If an orderly adjustment of the US economy is not achieved through a combination of increased saving (private and public), depreciation of the dollar and serious policies to reduce imports, for example through policies to reduce the consumption of imported oil, adjustment may take place in a more chaotic manner via a currency crisis (e.g. as a consequence of a speculative attack on the dollar similar to that on ERM currencies in 1992).

4 Japan: more than a decade of stagnation

The post-1990 Japanese economy provides a dramatic contrast to that of the United States. Growth in Japan has been half as fast as that of the USA and unemployment has been rising steadily since 1990, reaching rates above those in the USA for the first time since the war. As Table 17.7 makes clear, Japan grew very fast in the pre-1973 period; like the other big blocs, growth slowed sharply following the first oil crisis in 1973; but unlike the USA and the EU, the 1980s was a decade of fairly rapid growth for Japan. The 1990s therefore provides a contrast with Japan's previous dynamism as well as with the revival

Table 17.7 Comparative growth rates: Japan, USA, European Union, 1960–2002

	Real GDP growth (% p.a. growth rates)			Labour productivity growth Business sector (% p.a. growth rates)		
	Japan	USA	EU	Japan	USA	EU
1960–1973	9.7	4.0	4.7	8.4	2.6	5.4
1973–1979	3.5	2.9	2.6	2.8	0.3	2.5
1979–1989	3.8	3.0	2.2	2.8	1.3	2.0
1989–2002	1.4	2.8	2.1	1.3	1.9	1.6

Source: Calculated from OECD, *Economic Outlook*.

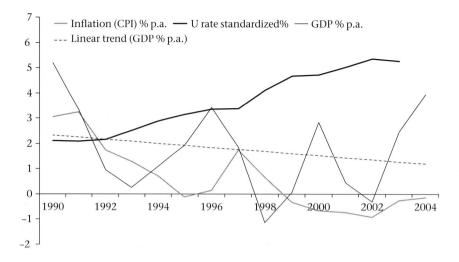

Figure 17.21 Japan: growth, unemployment, and inflation 1990–2004
Source: OECD.

of productivity growth in the USA. Europe's dynamism has drifted gently downwards period by period.

The strong growth at the end of the 1980s in Japan is generally viewed as representing a 'bubble' phenomenon in which asset prices—both stock market and property—increased well beyond levels consistent with the underlying fundamentals. This resulted in a wave of investment in projects with very poor returns. As a consequence, there was a substantial 'correction' in asset prices followed by a period of low investment. Whilst asset price bubbles have been observed in a number of the advanced economies (e.g. Sweden and the UK in the late 1980s, the USA in the late 1990s), they do not necessarily produce prolonged recession. The Japanese bubble and its aftermath have raised questions about the soundness of the Japanese financial system and the interconnections between the large corporate groups and the banks.[23] It has also raised questions about the soundness of macroeconomic policy making, which we focus on here.

The decline in growth over the post-1990 period is shown in Fig. 17.21 (the dashed line shows the trend). The steady rise in unemployment from the very low rates (of less than 3%) characteristic of the Japanese economy before 1990 is apparent; as is the emergence for the first time in an advanced economy in the post-war period of deflation, i.e. inflation rates below zero. Deflation was observed in 1995 and then from 1999 through to 2004.

The key macroeconomic features of the 1990s were weak aggregate demand on the part of the domestic private sector as investment and consumption spending were reduced by firms and households that suffered capital losses in the asset price crash. This was compounded by a negative trade shock in 1998 as a consequence of the Asian crisis. There was also a weakening of the supply side reflected in poor productivity growth, the opposite of the situation in the USA. The other notable macroeconomic development

[23] For an overview of the advantages and disadvantages of the Japanese financial system and its link with other specific characteristics of Japanese capitalism, see Boltho and Corbett (2000).

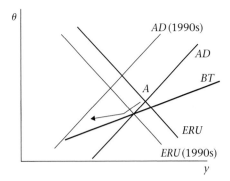

Figure 17.22 The 1990s in Japan

was the substantial nominal (50%) and real appreciation (40%) of the exchange rate between 1990 and 1995. Thereafter the exchange rate fluctuated but with little trend. The trajectory of the Japanese economy in the 1990s can be represented in Fig. 17.22. The economy began the period with a current account surplus (to the left of the *BT* curve) and with inflation and the real exchange rate stable so we can think of the economy as being on the *ERU* at point *A*. The weakness of aggregate demand is shown in the leftward shift of the *AD* curve, and the deterioration on the supply side by the leftward shift of the *ERU* curve, indicating that at any real exchange rate, equilibrium unemployment is higher. The strong appreciation of the yen drove the economy south-west as shown. Although the *ERU* shifted left, the combination of the appreciation and the extreme weakness of domestic demand meant that inflation was falling continuously through this period, taking it, as noted, into deflation.

What role has economic policy played in the Japanese slump?[24] We first consider monetary policy. In Chapters 2 and 5 we discussed how the presence of a liquidity trap or the attainment of the zero nominal interest rate bound inhibits the normal operation of monetary policy and we stressed the importance for the monetary authorities of setting their policy environment in a way that prevents deflation from emerging.[25] Once deflation sets in, monetary policy becomes much harder to use effectively. The Bank of Japan did not adopt an inflation-targeting regime; had it done so with a symmetric inflation target of, say 2%, it is possible that deflation may have been avoided.

However, as Fig. 17.23 illustrates, once deflation prevails, even an inflation target of 2% does not by itself provide a means for the economy to escape from the trap. The reason is that with weak aggregate demand, the *IS* curve is low (shown by '*IS* 1990s') and with deflation, the min *r* line showing the zero *nominal* interest rate is high (with deflation of 1%, the min *r* line is at a real interest rate of 1%). Thus unless the inflation target of 2% is incorporated in private sector expectations so that the min *r* line shifts down, the region of the *IS* curve that is shown as dashed is unattainable using the monetary policy rule because of the zero nominal interest rate bound. The most the central bank can do is to implement a zero interest rate policy, ZIRP, and attain point *B*. Since unemployment in the economy is above the equilibrium, deflation will worsen, which will push up the real

---

[24] For trenchant arguments as to the role of economic policy mistakes—especially in monetary policy—in the genesis of Japan's deflation, see Posen (2003) and Posen and Ito (2004).
[25] For an early analysis of Japan as a liquidity trap see Krugman (1998).

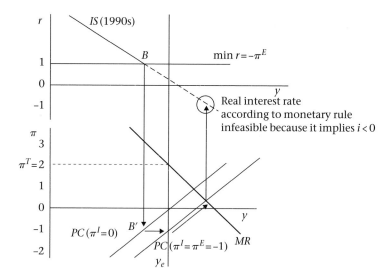

Figure 17.23 Japan: zero nominal interest rate bound

interest rate (i.e. the min *r* line will shift upwards), reducing activity further. As discussed in Chapter 5, deflation is likely to depress aggregate demand further because of its effect on balance sheets (deflation increases the real value of debts) and the consequent failure of businesses. This would shift the *IS* curve further to the left.

As argued in Chapter 5, it may not be easy to generate the positive inflation expectations to release the economy from a deflation trap. Notwithstanding these inherent difficulties, there has been much criticism of the Bank of Japan both for its failure to seriously attempt to prevent deflation from becoming established and then for failing to undertake the measures that would enhance the prospects for a return to positive inflation.[26] There appear to have been failures by the Bank of Japan:

- to consistently present the view that its inflation target is a rate of say 2% and in over-emphasizing the likelihood of 'runaway inflation' if it takes more determined steps to overcome deflation. In fact since its independence in 1998, the Bank of Japan has emphasized its mandate is price stability. The Governor of the Bank of Japan stated in 2000 that 'inflation is most likely uncontrollable once triggered'.[27]
- in stressing too much its 'independence' to the detriment of cooperation with the government in addressing Japan's problems. For example as noted in Chapter 5, a combined fiscal and monetary policy may be useful when there is a liquidity trap. For example, the central bank could directly fund tax cuts by monetizing the government debt: the government sells bonds to the central bank and sends out cheques to all citizens.
- More specifically it is argued that the Bank of Japan throttled the nascent recovery from the mid-1990s by raising the interest rate too soon. A second mistake was made in 2000 when the Bank of Japan having introduced a zero interest rate policy, ZIRP, in early

[26] For example, see Bernanke (2000). See also Posen and Ito (2004).
[27] Posen and Ito (2004 22).

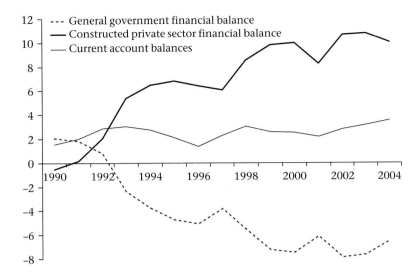

Figure 17.24 Japan financial balances, 1990–2004, % GDP
Source: OECD.

1999 lifted it in 2000, tightening policy in the face of deflation. The economy contracted and ZIRP was reintroduced.

Fiscal policy also appears to have been poorly judged in Japan. It was tightened in 1997, helping to prevent recovery from taking hold. Meanwhile the lengthy period of depressed growth has had the effect of producing large fiscal deficits and a rapid build-up in the share of government debt (from 68% in 1990 to 155% in 2003). Note that just as with private sector debt, the real value of government debt increases in a situation of deflation.

The striking character of Japan's evolution since 1990 is reflected in a different way in Fig. 17.24. In an economy with a chronic lack of demand, there is an *ex ante* excess of domestic savings over investment. This drives output down. Looking at the financial balances, there is a rising trend of the private sector financial surplus, which is mirrored by the absorption of those surpluses in the growth of the government deficit and a substantial, though stable, current account surplus. A revival of private investment is clearly needed as part of the solution to Japan's problems: this would raise the level of activity, reduce the private sector financial surplus, and by raising tax revenue reverse the trend of the public sector balance.

As noted above, the real appreciation in the early 1990s weakened activity in Japan by dampening net exports. From Fig. 17.22, it is clear that a real depreciation taking the economy to the north-east would help boost demand and many commentators have argued that one way to think about how monetary policy could contribute to Japan's recovery is in terms of creating inflation expectations as a way of weakening the currency. Fig. 17.22 also makes it clear that stronger domestic demand would need to accompany a depreciation if the current account surplus is not to widen further—a development likely to undermine attempts to achieve a sustained depreciation.

In the light of the analysis in section 4 on the US economy, where it was argued that a substantial depreciation of the dollar is required, we can see that a substantial depreciation of the Yen against the dollar is unlikely: the Bank of Japan had to intervene very heavily to prevent the Yen from appreciating in 2004. One source of the revival of growth in Japan from 2002 was the growth of exports to China. This is a new source of export demand and will generate faster growth in Japan as long as it is not extinguished by a large real appreciation (recall the analysis of a positive external trade shock: *AD* and *BT* shift right). The Chinese currency is fixed to the dollar but the substantially higher inflation in China than in Japan is helping to offset the effect of the nominal depreciation of the Chinese currency against the yen.

Signs of an end to Japanese stagnation and deflation are apparent in 2004–5. The strength of net exports has broadened beyond China and has been accompanied by the recovery of investment as is characteristic of 'normal' business cycle upswings. Fiscal and monetary policy mistakes have not been repeated and both the government and the Bank of Japan have made public commitments not to tighten policy prematurely. As supply-side reforms implemented over the past decade feed through, a sustainable recovery is possible. [28]

5 Conclusions

We have shown how the macro model can be used to interpret the role that has been played by

- external shocks,
- government policy, and
- institutional changes
- in a number of key episodes across Europe, the USA, and Japan in recent decades.

  We have made use of

- the 3-equation model to characterize monetary policy making,
- the open economy model to examine how economies adjusted to different shocks,
- the financial balances identity to track the relationship between private sector, public sector, and the external account,
- the analysis of fiscal sustainability, and
- growth accounting.

Descriptive data has been presented and linked with the key concepts in the models. We have seen how the data can be used to check whether the predictions of the model are broadly consistent with the facts. In the case of recent UK performance, we used the data to help refine our hypotheses.

---

[28] See Posen (2004).

In this book, we have sought to construct an integrated way of understanding how the macroeconomy works (i.e. a positive analysis) as well as identifying the policy implications (a normative analysis) and have emphasized the consensus that has emerged amongst economists on both of these dimensions. However by looking at the practice of macro policy in this chapter, we have noted some gaps between what would seem to be optimal policies and those that have been implemented. What might account for this?

• Political economy factors are evidently present in some cases. For example, there were common interests (in the short term) of the unions, employers' associations, and government in West Germany in pushing for wage convergence in East Germany. However, in other cases, the coalition of interests is harder to uncover such as in the refusal of the Bank of Japan to act in response to the danger of deflation or the unwillingness of the ERM members to realign their exchange rates following German unification. In both these cases, excessive weight seems to have been placed on the need to hold policy invariant.

• As is often the case, it is easier to diagnose the nature of shocks with the benefit of hindsight. This was true of the external supply shocks of the 1970s (as discussed in Chapter 11) and is also true of the German unification shock. Few economists recognized how very weak the productive base of the East German economy was. However, we have also seen an interesting case where a sensible policy framework seems to have allowed the policy maker to learn about the nature of the shock. In the late 1990s, the Federal Reserve was willing to experiment by allowing unemployment to keep falling below what was thought to be the equilibrium rate whilst inflationary pressures remained absent.

■ QUESTIONS FOR DISCUSSION

QUESTION A. 'Euro-zone growth is being throttled by monetary policy that is too tight and fiscal policy that is too loose.' Evaluate this claim, which was made in 2005.

QUESTION B. Under the pressure of political objectives and of the potential for migration of 'cheap labour' from East to West Germany, German unification took the form of extending to East Germany welfare benefits and collective bargaining wage rates from West Germany. The result was high and persistent unemployment in East Germany and a long-term burden on the German economy. In the light of this experience discuss the possible consequences of the removal of controls on the migration of workers from the EU accession countries to the rest of the EU. Note that average labour costs in the accession countries are about one-seventh those in West Germany. Evaluate alternative policies the non-accession EU member countries could implement. [Relevant reading: Sinn (2004).]

QUESTION C. Adapt the analysis of debt dynamics in Chapter 6 to show why a country cannot run a trade (i.e. goods and services) deficit indefinitely. What is the analogue in this case to the primary deficit in the case of the government's indebtedness? You may assume that the real rate of interest on foreign-owned assets is greater than the growth rate. Apply your analysis to developments in the US goods and services deficit and current account deficit.

QUESTION D. A report in the *Financial Times* in January 2005 said 'While Japan has enjoyed a period of decent growth, prices, bank lending and land values have continued to fall. Growth petered out in the second half of last year. Longer term, mounting public debt and an ageing population threaten fiscal disaster'. Explain the dangers posed by inappropriate macroeconomic policy to the sustained recovery of the Japanese economy.

QUESTION E. Choose an OECD country to analyse. Use the appendix tables for the OECD *Economic Outlook*, which are available from the OECD *Economic Outlook* page on the OECD website. Choose a five-year period (do not choose an EMU country after 1999) and analyse the role of the nominal exchange rate and the real exchange rate in the evolution of inflation and unemployment.

QUESTION F. The UK and Sweden have not joined EMU in the first round. Is the case for and against membership the same for each of these countries? [Refer to the resources on the UK Treasury's Euro website: **www.hm-treasury.gov.uk/documents/the_euro/ euro _index_index.cfm**]

QUESTION G. 'For a member of the eurozone, its economic performance no longer depends on the real exchange rate'. Comment on this statement first using theoretical arguments and, second, by looking at the data for a eurozone country of your choice since 1999.

18 Unemployment: Institutions, Shocks, and Policies

The aim of this chapter is to investigate an important issue of economic performance and policy using the models presented in this book to help organize and clarify the analysis. The rise of European unemployment starting in the early 1970s has been a major preoccupation for economists and policy makers. Unemployment represents a waste of economic resources if the unemployed are involuntarily jobless. Moreover recent research finds that unemployment is associated with substantial psychic costs over and above the loss of income.[1] Survey evidence also suggests that those who do not become unemployed are nevertheless unhappier when unemployment is higher: this is interpreted as support for the notion that the fear of unemployment affects well-being. Taking a broad view of utility and not simply counting the income and output cost associated with job loss emphasizes the importance of understanding the forces behind the trends and cross-country variations in unemployment.

During the European 'Golden Age' of the 1950s and 1960s when rapid growth in GDP per capita produced a clear catching up of living standards to those in the United States, unemployment rates were low in spite of rapid structural change. In this period rapid structural change took the form of the shift of labour out of the agricultural sector into industry; and the growth of the service sector's share of employment. As Table 18.1 illustrates, in Europe one-quarter of employment was still in agriculture in 1950 and this had fallen to 10% by 1973; in Japan, the shift was from just under one-half to 13% in

Table 18.1 Structural change 1950 to 1973 (% employment)

	1950			1973		
	Agriculture	Industry	Services	Agriculture	Industry	Services
EUR4	25.2	38.3	36.5	9.7	41.2	49.1
Japan	48.3	22.6	29.1	13.4	37.2	49.4
US	13.0	33.3	53.7	2.9	41.7	55.4

Note: EUR4 is the unweighted average of France, West Germany, Italy, and the UK.
Source: Maddison (1991), table C5.

[1] Survey evidence is from about a quarter of a million individuals in twelve European countries and the USA from the 1970s to the 1990s: di Tella, MacCulloch, and Oswald (2003).

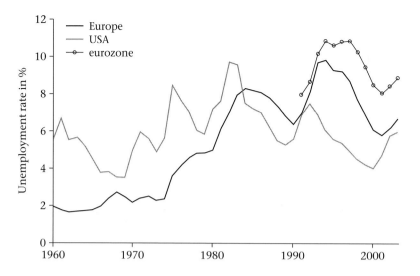

Figure 18.1 Unemployment in the USA, Europe, and the eurozone, 1960–2003

Note: Europe = 15 countries, unweighted average.

Source: OECD, *Economic Outlook*; IMF International Financial Statistics.

1973. Both Europe and Japan moved to an employment structure more like that of the USA by 1973. Once unemployment had fallen after the end of the Second World War in Europe, it remained very low through the 1960s and into the 1970s in spite of the large shifts in the pattern of employment across sectors. It was well below that of the United States. However, in the last thirty years, the trend has been upwards, reaching a higher peak after each successive recession as shown in Fig. 18.1. By contrast, in the USA, unemployment has fluctuated around a rate of 5–6%, with lower peak rates of unemployment after the mid-1980s. The line for Europe shows the unweighted average of European countries: the higher level of unemployment for the eurozone reflects both the absence of the low unemployment countries of the UK, Sweden, Norway, and Switzerland and the effect of weighting: it is the big eurozone countries that have higher than average unemployment.

This broad contrast between the trends in European and US unemployment fits that of some but not all European countries. It is characteristic, for example, of Germany, France, Italy, and Spain but not the UK or many of the small European countries. The worst period for British unemployment was the 1980s. In recent years, rates as low as the early 1970s have been achieved. By contrast, many of the small European countries were able to avoid the big rise in unemployment in the 1980s.

Fig. 18.2 provides a graphic illustration of the dispersion of unemployment rates across the OECD countries in the last forty years by plotting the five-yearly average unemployment rates for nineteen OECD countries. The OECD's standardized measure of unemployment is used. This is based on comparable labour market survey based definitions of unemployment, which allows cross-country comparisons to be made. The line goes through the data points for the USA and we can see that the cloud of countries below the

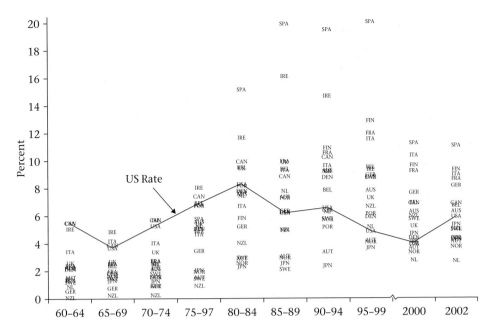

Figure 18.2 Trends and heterogeneity in unemployment across 19 OECD countries, 1960–2002
Source: Howell (2005), Fig. 1.1, p. 10.

USA up to the early 1980s moves above the USA thereafter. Nevertheless several European countries have had spectacular improvements in their unemployment performance in the 1990s: in addition to the UK, Ireland, the Netherlands, and Denmark are notable. Austria and Norway have very low rates throughout and Sweden and Finland have very low unemployment until the early 1990s: both improve strongly over the course of the 1990s. Spanish unemployment is the highest at 20% in the mid-1980s; it falls to less than 12% by the end of the period.

In this chapter, we begin by clarifying the key definitions relevant to the analysis of unemployment and some summary facts about labour market outcomes. We then turn to explanations for the broad trajectory of unemployment in the OECD countries: why did it rise in the 1970s, why did high unemployment persist in the 1980s, and what explains the cross-country variations? This entails using the macro models to systematize the determinants of changes in actual and equilibrium unemployment and to identify the role of shocks and institutions and how the two may interact. We look more closely at some examples of so-called employment miracles in the 1990s: the Netherlands, the UK, and Ireland. In Section 4, we investigate the question of whether increased European unemployment in the 1980s and increased wage inequality in the USA were two sides of the same coin: were common technology and trade shocks reflected in unemployment in Europe and inequality in the USA because of differences in labour market institutions in the two blocs? Section 5 examines whether the change in monetary arrangements in Europe with the formation of the European Monetary Union would be expected to affect unemployment. Finally, we conclude by examining the calls for labour market flexibility as the solution to Europe's unemployment problem and explanations for why such reforms are difficult to achieve.

1 Labour market outcomes

1.1 Definitions: employment, unemployment, and inactivity

There is not a one-for-one relationship between changes in employment and in unemployment. To see this, we need to note that the population of working age is divided into three labour market states: employed, unemployed (actively looking for work and able to begin), and inactive. Thus

$$Pop \equiv U + E + I$$
$$\equiv LF + I$$

where Pop is the population of working age, U is the number unemployed, E the number employed, I the inactive, and LF the labour force. The unemployment rate, u, is defined in terms of the labour force:

$$u \equiv \frac{U}{LF} \equiv \frac{U}{E + U} \qquad \text{(unemployment rate)}$$

whereas the employment rate, e, is normally defined in terms of the working age population:

$$e \equiv \frac{E}{Pop}. \qquad \text{(employment rate)}$$

The connection between the unemployment and employment rates is provided by the participation rate, which shows the proportion of the working age population active in the labour market:

$$PR \equiv \frac{LF}{Pop}. \qquad \text{(participation rate)}$$

These definitions imply:

$$e \equiv PR(1 - u)$$

and, equally, that

$$u \equiv 1 - \frac{e}{PR}.$$

Thus, a rise in the employment rate will only be reflected in a fall in the unemployment rate to the extent that it is not offset by a rise in participation as the economically inactive are brought back into the labour force. The participation rate is not fixed: during a recession, when unemployment rises, participation rates tend to fall. The opposite happens in upswings. There are also important long-run trends, as women's participation has risen over the last half-century and men's has tended to fall. In addition, policies affect participation. The most important from the perspective of interpreting trends in Europe have been sickness and disability regulations and retirement practices, especially the use of early retirement schemes.

Attempts to reduce the unemployment rate by lowering participation through early retirement schemes or easy access to disability benefits are likely to have serious consequences for macroeconomic management. Such measures can be counterproductive by reducing equilibrium employment through two channels: first, if these schemes have the effect of raising the tax burden, then equilibrium employment goes down because the price-setting curve shifts downwards. Second, measures to remove people from the labour force may reduce competition for jobs, which shifts the wage-setting curve upwards.

1.2 Who are the jobless?

Employment rates are lower for women and for older people: this is the outcome of a combination of lower participation rates and higher unemployment rates. As Table 18.2 shows, this is a common feature across the OECD countries. Nevertheless, there are interesting cross-country variations: the shortfall of the women's employment rate below that of men is least in the Nordic countries at around 10 percentage points or less; the shortfall is highest in the Catholic southern European countries and Ireland at nearly 30 percentage points or more. For older people (aged 55–64), the employment rate shortfall as compared with those between the ages of 25 and 54 is lowest in Japan and Switzerland (about 15 percentage points) and highest in the continental economies of Austria, Belgium, and the Netherlands (between 45 and 52 percentage points).

Unemployment rates for younger people (15–24 years) are higher than those for older workers across the OECD. The smallest excess unemployment rates for young people are in the European countries with well-established apprenticeship schemes (Austria, Germany, and Switzerland), in Japan and in Denmark, Ireland, and the Netherlands. In each case the gap is less than 5 percentage points. At the other end of the scale, we find Italy and Spain with unemployment rates for young people of between 17 and 22 points higher than for older workers.

Along the dimensions discussed so far, the USA does not stand out from the European countries. It does however, when we look at the weight of the long-term unemployed in total unemployment. Those unemployed for more than twelve months make up less than one-tenth of the unemployed in the USA. Only Norway is similar in Europe. All the other countries have much higher shares of long-term unemployment—ranging from around 30% in the UK, the Nordic countries, Austria, and Switzerland to 50% in Germany and 66% in Italy.

As we shall explore further in Section 4, the burden of joblessness has fallen unevenly according to levels of education. Although unemployment rates are much higher for those who have not completed secondary school, as compared with those with tertiary education (Table 18.3), even more striking is the difference in the *employment* rates of these groups: only one-half of the population of working age who have less than secondary education in the European Union are employed as compared with 80% of those with tertiary education. These numbers will be influenced by composition effects

Table 18.2 Patterns of joblessness, 1998

	Women's employment rate: shortfall with men's, % points	Older (55–64) employment rate: shortfall with 25–54 years, % points	Younger (15–24) unemployment rate: excess over 25–54 years, % points	Long-term unemployment, % of total
Europe	19	35	9	41
USA	14	23	7	8
Japan	20	15	4	20
Austria	18	52	3	28
Belgium	23	52	12	63
Denmark	11	33	3	29
Finland	7	43	12	29
France	18	44	15	44
Germany	19	38	2	52
Ireland	28	29	4	57
Italy	35	39	22	66
Netherlands	24	46	5	49
Norway	9	19	7	11
Spain	37	38	17	55
Sweden	4	18	9	33
Switzerland	18	14	3	28
UK	15	31	7	33

Note: Europe is the unweighted average of the European countries shown.
Source: OECD *Employment Outlook*.

Table 18.3 Difference in joblessness by educational group, EU 1998

	Less than completed secondary education	Completed tertiary education	Difference
Unemployment rate	10.6	6.0	4.6
Employment rate	52.0	82.1	30.1

Source: OECD *Employment Outlook*.

according to the factors in Table 18.2—i.e. those with less than secondary education are more likely to be women and to be older.

We can summarize the state of unemployment and employment in Europe as compared with the United States at the beginning of the twenty-first century by using the data in Table 18.4. The sixteen European countries are divided into two groups: high unemployment and low unemployment. Performance in the nine *low* unemployment European countries is comparable to the USA on all dimensions. The increase in the employment rates in the Netherlands and Ireland are striking and lend support to the term 'employment miracle', which has been used to describe their performance in the 1990s. This is discussed in more detail in section 3.

Table 18.4 Summary of employment and unemployment in Europe and the USA

	Unemployment 2002	ERU 2002	Employment rate 2001	Change in employment rate 1980–82 to 2001	Employment rate least ed. quartile 2001
USA	5.8	5.1	71.6	7.9	67.4
EU	7.6	7.4	63.9	3.3	55.6
Europe					
9 low *u*, of which	4.2	4.3	72.2	4.4	64.2
Ireland	4.4	5.9	65.0	10.9	50.5
Netherlands	2.7	3.5	74.1	11.5	57.7
Sweden	4.0	5.1	73.8	−5.0	71.7
UK	5.2	5.3	69.9	4.4	60.5
7 high *u*, of which	9.1	8.7	60.5	0.2	49.4
France	9.0	9.2	62.0	0.6	54.2
Germany	7.8	7.0	65.9	4.6	56.2
Italy	9.2	9.0	54.9	−1.8	35.1

Notes: Low unemployment group also includes: Norway, Denmark, Austria, Switzerland.
Final column uses background data for OECD Education at a Glance.
High unemployment group also includes: Spain, Greece, Finland, Belgium.
ERU is OECD's estimate of structural unemployment.
Source: OECD, *Employment Outlook*, various years.

The European high unemployment group of seven countries has higher actual and equilibrium unemployment and markedly lower employment rates—both on average and for the least educated. As discussed in Chapter 17, Germany's performance in the 1990s has been strongly influenced by unification and its aftermath. However France and Italy have no such 'excuse'. Especially worrisome are the low employment rates in France and Italy, and in Italy, the fact that only just over one-third of the least educated quartile are in work.

2 Trends and cross-country variation in European unemployment

2.1 Framework and overview

The ingredients that are useful in accounting for both the path of average European unemployment shown in Fig. 18.1, and for the cross-country variation in unemployment shown in Fig. 18.2 can be divided into the following.

(1) The determinants of shifts in actual unemployment around the equilibrium. These can arise from domestic aggregate demand policy, for example to push unemployment

up in order to reduce inflation (see Figs. 17.1 and 17.2). Alternatively, aggregate demand can fluctuate in response to *IS* shocks or from international shocks to trade, the interest rate or to world commodity prices (e.g. Figs. 17.3, 17.9, and 17.14).

(2) The determinants of equilibrium unemployment, as discussed in Chapter 4 and Chapter 11. These centre on factors shifting the wage-setting and/or price-setting curves or the unemployment/vacancy (Beveridge) curve[2] and hence, in the open economy, the *ERU* curve (see Fig. 11.7):

- The *WS* curve shifts up with a rise in union bargaining power; a fall in the cost of job loss (e.g. a rise in the unemployment benefit replacement rate). The degree of coordination of wage setting also affects the *WS* curve.
- The $PS(\theta)$ curve shifts down with a rise in taxes; a deterioration in the world terms of trade between manufactures and raw materials; an unanticipated fall in trend productivity growth; a rise in the real interest rate; a fall in the pressure of competition in the product market.
- The unemployment-vacancy (Beveridge) curve shifts to the right in unemployment-vacancy space when there is a rise in the mismatch between jobs available and potential employees (see Fig. 11.4).

(3) Interactions between shocks and institutions: this is where the effect on unemployment of a shock depends on the supply-side institutions in the country. For example, a supply-side shock such as an oil shock or a slowdown in productivity growth shifts the *PS* curve down: the impact of this on equilibrium unemployment depends on the slope of the *WS* curve, i.e. on how sensitive are real wages (of wage-setters) to unemployment. One way of characterizing a flexible labour market is one in which the *WS* curve is very steep—i.e. real wages are very responsive to changes in unemployment. If the *WS* is very flat, then for a given negative external terms of trade shock, a much larger rise in unemployment is required to bring about the necessary downward adjustment of real wage claims (see Fig. 18.3 for an illustration). The degree of wage coordination in the economy is also likely to influence the unemployment impact of productivity growth and external supply shocks. In particular, in a highly coordinated economy, since wage setters optimize by choosing the best position on the *PS* curve (i.e. the real wage is taken as a constraint), a downward shift in the *PS* curve leads only to higher voluntary unemployment (since the *WS* curve for the fully coordinated economy coincides with the labour supply curve).

(4) Hysteresis and persistence mechanisms: it is argued that a sustained period of high unemployment caused by weak aggregate demand can in turn cause a deterioration in the supply side of the economy so that the equilibrium unemployment rate is pulled up too. For example, weak aggregate demand raises unemployment, which leads to higher long-term unemployment resulting in the long-term unemployed becoming detached from the labour force. As a consequence, competition for jobs is less effective and the

---

[2] Refer back to Chapter 4 for an explanation of the Beveridge curve and how it relates to the *WS-PS* curve model.

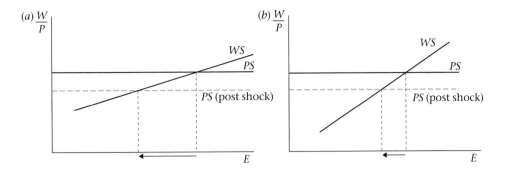

Figure 18.3 Common shock: interaction with flexible and inflexible real wages
(a) Inflexible real wages: large fall in E
(b) Flexible real wages: small fall in E

Table 18.5 Macroeconomic trends and unemployment, OECD 1960 to 1999 (five-year averages)

	U rate	Inflation	Productivity growth	Terms of trade	Tax wedge	Real interest rate
1960–64	2.1	3.6	4.0	0.7	19.2	2.1
1965–69	2.1	4.1	3.8	0.7	21.7	2.2
1970–74	2.5	8.2	3.1	−0.7	25.5	−0.2
1975–79	4.3	10.1	2.0	0.4	28.7	0.4
1980–84	6.9	9.0	1.6	−0.5	31.0	4.4
1985–89	7.7	4.0	1.5	1.3	31.4	5.2
1990–94	8.8	3.6	1.5	0.7	31.9	5.9
1995–99	8.2	1.8	1.5	0.1	31.9	3.7

Note: Unweighted data for 18 OECD countries. Productivity growth is Total Factor Productivity growth; Terms of trade is effect of changes in the terms of trade on living standards; Tax wedge as % GDP is sum of indiv. income tax, soc. security contributions (employer + employee), payroll tax, VAT (+ other indirect taxes); Real interest rate is long-run nominal interest rate minus consumer price inflation rate.
Source: Database used in Baker et al. (2005).

WS curve shifts upward. Simple models of hysteresis are set out in Chapter 4 (see e.g. Figs. 4.8–4.10).

Before looking at attempts to test the importance of one or other of these mechanisms, we set out a broad overview of the period from the late 1960s when the rise in unemployment began in Europe. Table 18.5 provides the key macroeconomic data for the OECD countries from 1960-4 to 1995-9.

1960-73. The 1960s was a period of especially low unemployment right across Europe, well below that in the USA. The roots of the rise in European unemployment are often traced to the years from 1968 to 1973, when bargaining power appears to have shifted away from employers toward workers (an upward shift in the *WS* curve as unions reduced the degree of bargaining restraint they exercised, see Chapter 4). This was reflected in a wave of strikes and wage explosions. This was also a period in which workers succeeded at the political level in getting an extension of the welfare state—taxation went up (pushing the price-setting curve down) and so did the generosity of welfare state benefits (wage-setting curve shifts up). The sharp increase in the tax wedge is shown in Table 18.5.

1973–79. The first oil shock plus a world commodity price hike occurred in 1973, bringing to an end two decades of modest improvements in the terms of trade for oil and commodity importing countries (see Fig. 18.4 and Table 18.5). This was an external supply-side shock that depressed output and employment, put upward pressure on inflation, and shifted the *ERU* curve to the left, reflecting higher equilibrium unemployment at a given real exchange rate (see Figs. 11.13 and 11.14). There was also a sharp slowdown in the growth rate of productivity, which also shifted the $PS(\theta)$ down (Table 18.5). It appears that the adjustment of wage claims in response to the productivity growth slowdown was extremely protracted, which had a lasting effect on equilibrium unemployment. The attempt of policy makers to use aggregate demand policy to offset rising unemployment left unemployment below the equilibrium, with the result that inflation was rising throughout this period.

1979 and 1980s. The second oil shock occurred in 1979 (see Fig. 18.4 and Table 18.5). As discussed in Chapter 11 (section 4.2), the response to the second oil shock was different from the first: countries sought to prevent the inflationary impact of the shock from feeding through to the economy. Monetary policy was tightened, as each country sought to dampen aggregate demand and use an appreciation of the exchange rate to mitigate the effects of the oil shock on inflation. The outcome was a rise in the world real interest rate (see Table 18.5), which shifted the $PS(\theta)$ down (see Chapter 4 section 2.2). This was followed by a lengthy period of tight macroeconomic policy aimed at bringing inflation rates down from double-digit levels.

Mid-1980s and thereafter. In the mid-1980s, there were some favourable shocks: there was a reversal in the oil and commodity prices (see Fig. 18.4 and Table 18.5) and in some countries, labour market and welfare state reforms were implemented that weakened unions and rolled back some of the gains of the early 1970s. The Single European Market programme was part of a broader move toward heightened competition in product

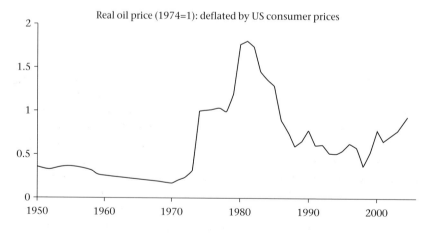

Figure 18.4 Oil prices, 1950–2004
Source: IMF Financial Statistics.

markets, which as we have seen should reduce equilibrium unemployment. Productivity growth and the tax share stabilized, preventing the need for further downward adjustment in expected real wage rises on the part of wage setters (Table 18.5).

Yet despite these reversals, unemployment did not return to its pre-1970s levels. As shown in Fig. 18.2, of particular concern is the persistence of high unemployment in the large European economies: unified Germany, France, Italy, and Spain. Following high unemployment in the 1970s and 1980s, the UK is the exception amongst the large countries in experiencing a sharp fall in unemployment in the 1990s and into the new century. In spite of facing common productivity slowdown and external trade shocks, many of the small economies were able to maintain low unemployment rates for much of the 25-year period.

2.2 Empirical studies

Starting from the *WS-PS* and matching models (Beveridge curve), many attempts have been made both in policy-related work and in academic articles to sort out the role of institutional factors and of shocks (technology; terms of trade; etc.) in explaining OECD unemployment. The OECD's *Jobs Study* of 1994 is a standard reference, which was followed in 1999 by *Implementing the Jobs Study*, the OECD's report on how the recommendations of the Jobs Study were implemented in each country. The framework of analysis used in the OECD's studies is broadly similar to that used in the academic papers that are reported in this section. The evolution of the institutional factors is shown in Table 18.6, which also provides an indication of the broad comparison of institutional characteristics as between continental European countries and an 'Anglo-Saxon' grouping that includes Ireland, Canada, Australia, and New Zealand. On average in continental Europe, trade union density increased from 1960 through to the early 1980s and then fell back. The extent to which employees are covered by trade union wage agreements is much higher than membership and although coverage rose with density to the early 1980s, it has remained stable since then at over 80%. Wage coordination has drifted very slowly downward across the period as a whole.

Turning to the lower part of Table 18.6, the comparison between continental Europe and the Anglo-Saxon group is clear: unions are much less important in the latter and coordination in wage bargaining is also much lower on average. As we know from the Calmfors–Driffill model (explained in Chapter 4 and in more detail in Chapter 15), coordination in wage setting can offset the effect on unemployment of higher unionization. The generosity of unemployment benefits has increased over time in continental Europe and is higher than in the Anglo-Saxon group. The duration of benefits has also gone up, but perhaps somewhat surprisingly is lower on average than is the case in the Anglo-Saxon group, as high initial benefits in many continental countries are scaled back for those that remain unemployed. The employment protection index for Europe peaked in the early 1980s and remains much higher than for the Anglo-Saxon countries. It has been argued that active labour market policies (ALMP) to keep the unemployed in touch with the labour market assist the matching process and maintain downward pressure on wages. On the other hand, ALMP that amount to providing subsidized employment in the public sector have been shown in micro studies to have the opposite effect, presumably because

Table 18.6 Trends and comparisons in labour market institutions

5-year ave.	Trade union density % employees	Coverage % employees	Wage Coord. Index	Unemp. Benefit Replacement rate %	Duration of UB Index	Employment protection Index	ALMP % GDP
(a) Continental European trends							
1960–64	39	77	2.5	26	0.18	0.97	
1965–69	40	77	2.4	31	0.20	1.06	
1970–74	43	78	2.4	35	0.24	1.26	
1975–79	48	81	2.4	45	0.35	1.42	
1980–84	48	82	2.3	49	0.39	1.47	
1985–89	45	82	2.2	56	0.42	1.46	0.86
1990–94	44	82	2.2	58	0.45	1.37	1.2
1995–99	43	83	2.1	58	0.50	1.17	1.2
(b) Continental European/Anglo-Saxon comparisons							
Cont. Eur.	43	83	2.1	58	0.50	1.17	1.2
Anglo-Saxon	30	49	1.4	31	0.69	0.43	0.7

Notes: Continental Europe covers eurozone plus Norway, Sweden, and Switzerland; Anglo-Saxon covers UK, Ireland, USA, Canada, Australia, and New Zealand.
Source: Database used in Baker et al. 2005.

such protected employment reduces the search intensity of these workers in the outside labour market. More resources are devoted to these in Europe than in the Anglo-Saxon countries.

Although the results of studies that attempt to confirm the role of the factors in Tables 18.5 and 18.6 are still disputed, it is useful to explain briefly the main strategies that have been undertaken in the empirical work. The simplest kind of study attempts to explain the cross-country variation in unemployment rates across the OECD countries. This focuses on the relative *position* of the *WS* and *PS* curves in different countries. A widely cited cross-section study is that of Nickell.[3] The second type of study, pioneered by Blanchard and Wolfers,[4] focuses on the idea that although institutions became less 'employment friendly' in the 1970s, the changes since then have tended to be in the opposite direction, yet unemployment has continued to rise in many countries. They therefore identify the interaction between broadly stable institutions and shocks as the likely source of the increased dispersion of unemployment rates: this focuses on a common shift in the *PS* curve that interacts with *WS* curves of differing slopes, as illustrated in Fig. 18.3. In more recent work, Nickell and co-authors attempt to identify the role of institutional *change* in accounting for the time-series variation in unemployment across the OECD countries: i.e. within country shifts in the *WS* or *PS* curve due to institutional changes.

[3] Nickell (1997). [4] Blanchard and Wolfers (2000).

2.2.1 Cross-country unemployment rates (Nickell 1997; Baker et al. 2005)

Nickell presents regression results for the unemployment rate in 20 OECD countries using data for two periods, 1983–8 and 1989–94. The equation that is estimated can be written as follows:

$$u_i = \alpha \Delta \pi_i + \beta_j X_{ij} + \gamma D_{89\text{-}94} + \epsilon_i$$

where i represents the country and j represents the institution. Let us look at each variable in turn: the first variable, $\Delta \pi_i$, is the change in inflation and captures the extent to which the country's unemployment is above or below the *ERU*. The second term, X_{ij}, is the set of variables that measure the institutions that are expected to shift the *ERU* (i.e. the wage- or price-push factors). The final term, $D_{89\text{-}94}$, is simply a so-called dummy variable that is included in the equation to allow for a shift in unemployment between the first period (1983–8) and the second period (1989–94). ϵ_i is the error term in the regression. The results can be summarized as follows: the only variable that is completely insignificant is the index of employment protection. Almost all the other variables are significant at conventional levels (i.e. at least 5%) and have the sign predicted by economic theory (the duration of unemployment benefit is weakly significant at the 10% level). A larger tax wedge raises unemployment. Higher unemployment benefits and longer duration of benefits raise unemployment; active labour market policy lowers it. Higher union density or coverage raises it and coordination lowers it. The results capture the idea that combinations of institutions can have off-setting effects: for example, a high degree of wage coordination (which reduces unemployment) can offset the effect of higher union density and/or coverage, which raises unemployment. Similarly, whilst a more generous unemployment system tends to raise unemployment, this can be offset by an active labour market policy.

Table 18.7 presents a summary of six studies, including that of Nickell (1997), in which the results can be compared.[5] Not all variables are included in each study and the studies use different time periods and methods of estimation. The most consistent results are for the effect of wage coordination and for taxes: in all studies, increased coordination is found to reduce unemployment and higher taxes, to raise it. However, the size of the estimated effects varies widely. In all but one study, stronger employment protection legislation raises unemployment, but by only a small amount in two of them. Wherever it was included, longer duration of unemployment benefits raises unemployment; a higher replacement rate also raises unemployment in most studies. A lesson from the comparison is that cross-country studies do not appear to give precise answers to the question of the likely magnitude of the effect of institutional and policy differences on unemployment outcomes.

2.2.2 Stable institutions; focus on interaction of shocks with institutions (Blanchard and Wolfers)

Although the evidence suggests that the cross-country relationship between institutions and unemployment rates is not very robust, explaining the time pattern of unemployment across countries poses an even greater challenge. Blanchard and Wolfers (2000) test

---

[5] The study by Baker et al. (2005) provides a systematic comparison of the cross-country empirical evidence.

Table 18.7 Estimated effects of institutions on unemployment: six studies

	Nickell 1997	Elmeskov et al. 1998	Belot & Van Ours 2002	Nickell et al. 2001	Blanchard/ Wolfers 2000	Bertola et al. 2001
Institutions:						
Employment Protection (+ 1 unit)	No effect	1.43	0.87	4.45	0.24	0.20
Unemp. Benefit Replacement Ratio (+ 10 PP)	0.88	1.29	0.10	1.24	0.70	No effect
UB Duration (+ 1 yr)	0.70	–	–	0.88	1.27	1.43
ALMP (+ 10 PP)	−1.92	−1.47	–	–	No effect	No effect
Union Density (+ 10 PP)	0.96	No effect	−1.06	No effect	0.84	No effect
Union Bargaining Coverage (+ 10 PP)	3.60	–	–	–	No effect	No effect
Bargaining Coordination (+ 1 unit) (scale 1–3)	−3.68	−1.48	−0.70	−11.64	−1.13	−1.11
Taxes (+ 10 PP)	2.08	0.94	1.79	1.69	0.91	0.97

Notes: For detailed discussion see Baker et al. 2005. PP means percentage points. 'No effect' means not statistically significant. – means variable not included.
Source: Baker, et al. 2005. Table 3.5.

the hypothesis that it was the interaction between different (stable) institutions and common shocks to which countries were subjected that accounts for the cross-country variation in unemployment rates over time. In short, the idea is that the institutions in some countries translated bad shocks (e.g. to productivity growth) into much more persistent unemployment problems than in others (as illustrated, for example in Fig. 18.3). They use five-year averages of unemployment rates and their baseline specification tests the interaction hypothesis by regressing unemployment on country (c_i) and time dummies (d_t) (to capture respectively, persistent differences in unemployment across countries and common trends in unemployment over the period) and on the interaction between the time dummy and a set of institutional variables (X_{ij}, like those used by Nickell). The time dummy can be thought of as shifting the *PS* curve each year in the same way in each country. The basic equation estimated by Blanchard and Wolfers can be written as follows:

$$u_{it} = c_i + d_t \left(1 + \sum_j b_j X_{ij} \right) + \epsilon_{it}$$

where ϵ_{it} is the error term.

Their results (Blanchard and Wolfers 2000, table 1) suggest, first, that the shocks themselves account for an average rise in the unemployment rate of 7.3% and, second, that higher replacement rates, longer duration of benefits, higher employment protection, a higher tax wedge, higher union coverage and density lead shocks to have a larger effect on unemployment; whereas more coordinated wage bargaining and active labour market policies result in a smaller effect. In contrast to Nickell, Blanchard and Wolfers find a role for stronger employment protection legislation in raising unemployment (see Table 18.7).

However, when the hypothesis is investigated more deeply by replacing the dummy variable for time as a measure of common 'shocks' affecting the OECD countries with measures of specific shocks that vary across countries such as measures of productivity growth, terms of trade changes etc., then the equation performs less well. This is worrying as it suggests that the interaction between the time dummies and the country institutions may be picking up some other mechanism than the one intended.

2.2.3 Changing institutions (Nickell et al. 2003)

A different empirical approach is taken by Nickell et al.,[6] whose idea is to use annual data and to estimate a dynamic model for unemployment. Variables are therefore included that would be expected to push unemployment away from equilibrium as well as determinants of the equilibrium itself. This is a useful exercise because it highlights the possible role of changes in institutions in the experience of different countries. But as the authors point out there are unsolved econometric problems associated with their approach. Although they do not use interaction terms between institutions and shocks, they do interact different institutions with each other (such as union density and wage coordination) to explore the idea that the presence of some institutions together in an economy can either reinforce or offset each other.

In Chapter 4 the connection between the matching efficiency of the economy as shown by the Beveridge curve and the *WS-PS* model is explained. Nickell et al. estimate a Beveridge curve equation and an unemployment equation. Their plots of Beveridge curves in each country are interesting because they show that for every country except Sweden and Norway there was an outward shift in the Beveridge curve between the 1960s and mid-1980s indicating a deterioration in the ability of the labour market to match the unemployed to vacancies. After the mid-1980s, countries can be divided into three groups (see Table 18.8): those with a further deterioration in matching with the Beveridge curve shifting further to the right; those where it has shifted back to the left; and a group where the situation is unclear (there is no vacancy data for Italy or Ireland). Fig. 18.5 shows the Beveridge curves for Sweden and the UK).[7]

Table 18.8 Shifts in the Beveridge curve

Beveridge curve shift	1960–mid-1980s	Mid-1980s–1999
No change	Nor, Swe	
Right	all others	Bel, Fin, Fr, G, J, Nor, Sp, Swe, Swi
Left		Can, Den, Neth, UK, US
Unclear		Aus, Austria, NZ, Por

Source: Nickell et al. 2003.

---

[6] Nickell et al. (2003).   [7] The data was kindly supplied by Luca Nunziata.

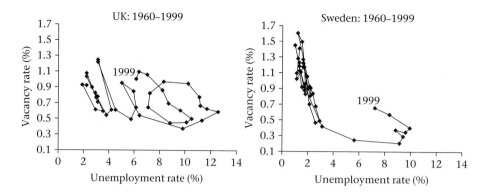

Figure 18.5 Beveridge curves for the UK and Sweden, 1960–1999

The Beveridge curve is estimated by regressing the annual unemployment rate on the vacancy rate, a proxy for the separation rate, and a set of shift factors. The downward-sloping Beveridge curve is obtained because there is a highly significant negative coefficient on the vacancy rate. The shift factors that appear to be empirically important in shifting the Beveridge curve to the right are

- longer benefit duration
- a higher owner occupation rate and
- higher union density

and to the left,

- higher employment protection.

It is argued that a higher owner occupation rate reduces worker mobility and therefore inhibits the matching process. The result that higher employment protection reduces mismatch is rather surprising and could indicate its role in increasing the incentive for firms to invest in policies to achieve better matching (because of the higher costs of severance). But a strong conclusion is hard to draw because other important variables such as active labour market measures that may be correlated with employment protection are omitted from the equation because of lack of data.pt

As explained in Chapter 4, the equilibrium unemployment rate will be affected both by shifts in the Beveridge curve and by *WS/PS* shifts and some factors will play a role in both (see Chapter 4, Fig. 4.13). In addition to the Beveridge curve, Nickell et al. estimate a dynamic unemployment equation and their results provide some support for the role of institutional change as an explanatory factor. The time-varying institutions that appear to be important are unemployment benefits and duration, the effect of which is intensified if generous benefits are accompanied by long durations, union density, and the tax wedge, the impact of each of which can be completely offset by wage coordination. Employment protection does not appear to be significant. By using time-series data and a dynamic estimation method for unemployment, Nickell et al. are able to produce country simulations: they show for each country the path of actual unemployment, unemployment that the model predicts, and the path that the model predicts if the institutional variables are held at their 1960 values. For some countries such as Australia, Belgium, France, the Netherlands, Spain, and the UK, the model fits actual unemployment pretty well and when simulated holding the institutions constant, it appears that institutional change has played a significant part in the pattern of unemployment. For some other countries such as Finland, Germany, and New Zealand, there is little difference between the simulated path with and without institutional change, which suggests that institutional change has not been important for their unemployment trajectories.

2.3 Country case-studies (UK and Netherlands; Ireland; Sweden and Finland; Germany)

One way to approach a country study of unemployment is to apply the results from a regression analysis, as was done by Nickell and Van Ours (2000) in a two-country study of the dramatic falls in unemployment observed in the UK and the Netherlands in the 1990s. Specifically, they use the coefficients from Nickell's 1997 cross-country equation to estimate the predicted effect on equilibrium unemployment in each country of *changes* observed in union density, coverage, coordination, active labour market policy, the benefit replacement ratio, and the tax wedge from the early 1980s to the mid-1990s. For the Netherlands, the predicted effects amount to a reduction in unemployment of 4.5% points as compared with an actual reduction of 5.7% and for the UK, the predicted fall is 3.8% as compared with an actual fall of 4.1%. For the Netherlands, the key contributing factors are a rise in wage coordination, a rise in active labour market policies and small contributions from a fall in the replacement rate and in the tax wedge. For the UK, the main contributions come from lower union density and coverage, with smaller contributions from a fall in the tax wedge and in the replacement rate. In terms of the Calmfors–Driffill model, the UK appears to move toward the decentralized pole (with lower unemployment) and the Netherlands toward the coordinated pole (also with lower unemployment).

This analysis places all the weight on supply-side factors, but it is illuminating to look at the broader picture including the external account. Table 18.9 provides macroeconomic data for each country for the mid-1980s and for the early 2000s.pt

As argued in Chapter 17 in the discussion of UK macroeconomic performance in the 1990s, it seems essential to include in the analysis of falling unemployment from 1997 the role played by the substantial and persistent real appreciation of the exchange rate. This is reflected in the deterioration of unit labour costs (the rise in RULC shown in Table 18.9) and the associated deterioration in the current account. The situation is different in the Netherlands, where the adjustment to lower unemployment takes place at a roughly constant real exchange rate and external balance. This suggests that whilst the Dutch unemployment miracle is predominantly a supply-side phenomenon, the UK one combines supply-side improvement with a more substantial element of an aggregate demand-led expansion via a consumption boom, where the associated exchange rate

Table 18.9 Three unemployment 'miracles' in Europe: key macroeconomic data

	Netherlands		UK		Ireland	
	1985	**2002**	**1985**	**2002**	**1985**	**2002**
U	9.2	2.8	11.6	5.1	16.5	4.4
ERU	7.5	3.7	8.1	5.3	13.2	5.9
change in inflation	falling	falling	stable	stable	falling	rising
RULC (1995=100)	102	94	109	145	158	73
Current account (% GDP)	3.2	2.1	0	−1.4	−3.7	−0.1

Notes: Change in inflation refers to the ave. of the annual change in inflation from 84–86 and 00–02 respectively.
RULC = relative unit labour costs: increase in RULC means fall in competitiveness.
ERU = OECD's 'structural unemployment' measure reported in *Economic Outlook* Annex Table 23.
Changes in RULC can be compared across countries. RULC data are for 2001. Current account deficit 00–02.
Source: OECD *Economic Outlook* tables.

appreciation helped contain inflation by boosting the real wage. Fig. 18.6 illustrates the contrast between the two cases. In a detailed analysis of the improvement in British economic performance, the extent of market-oriented supply-side reforms is documented. The authors note, however, that

the biggest problem in assessing the contribution of the reforms on employment from microstudies is, of course, that the macroperformance of the UK economy dominates overall employment patterns. ... If the market-oriented policy reforms in the labor market contributed to the length and extent of the economic expansion, they would indeed help explain the good performance of the United Kingdom in employment in this period, but such a contribution cannot be readily determined from microeconomic data.[8]

A third case of interest is Ireland, where unemployment fell from 16.5% in 1985 to 4.4% in 2002 (Table 18.9). The estimated ERU falls from 13.2% to 5.9% and inflation is falling in the first period in which actual unemployment is above the equilibrium and rising in the second, when it is below.

In their analysis of the 'Irish hare', Honahan and Walsh[9] identify supply-side improvements that would have shifted the *ERU* curve to the right: a dramatic rise in labour productivity growth, an increase in wage coordination (as discussed in Chapter 4) and some fall in trade union density. As a consequence of very strong inflows of foreign direct investment, Ireland experienced a massive improvement in its export performance: its export market share doubled between 1985 and 1999. As shown in the table, its relative unit labour costs more than halved. This is consistent with a strong rightward shift of the *ERU* curve as shown in Fig. 18.6. The sketches for each country in Fig. 18.6 show shifts in the relevant curves that are consistent with the macroeconomic data presented in Table 18.9 and with the narrative outlined in each case.

[8] Card and Freeman (2004: 53).   [9] Honahan and Walsh (2002).

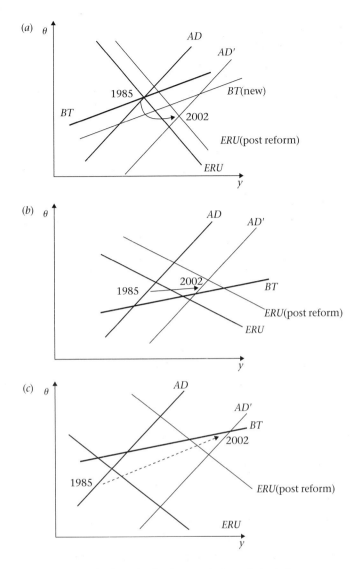

Figure 18.6 The UK, the Netherlands, and Ireland: unemployment 'miracles'
(a) UK
(b) Netherlands
(c) Ireland

The next two cases we consider are those of Finland and Sweden. Both countries had relatively low unemployment up to the end of the 1980s followed by a dramatic rise in the early 1990s and a subsequent decline. The top panel in Fig. 18.7 shows the paths of unemployment and inflation. Looking at unemployment first, in both countries, unemployment fell further at the end of the 1980s due to poorly timed macroeconomic policies. Financial liberalization and tax cuts were introduced at a time when the economies were already overheating.

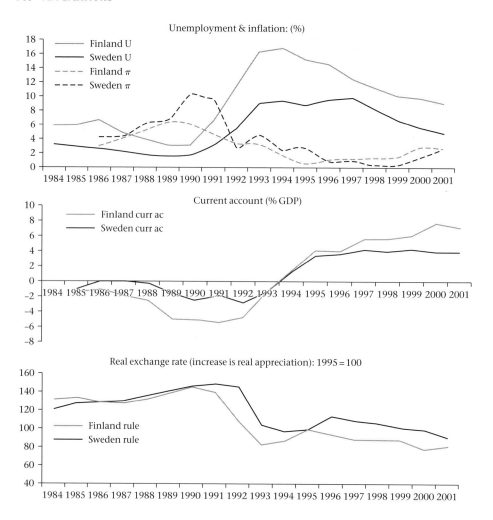

Figure 18.7 Macroeconomic developments in Sweden and Finland
Source: OECD, *Economic Outlook*, tables.

In the Swedish case,[10] there was a massive consumer boom associated with a housing asset price bubble. An indication of the extent of the boom is that the household savings ratio fell by 7% points between 1985 and 1988. The result was a sharp rise in inflation, which in Sweden went into double digits (unemployment had fallen to less than 2%). The boom was followed by a classic bust as macroeconomic policy was tightened—over-abruptly, which led to the collapse of consumption and investment and in the wake of this, of a number of banks. The savings ratio increased by 12 percentage points between 1989 and 1993 and investment fell by 40%. The Finnish 'bust' was exacerbated by an external trade shock due to the disintegration of the Soviet Union, which was a major trading partner (see the middle panel for the path of the current account balance). In

[10] For a more detailed account, see Calmfors (1993).

both countries, exchange rate devaluations in the early 1990s (shown by a fall in relative unit labour costs in the bottom panel) helped the recovery of aggregate demand and with unemployment well above equilibrium, inflation continued to decline.

With the recovery of internal and external demand, unemployment has gradually fallen in both countries. Strong external surpluses in both cases suggest that low unemployment is sustainable. Cost competitiveness has continued to improve, reflecting sound productivity growth and adequate wage restraint. These two cases illustrate that aggregate demand dynamics can have a dramatic effect on unemployment over a period as long as a decade and a half.

The final case study is Germany. As Fig. 18.2 shows, German unemployment was very low—below 4%—until the mid-1980s. From the mid-1980s to the mid-1990s, unemployment was similar to that in the USA and from the mid-1990s it has been higher. Whereas unemployment in the USA shows no trend since the 1960s, German unemployment trends have been strongly upwards. In the past decade and a half, German unemployment contrasts sharply with a number of European economies, such as the UK and the Netherlands, where it has fallen. The idea that German unemployment is a purely supply-side phenomenon rooted in its labour market and welfare state characteristics is explored in a detailed comparison of the Netherlands and Germany.[11] The comparison shows that

- incentives to work are greater in Germany than the Netherlands (with the exception of single-earner low income couples with children)
- taxes are generally higher in the Netherlands
- employment protection is similar in the Netherlands and in Germany.

The policy debate in Germany and in the reports on Germany by the OECD have stressed the importance of labour market and welfare state reform for improving Germany's unemployment performance. In line with their recommendations, the OECD reports that the following measures have been undertaken in Germany: improvement in active labour market policy, an overall reduction in the tax wedge, a reduction in employment protection for temporary contracts, a reduction in the duration of unemployment benefits and tightening work availability conditions, and the promotion of more decentralized wage setting. Yet unemployment has continued to increase. The UK experience with supply-side reforms suggests that it may take many years for such reforms to pay off. However, other evidence suggests that implementing labour market and welfare state reforms may not solve Germany's unemployment problem. The apparently limited effectiveness of the reforms implemented to date in Germany is consistent with both the cross-sectional evidence on Germany and the Netherlands and with the simulations reported in section 2.2.3, where changes in institutions were not found to account for the trajectory of unemployment in Germany.

The analysis of Germany's macroeconomic performance in Chapter 17 stressed the consequences of German unification. It was argued there that Germany needed to improve its competitiveness and to overcome the weakness in domestic aggregate demand. In principle, labour market and welfare state reforms of the kind that have been implemented should shift the *ERU* curve to the right and tax cuts should boost consumer spending,

---

[11] Schettkat (2003).

shifting the *AD* curve to the right and allow a non-inflationary expansion of activity and reduction in unemployment. However, analysis of the Dutch and Irish cases suggests that wage accords played a more important role in achieving the required real wage restraint there than did changes in replacement rates, tax wedges, or employment protection. By contrast, in the UK, it was a more traditional package of labour market and welfare state reforms that was implemented. Strong aggregate demand and a coherent macroeconomic policy framework were also present in the UK case (Chapter 17). There are several reasons why neither the Dutch/Irish approach nor the British one may work well or quickly in Germany.

Although wage setting in Germany has traditionally been at the more 'coordinated' end of the spectrum, the prospects for reinforcing coordination and achieving a rightward shift of the *ERU* through coordinated wage restraint (i.e. shifting *WS* down) may be limited. There are three reasons for this:

(1) Inflation in Germany is already very low and evidence suggests that it is more difficult to achieve real wage reductions through nominal wage cuts than through moderating money wage increases in the context of modest inflation. Moreover many of Germany's trading partners within EMU operate with coordinated wage-setting policies aimed at maintaining their cost competitiveness vis-à-vis Germany's.

(2) Section 3.2 highlights the fact that increased unemployment dispersion across regions has the effect of reducing wage restraint: the dispersion of unemployment went up in Germany in the 1990s, both because of the inclusion of the East German Länder, which have very high unemployment rates and because of increased dispersion across West German Länder.

(3) As we shall see in section 4, wage restraint in Germany may have been weakened by the move to EMU, as the disciplining role of the Bundesbank of reacting to increases in German inflation disappeared.

As noted above, a number of UK-type reforms to the labour market and welfare state have been introduced in Germany. Yet the German economy remains much more similar in its institutional arrangements to other continental European economies such as the Netherlands. On the one hand, some small countries in Europe appear to have been able to implement pro-employment reforms that have been broadly consistent with their pre-existing institutional arrangements, and on the other, the UK has implemented reforms to create a more coherent set of 'market-friendly' labour market and welfare state arrangements.[12] The prospects for Germany achieving either of these appear less rosy.

An unintended side-effect of the labour market and welfare state reforms that have been implemented in Germany may be to depress household consumption expenditure. In an economy such as Germany in which job tenure has typically been longer than,

---

[12] See the introduction and chapters in Card et al. (2004). In particular, Pencavel (2004: 225) provides evidence on the changes in British industrial relations over the 1980s and 1990s. He concludes that 'by the end of the 1990s, the association [in Britain] between unionism and low labor productivity appears to have been broken except in those workplaces where many unions bargain separately. Such fragmented bargaining is now unusual so that, in general, unions are no longer a factor depressing labor productivity.'

for example, in the UK, and in which the mid-career labour market is less developed, reforms may raise insecurity more and prompt higher precautionary savings. Domestic aggregate demand in Germany grew broadly in line with the rest of the European Union from 1991 to 1997 but weakened markedly thereafter. Germany recorded the largest negative gap between the annual growth in domestic demand and trend growth in GDP amongst eight large OECD countries in the 2000–3 period.[13] This reflects both weak private consumption and investment, and a highly constrained public sector and stands in sharp contrast to the role that buoyant household and public sector spending have played in both the UK and USA in sustaining aggregate demand over the past decade (see Chapter 17).

2.4 Hysteresis (Ball 1999a)

Lawrence Ball set out to test whether there was evidence that macroeconomic policy choices by governments and central banks influenced equilibrium unemployment by virtue of their effect on actual unemployment. His first claim was that some countries pursued excessively tight macroeconomic policies in the early 1980s, which led to pro-longed recessions and produced more long-term unemployment. As we have seen in Chapter 4, if the long-term unemployed are ineffective in dampening wage pressure, equilibrium unemployment is pushed up. 'Over-tight' policies became a self-fulfilling prophecy because the upward shift in the *WS* curve then requires tighter macro pol-icy to stabilize inflation. His second claim was that countries where unemployment fell substantially in the 1990s were those that undertook expansionary macro policies, i.e. hysteresis operated in reverse with strong aggregate demand reducing unemployment, which in turn brought down equilibrium unemployment.

This interpretation is clearly at odds with the econometric studies discussed above where the emphasis is on supply-side determinants of equilibrium unemployment. Ball demonstrates that the central banks in the USA and Canada cut interest rates much more vigorously and documents in central bank reports the apparently greater concern to impart a countercyclical stimulus than was the case in European countries in the early 1980s recession. However, it is extremely difficult to provide evidence that would confirm or refute the hysteresis hypothesis: how can the hypothesis that

- central banks pursued tight policy for longer in Europe because the supply side had deteriorated (i.e. tighter policy was needed to ensure disinflation)

be distinguished from Ball's hypothesis that

- the supply side deteriorated because the central banks in Europe failed to cut interest rates aggressively to promote recovery?

Although unresolved, this question remains an important one. In the context of EMU, member countries do not have control over monetary policy and, as, we have seen in Chapter 17, for countries with weak aggregate demand, low inflation perversely raises the real interest rate (since the nominal interest rate is common across EMU) and can reinforce stagnation.

---

[13] OECD, *Economic Survey of Germany* (2004): 25–6.

3 Trade, technology, and unemployment

The analysis in section 2 examined aggregate unemployment. In section 1.2, sharp differences in employment and unemployment rates by educational group were highlighted. In this section, we bring together these two issues. We begin with the analysis of the variation in unemployment rates between different groups within countries and then examine the connection between such differences and aggregate equilibrium unemployment. In the final part of this section, we look at recent developments in outsourcing and offshoring and their possible implications for unemployment.

3.1 Unemployment and the relative demand for skilled labour

One focus of research over the past decade has been on the variation in (un)employment rates between different education (or skill) groups (see Table 18.3) and on patterns of wage dispersion between the skilled and unskilled. In 1994, Paul Krugman suggested that the rise in unemployment in Europe and the rise in wage inequality in the Anglo-Saxon countries were 'two sides of the same coin' in which different labour market institutions produced contrasting outcomes in response to a fall in the relative demand for unskilled labour in the rich countries.[14] This is another example of the possible interaction between a common shock and different institutional arrangements. Two contending explanations for the fall in the relative demand for unskilled labour[15] relate to

- the role of increased competition from developing countries in the production of low-skill-intensive goods—the so-called 'trade' hypothesis and

- the emergence of a bias in technological progress toward skill-intensive innovation—the 'technology' hypothesis.

In the first round of empirical research, the facts were more consistent with the technology explanation. The pure trade hypothesis was based on the application of the standard model of comparative advantage (the famous Heckscher–Ohlin model). Following trade liberalization, the production of goods that are intensive in the use of the labour of workers with low education would be relocated to countries with a large endowment of unskilled labour and vice versa.[16] However, this was inconsistent with the following stylized facts:[17]

(1) the skill premium, i.e. the relative wage of skilled to unskilled workers, has risen in all sectors and in all countries, including less developed and newly industrializing countries as well as OECD countries.

---

[14] Krugman (1994). Many other authors have investigated these contrasting patterns, e.g. the chapters in Freeman (1994).

[15] There is a lively debate as to how important skill-biased shifts in labour demand have been and whether they—rather than, for example, falls in unionization and changes in minimum wages—were responsible for the rising inequality in the USA in the 1980s (e.g. Card and DiNardo (2002)).

[16] For an excellent presentation of the 'trade' argument, see Wood (1998).

[17] For an assessment of the trade hypothesis, see Desjonqueres, Machin, and Van Reenen (1999). For evidence on skill-biased technical progress, see Berman, Bound, and Machin (1998).

(2) along with the rise in the skill premium, there has been a rise in the ratio of skilled to unskilled employment in all sectors, both skilled- and unskilled-labour intensive.

(3) there has been no significant decline in relative prices for the products of low skilled industries outside the USA.

In this section, our focus is on establishing how a shift in relative demand for skilled labour—whatever its source—affects the employment, unemployment, and relative wages of skilled and unskilled workers. In the next section, we discuss how an increased dispersion of unemployment rates can affect equilibrium unemployment in the economy. To answer the first question, there are three important ingredients:

(1) the relative demand for skilled versus unskilled labour;

(2) the relative supply; and

(3) constraints on relative wage flexibility as a result, for example, of union wage-setting behaviour or a minimum wage.

Fig. 18.8 provides a very simple way of illustrating how relative demand, supply, and institutional wage rigidity interact. The demand for skilled labour is drawn from the left and the demand for unskilled labour from the right hand side. The total labour force is shown on the horizontal axis. The supply of labour is divided between high and low skilled workers as shown by the vertical line. In the initial situation, there is no unemployment and the higher demand for skilled labour relative to its supply means that high skilled workers receive a higher wage than do low skilled workers. This is labelled as the initial wage gap. A shift in labour demand toward skilled workers is shown by the upward shift in the D^H line and the downward shift in the D^L line. Relative supply of the different kinds of labour is held constant. If wages adjust flexibly to the demand shift, then the wage gap widens as shown. If, however, something prevents the wage of low

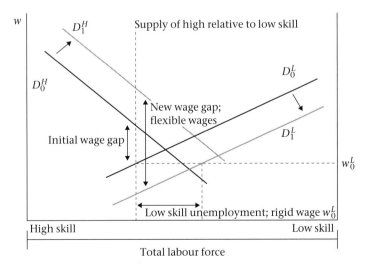

Figure 18.8 Shift in relative demand for skilled labour: rigid vs. flexible wages

skilled workers from falling, then unemployment of low skilled workers will emerge as shown. From this diagram, it is obvious that developments on the supply side will also influence the outcome. If, for example, the supply of high to low skilled labour goes up (shifting the line showing this to the right in Fig. 18.8), this will weaken the effect of the shift in relative demand.

The broad argument that a shift in the relative demand for skilled labour would be reflected in wage inequality in the countries with flexible wages and in unemployment inequality in those with inflexible wages has been influential in the policy debate but empirical studies have failed to confirm the predictions. For example, unemployment rates increased for all skill groups in European countries.[18]

3.2 Dispersion of unemployment rates and the *ERU*

It is clear that new technology and increasing global openness may affect wage inequality or unemployment inequality across educational groups or both. Policy makers are often concerned with increases in inequality whatever the form it takes but there is potentially an important difference between the situation in which the forces tending to raise inequality produce wage or unemployment inequality as the predominant outcome. It has been argued that increases in *unemployment* inequality can raise equilibrium unemployment. The logic of the argument hinges on the shape of the wage-setting curve. Evidence suggests that the wage-setting curve is non-linear: when employment is high and unemployment low, real wages respond strongly to changes in unemployment whereas when employment is low and unemployment high, an increase in unemployment tends to produce relatively little increase in wage moderation.

As Fig. 18.9 illustrates, a convex wage-setting curve implies that the *WS* for the economy as a whole is higher for a given average rate of unemployment in the economy when

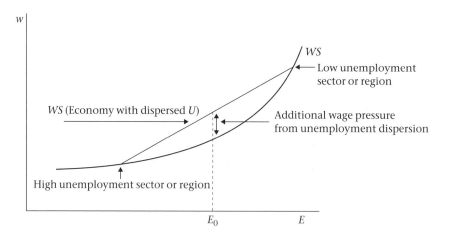

Figure 18.9 Dispersion of unemployment raises the *ERU*

---

[18] For example, Krueger and Pischke (1997) and Card, Kramarz, and Lemieux (1999).

unemployment rates are dispersed: in the example in the diagram, the comparison is between one economy in which unemployment is uniform across sectors and regions and another economy in which in half the sectors or regions, unemployment is higher than the average and in the other half, lower. If we take an average employment level of E_0 in each of these economies, the *WS* curve for the economy with dispersed unemployment rates lies above that for the economy with uniform unemployment. The reason is that high unemployment is especially ineffective in dampening wage claims whereas in the half of the economy with a tight labour market, wage pressure is disproportionately high. Since the *WS* for the economy as a whole is higher, equilibrium unemployment in the economy with greater unemployment dispersion will also be higher.

This effect highlights not only the consequences of any rise in unemployment differences by educational group but also of differences across regions. The role of the regional behaviour of unemployment in Europe as compared with the USA has been quite different over the 1990s. In the USA, regional unemployment rates have tended to converge, with one estimate suggesting that this has been responsible for a reduction of 2 percentage points in US equilibrium unemployment.[19]

By contrast, in Europe, regional unemployment rates have diverged. What has happened in the wake of increased European integration following the Single Market Act of 1986 is increased spatial concentration of economic activity in agglomerations that may cross national borders. Unemployment has become more polarized, with regions with unemployment initially near average for Europe shifting either to a position of high or low unemployment. The outcome is that, especially in the large continental economies, the dispersion of unemployment rates within countries has gone up. Research shows that between 1986 and 1996, the changes in unemployment of regions are more closely related to unemployment changes in their geographical neighbours (inside or outside the country) than to the average change in other regions in their country.[20] Wage setting continues to take place at a national level, with the consequence of higher equilibrium unemployment.

Overman and Puga also find that not only is the fall in unemployment in the surrounding geographical area important in accounting for falling regional unemployment but so is a lower share of low-skilled workers and a higher share of manufacturing industry at the outset of the period. The positive role of the initial level of manufacturing industry in keeping unemployment relatively low is presumably capturing the regions in Europe that had successfully moved out of heavy and low-skill manufacturing before the mid-1980s, yet retained a strong manufacturing base. The evidence on regional unemployment patterns within Europe highlights the impact that low levels of labour mobility both within and between countries plays in combination with national wage-setting systems. National fiscal systems operate to offset some of the impact of the divergent unemployment patterns on regional *living standards* but unless such transfers help the residents of the high unemployment regions to overcome the skill, structural, and other disadvantages characteristic of these regions, redistribution is not likely to promote sustainable convergence. The evidence about regional unemployment patterns may eventually provide the basis for a more conclusive evaluation of the role that labour market

[19] Wall and Zoega (2003).   [20] Overman and Puga (2002).

institutions play in Europe's unemployment puzzle than do the cross-national studies discussed in section 2.2.

3.3 New research in the 'trade and technology' debate

The previous subsection shows that if skill-biased technical progress or increased globalization through so-called outsourcing or offshoring interacts with labour market institutions to produce a greater regional or skill-related dispersion of unemployment, it can raise equilibrium unemployment. Against this must be set the possibility that developments in trade or technology raise productivity growth in the home economy, shifting the *PS* curve upwards and reducing equilibrium unemployment—at least for some years until wage claims adjust.

Outsourcing relates to the decision by the firm to shift from *in-house* production of inputs to the purchase of inputs from a separate supplier firm, which may be based abroad. Offshoring relates to a change in the *location* of the production of inputs used by the firm: establishing an affiliate abroad (foreign direct investment), switching from a domestic to a foreign supplier of inputs or deciding to outsource activities abroad are examples. Since outsourcing to a foreign supplier is subsumed in the definition of offshoring, we shall use the latter term.

In popular discussions of unemployment, much attention is paid to the idea that jobs are being lost in the OECD countries and gained in low wage countries through offshoring. In a recent detailed study of German and Austrian firms for the 1990s that covers 80% of German and 100% of Austrian direct investment in Eastern Europe, it is found that the opening up of Eastern European economies as a site for production has resulted in very little loss of jobs in Germany and Austria.[21] The firm-level data show that wages in their operations in Central and Eastern Europe are 16.5% of those in Germany and productivity is 60%, resulting in unit labour costs of 27.6%. In the case of Austrian firms, the wage differential is similar but productivity of only 30% of the Austrian level is achieved abroad, leaving unit labour costs one half those in Austria. The new source of cheap and abundant skilled labour has allowed firms to reduce their production costs and remain competitive in the face of increasing international competition. The data suggest that a reduction in costs in an affiliate firm in Central and Eastern Europe leads to an increase in employment in the parent firm. Similar results are reported for Swedish multinationals. Nevertheless, the question remains as to the dynamic consequences for future investment and employment in 'old Europe' of the availability of new production locations in 'new Europe'. As the levels of human capital accumulation and institutional quality in Central and Eastern Europe come to match those in their neighbours, the comparative advantage of Western European economies in producing high quality manufactured goods will be threatened.

Much recent debate has centred on the offshoring of service sector jobs. This phenomenon brings together developments in technology and in trade. New technologies have widened the possibilities for trade and for the relocation of employment abroad (e.g. in call centres, back-office operations, and software development). Imports of business services from abroad remain very small in quantitative terms, amounting to 0.4% of GDP in the USA and 1.2% of GDP in the UK in 2001. The USA and the UK are the largest

---

[21] Marin (2004). For similar evidence for Sweden, see Braconier and Ekholm (2000).

net *exporters* of business services with the UK's surplus rising strongly from the mid-1990s (as discussed in Chapter 17); Germany has run a small deficit throughout the 1980–2001 period, which has tended to widen somewhat in the 1990s.[22] The analysis of data at industry level for the UK shows no adverse effect of offshoring on employment. Indeed it has been argued that the ability to increase its comparative advantage in business services by offshoring may have helped the UK to overcome its productivity gap relative to France and Germany in this sector.[23]

Research on offshoring remains fragmentary and the impact on relative unemployment rates by skill level or by region has not been explored. The impact may also differ across countries. In the firm-level data from Germany and Austria discussed above, for example, it is argued that offshoring takes the form of creating high-skill jobs abroad whereas the focus in the USA and UK has been on the shift of low-skill jobs abroad.

Through the detailed analysis of the content of jobs and the use of computers, a more subtle version of the hypothesis of skill-biased technical progress has been developed.[24] Whereas the SBTP hypothesis predicts demand for skilled labour would rise relative to unskilled labour, it is now argued that it is the demand for non-routine cognitive and manual skills that would rise relative to the demand for routine skills that can be carried out by computers. Hence, technical progress depresses the demand for workers with middling levels of education who are employed doing routinized white or blue collar tasks (from accounting to machining) whereas it boosts the relative demand for the highly educated, whose skills are complementary to computers. With more rapid productivity growth in manufacturing and computer-related services, there is also a rise in the relative demand for unskilled workers who do *non-routine* service sector tasks, which cannot easily be carried out by machines. The latter is a version of the standard argument due originally to William Baumol that as an economy matures, the share of employment in services rises and 'deindustrialization' occurs.[25] This follows from two assumptions: that demand in constant prices grows for manufactures roughly in line with that for services and that productivity growth is faster in manufacturing. Evidence from the UK finds that between the 1970s and the late 1990s, there has been rapid growth in employment in professional and managerial jobs, some growth in non-routine service occupations such as stacking shelves and care work with old people and a decline in the so-called middling jobs (clerical and skilled manual jobs in manufacturing).[26] The interaction between the implementation of new technologies, institutional structures of the labour market, and wage and unemployment inequality by skill level remains to be investigated.

4 Unemployment and EMU

The increasing integration of the European economies following the Single European Market programme appears to have affected the location of economic activities, which in turn has influenced regional and equilibrium rates of national unemployment. This leads

---

[22] For details, see Amiti and Wei (2004).   [23] Abramovsky, Griffith, and Sako (2004).
[24] The key research is presented in Autor, Levy, and Murnane (2003).
[25] For further analysis of deindustrialization, see Baumol (2001); Rowthorn and Ramaswamy (1997); and Rowthorn and Coutts (2004).   [26] Goos and Manning (2003).

to the question of whether the change in *monetary arrangements* with the move to Economic and Monetary Union has played any role in European unemployment. Once again the comparison with the USA is a striking one: the USA has a single monetary policy, a single fiscal policy, and a labour market characterized by a combination of institutional arrangements and mobility that keeps the differences in unemployment rates between states quite low. In the eurozone, there is a single monetary policy, twelve national fiscal policies, and twelve national labour markets. As we have discussed in connection with analysing monetary policy in EMU (Chapters 11, 12, and 17) and in the fiscal policy chapter (Chapter 6), the intended policy assignment in EMU was:

- The ECB is responsible for maintaining low and stable inflation.
- National fiscal authorities are responsible for fiscal sustainability and subject to that to providing national level stabilization in the face of asymmetric shocks or asymmetric effects of common shocks. The Stability and Growth Pact was intended to prevent national fiscal authorities from pursuing policies that could threaten the inflation objective.
- National labour markets (and the supply side more broadly) determine equilibrium unemployment.

Three different arguments have been put forward to suggest that EMU could affect equilibrium unemployment in the member countries:

(1) Creation of a common currency area increases the transparency of relative labour costs across countries. This increases the elasticity of the labour demand curve that wage setters face. According to the Calmfors–Driffill model, this produces a lower *WS* curve and hence lower equilibrium unemployment (see Fig. 4.5 in Chapter 4). In the Calmfors–Driffill terminology, for countries with an intermediate level of wage setting, unemployment falls toward that associated with decentralized wage setting. The peak of the hump-shaped curve is flattened.

(2) Membership of a common currency area makes it more difficult to implement labour market reforms and therefore may make reductions in equilibrium unemployment harder to achieve. This argument centres on the political economy of reform: it may be easier to persuade important interest groups in the economy to accept reform if labour market reform (to shift the *WS* curve down or the *PS* curve up and hence the *ERU* curve to the right) is accompanied by cuts in interest rates and a currency depreciation. The logic is that depreciation takes the economy more swiftly along the *AD* curve to the north-east with rising employment than would be the case if the gains in competitiveness had to feed through via lower wage and price inflation than in other countries.

(3) Creation of a common currency area affects the way large wage setters interact with the central bank. If this produces a shift from 'coordinated' to 'intermediate' wage setting in the sense of the Calmfors–Driffill model, then equilibrium unemployment will rise. We examine this argument in more detail in this section.

Each of these arguments indicates that when wage setters are large, a change in monetary arrangements can affect the real side of the economy. In most EMU countries wages are set through collective bargaining at sectoral (industry) level with coordination at cross-sectoral level or economy-wide in some (see Table 4.2 in the Appendix to Chapter 4).

In the presence of union wage setting, how does the move to monetary union affect equilibrium unemployment? It can be argued that the replacement of a national monetary authority by a supra-national one such as the ECB may lead to a rise in equilibrium unemployment since the ECB does not 'punish' national wage setters by tightening monetary policy if they exert less restraint in wage setting. The simplest way to think about this is to imagine that without EMU wages are set at sectoral level in each country and the number of sectors in the economy is sufficiently small that each union is aware of the consequences of its wage decision in terms of the response of the central bank. Wage setters internalize the external effect of their wage decision because the anticipated reaction of the central bank creates the incentive for wage restraint. If we now consider the situation of the same unions facing the ECB, it is likely that they will anticipate less response to their wage decision and hence will exercise less restraint. The result is that the WS curve is higher under EMU (a shift from 'coordinated' to 'intermediate' in the Calmfors–Driffill model) and hence unemployment is higher. As we know from the Calmfors–Driffill model, the unions are worse off when they exercise less restraint: the real wage is the same, employment is lower, and there is a burst of higher inflation as the economy adjusts to the new equilibrium.

For this analysis to be relevant to the case of EMU, it is necessary to recognize that there was a monetary arrangement in place prior to EMU, namely the ERM.[27] As discussed in Chapter 17, Germany was de facto the key currency country in the ERM, which means that the Bundesbank was the ERM's monetary policy maker. One way of modelling the operation of the ERM is to treat all the countries other than Germany symmetrically and to assume that each wage setter maximizes utility by setting the wage at the tangency between the labour demand curve and the union indifference curve. This procedure is shown diagramatically in Fig. 18.10.[28] This produces the curve WS_0. Germany is different because German wage setters know that any increase in German inflation will lead the Bundesbank to tighten monetary policy. The Bundesbank's mandate related only to German inflation. If this 'external effect' is incorporated in German union behaviour, it can be represented in Fig. 18.10 by a flatter labour demand curve. The result is that the German WS curve, WS_1, is below that of the rest-ERM countries. Since the Bundesbank sets monetary policy for all ERM members, all countries must be on a labour demand curve indexed by the same level of aggregate demand. To make the analysis simpler, it is assumed that the countries (including Germany) are identical in every respect except in their relationship to the monetary policy maker. Equilibrium unemployment for the ERM system is shown by point B in Fig. 18.10. Given that the Bundesbank has set monetary policy so that the level of aggregate demand is y_2^D, then each of the rest-ERM countries optimizes by choosing point B and Germany optimizes by choosing point C. Turning this around, we know that the reason the Bundesbank chooses y_2^D is that this is consistent with constant inflation. The outcome is a constant inflation equilibrium for the ERM system

---

[27] This argument is set out in detail in Soskice and Iversen (1998). A more theoretical presentation is in Soskice and Iversen (2000). [28] For a formal model, see Chapter 15, section 3.

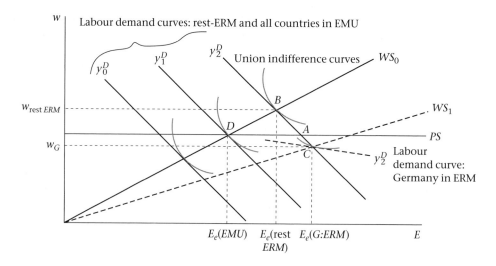

Figure 18.10 Equilibrium employment in ERM and in EMU

as a whole shown by point A: Germany has a lower real wage and higher employment than that of the rest-ERM countries and the weighted average for the ERM system as a whole is equal to the w^{PS} as shown by the PS curve in Fig. 18.10.

We now consider what happens when the Bundesbank is replaced by the ECB as the monetary policy maker. Germany ceases to be different from the other member countries, which means that WS_0 applies to them all. Without the additional wage restraint in Germany, the constant inflation equilibrium for the EMU system is at point D, with higher unemployment for rest-ERM countries and an even larger rise in unemployment for Germany. This analysis highlights an important difference between the way monetary union works in Europe, where large wage setters are present, and in the USA, where wage setting is decentralized and the wage setting curve therefore reflects highly elastic labour demand curves faced by wage setters (such as WS_1).

There is no firm empirical evidence available on how monetary union has affected unemployment in Europe. The discussion in this section provides a number of hypotheses and a framework for thinking about the forces at work but it is not possible to draw conclusions about which ones are having the most important impact.

5 Why is reform so difficult?

The OECD's 1994 *Jobs Study* has formed the basis for a decade of reform efforts designed to improve the functioning of labour markets and produce lower unemployment rates. The discussion of empirical studies in this chapter underlines the complexity of the determinants of unemployment and the empirical difficulties facing researchers with only a limited number of countries in their sample. Systematic comparison of the results of studies has shown that drawing firm conclusions about the size of the effects of different institutional arrangements and even about whether such effects are significant is premature. Country case studies highlight the importance of knowledge of institutional detail and of macroeconomic developments for understanding unemployment patterns. As the analysis in this chapter has shown, institutions, policies, and shocks interact in complex ways, which means that simple reform recipes are elusive.

5.1 Labour market policies interact

To take one example, the OECD has urged countries to reduce the extent of employment protection. As discussed in section 3, a survey of recent studies shows that in most, stricter employment protection raises equilibrium unemployment but the estimated size of the effect varies widely. In the estimates of the Beveridge curve presented in section 3, higher employment protection shifts the Beveridge curve to the left suggesting that stricter rules enhance the matching process between employer and employee. It is argued that both employment protection and unemployment benefits can play an efficiency role in a situation where workers are risk averse and where they cannot insure themselves against job loss—both of which seem reasonable assumptions. A private insurance market will not exist because of the moral hazard problem: since the worker's effort cannot be observed, it is not generally possible to distinguish between job loss due to poor performance and job loss due to a labour demand shock.[29] The view that 'unemployment and income insecurity create the demand for labour market institutions and regulations' can be contrasted with the one discussed at length in the chapter that 'labour market institutions and regulations create unemployment' (i.e. where wage- or price- push factors shift the *WS* curve upwards or the *PS* curve down).

When reviewing the evidence about the effect of employment protection on labour market performance in 1999[30] and again in 2004, the OECD reports mixed results. Reflecting an issue given prominence in this chapter is the conclusion of the OECD that:

some countries appear to have successfully reduced unemployment rates and maintained high employment to population ratios through the combined use of these instruments [employment protection provisions, active labour market policies (ALMP) and effective re-employment services]. Others seem to have equally enhanced labour market performance by reducing both EPL and unemployment benefits, with little recourse to ALMP. (OECD *Employment Outlook* (2004), 99)

Thus one reason why reform is so difficult is that reform packages are complicated by the way labour market institutions interact with each other and with other aspects of policy such as the tax and benefit regime.

5.2 Product and labour market regulation interact

Not only has the unemployment record of the large continental European economies been poor in comparison with that of the United States in the last twenty years but so

---

[29] Pissarides (2001) provides an accessible analysis of this issue against the backdrop of the emphasis on employment protection in the OECD's Jobs Study. Another useful article is Agell (2002).

[30] OECD (1999*a*).

too has their dynamism as measured by growth in per capita GDP or more narrowly by labour productivity growth in the business sector (see e.g. Table 17.6, Chapter 17). A recent strand of economic research suggests that one link between the two may be provided by the role played by product market regulation in the economy.[31] Product market regulation is used to refer to the extent of competition in the product market and to the ease with which new firms can enter and grow. A major effort is now underway (e.g. at the OECD, the World Bank, and Eurostat) to collect data on cross-country measures of regulatory barriers and to evaluate how they are related to the dynamics of firm entry, exit, and growth.[32]

An intuitive explanation of how product market regulation and labour market institutions may interact and be connected with macroeconomic outcomes is as follows: limited competition in the product market implies that there are monopoly rents available and this creates an incentive for employed workers to act collectively and bargain for a share of these rents. Equally when product market competition is intense, rents are smaller and the gains from collective action in the labour market are less. This line of argument suggests:

- that policies to shift the *PS* curve upwards by reducing product market regulation could have the effect of also pushing the *WS* curve downwards. This would reduce equilibrium unemployment.

- that the sequencing of reforms matters since effective product market reforms would bring in their wake a weakening of the incentives for workers to support some forms of labour market regulation.

However, arguments of this kind usually also rely on the role of new job creation from the entry and growth of new firms. Whilst in new firms (and industries encouraged by a more competitive environment where new entry is easier), workers may have less incentive to create or join unions, for example, employment in old firms will shrink and some old firms will exit from the market. This highlights the redistributive effects of deregulation. There will be losers as well as winners and this will create a further obstacle to reform: political opposition. Amongst the factors likely to generate opposition to reform, even if it were to raise aggregate welfare unambiguously, are the following:

- there are more losers than winners from the change (i.e. there may be no majority in support of the reform)

- existing losers are badly organized and are a minority (e.g. the unemployed)

- winners from the reform are heterogeneous (e.g. the unemployed and those at the top of the income distribution)

- there is uncertainty about who will win and who will lose.

---

[31] For a recent theoretical treatment, see Blanchard and Giavazzi (2003).
[32] For an early detailed study that has stimulated much recent work see Nicoletti, et al. (2001).

6 Conclusions

In this chapter, we have shown how the models presented in the book can be used to investigate the path of unemployment across the OECD since the 1960s and how unemployment varies across countries. Both aggregate demand and aggregate supply play a role in the analysis of unemployment. In the simplest case of a closed economy with a stable supply side (i.e. stable institutions and constant productivity growth), shocks to aggregate demand produce business cycle fluctuations in output and unemployment. A positive demand shock raises output and reduces unemployment. Inflation rises and this produces a response by an inflation-targeting central bank, which raises the real interest rate and guides the economy back to the constant-inflation equilibrium. In an open economy with a stable supply side, fluctuations in aggregate demand may have more persistent effects on output and unemployment because there is a range of constant inflation unemployment rates represented by the *ERU* curve.

The *ERU* curve shifts with changes in labour market policies and institutions, changes in the tax wedge, in product market competition, and with supply-side shocks such as changes in the real price of oil and in the growth rate of productivity. Empirical studies find that many of these factors help to explain both the cross-country pattern of unemployment and changes in unemployment over time. However, caution needs to be exercised when drawing policy conclusions because:

- the estimated magnitude of the effect of different wage- and price-push factors varies widely across studies,
- the effect on unemployment of some labour market institutions depends on the presence of other institutions, i.e. the interaction between institutions matters,
- labour and product market regulations may interact and changes in unemployment may therefore depend on the sequencing of reforms.

The country case studies draw attention to:

- fluctuations in aggregate demand as a major driver of long swings in unemployment (Sweden and Finland),
- the effectiveness of different combinations of supply-side policies along with the revival of aggregate demand (the Netherlands, Ireland, and the UK),
- the problems in designing and implementing a consistent set of supply-side reforms compounded by the context of a tightly constrained macroeconomic policy framework (Germany).

Global trends in trade and technology can affect the heterogeneity of unemployment within countries. We have also seen how the increased skill or regional dispersion of unemployment can raise equilibrium unemployment. This may be more problematic for large than for small countries and for those where labour market institutions tend to produce more compressed wage distributions.

A theme that has emerged in this chapter is that success in reversing lengthy adverse trends in unemployment appears to require that the reforms be coherent in a micro-institutional sense and that they are implemented in a supportive macroeconomic environment. This may be much more difficult to achieve in the large continental economies in EMU than in either the small ones or in the Anglo-Saxon countries.

■ QUESTIONS FOR DISCUSSION

QUESTION A. Does deindustrialization, i.e. the fall in the share of employment in industry, cause unemployment?

QUESTION B. Why is it misleading to assume that changes in the unemployment rate will be reflected directly in opposite changes in the employment rate? Suggest when it is more appropriate to analyse unemployment rates than employment rates and vice versa.

QUESTION C. Since the 1980s Swedish unemployment has followed a very different pattern from the average of European countries. Why?

QUESTION D. Adam Posen of the US Institute for International Economics has claimed that EMU is irrelevant for the German economy. In particular, he states: 'There is ample evidence that changes in monetary regimes induce little change in real economic structures such as labor or financial markets. . . . Most importantly, there is no good reason to believe that the ECB will behave any differently than the Bundesbank.' (Institute for International Economics Working Paper No. 99–5, April 1999.) Do you agree?

QUESTION E. 'Anyone who follows both mainstream macroeconomics and the newspapers knows that the textbook model of the wage-price-unemployment process is in trouble. By the textbook model, I mean the standard accelerationist Phillips curve centered on a stable NAIRU determining wage inflation.' (William Nordhaus, 'Comment', *Brookings Papers on Economic Activity*, No. 2 (1999), 241.) Explain Nordhaus's statement and evaluate it with reference to unemployment in OECD countries.

QUESTION F. Are institutional rigidities bad for economic performance? If so, why do they persist?

QUESTION G. In diagnosing Europe's unemployment problem, Nobel prize-winner James Heckman has claimed[33] that 'An economic order that was well adapted to the more stable and predictable economic environment of the 1950s and 1960s has become dysfunctional in the late twentieth and early twenty-first centuries.' He also argues that the new century requires 'new economics': 'The old economics focused on stable technologies where broad aggregates such as capital and labor were assumed to be homogeneous. The economics of the modern era focuses on models of matching and

---

[33] Heckman (2003).

sorting of heterogeneous individuals into trading and production units in the face of uncertainty about the suitability of any particular trading or production arrangement.' Do you agree with Heckman's assessment?

QUESTION H. The Italian unemployment rate was 11.6% in 1995 and 9.1% in 2001. Discuss the data on regional economic performance in Italy shown in Table 18.10, its implications for national economic performance, and suggest appropriate policy responses.

Table 18.10 Regional economic performance: Italy

	North-Centre		Mezzogiorno	
	1995	2001	1995	2001
GDP per worker	105.3	104.5	86.3	87.2
Employment rate (%)	60.9	65.3	51.1	53.2
Unemployment rate (%)	7.6	4.8	20.4	18.6

Note: GDP per worker for Italy as a whole is set equal to 100 in each period.
Source: OECD *Economic Survey of Italy* (2003), 42.

■ REFERENCES

ABRAMOVSKY, L., R. GRIFFITH, and M. SAKO (2004). 'Offshoring of Business Services and its Impact on the UK Economy'. Advanced Institute of Management Research (AIM Research), IFS, London.

ACEMOGLU, D., P. AGHION, and F. ZILIBOTTI (2002). 'Distance to Frontier, Selection and Economic Growth'. NBER Working Paper 9066.

AGELL, J. (2002). 'On the determinants of labour market institutions: rent seeking vs. social insurance', *German Economic Review*, 3/2: 107–35.

____ and LUNDBORG, P. (2003). 'Survey Evidence on Wage Rigidity and Unemployment: Sweden in the 1990s', *Scandinavian Journal of Economics*, 105/1: 15–29.

AGHION, P., and S. N. DURLAUF (eds.) (forthcoming 2005). *Handbook of Economic Growth*. Amsterdam: North Holland.

____ and P. HOWITT (1998). *Endogenous Growth*. Cambridge, Mass.: MIT Press.

____ ____ (2005). 'Growth with Quality-Improving Innovations: An Integrated Framework' in Aghion and Durlauf (eds.) (forthcoming 2005).

____ C. HARRIS, P. HOWITT, and J. VICKERS (2001). 'Competition, Imitation and Growth with Step-by-Step Innovation', *Review of Economic Studies*, 68/3: 467–92.

____ N. BLOOM, R. BLUNDELL, R. GRIFFITH, and P. HOWITT (2005). 'Competition and Innovation: An Inverted-U Relationship', *Quarterly Journal of Economics*, 120/2: 701–28.

AKERLOF, G. A. (1970). 'The Market for "Lemons": Quality Uncertainty and the Market Mechanism', *Quarterly Journal of Economics*, 84/3: 488–500.

____ (1982). 'Labor Contracts as Partial Gift Exchange', *Quarterly Journal of Economics*, 97/4: 543–69.

____ and J. L. YELLEN (1985). 'Can small deviations from rationality make significant differences to economic equilibria', *American Economic Review*, 75/4: 708–21.

ALESINA, A. (1987). 'Macroeconomic Policy in a Two-Party System as a Repeated Game', *Quarterly Journal of Economics*, 102: 651–78.

____ and S. ARDAGNA (1998). 'Tales of Fiscal Adjustments', *Economic Policy*, 27: 489–545.

____ R. PEROTTI, and J. TAVARES (1998). 'The Political Economy of Fiscal Adjustments', *Brookings Papers on Economic Activity*, 1: 197–266.

ALLEN, C., M. GASIOREK, and A. SMITH (1998). 'The Competition Effects of the Single Market in Europe', *Economic Policy*, 27: 441–86.

ALLSOPP, C., and D. VINES (2000). 'The Assessment: Macroeconomic Policy', *Oxford Review of Economic Policy*, 16/4: 1–32.

AMITI, M., and S.-J. WEI (2004). 'Fear of service outsourcing: is it justified?'. NBER Working Paper 10808.

ARROW, K. J. (1962). 'The economic implications of learning by doing', *Review of Economic Studies*, 29: 155–73.

ARTIS, M., and M. LEWIS (1993). 'Après le deluge: Monetary and Exchange Rate Policy in Britain and Europe', *Oxford Review of Economic Policy*, 9/3: 36–61.

ATTANASIO, O., and G. WEBER (1995). 'Is Consumption Growth Consistent with Intertemporal Optimization? Evidence from the Consumer Expenditure Survey', *Journal of Political Economy*, 103/6: 1121–57.

AUERBACH, A. J., and D. FEENBERG (2000). 'The Significance of Federal Taxes as Automatic Stabilizers'. NBER Working Paper No. 7662.

AUTOR, D. H., F. LEVY, and R. J. MURNANE (2003). 'The Skill Content of Recent Technological Change: An Empirical Exploration', *Quarterly Journal of Economics*, 118: 1279–333.

BAKER, D., A. GLYN, D. HOWELL, and J. SCHMITT (2005). 'Labor Market Institutions and Unemployment: A Critical Assessment of the Cross-Country Evidence', in D. R. Howell (ed.), *Fighting Unemployment: The Limits of Free Market Orthodoxy*. New York: Oxford University Press.

BALL, L. (1994), 'What Determines the Sacrifice Ratio?', in N. G. Mankiw (ed.), *Monetary Policy*. Chicago: University of Chicago Press, 155–82.

____ (1999a). 'Aggregate Demand and Long Run Unemployment', *Brookings Papers on Economic Activity*, 2: 189–251.

____ (1999b). 'Efficient Rules for Monetary Policy', *International Finance*, 2/1: 63–83.

Bank of England (1999). *The Transmission of Monetary Policy*, www.bankofengland.co.uk/montrans.pdf.

BANKS, J., and S. TANNER (1999). *Household Saving in the UK*, IFS Report, October 1999.

BARRO, R. J. (1974). 'Are Government Bonds Net Wealth?', *Journal of Political Economy*, 82/6: 1095–117.

____ and J.-W. LEE (2000). 'International Data on Educational Attainment: Updates and Implications'. CID Working Paper No. 42.

____ and X. SALA-I-MARTIN (2004). *Economic Growth* (2nd edn.). Cambridge, Mass.: MIT Press.

BAUMOL, W. J. (2001). 'Paradox of the Services: Exploding Costs, Persistent Demand', in T. ten Raa and R. Schettkat, *The Growth of Service Industries*. Cheltenham: Elgar, 3–28.

BEAN, C. (1998). 'The New UK Monetary Arrangements: A View from the Literature', *Economic Journal*, 108: 1795–809.

BELOT, M., and J. VAN OURS (2000). 'Does the Recent Success of some OECD Countries in Lowering their Unemployment Rate Lie in the Clever Design of their Economic Reforms?'. Institute for the Study of Labor (IZA) Discussion Paper No. 147.

BENHABIB, J., and M. SPIEGEL (1994). 'The Role of Human Capital in Economic Development: Evidence from Aggregate Cross-Country Data', *Journal of Monetary Economics*, 34/2: 143–73.

BERMAN, E., J. BOUND, and S. MACHIN (1998). 'Implications of Skill-Biased Technical Progress: International Evidence', *Quarterly Journal of Economics*, 113: 1245–80.

BERNANKE, B. S. (2000). 'Japanese Monetary Policy: A Case of Self-induced Paralysis?', in A. S. Posen and R. Mikitani (eds.), *Japan's Financial Crisis and its Parallels to US Experience*. Washington, DC: IIE.

BERTOLA, G. M., F. D. BLAU, and L. M. KAHN (2001). 'Comparative Analysis of Labor Market Outcomes: Lessons for the United States from International Long-Run Evidence'. NBER Working Paper No. w8526.

BEWLEY, T. (1999). *Why Wages Don't Fall During a Recession*. Cambridge, Mass.: Harvard University Press.

BHASKAR, V. (1990). 'Wage Relativities and the Natural Range of Unemployment', *Economic Journal*, 100/400: 60–6.

BILS, M., and P. J. KLENOW (2000). 'Does Schooling Cause Growth?, *American Economic Review*, 90/5: 1160–83.

BLANCHARD, O. (1984). 'The Lucas Critique and the Volcker Deflation', *American Economic Review*, 74/2: 211–15.

____ and F. GIAVAZZI (2002). 'Current Account Deficits in the Euro Area: The End of the Feldstein-Horioka Puzzle?' *Brookings Papers on Economic Activity*, 2: 146–87.

____ (2003). 'Macroeconomic Effects of Regulation and Deregulation in Goods and Labor Markets', *Quarterly Journal of Economics*, 118/3: 879–907.

____ and N. KIYOTAKI (1987). 'Monopolistic Competition and the Effects of Aggregate Demand', *American Economic Review*, 77/4: 647–66.

____ and P.-A. MUET (1993). 'Competitiveness through Disinflation: An Assessment of the French Macroeconomic Strategy', *Economic Policy*, 16: 11–56.

____ and T. PHILIPPON (2004). 'The Quality of Labor Relations and Unemployment'. NBER Working Paper No. 10590.

____ and L. SUMMERS (1986). 'Hysteresis and the European Unemployment Problem', *NBER Macroeconomics Annual*, 15–77.

____ and J. WOLFERS (2000). 'The Role of Shocks and Institutions in the Rise of European Unemployment: The Aggregate Evidence', *Economic Journal*, 110/462: 1–33.

BLINDER, A. S. (1998). *Central Banking in Theory and Practice: Lionel Robbins Lectures*. Cambridge, Mass.: MIT Press.

____ and R. M. SOLOW (1973). 'Does fiscal policy matter?', *Journal of Public Economics*, 2: 319–37.

____ ____ (1976). 'Does Fiscal Policy Matter? A Correction', *Journal of Public Economics*, 5: 183–84.

BLUNDELL, R., S. BOND, M. DEVEREUX, and F. SCHIANTARELLI (1992). 'Investment and Tobin's

Q: Evidence from Company Panel Data', *Journal of Econometrics*, 51/1–2: 233–57.

——— BROWNING, and C. MEGHIR (1994). 'A Microeconometric Model of Intertemporal Substitution and Consumer Demand', *Review of Economic Studies*, 61/1: 57–80.

BOLTHO, A., and J. CORBETT (2000). 'The Assessment: Japan's Stagnation: Can Policy Revive the Economy?', *Oxford Review of Economic Policy*, 16/2: 1–17.

BOND, S., and J. CUMMINS (2001). 'Noisy Share Prices and the Q Model of Investment'. IFS Working Paper W01/22.

——— and T. J. JENKINSON (1996), 'Investment Performance and Policy', *Oxford Review of Economic Policy*, 12/2: 1–29.

BRACONIER, H., and K. EKHOLM (2000). 'Swedish Multinationals and Competition from High- and Low-Wage Locations', *Review of International Economics*, 8/3: 448–61.

BRIOTTI, M. G. (2004). 'Fiscal Adjustment between 1991 and 2002: Stylised Facts and Policy Implications'. ECB Occasional Paper Series.

BUITER, W. (2001). 'Notes on "A Code for Fiscal Stability" ', *Oxford Economic Papers*, 53: 1–19.

——— (2003). 'Deflation: Prevention and Cure'. CEPR Discussion Paper No. 3869.

——— and C. GRAFE (2004). 'Patching up the Pact', *The Economics of Transition*, 12/1: 67–102.

——— and M. H. MILLER (1981). 'The Thatcher Experiment: The First Two Years', *Brookings Papers on Economic Activity*, 2: 315–79.

CABALLERO, R. (1999). 'Investment', in J. B. Taylor and M. Woodford (eds.), *Handbook of Macroeconomics*. Amsterdam: NorthHolland.

CAGAN, P. (1956). 'The Monetary Dynamics of Hyperinflation', in M. Friedman (ed.), *Studies in the Quantity Theory of Money*. Chicago: University of Chicago Press, 25–117.

CALMFORS, L. (1993). 'Lessons from the Macroeconomic Experience of Sweden', *European Journal of Political Economy*, 9: 25–72.

——— and J. DRIFFILL. (1988). 'Bargaining Structure, Corporatism and Macroeconomic Performance', *Economic Policy*, 6: 14–61.

CALVO, G. A. (1983). 'Staggered Prices in a Utility Maximizing Framework', *Journal of Monetary Economics*, 12/3: 383–98.

——— and C. REINHART (2002). 'Fear of Floating'. *Quarterly Journal of Economics*, 117/ 2: 379–408.

CAMPBELL, C. M., III, and K. S. KAMLANI (1997). 'The Reasons for Wage Rigidity: Evidence from a Survey of Firms', *Quarterly Journal of Economics*, 112/3: 759–89.

CAMPBELL, J. (1994). 'Inspecting the Mechanism: An Analytical Approach to the Stochastic Growth Model', *Journal of Monetary Economics*, 33: 463–506.

CARD, D., and J. DINARDO (2002), 'Skill Biased Technological Change and Rising Wage Inequality: Some Problems and Puzzles'. NBER Working Paper No. W8769.

——— and R. B. FREEMAN (2004). 'What Have Two Decades of British Economic Reform Delivered?' in Card, Blundell, and Freeman (2004).

——— R. BLUNDELL, and R. B. FREEMAN (eds.) (2004). *Seeking a Premier Economy: The Economic Effects of British Economic Reforms, 1980–2000*. Chicago: University of Chicago Press.

——— F. KRAMARZ, and T. LEMIEUX (1999). 'Changes in the Relative Structure of Wages and Employment: A Comparison of the United States, Canada and France', *Canadian Journal of Economics*, 32: 843–77.

CARLIN, W., and C. MAYER (2003). 'Finance, investment and growth', *Journal of Financial Economics*, 69/1: 191–226.

——— and D. SOSKICE (1990). *Macroeconomics and the Wage Bargain: A Modern Approach to Employment, Inflation and the Exchange Rate*. Oxford: Oxford University Press.

——— ——— (1997). 'Shocks to the System: The German Political Economy under Stress', *National Institute Economic Review*, 1/97: 57–76.

——— (2005). 'The 3-Equation New Keynesian Model-A Graphical Exposition', *Contributions to Macroeconomics* (forthcoming). www.bepress.com/bejm/contributions

——— A. GLYN, and J. VAN REENEN (2001). 'Export Market Performance of OECD Countries: An Empirical Examination of the Role of Cost Competitiveness', *Economic Journal*, 111/468: 128–62.

——— M. SCHAFFER, and P. SEABRIGHT (2004). 'A Minimum of Rivalry: Evidence from Transition Economies on the Importance of Competition for Innovation and Growth', *Contributions to Economic Analysis and Policy*, 32, Article 17. www.bepress.com/bejeap/contributions/vol3/iss1/art17.

CHECCHI, D., and C. LUCIFORA (2002). 'Unions and Labour Market Institutions in Europe', *Economic Policy*, 35: 363–401.

CHEUNG, Y.-W., M. CHINN, and I. MARSH (2000). 'How do UK Foreign Exchange Dealers Think their Market Operates'. NBER Working Paper 7524.

CHIANG, A. (2000). *Elements of Dynamic Optimization*. Prospect Heights: Waveland Press.

CHICK, V. (1977). *The Theory of Monetary Policy* (rev. edn.). Oxford: Blackwell.

—— (1992). 'The Evolution of the Banking System and the Theory of Saving, Investment and Interest', in P. Arestis and S. Dow (eds.) *Victoria Chick: On Money, Method and Keynes. Selected Essays*. New York: St Martins Press.

CHINN, M., and G. MEREDITH (2002). 'Testing Uncovered Interest Parity at Short and Long Horizons in the Post Bretton Woods Era'. University of California Santa Cruz Working Paper.

CHIRINKO, R. S. (1993). 'Business Fixed Investment Spending: Modeling Strategies, Empirical Results, and Policy Implications', *Journal of Economic Literature*, 31/4: 1875–911.

CHO, I.-K. and D. KREPS (1987), 'Signalling Games and Stable Equilibria', *Quarterly Journal of Economics*, 102: 179–222.

CHRISTIANO, L. J. , M. EICHENBAUM, and C. L. EVANS (2005). 'Nominal Rigidities and the Dynamic Effects of a Shock to Monetary Policy', *Journal of Political Economy*, 113/1: 1–45.

CLARIDA, R., and M. GERTLER (1997). 'How the Bundesbank Conducts Monetary Policy', in C. Romer and D. Romer (eds.), *Reducing Inflation: Motivation and Strategy*. Chicago: University of Chicago Press.

——J. GALI, and M. GERTLER (1999). 'The Science of Monetary Policy: A New Keynesian Perspective', *Journal of Economic Literature*, 37/4: 1661–707.

COLLINS, C., J. KENWAY, and J. MCLEOD (2000). 'Factors Influencing Educational Performance of Males and Females in School and their Initial Destinations after Leaving School'. Commonwealth of Australia, Ausinfo, Canberra.

CUMMINS, J. G., K. A. HASSETT, and R. G. HUBBARD (1994). 'A Reconsideration of Investment Behavior Using Tax Reforms as Natural Experiments' *Brookings Papers on Economic Activity*, 2: 1–74.

CUTHBERTSON, K., and D. GASPARRO (1993). 'The Determinants of Manufacturing Investment in the UK', *Economic Journal*, 103/421: 1479–92.

DEATON, A. (1992). *Understanding Consumption*, Oxford: Oxford University Press.

DE GRAUWE, P. (2003). *Economics of Monetary Union* (5th edn.). Oxford: Oxford University Press.

DE MELLO, L., P. M. KONGSRUD, and R. W. R. PRICE (2004). 'Saving Behaviour and the Effectiveness of Fiscal Policy'. OECD Economics Department Working Paper No. 397.

DESJONQUERES, T., S. MACHIN, and J. VAN REENEN (1999). 'Another Nail in the Coffin? Or Can the Trade Based Explanation of Changing Skill Structures Be Resurrected?', *Scandinavian Journal of Economics* (December), 101/4: 533–54.

DE VROEY, M. (2004a). *Involuntary Unemployment: The Elusive Quest for a Theory*. London: Routledge.

—— (2004b). 'Involuntary Unemployment: The Elusive Quest for a Theory', Université Catholique de Louvain Discussion Paper 2005–04.

DI TELLA R., R. J. MACCULLOCH, and A. J. OSWALD (2003). 'The Macroeconomics of Happiness', *Review of Economics and Statistics*, 85/4: 809–27.

DIXIT, A. (1992). 'Investment and Hysteresis', *Journal of Economic Perspectives*, 6/1: 107–32.

DORNBUSCH, R. (1976). 'Expectations and Exchange Rate Dynamics', *Journal of Political Economy*, 84/6: 1161–76.

—— (1996). 'The Effectiveness of Exchange Rate Changes'. *Oxford Review of Economic Policy*, 12/3: 26–38.

DOWRICK, S., and M. ROGERS (2002). 'Classical and Technological Convergence: Beyond the Solow-Swan Growth Model'. *Oxford Economic Papers*, 54: 369–85.

DOWNS, A. S. (1957). *An Economic Theory of Democracy*. New York: Harper & Row.

DUFLO, E., M. KREMER, and J. ROBINSON (2005). 'Understanding Technology Adoption: Fertilizer in Western Kenya: Preliminary Results from Field Experiments', Mimeo, MIT.

EGEBO, T., and A. S. ENGLANDER (1992). 'Institutional Commitments and Policy Credibility: A Critical Survey and Empirical Evidence from the ERM', *OECD Economic Studies*, 18: 46–84.

EICHENGREEN, B., and C. WYPLOSZ (1993). 'The Unstable EMS', *Brookings Papers on Economic Activity*, 1: 51–143.

ELMESKOV, M. J., and S. SCARPETTA (1998). 'Key Lessons for Labor Market Reforms: Evidence from OECD Countries' Experience', *Swedish Economic Policy Review*, 5/2: 205–52.

EMERSON, M. (ed.) (1992). *One Market, One Money*. Oxford: Oxford University Press.

ERICSSON, N. R., D. F. HENDRY, and K. M. PRESTWICH (1998). 'The Demand for Broad Money in the United Kingdom, 1878–1993', *Scandinavian Journal of Economics*, 100/1: 289–324.

ESTRELLA, A., and J. C. FUHRER (2002). 'Dynamic Inconsistencies: Counterfactual Implications of a Class of Rational-Expectations Models', *American Economic Review*, 92/4: 1013–28.

European Central Bank (2004). *The Monetary Policy of the ECB 2004*. Frankfurt: ECB.

FELDSTEIN, M., and C. HORIOKA (1980). 'Domestic Saving and International Capital Flows', *Economic Journal*, 90: 314–29.

FLANAGAN, R., D. SOSKICE, and L. ULMAN (1983). *Unionism, Economic Stabilization and Incomes Policies: European Experience*. Washington: Brookings Institution.

FISCHER, S. (2001). 'Exchange Rate Regimes: Is the Bipolar View Correct?', *Journal of Economic Perspectives*, 15: 3–24.

——— R. SAHAY, and C. A. VÉGH (2002). 'Modern Hyper- and High Inflations', *Journal of Economic Literature*, 40: 837–80.

FISHLOW, A. (1987). 'Gerschenkron, Alexander', in J. Eatwell, M. Milgate, and P. Newman (eds.), *The New Palgrave: A Dictionary of Economics*. London: Macmillan, 518–19.

FRANKEL, J. A., and P. R. ORSAG (eds.) (2002). *American Economic Policy in the 1990s*. Cambridge, Mass.: MIT Press.

FRANKEL, M. (1962). 'The Production Function in Allocation and Growth: A Synthesis', *American Economic Review*, 52/5: 995–1022.

FREEMAN, R. B. (ed.) (1994). *Working under Different Rules*. New York: Russell Sage Foundation.

FRENCH, E. (2004). 'The Labor Supply Response to (Mismeasured but) Predictable Wage Changes', *Review of Economics and Statistics*, 86/2: 602–13.

FRIEDMAN, M. (1968). 'The Role of Monetary Policy', *American Economic Review*, 58/1: 1–17.

——— (1969). *The Optimum Quantity of Money and Other Essays*. Chicago: Aldine.

——— (1997). 'John Maynard Keynes'. *Federal Reserve Bank of Richmond, Economic Quarterly*, 83/2: 1–23.

GÄCHTER, S., and E. FEHR (2001). 'Fairness in the Labour Market—A Survey of Experimental Results', in F. Bolle and M. Lehmann-Waffenschmidt (eds.), *Surveys in Experimental Economics: Bargaining, Cooperation and Election Stock Markets*. Heidelberg: Physica Verlag.

GERSCHENKRON, A. (1962). *Economic Backwardness in Historical Perspective*. Cambridge, Mass.: Harvard University Press.

GHOBARAH, H., P. HUTH, and B. RUSSETT (2003). 'Civil Wars Kill and Maim People—Long after the Shooting Stops', *American Political Science Review*, 97/2: 189–202.

GIAVAZZI, F., and C. A. FAVERO (2003). 'Revisiting "Immediate Challenges for the European Central Bank" ', in HM Treasury, *Submissions on EMU from leading academics: EMU study*. London: Stationery Office.

——— and M. PAGANO (1988). 'The Advantage of Tying one's Hands: EMS Discipline and Central Bank Credibility' *European Economic Review*, 32/5: 1055–75.

GIBBONS, R. (1992). *Game Theory for Applied Economics*. Princeton: Princeton University Press.

GODLEY, M., and A. IZURIETA (2001). 'As the Implosion Begins ...? Prospects and Policies for the U.S. Economy: A Strategic View', Levy Institute and later updates available on the Levy Institute website.

GOLDBERG, P., and M. KNETTER (1997). 'Goods Prices and Exchange Rates: What Have We Learned?' *Journal of Economic Literature*, 35: 1243–72.

GOODFRIEND, M., and R. G. KING (1997). 'The New Neoclassical Synthesis and the Role of Monetary Policy'. *NBER Macroeconomics Annual*, 12: 231–83.

GOODHART, C. (1989). 'The Conduct of Monetary Policy', *Economic Journal*, 99: 293–346.

——— (2002). 'The Endogenity of Money', in P. Arestis, M. Desai, and S. Dow (eds.), *Money, Macroeconomics and Keynes: Essays in Honour of Victoria Chick*. London: Routledge.

Goos, M., and A. Manning (2003). 'Lousy and Lovely Jobs: The Rising Polarization of Work in Britain'. CEP Discussion Paper No. 604.

Gordon, R. J. (2004). 'Five Puzzles in the Behavior of Productivity, Investment, and Innovation'. Mimeo, Northwestern University.

Groshen, E., and S. Potter (2003), 'Has Structural Change Contributed to a Jobless Recovery?' New York: Federal Reserve Bank of New York website.

Hall, P. A., and D. Soskice (2001). 'An Introduction to the Varieties of Capitalism', in P. A. Hall and D. Soskice (eds.), *Varieties of Capitalism: The Institutional Foundations of Comparative Advantage*. Oxford: Oxford University Press, 1–68.

Hall, R. (1978). 'Stochastic Implications of the Life-Cycle Permanent Income Hypothesis', *Journal of Political Economy*, 86/6: 971–87.

Ham, J. C., and K. T. Reilly (2002). 'Testing Intertemporal Substitution, Implicit Contracts, and Hours Restriction Models of the Labor Market Using Micro Data', *American Economic Review*, 92/4: 905–27.

Harsanyi, J. C. (1967–8). 'Games with Incomplete Information Played by Bayesian Players', Pts I–III, *Management Science*, 14: 159–82, 320–34, 486–502.

Heckman, J. J. (2003). 'The Labour Market and the Job Miracle', *CESifo Forum*, 2: 29–32.

Hibbs, D. (1977). 'Political Parties and Macroeconomic Policy', *American Political Science Review*, 71: 1467–87.

Hicks, J. (1937). 'Mr Keynes and the Classics: A Suggested Reinterpretation', *Econometrica*, 5: 147–59.

Holden, S., and J. Driscoll (2004). 'Fairness and Inflation Persistence'. *Journal of European Economic Association*, 2/2–3, *Papers and Proceedings*: 240–51.

Honahan, P., and B. Walsh (2002). 'Catching Up with the Leaders: The Irish Hare', *Brookings Papers on Economic Activity*, 1: 1–77.

Hoover, K. D. (1988). *The New Classical Macroeconomics*. Oxford: Blackwell.

Howard, J. W., and G. Zoega (2003). 'U.S. Regional Business Cycles and the Natural Rate of Unemployment'. St Louis Federal Reserve Working Paper 2003–030A.

Howell, D. R. (ed.) (2005). *Fighting Unemployment: The Limits of Free Market Orthodoxy*. New York: Oxford University Press.

Howitt, P. (2001). 'Learning about Monetary Theory and Policy'. Mimeo, Brown University.

Johnson, D., J. Parker, and N. Souleles (2004). 'How Households Responded to Tax Rebates of 2001'. NBER Working Paper No. 10784.

Jones, C. I. (1995). 'R&D-Based Models of Economic Growth', *Journal of Political Economy*, 103: 759–84.

____ (1997). 'On the Evolution of the World Income Distribution', *Journal of Economic Perspectives*, 11/3: 19–36.

____ (2005). 'Growth and Ideas' in P. Aghion, and S. N. Durlauf (eds.) (forthcoming 2005).

Kaplan, E., and D. Rodrik (2001). 'Did the Malaysian Capital Controls Really Work?'. NBER Working Paper No. w8142.

Keynes, J. M. (1936). *The General Theory of Employment, Interest and Money*. London: Macmillan.

King, M. A. (1997). 'Changes in UK Monetary policy: Rules versus Discretion in Practice', *Journal of Monetary Economics*, 39: 81–97.

Korten, D. (2001), *When Corporations Rule the World* (2nd edn.). Bloomfield, Conn.: Kumarian Press.

Kremer, M. (2004), 'On How to Improve World Health', *Daedalus*, 133/3: 120–3.

Krueger, A. B. (1991). 'Ownership, Agency, and Wages: An Examination of Franchising in the Fast Food Industry', *Quarterly Journal of Economics*, 106/1: 75–101.

____ and J.-S. Pischke (1997). 'Observations and Conjectures on the U.S. Employment Miracle'. NBER Working Paper No. 6146.

Krugman, P. (1994). 'Past and Prospective Causes of High Unemployment', *Economic Review*, Federal Reserve Bank of Kansas City, 23–43.

____ (1998). 'It's Baaack: Japan's Slump and the Return of the Liquidity Trap', *Brookings Papers on Economic Activity*, 2: 137–205.

Kydland, F. E., and E. C. Prescott (1977). 'Rules Rather than Discretion: The Inconsistency of Optimal Plans', *Journal of Political Economy*, 85/3: 473–92.

____ ____ (1982). 'Time to Build and Aggregate Fluctuations', *Econometrica*, 50/6: 1345–70.

LA PORTA, R., F. LOPEZ-DE-SILANES, A. SHLEIFER, and R. W. VISHNY (1997). 'Legal Determinants of External Finance', *Journal of Finance*, 52/3: 1131–50.

LAYARD, R., and S. NICKELL (1986). 'Unemployment in the UK', *Economica*, 53: S121–66.

LEBOW, D. E, R. E. SAKS, and B. A. WILSON (2003). 'Downward Nominal Wage Rigidity: Evidence from the Employment Cost Index', *Advances in Macroeconomics*: 3/1, Article 2. www.bepress.com/bejm/advances/vol3/iss1/art2.

LEIJONHUFVUD, A. (1987). 'IS-LM Analysis', in *The New Palgrave: A Dictionary of Economics*. Basingstoke: Macmillan.

LESCH, H. (2004). 'Trade Union Density in International Comparison', *CESifo Forum*, 4: 12–18.

LINDBECK, A., and D. J. SNOWER (1986). 'Wage Setting, Unemployment and Insider-Outsider Relation', *American Economic Review*, 76/2, *Papers and Proceedings*, 235–9.

LIPSEY, R. G., and K. I. CARLAW (2004). 'Total Factor Productivity and the Measurement of Technological Change', *Canadian Journal of Economics*, 37/4: 1118–50.

LJUNGQVIST, L., and T. SARGENT, (2004). *Recursive Macroeconomic Theory*. Cambridge, Mass.: MIT Press.

LONG, J. B., Jr., and C. I. PLOSSER (1983). 'Real Business Cycles', *Journal of Political Economy*, 91/1: 39–69.

LUCAS, R. E., Jr. (1972). 'Expectations and the Neutrality of Money', *Journal of Economic Theory*, 4: 103–24.

—— (1975). 'An Equilibrium Model of the Business Cycle', *Journal of Political Economy*, 83: 1113–44.

—— (1976). 'Econometric Policy Evaluation: A critique', *Carnegie-Rochester Conference Series on Public Policy*, 1: 19–46.

—— (1988). 'On the Mechanics of Economic Development', *Journal of Monetary Economics*, 22: 3–42.

MCCALLUM, B. T., and E. NELSON (1999). 'An Optimizing *IS-LM* Specification for Monetary Policy and Business Cycle Analysis', *Journal of Money, Credit and Banking*, 31/ 3/1: 296–316.

MCDONALD, I. M. (1995). 'Models of the Range of Equilibria', in R. Cross (ed.), *The Natural Rate of Unemployment: Reflections on 25 years of the Hypothesis*. London: Cambridge University Press, 101–52.

MADDISON, A. (1991). *Dynamic Forces in Capitalist Development: A Long-run Comparative View*. Oxford: Oxford University Press.

—— (1998). *Chinese Economic Performance in the Long-Run*. Paris: OECD Development Centre.

MANKIW, N. G. (1985). 'Small Menu Costs and Large Business Cycles: A Macroeconomic Model of Monopoly', *Quarterly Journal of Economics*, 101/2: 529–37.

—— (2002). 'US Monetary Policy during the 1990s', in J. A. Frankel and P. R. Orszag (eds.), *American Economic Policy in the 1990s*. Cambridge: MIT Press.

—— and R. REIS (2002). 'Sticky Information Versus Sticky Prices: A Proposal to Replace the New Keynesian Phillips Curve', *Quarterly Journal of Economics*, 117/4: 1295–328.

—— D. ROMER, and D. N. WEIL (1992). 'A Contribution to the Empirics of Economic Growth', *Quarterly Journal of Economics*, 107/2: 407–37.

MARIN, D. (2004). 'A Nation of Poets and Thinkers —less so with Eastern Enlargement? Austria and Germany'. CEPR Discussion Paper 4358.

MEGHIR, C. (2004). 'A Retrospective on Friedman's Theory of Permanent Income', *Economic Journal*, 114: F293–306.

MELTZER, A. H., and S. F. RICHARD (1981). 'A Rational Theory of the Size of Government', *Journal of Political Economy*, 89/5: 914–27.

MISHKIN, F. S. (1999). 'International Experiences with Different Monetary Policy Regimes', *Journal of Monetary Economics*, 43/3: 579–605.

MUELLBAUER, J. (1994). 'The Assessment: Consumer Expenditure', *Oxford Review of Economic Policy*, 10/2: 1–41.

—— and L. NUNZIATA (2004). 'Forecasting (and Explaining) US Business Cycles'. CEPR DP 4584.

MUTH, J. F. (1961). 'Rational Expectations and the Theory of Price Movements', *Econometrica*, 29/3: 315–35.

NELSON, R. E., and E. S. PHELPS (1966). 'Investment in Humans, Technological Diffusion, and Economic Growth', *American Economic Review*, 56/2: 69–75.

NEWBERY, D. M. (1987). 'Ramsey Model', *The New Palgrave: A Dictionary of Economics*, Vol iv. Basingstoke: Macmillan, 46–8.

NICKELL, S. (1997). 'Unemployment and Labor Market Rigidities: Europe Versus North America', *Journal of Economic Perspectives*, 11/3: 55–74.

NICKELL, S. (1997). and J. VAN OURS (2000). 'The Netherlands and the United Kingdom: A European Unemployment Miracle', *Economic Policy*, 30.

——— L. NUNZIATA, W. OCHEL, and G. QUINTINI (2001/2003). 'The Beveridge Curve, Unemployment and Wages in the OECD from the 1960s to the 1990s'. London: CEP, LSE (2001). Also in P. Aghion, R. Frydman, J. Stiglitz, and M. Woodford (2003) (eds.), *Knowledge, Information and Expectations in Modern Macroeconomics: In Honor of Edmund S. Phelps*. Princeton: Princeton University Press (2003).

NICOLETTI, G., A. BASSANINI, J. SÉBASTIEN, E. EKKEHARD, P. SANTIAGO, and P. SWAIM (2001). 'Product and Labour Market Interactions in OECD Countries'. OECD Economics Department Working Papers No. 312.

OBSTFELD, M. (2001). 'International Macroeconomics: Beyond the Mundell–Fleming model'. IMF Staff Papers, 47, Special Issue, 1–39.

—— and K. ROGOFF (2000*a*). 'Global Economic Integration Opportunities and Challenges'. Federal Reserve Bank of Kansas City Annual Monetary Policy Symposium.

——— ——— (2000*b*). 'New directions for Stochastic Open Economy Models', *Journal of International Economics*, 50: 117–53.

——— ——— (2004). 'The Unsustainable US Current Account Position Revisited'. NBER Working Paper 10869.

OECD (1994). *Jobs Study*. Paris: OECD.

—— (1999*a*). 'Employment Protection and Labor Market Performance', *Employment Outlook*. Paris: OECD.

—— (1999*b*) *Implementing the Jobs Study*. Paris: OECD.

—— (various years). *Economic Outlook*. Paris: OECD.

—— (various years). *Economic Survey* (of various OECD countries). Paris: OECD.

OFEK, E., and M. RICHARDSON (2002). 'The Valuation and Market Rationality of Internet Stock Prices', *Oxford Review of Economic Policy*, 18/3: 265–87.

OLINER, S. D., and D. E. SICHEL (2000). 'The Resurgence of Growth in the Late 1990s: Is Information Technology the Story?' *Journal of Economic Perspectives*, 14: 3–22.

ORPHANIDES, A., and J. C. WILLIAMS (2005). 'Imperfect Knowledge, Inflation Expectations, and Monetary Policy', in B. S. Bernanke and M. Woodford (eds.), *The Inflation-Targeting Debate*. Chicago: University of Chicago Press.

OVERMAN, H. G., and D. PUGA (2002). 'Unemployment Clusters across Europe's Regions and Countries', *Economic Policy*, 17/ 34: 115–47.

PAGAN, A. (2003). 'Report on Modelling and Forecasting at the Bank of England', www.bankofengland.co.uk/pressreleases/ 2003/paganreport.pdf.

PEMBERTON, M., and N. RAU (2001). *Mathematics for Economists*. Manchester: Manchester University Press.

PENCAVEL, J. (2004). 'The Surprising Retreat of Union Britain', in D. Card, R. Blundell, and R. B. Freeman (ed.), *Seeking a Premier Economy: The Economic Effects of British Economic Reforms, 1980–2000*. Chicago: University of Chicago Press.

PERSSON, T., and G. TABELLINI (1990). *Macroeconomic Policy, Credibility and Politics*. Chur, Switzerland: Harwood Academic Publishers.

PHELPS, E. S. (1967). 'Phillips Curves, Expectations of Inflation and Optimal Unemployment over Time', *Economica*, New Series, 34/135: 254–81.

—— (1994). *Structural Slumps: The Modern Equilibrium Theory of Unemployment, Interest and Assets*. Cambridge, Mass.: Harvard University Press.

PHILLIPS, A.W. (1958). 'The Relation between Unemployment and the Rate of Change of Money Wage Rates in the United Kingdom, 1861–1957', *Economica*, 25: 283–99.

PINDYCK, R. S. (1991). 'Irreversibility, Uncertainty and Investment', *Journal of Economic Literature*, 26/3: 1110–48.

PISSARIDES, C. (2001). 'Employment Protection', *Labour Economics*, 8: 131–59.

Poole, W. (1970). 'Optimal Choice of Monetary Policy Instruments in a Simple Stochastic Macro Model', *Quarterly Journal of Economics*, 84: 197–216.

Posen, A. S. (2003). 'It takes more than a Bubble to Become Japan'. IIE Working Paper 03–9.

Posen, A. S. (2004). 'What Went Right in Japan'. Policy Briefs in International Economics, IIE, November 2004.

—— and T. Ito (2004). 'Inflation Targeting and Japan: Why has the Bank of Japan not Adopted inflation targeting?'. NBER Working Paper 10818.

—— and R. Mikitani (eds.) (2000). *Japan's Financial Crisis and its Parallels to US Experience*. Washington, DC: IIE.

Putnam, R. D. (2000). *Bowling Alone: The Collapse and Revival of American Community*. New York: Simon & Schuster.

Qian, Y. (2003). 'How Reform Worked in China', in D. Rodrik (ed.), *In Search of Prosperity: Analytic Narratives on Economic Growth*. Princeton: Princeton University Press.

Quiggin, J. (2004). 'The Unsustainability of US Trade Deficits', *The Economists' Voice*, 1/3, Article 2.

Rau, N. (1985). 'Simplifying the Theory of the Government Budget Restraint', *Oxford Economic Papers*, 37/2: 210–29.

Robinson, J. (1953–4). 'Production Functions and the Theory of Capital', *Review of Economic Studies*, 25: 81–106.

Roed, K. (1997). 'Hysteresis in Unemployment', *Journal of Economic Surveys*, 11/4: 389–418.

Rogoff, K. (2002). 'Dornbusch's Overshooting Model after Twenty-Five Years'. Second Annual IMF Research Conference: The Mundell-Fleming Lecture. www.imf.org/external/np/speeches/2001/112901.htm.

Roland, G. (2000). *Transition and Economics: Politics, Markets, and Firms*. Cambridge, Mass.: MIT Press.

Romer, C., and D. Romer (eds.) (1997). *Reducing Inflation: Motivation and Strategy*. Chicago: University of Chicago Press,

Romer, P. M. (1986). 'Increasing Returns and Long-Run Growth', *Journal of Political Economy*, 94: 1002–37.

Romer, D. (2001). *Advanced Macroeconomics* (2nd edn.). New York: McGraw-Hill.

—— (1990). 'Endogenous Technological Change', *Journal of Political Economy*, 98: 71–102.

Rotemberg, J. J., and M. Woodford (1999). 'The Cyclical Behavior of Prices and Costs', in J. B. Taylor and M. Woodford (eds.), *Handbook of Macroeconomics*, Vol. ib. Amsterdam: Elsevier, ch. 16.

Rowthorn, R. E. (1999). 'Unemployment, Wage-Bargaining and Capital-Labour Substitution', *Cambridge Journal of Economics*, 23/44: 413–25.

—— and K. Coutts (2004). 'Commentary: De-industrialisation and the Balance of Payments in Advanced Economies', *Cambridge Journal of Economics*, 28/5: 767–90.

—— and R. Ramaswamy (1997). 'Deindustrialization: Causes and Implications'. IMF Working Paper WP/97/42.

Rubin, R. (2002). 'Comment' on 'Fiscal Policy and Social Security Policy during the 1990s' by D. W. Elmendorf, J. B. Liebman, and D. W. Wilcox in Frankel and Orszag (2002).

Schettkat, R. (2003). 'Are Institutional Rigidities at the Root of European Unemployment?', *Cambridge Journal of Economics*, 27: 771–87.

Schumpeter, J. A. (1934; 1961 edition). *The Theory of Economic Development*. New York: OUP Galaxy.

Seabright, P. (2004). *The Company of Strangers: A Natural History of Economic Life*. Princeton: Princeton University Press.

Seater, J. J. (1993). 'Ricardian Equivalence', *Journal of Economic Literature*, 31: 142–90.

Shapiro, C., and J. Stiglitz (1984). 'Equilibrium Unemployment as a Worker Discipline Device', *American Economic Review*, 74/3: 433–4.

Sinn, G., and H.-W. Sinn (1994). *Jumpstart: The Economic Unification of Germany*. Cambridge, Mass.: MIT Press.

Sinn, H.-W. (2004). 'EU Enlargement, Migration and the New Constitution', *CESifo Economic Studies*, 50/4: 685–707.

Solow, R. M. (1998). 'What is Labour-Market Flexibility? What is it Good for?'. The British Academy. www.britac.ac.uk/pubs/src/keynes97/text3.

—— (2000). *Growth Theory: An Exposition* (2nd edn.). Oxford: Oxford University Press.

Soskice, D. (1990). 'Wage Determination: The Changing Role of Institutions in Advanced

Industrialized Countries', *Oxford Review of Economic Policy*, 6/4: 36–61.

——— and T. IVERSEN (1998). 'Multiple Wage-Bargaining Systems in the Single European Currency area', *Oxford Review of Economic Policy*, 14/3: 110–24.

SOSKICE, D. and T. IVERSEN (2000). 'The Non-neutrality of Monetary Policy with Large Price or Wage Setters', *Quarterly Journal of Economics*, 115/1: 265–84.

STIGLITZ, J. E., and A. WEISS (1981). 'Credit Rationing in Markets with Imperfect Information', *American Economic Review*, 71/3: 393–410.

STOKEY, N., R. E. LUCAS, and E. C. PRESCOTT (1989). *Recursive Methods in Economic Dynamics*. Cambridge, Mass.: Harvard University Press.

SUTCLIFFE, B. (2004). 'World Inequality and Globalization', *Oxford Review of Economic Policy*, 20/1: 15–37.

SVENSSON, L. E. D. (1997). 'Inflation Forecast Targeting: Implementing and Monitoring Inflation Targets', *European Economic Review*, 41: 1111–46.

TAYLOR, J. B. (1993). 'Discretion Versus Policy Rules in Practice', *Carnegie-Rochester Conference Series on Public Policy*, 39/1: 195–214.

——— (1997). 'The Policy Rule Mix: A Macro Policy Evaluation'. Draft for Robert Mundell Festschrift. www.stanford.edu/~johntayl/Papers/mundell.pdf.

TOWNSEND, R. M. (1979). 'Optimal Contracts and Competitive Markets with Costly State Verification', *Journal of Economic Theory*, 21: 265–93.

US Government (2000). *Economic Report of the President 2000*, Washington, DC: GPO.

VANDENBUSSCHE, J., P. AGHION, and C. MEGHIR (2004). 'Growth, Distance to Frontier and Composition of Human Capital'. Mimeo, Harvard University.

VENKATARAMAN, P. (2002). *Applied Optimization with Matlab Programming*. New York: Wiley.

VICKERS, J. (1986). 'Signalling in a Model of Monetary Policy', *Oxford Economic Papers*, 38: 443–55.

WALL, H. J. and G. ZOEGA (2003). 'U.S. Regional Business Cycles and the Natural Rate of Unemployment', St Louis Federal Reserve Working Paper 2003–030A. http://research.stlouisfed.org/wp/2003/2003-030.pdf.

WEN, Y. (2004). 'What Does It Take to Explain Procyclical Productivity?', *Contributions to Macroeconomics*: 4/1, Article 5. www.bepress.com/bejm/contributions/vol4/iss1/art5.

WOOD, A. (1998). 'Globalisation and the Rise in Labour Market Inequalities', *Economic Journal*, 108/450: 1463–82.

WOODFORD, M. (1999). 'Evolution and Revolution in Twentieth Century Macroeconomics'. Mimeo, Princeton University.

——— (2003). *Interest and Prices: Foundations of a Theory of Monetary Policy*. Princeton: Princeton University Press.

World Bank. 'World Development Report 2000/2001: Attacking Poverty'.

▨ Index

Please note that page references to non-textual matter such as Figures or Tables are in *italic* print; references to footnotes have the letter 'n' following the page number.